Frommer's®

ITALY
FROM $70 A DAY

Here's what the critics say about Frommer's:

"Amazingly easy to use. Very portable, very complete."
—*Booklist*

♦

"The only mainstream guide to list specific prices. The Walter Cronkite of guidebooks—with all that implies."
—*Travel & Leisure*

♦

"Complete, concise, and filled with useful information."
—*New York Daily News*

♦

"Hotel information is close to encyclopedic."
—*Des Moines Sunday Register*

Other Great Guides for Your Trip:

Frommer's Italy 2000

Frommer's Rome 2000

Frommer's Born to Shop Italy

Frommer's Europe 2000

Frommer's Europe from $60 a Day 2000

Frommer's®

2nd
Edition

ITALY
FROM $70 A DAY

The Ultimate Guide to
Comfortable Low-Cost Travel

by Reid Bramblett, Stephen Brewer,
and Patricia Schultz

MACMILLAN • USA

ABOUT THE AUTHOR

Reid Bramblett has lived in Italy on and off since he was 11. When not penning guides such as this one, the *Complete Idiot's Guide to Europe,* and *Frommer's Tuscany & Umbria,* he splits his time between Italy, Columbia, Missouri, and his native Philadelphia.

Stephen Brewer has written many guidebooks and articles on Italy and spends as much time as he can traveling in Italy.

Patricia Schultz is the co-author of the shopping guide *Made in Italy,* as well as *Frommer's Europe from $60 a Day.* She's of Italian-American descent and returns to Italy regularly to visit family and explore all its nooks and crannies.

MACMILLAN TRAVEL

Macmillan General Reference USA, Inc.
1633 Broadway
New York, NY 10019

Find us online at **www.frommers.com**

ISBN 0-02862447-5
ISSN 1091-9430

Editor: Vanessa Rosen
Production Editor: Suzanne Snyder
Photo Editor: Richard Fox
Design by Michele Laseau
Staff Cartographers: John Decamillis, Roberta Stockwell
Additional Cartography: Raffaele DeGennaro, Vincent Aliberto
Page Creation: Melissa Auciello, Ellen Considine, John Bitter, and Sean Monkhouse
Cover Photo: Bay of Naples, Positano

SPECIAL SALES

Bulk purchases (10+ copies) of Frommer's and selected Macmillan travel guides are available to corporations, organizations, mail-order catalogs, institutions, and charities at special discounts, and can be customized to suit individual needs. For more information write to Special Sales, Macmillan General Reference, 1633 Broadway, New York, NY 10019.

Manufactured in the United States of America

5 4 3 2 1

Contents

Lists of Maps

An Invitation to the Reader

In researching this book, we discovered many wonderful places—hotels, restaurants, shops, and more. We're sure you'll find others. Please tell us about them, so we can share the information with your fellow travelers in upcoming editions. If you were disappointed with a recommendation, we'd love to know that, too. Please write to:

Frommer's Italy from $70 a Day
Macmillan Travel
1633 Broadway
New York, NY 10019

An Additional Note

Please be advised that travel information is subject to change at any time—and this is especially true of prices. We therefore suggest that you write or call ahead for confirmation when making your travel plans. The authors, editors, and publisher cannot be held responsible for the experiences of readers while traveling. Your safety is important to us, however, so we encourage you to stay alert and be aware of your surroundings. Keep a close eye on cameras, purses, and wallets, all favorite targets of thieves and pickpockets.

What the Symbols Mean

○ Frommer's Favorites

Our favorite places and experiences—outstanding for quality, value, or both.

The following abbreviations are used for credit cards:

AE	American Express	EURO	Eurocard
CB	Carte Blanche	JCB	Japan Credit Bank
DC	Diners Club	MC	MasterCard
DISC	Discover	V	Visa
ER	EnRoute		

The Following Abbreviations Are Used for Locations:

Borgo	B.	Riva	Rv.
Calle	C.	Ruga	R.
Campiello	Cplo.	Salizzada	Sz.
Campo	Cam.	Strada	S.
Corso	Cor.	Via	V.
Fondamenta	Fond.	Viale	Vle.
Largo	Lgo.	Vicola	Vc.
Piazza	Pz.	del/dei/delle	d.
Piazzale	Pzle.		

Find Frommer's Online

Arthur Frommer's Budget Travel Online (www.frommers.com) offers more than 6,000 pages of up-to-the-minute travel information—including the latest bargains and candid, personal articles updated daily by Arthur Frommer himself. No other Web site offers such comprehensive and timely coverage of the world of travel.

The Best of Italy from $70 a Day

Three authors. One country. A myriad of experiences. Deciding what to see and do in Italy is not easy. Especially on a budget. We've put our heads together and come up with the best of what this diverse country has to offer. This chapter will direct you to the most captivating museums, authentic wineries, hotel gems that are off the beaten path, and culinary delights that have been pleasing Italians and visitors alike for centuries. And this is only the beginning.

1 The Best Travel Experiences for Free (or Almost)

- **Enjoying Rome's Best Nighttime Panorama:** After a leisurely 3-hour dinner at a tiny trattoria in Rome's working-class neighborhood of Trastevere, stroll the cobblestone alleyways, then climb the Gianicolo hill for a moonlit panorama of the Eternal City. See chapter 4.
- **Listening to the Vespers in San Miniato** (Florence): This is one of the few places left in Italy where Gregorian chant is still sung. Here, in one of Florence's oldest churches, late afternoon vespers transport you back to the lost centuries of the hill-top Romanesque church's 11th-century origins. See chapter 5.
- **Biking Through the Town and Walls of Ferrara:** You can bike along the wide paths on Ferrara's medieval walls, which encircle the city with an aerie of greenery. The views are spectacular. Many hotels offer guests free use of bicycles. See chapter 7.
- **Taking a Vaporetto Ride on the Grand Canal** (Venice): For a fraction of the cost of a gondola ride, the no. 1 **vaporetto** plies the Grand Canal, past hundreds of Gothic and Byzantine palazzi redolent of the days when Venice was a powerful and wealthy maritime republic. Angle for a seat on the open-air deck up front. See chapter 8.
- **Cruising Lake Como** (Lake District): Board a lake steamer (4,500L/$2.65 each way) for the pleasant trip from Bellagio to other picturesque small villages on the section of the lake known as the Centro Lago. To the north, the lake is backed by snow-capped Alps, while the shorelines are lush with verdant gardens. As the steamer heads from one port to another, ochre- and pastel-colored villages will beckon you to disembark and explore their

ancient streets and piazzas—a good reason to purchase a day pass for 12,500L ($7.35) so you can get on and off the boat at as many stops as you wish. See chapter 11.

- **Climbing Up the Flanks of the Matterhorn in the Valle d'Aosta:** An excellent trail leads from Cervina-Breuil up the flank of this impressive mountain. A moderately strenuous uphill trek of 90 minutes will get you to the breathtaking Lac du Goillet, and from there it's another 90 minutes to the Colle Superiore delle Cime Bianche, a plateau with heart-stopping views. See chapter 12.

- **Walking in the Cinque Terre** (Italian Riviera): While away your time in the Cinque Terre by strolling from one lovely village to another along the Mediterranean on trails with views that'll take your breath away. See chapter 13.

- **Taking the Amalfi Coast Thrill Ride:** Hop on the local bus in Sorrento (2,210L/$1.30) for a 30-mile, white-knuckle ride down the breathtaking coastline of the Amalfi Drive. This two-lane road clings sometimes hundreds of feet up the cliff side, twisting and plunging past verdant gorges, tiny fishing villages, posh resort towns, and sparkling isolated beaches washed by bright azure waters. See chapter 14.

- **Exploring the Land of *Trulli*** (Apulia): The Valle d'Itria is a lush, surreal landscape carpeted with vineyards and speckled with one of Europe's oddest forms of vernacular architecture: the *trulli*, pointy whitewashed houses constructed without mortar and roofed by a cone of dark stones stacked in concentric circles. The capital of the region is Alberobello, a UNESCO World Heritage town made up of over 1,000 *trulli*—you can even spend the night in one (see "The Best Hotel Deals" below). See chapter 14.

- **Indulging in a Sunset Picnic at an Ancient Temple** (Sicily): Pack a picnic of fresh fruit, crusty bread, creamy cheese, assorted salamis, and a bottle of wine, and carry it all down into the Valley of the Temples below Agrigento, a city founded in the 5th-century B.C. by the Greeks. The archaeological park is free of charge, so all you have to do is pick a strategic spot to enjoy your feast fit for a god as you watch the sun set behind the honey-gold columns of the Temple of Concord, the world's most perfectly preserved ancient temple. See chapter 15.

2 The Best Bargain Destinations

- **Florence:** Meander in and out of the centuries of the Middle Ages and Renaissance when Florence was one of the richest, most vibrant and aesthetic cities in Western civilization. If you secure your modestly priced hotel in advance, you'll find that one of Italy's most expensive cities needn't break your budget. Choose your trattorias carefully, avoid the shopping temptations, wander its streets and savor a priceless vacation that can be orchestrated for not a lot of lire. See Chapter 5.

- **Chianti** (Tuscany): The very heartland of Tuscany stretches between Florence and Siena. Here the serendipity of lazy vineyard-hopping drives and spontaneous wine-tasting stops is heightened by the region's visually stunning landscape. Staring is free on the old **La Chiantigiana,** which links a string of picturesque wine towns that dot a history-rich area of forested hills, castles, stone farmhouses–turned–B&B and wine-producing estates. See chapter 6.

- **Ferrara** (Emilia-Romagna): This elegant city of rose-colored brick is much less expensive than nearby Bologna or Parma. You can take in all the Renaissance art and architecture, with a pass that provides discount admission to some of the best museums in town. It's not expensive to get around either—most hotels provide free bicycles. See chapter 7.

- **Venice:** A magnificent, and never-ending stage set, Venice is one of Italy's most expensive destinations, *unless* you go in the off-season when it's reclaimed by the Venetians during its empty winter months. Hotels can cost half as much, you'll have your pick, the local residents are less harried and the fog-cloaked corners of Venice promise mystery and mystique and million-dollar memories of a very special sojourn, even for the budget challenged. See chapter 8.
- **Piedmont Wine Country:** Getting and tasting Asti Spumante, Barbaresco, and Barolo wines at at-the-source prices is reason enough to call this area a bargain destination. Strolling through the medieval and Renaissance towns that rise from the vineyards, and finding low-country accommodations doesn't hurt either. See chapter 12.
- **The Cinque Terre** (Italian Riviera): You won't find a more beautiful coastline than the Cinque Terre lined with olive groves, vineyards, villages set above the sea, and hidden coves. The best part is that you can find low-cost accommodations (doubles run about 80,000L/$47 a night), excellent, inexpensive food, beaches, and free walking trails. See chapter 13.
- **Lecce** (Apulia): Intrepid travelers who make it all the way down into the stiletto tip of the heel on Italy's boot are often surprised to discover such an inexpensive, thriving, lively city and a stage set for some of the prettiest and most unique baroque architecture in Italy. Lecce's cafes serve delectable pastries, the city's artisan studios carry on the papier-mâché tradition that has made Lecce Italy's center for the craft. Since it's so out-of-the-way, prices stay rock-bottom. See chapter 14.
- **Cefalù** (Sicily): A Sicilian resort without the high price tag, Cefalù has the requisite beaches and succulent seafood dinners, but remains a fishing village at heart. And when you tire of the beach, Cefalù boasts one of Sicily's most gorgeously mosaicked medieval Norman cathedrals, a couple of heavyweight Renaissance pictures in the little local painting gallery, even a brooding pint-sized mountain to hike for outstanding vistas. See chapter 15.

3 The Best Small Towns

- **Lucca** (Tuscany): Protected from the new millennium within its remarkable swath of Renaissance ramparts (said to be among the best preserved in Europe), Lucca evokes the small-town charm of an elegant little town. Within these historical parameters, local matrons tool around on bicycles (a quaint hill town without the hill; little wonder bikes are so popular), young mothers with strollers walk the rampart-top promenade beneath the shade of centuries-old plane trees, and exuberant examples of Pisan-Romanesque architecture draw visitors to the Duomo and San Michele in Foro. Hometown boy Puccini would have no problem recognizing the city he always held close to his music-filled heart. See chapter 6.
- **Gubbio** (Umbria): This small, austere, proud no-nonsense mountain town has only recently figured on the maps of the intrepid off-the-beaten-path trekkers. Blessedly hard to get to, it has slumbered through the centuries and today offers up one of the country's best preserved scenarios of medieval architecture and ambience. Built into the side of the forest-clad Monte Igino, a funicular up to the Basilica of its beloved patron St. Ubaldo provides stunning panoramas and a

chance to understand something of the centuries-old serenity of the time-locked outpost poet Gabriele D'Annunzio called the "City of Silence." See chapter 6.

- **Bressanone** (South Tyrol): It's hard to believe that this quaint, small town was the center of a large ecclesiastical principality for almost 800 years. It's rich in history and natural beauty, and you can explore vineyards, mountains, and impressive museums and monuments, as well as amble through the town's pastel-colored houses and narrow cobblestone streets. See chapter 10.

- **Bellagio** (Lake District): The prettiest of all the towns in Italy's Lake Country, Bellagio was peaceful enough for Franz Liszt to use it as a retreat, and since it hasn't been inundated with throngs of tourist since, it's still tranquil today. See chapter 11.

- **Dolceacqua** (Liguira): This rustic, picturesque alternative to the fancier resorts on the Ligurian coast is crowned by the ruins of a 16th-century castle. For a taste of the local flavor, you can enjoy festivals from a forgotten era in January and August. See chapter 13.

- **Ravello** (Campania): Perched at the lip of the verdant Valley of the Dragon, high above the heat and tourist crush of the beachfront Amalfi Coast towns, Ravello revels in its quiet beauty, lush scenery, and spectacular gardens open to the public for concerts throughout the years. Come see how these pleasure gardens inspired Wagner's *Parsifal.* See chapter 14.

- **Alberobello** (Apulia): The capital of the land of *trulli*—those odd, pointy-roofed whitewashed houses unique to this region—is not only a sight to behold (the entire town has been declared a national monument), but is also one of the friendliest little burgs you'll ever have the pleasure of visiting. You might stop in a shop to ask a simple question and end up, two hours of broken conversation later, looking at pictures of grandchildren or being invited home for fresh pastries or an impromptu lesson in how to make *orecchiette* pasta by hand. See chapter 14.

- **Erice** (Sicily): This stony little cliff-top town riding high above the seedy port city of Trapani on Sicily's west coast looks like a medieval hill town of Tuscany. But Erice's roots go much deeper. This sacred city built in the shape of a triangle was renowned around the Mediterranean for its temple to the Earth goddess centuries before the Greeks and later Romans showed up and renamed her Venus. These days, most pilgrims come for Maria Grammatica's sinfully delicious marzipan pastries made famous by *Bitter Almonds,* a popular American cookbook she co-authored. See chapter 15.

4 The Best Cathedrals

- **The Vatican's St. Peter's** (Rome): The elaborately decorated capital of Christendom is world's second largest church and a monument to the Renaissance and baroque eras. It was designed by Bramante, capped with a dome by Michelangelo, and decorated by Bernini. St. Peter's includes among its treasures a *St. Peter* by Arnolfo di Cambio, and Michelangelo's *Pietà,* a haunting scene of Mary cradling the dead Christ, carved when the master was 19 years old. All that plus the chance to see the pope. See chapter 4.

- **Il Duomo di Firenze** (Florence): The red-tiled dome of Florence's magnificent Duomo dominates the skyline today just as it did when it was constructed 5 centuries ago. In its day it was the largest unsupported dome in the world, intended to dwarf the structures of ancient Greece and Rome. In true Renaissance style, built to be "il piu bello che si puo" (as beautiful as possible), it was and still is considered a major architectural feat and was the high point of architect Filippo Brunelleschi's illustrious career. In late 1996, an extensive and elaborate 15-year restoration was finally completed on the colorful 16th-century frescoes covering the inside of the cupola and depicting the world's largest painting of the Last Judgment. See chapter 5.

- **Duomo** (Tuscany): Begun in 1196, this black-and-white marble striped cathedral sits atop Siena's highest hill, and is one of the most beautiful and ambitious Gothic churches in Italy. Its exterior's extravagant zebra-striped marble bands borrowed from Pisan-Lucchese architecture continue indoors. Masterpieces here include a priceless pavement of masterful mosaics, 56 etched and inlaid marble panels created by more than 40 artisans, the octagonal pulpit, carved by master Tuscan sculptor Nicola Pisano, and the lavish Libreria Piccolomini, built in the late 15th century to house the important illuminated book collection of the Siena-born Pope Pius II, quintessential Renaissance man and humanist. See chapter 6.

- **Il Duomo** (Umbria): Begun in 1290 and with a bold, beautiful and intricate-ornamented facade that stands out among Italy's Gothic masterpieces, this Orvieto's Duomo is also known for one of the greatest fresco cycles of the Renaissance in its **Chapel of San Brizio.** The cycle, begun by Fra Angelico and completed by Luca Signorelli, depicts in vivid detail the Last Judgment, one that was said to have influenced Michelangelo in his own interpretation for the Sistine Chapel. See chapter 6.

- **Duomo** (Parma): Built in the 12th century, Parma's Duomo is one of the great achievements of Italian Romanesque architecture. The true star of the show however is Corregio's great masterpiece, his dramatic *Assumption of the Virgin,* which adorns the octagonal cupola. See chapter 7.

- **Basilica di San Marco** (Venice): Surely the most exotic and Eastern of the Western world's Christian churches, the onion-domed and mosaic-covered San Marco took much of its inspiration from ancient Constantinople's Hagia Sophia mosque. Somewhere inside the mysterious candle-lit cavern of the thousand-year-old church that began as the private chapel of the governing Doges are the remains of St. Mark, revered patron saint of Venice's ancient maritime republic. His "mascot," the winged lion, is as associated with the city as the "quadriga," the four magnificent chariot horses that decorate the open loggia of St. Mark's Basilica overlooking one of the world's great squares. See chapter 8.

- **Duomo of Milan:** It took 5 centuries to build this magnificent Gothic cathedral—the third largest church in the world. It's marked by 135 marble spires, a stunning triangular facade, and 2,000-some statues flanking the massive but airy, almost fanciful exterior. The interior, lit by brilliant stained-glass windows, is more serene. Lord Tennyson rapturously wrote about the view of the Alps from the roof. See chapter 11.

- **Cathedral of Monreale** (Sicily): When Palermo's secular king got into a fight with the city's bishop in the 11th century, the king decided to build his own cathedral in the hills above the city. Monreale stands as a testament to the craftsmanship of imported Greek artisans, who carpeted the interior with 68,472 square feet of glittering mosaics and filled the apse with a 66-foot-high, kindly eyed Christ. In the cathedral's quiet cloisters, high above the Palermo heat, you can while away the hours contemplating the wraparound arcade supported by hundreds of twisted and inlaid minicolumns. See chapter 15.

5 The Best Museums

- **Vatican Museums** (Rome): If you see only one museum in Italy, make it the Vatican's 12 galleries and papal apartments filled with a surfeit of art and history, everything from the Raphael Rooms with their *School of Athens* fresco to Michelangelo's incomparable Sistine Chapel ceiling with its fingers-almost-touching depiction of *God Creating Adam*. In between you'll find tens of thousands of Greek and Roman statues (including the *Apollo Belvedere* and *Laocoön*), medieval tapestries, illuminated manuscripts, ancient Egyptian and Chinese art, Etruscan artifacts, and a painting gallery covering everyone from Giotto and Leonardo Da Vinci to Caravaggio's *Deposition* and Raphael's final work, the magnificent *Transfiguration*. See chapter 4.
- **Galleria Borghese** (Rome): This is one of the great small museums of the world, recently fully reopened after a 14-year restoration that has returned vibrancy and life to the frescoes and decor of this 1613 palace. And that's merely the backdrop for the collections: masterpieces of baroque sculpture by a young Bernini—*David, Apollo and Daphne, The Rape of Persephone*—and paintings by masters like Caravaggio and Raphael. See chapter 4.
- **Museo Nazionale Romano** (Rome): The top collections of ancient Roman art anywhere languished for decades in the perennially closed Baths of Diocletian. But as of 1998, the collections have been broken up and displayed in several spaces: an ancient hall and two modern, well-curated museums converted from grand palaces—the 19th-century Palazzo Massimo and the frescoed, 16th-century Palazzo Altemps. These enormous collections of sculpture, mosaics, coinage and jewelry, and never-before-seen frescoes blow away anything else of their kind in Italy. See chapter 4.
- **Villa Giulia** (Rome): This is the single greatest museum devoted to the ancient, pre-Roman Etruscan culture. These guys left behind painted vases and some beautiful funerary art, including a terra-cotta sarcophagus lid bearing life-sized—and remarkably lifelike—full-body portraits of a husband and wife, smiling enigmatically and wearing their finest togas, sitting back to enjoy one final, eternal feast together. See chapter 4.
- **Galleria degli Uffizi** (Florence): When the Medici were the affluent men about town, this was the headquarters of the Duchy of Tuscany. For today's visitor, it is the riverside repository of the greatest collection of Renaissance paintings in the world, bequeathed to Florence with the understanding that it would never leave the city of the Medicis, nor these hallowed walls. The peculiar "Stendhal's Syndrome," the malaise of vertigo from the sheer overload of unparalleled culture, most likely was first experienced here. See chapter 5.
- **Museo Nazionale del Bargello** (Florence): The harsh, fortresslike Bargello, incarnated as the constable's headquarters and local prison among other things, is to Renaissance sculpture what the Uffizi is to Renaissance painting. Within this cavernous medieval shell lies a handsomely displayed collection without equal in Italy, with early works by Michelangelo and magnificent pieces by the master Donatello. See chapter 5.
- **Galleria dell' Accademia** (Florence): Here stands Michelangelo's *David*, one of the world's most recognized statues. Most remarkable is the fact that Michelangelo was just 29 years old at the time he created his "Giant." The *David* looms in stark perfection beneath the rotunda of the main room built exclusively for its display when it was moved here from the Piazza Signoria for safekeeping. After standing in awe before its magnificence, many visitors leave, drained, without seeing the museum's

other Michelangelos, particularly four never-finished *Prisoners* (or *Slaves*) struggling magnificently to free themselves from within. See chapter 5.

- **Palazzo Pitti and the Galleria Palatina** (Florence): The former residence of the Medici, the enormous Palazzo Pitti is home to seven museums, the largest collection of galleries in Florence under one roof. The **Galleria Palatina (Palatine Gallery),** 26 art-filled rooms on the first floor of the palazzo is the star attraction, home to one of the finest collections of Italian Renaissance and baroque masters in Europe and is the most important in Florence after the Uffizi's. The art of the 16th century is the forte of the Palatina, in particular that of Raphael and his many Madonnas. The museum's treasures also include a large collection of works by Andrea del Sarto, Fra Bartolomeo, some superb works by Rubens, canvases by Tintoretto, Veronese and a number of stunning portraits by Titian. See chapter 5.

- **Gallerie dell'Accademia** (Venice): The glory that was Venice lives on in the Accademia, the definitive treasure house of Venetian painting and one of Europe's great museums. Exhibited chronologically from the 13th through the 18th centuries, there is said to be no one hallmark masterpiece in this collection; rather, this is an outstanding and comprehensive showcase of works by all the great master painters of Venice, the largest such collection in the world. Most of all, though, the works open a window onto the Venice of 500 years ago. Indeed, you'll see in the canvases how little Venice, perhaps least of any city in Europe, has changed over the centuries. See chapter 8.

- **Collezione Peggy Guggenheim** (Venice): Considered to be one of the most comprehensive and important collections of modern art in the world and one of the most visited attractions in Venice, this collection of painting and sculpture was assembled by eccentric and eclectic American expatriate Peggy Guggenheim. She did an excellent job of it with particular strengths in Cubism, European Abstraction, Surrealism, and Abstract Expressionism since about 1910. See chapter 8.

- **Museo Archeologico** (Naples): If you only visit Pompeii without heading to Naples' archaeology museum, you're missing half the show. Everything that could have been carted off from the ruins of Pompeii (and hadn't already by looters) is kept here, including fantastic ancient mosaics and frescoes. But the collections don't stop there, and among the other ancient masterpieces is the *Farnese Bull,* a sculptural group 13 feet high and just as wide carved from a single gargantuan block of marble. See chapter 14.

6 The Best Ancient Ruins

- **The Roman Forum** (Rome): The standing columns, triumphal arches, and crumbling bits of architrave that fill the ancient Roman Forum mark the spot from which a small Latin tribe living on the Palatine Hill eventually extended their empire to rule the entire known world. See chapter 4.

- **The Colosseum** (Rome): The broken shell of the Colosseum was the grand sports arena of the Roman world, a 2,000-year-old entertainment complex where crowds of 50,000 Romans thundered their applause for bloody gladiator matches and wild beast massacres. This travertine amphitheater remains the world's largest, its jagged profile a study in the classical orders of architecture and the symbol of the Eternal City itself. See chapter 4.

- **Arena di Verona** (Verona): The best preserved Roman amphitheater in the world and the best known in Italy after Rome's Colosseum, the elliptical Arena was built in a slightly pinkish marble around the year A.D. 100 and stands in the very middle of town in the Piazza Brà. Its perfect acoustics have survived the millennia and make it one of the wonders of the ancient world and one of the most fascinating venues for live moonlit performances today, conducted without microphones. See chapter 9.

- **Buried by Vesuvius: Pompeii and Herculaneum** (Campania): In A.D. 79, Mt. Vesuvius blew its top 12 miles into the air, raining death and destruction on the Roman cities that had grown at its feet. A tidal wave of ash and superheated gases hurtled down the mountainside, burying the prosperous city of Pompeii and preserving its buildings—and the bodies of some 2,000 of its residents—for the ages. The nearby wealthy resort town of Ercolano (Herculaneum) was also buried, but by a river of scalding mud that seared the skulls of the unfortunate townsfolk and carbonized the wooden doors and furnishings of the houses, which were preserved along with wall frescoes, mosaics, and stuccoes. Pompeii and Herculaneum remain two of the world's most intact ancient cities, their ornate villas, everyday shops, even baths and brothels brought back to light and open for you to visit, wandering over the stone slab streets of these Roman ghost towns. See chapter 14.

- **The Greek Temples at Paestum** (Campania): Who said you had to go all the way to Greece to see ancient temples? Just an hour's train ride south of Naples, in the middle of nowhere in mozzarella country, stand three Doric temples and other ruins that mark the site of the 9th-century B.C. Greek colony of Paestum, founded back when southern Italy was part of *Magna Graecia,* or "Greater Greece." In fact, Paestum has something even Greece itself can't boast of: the only known examples of ancient Greek fresco in the world. See chapter 14.

- **The Greek Temples of Sicily** (Segesta, Agrigento, Selinute): Some of the most intact and beautifully sited ancient Greek temples in the world are not in Greece but in Sicily, many of whose cities were founded as Greek colonies in the age of *Magna Graecia,* the "Greater Greece" Mediterranean empire. At isolated **Segesta,** birds wheel between the columns of a giant Doric temple standing at the edge of a deep ravine and surrounded by a verdant amphitheater of hills. **Selinute,** too, sits in isolation, its ruinous temples and jumbled architecture overlooking the Mediterranean from two cliff tops on Sicily's southern shore above a laid-back little fishing village-cum-beach resort. In the Valley of the Temples below the thriving city of **Agrigento,** the 5th-century B.C. Greek colonists left a string of beautiful temples along a ridge awash in olive groves and pink almond blossoms in spring. One of these buildings, the exquisite Temple of Concord, ranks as one of the two best preserved Greek temples on earth. See chapter 15.

- **The Villa Romana del Casale at Piazza Armerina** (Sicily): The most extensive and best-preserved ancient Roman mosaics in the world carpet 37,800 square feet of the floor in this 4th-century villa. Set in the midst of Sicily's mountainous interior, these glorious polychrome and intricately detailed mosaics depict mythological stories, hunting scenes, and perhaps the first representation of bikinis in Western history. See chapter 15.

- **The Greek Theater in Siracusa** (Sicily): The world's largest Greek Theater occupies a rich archaeological park on the mainland of Siracusa, and ancient city that once defeated Athens itself to become the most powerful metropolis in the Greek world. The theater is in astoundingly good shape, and can still seat some 15,000 spectators for summertime performances of classical Greek dramas, music concerts, and modern plays. Siracusa also hosts Sicily's greatest archaeology museum. See chapter 15.

7 The Best Wine-Tasting Experiences

- **Montalcino and Montepulciano** (southern Tuscany): This less trod area south of Siena is sacred ground to wine connoisseurs for its unsurpassed **Brunello di Montalcino** and **Vino Nobile di Montepulciano.** Both of the picturesque hill towns have enotecas and cantinas in town. Montalcino's mighty Medici fortress has been reincarnated as a rustic wine bar, while those with a rental car can head out into the highly scenic countryside outside of Montalcino to the **Fattoria Barbi,** one of the area's most respected wine-producing estates, for a tasting and country-style dinner and even an overnight stay. See chapter 6.
- **Enoteca Italica Permanente** (Siena, Tuscany): Siena sits to the south of the Chianti-designated area, so there could be no better setting to showcase Italy's timeless wine culture. Set within the massive military fortress built by Cosimo dei Medici in 1560, this wine-tasting bar provides a wide selection of wines. The emphasis is on Tuscan wines—many made in the fabled Chianti area of Siena's backyard—but this enoteca is a national concern owned and operated by the government to support the Italian wine tradition. See chapter 6.
- **Torgiano** (Umbria): Ten miles to Perugia's southeast lies the small town of Torgiano, whose unique wine museum (and wonderful retail enoteca and osteria inn next door) is a must-do pilgrimage for serious wine lovers. With twenty well-organized, well-lit rooms that trace every aspect of viticulture, this is the only museum—unexpectedly interesting and certainly the most attractive—of its kind in Italy. The owners, the well-known wine-producing Lungarotti family, have become Umbria's most noted and some of the most celebrated in the Italian wine scene. See chapter 6.
- **Verona** (Veneto): The epicenter of the region's important viticulture (Veneto produces more DOC wine than any other region in Italy), Verona hosts the annual VinItaly wine fair held every April, a highly prestigious event in the global wine world. A number of authentic old-time wine bars still populate the medieval backstreets of the fair city of Romeo and Juliet fame. First opened in 1890, the **Bottega del Vino** boasts a wine cellar holding an unmatched 80,000-bottle selection, the largest in Verona. Belly up to the old oak bar and sample from five dozen good-to-excellent wines for sale by the glass, particularly the Veronese trio of bardolino and valpolicello (reds) and soave (white). **Masi** is one of the most respected producers, one of many in the Verona hills, whose cantinas are open to the public for wine-tasting visits. See chapter 9.
- **Barolo** (Piedmont Wine Country): This romantic town is full of shops selling the village's rich red wines. The highlight is the **Castello di Barolo,** which houses a wine museum and enoteca in its cavernous cellars. See chapter 12.
- **Monterosso** (Italian Riviera): At the **Enoteca Internazionale** in this small, charming town in the Cinque Terre, you can taste local wines from the vineyards that cling to the nearby cliffs. See chapter 13.

8 The Best Festivals

- **Carnevale, Venice** (Veneto) **and Viareggio** (Tuscany): Venice's Carnevale is the best known abroad of Italy's pre-Lenten celebrations. All of Venice becomes a stage and everyone is on it. A salute to the final years of the Serene Republic when unbridled gambling and gamboling went on for months before Shrove Tuesday, it is now confined to two events-packed weeks when the piazzas and streets are jam-packed with historical costumes and exquisitely theatrical getups that are nothing short of astounding. Music concerts from Baroque to salsa fill every imaginable venue in town, most of them free-of-charge, with a wild crescendo of private masked balls and a night of brilliant fireworks illuminating the Grand Canal. Tuscany's seaside resort of **Viareggio** hosts the runner-up to Venice, with enormous floats of mostly political figures of the moment, that parade through the crowds for the four Sundays of Lent. If anyone is in costume, they're usually under 10 and of the Zorro and cowboy set. See chapters 6 and 8.

- **Easter and Holy Week:** In **Rome,** the pope leads a stations-of-the-cross procession around the Colosseum on Good Friday, and tosses a blessing out his Vatican window on Easter Sunday to everyone in Piazza San Pietro below. Throughout **southern Italy and Sicily,** Easter Week brings out Spanish-influenced processions of hooded confraternity members and floats of the Passion and the Madonna, dressed in rich robes and trailing streamers of pinned-together 10,000L bills. There are especially fine processions in **Taranto,** Apulia, and **Trapani,** Sicily. See chapter 15.

- **Rome's Festa de' Noiantri:** Rome's archetypal working class neighborhood of Trastevere—across the Tiber River form the rest of the city, with its own dialect and proud folk and literary traditions—celebrates its uniqueness in mid-July in the "Feast of We Others," a week of communal banqueting at long tables set on the cobblestones of its alleyways, concerts and plays in the piazza, and a street fair on the main drag. See chapter 4.

- **Il Palio** (Siena): In July and August, this bareback, breakneck horse race between the ancient divisions of Siena's *comtrade* or neighborhoods turns the dirt-packed Piazza del Campo into an emotional sea of local fans and bewildered tourists who can't believe what they're seeing. The costumed pageantry before the two annual Palios and the victory and consolation feasts that take place afterward are just as entrancing. Tickets for the grandstands are pretty much impossible to get, but join the 100,000 crazies who fill the middle of the Campo for an experience they'll never forget. See chapter 6.

- **Giostra del Saracino** (Arezzo, Tuscany): The quirkily lopsided Piazza Grande is the timeless backdrop for the most entertaining of Italy's many jousting festivals in August and September. Here the target for the medieval tilting tournament is an "infidel" automaton that, when hit by a lance, hits back. The influence of Tuscan-born Franco Zefferelli can be seen in the fascinating costumes of the elaborate procession that wends through the town's evocative medieval streets. See chapter 6.

- **Spoleto Festival** (Umbria): Formerly known as the Festival of Two Worlds, this annual world-class bash held in June that celebrates music, dance and theater has long enticed major names, troupes and orchestras from all corners of the globe, with an arts-savvy audience to match. The ancient hill town offers a few unique venues such as an ancient Roman amphitheater and its extremely picturesque Piazza del Duomo. See chapter 6.

- **Corso dei Ceri** (Gubbio, Umbria): On May 15, three huge wooden towers called *ceri* (candles), weighing 880 pounds each, are raced around town by changing teams of burly young men in a fevered atmosphere akin to Pamplona's Running of the Bulls. This unique holiday is one of Italy's most ancient celebrations, loaded with pagan implications. Each tower is topped by the small statue of a saint, one of them the town's beloved 12th-century patron St. Ubaldo who always wins. See chapter 6.

- **Naples's Miracolo di San Gennaro** (Naples): St. Janarius was beheaded in the 4th century, but his followers preserved both the head and two vials of his blood.

Now, whenever those glass vials are brought near the skull, the coagulated blood in them liquefies and begins to boil in a standing miracle renowned the world over—not for nothing did southern Italian immigrants to New York City choose to honor San Gennaro in their biggest annual street festival. Back home in Naples, the liquefaction miracle is repeated several times throughout the year for the benefit of the devout, who attend the Byzantine masses held in the saint's honor in order to line up and kiss the vials for good luck. They honor the saint thusly on the first Saturday of May, September 19, and December 16. See chapter 14.

9 The Best Bargains for Serious Shoppers

- **Ceramics:** In southern Italy, you can find some excellent deals on hand-painted ceramics in the fishing town of **Vietri sul Mare** at the tail end of the Amalfi Coast (chapter 14), and even better ones in the Apulian town of **Grottaglie,** where some artisans still work in grottoes and the little city's proud rooster decorates the crockery (chapter 15). In northern Italy, ceramic buffs should head to the famous ceramic city, **Faenza,** located in the Emilia-Romagna region. In Umbria, **Gubbio** holds its own with a fair number of small quality shops reproducing local patterns that date back to the town's medieval importance. While entire dining room sets are pricey, you can often get single plates and bowls for as little as $3 to $10—put together enough of these "leftovers" and you have your own, colorful set of mix-and-match ceramics from all over Italy.
- **Glass:** Venetian glass has gotten a bad rap as tacky, gaudy, tawdry, and over-the-top. For those with a discerning eye, a visit to Venice will prove that the master artisans who keep the thousand-year-old torch burning haven't lost their artistic touch. Though it's fragile to transport, expensive to ship, and a hassle to carry, consider a small memento nonetheless: two slender flutes to toast in the millennium, a brightly colored Christmas-tree ball ornament you'll keep for life, an elegantly blown ashtray or table-top dish. See chapter 8.
- **Leather:** Since the Dark Ages, Italy's tanneries and leather workshops have turned out the best quality leather goods from saddles to shoes. The give-away deals of yesteryear are pretty much gone, but careful shoppers will have little trouble finding good selections at moderate-to-expensive price ranges in most cities, particularly **Florence,** still a leather-shopper's mecca after all these centuries. Low prices are hard to find, but the value-for-your-money makes a leather purchase in Florence a safe one. See chapter 5 for a listing of specific shops.
- **Fashion:** An inherent knack at effortlessly pulling it all together, compounded by the made-in-Italy quality guarantee of apparel designed and manufactured in the country, make Italy unparalleled fashion country. The high priests of fashion—Versace, Valentino, Armani, Dolce & Gabbana, Gucci —boast *alta moda* creations whose price tags make them all but inaccessible. But, at clothing stores throughout the country, you can find lots of lesser priced and less known houses and manufacturers who use quality textiles such as linen. Open-air markets such as **Florence's San Lorenzo** and **Mercato delle Cascine** markets and **Milan's market on Via Papiniano** (see chapter 11) can produce the odd bargain or good find, and twice yearly sales mean heavy discounts in most retail stores in August and January.
- **Gold:** You won't be stumbling upon too many offers you can't refuse: Government regulated prices have long been determined by the gram. But Italy's unrivaled art of goldsmithing can be traced to the ancient Etruscans 28 centuries ago.

Almost everything is 18-karat gold, something a teensy-tiny obligatory stamp on each item guarantees, and if you're looking for the quintessential memento or a family heirloom, Italy is still the place to shop. **Florence** has long been every shopper's favorite choice, but **Rome** and **Venice** have a reasonable selection of gold stores, while **Milan** stands out for contemporary design of fine jewelry.

- **Artisan crafts:** Pick up your old-fashioned ceramic **Neapolitan** *presepio* (Christmas crèche) figurines and props along Via San Gregorio Armeno in **Naples. Lecce,** in Apulia, is Italy's center for **papier-mâché.** You can pick up hand-crafted **Sicilian marionettes**—puppets of Charlemagne's heroes and Saracen warriors—from tourist shops all over, especially in Erice and Taormina. But one of the true centers of production is **Acireale** on Sicily's east coast, just north of Catania between Siracusa and Taormina.

10 The Best Hotel Deals

- **Coronet** (Rome; ☎ **06/679-0653**): The 15th-century Doria-Pamphilj palace contains one of Rome's top private painting museums, the apartments of the princely family itself, and, in one wing, this little hotel with baronially sized rooms scattered with Persian rugs run by the friendly Teresi family. Though you're only two blocks from the bus nexus of Piazza Venezia—not to mention mere steps away from the Pantheon and the evening *passeggiata* on the Corso— the Coronet resides on a quiet, hidden little piazza where Anna Magnani once lived. Doubles run as low as $60. See chapter 4.
- **Hotel Firenze** (Florence; ☎ **055/26-83-01**): A former student crash pad, and today a renovated two-star choice that appeals to all age levels, the Firenze is ideally situated between the Duomo and the Piazza della Signoria. A fresh overall look, great baths for this price range and an address that beats the best puts this hotel on every insider's short list. But don't expect a staff that's too professional or accommodating or you'll leave disappointed. Starting at $76 for a double with bathroom, this is Florence's centro storico's best value-for-your-money destination. See chapter 5.
- **Piccolo Hotel Puccini** (Lucca, Tuscany; ☎ **0583/55-421**): If you're planning a stay in Lucca, Giacomo Puccini's hometown, look no further than this charming three-star hotel in a 15th-century palazzo that sits just in front of the building where the great composer was born. Some of the hotel rooms overlook the small piazza and its bronze statue of Puccini. Paolo and Raffaella, the young and enthusiastic couple who have recently taken over the management, have lightened and brightened up the place and do everything to make this a perfect choice for those who appreciate tasteful attention and discrete professionalism. The Piazza San Michele, one of Lucca's loveliest squares, is two steps away. Doubles start at $73. See chapter 6.
- **Hotel Piccolo Etruria** (Siena, Tuscany; ☎ **0577/28-80-88**): This recently refurbished hotel is lovely enough to be your base in Tuscany—at $65 for a double, it's too great a find to be used as a mere one-night stop. The proud Fattorini family oversaw every painstaking detail in its recent renovation, and the taste and quality level is something one usually finds in hotels at thrice the cost. See chapter 6.
- **B&B Locanda Borgonuovo** (Ferrara, Emilia-Romagna; ☎ **0532/211-100**): Outstanding hospitality and charm is the name of the game here. Starting at $80, you can stay on a medieval palazzo in guest rooms decorated with an eclectic mix of antiques. The breakfasts served in the garden are a feast. See chapter 7.

- **Albergo Cappello** (Ravenna, Emilia-Romagna; ☎ **0544/219-813**): This hotel is a true deal considering what you get for a little over $100 for a double. The best rooms have been carved out of grand salons and are enormous; the bathrooms are clad in marble or highly polished hardwoods, with luxurious stall showers and tubs, and, like the bedrooms, lit with Venetian glass fixtures. See chapter 7.
- **Casa Verardo** (Venice; ☎ **041/52-86-127**): Hats off to the amiable Massimo and Sandra for the no-corners-cut metamorphosis of this quaint hotel around the corner from Venice's Piazza San Marco. From the moment you step inside the wood-paneled lobby, to your morning breakfast on the open-air breakfast terrace, you'll feel welcomed and relaxed. Thought and care are everywhere. All this for only $94 for a double. See chapter 8.
- **La Cascina del Monastero** (La Morra, Piedmont Wine Country; ☎ **0173/509-245**): What better way to spend your time in the wine country than to stay at a bed and breakfast at a farm that both bottles wine and harvests fruit? Housed in an converted, old, and charismatic farm building, the rooms have exposed timbers and brass beds. Doubles run for about $70. See chapter 12.
- **Albergo-Ristorante Da Cecio** (Cinque Terre, Italian Riviera; ☎ **0187/812-138**): After walking through the Cinque Terre, relax in your room at this old stone house in the countryside as you gaze out at the ocean, olive groves, and the nearby hilltop town of Corniglia. Doubles cost $47. See chapter 13.
- **Hotel Loreley et Londres** (Sorrento; ☎ **081-807-3187**): Set on a cliff top in the most central base town for exploring the entire Campania region, the Loreley retains the quirky, private home ambience and friendly family-management style that has made it a budget favorite for over 100 years. Some rooms have wraparound terrace patios, others a jumble of antiques on painted tile floors. Most have sweeping vistas of the Bay of Naples and its islands, and everyone gets to enjoy the view at the outdoor garden restaurant. Doubles cost only $77. See chapter 14.
- **Trullidea** (Alberobello, Apulia; ☎ **080/432-3860**): It isn't often you get to stay in a National Monument and UNESCO-protected heritage site, but that's what Trullidea offers: a *trullo* to call your own. This husband-and-wife company owns 10 *trulli*—unique, whitewashed cylindrical houses with the conical, drypoint stone roofs—right in the historic district of town. The interiors are peasant-simple and comfortably rustic, with rough-hewn beams across the ceiling, terra-cotta floors, modern kitchenettes, and working fireplaces. Best of all, it costs just $53 for a *trullo* and the chance to live like an Apulian for a few days. See chapter 14.
- **Gran Bretagna** (Siracusa, Sicily; ☎ **0931/68-765**): The furnishings are basic but solid and comfortable, and the family management ideal for Siracusa's only central budget inn. It's on historic Ortigia island, and from some rooms you can see the sea in both directions—or go for one of the accommodations with a frescoed ceiling. Doubles start at $50. See chapter 15.

11 The Best Rooms with a View

- **Albergo Abruzzi** (Rome; ☎ **06/679-2021**): The rooms are bare-boned and the piazza outside noisy, but all this dissolves away when you throw open your shutters to reveal the majestic portico of the ancient Pantheon a mere few dozen feet away. And what do you pay for this peerless vista and a fountain burbling beneath your window at night? A mere $75 per double. See chapter 4.

- **Hotel Torre Guelfa** (Florence; ☎ **055/2396338**). The breathtaking 360° view from this new hotel's medieval tower (hence the hotel's name) justifies beyond reasonable doubt the high end prices here. The riveting view from the tallest privately owned tower in Florence's *centro storico* is only one of many reasons to stay in this tastefully renovated landmark hotel. You can revel in a slightly less awesome view from your huge, private terrace if you're lucky enough to check into room no. 15. It's a splurge at $147 a night, but the views are worth it. See chapter 5.

- **Hotel ai do Mori** (Venice; ☎ **041/52-04-817**): The more accessible lower floors (there is no elevator and the hotel begins on the second floor with most rooms above) are slightly larger and offer interesting rooftop views, but the somewhat smaller top-floor rooms of this centrally sited hotel boast wonderful views that embrace San Marco's many domes and the nearby Torre dell'Orologio (Clock Tower) whose two bronze Moors ring the bells every hour. The atticlike top floor Artist's Room is cozy and charming, with its own private terrace and views that for $94 (for a double) beat anything offered by neighboring five-star hotels. See chapter 8.

- **Hotel Montana** (Cortina d'Ampezzo, Dolomites; ☎ **0436/862-126**. You can see a generous swath of spectacular mountain peaks from most of the cozy, paneled rooms at this pleasant Alpine-style hotel right in the center of town. Surprising in this often overpriced resort, rates start at 106,000L ($62.35) for a double and include a generous breakfast. See chapter 10.

- **Albergo Milano** (Varenna, Lake District; ☎ **0341/830-298**): The main point of coming to the Italian Lakes is enjoy the moody and romantic expanses of water backed by mountains and gardens, and the Albergo Milano offers vistas like this from all of its rooms, and some of them have large terraces hanging over the water as well. While a room with a view can come with a high price tag at the many lakeside hotels, at the homey, attractive Milano commodious, comfortable accommodations are a bargain at 175,000L ($102.95). See chapter 11.

- **Albergo Al Castello da Diego** (Novello, Piedmont Wine Country; ☎ **0173/744-011**): This Victorian castle is perched on the precipice of a summit with stunning views of the rolling vineyards and villages below. Plus, the large rooms are a delight, decorated with antiques of the claw-footed variety and equipped with bathrooms that are tucked into turrets. Many rooms have terraces, and with rates starting at 140,000L ($82.35) for a double, are very reasonably priced. See chapter 12.

- **Caesar Augustus** (Anacapri; ☎ **081/837-1421**): The Caesar Augustus is perched 1,000 vertiginous feet above the crashing surf, at the edge of a sheer cliff and the cusp of a stupendous panorama that encompasses the whole sweep of the Bay of Naples, from Ischia at the north end past Naples and Mt. Vesuvius to the Sorrentine Peninsula and the beginnings of the Amalfi Coast at the south. Doubles start at $118. See chapter 14.

- **Villa Athena** (Agrigento, Sicily; ☎ **0922/596-288**): This converted 18th-century villa is set within the confines of the "Valley of the Temples" archaeological park. From the pool, the terraced garden restaurant, and many of the rooms you get an unparalleled view, over bougainvillea and across an olive grove, of the exquisite 5th-century B.C. Temple of Concord not 2,000 feet away. You pay $147 to $176 per double for the pleasure, but you couldn't ask for a more perfectly sited room or a more romantic vista to wake up to than the world's best-preserved Greek temple framed in your window. See chapter 15.

12 The Best Affordable Hideaways by the Sea

- **Hotel del Capo** (Bordighera, Italian Riviera; ☎ **0184/261-558**): Location, location, location. The only hotel in the old city of Bordighera is stunningly located on a hilltop with views over the lower town and sea below. There always seems to be a cooling breeze here. From the balconies off the rooms, you can look up and down the coast as far as the eye can see. See chapter 13.
- **Albergo La Camogliese** (Camogli, The Riviera Levante; ☎ **0185/771-402**): Call this a hideaway by the seas. Not only is the hotel near a beach, but the owner will direct you to more hideaways along the nearby coast. This is especially convenient because this attractive hotel is also near the train station. See chapter 13.
- **Villa Eva** (Anacapri; ☎ **081/837-1549**): Eva and Vincenzo have crafted for themselves and a few lucky guests a little corner of Paradise on the famous Mediterranean's resort island of Capri. The little buildings and bungalows—with furnishings built by Vincenzo himself—are hidden amid the lush, exotic, jungle-thick vegetation and flowering vines of the Villa Eva's gardens. The sea may be a 20-minute walk away, but there is a secluded pool and bar, and Vincenzo, who knows the sea's humors better than most, may be willing to escort you down to the nearby Blue Grotto for a late-afternoon swim. See chapter 14.
- **La Tonnarella** (Sorrento; ☎ **081/878-1153**): Terraced below the quiet road leading out of town, La Tonnarella offers 19th-century ambience with 20th-century comforts. Oriental runners skip down the colorfully painted tiles of the stairs and halls, while the grounds feature pine-shaded terraces and gardens for wandering and a private beach with bar/restaurant accessible by elevator or a pretty, wooded path. Gorgeous views of the Sorrento headland and Bay of Naples spill put from most rooms and public spaces. See chapter 14.
- **Villa Rosa** (Positano; ☎ **089/811-955**): The large, echoey accommodations of this former *affittacamere* (rental rooms) are still being converted into hotel rooms, so the furnishings are spanking new. Aside from the great prices and kindly family management, the real attraction here is the view from your own bougainvillea-arbored sitting terrace across the inlet to a postcard-perfect shot of Positano's most photogenic quarter, the whitewashed and pastel cube houses climbing up the headland in a jumble of balconies and flowers. The best part is realizing that you're only paying $88 for your double but are getting a better view than the famous Hotel Sireneuse across the street for less than one-fifth the price. See chapter 14.
- **Villa Nettuno** (Taormina, Sicily; ☎ **0942/23-797**): The kindly Sciglio family have been keeping the rooms immaculate in this worn gem since 1953. It's one of the few hotels in overdeveloped Taormina that retains some of that genteel, dusty old 19th-century character and ambience, and the extensive gardens terrace fragrantly and colorfully up the hillside to some of the best vistas in town. Plus, you're right across the street from the cable car down to sparkling Mazzarò and Isola Bella beaches. See chapter 15.

13 The Best Affordable Restaurants

- **Fiaschetteria Beltramme** (Rome; no phone): This is one of the most genuine traditional trattorie in Rome, with a dark, hodgepodge decor and selection of wonderfully simple but hearty dishes that have changed little since 1886. It's like going home to your Italian Uncle Cesare's for lunch as you squeeze into a spot at the big round tables with neighborhood shopkeepers and office workers. All that and it's just 2 blocks from the Spanish Steps. See chapter 4.

- **Osteria del Caffe Italiano** (Florence; ☎ **055/289368**): The front room of this newly opened wine bar/trattoria is warmed by burnished wood paneling, and made even more welcoming with prices and hours so attractive that people stop in all day long. Housed in the stalwart 13th-century landmark Palazzo Salviati, the informal Osteria is the new brain child of Umberto Montano who proves he can do no wrong on the Florentine restaurant scene as long as he continues to think with his palate and heart. Beneath a magnificent wrought-iron chandelier hanging from the vaulted 20-foot ceiling, casual diners sample from the short and delicious lunch menu. Stop by at any time when they're not serving meals for a by-the-glass introduction to Montano's renowned wine cellar and an assortment of Tuscan *salumi* or cheeses. See chapter 5.

- **Da Giulio** (Lucca, Tuscany; ☎ **0583/55-948**): Delighted foreigners and locals of uncompromising allegiance agree that this big, airy, and forever busy trattoria is one of Tuscany's undisputed stars. Although casual, this is not the place to occupy a much-coveted table for just a pasta and salad. Save up your appetite and come for a full-blown home-style feast of *la cucina toscana,* trying all of Giulio's traditional rustic specialties. Waiters know not to recommend certain local delicacies to non-Italian diners, unless you look like the type who enjoys tripe, *tartara di cavallo* (horse meat tartare), or veal snout. See chapter 6.

- **Osteria le Logge** (Siena, Tuscany; ☎ **0577/48013**): This convivial and highly recommended Sienese trattoria is two steps off the gorgeous Piazza del Campo, a well-known destination for locals and well-informed visitors who join the standing-room-only scenario of those who keep this place packed. Its delicious *pasta fresca* (fresh homemade pasta) launches each memorable meal, with entrees that are all about the simple perfection of grilled meats. The excellent choice of extra-virgin olive oil is enough to confirm the affable owner's seriousness, seconded by a small but discerning wine list that is topped by his own limited production of Rosso and Brunello di Montepulciano. See chapter 6.

- **Olindo Facccioli** (Bologna; ☎ **051/223-171**): This intimate, inconspicuous restaurant has a limited, but delightful menu. The specials lean toward a light, vegetarian cuisine, but the starter of tuna carpaccio will satisfy fish-eaters as well. You can linger here as you decide which of the 400 vintages of wine will go best with your meal. See chapter 7.

- **Al Brindisi** (Ferrara; ☎ **0532-209-142**): This just may be the oldest wine bar in the world—it's been around since 1435. The two timbered dining rooms are stacked to the ceiling with wine bottles and for $1.75, you can choose a glass from this overwhelming selection. Have some appetizers, sausage, or pumpkin ravioli with your wine; or go for the whole shebang with the tourist menu, which includes a feast of appetizers, a special main course of the day, dessert and a carafe of wine, all for $17.95. See chapter 7.

- **Osteria dal Duca** (Verona; ☎ **045/59-44-74**): There are no written records to confirm that this 13th-century palazzo was once owned by the Montecchi (Montagues) family and, thankfully, the discreet management never considered calling this place the "Ristorante Romeo." But here you are in "fair Verona," nonetheless, dining in what is believed to be Romeo's house, a characteristic medieval palazzo, and enjoying one of the nicest meals in town in a spirited and friendly neighborhood ambience fueled by the amiable family that keeps this place always abuzz. It will be simple, it will be delicious, you'll probably make friends with the people sitting next to you, and you will always remember your meal at Romeo's Restaurant. See chapter 9.

- **Cantine Sanremese** (San Remo, Italian Riveria; ☎ **0184/572-063**): Since old habits die hard at the Cantine Sanremese, this is the place to sample traditional Ligurian cuisine. Everything is homemade. Instead of ordering main dishes, sample the *sardemaira,* the local foccacia-like bread, *torte verde* (a quiche of fresh green vegetables), or soups, including a minestrone thick with fresh vegetables and garnished with pesto. See chapter 13.

- **De Mananan** (Corniglia, Italian Riveria; ☎ **0187/821-166**): In this intimate restaurant, which is carved into an ancient stone cellar, the owners/chefs use only the finest ingredients to prepare homemade specialties such as pesto or *funghi porcini* (wild mushrooms), mussels, grilled fish, fresh anchovies stuffed with herbs, or *coniglio nostrano,* rabbit roasted in a white sauce. See chapter 13.

- **Donna Rosa** (Positano, Amalfi Coast; ☎ **089/811-806**): For gourmet food without the high prices, visit Donna Rosa in a little village halfway up the mountain from the posh Amalfi Coast resort town of Positano. The preparation, presentation, and flavors of every inventive dish are stupendous, while the atmosphere and prices remain that of a small, family trattoria, with mamma and papa laboring away under the hanging pots in the open kitchen and a trio of daughters serving tables—one of whom sits at the piano and breaks into song some evenings. See chapter 14.

- **Cucina Casareccia** (Lecce, Apulia; ☎ **0832/245-178**): Concettina Cantoro truly makes everybody feel like he's come home to her little osteria, a place of such wholesome simplicity and honest, full flavors that it comes as a shock to many—certainly it was for Signora Cantoro—that Concettina was asked to represent the entire Apulian region to a consortium of prestigious cooking schools in the United States. Let her put together a menu of her most traditional dishes—like fava beans with wild chicory or a salad of potatoes, mussels, and zucchini—and you can't go wrong, but be sure to arrive early, as many locals head here for lunch 6 days a week. See chapter 14.

- **La Forchetta** (Agrigento, Sicily; ☎ **0922/596-266**): La Forchetta is increasingly popular with the tourists, but still every inch the traditional neighborhood trattoria of yesteryear, with excellent Sicilian home cooking. Matriarch Mamma Giuseppa is a true Sicilian character, haranguing her sons/waiters out of one side of her mouth while welcoming you with a genuine sweet smile out of the other. If you're too stuffed to move after the meal, their hotel next door is by far the best budget inn in town. See chapter 15.

14 The Best Cafes

- **Tre Scalini** (Rome): Few places bother anymore to make their own *tartufi* (a gobstopper of an ice cream ball, with layers of vanilla and fudgey chocolate), preferring instead to serve the prepackaged variety. Not only does Tre Scalini craft its own *tartufo*—complete with maraschino cherry at the center—but its sidewalk tables have the most enviable position in Rome, at the center of Piazza Navona's long oval, overlooking Bernini's *Four Rivers* fountain and the carnival of life on the piazza. See chapter 4.

- **Caffè Rivoire** (Florence): The pudding-rich hot chocolate of Florence's premier historical cafe is second to the real reason for a visit: its dead-on view of the city's greatest piazza and a front-row seat for people watching is the first. The ambience is Old World inside and out: the stately Palazzo Vecchio looms in front of outdoor tables, and the piazza's most celebrated statue, a copy of Michelangelo's fabled *David.* Inside, it's cozy, elegant and no one raises an eyebrow if you nurse a tea for several hours. See chapter 5.

- **Bar Giuseppe** (Bologna): When you're tired of outdoor cafes, head underground to the Bar Giuseppe. It stretches for at least a block beneath historical arcades. And the ice cream here is pretty darn good. See chapter 7.
- **Historical Cafes of the Piazza San Marco** (Venice): The nostalgic 18th-century **Caffè Florian** is the best known of this stunning piazza, and the most famous. But the truth is, if the weather is lovely, and the other three cafes have moved their hundreds of tables outdoors, the piazza becomes one big bellini-sipping people-watching stage with St. Mark's Basilica as its singular backdrop. Around the corner, just in front of the Palazzo Ducale, is the **Cafe Chioggia,** the only cafe with a view of the water and the Watch Tower (whose bronze moors will be striking the hour in 1999 again after a 5-year renovation). Each of the piazza cafes has its own three- or four-piece **orchestrina,** but the music at the Chioggia is held to be the best and least commercial (no "New York, New York" here). See chapter 8.
- **Antico Caffè Dante** (Verona): The interior of Verona's oldest cafe is rather formal (and expensive), but set up camp here at an outdoor table in Verona's loveliest piazza, named after the early Renaissance man of letters whose statue commemorates his love for the city and ruling Scalageri family who hosted him during his years of exile from his hometown of Florence. If you're lucky enough to hold tickets for the opera in the city's 2,000-year-old Arena amphitheater, this is the traditional spot for an after-opera drink to complete, and contemplate, the evening's magic. See chapter 9.
- **Antica Pasticceria Gelateria Klainguti** (Genoa): Verdi enjoyed Genoa's oldest and best bakery. You probably will too for its *Falstaff* (a sweet brioche) and a stupefying selection of pastries and chocolates. See chapter 13.
- **Caffè Gran Gambrinus** (Naples): To recapture some of the elegance of courtly 19th-century Naples—in the company of a flaky *sfogliatella* cream-stuffed pastry—secure an outdoor table at this bastion of Neapolitan society across the street from the Royal Palace and Umberto I opera house. See chapter 14.

Getting to Know Italy 2

by Reid Bramblett & Stephen Brewer

Lord Byron called Italy his magnet; Robert Browning said Italy was engraved on his heart. Being poets, these fellows might have been given to hyperbole, but Italy does have a remarkably strong, and usually favorable, effect on visitors.

Part of the draw is Italy's cultural legacy—the country, after all, was the cradle of both ancient Rome and the Renaissance, two of the highest points of Western civilization. It is blessed with an endlessly varied and almost ridiculously seductive scenery of azure seas, silvery olive groves, stony hill towns, snow-capped mountains, and colorful fishing villages. The cuisine only seems to get better from region to region, and an enormous emphasis is placed on hospitality. Most appealing of all is the emphasis Italians place on enjoying life—from strolling through town on the evening *passaggiata* to lingering over a 3-hour dinner—and they seem determined to ensure their visitors do the same.

But Italy is not just a postcard: It has suffered its share of social and economic woes and has been riddled with political scandal. If you care to look, you'll find poverty, crime, unchecked urban development, and social injustice, just as there is in any other industrialized Western nation. But Italy offsets these realities with more grace notes than most other places manage, and in so doing rewards the traveler with a remarkable and enduring experience.

1 Regions in Brief

Italy, as we know it, was united only in the 1860s, and people still tend to identify themselves more as, say, Romans, Tuscans, or Sicilians than as Italians. Regional dialects are so diverse and strong that for a Neapolitan to converse with a Milanese, he has to resort to the common, "textbook Italian" learned in school.

PIEDMONT (*PIEMONTE*) Piedmont means "foot of the mountains," and the Alps are in sight from almost every parcel of Italy's northernmost province, which borders Switzerland and France. The flat plains of the Po River rise into rolling hills clad with orchards and vineyards. North of **Turin**—the historic, baroque capital of the region and, with its auto factories, a cornerstone of Italy's "economic miracle"—the plains meet the Alps head-on in the **Valle d'Aosta,** with its craggy mountains, craggy mountain folks, and year-round skiing.

LIGURIA   The Italian Riviera follows the Ligurian Sea along a narrow coastal band backed by mountains. At the center of this rocky coast is **Genoa,** the country's first port and still its most important—a fascinating city that greets visitors with a remarkable assemblage of Renaissance art and architecture. Some of Italy's most famous seaside retreats flank Genoa on either side: from the tony resort of **San Remo** on France's doorstep all the way down to the picturesque string of fishing villages known as the **Cinque Terre** that line the coast just above Tuscany.

LOMBARDY (LOMBARDIA)   Lombardy is Italy's wealthiest province, an industrial, financial, and agricultural powerhouse named for the Lombards, a Germanic people who migrated south over the Alps in the Dark Ages. Beyond its Po Valley factories and business cities, the scenic diversity of this prosperous region ranges from legendary lakes like **Como** and **Maggiore** backed by Alpine peaks to the fertile plains of the Po River. The region's capital, **Milan**—hotbed of high fashion, high finance, and avant-garde design—is a city of great art and architecture as well (Leonardo's *Last Supper* is but the beginning), and the region's Renaissance past is still much in evidence in **Cremona**, **Mantua**, and the other cities of the Lombard plains.

TRENTINO & THE DOLOMITES   Trentino is a region of mountains. The **Dolomites,** bordering Austria, cap the eastern stretches of the region with sharp pinnacles straight out of a fairy tale, while the peaks of the Alps crown the west. Trentino is home to legendary resorts like **Cortina d'Ampezzo** and **Merano,** as well as cities like **Trento** and **Bolzano** that lie at the crossroads of the German and Italian worlds.

VENICE & THE VENETO (VENEZIA E IL VENETO)   The Po River created the vast floodplain of the Veneto under the brow of pre-Venetian Alps to the north and the Dolomites in the west. What draws visitors to these agricultural flatlands are the art treasures of **Padua,** the Renaissance villas of **Palladio,** and—rising on pilings from a lagoon on the Adriatic coast—that year-round carnival and most serene city of canals, Venice.

EMILIA-ROMAGNA   History has left its mark on this central region riding along the north of the Appenine Mountains to the Po Valley. **Ravenna** was last capital of the empire and later the stronghold of the Byzantines and the Visigoths. **Ferrara** was a center of Renaissance art and culture, while **Parma,** one of the most powerful duchies in Europe under the Farnese family, is a famed producer of Parmigiano cheese and prosciutto ham. **Bologna** has been renowned for its university since the Middle Ages, and its fine cuisine throughout history.

TUSCANY (TOSCANA)   Beautiful, magically lit Tuscany was the cradle of the Renaissance, producing such artistic geniuses as Giotto, Leonardo, Michelangelo, and Botticelli. From the rolling vineyards of the Chianti and wide valley of the Arno River rise one wonder after another: **Florence,** capital of the Renaissance; **Siena,** city of Gothic painters and medieval palaces; **Pisa,** with its Romanesque cathedral and famously leaning tower; and dozens of other art-filled hill towns.

UMBRIA & THE MARCHES (UMBRIA E LE MARCHE)   St. Francis was born in Umbria, the green heart of Italy, and perhaps his gentle nature derived from the region's serene hills and valleys, a sun-blessed landscape similar to that of its neighbor Tuscany. The capital city of **Perugia** strikes a happy balance between medieval hill town, Renaissance art center, and bustling modern university city. Other Umbrian towns include such marvelously medieval centers as **Gubbio** and **Spoleto,** as well as that early Renaissance gem **Assisi.** The Marches borders the Adriatic and includes the ancient town of **Urbino,** birthplace of Renaissance greats Raphael and Bramante and a oft-forgotten jewel among Italy's great art cities.

The Regions of Italy

21

LATIUM *(LAZIO)* & ROME   Lazio and its capital, **Rome,** are at the center of Italy and, some say, of the Western world. Rome is where the philosophy and traditions of the ancient Greek east met the pragmatism and robust west to form one of the world's greatest empires. Rome is an intricate layering of ancient, medieval, Renaissance, baroque, and modern cities. You can scramble about the Colosseum and Forum, explore churches filled with baroque paintings by Caravaggio, gawk at Michelangelo's Sistine ceiling frescoes, or simply enjoy a gelato under the shade of a Bernini-designed fountain.

CAMPANIA   Welcome to the good life: Campania has been a refuge for the world-weary for over 2,000 years, from imperial Roman villas to modern resort towns. Campania wraps around **Naples**—that chaotic but beautiful city often overlooked on the grand tour—and is rimmed by the gorgeous **Amalfi Coast** with its necklace of comely villages: ravishing **Ravello,** historic **Amalfi,** and posh **Positano.** The seductive isle of **Capri** lies just offshore. In A.D. 79, Campania's menacing volcano Mt. Vesuvius rained tons of ash on the Roman port of **Pompeii,** preserving it as an evocative ghost town offering a unique glimpse into ancient civilization.

CALABRIA, APULIA & BASILICATA   This is the very sole of Italy, the bottom of the boot. Apulia, running the length of the boot heel, puts the lie to the "poor south" reputation of southern Italy—10% of the world's supply of olive oil comes from here, and its ports are some of the Mediterranean's busiest. The region's austerely beautiful scenery, whitewashed buildings, and serene beaches have begun attracting visitors in much larger numbers. The rocky scenery continues across Basilicata (the instep on Italy's boot) and forested Calabria (the elongated toe).

SICILY *(SICILIA)*   A mountainous triangle at the crossroads of the Mediterranean (and its largest island), Sicily sits just a few miles off the tip of Italy's toe—and only a few dozen from Tunisia, swept by both the cold *tramontana* winds from the north and the parched, sandy *scirocco* winds off the Sahara. A landscape at once fertile and foreboding, lush and harsh, Sicily has hosted every Mediterranean civilization from the Greeks and Islamic North Africans through the Spanish Bourbons to today's Italians (with the Romans, Normans, Austrians, and, yes, the Mafia, in between). The past 3,000 years have imparted upon this island of lemons, olives, and almonds a rich heritage to enjoy, from Greek temples to mosaicked Norman cathedrals, Moorish palaces to tony seaside resorts.

2 Italy Past & Present

Dateline

- Prehistory Neanderthal humans roam Italy; around 10,000 B.C., Cro-Magnon shows up.
- 1200 B.C. Etruscans begin to emigrate from Asia Minor, settling in Tuscany.
- 800 B.C. Greeks colonize Sicily and the peninsula's boot (collectively "Magna Graecia").
- 753 B.C. Romulus, says legend, founds Rome. In

continues

In its 3,000 years of history, Italy has endured emperors and kings, duchies and despots, fools and knaves, popes and presidents. Italy has been a definer of democracy, has fallen prey to dictators, and has sagged into anarchy. Italy knows triumph, and it knows loss, but above all, it knows how to survive.

PREHISTORY   Findings in caves around Isneria in the Abruzzi suggest that humans settled in Italy about a million years ago. Neanderthal man made a brief appearance, and Cro-Magnon, who knew how to fish and domesticate animals, showed up about 18,000 years ago.

MAGNA GRAECIA   *Magna Graecia,* "Greater Greece," describes Greek colonies established beginning in the 8th century B.C. in Sicily and on the mainland from Apulia northwest to Naples. The coastal land, never tilled, quickly turned out bumper crops. Abundant timber and wool production underpinned highly profitable trading. But these successful colonies fell to warring amongst themselves, and by the 4th century B.C. Greece was a fading influence in southern Italy. The best evidence of Magna Graecia exists in the temples at Paestum (in Campania), Agrigento, Segesta, and Selinute (all in Sicily), and amid the artifacts at the archeological museums of Paestum, Siracusa (in Sicily), and Crotone and Reggio di Calabria (both in Calabria).

THE ETRUSCAN ENIGMA The Etruscans were an innovative and influential people who settled primarily in what is today Tuscany, Umbria, and northern Lazio. Despite the great deal of excavated physical evidence we have, little is known about the origins of the Etruscans. The great Roman historian Herodotus (corroborated by most modern-day researchers), wrote that the Etruscans filtered into the Italian peninsula, probably from Asia Minor, as early as the 12th century B.C.

By the 8th century, there was a clearly delineated Etruscan culture, which reached a peak of power and wealth in the 6th century B.C. with the Tarquin dynasty, which ruled Rome itself (later to be ejected). Savaged by the Gauls (Celtic peoples from present-day France), the Etruscans began lose power. Their cities were slowly defeated and absorbed into the growing Roman Republic during the 1st century B.C.

The Etruscan political hegemony extended over Etruria (a loose association of city-states that were connected along religious rather than political lines). Key centers were such modern-day locations as Chiusi and Cortona in Tuscany, Cerveteri and Tarquinia north of Rome, Veio near Rome, and Orvieto and Perugia in Umbria. Etruscan artifacts are displayed in museums in Chiusi, Volterra, Florence, and Cortona; tombs at Tarquinia, Cerveteri, Veio, Cortona, and Chiusi; and the Etruscan walls and gateways preserved at Volterra and Perugia.

The Etruscans were highly skilled artisans who worked not only iron but also bronze, silver, copper, and gold. Etruscan potters threw handsome black *bucchero* vases with bas-relief figures, and later adopted Greek fashions to produce fine painted vessels. They were adept engineers, constructing walled cities astride hilltops and sophisticated canal systems that drained the enormous swampy lowlands of southern Tuscany and turned them into a

fact, Rome grows out of a strategically located shepherd village.

- **700 B.C.** Etruscans rise in power, peaking in the sixth century, and make Rome their capital.
- **509 B.C.** Republic of Rome is founded; power is shared by two consuls.
- **494–450 B.C.** Office of the Tribune established to defend plebeian rights. The Twelve Tablets stating basic rights are carved, the foundation of Roman law.
- **279 B.C.** Romans now rule all of the Italian peninsula.
- **146 B.C.** Rome defeats Tunisian power Carthage; the Republic now controls Sicily, North Africa, Spain, Sardinia, Greece, and Macedonia.
- **100 B.C.** Julius Caesar born.
- **60 B.C.** Caesar, Pompey, and Crassus share power in the First Triumvirate.
- **51 B.C.** Caesar triumphs over Gaul (France).
- **44 B.C.** March 15, Caesar assassinated, leaving all to his nephew and heir, Octavian.
- **27 B.C.** Octavian, now Augustus, is declared emperor, beginning Roman Empire and 200 years of peace and prosperity.
- **A.D. 29 (or 33)** Jesus is crucified in Roman province of Judea.
- **64–100** Nero persecutes Christians; a succession of military commanders restore order; Trajan expands the empire.
- **200** Goths invade from the north; the empire begins to decline.
- **313** With the Edict of Milan, Emperor Constantine I declares Christianity the official religion, establishes Constantinople as eastern

continues

- **476** Fall of the Roman Empire; the Dark Ages begin.
- **Late 6th century** Lombards sweep through much of Italy.
- **600–675** Church asserts political control as Pope Gregory I brings some stability to the peninsula.
- **774–800** Frankish king Charlemagne invades Italy, and is crowned emperor by Pope Leo III. Upon his death, Italy dissolves into a series of small warring kingdoms.
- **962** Holy Roman Empire founded under Otto I, king of Saxony; serves as the temporal arm of the church's spiritual power.
- **11th-century** Normans conquer southern Italy, introduce feudalism. The first Crusades are launched.
- **1309–77** Papacy abandons Rome for Avignon, France.
- **1350** The Black Death decimates Europe, reducing Italy's population by a third.
- **1450** City-states hold power; Venice controls much of the eastern Mediterranean. The Humanist movement rediscovers the art and philosophy of ancient Greece and gives rise to the artistic Renaissance.
- **1500** Peak of the High Renaissance. Brunelleschi's dome caps Florence's Duomo. Leonardo da Vinci completes *The Last Supper.* Lorenzo "The Magnificent" de' Medici (1449–92) of Florence becomes patron of artists like Michelangelo.
- **1508** Michelangelo begins the Sistine Chapel ceiling.
- **1550** Carlos I of Spain is crowned Holy Roman Emperor as Charles V; wages

continues

capital, splitting the empire in half.

breadbasket. The Etruscans also introduced that eventual favored vehicle of Ben-Hur, the chariot.

THE RISE OF ROME   Leaving aside the famous legend of a she-wolf nursing the abandoned twins Romulus and Remus (the former kills his brother and founds a village called Rome), and Virgil's *Aeneid* (Aeneas of Troy flees the burning city at the end of the Trojan War, makes his way to Romulus's little village, and turns it into an ancient superpower), Rome probably began as a collection of Latin and Sabine villages in the Tiber Valley. Rome was originally a **kingdom** ruled by the Etruscan Tarquin dynasty. In 509 B.C., the last Tarquin king raped the daughter of a powerful Roman. After the girl committed suicide, infuriated Romans ejected the king and established a **republic** ruled by two consuls (chosen from among the patrician elite), whose power was balanced by tribunes elected from among the plebian masses.

The young Roman Republic sent its military throughout the peninsula, and by 279 B.C. ruled all of Italy. Rome's armies trampled Grecian colonies throughout the Mediterranean, and after a series of brutal wars defeated Carthage (present-day Tunisia), a rival sea power and once Rome's archenemy. By 146 B.C., Rome controlled not only all of the Italian peninsula and Sicily, but also North Africa, Spain, Sardinia, Greece, and Macedonia.

Still, Rome wanted more. It invaded Gaulish lands to the north and added what we now call France and Belgium to its realm. Rome even crossed the English Channel and conquered Britain all the way up to the Scottish Lowlands (Hadrian's Wall still stands as a testament to how far north the Roman army got). However, so much military success so distant from Rome itself resulted in a severely weakened home front. With war booty filling the coffers, Rome ended taxation on its citizens. So much grain poured in from North Africa that the Roman farmer couldn't find a market for his wheat and simply stopped growing it. The booty had an additional price tag: corruption. Senators advanced their own lots rather than the provinces ostensibly under their care. Plebeians clamored for a bigger share, and the slaves revolted repeatedly. More reforms appeased the plebes while the slaves were put down with horrific barbarity.

HAIL CAESAR!   At the end of the 2nd century B.C., the Republic, sped along by a corrupt Senate, was corroding into near-collapse. Julius Caesar—successful general, skilled orator, and shrewd politician—stepped in to help maintain control over Rome's vast territories, but from the day Caesar declared himself "dictator for life," Rome, as a Republic, was finished. After sharing governmental power with others in a series of Triumverates, Caesar became the sole Consul in 44 B.C.

Caesar rose in popular influence partly by endearing himself to the lower classes though a life-long fight against the corrupt Senate. As his power crested, he forced many immoral senators to flee Rome, introduced social reforms, inaugurated the first of many new public building programs in the center of Rome (still visible as the Forum of Caesar), and added Gaul (France) to the dying Republic. But Caesar's emphasis on the plebians and their concerns (as well as his own thirst for power) did little to endear him to the old guard of patricians and senators. On March 15, 44 B.C., Caesar strolled out of the Baths of Pompey to meet Brutus, Cassius, and other "friends" who lay in wait with daggers hidden beneath their togas.

Caesar left everything to his nephew and heir, the 18-year-old Octavian. From the increasingly irrelevant Senate, Octavian eventually received the title *Augustus,* and from the people, lifetime tribuneship. And so Octavian became Emperor Augustus, sole ruler of Rome and most of the Western world.

THE EMPIRE Augustus' long reign ushered in *Pax Romana,* 200 years of peace under Roman rule. The new emperor, who preferred to be called "First Citizen," reorganized the military and the provincial governments, and reinstituted constitutional rule. Succeeding emperors were not so virtuous: Deranged Caligula, henpecked Claudius I, and Nero, who in A.D. 64 persecuted the Christians of Rome with a viciousness easily equal to the earlier slave repressions. Several of the military commanders who became emperors were exceptions to the tyrant mold. Late in the 1st century, Trajan expanded the empire's eastern boundaries and constructed great public works, including a vast series of markets (recently reopened to visitors in Rome).

At this peak, Rome knew amenities not to be enjoyed again in Europe until the 18th century. Citizens were privileged to have police protection, fire fighting, libraries, sanitation, huge public baths such as the Caracalla by the Appian Way, and even central heating and running water—if they could afford them.

The empire's decline began around A.D. 200. After sacking the city several times, Goths and other Germanic tribes set up their own leaders as emperors, and were more interested in the spoils of an empire than

war against Pope and Italian princes and city-states, occupying nearly all of Italy.

- **18th-century** Italy's darkest hour: brigands control the countryside, the Austrians and Spanish everything else.

- **1784** The French Revolution sparks Italian nationalism.

- **1796–1814** Napoléon sweeps through Italy, installing friends and relatives as rulers.

- **1814** Napoléon's defeat at Waterloo.

- **1830** Beginning of the *Risorgimento* national political movement and a new renaissance of literature and music.

- **1861** Kingdom of Italy is created under Vittorio Emmanuele II, Savoy king of Piemonte, and united through the military campaign of General Garibaldi. Turin and Florence both serve as interim capitals.

- **1870** Rome, last papal stronghold, falls to Garibaldi, and the city is declared Italy's capital.

- **Late 19th century** Mass emigration to America and other foreign shores, mostly from the impoverished, agricultural south.

- **1915** Italy enters World War I on Allied side.

- **1922** Mussolini marches on Rome and puts his Fascist Blackshirts in charge of the country, declaring himself prime minister.

- **1935** Mussolini defeats and annexes Ethiopia.

- **1939** Italy enters the war by signing an alliance with Nazi Germany.

- **1943** Italy switches sides as Allied troops push Nazis north up peninsula; by 1945, Mussolini and mistress executed by partisans.

continues

- 1946 A national referendum narrowly establishes the Republic of Italy.
- 1950–93 Fifty changes of government, yes, but also the "economic miracle" that has made Italy the world's fifth leading economy.
- 1993–99 Italy's Christian Democrat–controlled government dissolves amid corruption allegations. Silvio Berlusconi's right-wing coalition holds power for a few months, followed by center–left wing coalitions that introduce the most stable governments in decades under Prime Ministers Romano Prodi, then Massimo d'Alema.
- 1993–97 Series of disasters rock Italy's cultural roots: 1993 Mafia bombing of Uffizi Galleries, January 1996 fire at Venice's La Fenice opera; April 1997 conflagration in Turin's cathedral; September 1997 earthquakes in Umbria, which destroyed priceless frescoes in Assisi.

in actually running one. And while Gibbon's famous opus *The Decline and Fall of the Roman Empire* takes up an entire bookshelf to explain Rome's downfall, in the end it all boils down to the fact that the empire had gotten just too darn big to manage.

After embracing **Christianity** in his famous 313 Edict of Milan, Emperor Constantine I tried to resolve the problem by moving the capital of the empire from Rome to the city of Byzantium (later to be renamed Constantinople, and today known as Istanbul). The Roman empire was irrevocably split in half: a western Roman Empire comprising most of Europe and North Africa, and an eastern Roman Empire filling southeast Europe and the Near East.

CURTAIN GOING DOWN: THE DARK AGES
In 476, the last emperor (ironically, named Romulus) fell from power and the Roman Empire collapsed. It would be 1,500 years before Rome and Italy were once again united as capital and nation. As the 6th century opened, Italy was in chaos. Waves of barbarians from the north poured in while provincial nobles engaged in petty bickering and Rome became the personal fiefdom of the papacy. The Goths continued to rule nominally from Ravenna, but were soon driven out by Constantinople.

It was the Roman Catholic Church, beginning with Pope Gregory I late in the 6th century, that finally provided some stability. In 731, Pope Gregory II renounced Rome's nominal dependence on Constantinople and reoriented the Roman Catholic Church firmly toward Europe—in the process finalizing the empire's division into east and west.

During the **Middle Ages,** northern Italy fragmented into a collection of city-states. The papacy's temporal power shrunk considerably (mainly encompassing only Rome and its province), and its political concerns turned to arguing with the German (Gothic) emperors over the increasingly irrelevant office of Holy Roman Emperor. The southern half of the country went a different road when, in the 11th century, the Normans invaded southern Italy, wresting control from the local strongmen and, in Sicily, the Muslim Saracens who had occupied the region throughout the dark ages. To the south, the Normans introduced feudalism, a repressive social system that discouraged individual economic initiative, and the legacy of which accounts in large part for the social and economic differences between north and south that have continued into the 21st century.

In the mid–14th century the Black Death ravaged Europe, killing a third of Italy's population. Despite such setbacks, northern Italian cities grew wealthy from Crusade booty, trade with one another and with the Middle East, and banking. These wealthy principalities and pseudorepublics ruled by the merchant elite flexed their muscles in the absence of a strong central authority.

CURTAIN GOING UP: THE RENAISSANCE The Renaissance peaked in the 15th century as northern cities bullied their way to city-state status. Even while warring constantly with one another to extend their territories, such ruling families as the Medici in Florence, the d'Este in Ferrara, and the Gonzaga in Milan grew incredibly rich and powerful.

The princes, popes, and merchant princes who ruled Italy's city-states, spurred on by the Humanist philosophical movement, collectively bankrolled the explosion of poetic and artistic expression we now call the Renaissance (see the section on art and architecture below). But with no clear political authority or unified military, Italy was easy pickings and by the mid–16th century, Spain, courtesy of Charles V, occupied nearly all of the country.

THE SECOND FALL   From the mid–16th century until the end of the 18th century Italy suffered economic depression and foreign domination. As emphasis on world trade shifted away from the Mediterranean, Italy's influence diminished. Within Italy itself Spanish Bourbons controlled the duchies of the south, while Austria ruled those of the north. These foreign overlords kept raising taxes, farming declined, the birthrate sank, and bandits proliferated. The 18th century is viewed as Italy's nadir. In fact, only Europe's eager ear for Italian music and eye for art and architecture kept the Italian profile haughty and its cultural patrimony resplendent.

It was the late-18th-century French Revolution and the arrival of Napoléon that lit Italy's nationalistic fire, although it would be the mid–19th century before the *Risorgimento* movement and a new king could spread the flame.

THE SECOND RISE: THE 19TH CENTURY   Italians initially gave Napoléon an exultant *ciao* when he swept through the peninsula and swept out Italy's 18th-century political disasters (along with the Austrian army). But Napoléon, in the end, neither united Italy nor provided it with self-government—he merely set up his own friends and relatives as new princes and dukes. Many Italians, however, were fired up by the Napoleonic revolutionary rhetoric. The *Risorgimento* ("resurgence") nationalist movement—an odd amalgam of radicals, moderate liberals, and Roman Catholic conservatives—struggled for 30 years to create a single, united Italy under a constitutional monarchy.

You'll find *Risorgimento* heroes' names recalled in streets and piazze throughout Italy: Giuseppe Mazzini provided the intellectual rigor for the movement; the political genius of noble-born Camillo Cavour engineered the underpinnings of the new nation; and Gen. Giusseppe Garibaldi and his "Redshirts" soldiers did the legwork by conquering reluctant or foreign-controlled territories. In 1861, Vittorio Emanuele II, of the Piedmont House of Savoy, became the first King of Italy. By 1871, Garibaldi finally defeated the papal holdout of Rome and the great city once again became capital of a unified Italy.

FINALLY, A NATION UNITED   A united nation? On paper, yes, but the old sectional differences remained. While there was rapid industrialization in the north, the south labored under the repressive neofeudal agricultural ways of the late 19th century. Many southerners escaped economic hardship and political powerlessness by emigrating to the industrialized north, or to greener pastures abroad in America, South America, or northern Europe.

Italy entered World War I on the Allied side in exchange for territorial demands, and to vanquish that old foe, Austria. In the end the Austrian-Hungarian Empire was defeated, but at the Paris Peace Conference, Italy was granted much less territory than had been promised (though it did receive Trieste), which compounded the country's problems. As southerners abandoned the country in droves, the economy stagnated, and what remained of Italy's world importance seemed to be fading rapidly, along came Benito Mussolini, promising to restore national pride and bring order out of the chaos.

FASCISM REIGNS   Mussolini marched on Rome in 1922, forced the king to make him premier, nicknamed himself *Il Duce* (The Duke), and quickly repressed all other political factions. He put his Fascists "Blackshirts" in charge of the entire country: schools, the press, industry, and labor. Seeking, as Italian despot-hopefuls throughout history have done, to endear himself to the general populace, Mussolini instituted a vast public works program, most of which eventually failed. Mussolini fancied himself a second Caesar, and spent some time excavating the archaeological remains of ancient Rome—not always with the most stringent scientific methods—to help glorify his reign and lend it authority. The Great Depression of the 1930s made life considerably more difficult for Italians, and, to divert attention from his shortcomings as a ruler, Mussolini turned to foreign adventures, defeating and annexing Ethiopia in 1935.

Mussolini entered Italy into World War II as an Axis ally of the Nazis, but the Italian heart was not really in the war, and most Italians had little wish to pursue Hitler's anti-Semitic policies. Armed partisan resistance to the official government forces and to the Nazis remained strong. By 1945, the Italian people had had enough. They rose against Mussolini and the Axis, and the Fascists were disbanded. King Victor Emmanuel III, who had collaborated with the Fascists without much enthusiasm during the past two decades, appointed a new premier. At the end of the war Mussolini and his mistress were pictured in the world press hanging by their heels at a Milanese gas station after being shot by partisans.

DEMOCRACY AT LAST   After the war Italians narrowly voted to be a republic, and in 1946 a new republican constitution went into effect. Various permutations of the center-right Christian Democrat party ruled in a succession of more than 50 governments until 1993, when the entire government dissolved in a flurry of corruption and graft. The country's leaders were prosecuted (and many jailed) by what became known as the "Clean Hands" judges of Milan. The two main parties, the Christian Democrats and the Communists, both splintered in the aftermath, giving rise to some 16 major political parties and countless minor ones. The parties formed various coalitions, leading to such strange political bedfellows as the Forza Italia alliance, headed by media mogul Silvio Berlusconi, which filled the national power vacuum during 1994. It included both the nationalist *Alleanza Nazionale* party (the modern incarnation of the Fascist party) and the *Lega del Nord,* the separatist "Northern League," which wants to split Italy in half, making Milan capital of a new country in the north called "Padania," and leaving Rome to govern the poor south.

In 1994, the center-left Olive Tree coalition swept the national elections and Italy enjoyed a novelty: 3 years of stable rule under the government of Prime Minister Romano Prodi, recently replaced by a center-left government of Massimo D'Alema. Interestingly, given the stereotype among fellow Europeans of Italy as a nation prone to graft and political chaos, Prodi—an economist before becoming prime minister and the man who reigned in Italy's debt to qualify the country for the European economic union—was recently named to head the European Commission.

Politically, though, some things never change in Italy. The same mistrust among factions continues: cities are still paranoid about their individuality and their rights, and the division between north and south is as sharp as ever. The Mafia had by the late 19th century become a kind of shadow government in the south, and to this day controls a staggering number of politicians, national officials, even judges, providing one scandal after another. Even powerful Christian Democrat and senator-for-life Giulio Andreotti, who served seven terms as prime minister, was sentenced to 12 years in prison for corruption and Mafia collusion as this book went to press (though, given Italy's odd laws that exempt government officials from serving jail terms, it's unlikely Andreotti will ever actually end up behind bars).

Economically, it's a different story. The "economic miracle" of the north has worked around the political chaos (and often has even taken advantage of it) to make Italy the world's fifth largest economy. Even the south, while continuing to lag behind, is not in the desperate straits it once was.

The outsider looks and wonders how the country keeps going amid the political chaos, Byzantine bureaucracy, and deep regional differences. The Italian just shrugs and rolls his eyes. Italians have always excelled at getting by under difficult circumstances, and making the most of any situation. If nothing else, they're masters at survival.

3 Italy's Artistic Heritage

When you mention art in Italy, most people's thoughts fly first to the Renaissance, to Giotto, Donatello, Michelangelo, Raphael, and Leonardo. But Italy's artistic heritage actually goes back at least 2,500 years.

ARTS, ARTISTS & ARCHITECTS

ROME & THE ARTS   Today all, or almost all, design roads lead to Milan. In the beginning, though, all roads led from Athens. What the Greeks identified early on that captured the hearts and minds of so many others was classical rendering of form. To the ancients, "classic" or "classical" simply meant perfection—of proportion, balance, harmony, and form. To the Greeks, man was the measure of perfection, an attitude lost in the Middle Ages, and not rediscovered until the dawn of the Renaissance.

Although those early tourists to the Italian peninsula, the Etruscans, arrived with their own styles, by the 6th century B.C. they were borrowing heavily from the Greeks in their sculpture (and importing thousands of Attic painted vases). The Romans, in turn, made use of certain Greek innovations, particularly architectural ideas. The first to be adopted was post-and-lintel construction—essentially, a weight-bearing frame, like a door. Later came adaptation of Greek columns for supporting buildings, following the Classical orders of Doric column capitals (the plain ones) on the ground floor, Ionic capitals (with the scrolls on either end) on the next level, and Corinthian capitals (flowering with acanthus leaves) on the top.

Romans thrived on huge, complex problems for which they could produce organized, well-crafted solutions. Roman builders became inventive engineers, developing hoisting mechanisms and a specially trained workforce. They designed towns, built civic centers, raised grand temples and public baths, and developed the *basilica,* a rectangle supported by arches atop columns along both sides of the interior, and with an apse at one or both ends. Basilicas were used for courts of justice, banking, and other commercial structures. The design was repeated all over the Roman world, beginning around the 1st century A.D. Later, early Christians adapted the architectural style for the first grand churches, still called "basilicas."

Although marble is traditionally associated with Roman architecture, Roman engineers could also do wonders with bricks or even prosaic concrete, as still evident in Rome at the public baths of Caracalla, the Pantheon, and the Basilica of Maxentius. Concrete seating made possible such enormous theaters as Rome's 6-acre, 45,000-seat Colosseum.

Although painting got rather short shrift in ancient Rome (it was used primarily for decorative purposes) bucolic *frescoes,* the technique of painting on wet plaster, adorned the walls of the wealthy in Rome. Some of the best preserved of these frescoes are now on display in the new Museo Nazionale Romano (Palazzo Massimo in Rome) and at Pompeii (in the Villa dei Misteri).

Great Examples of Italian Art & Architecture

Architecture

- Ancient: Colosseum, Rome (late 1st century A.D.); Public arena sporting Classical order.
- Ancient: Pantheon, Rome (1st century B.C.); Hadrian's mathematically precise domed temple; considered the most architecturally significant Roman building.
- Ancient: Basilica of Maxentius in the Roman Forum (4th century A.D.); Basilican style originally used for law courts, adapted by Christians for churches.
- Ancient: Baths of Caracalla, Rome (3rd century A.D.); Public baths in an enormous brick and concrete structure.
- Ancient: Pompeii (1st century A.D.); Best intact example of Romans' exacting urban layout.
- Romanesque: Basilica of S. Ambrogio, Milan (11th–12th century).
- Romanesque: Pisa's Cathedral (11th–12th century).
- Gothic: Milan's cathedral (late 14th century).
- Renaissance: Palladio's Villa Rotunda, Vicenza (1570).
- Renaissance: Farnese Palace, Rome; completed by Michelangelo (1566).
- Baroque: Borromini's Sant'Ivo alla Sapienza, Rome (1640s).

Paintings, frescoes & sculptures

- Roman: marble bas-relief on the Arch of Constantine, Rome (1st century A.D.).
- Roman: sculpture and mosaic collections at the new Museo Nazionale Romano, Rome.
- Early Renaissance: Giotto, fresco cycles in Assisi's Basilica di San Francesco, and in Padua's Scrovegni (Arena) Chapel (late 13th/early 14th century).
- Early Renaissance: Masaccio, frescoes in Brancacci Chapel, Santa Maria del Carmine, Florence (1427).
- Early Renaissance: Botticelli, *The Birth of Venus*, Uffizi Gallery, Florence (1480).
- High Renaissance: Leonardo da Vinci, *Annunciation*, Uffizi Gallery, Florence (1481).
- High Renaissance: Raphael, *Pope Leo X and His Nephews Giulio de' Medici and Luigi de' Rossi*, Uffizi Gallery, Florence (1518).
- High Renaissance: Michelangelo, *Moses* statue, San Pietro in Vincoli, Rome (1513).
- Baroque: Caravaggio, *The Calling of St. Matthew*, San Luigi dei Francesi, Rome (1599).
- Baroque: Pietro da Cortona, *Glorification of the Reign of Urban VIII*, ceiling fresco, Palazzo Barberini, Rome (1635).
- Baroque: Bernini, *Fountain of the Four Rivers*, in Piazza Navona; sculptures in Galleria Borghese, Rome (1613–51).

Sculpture, so much more useful for aggrandizing, is another story. Regrettably, the Roman aesthetic was quite unadventurous, happily adapting Greek styles into original designs, but also setting up sculpture factories that churned out endless clones of Grecian classics. Bronze portraiture, a technique with both Greek and Etruscan roots, was polished to photographic perfection; the majestic, gilded equestrian statue of Marcus Aurelius in Rome's Capitoline Museums is a late, but excellent example.

ROMANESQUE, BYZANTINE & GOTHIC   When Pope Gregory the Great's strong hand brought some stability to Italy late in the 6th century, the rise of Catholicism created a demand for construction of new churches and cathedrals. The builders turned to the basilican form and the resultant style, called Romanesque, recalled the ancient building style of Rome. The word describes an architecture heavy and solid, with rounded arches—as opposed to the Gothic style whose spires would later thrust dramatically into the skies of France and Germany (and in Milan's Duomo). For an example of northern, or Tuscan, Romanesque, visit Pisa's cathedral buildings, with their stacked arcades of mismatched columns in the cathedral's facade and wrapping around the famous leaning cylindrical bell tower.

During the Dark Ages and early Middle Ages, painting languished under eastern, Byzantine traditions, which reproduced stylized Madonna and Child and Crucifixion paintings that remained eerily unchanged for centuries. In sculpture, the idiosyncratic Byzantine style gave way to the emotive Gothic carvings exemplified by the **Pisano** clan and their pulpits in Siena and Pisa cathedrals (and in the latter city's baptistery as well).

THE RENAISSANCE   From the 14th to 16th centuries, the popularity of the Humanist movement in philosophy prompted princes and powerful prelates to patronize a generation of innovative young artists. These painters, sculptors, and architects were experimenting with new modes in art and breaking with static medieval traditions to pursue a greater degree of expressiveness and naturalism. The term "Renaissance" was only later applied to this period in Florence (from which the movement spread to the rest of Italy and Europe).

The Renaissance also inspired a rediscovery and renewal of classical Greek and Latin literature and art, and a revitalized interest in exploring man's capabilities. To most of us since then, "Renaissance" has become a label for an era of explosion in science (Galileo), exploration (Columbus, among many others), politics (Machiavelli), religion (the growth of monastic orders in Italy and the Protestants in northern countries), and, most vividly, the arts.

Giotto, in the 1290s and early 1300s, charted a radical course change in Italian, and indeed all, painting when he insisted on rendering the human figure and face with life and warmth in his frescoes in Assisi's Basilica of San Francesco and Padua's Scrovegni (Arena) Chapel. It was probably an architect, **Filippo Brunelleschi,** in the early 1400s, who first truly grasped the concept of "perspective," and provided artists with ground rules for creating the illusion of three dimensions on a flat surface. Brunelleschi built Florence's Pazzi Chapel, the church of Santo Spirito, and, most famously, raised the dome over Florence's Duomo. His theories helped his contemporaries **Donatello** and **Ghiberti.** These sculptors achieved wonderful effects by using the nascent rules of perspective to produce evocative low reliefs. **Massacio,** who died at 27, drew upon Brunelleschi's findings to produce the first example of painted perspective in his *Trinità* fresco in Florence's Santa Maria Novella, as well as the famous fresco cycle in the Brancacci Chapel of Florence's Santa Maria della Carmine.

The High Renaissance of the late 15th and early 16th centuries lasted for only about 25 years. It was driven and dominated by the triumvirate of Michelangelo, Leonardo da Vinci, and Raphael, as each tried to outdo the other (Michelangelo claiming the other two were stealing his ideas, which in the case of the older Leonardo was a bit silly, but in the case of young Raphael probably wasn't far-fetched). **Raphael,** considered Western art's greatest draftsman, produced a body of work in his 37 short years that ignited European painters for generations to come. **Leonardo da Vinci** was a true "Renaissance Man," dabbling his genius in a bit of everything from art to philosophy to science (on paper, he even designed machine guns and rudimentary helicopters). Little of his remarkable painting survives, however, as he often experimented with new pigment mixes that proved to lack the staying power of traditional materials. Leonardo invented such painterly effects as the fine haze of *sfumato,* "a moisture-laden atmosphere that delicately veils . . . forms." Unfortunately, the best example of this effect, his fresco of *The Last Supper* in Milan, is sadly deteriorated, and even the ongoing multidecade restoration is saving but a shadow of the fresco's glory. See his early *Annunciation* in Florence's Uffizi Galleries for a better-preserved example.

Pope Julius II both funded **Michelangelo** and drove him to despair. Michelangelo's artistic focus was on the human figure, and he devoutly believed that sculpture was the only true expression of that belief, as he showed in his 13-foot *David* in Florence. Though he originally trained as a frescoist before turning to the chisel and marble, he tried everything to void the contract when Julius II ordered him to decorate the Sistine Chapel with paintings. Luckily for us, Michelangelo decided to give the commission his best, and the product influenced an entire generation of painters, inspiring Raphael to new heights and giving rise to the hyperstylized mannerist movement.

The peculiar coincidence of circumstances of the High Renaissance in Italy—the combined force of available money, a philosophy that stated that certain artists had a God-granted genius, and, of course, the spectacular talents of those geniuses—were never to be repeated. The next couple of hundred years brought little but variations on Renaissance themes. The late 16th-century *chiaroscuro* style of **Caravaggio** differed mainly in his insistence on working in a more realistic mode. His paintings reflect, with their renderings of the common man in dramatic contrasts of dark and light, his street-fighter origins.

By the mid–16th century Charles V of Spain occupied much of Italy. The Spanish laid the Inquisition on full bore and decreed that art was to serve the church alone. While there were indeed talented baroque artists, their heavy religious themes dominate any minor innovations they might have introduced to Italian art.

ON TO THE 20TH CENTURY   By the early 17th century, baroque (one definition says *baroque* is derived from the Portuguese word for "irregular, oversized pearl") influence was creeping in. Baroque architects, including Bernini and Maderno (who completed St. Peter's) were the pathfinders in European architecture for the next 150 years.

Except for a few rococo (baroque gone awry) architectural designs—de Sancticis' Spanish Steps (1726), and Salvi's Trevi Fountain (1762)—the 18th to the 20th centuries comprised one long decline in Italian painting, sculpture, and architecture. By the 19th century Italy had become a learning facility for eager students from all over the world who wanted to learn from the great masters, but Italy made few artistic innovations. In the early 20th century, Italian futurism, in its brief life, directly influenced cubism. Painters Modigliani and de Chirico drew international attention. Modigliani painted undulating, languorous figures, while Giorgio de Chirico, who called his work "metaphysical painting," inspired the early surrealists. In recent years, architect Pier Luigi Nervi has designed significant buildings, including his Exhibition Hall in Turin.

Today the Italian eye focuses, profitably for sure, on high fashion (Gucci, Armani, Versace, Ferragamo, Valentino), graphics, and industrial design (from Ferraris to whimsical Alessi coffee pots).

ITALY'S MUSIC

In the 14th century, Italy's music swept Europe. The country was an innovator in medieval music—**St. Ambrose,** Bishop of Milan in the 4th century, introduced to the

---

Andrea Palladio—Father of Neoclassicism

Order, balance, elegance, harmony with the landscape, and a human scale are all apparent in the creations of architect Andrea Palladio (1508–80). Palladio was working as a stonemason and sculptor when, at 30, inspired by the design of ancient buildings he studied on trips to Rome, he turned his hand to architecture and applied the principles of classical proportion to Renaissance ideals of grace, symmetry, and functionality. Vicenza, the little city near Venice where Palladio lived as a boy and where he returned in his prime, is graced with many Palladian palazzi and a church as well as his Teatro Olympico. In Venice, he designed the churches of San Giorgio Maggiore and Redentore.

Palladio is best known, though, for the villas he built on the flat plains of the Veneto for Venetian nobles yearning to escape the cramped city. Nineteen of these villas still stand, including what may be his finest, **La Rotunda,** outside Vicenza. The design of this and Palladio's other villas—square, perfectly proportioned, elegant yet functional—may well strike a note of familiarity with American and British visitors: Palladio influenced generations of architects who followed his lead when they designed neoclassical plantation houses in the American South and country estates in England.

---

church the custom of singing liturgical chants. In the 12th century, **Guido d' Arezzo** developed the basis of the musical notation that we use today. Blind **Francesco Landini** introduced sophisticated, varied rhythms. And in the mid–16th century, the first violin appeared. **Stradivari,** who learned his craft under the great master **Amati,** achieved a standard in violin design never improved upon.

Poets, who wanted a closer relationship between word and music, got their wish by the late 16th century. Until then, music had been but an incidental element in various entertainments, but a group in Florence wanted to adapt Greek drama, which they believed had been sung throughout, to a new kind of "musical drama." It came to be called "opera," a new form that caught on fast. The first great composer of opera was **Monteverdi,** of *Orfeo* fame, who is enjoying a new popularity today. Monteverdi managed to "translate human suffering into sound," lighting the way for succeeding generations of Italian composers.

Since Venice opened the first public opera house in 1637, it has continued to promote both operatic composers and productions. Venice's preeminent composer in the early 18th century was **Antonio Vivaldi,** who wrote more than 40 operas. The prolific **Scarlatti** (known mainly for his instrumental music), was also a composer of opera, turning out more than 100 in an exuberant, rococo style. It's also possible that Scarlatti played some of his music on **Bartolomeo Cristofori**'s 1709 invention the *pianoforte,* forerunner of the modern piano.

Italy has produced many fine composers, but **Giuseppe Verdi** was the unquestioned operatic master of the 19th century. Verdi, son of an innkeeper, understood dramatic form, wrote exquisite melodies, and his musicianship was unsurpassed. He achieved success early on with his third opera, *Nabucco,* a huge hit, then turned out *Rigiletto, Il Trovatore, Un Ballo in Maschera,* and *Aïda*—works that remain popular today. His powers continued unchecked as he grew older, maturing musically with such works as *Don Carlo* and his great *Otello* (written when the master was 73). At 80 years old he astonished the musical world with *Falstaff,* a masterpiece in *opera buffa* form, unlike anything he had composed before.

Opera buffa was Italy's most popular operatic form in the early 19th century, works of comedy with more surface than depth in which, unlike grand opera, individual musical numbers alternate with spoken dialogue. Opera buffa had its origins in the wisecracking comedians who had long entertained at fairs. **Rossini's** charming *The Barber of Seville,* and **Donizetti's** *Daughter of the Regiment* are examples of the form.

Rossini and Donizetti were also significant contributors to grand opera in the early and mid–19th century. **Puccini** came along a bit later, and his lyrical *La Bohème, Tosca,* and *Madama Butterfly* continue to please crowds.

Well known to today's international audiences is American-born **Gian-Carlo Menotti,** composer of *Amahl and the Night Visitors.* He is also the founder of Spoleto's **Festival of Two Worlds,** the international festival of music, drama, and dance which takes place in that Umbrian town annually in late June and early July.

4 Italy's Cuisine & Wine

For Italians, eating is not just something to do for sustenance three times a day. Food is an essential ingredient of the Italian spirit, practically an art form in a place that knows a lot about art. Even when Italy was a poor nation it was said that poor Italians ate better than rich Germans or English or Americans.

Italians pay careful attention to the basics in both shopping and preparation. They know, for instance, which region produces the best onions or choicest peppers, and when is the prime time of year to order porcini mushrooms, asparagus, truffles, or wild boar. If they're dining out, Italians expect the same care and pride they put into home cooking—and they get it. There are a lot of wonderful places to eat in Italy, from fancy *ristoranti* to neighborhood *trattorie.*

MEALS   **Breakfast** is treated lightly—a cappuccino and *cornetto* (croissant) at the corner bar. There are exceptions: many hotels, tired of hearing foreign guests grouse about the paltry morning offerings, have taken to serving sumptuous buffets like those offered in the United States and north of the Alps, complete with ham, cheese, and eggs.

At the big meal of the day (be it **lunch** or **dinner**) portions on a plate may be smaller than visitors are accustomed to, but a traditional meal gets you four full courses: *antipasto, primo, secondo* and *contorno.* The **antipasto** (**appetizer**) is often a platter of *salumi* (cold cuts), *bruschette* or *crostini* (toasted or grilled bread topped with pâté or tomatoes), and/or vegetables prepared in oil or vinegar, or perhaps melon and prosciutto. Next is the **primo** (**first course**), which may be a *zuppa* (soup), *polenta* (a cornmeal mush), *risotto* (a rice dish), or pasta. The **secondo** (**entree**) may include meat, fish, seafood, chicken, or game, and to accompany it you order a **contorno** (**side dish**) of vegetables or a salad. At the end of the meal, dig into a **dolce** (**dessert**)—fruit, gelato (ice cream), tiramisu (sweet cream atop espresso-soaked lady fingers), or *formaggio* (cheese) are traditionally offered.

Meals are usually accompanied by **wine** and a bottle of mineral water (*con gas* or *senza gas*/fizzy or still), and followed by an espresso. (One sure way to alienate an Italian waiter is to order cappuccino after dinner—it's usually drunk only in the morning.) Espresso is often followed by **grappa,** a fiery *digestivo* liqueur made from what's left over after the wine-making process.

Traditionally, a *ristorante* (restaurant) is a bit formal and more expensive than a family run *trattoria* or *osteria,* but the names are used almost interchangeably these days (trendy, expensive eateries often call themselves *osterie,* and little local joints may aggrandize themselves with the term *ristorante*). Snacks, perhaps a small plate of pasta, can be found in various *tavola calda* (literally "hot table," a kind of tiny cafeteria where

Coffee All Day Long

Italians drink coffee throughout the day, but only a little at a time and often while standing in a bar—and a "bar" in Italy is a place that serves coffee. There is usually liquor available, too, but it's the caffeine that draws the customers.

Five types of coffee are popular in Italy. The demitasse caffè is straight espresso, downed in one gulp. Cappuccino is espresso with an overlay of foamy steamed milk, usually sipped for breakfast with a pastry, and never as an after-dinner drink. Caffè macchiato is espresso with a wee drop of steamed milk, while latte macchiato is a glass of hot milk "stained" with a shot of espresso. Caffè coretto is espresso "corrected" with a shot of liquor. Caffe Hag is decaf. Most Italians hold in disdain the murky, watered-down coffee that percolates in offices and kitchens across America, but if you want a big mug like the stuff at home, you'll have to order "caffe Americano."

---

prepared hot dishes are sold by weight), *rosticcerie* (a tavola calda with chickens in roasting the window), and some trendy *enoteche* (wine bars).

PASTA   Aside from pizza, pasta is probably Italy's best-known export. It comes in two basic forms: *pastaciutta* (dry pasta), the kind most of us buy at the grocery store, and *pasta fresca* (fresh pasta), the kind that most self-respecting establishments in Italy, even those of the most humble ilk, will probably serve.

Pastasciutta comes in long strands including *spaghetti, linguine, trenette;* and in tubular *maccheroni* (macaroni) forms such as *penne* (pointed pasta quills) or *rigatoni* (fluted tubes), to name only a few. Pasta fresca is made in broad sheets, then cut into shapes used in lasagna, cannelloni, the stuffed pastas tortelloni and ravioli, or into noodles ranging from wide papparedelle to narrow fettuccine. If you sense that this is not even a dent in the world of pasta, you're right: There are more than 600 different pasta shapes in Italy.

ITALY'S REGIONAL CUISINES

Each Italian region has had thousands of years to develop its own culinary practices—and its own distinctive wines—and each still proudly sticks by its native dishes. Generally, northern cooking (areas north of Rome) is fancier, pricier, more elaborate, and with richer sauces; southern cooking is simpler, rougher, and cheaper. The north often uses cream and butter in its sauces, the south favors tomatoes and olive oil; the north eats red meat, the south sticks to chicken, pork, and fish. The south (and all of Italy south of Milan) eats pasta, the northernmost regions sometime substitute risotto (a delicate rice dish) or polenta (a cornmeal mush).

NORTHERN ITALY

PIEDMONT & VALLE D'AOSTA   As befits these regions of cold winters, meat roasts and hearty soups are served, often accompanied by thick slabs of polenta. Piedmont is blessed with strong-flavored white truffles (the lovely town of Alba is Italy's truffle center), and they're used in a favorite local dish, *fonduta,* a fonduelike cheese dip mixed with milk and eggs. Piedmont is also home to Gorgonzola cheese.

LIGURIA   This is the homeland of the seafarers of Genoa, who brought back from the New World many cooking ingredients now taken for granted. What, for instance, would Italian cooking be without tomatoes, potatoes, or peppers? The sea-skirted region is also famous for its seafood, including a shellfish soup called *zuppa di datteri,* and for pesto, a pasta sauce of ground basil, pine nuts, and olive oil. To the world of bread, Liguria has contributed focaccia—flat, delicious, and often topped with herbs or, when eaten as a snack, with cheese and vegetables.

LOMBARDY Like other northern regions, Lombardy favors butter over olive oil and seems not to be overly concerned with cholesterol. A specialty is *osso buco,* sliced veal sautéed with the bone and marrow. A fine starter for any meal is the region's vegetable soup with rice and bacon, *minestrone alla milanese,* or a risotto made from arboreal rice that grows on the region's low-lying plains and is often served in place of pasta. *Panettone,* the region's most popular dessert, is a local version of fruit cake that arrived from Vienna courtesy of Lombardy's 19th-century Austrian rulers. Austria also exported to Lombardy the breaded veal scallop of Wiener Schnitzle, in Italy called *cotoletta alla Milanese.* Remember, too, that Lombardy is blessed with the Italian lakes, and trout and perch find their way into ravioli and other pasta dishes as well as simply sautéed as a secondo.

VENICE & THE VENETO Venice gained fame and fortune as the spice market of the world beginning in the 12th century (when Marco Polo visited the Orient), which may help account for the amazing ways local chefs dress up the scampi, crab, squid, and other creatures they pluck from the Adriatic. The Venetians also have raised that humble combination of liver and onions (*fegato alla veneziana*) to an irresistible level of haute cuisine, and done the same with *risi e bisi* (rice and peas).

EMILIA-ROMAGNA This region counts cheese and ham as its two top specialties, most notably *Parmigiano-Reggiano* (Parmesan cheese) and *prosciutto di Parma.* They appear on just about every menu: *Prosciutto e melone* (ham draped over cantaloupe slices) is the ubiquitous appetizer here, and the sharp parmigiano cheese appears in and atop many dishes—often sprinkled atop the meat-and-tomato sauce termed *alla bolognese.* Other pastas include *tagliatelli* and *tortellini,* usually stuffed with meat and/or cheese, and almost all are topped in the creamy, buttery rich sauces for which the region is famous. Bologna, that wonderful old university city, is famous for its pork sausages, *salami,* and *mortadella* (its poor American descendant is baloney, a corruption of the city's name) as well as veal dishes.

CENTRAL ITALY

TUSCANY This is where Italian cooking, courtesy of the Medici, originated. *Bistecca alla florentina* is a thick T-bone sprinkled with olive oil, salt, and pepper and cooked very rare on a wood grill. Another Florentine dish is *pollo alla diavola,* chicken sprinkled with *pepperoncino* (hot pepper). Tuscany is also famous for its *fagioli* (beans), especially *cannellini* white beans, served simply with olive oil, or as the base—along with black cabbage and stale bread—of the thick, wintery *ribollita* vegetable soup.

UMBRIA & THE MARCHES This mountainous region dishes up robust fare like *porchetta* (roasted suckling pig), trout, game birds, and *cinghiale* (wild boar), often accompanied by black or white truffles, mushrooms, and pungently seasoned with wild herbs.

LAZIO/ROME Lazio is, of course, dominated by Rome, but the provincial Lazio mountain town of Amatrice contributed one of Rome's most famous dishes: *bucatini all'amatriciana,* thick, hollow spaghetti in a sauce of tomatoes, onion, pepperoncino (hot peppers) and pancetta (a kind of bacon). Other Roman staples include *spaghetti alla carbonara,* where black pepper–laden egg is cooked onto the hot spaghetti strands and then mixed with pancetta; *saltimbocca,* thin slices of veal skewered with sage and prosciutto and sautéed in white wine; and *gnocchi* potato dumplings (served in a tomato or a Gorgonzola sauce). These hearty dishes can be accompanied by *carciofi alla romana,* tender artichokes fried in oil.

SOUTHERN ITALY

Americans, and perhaps most foreigners, tend to think of "Italian food" as pasta in tomato sauce and other dishes common to southern cooking, which spread worldwide with the south's heavy emigration early in the 20th century.

CAMPANIA   Campania brings a lot to the table of world-renowned delights. Naples first made spaghetti famous in Europe, and long ago the ill-fated residents of Pompeii enjoyed something similar to the 19th-century Neapolitan delicacy called pizza. Pasta comes with every sauce you can think of and probably a few you haven't. Try it *alle vognole veraci,* with the diminutive clams of Naples's Bay, or with *calamari* (squid) or *cozze* (mussels)—or settle for simpler fare like *pasta e fagoli* (pasta and beans). Naples is primarily a fish and seafood town, but also popular is *bistecca alla pizzaiola,* a steak fillet topped with tomato sauce. *Mozzarella* is a delicate cheese made from the milk of the *bufala* (European bison) and best eaten fresh, perhaps with sliced tomatoes and a bit of oregano as a *caprese* salad.

APULIA   With Italy's longest coastline, Apulia's cuisine is seafood-based. Local dishes often incorporate oysters, lobster, mussels, and clams. Apulia also originated *orecchiette* (little ears) pasta, often served—especially in winter—with *cima di rape* (turnip greens). Another local dish is *cicoria e fave,* pureed chicory with fava beans. A *braciola* is a veal roll stewed, often overnight, in seasoned tomato sauce. Apulian olive oil is excellent.

SICILY   Sicily produces a bounty of citrus fruits, some of which go into one of the terrific Sicilian desserts, *cassata,* ice-cream cake with chocolate cream and candied fruits. *Cannoli,* a hard pastry shell stuffed with sweet ricotta, also originated here. The island's many cheeses, made mostly from goat's and sheep's milk, include *pecorino siciliano, caciocavello,* and *Siciliano pepato,* a spiced cheese. For an entree try *farsumagru,* a stuffed veal dish, or *pescespada,* swordfish, especially prized in Messina, and often served as an *involtino* roll around vegetables. The Sicilians' incorporate the *melanzana* (eggplant) into many a dish, including *pasta alla Norma,* with tomatoes, eggplant, and mozzarella.

WINE

Italy, with the right kind of terrain and the perfect amounts of sun and rainfall, happens to be ideal for growing grapes. Centuries ago the Etruscans had a hearty wine industry, and the ancient Greeks bolstered it by transplanting their vine cuttings to Italy's southlands. And it was Italy, under the Romans, that first introduced the vine and its possibilities to France and Germany.

Today, Italy exports more wine to the rest of the world than any other country. But there's plenty left at home from which to choose—more than 2,000 different wines are produced in Italy.

Wines of the north are generally drier than those of the south, which are usually sweeter and often quite a bit higher in alcohol volume (more sun equals more sugar). Each region has different growing conditions, and so each has its own special wines. **Piedmont** is known for its heavy reds, including Barolo, Barbaresco, Barbera, and Grignolino, as well as sparkling white Asti Spumante; the **Veneto,** for Valpolicella and Bardolino reds and, among whites, Pinot Grigio and Soave; **Emilia-Romagna,** for white Albano and red Lambrusco.

Tuscany is one of Italy's most important wine producers, with reds like Chianti, powerful Brunello di Montalcino, and refined Vino Nobile di Montepulciano (along with the famed white Vernaccia di San Gimignano); **Umbria** weighs in with Orvieto white and Montefiascone red; the Marches produce a compelling white called Verdicchio.

The DOC/DOCG/IGT System

More than 30 years ago, the Italian government instituted Denominazione di Origine Controllata, or **DOC,** a system that is akin to the French Appellation Controlée and certifies a wine's quality and place of origin. Some years later, a second, higher category was ordained, Denominazione di Origine Controllata e Garantita, or **DOCG,** to denote wines of particularly high quality. Recently **IGT** (Indicazione Geografica Tipica) was introduced so that modest local wines would be labeled as such. This leaves the title **vino da tavola** (table wine) to be used as it has for 30 years—on bottles of superior "super" wines, often made using foreign grape varietals like Merlot, Cabernet, and Chardonnay. Although highly complex and structured wines, these *supervini* fell outside the strict, traditional DOC or DOCG categories.

Montefiascone and Frascati, both whites, come from the vines that flourish on the hills around **Rome;** Ischia and Lacryma Christi have a delicate, somewhat sulfurous taste, due to the volcanic soil of **Campania; Apulia** is home to both white and red Locorotondo and the earthy red Salice Salentino. **Sicily** is known for its sweet Marsala, an aperitif, as well as Corvo whites and reds.

Throughout Italy, and especially in Tuscany, you are likely to encounter **Vin Santo** (sacred wine), made from grapes that are partly dried on the vine, then dried on racks before being pressed and aged in tiny oak *barriques*. This sweet wine may be drunk alone, but more often it is used for dunking hard almond cookies called biscotti as a dessert. **Grappa,** made from the skins, seeds, vines, and other remnants at the bottom of the pressing barrel, is a fiery digestivo drunk at the end of a meal. An **amaro** is a bitter liqueur drunk in midafternoon or before or after a meal.

5 Recommended Books

Italy has inspired natives and foreigners alike, and from their pens have flowed great literature, rich observations of the country's art, architecture, and history, and evocative writing on its food, wine, and other pleasures.

TRAVEL ACCOUNTS   Generations of travelers, among them some of Western civilization's most noted men and women of letters, have fallen under the spell of the peninsula. Still relevant are such classics as Goethe's *Italian Journey,* one of the most elegant travelogues ever written; Henry James's *Italian Hours,* full of youthful enthusiasm ("At last—for the first time—I live!"); D. H. Lawrence's *Etruscan Places* and *Twilight in Italy;* and John Ruskin's *The Stones of Venice,* required reading for anyone planning a visit to that city.

Jan Morris provides a marvelous 20th-century perspective in *The World of Venice,* which in turn is a fine companion piece to Mary McCarthy's *Venice Observed* (her *The Stones of Florence* is equally worthy). Other classics are *A Traveler in Italy, A Traveler in Rome,* and *A Traveler in Southern Italy* by H. V. Morton, whose 1930s observations still ring true, as do Norman Douglas's colorful accounts of travel through the south in the early days of this century, *Old Calabria.*

HISTORY   Werner Kerner's *The Etruscans* is a comprehensive and beautifully illustrated look at that civilization. Any history-minded traveler to Rome and Roman sights will want to tackle at least the Penguin abridged version of Edward Gibbons's classic *The History of the Decline and Fall of the Roman Empire.* Peter Gunn's *A Concise History of Italy* is as concise as this complex land will allow, and Giuliano Procacci's *History of the Italian People* provides another fine overview.

If you are going to read one work on Italy's Renaissance brilliance, make it Jacob Burkhardt's highly readable *Civilization of the Renaissance in Italy.* The autobiographical *Life of Benvenuto Cellini* richly captures the social background of the Renaissance, and Castiglione's *The Book of the Courtier* is a fascinating account and how-to manual regarding life in a Renaissance Court.

Two works that are rich with insight into the fabric of everyday Italian life are *The Italians,* Luigi Barzini's overview of centuries of social culture, and Barbara Grizutti Harrison's *Italian Days,* a memoir of her quest for her roots, mixed with wry observations on the Italian way of life. Tim Parks, an Englishman who has settled outside Verona, is quickly becoming the favorite chronicler of late-20th-century Italian life with his *Italian Neighbors* and *An Italian Education.* And American poet Frances Mayes recently topped the *New York Times* best-seller list for months with *Under the Tuscan Sun,* an account of renovating her dream villa outside Cortona interspersed with a handful of recipes based on Tuscany's bounty.

ART & ARCHITECTURE   *Roman Italy,* by T. W. Potter, is a comprehensive and heavily illustrated guide to Italy's vast archaeological heritage. Giorgio Vasari's *Lives of the Artists* was the first art history book and provides a veritable Who's Who of Renaissance artists, with essays on Giotto, Brunelleschi, Michelangelo, Botticelli, and others. Some of the most thorough and thoroughly enjoyable works on Italian painting are Bernard Berenson's *Italian Pictures of the Renaissance* and James Beck's *Italian Renaissance Painting.*

For an equally knowledgeable—and remarkably entertaining and readable— overview of sculpture, consult John Pope-Hennessy's *Italian Gothic Sculpture, Italian Renaissance Sculpture,* and *Italian High Renaissance and Baroque Sculptures.* James Ackerman's *Palladio* is one the best works written on the architect, while Peter and Linda Murray's *The Architecture of the Italian Renaissance* provides a concise and all-encompassing look at some of the country's most important buildings.

LITERATURE   Dabbling in ancient Roman literature can be an insightful and downright juicy experience. For the most colorful accounts of the empire, consider Livy's lively *Early History of Rome,* Petronius's *Satyricon,* about Rome under Nero, and Seutonius's *The Twelve Caesars.* Of recent vintage are *I, Claudius* and *Claudius, the God,* Robert Graves's enjoyable and informative fictional accounts of life in the Empire.

A brief perusal of other classics might include Giovanni Boccacio's *The Decameron,* the collection of 100 tales that capture the essence of 14th-century Italian life, and, of course, Dante's *The Divine Comedy* and Machiavelli's *The Prince.* Giuseppe Lampedusa's *The Leopard* is an exquisite novel evoking 19th-century Sicily, while a wealth of other literature captures aspects of Italy's turbulent 20th-century.

Christ Stopped at Eboli, by Carlo Levi, depicts the hardships of life in the south; *Bread and Wine* is Ignazio's Silone's hard-biting account of the his native Abruzzo. Giorgio Bassani's *Garden of the Finzi-Continis* is the story of Ferrara and the fate of its Jewish population during World War II, and Alberto Moravia's *Roman Tales* and *The Woman of Rome* are accounts of the dark side of one of the world's most fascinating and sensual cities. Travelers planning on visiting Il Vittorale, the home of the poet Gabriele D'Annunzio on Lago di Garda, might want to acquaint themselves with what is considered to his most lyrical work, *Halcyon.*

3

Planning an Affordable Trip to Italy

by Patricia Schultz

The days when Italy was an idyllic inexpensive destination of good food and countless treasures may be a thing of the past, but there are still a myriad of inexpensive ways to enjoy its remarkable wonders and the incomparability of its *dolce vita*. With some flexibility and advance planning, a moderate budget can go a long way. Remember, this is the country where for $3 you can get a gelato and a front-row table at an outdoor cafe in just about any ancient open-air piazza. The colorful street theater that'll stroll and preen before you is free. But before you hit the piazzas, read on. This chapter shows you how to organize and get your trip together and on the road.

1 How This Guide Can Save You Money

Italy encourages the art of serendipity, but don't underestimate the importance of advance planning. This chapter is full of money-saving hints, insider information, contacts, and expertise accumulated over our innumerable fact-finding trips—you won't even know you're stretching your dollars. In fact, you'll enjoy your trip even more knowing you're getting the biggest bang for your buck, easily keeping your accommodation cost (let's say breakfast is included) and two meals a day to as little as $70 a day. (We assume that two adults are traveling together and that between the two of you, you have $140 to spend. Traveling alone has other pluses and drawbacks, but usually turns out to be slightly more expensive mostly due to the hotel factor.) The cost of transportation, activities, sightseeing, and entertainment are extra, but we have plenty of insider tips to save you money on those activities as well. Luckily for travelers on a limited budget, Italy is one of the world's great countries whose spectacular wonders—both natural (think the Dolomite mountains, or Sicily's smoldering Mt. Etna, the only active volcano in Europe) and manufactured (who can forget an evening *passeggiata* around Rome's Piazza Navona, or the outdoor orchestras whose music fills Venice's unique Piazza San Marco?)—are yours to enjoy for free.

2 Fifty Money-Saving Tips

Don't fret about spending too much in Italy: Worry about spending too little time. Yes, it costs more than yesteryear, but here you can revel in that same plate of delicious *pasta fatta a casa* (homemade pasta) for a palatable $5 that your hotshot neighborhood restaurant puts on their menus back home for $18. Piazza life is colorful, outrageous, comical, heart-warming, and yours for the price of a cappuccino. You might even pay less during after-Christmas sales for the cashmere sweater you thought was a bargain in Florence, but it will make you smile every time you wear it for the next 20 years. And can you even put a price on the atmospheric mansard room with your own private balcony overlooking the cupolas of St. Mark's Basilica? A million dollar memory for under $100.

It's hard to go wrong in Italy, but very easy to go right if you give some heed to the following:

WHEN TO GO

1. So the weather isn't a perfect 75°, and the skies aren't always cloud-free. But off-season Italy promises the biggest cuts in airfare, the beauty of popping up at small hotels (more discounted rates) without needing a reservation confirmed three months in advance, the blessed absence of no lines at the museums and the local people less harried and more accommodating. For more details on high versus low season travel, see "When to Go" later in this chapter.

PACKAGE DEALS, INTERNATIONAL & DOMESTIC TRAVEL

2. An enjoyable, affordable trip begins way before leaving home. Do your cyber homework: Surf the Internet and save. There are lots and lots of Web pages and on-line services designed to clue you in on discounted airfares, accommodations, and car rentals. See the sidebar "CyberDeals for Net Surfers" for some sites that offer real deals.

3. No computer? No problem. Visit a travel agent and see what bargains or deals they offer you that you wouldn't have access to independently. It doesn't cost you a thing, and there's no obligation to buy. It never hurts to ask. See page 61 later in this chapter for a list of agencies that specialize in trips to Italy.

4. When calling the airlines directly, always ask for the lowest possible fare. Be flexible in your schedule—flying on weekdays versus weekends can make a difference. Find out the exact dates of the seasonal rates; these differ from airline to airline even though the destination stays the same. Some flights into or out of Rome versus Milano may differ in price. Don't forget to ask about discounts for seniors, students or children.

5. Buy your ticket well in advance. Most airlines discount tickets purchased 7, 14 or 21 days before the departure dates.

6. Or buy it at the last minute—something best recommended if you have a flexible schedule and are traveling off-season when availability is more probable.

7. Be an educated traveler. Read the travel section of your local newspaper (especially weekend editions) for special promotional fares and discounts and know who's offering what and for how much.

8. Check your newspaper for consolidators, wholesalers once more frequently known as "bucket shops." These companies operate by alleviating blocks of unsold tickets from the major international airlines. It's still not a bad idea to check their records first with the Better Business Bureau. Most operate firmly aboveboard and offer substantial savings, particularly off-season: See those we list in the section "Getting There Without Going Broke," page 67.

9. You may not be a groupie, but check package deals and escorted trips before deciding if they are or are not for you. You might find the air and hotel savings alone make them worth considering; many trips are unstructured enough to let you split from the group and do your own thing. You might even wind up preferring the companionship of the others on board and the luxury of having every day's bothersome details prearranged. Air/hotel packages (often offered by the

CyberDeals for Net Surfers

It's possible to get some great deals on airfare, hotels, and car rentals via the Internet. The Web sites we've highlighted below are worth checking out, especially since all services are free.

Travelocity (www.travelocity.com)   This is one of the best travel sites out there. In addition to its "Personal Fare Watcher," which notifies you via e-mail of the lowest airfares for up to five different destinations, Travelocity will track the three lowest fares for any routes on any dates in minutes. You can book a flight right then and there, and if you need a rental car or hotel, Travelocity will find you the best deal via the SABRE computer reservations system (a huge database used by travel agents worldwide). Click on "Last Minute Deals" for the latest travel bargains.

Microsoft Expedia (www.expedia.com)   The best part of this multipurpose travel site is the "Fare Tracker": You fill out a form on the screen indicating that you're interested in cheap flights to whatever your destination may be in Italy, from your hometown, and, when prices change, you'll get an e-mail indicating how the price has changed. The site's "Travel Agent" will steer you to bargains on hotels and car rentals, and you can book everything, including flights, right online. This site is even useful once you're booked: Before you go, log on to Expedia for oodles of up-to-date travel information, including weather reports and foreign exchange rates.

Preview Travel (www.reservations.com and www.vacations.com)   Another useful travel site, "Reservations.com" has a "Best Fare Finder," which will search the Apollo computer reservations system for the three lowest fares for any route on any days of the year. Say you want to go from Chicago to Rome and back between December 6 and 13: Just fill out the form on the screen with times, dates, and destinations, and within minutes, Preview will show you the best deals. If you find an airfare you like, you can book your ticket right on line—you can even reserve hotels and car rentals on this site. If you're in the preplanning stage, head to Preview's "Vacations.com" site, where you can check out the latest package deals for Hawaii and other destinations around the world by clicking on "Hot Deals."

Trip.Com (www.thetrip.com)   This site is really geared toward the business traveler, but vacationers-to-be can also use Trip.Com's valuable fare-finding engine, which will e-mail you every week with the best city-to-city airfare deals on your selected route or routes.

Priceline.com   On this auctionlike Web site, you decide what you want to pay for your airline ticket or hotel room. Input when and where you want to fly to, the price you want to pay, and your credit card number. Priceline then does a

airlines themselves) also offer great savings though hotels are sometimes on the outskirts of towns (hence the big discounts); check their location first if this is important to you.

10. Domestic or one-way flights within Italy (or Europe) can be killers. The most distant flights within Italy (Venice to Palermo, for example) might be a contender for air travel, but opt for the train at a fraction of the cost, breaking up your travel times with overnight stops planned along the way. There is never a shortage of sites awaiting you between any two points.

search to determine if any supplier will accept the price; if the price is accepted the ticket is immediately bought and charged to your credit card. The Web site offers a similar deal for hotel rooms.

Discount Tickets (www.discount-tickets.com)   Operated by the ETN (European Travel Network), this site offers discounts on airfares, accommodations, car rentals, and tours. It deals in flights between the United States and other countries, not domestic U.S. flights, so it's most useful for travelers coming to Hawaii from abroad.

www.moments-notice.com   This site is a bargain-hunter's dream. Updated each morning, many of the deals offered are snapped up by the end of the day. A drawback is that many of these vacations require you to drop everything and go almost immediately.

www.180096hotel.com   Here you'll find budget reservations at prestigious hotels all over the world—many accommodations are offered for up to 65% off.

E-Savers Programs   Several major airlines offer a free e-mail service known as **E-Savers,** via which you'll receive the best bargain airfares on a weekly basis. Here's how it works: Once a week (usually Wednesday), subscribers receive a list of discounted flights to and from various destinations, both international and domestic. Now here's the catch: These fares are only available if you leave the very next Saturday (or sometimes Friday night) and return on the following Monday or Tuesday. It's really a service for the spontaneously inclined and travelers looking for a quick getaway (better a few days in Italy than none at all). But the fares are cheap, so it's worth taking a look. If you have a preference for certain airlines (in other words, the ones you fly most frequently), sign up with them first. Another caveat: You'll get frequent-flier miles if you purchase one of these fares, but you can't use miles to buy the ticket.

Here's a list of airlines and their Web sites, where you can not only get on the e-mailing lists, but also book flights directly:

- **American Airlines:** www.americanair.com
- **Continental Airlines:** www.flycontiental.com
- **TWA:** www.twa.com
- **Northwest Airlines:** www.nwa.com
- **US Airways:** www.usairways.com

Epicurious Travel (travel.epicurious.com), another good travel site, allows you to sign up for all of these airline e-mail lists at once.

—*Jeanette Foster*

All major airports have rail or bus service to get you to and from downtown—Rome and Pisa's ultraconvenient trains pull right into the airport itself. Taxis are expensive though tempting to jet-lagged travelers laden with luggage.

11. Which reminds us: Travel lightly! You'll never wear or need half of the stuff you're convinced you can't live without. What you'll save on cabs, porters, and energy can be considerable. But it's the inconvenience you'll find at every turn that you'll remember long afterward! Never take more than you can carry single-handedly when running for a bus or train.

12. Train travel in Italy has improved immeasurably since the 1970s and 1980s. The relatively new **"InterCity"** trains are clean and efficient enough to make second-class travel a near first-class experience. The fancy, fast-paced **EuroStar** trains can cut speed, but is a 1-hour (or less) difference worth the extra cost?

13. Map out your strategy before leaving to see if a **Eurail pass** will save you or cost you money. On long international stretches of train travel, the former is usually true. Within Italy, buying second class point-to-point tickets as you go may save you money. The Eurail pass is cheapest when bought at home before leaving.

14. Use public transportation in cities rather than taxis. It also offers a peak into the daily lifestyles of the local residents. Most concentrated historical districts make sightseeing most enjoyable when done by foot; in the large cities like Rome or Milan, consider daily or weekly passes for unlimited travel on buses or subways.

CAR RENTALS

15. Call around to all the major car-rental agencies; promotional rates sometimes make the big boys the best. Make a reservation before leaving home, but make one last inquiry before getting on the plane to see if any new lower rates have been introduced in the meantime. Making your reservation before leaving for Italy is almost always a guaranteed money saver.

16. Ask questions about waivers and insurance suggested and required by the rental agency and then check with your **credit card company** to see what they offer before booking. Don't wind up paying for the same coverage twice, or charged for extraneous coverage that is recommended but not obligatory.

17. Aim at the least expensive economy car category (unless you'll be making long autostrada stretches when it will seem you're standing still as virtually every other vehicle zips by). If you're told they're unavailable in an attempt to have you book the next most expensive model, call elsewhere. Know in advance that almost all rental cars in Italy are stick shift; to book an automatic will hike the price considerably—if any are available. Air-conditioning will also cost extra. Consider the weather you'll be encountering.

18. Book the weekly rates to save. To book a car for just a day or two for a tool in the country is an expensive venture. However, to book for a longer period, only to have the car sit in an (expensive) parking lot (almost all historical centers now ban car traffic entirely) doesn't make sense either. Have a loose idea of what your vacation's schedule will be, and work around that.

19. Parking is a nightmare in Italy and the police are serious about enforcing tow-away zones. Don't try to conserve parking lot costs by parking on the streets if you're not sure just what the streets signs say (most are an icon of a car with a slash through it). The cost of retrieving a towed car is only half as bad as the hassle of trying to find it and getting it back without the incident ruining your entire trip.

20. If you decide to rent once you're already in Italy, check out the prices and then call a friend back home and ask them to book for you from there if the rates are less; they almost always are.

21. Always return your rental car full of gas, or the rental agency will charge you for it, usually at top lire. Don't have heart failure at the cost of gas *(benzina)* in Italy: it is some of Europe's most expensive. The cars get excellent mileage, however, and you won't have to fill up often.

22. The largest cities may have car-rental offices at both the airport and downtown. There is often an extra charge to pick up at one and drop off at the other. To pick

up and drop off in two different cities is even worse. In two different countries—better take the train.

ACCOMMODATIONS

23. If you're traveling during high season (summer), book early. You won't get any discounts, but you won't be forced to spend more by upgrading just to find a vacancy in town.

24. If the idea doesn't faze you, consider a less expensive room with a shared bathroom instead of an "en suite" private bathroom. Ask how many rooms will be sharing the bathroom—sometimes it is as few as two; if the other room is vacant, the bathroom will be yours alone.

25. Many of the hotels listed in this book don't advertise seasonal rates, but there's usually some discount offered during the slow months. Always ask. The more nights you stay, the more you're likely to get a discount. The way you approach the subject is very important: a smile and a pretty-please upon check-in is always more successful than a hard-nosed demand. If it's a slow month and late afternoon, the advantage is yours.

26. Don't underestimate the power of Frommer's. Mention of this book in your faxed request or a flash of the book upon check-in will notify the hotel from whence you come. Most of our hotels have repeatedly proven to be very appreciative of the volume and quality of travelers that we bring to their establishment and they're apt to do their best to accommodate you when and if possible.

27. Is your room so dismal you could just cry? Keep cool and polite, but voice your disappointment and ask if you might be shown another room. Be specific about what bothers you—the soft mattress or lack of light might not be something found in all rooms. You might even get upgraded at no extra cost. Don't resort to drama and histrionics.

28. Single rooms in Italy can be downright teensy tiny miniscule. If you're traveling alone and it's off-season, ask if the management might be so kind to offer you a double room at a single occupancy rate. Many of them will if the rooms are available; always ask.

29. Before you go arranging your own parking, check first with your hotel. Hotels often have a standing deal with a nearby parking facility. In Venice, hotels will give you a voucher to present at the parking lots on the outskirts of town.

30. Breakfast. Is it included, or not? Always ask, and ask if it is continental or buffet. When you're paying $5 per person (for example) for a prepackaged month old *cornetto* (croissant) and cup of mediocre coffee, check out the charming outdoor cafe down the block. If the self-service, all-you-can-eat buffet of cold cuts, fresh rolls, juice, yogurt, and—well, you've caught the drift—is offered in a simpatico setting and will keep you going till dinner, dig in, enjoy yourself, and grab an apple for the road.

31. Don't make long distance telephone calls from your room if you can avoid it. The service charge and taxes tagged on to the briefest call home will ruin the moment of enjoyment it brought. Use calling cards at public phones or arrange to have your family call you at designated hours.

32. The "frigo bar" (minibar) is a mixed blessing. That Diet Coke *(Coca Cola Lite)* and Toblerone candy bar can set you back and easy $10. Check the price list before giving in to hunger pangs, and know what you're about to eat—it might not taste so good.

33. Each hotel's policy regarding children is different so be specific regarding the children's ages when booking: generally speaking, children under 12 (sometimes 10)

stay for free in the parents' room. There's no fudging the children's age, with the obligatory presentation of the passport upon check-in.

EATING

34. Take advantage of Italy's cornucopia of excellent bakeries and food stores and make every lunch a picnic. Yes, you'll save more to spend on dinner, but you'll also wind up enjoying a million-dollar lunch in an opera-set piazza.

35. It's lunch time and it's rainy or cold, or you just need to sit indoors for awhile, but an expensive meal is out of your budget. Italy is slowly leaning towards the affordable quick lunch. Bars and cafes are serving informal lunches of pastas and salads as much to local merchants and workers as to cost-conscious travelers, usually for $6 to $7 or less.

36. If you're running over your day's budget (couldn't resist the calfskin attaché case?), remember that this is the country that gave us pizza and wine. Find a pizzeria with outdoor seating, order a carafe of the house wine *(vino della casa)* and eat like a king, spend like a poor man. Save your three-course trattoria meal for a more solvent day.

37. Tourist menus *(menu turistico)* or fixed-price menus *(menu a prezzo fisso)* sound like a good deal, and often are. But portions may be smaller, choices less varied or uninspired (expect the ubiquitous spaghetti with tomato sauce and roast chicken). Menus are usually posted in the window, so peruse your choices before entering and ordering.

38. If you aren't accustomed to eating so much but want to taste it all, order a *mezza porzione* (half portion) of pasta for your first course, so you have room left for your second course—and be charged accordingly. Most restaurants will gladly oblige.

39. The rule of thumb in this cafe society: Always expect to pay more at a table than at the bar; more at an outdoor table (consider it your cover charge for the free piazza-life entertainment). That said, don't expect to be rushed: For the cost of an iced-tea or mineral water, you can sit and write post cards for hours and you'll never overstay your welcome.

40. If you've been snacking all day and would be happy with just a good plate of pasta and not a full-blown repast, make sure you choose your restaurant well. You might anger some establishments if you occupy a table for a single course dinner and not the full nine yards. Casual, informal neighborhood joints won't give a second thought to you lingering over a simple pasta, salad, and glass of wine.

    House wines can be surprisingly good and inexpensive. Enjoying a good bottled wine will bring your bill up a notch but hey, that's probably what you're visiting Italy for anyway. Stick with wines of the region, and experiment with some of the small-time, lesser-known (but not necessarily less sophisticated) wine producers of the area. For the wallet-challenged, go with the mineral water, and stop off at a wine bar after dinner and choose one very special cru by-the-glass in a convivial *ambiente*.

SIGHTSEEING

41. Make a beeline for the **Tourist Information Office** to check out special events, free concerts, arts festivals, and so on to maximize your (always too brief) stay in town. Some museums offer one evening a week free; outdoor evening or church concerts are free, not infrequent and lovely. Sometimes your hotel staff can be twice as helpful and informed than the tourism people.

42. To get the most on always increasing museum admissions, see if you can buy tickets in advance to eliminate waiting in line. Always ask about possible senior and student discounts. Extended hours for summer months are often confirmed at the last minute (therefore not reflected in guidebooks) and are not widely publicized: if you're in-the-know, you might have Florence's Uffizi Galleries to yourself at 10 o'clock in the evening—put a price on that!

43. More and more cities are offering joint tickets or passes for both major and minor museums. You might be able to get admission to as many as 10 museums over an open period of time. But study which museums are included—they are often obscure and esoteric collections that are of little interest or inconveniently located for the tourist on a tight schedule.

44. Free, do-it-yourself walking tours are a viable substitute for the expensive, escorted tours. But the latter are worth your while if your time in town is extremely limited and the sites are many. Before signing up for a half or full day tour, see exactly which sites will be visited so you don't miss those of most interest to you.

45. Don't short-change yourself on people watching in Italy, the single great pastime that has been perfected here as an art form, and the best free entertainment you're bound to see anywhere. Pull up a cafe chair and settle in; to avoid any charge at all, a piazza bench will do fine.

SHOPPING

46. Before splurging on that fragile glassware from Venice or hand-painted ceramic platter from Deruta, consider the cost of shipping, which can double the otherwise respectable price. Do you really want to carry it around for the rest of your trip? Some stores don't offer the amenity of shipping and to package and send it yourself is troublesome and time consuming. Insurance hikes the cost even further.

47. Pay by credit card as often as possible: The fewer transaction fees (incurred by ATMs or changing travelers checks or cash) needed, the more saved.

48. Alas, **bargaining** in Italy, once a theatrical and generally enjoyable part of every purchase, is fast becoming a dying animal. But if you're buying more than one item, paying by cash or travelers checks, and have struck up a friendly banter with the merchant, give it a shot. The best time to test your talents is during the slow months, when the market or shop looks like it's hungry for business.

49. Don't forget to cash in on your **value-added tax (VAT)** (See "Tips on Shopping," below) if you qualify. Million of dollars of unclaimed refunds is the result of forgetful or uninformed tourists.

50. By now the world is a village. Be realistic about what you can and cannot find back home of the legion made-in-Italy souvenirs you're dying to snatch up. Do you really want to spend a precious afternoon in Florence tracking down a pair of black leather gloves that are a dime-a-dozen at home, when it could be time far better spent gazing upon the wonder of Michelangelo's David?

3 Visitor Information & Entry Requirements

VISITOR INFORMATION

TOURIST OFFICES   For information before you go, contact the **Italian National Tourist Office (Ente Nazionale Italiano per il Turismo, or ENIT)**. The Web address is **www.enit.it**. You can also write directly (in English or Italian) to the provincial or local tourist boards of areas you plan to visit, but don't expect Swiss efficiency with a return response. These provincial tourist boards, **Ente Provinciale per il Turismo (E.P.T.),** operate in the principal towns of the provinces. The local tourist boards, occasionally referred to as **Azienda Autonoma Soggiorno** or more simply **Ufficio di Informazione,** operate in all places of tourist interest, and you can get a list from the Italian government tourist offices. When trying to contact the offices themselves, **be aware** that readers have complained the office isn't as helpful as it could be. Here are the foreign branches:

- **United States**   630 Fifth Ave., Suite 1565, New York, NY 10111 (☎ 212/ **245-4822;** fax 212/586-9249); 500 N. Michigan Ave., Suite 2240, Chicago, IL 60611 (☎ **312/644-0990** or 312/644-0996; fax 312/644-3019); 12400 Wilshire Blvd., Suite 550, Los Angeles, CA 90025 (☎ **310/820-0098;** fax 310/ 820-6367).
- **Canada**   1 place Ville Marie, Suite 1914, Montréal, Québec H3B 2C3 (☎ **514/866-7667;** fax 514/392-1429).
- **United Kingdom**   1 Princes St., London W1R 8AY (☎ **0171/408-1254;** fax 0171/493-6695).

INTERNET RESOURCES   Major Internet sites like Yahoo (**www.yahoo.com**), Excite (**www.excite.com**), Lycos (**www.lycos.com**), and Infoseek (**www.infoseek.com**) contain subcategories on travel, country/regional information, and culture—search these for links to Web sites specializing in Italy.

General Information   One of the best resources for general travel and destination-specific information is Excite's City.Net (**www.city.net/countries/italy**). Other good general sites are Travel Italy (**www.travel.it**), which includes updated tourist information as well as details about hotels and house rentals, spas, transportation services, tour operators, and more; In Italy On-line (**www.initaly.com**), with details on accommodations, tours, festivals, shopping, and more; Hello Italy (**www.gatourism.it**), a hotel reservations service; the Italian Tourist Web Guide (**www.itwg.com**), with on-line hotel reservations and information on art and history; Italy in a Flash (**www.italyflash. com**), offering hotel information, railway and airline schedules, latest exchange rates, weather, and current news; and Let's Roam Italy (**http://tqd.advanced.org/2838**), a great site for students and younger travelers, with travel tips, information about Italian culture and history, and a list of e-mail addresses for English-speaking students in Italy so you can find an e-mail pal who can tell you more about the country.

Rome   Gearing up for the year 2000 and its much awaited Jubilee, Rome boasts the most sites of any Italian city (no surprise). One of the best is run by Travelocity (**www.travelocity.com**). From the home page, click on the "Destinations & Interests"

The Best of Budget Travel from the King of Budget Travel

Forget the usual travel magazines: They generally focus on high-end vacations, and even when they boast about "deals" the savings they claim are really negligible. However, now there's the bimonthly *Arthur Frommer's Budget Travel,* available for $14.95 per year. This full-color magazine is filled with all the details concerning "vacations for real people." In the premiere issue were articles like "The Cheapest Places on Earth" and "This Spring's 40 Best Bargain Vacations." You can find individual issues on the shelves (beware, though—it sells out fast), or you can order a subscription by calling ☎ **800/829-9121** or by checking out Arthur Frommer's Web site at **www.frommers.com**.

button, then navigate your way to "Rome and Environs." It has hundreds of listings—full-fledged write-ups in most cases—for everything from sights, hotels, and restaurants to shopping, nightlife, tour companies, and an excellent festivals and events calendar. Roma 2000 (**www.roma2000.it**) is very graphics-heavy with a wealth of information on sightseeing, including some walking tours. It also lists dozens of hotels, restaurants, and shops, but mostly gives just the addresses and phone numbers. Try Nerone: The Insider's Guide to Rome (**www.xplore.it/nerone/index.htm**), with visitor as well as cultural and sightseeing information. You can search for general info at **www.romeguide.it** or download the latest issue of Time Out Rome at **www. timeout.co.uk**. For an unrelentingly religious site with a wonderful armchair photo tour of the Vatican and its art treasures, head to Christus Rex (**www.christusrex.org**).

Florence   Welcome to the Incredible City of Florence, Italy (**www/tiac.net/users/ pendini/index.html**), includes details on hotels, museums, music, "hidden corners," and lots more; at Your Way to Florence (**www.arca.net/florence.htm**), you'll find info about art, history, museums and monuments, churches, hotels, and theaters.

Venice   Venice Today (**www.iuave.it/~juli/ventoday.htm**), provides weekly updated details on the city and its events, news, and tourism, plus links to other Venice sites. There's more on Venice at **www.doge.it**, where you'll find everything from the latest happenings to the most affordable hotel rooms.

ENTRY REQUIREMENTS

Citizens of the United States, Canada, Great Britain, Ireland, Australia, and New Zealand with a **valid passport** do not need a visa to enter Italy if they don't expect to stay more than 90 days and don't expect to work there. Those who want to stay longer can apply for a permit for an additional stay of 90 days, which as a rule is granted immediately. Applicants for such an extension should bring their passport to the nearest police headquarters *(questura)* or inquire at their home country's consulate or embassy.

4 Money

There are no restrictions as to how much foreign currency you can bring into Italy, though if it's substantial you should declare the amount brought in so that, if there's a question, you can prove to the Italian Customs office on leaving that the currency came from outside the country. Italian currency taken into or out of Italy may not exceed 200,000L in denominations of 50,000L or lower.

CURRENCY   The basic unit of Italian currency is the **lira** (plural: **lire**), abbreviated as **L** in this book. Coins are issued in denominations of 50L, 100L, 200L, and 500L (with 10s and 20s rarely found), and bills come in denominations of 1,000L, 2,000L, 5,000L, 10,000L, 50,000L, 100,000L, and 500,000L. Coins for 50L and 100L come in two sizes each, the newer ones both around the size of a dime (which can't yet be used in any coin-accepting machines or public phones).

CURRENCY EXCHANGE   With the arrival of the euro fast upon us (see below), things will change considerably. Until then, interbank rates are established daily and listed in most international newspapers. To get a transaction as close to this rate as possible, pay for as much as possible with credit cards. ATM machines and bank cards offer close to the same rate, plus an added-on fee for cash transaction.

Although exchange rates are more favorable at the point of arrival, it is often helpful to exchange at least some money before going abroad (standing in line upon your arrival at the Milan or Rome airport's *cambio* may make you miss the next bus leaving

Currency Converter

All the prices in this book were calculated at the rate of 1700L to $1. However, the exchange rate constantly fluctuates. If you have access to the Web, you can get an instant exchange rate by logging onto the site: **www.x-rates.com/calculator.html**.

for downtown). Check with any of your local American Express or Thomas Cook offices or major banks. Or order Italian lire in advance from the following: American Express (cardholders only) (☎ **800/553-6782**), Thomas Cook (☎ **800/287-7362**), Chase Manhattan Bank (☎ **800/935-9935**), or International Currency Express (☎ **888/842-0880** or 888/287-6628).

When exchanging money in Italy, it's best to exchange currency or traveler's checks at a bank, not a *cambio* (exchange bureau), hotel, or shop. Currency and traveler's checks (for which you'll receive a better rate than cash) can be changed at all principle airports and some travel agencies, such as American Express and Thomas Cook. Note the rates and ask about commission fees; it can sometimes pay to shop around and ask the right questions.

Rarely will Italian hotels accept a dollar-denominated check from your hometown bank as a deposit sent in advance; if you find a hotel that does, it'll probably charge dearly for the conversion. Some hotels accept countersigned traveler's checks sent by mail or a credit card (the latter more commonly done in the larger or higher-grade hotels, but more and more by the smaller hotels such as those suggested in this book) given over the phone.

A few of the smaller hotels still demand a check drawn on an Italian bank when reserving a room from overseas. This can be arranged by a large commercial bank or by a currency specialist like **Ruesch International,** 700 11th St. NW, Suite 400, Washington, DC 20001 (☎ **800/424-2923** or 202/408-1200; www.ruesch.com). Ruesch maintains additional offices in New York, Los Angeles, Chicago, Atlanta, and Boston, though the Washington, D.C., office can supply the bank draft through phone orders.

CREDIT CARDS   Never rely entirely on credit cards alone, although they can be used almost everywhere as plastic becomes more commonly accepted throughout the country. Visa and MasterCard are accepted at most hotels, restaurants, and shops, with American Express trailing behind. Diner's Club is also a favorite. Once you leave the larger or less-visited cities or in some of the smaller, family run hotels and shops and trattorias, a cash/traveler's-checks-only policy still prevails.

A cash advance against your credit cards, whether from a bank or an ATM, is costly, and usually combines three charges—the surcharge above the interbank rate, the transaction fee, and the financing charge on the loan, which is what a cash advance is (see below).

ATM NETWORKS   The ATM revolution is being felt throughout Italy, rapidly taking hold in both smaller towns as well as larger cities. Although **Bancomat** is the name of a privately owned Italian company, its name has become the generic word for ATMs in Italy where you can withdraw money from your account at home or, more expensively, against your credit card as a cash advance. American Express cardholders can use the ATMs of **Banco Popolare di Milano** throughout Italy or at any American Express office in Italy.

Old worries about PIN numbers not working abroad rarely hold any more, but double-check before leaving home to be sure. On the Internet, check

The Italian Lira, the U.S. Dollar & the British Pound

At this writing, US$1 = approximately 1,700L, and this was the rate of exchange used to calculate the dollar values throughout this book. The rate fluctuates from day to day, depending on a complicated series of economic and political factors, and might not be the same when you travel to Italy.

Likewise, the ratio of the British pound to the lira fluctuates constantly. At press time, £1 = approximately 2,700L, an exchange rate reflected in the table below.

Lire	US$	UK£	Lire	US$	UK£
1,000	0.59	0.37	35,000	20.59	12.96
1,500	0.88	0.56	40,000	25.53	14.82
2,000	1.18	0.74	45,000	26.47	16.67
3,000	1.76	1.11	50,000	29.41	18.52
4,000	2.35	1.48	100,000	58.82	37.04
5,000	2.94	1.85	125,000	73.53	46.30
7,500	4.41	2.78	150,000	88.24	55.56
10,000	5.88	3.70	200,000	117.65	74.08
15,000	8.82	5.56	250,000	147.06	92.60
20,000	11.76	7.41	500,000	294.12	185.20
25,000	14.71	9.26	1,000,000	588.24	370.40
30,000	17.65	11.11			

www.mastercard.com/atm or **www.visa.com/cgi-bin/vee/main.html** to find ATMs where you'll be visiting.

TRAVELER'S CHECKS   Although going the way of the dinosaur, traveler's checks are a safe method of carrying money, since in the event of theft, the value of your checks will be refunded if properly documented. Most large banks sell traveler's checks, charging fees averaging 1% to 2% of the value of the checks you buy. If your bank wants more than a 2% commission, it sometimes pays to call the traveler's check issuers directly for the address of outlets where the commission will cost less.

Issuers sometimes have agreements with groups to sell checks commission-free. For example, **Automobile Association of America (AAA)** clubs sell American Express checks in several currencies without commission.

American Express (☎ **800/221-7282** in the U.S. and Canada; www.americanexpress.com) is one of the largest and most immediately recognized issuers of traveler's checks. The commission is waived for holders of certain types of American Express credit cards.

Citicorp (☎ **800/645-6556** in the U.S. and Canada, or 813/623-1709, collect, from anywhere else in the world; www.citicorp.com) issues its own checks. **Thomas Cook** (☎ **800/223-7373** in the U.S. and Canada; otherwise call 609/987-7300 collect from other parts of the world; www.thomascook.com), issues MasterCard traveler's checks. And **Interpayment Services** (☎ **800/732-1322** in the U.S. and Canada; call 44-17-33-31-89-49 collect from other parts of the world) sells Visa checks, which are issued by a consortium of member banks and the Thomas Cook organization.

The Debut of the Euro

In a big step toward European unification, a single European currency, called the **euro,** is slowly going into effect in Europe. Austria, Belgium, Finland, France, Germany, Ireland, Italy, Luxembourg, the Netherlands, Portugal, and Spain have all agreed to accept this currency. For the traveler, the introduction of the euro will have a significant impact—making foreign exchange (eventually) less confusing and expensive. Several countries—including Britain, Denmark, and Sweden—have opted out from switching over just yet (they may do so in 2002); Greece hasn't yet met the economic requirements to join.

As a visitor, you don't have to worry about dealing with euro coins and notes until 2002. Although the changeover took effect on paper on January 1, 1999, it is a "virtual currency" that basically applies only to financial and electronic transactions between businesses in Europe. You'll likely see prices in shops, hotels, and restaurants quoted in both the local currency and euros beginning in 1999 to ease the world into euro-speak. Like the American dollar, the euro is made up of 100 cents. It started at US$1.18 to 1 Euro, but in the first six months, it has fallen to $104. Some experts believe it may one day replace the almighty dollar as the globe's most powerful currency.

However, according to Henri Ruff, head of the euro at Visa International in London, euro traveler's checks are now available, and he suggests people begin paying in euros whenever possible on their charge cards. Check with each credit card company first to see if it's accepting euros as payment beginning in 1999.

For more information on the euro, check out **www.europa.eu.int/euro**.

WIRE SERVICES   If you find yourself out of money, a wire service can help you tap willing friends and family for funds. Through **MoneyGram,** 6200 S. Quebec St., P.O. Box 5118, Englewood, CO 80155 (☎ **800/945-2264**), money can be sent around the world in less than 10 minutes. Cash and Visa or MasterCard are the only acceptable forms of payment (American Express cards aren't accepted). MoneyGram's fee for the service is $20 for the first $200 and $30 for up to $400, with a sliding scale for larger sums. The beneficiary can pick up the transaction in US$ traveler's checks at any of the American Express offices in Milan, Florence, Rome, or Venice and must present a photo ID (like a passport) to receive money.

A similar service is offered by **Western Union** (☎ **800/325-6000**), which accepts cash and Visa, MasterCard, or Discover. You can arrange for the service over the phone or at a Western Union office. A sliding scale begins at $15 for sums paid for by cash ($33 when paid by credit card), for the first $100. When picking up the goods, you should note that in Italy, you don't have to go to a Western Union office. You just need to find a Western Union affiliate, which in the big towns can be bars, supermarkets, exchange bureaus, banks, and so on.

5 When to Go

May to **June** and **September** and **October** are the most pleasant months for touring Italy—temperatures are usually mild and the hordes not so intense. But starting in mid-June, the summer rush really picks up, and from July to mid-September the country teems with visitors. **August** (with July a close runner up) is the worst month—not only does it get uncomfortably hot, muggy, and crowded, but the entire country goes on vacation at least from August 15 to the end of the month, and a good percentage of Italians take off the entire month, leaving the cities to the tourists. Many hotels, restaurants, and shops are closed—except along the coast and on the islands, which is where most Italians head. From **late October to Easter,** most sights go on shorter winter hours or are closed for renovation, many hotels and restaurants take a month or two off between November and February, beach destinations become padlocked ghost towns, and it can get much colder than you'd expect (it may even snow).

High season on most airlines' routes to Rome usually stretches from June to the end of September and Christmas week. This is the most expensive and most crowded time to travel. **Shoulder season** is from Easter time (usually late march or April) to May, late September to October, and December 15 to 24. **Low season** is generally January 6 to mid-March, November 1 to December 14 and December 25 to March 31.

WEATHER   It's warm all over Italy in summer, especially inland. The high temperatures (measured in Italy in degrees Celsius) begin in Rome in May, often lasting until some time in late September. July and August can be impossible and explain why life in the cities slows down considerably (and life in the coastline resorts comes alive). Winters in the north of Italy are cold with rain and snow, and December and January are generally unpleasant unless you're skiing in Cortona. In the south, the weather is mild in the winter months, averaging in the 40s. Sicily's citrus and almond trees are already in bloom in February—but nights can be cold, and hotels don't pay much attention to heat.

For the most part, it's drier in Italy than in North America. Since the humidity is lower, high temperatures don't seem as bad; exceptions are cities known for their humidity factor, such as Florence and Venice. In Rome, Naples, and the south, temperatures can stay in the 90s for days, but nights are most often comfortably cooler. It's important to remember that this is not a country as smitten by the notion of air-conditioning and central heating as, say, the United States. And remember that the inexpensive hotels we list in this book are often the very places that will remind you of the pros and cons of ancient stone palazzi built with 3-foot-thick walls. Don't expect the comfort of the Ritz.

Italy's Average Daily Temperature & Monthly Rainfall

Florence

	Jan	Feb	Mar	Apr	May	June	July	Aug	Sept	Oct	Nov	Dec
Temp. (°F)	45	47	50	60	67	76	77	70	64	63	55	46
Rainfall (in.)	3	3.3	3.7	2.7	2.2	1.4	1.4	2.7	3.2	4.9	3.8	2.9

Naples

	Jan	Feb	Mar	Apr	May	June	July	Aug	Sept	Oct	Nov	Dec
Temp. (°F)	50	54	58	63	70	78	83	85	75	66	60	52
Rainfall (in.)	4.7	4	3	3.8	2.4	.8	.8	2.6	3.5	5.8	5.1	3.7

Rome

	Jan	Feb	Mar	Apr	May	June	July	Aug	Sept	Oct	Nov	Dec
Temp. (°F)	49	52	57	62	72	82	87	86	73	65	56	47
Rainfall (in.)	2.3	1.5	2.9	3.0	2.8	2.9	1.5	1.9	2.8	2.6	3.0	2.1

HOLIDAYS   Offices and shops in Italy are closed on the following dates: **January 1** (New Year's Day), **Easter Monday, April 25** (Liberation Day), **May 1** (Labor Day), **August 15** (Assumption of the Virgin), **November 1** (All Saints' Day), **December 8** (Feast of the Immaculate Conception), **December 25** (Christmas Day), and **December 26** (Santo Stefano).

Closings are also observed in the following cities on feast days honoring their patron saints: Venice, **April 25** (St. Mark); Florence, Genoa, and Turin, **June 24** (St. John the Baptist); Rome, **June 29** (Sts. Peter and Paul); Palermo, **July 15** (Santa Rosalia); Naples, **September 19** (St. Gennaro); Bologna, **October 4** (St. Petronio); Cagliari, **October 30** (St. Saturnino); Trieste, **November 3** (San Giusto); Bari, **December 6** (St. Nicola); and Milan, **December 7** (St. Ambrose).

ITALY CALENDAR OF EVENTS

All of Italy, and particularly Rome, is preparing for the arrival of the **Jubilee Year,** the year 2000, the Catholic Church's celebration of the millennium. In typical Italian fashion, a flurry of events, concerts, and festivals that will be concentrated in Rome, but spill over into every city on the peninsula, are far from being confirmed at press time. The jubilee will officially begin with midnight mass on December 24, 1999, celebrated by the pope at St. Peter's in Rome.

For more information about the jubilee and other events that follow, contact the **Italian National Tourist Office** (see "Visitor Information & Entry Requirements," earlier in this chapter) or check the regularly updated Web sites listed above (see page 42) as dates often vary from year to year.

January

- **Epiphany celebrations, nationwide.** All cities, towns, and villages in Italy stage Roman Catholic Epiphany observances. One of the most festive celebrations is the Christmas/Epiphany Fair at Rome's Piazza Navona. From Christmas to January 6.
- **Festival of Italian Popular Song, San Remo (the Italian Riviera).** A 3-day festival when major artists perform the latest Italian song releases. Late January.
- **Foire de Saint Ours, Aosta, Valle d'Aosta.** Observing a tradition that's existed for 10 centuries, artisans from the mountain valleys come together to display their wares—often made of wood, lace, wool, or wrought iron—created during the long winter months. Late January.

February

- **Carnival (English) or *Carnevale* (Italian), Viareggio, on the Tuscan coast.** Fireworks, pageants, parades of papier-mâché floats, and a flower show. Popular with kids and not as theatrical and culturally inclined as Venice's rendition. Dates vary; parades take place three consecutive weekends, culminating on Shrove Tuesday *(Martedi Grasso)*, the day before Ash Wednesday.
- ✪ **Carnevale, Venice.** Venice's Carnival evokes the final theatrical 18th-century days of the Venetian Republic. Historical presentations, elaborate costumes, and music of all types in every piazza cap the festivities. The balls are by invitation, but the cultural events, piazza performances, and fireworks (Shrove Tuesday) are open to everyone. Culminates the week before Shrove Tuesday.
- **Almond Blossom Festival, Agrigento (Sicily).** This folk festival includes song, dance, costumes, and fireworks. First half of February.

April

- **Holy Week (*Settimana Santa*), Rome.** The most notable procession is led by the Pope, passing the Colosseum and Roman Forum up to Palatine Hill. A torch-lit parade caps the observance. Sometimes at the end of March, but often in April.

Hot Tickets

For major events where tickets should be procured well before arriving on the spot, check with **Edwards & Edwards** (☎ **800/223-6108** in the U.S.).

- **Good Friday and Easter Week observances, nationwide.** Processions and age-old ceremonies—some from pagan days, some from the Middle Ages—are staged. The most colorful and evocative are in **Trapani** and other towns throughout **Sicily.** Beginning on the Thursday or Friday before Easter Sunday, usually April.
- **Easter Sunday** (*Pasqua*), **Piazza di San Pietro, Rome.** In an event broadcast around the world, the Pope gives his blessing from a balcony overlooking a packed St. Peter's Square.
- **Scoppio del Carro (Explosion of the Cart), Florence.** An ancient observance: A cart laden with flowers and fireworks is drawn by three white oxen to the duomo, where at noon mass a mechanical dove detonates it from the altar by means of a wire that passes through the duomo's open doors. Easter Sunday.
- **Festa della Primavera, Rome.** The Spanish Steps are decked out with banks of azaleas and other flowers, and later orchestral and choral concerts are presented in Trinità dei Monti. Dates vary.

May
- **Calendimaggio (Celebration of Holy Week), Assisi.** This pagan celebration of spring is held according to rites dating back to medieval times. First weekend after May 1.
- **International Horse Show, Piazza di Siena in the Villa Borghese, Rome.** Usually May 1 to 10, but dates can vary.
- **Sagra di Sant'Efisio (Festival of St. Efisio), Cagliari (Sardinia).** At one of the biggest and most colorful processions in the world, several thousand pilgrims (wearing costumes dating from 1657) accompany the statue of the saint on foot, on horseback, or in a cart. May 1 to 4.
- **Corso dei Ceri, Gubbio.** In this centuries-old ceremony, 1,000-pound 30-foot wooden "candles" (*ceri*) are raced through the streets of this perfectly preserved medieval hill town in Umbria. Celebrating the feast day of St. Ubaldo, the town's patron saint, the candles are mounted by statues of the patron saints of the town's medieval guilds and are raced through the narrow streets and up a steep hill to the monastery. May 15.
- ✪ **Maggio Musicale Fiorentino (Musical May Florentine), Florence.** Italy's oldest and most prestigious festival presents opera, ballet, and concerts. It takes place at the Teatro Comunale, the Teatro della Pergola, and various other venues, including Piazza della Signoria and the courtyard of the Pitti Palace. Schedule and ticket information is available from Maggio Musicale Fiorentino/Teatro Comunale, V. Solferino 16, 50123 Firenze (☎ **055/27-791**). Late April through June.
- **Cavalcata Sarda (Sardinian Cavalcade), Sassari.** Traditional procession with over 3,000 people in Sardinian costumes, some on horseback. Next to last Sunday in May.

June
- **Calcio in Costume (Ancient Football Match in Costume), Florence.** Revival of a raucous 16th-century football match between the four teams representing

the historical districts in medieval costumes preceded by an elaborate procession. Four matches, usually culminating between June 24, feast day of San Giovanni (St. John) beloved patron saint of Florence.

- **L'Infiorata, Genzano, Lazio.** A religious procession along streets carpeted with flowers in splendid designs, often copies of famous artworks. Details are available from Azienda Autonoma di Soggiorno e Turismo dei Laghi e Castelli Romani, Via Risorgimento.
- **San Raineri and the Gioco del Ponte (Bridge Game), Pisa.** Pisa honors its own saint Raineri with candlelit parades followed the next day by eight-rower teams competing in 16th-century costumes. June 16 and 17. The Gioco del Ponte takes place the first Sunday of June, with teams in Renaissance garb taking part in a hotly contested tug-of-war on the Ponte di Mezzo spanning the Arno River.
- ✪ **Festival dei Due Mondi (Festival of Two Worlds), Spoleto.** Dating from 1958, this festival was the creation of American-born Maestro Gian Carlo Menotti whose 86th birthday was celebrated in 1998. It's now the country's biggest and most prestigious arts festival. International performers convene in this lovely Umbrian hill town for 3 weeks of dance, drama, opera, concerts, and art exhibits. Last week of June to mid-July. Tickets and information are available from Festival dei Due Mondi, V. Cesare Beccaria 18, 00196 Roma (☎ 06/32-10-288).
- **Festa di San Pietro, St. Peter's Basilica, Rome.** The most significant Roman religious festival, observed with solemn rites in St. Peter's. Usually around June 29.

Events That Last Throughout the Summer

- **Biennale, Venice.** This is Europe's most prestigious—and controversial—International Exposition of Modern Art, taking place in odd-numbered years only from June to October. More than 50 nations take part, with art displayed in permanent pavilions in the Public Gardens and elsewhere about town. June to September.
- **Son et Lumière, the Roman Forum and Tivoli, Rome.** These areas are dramatically lit at night. Early June to the end of September.
- **Shakespearean Festival, Verona.** Ballet, drama, and jazz performances are included in this festival of the Bard with a few performances in English. June to September.
- ✪ **Il Palio, Piazza del Campo, Siena.** Palio fever grips this Tuscan hill town for a wild and exciting horse race from the Middle Ages. Pageantry, costumes, and the celebrations of the victorious contrada mark the well-attended spectacle. It's a no-rules event: Even a horse without a rider can win the race. Details are available by writing Azienda di Promozione Turistica, Pz. d. Campo 56, 53100 Siena (☎ 0577/28-05-51). Tickets (impossible to come by for non-Sienese) usually sell out by January, but consider joining the nonticket-holding crowd that stands in the middle of the square. July 2 and August 16.
- **Arena di Verona (Outdoor Opera Season in Verona), Verona.** Culture buffs flock to the open-air, 20,000-seat Roman amphitheater, one of the world's best preserved. The season lasts from early July to August for awesome productions of *Aïda* and others.
- **Music and Drama Festival, Taormina, Sicily.** July and August are the most important months for performances held in the resort town's gorgeously sited ancient Greek amphitheater, with Mt. Etna looming in the distance. The local tourism board distributes tickets.

Travel Tip

Try to avoid traveling to Italy in August, as this is when most Italians take their vacations *(ferie)* and many shops and restaurants will be closed. Keep in mind that many of the less expensive hotels we list don't have air-conditioning, and nights can be intolerable.

July

- **World Pride 2000, Rome.** The first-ever World Pride will honor gays, lesbians, bisexuals, and transgender peoples from throughout the world and focus on international civil rights. A host of art exhibits, performances, and cultural and political events will take place, culminating in a demonstration in downtown Rome. For comprehensive information, call ☎ **06-541-3985** or visit www.mariomieli.it or www.interpride.org on the Web. July 1 to 8, 2000.
- **La Festa di Nolantri, Trastevere, Rome.** The most colorful quarter of Old Rome becomes a gigantic outdoor restaurant, as tons of food and drink are consumed at tables lining the streets. Merrymakers and musicians provide the entertainment that has lost some of its authenticity as more and more tourists replace the locals. Mid-July.
- **Umbria Jazz, Perugia.** The Umbrian region hosts the country's (and one of Europe's) top jazz festival featuring world-class artists. Mid- to late July.
- **La Festa del Redentore (Feast of the Redeemer), Venice.** Marks the lifting of the plague in July 1578, with fireworks, pilgrimages, and boating on the lagoon. Third Saturday and Sunday in July.
- **Festival Internazionale di Musica Antica, Urbino.** A cultural extravaganza, as international performers converge on Raphael's birthplace for 10 days. It's the most important Renaissance and baroque music festival in Italy, focusing on music written before 1750. Details are available from Urbino's local A.P.T. (☎ **0722/2613**). Ten days in late July.

August

- **Torre del Lago Puccini, near Lucca.** Puccini operas are performed in this Tuscan lakeside town's open-air theater, near the celebrated composer's former summertime villa. Contact tourist office in Lucca. Throughout August.
- **Rossini Opera Festival, Pesaro.** The world's top bel canto specialists perform Rossini's operas and coral works at this popular festival on the Italian Adriatic Riviera. Mid-August to late September.
- ✪ **Venice International Film Festival.** Ranking after Cannes, this film festival brings together stars, directors, producers, and filmmakers from all over the world. Films are shown both day and night to an international jury as well as to the public, at the Palazzo del Cinema, on the Lido, and other venues. Contact the Venice Tourist Office or the Venice Film Festival (☎ **041/52-18-838**). Two weeks in late August to early September.

September

- **Regata Storica, the Grand Canal, Venice.** All seaworthy gondolas and other craft in Venice participate in the spectacular maritime procession down the Grand Canal that's followed by the much awaited race. First Sunday in September.
- **Giostra del Saracino (Joust of the Saracen), Arezzo.** A colorful procession in full historical regalia precedes the tilting contest of the 13th century with knights in armor in the town's main piazza. First Sunday in September.

Riding in Italy

The Italian countryside has always been legendary for its beauty and architectural richness. Tuscany and Umbria are longtime designated favorites. Several companies specialize in horseback treks and bicycle tours. As a budget traveler, you may want to make your own arrangements through local tourist offices.

CYCLING TOURS   Cycling tours are a good way to see Italy at your own pace. Some of the best are featured by the **Cyclists' Touring Club,** 69 Meadrow, Godalming, Surrey GU7 3HS (☎ **01483/41-72-17;** www.ctc.org.uk; e-mail cycling@ctc.org.uk). It charges £25 a year for adults and £12.50 for those 17 and under for membership, part of which includes information and suggested cycling routes through most European countries. One of the oldest in the United States specializes in walking as well as cycling tours: **Ciclismo Classico** (☎ **800/866-7314;** www.ciclismoclassico.com).

If you want to cycle on your own, head to the Web site of Florence Bike Pages (**www.abeline.it/fbp.htm**). You'll find bike maps of Florence and Tuscany, instructions on how to bike solo, and information on bike supplements for the trains (many trains have a cargo car for bikes; look for a bike icon on train schedules that designates these trains).

For a guided 1-day bike trip, **I Bike Italy** (in Florence ☎ **055/234-2371;** www.ibikeitaly.com; e-mail IBikeItaly@compuserve.com) explores the idyllic Tuscan countryside surrounding Florence (walking tours are also arranged). Bikes, a guide, a picnic lunch, and car transfer in and out of the city center are provided.

The Perugia-based **Porta Sole** (☎ **39/075-573-6364;** www.promoumbria.it/vvs; e-mail vvs@promoumbria.it) is a helpful source for cycling, walking, and gourmet tours throughout the region of Umbria, including cooking courses and villa rentals as well.

HORSEBACK RIDING   High in the Chianti hills southeast of Florence outside Arezzo, Englishwoman Jenny Bawtree has been running a 12-acre farm and riding school for 30 years. **Rendola Riding** has 20 horses (for English riding only) that take both novices and experts into the surrounding countryside for organized trips of a few hours or many days. Flexible and varied 1-week tours and destinations are available. Using Rendola as a nightly base (eight rustic guests rooms are available) costs 1,694,000 to 1,892,000L ($996 to $1,113) per person on a double occupancy basis; a Chianti camping tour by horseback costs 1,450,000L ($853) per person. Short stays (minimum of 2 nights) cost 120,000L

- **Partita a Scacchi con Personnagi Viventi (Living Chess Game), Marostica.** This chess game is played in the town square by living pawns in period costume. The second Saturday/Sunday of September during even-numbered years.

October

- **Sagra del Tartufo, Alba, Piedmont.** Honors the expensive truffle in Alba, the truffle capital of Italy, with contests, truffle-hound competitions, and tastings of this ugly but precious and delectable fungus. Two weeks in mid-October.

December

- ✪ **La Scala Opera Season, Teatro alla Scala, Milan.** At the most famous opera house of them all, the season opens on December 7, the feast day of Milan's

($70.60) per person, double occupancy basis, full board with riding extra at 25,000L ($14.70) per hour. ☎ and fax **055/9707045;** e-mail bawtree@ats.it; www.freeweb.org/hobby/silicito/rendola/index.html.

Southwest of Siena the Italian-Austrian Paradisi family has been running the **Rifugio Prategiano** for more than 30 years in this little-visited area of Tuscany called the Maremma (☎ **0566/997700;** fax 0566/997891; e-mail prategian@ bigfoot.com; prategiano.heimatseite.com). Mountain bikers and hikers will also be happy here, but it's the Rifugio's 20 horses (with English or trail saddles) that are the draw, and the many different outings they offer to nearby points of a interest: Etruscan tombs, Tuscany's nearby white sandy beaches, through olive groves to castle ruins and natural hot springs. There's a pool and the choice of three-star accommodation (weekly rate of $454 per person, double occupancy, full board) or in less fussy quarters over the stables with shared bathrooms (weekly rate of $317 per person, double occupancy, full board). Riding is additional, with six full-day rides at $332.

One of Tuscany's top riding clubs is **Il Paretaio** (☎ **055/8059218;** fax (055)8059231; e-mail: ilparetaio@dada.it), located 30 minutes south of Florence in the heart of Chianti in Barberino Val d'Elsa. In addition to lessons, riders can opt for half- and full-day outings (English-style) through the Tuscan countryside, choosing from any of the 20 horses available. Riders stay in six guest rooms with shared facilities in an early 18th-century stone farmhouse with a view—even the pool is beautifully sited. Dressage lessons cost 45,000L ($26.50) per hour; full-day trail riding with picnic is 130,000L ($76.50), no room or board; 1-week all-inclusive packages with 6 half-days of trail riding and half-board on a double occupancy basis costs 1,170,000L ($688.20) per person.

Even closer to Florence (20km/12.6 mi.) in Pontassieve but in countryside that is quintessentially Tuscan is the **Vallebona Ranch** (☎055/8397246; fax 055/8398518; e-mail vallebona@iol.it). English riding is available, but Western is the tradition here and guests can choose from lessons, full-day treks returning daily to the six guest bedrooms (with shared bathrooms) at the centuries-old farmhouse, or weeklong inn-to-inn itineraries that begin and end at Vallebona. One-week all inclusive with full board and lodging at Vallebona is 850,000L ($500) per person double occupancy; 1-week inn-to-inn treks are 1,100,000L ($647.05) per person double occupancy, all inclusive.

patron St. Ambrogio, and runs into July. Though it's close to impossible to get opening-night tickets, it's worth a try; call ☎ **02/80-70-41** for information or 02/80-91-26 for reservations. Restoration of the opera house is scheduled to be finished in time for the opening of the 1999 season.

- **Midnight Mass, Christmas**, **Assisi.** The pope inaugurates the opening of the Jubilee Year on December 24, 1999, in the Basilica of St. Francis, by special invitation only. December 31, New Year's Eve 1999, in Rome should prove to be one massive street *festa* as the city rings in the 2000-year anniversary of the Catholic Church.

- **Christmas Blessing of the Pope, Piazza di San Pietro.** Delivered at noon from a balcony of St. Peter's Basilica. It's broadcast around the world. December 25.

6 Learning & Special Interest Vacations

The inclusion of an organization in this section is in no way to be interpreted as a guarantee. Information about the organization is presented only to point you toward possibilities for your own investigations.

CULTURAL EXCHANGE

Italy doesn't have an established "Meet the Italians" program, but cities and most towns have an official tourist office (called either **EPT, Ente Provinciale per il Turismo,** or **AAST, Azienda Autonoma di Sogiorno e Turismo**) that might arrange for you to stay with or just meet an Italian family. Such arrangements are usually made for those staying for several weeks or more in an Italian city. Requests should be sent several months before your trip to Italy by writing to the official tourist office of the town.

The Friendship Force, 57 Forsyth St. NW, Suite 900, Atlanta, GA 30303 (☎ **800/554-6715** or 404/522-9490), is a nonprofit organization existing to foster friendship among peoples around the world. Each participant is required to spend 1 to 2 weeks in the host country with 1 full week in the home of a family as a guest. You can then spend the second week traveling in the host country.

Servas (an Esperanto word meaning "to serve"), 11 John St., Room 407, New York, NY 10038 (☎ **212/267-0252;** www.servas.org), is a nonprofit, nongovernmental, international, interfaith network of travelers and hosts whose goal is to help build world peace, goodwill, and understanding. They do this by providing opportunities for contacts among people of diverse cultures and communities worldwide through 2-day home visits or single-day visits (meeting for tea or sightseeing, for example). Travelers pay a $65 annual fee and a $25 list deposit, fill out an application, and are interviewed for suitability. Hosts also are interviewed, make a voluntary contribution of $25, and are contacted by travelers who arrange for their visit.

Language Programs Schools and programs offering courses in the Italian language, always throw in a few featuring fine arts, cooking, history, literature, and Italian culture. Courses are available at several centers throughout the Italian peninsula, with the most varied and best-recommended usually headquartered in what most Italians refer to as their nation's intellectual and cultural capital, Florence. It is here, the descendants of Dante defend, that perfect Italian is spoken.

You can call or fax any of the following for information about programs located across Italy, varying in length, location (city versus rural), short or long term and varying greatly in price: The **Italian Cultural Institute** in New York (☎ 212/879-4242); **The American Institute for Foreign Study** (☎ 800/727-AIFS; www.aifs.org); **Institute of International Education** (☎ 800/445-0443 or 212 984-5413; www.iie.org).

Language Study Abroad, 1301 N. Maryland Ave., Glendale, CA 91207 (☎ 818/242-5263; e-mail cdoo2380@mindspring.com; www.languagestudy.com/italy2.htm),

A Great General-Interest & Educational Website

At the InfoHub Specialty Travel Guide (**www.infohub.com**) you can find tours in Italy (as well as other countries) centered around just about everything: antiques, archaeology, art history, churches, cooking, gay life, nudism, religion, wineries, and much more. If this sounds expensive to you, don't worry—while searching the site, you can even set your own price limit.

is associated with the Centro di Lingua e Cultura Italiana in Rome; its 2-week, 40-hour program costs 480,000L ($282.). Private lessons are an option at 500,000L ($295.) for 10 hours. **The British Institute of Florence,** offers courses on Italian Language and Culture from 3 days to 4 weeks, Palazzo Lanfredini, Lungarno Guicciardini 9, 50125 Firenze (☎ 055/284031; fax 055/289557). You can also contact the **Centro di Lingua e Cultura Italiana per Stranieri,** Pz. Santo Spirito 4, 50134 Firenze (☎ **055/23-96-966;** fax 055/28-08-00); and the **Centro Linguistico Italiano Dante Alighieri,** V. de'Bardi 12, 50125 Firenze (☎ **055/2342984;** fax 055/2342766), with branches in Siena, Rome and other cities.

AN ARCHAEOLOGICAL DIG   With digs hardly as available as those in Israel or Egypt, Italy offers the occasional dig for those who dig archaeology—but they don't come cheaply: contact the **Poggio Colla Field School** (☎ **214/768-2783** or 214/768-2698; e-mail gwarden@mail.smu.edu; www.upenn.edu/museum_pubs/poggio/field_school.html). Poggio Colla, an Etruscan hilltop settlement about 22 miles northeast of Florence, is being excavated by a team of archaeologists sponsored by the Southern Methodist University and the University of Pennsylvania Museum of Archaeology and Anthropology. A limited numbers of volunteers are allowed to participate for 6 weeks from mid-June to late July at a cost of $4,000, which includes tuition, lodging in excavation houses, meals, and local commute.

PROGRAMS FOR SENIORS   One of the most dynamic organizations for seniors over 55 is **Elderhostel,** 75 Federal St., Boston, MA 02110 (☎ **617/426-7788** or 877/426-8056; www.elderhostel.org). It offers informal educational programs throughout Europe, most lasting around 3 weeks. These trips are a good value, considering airfare, hotel accommodations in student dorms or modest inns, all meals, and tuition are included. Courses are especially focused in the liberal arts. Elderhostel's offerings in Italy include a historic and artistic overview of Sicily from headquarters in the fishing village of Mondello (outside of Palermo) and an introduction to the art and architecture of Umbria and Tuscany. Contact the address above for Elderhostel's free catalog and a list of upcoming courses and destinations.

7 Organized Tours, Package Tours & Tour Operators

Before you start your search for the lowest airfare, you may want to consider booking your flight as part of a travel package such as an escorted tour or a package tour. What you lose in adventure, you'll gain in time and money saved when you book accommodations, and maybe even food and entertainment, along with your flight. If you're planning on visiting a lot of different destinations throughout Italy, a good tour operator will make sure that you don't have to worry about the logistics of connections, transportation in places where language might be a problem or looking after your own luggage, coping with reservations and payment at individual hotels, and facing other nuts and bolts of travel in a foreign culture. Some travelers may find the biggest compromise is the hotel factor. Most lodging is found in large modern facilities (sometimes on the outskirts of town), not in the small charming places in the *centro storico.* Although several of the best-rated moderately priced companies are described below, check as well with a good travel agent, on the Internet or in your newspaper for the latest offerings and advice.

One of the more moderately priced package-tour operators for travel in Italy is **Italiatour,** part of the Alitalia Group (☎ **800/845-3365** or 212/765-2183; www.italiatour.com), which offers a wide variety of tours at great savings in the off season. The company appeals to the free-at-heart and specializes in tours for independent travelers who ride from one destination to another by train or rental car. In most cases, the company sells prereserved hotel accommodations that are usually less expensive than if you had reserved yourself. The range of accommodations provided begins with three-star hotels that, when booked with their bulk discount, can account for a very attractive bottom line. Because of the company's close link with Alitalia, the prices quoted for air passage are sometimes among the most reasonable on the retail market.

Also working with volume and affiliated with Alitalia—and therefore promising big-volume discounts—is the reputable **Central Holidays Tours (CHT)** (☎ **800/ 935-5000;** www.centralholidays.com), which offers low- and high-season package tours that are escorted, hosted, or independent. This outfitter is also a good choice if you want to mix and match your own arrangements: they'll help with air, hotel, and car rental according to your needs.

There are smaller, equally established agencies that specialize in Italy and often come up with rates comparable to the big guys. **Pino Travel** (☎ **800/247-6578** or 212/682-5400; www.pinotravel.com) and **Penem Travel** (☎ **800/628-1345** or 212/ 730-7675) offer a pick-and-choose menu of car rental, air, and hotel; **Maiellano** (☎ **800/223-1616**) specializes in discount car rental but has successfully expanded into all aspects of travel in Italy.

The London headquarters of the **IATA (International Association of Travel Agencies)** (☎ **0181/74-49-280**) can provide the names and addresses of tour operators who specialize in travel relating to your particular interest or destination in Italy.

8 Health & Insurance

STAYING HEALTHY   You'll encounter few health problems traveling in Italy. Aside from the occasional sign **ACQUA NON POTABILE** (do not drink the water), Italy's tap water is generally safe to drink (though complaints often have to do with what it tastes like), the milk pasteurized, and health services good.

Bring along copies of your prescriptions that are written in the generic, not brand-name, form. If you need a doctor, your hotel can recommend one or you can contact your embassy or consulate. You can also obtain a list of English-speaking doctors before you leave from the **International Association for Medical Assistance to Travelers (IAMAT),** in the United States at 417 Center St., Lewiston, NY 14092 (☎ **716/ 754-4883**), or in Canada at 40 Regal Rd., Guelph, ON N1K 1B5 (☎ **519/ 836-0102**). Its Web address is **www.sentex.net/~iamat.**

If you suffer from a chronic illness or special medical condition, consider purchasing a Medic Alert identification bracelet or necklace, which will immediately alert any doctor to your condition and will provide Medic Alert's 24-hour hot line phone number so that foreign doctors can obtain medical information on you. The initial membership is $35, and there's a $15 annual fee. Contact the **Medic Alert Foundation,** 2323 Colorado Ave., Turlock, CA 95381-1009 (☎ **800/432-5378;** www. medicalert.org).

INSURANCE   Before purchasing any additional insurance, check your homeowner's, automobile, and medical insurance policies, as well as the insurance provided by your credit card companies and auto and travel clubs. You may have adequate off-premises theft coverage or your credit card company may even provide cancellation coverage if your airline ticket is paid for with a credit card.

Remember, Medicare covers only U.S. citizens traveling in Mexico and Canada, not in Italy or other European countries. Also note that to submit any insurance claim you must always have thorough documentation, including all receipts, police reports, and medical records.

Travel Guard International, 1145 Clark St., Stevens Point, WI 54481 (☎ **800/ 826-1300;** www.travelguard.com), features comprehensive insurance programs starting as low as $48. The program covers basically everything: trip cancellation and interruption, lost luggage, medical coverage abroad, emergency assistance, accidental death, and a 24-hour worldwide emergency hot line. A preexisting medical conditions waiver is included.

With **Travel Insured International,** P.O. Box 280568, East Hartford, CT 06128-0568 (☎ **800/243-3174** in the U.S., or 203/528-7663 outside the U.S. between 7:45am and 7pm EST), trip cancellation and emergency evacuation costs $5.50 for each $100 of coverage. Travel accident and illness insurance goes for $10 for 6 to 10 days, and $500 of insurance for lost, damage, or delayed luggage is $20 for 10 days. The insurance is underwritten by The Travelers Group.

Travelex Insurance Services (☎ **800/228-9792**) offers cruise and tour insurance packages that include travel-assistance services and financial protection against trip cancellation, trip interruption, flight and baggage delays, sickness, accident-related medical costs, accidental death and dismemberment, and medical evacuation coverage. Application for insurance packages beginning at $67 per person can be made over the phone with a major credit card.

In London you can call **Columbus Travel Insurance** (☎ **171/375-0011;** www.columbusdirect.co.uk) or **Endsleigh Insurance** (☎ **171/436-4451;** www. endsleigh.co.uk). In Sydney contact the **Australian Federation of Travel Agents (AFTA)** (☎ **02/9264-3299;** www.afta.com.au).

9 Tips for Travelers with Special Needs

FOR TRAVELERS WITH DISABILITIES

If you're flying around Europe, the airlines and ground staff will help you on and off planes and reserve seats for you with sufficient legroom, but it's essential to arrange for this assistance in advance by contacting your airline.

Recent laws in Italy have compelled rail stations, airports, hotels, and most restaurants to follow a stricter set of regulations about wheelchair accessibility to rest rooms, ticket counters, and so on. Many museums and other sightseeing attractions have conformed to these regulations. **Alitalia,** as Italy's most visible airline, has made a special effort to make its planes, public areas, rest rooms, and access ramps as wheelchair-friendly as possible.

RESOURCES IN THE UNITED STATES   Several agencies can provide advance-planning information. One is the **Travel Information Service,** MossRehab Hospital, 1200 W. Tabor Rd., Philadelphia, PA 19141, which provides information to telephone callers only: Call ☎ **215/456-9600** (voice) or 215/456-9602 (TDD). Its Web address is **www.mossresourcenet.org**.

You may also want to consider joining a tour for visitors with disabilities. You can get names and addresses of such tour operators and miscellaneous travel info by contacting the **Society for the Advancement of Travel for the Handicapped,** 347 Fifth Ave. Suite 601, New York, NY 10016 (☎ **212/447-7284**). Annual membership dues are $45 or $25 for seniors and students. Send a self-addressed stamped envelope.

For the blind or visually impaired, the best source is the **American Foundation for the Blind,** 11 Penn Plaza, Suite 300, New York, NY 10001 (☎ **800/232-5463,** or 212/502-7600 for ordering information booklets; www.afb.org). It offers information on travel and the various requirements for the transport of and border formalities for Seeing Eye dogs.

Contact **Twin Peaks Press** (☎ **800/637-2256** or (206)694-2462; www.pacifier. com/~twinpeak), publisher of the **Directory of Travel Agents for the Disabled** ($19.95), for a list of more than 370 agencies worldwide. Two of the many U.S. agencies that cater to disabled travelers are **Access First Traveler** (☎ **800/557-2047;** e-mail accessfir@aol.com) and **Flying Wheels** (☎ **800/535-6790;** www.flyingwheels. com).

Accessible Italy (www.tour-web.com/accitaly/index,html) concentrates on info pertinent to Rome, Florence, Venice, and Milan for the traveler with reduced mobility. This operator can help plan itineraries to a host of other Italian cities as well.

Armchair World: The Well Informed Traveler (www.armchair.com/info/ netinfo/html) targets U.S. citizens traveling abroad with information about (but not limited to) passengers with disabilities.

Yahoo! Travel Agents: Special Needs (www.yahoo.com/business_and_economy/ companies/travel/agents/special_needs/index.html) provides information listing travel agents who specialize in planning trips for the disabled.

RESOURCES IN THE UNITED KINGDOM   **RADAR** (Royal Association for Disability and Rehabilitation), Unit 12, City Forum, 250 City Rd., London EC1V 8AF (☎ **0171/250-3222;** www.radar.org.uk), publishes holiday fact packs—three in all—which sell for £2 each or £5 for all three. The first one provides general information, including planning and booking a holiday, insurance, and finances. The second outlines transport and equipment, transportation available when going abroad, and equipment for rent. The third deals with specialized accommodations.

Another good resource is **Holiday Care Service,** 2nd Floor, Imperial Building, Victoria Road, Horley, Surrey RH6 7PZ (☎ **01293/77-45-35;** fax 01293/78-46-47), a national service organization that advises on accessible accommodations. Annual membership costs £25. Once you're a member, you can receive a newsletter including information about hotels throughout Europe.

FOR GAY & LESBIAN TRAVELERS

Since 1861, Italy has had liberal legislation regarding homosexuality, but that doesn't mean it's always looked on favorably in a Catholic country, especially in Sicily (though Taormina has long been a gay mecca). Homosexuality is much more accepted in the north than in the deep south, particularly the smaller provincial towns. However, all major towns and cities have an active gay life, especially Florence, Milan, Rome, and Bologna. Milan considers itself the gay capital of Italy (Bologna is a proud contender) and is the headquarters of **ARCI Gay,** the country's leading gay organization, with branches throughout Italy. **Capri** is the gay resort of Italy, with a predominant Milanese following, with the Amalfi Coast's resort town of Positano (just across the Bay of Naples) just a boat ride away. A gay-operated, English-speaking travel agency in Rome, **Zipper Travel** (V. Francesco Carletti 8, Rome 00154, ☎ **06/488-2730;** fax 06/488-2729; e-mail tptravel@aconet.it) can help create itineraries in both large and small cities, as well as make reservations for travel and hotel.

To learn more about gay and lesbian travel in Italy, you can secure publications and join data-dispensing organizations before you go. Men can order *Spartacus,* the international gay guide ($32.95), or *Odysseus,* a guide to international gay accommodations ($27). Both lesbians and gay men might want to pick up a copy of *Gay Travel A to Z* ($16), which specializes in general information, as well as listings of bars, hotels, restaurants, and places of interest for gay travelers throughout the world.

Macmillan Travel has just published its first guide especially for gays and lesbians, *Frommer's Gay & Lesbian Europe* ($21.95), which includes Rome, Florence,

Venice, and Milan among its offerings. These books and others are available from **A Different Light,** 151 W. 19th St., New York, NY 10011 (☎ **800/343-4002** or 212/989-4850; www.adlbooks.com), and **Giovanni's Room,** 1145 Pine St., Philadelphia, PA 19107 (☎ **215/923-2960;** fax 215/923-0813).

Our World, 1104 North Nova Rd., Suite 251, Daytona Beach, FL 32117 (☎ **904/441-5367;** www.pimps.com/ourworld), is a magazine devoted to options and bargains for gay and lesbian travel worldwide. It costs $35 for 10 issues in the States. The upscale *Out and About,* 8 West 19th St., Suite 401, New York, NY 10011 (☎ **800/929-2268;** www.outandabout.com), has been hailed for its straight reporting about gay travel. It profiles the best gay or gay-friendly hotels, gyms, clubs, and other places throughout the world. It costs $49 a year for 10 information-packed issues. Both publications are available at most gay and lesbian bookstores.

The **International Gay & Lesbian Travel Association (IGLTA),** P.O. Box 4974, Key West, FL 33041 (☎ **800/448-8550;** www.iglta.com), encourages gay and lesbian travel worldwide. With around 1,300 member travel agencies, it specializes in networking travelers with the appropriate gay-friendly service organizations or tour specialists. It offers a quarterly newsletter, marketing mailings, and a membership directory that is updated four times a year.

In the United States, the following travel agencies specialize in gay and lesbian travel and offer frequent though erratically scheduled tours to Italy: **Yellowbrick Road Travel** (☎ **800/642-2488** or 312/561-1800); **Kennedy Travel** (☎ **800/988-1181** or 212/242-3222); and **Advance-Damron Vacations** (☎ **800/695-0880**).

In London, travel agencies offering similar services include: **Alternative Holidays** (☎ **171/701-7040;** fax 171/708-5668; e-mail info@alternativeholidays.com); **In Touch Holidays** (☎ **181/742-7749;** fax 181/742-7407; www.bogo.co.uk/alternatives); **London Handling Ltd.** (☎ **171/589-2212;** fax 171/225-1033); and **Zone One** (☎ 171/730-2347; fax 171/730-9756).

FOR SENIORS

Many senior discounts are available, but note that some may require membership in a particular association.

For information before you go, obtain the free booklet *101 Tips for the Mature Traveler,* from **Grand Circle Travel,** 347 Congress St., Boston, MA 02210 (☎ **800/221-2610** or 617/350-7500; www.gct.com).

SAGA International Holidays, 222 Berkeley St., Boston, MA 02116 (☎ **800/343-0273;** www.saga.com), runs all-inclusive tours for those 50 years old or older. Insurance is included in the net price of their tours.

AARP (American Association of Retired Persons) is the leading organization in the United States for seniors. It offers discounts on car rentals and hotels. For more information, contact AARP at 601 E St. NW, Washington, DC 20049 (☎ **800/424-3410** or 202/434-AARP; www.aarp.org).

Information is also available from the **National Council of Senior Citizens,** 8403 Colesville Rd., Suite 1200, Silver Spring, MD 20910 (☎ **301/578-8800;** www.ncscinc.org), charging $13 per person or per couple. You receive a bimonthly magazine, part of which is devoted to travel tips, as well as discounts on hotel and auto rentals.

If you're 45 or older and need a companion to share your travel and leisure with, consider contacting **Golden Companions,** P.O. Box 5249, Reno, NV 89513 (☎ **702/324-2227**). Founded in 1987, this helpful service has found companions for hundreds of mature travelers from all over the United States and Canada. Members meet through a confidential mail network.

FOR FAMILIES

IN THE UNITED STATES *Family Travel Times* is published bimonthly and includes a weekly call-in service for subscribers. Subscriptions cost $39 a year and can be ordered by writing to Family Travel Times, P.O. Box 14326, Washington, DC 20044-4326 (☎ **888/822-4388**).

Families Welcome! Great Destinations Incorporated, 92 Main St., Ashland, OR 97520 (☎ **800/326-0724** or 541/482-5806; e-mail europalet@wave.net), is a travel company specializing in worry-free vacations for families and can help with apartment rentals in Rome, Florence, and Venice.

IN THE UNITED KINGDOM The best deals for families are often package tours put together by some of the giants of the British travel industry. Foremost among these is **Thomsons Tour Operators** (☎ **0171/387-9321**), which offers dozens of air/land packages to Italy, where a designated number of airline seats are reserved for the free use of children under 18 who accompany their parents. To qualify, parents must book airfare and hotel accommodations lasting 2 weeks or more, as far in advance as possible. Savings for families with children can be substantial.

FOR STUDENTS

IN THE UNITED STATES **Council Travel Service (CTS)** (a subsidiary of the Council on International Educational Exchange) is America's largest student, youth, and budget travel group, with more than 60 offices worldwide. The main office is at 205 E. 42nd St., New York, NY 10017 (☎ **800/226-8624** or 212/822-2700; www. counciltravel. com). International Student Identity Cards **(ISIC)**, issued to all bona fide students for $19, entitle holders to generous travel and other discounts. Discounted international and domestic air tickets are available (nonstudents under 25 are eligible for similar but limited discounts), as well as Eurail passes, YHA (Youth Hostel Association) passes, weekend packages, and hostel/hotel accommodations are also bookable.

Since youth hostels are the place to stay if you're a student or, in some cases, if you're traveling on an ultratight budget, budget travelers should consider joining **Hostelling International/American Youth Hostels (HI-AYH).** For information, contact Hostelling Information/American Youth Hostels, 733 15th St. NW, No. 840, P.O. Box 37613, Washington, DC 20013-7613 (☎ **202/783-6161**; www.hiayh.org). Membership costs $25 annually, but those age 17 and under pay $10 and those 55 and older pay $15.

IN THE UNITED KINGDOM & ABROAD **CTS's** (see above) U.K. office is at 28A Poland St. (Oxford Circus), London WIV 3DB (☎ **0171/437-7767**); the **Italy office** is in Rome, near the train station at V. Genova 16, 00184 Roma (☎ **06/ 46791**). In Canada, **Travel CUTS,** 187 College St., Toronto, Ont. M5T 1P7 (☎ **416/798-2887**), offers similar services.

USIT Campus Travel, 52 Grosvenor Gardens, London SW1W OAG (☎ **0171/ 730-3402**), opposite Victoria Station (and with a dozen branches throughout England), open daily, is Britain's leading specialist in student and youth travel. It provides a comprehensive service specializing in low-cost rail, sea, and airfares, holiday breaks, and travel insurance, plus student discount cards.

The International Student Identity Card **(ISIC)** is an internationally recognized proof of student status that entitles you to savings on flights, sightseeing, food, and

Travel Tip

Most youth hostels fill up in the summer, so be sure to book ahead.

accommodation. It sells for £5 and is well worth the cost. Always show your ISIC when booking a trip—you may not get a discount without it.

If you're planning on staying in hostels, you'll need an **International Youth Hostels Association** card, which you can purchase from either of London's youth hostel retail outlets, near Covent Garden at 14 Southampton St., London WC23 7HY (☎ **0171/83-68-541**), and at 52 Grosvenor Gardens, London SW1W OAG (☎ **0171/82-34-739**; in the same building as Campus Travel). The outlets sell rucksacks, hiking boots, maps, and all the paraphernalia a camper, hiker, or shoestring traveler might need. To apply for a membership card, take your passport and some passport-size photos of yourself, plus a membership fee of £9.30. For more information, contact **Youth Hostels Association of England and Wales (YHA),** 8 St. Stephen's Hill, St. Albans, Hertfordshire AL1 2DY (☎ **01727/855-215**).

The Youth Hostel Association puts together a *YHA Budget Accommodations Guide* (Volumes 1 and 2), which lists the address, phone number, and admissions policy for every youth hostel in the world. (Volume 1 covers Europe and the Mediterranean, Volume 2 the rest of the globe.) They cost £6.99 each and can be bought at the retail outlets above. If ordering by mail, add 61p for postage in the United Kingdom.

10 Getting There Without Going Broke

BY PLANE
The upheavals that shook the airline industry during the early 1990s have subsided a bit, but despite relative calm, the industry may still undergo some changes during the life of this edition. For up-to-date conditions, check with a travel agent, consolidators, the various Web sites we suggest or directly with the individual airlines for promotional discounts.

Flying time to **Rome** from New York, Newark, and Boston is 8 hours, from Chicago 10 hours, and from Los Angeles 12½ hours. Flying time to **Milan** from New York, Newark, and Boston is 8 hours, from Chicago 9¼ hours, and from Los Angeles 11½ hours. Consider flying into Rome and out of Milan (or vice versa) if it facilitates your travel arrangements; there is usually no additional cost.

Fares to Italy are constantly changing, but you can expect to pay as low as $400 during winter months and in the range of $800 to $1,000 for a direct round-trip ticket during peak months from New York to Rome in coach class. Consolidators may undercut these rates.

Those interested in an attractive deal combining a stop of a few hours or a few days (or more) in a major European city en route to Italy should consider one of the European carriers below. In order to encourage the public to choose a nondirect alternative, round-trip rates are often handsomely discounted and direct connections sometimes involve no more than an hour or two (check for details and avoid change of airports in London and Paris where possible). By connecting in major European hubs, you may also be able to avoid Milan and Rome by flying into Italy's secondary international airports, like Venice, Pisa, Florence, Naples, or Palermo. **British Airways** (☎ **800/AIRWAYS;** www.british-airways.com) stops over in London, **Lufthansa** (☎ **800/645-3880**) in Frankfurt, **Air France** (☎ **800/237-2747;** www.airfrance. com) in Paris, and **KLM** (☎ **800/374-7747;** www.klm.nl) in Amsterdam.

FROM THE UNITED STATES & CANADA
The major Italian carrier, **Alitalia** (☎ **800/223-5730** in the U.S., or 514/842-8241 in Canada; www.alitalia.it/english/index.html), offers the most extensive flight schedule. It flies nonstop to both Rome and Milan from a number of North American cities, including New York's JFK, Newark, Boston, Chicago, Miami, and Los

Angeles. Schedules are designed to facilitate easy transfers to all the major Italian cities. Unlike American carriers, Alitalia may add on a small leg to your flight, if your final destination is a secondary airport, for no extra cost (this doesn't apply to all fares). For example, on direct flights from New York to Milan, you may connect and fly on to Venice for the same rate. Many European airlines, including Alitalia, offer students or anyone 12 to 24 a youth fare, which you can buy only within 72 hours of departure; its primary advantage is that it's good for up to 12 months. Infants under 2 fly for 10% of an adult fare and children under 12 fly for 75% of an adult fare. Unlike most other international carriers, Alitalia doesn't forbid smoking, although its smoking section has been cut back to just a few rows.

Canada's second largest airline, Calgary-based **Canadian Airlines International** (☎ **800/426-7000;** www.cdnair.ca), flies every day of the week from Toronto to Rome.

Finding the Best Fare

HIGH & LOW SEASON   **January** and **February** are low-season months when last-minute rates can be remarkably low. **November** and **preholiday December** have recently become as favorable a period for minimum fares. The beginning and cutoff dates designating high season—usually June 1 through September—may vary a little among some airlines. Shoulder season may be April through May, October, and December 15 to 24. Low season is generally November 1 to December 14 and early January to March 31.

APEX FARES   Advance-purchase booking (still referred to as APEX by some lines) is often, but not always, the key to getting the lowest fare. Policies may differ from one airline to the next. You generally must be willing to make your plans and buy your tickets as far ahead as possible: The **21-day APEX** is seconded only by the **14-day APEX,** with a stay in Italy of 7 to 30 days. Moreover, since the number of seats allocated to APEX fares is severely limited (sometimes to less than 25% of the capacity of a particular plane), the early bird gets the low-cost seat. There's often a surcharge for flying on a weekend in either direction, and be aware that the peak season may have a shoulder season, comprising those weeks before and after the peak season, with only slightly slower rates. Cancellation and refund policies can be strict. Absolute freedom is given to those who buy a regular economy fare that has no restrictions and is naturally the most expensive item on the market. One-way tickets are so extreme, it is almost always worth buying a discounted round-trip ticket, and forfeiting the return half.

CONSOLIDATORS   Also called "bucket shops," consolidators act as clearinghouses for blocks of excess-inventory tickets that major international airline carriers discount to a wholesaler or consolidator. These aren't charters, and the service is now available in peak periods (when discounts are moderate) as well as in the slow season (when savings can be major). You might even be able to accrue frequent-flier miles. This is the factory-outlet approach to ticket shopping; when using the established and trustworthy agencies, the risk is extremely low. Tickets are sometimes priced at up to 35% (and more) off the full fare. Terms of payment can vary—say, anywhere from 45 days prior to departure to last-minute sales offered in a final attempt by an airline to fill an empty aircraft. Restrictions may apply: Inquire about the conditions involved in cancellations, refunds, and reendorsing to another airline should your carrier delay or cancel. Ask about those frequent-flier miles. Paying by credit card should be your preference, if allowed, to guarantee further protection.

Since dealing with unknown bucket shops still carries some risk, it's wise to call the Better Business Bureau in your area to see if complaints have been filed against the company from which you plan to purchase a ticket. After booking with the agency, call the airline the agency has booked you on to see if you appear on their confirmed passenger list.

One of the biggest U.S. consolidators is **Travac,** 989 Sixth Ave., 16th Floor, New York, NY 10018 (☎ **800/TRAV-800** or 212/563-3303; www.the travelsite.com), which offers discounted seats throughout the United States to most cities in Europe on commercial airlines. Another branch office is at 2601 E. Jefferson St., Orlando, FL 32803 (☎ **407/896-0014**).

In New York try **TFI Tours International,** 34 W. 32nd St., 12th Floor, New York, NY 10001 (☎ **800/745-8000** or 212/736-1140), which offers services to well over 150 cities worldwide.

We've also had good service and good deals by using **1-800-FLY-4-LESS, 1-800-FLY-CHEAP** or Cheap Tickets at **1-800-377-1000** with a Web site at www.cheaptickets.com.

From the Midwest, explore the possibilities of **Travel Avenue,** 10 S. Riverside Plaza, Suite 1404, Chicago, IL 60606 (☎ **800/333-3335;** www.travelavenue.com), a national agency with tickets that keeps up with the best.

Another possibility is **TMI (Travel Management International),** 3617 Dupont Ave. S, Minneapolis, MN 55409 (☎ **800/245-3672**), offering a wide variety of discounts, including youth fares, student fares, and access to other kinds of air-related discounts. **UniTravel,** 11737 Administration Dr., Suite 120, St. Louis, MO 63146 (☎ **800/325-2222**) is your best choice for last-minute and short-notice flights to Europe.

The ultimate free-spirited traveler should contact **Airhitch,** 2641 Broadway, 3rd Floor, New York NY 10025 (☎ **800/326-2009** or 212/864-2000; www.airhitch.org). Just pick a 5-day period during which you can fly to a general area of Europe (northern versus southern); most passengers are booked within their first or second day. Here are typical one-way fares: from the northeast United States to Europe $159, Midwest to Europe $209, southeast to Europe $189, West Coast or Northwest to Europe $239.

Similar rates are available to flexible travelers from **Airtech** (☎ **212/219-7000;** www.airtech.com), which caters to care-free travelers who don't mind landing in Zurich instead of Milan on Monday instead of Wednesday. You can get discounted hotel prices on budget accommodations that are potentially short on atmosphere but big on savings.

A California company has started a EurailPass-like approach to air travel within Europe called **EurairPass** (☎ **888/387-2479;** www.europeflightpass.com) for U.S. citizens. More than 60 European cities are linked by 13 participating airlines in 20 countries including Italy. Coupons represent one flight, each costing $90 and valid for 120 days. A minimum of three segments must be purchased.

CHARTER FLIGHTS   Strictly for reasons of economy (and rarely for convenience), some travelers are willing to accept the possible uncertainties of a charter flight to Italy, a dying breed of travel as the major airlines now match charter prices when booked through consolidators.

In a strict sense, a charter flight occurs on an aircraft reserved months in advance for a one-time-only transit to some predetermined point (and often arrives in a major city's secondary airport, such as Rome's Ciampino Airport). Before paying for a charter, check the restrictions. You can wind up paying a stiff penalty or forfeit the ticket entirely if you cancel or change dates. Charters are occasionally canceled when the plane doesn't fill up (more frequent in low season). In some cases, the charter-ticket seller will offer you an insurance policy in case you must cancel (for hospitalization, death in the family, and so on). Don't even think about frequent-flier miles.

There's no way to predict whether a proposed flight to Rome (very few charters arrive in Milan) will cost less on a charter or less through a consolidator. You'll have to investigate at the time of your trip.

GOING AS A COURIER This option isn't for everyone. The free tickets of the past offered by courier services now cost a minimum of $150 round-trip from New York to Italy with little notice (with a yearly membership cost often thrown in). Least expensive rates require that you leave within, let's say, 1 to 2 days' notice; otherwise, during peak season and advance booking, you may be paying rates not much less than some consolidator's rates (courier rates sometimes top $499 from New York to Milan); you may also be locked into dates and restrictions imposed by the courier service as they need to be assured of your services to deliver their goods. Couriers must waive their two-piece check-in luggage allowance, which is used by the courier service to transport goods; you travel alone, so flying with a companion becomes problematic. Sometimes when the courier's representative meets you at the airport things go ultra-smoothly, sometimes they don't, and you may spend unnecessary hours at the airport. Some long-time couriers would fly no other way. Only the patient, flexible, light-packing, and adventurous should contact **Halbart Express** (☎ **718/656-8189** 10am to 3pm) or **Now Voyager,** 74 Varick St., Suite 307, New York NY 10013 (☎ **212/ 431-1616** 10am to 6pm; at other times you'll get a recorded update of destinations and availabilities). Unless you intend to fly with them regularly, yearly membership costs don't make sense.

FROM THE UNITED KINGDOM

Getting to Italy from the United Kingdom has become less expensive in recent years, but savvy folks usually still rely on travel agents for a deal. Charter flights and special air-travel promotions are still the best alternative.

If a special air-travel promotion isn't available or feasible at the time of your visit, then an **APEX ticket** might be the way to keep costs trimmed. These tickets must be reserved in advance. However, an APEX ticket offers a discount without the usual booking restrictions. You might also ask the airlines about a **Eurobudget ticket,** which imposes restrictions or length-of-stay requirements.

British newspapers are always full of classified ads touting slashed fares to Italy. One good source is the magazine *Time Out,* published in London. London's *Evening Standard* has a daily travel section, and the Sunday editions of almost any newspaper will run many ads. Although competition is fierce, one well-recommended company that consolidates bulk ticket purchases and then passes the savings on to you is **Trail-finders** (☎ **0171/93-75-400** in London; fax 0171/937-0555). It offers access to tickets on such carriers as SAS, British Airways, and KLM to Milan and Rome as well as Pisa, Florence, Venice, and other cities.

In London, there are many consolidators or **bucket shops** around Victoria and Earls Court that offer cheap fares on major lines. Make sure the company you deal with is a member of the IATA, ABTA, or ATOL. These umbrella organizations will help you out if anything goes wrong.

CEEFAX, a television information service included on many home and hotel TVs, runs details of package holidays and flights to Italy and beyond. Just switch to your CEEFAX channel and you'll find a menu of listings that includes travel information.

Make sure you understand the bottom line on any special deal you purchase—that is, ask if all surcharges, including airport taxes and other hidden costs are cited before committing yourself to purchase. Upon investigation, some of these deals are not as attractive as advertised. Also, make sure you understand what the penalties are if you're forced to cancel at the last minute.

Both **British Airways (BA)** (☎ **0181/89-74-000;** www.british-airways.com) and **Alitalia** (☎ **0181/74-58-200;** www.alitalia.it/english/index.html) have frequent flights from London's Heathrow Airport to Rome, Milan, Venice, Pisa, Florence, and Naples. Flying time from London to these cities is anywhere from 2 to 3 hours. BA also has one direct flight a day from Manchester to Rome. A new subsidiary of British Air, **Go,** opened in 1998, services flights from London to Rome and Milan (☎ **08456/054-321;** www.go-fly.com.) Virgin Air has also introduced a subsidiary called **Virgin Express** (☎ **0322/752-0505;** www.virgin-express.com) from London to Rome or Milan.

BY TRAIN

If you plan to travel a lot on the European and/or British railways, you'll do well to secure the latest copy of the definitive *Thomas Cook European Timetable of Railroads.* This 500-plus-page timetable documents all of Europe's mainline passenger rail services with detail and accuracy. It's available from **Forsyth Travel Library,** 226 Westchester Ave., White Plains, NY 10604 (☎ **800/FORSYTH;** www.forsyth.com), at a cost of $27.95 (plus $4.95 shipping in the U.S., $6.95 in Canada). The timetable is also available at some travel-specialty bookstores such as **Rand McNally,** 150 E. 52nd St., New York, N.Y. 10022 (☎ 212/758-7488).

TIPS FOR TRAVELERS FROM THE UNITED STATES

EURAILPASSES   One of Europe's greatest bargains, the **EurailPass** permits unlimited first-class rail travel (second-class travel available to those under 26) in any country in western Europe (except the British Isles). It does *not* include travel on the rail lines of Sardinia, which are organized independently of the lines of the rest of Italy.

Here's how it works: The pass is sold only in North America. It costs $554 for 15 days, $718 for 21 days, $890 for 1 month, $1,260 for 2 months, and $1,658 for 3 months. Children under 4 travel free, providing they don't occupy a seat (then they're charged half-fare); children under 12 pay half-fare.

The advantages are tempting: No tickets; simply show the pass to the ticket collector, then settle back to enjoy the scenery. Seat reservations are required on some trains. Many of the overnight trains have *couchettes* (sleeping cars for four or six) or *wagons lits* (for two), for which an additional fee is charged and paid for before boarding.

Obviously, the heavily peripatetic 2- or 3-month traveler gets the greatest economic advantage—whereas with a 15-day pass, you'd have to spend a great deal of time on the train to get your money's worth. Know in advance what kind of territory you realistically intend to cover to weigh the savings.

EurailPass holders are entitled to considerable reductions on certain buses and ferries. You'll get a 20% reduction on second-class accommodations from certain

---

Train Travel

Are you thinking of buying a EurailPass, but just not sure if it'll make financial sense? Here are some examples of how much you'd have to pay if you opt not to use the pass. **Rome/Paris** (16 hours) first class costs $207; second class is $147. **Rome/Amsterdam** (20 hours) first class is $365; second class costs $236. **Rome/Munich** (13.5 hours) first class is $141; second class costs $90. For Italian and European rail information, visit the Web site of **CIT Travel** (the official representative of Italian State Railways) at www.fs-on-line.com or call ☎ **800/CIT-RAIL.**

companies operating ferries between Naples and Palermo or for crossings to Sardinia and Malta.

Travel agents in all towns and railway agents in such major cities as New York, Montréal, and Los Angeles sell these tickets. A EurailPass is available at the North American offices of CIT Travel Service, the French National Railroads, the German Federal Railroads, and the Swiss Federal Railways.

Eurail Saverpass is a money-saving ticket offering discounted 15-day first-class travel for groups of two to five people traveling together between April and September or two people traveling together between October and March. The per-person price of a Saverpass, valid all over Europe, is $470 for 15 days, $610 for 21 days, and $756 for 1 month.

Eurail Flexipass is valid in first class and offers the same privileges as the Eurail-Pass. However, it gives you a number of individual travel days you can use over a much longer period. That makes it possible to stay in one city and yet not lose a single day of travel. There are two passes: 10 days of travel in 2 months for $654 and 15 days of travel in 2 months for $862. There's also a **Eurail Saver Flexipass** for two to six people, costing per person $556 for 10 days of travel in 2 months and $732 for 16 days of travel in 2 months.

If you're under 26, you can purchase a **Eurail Youthpass** entitling you to unlimited second-class travel wherever the EurailPass is honored. The pass costs $388 for 15 consecutive days, $623 for 1 month, or $882 for 2 months. There's also a **Eurail Youth Flexipass** for travelers under 26. Two passes are available: 10 days of travel in 2 months for $458 and 15 days of travel in 2 months for $599.

EUROPASSES   Introduced by the EurailPass folks, the **EuroPass** lets you travel in five EuroPass countries: Italy, France, Germany, Spain, and Switzerland with the purchase of a 5-, 6-, or 8-day pass of unlimited first-class train travel in a 2-month period; discounts available for two adults traveling together. A 5-day pass costs $298 for each of two adults, $348 traveling alone; a 6-day pass $314 for each of two adults, $358 traveling alone; an 8-day pass $382 for each of two adults, $448 traveling alone. You can opt for a 10- or 15-day pass or extend your range of travel by adding a sixth or seventh country.

For travelers under 26, the **Euro Youth Pass** (available in the U.S.) allows unlimited second-class travel (not an option for those over 26) in these same five countries. A 5-day pass in a 2-month period costs $233, a 6-day pass $253, an 8-day pass $313, and so on. Also available are a 10-day ($383) and 15-day ($513) pass in a 2-month period, and the chance to add a sixth or seventh country. All EuroPasses offer the option of purchasing an associated country, such as Austria, Benelux, Greece, or Portugal—each additional country costs $45, two additional countries will run you $78.

TIPS FOR TRAVELERS COMING FROM THE UNITED KINGDOM

Train travel is not the least expensive manner to get to Italy, but it is one of the most leisurely, allowing the opportunity to stop off along the way. It's about a 20-hour rail ride from London to Milan, direct.

Many rail passes are available in the United Kingdom for travel within Europe or direct to Italy; point-to-point tickets are the alternative for those on time-restricted itineraries. **Italian State Railways** Marco Polo House, 3–5 Landsdowne Rd, Croydon, Surrey (☎ **0181/686-0677;** e-mail ciao@citalia.co.uk), books all manner of train travel to and from Italy as well as within Italy. So does **European Rail Ltd.,** phone sales only at ☎ **0171/387/0444.** General information can be acquired from **European Rail Inquires** (☎ **0171/803-4800**).

The popular **International** has been absorbed by its former competition, **Wasteels,** just next door, adjacent to platform 2, Victoria Station, London SW1V 1JY (☎ **0171/83-47-066;** fax 0171/630-7628). All of the most popular rail passes are available, including the **EurailPass** and **EuroYouth** (available in Europe) offered only to travelers under 26 (see above), entitling them to unlimited second-class travel in 26 European countries. The unlimited travel 15-day pass for £265 is the least expensive. These passes can be issued only to those who have been in the United Kingdom or Europe for less than 6 months, and so are appropriate for U.S. citizens on their way to Italy.

Citizens of the United Kingdom under 26, or anyone under 26 who can prove they have been in the United Kingdom for more than 6 months, will do as well with the **Inter-Rail Pass** (The Inter-Rail+26 is not valid for travel to or within Italy). It permits unlimited travel to and within Italy for 22 days for £159, or 1 month £209.

Call **Campus Travel** (☎ **0171/730-3402;** www.usitcampus.co.uk) or any of its many branches throughout the United Kingdom for direct London to Italy train travel for those under (or over!) 26. Through Campus Travel, you can get all the variations of the EurailPass and its cousin passes and the Inter-Rail passes.

Wasteels (see above), will sell a **Rail Europe Senior Pass** to bona fide U.K. residents for £5. With it, a British resident over 60 can buy discounted rail tickets on many of the rail lines of Europe. To qualify, you must present a valid British Senior Citizen rail card, available for £16 at any BritRail office if proof of age and British residency is presented.

BY BUS

Eurolines is the leading operator of scheduled coach services across Europe. Its comprehensive network of services includes regular departures to destinations throughout Italy, including Turin, Milan, Bologna, Florence, and Rome—plus summer services to Verona, Vicenza, Padua, and Venice.

Eurolines' services to Italy depart from London's Victoria Coach Station and are operated by modern coach, with reclining seats and a choice of smoking or no-smoking areas. Departures are 9am Wednesday and Saturday (with extra departures added during summer months) arriving in Rome 6:30pm the next evening and can be booked up until the day of departure (one week advance purchase is recommended during high season). Return tickets are valid for up to 6 months, and passengers may leave the return date open. For information and reservations by credit card, call ☎ **01582/40-45-11** or book in person at Eurolines, 52 Grosvenor Gardens, Victoria, London SW1 (opposite Victoria Rail Station; an additional Eurolines desk can be found within Victoria Station in The Ticket Hall; no phone). A round-trip ticket from London to Rome using as direct a route as possible costs £125 (£112 under 26) and from £88 (£78 under 26) one-way, depending on the season. Passengers can interrupt their journey, pending available space on subsequent legs of their trip, in Paris or Milan en route.

In the United States, Eurolines is represented by **DER Travel** (☎ **800/782-2424**), which offers Eurolines 1-month passes but not point-to-point. Peak-season passes cost $359 for 30 days ($309 for youth and senior passes); 60-day passes $439 ($389 for youth and senior passes). These passes offer unlimited travel to 30 cities within 16 European countries including Italy.

BY CAR

If you're already on the Continent or are based in London, you may want to drive to Italy. London to Rome is 1,124 miles via Calais/Bologna/Dunkirk or 1,085 miles via Oostende/Zeebrugge, not counting Channel crossings, by either Hovercraft, ferry, or the Chunnel. Milan is some 400 miles closer to Britain than Rome. Once you've arrived at one of the continental ports, you still face a 24-hour drive. Most drivers play it safe and budget 3 days for the journey, 5 for a only marginally more leisurely tool along some of Europe's most scenic highways.

Most of the roads from western Europe leading into Italy are toll-free, with some notable exceptions. If you use the **Swiss superhighway network,** you'll have to buy a special tax sticker at the border. You'll also pay to go through the **St. Gotthard Tunnel** into Italy. Crossings from France can be made through the **Mont Blanc Tunnel,** which also has a toll charge, or you can leave the French Riviera at Menton (France) and drive directly east than south into Italy along the Italian Riviera in the direction of San Remo. The latter is the most popular and least grueling route from London or northern France—who wouldn't welcome a little R&R en route in any of the small towns along the Côte d'Azur?

11 Getting Around

BY PLANE

Italy's domestic air network on **Alitalia** (see "Getting There Without Going Broke") is one of the largest and most complete in Europe. Some 40 airports are serviced regularly from Rome, and most flights take less than an hour. Fares vary, but some discounts are available. Tickets are discounted 50% for children 2 to 12; for passengers 12 to 24, there's a youth fare. Prices are still astronomical for domestic flights and you're almost always better off taking a train, except for long-distance hauls (like Palermo to Venice) where you'd rather spend the money than the time—unless can stop off along the way: in Italy there's never a shortage of major sites to see.

BY TRAIN

Trains provide a medium-priced means of transport, even if you don't buy the Eurail-Pass/Europass or one of the special Italian Railway tickets (see below). As a rule of thumb, second-class travel regardless of the destination usually costs about two-thirds the price of an equivalent trip in first class, and the difference in quality is minimal. The relatively new **InterCity trains** (designated **IC** on train schedules) are modern air-conditioned trains that make limited stops; compared to the far slower direct or regional trains, the supplement can be steep, but a second-class IC ticket will provide a first-class experience. Seat reservations are highly recommended during peak seasons and on weekends or holidays; they must be booked in advance. Minimal in cost, they're sometimes included in the cost of your ticket. Children 4 to 11 receive 50% off the adult fare, and children under 4 travel free with their parents.

Travel Times Between the Major Cities

Cities	Distance	Air Travel Time	Train Travel Time	Driving Time
Florence to Milan	298km/185 mi	55 min	2½ hr	3½ hr
Florence to Venice	281km/174 mi	2 hrs, 5 min	4 hr	3 hr, 15 min
Milan to Venice	267km/166 mi	50 min	3½ hr	3 hr, 10 min
Rome to Florence	277km/172 mi	1 hr, 10 min	2½ hrs	3 hr, 20 min
Rome to Milan	572km/355 mi	1 hr, 5 min	5 hr	6 hrs, 30 min
Rome to Naples	219km/136 mi	50 min	2½ hr	2½ hr
Rome to Venice	528km/327 mi	1 hr, 5 min	5 hr, 15 min	6 hrs
Rome to Genoa	501km/311 mi	1 hr	6 hr	5 hr, 45 min
Rome to Torino	669km/415 mi	1 hr, 5 min	9–11 hr	7 hr, 45 min

Fly by Night

When traveling on domestic flights in Italy, you can get a 30% reduction by taking a flight that departs at night.

Seniors get a break, too. Anyone 60 and over can buy a **Silver Card (Carta d'Argento)** by presenting proof of age at any rail station. The card, which can be purchased only in Italy, allows a 20% discount off the price of any ticket between points on the Italian rail network. It's good for 1 year and costs about 45,000L ($26.50). It's not valid on Friday, Saturday, or Sunday between late June and late August or anytime during Christmas week. The Italian rail system also offers a *cartaverde,* good for anyone under 26. Valid for a year, the card costs 45,000L ($26.50) and entitles a passenger to a 20% reduction off any state train fare. This pass can be purchased only in Italy.

An **Italian Railpass** (known within Italy as a **BTLC Pass**) allows non-Italians to ride as much as they like on the entire rail network of Italy. Buy the pass in the United States, have it validated the first time you use it at any rail station in Italy, and ride as frequently as you like within the time validity. An 8-day pass costs $273 in first class and $182 in second, a 15-day pass $341 in first class and $228 in second, a 21-day pass $396 in first class and $264 in second, and a 30-day pass $478 in first class and $318 in second.

With the Italian Railpass and each of the other special passes, a supplement must be paid to ride on certain express trains. The brand-new, super fast trains **ETR-450** or **EUROstar trains** (formerly known as Pendolino trains) are understandably the most expensive, servicing only the principle cities. The rail systems of Sardinia are administered by a separate entity and aren't included in the Railpass or any of the other passes mentioned.

Another option is the **Italian Flexirail Card,** entitling holders to a predetermined number of days of travel on any rail line of Italy within a certain period. It's ideal for passengers who plan in advance to spend several days sightseeing before boarding a train for another city. A pass giving 4 possible travel days out of a block of 1 month costs $216 in first class and $144 in second, a pass for 8 travel days in 1 month costs $302 in first class and $202 in second, and a pass for 12 travel days in 1 month costs $389 in first class and $259 in second.

In previous years, Italian Railway authorities have required that many of the above passes be bought only outside Europe. These rules have relaxed considerably, and at press time you could buy some passes in Italy. (Check with CIT, below, before your departure, as this might change at any time.) So far, the only exception is the **Italian Flexirail Card,** which requires purchase in North America. You can buy any of these passes in the United States from a travel agent or at **CIT Tours,** the official representative of Italian State Railway, with offices at 15 W. 44th St., 10th Floor, New York, NY 10173 (☎ **800/248-7245** or 212/730-2121; fax 212/730-4544), and 6033 West Century Blvd., Suite 980, Los Angeles, CA 90045; ☎ **310/338-8616;** fax 310/670-4269). Its Web address is **www.cittours.com.**

BY BUS

Italy has an extensive and intricate bus network, covering all regions. But because rail travel is inexpensive, the bus isn't the preferred method of travel. You're better off getting bus transportation through your hotel or a local tourist agency upon your arrival. You cannot book or pay for your ticket in advance or over the phone; in fact, you're lucky if anyone answers when you call. If they do, it will be only in Italian.

SITA, Via Santa Caterina da Siena, in Florence (☎ **055/48-36-51**), and **ANAC,** Pz. Esquilino 29, in Rome (☎ **06/44-82-05-31**), are two companies that blanket the country with air-conditioned coaches. Other bus companies are **Autostradale,** Piazzale Castello, in Milan (☎ **02/80-11-61**), which serves a large chunk of northern Italy, and **Lazzi,** Pz. d. Stazione 4–6, in Florence (☎ **055/21-51-54**), which goes through Tuscany, including Siena and much of central Italy.

Where these nationwide services leave off, local bus companies operate in most regions, particularly in the hill sections and in the alpine regions where travel by rail is not possible. For more information about local services, refer to the "By Bus" sections under "Getting There" in the various destinations.

BY CAR

Driving can be very expensive in Italy. However, there are several strategies you can pursue to make renting a car more affordable, especially for a group of several people.

RULES & REGULATIONS   Technically, U.S. and Canadian drivers must carry an **International Driver's Permit** when touring Italy or obtain a declaration from the Automobile Club d'Italia (ACI) that entitles them to drive on Italian roads on presentation of a valid U.S. or Canadian driver's license (with Italian translation). Although rarely requested to be seen, the declaration is available from any ACI frontier or provincial office. Several organizations, including AAA, can provide an Italian-language translation of a U.S. or Canadian driver's license. The possession of such a translation is intended to facilitate procedures with Italian police personnel, who don't necessarily understand English text. In practice, however, the translation is often not even looked at, but those wanting to follow the letter of the law should have it. Car-rental agencies are happy to see nothing more than a foreign driver's license with photo.

You can apply for an international driver's license at any **American Automobile Association (AAA)** branch. You must be at least 18 and have two 2-by-2-inch photographs, a $10 fee, and a photocopy of your U.S. driver's license with an AAA application form. To find the AAA office nearest you, check the local phone directory or contact AAA's national headquarters at 1000 AAA Dr., Heathrow, FL 32746-5063 (☎ **407/444-7000**). Remember that an international driver's license is valid only if physically accompanied by your original driver's license. In Canada, you can get the address of the **Canadian Automobile Association** closest to you by calling its national office at ☎ **613/247-0117.**

The **Automobile Club d'Italia (ACI)** is the equivalent of the AAA. It has offices throughout Italy, including the head office, V. Marsala 8, 00185 Rome (☎ **06/ 499-81**), open Monday to Saturday 8am to 2pm. The 24-hour **Information and Assistance Center (CAT)** of the ACI is at V. Magenta 5, 00185 Roma (☎ **06/ 44-77**). Both offices are near the main rail station (Stazione Termini).

RENTALS   Many of Italy's most charming landscapes lie far away from the rail network. For that, and for sheer convenience, renting a car is usually the best way to explore the country. It's also the most expensive (Italy's rates have always been some of the highest in Europe) and is usually a consideration only for the budgeteer traveling with one or more companions to split the cost. Also, note that it's much cheaper to book a rental car in your home country than it is once you get to Italy. If you're already in Italy, and you need a car immediately, have someone back home reserve it for you.

The legalities and contractual obligations of renting a car in Italy (where accident and theft rates are very high) are more complicated than those in almost any other country in Europe. You must have nerves of steel, a sense of humor, a valid driver's license (with photo), a valid passport, and be over 25 (some places accept 21). Payment and paperwork are much easier if you present a valid credit card with your completed rental contract (many companies won't even consider a noncredit card payment). If that isn't possible, you'll likely be required to pay a substantial deposit, sometimes in cash. Insurance on all vehicles is compulsory, though what kind and how much is up to you and your credit card company: ask the right questions and check with your credit card company before leaving home.

The three major rental companies in Italy are **Avis** (☎ 800/331-2112; www.avis. com), **Budget** (☎ 800/472-3325; www.budgetrentacar.com), and **Hertz** (☎ 800/ 654-3001; www.hertz.com). Smaller U.S.-based companies specializing in European car rentals are **Auto-Europe** (☎ 800/223-5555; www.autoeurope.com); **Europe by Car** (☎ 800/223-1516, 800/252-9401 in California, or 212/581-3040 in New York; www.europebycar.com); **Kemwel** (☎ 800/678-0678; www.kemwel.com) and **Maiellano** (☎ 800/223-1616). Although they're most frequently contacted for package deals and air travel, see any of the tour operators under "Organized Tours, Package Tours & Tour Operators" that specialize in discounted car rental you can buy independently. You'll have to do your homework in this area, as the three major agencies can be far more or far less expensive than the smaller agencies or some of the tour operators, depending on special promotions and seasonal rates being offered at the time. Never settle for the first figures quoted: Prices can vary greatly from agency to agency.

Rates for the least expensive vehicle (manual drive and no air-conditioning), vary from $290 to $450 for a weeklong midsummer rental of a cramped but peppy Fiat Fiesta or Opel Corsa (though there's always a possibility of a seasonal promotion). In some cases, slight discounts may be offered to members of the American Automobile Association (AAA) or the American Association of Retired Persons (AARP).

Each company offers a collision-damage waiver (**CDW**) costing $14 to $21 per day (depending on the value of the car). Some companies include CDWs in the prices they quote; others don't. In addition, because of Italy's rising theft rate, all three of the major U.S.-based companies offer theft and break-in protection policies (Avis and Budget require it). For pickups at most airports in Italy, all three impose a 12% government tax (called an airport tax or surcharge). To avoid that, consider picking up your car at an inner-city location if this is convenient to you. There's also an unavoidable 20% government value-added tax (VAT) (called IVA in Italy), though more and more companies are including this in the rates they quote; ask to avoid last minute surprises. Automatic shift (the vast majority of available cars are standard/stick shift only) and air-conditioning will raise your rates, as will the option of picking up your car in one city and dropping off in another. Principal cities have both airport and downtown locations; picking up your car at one and dropping it off at the other, even though within the same city, will most likely cost you. Dropping off outside Italy is even more expensive: Make sure you ask all the right questions when calling around.

GASOLINE Gasoline (known as *benzina*) is expensive in Italy, as are *autostrade* tolls. Carry enough cash if you're going to do extensive motoring. Filling the tank of a medium-size car with super *benzina*, the octane rating appropriate for most of the cars you'll be able to rent, will usually cost around 65,000L ($38.25) but will last for days.

Gas stations (*distributori di benzina*) on *autostrade* are often open 24 hours, but on regular roads gas stations are rarely open on Sunday, may close between noon and 3pm for lunch, and shut down after 7pm. Others will have self-service machines accepting 10,000L bills/notes. Make sure the pump registers zero before an attendant starts refilling your tank. A popular scam, particularly in the south, is to fill your tank before resetting the meter so you pay not only your bill but also the charges run up by the previous motorist.

ROAD MAPS   The best touring maps are published by the Automobile Club d'Italia (ACI) and the Italian Touring Club, or you can buy the maps of the Carta Automobilistica d'Italia, covering Italy in two maps on the scale of 1:800,000 (1cm = 8km). These two maps should fulfill the needs of most motorists. If you plan to explore one region of Italy in depth, consider one of 15 regional maps (1:200,000; 1cm = 2km), published by Grande Carta Stradale d'Italia.

All maps mentioned above are sold at some autostrada gas stations, certain newsstands, and all major bookstores, especially those with travel departments. Many travel bookstores in the United States also carry them. If U.S. outlets don't have these maps, they often offer Michelin's red map (no. 988) of Italy, which is on a scale of 1:1,000,000 (1cm = 10km). This map covers all of Italy in some detail.

BREAKDOWNS/ASSISTANCE   In case of car breakdown or for any tourist information, foreign motorists can call ☎ **116** (nationwide telephone service). For road information, itineraries, and all sorts of travel assistance, call the Rome headquarters ☎ **06/49-98-234** of **ACI/Automobile Club d'Italia,** a branch of the Touring Club Italiano.

12 Tips on Accommodations

Italy and its regional boards control the prices of its hotels, designating a minimum and a maximum rate. Many hotels are opting to go with one year-round rate to avoid confusion; others maintain two separate high and low season tariffs. Any difference in price may be the result of the room's location, size and if it offers a private or shared bathroom. Italian hotels are classified by **stars,** indicating their category of comfort: five stars for deluxe, four for first class, three for second, two for third, and one for fourth. Government ratings don't depend on the decoration, quality of the mattresses or on frescoed ceilings but rather on facilities, such as elevators, the presence of an in-house restaurant, amenities, and the like. Many of the finest hostelries in Italy are rated second class because they serve only breakfast (a blessing for those seeking to escape the board requirements, a dying obligation in European hotels these days). Generally speaking, this guide book concentrates on three- and two-star hotels to keep prices comfortable, but remember you might pay the same for a two-star hotel in Venice off-season as you will pay for a three-star hotel in Lucca in high season (almost all of which do not have garages by the way, but maintain an agreement with nearby parking lots).

Government regulation stipulates that breakfast is not mandatory and must be charged separately. Almost all hotel owners, however, include it in the cost of the room. It can be a welcomed convenience—many of the all-you-can-eat buffet breakfasts are well worth the cost. Check it out before you insist on having breakfast elsewhere.

The Italian term *albergo* is more and more commonly being replaced by the international word *hotel. Locanda* once meant a rustic inn or carriage stop, though it's now used to sometimes refer to a place quite charming or fancy. The **pensione** system of yesteryear has pretty much disappeared, and with it the obligation to share bathrooms and eat three meals a day prepared by the families that once owned them. They are now one- and two-star hotels, with many of them retaining the **pensione** in their names to connote a hotel of character or charm (not always the case!). Single travelers stand to be the most disappointed: Rarely are single rooms anything to write home about. Closet-size rooms are not uncommon; if it is a slow month, see if the hotel owner will consider renting (an otherwise empty) double room at a single-occupancy rate.

Reservations are always advised, even in the so-called slow months of November to March when you might find towns such as Verona and Bologna (not to mention the large cities) booked solid with conventions and trade fairs. Travel to Italy peaks from May through October, when moderate and budget hotels are full.

Italy's keeping-up-with-the-Jones's approach to approval by its Common Market neighbors and government-imposed restrictions have done a tremendous amount to improve the status of its hotel situation—and it accounts for soaring prices. Many of the small guys have fallen between the cracks however. The clean-as-a whistle conditions that are a given in Switzerland or Germany's least expensive hostelries are not such a guarantee as you head south. All the more reason to rely on our suggestions.

APARTMENTS, VILLAS & PALAZZI   Local tourist boards or provincial tourist office in the city or town where you expect to stay are not much help. Information on villas and apartments is available in daily newspapers or through local real-estate agents in Italy and some international travel publications. Millions of properties are put up for rent by their Italian owners—you'll have to do your homework and legwork. Single travelers will find the option of rentals expensive; couples less so. Groups or families of four to six people (the more the merrier) may find villa or apartment rental an enjoyable savings. Everyone fantasizes about that dream villa in Tuscany; but remember that photos do not always 1,000 words tell.

These organizations rent villas or apartments, generally on the pricey side, but stipulate your price range when inquiring. Least expensive will be an Italian B&B organization that offers more than 60 historic palazzos and villas in ten regions where rooms range from $30 to $95 per person: order their guidebook from **Caffeletto,** 23 Marciola, 50020 San Vicenzo a Torri, Florence (☎ **055/730-9145;** fax 055/768-121). Pricier possibilities include some lower-end choices through **Hideaways International,** 767 Islington St., Portsmouth, NH 03801 (☎ **800/843-4433** or 603/ 430-4433); **At Home Abroad,** 405 E. 56th St., Suite 6H, New York, NY 10022-2466 (☎ **212/421-9165;** fax 212/752-1591); **Rent a Vacation Everywhere (RAVE),** 135 Meigs St., Rochester, NY 14607 (☎ **716/256-0760;** fax 716/256-2676); **Hometours International,** P.O. Box 11503, Knoxville, TN 37939 (☎ **800/367-4668**); and **Rentals in Italy,** 1742 Calle Corva, Camarillo, CA 93010 (☎ **800/726-6702** or 805/987-5278; fax 805/482-7976) is one of the largest. **Vacation, Inc.** (☎ **800/ 700-9549** or (212)460-9878) also has a Web site at www.vacation-inc.com/home.html.

FARMHOUSES   Another option is to stay in a farmhouse, an apartment, or a bedroom on a working Italian farm (wine-producing estates make up a large part of these) as part of a nationwide program known as *agriturismo.* Most of the farms lie in rural areas within easy reach of town centers or principal cities, such as those in Umbria, Tuscany, and Lazio. You can share the setup with the owners (staying in a guest bedroom in the main house) or have the place to yourself (free-standing converted stalls, mills, worker's quarters on the grounds offering more privacy), the former being the less expensive of course. Contact boards of tourism for listings of *agriturism* situations for a do-it-yourself reservation and daily double rates that usually start at 45,000L ($26.50) with breakfast.

The U.S.-based **Italy Farm Holidays (IFH),** 547 Martling Ave., Tarrytown, NY 10591 (☎ **914/631-7880;** fax 914/631-8831), represents about 50 working farms (a number owned by Americans or foreigners) scattered for the most part in the Piedmont, Tuscany, Umbria, Veneto, and Puglia, any of which would be suitable as a base for touring the region's art cities. Each farm or cooperative has passed inspection, and some of the most desirable ones lie just a few miles from the heart of Florence and

Siena. Most properties require minimum stays of 3 to 7 days and payment in full in advance. Many offer meals (usually breakfast) as part of the arrangement; others provide amenities like free use of bikes or optional horseback riding. Only a few of the places contain more than seven rentable accommodations, most have private bathrooms, and many contain kitchens of their own.

Weekly rates for two begin at around $600 in low season in a modest apartment or B&B, and go way up for high season villas or castles that accommodate up to 10 occupants.

In the United Kingdom, call or check the Web site of **Interhome,** with vacation homes all over Italy (and other countries) (☎ **0181/891-1294;** www.interhome.uk). You'll also find interesting last-minute discounts for 1-week advance bookings. **Italiatour** in London (☎ **0171/605-7500**) specializes in all phases of travel to Italy, including villa and country home rentals.

RELIGIOUS INSTITUTIONS   Convents, monasteries, and other religious institutions in Italy offer accommodations, generally of the fourth-class (one-star) hotel or former *pensioni* category. Some are just for men; others are for women only. Many, however, accept married couples. Italian tourist offices generally have abbreviated listings of these places, which are most commonplace in cities of religious pilgrimage such as Rome or Assisi. They'll be working at full scale during the jubilee year to accommodate the unprecedented numbers of tourists expected.

Ranging from very comfortable convents to bare-bones monastic cells, one of the main reasons to stay in a religious institution is economy, as the rooms are invariably cheaper than those in most hotels. Contact the local tourist offices for a listing.

13 Tips on Dining

For a quick bite, go to a *bar*—while it does serve alcohol, it functions mainly as a cafe. Prices here have a split personality: *al banco* is standing at the bar, while *à tavola* means sitting at an indoor or outdoor table where you'll be waited and charged two to four times as much—but consider it rent, and you won't be rushed even after reading the newspaper and finishing your postcards. In bars you can find *panini* sandwiches on various rolls and *tramezzini* (giant triangles of white-bread sandwiches with the crusts cut off). These both run 2,000 to 6,000L ($1.20 to $3.50). A *toast* is a grilled ham-and-cheese Italian style, stuck in a kind of tiny press to flatten and toast it so the crust is crispy and the filling hot and gooey; microwaves have invaded and are everywhere, and many bars now offer quick one-course hot lunches of a pasta or mixed salads for 5,000 to 7,000L ($2.95 to $4.10).

Pizza a taglio or *pizza rustica* indicate a place where you can order pizza by the slice—though the quality can vary wildly. You'll fare somewhat better at a *pizzeria,* a casual sit-down restaurant that cooks large, round pizzas with very thin crusts in wood-burning ovens with lots of toppings and varieties to keep you coming back. A *tavola calda* (literally "hot table") serves ready-made hot foods you can either take away for a picnic or eat at one of the few small tables often available. The food is usually very good, and you can get away with a full meal at a *tavola calda* for well under 20,000L ($11.75). A *rosticceria* is the same type of place with some chickens roasting on a spit in the window and the smell of *arrista* (roast pork with rosemary) and roast potatoes luring you in.

Eating lunch (*pranzo*) or dinner (*cena*) in Italy can be a pretty elaborate affair, although the serious three-course lunch is fast being reduced to the American standard of a quickie. Where you choose to sit (if you occupy a table and eat less than a full meal) will determine the type of welcome that you receive. Full-fledged restaurants go by the names *osteria, trattoria,* or *ristorante.* Once upon a time, these terms meant something—*osterie* were basic tavernlike inns where you could get a plate of spaghetti and a glass of wine; *trattorie* were casual family run places serving simple full meals of filling, simple fare; and *ristoranti* were fancier places, with waiters in bow-ties, printed menus, linen table cloths, a wine list, and hefty prices. Nowadays, fancy restaurants often go by the name of *trattoria* to cash in on the associated charm factor, trendy spots use *osteria* to show they're of-the-moment hip, and casual inexpensive places sometimes tack on *ristorante* to ennoble themselves. The more casual the ambience, the less you'll feel inclined to order the full-blown Italian repast. Put your nose to the window and see for yourself. Better yet, follow our suggestions and eliminate the suspense. It's hard not to eat well in the country that gave us pasta and Chianti.

SET-PRICE MENU You'll find at many restaurants, especially larger ones and in cities, a *menù turistico* (tourists' menu), costing anywhere from 10,000 to 35,000L ($5.90 to $20.60), sometimes called *menu del giorno* (menu of the day). This set-price menu usually covers all meal incidentals—including table wine, cover charge, and 15% service charge—along with a first course (*primo*) and second course (*secondo*), but it almost always offers an abbreviated selection of uninspired dishes (with portions that may be less than the standard): spaghetti in tomato sauce and roast chicken. Sometimes better is a *menu à prezzo fisso* (fixed-price menu). It usually doesn't include wine but sometimes covers the service and *coperto* (cover charge from 1,500 to 5,000L/90¢ to $2.95)—the unavoidable privilege of sitting at the table—and often offers a wider selection of better dishes, occasionally house specialties and local foods. Ordering à la carte, however, offers you the best chance for a memorable meal for a price that needn't be too much more. Regardless of where you eat, check the bill to see if service is included (*servizio incluso*); at 15%, it is usually added. If not, leave 10% to 15% on the table if service was satisfactory.

FOOD & WINE The *enoteca* wine bar is a growingly popular marriage of a wine bar and *osteria,* where you can sit and order from a host of local and regional wines by the glass (usually from 2,500 to 8,000L/$1.50 to $4.70) while snacking on finger foods (and usually a number of simple first-course possibilities) that reflect the region's fare. Relaxed, full of ambience and good wine, these are great spots for light and inexpensive lunches, and the perfect venue to educate your palate and recharge your batteries.

FOOD STORES It's also possible and inexpensive to go into one of hundreds of general food stores (*alimentari*) throughout the country and have sandwiches prepared on the spot or buy the makings for a picnic lunch to be enjoyed in a park or shady piazza.

14 Tips on Shopping

Italy is one of the world's great shopping meccas. The **Made in Italy** concept of centuries-old craftsmanship and dead-on style and fashion sensibility make just about everything too tempting to overlook. But this is not the Italy of the '70s when leather goods and gold jewelry were yours for a song. That kidskin bag, hand-painted ceramic bowl, and designer-label overcoat are worth a Medici's ransom, and not much less expensive than what you'd find them for back home now that import-export has shrunk the globe and never-pay-retail after-Christmas sales make Italian fashion more accessible.

Outdoor markets like Florence's unrivaled **Mercato San Lorenzo** still make bargain hunting fun, though much of the T-shirts and marbleized-paper-covered goods are made in China. Woolen scarves, handsome knitwear, trendy shoes, and food items

How to Get the VAT Back

If you make a purchase in Italy and your bill at any one store totals 300,000L ($176.50), you're eligible for a value-added tax (**VAT;** called IVA in Italy) rebate up to 19% (the IVA varies according to item and is already included in the price). Ask the store for a formal receipt, and before leaving Italy, bring your receipt and purchase (the item must be available for inspection) to Italian Customs at the airport before check-in. The Customs agent will stamp your receipt and give you further directions. The stamped receipt gets sent back to the store and your reimbursement will be credited against your credit card or sent to you by check; either can take months. Be sure to allow enough time before you board your flight home. If you're intending to shop, check with **Global Refund** in the United States (☎ **800/566-9828;** www.taxfree.se) for details.

won't break your budget and still make the quintessential Italian memento, whether for yourself or your loved ones left behind. Instant family heirlooms like gold necklaces or earrings, and quality leather outerwear are more serious investments, but Italy is still the place to make them if you've saved accordingly.

SENDING YOUR GOODIES HOME　Shipping (see "Fifty Money-Saving Tips," p. 40) hikes the cost of the most inexpensive Murano glass object. It can double the cost of a fragile purchase—do you really want to pay for shipping and insurance? Do you want the hassle of wrapping it and doing it yourself when the store doesn't offer the service? Is the option of carrying your purchase around for the duration of your trip looking less attractive? Think first about purchasable items that are heavy, cumbersome, or fragile and shop accordingly. When flights are full, airlines can be unflinchingly strict about carry-on restrictions and the number and size of pieces they allow you to check in.

CUSTOMS

Overseas visitors can bring along most items for personal use duty-free, including fishing tackle, a sporting gun and 200 cartridges, a pair of skis, two tennis racquets, a baby carriage, two hand cameras with 10 rolls of film, and 400 cigarettes (two cartons) or a quantity of cigars or pipe tobacco not exceeding 500 grams (1.1 lb.). There are strict limits on importing alcoholic beverages. However, limits are much more liberal for alcohol bought tax-paid in other countries of the European Union.

For U.S. Citizens　Returning U.S. citizens who've been away for 48 hours or more are allowed to bring back, once every 30 days, $400 worth of merchandise duty-free. You'll be charged a flat rate of 10% duty on the next $1,000 worth of purchases. Be sure to have your receipts handy. On gifts, the duty-free limit is $100. For more specific guidance, contact the **U.S. Customs Service,** P.O. Box 7407, Washington, DC 20044 (☎ **202/927-6724**), to request the free pamphlet *Know Before You Go.* You can download it from the Internet at **www.customs.ustreas.gov/travel/kbygo.htm**. If you make purchases in Italy, it's important to keep your receipts. For refunds of the value-added tax (IVA in Italy), see the VAT box earlier in this chapter.

For EU Citizens　On January 1, 1993, the borders between European countries were relaxed as the European markets united. When you're traveling within the EU, this will have a big impact on what you can buy and take home for personal use.

　If you buy your goods in a duty-free shop, then the old rules still apply—you're allowed to take home 200 cigarettes and 2 liters of table wine, plus 1 liter of spirits or

Size Conversion Chart

Women's Clothing

American	6	8	10	12	14	16			
Continental	36	38	40	42	44	46			
British	8	10	12	14	16	18			

Women's Shoes

American	5	6	7	8	9	10			
Continental	36	37	38	39	40	41			
British	4	5	6	7	8	9			

Children's Clothing

American	3	4	5	6	6X				
Continental	98	104	110	116	122				
British	18	20	22	24	26				

Children's Shoes

American	8	9	10	11	12	13	1	2	3
Continental	24	25	27	28	29	30	32	33	34
British	7	8	9	10	11	12	13	1	2

Men's Suits

American	34	36	38	40	42	44	46	48	
Continental	44	46	48	50	52	54	56	58	
British	34	36	38	40	42	44	46	48	

Men's Shirts

American	14½	15	15½	16	16½	17	17½	18	
Continental	37	38	39	41	42	43	44	45	
British	14½	15	15½	16	16½	17	17½	18	

Men's Shoes

American	7	8	9	10	11	12	13		
Continental	39½	41	42	43	44½	46	47		
British	6	7	8	9	10	11	12		

2 liters of fortified wine. But if you buy your wine, spirits, or cigarettes in an ordinary shop in Italy, for example, you can take home almost as much as you like. (U.K. Customs and Excise doesn't set theoretical limits.) If you're returning from a non-EU country, the allowances are the standard ones from duty-free shops. You must declare any goods in excess of these. For details, get in touch with **Her Majesty's Customs and Excise Office,** New King's Beam House, 22 Upper Ground, London, SE1 9PJ (☎ **0171/620-1313**) for more information.

FAST FACTS: Italy

American Express Offices are found in **Rome** at Pz. di Spagna 38 (☎ **06/67-641**); in **Florence** at Via Dante Alighieri (☎ **055/50-981**); in **Venice** at Salizzada San Moisè, San Marco 1471 (☎ **041/52-00-844**); and in **Milan** at V. Brera 3 (☎ **02/72-85-571**).

Banks They're open Monday to Friday 8:30am to 1 or 1:30pm and 2 or 2:30 to 4pm and closed all day Saturday, Sunday, and national holidays. Hours change slightly from city to city.

Business Hours   Local business hours can vary greatly and change seasonally. Regular business hours are usually Monday to Friday 9am (sometimes 9:30am) to 1pm and 3:30 (sometimes 4) to 7 or 7:30pm, with Saturdays being half or full days depending on the season or type of business in question. In July or August, some offices, stores, and businesses may not open in the afternoon until 4:30 or 5pm. An exaggerated siesta (*riposo*) closing is often observed in Rome, Naples, and most cities of southern Italy; however, in Milan and other northern and central cities the custom has been cut back considerably. Most shops are closed on Sunday, except for pastry stores/bars and certain barbershops that are open on Sunday morning. Some tourist-oriented stores are now permitted to stay open during high season.

Camera/Film   U.S.-brand film is available in Italy but is expensive. Take in as much as Customs will allow if you plan to take a lot of pictures.

Currency   See "Money," earlier in this chapter.

Customs   See "Tips on Shopping," earlier in this chapter.

Driving Rules   See "Getting Around," earlier in this chapter.

Drug Laws   Penalties are severe and could lead to either imprisonment or deportation. Selling drugs to minors is dealt with particularly harshly.

Drugstores   *Farmacia* take turns staying open at night and on Sunday. At every *farmacia* a list is posted of those that are open in off-hours.

Electricity   The electricity in Italy varies considerably. It's usually alternating current (AC), varying from 42 to 50 cycles. The voltage can be anywhere from 115 to 220. It's recommended that any visitor carrying electrical appliances obtain a transformer and an adapter plug. Check the exact local current with your hotel. Plugs have prongs that are round, not flat.

Embassies/Consulates   The Embassy of the **United States** is in **Rome** at V. Vittorio Veneto 119/A (☎ **06/46-741;** fax 06/488-26-72). U.S. consulates are in **Florence** at Lungarno Amerigo Vespucci 38 (☎ **055/23-98-276;** fax 055/284-088) and in **Milan** at V. Principe Amadeo 2/10 (☎ **02/29-03-51;** fax 02/29-00-11-65). These offices are open Monday to Friday 8:30am to 4:30pm. There's also a consulate in **Naples** at Piazza della Repubblica (☎ **081/ 761-43-03;** fax 081/761-18-69), open Monday to Friday 8am to noon. The consulate in Genoa is closed; however, there's an office of the U.S. Foreign Commercial Service, Pz. Portello 6 (☎ **010/54-38-77**), open Monday to Friday 8:30am to 12:30pm.

Consulate and passport services for **Canada** are in Rome at V. Zara 30 (☎ **06/44-59-81**), open Monday to Friday 10am to 12:30pm. The office of the **United Kingdom** is in Rome at V. XX Settembre 80A (☎ **06/48-25-441;** fax 06/487-3324), open Monday to Friday 9:15am to 1:30pm. The Consulate General's office in Florence is at Lungarno Corsini 2 (☎ **055/284-133**), open Monday to Friday 9:30am to 12:30pm and 2:30 to 4:30pm. The Naples office is at V. Francesco Crispi 122 (☎ **081/66-35-11**), open Monday to Friday 9am to 12:30pm and 2 to 4:30pm. In Milan, contact the office at V. San Paolo 7 (☎ **02/72-30-01**), open Monday to Friday 9:15am to 12:15pm and 2:30 to 4:30pm. The **Australian** Embassy is in Rome at V. Alessandria 215 (☎ **06/ 85-27-21;** fax 06/852-723-00), open Monday to Thursday 8:30am to noon and 2 to 4pm and Friday 8:30am to noon. The consular services for Australia are in Rome at Cor. Trieste 25 (☎ **06/85-22-721**), open Monday to Thursday 8:30am to noon and 2 to 4pm and Friday 9am to noon. For **New Zealand,** the office in Rome is at Via Zara 28 (☎ **06/44-02-928;** fax 06/440-29-84), open Monday to Friday 8:30am to 12:45pm and 1:45 to 5pm. In case of emergency, embassies have a 24-hour referral service. For **Ireland,** the office in Rome is at Pz. di Campitelli 3 (☎ **06/697-91-21;** fax 06/679-2354), open Monday to Friday 9:30am to 12:30pm and 2 to 4pm. For consular queries, dial ☎ **06/697-91211.**

Emergencies   Dial ☎ **113** for an ambulance, police, or fire. In case of a breakdown on an Italian road, dial ☎ **116** at the nearest telephone box; the Automobile Club of Italy (ACI) will be notified to come to your aid.

Holidays   See "When to Go," earlier in this chapter.

Information   See "Visitor Information & Entry Requirements," earlier in this chapter, and specific cities for local information offices.

Legal Aid   The consulate of your country is the place to turn, though offices can't interfere in the Italian legal process. They can, however, inform you of your rights and provide a list of attorneys. You'll have to pay for the attorney out of your pocket, as there's no free legal assistance. If you're arrested for a drug offense, about all the consulate will do is notify a lawyer about your case and perhaps inform your family.

Liquor Laws   Wine with meals has been considered a normal part of family life for hundreds of years in Italy. Children are exposed to wine at an early age, and alcoholic consumption isn't considered anything out of the ordinary. There's no legal drinking age for buying or ordering alcohol. There are no restrictions on the sale of wine or liquor in Italy.

Mail   At post offices, General Delivery service is available in Italy. Correspondence can be addressed c/o the post office by adding *Fermo Posta* to the name of the locality. You can pick up mail at the local central post office by showing your passport. In addition to the post offices, you can buy stamps at little *tabacchi* (tobacco) stores throughout any city.

Mail delivery in Italy is notoriously bad and doesn't seem to be improving. If you're writing for hotel reservations (bad idea), it can cause much confusion—visitors may arrive in Italy long before their hotel deposits do. Fax machines speed up the process tremendously, e-mail better yet. Postcards, aerogrammes, and letters weighing up to 20 grams to the United States and Canada cost 1,300L (75¢), to the United Kingdom and Ireland 800L (45¢), and to Australia and New Zealand 1,400L (80¢).

Maps   See "Getting Around," earlier in this chapter. Also see certain map recommendations in the city listings for such cities as Rome, Florence, and Venice.

Newspapers/Magazines   In major cities, it's possible to find the *International Herald Tribune, USA Today, Time,* and *Newsweek,* as well as other English-language newspapers and magazines at hotels and news kiosks.

Pets   A veterinarian's certificate of good health is required for dogs and cats and should be obtained by owners before entering Italy. Dogs must be on a leash or muzzled at all times. Other animals must undergo examination at the border or port of entry. Certificates for parrots or other birds subject to psittacosis must state that the country of origin is free of disease. All documents must be certified first by a notary public, then by the nearest Italian consulate.

Police   Dial ☎ **113,** the all-purpose number for police emergency assistance in Italy.

Radio/TV Most radio and TV broadcasts are on **RAI,** the Italian state radio/TV network. Occasionally, especially during the tourist season, the network will broadcast special programs in English. Announcements are made on the radio and TV guide sections of local newspapers. Vatican Radio also carries foreign-language religious news programs, often in English. Short-wave transistor radios pick up broadcasts from the BBC (British), Voice of America (United States), and CBC (Canadian). RAI TV and private channels broadcast only in Italian. Even some of the less expensive hotels with TVs in the guest rooms are beginning to carry CNN.

Rest Rooms All airport and rail stations have rest rooms, often with attendants, who expect to be tipped. Bars, nightclubs, restaurants, cafes, and all hotels have facilities; public toilets are found near many of the major sights.

Usually rest rooms are designated as W.C. (water closet) or toilette and marked as *donne* (women) or *uomini* (men). The most confusing designation is *signori* (gentlemen) and *signore* (ladies), so watch those final i's and e's!

Safety Violent street muggings are uncommon in Italy, though these are increasing everywhere. The most usual menace, especially in all large cities (particularly Rome) is the plague of pickpockets and the roving gangs of gypsy children who virtually surround you, distract you, and in all the confusion, steal your purse or wallet. Never leave valuables in a car (even unseen in a locked trunk) and never travel with your car unlocked.

Taxes As a member of the European Union, Italy imposes a tax on most goods and services that's already included in the price. It's a **value-added tax,** called **IVA** in Italy. The tax affecting most visitors is that imposed at hotels, which, at about 9% in first- and second-class hotels, is usually incorporated into the bill.

Telegrams/Telephone/Telex/Fax A **public telephone** is always near at hand in Italy. Local calls cost 200L, and you can use 100L, 200L, or 500L coins. Most phones, especially in the cities, accept a multiple-use precharged phone card called a *carta telefonica* or scheda, which you can buy at all tabacchi and bars in increments of 5,000L, 10,000L, or 20,000L. To use this card, insert it into the slot in the phone and then dial. A digital display will keep track of how many lire you use up. The card is good until it runs out of lire, so don't forget to take it with you when you hang up.

International calls to the United States and Canada can be dialed directly. Dial **00** (the international code from Italy), then the country code (1 for the United States and Canada), the area code, and the number you're calling. Calls dialed directly are billed on the basis of the call's duration only. A reduced rate is applied 11pm to 8am Monday to Saturday and all day Sunday. Other country

---

Calling Italy

To call Italy from the United States, dial the **international prefix, 011;** then Italy's **country code, 39;** then the **city code** (for example, **06** for Rome and **055** for Florence); then the actual **phone number.**

Note that numbers in Italy do indeed range from four to eight digits in length. Also note that as of late 1998, when calling from outside Italy, you must now include the initial zero in the city code (previously you had to drop the zero). This also applies when you call anywhere within Italy—even when you're calling within the town you're visiting.

codes are as follows: the United Kingdom 44, Ireland 353, Australia 61, New Zealand 64.

If you wish to make a **collect call** from a pay phone, simply deposit 200L (you get it back when you're done), dial **170,** and an international (and usually English-speaking) operator will come on the line. For calling-card calls, drop in the refundable 200L, then dial the appropriate number for your card's company to be connected with an operator in the United States: for AT&T, **172-1011;** for MCI, **172-1022;** and for Sprint, **172-1877.**

Don't count on all Italian phones having Touch-Tone service! Even in some of the larger and more expensive hotels you'll find rotary dials: You may not be able to access your voice mail or answering machine if you call home from Italy.

If you make a **long-distance call** from a public phone, there's no surcharge. However, hotels have been known to double or triple the cost of the call with taxes and surcharges, so be duly warned. Direct-dial calls from the United States to Italy are much cheaper, so arrange for whomever to call you at your hotel at a prearranged hour if possible.

Chances are your hotel will send or receive a **telex** or **fax** for you, sometimes at inflated prices per page or minute. You can send a fax from the post office to any country in the world, with the exception of the United States. Otherwise, most *cartolerie* (stationery stores), *copisti* or *fotocopie* (photocopy shops), and some *tabacchi* (tobacconists) offer fax services: look for SERVIZIO FAX signs in their windows. For **telegrams,** ITALCABLE operates services abroad, transmitting messages by cable or satellite. Both internal and foreign telegrams may be dictated over the phone (dial ☎ **186**).

Time   In terms of standard time zones, Italy is 6 hours ahead of eastern standard time in the United States. Daylight savings time goes into effect in Italy each year from the last Sunday in March through the last Sunday in October.

Tipping   This custom isn't practiced with the same flair in Italy as in the States, even though many people depend on tips to supplement their livelihoods. In hotels, the service charge is already added to a bill. In addition, it's customary to tip the chambermaid a minimum of 1,000L (60¢) per day and the bellhop or porter 2,000L ($1.20) per bag. If your concierge has helped to resolve a problem, procure a ticket to a sold-out concert, or find an overnight parking space, acknowledge this effort with 5,000L ($3.30) or more.

In restaurants, 15% is almost always added to your bill (*servizio incluso*). An additional tip for good service is expected in upscale eateries. It's customary in restaurants in more cosmopolitan establishments to leave an additional 5% to 10%, which, combined with the assessed service charge, is a very high tip indeed. Washroom attendants expect at least 300 to 500L, more in nicer restaurants and hotels. Restaurants are required by law to give customers official receipts. Taxi drivers expect at least 10% to 15% of the fare from foreign customers, though Italians tip infrequently.

Tourist Offices   See "Visitor Information & Entry Requirements," earlier in this chapter, and also specific city chapters.

Water   It's generally safe to drink the water, though the taste may be different from what you're accustomed to. However, in the south of Italy, particularly the Naples region, it's best to stick to bottled water.

4 Rome

by Reid Bramblett

As monuments of ancient Rome—the Colosseum, the Pantheon, and the Forum—stand amid a sea of sputtering Fiats, milling visitors, and hurried locals, the Romans have found a way to meld the old with the new. New museums and archaeological sites are opening every year, and monuments and galleries that have spent decades languishing under scaffolding are emerging sparkling clean and equipped with the latest sightseeing technologies. There are now visitor information kiosks all over town, and the city's orchestras, opera, and theaters have come roaring out of the doldrums after years of mismanagement and mediocre talent to inaugurate fabulous new seasons. Sights are staying open longer, monuments and palaces hosting more exhibitions and concerts, and hotels are busily renovating.

Still, modern initiatives aside, Rome is a place that turns most people's attention to the distant past.

It's a city whose layout is still echoed in baroque squares like cafe-lined and fountain-studded **Piazza Navona,** in the **papal Castel Sant'Angelo** built atop Hadrian's tomb, in the curve of a medieval building whose foundations rest on the tiers of an ancient amphitheater, or the antique vaulting of the restaurant where you settle back for a sumptuous 3-hour dinner for under $25.

But Rome is also the seat of another great empire. From the day in A.D. 312 when the emperor Constantine converted to Christianity, the Mother Church has focused its religious, political, and artistic powers on this double bend of the Tiber River. These Christians changed the face of Rome and the fate of the Western world, covering the city with grandiose medieval, Renaissance, and baroque churches designed by the likes of Bramante, Bernini, and Borromini. These hallowed structures were enriched by Byzantine-era mosaics, or the frescoes, sculpture, and paintings by the finest artists of the Renaissance and baroque: Giotto, Michelangelo, Raphael, Da Vinci, Caravaggio. St. Peter's with its vast Vatican Museums and the fingers-almost-touching artistic icon of *God Creating Adam* on Michelangelo's Sistine Chapel ceiling is but the beginning.

However, it is not the past, but the future that is on the mind of everybody in the Eternal City today. The immediate future: A.D. 2000, a Holy Year and Papal Jubilee that will bring more pilgrims and travelers to Rome than there are citizens in all of Italy—more than 29 million visitors are expected. And although a great number of monuments have emerged from the scaffolding, many remain wrapped in protective covering, while the black veil of pollution is sandblasted away.

Predictably, prices on everything have been rising at an alarming rate as the city gears up for Jubilee Year 2000. That being said, good values are difficult to find. But, I've already done the work for you. The hotels, restaurants, and money-saving tips listed in this chapter will leave you with enough lire to enjoy the Eternal City and all that its many epochs have to offer.

1 Arriving

BY PLANE   Most international flights land at **Leonardo da Vinci International Airport,** also called **Fiumicino** (☎ **06/659-51**), 30 kilometers (18 mi.) west of the city. Beyond customs you'll find a visitors' information booth with good, free maps and brochures, open from 8:30am to 7pm.

To get downtown, follow the signs marked *treni* for hourly nonstop trains to the main rail station, **Stazione Termini** (30 min.; 15,000L/$8.80). There's a train ticket office in the tiny airport station, or try your luck at one of the temperamental ticket machines. If you're really pinching lire, you can take a local train every 20 minutes toward Rome's **Tiburtina** station (45 min.; 9,500L/$5.60) from the same tracks (get off at Ostiense and walk to the Piramide Metro stop to catch the B line to Termini; if you miss the Ostiense stop, stay on the train all the way to Tiburtina where you can also get the B line). I find the longer train ride doesn't really justify the small savings, but it is convenient if your hotel is in Trastevere (get off at the Trastevere stop) or the Aventine (get off at Ostiense).

Many charter and continental flights land at **Ciampino** airport (☎ **06/7934-0297**). Outside the terminal, a COTRAL bus (2,000L/$1.20) leaves about twice an hour for the 20-minute trip to Anagnina, the terminus of Metro line A, where you can grab a subway to Termini (1,500L/90¢).

Taxis to or from either airport cost about 70,000L ($41.20), plus around 5,000L ($2.95) for bags.

Getting to Fiumicino from Rome   There's a special **Alitalia/Fiumicino desk at Termini,** Rome's main train station, at track no. 22 open 6:30am to 9pm. The first airport train (30 min.; 15,000L/$8.80) leaves Termini at 6:50am (arriving 7:23am), but most run hourly on the 20-minute mark. If you have no luggage to check, you can check in for most Alitalia flights here as well (*except* flights AZ640/AZ642 to Newark or AZ650 to Toronto).

If you have an **early flight,** catch a taxi or take a local airport train from Rome's Tiburtina rail station, which leaves starting at 5am (48 min.; 7,000L/$4.10). To get **to the airport late at night,** take a taxi, or night bus 42N (every 20 to 30 minutes) from Termini to Tiburtina, where you can catch a COTRAL bus to the airport (30 min.; 7,000L/$4.10) at 12:30, 1:15, or 2:30pm and 3:45am.

Travel Tip

If you're landing at Rome's Fiumicino but plan to head straight to, say, Florence or some other city the instant you get to Termini (Rome's downtown train station), you can save loads of time by using the airport train terminal's ticket desk to buy your Rome-to-Florence rail ticket rather than braving the ludicrously long lines at Termini.

Jubilee 2000

The year 2000 will not be just another year in Rome, nor merely the start of a new millennium. It will be a Jubilee Year, and that means all heaven's gonna break loose across the city. Pope Boniface VIII adapted the Holy Year tradition from Judaism in A.D. 1300. He declared a Papal Jubilee (*Giubileo* in Italian), a year during which pilgrims who came to Rome and made the rounds of all four of the great Basilicas—San Giovanni in Laterano, Santa Maria Maggiore, San Paolo Fuori le Mura, and St. Peter's—would receive a plenary indulgence (sort of like the Super Bowl of going to confession). At first Holy Years were held every century, then every 33 years, and finally every 25 years, which brings us up to the year 2000 and the hundreds of ambitious city plans and projects that are now underway. To officially kick off the Jubilee Year on Christmas Eve 1999, the Pope will knock his hammer on the perennially closed, right-hand door of St Peter's (which will stay open for the duration of the year).

But, what will the year 2000 specifically mean to the visitor? Well, first of all, you'll be in good company. More than 29 million visitors (it's estimated that 10 million will be foreigners) are expected. To the some 400,000 beds already available in the Lazio region, the city of Rome will add approximately 4,000 new ones—there are even plans to dock old cruise ships at Anzio and Fiumicino and park train sleeper cars on unused tracks at main rail station, together opening up some 9,000 more sleeping spaces for the pilgrims.

There are also plans to increase normal city bus service by 120%. The creation of various reception centers, megahotels, food distribution centers, and other structures specifically for pilgrims are also in the works. Visitors will find metal detectors in all the basilicas and airport-style X-ray machines at the enormous new Vatican Museums entrance.

The Vatican is nearing completion on a vast new public parking lot to accommodate cars and tour buses that's been hollowed out of the Gianicolo hill just downriver from St. Peter's. As this book went to press, the city was breaking ground to install another lot under Tiburtina train station (which is planned to

BY TRAIN   There are at least three trains an hour from **Florence** (1.5 to 3.5 hr.; 25,500L/$15). There are 13 direct trains daily from **Venice** (4.5 to 7 hr.; 45,500L/$26.75); and hourly runs from **Milan** (4.5 to 9 hr.; 49,000L/$28.80). There are two to three runs hourly (at least once an hour Sunday) from **Naples** (2 to 2.5 hr.; 18,000L/$10.60).

Rome's **main train station** is **Stazione Termini** (although a few long-haul trains stop only at Rome's secondary Tiburtina station in the southern part of the city), at the northeast corner of the *centro storico* (historic center) (☎ **1478/88-088** toll-free, or 06/4730-6599). The station is divided into three sections: the **tracks,** beyond which is the **main hall**—filled with shops and services like newsstands, eateries, banks, the **Metro** entrance, and a 24-hour pharmacy—and beyond that, the **ticketing hall.** Beyond the ticketing hall is Piazza del Cinquecento, a huge square containing taxi stands and Rome's major bus terminus where some two dozen routes converge.

Termini has always been a chaotic station, and this has only worsened as it busily renovates itself for the year 2000. Most of the services like ticketing and information are frequently moved around to temporary clapboard structures inside the complex. The "ticketing" hall has recently only hosted the **train information booth** (always be put into more active service—taking some of the strain off the main rail station, Termini). Interestingly, while these new parking lots are popping up all over the place, the rules against vehicles in the city center are becoming more stringent. More and more pedestrian zones are being created, including around Piazza Risorgimento, which is a major bus stop and traffic square tucked into the Vatican Walls between St. Peter's and the Museums' entrance (no one I talked to seemed entirely sure where all the traffic was gong to go now).

And of course, you can't have a jubilee without art and music. The **Accademia di Santa Cecilia musical conservatory** is commissioning celebratory works from Italian and international composers, and will hold several series of concerts throughout the year. The **Rome Opera** is planning a special series of year-long spectacles, and countless less high-profile groups will be getting in on the action, with hundreds of exhibitions and shows scheduled in almost every free space available in the city. A special Easter celebration will have Barbra Streisand and Placido Domingo singing Leonard Bernstein's *Mass.*

Expect monuments and museums to stay open much longer, lines to take forever, crowds to be thicker than you'd ever imagined them, prices to soar, tempers to be short, and spirits to be high. Jubilee 2000 will be far from a typical year in which to visit Rome, but if nothing else it's bound to be a memorable one.

For details, you can check the Iternet site **www.romagiubileo.it** or visit the **information office/Cyberpoint** installed around the back left side of the Vittorio Emanuele monument (just beyond the Risorgimento museum) off Via dei Fori Imperiali on Via San Pietro in Carcere (☎06-6992-4600; fax 06-6992-4664). It's open Tuesday to Sunday 9:30am to 6:30pm. There will also be offices opening on Via della Conciliazione, the main drag to the Vatican, and on Via Giolitti, along the south flank of Termini train station. You can also contact the **Comitato Centrale del Grande Giubileo del 2000** at Borgo Sant'Angelo 23, 00193 Roma (☎06-6988-1561; fax 06-6988-2181), for a list of events in English.

good for an agonizingly long, take-a-number wait), a Rome **city information booth** (also comically crowded, but good for a free map), and the **budget travel agencies** Wasteels and CIT. At press time, the perennially packed **ticket windows** were temporarily housed next to track no. 1, with some of the most miserable lines in Italy (plan to wait at least an hour).

Luggage storage is at track no. 22, open 5:15am to 12:20am. It costs 5,000L ($2.95) per 12 hours per bag, and you must pay for the first 12 hours when you drop the luggage off. Lockers, open the same hours, cost 3,000 to 5,000L ($1.75 to $2.95) per 6 hours. Lockers are emptied after 24 hours, and you'll have to go through lots of red tape to get your stuff back. There's an **Alitalia office** at track no. 22 where you can buy tickets for the direct train to Fiumicino airport (*don't waste time waiting in the regular ticket lines*). See above under "By Plane" for details on how to get to the airport.

BY BUS   Rome has coach connections with every major Italian city, but it's preferable to travel by train as buses invariably take longer, are less comfortable, and cost about the same. They can, however, be handy (but crowded) when the rail system goes on strike (a frequent occurrence). For 24-hour info on all bus lines into and out of

Rome, call ☎ **166/845-010.** Most intercity buses arrive either near Termini or at one of several suburban bus stations (each near a Metro stop).

BY CAR   The saying "all roads lead to Rome" still rings true in Italy, where the capital is at the convergence of a dozen highways, including the **A1 autostrada,** which connects Rome with Florence, Milan, and Naples. The *Grande Raccordo Annulare,* called the **"GRA,"** is a highway ring around the greater Roman urban area into which all incoming roads feed. Rome's a headache to drive in, so use the GRA to circle around to the side of the city closest to your final destination rather than trying to cut across downtown. For **parking,** see "Getting Around: By Car" below.

2 Orientation

VISITOR INFORMATION

TOURIST OFFICES   The **main office** (☎ 06/4889-9253; fax 06/4889-9228; www.informaroma.it) is at V. Parigi 5, about a 5-minute walk straight out from the station and across several bus-choked piazze and traffic circles. It's open Monday to Saturday 8:15am to 7pm. There's also a dinky **tourist information** office inside Termini station (☎ **06/4890-6300**), usually crowded with more people than information. It's most useful on Sundays, when the main office is closed. There's another info desk at Fiumicino airport, open daily. For the lowdown on **events,** see "Newspapers & Magazines" under "Fast Facts," below.

INFO KIOSKS   Rome has recently added helpful information kiosks peppered about town. In addition to the usual pamphlets and maps, museum hours, hotel help, event information, exhibitions, and public transportation, these kiosks also have computers (sporadically linked into a database) you can use to find out even more information. They are at: Largo Goldoni/Via del Corso (☎ **06/6813-6061**); Via Nazionale (☎ **06/4782-4525**); Piazza Tempio della Pace, near the Roman Forum (☎ **06/6992-4307**); Piazza d. Cinque Lune, off Piazza Navona (☎ **06/6880-9240**); Lungotevere Castel Sant'Angelo (☎ **06/6880-9707**); Via del Tritone, at La Rinascente department store (☎ **06/6920-0435**); and Piazza San Giovanni in Laterano (☎ **06/772-3598**).

ENJOY ROME   The private firm of **Enjoy Rome,** 3 blocks north of Termini at V. Varese 39 (☎ **06/445-1843**; fax 06/445-0734; www.enjoyrome.com; e-mail info@enjoyrome.com), started as a walking tour outfit in the early 1990s but soon became the first stop in Rome for budget travelers, students, and backpackers. In addition to running year-round foot and bike tours of the city—and a convenient bus directly to Pompeii—Enjoy Rome's young staff, which hails from English-speaking countries, will also provide lots of info on the city, and a free room- and apartment-finding service (see "Where to Stay" below). It's open Monday to Friday 8:30am to 1pm and 3:30 to 6pm, Saturday 8:30am to 1pm.

WEB SITES   Although Rome's official Web sites are **www.comune.roma.com** and **www.informaroma.it**, there are several good privately maintained sites, including **www.roma2000.it**, **www.nettuno.it/electric-italy/metropolitan.html**, and **www. des.it/roma/roma.html**. The Vatican maintains its own Web site at **www.vatican.va**.

CITY LAYOUT

Rome is strung along an S-shaped bend of the **Tevere (Tiber River).** The bulk of the *centro storico,* or historic center, lies east of the Tevere. While there are official administrative districts, the Romans themselves think in terms of an address being near this *piazza* (square) or that major monument, so we'll do the same.

The north end of the centro storico is the oval **Piazza del Popolo.** From this obelisk-sporting square, three major roads radiate south: Via del Babuino, Via del Corso, and Via di Ripetta. The middle one, **Via del Corso** (usually just called the **Corso**), divides the heart of the city in half.

To the east of the Corso lie the **Spanish Steps** (which is where Via del Babuino ends) and **Trevi Fountain.** Surrounding these monuments are Rome's most stylish shopping streets—including the boutique-lined **Via dei Condotti,** which runs straight from the Spanish Steps to the Corso. To the west of the Corso spreads the medieval Tiber Bend area, home to landmarks like the long, bustling **Piazza Navona** square, the ancient **Pantheon,** the market square of **Campo de' Fiori,** countless churches, a few small museums, and the medieval **Jewish Ghetto.**

The Corso ends at about Rome's center in **Piazza Venezia.** This major traffic circle and bus juncture is marked by the enormous, overbearing, and garish white **Vittorio Emanuele Monument.** Leading west from Piazza Venezia is **Via Plebescito,** which, after passing through the archaeological site and major bus stop **Largo di Torre Argentina,** becomes **Corso Vittorio Emanuele II.** Corso V. Emanuele is a wide street that effectively bisects the Tiber Bend as it heads toward the river and the Vatican. (Piazza Navona and the Pantheon lie to the north, Campo de' Fiori and the Jewish Ghetto to the south.)

Back at Piazza Venezia and facing south, if you go to the right around the Vittorio Emanuele Monument—directly behind which stretches the archaeological zone of the **Roman Forum**—you'll see stairs leading up behind it to **Capitoline Hill,** Rome's seat of government. Around the left side of the monument is **Via dei Fori Imperiali,** a wide boulevard that makes a beeline from Piazza Venezia to the **Colosseum,** passing the famous **Roman Forum** on the right (slung into the low land between the Capitoline and **Palatine Hills**) and the **Imperial Forums** on the left. South of the Forum and Colosseum rises the shady residential **Aventine Hill,** beyond which is another hill, the old working-class quarter **Testaccio,** which has recently become a trendy restaurant and nightclub district.

Those are the areas of Rome where you'll spend most of your time. But, the grid of 19th-century streets surrounding the main train station, **Termini,** defines the eastern edge of the centro storico. You might also want to venture out at mealtimes to the area east of Termini to the University and intellectuals' district of **San Lorenzo,** home to some fantastic restaurants.

To the northwest of Termini (east of the Spanish Steps area) is a boulevard zone where many foreign embassies lie, the highlight being the lazy S-curve of the cafe-lined **Via Veneto,** of the fashionable 1950's *La Dolce Vita* fame. Via Veneto ends at the southern flank of the giant **Villa Borghese** park, studded with museums and expanding northeast of the centro storico (it's also accessible from Piazza del Popolo, where we began this orientation discussion).

Across the Tiber River are two major neighborhoods we're interested in. Mussolini razed a medieval district to lay down the wide **Via della Conciliazione** linking the Ponte Vittorio Emanuele bridge with **Vatican City and St. Peter's.** South of here, past the long, parklike **Gianicolo** hill, lies the once medieval working-class, then trendy, and now touristy district of **Trastevere,** with lots of bars and restaurants.

Street Maps   The maps in this chapter will help you orient yourself and find sights, hotels, and restaurants. For more detailed city plans, take along the handy, pocket-sized, laminated "Streetwise Rome," which covers central Rome very well and includes a street index; it's available at your local bookstore or travel shop for $5.95. For wider coverage and even more detail, get the brand-new Michelin map no. 38, a large sheet map of Rome with a street finder and indicators for one-way roads ($12.95).

Available in Rome at newsstands and book stores, the De Agostini 1:12,000 scale fold-out map is very complete and comes with a street index (9,000L/$5.30). If you're searching for an address, stop into any bar or ask your hotel if you can look at their *Tuttocittà*, a magazine that maps every little alleyway but unfortunately only Rome residents can obtain (it comes with their phone books).

NEIGHBORHOODS IN BRIEF

AROUND ANCIENT ROME   This catchall category covers the heart of the ancient city, from the **Colosseum** through the Roman and Imperial Forums to the **Capitoline** and **Esquiline Hills, Piazza Venezia,** and the streets surrounding them to the river. Antiquity buffs will want to spend a lot of their visit in this vast archaeological zone, but it offers few good hotels and even fewer decent restaurants (most cater to entire tour buses with bad food at high prices).

AROUND CAMPO DE' FIORI & THE JEWISH GHETTO   This working-class neighborhood of the Tiber Bend, strung between the river and Corso V. Emanuele, has lots of good restaurants, a daily market on Campo de' Fiori, Renaissance palaces lining the Via Giulia, and a burgeoning nightlife scene. The eastern half of the area—between Via Arenula and Via di Teatro Marcello, and below Largo di Torre Argentina—has been home to Europe's oldest Jewish population ever since it was a walled ghetto in the 16th century. Roman Jewish cooking is some of the city's best, and you'll find delicious and relatively inexpensive examples in trattorie scattered throughout this zone.

AROUND PIAZZA NAVONA & THE PANTHEON   This is the true heart of Medieval Rome, with a host of sights and monuments like the lively **Piazza Navona,** the ancient and beautiful **Pantheon,** churches hiding Caravaggio paintings or Michelangelo sculptures, and plenty of pedestrian-only elbow room. It has a host of excellent restaurants, lots of nightlife possibilities, and a few choice hotels that won't break the bank. You're also within easy walking distance of both the Vatican and the ruins of ancient Rome. It's a toss-up between this and the Spanish Steps area when it comes to choosing the absolute best place to base yourself in Rome (sightseeing fanatics will want to book here; shoppers nearer the Spanish Steps).

AROUND THE SPANISH STEPS & PIAZZA DEL POPOLO   Since the 18th century, this has been one of the most popular expatriate areas of Rome, full of Brits and Germans and lots of *passeggiata* (evening stroll) action. Today the streets around Piazza di Spagna comprise the heart of Rome's shopping scene, with boutique-lined streets like Via de' Condotti sporting the biggest names in Italian and international fashion. It's also one of the most touristy areas of the center, with "public living rooms" and patented tourist draws like the graceful baroque off-center sweep of the Spanish Steps and the gushing mountain of white marble called the Trevi Fountain. It's no coincidence that Rome's top hotels cluster at the Spanish Steps' summit, or that the American Express is on Piazza di Spagna itself (and that Italy's first McDonald's opened a few doors down in 1986, nearly inciting a riot by Italian food traditionalists). Moving about this neighborhood is often an exercise in weaving between large clots of camera-clicking tour groups, but the area certainly stays animated and most roads are blessedly closed to cars.

AROUND VIA VENETO & PIAZZA BARBERINI   In the 1950s, this was the heartbeat of *La Dolce Vita* ("the sweet life") made famous by Fellini films. Via Veneto still has the cafes of its heyday, but today they're overpriced and patronized mainly by tourists, and its grand old hotels are similarly expensive and booked mostly by guided and packaged tours. The area around Via Veneto and Piazza Barberini is also full of baroque and 19th-century palazzi, today home to everything from embassies to one of Rome's best painting galleries (in Palazzo Barberini) to newspaper headquarters.

TERMINI   Aside from some churches and a great museum, the 19th-century neighborhood around the train station is a pretty boring part of town and too far from the bulk of Rome's sights to walk. Although it has an abundance of cheap hotels and has actually improved dramatically in recent years, the Termini area is still rather unattractive overall, and it's the least safe area in central Rome, with a higher rate of pickpocketing and mugging. However, the old rule of thumb has flip-flopped: Now the streets just to the **North of Termini** are the cleanest and safest, while those to the **South of Termini** have become even more decrepit and dangerous. Unless you're concerned about catching a train to make an early flight, I'd find a hotel in a safer, more interesting, and central part of town.

THE AVENTINE & TESTACCIO   The **Aventine Hill** south of the Palatine and next to the river is one of central Rome's quietest, leafiest, and most posh residential sections, with a couple of ancient churches set on curving roads. Few tourists venture here and the views somehow overlook most of Rome's urban sprawl to encompass only the leafiness around you and the mountains in the distance. It's a good place to stay if you want a vacation from the urban chaos but still to be only a stroll from the nearest bus or Metro stop.

South of the Aventine and up against the river where it turns south again is one of Rome's greatest working-class neighborhoods, **Testaccio,** home of the old city slaughterhouse and once Rome's port on the Tiber. Its name means "ugly head" and refers to the small man-made hillock that hems in the neighborhood on the east. As the Tiber docklands in ancient times (before recycling was invented), Testaccio received countless barges carrying amphorae full of wine and olive oil. These ceramic vases were offloaded, their merchandise measured into smaller, more salable containers, and then the amphorae were discarded onto a pile, which eventually grew into the 165-foot hill of Testaccio, now covered with grass. Since all that ceramic keeps constant temperature and moisture levels, grottoes were dug into the mound for storing wine and food, and many of Rome's most authentic restaurants still line Testaccio, their dining rooms and cellars burrowed back into the artificial hill of pot shards and their kitchens turning out ultratraditional cuisine in the city. The area's also become rather fashionable, and most of Rome's hottest nightclubs appear in old warehouses here (and often disappear after a few months).

TRASTEVERE   Trastevere, which means "Across the Tiber," was another of Rome's great Medieval working-class neighborhoods, one that spoke its own distinct dialect and had a tradition of street fairs and poetry—still echoed in the July ✪ **Festa de' Noiantri,** or "Feast of We Others." But after Trastevere became trendy in the 1970s and 1980s, popular with both the Roman upper middle class and lots of expatriate Americans, it became touristy in the 1990s. It always had lots of restaurants and excellent tiny trattorie, but this boom in popularity has filled it beyond bursting with eateries, pubs, dance halls, funky boutiques, sidewalk vendors and fortune tellers, and a constant, stifling crush of "trendoids" and tourists. Trastevere has become a requisite stop for coach tours and a guided walk in travel books. It's still one of Rome's most colorful quarters, and the best place to come if you just want to wander into a good restaurant at random, but, like the Latin Quarter in Paris or SoHo in New York, it really has degraded into a parody of itself.

AROUND THE VATICAN   Called the *Borgo,* the area surrounding the Vatican is full of tour buses and the restaurants and businesses that cater to them, but also many modestly priced (if mostly boringly modern) hotels. Expanding north and northeast

Rome Orientation

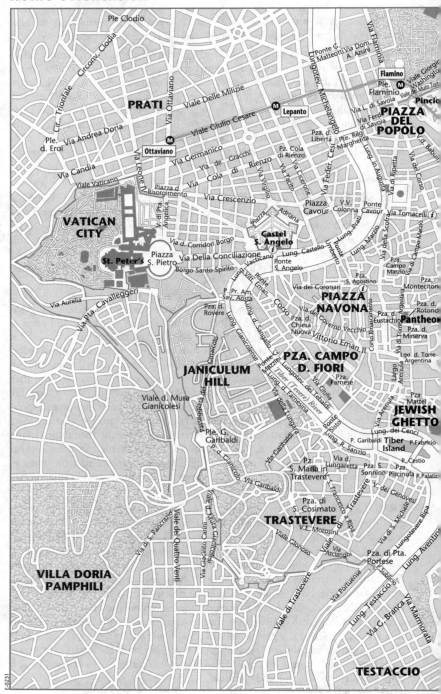

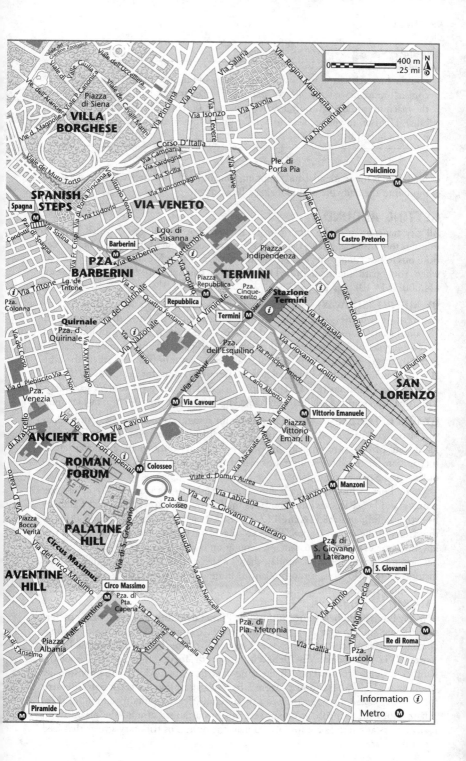

Metro Tips

You can buy tickets and passes for buses, trams, and the Metro from *tabacchi* (tobac-conists), most newsstands, Metro stations, or machines at major bus stops (**Note:** the machines annoyingly only accept coins and 1,000 or 10,000L notes, not 5,000L bills). Hold on to your ticket until you're off the bus or out of the station to avoid paying a huge fine.

of the Borgo is the residential and shopping zone of **Prati**—no sightseeing, just a good glimpse into the daily life of middle-class Romans.

GETTING AROUND

All city transport uses the same *biglietto* (**ticket**). For 1,500L (90¢), you'll have 75 minutes to transfer as often as you'd like (you can enter the Metro system only once) from bus to bus. Stamp one end on the first bus (or tram or Metro), and the other end when you board the final bus. There are also daily (6,000L/$3.55) and weekly (24,000L/$14.10) passes.

BY METRO (SUBWAY)   Rome's *Metropolitana* (Metro) isn't very extensive. The city has only two lines—the orange "A" line and the blue "B" line—that etch a rough "X" on the city map with Termini at the intersection. **Line A** runs from Ottaviano (a dozen blocks from the Vatican), through such stops as Flaminia (near Piazza del Popolo), Spagna (Spanish Steps), Termini, and San Giovanni (Rome's cathedral). **Line B** is most useful to shuttle you quickly from Termini to stops for the Colosseo (Colosseum), Circo Massimo (the Circus Maximus), and Piramide (at Rome's secondary, Tiburtina train station and near Testaccio). The Metro runs from 8:30am to 11:30pm.

BY BUS & TROLLEY   Rome's bus and tram system is much more extensive than the Metro, and you usually don't have to walk far for a connection. The tourist office hands out a free bus route map, but with massive city infrastructure renovations in preparation for the Jubilee, lines are created, diverted, or retired with annoying frequency, so be prepared for detours.

Useful lines include the **64,** a beeline from Termini to the Vatican (heavily used by tourists, and hence thieves, and known as the Pickpocket Express or Wallet Easter, so be extra careful); and the **116** and **117,** two teensy electric buses that trundle through the streets of the centro storico. There's also a **116T** line that runs evenings and follows to some extent the 116 route, diverging on occasion to pass by Rome's various performing arts theaters. On Sunday, there's a special line **204** that hits much of the historic center. Most buses run 5:30am to midnight, with a separate series of night buses whose route numbers are prefaced by an "N." For bus information, call ☎ **167/ 431-784.**

Many buses start their routes at the large **Piazza dei Cinquecento** in front of Termini. There are also four major spots in the centro storico where multiple bus lines converge for easy transfers. They are: **Largo di Tritone/Piazza Barberini; Piazza Venezia/Via Plebescito; Via Plebescito/Largo di Torre Argentina** (south of the Pantheon; due to construction at the time of writing, many buses are provisionally stopping on Via Plebescito just before Largo Argentina); and **Piazza San Silvestro** (just off the Corso, between the Spanish Steps and Trevi Fountain). For all of these squares, some buses pause at one of several stops arranged around the piazza itself, many others at a series of stops located near the outlets of tributary streets that feed into the square.

Driving Tip

If you plan to rent a car in Italy and are starting in Rome, wait to pick up the car until the day you set out into the countryside; if you're flying home from Rome, drop the rental off the instant you drive into town and spend your days in the capital blissfully car-free.

ON FOOT   Rome is a town to explore on foot. From little baroque churches with ancient columns to a roving knife sharpener working the pedal of his portable grindstone, you never know what you might come across while walking down a Roman street. Rome, however, is not quite a walker's paradise—the sidewalks are too narrow (or, in many cases, nonexistent) and the traffic far to heavy. Fortunately, much of the historic center has now been pedestrianized save for a few main thoroughfares. Beware: Hard, uneven cobblestones are rough on your feet, your shoe soles, and your ankles.

BY TAXI   Although you can reach most of Rome's sights easily by bus or foot, trips from the airport or train station to your hotel may be more comfortable in a taxi. Taxi stands are located at major piazze, including Piazza Venezia, Largo Argentina, at the Pantheon, and in front of Termini. You can also call a taxi at ☎ **3570** or 4994, but the meter begins running when the driver picks up your call. The initial charge is 4,500L ($3.85), plus 200L (20¢) per kilometer. There are additional charges for luggage (2,000L/$1.20 per bag) and travel at night (5,000L/$2.95) or on Sundays (2,000L/$1.20).

BY CAR   If you have a choice, don't drive in Rome. Having a car here is a royal pain. Not only are Italian drivers even more manic in the city—and parking near impossible—but the system of one-way roads seems specially designed to keep you from driving anywhere near your intended direction. Much of the historic center is pedestrian-only, but you are allowed to drive in to your hotel to drop off luggage.

Parking   Your hotel may have a garage or an arrangement with one, or you may be lucky enough to be staying in one of the few scraps of the historic center that have not yet been designated a *zona blu*—as part of a new initiative, most of the city's parking spaces have been painted with blue stripes, which means you must pay a parking meter (usually a box at the end of the block; you feed it coins and it gives you a slip to leave on the dashboard). The cheapest and biggest **public garage** is **Parcheggio Borghese** under the Villa Borghese park in the northeast corner of town. Its entrance is on Viale del Muro Torto, which leads off into the park from the traffic circle at Porta Pinciana, where Via Veneto, Corso d'Italia, and Via Pinciana converge.

BY BICYCLE OR SCOOTER   The three best prices on rental bikes or scooters are at **Treno e Scooter,** at track 1 inside Termini train station—pick up bikes outside the station on the right (☎ **06/4890-5823**); **I Bike Rome,** V. Veneto 156, in section 3 of the underground parking lot (☎ **06/322-5230**); and **Roma Solutions Rent A Scooter,** locations at V. F. Turati 50 near Termini (☎ **06/446-9222**) and Cor. V. Emanuele II 204 near Piazza Navona (☎ **06/687-6922**). Rates at all are about 4,000L ($2.35) per hour or 10,000 to 13,000L ($5.90 to $7.65) per day for a regular bike; 7,000L ($4.10) per hour or 18,000 to 20,000L ($10.60 to $11.75) per day for a 10-speed; 30,000 to 70,000L ($17.65 to $41.20) for 4 hours or 35,000 to 100,000L ($20.60 to $58.80) for a day with a scooter (depending on engine size). Scooters come with a *casco* (helmet) and lock.

FAST FACTS: Rome

American Express American Express (☎ **06/67-641**) is just to the right of the Spanish Steps at Pz. di Spagna 38. It's open May to September, Monday to Friday 9am to 7:30pm and Saturday 9am to 3pm; October to April, Monday to Friday 9am to 5:30pm and Saturday 9am to 12:30pm. To report lost or stolen traveler's checks, call ☎ **1678/72-000,** lost or stolen AMEX cards ☎ **722/80-371.**

Business Hours As in most of Italy, almost all shops and offices, most churches, and many museums observe a siesta-like midafternoon shutdown called *riposo,* which lasts roughly from noon or 1pm to 3 or 4pm. It's a good idea to figure out the few sights in town that remain open during *riposo* so you can save them—and a leisurely lunch—to fill this time.

Most shop hours are Tuesday to Saturday 8am to noon or 1pm and 3 or 4pm to 8pm, Monday 3 or 4pm to 8pm. Food shops are generally also open Monday mornings, but closed Thursday afternoons. However, more and more stores are posting *orario continuato* or "no-stop" signs, meaning they've given into the pressures of the Americanized capitalist world and are staying open through the riposo.

Doctors & Dentists First aid is available 24 hours a day in the emergency room *(pronto soccorso)* of major hospitals; see "Hospitals" below. Also try the **International Medical Center** at V. Giovanni Amendola 7 (☎ **06/488-2371**). Call the **U.S. Embassy** (☎ **06/46-741**) for a list of English-speaking doctors and dentists.

Embassies & Consulates The **U.S. Embassy** is at V. Vittorio Veneto 121 (☎ **06/46-741**). For passport and consular services, head to the consulate, left of the embassy's main gate, open Monday to Friday 8 to 11:30am and 1:30 to 3pm. The **Canadian** consulate is at V. Zara 30, on the fifth floor (☎ **06/445-0981** or 06/440-3028), open Monday to Friday 10am to noon and 2 to 4pm. Citizens of the **United Kingdom** will find their consulate at V. XX Settembre 80A (☎ **06/852-721** or 06/482-5441; fax 06/487-3324), open July 15 to August 31, Monday to Friday 8am to 1pm; September to July 14, Monday to Friday 9:30am to 12:30pm and 2 to 4pm. The **Australian** consulate is at V. Alessandria 215 (☎ **06/852-721;** fax 06/8527-2300), open Monday to Thursday 9am to noon and 1:30 to 5:30pm, Friday 9am to 1:30pm. The **New Zealand** consulate is at V. Zara 28 (☎ **06/440-2028;** fax 06/440-2984), open Monday to Friday 8:30am to 12:45pm and 1:45 to 5pm.

Emergencies Dial ☎ **113** in any emergency. You can also call ☎ 112 for the *carabinieri* (the military-trained and more useful of the two police forces), ☎ 118 or 5100 to summon an ambulance, or ☎ 115 for the fire department. *Pronto Soccorso* means first aid, and is also the word used for emergency rooms. Call ☎ 116 for roadside assistance (not free).

Hospitals In an emergency, go the nearest emergency room *(pronto soccorso)* of any hospital *(ospedale).* Convenient ones in the historic center include **San Giacomo,** V. Canova 29, off V. d. Corso, 2 blocks from Piazza del Popolo (☎ **06/36-261**); **Fatebenefratelli,** on Tiber Island (☎ **06/68-371**); and **Ospedale S. Spirito in Sassia,** Lungotevere in Sassia 1 on the river just south of Castel Sant'Angelo (☎ **06/68-351**). The new "H" bus line makes a circular route of all the major hospitals.

English-speaking doctors are always on duty at the **Rome American Hospital,** V. Emilio Longoni 69 (☎ **06/22-551**), and at the privately run **Salvator Mundi**

Two-Wheel Deals

If you arrive in Rome by train and bring your canceled train ticket to Treno e Scooter, you get a 30% (bicycle) or 10% (scooter) discount on your first day of rental (valid only on the day you arrive in town). However, Rome's chaotic traffic and widespread pedestrian zones make trying to get around by scooter dangerous, frustrating, and often untenable.

International Hospital, Vle. d. Mura Gianicolensi 67 (☎ **06/586-041**). Most hospitals will be able to find someone to help you in English, and with Italy's partially socialized medical system, you can usually pop into an emergency room, get taken care of speedily without dealing with insurance forms and the like, and be sent on your way with a prescription and a smile.

Laundry   Self-service *lavanderie* (Laundromats) are all over town. Try the **Bolle Blu** at V. Milazzo 20, where they do the wash for you in an hour for 14,000L ($8.25), soap included. For coin-op Laundromats, hit the **Ondablu chain,** with central locations at V. Principe Amadeo 70b (south of Termini) and V. Vespasiano 50 (near the Vatican). The cost is 13,500L ($7.95), soap included.

The bulk of *lavanderie,* though, are full-service, charging ridiculous by-the-piece rates (4,000L/$2.35 for a pair of pants, 2,000L/$1.18 for socks) to wash, dry, press, and wrap up your T-shirts and undies like a Christmas present. Always ask first if service is *à peso* (by weight, the cheap way) or *al pezzo* (by the piece). However, these full-service joints also usually provide *lavasecco* (dry-cleaning) service at prices comparable to those in the United States. Your hotel will be able to point out the nearest one.

Lost & Found   The *Ufficio Stranieri* (foreigners' office) of Rome's *Questura* (police headquarters) is at V. S. Vitale 15 (☎ **06/4686-2102**). Termini **train station**'s *Oggetti Rivenuti* office is open 7am to 11pm (☎ **06/4730-6682**).

Luggage Storage & Lockers   See "Getting Here: By Train" above.

Mail & E-Mail   The Italian mail system is notoriously slow, and friends back home may not receive your postcards for anywhere from 1 to 8 weeks (sometimes longer). The **main post office** is at Pz. San Silvestro 19, 00187 Roma, Italia (off Via del Corso, south of the Spanish Steps). It's open Monday to Friday 9am to 6pm, Saturday 9am to 2pm, Sunday 9am to 6pm. Enter and head around to the right to buy *francobolli* (**stamps**) at windows 22 and 23. You can also pick up stamps at any *tabacchi* (tobacconists; signs have a white "T" on a brown or black background) around town.

If you want your letters to get home before you do, use the **Vatican post office** instead. It costs the same—but you must use Vatican stamps, available only at their post offices—and is much quicker and more reliable. There are three offices: to the left of the basilica steps, just past the information office; a less crowded branch behind the right-hand colonnade of Piazza San Pietro (where the alley dead-ends beyond the souvenir stands); and upstairs in the Vatican Museums entrance, near the gift shop.

To receive mail while in Rome (for a modest pick-up fee), have it sent to the main post office above, addressed to Your Name/FERMO POSTA/Roma, Italia/ITALY. Holders of AMEX cards can get the same service for free by having their mail sent to Your Name/CLIENT MAIL/American Express/Piazza di Spagna 38/Roma, Italia/ITALY.

You can log onto the **Internet** in central Rome at **Thenetgate,** Pz. Firenze 25 (☎ **06/689-3445**), open in summer Monday to Saturday 10:30am to 12:30pm and 3:30 to 10:30pm, in winter daily 10:40am to 8:30pm. A single 20-minute visit costs 5,000L ($2.95); 1 hour (including mailbox) costs 10,000L ($5.90). On Saturday there are happy half-hours 10:30 to 11am and 2 to 2:30pm when Internet access is free.

Newspapers & Magazines   Expatriate magazines *Wanted in Rome* (1,500L/90¢; www.wantedinrome.com) and the more British *Metropolitan* (1,500L/90¢; www.nettuno.it/electric-italy/metropolitan.html) have calendar-of-events sections along with classified ads and articles on Rome and Italy from the foreigner's point of view. You'll find them at most newsstands, especially around tourist areas such as the Vatican. If you want to try your hand at Italian, the Thursday edition of the newspaper *La Repubblica* contains the magazine insert *TrovaRoma* (www.repubblica.it), with ultra-complete entertainment, event, gallery, and show listings. Two other prime resources are the excellent weekly magazine *Roma C'è* (2,000L/$1.20), which has a "This Week in Rome" section at the end in English, and the Rome edition of *Time Out* magazine (4,500L/$2.65), which comes out every 2 months; both are available at newsstands.

Pharmacies   *Farmacie* follow a rotation schedule so that several remain open all night and on Sundays and holidays. This schedule is posted outside each pharmacy. The **Farmacia Internazionale,** at Pz. Barberini 49 (☎ **06/679-4680**), and the **Station International Pharmacy,** at Termini train station (☎ **06/ 488-0019**), are both open 24 hours.

Police   Dial ☎ **113** in emergencies (see also "Emergencies" above).

Safety   Random violent crime is extremely rare in Rome, but pickpockets— especially gypsy children; see below—target tourists. Thieves favor buses that run between Termini and the major tourist sites (particularly bus 64, the Pickpocket Express, to the Vatican). Watch your wallet in Termini, near the Forums and Colosseum, in Piazza del Popolo, and around the Vatican in particular.

Gypsy children work in packs around tourist areas, especially the Colosseum/ Forum region and subway tunnels. They aren't physically dangerous, but whenever they're around, a tourist and his money will soon be parted. They approach looking pitiful, begging, and waving scraps of cardboard, occasionally scrawled with a few words in English. This flurry of cardboard is merely a distraction beneath which their fingers will be busy relieving you of everything in your pockets. If you see a group of dirty kids dressed in colorful but filthy rags headed your way, yell *Va via!* (scram!), or loudly invoke the *polizia.* If they get too close, shove them away violently—don't hold back just because they're kids.

Gypsy mothers usually stick to panhandling, but aren't above picking your pocket—one scam is to suddenly toss their swaddled baby through the air at you (usually it's a doll in blankets, but sometimes they toss the real thing!), and while you in your surprise rush to catch it, they or their waiting brood fleece you in the blink of an eye.

For women: There is an occasional drive-by purse snatching by young Vespa-riding thieves. Keep your purse on the wall side of the sidewalk, wear the strap diagonally across your chest, and try to keep from walking along the sidewalk's edge. Also, if your purse has a flap, keep the clasp side facing your body to deter pickpockets. **For men:** Keep your wallet in your front pocket rather than the rear and your hand on it while riding the bus.

Getting the Best Deal on Accommodations

- Reserve in advance to get the best budget room. None of the centrally located bargains are secrets, and they fill up quickly, especially in summer.
- If you didn't book ahead, call for a room as soon as you arrive at the station, rather than walking around to hotels, bags in tow.
- Always ask for off-season rates from October to Easter, or for other special rates for students, teachers, professionals—you never know what might work.
- Ask for the cheapest rooms, as prices often vary according to size, view, amenities, and so on.
- Settle for a room without private bathroom—invariably cheaper.
- This is a vanishing phenomenon, but a double bed (*letto matrimoniale*) is still sometimes cheaper than two twin beds (*due letti*) in a double room.
- Never, ever make a phone call from your hotel room. You'll pay two or three times more than at a pay phone.
- If at all possible, opt to eat outside of the hotel ; you can get the same *cornetto* and cappuccino at the corner bar for a third of the hotel's price.
- Agree on all charges when you check in. Make sure the rate is *per room,* not per person. That way you'll have no unpleasant surprises upon checkout.

Taxis   See "Getting Around: By Taxi," earlier in this chapter.

Transit Info   For information on **ATAC** (city buses) call ☎ **06/4695-4444.** For **COTRAL** (suburban buses) call ☎ **06/591-5551.**

Travel Agencies   In Termini train station you'll find desks for **Wasteels** (☎ **06/ 482-5537**) and **CTS** (☎ **06/467-9254**), both open 8:30am to 8:30pm to offer discounts (under 26) and assistance (all ages), but only for *international* train travel. Their main offices are: **Wasteels,** V. Milazzo 8c (☎ **06/445-6679**); **CTS,** Cor. V. Emanuele II 297 (☎ **06/687-2672**).

3 Accommodations You Can Afford

Even as a frugal traveler, you don't have to settle for the cheap, often squalid rooms surrounding the train station. (Although there are several good ones recommended below, the location leaves something to be desired.) You can still stay well within budget in a small but comfortable room overlooking the Pantheon, near the Spanish Steps, or hidden in Trastevere.

In the list of buses that pass near each hotel, boldface indicates lines you can take directly from the main train station, Termini (either from the bus terminus on Piazza del Cinquecento directly out front or from a stop on the streets ringing the piazza). Parking rates usually apply for small to midsized cars; you may have to pay more for larger models.

ROOM-FINDING SERVICES   The **tourist offices** (in the train station and at V. Parigi 5; see "Visitor Information," earlier in this chapter) will help you track down a room, but are often loathe to do so when there's a long line behind you. Tourist offices are not allowed to play favorites regarding specific hotels, so the employees will look for any available room in your vague price range. (Some people are kind enough to try and stick you close to the center).

Rome Accommodations

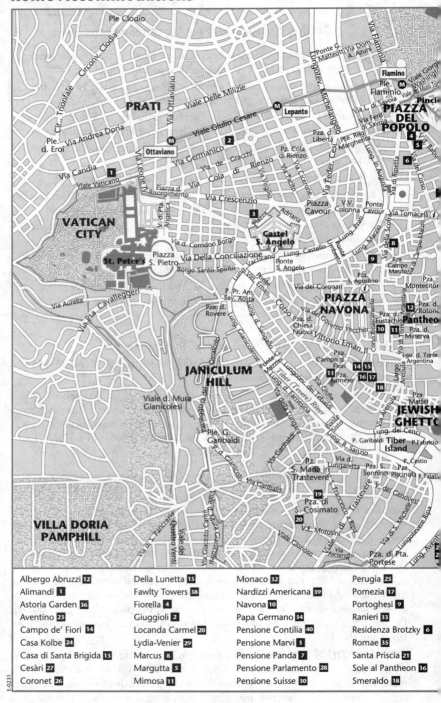

Albergo Abruzzi **12**
Alimandi **1**
Astoria Garden **36**
Aventino **23**
Campo de' Fiori **14**
Casa Kolbe **24**
Casa di Santa Brigida **13**
Cesàri **27**
Coronet **26**

Della Lunetta **15**
Fawlty Towers **38**
Fiorella **4**
Giuggioli **2**
Locanda Carmel **20**
Lydia-Venier **29**
Marcus **8**
Margutta **5**
Mimosa **11**

Monaco **32**
Nardizzi Americana **39**
Navona **10**
Papa Germano **34**
Pensione Contilia **40**
Pensione Marvi **3**
Pensione Panda **7**
Pensione Parlamento **28**
Pensione Suisse **30**

Perugia **25**
Pomezia **17**
Portoghesi **9**
Ranieri **33**
Residenza Brotzky **6**
Romae **35**
Santa Priscia **21**
Sole al Pantheon **16**
Smeraldo **18**

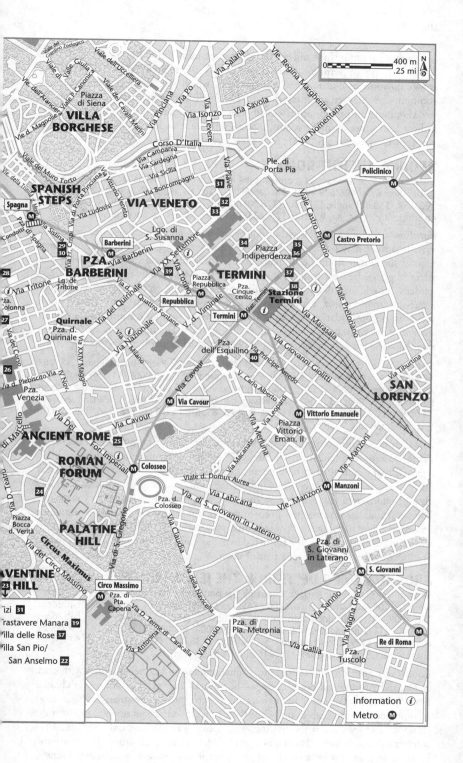

400 m
.25 mi

VILLA BORGHESE

Viale del Giardino Zoologico
Viale di Valle Giulia
Viale P. Canonica
Piazza di Siena
Viale dei Cavalli Marini
Viale dell'Uccelliera
Vle. dell'Arancera
Viale P. Canonica
Vle. d. Magnolie
Viale della Trinità d. Monti
Vle. della Trinità d. Monti
Viale del Muro Torto
Via Salaria
Viale Regina Margherita
Via Po
Via Pinciana
Via Isonzo
Via Savoia
Via Tevere
Via Nomentana

Corso D'Italia
Via Campania
Via Sardegna
Via Sicilia
Via Boncompagni
Via Piave
Via Pinciana

Ple. di Porta Pia

Policlinico **M**

SPANISH STEPS

VIA VENETO

Spagna **M**

Pza. di Spagna
Via Condotti
Via Fr. Crispi
Via Sistina
Via di Porta Pinciana
Vittorio Veneto
Via Ludovisi
Via di P. Pinciana

Via Castro Pretorio
Castro Pretorio **M**

Barberini **M**
Lgo. di S. Susanna
PZA. BARBERINI
Via Tritone
Lg. de Tritone
Pza. Colonna
Via XX Settembre
Via Barberini
Via Torino
Piazza Repubblica
34
31
32
33
35
36
Piazza Indipendenza
37

28
29
30
39
TERMINI
38
Stazione Termini
Staz. Termini

27
Quirinale
Pza. d. Quirinale
Via del Quirinale
Quattro Fontane
V. d. Viminale
Pza. Cinque-cento
Repubblica **M**
Termini **M**
Via Marsala

Via del Corso
Via d. Plebiscito
Via IV Nov.
Via Nazionale
Via Milano
Pza. dell'Esquilino
40
V. Principe Amedo
Via Giovanni Giolitti
Via Tiburtina

26
Via XXIV Maggio
Pza. Venezia
Via Cavour
V. Carlo Alberto
SAN LORENZO

Via d. Teatro di Marcello
ANCIENT ROME
25
Fori Imperiali
Via Cavour **M**
Via Merulana
Via Leopardi
Piazza Vittorio Eman. II
Vittorio Emanuele

ROMAN FORUM
Colosseo **M**
Viale d. Domus Aurea
Via Labicana
Via Macanate
Vle. Manzoni
Manzoni **M**

24
Pza. d. Colosseo
Via di S. Giovanni in Laterano

PALATINE HILL
Via di S. Gregorio
Via Claudia
Via della Navicella
Pza. di S. Giovanni in Laterano
S. Giovanni **M**

Piazza Bocca d. Verità
Circus Massimo
Via del Circo Massimo

AVENTINE HILL
23
Circo Massimo **M**
Pza. di Pta. Capena
Via D. Terme di Caracalla
Via Sannio
Via Magna Grecia

Pza. di Pla. Metronia
Via Druso
Via Antonina di Caracalla
Via Gallia
Pza. Tuscolo
Re di Roma **M**

izi **31**
rastavere Manara **19**
illa delle Rose **37**
illa San Pio/
    San Anselmo **22**

Information **ⓘ**
Metro **M**

105

You may have more luck and certainly better service at **Enjoy Rome,** a private outfit 3 blocks north of Termini at V. Varese 39 (☎ **06/445-1843;** fax 06/445-0734; www.enjoyrome.it; e-mail: info@enjoyrome.it), which specializes in finding budget accommodations, even at the last minute. The English-speaking staff will help you for free via phone, in person, or via e-mail. The clerks often try to convince you to stay in hostels or other dormlike rooms, especially if you're under 30—just remind them you are willing to pay a bit more for a private room.

AROUND ANCIENT ROME

Casa Kolbe. V. S. Teodoro 44 (bordering the east side of the Palatine archaeological zone), 00186 Roma. ☎ 06/679-4974. Fax 06/6994-1550. 63 units, all with bathroom. TEL. 100,000L ($58.80) single; 130,000L ($76.50) double. 7,000L ($4.10). AE, MC, V. Free parking on street. Bus: H, 44, 81, 95, 160, 170, 628, 715, 716, 780 (to Pz. Bocca d. Verità).

For those who love archaeology but don't need many hotel amenities, this huge converted convent may be perfect. It's as hidden as you can get in the heart of Rome, around the corner from the Roman Forum's "back door" on the little-traveled side street hugging the west flank of the Palatine Hill. Most rooms overlook palm-filled gardens in back, and all are monastically quiet, even those on the street. Second-floor street-side rooms enjoy a low panorama of the Palatine's ruins and a few Forum columns. Accommodations are large and fairly basic, with an institutional feel reminiscent of the convent that still occupies the top floor. The furnishings are unmemorably modular, bathrooms are nice, and beds could be firmer but aren't bad.

Perugia. V. d. Colosseo 7 (near corner of V. d. Tempio di Pace), 00184 Roma. ☎ **06/679-7200.** Fax 06/678-4635. 13 units, 7 with bathroom. TEL. 70,000L ($41.20) single without bathroom, 90,000L ($52.95) single with bathroom; 95,000L ($55.90) double without bathroom, 125,000L ($73.50) double with bathroom. AE, DC, MC, V. Parking 20,000–30,000L ($11.75–$17.65); free on street. Bus: **75,** 85, 87, **115,** 117, **175,** 186, 810, 850 (to V. d. Fori Imperiali). Metro: Colosseo.

A well-run but rundown inn a block behind the Forum entrance, the side-street Perugia is a study in trade-offs. The funky '70s-reject furnishings are on their last disco legs and that single 40-watt bulb doesn't quite illuminate your room, but the street's fairly quiet so you can open the windows for light, and everything's kept tolerably clean. Bounce on a few beds before choosing, as some will be kinder to your spine. You won't find the best mattress in room no. 26, but the room overlooks a minuscule courtyard full of hanging ivy. Private bathrooms are nicer than shared ones. Compared with Casa Kolbe (above), it's further down the comfort scale, equidistant from a Forum entrance, but in a livelier part of town.

AROUND CAMPO DE' FIORI & THE JEWISH GHETTO

Campo de' Fiori. V. d. Biscione 6 (just off the northeast corner of Cam. de' Fiori), 00186 Roma. ☎ **06/687-4886** or 06/6880-6865. Fax 06/687-6003. 27 units, 9 with bathroom. TEL. 170,000L ($100) single with bathroom; 140,000L ($82.35) double without bathroom, 200,000L ($117.65) double with bathroom; 200,000–250,000L ($117.65–$147.05) double apt., 50,000L ($29.40) extra person. MC, V. Parking 30,000L ($17.65). Bus: 46, 62, **64** (to first stop on Cor. V. Emanuele); 116, 116T (to Cam. de' Fiori).

Rooms vary greatly at this central inn—some modern and carpeted, others with brick arches and rustic wood-beam ceilings—but overall they're a cut above the cheaper Hotel Sole across the way. Although a couple aren't much larger than the beds, most accommodations are sizable, and while there's no elevator, room no. 602 is worth the climb for its views across the rooftops and domes—a vista beat only by that of the communal roof terrace. The nightly party noise wafting up from the streets can be annoying, so request a room off the front if you want to sleep more soundly.

Long-Term Accommodations in Rome

If you plan on staying in Rome for more than a few days, here are some tips. First off, bargain with any hotel for stays longer than 3 nights; bargain even harder for stays of 7 nights or more. **Enjoy Rome** (p. 178) might have a few leads on inexpensive apartments for rent. Of the hotels I've recommended, the **Campo de' Fiori** also rents apartments at reasonable rates, and the **Navona** has a few efficiency units with kitchenettes for long-term rental. Otherwise, check out the classifieds of the English-language weeklies *Wanted in Rome* and *Metropolitan* (if you can read Italian, the Roman circular *Porta Portese* is another good resource). Also stop by **CTS,** V. Genova 16 (☎ **06/46-791**), a student travel agency that often has rental rooms posted (and, especially if you're younger, may help you find a place).

Bathrooms, shared or private, are clean. The owners also rent eight apartments in nearby buildings if you're staying longer. If you don't believe us, a wide range of travelers consistently cite this as their favorite hotel of the *centro storico*.

Della Lunetta. Pz. d. Paradiso 68 (off V. d. Paradiso, a block from Cor. V. Emanuele), 00186 Roma. ☎ **06/686-1080.** Fax 06/689-2028. 35 units, 15 with bathroom. TEL. 90,000L ($52.95) single without bathroom; 110,000L ($64.70) double without bathroom, 150,000L ($88.25) double with bathroom. MC, V. Free parking on piazza (if you can find a spot). Bus: 46, 62, **64** (to first stop on Cor. V. Emanuele); 116, 116T (to Cam. de' Fiori).

The mumbling manager seems terminally cranky, and the accommodations feel a bit institutional with ranks of two to three cots (a little lumpy, but not bad) and modular furnishings, but this hotel has the best prices in the neighborhood. Most bathrooms are new with box showers, but a few suffer from the curtainless spigot in the wall and drain in the floor arrangement. In all, it'd be my last choice amid this cluster of hotels above Campo de' Fiori, although it is quieter than those closer to the Campo itself.

Pomezia. V. d. Chiavari 12 (between Lgo. d. Pollaro and V. Giubbonari), 00186 Roma. ☎ and fax **06/686-1371.** 24 units, 12 with bathroom. TEL. 90,000L ($52.95) single without bathroom, 130,000L ($76.50) single with bathroom; 130,000L ($76.50) double without bathroom, 180,000L ($105.90) double with bathroom. Rates 20% lower in winter. Rates include breakfast. AE, DC, MC, V. Bus: 46, 62, **64** (to first stop on Cor. V. Emanuele); 116, 116T (to Cam. de' Fiori).

This spare but comfortably furnished inn has been in the same family since 1932, and the current generation of three brothers keeps it in decent shape. Beds could be stiffer, and some bathrooms give new meaning to the word *cramped,* but it's all squeaky clean. The dismal shared bathrooms are not the hotel's best feature. Keep in mind that the rooms with private bathrooms were also renovated in the mid-1990s, and it's worth springing for them. You may not have an elevator to help you reach the top-floor rooms, but they do catch some rooftop views and less street noise. In fact, the double-paned windows don't do much good, and the walls are thin, so a room on the *cortile* air shaft is best for light sleepers. In winter you may be able to talk to them about the off season discount and save 10,000L ($5.90) a head.

Smeraldo. Vc. d. Chiodaroli (between V. Chiavari and V. Monte d. Farina), 00186 Roma. ☎ **06/687-5929.** Fax 06/6880-5495. 50 units, 42 with bathroom. A/C TV TEL. 95,000L ($55.90) single without bathroom, 130,000L ($76.50) single with bathroom; 125,000L ($73.50) double without bathroom, 160,000L ($94.10) double with bathroom. 8,000L

($4.70). AE, MC, V. Parking 25,000–35,000L ($14.70–$20.60). Bus: **H,** tram 8 (to V. Arenula); 56, 60, **70,** 81, 87, **115,** 186, **492,** 628, **640** (to Lgo. di Torre Argentina); 46, 62, **64** (to first stop on Cor. V. Emanuele); 116, 116T (to Cam. de' Fiori).

Smeraldo offers the utmost comfort and lots of amenities at reasonable prices. Most rooms have fresh and comfortable mattresses, spanking new bathrooms, and functional but pleasant built-in furnishings, although the pebbly stone tile floors should probably be replaced. Most of the rooms are extremely quiet, save for some distant traffic rumble on the Via Monte della Farina side. There's a fourth-floor terrace for shade and quiet and a rooftop that offers sun and a panorama of Rome's rooftops.

Sole al Pantheon. V. d. Biscione 76 (half a block north of Cam. de' Fiori), 00186 Roma. ☎ **06/6880-6873.** Fax 06/689-3787. 62 units, 40 with bathroom. TEL. 85,000–95,000L ($50–$55.90) single without bathroom, 115,000–120,000L ($67.65–$70.60) single with bathroom; 130,000–140,000L ($76.50–$82.35) double without bathroom, 160,000–180,000L ($94.10–$105.90) double with bathroom. No credit cards. Parking 30,000–40,000L ($17.65–$23.55). Bus: 46, 62, **64** (to first stop on Cor. V. Emanuele); 116, 116T (to Campo de' Fiori).

The pillows are rock hard, cots swaybacked, and the wall's linoleum is peeling in spots, but that's as bad as it gets in Rome's oldest hotel (founded 1462). In fact, many accommodations are in better shape than that—most rooms aren't minuscule, and the big old-fashioned wood furnishings are nicely tooled or inlaid. But even double-glazed windows on the streetside rooms can't block out the late-night revelers, so request one overlooking the garden courtyard. Rooms on the fourth floor even get a Roman rooftop view that encompasses a few domes and hundreds of TV aerials. If you get a chance, check out the basement garage, where bits of Pompey's Theater (55 B.C.) remain. This inn is popular—notwithstanding the recent and unjustified rise in prices—so book ahead.

WORTH A SPLURGE

✪ **Casa di Santa Brigida.** V. Monserato 54 (just off Pz. Farnese). Postal address: Pz. Farnese 96, 00186 Roma. ☎ **06/6889-3596.** Fax 06/6889-1573. www.brigidine.org. E-mail: brigida@mclink.it. 20 units, all with bathroom. TEL. 145,000L ($85.30) single; 250,000L ($147.50) double. Rates include breakfast. DC, MC, V. Bus: 46, 62, **64** (to first stop on Cor. V. Emanuele); 116, 116T (to V. Farnesi/Pz. Farnese).

Rome's best (and poshest) convent hotel is run by the sweet and friendly sisters of St. Bridget in the house where that Swedish saint died in 1373. It's got a stellar location across from the Michelangelo-designed Palazzo Farnese on a quiet square just a block from the daily market and nightlife of Campo de' Fiori. The splurge prices are a bit high, but justified by the comfy and rather roomy Old World accommodations outfitted with antiques or reproductions on parquet (lower level) or carpeted (upstairs) floors. Bathrooms are a little old, but at least have shower curtains, and the beds are heavenly firm. There's a roof terrace, library, and church, and air-conditioning may arrive by the end of 1999. This retreat is very highly requested, so reserve as far in advance as possible.

AROUND PIAZZA NAVONA & THE PANTHEON

✪ **Albergo Abruzzi.** Pz. d. Rotonda 69, 00186 Roma. ☎ **06/679-2021.** No fax. 26 units, none with bathroom. 93,000L ($54.70) single; 130,000L ($76.50) double. No credit cards. Bus: 116, 116T (to Pz. d. Rotunda); 46, 56, 60, 62, **64, 70,** 81, 87, **115,** 186, **492,** 628, **640** (to Lgo. Argentina and walk 4 blocks north).

When, for well under $100, you can look out your window and the Pantheon is less than 100 feet away, you've found something special. Of course, a cheap hotel this perfectly placed is no secret, and you need to book ahead—and send an international money order with 1 night's deposit. Although not all rooms are blessed with the vista, most are still large, clean, and utterly basic. Shared bathrooms are a bit decrepit, but the beds are thankfully brand-new and very firm. Since the piazza is a popular hangout until late, the noise can get annoying, but with this location and that view, who cares?

✪ Coronet. Pz. Grazioli 5, 00186 Roma. ☎ **06/679-0653.** Fax 06/6992-2705. 13 units, 10 with bathroom. TEL. 80,000–120,000L ($47.05–$70.60) single without bathroom, 100,000–150,000L ($58.80–$88.25) single with bathroom; 100,000–160,000L ($58.80–$94.10) double without bathroom; 140,000–190,000L ($82.35–$111.75) double with bathroom. Rates include breakfast. AE, MC, V. Free parking on piazza (ask hotel for permit). Bus: 46, 56, 60, 62, **64, 70,** 81, 87, **115,** 186, **492,** 628, **640** (to V. Plebescito. From V. Plebescito, turn up V. d. Gatta).

Here's your chance to live in high-ceilinged rooms in a 15th-century Roman palace (now the Galleria Doria-Pamphilj). Simona Teresi and her son preside over baronially sized rooms with modest, worn, but comfy mismatched furnishings—some functional, others antique-styled. Some beds are a little lumpy, but most have orthopedic mattresses, and there are three hall bathrooms for the trio of rooms without. Rooms no. 34, 35, and 45 have wood ceilings and sitting corners with sofas. The piazza isn't very noisy, but for absolute quiet ask for a room overlooking the gravely private gardens. Call for reservations, but confirm by fax if possible. The price range reflects a high season of March to May and September to October.

Mimosa. V. S. Chiara 61, 00186 Roma. ☎ **06/6880-1753.** Fax 06/683-3557. 12 units, 2 with bathroom. 85,000L ($50) single without bathroom; 110,000L ($64.70) double without bathroom, 140,000L ($82.35) double with bathroom. 10% discount in slow periods of winter. 5,000L ($2.95). No credit cards. Parking 30,000L ($17.65). Bus: **H,** tram 8, 46, 56, 60, 62, **64, 70,** 81, 87, **115,** 186, **492,** 628, **640** (to Lgo. Argentina). About 2 blocks behind the Pantheon; from Lgo. Argentina, turn up V. d. Torre Argentina, then left on V. S. Chiara.

This friendly little pensione offers a fantastic price for such a central location. It's a bit threadbare but very well cared for by Riccardo and Michele Cappelletto and sons. Room furnishings are built-in or modular—nothing special, but most accommodations are actually pretty huge, with multiple beds for families on a budget (a few singles are cramped). Beds are springy, firm, and covered with attractive comforters—quality touches that separate this caring modest inn from the student dives. The communal bathrooms are clean, and it's rather popular, so book ahead; if you don't get a response to your fax within 48 hours, it means the hotel's full.

✪ Marcus. V. d. Clementino 94 (in the renamed final block of V. Fontanella Borghese before Pz. Nicosia, just south of Augustus' Mausoleum), 00186 Roma. ☎ **06/6830-0320.** Fax 06/6830-0312. 18 units, 17 with bathroom. MINIBAR TV TEL. 120,000L ($70.60) single; 170,000L ($100) double. Rates include breakfast. AE, MC, V. Bus: **70,** 87, 116, 116T, 186 (to V. di Monte Brianzo); 70, 81, **115,** 186, 628 (to Lungotevere Marzio).

This updated pensione located in a central 18th-century palazzo is easily one of the best two-star hotels in Rome. This place has it where it counts: friendly management by Frommer's-loving Salvatore and his wife, firm beds, decent bathrooms, Persian rugs on the patterned tile floors, the occasional classy antique furnishing, and walls hung with Roman prints and art deco lights. Salvatore believes in running a hotel he would want to stay in, so since he hates noise, the windows have formidable double glazing. Larger rooms have futon chairs that can sleep one more. Only half the accommodations have air-conditioning, which costs an extra 20,000L ($11.75); those without have ceiling fans.

Navona. V. d. Sedari 8 (off Cor. d. Rinascimento, between Pz. Navona and the Pantheon), 00186 Roma. ☎ **06/6821-1391.** Fax 06/6880-3802. 30 units, 26 with bathroom. 85,000L ($50) single without bathroom, 100,000L ($58.80) single with bathroom; 125,000L ($73.50) double without bathroom, 140,000L ($82.35) double with bathroom; 200,000L ($117.65) top-floor units. Rates include breakfast. No credit cards. Free parking on street (ask hotel for permit). Bus: **70,** 81, 87, **115,** 116, 186, **492,** 628 (to Cor. d. Rinascimento).

The Australian architect who owns the Navona is busy overhauling with an eye toward four-star status, so get here while the prices are still low. The top floor used to be Shelley's apartment, restructured in 1998 with terra-cotta/wood slat ceilings, Valentino tiles in the bathrooms, and wonderfully firm beds. The wicker and bamboo furnishings are just as new, and although the as-yet unrenovated lower floor rooms have worn furnishings and old stone floors, the workers are setting into those as this book goes to press. There's also a top-floor suite with kitchenette available on a weekly basis. The hotel might begin accepting credit cards in 1999.

WORTH A SPLURGE

Cesàri. V. di Pietra 89A (just off the Cor., a block south of Pz. Colonna). ☎ **06/679-2386.** Fax 06/679-0882. 47 units, all with bathroom. A/C TV TEL. 180,000–215,000L ($105.90–$126.50) single; 230,000–300,000L ($135.30–$176.50) double. Rates include breakfast. DC, MC, V. Parking 50,000–60,000L ($29.40–$35.30). Bus: 116, 116T (to V. d. Burro); 56, 60, 62, 81, 85, 95, 117, 160, **175, 492,** 628, 850 (to V. d. Cor.).

You couldn't ask for a location more central than just off the Corso, halfway between the Pantheon and the Trevi Fountain, the Spanish Steps and the Roman Forum. In the Cesàri's 200-plus years, it has hosted the likes of Stendhal and Garibaldi, but a 1990s remodeling has left it with a modern style that hums with standardized comforts. The furnishings are built-in, the double-glazed windows particularly effective in blocking street sounds, the bathrooms *modernissimo* (heated towel racks, hair dryers), and the waxed hardwood floors scattered with Persian rugs. Most rooms are modestly sized, but a few are big enough for families. The price range reflects season.

Portoghesi. V. d. Portoghesi 1 (1 block west of V. d. Scrofa), 00186 Rome. ☎ **06/686-4231.** Fax 06/687-6976. 28 units, all with bathroom. 170,000–190,000L ($100–$111.75) single; 230,000–270,000L ($135.30–$158.80) double; from 350,000L ($205.90) suite. Rates include breakfast. MC, V. Parking 40,000L ($23.55). Bus: **70,** 87, 116, 116T, 186 (to V. di Monte Brianzo, then turn down V. d. Cancello and hotel is on left).

This is a great central splurge with full amenities, antiques in the halls, and a killer location. It's a few minutes' walk from Piazza Navona in a picturesquely Roman corner of the city: on a little-trafficked fork in the medieval streets, next door to a Baroque church and across from a medieval tower (the best views are of this ensemble, from rooms 4, 20, 22, 24, 38, 40, and 42). The comfy rooms are carpeted, with built-in wood or lacquer units. Except for the larger, antique-accented suites, accommodations are meanly sized without being too cramped. The space-efficient bathrooms are very modern. The inn is small and has a roster of devoted regulars, so reserve well in advance.

AROUND THE SPANISH STEPS & PIAZZA DEL POPOLO

Fiorella. V. d. Babuino 196 (½ block from Pz. d. Popolo), 00187 Roma. ☎ **06/361-0597.** 8 units, none with bathroom. 65,000L ($38.25) single; 105,000L ($61.75) double. Rates include breakfast. No credit cards. Parking 30,000L ($17.65). Bus: 117 (to the end of V. d. Babuino); 628, 926 (to Pz. d. Popolo). Metro: Flaminio (not the closest, but most direct from Termini).

The tiny Fiorella has long been a budget traveler's staple with its eye-popping green-and-orange tiling, 1960s port-a-lamps, basic stucco decorations on the high ceilings, sleepable beds, and lamentable 1am curfew. The shared bathrooms are large and clean, and the modular furniture is definitely showing its age, but fresh paint and general tidiness keep it all looking nice. However, the family that's run it for years is retiring and who knows what the new owners will bring? For the time being at least, my favorite room remains no. 8, quietly off the street side with a desk in a sunny sitting nook.

Lydia-Venier. V. Sistina 42 (almost a block from Pz. Trinità d. Monti), 00187 Roma. ☎ **06/679-1744.** Fax 06/679-7263. 28 units, 14 with bathroom. TV TEL. 90,000–120,000L ($52.95–$70.60) single without bathroom, 120,000–170,000L ($70.60–$100) single with bathroom; 130,000–200,000L ($76.50–$117.65) double without bathroom, 180,000–220,000L ($105.90–$129.40) double with bathroom. Rates include breakfast. AE, DC, MC, V. Parking 24,000L ($14.10). Bus: 52, 53, 56, 58, 58/ 60, 61, 62, 95, 116, **175, 492** (to Pz. Barberini); 117 (to V. Capo le Case). Metro: Spagna (exit Pz. Trinità d. Monti), Barberini.

The Lydia-Venier has some high points and some low ones—that is, low prices on high-ceilinged rooms. Another high point: It's located a block from the top of the Spanish Steps. A sweeping marble staircase leads to the first floor and the spick-and-span rooms. The built-in furnishings are brand-new, the fresh mattresses are some of the firmest in town, and a shower and sink grace even the rooms without bathrooms (full bathrooms are ugly stuck-in-the-corner modular jobs, but at least they're new and clean). There's a lavishly frescoed 18th-century room, and remnants of this decor spill over into a few guest quarters—no. 208 and 209 share a ceiling of gilded stuccoes, and no. 105 has a frescoed ceiling and windows on three sides (great light; a bit noisy). Wall carpeting helps dampen noise, but rooms on the back are quietest. See a few accommodations before choosing; most are huge, but a few feel downright cramped. Prices reflect a high season of March 15 to May and September to October.

Margutta. V. Laurina 34 (2 blocks from Pz. d. Popolo between V. Babuino and V. d. Cor.), 00197 Roma. ☎ **06/322-3674.** Fax 06/320-0395. 24 units, all with bathroom. TEL. 156,000L ($91.75) single or double. Rates include breakfast. AE, DC, MC, V. Bus: 117 (to the end of V. d. Babuino); 628, 926 (to Pz. d. Popolo). Metro: Flaminio (not the closest, but most direct from Termini).

The Margutta is not for those who need a lot of elbow room, but it offers reliability and a touch of style for an inexpensive central choice. The hardworking management likes to joke around, providing efficient service with a smile in rapid-fire English. Curly, wrought-iron bed frames give the place a classy feel, but the lumpy beds barely pass muster for firmness. Most rooms are immaculate, but on the small side of cozy, and some bathrooms are positively minuscule. Double-glazed windows keep street noise down, but since you're already on a side street, things are pretty tranquil.

Pensione Panda. V. d. Croce 35, 00187 Rome. ☎ **06/678-0179.** Fax 06/6994-2151. 20 units, 3 with bathroom. 60,000L ($35.30) single without bathroom, 80,000L ($47.50) single with bathroom; 95,000L ($55.90) double without bathroom, 110,000–130,000L ($64.70–$76.50) double with bathroom. AE, MC, V. Bus: 116, 116T, 117 (to Pz. di Spagna). Metro: Spagna.

This hotel is just 2 blocks from the Spanish Steps, in the heart of Rome's shopping district. The secret here is to request a room on the first floor (which includes fine touches like frescoed ceilings, wrought-iron fixtures, and firm beds set on terra-cotta floors). The linoleum-floored second-story rooms are decidedly inferior and no-frills, but clean. None, however, are very large. The lack of phones or private bathrooms keeps prices way down for this prime location. Rooms facing the (mostly pedestrian) street have double-glazed windows.

Pensione Suisse. V. Gregoriana 54 (near intersection with V. Capo le Case), 00187 Roma. ☎ **06/678-3649.** Fax 06/678-1258. 13 units, 11 with bathroom. TEL. 115,000L ($67.65) single without bathroom, 135,000L ($79.40) single with bathroom; 140,000L ($82.35) double without bathroom, 190,000L ($111.75) double with bathroom. Rates include breakfast. MC, V. Bus: 116, 116T, 117 (to V. Due Macelli); 52, 53, 56, 58, 58/, 60, 61, 62, 95, **175, 492** (to V. d. Tritone/Lgo. Tritone). Metro: Barberini.

Just 1 (very long) block down a quiet street from the astronomically priced hotels atop the Spanish Steps, the clean Suisse is a comfy, small third-floor hotel. The furnishings may be a bit worn, but are serviceable and tasteful, with stiff mattresses on wooden boards. A few of the roomy accommodations retain old ceiling stuccoes. Only a few bathrooms are new, but even the older ones are in good shape. You share the dowdy old shoe of a TV/sitting room with the family, and they'll sell you cheap sodas and water from a little fridge. The Suisse is popular, so book ahead. You can only pay half your bill with credit card, and there's no one at the desk to buzz you in from 2 to 6am.

Residenza Brotzky. V. d. Cor. 509 (between V. A. Canova and V. d. Vantaggio), 00186 Roma. ☎ **06/361-2339.** Fax 06/323-6641. 25 units, all with bathroom. 70,000L ($41.20) single; 150,000L ($88.25) double. Discount for longer stays. 8,000L ($4.70). No credit cards. Parking 40,000L ($23.55). Bus: 117 (to V. d. Cor.); 32, 81, **115**, 628, 913, 926 (to Pz. A. Imperatore).

To enter this old-fashioned pensione, you need to take a rickety courtyard elevator to the third floor then skirt a vertiginous narrow terrace. Although the hotel is in the throes of restructuring, the downstairs rooms are still outfitted with high ceilings, hard beds (foam on board), and worn furnishings hung with the ghost of elegance. Some accommodations are small, and the walls are stained in spots. The choice rooms are on the fourth floor, rebuilt in 1998 with lower sloping ceilings, newer furniture, and a few views across the rooftops and domes of central Rome. Everyone gets to enjoy the cityscape panorama from the rooftop terrace. Most rooms have a TV, and all should soon have phones. It's possible that credit cards will be accepted in 1999. Rooms on the Corso are considerably noisier.

✪ **Pensione Parlamento.** V. d. Convertite 5 (at intersection with V. d. Cor., near Pz. San Silvestro), 00187 Roma. ☎ **06/679-2082.** Fax 06/6992-1000. 23 units, all with bathroom. TV TEL. 140,000–160,000L ($82.35–$94.10) single; 170,000–180,000L ($100–$105.90) double; 216,000–235,000L ($127.05–$138.25) triple; 240,000–270,000L ($141.20–$158.80) quad. Rates include breakfast. AE, DC, MC, V. Parking 40,000L ($23.55). Bus: 52, 53, 58, 58/; 61, 71, 85, 116, 116T, 160, 850 (to Pz. San Silvestro); 56, 60, 62, 95, **115, 175**, 492 (to Lgo. Chigi/V. Tritone).

The Parlamento has four-star class at two-star prices. After a few stairs, there's an elevator to the third floor and a friendly, professional reception. A *double set* of double-glazed windows effectively blocks out the heavy street traffic. The furnishings are antiques or good reproductions, and the firm beds are backed by carved wood or wrought-iron headboards. Fifteen rooms have air-conditioning, and the bathrooms were recently redone with hair dryers, heated towel racks, phones, and, in a few, even marble sinks. You can enjoy the chandeliered and trompe l'oeil room or carry your cappuccino up to the small roof terrace with its view of San Silvestro's bell tower (several upper-floor rooms share this vista). Some larger accommodations are great for families, including the triple no. 82 with big old antiques and no. 108, with two bedrooms and a small private terrace. Rates reflect season.

AROUND VIA VENETO & PIAZZA BARBERINI

Monaco. V. Flavia 84 (parallel to V. XX Settembre, near V. S. Tullio.), 00187 Roma. ☎ and fax **06/474-4335.** 12 units, 2 with bathroom. 50,000L ($29.40) single; 75,000L ($44.10) double with or without bathroom. No credit cards. Valet parking 30,000–40,000L ($17.65–$23.55); free on street. Bus: **3, 4, 38, 38/, 319** (to the first stop on V. Piave, after crossing V. XX Settembre); 37, 60, 61, 62, 910 (to V. XX Settembre); **16**, 136, 137 (to the end of the line at V. XX Settembre).

Maria Tomassi, her sister Elena, and her grown children run this bare-bones hotel at the edge of an upscale neighborhood. Most rooms are quite sizable, with just a few pieces of mismatched functional furnishings and closet-sized private bathrooms without shower curtains. Beds range from thin and stiff to soft and springy, but sagging is kept to a minimum. It's all a bit institutional—I had college-dorm flashbacks when I saw the shared bathrooms—but the Tomassis keep it tidy and clean, the prices are fantastic, and the welcome is friendly. The streets can be noisy by day, but quiet down at night. They sometimes impose a midnight curfew, so ask before heading out.

Tizi. V. Collina 48 (east of Pz. Sallustio and west of V. Piave), 00187 Roma. ☎ **06/482-0128.** Fax 06/474-3266. 20 units, 7 with bathroom. 50,000L ($29.40) single without bathroom; 70,000L ($41.20) double without bathroom, 90,000L ($52.95) double with bathroom. No credit cards. Parking 30,000L ($17.65). Bus: **3, 4, 38, 38/, 319** (to the first stop on V. Piave, after crossing V. XX Settembre); 56, 58, 58/ (to V. Boncompagni); 490, 495 (to V. Lucania).

The very clean Tizi is run by an amicable family and its very fluffy cat on two floors in a quiet, posh neighborhood just south of Villa Borghese park. It's an inn favored by young travelers who'd rather have peace, quiet, and a family atmosphere than beer and parties. A few antique-style pieces in the reception hall give way to mostly brand-new modular furnishings in the rooms, but the new orthopedic foam mattresses rest on old-fashioned metal tube bed frames. Ceilings are high and airy, some with stucco work, and the private bathrooms are in good working order with box showers. Shared bathrooms are mostly large and there's one for every two rooms, so no waiting.

WORTH A SPLURGE

Ranieri. V. XX Settembre 43 (near V. S. Tullio), 00187 Roma. ☎ **06/481-4467.** Fax 06/ 481-8834. www.venere.it/roma/ranieri. E-mail: hotel.ranieri@italyhotel.com. 47 units, all with bathroom. A/C MINIBAR TV TEL. 180,000–195,000L ($105.90–$114.70) single; 240,000–260,000L ($141.20–$152.95) double. Rates include breakfast. AE, DC, MC, V. Valet parking 28,000–40,000L ($16.50–$23.55). Bus: **3, 4, 38, 38/, 319** (to the first stop on V. Piave, after crossing V. XX Settembre); 37, 60, 61, 62, 910 (to V. XX Settembre); **16,** 136, 137 (to the end of the line at V. XX Settembre).

The staff at this large, modern hotel loves Frommer's readers. The carpeted rooms were renovated in the mid-1990s with lots of built-in wood-and-marble units. Pebbly fabric pads the walls, keeping rooms tomb quiet. The double-paned windows do battle with the traffic noise from Via XX Settembre below (rooms on the back, of course, manage to be even quieter). Bathrooms are highly modernized, and extra amenities abound, such as trouser presses, international outlets you can plug anything into, and phone jacks for computer hookups. The room and bar/lounge are done in postmodern '80s style. The price range reflects season.

NORTH OF TERMINI

Note: I've given bus information for each of these hotels below, but you'll notice none are boldface. Each hotel is within a few easily walked blocks of Termini train station.

Astoria Garden. V. V. Bachelet 8, 00185 Roma. ☎ **06/446-9908.** Fax 06/445-3329. E-mail: astoria-garden@flashnet.it. 34 units, 28 with bathroom. TV TEL. 80,000L ($47.05) single without bathroom, 120,000L ($70.60) single with bathroom; 150,000L ($88.25) double without bathroom, 180,000L ($105.90) double with bathroom. AE, DC, MC, V. Rates include breakfast. Parking 20,000L ($11.75); a few free spots on street. Bus: 75 (to Pz. Indipendenza); H, 3, 4, 9, tram 14, 16, 36, 36/, 38, 38/, 64, 70, 105, 115, 157, 170, 175, 310, 317, 319, 492, tram 516, 640, 714, 910 (to Termini area). Metro: Termini or Castro Pretorio. 3½ blocks north of Termini; this street is actually the final block of V. Varese just SE of Pz. Indipendenza.

The prices are fantastic considering what you get at this hotel in a late 19th-century palazzo with stucco ceilings and Old World atmosphere. However, until the restructuring is completely finished, accommodations will continue to vary greatly. The old rooms have squishy beds and chipping lacquer on modular furnishings. These just don't compare to the reproduction furnishings and soft carpets in the High Turin–style guest quarters of one wing. Rooms with bathrooms also have air-conditioning. There's a garden shaded by palm, banana, and orange trees with a glassed-in veranda for year-round. The quiet garden rooms enjoy the best views. For optimal tranquillity, opt for one of the several bungalow-like accommodations across the garden. If you'll be staying several days, tell manager Francesco Cusato you're traveling with Frommer's and you may get a discount.

Fawlty Towers. V. Magenta 39 (1 block north of Termini, between V. Milazzo and V. Marghera), 00185 Roma. ☎ and fax **06/445-0374.** www.enjoyrome.it/ftytwhtl.htm. 12 units, 3 with bathroom; 3 shared rooms, none with bathroom. 60,000L ($35.30) single without bathroom, 75,000L ($44.10) single with bathroom; 85,000–100,000L ($50–$58.80) double without bathroom, 110,000L ($64.70) double with bathroom; 30,000–35,000L ($17.65–$20.60) bed in shared room. No credit cards. Bus: H, 3, 4, 9, 16, 36, 36/, 38, 38/, 64, 70, 75, 105, 115, 157, 170, 175, 310, 317, 319, 492, 640, 714, 910. Tram: 14, 516. Metro: Termini.

This hotel-and-hostel is a fave of students and the younger international set who, like the inn itself, are primarily of the clean-scrubbed variety. It's owned by the Enjoy Rome people, staffed by friendly young folk from English-speaking countries, and has the cleanest, most comfy, and well-located hostel-style accommodations in town. The shared dorms are on the fifth floor (there's an elevator), private rooms on the sixth. Hostel rooms sleeping three or four are as bare as you'd expect, but not squalid or crowded like most (no bunk beds here, just squishy cots). The simple singles and doubles have much firmer mattresses, functional furnishings, and paisley bedspreads. Four of the bathless rooms have at least a sink and a shower, and there's a solarium with TV, fridge, and microwave as well as a small outdoor terrace, and no curfew.

Papà Germano. V. Calatafimi 14a, 00185 Roma. ☎ **06/486-919.** 17 units, 7 with bathroom. TEL. 45,000L ($26.50) single without bathroom; 70,000L ($41.20) double without bathroom, 90,000L ($52.95) double with bathroom; 30,000L ($17.65) bed in shared room without bathroom. MC, V. Parking 20,000L ($11.75). Bus: 3, 4, 16, 36, 36/, 37, 38, 38/, 317, 319 (to V. Volturno; or to V. Goito—except 16 and 37—if heading toward Termini); 60, 61, 62, 136, 137 (to V. Cernaia); 75 (to Pz. Indipendenza). Metro: Repubblica. Four blocks west of Termini; it's a dead-end street off V. Volturno, behind the baths of Diocletian, between V. Gaeta and V. Montebello.

Gino holds cleanliness in the highest regard and repaints or repapers his hotel every year or two. He's also a terrifically friendly guy who loves to help visitors settle into Rome, handing out advice as freely as smiles. The mattresses under attractive spreads are firm to the point of being hard, but just about everything—from the built-in units and box showers to the double-glazed windows and hair dryers in every room (even bathless ones!)—is spotless and either brand-new or kept looking that way. The shared bathrooms are great, but accommodations with private bathrooms also have satellite TV (which should soon spread to every room). Gobs of guidebooks list this perfectly modest inn, so call ahead. Six of the bathless rooms can become shared dorms (if you ask, you can save by bunking with two or three strangers).

Romae. V. Palestro 49 (4 blocks north of Termini; near the corner with V. Vicenza), 00185 Roma. ☎ **06/446-3554.** Fax 06/446-3914. E-mail: htlromae@flashnet.it. 28 units, all with bathroom. TV TEL. 130,000L ($76.50) single; 160,000L ($94.10) double. Rates include breakfast. AE, MC, V. Parking 40,000L ($23.55). Bus: 75 (to Pz. Indipendenza); H, 3, 4, 9, tram 14, 16, 36, 36/, 38, 38/, 64, 70, 105, 115, 157, 170, 175, 310, 317, 319, 492, tram 516, 640, 714, 910 (to Termini area). Metro: Castro Pretorio.

This simple, pleasant hotel is kept all in the family—the Boccaforno family commanded by Lucy and Francesco. Built-in closets help the midsized accommodations seem that much roomier, and the beds aren't too bad on your back. All the rooms have fans. Prints or oils in the walls and curving ceilings in some rooms (others have acoustic tiles) lend a touch of class, but in most respects this is a basic (and clean) inn at basic prices. The rates listed above are special to Frommer's readers, so let them know you've got this book.

WORTH A SPLURGE

Villa delle Rose. V. Vicenza 5 (1½ blocks north of Termini; between V. Magenta and V. d. Mille), 00185 Roma. ☎ **06/445-1795.** Fax 06/445-1639. www.villarose.it. 38 units, all with bathroom. TV TEL. 135,000–175,000L ($79.40–$102.95) single; 180,000–200,000L ($105.90–$117.65) double. Rates include breakfast. AE, DC, MC, V. Free parking (just a few spots; first-come, first-served). Bus: H, 3, 4, 9, tram 14, 16, 36, 36/, 38, 38/, 64, 70, 105, 115, 157, 170, 175, 310, 317, 319, 492, tram 516, 640, 714, 910 (to Termini area); 75 (to Pz. Indipendenza). Metro: Termini.

Isn't a dose of faded grandeur in an 1870s villa set amid modest gardens with a location less than 2 blocks from Termini worth a little extra? The threadbare rugs and frescoed ceiling of the lounge set the tone for the rooms, some of which have high, stucco ceilings and Oriental rugs. Most accommodations are more basic, bland modular units (which infest even the more nicely styled rooms), older bathrooms, and soft mattresses. Rooms overlooking either the flagstone sitting terrace or small, overgrown gardens are marginally quieter than those facing a street (plus, some have terraces). Three of the rooms have lofts to sleep up to five—great for families. Seven rooms currently have air-conditioning, but there are plans to install it in the rest of them. Room rates reflect season.

SOUTH OF TERMINI

✪ **Nardizzi Americana.** V. Firenze 38 (just off V. XX Settembre), 00184 Roma. ☎ **06/ 488-0368.** Fax 06/488-0035. 19 units, all with bathroom. A/C TV TEL. 77,000–110,000L ($45.30–$64.70) single; 105,000–150,000L ($61.75–$88.25) double. Rates include breakfast. AE, DC, MC, V. Parking 25,000L ($14.70). Bus: 37, 60, 61, 62, 136, 137, **175, 492, 910** (to Lgo. S. Susanna/V. V.E. Orlando); **64, 70, 115, 170,** 116T, **640** (to V. Nazionale/Pz. d. Repubblica). Metro: Repubblica.

Nardizzi Americana has always been a steal of a hotel. When I visited in late 1998, Nik and Fabrizio were busily restructuring everything, but they promise to keep the rates way down while transforming their hotel into one of the best two-stars in town. The new style is inspired by ancient Rome, with street lamps on the narrow terrace where you can in nice weather, and a patterned tile decor giving an inlaid stone look to the walls and floors of public areas. The rooms now have tiled floors, and a few have wood-beam ceilings. All the bathrooms are brand new, and while smaller rooms have built-in dressers the larger ones get walk-in closets. Rates represent a high season of April to October. In July and August you get 4 nights for the price of 3.

WORTH A SPLURGE

Pensione Contilia. V. P. Amadeo 79d–81, 00185 Roma. ☎ **06/446-6942.** Fax 06/ 446-6904. E-mail: contilia@tin.it. 37 units, 34 with bathroom. TV TEL. 100,000–150,000L ($58.80–$88.25) single; 150,000–200,000L ($88.25–$117.65) double. Rates include breakfast. AE, DC, MC, V. Parking 30,000L ($17.65); free on street. Bus: 4, 9, tram 14, 16, 70, 71, 75, tram 516, 714 (to V. Gioberti); 105 (to V. F. Turati). Metro: Termini. Near V. Gioberti, just 2 blocks from Termini, so it's best to walk.

As the automatic doors part to reveal a stylish marble lobby of Persian rugs and antiques, you might step back to double-check the address. The sturdy, popular old-fashioned pensione Tony-Contilia of yesteryear has taken over this building's other small hotels and gentrified itself in an agreeable way. It's the best choice in the diciest neighborhood of the center. Rooms have been redone in modern, midscale comfort with floral quilted spreads on perfectly firm beds and built-in units. Double-glazed windows keep out traffic noise, and rooms overlooking the cobblestone courtyard are even more quiet. The only drawback to the fresh, contemporary bathrooms are their smallish size and lack of shower curtains. Currently only 11 rooms have air-conditioning, and three are bathless, but the whole hotel should be standardized soon.

THE AVENTINE

To get to these hotels from the airport, take the *local* train into Rome (not the express to Termini) and get off at "Ostiense" station, just several trafficky blocks from the Aventine. For the trio of S. Anselmo/Aventino hotels, no bus saves you from a long walk uphill, so it might be worth it to take a taxi from Ostiense.

WORTH A SPLURGE

Aventino. V. S. Domenico 10 (address correspondence to, and check in at, the nearby San Anselmo hotel; see below). ☎ **06/574-3547.** Fax 06/578-3604. 23 units, all with bathroom. TV TEL. 140,000L ($82.35) single; 210,000L ($123.50) double. Rates include breakfast. AE, DC, MC, V. Free parking at hotel (first-come, first-served) or on street. Bus: 13, 23, 715, 716, 719 (to V. Marmorata). Metro: Piramide.

More downscale than its sister hotels on this hill (see below), the Aventino's exterior is also a bit more decrepit—the shutters and walls could use a good scraping and paint job—but the interior is tidier, and it's still got that Aventine villa style and at much lower rates. It's set in a bit of gardens, and the rooms have parquet or tile floors, mushy cots beds, and eclectic furnishings—but still plenty of antique pieces. No. 346 has a long columned balcony overlooking the road and surrounding mansions.

Villa San Pio/San Anselmo. Pz. S. Anselmo 2 (where V. S. Domenico and V. S. Anselmo end at V. Porta Lavernale), 00153, Roma. ☎ **06/574-3547.** Fax 06/578-3604. 110 units, all with bathroom. TV TEL. 180,000L ($105.90) single; 270,000L ($158.80) double. Rates include breakfast. AE, DC, MC, V. Parking first-come, first-served at hotel or free on street. Bus: 13, 23, 715, 716, 719 (to V. Marmorata). Metro: Piramide.

These inns retain distinct flavors even though both hotels (and the Aventino, above) share a single management that considers it a single hotel spread across three former villas—they won't let you book into one specifically, but you can always ask when you check in. The San Anselmo is the posh, showy centerpiece; the Villa San Pio the stylish hideaway; and the separately reviewed Aventino the budget gem. Of these two pricier inns, Villa San Pio is the best buy, for while the San Anselmo has more consistently classy accommodations, the best rooms at the friendlier San Pio definitely outshine.

The public salons and halls of the **San Anselmo** are fitted with Oriental rugs, chandeliers, embroidered drapes, and other accouterments of the 18th and 19th centuries. The bedrooms feature antiques or reproductions, embroidered headboards, rich wall fabrics, modernized bathrooms, firm beds, and marble panel or stone tile floors. Third-floor accommodations also have air-conditioning. **Villa San Pio** consists of two buildings bridged by a magnolia-shaded garden and solarium. Room decor varies widely, some with tasteful modular furnishings, others in grand 19th-century style, all with excellent firm beds. The choice rooms are in the structure beyond the gardens, where especially up on the first floor you're most likely to find the best combination of reproduction furnishings, Persian rugs on hardwood floors, painted ceilings, and ultramod bathrooms with Jacuzzis (or perhaps a claw-footed tub). The roof terrace has splendid tranquil views that encompass the Aventine and mountains in the distance.

IN TRASTEVERE

To get to your Trastevere hotel from the airport, hop on the local train toward Tiburtina (instead of the express into Termini), which will stop at Trastevere's train station where you can catch tram 8 up Viale Trastevere.

Locanda Carmel. V. G. Mameli 11 (the continuation of V. E. Morosini off Vle. Trastevere), 00153 Roma. ☎ and fax **06/580-9921.** 8 units, all with bathroom. 90,000L ($52.95) single; 120,000L ($70.60) double. Rates include breakfast. No credit cards. Free parking on street. Bus: **H,** tram 8 to Vle. Trastevere; coming from the center, get off after you pass Standa department store on the right.

The Carmel is a kosher inn 2 blocks beyond the daily food market of Piazza San Cosimato, a 6-minute walk from the heart of Trastevere. A 1997 renovation significantly freshened up the place, adding pine headboards and new modular furnishings, fresh floor tiles, and spiffy soft quilts in a few rooms, such as no. 8 and 9. It's on a shady but rather trafficked residential road, so book a room on the back for quiet. Bathrooms could stand to be upgraded, and definitely could be kept cleaner. Unfortunately, noise also carries within the hotel itself (your door may shake every time another one closes, and you can hear other guests' alarms go off in the morning). But for budget sleeps in trendy Trastevere, the Carmel is a good bet.

✪ **Trastevere Manara.** V. L. Manara 24a–25, 00153 Roma. ☎ **06/581-47-13.** 8 units, all with bathroom. TV TEL. 90,000L ($52.95) single; 120,000L ($70.60) double. Rates include breakfast. AE, MC, V. Free parking on street. Bus: **H,** tram 8 (to Vle. Trastevere; coming from the center, get off at the second stop after you cross the river. It's just behind Pz. San Cosimato; the continuation of V. di Fratte s. Trastevere off Vle. Trastevere).

Get here while it's still one of Rome' best bargains: cushy, brand-new amenities at fantastic prices, a location right at the heart of Trastevere's restaurants and nightlife, and a daily market at your doorstep for incredibly fresh picnic pickings. In 1998, what was once the dingiest hotel in Trastevere renovated itself into the classiest. These newly gentrified rooms are still pensione cavernous, but with fresh tiles and painted stucco, massive modular wood furnishings, and spanking new private bathrooms. All except smaller (and dreary) no. 1 and 2 overlook the neighborhood market square of San Cosimato—colorful, but rather noisy rather early. With all these improvements, I can't imagine the rates will stick this low for long.

AROUND THE VATICAN

Note: Take the buses listed for each hotel below with a huge shaker of salt; the transportation reroutings and upsets caused by Rome's preparations for the Jubilee Year 2000 affect no neighborhood more than the area around the Vatican, where it seems every week they issue a new list of changed bus routes.

Alimandi. V. Tunisi 8 (at V. Veniero and the base of the steps up to Vle. Vaticano), 00192 Roma. ☎ **06/3972-3941.** Fax 06/3972-3943. www.travel.iol.it/alberghi/alimandi. E-mail: alimandi@tin.it. 35 units, all with bathroom. A/C TV TEL. 130,000L ($76.50) single; 175,000L ($102.95) double. 15,000L ($8.80). AE, DC, MC, V. Parking 30,000L ($17.65). Bus: 49 (to Vle. Vaticano, at the Vatican Museums entrance; take bus 492 from Termini to any stop on V. Crescenzio, after Pz. Cavour, to transfer to the 49). Metro: Ottaviano.

It's a tour group–style hotel, but one of the better ones, with a great location for the district, 3 blocks from Rome's best daily food market (on Via Andrea Doria) and just a short staircase down from the entrance to the Vatican Museums. The rooms are standardized, modern, and comfortable, holding few surprises in the built-in wood units and newish bathrooms. The firm beds sport fresh foam mattresses. There's a faux medieval bar, billiards room, and pleasant roof terrace with no particular view but good sun and caged exotic birds for atmosphere. Although there are plenty of bus stops a few long blocks in any direction, it *is* inconvenient to reach with luggage, but an airport shuttle is planned to begin in 1999 (book it in advance).

Giuggioli. V. Germanico 198 (between V. Principe Emilio and V. F. Massimo.), 00192 Roma. ☎ **06/324-2113.** 5 units, 1 with bathroom. 100,000L ($58.80) single; 120,000L ($70.60) double without bathroom, 140,000L ($82.35) double with bathroom. No credit cards. Free

---

Hostel Takeovers

Fawlty Towers remains the best hostel in town, which is why it gets a full listing above (see p. 114). Rome's main IYH hostel, **Ostello Foro Italico,** is rather removed from the action north of the center at Vle. d. Olimpiadi 61 (☎ **06/ 323-6267;** fax 06/324-2613). It's institutional, with 334 beds spread across rooms sleeping two to six plus several single-sex dorms. A bed costs 24,000L ($14.10), there's a lockout until 2pm, and curfew's midnight. Take bus 910 from Termini to the end of the line at Piazza Mancini, then bus 280 to the third stop (at the hostel); or, take Metro A to the Ottaviano end of the line, then bus 32 to Foro Italico.

---

parking on street. Bus: 32, 81 (to V. Cola di Rienzo); 994, 999 (to V. Dalla Chiesa/Vle. G. Cesare); **70,** 186, 280, 913 (to V. M. Colonna). Metro: Lepanto.

Signora Gasparina Giuggioli has been running her little pensione for more than 50 years, and although she talks of retiring, she loves the job too much to quit. She keeps her big rooms squeaky clean. To go with the high ceilings, patterned rugs on tile floors, and the firmest of mattresses, most accommodations have sturdy old functional furnishings, although enormous no. 6 (the one with a bathroom) enjoys classier antique pieces. No. 4 features a balcony jutting into the profusion of leafy branches that block the boring street from view (it's a bit trafficky, but the new double-glazed windows help cut down on noise). Signora Giuggioli smiles as she pours you a cup of stovetop espresso or a *digestivo* (digestive liqueur) when you return home from dinner. With a sigh, she remarks "When I'm reincarnated, I hope I come back as a hotelier again." So do we.

Pensione Marvi. V. Pietro d. Valle 13 (off V. Crescenzio a block west of "Pz. Adriana," the north arm of Castle Sant'Angelo's star-shaped park), 00193 Roma. ☎ **06/6880-2621.** Fax 06/686-5652. 8 units, all with bathroom. TEL. 80,000L ($47.05) single; 130,000L ($76.50) double. Rates include breakfast. No credit cards. Parking 25,000L ($14.70). Bus: 34, 49, **492,** 990 (to V. Crescenzio); 23 (to V. P. Castello); 49, **70,** 87, 186, 280, 913, 926 (to Pz. Cavour).

Since 1969, a friendly guy from Orvieto has run this clean little hotel on a side street of the Borgo (the zone between the Vatican and the river). His rooms are simple, but some of the hodgepodge furnishings are actually quite nice; the bathrooms, though, are tiny. Brand-new cot springs support stiff foam mattresses covered by fashionable bedspreads. No. 10 and 14 have stucco decorations on the ceiling, and no. 11 gets lots of light from windows on two sides. Rooms on the third floor tend to be pretty quiet. The hotel may start accepting credit cards by 2000.

4 Great Deals on Dining

You could spend a lot on dining in Rome, dropping upwards of 70,000L ($41.20) in the many fine ristorante and overpriced tourist-oriented trattorie of the center, but you don't have to. Plenty of *osterie* (cheap eateries frequented by locals) and old-fashioned *fiaschetterie* (old-fashioned wine bars serving a few inexpensive dishes) where you can get basic, filling Roman meals for under 35,000L ($20.60) still abound, many just steps away from the most touristy sights of the centro storico. If you just want to wander and find a restaurant on your own, the strongest concentration of eateries is in Trastevere. Also, trendy **"Wine Bars"** (called that even in Italian) have been popping up all over town for the past several years, places where you can drink remarkable wines by the glass and nibble on cheese platters, salamis, and small, often inventive dishes all pretty cheaply.

As for typical Roman dishes, you start off with an antipasto (appetizer), which in Rome most often means a simple **bruschetta** (a slab of peasant bread grilled, rubbed with garlic, drizzled with olive oil, and sprinkled with salt; al pomodoro adds a pile of cubed tomatoes on top). If you see *carciofi* (artichokes), *alla giudea* or otherwise (especially if you're in the Jewish Ghetto), snap up one of Rome's greatest specialties— ever so tender and lightly fried in olive oil. One fave that's recently been exported is *prosciutto e melone,* a surprisingly good combination of salt-cured ham draped over a slice of sweet cantaloupe (in the summer, it may be figs instead of melon).

Your *primo* (first course) could be a soup—try ***stracciatella*** (egg and Parmesan in broth)—or a pasta. Available on just about every Roman menu are such traditional favorites as spaghetti or bucatini ***all'Amatriciana*** (in a spicy tomato sauce studded with pancetta bacon and dense with onions), ***spaghetti alla carbonara*** (steaming hot spaghetti mixed with eggs, bacon, and loads of black pepper—the heat of the pasta cooks the eggs), or ***pasta al pomodoro*** (in a plain tomato sauce). Also try ***penne all'arrabbiata*** ("hopping mad" pasta quills in a spicy tomato sauce), ***tagliolini alla gricia*** (thin egg noodles with Parmesan and pig's jowl, which is sort of like bacon), tagliolini or spaghetti *cacio e pepe* (simply prepared with black pepper and grated pecorino cheese), the ever-popular poor man's ***pasta e fagioli*** (pasta with beans), ***pasta e ceci*** (pasta with chickpeas), or **gnocchi** (potato-based pasta dumplings).

Secondi (second courses) include such ultratraditional local dishes as the eyebrow-raising but delicious ***coda alla vaccinara*** (braised oxtail with tomatoes), ***pajata*** (made of calves' intestines still clotted with mother's milk and often put in tomato sauce on rigatoni pasta), and ***trippa*** (good old-fashioned tripe). Less adventurous main courses include ***involtini*** (veal layered with prosciutto, cheese, and celery then rolled up and cooked with tomatoes), ***polpette*** (meatballs), ***bocconcini di vitello*** (veal nuggets, usually stewed with potatoes and sage), ***pollo arrosto*** (roast chicken, usually one of the cheapest entrees on the menu and often excellently sided *con patate,* with roast potatoes), ***pollo e peperoni*** (chicken smothered in roast red and yellow peppers), ***straccetti con rughetta*** (strips of beef tossed with torn rughetta lettuce), ***arrosto di vitello*** (simple roast veal steak), or ***abbacchio a scottadito*** (grilled tender Roman spring lamb chops; so good the name declares you'll "burn your fingers" in your haste to eat them). One of the best Roman secondi is ***saltimbocca,*** which means "jumps-in-the-mouth." It's a tender veal cutlet cooked in white wine with sage leaves and a slice of prosciutto draped over it.

Roman **pizza**—the kind from a cheap, sit-down pizzeria or *pizza al forno*—is large, round, flat, and crispy (unlike its softer Neapolitan cousin). A "plain" tomato sauce, mozzarella, and basil pie is called *pizza margherita.* The adventurous may want to try a *cappriciosa,* a capricious selection of toppings that often includes anchovies, prosciutto, olives, and an egg cracked onto the hot pizza where it fries in place. You can also get the Roman version of pizza by the slice, ***pizza rustica*** (aka *pizza à taglio)* from hole-in-the-wall joints (see the "Quick Bites" box later in this section).

The *contorni* on the menu are vegetables and side dishes (*melanzana* is eggplant, *fagioli* are beans, *patate* are potatoes, and *zucchini* are obvious). Round off your meal with a ***tiramisu*** (a layer cake of espresso-soaked lady fingers and sweetened, creamy mascarpone cheese dusted with cocoa), a ***tartufo*** (the mother of ice-cream balls—a fudge center, then vanilla, then chocolate, dusted with cocoa or bittersweet chocolate chunks), or simple ***biscotti*** (hard, twice-baked almond cookies).

Although the capital's restaurants are usually blessed with wine cellars that draw on the best vineyards throughout Italy, table wine in Rome is usually a light, fruity white

---

Getting the Best Deal on Dining

- Some more expensive restaurants have cheaper lunch menus, which offer you a chance to sample their fine cuisine at two-thirds the cost.
- Take lunch in a less-expensive *tavola calda* or pizzeria instead of a restaurant.
- Don't just go for any *menu turistico*. Look for good value menus that offer choices within each course and include wine and cover charge.
- Eat anywhere that is full of locals. Empty restaurants and those crowded with tourists are places locals steer clear of—you would be wise to follow their example.
- Order the *vino di casa* (house wine); it will usually be excellent and always cheaper than any bottle on the wine list.
- Stand at bars and cafes rather than taking a table where the same food costs twice as much.
- Check your bill to see if service is included in the total (*servizio incluso*). You wouldn't want to tip twice.

---

from the hills south of the city, either a **Frascati** or the often slightly inferior **Castelli Romane.**

AROUND ANCIENT ROME

Birreria Peroni. V. S. Marcello 10 (north of Pz. SS. Apostoli). ☎ **06/679-5310.** Reservations not accepted. Dishes 5,500–18,500L ($3.25–$10.90); buffet items 3,800–11,400L ($2.25–$6.70). MC, V. Mon–Fri 12:30–11:30pm, Sat 8pm–midnight. Closed up to 4 wk. in Aug. Bus: H, 64, 70, 170, 640 (to V. IV Novembre); 56, 60, 62, 81, 85, 95, 117, 160, 175, 492, 628, 850 (to V. d. Cor.). ROMAN/GERMAN/BUFFET.

Long one of my favorites, this 1906 Italian beer hall is the haunt of local businesspeople who pack in for good food at ridiculously low prices. Few meals in the historic center are so cheap, fast, and filling. The edges of the fan-cooled vaulted ceilings were frescoed in the 1940s with art nouveau sportsman drinking beer and espousing brewery homilies like "Beer makes you strong and healthy." Plates run the gamut from *bucatini all'amatriciana, trippa,* and *pollo arrosto con patate,* to the *arrosto misto alla Peroni* (a huge mix of lots of German beer hall–style eats, like sausage with sauerkraut and goulash with potatoes). The buffet includes prosciutto, goose salami, stuffed or piccante olives, beans with tuna, and marinated artichokes. To wash it all down, of course, order a Peroni beer or the "blue ribbon" Nastro Azzurro label.

✪ **Shawerma.** V. Ostilia 24 (at the corner with V. Capo d'Africa). ☎ **06/700-8101.** Reservations recommended. Appetizers 6,000–8,000L ($3.55–$4.70); main courses 12,000–18,000L ($7.05–$10.60). Light menu 15,000L ($8.80, no wine); *menu economico* 25,000L ($14.70, with wine); *menu completo* 30,000L ($17.65, with wine), 40,000L ($23.55, with wine) on show days. No credit cards. Tues–Sun noon–3pm, 5pm–midnight. Bus: tram 30/, 75, 81, 85, 87, 117, 175, 186, 673, 810, 850 (to Pz. d. Colosseo). Metro: Colosseo. EGYPTIAN/ARAB.

Want a break from Italian? Oriental rugs on the sidewalk herald this excellent Egyptian restaurant. An exotic kaleidoscope of Egyptian artifacts covers the walls, but on balmy days people sit out in front. Friday nights (and sometimes Saturday and Sunday) you get an Egyptian dancer floor show. The *menu completo* is a Middle Eastern feast at supercheap prices. *Meza* (appetizers) include falafel, dolamdes (grape leaves wrapped around rice and minced meat), hummus and other dips like *foul masty* (better than it sounds, it's made of fava beans with lemon and cumin). Main courses include *shawerma* (slow roasted veal carved in strips and mixed with torn lettuce and cubed tomatoes), couscous *di verdure* (with vegetables) or *di carne e verdure* (with veggies and lamb), and *riso lebanese* (rice with pine nuts, almonds, and minced meat). There's Egyptian beer to accompany it, and don't miss the pastries and puddings like *muhalagia* for dessert.

AROUND CAMPO DE' FIORI & THE JEWISH GHETTO

Vegetarians looking for monstrous salads—or if you just want to lay off the heavy Italian for a meal—can find great food at **Insalata Ricca,** Lgo. d. Chiavari 85, ☎ 06/ 6880-3656 (see the review under " Around Piazza Navona & the Pantheon," later in this section).

Ai Banchi Vecchi. V. d. Banchi Vecchi 129 (near Vc. Sugarelli). ☎ **06/683-2310.** Primi 8,000–13,000L ($4.70–$7.65); secondi 9,000–23,000L ($5.30–$13.50); pizza 9,000–13,000L ($5.30–$7.65). AE, DC, MC, V. Mon–Sat noon–2:30pm, 7pm–midnight. Closed Aug. Bus: 116 (to V. d. Banchi Vecchi); 46, 62, 64 (to Pz. S. Cesarini on Cor. V. Emanuele II). ROMAN/PIZZA.

This agreeable hosteria/pizzeria lies on one of the main streets of the workaday neighborhood west of Campo de' Fiori. The decor is traditional trattoria, with wine bottle–lined shelves, stucco walls, ladderback chairs, and a time-worn coffered wood ceiling. Local shopkeepers gather here for a lunch of rigatoni al Gorgonzola, ravioli in salsa *di noci* (in a nut sauce), pasta *e ceci* (pasta with garbanzo beans), or a killer *bucatini all'Amatriciana*. Secondi include *straccetti con rughetta* (bitter lettuce), *scamorza con prosciutto* (smoked cheese melted with prosciutto), and *filette al curry* (beef fillets in a curry sauce). Evenings they also offer pizza and a bargain *fritto misto* of potato croquettes, *supplì* rice balls, fried zucchini flowers, and other fried goodies.

✪ Da Giggetto. V. d. Portico d'Ottavia 21–22. ☎ **06/686-1105.** Reservations recommended. Primi 8,000–16,000L ($4.70–$9.40); secondi 12,000–24,000L ($7.05–$14.10). AE, MC, V. Tues–Sun 12:30–3pm, 7–11pm. Closed Aug. Bus: H, 44, 81, 95, 170, 160, 628, 715, 716, 780 (to V. d. Teatro di Marcello); 23, 280 (to Lungotevere d. Cenci). ROMAN JEWISH.

This third-generation, classic eatery of Rome's old Jewish quarter rambles back in wood-beamed room after room hung with drying herbs and spices. But if you want one of the coveted tables wedged in between the ancient Roman temple columns sprouting out of the sidewalk in front, call ahead. Since 1923, neighborhood cronies have rubbed elbows with a healthy share of tourists digging into Roman Jewish specialties like perfectly fried *carciofi alla giudia* (flattened, tender fried artichokes), and *fiori di zuccine ripieni* (fried zucchini flowers stuffed with mozzarella and anchovies), as well as well-prepared typical Roman dishes *bucatini all'amatriciana, penne all'arrabbiata,* saltimbocca, and *costolette di abbacchio a scottaditto*. With so many excellent dishes, it's easy to go overboard here, so keep an eye on that mounting bill.

Da Pancrazio. Pz. d. Biscione 92 (just off the northeast corner of Cam. de' Fiori). ☎ **06/ 686-1246.** Reservations highly recommended. Primi 12,000–18,000L ($7.05–$10.60); secondi 16,000–30,000L ($9.40–$17.65). *Menu tipico* 43,000L ($25.30, with wine). AE, DC, MC, V. Thurs–Tues 12:30–2:30pm, 7:30–11pm. Closed 25 days in Aug. Bus: 46, 62, 64 (to first stop on Cor. V. Emanuele); 116 (to Cam. di Fiori). ROMAN/ITALIAN.

It doesn't get more atmospheric than this, a restaurant whose basement rooms are set into the restored arcades of Pompey's 55 B.C. theater. It's like dining in a museum. Although these historic downstairs rooms are often booked by tour groups, try your darndest to get a seat there—though there's nothing wrong with the coffered wood

Rome Dining

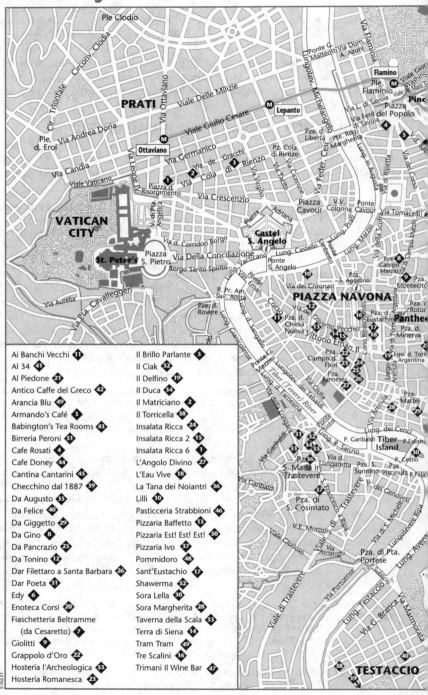

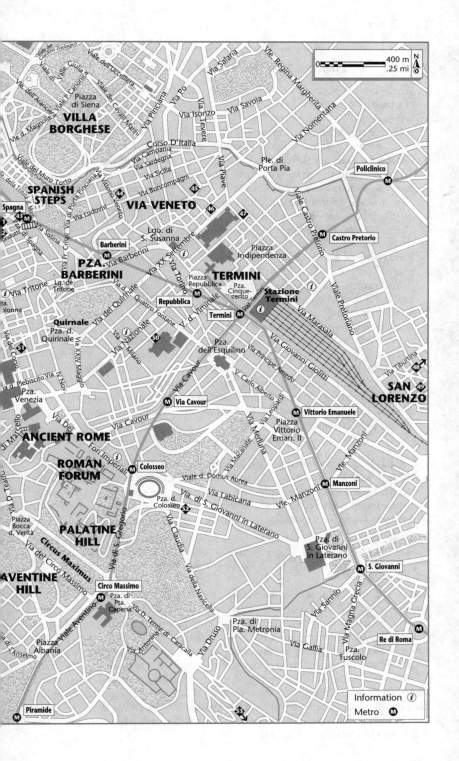

Picnicking on the Freshest Food in Rome

Whether you're planning a day trip, want to dine al fresco around the fountain of a piazza, or simply eat in your hotel room, it's not hard to find perfect picnic fare in Rome.

For the absolute best and freshest in raw ingredients, and a true Roman experience, nothing beats the stalls of an **outdoor food market.** In the centro storico, **Campo de' Fiori** has flower stalls at one end, but food throughout the rest. In Trastevere, head to rectangular **Piazza San Cosimato.** North of the Vatican there's an **indoor market at Via Cola di Rienzo 53/Piazza dell'Unità,** but I prefer the **Via Andrea Doria** market a short walk north and west that occupies the block between Via Santamaura and Via Tunisi (just past Largo Trionfale). The stalls on **Piazza Testaccio** fuels the kitchens of the neighborhood's working-class trattorie. The largest Roman market by far is in the process of moving from **Piazza Vittorio Emanuele** to nearby Via G. Giolitti (which runs along the south edge of Termini).

Markets tend to open Monday through Saturday around 7am. The best pickings are in the earliest hours, when you might bump into your trattoria owner from the night before selecting the ingredients for this evening's bounty. Don't expect to find anything worthwhile after noon.

Once you find the perfect delicacy, you can order it by the kilo (2.2 lb.) or *mezzo kilo* (half a kilo), but most people order their foods in grams. One hundred grams is nicknamed *un etto,* slightly less than a quarter pound. When you're throwing together a picnic for two to four people, usually one etto each of these two cheeses, another etto of prosciutto, and an etto of those olives over there—added to a loaf of bread, bottle of vino, and some fruit—somehow ends up being just the right amount.

---

ceiling and brick arches upstairs. For a touristy restaurant, the cooking is surprisingly excellent. Among their top dishes are spaghetti alla carbonara, delicious cannelloni alla *"Pancrazio"* (pasta tubes stuffed with meat and cheese), and spaghetti *con la bottarga* (with gray mullet eggs). Follow up with *involtini, abbacchio al forno con patate, tournedos di filetto alla Rossini* (beef tournedos in a Madeira sauce with liver pâté), or fresh fish.

Grappolo d'Oro. Pz. d. Cancelleria 80 (across from Pz. S. Pantaleo). ☎ **06/686-4118.** Primi 9,000–14,000L ($5.30–$8.25); secondi 11,000–18,000L ($6.50–$10.60). Mon–Sat noon–3pm, 7:15–11pm. AE, DC, MC, V. Closed Aug. Bus: 46, 62, 64 (to Pz. S. Pantaleo); 116 (to V. Baullari). ROMAN.

Andrea and son Paolo still oversee this upscale hosteria in the heart of Rome, but quality has slipped somewhat and prices have risen steadily since their restaurant became the star of an 11-page *New Yorker* story, prompting every travel publication under the sun to review the joint. But if you stick to their famed specialties, you can still dine wonderfully. Some Roman dishes like saltimbocca alla romana or rigatoni all'amatriciana can be hit or miss, but still superb are the judiciously spicy penne all'arrabbiata, fettuccine *alla greca* (noodles with tomatoes and olives), lasagna, and trippa alla romana. Although the elbow-to-elbow tables in the rustic interior are agreeable, on sunny days reserve ahead for a table on the little piazza. At dinner it's taken over by tourists, but lunch is still a healthy mix of intellectuals, visitors, and the journalists who put this place on the map.

If It's Tuesday

In addition to their regular offerings, the menus of many smaller Roman eateries still follow the traditional weekly rotation of dishes: Tuesday *zuppa di farro* (barley-like emmer soup), Wednesday trippa, Thursday gnocchi, and Friday baccalà and/or pasta e ceci.

✪ **Hosteria Romanesca.** Campo de' Fiori 40. ☎ **06/686-4024.** Reservations recommended. Primi 11,000–12,000L ($6.50–$7.05); secondi 12,000–18,000L ($7.05–$10.60). No credit cards. Tues–Sun noon–4pm, 7pm–midnight. Closed 20 days in Aug. Bus: 46, 62, 64 (to first stop on Cor. V. Emanuele); 116 (to Cam. di Fiori). ROMAN CASARECCIA.

If you're looking to buck the tourists that pack into the famous but much-declined La Carbonara, but still want a seat on the cobbles of lively Campo de' Fiori, head to Armando and Enzo's little 110-year-old osteria to line up for a table. It's the piazza atmosphere and well-tuned traditional dishes you come for, not the service, which some evenings seems nonexistent (they work hard, but there are just too many diners for two waiters and two cooks to handle). Wine is from Frascati, and dishes include tried-and-true Roman faves like an excellent pasta all'amatriciana, saltimbocca alla romana, flawless abbacchio scottaditto, and *cervello d'abbacchio* (fried lamb's brains). In colder weather, they retreat under the wood beams of the tiny interior room.

L'Angolo Divino. V. d. Balestrari 12 (1 block southeast of Campo de' Fiori). ☎ **06/686-4413.** Reservations not accepted. Dishes 5,000–15,000L ($2.95–$8.80). MC, V. Tues–Sun 10am–2:30pm, 5:30pm–1am. Bus: 116 (to Campo de' Fiori). WINE BAR/LIGHT MEALS.

Massimo Crippa and his brothers successfully transformed their grandmother's old wine shop into a fashionable and lovable wine bar just off Campo de' Fiori. Although old-fashioned in style with wood ceilings and shelves of vino, it's trendy in concept with its culinary offerings. That the menu's translated into English may be due to its location, for the clientele remains overwhelmingly Roman. Like most wine bars, it offers mixed platters of cheeses, salamis, smoked fish, and bruschetta, but also daily dishes like lasagna, *rustica ripiena* (a cousin to quiche), salads, and delectable vegetable terrines. There's a vast selection of wines by the glass, particularly strong in Italian vintages but with a good number of select foreign labels as well.

✪ **Sora Margherita.** Pz. Cinque Scole 30 (east of V. Arenula). ☎ **06/686-4002.** Reservations not accepted. Primi 10,000L ($5.90); secondi 13,000L ($7.65). No credit cards. Mon–Fri noon–3pm. Closed Aug 7–Sept 6. Bus: H, 23, 280 (to Lungotevere dé Cenci); tram 8 (to V. Arenula). ROMAN JEWISH.

Margherita Tomassini opened this signless, nine-table osteria 40 years ago as an outlet for her uncle's Velletri wine. The vino still comes from Velletri, as does the olive oil from the family farm, and Margherita keeps busy in the kitchen making the fresh *agnolotti* (meat-stuffed ravioli in ragout), fettuccine (best sauced *cacio e pepe*, with pecorino and pepper), and on Thursdays, gnocchi. She began serving her legendary *polpette* (meatballs) almost 20 years ago so her infant son would have something soft to eat—patrons were soon clamoring for them to be included on the menu. *Baccalà* (salt cod) is offered more often than on de rigueur Fridays. Try the heavenly parmigiana *di melanzane*—no frying of the eggplant slices here; she just loads them down with mozzarella and bakes them in tomato sauce long and slow.

AROUND PIAZZA NAVONA & THE PANTHEON

Al Piedone. V. d. Piè di Marmo 28 (southeast of the Pantheon). ☎ **06/679-8628.** Reservations recommended. Primi 7,000–9,000L ($4.10–$5.30); secondi 10,000–19,000L ($5.90–$11.20). Mon–Sat noon–3pm, 7–11pm. Closed 2 wk. in Aug. Bus: 56, 60, 62, 81, 85, 95, 117, 160, 175, 492, 628, 850 (to south end of V. d. Cor.); 46, 64, 70, 87, 115, 186, 640 (to V. Plebescito). ROMAN.

I tracked down this true Roman-style eatery based on a cookbook recipe that came from its kitchens, an amatriciana bianca sauce that predates the 16th-century advent of tomatoes from the New World. In wood-paneled rooms filled with businesspeople and a few British expatriates you can discover the simple joy of this powerful sauce made from pancetta fried with garlic cloves in pepperoncino-spiked olive oil, tossed with fresh ribbons of pasta and dusted with Parmesan. Other worthy dishes include tortelloni ricotta e spinaci (fresh leaves of white and green pasta wrapped around ricotta and spinach in a light tomato sauce), fettuccine al porcino (noodles with porcini mushrooms), and involtini alla romana.

Da Gino. Vc. Rosini (an alley off Pz. d. Parlamento). ☎ **06/687-3434.** Reservations not accepted. Primi 6,500–10,000L ($3.80–$5.90); secondi 12,000–17,000L ($7.05–$10). No credit cards. Mon–Sat 1–3pm, 8–10pm. Closed Aug. Bus: 116 (to Pz. de. Parlamento); 81, 115, 117, 492, 628 (to V. d. Cor.). ROMAN.

Da Gino remains a local trattoria to which few tourists venture despite its central, if hidden, location. The jammed lunch hour is a rapid affair, when a crowd of politicos and journalists from Parliament across the street crowd under the trompe l'oeil frescoed vaults. They sink their forks with zeal into such primi as ravioli *burro e salvia* (cheese-stuffed pasta prepared simply with butter and sage), spaghetti all'amatriciana, or Gino's specialty *tonnarelli alla ciociara* (pasta with peas and pancetta bacon). For an encore, try the *coniglio al vino* (rabbit cooked in white wine), agnello all cacciatora, or, on Fridays, fish. Don't pass up the heavenly tiramisu for dessert.

✪ Da Tonino. V. d. Governo Vecchio 18 (no sign; at the corner with Vico d'Avila). ☎ **06/241-693.** Reservations not accepted. Primi 7,000–8,000L ($4.10–$4.70); secondi 10,000–11,000L ($5.90–$6.50). No credit cards. Mon–Sat noon–3pm, 7:30–11:30pm. Bus: 46, 62, 64 (to Pz. d. Chiesa Nuova on Cor. V. Emanuele II). ROMAN.

This traditionalists' trattoria's been satisfying a full house of Romans for three generations. Its name is Trattoria Antonio Bassetti, but everybody calls it "Tonino"—not that there's a sign to even let you know it's there. Look for the beads hanging in a doorway and follow the sounds of Roman dialect and clinking plates. It's the sort of scene Fellini liked to film—a whitewashed room divided by a double arch, brown paint slapped on an uneven wood ceiling, paper on the tables, local antique workers and shopkeepers squeezed elbow-to-elbow, and Tonino racing around by himself, keeping everyone flush with the staples of Roman cookery. The menu holds few surprises but plenty of good, honest flavors: pasta e fagioli; pasta all'Amatriciana, alla carbonara, or *al melanzane* (with eggplant), ravioli; straccetti con rughetta; arrosto di vitello; involtini; and polpette. You have to struggle to spend more than 30,000L ($17.65) a head here.

✪ Enoteca Corsi. V. d. Gesù 88 (off V. d. Plebescito). ☎ **06/679-0821.** Reservations not accepted. Primi 8,000L ($4.70); secondi 12,000L ($7.05). AE, DC, MC, V. Mon–Sat noon–3:30pm. Closed Aug. Bus: 46, 56, 60, 62, 64, 70, 81, 87, 115, 186, 492, 628, 640 (to V. d. Plebescito). ROMAN.

It isn't often you find a dirt-cheap, old-fashioned wine-shop-with-food that accepts Diner's Club. Corsi has kept up with the times, but luckily not the prices, so while the enoteca inside the main entrance is every inch the *vini olii* shop of yesteryear (1937, to be specific), behind it and next door are large, fan-cooled rooms to accommodate the lunchtime crowds of local workers at long tables. Your choices are limited to three primi and half a dozen secondi, but every one is excellent in its simplicity. The chalkboard menu changes daily but may run the mill from penne all'arrabbiata, saltimbocca, trippa, and arrosto di vitello, to such delectable dishes as tepid pasta e patate soup or *zucchine ripiene* (zucchini flowers stuffed with minced meats then baked).

Il Delfino. Cor. Vittorio Emanuele 67 (at the corner of Lgo. Argentina). ☎ 06/686-4053. Reservations not accepted. Primi 4,000–8,000L ($2.35–$4.70); secondi 10,000–13,000L ($5.90–$7.65). Fixed-price menus 14,000–16,000L ($8.25–$9.40). AE, DC, MC, V. Tues–Sun 11am–9pm. Bus: 46, 56, 60, 62, 64, 70, 81, 87, 115, 186, 492, 628, 640 (to Lgo. di Torre Argentina). Tram: 8. ROMAN FAST FOOD.

Fast, cheap, reliable, open through riposo, and perfectly placed. That's what cafeteria-like Il Delfino has offered for years to visitors determinedly tramping about the heart of the centro storico: a glorified *tavola calda* (minicafeteria) with self-service hot foods and pizza and a fantastically convenient location on Largo Argentina, just 2 blocks south of the Pantheon. While the food is but mediocre by Roman standards, it's still several cuts above American-style fast-food chains. The steaming trays behind the glass counters usually offer an array of dishes like *risotto alla pescatora* (seafood-studded rice), *carciofi alla romana* (Roman-style artichokes), *cotoletta di pollo* (chicken cutlet), and *patate al forno* (oven roasted potatoes), as well as pizza, calzone, and panini.

Insalata Ricca 2. Pz. Pasquino 72 (southwest of Pz. Navona). ☎ 06/6830-7881. Reservations recommended. Primi 8,000–14,000L ($4.70–$8.25); secondi 8,000–25,000L ($4.70–$14.70); salads 7,000–14,000L ($4.10–$8.25). AE, MC, V. Daily 12:15–3:15pm, 7pm–12:30am. Bus: 46, 62, 64 (to Paizza S. Pantaleo); 70, 81, 87, 115, 116, 116T, 186, 492, 628 (to first stop on Cor. d. Rinascimento). ITALIAN/SALADS.

A need for more vegetarian restaurants and lighter, low-fat fare in Rome helped a single little postmodern trattoria hawking entree-size salads quickly grow into a Roman chain of seven perennially filled restaurants. At the no. 2 branch, most people call ahead for an outdoor table, though on summer days you may prefer the smoke-free air-conditioning of the high-ceilinged rooms within. Some of the more popular oversized salads include the *baires* (lettuce, rughetta, celery, walnuts, apples, Gorgonzola), *siciliana* (lettuce rughetta, sun-dried tomatoes, green olives, corn, hard salted ricotta), and *ricca 2* (lettuce, tomato, ham, cucumbers, olives, carrots, corn). Dishes like gnocchi verdi al Gorgonzola (spinach gnocchi with Gorgonzola sauce) and pasta integrale (whole wheat pasta in a tomato and basil sauce) are also available. The branches near **Campo de' Fiori** and near the **Vatican** (the only other two not out in the burbs) have more or less the same menu; I'll list them under their respective neighborhoods.

Lilli. V. Tor di Nonna 26 (at the base of steps down from Lungotevere Tor di Nonna). ☎ 06/686-1916. Reservations recommended (but sometimes not accepted). Primi 12,000–13,000L ($7.05–$7.65); secondi 13,000–14,000L ($7.65–$8.25). AE, MC, V. Mon–Sat 1–3pm, 8–11:30pm. Closed 15 days in Aug. Bus: 280 (to Lungotevere Tor di Nonna). ROMAN.

Whenever it's warm enough, the crowds abandon the tiny room filled with mementos of owner Silvio Ceramicola's sporting past to sit out on the cobbles of this peaceful, dead-end alley sunk below the Lungotevere. The clientele is mainly local—shopkeepers who don't mind the long waits between courses while the staff huddles around the kitchen TV to catch up on the soccer match. With Trebbiano wine on tap and time-tested primi such as tagliolini cacio e pepe, penne all'arrabbiata, and bucatini all'amatriciana, it's hard to go wrong, and if you stick to the cheaper dishes you can easily make this an especially affordable meal. Entrees include trippa alla romana, pollo con peperoni, and the hearty *polpettine in umida con fagioli* (tiny meatballs stewed with beans), but the true specialty is a delicious *fornata con patate al forno* (oven-roasted veal breast with potatoes).

✪ **Pizzaria Baffetto.** V. d. Governo Vecchio 114 (at the corner with V. Sora). ☎ **06/686-1617.** Reservations not accepted. Pizza 6,000–11,000L ($3.55–$6.50). No credit cards. Mon–Sat 6:30pm–1am. Open daily Mar–Oct. Closed Aug 10–30. Bus: 46, 62, 64 (to Cor. V. Emanuele II). PIZZA.

The pizzaria of Rome, where the service is fast and furious and the thin-crust wood-oven pizza sublime and bubbling hot. People line up early to squeeze in for a paper-spread table surrounded by photos of the directors, artists, and other international types who've shown up nightly over the past 40 years to slum it with businessmen, locals, and packs of youngsters. The night's pizzas are chalked up on a board, so when the waiter whisks past be ready to order a *piccolo* (small), *media* (medium), or *grande* with the toppings of your choice; "plain" margherita is overwhelmingly the most popular, perhaps after a plate of bruschetta. Though you can order dessert, don't dawdle over it—there's a long line outside until well past midnight just waiting for that table and a chance at this Roman legend.

Terra di Siena. Pz. Pasquino 77–78 (southwest of Pz. Navona). ☎ **06/6830-7704.** Reservations highly recommended. Primi 13,000–16,000L ($7.65–$9.40); secondi 14,000–28,000L ($8.25–$16.50). MC, V. Tues–Sun 11:30am–3pm, 7:30–11:30pm. Closed 3 wk. in Aug. Bus: 46, 62, 64 (to Pz. S. Pantaleo); 70, 81, 87, 115, 116, 116T, 186, 492, 628 (to first stop on Cor. d. Rinascimento). TUSCAN.

The family that runs the capital's best Tuscan restaurant celebrates the cooking from their homeland in the hills south of Siena. You can dine under rustic wood beams and softly lit goldenrod walls, or in nice weather, a communal table set on the lively piazza. The menu changes seasonally with the hunter-and-harvest cuisine, but you can always start off with *crostini misti* (toast rounds spread with liver pâté, spicy tomato sauce, or mushrooms), followed by Sienese standard *pici all'aglione* (fat, hand-rolled spaghetti in a spicy, garlicky tomato sauce), or traditional *pappardelle al sugo di cinghiale* (wide noodles in wild boar sauce). In winter, dig into a hearty *ribollita* (stewlike vegetable and bread soup). Your secondo could be the pungent *cinghiale alla maremmana* (wild boar stewed with tomatoes) or a lighter *cacio toscano con le pere* (pears with Siena province's famous ewe's milk cheese, which the restaurant gets from a Radicofani peasant). Stick with the quite good house wines—the bottled vintages are overpriced.

WORTH A SPLURGE

✪ **L'Eau Vive.** V. Monterone 85 (off Pz. Sant'Eustachio). ☎ **06/6880-1095.** Reservations highly recommended. First courses 6,000–20,000L ($3.55–$11.75); entrees 10,000–30,000L ($5.90–$17.65); complete menu 15,000–50,000L ($8.80–$29.40; with wine). MC, V. Mon–Sat 12:30–2:45pm, 7:30–10:30pm. Closed Aug. Bus: 116, 166T (to V. d. Dogana Vecchia); 46, 62, 64 (to first stop on Cor. V. Emanuele II). FRENCH/INTERNATIONAL.

This is the most elegant dining experience in Rome, definitely worth the splurge for its unique food, atmosphere, and service. Fine French cuisine and a daily exotic dish are prepared and served by a lay sisterhood of missionary Christians from five continents who dress in their countries' traditional costumes. Nonsmokers get to skip the plain stuccoed vaulting downstairs and climb to the *piano nobile* of this 16th-century palazzo, where the high ceiling is gorgeously frescoed and the air smoke-free. First courses include the specialty *soupe à l'oignon gratinée* (French onion soup), and scrumptious *chèvre chaus aux aumandes* (toasted goat cheese coated with mustard and almond slivers). Entrees include *langouste Thermidor* (lobster thermidor), and *magret de canard à l'orange* (duck fillet in Grand Marnier sauce with puff-fried potatoes).

Most wines hail from France, with plenty of half-bottles available. At 10pm, the classical music is interrupted so the sisters can sing the "Ave Maria of Lourdes" (you're handed a lyrics sheet to join in), and some weekend evenings they perform a short Bible story in ballet. Only then will they bring out your chocolate mousse or crepes flambé (crepes cooked in Grand Marnier sauce). Tip well; the profits go to charity.

AROUND THE SPANISH STEPS & PIAZZA DEL POPOLO

For a super cheap eat, head to **Il Brillo Parlante** at Via d. Fontanella 12 (one block south of Piazza del Popolo; ☎ 06-324-3334), where you can choose from over 1000 bottles of wine and a menu of creative Italian cuisine.

Edy. Vc. d. Babuino 4 (off V. d. Babuino, 3 blocks from Pz. d. Popolo). ☎ **06/3600-1738.** Reservations highly recommended. Primi 9,000–16,000L ($5.30–$9.40); secondi 9,000–23,000L ($5.30–$13.50). DC, MC, V. Mon–Sat noon–3:30pm, 7–midnight. Closed 1 wk in Aug. Bus: 117 (to V. d. Babuino). ROMAN/SEAFOOD.

Edmondo and Luciana run this comfy trattoria near Rome's toniest shopping zone, offering downscale prices, especially on the fish half of the menu, in an otherwise terminally upscale area. Under an old coffered and painted ceiling inside or at candlelit tables out on the cobblestones, you can sample their ravioli agli asparagi (ravioli with asparagus), excellent tagliatelle con ricotta e carciofi (in a ricotta and artichoke sauce), or specialty spaghetti al cartoccio (pasta and seafood baked in foil). For secondo try their popular *abbacchio Romanesco con patate* (spring lamb with potatoes), *bocconcini di vitello* (veal nuggets stewed with tomatoes, peas, and couscous), or *rombo alla griglia con patate* (grilled turbot with potatoes). Don't leave without ordering one of their homemade desserts.

☺ Fiaschetteria Beltramme (da Cesaretto). V. d. Croce 39 (4 blocks from the Spanish Steps). No phone. Reservations not accepted. Primi 14,000L ($8.25); secondi 18,000L ($10.60). No credit cards. Mon–Sat noon–2:30pm, 7–10:30pm. Bus: 117 (to V. d. Cor.). Metro: Spagna. ROMAN.

A *fiaschetteria* refers to the flasks from which they once poured your wine, to be accompanied by a simple plate of pasta or maybe roast meat. Little has changed here since 1886—although the menu's a tad longer now and the place has been declared a national monument. Cesare and his hardworking staff keep the lucky 30 or so diners happy in this hole-in-the-wall. At lunch, businesspeople and local workers line up to cram into communal tables under whirling fans and framed whatnot on the walls. Dinnertime is just as crowded, but there are more families and tourists. The antipasto misto is good, as are *rigatoni al cesareto* (perfectly al dente pasta topped with arugula, cherry tomatoes, mozzarella, olive oil, and herbs) and *tagliatelle ai funghi* (noodles with mushrooms). Secondi are traditionally basic: a *bollito misto* (mix of boiled meats) or abbacchio scottaditto.

WORTH A SPLURGE

Al 34. V. Mario de' Fiori 34 (a block from the Spanish Steps). ☎ **06/679-5091.** Reservations highly recommended. Primi 13,000–28,000L ($7.65–$16.50); secondi 15,000–32,000L ($8.80–$18.80). Fixed-price menus 55,000–68,000L ($32.35–$40). AE, MC, V. Tues–Sun 12:30–3pm, 7–11:30pm. Closed Aug 10–31. Bus: 116, 117 (to near Pz. di Spagna). Metro: Spagna. ROMAN/INNOVATIVE ITALIAN.

This is a fashionable and classic postshopping restaurant, with such flavorful food and atmosphere we can forgive the splurge prices. The most coveted tables are on out the cobblestones, but the interior is a pleasant mix of rustic wood beams, brick arches, and Liberty-style mirrors and prints. The set-price menus are great deals, covering everything from antipasto to tiramisu. The Sicilian-inspired "Oscar" menu gets you

---

Quick Bites

At **Dar Filettaro a Santa Barbara,** just off the southeast corner of Campo de' Fiori at Lgo. d. Librari 88 (☎ **06/686-4018**), you can join the line of people threading to the back of the bare room to order a fillet of *baccalà* (salt-cod) fried golden brown *da portar via* (wrapped in paper to eat as you *passeggiata*). It costs 4,500L ($2.65). The restaurant is closed on Sunday.

Lunchtime offers you the perfect opportunity to savor Roman fast food— *pizza rustica,* by the slice (often called *pizza à taglio),* half wrapped in waxed paper for easy carrying. You can find joints all over the city that sell this stuff. Just point to the bubbling, steaming sheet with your preferred toppings behind the counter and hand over a few thousand lire; 2,000L ($1.20) buys a healthy portion of "plain" tomato sauce–basil-and-cheese pizza margherita. *Pizza rossa* (just sauce) and *pizza con patate* (with cheese and potatoes) cost even less, as does the exquisitely simple *pizza bianca*—plain dough brushed with olive oil and sprinkled with salt and sometimes rosemary. **Anchovy lovers** should order the *pizza napoletana.*

A *rosticceria* is a *pizza à taglio* with spits of chickens roasting in the window and a few pasta dishes kept warm in long trays. You can also sit down for a quick pasta or prepared meat dish steaming behind the glass counters at a *tavola calda* (literally "hot table") for about half the price as in a trattoria yet nearly as good. A Roman **bar,** although it does indeed serve liquor, is more what we would call a cafe, a place to grab a cheap *panino* (flat roll stuffed with meat, cheese, and/or vegetables) or *tramezzini* (large, triangular sandwiches on white bread with the crusts cut off—like giant tea sandwiches).

---

spaghette al pesto di Trapani (short pasta in a pesto of basil and almonds), *maccheroni alla Positano* (with eggplant and provolone cheese), and steak or Messina-style *involtini di pesce spada* (swordfish rolls). If you prefer Roman delights, the "Roma" menu offers tastes of *bombolotti* (thin pasta tubes) alla amatriciana, and rigatoni con pagliata, followed either by trippa alla romana and coda alla vaccinaara, or a less adventurous but enormous serving of abbachio al forno.

AROUND VIA VENETO

Cantina Cantarini. Pz. Sallustio 12 (east of V. Veneto; turn up V. S. Tullio from V. XX Settembre and bear left). ☎ **06/485-528.** Reservations recommended. Primi 6,000–14,000L ($3.55–$8.25); secondi 12,000–18,000L ($7.05–$10.60). AE, DC, MC, V. Mon–Sat 12:30–3:30pm, 7:30–10:30pm. Closed 3 wk. in Aug, last wk Dec/1st wk Jan. Bus: 910 (to V. Q. Sella); 16, 37, 60, 61, 62, 136, 137 (to V. XX Settembre). MARCHIGIANA/ROMANA.

Courteous, fast service and a good culinary balance of Roman faves and specialties from the Marches region define this 100-year-old trattoria in an upscale neighborhood. You literally rub elbows with the throng of local regulars at simple wooden tables, or sit out on the sidewalk in fine weather. Spaghetti alla carbonara and alla Matriciana (very good) make their appearance alongside fettuccine al salmone or, in season, ai funghi porcini. The archetypal secondo is *fegato marchigiana* (breaded veal liver sautéed with sage), but you can also order a *bollito misto* (mix of boiled meats) or *coniglio alla cacciatore* (hunter's style rabbit). For variety, stop by on Thursday evening through Saturday when fresh fish is added to the menu. The house wines are a white Verdicchio and a Kylix rosso from the Marches.

NORTH OF TERMINI

✪ **Trimani Il Wine Bar.** V. Cernaia 37b (at V. Goito). ☎ **06/446-9630.** Primi 8,000–14,000L ($4.70–$8.25); secondi 12,000–36,000L ($7.05–$21.20); salads and cheeses 12,000–18,000L ($7.05–$10.60). AE, DC, MC, V. Mon–Sat 11:30am–3pm, 5:30pm–12:30am. Closed Aug. Bus: 60, 61, 62, 136, 137 (to V. Cernaia); 37, 116T, 175, 492, 910 (to V. E. Orlando/Pz. d. Repubblica). Metro: Repubblica. ITALIAN/WINE BAR/LIGHT MEALS.

For a gourmet experience that won't break the bank (but may bend it to 50,000L/$29.40, depending on your wines), head to this postmodern wine bar. For Marco and Carla Trimani, serving fine foods to accompany glasses of wine chosen from among their thousands of labels is merely an extension of the family's 170-plus years in the vino trade. The wine bar's tiny rooms, long stylish bar, and outdoor gazebo are tinged with elegance and popular with intellectuals and journalists. The food is excellent, from cheese assortments or Italian salamis to dishes such as *carrè d'agnello alle erbe con cavolo rosso* (herbed loin of lamb with red cabbage). The daily changing menu might include Andalusian gazpacho or the strongly flavored *trittico di crostini,* a trio of bread slices generously topped with Gorgonzola, stilton, and Roquefort, then baked and drizzled with chestnut honey.

IN SAN LORENZO

✪ **Arancia Blu.** V. d. Latini 65 (at V. Arunci). ☎ **06/445-4105.** Reservations highly recommended. Appetizers 7,000L ($4.10); main courses 12,000–16,000L ($7.05–$9.40). No credit cards. Mon–Fri 12:30–3pm, 8pm–midnight; Sat–Sun 8pm–midnight. Bus: 71 (to V. Tiburtina). INVENTIVE VEGETARIAN ITALIAN.

Fabio Bassan and Enrico Bartolucci offer the best vegetarian cuisine in Rome. Under soft lighting and wood ceilings, surrounded by wine racks and university intellectuals, the friendly waiters will help you compile a menu to fit any dietary need. The dishes at this trendy spot are inspired by peasant cuisines from across Italy and beyond, and everything's made with organic and natural ingredients. Appetizers range from hummus and tabbouleh to a zucchini and saffron quiche or insalata verde con mele, *Gorgonzola naturale e aceto balsamico* (salad with apples, Gorgonzola, and balsamic vinegar). Main courses change seasonally and may include a lasagna with red onions, mushrooms, zucchini, and ginger; couscous *con verdure* (vegetable couscous), or *ravioli ripieni di patate e menta* (ravioli stuffed with potatoes and mint served under fresh tomatoes and Sardinian sheep's cheese). They offer almost 100 wines, cheese platters, and inventive desserts like *pere al vino* (pears cooked in wine, scented with juniper, and served with a semifreddo of orange honey).

Pommidoro. Pz. Sanniti 44 (turn off V. Tiburtina onto V. degli Ansoni). ☎ **06/445-2692.** Reservations highly recommended. Primi 10,000–15,000L ($5.90–$8.80); secondi 7,000–18,000L ($4.10–$10.60). AE, MC, V. Mon–Sat noon–3pm, 7:30pm–midnight. Closed Aug. Bus: 71, 492 (to V. Tiburtina). ROMAN.

The Bravi family—these days Anna (cook), Aldo (hunter) and their brood—have for four generations been satisfying everyone from downtown cognoscenti and neighborhood cronies to intellectuals and celebrities like Pier Pasolini and Maria Callas. There's a glassed-in deck on the piazza, but the inside's more atmospheric with a huge old fireplace grill. Or, head downstairs to dine under low arches of hand-cast brick. Roman specialties reign supreme, from amatriciana and the excellent carbonara to spaghetti alla gricia and rigatoni con pajata. When porcini mushrooms are in season, try them tossed with fettuccine, or order *pappardelle al sugo cinghiale* (wide noodles in boar sauce). Secondi include truly Roman trippa, coda alla vaccinara, *animelle alla cacciatore* (sweetbread stew), and, Pasolini's old favorite, a simple *bistecca di manzo* (beefsteak).

Tram Tram. V. d. Reti 44–46 (at the corner with V. d. Piceni). ☎ **06/490-416.** Reservations highly recommended. Primi 9,000–16,000L ($5.30–$9.40); secondi 15,000–22,000L ($8.80–$12.95). DC, MC, V. Tues–Sun 12:30–3pm, 7:30pm–12:30am. Closed 2–3 wk. in Aug. Bus: tram 19, tram 30/, 71, 492, (to V. Tiburtina). SOUTHERN ITALIAN/ROMAN.

Rosanna di Vittorio and daughters Antonella and Fabiola run this eternally crowded trattoria. Don't get worried if the silverware and glasses tinkle—it's just the trams rumbling by. These trams inspired both the name and the decor: old trolley signs and photos, even tram benches as seats. The excellent pan-Italian wine list and menu (well balanced between meat and fish), Roman cuisine, and the cooking of Rosanna's native Apulia, have made this old factory worker's eatery trendy (director Nanni Moretti drops by, among others). But the nearby university, reasonable prices, and happy leftist air of the neighborhood keeps it a populist trattoria. Primi include *cavatelli alla siciliana* (short pasta with swordfish and eggplant), handmade *orecchiette broccoli e vongole* (ear-shaped pasta with broccoli and clams) or *alla norma* (with tomato, eggplant, and hard ricotta), and rigatoni alla paiata. For secondo, the abbacchio scottaditto is among the most tender in Rome, or try the *alici fritte dorate* (golden fried anchovies), or *filetti di cernia* (grilled grouper fillet).

SOUTH OF TERMINI

Pizzaria Est! Est! Est! V. Genova 32 (off V. Nazionale). ☎ **06/488-1107.** Reservations recommended. Pizza 9,500–17,000L ($5.60–$10). MC, V. Tues–Sun 7pm–midnight. Closed Aug. Bus: H, 64, 70, 71, 115, 116T, 170, 640. PIZZA.

You can sit outside at the box canyonlike end of the road as part of an old-fashioned Roman street dining scene, or opt for the Liberty-style interior of the Ricci family's 100-year-old pizzaria. The starched-shirt service and small pies of Est! Est! Est!—named after a sweet white wine from northern Lazio—have long been popular with the nearby police station and other locals as well as visitors. Order an appetizer of *supplì* (gooey fried balls of rice and mozzarella) and *olive ascolane* (green olives stuffed with minced meat, breaded, and fried) before your pizza. If regular is too small, you can order any pie *gigante* for twice the price. The pizza is excellent, with a soft Neapolitan-style crust; try it with funghi porcini or *capricciosa* (mushrooms, prosciutto, mozzarella, tomatoes, and a fried egg).

IN TESTACCIO

Da Felice. V. Maestro Giorgio 29 (at the corner of V. A. Volta). ☎ **06/574-6800.** Reservations highly recommended. Primi 6,500–8,000L ($3.80–$4.70); secondi 11,000–18,000L ($6.50–$10.60). No credit cards. Mon–Sat 12:30–2:30pm, 8–10:30pm. Closed Aug. Bus: 27, 673, 719 (to V. Galvani); 13, 23, 75, 715, 716 (to V. Marmorata). Metro: Piramide. ROMAN.

The cloth napkins give the appearance of a classy joint, but for more than 50 years this has been as traditional a Roman osteria as they come. There's no sign or menu, and every table's marked *"riservato"* so Felice can look you over as you enter and decide whether you're serious enough about wanting to eat here to deserve a table. Every seat fills up anyway, and solo travelers may find themselves sharing with one of the regulars who lunch here every day. It's a family affair—Felice himself ambles around the single high-ceilinged room in his waiter's jacket, his son mans the kitchen, and his grandson helps serve. The dishes change with the days of the week, made from the freshest ingredients from the nearby market. Primo is usually a toss-up between minestrone and a remarkable *tonarelli cacio e pepe* or *al sugo*. The most popular secondi—*involtino al sugo* and *spezzatino di vitello con peperoni* (veal smothered with bell peppers)—are equally good, or try *spigola in bianco* (fresh sea bass).

○ **Il Torricella.** V. E. Torricelli 2–12 (at V. G. B. Bodoni, just off the Lungotevere a few blocks up from Ponte Testaccio). ☎ **06/574-6311.** Primi 8,000–14,000L ($4.70–$8.25); secondi 9,000–20,000L ($5.30–$11.75). MC, V. Tues–Sun 12:30–3:30, 7:30–11:30. Closed a few days in Aug. Bus: 27, 719 (to Lungotevere Testaccio/V. A. Manuzio); 95, 673 (to V. N. Zabaglia). Metro: Piramide. ROMAN/SEAFOOD.

This is another ultratraditional Testaccio osteria, set in the echoey tiled rooms of what appears to be an old dock warehouse, with tall arches, soccer team photos lining the walls, and a die-hard clientele of neighborhood families. It ain't fancy, and gets a star for its genuineness and hugely abundant portions. The menu has only Roman faves like *spaghetti ai frutti di mare* (spaghetti with seafood), homemade gnocchi (on Thursdays), great rigatoni con pagliata, tasty bucatini all'amatriciana, saltimbocca alla romana, abbacchio à scottadito, *bistecca di manzo ai pepi verdi* (steak covered by a cream sauce with green peppercorns), and fresh *sogliole* (sole), *spigola* (sea bass), *rombo* (turbot), and other fish.

WORTH A SPLURGE

○ **Checchino dal 1887.** V. di Monte Testaccio 30 (at the southerly end of Testaccio). ☎ **06/574-6318.** www.checchino-dal-1887.com. Reservations required. Primi 7,000–21,000L ($4.10–$12.35); secondi 12,000–35,000L ($7.05–$20.60). AE, DC, MC, V. Tues–Sat 12:30am–3pm, 8–11pm, Sun 11am–3pm. Closed Aug, 1 wk at Christmas, and Sun–Mon June–Sept. Bus: 27, 719 (to V. Monte Testaccio). Metro: Piramide. ULTRAROMAN.

Checchino is the single greatest splurge in Rome, the city's premier mecca for international foodies. The Mariani family started Rome's elegant temple of traditional cuisine six generations ago as a blue-collar wine shop, patronized by workers from the slaughterhouse across the street. These men received the undesirable "fifth fourth" of the day's butchering: offal, tails, feet, and so on. Checchino turned these remains into culinary masterpieces of poor man's food, like rigatoni con pajata, *insalata di zampe* (salad with jellied trotters), and bucatini alla gricia. This is the family that nearly 100 years ago managed to make an oxtail appetizing by inventing *coda alla vaccinara* (it's stewed with tomatoes, celery, white wine, bittersweet chocolate, pine nuts, and raisins). They also offer plenty of flawlessly prepared but less adventurous Roman and Italian dishes, including the specialty *abbacchio alla cacciatore* (spring lamb browned in olive oil and flavored with anchovies, vinegar, and pepperoncini), which comes with a commemorative plate. Don't end you meal without sampling from some two dozen cheeses, or a homemade dessert. Each is accompanied by the perfect glass of wine or dessert wine from among the 500 labels of Rome's most extensive wine cellar.

IN TRASTEVERE

Da Augusto. Pz. de' Renzi 15 (between Vc. d. Cinque and V. d. Moro). ☎ **06/580-3798.** Reservations not accepted. Primi 3,500–8,500L ($2.05–$5); secondi 6,000–12,000L ($3.55–$7.05). No credit cards. Mon–Fri noon–3pm, 7–midnight; Sat noon–3pm. Bus: 23, 280 (to Lungotevere Sanzio just past Pz. Trilussa). ROMAN.

The Silvestri family's modest eatery has found its way into virtually every guidebook as a poster child Trastevere osteria. But the bulk of patronage remains neighborhood cronies who pack into the pair of rooms and few tables squeezed into the triangular piazza. Perhaps visitors just can't find the place, tucked into a forgotten corner of Trastevere on a tiny square used as a parking lot. The lucky few sit elbow-to-elbow to dig into standbys like rigatoni all'amatriciana, *fettuccine cacio e pepe, trippa alla romana, involtini,* and succulent *abbacchio.* They get rather busy, so don't expect solicitous service; just excellent home cooking.

Dar Poeta. Vc. d. Bologna 45 (off Pz. S. Maria d. Scala, not to be confused with V. d. Bologna, off which it branches) ☎ **06/588-0516.** Reservations recommended. Pizza 6,000–14,000L ($3.55–$8.25). AE, DC, MC, V. Tues–Sun 8pm–midnight. Bus: 23, 280 (to Lungotevere Sanzio just past Pz. Trilussa). PIZZA.

This crowded pizzaria with brick ceilings and some shaky tables out on the cobble-stones is part of a small but devoted movement to offer an alternative to thin crust Roman-style pizza. Regular pizza dough rises an hour at most; Dar Poeta's leavened version gets 24 hours. The result is a crust still very thin, but much lighter and airier, and the toppings are piled on without making the pie to heavy. The *Dar Poeta* has zuc-chini, garlic, mozzarella, and sausage sprinkled with hot pepper, while the popular *campagnola* is topped with uncooked cherry tomatoes and miniature mozzarella balls then strewn with rughetta leaves (a bitter lettuce). For an even more economical meal, the bruschetta—thick slabs of peasant bread broiled and slathered with veggie top-pings—are more enormous than their 3,000L price tag would let on.

✪ **Il Duca.** Vc. d. Cinque 52–56 (just around the corner from Pz. S. Egidio, behind Pz. S. Maria in Trastevere). ☎ **06/581-7706.** Reservations recommended. Primi 11,000–16,000L ($6.50–$9.40); secondi 10,000–22,000L ($5.90–$12.95); pizza 8,000–11,000L ($4.70–$6.50). AE, DC, MC, V. Tues–Sat 7pm–midnight; Sun noon–3pm, 7pm–midnight. Bus: 23, 280 (to Lungotevere Sanzio). ROMAN/PIZZA.

The rustic, wood-ceilinged interior and walls whose brick arches are muraled with Roman scenes in this many-roomed Trastevere institution are as much of an attraction as the noisy banter—plenty of Trasteverino and Roman dialect still mixed in with the tourist languages here—and excellent cooking. But this place gets the star for the out-standing, melt-in-your-mouth lasagna, the only version on the face of the planet better than my mother's (Mom, incidentally, agrees). Since everyone at the table can't order the same thing, they also offer spaghetti alla carbonara (my old standby back in the days when lasagna was only an occasional daily special and not permanently on the menu), spaghetti alla gricia, or gnocchi alla gorgonzola. For secondo, the saltimbocca alla romana is divine, or try pollo arrosto con patate, or abbacchio à scottaditto.

La Tana d. Noiantri. V. d. Paglia 1–3 (the street leading west out of Pz. Santa Maria in Traste-vere). ☎ **06/580-6404.** Reservations highly recommended. Primi 7,000–14,000L ($4.10–$8.25); secondi 15,000–25,000L ($8.80–$14.70); pizza 11,000–15,000L ($6.50–$8.80). AE, MC, V. Wed–Mon noon–3pm, 7:30–11:30pm. Bus: 23, 280 (to Lungotevere Sanzio); H, tram 8 (to Pz. Sidney Sonnino). ROMAN/ITALIAN/PIZZA.

La Tana dei Noiantri has a vast menu with seemingly limitless offerings of quite good food, impeccable service by crisply bow-tied waiters who've been here forever, and an enviable location just off Piazza Santa Maria. But everybody really comes here for the romance of dining out on the cobblestones, under the tentlike umbrellas of a pocket-sized piazza cupped by the brick walls of Santa Maria in Trastevere. The interior is a bit more formal with wood ceilings and painted coats of arms hanging above baronial fireplaces. Open with tasty *stracciatella romana* (egg-drop soup with Parmesan), *riga-toni con pajata*, or the wonderfully hot penne all'arrabbiata. The best among the sec-ondi are abacchio arrosto con patate and *fritto cervello di abbacchio* (fried lambs brains and zucchini), though the *bistecca di manzo* (beefsteak) is fine as well. There's also a sizable selection of fresh fish and seafood, including *cozze alla marinara* (mussels in tomato sauce).

Pizzaria Ivo. V. San Francesco a Ripa 158 (from Vle. di Trastevere, take a right onto V. Fratte di Trastevere, then left on V. S. Francesco a Ripa). ☎ **06/581-7082.** Reservations not usually necessary. Primi 10,000–12,000L ($5.90–$7.05); secondi 9,500–15,000L ($5.60–$8.80); pizza 8,000–16,000L ($4.70–$9.40). AE, DC, MC, V. Wed–Mon 5:30pm–1:30am. Bus: H, tram 8 (to Vle. Trastevere); 44, 75 (to V. Tavolacci/V. E. Morosini). PIZZA/ROMAN.

Trastevere's huge, famed, bustling pizza parlor is always thronged with locals and foreign visitors (is there any guidebook that doesn't list it?), but the hordes haven't led it to compromise taste or prices. It's changed little since I first sat down here 15 years ago. Tables outside are hard to come by, but the street's fairly trafficked, so I always choose the crowded, closely spaced tables inside. Service is swift and brusque in true Trastevere style, and despite its almost terminal popularity, Ivo remains an excellent place to introduce your yourself to genuine, Roman style wood-oven pizza. My fave is the "plain" margherita, but also good are al prosciutto and *capricciosa* (at the whim of the chef, but likely to include anchovies, prosciutto, olives, and a fried egg). There are plenty of pastas to choose from as well.

Taverna della Scala. Pz. d. Scala 19. ☎ **06/581-4100.** www.iceberg-usa.com/tavernascala.htm. Reservations recommended. Primi 9,000–12,000L ($5.30–$7.05); secondi 12,000–22,000L ($7.05–$12.95); pizza 7,000–13,000L ($4.10–$7.65). AE, MC, V. Wed–Mon 12:30–3pm, 7:30–midnight. Bus: 23, 280 (to Lungotevere Sanzio). ROMAN/PIZZA.

This basic and ever-popular trattoria has a few tables set on the out-of-the-way piazza, but most diners end up in the small, trattoria-style dining room on the ground floor or in the stuccoed basement surrounded by odd modern art. All the Roman staples are here: bucatini all'amatriciana, penne all'arrabbiata, and the titillatingly named spaghetti alla puttanesca ("whore's pasta," spicy and thrown together quickly with black olives, capers, garlic, and anchovies) and *farfalle alle mutandine rose* (bow-tie pasta "pink panties," in a rosé tomato-and-cream sauce). For secondo sample the *ossobuco romano* (veal shank cooked with tomatoes; the marrow is considered a delicacy), *scaloppina al vino* (veal scallop in wine), or fresh fish like *spigola* (sea bass) or *orata* (sea bream) grilled.

WORTH A SPLURGE

Il Ciak. Vc. d. Cinque 21 (just south of Pz. Trilussa, north of Pz. S. Maria in Trastevere). ☎ **06/589-4774.** Reservations highly recommended. Primi 10,000–15,000L ($5.90–$8.80); secondi 14,000–23,000L ($8.25–$13.50). AE, MC, V. Tues–Sun 8pm–midnight. Bus: 23, 280 (to Pz. Trilussa/Lungotevere Sanzio). TUSCAN/GAME.

The decor is amalgamated Tuscan rustic spruced up with movie stills from owner Paolo Celli's former life as an actor. Celli hails from Lucca, a genteel Tuscan city renowned for its olive oil, wines, and hearty barley soup. There's big old bottle of pay-what-you-drink Chianti on the table to accompany the wonderfully flavored, stick-to-your-ribs food. For primo try *papardelle al sugo di cinghiale* (wide noodles in wild boar sauce), *minestra di farro con fagioli* (that barleylike emmer soup with beans), or *ribollita* (vegetable soup made thick with bread). Secondi include *braciole di maiale* (pork shop) and the mighty *Fiorentina originale* (a heavenly grilled steak; if you can't handle this 800-gram/1.75-pound slab of beef, you can order the 400-gram *mezza*). There's also game on the menu like *cinghiale alla boscaiola* (woodsman's-style wild boar) and *starna al crostone* (partridge on toasted bread).

۞ Sora Lella. V. Ponte Quattro Capi 16 (on Tiber Island, at the foot of Ponte Fabricio). ☎ **06/686-1601.** Reservations highly recommended. Primi 14,000–18,000L ($8.25–$10.60); secondi 18,000–28,000L ($10.60–$16.50). AE, DC, MC, V. Mon–Sat 1–2:30pm, 8–10:30pm. ROMAN/INVENTIVE ITALIAN.

You Get What You Pay for

At Rome bars, cafes, and gelaterie, don't just saunter up to the bar and order two fingers of vino. Go first to the cashier, order what you want, pay for it, and take the receipt to the counter where you can order your cappuccino or your *coppa* (cup) or *cono* (cone) or gelato, putting the receipt down with a 100L or 200L piece as a tip.

The Best Roman Ice Cream & Cafes

Although Rome isn't quite the ice-cream mecca that Florence is, Rome's **gelato** is still heavenly. Any place that advertises *produzione propria* (homemade) will have a high-quality, tasty stock, but *the* parlor in which to enjoy this sweetly sinful snack is the 19th-century **Giolitti** (☎ **06/699-1243;** www.giolitti.it), a few long blocks north of the Pantheon at V. Uffici d. Vicario 40. Another Roman institution that's as vital to visit as the Colosseum or Vatican is the bar ✪ **Tre Scalini,** Pz. Navona 28–32 (☎ **06/6880-1996**), where you can sit outside watching the carnival of life on the piazza while indulging in a homemade tartufo ice-cream ball (a ball of chocolate ice cream rolled in chocolate chunks with a cherry in the middle).

Aside from Tre Scalini, you may want to pop into these other historic cafes. The **Antico Caffè del Greco,** V. Condotti 96 (☎ **06/679-1700**), was established in 1760, just in time for Casanova to while away the hours waiting to meet in secret with his lovers, and for the German author Goethe to become a regular during his prolonged stay in the city as Rome's first Grand Tourist. Nearby, just to the left of the Spanish Steps, is one of Rome's bastions of the Anglo-American expatriate scene, **Babington's Tea Rooms,** Pz. di Spagna 23 (☎ **06/678-6027**), started by two little old ladies in 1893. Stop in to raise your pinkies to a very proper (and *very* expensive) high tea in this staunchly British reminder of the genteel 19th century. A pot of tea runs from 12,000L ($7.05) on up, but excellent British cakes, sandwiches, and dishes are also available.

Near the Pantheon lies the cafe of **Sant'Eustachio,** Pz. Sant'Eustachio 82 (☎ **06/686-1309**), a traditional Italian stand-up bar serving since 1938 what is widely held to be Rome's best cappuccino (2,200L/$1.30), made with water carried into the city on an ancient aqueduct. The **Pasticceria Strabbioni,** V. Servio Tullio 2 (☎ **06/487-3965**), is a cafe and pastry shop with fancifully decorated vaults, a courteous staff, and excellent pastries.

On Piazza del Popolo, the place to see and be seen—and catch a nightly parade of cruisin' Ferraris and Maseratis—is **Cafe Rosati,** Pz. d. Popolo 4–5 (☎ **06/322-5859**), which still retains its 1922 art nouveau decor. Its outdoor tables and (overpriced) upstairs restaurant are preferable to those of its rival Canova across the square. If you want to capture some of that lingering *La Dolce Vita* spirit on the Via Veneto, head to its old queen of Roman bars, the **Cafe Doney,** V. Veneto 145 (☎ **06/482-1788**), which in its heyday was the epicenter of the glamour crowd (Marcello Mastroianni, Ava Gardner, Anita Ekberg).

This classic is best described as refined rustic, with rough hewn beams, classy place settings, cozy rooms, elegant service, and a great wine list. Aldo Trabalza and his sons honor the memory of Aldo's mother, Sora Lella Fabbrizi—cook, unlikely star of Italian TV, and archetypal Roman character—by serving rigorously traditional faves, innovative lighter fare, and half-forgotten Roman dishes with centuries of pedigree. The specialty primo is *tonnarelli alla cuccagna* (fresh pasta with sausage, eggs, walnuts, cream, and a dozen other ingredients), but also good are *bombolotti alla ciafruiona* (pasta with tomatoes, artichokes, peas, and tuna), or rigatoni con pagliata. For secondo try the rarely found *abbacchio brodettato* (veal pieces sautéed with eggs, lemon, Parmesan, and parsley), or the typical *maialino al forno "antica romana"* (sweet-and-sour suckling pig with prunes, raisins, pine nuts, almonds, and baby onions). At these prices, portions could be larger, but the quality is impeccable.

AROUND THE VATICAN

The no. 6 branch of the wildly popular Roman chain of salad-and-light-meals restaurants called **Inslata Ricca** is located across from the Vatican walls at Pz. d. Risorgimento 5–6, ☎ **06/3973-0387** (see the review under "Around Piazza Navona & the Pantheon," earlier in this section). If you're looking for an Italian pub with food, head to **Armando's Cafe** at Via Paolo Emilio 17 (at Via Cola di Rienzo; ☎ **06-324-3111**).

Il Matriciano. V. d. Gracchi 55 (at the corner with V. Silla). ☎ **06/321-3040.** Reservations highly recommended. Primi 15,000L ($8.80); secondi 18,000–26,000L ($10.60–$15.30). AE, DC, MC, V. May–Oct Sun–Fri 12:30–3pm, 8–11:30pm; Nov–Apr Thurs–Tues 12:30–3pm, 8–11:30pm. Closed Aug 6–21. Bus: 32, 81 (to V. Cola di Rienzo); tram 19, 51, 81, 492, 907, 990, 991, 982 (to Pz. d. Risorgimento). Metro: Ottaviano. ROMAN.

This classic and classy Roman ristorante has for more than 80 years been beloved by Rome cognoscenti, Prati residents, and film directors for business lunches. There are broad paneled walls, colored prints, and bow-tied waiters inside and tables on the sidewalk when weather permits. At these prices, portions could be larger and sauces more ample, but the cooking is impeccable. It would be a sacrilege if at least one person didn't order the namesake bucatini alla matriciana (the restaurant sometimes skimps on the meat). Other good primi include fettuccine *casarecce* (basic, with tomatoes and basil) and tagliolini alla gricia. The pride of the secondi is *abbacchio al forno con patate* (lamb with tasty oven-roasted potatoes), or try *ossobuco cremoso con funghi* (ossobuco under a mushroom cream sauce), or a *filetto di bue* (ox steak).

ON THE VIA APPIA ANTICA

Hosteria l'Archeologica. V. Appia Antica 139 (across the street from San Sebastiano catacombs, at corner with Vc. d. Basilica). ☎ **06/788-0494.** Reservations recommended. Primi 10,000–17,000L ($5.90–$10); secondi 10,000–26,000L ($5.90–$15.30). AE, DC, MC, V. Fri–Wed 12:15–3pm, 8–11pm. Bus: 660 (to San Sebastiano catacombs); 760 (Sun only, to San Sebastiano); 218 (to Lgo. M.F Ardeatine, then a 10-min walk down V. d. Sette Chiese). ROMAN/ITALIAN.

Perfectly placed for a postcatacombs lunch, this is one of Rome's few remaining countryside trattorie, where entire extended families gather for Sunday lunch under masses of wisteria. This garden seating extends back from the original roadside inn, with its tightly spaced tables under cozy wood-beam ceilings and painting-covered walls. Kick off with bucatini all'amatriciana, gnocchi *al cinghiale* (homemade gnocchi in a hearty tomato sauce enriched with chunks of wild boar), or *rigatoni al cuore di carciofo* (pasta with artichoke hearts). Secondi are simple, often grilled meats, and include *bistecca di manzo all griglia* (grilled steak) and a good abbacchio alla scotta ditto.

A Note About Hours

When trying to plan your day to explore all of Rome, remember that because so many museums, monuments, and archaeological sites are reopening after restorations (sometimes years of it) and others are opening for the first time ever, many still don't have year-round hours worked out yet. Be especially wary in winter of any sight in this chapter with open hours that last into the late evening; many of these hours were from a museum's first summer, and although neither the Rome tourist office nor the museum offices could guess what the slower winter season would bring, I strongly suspect hours will shorten and many sights may close as early as 2pm.

Cheap Thrills: Exploring Rome for Free (or Almost)

- **Visit a church.** All of the city's 900-odd churches are free. Many seem to be nothing more than consecrated walls that serve as backdrops to Renaissance and baroque masterpieces by Caravaggio, Pinturrichio, Filippo Lippi, Michelangelo, and Bernini.

- **Step back in time. The Pantheon,** one of the most perfectly preserved ancient temples in the world and a masterpiece of architeture and aesthetic beauty, won't cost you a lire. **The Roman Forum,** the heartbeat of the ancient city that controlled Europe, North Africa, the Near East, and parts of Asia 2,000 years ago, is gratis.

- **Wander through the piazzas and fountains.** There's no charge to sip a cappuccino in Piazza Navona while admiring Bernini's *Fountain of Four Rivers*. Or join the throngs at the Trevi Fountain (cost: 200L tossed into the basin to ensure you'll return to Rome).

- **Window shop.** You can wander down chic streets like **Via dei Condotti** off Piazza di Spagna, lined with stylish outlets showing off the latest from Armani, Ferragamo, and Gucci. How "free" this is depends on the willpower of whomever's holding the credit cards.

- **Join the museum crowds. The Vatican** and **Capitoline Museums** are both free on the last Sunday of every month. However, since this is common knowledge, be prepared to be get crushed. Pay full price instead and go on a Wednesday morning to truly enjoy it.

- **Enjoy nighttime panormas.** Wander around the backside of the mayor's palace on Piazza del Campidoglio to see the Rome of the Caesars floodlit in a solemn and shadowy light. Or end your evening (after a hearty Trastevere dinner) with a walk along the walls of the Gianicolo hill stretching north toward the Vatican with a sweeping vista of the city.

5 Exploring the Vatican & St. Peter's

✪ **St. Peter's Basilica.** Pz. San Pietro (there's an information office/bookshop on the left [south] side of the steps up to the basilica). ☎ **06/6988-4466.** Admission free to the church, sacristy, and crypt; Dome 5,000L ($3) adults, 1,000L (60¢) students, or 6,000L ($3.60) for elevator most of the way up; Treasury 5,000L ($2.95). Appropriate dress required (see "Travel Tip" on p. 139). Church Apr–Aug daily 7am–7pm, Sept–Mar daily 7am–6pm. Dome Mar–Sept daily 8am–6pm, Oct–Feb daily 8am–4:30pm. Crypt Apr–Sept daily 7am–6pm, Oct–Mar daily 7am–5pm. Treasury Apr–Sept daily 9am–6:30pm, Oct–Mar daily 9am–4pm. Bus: tram 19, 23, 32, 34, 46, 46/,49, 51, 62, 64, 81, 98, 492, 881, 907, 982, 990, 991. Metro: Ottaviano.

St. Peter's is one of the holiest basilicas in the Catholic faith, the pulpit for a parish priest we call the pope, one of the grandest creations of Rome's Renaissance and baroque eras, and the largest church in Europe (it was biggest in the world until an ugly barn of a place was recently completed in Africa).

St. Peter's is absolutely huge, longer than two football fields and 145 feet high inside, but since every part of it is oversized (even the cherubs would dwarf a 6-foot man) it doesn't appear nearly that large—until you look 614 feet down to the opposite end and see the specks of people walking about. Mocking bronze plaques set in the floor of the central nave mark just how short the world's other great cathedrals come up. The basilica itself takes at least an hour to see—not because there are many specific sights; it just takes that long to walk down to one end of it and back. A more complete visit will take 2 to 3 hours, including climbing Michelangelo's dome and descending to the papal crypt.

THE PIAZZA You approach the church through the embracing arms of Bernini's oval colonnade, which encompasses **Piazza San Pietro.** Actually, this "oval" is a perfect ellipse described by the twin arms of 284 Doric columns, arranged in four rows and topped with 96 statues of saints. The ellipse creates a neat special effect: Between either of the two fountains and the Egyptian obelisk in the piazza's center is a marble disk in the ground. Stand here to see the rows of the colonnade closest to you line up, appearing to be only one column deep.

THE BASILICA The basilica, which replaced a crumbling 4th-century version, went through many architects, each attempting to realize a personal vision. It was started by Bramante in 1506 (on a Greek Cross floor plan), continued by Raphael (who chose to adapt it to a Latin Cross plan), then by Peruzzi (back to Greek Cross), Antonio Sangallo the Younger (Latin Cross again), Michelangelo (guess what: Greek Cross, although his major contribution was raising the dome), and Giacomo della Porta and Carlo Fontana (who completed it in 1590 more or less in line with Michelangelo's designs). Then in 1605, they tore down the facade and brought in Carlo Maderno who—tell me you didn't see this coming—lengthened the nave so as to finish it off in a Latin Cross plan by 1626. For a baroque flourish, Bernini, in addition to creating the piazza out front, took care of much of the interior decor from 1629 through the 1650s.

To the right as you enter the basilica is the greatest single sight, **Michelangelo's** *Pietà* (1500). The beauty and unearthly grace of sweet-faced Mary and her dead son, Jesus, with details that seem exactingly perfect and yet are exaggerated for effect—the Virgin's lap is mountainously large in order to support the body of a full-grown man without seeming unbelievable—led some critics of the day to circulate a rumor that the 25-year-old Florentine sculptor could never have carved such a work himself. An indignant Michelangelo returned to the statue and did something he never did before or after: He signed it, chiseling his name unmistakably right across the Virgin's sash. The *Pietà* has been behind protective glass since the 1970s when a hammer-wielding lunatic attacked it.

Under the dome is Bernini's twisty-columned *baldacchino* (1524), a 96-foot-high and ridiculously fancy altar canopy that was constructed with bronze taken from the Pantheon. Of the four great piers that support the dome, the first on your right is a backdrop for a late 13th-century bronze statue of *St. Peter* by **Arnolfo di Cambio.** This architect of Florence's Gothic *palazzi* was also an underrated sculptor, and his greatest work in Rome does double duty as a piece of art and a holy good luck talisman for the faithful—you'll often see a line of people sidling up to touch or kiss his outstretched foot, by now worn to a shiny nub.

Alongside the usual collection of embroidered vestments, gilded chalices, and other bejeweled accouterments of the faith in the **Treasury** (entrance just before the left

---

Papal Audiences

It is possible to the see the pope when you visit the Vatican. If the pope is at home (and has time), he holds a public audience every Wednesday at 11am (sometimes as early as 9am in the heat of summer). This basically means you get to attend a short service performed by the pope, either in the Vatican's large Paolo IV Hall or, when it's really crowded, out on the piazza itself. You need a ticket for this (see below), but not for the brief Sunday noon blessing the pope tosses out his office window to the people thronging Piazza San Pietro below.

Tickets are free, but you must get them ahead of time (before Tuesday would be wise). Apply in person at the Prefecture of the Papal Household (☎ 06/6988-3273), located through the bronze door where the curving colonnade to the right of the church begins on Piazza San Pietro. It's open Monday to Saturday 9am to 1pm. You can also obtain tickets by writing at least two weeks beforehand to Prefettura della Casa Pontifica/Città del Vaticano/00120 ITALIA. Specify your nationality, the number of tickets, and date you'd like (remember: Wednesday only). Mid-July to Mid-September, His Holiness is often cooling his heels at his summer estate Castelgandolfo, so there are few audiences at the Vatican.

---

transept) is the enormous bronze slab tomb of Pope Sixtus IV, cast by early Renaissance master Antonio del Pollaiuolo in 1493 and edged with relief panels personifying the scholarly disciplines.

THE CRYPT   Recessed into that pier with the statue of St. Peter are the steps down to the **Papal Crypt** (aka **Vatican Grottoes**); sometimes the entry is moved to another of the central piers. Along with the tomb chapels of lots of dead popes (plus Queen Christina of Sweden), you get to see 15th-century bronze plaques on the lives of Saints Peter and Paul by Antonio del Pollaiuolo and remaining bits of Constantine's original basilica. See the crypt last, as they usually route you right from this up to the dome, then out onto the piazza, ending your visit.

THE DOME   The last great thing to do at the Vatican is climb (you can ride an elevator for parts of the ascent) **Michelangelo's Dome,** 450 feet from the ground at its top and 138.6 feet in diameter—in deference to the Pantheon, Michelangelo made his dome 5 feet shorter across. From the dome base, you wander a little village of souvenir shops to the backside of the facade for a view over Piazza San Pietro. More stairs lead up to Carlo Maderno's lantern for a fantastic and dizzying ✪ **panorama** of Rome laid out at your feet, sheltered by the huge sky of the Roman campagna. On a clear day, from this perch you can see far beyond the city to the low mountains and countryside beyond.

THE SUBCRYPT   If the Papal Crypt wasn't enough, you can also tour the **subcrypt around St. Peter's tomb,** with tombs and a necropolis dating all the way back to the origins of Christianity. St. Peter was probably martyred in the Circus of Nero, which lies under part of the current St. Peter's, but the actual site of his grave was argued over for centuries. Then excavations in the 1940s uncovered here what many thought was merely a medieval myth: the Red Wall, behind which St. Peter was known to be buried and upon which early Christian pilgrims scratched prayers, invocations, thanks, and "Killroyus was here" in Latin. Sure enough, behind this wall a small pocket of a tomb was found in which doctrine now holds the first pope was buried (however there's no evidence other than circumstantial that the disturbed set of human bones found here

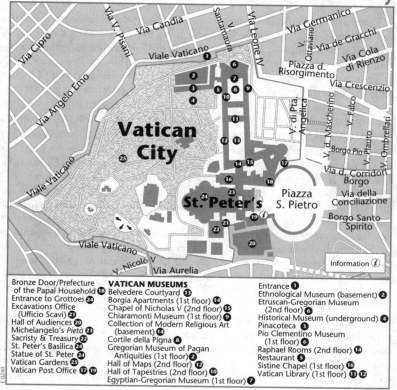

Bronze Door/Prefecture of the Papal Household 18
Entrance to Grottoes 24
Excavations Office (Ufficio Scavi) 21
Hall of Audiences 20
Michelangelo's Pietà 23
Sacristy & Treasury 22
St. Peter's Basilica 24
Statue of St. Peter 24
Vatican Gardens 25
Vatican Post Office 17 19

VATICAN MUSEUMS
Belvedere Courtyard 13
Borgia Apartments (1st floor) 14
Chapel of Nicholas V (2nd floor) 15
Chiaramonti Museum (1st floor) 9
Collection of Modern Religious Art (basement) 14
Cortile della Pigna 8
Gregorian Museum of Pagan Antiquities (1st floor) 2
Hall of Maps (2nd floor) 12
Hall of Tapestries (2nd floor) 10
Egyptian-Gregorian Museum (1st floor) 7

Entrance 1
Ethnological Museum (basement) 2
Etruscan-Gregorian Museum (2nd floor) 6
Historical Museum (underground) 4
Pinacoteca 3
Pio Clementino Museum (1st floor) 6
Raphael Rooms (2nd floor) 14
Restaurant 5
Sistine Chapel (1st floor) 16
Vatican Library (1st floor) 11 12

actually belonged to Heaven's Gatekeeper).

Although renovations are underway in the subcrypt to improve the lighting and climate-control systems in anticipation of the Jubilee 2000 hordes, at least for now the old system holds: The only way to get here is by tour. Apply in advance (4 or 5 days before you plan to visit) at the Ufficio Scavi (☎ 06/6988-5318), through the arch to the left of the stairs up the Basilica. You specify your name, number in your party, language, and dates you'd like to visit. They'll notify you by phone of your admission date and time. Guided tours cost 15,000L ($8.80), audio tours 6,000L ($3.55).

✪ **Vatican Museums & Sistine Chapel.** Vle. Vaticano (on the north side of the Vatican City walls, between where V. Santamaura and the V. Tunisi staircase hit Vle. Vaticano; about a 5–10-min. walk around the walls from St. Peter's). ☎ 06/6988-3333. Admission 15,000L ($8.80) adults, 10,000L ($5.90) students under 26 and kids under 14. Free (but crowded!) last Sun of each month. Apr–June 15 and Sept–Oct Mon–Fri 8:45am–4:30pm, Sat 8:45am–1:45pm. June 16–Aug and Nov–Mar Mon–Sat 8:45am–1:45pm. Last admission 30 min. before closing. Closed: Jan 1 and 6, Feb 11, Easter Mon, May 1, June 29, Aug 15, Nov 1, Dec 8 and 25, and many other religious holidays. Bus: 49 (or tram 19, 23, 32, 49, 51, 64, 81, 492, 907, 982, 990, 991). Metro: Ottaviano.

The Vatican harbors one of the world's greatest museum complexes, a series of some 12 collections and apartments whose highlights include Michelangelo's incomparable Sistine Chapel and the Raphael Rooms. It's a good idea to get up extra early and be at the grand new monumental museum entrance (next door to the old one) before it opens—30 minutes before in summer—or be prepared to wait behind a dozen busloads of tourists.

There are four color-coded itineraries you can follow, depending on your interests and amount of time (it would be impossible to try to see it all in one day). Plan "A" takes about 90 minutes—it shuttles you through the Raphael Rooms to the Sistine—plan "D" takes upwards of 5 hours and hits most of the highlights. To any tour add 30 to 45 minutes for waiting in lines. My suggestion for the best *short* visit (2.5 hours total): Before you hop on the plan "A" route, head to the right when you get to the end of the awning-covered corridor to run quickly (20 to 30 minutes) through the *pinacoteca* (picture gallery), which isn't included on the short itinerary but really should be.

✪ **PINACOTECA (PICTURE GALLERY)**   One of the top painting galleries in Rome shelters Giotto's *Stefaneschi Triptych* (1320), a Perugino *Madonna and Child with Saints* (1496), Leonardo da Vinci's unfinished *St. Jerome* (1482), Guido Reni's *Crucifixion of St. Peter* (1605), and Caravaggio's *Deposition from the Cross* (1604), alongside works from Simone Martini, Pietro Lorenzetti, Gozzoli, Fra' Angelico, Filippo Lippi, Melozzo da Forlì, Pinturicchio, Bellini, Titian, Veronese, and Il Guercino.

But the most famous name here is Raphael, the subject of room VIII, where you'll find his *Coronation of the Virgin* (1503) and *Madonna of Foligno* (1511) surrounded by the Flemish-woven tapestries executed to the master's designs. In the center of the room hangs Raphael's greatest masterpiece, the ✪ *Transfiguration* (1520). This 13.5-foot-high study in color and light was discovered almost finished in the artist's studio when he died suddenly at the age of 37, and mourners carried it through the streets of Rome during his funeral procession.

✪ **STANZE DI RAFFAELLO (RAPHAEL ROOMS)**   Pope Julius II didn't like his predecessor's digs (the Borgia Apartments; see below), so in 1508—just a few months after commissioning Michelangelo to paint the ceiling of the Sistine Chapel down the hall—Julius hired Raphael to decorate these new chambers. As Raphael's fame and commissions grew, he turned more of his attention away from this job and his assistants handled much of the painting in the first and last rooms you visit. But in the Stanza della Segnatura and Stanza d'Eliodoro (the first two actually painted), the master's brush was busy. Since 1993, these frescoes have been under restoration, two walls at a time, but it should all be finished by the time this book hits the shelves (or at least by 2000). The order in which you visit the rooms is also occasionally rearranged.

The first room, the **Stanza dell'Incendio,** was actually the third one painted (1514–17), during the reign of Pope Leo X (also a Raphael fan), which explains why the frescoes detail exploits of previous popes named Leo. The best is the *Borgo Fire,* which swept the neighborhood around the Vatican in A.D. 847 and was extinguished only when Pope Leo IV hurled a blessing at it from his window in the background. The setting, though, is classical, showing Aeneas carrying his jaundiced father, Anchises, and leading his son, Ascanius, as they escape the fall of Troy (eventually, according to Virgil, Aeneas will make it the village started by Romulus and found the city of Rome). Although pupils like Giulio Romano painted most of this fresco, some experts see the master's hand at work in the surprised woman carrying a jug on her head and possibly in the Aeneas group.

The second room is perhaps the highlight, the **Stanza della Segnatura** (1508–11), containing Raphael's famous *School of Athens.* This mythical gathering of the philosophers from across the ages is also a catalog of the Renaissance, with many philosophers actually bearing portraits of Raphael's greatest fellow artists, including his mentor the architect Bramante (on the right as balding Euclid, bent over as he draws on a chalkboard), Leonardo da Vinci (as Plato, the bearded patriarch in the center pointing heavenward), and Raphael himself (looking out at us from the lower right corner next to his white-robed buddy Il Sodoma). In the midst of painting this masterpiece, Raphael took a sneak peek at what his heretofore rival Michelangelo was busy painting on the ceiling of the Sistine Chapel down the hall. He was so impressed that he returned to the *School of Athens* and added in a sulking portrait of Michelangelo (as Heraclitus) sitting on the steps in his stonecutter's boots. It was a true moment of growth for the cocky young master, who realized even he could learn from the genius of another (in fact, he soon adapted his style and color palate, reflecting Michelangelo's influence).

Another important fresco here is the *Disputation of the Sacrament,* with three more portraits. Toward the middle of the right side, half hidden behind a golden-robed church dignitary, stands a dour-looking man in red with a laurel-leaf crown—the Tuscan poet Dante, whose *Inferno* revolutionized Italian literature by using the Tuscan vernacular rather than Latin, and became the basis for the Italian language. Look also on the far left for a pious-looking man in black with just a wisp of white hair remaining—it's a portrait of the monastic painter Fra' Angelico, whose great work in Rome lies just after these rooms. Bramante (again) bends over the railing in front and thumps a book (probably arguing some finer point of architecture).

The third room, the **Stanza di Eliodoro,** was painted from 1510 to 1514. The title fresco, *Heliodorous Expelled from the Temple,* shows the king's lackey trying to carry out orders to steal a Hebrew temple's sacred objects; a heavenly knight appears to help the faithful chase him off while a time-traveling Pope Julius II—a warrior pope whose own battle against enemies of the Church this fresco is metaphorically celebrating— looks on from his litter to the left. There's also the darkly dramatic *Freeing of St. Peter from Prison,* a Renaissance example of using "special effects" (the angel's brilliant glow would be enhanced by the natural light streaming through the window below).

Another scene shows Pope Leo I (bearing Julius II's face) calling forth the armed and floating Saints Peter and Paul in A.D. 452 to scare off a marauding Attila the Hun—the miracle actually happened at Mantua, but Raphael painted a Roman aqueduct and the Colosseum into the background! Pudgy-faced Cardinal Giovanni de' Medici, a Raphael patron and soon-to-be successor to Julius as Pope Leo X, looks on from his horse at the far left.

The Miracle of Bolsena depicts the origin (1264) of the feast of Corpus Christi, when a Bohemian priest who doubted transubstantiation (the miraculous transformation of wafer and wine into the body and blood of Christ) was saying mass in the town of Bolsena and the Eucharist wafer suddenly began to drip blood onto the altar cloth. Attending the scene at the lower right are members of the papal Swiss Guards; this detail provided some of the historical evidence upon which the Guards' current retro-Renaissance outfits are based.

The fourth room, the **Stanza di Constantino** (1517–24), is the least satisfying and was largely painted after Raphael's death according to his hastily sketched designs. Giulio Romano and Rafaellino del Colle adapted some of their master's cartoons into the newly fashionable Mannerist style of painting. They probably did most of the *Battle at the Milvian Bridge* (Emperor Constantine the Great fights his would-be deposer Maxentius), the *Vision of the Cross* (under whose miraculous sign the emperor wins), and the *Donation of Rome* (the now-converted Emperor Constantine gives princely power over Rome to Pope Silvester I), while a less apt pupil of Raphael's finished off the cycle with a weak *Baptism of Constantine.*

BORGIA APARTMENTS/CHAPEL OF NICHOLAS V After visiting the Raphael Rooms' Sala di Constantino, you pop out into the **Sala dei Chiaroscuro,** with a 16th-century wooden ceiling bearing the Medici arms and a little doorway in the corner many people miss and most tour groups skip. Their loss. Through this doorway is the Vatican's most gorgeous hidden corner, the closet-size ✪ **Chapel of Nicholas V** (1447–49), colorfully frescoed floor-to-ceiling with gentle, early Renaissance Tuscan genius by that devout little monk of a painter, Fra' Angelico.

The **Borgia Apartments** downstairs from the Raphael Rooms were occupied by the infamous Spanish Borgia pope Alexander VI, and are now hung with bland pieces of modern art. But the walls and ceilings retain their rich frescoes, painted by Pinturicchio with wacky early Renaissance Umbrian fantasy. A co-pupil of Raphael's under master Perugino, Pinturicchio had a penchant for embedding fake jewels and things like metal saddle studs in his frescoes rather than painting these details in. And while his art is not necessarily at its top form in these rooms, it's worth a run-through. From here you can climb back up and head straight to the Sistine Chapel, or continue downstairs to visit the Modern Art Museum first.

✪ **SISTINE CHAPEL**   The pinnacle of Renaissance painting and masterpiece of Michelangelo covers the ceiling and altar wall of the Sistine Chapel, the grand hall where the College of Cardinals meets to elect a new pope. Photography and talking are not allowed (which is why tour groups clot the long Hall of Maps and Hall of Tapestries leading here as their guides discuss what they're about to see).

Pope Sixtus IV had the Sistine's walls frescoed with scenes from the lives of Moses (left wall) and Jesus (right wall) by the greatest masters of the early Renaissance: Botticelli, Ghirlandaio, Perugino, Pinturicchio, Roselli, and Signorelli. Each of these would be considered a masterpiece in its own right, if they weren't literally overshadowed by the famous ceiling.

Pope Julius II had hired Michelangelo to craft a grand tomb for him, but then pulled the sculptor off the job and asked him instead to decorate the chapel ceiling—which at that time was done in the standard Heavens motif, dark blue with large gold stars. Michelangelo complained that he was a sculptor, not a frescoist, but a papal commission cannot be ignored.

Luckily for the world, Michelangelo was too much of a perfectionist not to put his all into his work, even at tasks he didn't much care for, and he proposed to Julius that he devise a whole fresco cycle for the ceiling rather than just paint "decorations" as the contract called for. At first Michelangelo worked with assistants as was the custom, but soon found that he was not a good team player and fired them all. And so, grumbling and irritable and working solo, he spent 1508 to 1512 daubing at the ceiling, craning his neck, arching his back, with paint dripping in his eyes and an impatient pope looking over his shoulder.

When the frescoes were unveiled, it was clear that they had been worth the wait. Michelangelo had turned the barrel-vaulted ceiling into a veritable blueprint for the further development of Renaissance art, inventing new ways to depict the human body, new designs for arranging scenes, and new uses of light, form, and color that would be embraced by several generations of painters.

The scenes along the middle of the ceiling are taken from the Book of Genesis and tell the stories of Creation (the first six panels) and of Noah (the last three panels, which were actually painted first and with the help of assistants). In thematic order, they are: *Separation of Light from Darkness; Creation of the Sun, Moon, and Planets* (scandalous for showing God's behind and the dirty soles of his feet); *Separation of the Waters from the Land;* the fingers-almost-touching artistic icon of the ✪ *Creation of Adam; Creation of Eve; Temptation and Expulsion from the Garden* (notice how the idealized Adam and Eve in paradise become hideous and haggard as they're booted out of Eden); *The Sacrifice of Noah; The Flood;* and *The Drunkenness of Noah.*

These scenes are bracketed by a painted false architecture to create a sense of deep space (the ceiling is actually nearly flat), festooned with chubby cherubs and 20 *ignudi,* nude male figures reaching and stretching, twisting and turning their bodies to show off their straining muscles and male physiques—Michelangelo's favorite theme. Where the slight curve of the ceiling meets the walls, interrupted by pointed lunettes, Michelangelo ringed the ceiling with Old Testament prophets and ancient Sibyls (sacred fortune-tellers of the classical age in whose cryptic prophecies medieval and Renaissance theologians liked to believe they found specific foretellings of the coming of Christ). The triangular lunettes contain less impressive frescoes of the Ancestors of Christ, and the wider spandrels in each corner depict Old Testaments scenes of salvation.

A lengthy and politically charged cleaning from 1980 to 1990 removed centuries of dirt and smoke satins from the frescoes, although the merits of the restoration are still hotly debated. The techniques used and the amount of grime—and possibly paint—taken off are bones of contention among art historians; some even maintain that later additions, detailing, or shading by Michelangelo were lost during the cleaning.

In 1535, at the age of 60, Michelangelo was called in to paint the entire end wall with a ✪ *Last Judgment,* a masterwork of color, despair, and psychology finished in 1541. The aging master carried on the medieval tradition of representing saints holding the instruments of their martyrdom—St. Catherine carries a section of the spiked wheel with which she was tortured and executed; St. Sebastian clutches some arrows.

Look for St. Bartholomew holding his own skin and the knife used to flay it off. St. Bart's face (actually a portrait of the poet Pietro Aretino) doesn't match that of his skin's. Many hold that the droopy, almost terminally morose face on the skin is a psychological self-portrait of sorts by Michelangelo, known throughout his life to be a sulky, difficult character (and most likely a severe manic-depressive). The master was getting old, Rome had been sacked by barbarians a few years earlier, and both he and the city were undergoing religious crises—not to mention that Michelangelo was weary after years of butting his artistic head against the whims and directives of the Church and various popes who were his patrons.

In the lower right corner is a political practical joke—there's a figure portrayed as Minos, Master of Hell, but it is in reality a portrait of Biagio di Cesena, Master of Ceremonies to the pope and a Vatican bigwig who protested violently against Michelangelo's painting all these shameless nudes here (although some of the figures were partially clothed, the majority of the masses were originally naked). As the earlier Tuscan genius Dante had done to his political enemies in his poetic masterpiece *Inferno,* Michelangelo put Cesena into his own vision of Hell, giving him jackass ears and painting in a serpent eternally biting off his testicles. Furious, Cesena demanded that the pope order the artist to paint his face out, to which Pope Paul III reportedly replied "I might have released you from Purgatory, but over Hell I have no power."

Twenty-three years and several popes later, the voices of prudence (in the form of Pope Pius IV) got their way and one of Michelangelo's protégés, Daniele da Volterra, was brought under protest in to paint bits of cloth draped over the objectionable bits of the nude figures. These loincloths stayed modestly in place until many were removed during a recent and, yes, controversial cleaning that ended in 1994. Some critics of this restoration claim, among other things, that Michelangelo himself

Impressions

Until you have seen the Sistine Chapel, you can have no adequate conception of what man is capable of accomplishing.

—Goethe

A Trip to Another Country

Rome's greatest museum is technically not even in Italy. The Vatican is the world's second smallest sovereign state, a theocracy ruled by the pope with about 1,000 residents (some 550 of whom are Vatican citizens) living on 44 hectares of land. It's been that way ever since the 1929 Lateran Pact with Italy's government. But don't worry, your lire are still good here (though the efficient Vatican post office does use different stamps).

painted some of the cloths on after he was done and that too many were removed; others wanted all of the added draperies stripped from the work. It seems that the compromise, with the majority of figures staying clothes but a few bare bottoms uncovered, pleased nobody.

One thing is for certain. Since the restorations of both the ceiling and the *Last Judgment*, Michelangelo's colors just pop off the wall in warm yellows, bright oranges, soft flesh-tones, and rich greens set against stark white or brilliant azure backgrounds. Many still prefer the dramatic, broodingly somber and muddled tones of the precleaning period. For all the controversy, the revelations provided by the cleanings have forced artists and art historians to reevaluate everything they thought they knew about Michelangelo's color palette, his technique, his painterly skills, and his art.

THE PIO-CLEMENTINO MUSEUM   This is the best of the Vatican's ancient Greek and Roman sculpture collections. In the octagonal Belvedere Courtyard—the original core of the Vatican museums—you'll find the famed *Laocoön* group, a 1st-century B.C. tangle of a man and his two children losing a struggle with giant snakes (their fate for warning the Trojans about the Greeks' tricky wooden horse); and the *Apollo Belvedere,* an ancient Roman copy of a 4th-century B.C. Greek original that for centuries continued to define the ideal male body (as late as the baroque era, a young Bernini was basing his own Apollo in the Borghese Gallery on this one). In the long Room of the Muses you'll find the muscular *Belvedere Torso,* a 1st-century B.C. fragment of another Hercules statue that Renaissance artists like Michelangelo studied to learn how the ancients captured the human physique.

OTHER VATICAN COLLECTIONS   The Vatican has many more museums; it would take months to go through them all. Among them are good collections of **Egyptian, Etruscan, Paleochristian,** and **Ancient Roman artifacts,** including the **Gregorian Musuem of Pagan Antiquities** with a fantastic floor mosaic from an ancient Roman dining room "littered" with banquet leftovers.

The **Modern Religious Art** gallery features papal robes designed by Matisse, while the **Ethnological Museum** covers 3,000 years of history across all continents (the Chinese section is particularly good). There's also a two-hour foot-and-bus tour of the 16th-century **Vatican Gardens.** Book this a day or two in advance at the Vatican Information office to the left of St. Peter's entrance (☎ **06-6988-4466** or 06-6988-4866). Visits generally run at 10am Monday, Tuesday, and Thursday to Saturday; tickets are 18,000L ($10.60.)

Castel Sant'Angelo. Lungotevere Castello. ☎ **06/681-9111.** Admission 8,000L ($4.70) adults, free under 18 and over 60. Tues–Sat 9am–10pm, Sun 9am–8pm. Closed 2nd and 4th Tues of each month. Bus: 32, 34, 49, 87, 70, 186, 280, 492, 913, 926, 990.

Hadrian's massive brick cylindrical tomb was transformed in the Middle Ages into Rome's greatest castle and papal military stronghold (it's still connected to the Vatican by a raised brick viaduct so the Pope could move back and forth in safety).

Today, beyond Hadrian's burial chamber and the original 2nd-century brick-walled spiraling ramp, the castle is a museum with a hodgepodge of exhibits and wonderful **views** of the Tiber and the statue-lined Ponte Sant'Angelo from the ramparts. The collections range from 16th-century ceiling frescoes to a small **arms and armor** museum covering everything from a 6th-century B.C. Etruscan gladiator's helmets to an officer's uniform of 1900, with some deadly swords, daggers, spears, guns, pikes, halberds, and the likes in between. The castle is slowly being transformed into a space for temporary exhibitions.

6 The Forum, Colosseum & Best of Ancient Rome

✪ **Foro Romano (Roman Forum).** V. d. Fori Imperiali (across from the end of V. Cavour), or V. d. Foro Romano (just south of the Campidoglio). ☎ **06/699-0110.** Free admission (only for Forum area; see Palatine listing, below). Apr–Sept Mon–Sat 9am–6pm, Sun 9am–1pm; Oct–Mar Mon–Sat 9am–3pm, Sun 9am–1pm. Bus: 75, 85, 87, 115, 117, 175, 186, 810, 850. Metro: Colosseo.

Slung between the Palatine and Capitoline Hills, the Forum was the cradle of the Roman Republic, a low spot whose buildings and streets became the epicenter of the ancient world. It takes a healthy imagination to turn what are now dusty chunks of architrave jumbled on the ground, crumbling arches, and a few shakily re-erected columns into the glory of Ancient Rome, but this archaeological zone is fun to explore nonetheless. You could wander through in an hour or two, but many people spend 4 or 5 hours and pack a picnic lunch to eat on the Palatine. It gets hot and dusty in August, so visit in the cool morning, wear a brimmed hat, and bring bottled water. You can rent audio guides in English for 7,000L ($4.10); English guided tours set out once daily, usually at 10:45am or noon (call to confirm) and cost 6,000L ($3.55).

The early Etruscan kings drained this swampy lowland, and under Republican rule it became the heart of the city, a public "forum" of temples, administrative halls, orators' podiums, markets, and law courts. There are standing ranks of columns here and there marking the sites of once-important temples and buildings. Much of it means little to those of us who aren't fresh from a class in ancient history, so I'll highlight a few of the more visually spectacular sights.

As you walk down the sloping entrance road, on your left is a medieval church grafted onto and above the **Temple of Antonius & Faustina,** the eight columns still standing free of the church fabric at the top of some steps (it was built in A.D. 141 by Antonius Pius in honor of his late wife, Faustina). Turn right at the bottom of the entrance slope to walk west along the old **Via Sacra,** or "Holy Way" (the Broadway of ancient Rome, down which triumphal military parades and imperial procession marched) toward the arch. Just before the arch on your right is the large brick **Curia** built by Julius Caesar, the main seat of the Roman Senate and remarkably well preserved (partly from being transformed in the Middle Ages into a church; if it's unlocked pop inside to see the marble inlay floor, an A.D. 3rd-century original).

The triumphal **Arch of Septimius Severus** (A.D. 203) displays time-bitten reliefs of the emperor's victories in what are today Iran and Iraq. During the Middle Ages, Rome became a provincial backwater, and frequent flooding of the nearby river helped rapidly bury most of the Forum. This former center of the empire became, of all things, a cow pasture. Some bits of it did still stick out aboveground, including the top half of this arch, which was used to shelter a barbershop! It wasn't until the 19th century that people really became interested in excavating these ancient ruins to see what Rome in its glory must once have been like.

Factoid

Faith aside, there's only a 1-in-365 chance that Jesus was actually born on December 25; part of Christianity's early success was its savvy leaders' ability to graft their new cult on to existing pagan ones, taking things like the popular holiday of *Saturnalia* and making it their own so as to render Christianity more familiar and palatable to potential converts.

Just to the left of the arch you can make out the remains of a cylindrical lump of rock with some marble steps curving off it. That round stone was the **Umbilicus Urbus,** considered the center of Rome and of the entire Roman empire, and the curving steps of the **Imperial Rostra,** where great orators and legislators stood to speak and the people gathered to listen.

Against the back of the Capitoline Hill—the modern building of which is raised upon a foundation of the ancient **Tabularium,** where the ancients stored their State Archives—you'll see the much-photographed trio of fluted columns with Corinthian capitals supporting a bit of architrave to form the corner of the **Temple of Vespasian and Titus** (emperors were routinely turned into gods upon dying).

Start heading to your left toward the eight standing Ionic columns comprising the front and corners to the **Temple of Saturn** (rebuilt 42 B.C.), which housed the first treasury of Republican Rome. It was also where one of the Roman year's biggest annual blowout festivals took place—the December 17 feast of *Saturnalia* which, after a bit of tweaking, we now celebrate as Christmas (see Factoid).

Here you turn left to start heading back east, walking along the Forum's southern side past the worn steps and stumps of brick pillars (19th-century reconstructions) that outline the enormous **Basilica Julia,** built by Julius Caesar. Past it are three standing Corinthian columns of the **Temple of the Dioscuri,** dedicated to the original Gemini twins, Castor and Pollux. Actually, these identical twin gods were part of a fraternal triplet, all born out of the divine egg laid by Leda, whose transformation into a swan didn't do much to dampen Zeus amorous advances. Who was the other triplet? Helen of Troy, a woman so beautiful the ancient Greeks went to war with the Trojans over her.

Beyond the bit of curving wall that marks the site of the little round **Temple of Vesta** (rebuilt several times after fires started by the sacred flame housed within), you'll find the partially reconstructed **House of the Vestal Virgins** (A.D. 3rd to 4th centuries) against the south side of the grounds. This was home to the consecrated young women who tended the sacred flame in the Temple of Vesta. Vestals were young girls selected between ages 6 and 10 from patrician families to serve as priestesses for 30 years. During their tenure they were among Rome's most venerated citizens, with unique powers such as the ability to pardon condemned criminals. The cult of the goddess Vesta was quite serious about the "virgin" part of the job description. If any of Vesta's earthly servants were found to have "misplaced" their virginity, the miscreant Vestal was summarily buried alive. (Her amorous accomplice was merely flogged to death.)

The overgrown rectangle of their gardens has lilied goldfish ponds and is lined with broken, heavily worn statues of senior Vestals on pedestals (and, at any given time when the guards aren't looking, two to six visitors posing as Vestal Virgins on the empty pedestals).

The path now dovetails back to join the Via Sacra at the entrance. Turn right, climbing between some overgrown ruins and medieval additions under the shade

Ancient Rome & Attractions Nearby

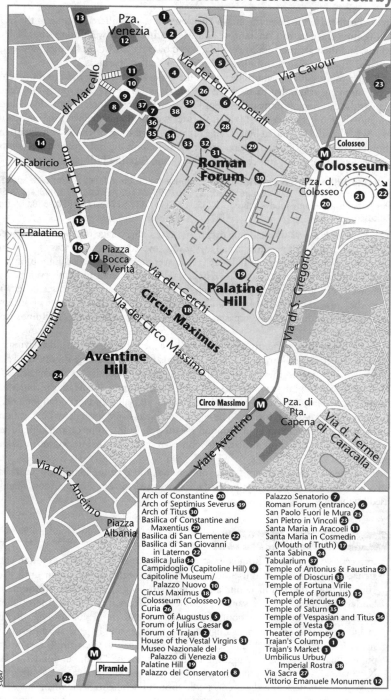

Arch of Constantine **20**
Arch of Septimius Severus **39**
Arch of Titus **30**
Basilica of Constantine and
  Maxentius **29**
Basilica di San Clemente **22**
Basilica di San Giovanni
  in Laterno **22**
Basilica Julia **34**
Campidoglio (Capitoline Hill) **9**
Capitoline Museum/
  Palazzo Nuovo **10**
Circus Maximus **18**
Colosseum (Colosseo) **21**
Curia **26**
Forum of Augustus **5**
Forum of Julius Caesar **4**
Forum of Trajan **2**
House of the Vestal Virgins **31**
Museo Nazionale del
  Palazzo di Venezia **13**
Palatine Hill **19**
Palazzo dei Conservatori **8**

Palazzo Senatorio **7**
Roman Forum (entrance) **6**
San Paolo Fuori le Mura **25**
San Pietro in Vincoli **23**
Santa Maria in Aracoeli **11**
Santa Maria in Cosmedin
  (Mouth of Truth) **17**
Santa Sabina **24**
Tabularium **37**
Temple of Antonius & Faustina **28**
Temple of Dioscuri **33**
Temple of Fortuna Virile
  (Temple of Portunus) **15**
Temple of Hercules **16**
Temple of Saturn **35**
Temple of Vespasian and Titus **36**
Temple of Vesta **32**
Theater of Pompey **14**
Trajan's Column **1**
Trajan's Market **3**
Umbilicus Urbus/
  Imperial Rostra **38**
Via Sacra **27**
Vittorio Emanuele Monument **12**

trees, then head left to enter the massive brick remains and coffered ceilings of the A.D. 4th-century **Basilica of Constantine and Maxentius**. These were Rome's public law courts, and their architectural style was adopted by early Christians for their houses of worship (the reason so many ancient churches are called "basilicas").

Return to the path and continue toward the Colosseum, veering right to the second great surviving triumphal arch, the **Arch of Titus** (A.D. 81), on which one relief depicts the carrying off of treasures from Jerusalem's temple—look close and you'll see a menorah among the booty. This arch glorifies the war that ended with the expulsion of Jews from the colonized Judea, signaling the beginning of the Jewish Diaspora throughout Europe. From here you can enter and climb the only part of the Forum archaeological zone that still charges admission, the **Palatine Hill** (see below).

Palatine Hill & Museo Palatino. Main entrance inside the Roman Forum (see above); second entrance at V. di S. Gregorio 30. ☎ **06/699-0110.** Admission 12,000L ($7.05). Hours same as Forum (above). Bus: 75, 85, 87, 115, 117, 175, 186, 810, 850. Metro: Colosseo.

The Palatine Hill was where Rome began as a tiny Latin village (supposedly founded by Romulus) in the 8th century B.C. Later it was covered with the palaces of patrician families and the early emperors. Today it's an overgrown, tree-shaded hilltop of gardens and fragments of ancient villas that few visitors bothered to climb even before there was a charge for admission. As such, it can make for a romantic, scenic escape from the crowds, a place where you can wander across the grassy floors of ancient palaces and peer down the gated passageways that were once the homes of Rome's rich and famous.

In 1998, the **Museo Palatino** up here finally reopened after 13 years, displaying an excellent collection of Roman sculpture and finds from the ongoing digs in the Palatine villas. In summer, there are guided tours in English Monday to Sunday at noon for 6,000L ($3.55); call in winter to see if they're still running. If you ask the museum's custodian, he may take you to one of the nearby locked villas and let you in for a peek at surviving frescoes and stuccoes. The entire Palatine is slated for renewed excavations and a general prettying up in preparation for the year 2000, so be on the lookout for many areas to be roped off at first, but soon even more than before will open to the public.

From the Palatine's southern flank, you can look out over the long grassy oval that was the **Circus Maximus,** where Ben-Hur types used to race chariots (now mainly used by joggers).

Seeing the Sights at Night

In recent years, some of Rome's most popular (and newly renovated) monuments, archaeological sites, and museums have not only begun staying open until 8 or 10pm during the summer, but also begun engaging in "**Art and Monuments Under the Stars,**" special summer schedules wherein they reopen one or more nights a week for evening hours from around 8:30 to 11:30pm. The offering include guided tours (often in English), concerts, or simply general admission to sights for night owls, including tours of some ancient sites usually closed to the public, like the Tomb of Augustus or the Stadium of Domitian (under Piazza Navona). This is a developing phenomenon, so I can't give you many specifics, but keep your eyes peeled in the events guides from mid-June to September.

(say yes)

u pop the question in Paris, you better have an **AT&T Direct**® Service wallet guide in your pocket. It's a list of access

numbers you need to call home fast and clear from around the world, using an AT&T Calling Card or credit card.

So you can give everyone back home a ring.

For a list of **AT&T Access Numbers,** take the attached wallet guide.

I t ' s   a l l   w i t h i n   y o u r   r e a c h .

◑ Colosseo (The Colosseum). Pz. d. Colosseo. ☎ **06/700-4261.** Admission 10,000L ($5.90); free under 18 and over 60. Summer Mon–Sat 9am–6pm, Sun 9am–1pm; winter daily 9am–3pm. Metro: Colosseo. Bus: tram 30/, 75, 81, 85, 87, 117, 175, 186, 673, 810, 850.

This wide, majestic oval with the broken-tooth profile is the world's most famous sports arena, even though it's been well over 1,500 years since gladiators battled with exotic wild beasts and fought each other to the death. Since then, the most impressive aspect of the Colosseum has been viewing it from afar, admiring that unmistakable silhouette, symbol of Rome itself, as you walk up Via dei Fori Imperiali. I warn you, though, the Colosseum fell into disuse as the empire waned, earthquakes caused considerable damage, and later generations used its stones and marble cladding as a mine of precut building materials.

The interior of the Colosseum was always a bit disappointing, and is even more so now that there's a hefty admission price. The seats are gone, as is the wooden floor, making it look like a series of nested broken eggshells of crumbling brick, littered with lazing cats and cupping a maze of walls in the center that once supported the floor (these walls mark the corridors and holding pens for the animals, equipment, and gladiators).

The Colosseum has also become the turnstile for Rome's largest traffic circle, around which thousands of cars whip daily, spewing exhaust all over this venerable monument. Until close to the year 2000, parts of the exterior will remain swathed in scaffolding as workers attempt to scrape off this black patina of pollution. Ambitious plans are also underway to rebuild 500 square meters of the flooring and install an elevator to allow visitors to explore more fully the interior by 2002. For now, you can rent an audio guide for 7,000L ($4.10), or take an English guided tour Monday to Sunday (six daily).

Started in A.D. 70 on the filled-in site of one of Nero's artificial fish ponds, this grand amphitheater was the "bread and circus" of the Roman Empire, an arena of blood and gore to amuse 50,000 of the masses at a time—the inaugural contest in A.D. 80 lasted 100 days and killed off 5,000 beasts and countless gladiators. These contests eventually drove to extinction several creatures, including the Middle Eastern lion and North African elephant.

As for man-to-man (or woman) combat, professional gladiators were young men who, either poor or ruined, slaves or criminals, were lured by the promise of prize riches to sell themselves into a kind of slavery to the trainers and lead brutish, dangerous lives. If a gladiator was seriously wounded but not mortally, he stretched out on the ground and raised his left arm for mercy. The victor then decided his opponent's fate, but when the emperor was around, he made the call, giving us a gesture we still use today. Gauging the crowd's reaction, he judged whether to spare the loser by flashing the thumbs up signal, or give the order to finish him off by gesturing thumbs down. The only release from gladiatorial life was death in the ring or the granting by the emperor of the *rudis,* a wooden sword that signaled a dignified, well-earned retirement from the games.

Architecturally, the Colosseum is a poster child for classical order, built of three levels of arcades whose niches were once filled with statues and whose columns became more ornate with each level, following the Greek order of Doric, Ionic, and Corinthian respectively. A fourth level, plainer in design, supported an apparatus of pulleys, beams, and canvas that created a retractable roof, winced out by a specially trained troupe of sailors to shade the seats from sun and rain (Astrodome, eat your heart out).

Standing next to the Colosseum is the **Arch of Constantine,** one of the largest of Rome's ancient triumphal arches, celebrating Emperor Constantine the Great's A.D. 312 victory over Maxentius at the Milvian Bridge. Though the arch's reliefs were primarily pirated from earlier sites and make no mention of the battle itself, it was perhaps one of the most significant of all ancient Rome's wars. It was during this battle that the emperor asked for a sign from the gods favoring him and had a vision of a Cross. After winning his battle, Constantine dutifully converted himself—and later the Roman Empire—to Christianity.

Imperial Fori. V. d. Fori Imperiali/V. Alessandrina. No Admission. Bus: 75, 85, 87, 117, 175, 186, 850. Metro: Colosseo.

As late Republican Rome grew into the metropolis of the Empire, the growing population began to crowd the public buildings and temples of the Roman Forum. A succession of leaders and emperors, starting with Julius Caesar, began building new forums and markets east of the original Forum in ambitious bouts of urban expansion that provided for the populace, curried favor with the elite, and improved the city infrastructure all at once. Much of this area is still only visible from above on the sidewalk as you walk past, but the Markets of Trajan (see below) are now open, and plans are afoot to create a much larger archaeological park that will link the entire area together.

The **Forum of Caesar** is the only one on the west side of Via dei Fori Imperiali, tucked between the Vittorio Emanuele monument, the Capitoline, and the Roman Forum. It was the first of these new fori, built by Julius Caesar in the 1st century B.C. The popular general (with his eye on the dictatorship) used the money he made during his successful Gaulish wars to buy up all the private property flanking the Roman Forum at this spot, tear down the houses, and build public temples and markets in their stead. Those three standing Corinthian columns belonged to his self-serving Temple to Venus Genetrix, a goddess from whom Caesar claimed direct descent through Rome's legendary founder Aeneas.

Walking from the Colosseum north and branching onto Via Alessandrina, the first major forum on your right is the **Forum of Augustus.** The stairs and column stumps in the center once belonged to the 2nd-century B.C. Temple of Mars Ultor. When it's open, you can follow a catwalk running along the forum's edge to get a better view. More dramatic are the next set of ruins, the **Markets of Trajan** and, across Via Alessandrina, **Trajan's Forum,** both now open to the public and reviewed separately below.

Markets of Trajan/Trajan's Forum. V. IV Novembre 94 (at the end of V. Nazionale). ☎ 06/679-0048. Admission 3,750L ($2.20) adults, 2,500L ($1.50) students, free under 18 and over 60. Free last Sun of each month. Summer Tues–Sat 9am–6:30pm, Sun 9am–1:30pm; winter Mon–Sun 9am–4pm. Bus: 64, 70, 170, 640.

The Emperor Trajan built his **markets** in the A.D. 2nd century, and after being closed for years they've become the first of the Imperial Fori to reopen to the public (in 1998). You enter around the back side (on Via IV Novembre), into a grand bazaar hall lined by former market stalls with marble porticos and barrel-vaulted ceilings. These now contain informative placards (in English) on each of the Imperial Fori plus some sculptural bits—most just fragments, but a few with remarkably sharp and well-preserved detailing.

You get to wander the brief but evocative sections of the most intact ancient Roman streets in the city, clamber up to the top terrace for a bird's eye panorama of the curving market and forums of Trajan and Caesar across the street, and explore the four stories of 150 empty *tabernae* (shops) that made up the world's first multilevel shopping mall.

When it's open, you can also duck through a tunnel that leads under Via de Fori Imperiali to **Trajan's Forum** (if the tunnel's closed, you can still see it well from the road. This site is marked by several rows of re-erected columns that comprised merely the central part of the huge Basilica Ulpia, Rome's largest basilican law courts. Behind them rises the Imperial Fori's most stunning sight, the 98-foot ✪ **Trajan's Column,** today topped by a 16th-century statue of St. Peter. Around the column wraps a cartoon strip of deep relief carvings that would measure some 660 feet if stretched out. It uses a cast of 2,500 to tell the story of Trajan's victorious A.D. 101–06 campaigns to subdue the Dacians (modern-day Romania). A spiral staircase inside leads to the top (closed), and the emperor's ashes were kept in a golden urn entombed at the base. It's hard to see the carvings well (casts are kept at the Museo della Civiltà Romana; see "The Aventine & South" below), but you can get a better glimpse from the street level.

✪ **Pantheon.** Pz. d. Rotonda. ☎ **06/6830-0230.** Admission free. Mon–Sat 9am–6:30pm, Sun 9am–1pm. Bus: 116; H, tram 8, 46, 56, 60, 62, 64, 70, 75, 81, 87, 115, 186, 492, 628, 640.

"Simple, erect, severe, austere, sublime..." That's the poet Byron groping for words to capture the magic and power of Rome's best-preserved ancient building, a "pantheon," or temple to all the gods. This may sound strange, but it's the empty space inside that makes the Pantheon so awe-inspiring, an architectural achievement like no other. Emperor (and accomplished architect) Hadrian built it in the early 2nd century A.D., and his engineering skills allowed him to create a mathematically exacting and gravity-defying space inside. (Hadrian constructed the Pantheon over a previous temple erected by the general Marcus Agrippa, but modestly kept the dedicatory inscription from Agrippa on the architrave of the monumental porch's pediment.)

The bronze entrance doors—1,800-year-old originals—weigh 20 tons each. The interior is circular and the entire coffered ceiling a perfect half-sphere of a dome, with an 18-foot oculus, or eye, in the center that lets sunlight and rain stream in. The dome is 143 feet across and the building 143 feet high—in other words, if you could find a basketball big enough, it would fit perfectly in this space. Such an engineering marvel remained unduplicated until the Renaissance, and it was only relatively recently that that Hadrian's secrets were revealed. For one thing, the roof is made of poured concrete (a Roman invention) composed of light pumice stone, and the weight of it, rather than bearing down, is distributed by brick arches embedded sideways into the fabric of the walls and channeled into a ring of tension around the lip of that oculus. It also helps that the walls are 25 feet thick.

The decoration is spare, but includes the tombs of Italy's short-lived 19th-century monarchical dynasty (three kings total, only two are here), and that of the painter Raphael. The Pantheon has survived the ages because it was left alone by the barbarians, who recognized its beauty, and by zealous, temple-destroying Christians, who reconsecrated it as a church in 609. Later Christians weren't as charitable. When Pope Urban VIII, a prince of the Barberini family, removed the bronze tiles from the portico and melted them down to make 80 cannons and the baldacchino in St. Peter's, it prompted one local wit to quip, "What even the barbarians wouldn't do, Barberini did." Interestingly enough, as a church it is dedicated to Santa Maria ad Martyres, or Saint Mary of the Martyrs—and since the martyrs are the saints, and the saints (especially here in the Catholic Mediterranean) are the "gods" of Christianity, it's *still* a temple to "all the gods."

7 Attractions Near Ancient Rome

Musei Capitolini (Capitoline Museums)/Capitoline Hill. Pz. d. Campidoglio. ☎ **06/ 6710-2071.** Admission (covers both museums) 10,000L ($5.90) adults, 5,000L ($2.95) students, free under 18 and over 60. Admission is free (and crowded) the last Sun of the month. Tues–Sun 9am–7pm. Bus: 44, 56, 60, 70, 75, 81, 87, 95, 160, 170, 628, 640, 715, 716, 780, 810.

The **Capitoline Hill,** behind Piazza Venezia's Vittorio Emanuele monument, has been the administrative seat of Rome's civic government since the 11th century, and was a highly venerated spot used for the highest of state occasions in ancient Republican Rome. The trapezoidal **Piazza del Campidoglio** at its top, reached by a long set of low sloping steps meant to accommodate carriages, was laid out by an elderly Michelangelo, who also designed the palace facades on its three sides. It is one of Rome's most unified open spaces and a prime example of High Renaissance ideals in aesthetics, architecture, and spatial geometry by one of the era's great masters. It's centered on a copy of the A.D. 2nd-century bronze equestrian statue of Marcus Aurelius, his outstretched hand seeming to bless the city of Rome (the original's in the Palazzo Nuovo, below). The central **Palazzo Senatorio** houses the Mayor's office; the side palaces house two of Rome's top museums.

On the left, you have the **Palazzo Nuovo,** filled with ancient sculpture like the *Dying Gaul,* busts of ancient philosophers, the *Mosaic of the Doves,* and the original horseback statue of Marcus Aurelius (the regilded bronze statue had been tossed into the Tiber, and when Christians later fished it out, they mistakenly thought it was Constantine the Great, the first Christian emperor, a misinterpretation that saved it from being hacked to pieces). **Note:** As this book went to press, this part of the museum was closed for renovations until sometime in the year 2000.

But if you only have time for one museum, make it the one on the right, the **Palazzo dei Conservatori.** The entrance is to the left of a courtyard filled with the oversized marble head, hands, foot, arm, and kneecap of what was once a 40-foot-high colossal statue of Constantine II. The collections have their share of antique statuary—including the A.D. 1st-century *Spinario,* a little bronze boy picking a thorn out of his foot, and the Etruscan bronze *She-Wolf,* crafted in the late 6th century B.C. (the suckling toddlers were added in the 16th century; see Factoid below)—but the paintings are the stars. The upstairs gallery houses works by Guercino, Veronese, Titian, Rubens, Pietro da Cortona, and two by Caravaggio—the *Gypsy Fortune Teller* and the scandalously erotic *St. John the Baptist,* where the young, nubile saint twists to embrace a ram and looks out at us coquettishly.

Santa Maria in Aracoeli. V. d. Teatro di Marcello (up many steps, between Pz. Venezia's VEII Monument and Pz. d. Campidoglio). ☎ **06/679-8155.** Admission free. Daily 7am–noon, 3:30–5:30pm. Bus: 44, 56, 60, 70, 75, 81, 87, 95, 160, 170, 628, 640, 715, 716, 780, 810.

Travel Tip

Standing on Piazza del Campidoglio, walk around the right side of Palazzo Senatorio to a terrace that overlooks the city's best panorama of the Roman Forum, with the Palatine Hill and the Colosseum as a backdrop. Return to the square and walk around the left side of the Palazzo Senatorio and you'll find a stair that winds down past the Forum wall, passing close by the upper half of the Arch of Septimius Severus, and then out around to the Forum's main entrance—a nifty little shortcut.

Factoid

Rome was legendarily founded by twin brothers, Romulus and Remus, who had been abandoned in the woods and raised by a she-wolf. Romulus later quarreled with and killed Remus à la Cain and Abel—which is why you're visiting Rome and not Reme—but that heroic she-wolf with the overactive motherly instincts became the most famous of the trio, and since ancient times has been the symbol of Rome and all it stands for.

Santa Maria in Aracoeli is an ancient church, old when it was first mentioned in the 7th century, but its current incarnation dates from the Franciscans and A.D. 1250. Legend holds that the Tiburtine Sibyl told Emperor Augustus that on this lofty spot would be an "altar to the first among gods," whereupon the emperor had a vision of the heavens opening up and a woman bearing a child in her arms alight on the hilltop. Augustus dutifully built an *arcoeli*, or "Altar in the Sky" up here, but Christians later interpreted the prophecy as a reference to their God and replaced it with a church.

Past the unfinished facade of rough brick is a Romanesque interior hung with chandeliers and slightly baroqued, but retaining a Cosmatesque pavement and 22 mismatched antique columns recycled from pagan buildings. The elegant wood ceiling is carved with naval emblems and motifs to commemorate the great naval victory at Lepanto (1571). The worn tomb of Giovanni Crivelli to the right of the door was cast by Donatello, and the first chapel on the right was frescoed by Umbrian Renaissance master Pinturicchio, one of his greatest masterpieces.

To the left of the altar with its 10th-century *Madonna d'Aracoeli* painting, is the chapel that once housed a highly venerated statue of the baby Jesus called the *Santo Bambino,* supposedly carved from an olive tree in the Garden of Gethsemane and imbued with miraculous powers to heal the sick (he spent half his time making the rounds of Rome's hospitals to visit the sickbeds of the terminally ill), and answer the prayers of children. The Bambino received thousands of letters from around the world every year—most addressed simply "Santo Bambino, Roma"—which were left in his chapel, unopened, until they were burned so the prayers in them could waft heavenward. Roman children came to recite little speeches or sing poetry in front of the holy little statue, especially at Christmastime. The *Santo Bambino* was stolen in 1994.

Santa Maria in Cosmedin/Mouth of Truth. Pz. Bocca d. Verità 18. ☎ **06/678-1419.** Admission free. Church daily 10am–1pm, 3–5pm; portico (containing Mouth of Truth) daily 10am–5pm (in summer they *sometimes* leave the gates open as late as 8pm for tourists). Bus: H, 23, 44, 81, 95, 170, 160, 280, 628, 715, 716, 810.

At the western foot of the Palatine Hill sit two small 2nd-century B.C. temples—the square **Temple of Portunus** and the round **Temple of Hercules Victor,** the oldest marble structure surviving in Rome—and **Santa Maria in Cosmedin,** with its early 12th-century bell tower and Cosmatesque floors.

But it's the front porch of this church that draws the crowds to stick their hands inside the **Mouth of Truth,** a 4th-century B.C. sewer cover carved as a bearded face with a dark slot for a mouth. Medieval legend holds it that if you stick your hand in its mouth and tell a lie, it will clamp down on your fingers (apparently, a priest once added some sting to this belief by hiding behind the Mouth with a scorpion, dispensing justice as he saw fit).

Up Via di Teatro Marcello from the piazza out front you can see the outer wall of what looks like a midget Colosseum with a 16th-century palace grafted atop its curve.

This was actually the model for the Colosseum, the **Teatro di Marcello,** built by Augustus in 11 B.C. and dedicated to his nephew Marcellus.

San Pietro in Vincoli (St. Peter in Chains). Pz. S. Pietro in Vincoli 4 (just south of Pz. Cavour). ☎ **06/488-2865.** Admission free. Daily 7am–12:30pm, 3:30–6pm. Metro: Cavour. Bus: 75, 115, 117.

Besides the chains that supposedly once bound St. Peter in prison (now on display under the altar), this 5th-century church with the Renaissance portico facade is famous for containing one of Michelangelo's greatest masterpieces—and one of his most bitter failures. In 1505, Pope Julius II commissioned Michelangelo to create for him a monumental tomb, and the master came up with a grandiose mausoleum festooned with 40 statues. The pope sent the sculptor off to the mountains of Carrara to search for marble, but when Michelangelo returned Julius set him to work painting the Sistine Chapel ceiling instead.

Doggedly trying to continue work on the tomb over the next several decades, Michelangelo kept reducing his plans as other projects took up his time and the descendants of Julius squabbled over how much they would invest in a tomb for their late, illustrious relative. The master managed to finish two *Slaves*, which now reside in the Louvre in Paris, and roughed out five more, now in Florence's Accademia Gallery. He also crafted one of the grand figures who was to sit above our heads at the corners of the tomb, a muscle-bound ✪ *Moses* with satyrs horns in his head (symbolizing the holy rays of light from medieval iconography), the Commandments tablets clutched in one hand, and a portrait of Michelangelo hiding in Moses' flowing beard.

And that's pretty much all poor old Julius got in the end. This (relatively) modest wall monument, with a few other niched statues, was mostly executed by Michelangelo's assistants (though the master probably had a hand in the more delicate Rachel and Leah figures flanking Moses). In a final twist of fate, this is a monument only, not a tomb. Julius himself lies buried and forgotten in an unassuming grave in a corner of the Vatican.

Basilica di San Clemente. V. San Giovanni in Laterano/V. Labicana 95. ☎ **06/7045-1018.** Admission to church free; 4,000L ($2.35) to excavations. Mon–Sat 9am–12:30pm, 3:30–6pm; Sun 10am–12:30pm, 3:30–6pm. Bus: 30/, 85, 87, 117, 186, 810, 850. Metro: Colosseo.

Nowhere else in this city is the layering effect of Rome's history more evident than in this 12th-century church built atop a 4th-century church built atop a late 2nd-century pagan temple. This situation is far from unique in Rome—almost the entire city is built directly on top of the ancient one—but what's special about San Clemente is that you can actually clamber down into those lower levels to explore Rome's sandwich of history.

Even without that, the **upper church**—built in 1108 and run by the convent of Irish Dominican monks who rediscovered the lower levels in the 19th century—is beautiful enough to stand out on its own. It features a pre-Cosmatesque pavement, ornate marble choir (a 6th- to 9th-century piece that came from the lower church), recently restored frescoes of the *Life of St. Catherine* (1228) by Masolino and his young disciple Masaccio in the first chapel on your right, and a 12th-century mosaic filling the apse with a *Triumph of the Cross.* This shows a crucified Christ in the center with the Tree of Life growing in twisting vine tendrils all around, loaded with medieval symbolism (Christ and the Apostles pose as sheep along the bottom, the Rivers of Paradise flow from the base of the cross from which the faithful, represented by stags, drink, doves flutter about, and the Hand of God reaches down from the canopy of the Heavens).

Off the right aisle is a postcard-lined passageway and the entrance down to the **lower church,** built in the 4th century and largely demolished by Barbarian sackings in 1084. It preserves a few crude frescoes, including the *Life of St. Clement* on the wall before you enter the nave and the *Story of St. Alexis* on the left wall of the nave itself. After you've had your fill of this Dark Ages church, you can descend another flight of stairs to the ancient pagan **Mithraic temple** and adjacent **Roman** *palazzo* of the A.D. 1st century. Both later church's altars are placed directly above this pagan one to Mithras, which depicts the god sacrificing a bull. As you wander in and out of the brick vaulted rooms of Flauvius Clemens grand palazzo, you'll hear the sound of rushing water, and in one room you can even take a drink from the sweet spring water gushing out of an ancient pipeline to be routed along a small aqueduct set into the wall.

Basilica di San Giovanni in Laterano (Saint John Lateran). Pz. S. Giovanni in Laterano. ☎ **06/6988-6433.** Admission free. Daily 7am–5:45pm. Bus: 16, tram 30/, 81, 85, 87, 117, 186, 218, 650, 850. Metro: S. Giovanni.

The cathedral of Rome (St. Peter's is merely a holy basilica on Vatican property) is oddly one of the least interesting of the city's grand churches. San Giovanni in Laterano has an illustrious history—founded by Constantine himself as the first Christian basilica in Rome in A.D. 314, and the model for all Christian basilicas—but after going through some seven cycles of destruction and rebuilding (due to fires, earthquakes, barbarians, or simple wholesale remodeling), today's basilica is primarily a Borromini construction of the 1640s—and even parts of that were destroyed and are currently being restored after a 1993 bombing.

The massive facade by Alessandro Galilei is made of stacked porticoes with a line of colossal saints, apostles, and Christ standing along the top. The gargantuan interior (230 feet long) has a unified decorative scheme designed by Borromini and a fine medieval Cosmatesque floor. On the aisle side of the first pillar on the right is a fresco by the proto-Renaissance genius Giotto (all that survives of a series of frescoes the master painted here in the early 14th century). The scene shows Boniface VIII proclaiming the first Jubilee Holy Year on this spot in 1300. The cloisters off the left transept are a peaceful oasis amid the bustle of Rome, a quadrangle of twisty columns inlaid with Cosmati stoneworks and the walls lined with fragments from earlier incarnations of this cathedral.

8 Attractions Around Campo de' Fiori & the Jewish Ghetto

Campo de' Fiori. Just south of Cor. Vittorio Emanuele II. Bus: 116, 116T.

Once a meadow (campo) filled with flowers (fiori), this piazza, surrounded by tall medieval buildings, is a veritable theater of life. In 1869 the fresh produce market moved here from Piazza Navona, and it continues to fill the square every morning with a colorful collage of sun-beaten canvas awning shading piles of fruits, vegetables, cheeses, and flowers. Between the raising of the buildings in the 15th century and the residency of the marketplace, though, the square did dark duty as an execution site. The bronze statue of a grim Giordano Bruno scowling under his cowl reminds us that even a great Renaissance philosopher such as he was not safe from persecution—this is where he was burned at the stake for heresy in 1600.

Largo di Torre Argentina. Bus: H, tram 8, 46, 56, 60, 62, 64, 70, 81, 87, 115, 186, 492, 628, 640.

The center of one of Rome's busiest intersections is sunk a good 15 feet below the street to what was ground level in ancient Roman times. Umbrella pines shade the remains of three small Republican-era temples around which hundreds of cats hide like Easter eggs among the grasses. Behind the circular one (on the western, Via di Torre Argentina side) is a jumble of brick walls and podium that belonged to Pompey's Curia. This was likely the spot (or close enough) where Julius Caesar was exiting that building when Brutus and the other conspirators approached Caesar and stabbed him to death.

9 Attractions Near Piazza Navona & the Pantheon

Note that this neighborhood's greatest sight, the Pantheon, is covered under "The Forum, Colosseum & Best of Ancient Rome," above.

✪ **Piazza Navona.** North of Cor. V. Emanuele II. Bus: 46, 62, 64, 70, 81, 87, 115, 116, 116T, 186, 492, 628.

Closed to traffic, studded with fountains, lined with cafes, and filled with tourists, street performers, artists, kids playing soccer, and couples smooching on benches, Piazza Navona is one of Rome's archetypal open spaces. It's also one of the best places to kick back and relax in the heart of the city. The piazza owes its long, skinny, round-ended shape to the **Stadium of Domitian,** which lies mostly unexcavated underneath (though you can see one travertine entrance arch from the north curve of the stadium buried under a bank on Piazza di Tor Sanguigna, just outside the piazza).

The **Fountain of the Moor** on the piazza's south end was designed by Giacomo della Porta (1576), the **Fountain of the Neptune** at the north end by Antonio della Bitta and Gregorio Zappalà (1878), and the soaring ✪ **Fountain of Four Rivers** in the center by Gianlorenzo Bernini (1651). This last is a roiling masterpiece of rearing mer-horses, sea serpents, and muscle-bound figures topped by an obelisk. The giant figures at the four corners represent the world's four great rivers (or at least those known in the 1650s): the Danube (Europe), the bearded Ganges (Asia), the bald Plate (Americas), and the Nile (Africa, shrouding his head since the source of the Nile was unknown at the time). Borromini's curvaceous facade of **Sant'Agnese in Agone** church rises next to the fountain, and tour guides love to tell the legend that Bernini carved a slight to Borromini in the figure of Plate, rearing back and throwing his arm up as a guard against the church facade falling on him. While it's true that the two architects were archrivals, the facade was started in 1653—2 years after Bernini finished the fountain.

The stadium's tradition as a place for chariot races and games was kept alive throughout the ages with medieval jousts, Renaissance festivals, and the 17th- to 19th-century practice of flooding it on August weekends for the populace to wade and the nobles to parade around on the shallow pools in their carriages. It was a market from 1477 to 1869, and for ages has hosted a Christmastime fair selling traditional crèche figurines and statues along with toys and dolls of the Christmas Witch *La Befana*, who traditionally brings Italian children presents on January 6.

✪ **Santa Maria Sopra Minerva.** Pz. d. Minerva (southeast of the Pantheon). ☎ **06/ 679-3926.** Admission free. Daily 7am–noon, 4–7pm. Bus: 116; H, tram 8, 46, 56, 60, 62, 64, 70, 81, 87, 115, 186, 492, 628, 640.

Rome's only Gothic church was built in 1280 over the site of a Temple to Minerva (hence the name "St. Mary Over Minerva"). The piazza out front sports a whimsical statute by Bernini of a **baby elephant** carrying a miniature Egyptian obelisk on its back (1667). The interior was heavily restored in the 19th century, and contains some

Attractions Near Campo de' Fiori & Piazza Navona

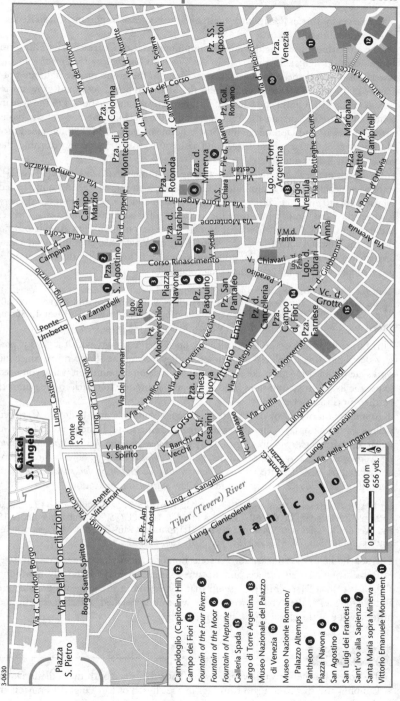

Campidoglio (Capitoline Hill) 12
Campo dei Fiori 14
Fountain of the Four Rivers 5
Fountain of the Moor 6
Fountain of Neptune 3
Galleria Spada 15
Largo di Torre Argentina 13
Museo Nazionale del Palazzo di Venezia 10
Museo Nazionale Romano/ Palazzo Altemps 1
Pantheon 8
Piazza Navona 6
San Agostino 2
San Luigi dei Francesi 4
Sant' Ivo alla Sapienza 7
Santa Maria sopra Minerva 9
Vittorio Emanuele Monument 11

3-0630

159

masterpieces by Tuscan Renaissance artists and the bodies of important Tuscan Renaissance personalities.

The last chapel on the right retains a sumptuous cycle of ✪ **frescoes** by **Filippino Lippi** (coin-op lights). In the scene of *St. Thomas Condemning the Heretics* on the lower half of the chapel's right wall, the two boys in the group on the right are portraits of Giovanni de' Medici and Giulio de' Medici. These two would grow up to become Pope Leo X and Pope Clement VII, respectively, and are buried in the apse in tombs by Antonio Sangallo the Younger. Under the altar lies the body of the pious medieval activist and Dominican nun St. Catherine of Siena (1347–80), a skilled theologian and diplomat whose letters and visits were instrumental in returning the papacy from Avignon to Rome.

To the left of the altar steps is ✪ **Michelangelo's** muscular *Risen Christ* (1514–21), leaning nonchalantly on a diminutive Cross (such a strong, virile, and quite naked Christ wasn't to everyone's taste, and the church later added a sweep of bronze drapery to cover the Lord's loins). In a corridor to the left of the choir, behind a small fence, is the tomb slab of the early Renaissance master and devout monk **Fra' Angelico,** who died in the attached convent in 1455. Pope Nicholas V, who had commissioned a Vatican chapel from the painter 10 years earlier and was touched by the little monk's piety, modesty, and skill, wrote the epitaph himself.

Galleria Doria-Pamphilj. Pz. d. Collegio Romano 1A (off V. d. Cor. near Pz. Venezia). ☎ **06/679-7323.** Admission 13,000L ($7.65) adults, 9,000L ($5.30) students and over 60; tour of apts. 5,000L ($2.95). Gallery Fri–Wed 10am–5pm; Apts. Fri–Wed 10:30am–12:30pm. Closed Aug 15–31. Bus: 56, 60, 62, 81, 85, 95, 117, 160, 175, 492, 628, 850.

This formerly private art collection is now open to the public, with the layout preserved and paintings displayed more or less as they were in the 19th century. Since the works are jumbled together like a giant jigsaw puzzle on the dimly lit walls, you need to use the list of artists and titles handed out at the entrance to match to the numbers on the works themselves.

Among masterworks by Tintoretto, Correggio, Annibale and Lodovico Carracci, Bellini, Parmigianino, Jan and Pieter Brueghel the elders, and Rubens, you'll find two stellar ✪ **paintings** by Caravaggio, *Mary Magdalen* and the *Rest on the Flight into Egypt*, as well as a copy he made of his *Young St. John the Baptist* now in the Capitoline Museums. Also here are Titian's *Salome with the Head of St. John the Baptist*, and Bernini's *Bust of Innocent X*, whose sister-in-law started this collection.

✪ **Museo Nazionale Romano—Palazzo Altemps.** Pz. di Sant'Apollinare 44 (2 blocks north of Pz. Navona). ☎ **06/683-3759.** Admission 10,000L ($5.90) adults, free under 18 and over 60. Tues–Fri 9am–9:45pm, Sat 9am–11:15pm, Sun 9am–7:45pm. May keep shorter hours in winter. Bus: 70, 81, 87, 115, 116, 116T, 186, 492, 628.

The new home to the famed Ludovisi collection of ancient sculpture is a crown jewel in Rome's touristic renaissance, and a prime example of Italy's seemingly newfound ability to craft a 21st-century museum that respects both the gorgeous architecture and the frescoes of the Renaissance space in which it is installed, and the aesthetic and historic value of the classical collection it contains.

Travel Tip

Try not to hit the Piazza Navona area on Thursday, since both the Galleria Doria-Pamphilj and the Caravaggio paintings in the church of San Luigi dei Francesi are closed.

What was once a single museum—one that languished for decades in a quasi-mythical state inside the eternally closed Baths of Diocletian—has split up across the city in four "Museo Nazionale Romano" collections: The Ludovisi, Mattei, and Altemps Collections of Classical statuary here; more statues plus exquisite ancient Roman mosaics, bronzes, frescoes, coins, and jewelry at the Palazzo Massimo alle Terme; bathhouse art and colossal statuary in the Aula Ottagona just off Piazza della Repubblica (both listed under "Near Termini," below); and an as-yet-to-be-reopened collection in the original Baths of Diocletian space.

Rather than stuff lots of statues into every nook and cranny of this Altemps space, a few choice pieces have been placed in each room, allowing and encouraging you to examine each statue carefully, walk around it, and read the accompanying placard in English and Italian that explains its significance and shows which bits are original and which were "restored" in the 17th century. The 16th- to 18th-century palazzo itself is gorgeous, with a grand central courtyard and many surviving frescoes and original painted wood ceilings, especially upstairs where you can wander onto a bust-lined, Alberti-inspired loggia frescoed as a "Garden of Delights" in the 1590s.

Among the collections, be on the lookout for an A.D. 2nd-century giant *Dionysus with Satyr;* a 1st-century B.C. copy of master Greek sculptor Phidias's most famous statue (now lost), the 5th-cenutry B.C. *Athena* that once held the place of honor in Athens's Parthenon; 2nd-century B.C. Ptolemaic Egyptian statuary; a pair of lute-playing *Apollos;* plenty of Imperial busts; and an A.D. 3rd-century sarcophagus carved from a single block of marble and depicting in incredible, unrestored detail the Roman legions fighting off invading Ostrogoth Barbarians. Audio guides cost 7,000L ($4.10), and guided tours on summer evenings run 6,000L ($3.55).

San Luigi d. Francesi. Pz. S. Luigi d. Francesi 5 (just east of Pz. Navona). ☎ **06/688-271.** Admission free. Fri–Wed 7:30am–12:30pm, 3:30–7pm. Also sometimes open Thurs mornings. Bus: 70, 81, 87, 115, 116, 116T, 186, 492, 628.

France's national church in Rome is an unmissable stop for Caravaggio fans, for in the last chapel on the left (coin-gobbling lights) is his famous St. Matthew cycle of paintings. These huge canvases depict ◗ *The Calling of St. Matthew* on the left, the best of the three and amply illustrating Caravaggio's mastery of light and shadow to create mood and drama; *The Martyrdom of St. Matthew* is on the right; and *St. Matthew and the Angel* is over the altar.

Interestingly, that scene with the angel inspiring St. Matthew to write his Gospel is not the one Caravaggio had originally painted for the chapel. The church objected to that first version, which showed the saint as a rough, illiterate peasant, the angel directly guiding his hand as he wrote. A wise collector not affiliated with the church bought that version (now destroyed), but its legacy appears here—Matthew's stool tips over the edge of the painting, as though about to tumble onto the altar. Before you leave, check out the Domenichino frescoes in the second chapel on the right aisle.

San Agostino. Pz. S. Agostino (northeast of Pz. Navona). ☎ **06/6880-1962.** Admission free. Mon–Sat 4:30–7:30pm; Sun 7:45am–12:45pm, 4:30–7:30pm. Bus: 70, 81, 87, 115, 116, 116T, 186, 492, 628.

Around the corner from San Luigi dei Francesi is another stop on the Caravaggio tour, the early Renaissance church of San Agostino. The first altar on the left inside contains Caravaggio's almost Mannerist ◗ *Madonna del Loreto*, with pair of dirty-footed pilgrims kneeling before the willowy, velvet-robed Virgin who's carrying a ridiculously oversized (if marvelously lifelike) Christ child. The picture's beautiful, but a bit weird. Against the entrance wall is a shrine to the *Madonna del Parto*, a pregnant Virgin Mary (carved by Jacopo Sansovino in 1521) surrounded by thousands of votive offerings sent in supplication, especially by women who want to ensure a safe childbirth. The third pillar on the right side has a fresco by Raphael of *Isaiah* showing the influence of Michelangelo on the young painter.

Sant'Ivo alla Sapienza. Cor. Rinascimento 40 (it's a plain doorway; the church is in the courtyard beyond). ☎ **06/686-4987.** Admission free. Sat 9am–noon, 6–8pm; Sun 9am–noon. Bus: 70, 81, 87, 115, 116, 116T, 186, 492, 628.

Borromini designed the courtyard of Giacomo della Porta's Palazzo della Sapienza in the 1640s, surrounding three sides with porticoes and the back with the magnificent glowing white facade of Sant'Ivo church. This geometrically complex and highly influential baroque playground of concave and convex curves is topped by a remarkable spiraling oval dome that became a favorite feature on baroque churches in northern Europe. Although the light-filled oval interior is fine as well, don't let the church open hours put you off, because the best part really is that facade.

10 The Spanish Steps, Piazza del Popolo & Nearby Attractions

Fontana d. Trevi (Trevi Fountain). Pz. Trevi, 1 block south of V. Tritone. Bus: 52, 53, 56, 58, 58/, 60, 61, 62, 71, 95, 115, 116, 116T, 175, 492.

This huge baroque confection of thrashing mer-horses, splashing water, and striding Tritons all presided over by a muscular Neptune is one of Rome's most famous and visited sights. It was sculpted in 1762 by Nicolà Salvi to serve as an outlet for the waters carried into Rome by the 13-mile *Acqua Vergine* aqueduct, built in 19 B.C. and still running (it also supplies the fountains in Piazza Navona and Piazza di Spagna). Tourists and young folk just hanging out on the curving steps throng the cramped little piazza from early morning until after midnight, making it one of the most densely crowded but scenic spots to squeeze into a marble seat and people-watch.

Legend and a host of silly American movies hold that if you toss a coin into this fountain, you are guaranteed to return to Rome some day. General weathering and the chemical damage from all those rusting coins forced its restoration in 1990, and now the monies are collected regularly and donated to the Red Cross. Some say you must lob the coin with the right hand backward over the left shoulder. Others insist you must use three coins. Historians point out the original tradition was to drink the fountain's water, but unless you like chlorine, I'd stick to tossing lire.

Spanish Steps. From Pz. di Spagna to Pz. Trinità d. Monti. Metro: Spagna. Bus: 116, 116T, 117.

The off-center, yet graceful curves of the **Spanish Steps** rising from the hourglass-shaped Piazza di Spagna are covered with bright azaleas in spring and teeming with visitors, Roman teens, and tour groups year-round. It's capped at the top by the twin-towered French **Trinità dei Monti** church—with paintings by Michelangelo protégé Daniele da Volterra and frescoes by Raphael's pupil Giulio Romano inside—and at the bottom by the beloved *Barcaccia* ("Ugly Boat") fountain. The *Barcaccia* was sculpted by a teenage Bernini and his pop Pietro (they solved the dilemma of low water pressure at this point in the Acqua Vergine aqueduct system by forgoing the usual dramatic sprays and jets and instead crafting a sinking boat overflowing with water).

The steps themselves were built in the 18th century by the French to lead up to their church, and in Italian this monumental baroque staircase is called the *Scalinata di Trinità dei Monti;* the piazza at the bottom is called the "Spanish Square" after the nearby residence of the Spanish Ambassador to the Vatican.

The Spanish Steps, Piazza del Popolo & Nearby Attractions

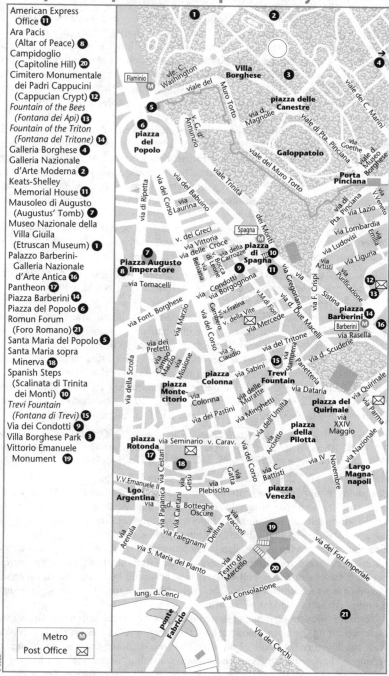

Metro Ⓜ
Post Office ✉

3-0632

163

Historically, Piazza di Spagna is the Anglo-American and commercial center of Rome. English and American artists lived or had studios (many still do) on Via Margutta (parallel to Via del Babuino, which empties into the piazza); the Anglican church is just down the road; the Grand Tour's most posh hotels still huddle expensively at the top of the Steps; Italy's first McDonald's and the American Express office are just a few yards up the piazza; and flanking the steps themselves are the British 19th-century bastions of Babington's Tea Rooms and the house where Keats spent his final months with Joseph Severn by his side.

Inside the young Romantic poet's former apartment at Pz. di Spagna 26 is the **Keats-Shelley Memorial** (☎ **06/678-4235**). It was here, with a view over the steps, that John Keats died of consumption (tuberculosis) in 1821 at the age of 25. The rooms are stuffed with mementos, letters, Keats's death mask, portraits, and around 10,000 books by Romantic greats Shelley, Byron, Leight Hunt, and of course Keats. It's open Monday to Friday, in summer 11am to 2pm and 3 to 6pm, in winter 9am to 1pm and 3 to 6pm. Admission is 5,000L ($2.95).

Leading out from the bottom of the steps is the fashionable **Via dei Condotti,** the centerpiece for Rome's toniest boutique shopping scene and home to the top names in Italian fashion. (See "Shopping" in section 17, below.)

Mausoleo di Augusto (Augustusí Tomb). Pz. Augusto Imperatore. ☎ **06/6710-3819.** Admission only by appointment. Sat–Sun 10am–1pm, 5–7pm; guided tours 9pm–11pm in summer. Bus: 32, 81, 115, 628, 913, 926.

In one of Rome's most hideous, Fascist-designed piazze lie the rotund brick remains of Augustus's tomb, which once housed the remains of Rome's first emperor, his family, his general, Agrippa, and every Roman emperor up to Nerva (d. A.D. 98). This ring of brick 287 feet in diameter was once crowned with a dirt mound and cypress trees, but has been so abused throughout the centuries—in the Middle Ages it was a fortress, then became an amphitheater in the baroque era for cockfights and bear baiting, and finally was used as a concert hall until 1936—that we're lucky the body survives with a few plaques of the old marble cladding still in place.

Ara Pacis. Lungotevere in Augusta/Pz. Augusto Imperatore. ☎ **06/6880-6848.** Admission 3,750L ($2.20) adults, 2,500L ($1.50) students. Summer Tues–Sat 9am–7pm, Sun 9am–1pm; winter Tues–Sun 9am–4pm. Bus: 32, 81, 115, 628, 913, 926.

Augustus had his "Altar of Peace" built from 13 to 9 B.C. to celebrate the peace his campaigns to unify the new Empire had brought to Europe, northern Africa, and the Near East. It's been reconstructed and placed in a huge aquarium along the Lungotevere, and though you can admire it from without through the glass walls, it's worth the low admission to go inside and examine up close the decorative relief panels that ring the entire exterior. These depict mythological figures and long processions of prominent citizens from Rome's history above a Greek key band and lower frieze of acanthus leaves and swans. Not only are they beautiful, but these carvings represent the point at which Roman art finally significantly broke from Greek models to make a strong, classical statement all its own.

Since the 16th century, bits of decorative frieze have been recovered from beneath buildings lining the Corso, most making their way to collections in the Louvre, Vatican, and Florence. The bulk of the altar, however, lay under the water table and was serving as the foundation for several *palazzi*. Mussolini, who was always looking for ways to link the concept of his new, Fascist empire with that of ancient Rome, ordered the rest excavated in 1937. His archaeologists came up with the brilliant plan of freezing the water in the soil, building new supports for the palaces above, and extracting the chunks of marble altar before the ground thawed again. The reconstituted Ara Pacis is very close to complete, with casts replacing the bits Rome hasn't been able to repatriate from museums. There are (as-yet vague) plans to renovate the display space for the Jubilee 2000, so be prepared for scaffolding.

Santa Maria d. Popolo. Pz. d. Popolo 12 (at the Porta d. Popolo). ☎ **06/361-0836.** Admission free. Mon–Sat 7am–noon, 4–7pm, Sun 8am–2pm, 4:30–7:30pm. Bus: 95, 117, tram 225, 490, 495, 628, 926. Metro: Flaminio.

Although the first church on this site was built in 1099 to exorcise Nero's ghost from some local walnut trees, the current Renaissance and baroque structure dates from the 1470s. You'll have to search out light switches and lire-gobbling light boxes in this shadowy church, but it's worth it.

The much-restored frescoes in the first chapel on the right are by the Umbrian early Renaissance master Pinturicchio. For a hidden delight, duck behind the altar to the coffered, shell-motif apse—one of Bramante's earliest works in Rome (flip on the lights at the fuse box to your left). Andrea Sansovino carved the two tombs here from 1505 to 1507, combining classical triumphal arches with surprising sarcophagal depictions of the deceased. This is much peppier than the lying-in-state look of medieval tombs—these Renaissance cardinals recline comfortably on cushions, only half asleep. Set higher in the walls are Rome's first stained-glass windows, commissioned in 1509 from the supreme French master Guillaume de Marcillat. The frescoes on the vault are again by Pinturicchio; the apse has been filled with scaffolding for the past few years, but should reopen before 2000.

In the first transept chapel to the left of the altar, you're treated to a unique juxtaposition of the two rival baroque masters, Annibale Carracci and Caravaggio. Crowd-pleasing Annibale was more popular in his day, as the colorful, highly modeled ballet of his *Assumption of the Virgin* in the center might suggest, but posterity has paid more attention to the moody chiaroscuro of Caravaggio's tensely dramatic, original style. He used overly strong and patently artificial light sources to enhance the psychological drama of *The Conversion of St. Paul* and *The Crucifixion of St. Peter,* and to draw the viewer right into the straining muscles, wrinkled foreheads, dirty feet, and intense emotions of his figures.

When banking mogul Agostino Chigi commissioned his favorite artist, Raphael, to design a memorial chapel tomb for him, he had no idea he'd need it so soon. Both patron and artist died in 1520, by which time Raphael had barely begun construction on the pyramid-shaped tombs of Agostino and his brother for the **Chigi Chapel** (second on the left). Chigi Pope Alexander VII later hired other artists to complete the chapel and ceiling mosaics to Raphael's designs, with God in the center of the dome seeming to bless Agostino's personal horoscope symbols, which surround him. Lorenzetto carved the smoother-bodied statues of Jonah and Elijah to match Raphael's sketches, but Bernini stuck to his own active, detailed style to depict Habakkuk with the angel and Daniel getting his foot licked by a rather bemused-looking lion. (Actually, Bernini is using the chapel space to tell a Bible story here; the angel is about to carry Habakkuk and his picnic basket across the chapel to feed Daniel, starving in the lion's den). The chapel's altarpiece is by Sebastiano del Piombo, and the macabre flying skeleton in the floor is an addition by Bernini.

✪ **Galleria Borghese.** In the northeast corner of Villa Borghese park, off V. Pinciana. ☎ **06/ 328-101** for ticket reservations, 06-841-7645 for the main desk. Admission 10,000L ($5.90), free under 18 and over 60. There's also a 2,000L ($1.20) surcharge (for all ages) to reserve in advance; you can arrive without a reservation, but it's risky. Summer Tues–Sat 9am–10pm, Sun 9am–8pm. Winter Tues–Sun 9am–5pm, Sun 9am–1pm. Bus: 95, 490, 495 (to the middle of the park); 52, 53, 910 (to V. Pinciana). Metro: Spagna.

Fully reopened in late 1997 after a 14-year restoration, this is my favorite small museum in the world. You could spend 45 to 90 minutes walking around this frescoed 1613 villa admiring classical statues and mosaics, Renaissance paintings, and some of the finest marble sculptures of the baroque, most acquired by the villa's original owner, Cardinal Scipione Borghese (who bought Caravaggio's works when no one else wanted them). The new ticket reservation policy is annoying, but in summer the museum can be sold out for days, so try to book at least a day beforehand (earlier if possible) to ensure you get the entry time you want.

Neoclassical master Canova's sculpted portrait of Napoleon's sister *Pauline Bonaparte as Venus* (1805) reclining on a couch was quite the scandal in its time. When asked whether she wasn't uncomfortable posing half-naked like that, Pauline reportedly responded, "Oh, no—the studio was quite warm."

Four rooms are each devoted to an early masterpiece by the baroque's greatest genius, Gianlorenzo Bernini. On the ground floor are his *Aeneas and Anchises* (1613), chipped out at the age of 15 with the help of his father, Pietro, and the *Rape of Persephone* (1621). Also here is the *Apollo and Daphne* (1624), in which the 26-year-old sculptor captures the moment the nymph's toes take root and her fingers and hair start sprouting leaves as her river god father sympathetically transforms her into a laurel tree to help her escape from a Cupid-struck Apollo hot on her heels.

Bernini's vibrant *David* (1623–24) is a resounding baroque answer to Michelangelo's Renaissance take on the same subject in Florence. The Renaissance *David* was pensive, all about proportion and philosophy. This baroque *David* is a man of action, twisting his body as he is about to let fly the stone from his sling. Bernini modeled the furrowed brow and bitten lip of *David's* face on his own mug.

Also on the ground floor is a room with (count 'em) five Caravaggio paintings, including the powerful *Madonna of the Serpent,* aka *Madonna dei Palafrenieri* (1605); the *Young Bacchus, Ill* (1653), the earliest surviving Caravaggio and said to be a self-portrait from when the painter had malaria; and the creepy *David with the Head of Goliath* (1610), in which Goliath may be another self-portrait.

The second floor contains the rest of the painting collection, starring good works by Andrea del Sarto, Titian, Dürer, Rubens, Antonella Messina, Pinturicchio, Corregio, and a large, masterful 1507 *Deposition* by the young Raphael.

✪ **Museo Nazionale di Villa Giulia (Etruscan Museum).** Pzle. di Villa Giulia (on Vle. d. Belle Arti, in the northern reaches of Villa Borghese park). ☎ **06/320-1951.** Admission 8,000L ($4.70) adults, free under 18 and over 60. Tues–Sat 9am–7pm, Sun 9am–1:30pm. Bus: tram 19, tram 30/, 95, tram 225, 490, 495, 926.

Housed in a 16th-century Mannerist villa built for Pope Julius III by Ammanati, Vasari, and Vignola, this museum is dedicated above all to the Etruscans. The Etruscans, who may have immigrated to Italy from Turkey in the 9th century B.C., were the peninsula's first great culture, concentrated in what are today the provinces of Tuscany, Umbria, and the north half of Lazio (Rome's province). The height of their power as an association of loosely organized city states was from the 7th to 5th centuries B.C., when their Tarquin dynasty even ruled Rome as her first kings. Etruscan society is something of a mystery to us since what little we know of it comes down mainly through vases and funerary art (and it's hard to reconstruct an entire culture based solely by looking at its cemeteries), but from what we can gather they enjoyed a highly developed society, a great deal of equality between the sexes, and appreciated the finer things in life like banqueting, theater, and art.

This museum houses the most important Etruscan collection in Italy, unrivaled by anything even in Tuscany. The greatest piece is the touching and remarkably skilled 6th-century B.C. terra-cotta ✪ **sarcophagus** from Cerveteri, whose lid carries full-size likenesses of a husband and wife sitting down to their final, eternal banquet together. Also look for the 4th-century B.C. Ficoroni Cist, a bronze marriage coffer richly engraved with tales of the Argonauts, and a large painted terra-cotta ✪ **statue of Apollo** (c. 500 B.C.), which once topped a temple to Minerva at Veii.

The Castellani collection of ancient jewelry spans Minoan civilization through the Hellenistic and Roman eras as well as some Asian pieces. But what strikes most visitors about the Villa Giulia are the miles upon miles of pots, ranging from native pre-Etruscan styles through the Etruscan and Greek eras to the Roman one, many beautifully painted. Be sure to seek out the Faliscan Krater, with a scene of Dawn riding her chariot across the sky, and the early 7th-century B.C. Chigi Vase showing hunting scenes and the Judgment of Paris.

Galleria Nazionale d'Arte Moderna. Vle. d. Belle Arti 131 (in the Villa Borghese park). ☎ **06/322-981.** Admission 8,000L ($4.70) adults, free under 18 and over 60. Tues–Sat 9am–10pm, Sun 9am–8pm (sometimes closes 2pm in winter). Bus: 95, 490, 495.

In the heart of Villa Borghese park, Rome's main modern art gallery concentrates on late 19th- and early 20th-century European and Italian art. There's art nouveau by Galileo Chini, Futurism by Gino Severini, and *Macchaioli* (a Tuscan variant on Impressionism) by Giovanni Fattori and Silvestro Lega. Assorted foreign schools are represented by Gustav Klimt, Marcel Duchamp, Mondrian, Cézanne, Degas, Van Gogh, Modigliani, Goya, Ingres, Gauguin, Whistler, and Münch.

11 More Attractions

AROUND VIA VENETO & PIAZZA BARBERINI

Via Veneto and Piazza Barberini. V. Vittorio Veneto. Metro: Barberini. Bus: 52, 53, 56, 58, 58/, 60, 61, 62, 95, 116, 116T, 175, 492.

The broad lazy S-curve of the tree-shaded **Via Veneto** was laid out in 1866. Lined with extravagant hotels, mansions, and the first grand cafes, it later garnered international fame as the epicenter of 1950s and 1960s *La Dolce Vita* ("The Sweet Life"). In this era of "Hollywood on the Tiber," Via Veneto became a hot spot for celebrities, the jet set, and European nobility. This phenomenon, and the street, were immortalized in Fellini's film *La Dolce Vita,* which also introduced a new word into modern vocabulary: *Paparazzo* was the name of the photographer who worked this street getting candid shots of celebrities.

The base of Via Veneto is **Piazza Barberini,** today a traffic-choked circle of cars around one of Bernini's masterpieces, the travertine ✪ **Triton Fountain,** built for the princely Barberini family in 1643 and restored in 1998. Four serpentine dolphins (saddled with stemma of Barberini bees) raise their tails to support an open oyster shell atop which kneels the God of the Seas, blowing mightily through his conch shell a jet of water that falls back to splash off his muscular shoulders.

A few feet up Via Veneto from this piazza you'll see an example of Barberini largess—the small sidewalk **Fountain of the Bees,** crafted by Bernini with a few emblematic bees clinging to a scallop shell. An inscription dedicates the use of the fountain to "the public and their animals."

Cimitero Monumentale d. Padri Cappuccini (Capuchin Crypt). In Santa Maria Immacolata Concezione church, V. Veneto 27. ☎ **06/487-1185.** Donation of 2,000L ($1.20) expected. Daily 9am–noon, 3–6pm. Metro: Barberini. Bus: 52, 53, 56, 58, 58/, 60, 61, 62, 95, 116, 116T.

The cappuccini are monks with a death wish—or, depending on how you look at it, a healthy attitude toward their own mortality. They're a weird lot, very polite but with a penchant for making mosaics out of the bones of their deceased brethren. That's what happened in the crypt of this church, where five chambers were filled between 1528 and 1870 with mosaics made from over 4,000 dearly departed cappuccini (first dried out by temporary burial in the floors filled with dirt from Jerusalem).

These fantastic displays form morbid patterns and baroque decorative details, from rings of knucklebones and garlands of pelvises to walls made from stacked skulls and scapulae used to create butterflies or hourglasses in an all-too-fitting *memento mori* motif. A few bodies lean against the walls in varying states of advanced desiccated decay, and the full skeletons of two Barberini princelings adorn the last chamber, near a placard that drives home the ashes-to-ashes point, in several languages, "What you are, we used to be. What we are, you will become."

✪ **Palazzo Barberini—Galleria Nazionale d'Arte Antica.** V. Quattro Fontane 13 (just up from Pz. Barberini). ☎ **06/481-4591.** Admission 8,000L ($4.70) adults, free under 18 and over 60. Tues–Sat 9am–10pm, Sun 9am–8pm. Metro: Barberini. Bus: 52, 53, 56, 58, 58/, 60, 61, 62, 95, 116, 116T, 175, 492.

When a Barberini finally made pope (Urban VIII), the fabulously wealthy family celebrated by hiring Carlo Maderno in 1624 to build them a huge palace, which both Borromini and Bernini later embellished with window frames and doorways. Since 1949, it has housed half of Rome's National Gallery of paintings, works that span the 13th to 17th centuries (the other half's in Trastevere's Palazzo Corsini). The collection is currently being rearranged following a lengthy restoration of the *palazzo*.

The masterpieces are numerous, but while you're admiring the paintings hung on the walls, don't fail to look up at the ceilings, many of which were decorated by one of the masters of Roman baroque frescoes, Pietro da Cortona. Keep an eye out especially for the Great Hall, where Pietro frescoed his masterpiece, the allegorical ✪ *Triumph of Divine Providence* (1633–39). It celebrates the Barberini dynasty in a sumptuously busy but masterful trompe l'oeil space open to the heavens with the Barberini bees swarming up to greet Divine Providence herself, who's being crowned by Immortality (most baroque pontiffs were not known for their modesty).

As for the works on the walls, you'll pass icons of art like Filippo Lippi's *Annunciation* and his *Madonna and Child;* Andrea del Sarto's *Holy Family;* Peruzzi's *Ceres;* Bronzino's precision *Portrait of Stefano Colonna;* Guido Reni's *Portrait of a Lady* believed to be Beatrice Cenci (who was condemned for the murder of her own father); and three Caravaggios, including a *Narcissus* and a gory, action-packed *Judith beheading Holofernes,* along with an attributed *St. Francis in Meditation.*

But the star painting has to be Raphael's bare-breasted ✪ *Fornarina,* held to be a (rather racy) portrait of the artist's girlfriend, a baker's daughter named Margherita. Some critics say it's actually a painting of a courtesan by Raphael's pupil Giulio Romano, but this would not explain why the lass wears an armband bearing Raphael's name. Other great artists represented here include Filippino Lippi, Sodoma, Beccafumi, El Greco, Tintoretto, Titian, Paul Brill, and Luca Giordano.

Santa Maria d. Vittoria. V. XX Settembre 17 (at Lgo. S. Susanna). ☎ **06/482-6190.** Admission free. Daily 6:30–11:30am, 4:30–7pm. Bus: 60, 61, 62, 116T, 175, 492. Metro: Repubblica.

The interior of this small church is one of Rome's most successful examples of unified baroque decoration, nicely restored in the early 1990s. The star of the show is in the last chapel on the left, where Bernini used full sculpture and tricky optical reliefs to turn the shallow chapel into a tiny opera house for his rendition of ✪ *St. Theresa in Ecstasy.* On either side of the chapel are "box seats" so that the members of the Cornaro family, who paid for the chapel, could look on as bas relief portraits (on the left side, the half-hidden figure on the right end is said to be a self-portrait by Bernini).

Attractions Near Termini & Via Veneto

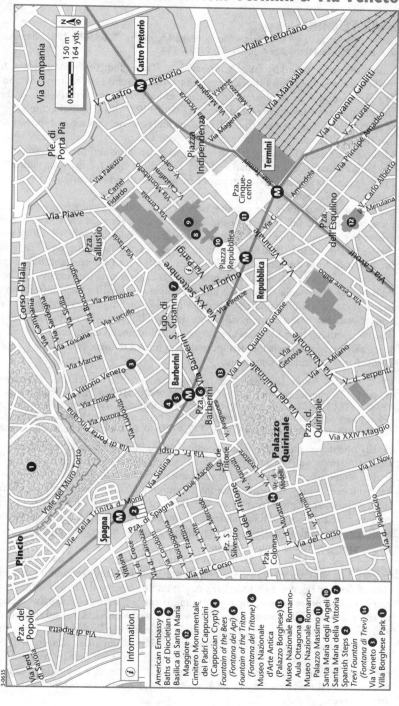

Information

American Embassy 3
Baths of Diocletian 9
Basilica di Santa Maria
  Maggiore 12
Cimitero Monumentale
  dei Padri Cappuccini
  (Cappucian Crypt) 4
Fountain of the Bees
  (Fontana dei Api) 5
Fountain of the Triton
  (Fontana del Tritone) 6
Museo Nazionale
  d'Arte Antica
Museo Nazionale Romano—
  Aula Ottagona 8
Museo Nazionale Romano—
  Palazzo Massimo 11
Santa Maria degli Angeli 10
Santa Maria della Vittoria 7
Spanish Steps 2
Trevi Fountain
  (Fontana di Trevi) 14
Via Veneto 3
Villa Borghese Park 1

Museo Nazionale Romano- 13

3-0635

169

NEAR TERMINI

Basilica di Santa Maria Maggiore. Pz. S. Maria Maggiore. ☎ **06/483-195.** Admission free. Daily 7am–6:45pm. Bus: 4, 9, 16, 70, 71, 75, 714.

This is the greatest, and by far best preserved, of Rome's four basilican churches. It marks the city skyline with Rome's tallest bell tower, a graceful 14th-century addition. The main facade is a baroque mask that uses arcades and loggias to partially hide the fantastically mosaicked earlier facade from 1294 to 1308. Often, you can climb a set of stairs to view these mosaics from up close, including scenes that recount the legend that this basilica was founded in the 350s by Pope Liberius, who had a vision of the Madonna one night in August telling him to raise the church on the spot and along the outlines that would be demarcated by a miraculous snowfall the next morning. Every August 5 a special Mass takes place here with the snowfall beautifully reenacted using pale flower petals.

Entering the basilica is like stepping back in time, with its basic design and decor preserved from the 6th century. The gargantuan space is some 284 feet long, a dark echoey environment suited to religious pilgrimages. The glowing coffered ceiling was the work of Giuliano da Sangallo, said to be gold leafed using the very first gold brought back from the Americas by Columbus (a gift from Ferdinand and Isabella to the pope). The floor was inlaid with marble chips in geometric patterns by the Cosmati around 1150, while the mosaics lining the nave and covering the triumphal arch before the altar are glittering testaments to the skill of 5th-century craftsmen (the apse's *Coronation of the Virgin* mosaics were designed by Iacopo Torriti in the 1290s). The most striking later additions are the two magnificent and enormous late Renaissance and baroque chapels that flank the altar to form a transept (the Sistina Chapel on the left is particularly sumptuous).

✪ **Museo Nazionale Romano—Palazzo Massimo alle Terme.** Lgo. di Villa Peretti (where Pz. d. Cinquecento meets V. Viminale). ☎ **06/4890-3500** or 06/520-726. Admission 12,000L ($7.05) adults, free under 18 and over 60. (Admission also covers Aula Ottagona, below.) Tues–Sat 9am–10pm, Sun 9am–8pm. Winter hours may be Tues–Sat 9am–2pm, Sun 9am–1pm. Bus: H, 64, 70, 115, 116T, 170, 175, 492, 640, 910. Metro: Termini, Repubblica.

Finally opened in June 1998, this museum (paired with its sister collection in the Palazzo Altemps near Piazza Navona; above) simply blows away anything else you'll find in Rome when it comes to classical statues, frescoes, and mosaics. It's a "where have you been all my life" experience for antiquities buffs, and promises an aesthetically pleasant and informative afternoon even for the mildly curious. The 19th-century palazzo houses a fully modernized museum of advanced lighting systems, explanatory placards in English, and a curatorial attention to detail heretofore unseen on the dusty old Roman museum scene.

There are no boring ranks of broken marble busts here—portrait busts are aplenty, but most are masterworks of expression and character, representing famous Romans and giving you an opportunity to put marble faces to the names of all those emperors and other ancient bigwigs. Among them is a statue of Augustus Caesar wearing his toga pulled over his head like a shawl, a sign he had assumed the role of a priest (actually, of the head priest, which in Latin is *Pontifex Maximus*, a title the Christian popes would later adopt). Also on the ground floor are an altar from Ostia Antica whose reliefs bear a striking resemblance to 15th-century frescoes of the Nativity, and a hauntingly beautiful 440 B.C. statue of a wounded Niobid, collapsing as she reaches for her back where one of Apollo and Artemis's spiteful arrows struck.

Among the masterpieces up on the first floor are a discus thrower, a bronze Dionysus fished out of the Tiber, bronze bits from ancient shipwrecks on Lake Nemi, and an incredibly well-preserved sarcophagus featuring a tumultuous battle scene between Romans and Germanic barbarians (all from the A.D. 2nd century).

Up on the second floor are Roman frescoes, stuccoes, and mosaics spanning the 1st century B.C. to the A.D. 5th century, most never seen by the general public since they were discovered in the 19th century. You can visit only via a 45-minute guided tour, which is included in the price of your admission (when you enter the museum, your ticket will have a time printed on it; be on the second floor at that time for the tour; you can return to visit the rest of the museum afterwards). The ✪ **frescoes and stuccoes** are mainly countryside scenes, decorative strips, and a few naval battles, all carefully restored and reattached into spaces that are faithful to the original dimensions of the rooms from which they came.

Also up here are halls and rooms lined with incredible **mosaic** scenes, among them the famous ✪ *Four Charioteers* standing with their horses in the four traditional team colors (red, blue, green, and white) that would run the races around the Circus Maximus. There are also several rare, A.D. 4th-century *opus sectile* (marble inlay) scenes from the Basilica of Giunio Bassa.

The basement, still being installed as of late 1998, has two sections. The first contains **ancient jewelry,** gold hair nets, ivory dolls, didactic CD-ROM consoles, and the mummy of an 8-year-old girl. The second is an oversized vault containing Rome's greatest **numismatic collection.** It traces Italian coinage from ancient Roman Republic monies through the pocket change of Imperial Rome, medieval Italian empires, and Renaissance principalities, to the Italian lira, the euro, and a computer live feed of the Italian stock exchange. Several daily guided tours of the entire museum, in English cost 6,000L ($3.55).

Museo Nazionale Romano—Aula Ottagona. V. G. Romita 3 (between Pz. d. Repubblica and the tourist office on V. Parigi). ☎ **06/488-0530.** Admission on ticket from Palazzo Massimo (see previous review). Tues–Sat 9am–2pm, Sun 9am–1pm. Bus: 60, 61, 62, 136, 137. Metro: Repubblica.

The only section of the Museo Nazionale Romano still housed in the Baths of Diocletian, this "octagonal hall" is ringed with statues that came from various bath complexes throughout the empire, from the A.D. 2nd-century *Lyceum Apollo* found near the Baths of Trajan here in Rome to the A.D. 1st-century *Aphrodite of Cyrene*, a Hellenistic work from Libya.

THE AVENTINE & SOUTH

Santa Sabina. Pz. Pietro d'Illiria/V. S. Sabina. ☎ **06/574-3573.** Admission free. Daily 7am–12:30pm, 3:30–6pm. Bus: 81, 160, 628, 715.

This is one of Rome's best surviving paleochristian churches. It was built between A.D. 422 and 32 and still retains its original ✪ **5th-century wooden doors**, beautifully carved with Biblical scenes including one of the earliest Crucifixions in western art (the door is located at the end of the 15th-century porch filled with sarcophagus lids you can spin to examine both sides). At first glance, the gorgeous and shadowy interior seems almost perfectly preserved, with giant Corinthian columns pirated from a nearby ancient structure and the original *opus sectile* marble inlay above the arches. Most of the chapels, however, have been baroqued, though this impacts little on the overall effect. If it's open, pop into the pretty 13th-century cloister off the porch.

Just down the road—at no. 3 of the Piazza dei Cavaliere di Malta, a square designed in 1765 by Piranesi—is the massive **Knights of Malta gate** with a large **keyhole,** and often a tourist bent over peering through it. This peeping view is a staple of Roman postcard stands, for the keyhole and the avenue of trees marching straight out behind it perfectly frame the dome of St. Peter's in the hazy distance.

Terme di Caracalla (Baths of Caracalla). V. d. Terme di Caracalla. ☎ **06/575-8626.** Admission 8,000L ($4.70). Summer Mon–Sat 9am–6pm, Sun 9am–1pm; winter 9am–3pm. Bus: 628, 760. Metro: Circo Massimo.

Public baths complexes were meant to exercise the minds and the bodies of ancient Roman citizens. These built by Emperor Caracalla in A.D. 212 could hold up to 1,600 bathers at a time and are among the largest to survive from the Imperial age. The plan of the visit changes regularly as sections close for restoration, but you usually start where the ancient bathers did, in the *palestra* (gym). After your exercises, you proceeded to the *laconicum* (Turkish bath) to scrape your sweaty body clean, then the boiling hot *calidarium,* followed by a spell soaking in the lukewarm *tepidarium,* and finally a pore-closing dip in the cold waters of the *frigidarium.* After this you could get a rub down, continue to the open-air *natatio* (swimming pool), or visit the on-site library or art gallery.

Montemarini/Art Center Acea. V. Ostiense 106. ☎ **06/574-8030.** 12,000L ($7.05) adults, 8,000L ($4.70) ages 6–18 and over 60. July 15–Sept 15, Tues–Fri 10am–2pm, 5–10pm, Sat–Sun 10am–10pm; Sept 16–July 14, Tues–Sun 10am–6pm. Bus: 128, 170, 670, 707, 761, 766.

The Acea Art Center is a bona fide *deus ex macchina* experience. The spruced-up, old Montemarini power plant houses more than 400 gorgeous ancient Roman sculptures from the Capitoline Museums collections that haven't been seen by the public in decades. They're displayed evocatively against a backdrop of the power plant's inky black iron machinery, much of it so massive and muscularly mechanical that it looks more like a metaphor of early industry than actual working devices, like it came from a Fritz Lang movie set.

Past the ticket desk is an excellent Roman replica of a rather sexy 5th-century B.C. Greek *Aphrodite,* posing in front of a wood-burning kiln. The first rooms, devoted mainly to art that once decorated public areas, contain fragments of terra-cotta pediments and friezes, marvelous small bronzes, marble busts, and statues—many from the Roman Forum area—as well as remains of a litter and sofa, fishy mosaics from the 2nd and 1st centuries B.C., and the well-preserved ✪ *Togato Barberini.* This berobed patrician hails from the 90s B.C. and is carrying what appear to be two heads. In Republican Rome, prominent citizens kept hollow wax portrait busts of their illustrious ancestors—in this case, Grandpa in the left hand and Dad in the right—and wore them during important occasions and ceremonies so as to serve as symbolic stand-ins for their deceased progenitors.

In the *macchine* (machines) room upstairs, there are two preserved enormous diesel engines. Around these engines, you'll see late Republican statues, which are excellent Roman copies of Greek originals, and the arm, head, and feet of what was a 26-foot-tall colossal goddess statue (101 B.C.) from the Temple of Fortuna in Largo di Teatro Argentina. In the *caldai* (boiler) room up the next set of steps is the collection of pieces that once decorated private Roman homes. These range from a delicate early Hellenistic *Niobe's Son* about to get shot by Apollo's and Artemis's arrows and the early Imperial *Esquiline Venus,* to a floor mosaic of a hunting scene and a copy of 2nd-century B.C. *Muse* carved with a symbolist touch that looks almost modern.

San Paolo Fuori le Mura (St. Paul's Outside the Walls). Vle. di S. Paolo/V. Ostiense. ☎ **06/541-0341.** Admission free. Daily 7am–6:30pm (cloisters close 1–3pm). Metro: S. Paolo.

Another of Rome's four grand grand pilgrimage basilicas, St. Paul Outside the Walls burned down in 1873, but it has been faithfully reconstructed using as many elements as possible from the original structure. The **Byzantine doors,** with incised bronze panels from the 11th century, were badly damaged in the fire, but survived to be preserved on the inside of the west wall, between the central and south portals. The altar is said to mark the spot of St. Paul's burial (an A.D. 1st-century tomb discovered underneath would seem to support this tradition), and sheltering the altar is a late-13th-century *ciborium* by Arnolfo di Cambio. Nearby is a weird, giant **marble candlestick** carved in the 12th century with a whirl of medieval scenes. The restored **apse mosaics** were executed by Venetian craftsmen in the 1220s.

The one part of the church to survive the fire almost intact is still its greatest draw, the lovely and peaceful early 13th-century ✪ **cloisters,** whose columns are a cornucopia of variety, many twisted or paired and inlaid with gems, mosaics, or colored marble chips in glittering patterns.

Museo della Civiltà Romana (Museum of Roman Civilization). Pz. G. Agnelli 10 (in EUR, south of the city center). ☎ **06/592-6041.** Admission 5,000L ($2.95). Mon–Sat 9am–7pm, Sun 9am–1pm. Metro: EUR-Fermi.

Six kilometers/3.6 miles south of the city center, **EUR** is Rome's great model of early 20th-century urban planning. It showcases the Fascist-era architecture that tried to weave together modern engineering and planning principles with the monumental marble-clad building style of ancient Rome (whose vast empire Fascist dictator Mussolini was trying to re-create for modern Italy with the help of his Nazi buddy Hitler).

EUR is a sight in and of itself—that tall, stark marble building with the relentless rows of oversized window arches is the Palazzo del Lavoro, better known as **"The Square Colosseum"**—and contains several history and ethnographic museums of the sort Roman grammar school students make field trips to see. But most visitors make the trip down here to visit the ✪ **Museum of Roman Civilization.** In it are housed two scale models that accurately reproduce ancient Rome at two time periods, a 1:1000 model that re-creates early Republican Rome, and a 1:2500 model that shows how Rome looked at the time of Emperor Constantine in the A.D. 4th century. The museum also houses plenty of late Imperial and Paleochristian art, among them 125 casts of the reliefs that spiral up Trajan's Column in the Imperial Fori. Unlike the originals, these are displayed at eye level so you can admire the artistry and follow the cartoon strip–like story of Trajan's victorious Dacian campaign.

TRASTEVERE

Santa Maria in Trastevere. Pz. S. Maria in Trastevere. ☎ **06/581-9443.** Admission free. Daily 8am–12:30pm, 4–7:30pm. Bus: H, tram 8, 23, 280.

Rome's oldest church dedicated to the Virgin was established before A.D. 337 on the site of an inn where a well of olive oil sprang from the floor at the precise moment Christ was born (look for this detail in the mosaics of the apse inside). The current structure was raised in 1140, with a Romanesque bell tower and a 12th- to 13th-century mosaic on the facade (lit at night) of the Madonna and ten women. The interior preserves a gorgeous Cosmatesque-like *opus sectile* floor, 21 columns pilfered from nearby ancient buildings, and a 1617 wood ceiling by Domenichino.

Filling the apse are some of Rome's most beautiful mosaics, the half dome picturing Christ and the Madonna (1140) and below that, ✪ **six scenes** from the *Life of the Virgin* by Pietro Cavallini (1291). These show the artist's remarkable use of color tones and foreshortening to create depth and facility with expressing character psychology and story line. (Cavallini was really the only artist in Rome who, as a slightly earlier contemporary of Florence's Giotto, was helping break art from its static Byzantine traditions to plunge it into a vibrant, proto-Renaissance mode.)

Santa Cecilia in Trastevere. Pz. di Santa Cecilia 22. ☎ **06/589-9289**. Admission to church free; excavations 2,000 lire; donation expected for Cavallini fresco. Daily 10am–noon, 4–6pm (sometimes closes early in winter). Cavallini fresco open Sun 11:30–noon, Tues and Thurs 10–11:30am. All hours subject to change. Bus: H, tram 8, 23, 44, 280.

The rather bland, 18th-century interior of his convent church hides the fact that it dates from 824, and contains not only one of the greatest frescoes from late Medieval Rome, but also the ruins of a Roman patrician house underneath. The house was, ostensibly, the home of St. Cecilia, killed in A.D. 230 for political reasons and—since the Roman prosecutors used her practice of the illegal cult of Christianity as the chief accusation against her—an early martyr.

The mosaic **apse** dates from the 9th century, when Pope Paschal I rebuilt the church and brought Cecilia's body from the catacombs to rebury her beneath the altar. Under the present **altar,** with its Guido Reni painting and beautiful Arnolfo di Cambio *baldacchino* (1283), lies Stefano Maderno's touching 17th-century statue of *St. Cecilia.* Maderno was on hand to make sketches when Cardinal Sfondrati opened the saint's tomb in 1599, and they found Cecilia perfectly preserved under a gold funeral shroud. The cut across her neck tells of her famous martyrdom: After locking her in her own steam room for 3 days failed to do her in—indeed, Cecilia came out singing, for which she later was declared the patron saint of music—the executioners tried decapitating her. The three allowed strokes of the axe failed to finish the job however, and Cecilia held on for another 3 days, slowly bleeding to death and converting hundreds with her show of piety (and this obvious evidence of the power of the God protecting her).

You can descend to those **Roman ruins** beneath the church, but be sure afterward to ask the nun on duty if you can please see the *ìaffreschi di Cavalliniî* (if no one is on duty, ring the bell at the door on the left aisle; you'll have to bribe the nun a few thousand lire to walk you up to the frescoes). The 18th-century interior redecorators slapped plaster over most of the bottom half of Cavallini's masterful ✪ *Last Judgment* on the entrance wall, but had to leave room for a large built-in balcony so that the cloistered nuns could attend Mass unseen. In doing so, they unintentionally preserved the fresco's top half, and what remains here of Christ, the angels, and apostles is stunning. Cavallini painted this in 1293 in a magnificent break from formulaic Byzantine painting. For the first time, each character has a unique face and personality, and all are highly modeled with careful shading and color gradients.

Farnesina. V. d. Lungara 230. ☎ **06/6880-1767**. Admission 6,000L ($3.55) adults, 4,000L ($2.35) age 14–18, free under 14 and over 60. Tues–Sun 9am–1pm. Bus: 23, 280.

Baldassare Peruzzi built this modestly sized but sumptuously decorated villa for banking mogul Agostino Chigi from 1508 to 1511. Chigi loved to show off his vast wealth. He also had good taste in artists, and hired Raphael, Sodoma, and Peruzzi to decorate the interior of his new villa. The **Loggia of Galatea** has a ceiling painted by Peruzzi with Chigi's horoscope symbols, lunettes by Sebastiano del Piombo featuring scenes from Ovid's *Metamorphosis,* and the famous ✪ *Galatea* by Raphael. This perfectly composed Renaissance fresco depicts the nymph and her friends attempting to flee on the backs of pug-nosed dolphins from their mermen admirers.

The ceiling in the **Loggia of Cupid and Psyche** is frescoed as an open pergola of flowers and fruit that frame scenes from the myth of Psyche, a woman so beautiful Cupid himself fell in love with her. The fresco cycle was executed between 1510 and 1517 (restored in the 1990s) by Raphael's students Giulio Romano, Raffaellino del Colle, and Francesco Penni.

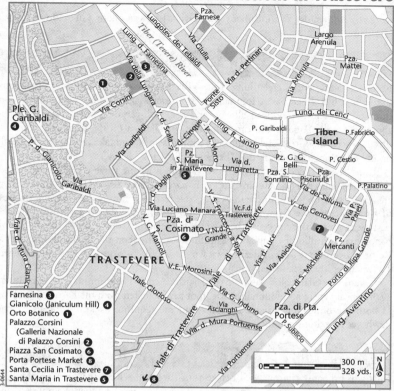

Farnesina ❸
Gianicolo (Janiculum Hill) ❹
Orto Botanico ❶
Palazzo Corsini
  (Galleria Nazionale
  di Palazzo Corsini) ❷
Piazza San Cosimato ❻
Porta Portese Market ❽
Santa Cecilia in Trastevere ❼
Santa Maria in Trastevere ❺

In the grand **Sala delle Prospettive** upstairs, Peruzzi frescoed every inch of the walls to masterfully carry trompe l'oeil to its extremes and allow Chigi to glimpse an imagined outside world of Roman countryside and cityscapes between the painted marble columns of a (fake) open loggia. Even with the frescoes faded by time, Peruzzi's painterly and architectural tricks create a pretty convincing optical illusion. Notice how, from the correct angles, the room's real flooring and coffered ceiling are continued into the painted space with perfect perspective. The imperial army of Charles V, sacking the city in 1527, didn't seem to have much respect for this talent, scratching into the frescoes' plaster antipapal epithets in gothic German script and signing their names and in one place the date (at the time it was vandalous graffiti; time has turned it into a precious historical record to be preserved behind Plexiglas shields). The small **bedchamber** off this room was frescoed with a delightful scene of the *Wedding Night of Alexander the Great* by Sodoma.

Galleria Nazionale di Palazzo Corsini. V. d. Lungara 10. ☎ **06/6880-2323.** Admission 8,000L ($4.70) adults, free under 18 and over 60. Tues–Fri 9am–7pm, Sat 9am–2pm, Sun 9am–1pm. Bus: 23, 280.

This 15th-century palace houses the original half of Rome's National Gallery of paintings (the other half's in the Palazzo Barberini, near Via Veneto). The paintings are hung sort of all squished together, but search out especially Murillo's *Madonna and Child,* Caravaggio's *St. John the Baptist,* a triptych by Fra' Angelico, and Guido Reni's *Salome with the Head of St. John the Baptist.* Also be on the lookout for fine works by Andrea del Sarto, Rubens, Van Dyck, Joos van Cleve, Guercino, and Luca Giordano.

12 Rome's Parks & Gardens

Rome's greatest central green lung is the **Villa Borghese** park, 226 acres of gardens, statue- and bust-lined paths, fountains, and artificial lakes containing a biopark zoo, three top museums (reviewed above), and the 19th-century Pincio Gardens rising above Piazza del Popolo. You can rent bikes, paddleboat on the small lake (there's a tiny 19th-century Greek-style temple on a mini-island), and take the kids to the newly revamped zoological biopark (see "Especially for Kids," below).

Rising above Trastevere, south of the Vatican, is a long ridge paralleling the Tiber called the **Gianicolo** (Janiculum), famously *not* one of the Seven Hills of Rome. There are a few sights up here, but the most attractive feature is simply the sweeping ✪ **view of Rome across the river,** taking in everything from the Pincio gardens on the left past the domes of the city center beyond the curve of the Colosseum on the right. This panorama is thrilling by day and beautiful by night, when the Gianicolo doubles as Rome's Lover's Lane (lots of steamy Fiat windows and lip-locked lovers stationed every 10 feet along the vista-kissed walls).

Toward the Gianicolo's southerly end is the Acqua Paolo fountain, a gargantuan 17th-century basin and fountain made from marble taken from the Forum that serves as both the outlet for Trajan's aqueduct and the requisite backdrop for all Roman newlyweds' wedding photos.

13 Especially for Kids

Kids will probably tire out well before you. Pace yourselves, and keep up the kids' interest with breaks, picnics, a few sights just for them (more on that in a minute), and generous amounts of gelato.

There are several sights and museums that seem to fire children's enthusiasm and imagination more than others. Some of my favorites from when I was 11 years old and living in Rome included the arms and armor collection in **Castel Sant'Angelo,** the gruesome bone mosaics of the **Capuchin Crypt,** the miles of tunnels of the **catacombs,** the **Mouth of Truth,** the **mummies** in the Egyptian wing of the Vatican, some of the **fountains** and statues like **Bernini's baby elephant obelisk,** and the explorable ruins of the **Roman Forum** and **Trajan's Markets.** And few people, regardless of their age, aren't seriously impressed by the **Colosseum** and the **Sistine Chapel.**

Several museums even have separate spaces or programs for kiddies, including the **Montemarini/Art Center Acea,** which Sundays from 10am to 7pm will give them crayons and paper and accompany them around the museum of colossal machines and ancient statuary. The **Museii Capitolini** have a didactic multimedia area (in English) aimed at kids ages 7 to 13 to teach about the ancient city and its history and art. The ✪ **Galleria Borghese** runs a didactic program Saturdays at 5pm and Sundays at 11am.

As for kid-specific sights, you can have lots of fun in the **Villa Borghese** park for all ages: renting bikes, riding the merry-go-round on the Pincio, paddling boats on the Giardino del Lago lake to the little faux-temples at its center, and visiting the revamped zoo.

This new **Bioparco,** Pzle. d. Giardino Zoologico 1 (☎ **06/360-8211**), has been retooled from a zoo of cages to a biological garden of natural habitat enclosures, which primarily house endangered species and injured animals that are being rehabilitated to return to the wild. It has become a teaching zoo, with placards at each endangered or threatened animal's enclosure that show via pictograms what threat the animal faces in the wild (climate changes, pollution, habitat destruction, hunting); the bears, wolves, lions, and apes are especially popular. Admission is 10,000L ($5.90) adults, 7,000L ($4.10) ages 6 to 12. It's open daily 9:30am to 7pm (5pm November to February).

The **Gianicolo Hill** has great city panoramas, a merry-go-round, and on Piazzale del Gianicolo the **✪ Teatrino di Pulcinella al Gianicolo** (☎ **06/582-7767**), an open-air puppet theater featuring the Neapolitan hand-puppet Pulcinella (known to Americans as Punch, of Punch and Judy fame). Shows of this traditional Italian entertainment run every afternoon between 3 and 8pm (whenever enough kids show up), and Sunday mornings as well. It's free, but you're welcome to leave a donation.

14 Exploring the Catacombs of the Appian Way

The arrow-straight Via Appia was the first of Rome's great consular roads, completed as far as Capua by 312 B.C. and soon after extended the full 370 kilometers (222 mi.) all the way to Brindisi in Apulia, the heel of Italy's boot. Its initial stretch in Rome is lined with ancient tombs of Roman families—burials were forbidden within the city walls as early as the 5th century B.C.—and, beneath the surface, miles of tunnels hewn out of the soft tufa stone.

These tunnels, or **catacombs,** were where early Christians buried their dead and, during the worst times of persecution, held church services discreetly out of the public eye. A few of them are open to the public, so you can wander through mile after mile of musty-smelling tunnels whose soft walls are gouged out with tens of thousands of burial niches—long shelves made for two to three bodies each. The requisite guided tours, hosted by priests and monks, feature a smidgen of extremely biased history and a large helping of sermonizing.

The Via Appia Antica has been a popular Sunday lunch picnic site for Roman families following the half-forgotten pagan tradition of dining in the presence of one's ancestors on holy days. This practice was rapidly dying out in the face of the traffic fumes that for the past few decades have choked the venerable road, but a 1990s initiative has closed the Via Appia Antica to cars on Sundays, bringing back the picnickers and bicyclists—along with in-line skaters and a new Sunday-only bus route to get out here.

Getting Here   You can take bus 218 from San Giovanni Metro stop, which follows the Via Appia Antica for a bit, then veers right onto Via Ardeatina at Domine Quo Vadis? church. After another long block, the 218 stops at the square Largo M. F. Ardeatine, near the gate to San Callisto catacombs. From here, you can walk right on Via d. Sette Chiese to the San Domitilla catacombs; or walk left down Via d. Sette Chiese to San Sebastiano catacombs.

Alternately, you can ride the Metro to the Colli Albani stop and catch bus 660, which wraps up the Via Appia Antica from the south, veering off it at the San Sebastiano catacombs (if you're visiting all three, you can take the 218 to the first two, walk to San Sebastiano, then catch the 660 back to the Metro). On Sundays the road is closed to traffic, but bus 760 trundles from the Circo Massimo Metro stop down the Via Appia Antica, turning around after it passes the Tomb of Cecilia Metella.

Catacombe di San Sebastiano (Catacombs of St. Sebastian). V. Appia Antica 136. ☎ **06/785-0350** or 06/788-7035. Admission 8,000L ($4.70), 4,000L ($2.35) age 6–14. Mon–Sat 8:30am–noon, 2:30–5pm. Closed Nov. Bus: see "Getting Here," above.

Though the tunnels run for 7 miles and the venerable bones of Saints Peter and Paul were once hidden here for safekeeping, the St. Sebastian tour is one of shortest and least satisfying of all the catacombs visits. The highlight is a chance to see a few well-preserved Roman (not Christian) tombs from what used to be an aboveground necropolis adjacent to the catacombs. Since this pagan graveyard was buried by the centuries, the stucco decorations on the ceilings and frescoes inside were almost perfectly preserved.

Catacombe di San Callisto (Catacombs of St. Callixtus). V. Appia Antica 110. ☎ **06/5130-1580** or 06/513-6725. Admission 8,000L ($4.70), 4,000L ($2.35) age 6–14. Thurs–Tues 8:30am–noon, 2:30–5pm. Closed Feb. Bus: see "Getting Here," above.

This catacomb has the biggest parking lot, and hence the largest crowds of tour bus groups—and the cheesiest, most Disneyesque tour, full of canned commentary and stilted jokes. Some of the tunnels, however, are phenomenal, 70 feet high and less than 6 feet wide, with elongated tomb niches pigeonholed all the way up to the top. Of all the catacombs, these are among the oldest and certainly the largest (12 miles of tunnels more than 33 acres and five levels that house the remains of half a million Christians), and were the final resting place of 16 early popes. You also get to ogle some of the earliest Christian art—frescoes, carvings, and drawings scratched into the rock depicting ancient Christian symbols like the fish, the anchor, the dove, and images that tell some of the earliest popular Bible stories.

✪ **Catacombe di San Domitilla.** V. d. Sette Chiese 283. ☎ **06/511-0342.** Admission 8,000L ($4.70), 4,000L ($2.35) age 6–14. Wed–Mon 8:30am–noon, 2:30–5pm. Closed Jan. Bus: see "Getting Here," above.

This oldest of the catacombs is also hands-down the winner for most enjoyable catacomb experience. Groups are small, most guides are genuinely entertaining and personable, and depending on the mood of the group and your guide the visit may last 20 minutes or over an hour. You enter through a sunken 4th-century church. There are fewer "sights" than in the other catacombs—although the 2nd-century fresco of the *Last Supper,* is impressive—but some of the guides actually hand you a few bones out of a tomb niche so you can rearticulate an ancient Christian hip. (Incidentally, this is the only catacomb where you'll get to see bones; the rest have emptied their tombs to rebury the remains in ossiaries on the inaccessible lower levels.)

15 Organized Tours

Enjoy Rome, V. Varese 39 (☎ **06/445-1843;** www.enjoyrome.it), has a young staff from various English-speaking countries who run both 3-hour **walking tours** (maximum 15 to 20 people; those of Ancient Rome and Rome at Night run daily, of the Vatican about three times weekly) and daily 4-hour **bike tours** (bike and helmet included; maximum 10 people). They cost 30,000L ($17.65), or 25,000L ($14.70) for the walking tours if you're under 26.

What kind of **guided bus tour** you get depends on how much you spend. For 15,000L ($8.80), city-run **ATAC bus 110** (☎ 06/4695-2252) runs on a 3-hour circuit on an old-fashioned bus where your only "guide" is an information leaflet. It leaves from outside Termini daily at 10:30am, and 2, 3, 5, and 6pm and costs 15,000L ($8.80). **Green Line Tours** (☎ 06/483-787) gives you an audio guide in the language of your choice for the hop-on, hop-off bus tour that costs 30,000L ($17.65) for a day ticket (10am to 3pm). If you want live commentary, you'll have to pony up 53,000 to 60,000L ($31.20 to $35.30) to **American Express** (☎ 06/6764-2413), Pz. di Spagna 38, for their 4-hour introductory tours, which depart at 9:30am and/or 2:30pm daily, depending on the season. One tour gives a general overview of all Rome and the Vatican, another focuses mainly on ancient Rome.

16 Special & Free Events

The week before Lent is **Carnevale,** when everyone eats *frappe* (pastry leaves coated with powered sugar) and the kiddies go around dressed in costume for their own version of Halloween (only without the candy). The final Tuesday, *Martedi Grasso* (Fat Tuesday), is a night for big private parties, but little goes on out in the streets. At the end of April/beginning of May, the Spanish Steps are covered with azaleas for the **Festa di Primvera,** or feast of spring.

During **Holy Week,** pilgrims flood the city to attend church and glimpse the pope saying Mass at the Colosseum on **Good Friday,** after which he leads a procession around the ancient amphitheater pausing for each of the Stations of the Cross. On **Easter Sunday,** the pope speaks a blessing from his balcony in the Vatican overlooking St. Peter's square, and on *Pasquetta* (**Easter Monday**), everyone leaves town for his first picnic of spring.

April 21 is **Rome's Birthday** (officially founded 753 B.C.) celebrated every year with ceremonies on the Campidoglio and little shallow basin candles that are set to flicker all along the city's stairways and palazzo rooftops. In late April or early May, there's an **International Horse Show** of equestrian skill held in the Villa Borghese's Piazza di Siena. **May Day** (May 1) is celebrated by the city's left-leaning citizens with a huge free rock concert on the piazza in front of San Giovanni in Laterano that lasts all afternoon and night. At the end of May (and again in late October) there's an **antiques fair** sponsored by the dealers along Via de' Coronari, and an **art fair** at the galleries lining Via Margutta.

Rome's **Estate Romana** summer has been drawing countless concerts, programs, exhibitions, and performers to numerous venues across the city in recent years. Summer is also when the **Rome Opera heads outdoors** to perform a roster of popular favorites at various venues that may include on any given year performances of *Aida* in the ancient Baths of Caracalla and other evocative settings.

For a slightly more religious good time, the June 23 **Festa di San Giovanni** is still celebrated with throngs of people singing and dancing and consuming large amounts of stewed snails and artery-clogging *porchetta* pork on Piazza San Giovanni in Laterano. On June 29, the two Big Saints are honored in the **Festa di San Pietro e Paolo** with a street fair on Via Ostiense and Masses at St. Peters and St. Paul's Outside the Walls.

The Trastevere district celebrates, well, itself during the mid-July **Festa dei Noiantri,** or "Feast of We Others," immortalized near the end of Fellini's film *Roma* (the scene in which he interviews Gore Vidal). This festival basically consists of everyone eating outside at long communal tables with a street fair on Viale Trastevere and concerts and plays performed on Piazza Santa Maria in Trastevere.

August 5 is the **Festa della Madonna della Neve** in the Basilica of Santa Maria Maggiore, wherein the church's legendary founding is reenacted with a pretty "snowfall" of rose petals over the congregation during Mass. August 15 marks the start of the **Ferr'agosto.** It is not a holiday; it is an exodus. It's when most Romans (and Italians across the country) leave for their 2 weeks at the beach. The city is deserted, museums and public services like buses go on restricted hours, almost every shop not directly catering to tourists shutters up for the duration, and it tends to be hotter than the "Damned in Hell" side of a *Last Judgment* fresco. Try by any means possible *not* to be in Rome for the final 2 weeks of August.

In the first week of September, grape growers from the region come to the Basilica of Maxentius in the Roman Forum to hold a **Sagra dell'Uva,** or "Festival of the

Grape," in the shade of its half-ruined vaults. This harvest festival of half-price grapes is accompanied by costumed musicians and other market stalls.

You've seen it on TV, now you can come in person to watch the pope give his annual **December 25** *Urbi et Orbi* blessing from his Vatican window overlooking St. Peters, repeating the words in as many languages as the polyglot pontiff can manage. For a more consumerism (but traditional) take on the holiday season, visit the **Christmas fair on Piazza Navona** between mid-December and January 6, where the market stalls of handmade crèche figurines and *La Befana* Christmas Witch dolls still pepper the square between stands hawking mass market toys and trailers housing carney games of chance.

17 Shopping

THE SHOPPING SCENE & BEST BUYS

Rome's best buys are in antiquities, high fashion, wine, ecclesiastical knickknacks, designer housewares, and flea-market bargaining. The capital's toniest boutique zone radiates out from the **Spanish Steps,** centered on the matriarch of high fashion streets, **Via dei Condotti.** Condotti runs arrow-straight from the base of the Steps and has become rather too famous for its own good, sprouting such downscale abominations as a Footlocker and other international chain outlets. This zone is bounded by **Via del Corso,** ground zero for Rome's most fashionable see-and-be-seen *passeggiata* evening stroll. It, too, is lined with generally expensive bigger stores—great for window shopping, but look elsewhere for good prices.

Via dei Coronari, running west off the north end of Piazza Navona, has always been the heart of Rome's antiques district. Almost every address here is a dealer or restorer, and many of their wares or works-in-progress spill out onto the narrow cobbled street. For art, the highest concentration of dealers and studios lies along **Via Margutta,** a side street parallel to Via del Babuino.

But while the locals do turn out to passeggiata on the Corso and window shop on Via dei Condotti, the actual shopping in these parts is pretty touristy. To the Romans, the true shopping nexus of the city is the upper-middle-class residential zone of **Prati,** just northeast of Vatican, with the economic activity centered on wide **Via Cola di Rienzo.** Here you'll find generally lower prices, more down-to-earth stores, and a much better opportunity to see how the citizens of Rome really live and shop.

SHOPPING A TO Z

ANTIQUITIES   How much is a Grecian urn? Anywhere from 200,000 to 9.5 million L ($117.65 to $5,588.25) at **M. Simotti Rocchi,** Lgo. Fontanella Borghese 76 (☎ 06/687-6656), a dealer in Etruscan, Greek, and Roman antiquities. That cheapest painted vase would be a 4-inch piece from the ancient equivalent of a child's tea set. Thought only museums and the very rich could own a piece of the ancient world? Here you can pick up Roman coins, tiny terra-cotta ex-voto heads, or an oil lamp starting at 150,000L ($88.25). Marble statues can cost up to 150 million L— still, it's about one-third the price you'd find at Sotheby's in New York or London.

For even lower prices, visit **Gea Arte Antica,** V. d. Coronari 233A (☎ 06/6880-1369), where small oil lamps go for as little as 120,000 to 200,000L ($70.60 to $117.65)—although the more nicely decorated ones, not to mention larger vases, start around 900,000L ($529.40). It is hoped that Tullio Diamanti got a license to carry coins as well at his shop in 1999. If you'd prefer to wear your classical acquisitions, check out **Massimo Maria Melis,** under "Jewelry," below.

BOOKS   Among the better English-language bookstores are the venerable **Lion Bookshop,** in its new digs at V. d. Greci 33–36 (☎ 06/3265-4007); the large **Anglo-American,** beyond the Spanish Steps at V. d. Vite 102 (☎ 06/679-5222); and the even larger **Economy Bookshop,** just below Termini at V. Torino 136 (☎ 06/474-6877), which also offers a wide selection of cheap, used paperbacks (trade in that already read novel for another) and a free "Rome Travel Pack" with map and guides to the city's services.

Italy's version of Barnes & Noble is the Feltrinelli chain, and you'll find a wide selection of books in English at the huge branch off Piazza d. Repubblica, **Feltrinelli International**, V. V. E. Orlando 84–86 (☎ 06/487-0999; www.feltrinelli.it). Other branches are at Lgo. di Torre Argentina 5A (☎ 06/6880-3248), V. d. Babuino 49–40 (☎ 06/3600-1873), and a shop next door to the "International" one at V. V. E. Orlando 78–81 (☎ 06/487-0171).

A newcomer to this multilevel megabookshop scene is **Mel Bookstore,** V. Nazionale 254–255 (☎ 06/488-5405), worthwhile for carrying both new and discounted used books and CDs. There's a tiny cafe upstairs next to the art books (some of which are marked down 50%), and a small selection of English books.

Remainders, Pz. S. Silvestro 27–28 (☎ 06/679-2824), is what the name says—a shop selling overstock books up to 50% off, including lots of glossy art and coffee-table books. **La Grotta del Libro,** V. d. Pellegrino 172 (☎ 06/687-7567), and **Libreria Vecchia Roma,** V. d. Pellegrino 94, both look like garages piled to the ceiling with books, advertising even cheaper "they fell off the back of the truck" coffee-table books at 50 to 80% off, but not as consistent a selection. **Le Pleiadi Librerie,** V. d. Giubbaonari 76–77 (☎ 06/6880-7981), is classier, with a wider selection of recently printed books on art and the city of Rome up to 50% off. Also don't miss the **antiquarian book and print market** on Piazza Borghese with good deals on dated art books as well as spiffy Roman prints.

DEPARTMENT STORES   The top two national department store chains in Italy are both a bit pricey. The huge, designer label–driven **La Rinascente,** Via del Corso/Piazza San Silvestro (☎ 06/679-7691), is set apart by its cover-all-bases selection, English-language information and tax-free shopping desk, and central location in its own 19th-century high rise. **Coin,** above San Giovanni Metro stop at Pzle. Appio 7 (☎ 06/708-0020), has recently been muscling in on La Rinascente territory by going more upscale in look and attitude, with stylish displays of upper-middle-class fashions—a chic Macy's.

For more everyday shopping, head to **Standa,** locations at Vle. Trastevere 62–64 (☎ 06/589-5342) and V. Cola di Rienzo 173 (☎ 06/324-3319), the chain where Italians buy their socks and underwear. It's the place that runs back-to-school specials and carries bulk dish detergent, frying pans, lamps, cake mix, and other everyday items and clothes—a sort of upscale Kmart with a supermarket in the basement. **Upim,** Piazza di S. Maria Maggiore (☎ 06/446-5579), is another national chain that sits perhaps one hair's width above Standa (we're in Sears/JCPenney territory now).

DESIGN & HOUSEWARES   Italians are masters of industrial design, making the most utilitarian items into memorable pieces of art. Rather than a percolator, they create the Pavoni espresso machine, and the lowly teapot becomes a whimsical Alessi masterpiece that MOMA is proud to display.

If you're willing to take your budget above the $70 a day point—or you just want to browse among the bounty—**Spazio Sette,** hidden at V. d. Barberi 7 off Largo di Torre Argentina (☎ 06/686-9747), is far and away Rome's best housewares emporium, a design boutique of department store proportions. It goes way beyond the requisite Alessi tea kettles to fill three huge stories with the greatest names, and latest word, in Italian and international design. Even if you aren't in the market for the living-room furnishings up on the top floor, climb up anyway to gawk at the frescoed ceilings. Another good bet is **Bagagli,** V. Cam. Marzio 42 (☎ **06/687-1406**). It's not the cheapest in town—though there is a discount section at the back—but there's a good selection of Alessi, Rose and Tulipani, and Villeroy & Boch china in a pleasantly kitschy old Rome setting (cobblestone floors and so on).

Bargain hunters should head to one of **Stock Market's** two branches, at V. d. Banchi Vecchi 51–52 (☎ **06/686-4238**) or near the Vatican at V. Tacito 60 (☎ **06/3600-2343**). You'll find mouthwatering prices on last year's models, overstock, slight irregulars, and artistic misadventures in design that the pricier boutiques haven't been able to move. Most is moderately funky household stuff, but you never know when you'll find a gem of design hidden on the shelves.

If the big names don't do it for you, you may prefer **c.u.c.i.n.a.,** V. d. Babuino 118A (no phone), a stainless steel shrine to everything you need for a proper Italian kitchen, sporting designs that are as beautiful in their simplicity as they are utilitarian.

FASHION AT A DISCOUNT   Rome has several stock houses selling last year's fashions, irregulars, and overstock at cut-rate prices. One of the best is **Il Discount dell'Alta Moda,** with branches near the Spanish Steps at V. di Gesù e Maria 16A (☎ **06/361-3796**) and near Termini at V. Viminale 35 (☎ **06/482-3917**). The honest and genuinely helpful staff will help you pick through the constantly shifting racks of clothing (men's and women's) at up to 50% off from such labels as Versace, Donna Karan, Armani, Dolce & Gabbana, Venturi, Krizia, and Ferré.

Tiny **Firmastock,** V. d. Carrozze 18 (☎ **06/6920-0371**), carries everything from Levi's and Hugo Boss to Valentino, Armani, and Max Mara all from 50 to 70% off. The small, eclectic, and ever-changing inventory includes men's and women's suits, dresses, overcoats, and shoes. It's perfect if you want to slip into a pair of Armani pants for under $80.

New Fashion, in Prati at V. Simone de Saint Bon 85–87 (☎ **06/3751-3947**), carries women's suits and skirts from top designers such as Moschino, Valentino, Max Mara, and Dolce & Gabbana as well as lesser-known "Made in Italy" labels, usually from the past few seasons. Prices are not as low as at the other stock houses listed here, but the discounts are honest and the outfits tend to be more consistently fashionable.

It's not a stock house, but **Emporio Armani,** V. d. Babuino 140 (☎ **06/322-1581**), is a sizable shop carrying the famed designer's downscale line—clothing less chichi, slightly less well made, and designed especially for us budget-minded plebes to be sold at prices less (this is a relative term) heart-stoppingly expensive than Armani's haute couture garments.

FOOD   Rome's top food emporium—after the fresh **food markets** described in the "Picnicking" box of the dining section earlier in this chapter—is undoubtedly **Castroni,** a legend since 1932 with the main shop in Prati at V. Cola di Rienzo 196 (☎ **06/687-4383**), and an offspring store just north of Piazza del Popolo at V. Flaminia 28–32 (☎ **06/361-1029**). Castroni carries a stupefying collection of the best foods, both fine and common, from around the world, including such exotic concoctions as American peanut butter.

Next door to the main Castroni is **Franchi,** V. Cola di Rienzo 204 (☎ **06/687-4651**; www.franchi.it), a more traditional Italian-style alimentari, and one of the highest caliber. The excellent prepared foods include, starting at 5pm, *calzoni fritti* and *calzoni al forno* (fried and baked versions of pizza pockets wrapped around cheese and ham)—the best in town by a long shot, with the daily long lines awaiting that magical 5pm to prove it.

Romans come from all over town and the burbs to buy their cheeses and milk products from among the fantastic selection at **Latteria Micocci,** V. Collina 16 (☎ 06/474-1784). For some offbeat food shopping in Trastevere, hit **Drogheria Innocenzi,** Pz. San Cosimato 66 (☎ 06/581-2725), an old-fashioned bit-of-everything grocery store with a newfangled eclectic stock. Part natural health food emporium, part gourmet international foods shop, and part medieval spicery, it's the only place I've ever been able to find all the odd ingredients called for by the recipes in Apicius's ancient Roman cookbook.

GIFTS   I've always been of the opinion that the greatest Roman gifts come from the combination of kitschy and holier-than-thou **Vatican gift shops** and souvenir stands that encircle St. Peter's and the Vatican in a most unreligious capitalist swarm. You'll find everything from a plastic, light-up Michelangelo's *Pietà* and pictures that show a smiling Christ from one angle and a crucified one from another, to models of the Virgin Mary that weep on command, your-name-here papal indulgences, and the oft-sought but seldom found "Pope-ener" (an anthropomorphic corkscrew; by twisting the medallion printed with the Pope's head, you cause his "arms" to raise slowly in benediction).

The more astrologically minded can visit **Guaytamelli,** in Trastevere at V. d. Moro 59 (☎ 06/588-0704), where Argentinean Adrian Rodriguez crafts singular time-pieces—hour candles, hourglasses, and sundials in the form of rings, sticks, pendants, and flip-top boxes—of beautiful and quality workmanship at rather low prices (from 15,000L/$8.80 for a sundial ring). There's even a tiny flat pendant sextant; turn the sandwich of engraved disks until they align with the stars and it'll tell you the time at night.

JEWELRY   For traditional pieces, **Tresor,** V. d. Croce 71B–72 (☎ 06/687-7753), crafts classically worked 18-karat gold jewelry at prices not much higher than the market value of the raw material. At **Massimo Maria Melis,** V. dell'Orso 57 (☎ 06/686-9188), 21-karat gold is hand worked to encase genuine coins and pieces of glass or carved stone from the Etruscan, Roman, and medieval eras. A pair of earrings set with Imperial Roman coins will set you back about 500,000L ($295.10).

MARKETS   The mother lode of Roman bazaars is **Porta Portese,** a flea market off Piazza Ippolito Nievo that began at the close of World War II as a black and gray market but has grown to be one of Europe's premier permanent garage sales. You'll find everything here from antique credenzas to used carburetors, bootleg CDs to birds that squawk "Ciao," previously owned clothes to Italian comic books to used Leicas, all in a carnival atmosphere of haggling and hollering, jostling and junk jockeying, beggars, pickpockets, and shrewd stall owners, swirling around auditory pockets of badly dubbed dance music and the scents of sweet roasting corn. It runs every Sunday, dawn to lunchtime. Hang on to your wallet.

Snuggled up along a stretch of the Aurelian Wall off Via Sannio are the half-covered stalls of the **San Giovanni clothing market,** the best place to pick up inexpensive new and cut-rate used clothing and outfit yourself like a true Roman (or cheap army surplus in case you need an extra pack, sleeping bag, or tent). It runs Monday to Friday 10am to 1pm, Saturday 10am to 5pm.

Campo dei Fiori, once the site of medieval executions, is today one of Rome's most lively squares—a cobblestoned expanse that starts bustling in the pre-dawn as the florists arrange bouquets and fruit and vegetable vendors set up their stalls, imbuing the piazza with a burst and swirl of color and scents that winds down after lunch but is echoed later in the evening as the square comes to life again in a carnival of dining and nightlifing Romans and tourists. For other **food markets,** see the box on "Pick-nicking" in the dining section earlier in this chapter.

MUSIC   Italy's biggest chain of record stores is **Ricordi,** with major branches in Rome at V. d. Corso 506 (☎ 06/361-2370), V. C. Battisti 120D (☎ 06/679-8022), and on Piazza Indipendenza (☎ 06/444-0706). All have a wide selection of Italian and international music and listening stations, as does **Messaggeri Musciali,** V. d. Corso 123 (☎ 06/679-3948). For a good selection of used and new CDs, tapes, and vinyl visit **Millerecords** (☎ 06/495-8242), with two shops on V. d. Mille at no. 29 (jazz, rock, and pop) and no. 41 (classical).

SHOES & ACCESSORIES   If you're scared away by all those zeros on the tags at designer footwear boutiques, try **Rocco Shoes,** V. Gioberti 22–26 (☎ 06/446-7299), where you'll find good quality control on minor "Made in Italy" brands you've prob-ably never heard of at prices ranging from 10,000L ($5.90) for women's canvas slip-pers to 110,000L ($64.70) for men's dress leather shoes. Similar discount shoe shops line this street, all the way down to the rock-bottom prices on cheap knock-offs avail-able at outdoor stands around Santa Maria Maggiore at the end of the block.

For classically inspired and beautifully crafted shoes, sandals, and half-boots starting around 300,000L ($176.50), check out the boutique of **Fausto Santini,** V. Frattina 120 (☎ 06/678-4114). They also do purses and bags along clean, modernist lines. If you like Santini's style but not the prices, head over to V. Cavour 106 (☎ 06/488-0934), the designer's discount outlet for last year's models ranging from 100,000 to 200,000L ($58.80 to $117.65), and remainders as low as 20,000 to 70,000L ($11.75 to $41.20).

Want a wider range of accessories at stock shop prices? **Il Discount delle Firme,** on the tiny road off Largo del Tritone called V. d. Serviti 27 (☎ 06/482-7790), carries perfumes, purses, ties, scarves, shoes, wallets, and belts from all the top names (and a few lesser-known Italian designers) at 50% off. Near the Vatican your best bet is **Grandi Firme,** V. Germanico 8 (☎ 06/3972-3169), with a rotating accessory stock of purses, ties, belts, scarves, and shoes also up to 50% off from names like Fendi, Christian Dior, Missoni, and Ferré.

Windsor knot fans should make a stop at **Cravatterie Nazionali,** V. Vittoria 62 (☎ 06/6992-2143). It's a boutique, not a stock shop, but it sports a good selection of Givenchy, Zenga, Valentino, Gucci, Missoni, Krizia, and other major label ties at rea-sonable (for designer) prices and all in one spot.

If you want to hook yourself up with one of those colorful **Invicta** backpacks that seem a required part of every school uniform for Italian students from kindergarten through grad school, visit their showroom at V. d. Babuino 27–28 (☎ 06/3600-1737).

TOYS   Rome's best toy store is **La Città del Sole,** V. d. Scrofa 65 (☎ 06/6880-3805). Since 1977, this owner-operated branch of the national chain has sold old-fashioned wooden brain teasers, construction kits, hand puppets, 3-D puzzles, and science kits. There's even a tot's book section in case you want to start junior on his Italian early. And there's nary a video game in sight. These are the sorts of toys that, while being gobs of fun, also help youngsters push and stretch their minds, encour-aging creativity and imagination. Heck, a lot of this stuff is fun for adults, too.

For slightly more mass-market toys—but still fantastic and largely European-made—visit one of the **Giorni** branches in Prati. At V. d. Gracchi 31–33 (☎ 06/321-7145), you'll find only models, from build-it-yourself to ready out of the box, including the Bburago series of cast-metal cars—in case you can't afford a full-scale

Ferrari or Fiat. The softer side is at V. M. Colonna 26 (☎ 06/321-6929), where you'll find dolls, stuffed animals, and music boxes. For a more general selection, visit their V. Pompeo Magno 86 shop (☎ 06/321-3540), where the playthings are appropriate for ages up to 10, or head next door to V. Pompeo Magno 84 (☎ 06/321-4736), the toy outlet "for ages 8 to 99."

WINE & LIQUOR   Rome's most peculiar inebriatory experience has to be **Ai Monasteri,** of the north corner of Piazza Navona at Pz. d. Cinque Lune 76 (☎ 06/ 6880-2783). Here are gathered together the liqueurs, elixirs, *digestivi,* extracts, apéritifs, and other alcoholic ingestibles that are concocted by industrious monks at various monasteries, abbeys, and convents across Italy. Sort of a central outlet shop for the country's collective monastic liquor cabinet.

The granddaddy of Rome wine stores is **Trimani,** V. Goito 20 (☎ 167/014-625 toll-free, or 06/446-8351), a family business since 1821 with literally thousands of bottles in a huge shop and even more down in the cellars. This place ain't cheap, but it isn't unreasonable either. You'll find plenty of quaffable stuff for under 10,000L ($5.90)—you just have to search it out between lots of classy, aged, high-profile bottles that can easily run upwards of 200,000L ($117.65).

For those looking for a deal, **La Vecchia Cantina,** V. Viminale 7B (☎ 06/ 460-737), is a good spot to pick up a cheap but decent bottle of *vino* for that picnic. For more atmosphere and selection, try **Enoteca al Parlamento,** V. d. Prefetti 15 (☎ 06/687-3446), a stylish and old-fashioned wood-lined wine emporium where you rub shoulders with politicians and other business suits as you sample wine by the glass at the counter and choose from the select stock, which also includes liqueurs, champagnes, honeys, and marmalades. Another historic wine shop is **Buccone,** V. di Ripetta 19–20 (☎ 06/361-2154), with more bottles that you'd know what to do with and tastings as well.

18 Rome After Dark

The true Roman nightlife experience consists of lingering over a full restaurant meal until after midnight, with lots of good wine and good conversation among friends. For a more high culture evening, or a late night or bar hopping, check out the listings below and the events guides described under "Newspapers & Magazines" in the "Fast Facts" of section 2, earlier in this chapter.

THE PERFORMING ARTS

CLASSICAL MUSIC   Always check the events listings (see "Newspapers & Magazines" section of "Rome Fast Facts" on p. 102) for information about concerts being held in Rome's medieval and baroque churches and, in summer especially, outdoor evening performances in evocative, archaeological settings surrounded by ancient columns and ruins.

One of Italy's premier musical associations, the **Accademia Nazionale di Santa Ceclia,** finally has a permanent seat at the Auditorio V. d. Concilliazione 4 (☎ 06/ 6880-1044, or contact their V. Vittoria 6 office at **06/361-1064; for tickets call 06/3938-7297**). The season runs October to May, with symphonic concerts Saturday to Tuesday, and soloist and ensemble chamber music Fridays. In summer, there are outdoor concerts in the Villa Giulia's theatrical *nymphaeum.*

The **Accademia Filarmonica Romana,** which performs in the Teatro Olimpico north of the center at Pz. G. da Fabriano 17 (☎ **06/323-4890,** or 06/3938-7297 ticket sales), was founded in 1821 and puts on Thursday night concerts from October to June that range from chamber music and classical hits to folk and ethnic music. The Accademia also hosts international ballet and dance companies.

The **Orchestra Regionale del Lazio** performs at the Teatro Nazionale, V. Viminale 51 (☎ **06/485-494** or 06/487-0614) from January to June, with a program from baroque classics to contemporary composers directed by mainly young, up-and-coming Italian and international conductors and musicians.

OPERA & BALLET   After years of languishing without funding or respect, Rome's **Teatro dell'Opera** finally has a new superintendent (as of 1997) and a new musical director (as of 1998) who have turned the outfit around and are attracting fine musicians, conductors, and performers for their opera and ballet seasons. In Rome's newly restored late 19th-century opera house, **Piazza B. Gigli** at the intersection of Via Torino and Via Viminale (☎ **167/016-665** toll-free information, 06/481-601 office, or 06/4816-0255 box office; www.themix.it), the preseason runs October to December, the official season January to June. The summer season of July and August changes venue every year (there's a rumor they may even start putting on *Aida* in the Baths of Caracalla again). You can buy tickets at the box office (closed Monday), any Banca di Roma bank, or by phone at ☎ **147/882-211.**

THE CLUB & MUSIC SCENE

DISCOS & CLUBS   Dam Dam, V. Benedetta 17 (no phone), has been a survivor on Rome's fickle after-dark scene for 15 years, and is still a required stop during any Trastevere night of clubbing. These days there's a variety of musical styles, including salsa and Latin Tuesdays; disco, '80s, and R&B Thursdays; and rap, hip-hop, and reggae Saturdays. There's live music at least once a week, and a non-smoking room. Best of all, admission is free and it's open every night from 8pm to 2am.

Clochard, V. d. Teatro Pace 29–30 (☎ **06/6880-2029**), is a restaurant and nightclub in a 15th-century palazzo with a disco floor spinning funk and '70s flashback tunes and featuring a live band most evenings. It opens early, 8:30pm to 3:30am; it's closed Monday, and you'll only have to pay 15,000L ($8.80) for that obligatory drink from Thursday through Saturday.

Rome's attempt at a major Manhattan- or London-style disco is **Alien,** V. Velletri 13–19 (☎ **06/841-2212**), with a funky sci-fi decor in an underground and garage music setting, with (mainly 20-something) pumping bodies dancing. Tuesdays it does an about-face to become a New Age club. It's open Tuesday to Sunday 11pm to 4am, with an admission charge of 10,000 to 30,000L ($5.90 to $17.65).

In the heart of the center is the slightly creepy **Gilda,** V. Mario de' Fiori 97 (☎ **06/678-4838**), a famous disco and nightclub patronized by a fair lot of politicians (hence the creepiness factor) but also plenty of Romans of all ages, and lots of visitors, who arrive in droves to this club to act excruciatingly trendy but seemingly with no clear idea why, or indeed agreement on just exactly what trendy *is* these days. The admission charge with obligatory first drink is a scandalous 40,000L ($23.55); they're open 10:30pm to 4am Tuesday to Sunday.

LATIN RHYTHMS   Romans go crazy for Latin music (no pun intended), and two of the best clubs where you can enjoy it are in Trastevere. **Berimbau,** V. d. Fienaroli 30B (☎ **06/581-3249**), is a South American club devoted to samba, cocktails, and live music every night, with free Latin dance lessons and a DJ for dancing after the live concert. It's open 10:30pm to 3am. Obligatory first drink is 10,000L ($5.90) Wednesday, Thursday, and Sunday; 15,000L ($8.80) Friday; and 20,000L ($11.75) Saturday. You can also get free dance lessons Tuesday nights at **Bossa Nova,** V. Orti di Trastevere 23 (☎ **06/581-6121**), a Brazilian joint with live music every night. Obligatory first drink is 10,000L ($5.90). It's open Tuesday to Sunday 10:30pm to 3am.

The open-air **Sela Rum,** V. d. Fienaroli 12 (☎ **06/581-9130**), isn't exactly a Latin American dance club, but it does try to recreate a relaxed, laid-back Caribbean beach bar with bamboo screens and low-key live music (mainly guitar, folk, or slightly more jumpy Latin or classical Spanish tunes). Admission is free; it's open May to September from 10pm to 2am.

JAZZ, SOUL & BLUES If you make time for only one jazz club, make it **Alexanderplatz,** in Prati at V. Ostia 9 (☎ **06/3974-2171**). It's really Rome's only club with a heavy dose of respect on the international jazz circuit, drawing names like Winton Marsalis, Lionel Hampton, and George Coleman along with top Italian players. Meals are served starting at 9pm, with the concert beginning at 10:30pm and lasting to 1:30am or later. They close Mondays, and a pass good for 2 months costs 12,000L ($7.05).

Two other solid choices on the Rome jazz scene for live performances are **New Mississippi Jazz Club,** B. Angelico 18a (☎ **06/6880-6348**), open Thursday to Saturday 9:30pm to 2am; and **Colosseum Jazz Live,** V. P. Verri 17 (☎ **06/7049-7412**), where you can hear some of Italy's top artists Thursday to Sunday 9pm to 2am. Both charge one-time admission passes costing 10,000L ($5.90).

The Roman home of the blues is in Trastevere at **Big Mamma,** Vc. S. Francesco a Ripa 18 (☎ **06/581-2551**), which since 1984 has been hosting some of the world's top blues musicians when they come to Rome, sprinkling the offerings with funk and jazz as well. A monthly pass costs 10,000L ($5.90), but the prices sometimes go up for particular shows. The music is strictly live, so it's only open when there's someone on the ticket (call ahead).

BARS, PUBS & ENOTECHE BY NEIGHBORHOOD

AROUND CAMPO DE' FIORI On happenin' Cam. de' Fiori you'll find a full gamut of alcohol-oriented nightspots. The exceedingly popular but rigorously old-fashioned wine bar called **Vineria** (no. 15; no phone) is still holding its own amid the nightly crowds of this newly trendy piazza. There's a crowded **Taverna del Campo** snack stop with crostini, panini, and beer next door (no. 16; ☎ **06/687-4402**), and a few more doors down you can groove to the live-DJ spun music (and air-conditioning) of the American-style bar **The Drunken Ship** (no. 20–21; ☎ **06/6830-0535**). Off the Campo itself, things chill out quickly, although if you want some smooth, understated modernist digs with cocktails, pop 2 blocks over to trendy **Chiavari,** V. d. Chiavari 4–5 (☎ **06/683-2378**).

NEAR PIZZA NAVONA/THE PANTHEON In the Tiber Bend around Piazza Navona and the Pantheon, steer your beer cravings toward the basement rooms of the **Black Duke** (☎ **06/6830-0381**), an Irish pub complete with pub grub just north of the Pantheon at V. d. Maddalena 29B. Similar is the **Abbey Theatre Irish Pub,** V. d. Governo Vecchio 51–53 (☎ **06/686-1341**), a "Guinness bar"—the Irish beer company sells prefab rustic-style pubs, complete from the woodsy decor down to the kitschy Brit paraphernalia and dart board. Of course, Kilkenny and Guinness are on tap.

Even more genuine is the **St. Andrew's Pub,** Vc. D. Cancelleria 36 (☎ **06/683-2638**), so Scottish it's got tartan on the walls. There's Tennent's on tap along with that excellent Edinburgh double malt red ale Devil's Kiss, and Caffrey's stout (that one's Irish, but it's still good). There are simple dishes like hamburgers, but sadly (fortunately?) no haggis.

The most unique nightspot in the area without a doubt ✪ **Jonathan's Angels**, V. d. Fossa 16 (☎ **06/689-3426**), down a side street strung with colored Christmas lights and a temple to kitsch and one man's artistic vision. The owner was a circus acrobat and restaurateur before opening this funky, dark, casual bar and turning his energies to painting and sculpting to decorate the place. If nothing else, come to use the over-the-top bathroom, complete with its own fountain and thematic putti.

Henry's Pub, V. Tor Millinia 34a (☎ 06/686-9904), is a small joint with outdoor seating on the heart of the action off Piazza Navona's northwest end and a sangria punch bowl into which the barman dumps the leftovers from mixing drinks. Next door at no. 32 is the **Vineria La Botticella** (☎ 06/686-1107), a little vineria-cum-American-style bar with Devil's Kiss on tap. Down on Piazza S. Andrea della Valle at Cor. V. Emanuele II 107 is the ever-popular and crowded **John Bull Pub** (☎ 06/687-1537) serving John Bull ale and Strongbow cider to a mainly young crowd (lots of American students).

NEAR THE SPANISH STEPS & PIAZZA DEL POPOLO   The **Birreria Viennese,** V. d. Croce 21 (☎ 06/679-5569), is a Bavarian-tinged Viennese *bierhaus* with a woodsy dark interior and pretzels hanging at each table where you can order Austrian grub and beer by the liter mug. Down the block, **L'Enoteca Antica di Via della Croce,** V. d. Croce 76b (☎ 06/679-0896), is a friendly and relaxed spot, sort of a traditional *enoteca* gone trendy, now offering wine bar fare like salads and sampler platters of cheese and salamis along with wine by the glass, beer, and harder drinks.

True to its name, the **Victoria House Pub,** V. Gesù e Maria 18 (☎ 06/320-1698), is a genuine English Victorian–style pub—though most of the ale on tap is Scottish (Tennent's) or Irish (Cafferey's). There's also shepherd's pie and other pub grub at lunch and in the evenings, plus (minor miracle in nicotine-saturated Italy) a no-smoking bar and sitting room at the back. If you fancy a spot of pool in a contemporary pub on a busy road near the Trevi Fountain (just before the tunnel off Piazza Trionfale), head to **The Albert,** V. d. Traforo 132 (☎ 06/481-8795).

IN TRASTEVERE   New bars and clubs open in Trastevere every month—and about half are closed by the next one (yes, this leaves half of the newbies still functioning; Trastevere seems to know no limit of critical mass when it comes to nightlife). The following places seem here to stay. **Birreria della Scala,** Pz. d. Scala 60 (☎ 06/580-3763), is a somewhat raucous Italian-style beer hall, with lots of good food, snacks, desserts, and a good selection of beers and wines. There's live music Tuesday, Thursday, and Sunday (preceded on Thursday and Sunday by a magic show). **Molly Malone Pub,** V. dell'Arco di San Calisto 17 (☎ 06/5833-0904), is more of an American bar; small, but it's got a dart board.

One of Trastevere's greatest stops for traditionalists doesn't even have a name or a sign at V. d. Scala 64, just the moniker **Vini Olii** (wines and oils) spray-painted on the concrete door lintel. Come for cheap glasses of vino while you stand at the minuscule counter with the neighborhood's old men. The **Bar San Callisto,** Pz. S. Callisto 3–4 (no phone), is just your run-of-the-mill *bar* (in the Italian sense of the word), a bit dingier than most, that somehow has become a requisite nightly stop for everyone from trendoids to tourists to Trasterini (and representing a spectrum of characters from scuzzoid to chic).

THE GAY SCENE

The hottest gay club in Rome these days is **Albi,** V. Monte Testaccio 40–44 (☎ 06/574-3448), with a rotating schedule of DJs that give each night a different spin (Wednesday '70s disco; Thursday garage music; Friday underground tunes; Saturday a mix of pop and dance hits; Saturday house music and surprise festas). Admission ranges from 10,000 to 20,000L ($5.90 to $11.75) and it's open Thursday to Sunday 11pm to 4am.

The Hanger, Via in Selci 69 (☎ 06/488-1397), is Rome's oldest gay club, run by an American/Italian gay couple and these days frequented mainly by the under-30 crowd and Anglo-American visitors. Monday nights draw the biggest crowds with high quality gay skin flicks; this is the only night women are not allowed. Admission is free, and they open Wednesday to Monday 10:30pm to 2am. In the heart of Trastevere is a classic men-only disco called **Angelo Azzurro,** V. Cardinal Merry del Val 13 (☎ 06/580-0472), with guys of all ages dancing to the DJ mix of dance, house, and pop. Admission's free; they open Friday to Sunday only, midnight to 4am.

Strangely, only one club on one night in all of Rome is devoted to lesbians: **New Joli Coeur,** V. Sirte 5 (☎ 06/8621-5827), is a women-only disco open Saturdays 11pm to 4am. It's divided into three sections: a games room, a cabaret or floor show, and a dance hall. Admission ranges from 15,000 to 20,000L ($8.80 to $11.75).

MOVIES

Newly reincarnated from the dingy old movie house that expatriates have loved for decades, the **Pasquino,** now entered from Piazza S. Egidio (☎ 06/580-3622), has three screens showing original-language films (which almost always means English). Screen 1 shows first-run Hollywood movies a month or two after they open in the States; screen 2 leans a bit more toward art house and independent film; while dinky screen 3 is for experimental movies. Tickets are 12,000L ($7.05), 8,000L ($4.70) matinees, Wednesdays, under age 10, and over 60. For screen 2, you must also buy a club pass, good for two months, for 2,000L ($1.20); shows at Pasquino 2 are then 8,000L ($4.70) weekdays, 12,000L ($7.05) weekends.

19 Side Trips: Ostia Antica & Tivoli

OSTIA ANTICA

The ruins of Rome's ancient sea port, 23 kilometers (14 mi.) west of the city, are just as important and almost as fascinating as those of Pompeii, but without the crowds and just a metro ride from Rome. **Ostia Antica** (☎ 06/5635-8099) is only partly excavated, much of it overgrown with tall grasses and umbrella pines that give the place that romantic touch missing from so many dusty, tourist-ridden archaeological sites these days. Bring a picnic and make a day of it.

Most of the buildings date from between the A.D. 1st and 4th centuries, though the city was founded in the 4th century B.C. The site plan handed out at the gate is very good, and most of the structures inside the park are now placarded in English. Most visitors follow the *Decumanus Maximus* (Latin for Main Street) from beginning to end, but take the time to explore the side streets where you'll find lots of intact shops, black and white floor mosaics, a few frescoes clinging to walls, and millstones hiding in the weeds behind baker's shops.

Make sure you stop at the well-preserved **Theater,** built in the A.D. 1st and 2nd centuries, which could seat 2,700 people. Several giant marble theater masks still survive on tufa columns at the stage. The **Casa di Diana** is a typical three-story house with shops on the ground floor, some frescoes on the walls inside, and a courtyard fountain of the huntress goddess that gave the house its name. Don't miss Ostia's on-site museum (☎ 06/563-5801), which houses all the bits that unscrupulous types might try to carry off (as the Dark Ages barbarians and early baroque-era excavators did with wild abandon).

On the town's Forum you'll find the **Capitolum,** an important temple with an imposing flight of steps and most of the brick cella still standing. Finally, search out the **Terme dei Sette Sapienti,** a well-preserved baths complex named for the seven "sages" painted on the wall and spouting bath-house homilies. The central hall here retains its magnificent floor mosaic of hunting scenes.

Admission to the site is 8,000L ($4.70). It's open Tuesday to Sunday 9am to 6pm (4pm in winter); the museum 9am to 1:30pm. Take Rome's B Metro to S. Paolo stop, where you can catch a twice-hourly local train to the *Ostia-Scavi* stop (1,500L/90¢). You can also ride this metro line to its end, *Ostia-Lido,* if you fancy a day at Rome's very crowded (and not perfectly clean) **beach.**

TIVOLI

GETTING HERE　To get to Tivoli, take Rome's B Metro to Ponte Mammolo stop, where you catch the COTRAL bus (3,000L/$1.75) to Tivoli-Villa d'Este (every 30 min.) or Tivoli-Villa Adriana (every hour).

EXPLORING THE AREA　This little city, 32 kilometers (19 miles) from Rome, was already 4 centuries old when the Eternal City itself was founded, and it became a popular spot for countryside villas both during the Imperial period and the Renaissance.

In the center of town is the **Villa D'Este** (☎ 0774/312-070), started by Piero Ligorio for the Humanist and fabulously wealthy Cardinal Ippolito II D'Este in 1550 (the construction outlived both of them and the gardens were added to up until 1927). This pleasure palace is renowned less for the (relatively) modest villa itself than for the spectacular ✪ **gardens,** a baroque fantasy of some 500 fountains terraced down a hillside and surrounded by artificial grottoes and scads of umbrella pines, cypress, ilex, elm, and cedar.

Call before making the trip out here to be sure the fountains will be going at full blast that day, for the play of water against the sunlight is what the Villa D'Este is all about (the fountain is usually going full blast on sunny weekends). Though what's here is spectacular—including the high jets of the Neptune Fountain and the long wall of One Hundred Fountains whose decorative frieze is romantically overgrown with mosses—imagine what it must have been like when the famous Water Organ fountain was still working and playing its songs, or the Fontana della Civitta that created birdsong and the screech of an owl. Admission is 8,000L ($4.70). It's open daily 9am to 6:30pm (4pm in winter).

Five kilometers (3 mi.) before the town on the road to Rome lie the ruins of the most fabulous palace built during the Roman Empire, the ✪ **Villa Adriana** (☎ 0774/530-203). The Emperor Hadrian was quite an accomplished architect, designing not only Rome's Pantheon but also his own lavish Imperial palace in A.D. 118, a countryside retreat within easy reach of the capital and from which he could rule the Empire (and so architecturally advanced that it even included central heating).

Hadrian was a well-traveled man, and picked up so many architectural ideas from his voyages throughout the Empire that he decided to recreate his own versions of famous buildings here at his villa. This is why today you can wander the long pool of the **Canopus,** and Egyptian-inspired piece lined by statues with a beautiful curved colonnade at one end and a Temple of Serapis at the other. Recent reinterpretation of the statues lining this canal suggest that the whole ensemble might be meant to represent the Mediterranean world, with the temple at the end portraying Egypt, the statues that imitate the caryatids from Athens's Acropolis in the middle symbolizing Greece, and the statues of Amazons at the other end standing for Asia.

To honor the genius of the ancient Greeks, Hadrian built himself a peristyle—sort of like a giant cloister measuring 766 by 320 feet—called the **Pecile,** loosely modeled after the Stoa Poikile, or "painted porch," of Athens under which the great philosophical school of Stoicism was founded. **The Teatro Marittimo** was a retreat for the

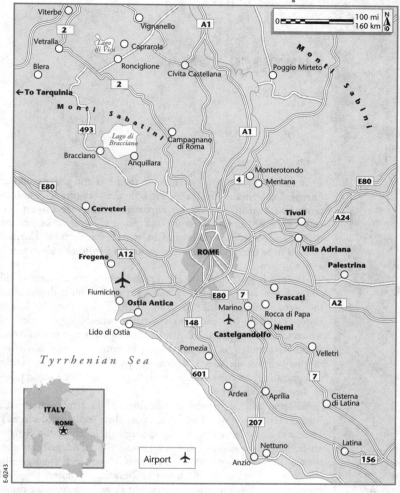

emperor, who could escape with his thoughts to this circular structure in the middle of a pond and pull the wooden bridges after him for seclusion.

The **Imperial Palace** is grouped around four courtyards. In the staff wing are preserved some fine mosaics, and you can see some good portions of both the Small Baths and the Large Baths still standing at the west end of the compound. The grounds of this archaeological park are vast, and parts are still being excavated. Wander for as long as you can, looking for the Greek Theater and the ruins of the Accademia, and pausing in the two small museums to get a better grip on the original layout of the palace. Bring a picnic lunch and stay the whole day. Admission is 8,000L ($4.70). It's open daily 9am to 6:30pm (4pm in winter).

5

Florence

by Patricia Schultz

Five hundred years ago, Florence was the heart and nerve center of European culture and life. It was here from the 14th through the 16th centuries that many of the most important developments in art, science, literature, and architecture took place. Considered one of the richest and most beautiful cities in western civilization, Florence remains to be seen and experienced by today's awestruck visitors much as it was then.

Florence is no longer the axis around which the cultural world revolves, but the taste, elegance, and aesthetic sensibility that marked the Renaissance are still alive and well. Today, the city boasts Europe's richest concentration of artistic wealth, a great deal of which can be seen or sensed without even entering any of its myriad world-class museums. Elegant young Florentines hurry down the narrow cobblestone streets, across the spacious stone-paved piazze, and past the great august palazzi with the same confidence and pride as their forebears.

Europe's cultural revolution was financed in large part by the Medicis (and those who flourished under their commercial success), Florence's unrivaled ruling family throughout much of the Renaissance. They came to power as shrewd bankers and used their unprecedented acumen and wealth to foster artistic and intellectual genius. The city is filled with this heritage: Fully half a dozen principal museums, as well as myriad churches and palazzi, house major paintings and sculpture of that golden period when Florence was, as D. H. Lawrence described it, "Man's perfect center of the Universe."

However, it's not only sights and history that make Florence a special place for visitors. The nuts and bolts of where you stay and what you eat will make this city special in and off-season. Many of the affordable hotels I've listed are housed in imposing palazzi that date from the time of the Medicis and Michelangelo and his peers. You may find yourself sleeping beneath a ceiling decorated with colorful frescoes whose origins reach back into the centuries, or sampling a glass of Chianti in the cantina of a palazzo built before the locally born Giovanni da Verrazzano set eyes on New York Harbor. The rustic though delicious cuisine of this region, *la cucina toscana,* from the heart of the nation's wine- and olive-producing farmland, is one of the finest in Italy—certainly one of the most sought after in the world. But don't worry, it is possible to get a dinner fit for a Florentine duke for a song.

1 Orientation

ARRIVING

BY PLANE Alitalia, British Air, Lufthansa, and many other European airlines service Florence's newly expanded **Amerigo Vespucci Airport** (☎ 055/37-34-98) (also called **Peretola** after the zone in which it's located), although to date there are no direct flights from the United States. The regularly scheduled city bus no. 62 connects the airport with the Piazza Stazione in downtown Florence, making the journey in about 30 minutes, and costs 1,500L (90¢) each way. Slightly more expensive but without the local stops is the hourly **SITA bus** to and from downtown's **bus station** on V. Santa Caterina 15r (☎ 21-47-21) behind the train station, costing 6,000L ($3.50). Metered taxis line up outside the airport's arrival terminal and charge about 25,000L ($14.70) to most hotels in the city center.

From the Pisa Airport A greater number of flights from the United States connect in European cities such as London, Paris, and Frankfurt for Pisa's **Galileo Galilei Airport** (☎ 050/50-07-07). A frequent 1-hour train service to Florence S.M.N. train station costs 7,400L ($4.35). When departing from the Pisa airport, you can check in your baggage for all flights and receive your boarding pass at the **Air Terminal** on track five in Florence's train station. Early morning flights might make train connections to the airport difficult, although the regular train into downtown Pisa Centrale is the alternative, with a 5,000L ($2.95) hop from the Pisa train station to the nearby Pisa Airport.

BY TRAIN Most Florence-bound trains roll into the **Stazione Santa Maria Novella** (☎ 147/888-088 toll free, or 055/28-87-65), which you'll often see abbreviated as "**S.M.N.**" The station is on the western edge of the city's compact *centro storico* or historical center, a leisurely 10-minute walk from the Duomo and 15 minutes from Piazza della Signoria and the Uffizi Galleries. With your back to the tracks, you'll find an **Ufficio Turismo** information and hotel accommodations service office toward the station's left exit (See "Visitor Information" and "Accommodations You Can Afford," below). The train information office is near the opposite exit to your right. Walk straight through the large glass doors into the outer hall for tickets at the *biglietteria* and a bank that changes money Monday to Saturday from 8:20am to 7:20pm. Adjacent to track 16 is an **Albergo Diurno,** or day hotel, where you can wash up or take a shower after a long train ride. There's also a 24-hour **luggage depot** at the head of track 16 where you can drop your bags while you search for a hotel. It charges 5,000L ($2.95) per piece per 12-hour period.

Trains arriving from the principal cities in Italy are frequent (the following prices are for **I.C. trains second class**): **Milan** (3 hr.; 42,500L/$25), **Bologna** (1 hr.; 17,000L/$10), **Rome** (2 hr.; 51,000L/$30), and **Venice** (3½ hr.; 48,000L/$28.25). The occasional train may bypass the Santa Maria Novella station to stop at the outlying **Stazione Campo di Marte** or **Stazione Rifredi,** which can be inconvenient and is worth avoiding. Although there's 24-hour bus service between these satellite stations and the principal S.M.N. station, departures are not always frequent and taxi service is erratic and expensive.

BY BUS Dozens of companies run frequent service to Florence from cities within Tuscany and Umbria to two bus hubs one on either side of the main Train Station of Santa Maria Novella: **SITA** (V. Santa Caterina da Siena 17r; ☎ 055/214721) is important for those bussing to San Gimignano or Siena; **Lazzi** (Pz. d. Stazione 4–6; ☎ 166-856010 toll-free within Italy) specializes in service to Lucca, Pisa, and the coast (Viareggio, Forte dei Marmi).

BY CAR Florence, because of its central location, enjoys good autostrada connections with the rest of Italy. **Autostrada 1** connects Florence with both the north and south. Take **A11** from Florence if you want to travel west through Prato to Lucca and Pisa; follow signs for Firenze-Mare (Florence in the direction of the coast). When you pick up your rental car, agencies will explain both the fastest or most scenic routes to take. Florence lies 172 miles north of **Rome** (approximately 3 hr.), 65 miles west of **Bologna** (1 hr.) and 185 miles south of **Milan** (3 hr.). Driving to Florence is easy; the problems begin once you arrive. Almost all automobiles are banned from the city's centro storico—only those with special permits are allowed in. You will most likely be stopped at some point by the traffic police who will assume from your rental plates that you're a tourist heading to your hotel. Have the name and address of your hotel ready and they'll wave you through. You can drop off baggage at your hotel (the hotel staff will give you a sign for your car advising traffic police that you are unloading), then you must relocate to a parking lot. See "Getting Around" (by Car), below, for information about parking in the centro storico.

VISITOR INFORMATION

Before you arrive, do your homework and visit the A.P.T. Web site at **www.firenze. turismo.toscana.it**; e-mail: firenze@mail.turismo.toscana.it.

The main train station's **Ufficio Informazioni Turistiche** (I.T.A.) information office distributes fairly good free city maps, answers simple questions just outside the station: With your back to the tracks, take the left exit, cross onto the concrete median, and turn right; the office will be about 100 feet ahead. This small tourist information office (☎ 055/28-28-93) distributes a wide variety of government tourist publications, including *Firenze Oggi (Florence Today),* a helpful 2,000L ($1.30) bimonthly. It's usually open daily from 8am to 7:30pm.

The city's largest **A.P.T. tourist office** is at V. Cavour 1r (☎ **055/29-08-32;** fax 055/2760383), about 3 blocks north of the Duomo. This office is slightly less harried than the busy station offices, offers lots of literature, with a sometimes helpful staff that can use more training and patience. The office is usually open Monday through Saturday from 8:15am to 7:15pm in the summer, 8:15am to 1:45pm in the winter. Replacing the once-conveniently located tourist office off the Piazza Signoria is the new office on the little-trafficked side street, Bor. Santa Croce 29r, just south of the Piazza Santa Croce (☎ **055/23-40-444;** fax 055/2264524). It has all general information, including up-to-the-minute info on museum hours, concert schedules, and a list of *affittacamere,* or boarding-house situations, usually available by the week. Hours are the same as at the Via Cavour office.

The bilingual *Concierge Information* magazine, available free from the concierge desks of top hotels, contains a monthly calendar of events, as well as information on museums, sights, and attractions. *Firenze Spettacolo,* a 3,000L ($1.75) Italian-language monthly sold at most city newsstands, lists the latest in nightlife, arts, and entertainment.

CITY LAYOUT

Florence is a compact city that's best negotiated on foot. No two sights are more than a 20- or 25-minute walk apart, and all the hotels and restaurants listed in this chapter are located in the downtown area, a quasi traffic-free with the exception of principal routes for buses and taxis.

The city's relatively small, beautiful, and touristy centro storico (historic center) is loosely bounded by the **S.M.N.** Train Station to the northwest, **Piazza della SS. Annunziata** to the northeast, **Piazza Santa Croce** to the east, and the **Arno River** to

Finding an Address

Traditionally, two systems of street numbering have been used in Florence: *nero* (black) and *rosso* (red). Black numbers are used for residential and office buildings, including hotels, while red numbers are used to identify all commercial enterprises, including restaurants and stores. A residential building at V. Por Santa Maria 15 may be found just next door to a commercial building at V. Por Santa Maria 89r. But, as of mid-1996 a regulation was passed to eliminate all red numbers and renumber in black. However, this is being protested by merchants who want to keep their red numbers—the situation is at the moment in a state of impasse, as of 1999 still in a no-action holding pattern. In this chapter, red-numbered addresses are indicated by a lowercase "r" following the number.

---

the south. South of the river is the **Oltrarno** (literally meaning "on the other side of the Arno"), generally considered an adjunct to the centro storico.

Piazza del Duomo, dominated by Florence's magnificent cathedral and ancillary baptistery, is at the geographic center of the tourist's city. During your stay, you'll inevitably walk along many of the streets radiating from this imposing square, the geographic nucleus of the city.

Borgo San Lorenzo, a narrow street running north from the Baptistery, is best known for the excellent outdoor **Mercato San Lorenzo** at its far end; it sells everything from marbleized paper-wrapped pencils and boxes to leather bags and jackets. It borders the train station neighborhood, home to a cluster of the city's cheapest hotels.

Via Calzaiuoli, Florence's most popular pedestrian thoroughfare and shopping street, runs south from the Duomo, connecting the church with the romantic, statue-filled **Piazza della Signoria.** West and parallel to this is **Via Roma,** which becomes **Via Por Santa Maria,** more excellent pedestrian shopping territory. Midway between the two is the **Piazza della Repubblica,** a busy shop- and cafe-ringed square surrounded by expensive upscale shopping streets. Farther west still, and you're on **Via Tornabuoni,** the designer-lined Fifth Avenue of Florence and its offshoots.

Exit the Piazza della Signoria by the Via Vacchereccia, then turn left for 2 blocks to the **Ponte Vecchio (Old Bridge),** the Arno's oldest and most famous span. Topped with dozens of tiny gold and jewelry shops, the bridge crosses over to the **Oltrarno** area, a section of artisans and shopkeepers that's best known for the Pitti Palace, just a few blocks past the bridge and the green Boboli Gardens behind it, and the Piazza Santo Spirito west of that.

Confused? Climb the 414 steps to the top of **Giotto's Campanile** (Bell Tower) that flanks the Duomo and you'll be rewarded with a beautiful eagle's-nest view of Florence that will help you navigate your way around. For a sunset memory that will stay with you for life, view Florence from afar at the Piazzale Michelangiolo in the Oltrarno section of town.

NEIGHBORHOODS IN BRIEF

Florentines generally divide their city into the two different banks of the Arno River, the northern bank around the Duomo and Piazza Signoria and the southern bank around the Palazzo Pitti. We have broken it down further, mostly into the visitor-oriented neighborhoods surrounding particular sites or churches, to facilitate the location of hotels, restaurants, and so on. It is a loose and arbitrary designation to help you understand the flavor of each, decide where you want to stay, and plan your days.

AROUND THE DUOMO & PIAZZA SIGNORIA   This is as central as you can get, and consequently offers the greatest concentration of attractions, restaurants, hotels, and so on, that you'll find in this chapter. Real estate is understandably the most expensive and visitors help pay for this. **The Duomo** has been Florence's religious hub for centuries, the **Piazza della Signoria** its civic hub: Together, they have been the uncontested heart of the city and continue to remain so. Many streets still follow the ancient grid pattern laid down by the Romans, and the narrow, back streets of truncated medieval towers and stalwart palazzi are some of the most picturesque and evocative. While shops along the neighborhood's western boundary of the boutique-lined **Via Tornabuoni** belong to the high priests of made-in-Italy glamour, the area generally offers something for everyone: The same is true of hotels and restaurants that can range from the refreshingly unpretentious to the over-the-top-priced tourist traps. With a handful of exceptions, the city's principal attractions are all here: the Duomo, the Uffizi, the Bargello, the Palazzo Vecchio in the Piazza della Signoria, and others.

NEAR THE TRAIN STATION, THE MERCATO SAN LORENZO & SANTA MARIA NOVELLA   North and northwest of the Duomo area, but still easily accessible by foot, this neighborhood is one of the busiest due to train-station traffic and marketplace shoppers. Colorful, yes; peaceful, hardly. However, it does not carry the stigma of Rome's train station area (often seedy) or that of Venice (inconvenient to most sites). The budget-hotel strips of Via Faenza and Via Fiume are nondescript but passable for those looking to cut costs in accommodations. There is no danger to speak of. The blocks surrounding the **Medici Chapels, Church of San Lorenzo,** and the vast indoor **Mercato Centrale** are overwhelmed by hundreds of pushcart stalls, a potential plus for the shopping fiend; this is also where restaurant chefs and Florence's housewives do their daily shopping. The 13th-century **Church of Santa Maria Novella** lends a note of quiet grace to the otherwise commercial and bustling area.

NEAR SAN MARCO & SANTISSIMA ANNUNZIATA   Defining the northern limits of the centro storico, the Piazza San Marco is light years away from the square by the same name found in Venice. Traffic has taken over this square, and nearby high schools and university buildings keep it people-busy, too. It is home to the important **Museo San Marco** dedicated to the work of Fra' Angelico, and the expansive **Piazza SS. Annunziata,** said to be one of the Renaissance's most beautiful. But make no mistake that the area's greatest magnet is Michelangelo's David in the **Galleria dell'Accademia.** The relatively quiet side streets are removed enough from the Duomo crush to make this a preferred area for alternative hotel choices, though the walk to and from Duomo-area sites can be tiresome.

NEAR SANTA CROCE   This large, neighborhoody area east of the busy Via Proconsolo (and east of the Bargello and Uffizi Museums found in the Duomo/Signoria area) is dominated by the Gothic **Church of Santa Croce**—by far the most visited of this neighborhood's sites. Nonetheless, it is an area that offers its fair share of genuine, residential character in a city fast succumbing to fast-food bars and tourist shops. An alluring choice of restaurants and quiet side streets and a must-do visit to the Pantheon-like burials and frescoes for which Santa Croce is famous means you'll probably visit this eastern end of the centro storico at least once.

THE OLTRARNO   "The Other Side of the Arno" is often referred to as the city's Left Bank. Escaping the prohibitive costs of the Duomo-dominated scenario north of here, it has long been the alternative location for artists and artisans for centuries, but escalating costs today are slowly changing the neighborhood's dynamics—something

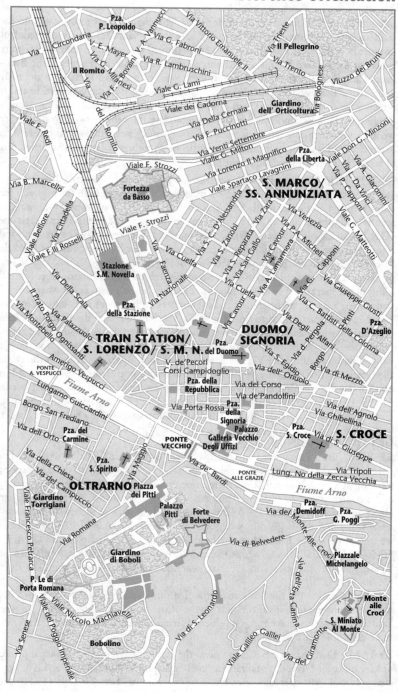

Florence Orientation

Pza. P. Leopoldo

Via Circondaria

Via Vittorio Emanuele II

Via Trieste

Il Pellegrino

Via E. Mayer

V. A. Vannucci

Via G. Fabroni

Via Trento

Il Romito

Via G. Milanesi

Via R. Lambruschini

Viuzzo dei Bruni

Viale F. Redi

Viale G. Lami

Viale dei Cadorna

Giardino dell' Orticoltura

Via Della Cernaia

Via Bolognese

Viale F. Strozzi

Via F. Puccinotti

Via Venti Settembre

Viale G. Milton

Pza. della Libertà

Viale Don G. Minzoni

Via A. Giacomini

Via Lorenzo Il Magnifico

Fortezza da Basso

Viale Spartaco Lavagnini

S. MARCO/
SS. ANNUNZIATA

Via L. Da Vinci

Via P. Capponi

Via B. Marcello

Viale Belfiore

Via Cittadella

Viale F.lli Rosselli

Viale F. Strozzi

Via S. C. D'Alessandria

Via S. Zanobi

Via S. Reparata

Via Zara

Via S. San Gallo

Via Cavour

Via P. A. Micheli

Via Venezia

Viale G. Matteotti

Stazione S.M. Novella

Via Della Scala

Via Faenza

Via Cuella

Via A. Lamarmora

Capponi

Via Giuseppe Giusti

Via Palazzuolo

Via Nazionale

Via Cuella

Via Cavour

Via G.

Via C. Battisti

Via degli Alfani

Pza. D'Azeglio

Il Prato

Borgo Ognissanti

Via Montebello

Pza. della Stazione

TRAIN STATION/
S. LORENZO/ S. M. N.

Pza. del Duomo

DUOMO/
SIGNORIA

Via S. Egidio

Borgo Pinti

Via di Mezzo

PONTE A. VESPUCCI

Amerigo Vespucci

V. de'Pecori

Corsi Campidoglio

Via dell' Oriuolo

Via di Pergola della Colonna

Fiume Arno

Lungarno Guicciardini

Pza. della Repubblica

Via del Corso

Via de'Pandolfini

Via dell'Agnolo

Borgo San Frediano

Via Porta Rossa

Pza. della Signoria

Via Ghibellina

Via dell'Orto

Pza. del Carmine

Palazzo Vecchio

Pza. S. Croce

S. CROCE

PONTE VECCHIO

Galleria Vecchio Degli Uffizi

Via di S. Giuseppe

Via della Chiesa

Pza. S. Spirito

Via Maggio

Via de' Bardi

PONTE ALLE GRAZIE

Via Tripoli

Via del Campuccio

OLTRARNO

Piazza dei Pitti

Lung. No della Zecca Vecchia

Giardino Torrigiani

Palazzo Pitti

Forte di Belvedere

Fiume Arno

Pza. Demidoff

Pza. G. Poggi

Viale Francesco Petrarca

Via Romana

Via del Monte Alle Croci

Giardino di Boboli

Via di Belvedere

Piazzale Michelangelo

P. Le di Porta Romana

Viale Niccolo Machiavelli

Via dell'Erta Canina

Monte alle Croci

Via Seneste

Bobolino

Via di S. Leonardo

Viale Galileo Galilei

S. Miniato Al Monte

Via del Poggio Imperiale

197

not immediately obvious to the outside visitor. The nightlife that revolves around the outdoor bars and restaurants of the tree-shaded Piazza Santa Spirito are still redolent of those bohemian days. Its historical sites are limited though important: The picture gallery at the **Palazzo Pitti** is second only to the Uffizi, and the frescoes of the **Brancacci Chapel at the Carmine Church** were some of the most seminal in the early years of the Renaissance. The Oltrarno was once the edge of the countryside and it retains a sense of separateness and removal from the northern bank of the Arno, a 5-minute walk away. Side streets still accommodate the centuries-old workshops of wood carvers, furniture restorers, leather workers, and jewelry makers. Together with Santa Croce, this is one of the more residential neighborhoods, but with a spirited mix of restaurants, small shops, and wine bars.

IN THE HILLS The oppressive weather of valley-trapped Florence has residents and visitors alike taking to the hills for a moment's respite from both the heat and the crowds. Although Fiesole (to the north) is considered a city in its own right, it is often seen as a suburb of Florence and its views and restaurants make it a favorite escape (see "Day Trip to Fiesole," in section 9). On the southern "Oltrarno" bank of the Arno and across from the area of the Church of Santa Croce, is the lofty perch of the **Piazzale Michelangiolo** and its postcard-perfect view of Florence and the Duomo (and Fiesole beyond). A visit to the lovely **Romanesque Church of San Miniato,** an easy stroll south of the Piazzale, is recommended for a late-afternoon gelato break when Gregorian vespers are sung at the church and the sun sets on Florence's terra-cotta rooftops. Those in shape can walk here from the Ponte Vecchio by taking the **Via San Nicolo** that initially runs parallel to the river, then turns south and passes through the ancient gate of the city, Porta San Nicolo, and heads up towards the Piazzale, becoming a stepped pathway called the **Via del Monte alle Croci.** Alternatively, from the Ponte alle Grazie, east of the Ponte Vecchio on the Oltrarno side of the river, take the **bus no. 13** for the 10-minute trip. A taxi from the center of town will probably cost around 15,000L ($8.80), but you may risk being stuck without return transportation—they usually won't wait unless paid (but you can always take a bus or walk back).

GETTING AROUND

BY BUS You'll rarely need to take advantage of Florence's efficient A.T.A.F. bus system, since the city is so wonderfully compact. Don't overestimate the distances by glancing at a map: You might get there more quickly by foot (inquire before setting off). Bus tickets cost 1,500L (90¢) and must be purchased before you board (you can buy it on board for 3,000L/$1.75 exact change). A four-pack of tickets (*biglietto multiplo*) will run 5,800L ($3.40), while a 24-hour pass costs 6,000L ($3.50). Tickets are sold at the **A.T.A.F. booth** at the head of track 14 in the train station (☎ 055/56-50-222) and at tobacco shops (*tabacchi*), bars, and most newsstands. Once on board, validate your ticket in the box near the rear door or you could be fined (76,000L/$44.70).

If you intend to use the bus system, the first thing you should do is pick up a bus map at any of the tourist offices. Since most of the historical center is *zona blu* with limited traffic, buses make runs on principal streets only, making the rest of the city a more enjoyable place to stroll.

BY TAXI Don't hail a cab. Catch one at the taxi stands in or near principal piazze, or have one called to your restaurant or hotel by dialing ☎4242, 4798, or 4390. Taxis charge 1,500L (90¢) per kilometer, but there's a minimum fare of 6,500L ($3.80) and most hops around the city average about 10,000 to 15,000L ($5.90 to $8.80); don't forget to include a 10% tip. Taxis are especially worthwhile when you need to get to and from the train station with your luggage. Otherwise, the harrowing tangle of one-way side streets makes daytime hops hither and yon more easily accomplished by foot.

BY BICYCLE   Florence is becoming a relatively traffic-free historical center, and the city is doing its utmost to introduce the alternative of biking: It's slowly catching on. The city has set up temporary sites about town during summer months (look for stands at the train station, Piazza Mercato Centrale, Piazza Strozzi, and on Via della Nina along the south side of the Palazzo Vecchio to name a few) where bikes are furnished free from 8am to 8pm. If the supply is *esaurito* (sold out), you'll have to pay: Check out any of the permanent shops such as **Alinari** on V. Guelfa 85r (☎ **055/28-05-00**), which rents bikes by the hour (4,000L/$2.35) and day (20,000L/$11.75). You can also rent Vespas and Honda *motorinos* by the hour or day there.

ON FOOT   With its medieval and 15th-century palazzi lining cobblestone streets that are even older, Florence is one of the most delightful cities in Europe to explore on foot. Since the city is so compact, a leisurely walk will take you from one end of the tourist area to the other—from the train station to Piazza Santa Croce—in about 40 minutes, or perhaps 5 hours if you give in to window-shopping. The free map handed out by the tourist office lacks a street index, but may be all you need. The best full map of the city is the yellow-jacketed map by Studio F.M.B. Bologna, available at most newsstands for 7,000L ($4.10).

BY CAR   Driving in Florence's historic center, where most hotels are located, is strictly off-limits to all vehicular traffic, except that of local residents. Standard rates for parking near the center are 2,000 to 4,000L ($1.20 to $2.35) per hour; many lots offer a daily rate of 25,000 to 35,000L ($14.70–$20.60). Least expensive is the new, vast underground **Parterre** at the Piazza della Liberta at 15,000L ($8.80); they'll supply a free bike or give you a taxi voucher worth 5,000L ($2.95) to put you on your way. When booking, check first with your hotel, as many of them have standing agreements with their neighborhood lots—many of the small hotels have begun to offer valet parking at no extra charge.

FAST FACTS: Florence

American Express   A relatively new office is east of the Piazza della Repubblica on the narrow V. Dante Alighieri 22r (☎ 055/50-981). It exchanges all traveler's checks without a commission and will issue train tickets at no fee, letting you avoid train station lines. Open Monday to Friday from 9am to 5:30pm.

Baby-Sitting   There is no official organization, but ask at your hotel and give advance notice.

Bookstores   The **BM Libreria Book Shop,** Bgo. Ognissanti 4r (☎ 055/29-45-75), is the best place in town for books in English. The best travel bookstore in town is **Libreria Il Viaggio,** Bgo. degli Albizi 41r (☎ 055/24-04-89) with a sizeable selection of books in English. For more bookstores, see section 7, "Shopping."

Business Hours   In summer, most **businesses and shops** are open Monday to Friday from 9am to 1pm and 4 to 7:30 or 8pm; on Saturday, most shops are open in the morning only. From mid-September through mid-June, most shops are open Tuesday to Saturday from 9am to 1pm and 3:30 to 7:30pm; on Monday during winter, shops don't open until the afternoon. (More and more stores in the heart of town are staying open during lunch break.) The exception to this winter rule are *alimentari* (small grocery stores), which are open on Monday morning in low season but closed Wednesday afternoon. In Florence, as through-out Italy, just about everything is closed on Sunday except touristy shops in the center of town with special permits. Restaurants are required to close at least 1 day per week (known as their *giorno di riposo*), though the particular day varies from one trattoria to another. Many serve lunch on Sunday but close for Sunday dinner.

Climate The city's position in the Arno Valley, guarantees still, humid sum-mers where mid-July through mid-August can be unbearable with temperatures in the high 90s (and little to no air-conditioning). May and September are the nicest months to visit, with weather in the 60s, but huge crowds can dampen your spirits. October is cooler, in the 50s, but can be very wet. January and Feb-ruary are the coldest with days in the 30s to 40s, with regular rainfall (but rarely snow). You'll never wait in line at the Uffizi, however.

Consulates The consulate of the **United States** is at Lungarno Amerigo Vespucci 38 (☎ 055/23-98-276), near its intersection with Via Palestro; it's open Monday to Friday from 9am to noon and 2 to 4pm. The Consulate of the **United Kingdom** is at Lungarno Corsini 2 (☎ 055/28-41-33), near Piazza Santa Trinita; it's open Monday to Friday from 9:30am to 12:30pm and 2:30 to 4:30pm.

Crime Petty thefts are performed deftly and swiftly by Florence's gypsy (*zingari*) population, despite the efforts of plainclothes police. They show up in small groups at the most touristed spots, and will jostle or distract you while relieving you of your valuables. Groups of gypsy children are the most clever; they'll be gone before you know what you're missing and police seem to be able to do little to stop them. Gypsy and nongypsy incidents are known to happen at the crowded markets or on public buses.

Currency Exchange Standard bank hours are Monday to Friday from 8:30am to 1:30pm and some of them reopen 2:45 to 3:45pm; only a few banks are open on Saturday. There is an ATM at the train station and quite a few throughout the center of town. Privately owned *cambios* (exchange bureaus) can also be found around town; their rates are often good but the fine print confesses they charge 3% to 7% commission—up to 10% if you're exchanging low sums such as $20!

Dentists/Doctors For a list of English-speaking dentists or doctors, ask at the American or British consulate, the American Express office or at your hotel. Vis-itors in need of medical care and English-speaking help can call Volunteer Hos-pital Interpreters (Associasione Volontari Ospedalieri/AVO) (☎ **055/23-44-567** or 055/425-0126) day or night. The interpreters are always on call and offer their services free of charge.

Emergencies As throughout Italy, dial ☎ **113** for the police. Some Italians recommend the military-trained *Carabinieri* (call ☎ **112**), whom they consider a better police force. To report a fire, dial ☎ **115.** For an ambulance, dial ☎ **118** and for a mechanical breakdown and road service call ☎ **116.**

Fax Fax service is available from the post office (see "Mail," below) to almost every destination with the exception of the United States. Ask your hotel if they can provide the service, or look for stationery and office supply stores with "servizio fax" posted in their windows.

Holidays Florence's patron saint, San Giovanni (John the Baptist), is honored on June 24. Watch for the fireworks and expect many stores to close. See chapter 2 for more details about holidays in Italy.

Hospitals   **Ospedale di Santa Maria Nuova** (☎ 055/27581) at Pz. di S. Maria Nuova 1 (3 blocks east of Duomo) always has some form of English-speaking doctors, nurses, or staff on hand.

Internet   The **Internet Train** at V. dell'Oriuolo (one block east of the Duomo), ☎055-263-8968, fax 055/263-8968, E-mail: info@fionline.it, www.fionline.it, offers free startup (pay by the time you use). If you bring a friend you can get 1 hour free. It's open late 7 days a week. **Cyberoffice** at V. San Gallo 4r (one block north of Duomo, past the Mercato San Lorenzo), ☎/fax **055/211103**) gives out free E-mail accounts. You pay by the minute.

Laundry/Dry Cleaning   North of the Duomo is one of four modern, self-service locations of the American-owned **Wash & Dry,** V. d. Servi 105r (☎ 055/580480 for seven other locations in town or ask your hotel). They charge about 12,000L ($7.05) for a wash and dry and are open daily from 8am to 10pm. Dry cleaning (*lavasecco*) is much more costly but more commonly found; ask at your hotel for a neighborhood location.

Lost & Found   All objects handed over to the police and railroad officials wind up at **Oggetti Smarriti** (Lost Property), V. Circondaria 19 (☎ 055/36-79-43), in the area behind the train station. The Santa Maria Novella train station has its own lost and found next to track 16.

Luggage Storage— There's also a 24-hour **luggage depot** at the head of track 16 at S.M.N. train station.

Mail   Florence's **main post office** is on V. Pellicceria 3, off the southwest corner of Piazza della Repubblica. You can purchase stamps (*francobolli*) and pick up letters sent "Fermo Posta" (Italian for General Delivery) or *Poste Restante* upon showing identification. The post office is open Monday through Friday from 8:15am to 7pm and Saturday from 8:15am to 12:30pm.

All packages heavier than 1 kilo (2¼ lb.) and up to 20 kilos (44 lb.) must be properly wrapped and brought around to the **parcel office** at the back of the building (enter at V. d. Sassetti 4, also known as Piazza Davanzati). If you're uncertain about Italy's complex parcel-post standards, take your shipment to **Olica,** B. SS. Apostoli 27r (☎ 055/23-96-917), off Via Por Santa Maria and south of the post to 15,000L ($2.65 to $8.80) according to size (they follow regular store hours).

Pharmacies   Two addresses offering 24-hour schedules are the **Farmacia Communale,** at the head of track 16 in the train station (☎ 055/21-67-61), and **Molteni** on V. Calzaiuoli 7r just north of the Piazza Signoria (☎ 055/21-54-72). Both manage to deal efficiently with English-speaking requests in person.

Rest Rooms   There are public rest rooms at the train station, on the ground floor of the Palazzo Vecchio, and in all museums. The cost of a coffee or mineral water will give you access to any bar's facilities, which are reserved for the use of patrons only. With a modicum of attitude, you can use the decent facilities at the **Caffe Rivoire** in Piazza della Signoria—everyone else does.

Shoe Repair   East of the Duomo, the one-man show **at Heel Express,** at V. Oriuolo 29r (no phone), repairs while you wait. He's of a dying breed: Hope he's still there if you need him. Rising rents have forced his competition out of the centro storico.

Student Networks & Resources   Florence's university is between the Mercato Centrale and Piazza San Marco, the latter being the center of student activity in

Florence. The *mensa*, or cafeteria, where students congregate at mealtimes is at V. San Gallo 25a. There's a sizable community of American students in Florence enrolled in over 32 study-abroad programs.

The **Centro Turistico Studentesco (C.T.S.)**, at V. d. Ginori 25r (☎ 055/ 28-95-70; fax 055/292150), just north of the San Lorenzo Market, is the best budget travel agent in Florence, selling reduced-price train, air, and ferry tickets and will book all-category discounted hotel accommodations in Italy and abroad. This agency specializes in youth and student fares but in some cases is helpful to thrifty travelers of all ages. Note that the staff doesn't make train reservations and may or may not accept credit or charge cards in 1999. It's open Monday through Friday from 9am to 1pm and 2:30 to 6pm and Saturday from 9am to noon.

Also worth checking out is **S.T.S. (The Youth and Student Travel Service)** at V. Zannetti 18r (just off Via Cerretani; ☎ 055/28-41-83), which offers many of the same services but accepts credit cards.

Taxis   There are taxi stands in or near all the major piazze. Or call a taxi at ☎ **4242,** 4390, or 4798. Taxis are metered and there are supplements for Sunday, nighttime travel and luggage.

Telephone   The telephone area code for Florence is 055 and must now be dialed as part of each number even when dialing from within the city.

Travel Agencies—See "Student Networks & Resources" and "American Express," above.

2 Accommodations You Can Afford

Florence is not the place to arrive during the peak summer months without a confirmed reservation. If you do, it's important to arrive early, as many hotels fill up for the next night even before those guests checking out have packed. If you have trouble with or are intimidated by the language barrier, try the **Informazioni Turistiche e Alberghiere** (room-finding office) in the train station, near the track 16 exit (see "Arriving," earlier in this chapter). Indicate which category you want (two-star, and so on) or how much you want to spend, and the staff will do its best to accommodate you, charging you 4,500 to 7,500L ($2.65 to $4.40) for the reservation. **Peak season** is generally considered mid-March through mid-July, September through early November, and December 23 through January 6. May and September are particularly popular both in the city and the surrounding Tuscan hills.

NEAR THE TRAIN STATION, MERCATO SAN LORENZO & SANTA MARIA NOVELLA

Being within easy striking distance from the train station explains the proliferation of cheap and inexpensive hotels in this general area, particularly on **Via Fiume** and **Via Faenza** where some buildings house as many as six pensiones. Logistically it makes more sense to walk to some of these hotels than to take public transportation (or, since the distance is short, taxis should be considered by those weighed down with luggage). Exit the train station near the 24-hour pharmacy and turn right toward the Via Nazionale where you take a left. The popular Via Faenza is the second intersection (Via Fiume is the first left) on Via Nazionale. This is the bustling area of the sprawling open-air Mercato San Lorenzo and is generally safe though short on picturesque charm.

Albergo Azzi. V. Faenza 56 (1st floor), 50123 Firenze. ☎ **055/21-38-06.** Fax 055/ 21-38-06. 12 units, 3 with bathroom. 49,000L ($28.80) single without bathroom; 80,000L

($47.05) double without bathroom, 105,000L ($61.75) double with bathroom; 105,000L ($61.75) triple without bathroom, 115,000L ($67.65) triple with bathroom; 114,000L ($67.05) quad without bathroom, 130,000L ($76.50) quad with bathroom. Breakfast 5,000L ($2.95). Rates discounted approximately 20% low season. DC, MC, V. Parking at nearby private garage 20,000L ($11.75).

Sandro and Valentino, the new owners of this pensione, also known as the Locanda degli Artisti (the Artists' Inn), are themselves musicians and are slowly creating a home away from home for thrift-minded traveling artists, artists manqués, and student types. Not for the fastidious or fussy, this venerable place exudes a relaxed bohemian feel—not all doors hang straight, not all bedspreads match. A little down at the heels, the young owners are slowly but surely bringing it around. In the meantime, no one can complain about the lovely open terrace with a view, where breakfast is served in warm weather. The Albergo Anna (eight rooms, four without bathroom) is located in the same building (☎ **055/2398322**); same management, similar rates.

✪ **Albergo Centrale.** V. d. Conti 3 (2nd floor; off V. Cerretani), 50123 Firenze. ☎ **055/ 21-57-61.** Fax 055/21-52-16. 18 units, 15 with bathroom. TV TEL. 140,000L ($82.35) single with bathroom; 150,000L ($88.25) double without bathroom, 180,000L ($105.90) double with bathroom; 190,000L ($111.76) triple without bathroom, 230,000L ($135.30) triple with bathroom. Rates include continental buffet breakfast. These are special rates for Frommer's readers. Rates further discounted low season Dec 1–27, and Jan 1–Feb 28. AE, DISC, MC, V.

If you appreciate attention to detail, you'll certainly appreciate the Centrale's bright, spacious rooms freshly painted in soothing pastel shades and outfitted with matching antique armoires and headboards. Chenille bedspreads and tasteful choice of floral wallpaper, attentive housekeeping, and the thoughtful touch of white lace doilies or dried-flower arrangements sets this hotel well apart from the ho-hum decor normally found at hotels at this price range. The presence of Normandy-born manager Marie-Thérèse Blot is everywhere in this welcoming and comfortable pensione housed in the former 14th-century patrician residence known as the Palazzo Malaspina, many of whose rooms overlook the cupola of the Medici Chapels. A perfect choice for families or for off-season travelers who can stay for a minimum of 4 nights and need only pay for three. A nod goes to one of the most ample buffet breakfasts in town at these rates.

Albergo Merlini. V. Faenza 56 (3rd floor), 50123 Firenze. ☎ **055/21-28-48.** Fax 055/ 28-39-39. 10 units, 2 with bathroom. 60,000L ($35.30) single without bathroom; 100,000L ($58.80) double without bathroom, 120,000L ($70.60) double with bathroom; 130,000L ($76.50) triple without bathroom. Breakfast 9,000L ($5.30). Off-season rates approximately 15% less. MC, V.

Family run (with the English-speaking Signora Mary at the helm for more than 40 years) and cozy, this small place is proudly appointed with wooden-carved antique headboards and furnishings that set it apart. Breakfast (optional) is served on a glassed-in terrace decorated with frescoes by talented American art students who lived here in the 1950s. Enjoy your cappuccino with a view of the Medici Chapel's cupola, Florence's different bell towers, and the city's terra-cotta roofscape. Guests of a certain age and budget seem to feel at home as the younger crowd who hold the majority rule.

Albergo Monica. V. Faenza 66 (1st floor; at V. Cennini), 50123 Firenze. ☎ **055/28-38-04.** Fax 055/28-17-06. 15 units, 10 with bathroom. TEL TV A/C. 100,000L ($58.80) single without bathroom, 120,000L ($70.60) single with bathroom; 160,000L (94.10) double without bathroom, 190,000L ($111.75) double with bathroom; 210,000L ($123.50) triple with shower only (no toilet), 240,000L ($141.20) triple with bathroom; 280,000L ($164.70) quad with bathroom. Rates include continental breakfast. Rates are discounted 5% in high season for Frommer's readers. Rates are discounted an additional 40% in low season, which includes Frommer's discount. AE, DC, MC, V.

Florence Accommodations

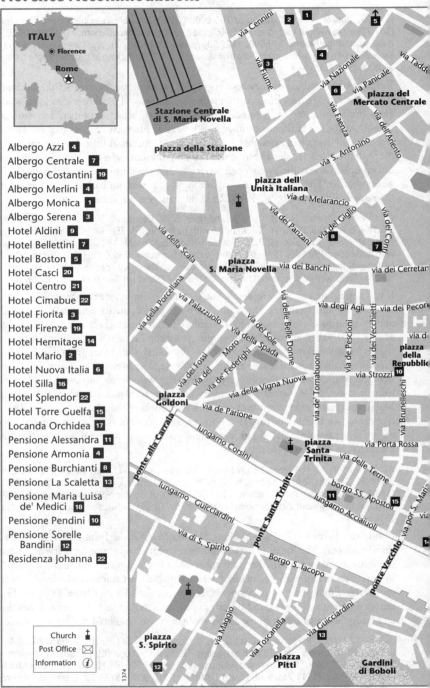

Albergo Azzi **4**
Albergo Centrale **7**
Albergo Costantini **19**
Albergo Merlini **4**
Albergo Monica **1**
Albergo Serena **3**
Hotel Aldini **9**
Hotel Bellettini **7**
Hotel Boston **5**
Hotel Casci **20**
Hotel Centro **21**
Hotel Cimabue **22**
Hotel Fiorita **3**
Hotel Firenze **19**
Hotel Hermitage **14**
Hotel Mario **2**
Hotel Nuova Italia **6**
Hotel Silla **16**
Hotel Splendor **22**
Hotel Torre Guelfa **15**
Locanda Orchidea **17**
Pensione Alessandra **11**
Pensione Armonia **4**
Pensione Burchianti **8**
Pensione La Scaletta **13**
Pensione Maria Luisa
  de' Medici **18**
Pensione Pendini **10**
Pensione Sorelle
  Bandini **12**
Residenza Johanna **22**

Church †
Post Office ✉
Information ⓘ

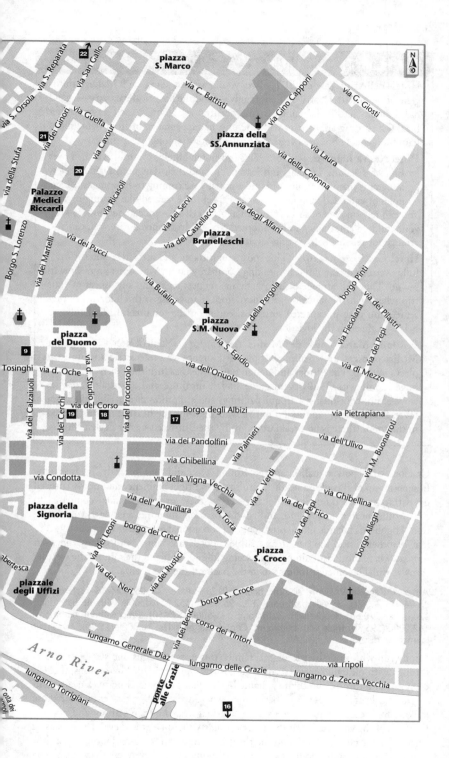

205

⊕ Family-Friendly Hotels

Hotel Bellettini *(see p. 207)* Two young sisters, Gina and Marzia, third-generation hoteliers, carry on their family's—and the historical palazzo's—legend of hospitality in this charming extremely central small hotel. A self-service buffet breakfast is a big affair here, with the unusual appearance of fresh fruit, sliced ham, homemade breads, sweets, and baked goods, among other things.

Hotel Nuova Italia *(see p. 208)* This top-notch hotel is carefully watched over by English-speaking Luciano and Eileen Viti and their daughter, Daniela. New grandparents themselves, the Vitis are especially welcoming to Frommer's readers (couples or extended families), who can expect to be treated like visiting royalty. You can rely on American-born Eileen as an excellent source about how to keep your children entertained in her adopted city. With advance notice, you can also arrange for reliable baby-sitting service.

Hotel Casci *(see p. 210)* This most comfortable and attractive hotel is carefully overseen by the English-speaking Lombardy family who don't know how to say no. They can arrange or help with any request regarding any aspect of your trip whether in Florence or your next stop. If traveling with children has presented you with unexpected scenarios, count on the resourceful Lombardys to help you through the logistics.

Pensione Maria Luisa de' Medici *(see p. 211)* Named after the very last Medici princess, this pensione is one of Florence's more eclectic and unusual places to sleep. The history and design buff owner has furnished each of the nine huge rooms with 1960s avant-garde Italian furniture and a veritable treasure trove of museum-quality baroque paintings and sculptures displayed in the main foyer. Rooms sleep families up to five who welcome the hearty breakfast served in the room (there is no breakfast room) by the British co-owner Evelyn Morris.

Gracious and polylingual, manager Rhuna Cecchini has recently overseen the freshening-up of this pleasant hotel, resulting in a bright ambience and newly spruced up bathrooms. Its train-station location keeps these prices contained compared to competitors nearer the Duomo, and good off-season discounts are worth your attention. Highlights include terra-cotta floors, the occasional exposed-brick archway redolent of other times, the bar area's marble-topped cafe tables, and a large open-air terrazza where breakfast (and postsightseeing idling) is offered the minute the weather turns warm. The quietest rooms are in the back off the Via Faenza.

Albergo Serena. V. Fiume 20 (2nd floor), 50123 Firenze. ☎ **055/21-36-43.** Fax 055/ 28-04-47. 7 units, 3 with bathroom. TEL. 95,000L ($52.95) double without bathroom, 120,000L ($70.60) double with bathroom; 121,500L ($71.50) triple without bathroom, 162,000L ($95.30) triple with bathroom. Continental breakfast 10,000L ($5.90). Ask about low-season discounts. AE, MC, V.

Family run with pride by the Bigazzi family, this unpretentious one-star place comes through with pleasant surprises: some brand-new and nicely tiled bathrooms, molded ceilings, and turn-of-the-century stained-glass French doors. Rooms are airy and bright and kept clean as a whistle by the owner's wife. A dignified choice for those looking for a comfortable place to hang their hat near the train station, and not just for those of the younger set. If this place is full, try the smaller and even less expensive Otello Tourist House upstairs on the third floor next to the Hotel Fiorita. It has just four simple but lovely rooms, two with bathroom, at rates even less than the Serena

(☎ and fax **055/23-96-159**) and is run by the gracious owners, English-speaking Anna and her husband, Otello.

✪ Hotel Bellettini. V. de' Conti 7 (off V. d. Cerretani), 50123 Firenze. ☎ **055/21-35-61.** Fax 055/28-35-51. www.firenze.net/hotelbelletini. E-mail: hotel.bellettini@dada.it. A/C TV TEL. 27 units, 23 with bathroom. 115,000L ($67.65) single without bathroom, 135,000L ($79.40) single with bathroom; 150,000L ($88.25) double without bathroom, 185,000L ($108.80) double with bathroom; 245,000L ($144.10) triple with bathroom; 310,000L ($182.35) quad with bathroom. Rates include breakfast. AE, DC, MC, V. Nearby parking 35,000L ($20.60).

In the wooden-beamed breakfast salon, a *pietra serena* stone plaque states that there has been a hotel in this Renaissance palazzo since the 1600s. Two young sisters, Gina and Marzia, third-generation hoteliers, arrived in 1993 to carry on the building's legend of hospitality in this gem of a small hotel. Terra-cotta tiles, chenille bedspreads, and wrought-iron beds decorate most rooms, and a mix of handsome antique pieces found throughout the two-floor hotel as well as the palazzo's architectural elements (stained-glass windows, hand-painted wood-coffered ceilings) guarantee its distinctive air. Room no. 44 has a tiny balcony with jasmine and geranium blooms, second-best to room no. 45, with its view of the Medici Chapels, Florence's terra-cotta rooftops, and the Duomo's cupola. A self-service buffet breakfast is a big affair here, with the unusual appearance of fresh fruit, sliced ham, homemade breads, sweets, and baked goods, among other things. Since late 1998, the hotel shares the same management with the small two-star Hotel Le Vigne in Pz. Santa Maria Novella 24 (☎ **055/ 29-44-49;** fax 055/23-02-263), which is intended to absorb some of the overflow from the ever-in-demand Belletini.

Hotel Boston. V. Guelfa 68 (west of V. Nazionale), 50129 Firenze. ☎ **055/49-67-47.** Fax 055/47-09-34. 20 units, 16 with bathroom. A/C TV TEL. 80,000L ($47.05) single without bathroom, 120,000L ($70.60) single with bathroom; 170,000L ($100) double with bathroom; 220,000L ($129.40) triple with bathroom 270,000L ($158.80). Rates include continental breakfast. These are special rates for Frommer's readers. Ask about low-season 15% discounts. MC and V accepted for 50% of room payment. Valet parking 30,000L ($17.65).

The Boston is a peaceful, dignified place filled with original art and blessed with an outside shaded patio where breakfast becomes an idyllic way to start your day. The first two floors were built in the 17th century and have exposed wooden beams and plenty of charm (rooms on the newer third floor, equally recommended, are accessible by elevator). The Via Guelfa gets moderate traffic, so ask for a quiet room overlooking the back patio garden whose only noise is the clink of breakfast china that will serve as your wake-up call. When booking with the amenable Viti family, make sure you mention that you're a Frommer's reader to be eligible for their special discounted rates.

Hotel Centro. V. Ginori 17 (north of Pz. San Lorenzo), 50123 Firenze. ☎ **055/23-02-901.** Fax 055/212706. www.travelita.com/hotelcentro. E-mail: centro@pronet.it. 16 units, 12 with bathroom. TV TEL. 90,000L ($52.95) single without bathroom, 120,000L ($70.60) single with bathroom; 140,000L ($82.35) double without bathroom, 190,000L ($111.75) double with bathroom; 250,000L ($147.05) triple with bathroom; 280,000L ($164.70) quad with bathroom. Rates discounted approximately 20% in low season. Rates include buffet breakfast. AE, MC, V. Nearby parking available for 35,000L ($20.60). Bus: 7, 14 or 1 to Pz. Duomo.

Just 1 block north of the sprawling outdoor Mercato San Lorenzo, this newly refurbished hotel is housed in an old Florentine palazzo that was the preferred home of the Renaissance master painter Raphael of Urbino from 1505 to 1506. There is precious little he would recognize in its contemporary and bright reincarnation, with ample-sized rooms outfitted in pastel-colored bedspreads and blond-wood furnishings. Bathrooms are new, tiled in white and brightly lit. If you're looking for a cozy, old-world ambience, you better keep looking. The new owners, Andrea and Sandra Vendali, continue to upgrade and modernize with amenities such as hair dryers, CNN, safes in every room and, beginning in 1999, air-conditioning in a select few (ask when booking). They also discount 10% any stay longer than 3 nights—like you needed another reason to stay on in Florence.

Hotel Fiorita. V. Fiume 20 (3rd floor), 50123 Firenze. ☎ **055/28-31-89.** Fax 055/27-28-153. E-mail: htlfior@tin.it. 13 units, 10 with bathroom. A/C MINIBAR TV TEL. 90,000L ($52.95) single without bathroom, 110,000L ($64.70) single with bathroom; 170,000L ($100) double with bathroom; 220,000L ($129.40) triple with bathroom; 300,000L ($176.40) quad with bathroom. Rates include continental breakfast. Low-season discount 25%. AE, DC, MC, V. Nearby parking 30,000L ($17.65).

The friendly Maselli family is continuing to gussy up its one-star establishment to meet two-star standards, and I found it scheduled to reopen in the spring 1999. It is hoped that the addition of welcomed amenities will not encroach upon the venerable charm inherent in the original, stained-glass doors and windows that hint of the palazzo's late 19th-century origins. Approximately half of the rooms and bathrooms are being refurbished and, although they haven't yet been seen, will probably be the ones to opt for.

✪ Hotel Nuova Italia. V. Faenza 26 (just off the V. Nazionale), 50123 Firenze. ☎ **055/26-84-30** or 055/28-75-08. Fax 055/21-09-41. 20 units, all with bathroom. A/C TEL. 120,000L ($70.60) single; 180,000L ($105.90) double; 230,000L ($135.30) triple; 270,000L ($158.80) quad. Rates include continental breakfast. These are special rates for Frommer's readers. Ask about low-season rates. AE, MC, V. Private parking nearby 30,000L ($17.65).

This top-notch hotel is carefully watched over by English-speaking Luciano and Eileen Viti and their daughter, Daniela. Eileen met Luciano more than 30 years ago, when she stayed at his family's hotel on the recommendation of *Europe on $5 a Day.* Today, the Vitis are especially welcoming to our readers who can expect to be treated like visiting royalty (this is also an ideal selection for traveling families). The improvement of their already lovely hotel is a work in progress: One season, triple-paned soundproof windows and rarely found mosquito screens were installed, the next season bathrooms were all retiled and air-conditioning installed. Expected sometime in 1999: TV (and CNN) and new furniture custom designed by Eileen herself. The family's love of art is manifested in the framed posters and paintings found everywhere; you can rely on Eileen being a far more knowledgeable source about the art scene than the board of tourism. The location of the very good Trattoria Antichi Cancelli (V. Faenza 73r; ☎ 055/218927) directly across the street couldn't be any more convenient; the menù turistico is a steal at 19,000L ($11.20) with an à la carte meal averaging 30,000L ($17.65).

Pensione Armonia. V. Faenza 56 (1st floor), 50123 Firenze. ☎ **055/21-11-46.** 7 units, none with bathroom. 60,000L ($35.30) single; 95,000L ($55.90) double; 135,000L ($79.40) triple; 175,000L ($102.95) quad. Breakfast 7,000L ($4.10). Rates discounted approximately 30% low season. No credit cards.

Owned by Mario and Marzia, a young, accommodating English-speaking brother and sister act, this small pensione is a reliable no-frills one-star choice when your budget keeps you near the train station. An occasional touch sets it apart from the pack: Some whitewashed, tiled rooms have nice bedspreads and breakfast is served in your room at no extra charge. You'll have the key to the front door, so you won't need to apologize to the night porter for waking him after hours. The three rooms in the back are the quietest.

✪ Pensione Burchianti. V. d. Giglio 6 (off V. Panzani), 50123 Firenze. ☎ and fax **055/21-27-96.** 11 units with shower only, 6 with complete bathroom. 65,000L ($38.25) single without bathroom, 75,000L ($44.10) single with bathroom; 110,000L ($64.70) double without bathroom, 150,000L ($88.25) double with bathroom; 150,000L ($88.25) triple without bathroom, 190,000L ($111.75) triple with bathroom. Rates include continental breakfast; not mandatory (deduct 5,000L/$3.30 from room rate). Ask about low season discounts. No credit cards. Nearby parking approximately 50,000L ($29.40).

Rich with history and redolent of a grand lifestyle past, this is a most unusual find for lovers of high drama and low prices. This once renowned pensione was established in the late 19th century by the Burchianti sisters (the last of whom died in 1973) in the noble 16th-century Salimbeni palazzo near the Duomo. During its golden days, it hosted royal and VIP guests (you might wind up in Benito Mussolini's room). Most of that same historical grandeur is still intact throughout—leaded and stained-glass windows and doors, beautifully frescoed walls and ceilings, hand-painted wooden coffered ceilings, and here and there remnants of valuable antique furniture left behind by the former owners (steer clear of the two rooms as painstakingly plain as the others are theatrical). Prohibitive costs forbid a much deserved restoration, but if you love such nostalgic threadbare romance, you'll be in heaven here. Imaginative plumbing results in the eyesore addition of prefabricated shower stalls insensitively stuck in corners and sinks bolted directly onto precious 19th-century frescoed walls (some rooms have shower stalls only but not a full bathroom). A pretty sun-filled salon and handsome breakfast room seems pulled out of an E. M. Forster movie.

WORTH A SPLURGE

✪ **Hotel Mario.** V. Faenza 89 (1st floor; near V. Cennini), 50123 Firenze. ☎ **055/ 21-68-01.** Fax 055/21-20-39. www.webitaly.com/hotel.marios. E-mail: hotel.marios@webitaly. com. 16 units, all with bathroom. A/C TV TEL. 210,000L ($123.50) single; 260,000L ($152.95) double; 330,000L ($194.10) triple. Rates discounted approximately 40% in low season. Rates include continental breakfast. AE, DC, DISC, MC, V. Valet parking 32,000L ($18.80).

In a traditional Old Florentine atmosphere, owner Mario Noce and his wife run a first-rate ship that has been a long-enduring favorite with our readers. Rooms are furnished with wrought-iron headboards and massive reproduction antique armoires, some looking over a peaceful garden; others facing the street are soundproofed with double paned windows. Included are amenities such as CNN, hair dryers, and air-conditioning at no extra charge. Details like stained-glass windows and a homelike warmth keep guests coming back time and again (very attractive low rates during slow months help). The beamed ceilings in the common areas date from the 17th century, though the building became a hotel "only" in 1872. The youthful Mario confides that he feels he's been around twice as long as that, first opening his doors to the backpack set when he himself was an industrious youth with an innate yen for hospitality. Those backpackers are now return guests from the baby-boomer age.

NEAR THE DUOMO & PIAZZA SIGNORIA

Albergo Costantini. V. Calzaiuoli 13 (2nd floor; near Pz. Duomo), 50122 Firenze. ☎ **055/ 21-39-95;** ☎ and fax 055/21-51-28. 14 units, all with bathroom. A/C TEL. 120,000L ($70.60) single; 190,000L ($111.75) double; 280,000L ($164.70) triple; 370,000L ($217.65.85) quad. Rates include breakfast. AE, DC, MC, V.

This formerly nondescript two-star hotel with a 10-star location was always a favorite choice of mine for its rock-bottom prices. It was closed during my last visit, and one can only hope that the doubled prices are justified by promising improvements. Housed in what is left of the two 13th-century towers long ago joined together to create this palazzo just south of the Piazza Duomo, its biggest draw had been the six spacious rooms with a view of Giotto's slender Campanile (bell tower) and the tricolored Duomo that seem within reach. For those who found the proximity of the Campanile's frequent bells glorious and not annoying, and for whom cleanliness was paramount (thanks to the impeccable housekeeping of owner Anna Mollica), this made an excellent choice. Breakfast tasted especially wonderful underneath period frescoes that could also be found in two of the guest rooms. For a few dollars more, the upstairs Hotel Aldini (see "Worth a Splurge," below) shares the same pivotal location though the Costantini's new reincarnation might steal some of its thunder.

✪ **Hotel Casci.** V. Cavour 13 (between V. de'Gori and V. Guelfa), 50129 Firenze. ☎ **055/ 21-16-86.** Fax 055/23-96-461. www.venere.it/firenze/casci. E-mail: casci@pn.itnet.it. 25 units, all with bathroom. TV TEL. 120,000L ($70.60) single; 170,000L ($100) double; 225,000L ($132.35) triple; 280,000L ($164.70) quad. Rates include buffet breakfast. Rates discounted 30%–40% during low season. AE, DC, MC, V. Valet parking 40,000L ($23.50). Bus from station: 11 or 17 to Piazza Duomo.

The industrious Lombardi family has deftly transformed this former pensione from student crash pad into a most comfortable and attractive hotel that aims to please an older and more discerning guest. Firm new mattresses are draped in bedspreads of paisley or floral designs, with green-stained wooden headboards matching freestanding armoires. The attentive Signora Lombardi is a stickler for cleanliness and it's obvious: Most bathrooms are brand-new and even those that aren't literally gleam. Rooms overlooking the busy Via Cavour that heads north out of Piazza Duomo have double-paned windows to ensure quietness, but ask for a room overlooking the inner courtyard's four-story magnolia tree to be safe. A large breakfast buffet is served in a spacious frescoed room, one of the many throwbacks to the 1850s when this 15th-century building was the home of Gioacchino Rossini, legendary composer of Barber of Seville and The William Tell Overture. Air-conditioning was expected to be added in 1999.

Hotel Chiari Bigallo. Vc. degli Adimari 2 (off the V. Calzaiuoli near the Piazza Duomo), 50122 Firenze. ☎ **055/21-60-86.** Fax 055/21-44-96. 27 units, all with bathroom. A/C TV TEL. 100,000L ($58.80) single with bathroom; 180,000L ($105.90) double with bathroom. Rates include continental breakfast. AE, MC, V. Nearby parking 27,000L ($15.90). Bus from station: no. 22, 36, 37.

As they say in the business, the Chiari-Bigallo isn't going to win any awards for its interior design (albeit a clean and refurbished atmosphere); in the location competition, however, it has few contenders (runners-up would be the neighboring Albergo Costantini and Hotel Aldini, see above and below). If you get one of the few rooms facing the Duomo, I'd venture to say that you will have a view like no other, within poking distance of Giotto's magnificent bell tower. The traffic-free zone doesn't mean you won't have pedestrian noise that drifts up from the cobbled street below, one of the city's most trammeled. A few blocks away on Via delle Oche and with side views of this living postcard, the **Hotel de' Lanzi** is a quieter alternative that shares the same ownership, with rates (doubles are 260,000L/$152.95) qualifying for our splurge category, but who can get more central than this, short of camping out on the Duomo's steps?

✪ **Hotel Firenze.** Pz. Donati 4 (on the V. d. Cor., off V. Calzaiuoli), 50122 Firenze. ☎ **055/ 26-83-01** or 055/21-42-03. Fax 055/21-23-70. 61 units, all with bathroom. TV TEL. 90,000L ($52.95) single; 130,000L ($76.50) double; 180,000L ($105.90) triple; 225,000L ($132.35) quad. Rates include continental breakfast. No low-season rates. No credit cards. Bus: any of the many lines from the train station that stop in the Piazza Duomo.

For years this perfectly located hotel was a favorite student's choice, but a multiple-year renovation completed in 1997 has transformed it into a shining two-star establishment with little impact on its consistently low rates—some of the most attractive in town. Sitting on its own little piazza in the middle of the centro storico's pedestrian zone of shops, museums, and monumental buildings, the hotel is actually two adjoining historical palazzi now boasting brightly tiled, sunlit guest rooms, and the best bathrooms in this price range in town. These prices encourage a revolving-door traffic of independent travelers who demand little (and often get less) from the staff of young international personnel who range from well-meaning and accommodating to distant and inexperienced.

Pensione Alessandra. B. SS. Apostoli 17 (east of V. Tornabuoni and the Piazza Santa Trinita), 50123 Firenze. ☎ **055/28-34-38.** Fax 055/21-06-19. www.hotelalessandra.com. E-mail: htla-lessandra@mclink.it. 25 units, 17 with bathroom. A/C TV TEL. 100,000L ($58.80) single without bathroom, 150,000L ($88.25) single with bathroom; 150,000L ($88.25) double without bathroom, 200,000L ($117.65) double with bathroom; 220,000L ($129.40) triple without bathroom, 270,000L ($158.80) triple with bathroom; 260,000L ($152.95) quad without bathroom, 330,000L ($194.10) quad with bathroom. Rates include buffet breakfast. Ask about low-season rates. AE, MC, V. Parking at nearby garage 30,000L ($17.65).

This special pensione is located between two principal shopping streets on a narrow cobblestone street, lined with medieval towers and early Renaissance palazzi and running parallel to the Arno River. Street-level, etched-glass doors hint of the architectural and historical significance of the Alessandra's palazzo *nobile*, designed in 1507 by Baccio d'Angnolo, a pupil of Michelangelo. The antiquity of high ceilings and spacious rooms is appreciated, but so is the modernity of new bright bathrooms. This is a good spot to opt for a room without a bathroom, since only seven rooms share four large, communal bathrooms. Good housekeeping and the simplicity of tasteful floral bedspreads and sheer white curtains are much welcome, as is the free-of-charge air-conditioning—but request it upon reserving, as not all rooms are equipped. Signora Anna runs a lovely operation that attracts discerning guests.

Pensione Maria Luisa de' Medici. V. d. Cor. 1 (2nd floor; between V. Calzaiuoli and V. Proconsolo), 50122 Firenze. ☎ and fax **055/28-00-48.** 9 units, 2 with bathroom. 101,000L ($59.40) double without bathroom, 129,000L ($75.90) double with bathroom; 140,000L ($82.35) triple without bathroom, 179,000L ($105.30) triple with bathroom; 179,000L ($105.30) quad without bathroom, 227,000L ($133.50) quad with bathroom. Rates include breakfast. No credit cards. Nearby parking approximately 30,000L ($17.65). Bus from train station: no. 14 or 23 to V. Proconsolo.

This pensione, named after the very last Medici princess and located around the corner from Dante's house is one of Florence's more eclectic and unusual places to sleep. Rooms are named after the different members of the Medici clan whose portraits grace their walls. The owner, Dr. Angelo Sordi—physician, collector, history, and design buff—has furnished each of the nine huge rooms with 1960s avant-garde Italian furniture—an unexpected collection that contrasts (purists might find it jarring) with a veritable treasure trove of museum-quality baroque paintings and sculptures displayed in the main foyer that are more compatible with the 17th-century palazzo. With enormous rooms sleeping up to five people, the Maria Luisa is a good choice for traveling families, which will also relish the breakfast served in the room (there is no breakfast room) by Dr. Angelo or his Welsh partner, Evelyn Morris. Sustained by eggs, cereal, and juice, you shouldn't mind the three-story walk up or down.

WORTH A SPLURGE

Hotel Aldini. V. Calzaiuoli 13 (south of Piazza Duomo), 50122 Firenze. ☎ **055/21-47-52.** Fax 055/29-16-21. www.pronet.it/hotelaldini. E-mail: hotelaldini@pronet.it. A/C TV TEL. 14 units, all with bathroom. 130,000L ($76.50) single; 210,000L ($123.50) double; 270,000L ($158.80) triple; 320,000L ($188.25) quad. Rates include continental breakfast. Rates discounted 20% low season. AE, DC, MC, V. Nearby parking 30,000L ($17.65).

There's little hyperbole in the Aldini's claim to being near the Duomo (it will sound as if the bells are under your pillow). If such convenience is your idea of heaven (it is mine), the Aldini will be worth your extra lire. Within centimeters of the magnificent tricolored marble Duomo and its slender 14th-century campanile designed by Giotto, the Aldini is found in the same palazzo above the marginally less expensive Hotel Costantini (see above). But, the Aldini is more distinguished—a handsome, comfortable place with rich terra-cotta floors covered by Persian runners and large rooms whose fresh floral bedspreads, matching drapes, and spacious bathrooms reflect a recent renovation. The front rooms have windows with a partial view of the Duomo through which the clip-clop of horse-drawn carriages and the chatter of late-night strollers from the heart of Florence's pedestrian area drift in.

○ **Hotel Hermitage.** Vc. Marzio 1 (in Piazza del Pesce near the Ponte Vecchio and east of V. Por Santa Maria), 50122 Firenze. ☎ **055/287216.** Fax 055/212208. www.italthotel.com/ firenze/hermitage. E-mail: hermitage@italyhotel.com. 28 units, all with bathroom. A/C TEL TV. 330,000L ($195.10) double; 410,000L ($241.20) triple; 470,000L ($276.50.90) quad. Inquire about single rates. Rates include continental breakfast. Ask about low-season discounts. MC, V. Valet parking 35,000L ($20.60).

This is it, the ultimate splurge for location, location, location and charm, charm, charm. The Hermitage is a very romantic choice two steps from the Ponte Vecchio and with rooms with a view as E. M. Forster meant them to be. Breakfast under the leafy arbor on the flower-filled 6th-floor terrace will make every day in Florence the best of your trip. Breathtaking views from atop this 13th-century palazzo/tower are close to 360°—and what an unmatched tableau, composed of the covered Ponte Vecchio, the Arno River, the terra-cotta cupola of the Duomo, the neighboring Church of Santo Stefano, and Florence's beloved bell towers and encroaching green hills. Most of the smallish well-manicured rooms (some with Jacuzzis for a nominal increase) either look south over the river or north toward the Duomo. Two on the rooftop sound like heaven, until early risers make breakfast, noise annoying for late sleepers. Book in advance: The Hermitage's fans are legion, many as swayed by the warmth of the English-speaking owner Vicenzo Scarcelli as by his homelike decor whose charm is evident at every turn.

○ **Hotel Torre Guelfa.** B. SS. Apostoli 8 (between V. Tornabuoni and V. Por Santa Maria), 50123 Firenze. ☎ **055/2396338.** Fax 055/2398577. www.firenzealbergo.it. 12 units, all with bathroom. A/C MINIBAR TV TEL. 160,000L ($94.10) single; 250,000L ($147.05) double; 320,000L ($188.25) triple; 350,000L ($205.90) quad. Rates include continental breakfast. Ask about low-season discounts. AE, MC, V.

The high-end prices at this new hotel are justified beyond a reasonable doubt by the privilege of experiencing the breathtaking 360° view from the medieval tower (the tallest privately owned tower in Florence's centro storico). Book now, before the hotel applies for three-star category and raises its rates completely out of your sphere. Cozy guest rooms with canopied iron beds, inviting warm-colored walls, and rich paisley carpeting make it hard to get motivated to take advantage of the ultracentral location that awaits outdoors (you can view it all from your huge, private terrace if you're lucky enough to check into room no. 15—but you didn't hear it from me). Follow the wafting strains of classical music to the salon, whose vaulted ceilings and lofty proportions hark back to the palazzo's 14th-century origins. If you love it here, and what's not to love, then ask the young owners about their Tuscan hideaway in the heart of Chianti, the Villa Rosa in Panzano, an idyllic 35-kilometer (22-mi.) drive from Florence whose 15 doubles with bathroom cost 180,000L ($105.90).

Pensione Pendini. V. Strozzi 1 (Pz. d. Repubblica), 50123 Firenze. ☎ **055/21-11-70.** Fax 055/28-18-07. www.tiac.net/users/pendini/hotel.html. E-mail: pendini@dada.it. 40 units, all with bathroom. A/C TV TEL. 170,000L ($100) single; 250,000L ($147.05) double; 350,000L ($205.90) triple; 410,000L (241.20) quad. Rates discounted low season. Rates include continental breakfast. AE, DC, MC, V. Valet parking 35,000L ($20.60).

New owners David and Emmanuele Abolaffio have found a way to keep the old-fashioned hominess of this century-old, refurbished pensione intact. With a location in one of Florence's most central and important squares, it's to be expected that the nine spacious rooms overlooking the Piazza della Repubblica are the most popular; guests don't seem to mind the music fest that takes place in the outdoor cafes that ring the square, featuring live music into the wee hours during warm-weather months. Rooms overlooking an inner courtyard are quieter, these too refurbished in a countrylike style: The owners rescued the original period pieces that deserved it, supplementing them with convincing reproductions where necessary. A long, buffed corridor of rich parquet flooring covered with Persian runners leads to the inviting sitting room and the sunny breakfast room with a view of the whole of Via Strozzi. The Pendini has been revitalized but still exudes its 19th-century elegance in a quasi-British, proper kind of way. The concept of the classic family-run pensione, quickly disappearing in Italy, is alive and well here.

NEAR SAN MARCO

✪ **Hotel Cimabue.** V. Benifacio Lupi 7 (west of V. San Gallo), 50129 Firenze. ☎ **055/ 47-19-89.** Fax 055/47-56-01. 16 units, all with bathroom. TV TEL. 140,000L ($82.35) single with bathroom; 190,000L ($111.75) double with bathroom; 240,000L ($141.200) triple with bathroom; 280,000L ($164.70) quad with bathroom. Rates include buffet breakfast. Rates are discounted approximately 15% off-season. AE, DC, MC, V. Nearby parking 22,000L ($12.95). Bus from station: no. 17, Piazza San Marco stop.

Looking for a home away from home with lots of charm and character and a spirited polylingual couple that runs it all with warmth and pride? This small hotel may only have two stars, but they are two shining stars, from the firm orthopedic mattresses to the best freshly ground breakfast cappuccino to jump-start your morning. When Igino Possi and his Belgian wife, Daniele Dinau, renovated their new acquisition in 1993, they saved what they loved best in this 1904 palazzo, and renovated around it: the original terra-cotta pavement, ceiling frescoes in six lucky rooms, suites of art nouveau (called liberty in Italy) headboards, and mirrored armoires. During a recent visit, the guests were an interesting mix of two retired British professors, an American priest, a young Canadian couple on their honeymoon, and a stylish German art historian. Igino enveloped them all underneath his umbrella of hospitality with a heartfelt smile, answering every question, making sure the disparate mélange of guests was comfortable and happy.

Residenza Johanna. V. Bonifacio Lupi 14 (east of Spartaco Lavagnini), 50129 Firenze. ☎ **055/48-18-96.** Fax 055/48-27-21. 11 units, 9 with bathroom. 75,000L ($44.10) single without bathroom; 120,000L ($70.60) double with bathroom; 145,000L ($85.30) triple with bathroom. Rates include breakfast. No credit cards.

A friendly family atmosphere is encouraged by the Italian/French co-owners who have created a stylish refuge for a certain class of tourism. The lack of television and phones in the rooms keep the prices down, and the clientele of those in the arts and in the know don't seem to notice. What they *do* notice are the silk flower arrangements, minilibrary of coffee-table books left for their enjoyment and the quiet level of *buon gusto* throughout. Rooms are very tastefully done, with quiltlike comforters, coordinated wall-to-wall carpeting, and electric kettles for a do-it-yourself tea break. You'll have your own keys to come and go in this handsome 19th-century residential palazzo built around a gravel courtyard with a towering three-story magnolia tree at its center. This quiet neighborhood is just far enough away (with a walking distance to the Duomo clocked at 30 minutes) to justify lower prices. You won't be central enough to come and go in the middle of the day, but then again, try to beat these prices.

IN THE OLTRARNO

Much more convenient than the remote though beautiful IYHF youth hostel in the hills of Fiesole (Ostello Villa Canerata, Vle. Augusto Righi 2/4, 50137 Firenze; ☎ 055/60-14-51; fax 055/61-03-00), the privately run **Ostello Santa Monaca** (V. Santa Monaca 6, 50124 Firenze. ☎ **055/26-83-38** or 055/23-96-704. Fax 055/ 28-01-85. www.ostello.it. E-mail: info@ostello.it.) is a lively gathering spot for the collegiate and newly graduated crowd, as well as a great place to trade budget tips and meet travel companions.

✪ **Hotel Silla.** V. d. Renai 5 (on the Piazza Davidoff, east of Ponte delle Grazie), 50125 Firenze. ☎ **055/23-42-888.** Fax 055/23-41-437. 35 units, 33 with bathroom. A/C MINIBAR TV TEL. 180,000L ($105.90) single with bathroom; 180,000L ($105.90) double without bathroom, 250,000L ($147.05) double with bathroom; 300,000L ($176.50) triple with bathroom. Rates include continental breakfast. Rates are discounted off-season. AE, DC, MC, V. Parking in hotel garage 25,000L ($14.70). Bus from station: no. 23, Ponte alle Grazie stop.

You can sidestep the Silla's splurge-category prices if you succeed in nabbing either of the two shared-bathroom doubles, and the chance to experience the seignorial life in a proper 15th-century palazzo. The hotel, situated on a quiet shaded riverside piazza, offers a spacious patio-terrace on the palazzo's second floor that is one of the city's nicest breakfast settings (during winter months the elegant breakfast salon replete with crystal chandelier, reproduction period furniture, and marble floors is enough to lure you indoors and allay the whimpering). The Silla's most recent renovation was in 1997 with a few rooms redone earlier in 1994. Many overlook the Arno River and the spire of Santa Croce on the opposite bank. The all-around attention to freshness and detail, and a friendly but skilled staff should make this hotel worthy of being better known, but word-of-mouth keeps it regularly full in pricey Florence despite its refreshing low profile.

✪ **Pensione La Scaletta.** V. Guicciardini 13 (2nd floor, near Piazza Pitti), 50125 Firenze. ☎ **055/28-30-28** or 055/21-42-55. Fax 055/28-95-62. www.italyhotel.com/firenze/ lascaletta. E-mail: lascaletta.htl@dada.it. 12 units, 11 with bathroom. TEL. 80,000L ($47.05) single without bathroom, 140,000L ($82.35) single with bathroom; 140,000L ($82.35) double without bathroom, 200,000L ($117.65) double with bathroom; 180,000L ($105.90) triple without bathroom, 240,000L ($141.20); 260,000L ($152.95) quad with bathroom. Rates include continental breakfast. Ask about low-season rates. There's a 10,000–15,000L ($5.90–$8.80) discount for Frommer's readers who pay in cash (ask on arrival). MC, V. Nearby parking approximately 35,000L ($20.60). Bus: "D" from train station.

Bring your travel journal, order an iced tea, and head for this pensione's two-tiered, umbrellaed terrace at sunset—then try to put down in words the stunning 360° panorama that surrounds you and qualifies this pensione for a star. Overlooking the stalwart Pitti Palace and housed in one of only two historical palazzi on this street to survive World War II bombing, this comfortable top-floor spot is efficiently run by owners Barbara Barbieri and her enthusiastic son Manfredo. Rooms are clean, spacious, and vary greatly in decor. Those that front the very busy Via Giucciardini have double-paned windows to cut the noise, but the ones in back overlook the verdant Boboli Gardens that fan up the hill. Young Manfredo himself whips up a fixed-price dinner of 20,000L ($13.15) upon request. He peruses the daily marketplace before creating the menu that includes antipasto, pasta, a meat-based entree, vegetable, and dessert; repair afterward to the terrace for your après-dinner *vin santo*.

Pensione Sorelle Bandini. Pz. Santo Spirito 9, 50125 Firenze. ☎ **055/21-53-08.** Fax 055/ 28-27-61. 14 units, 5 with bathroom. TEL. 159,000L ($93.50) double without bathroom, 190,000L ($111.75) double with bathroom; 220,000L ($130.60) triple without bathroom, 250,000L ($147.05) triple with bathroom. Inquire about single and quad rates and availability.

Rates include continental breakfast. Should accept V by 2000; check when booking. Personal checks from U.S. banks accepted.

Guests either love or hate this old-time pensione in a landmark Renaissance palazzo in Piazza Santo Spirito, one of Florence's most authentic squares. If you step back when standing in the piazza, on the top floor you can see the massive open-air loggia that wraps around the landmark building: This is your chance to live like the noble families of yore. With 15-foot ceilings, the 10-foot windows and oversized pieces of antique furniture are proportionately appropriate. But upon closer inspection, you'll see that the resident cats have left their mark on common-area sofas, and everything seems just a little ramshackle, musty, and uneven. But that seems to be the point—or so the return guests will have you believe, judging from the students, older folks, and families who love the huge lofty-ceilinged rooms (room no. 9 sleeps five and offers a view of the Duomo from its bathroom window) and hallways dripping with history. And don't forget that monumental terrace where Mimmo, the English-speaking manager, oversees breakfast and encourages brown-bag lunches and the chance to relax and drink in the view especially during the bewitching hours of sunset.

3 Great Deals on Dining

Judging from the innate elegance of the Florentine people and the tony stores from which they fill their wardrobes, you'd never think the local **cucina toscana** would be so rustic and simple. In true Tuscan style, when they tell you theirs is the best and most genuine, you'll be hard pressed to find reason to disagree.

There's no one dish or neighborhood that equals good budget dining in Florence. For light meals, your best bet is to choose an eatery that you know will allow you to order just one course (easier done at lunch than dinner) though whether a modest pasta dish will satisfy your appetite may be another matter—the portion is not meant to be your entire meal. While not always the cheapest way to dine, the commonly found *menù turistico* (a three-course fixed-price meal) is a good way to contain costs, but check out what the day's menu consists of first. My personal suggestion is to frequent the cafes and bars where a pasta primo or sandwich will keep you happy, and look forward every evening to a lovely and leisurely Tuscan meal in any one of the great trattorias listed below.

REGIONAL CUISINE Almost all of the eating establishments that follow specialize in the poor man's *cucina povera,* based on the region's agricultural role in history. Slabs of crusty bread are used for *crostini,* spread with chicken-liver pâté as the favorite Florentine antipasto. Hearty Tuscan peasant soups often take the place of pasta, especially *ribollita,* a rich soup of twice-boiled cabbage, beans, and bread, or *pappa al pomodoro,* a similar soup made from tomatoes, thickened with bread, and drizzled with olive oil. Look for *pasta fatta in casa* (the homemade pasta of the day), or the typically Tuscan *pappardelle,* thick flat egg noodles often covered with a simple

Dining Calendar

Despite Florence's importance as a modern-day Grand Tour destination, almost all restaurants (stores and offices) close *per ferie* (for vacation) at some point in July or August from 2 to 6 weeks. The date may vary from year to year, so call any of the following choices during this period before showing up: Your hotel will always know of a reliable choice in the neighborhood. In August, no one ever goes hungry, but your choice is considerably diminished.

Florence Dining

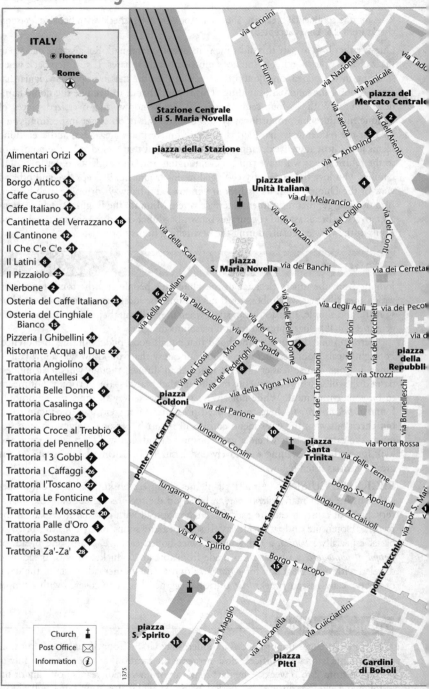

Alimentari Orizi ⑩
Bar Ricchi ⑬
Borgo Antico ⑬
Caffe Caruso ⑯
Caffe Italiano ⑰
Cantinetta del Verrazzano ⑱
Il Cantinone ⑫
Il Che C'e C'e ㉑
Il Latini ⑧
Il Pizzaiolo ㉕
Nerbone ②
Osteria del Caffe Italiano ㉓
Osteria del Cinghiale
 Bianco ⑮
Pizzeria I Ghibellini ㉔
Ristorante Acqua al Due ㉒
Trattoria Angiolino ⑪
Trattoria Antellesi ④
Trattoria Belle Donne ⑨
Trattoria Casalinga ⑭
Trattoria Cibreo ㉕
Trattoria Croce al Trebbio ⑤
Trattoria del Pennello ⑲
Trattoria 13 Gobbi ⑦
Trattoria I Caffaggi ㉖
Trattoria l'Toscano ㉗
Trattoria Le Fonticine ①
Trattoria Le Mossacce ⑳
Trattoria Palle d'Oro ③
Trattoria Sostanza ⑥
Trattoria Za'-Za' ㉘

Church †
Post Office ⊠
Information ⓘ

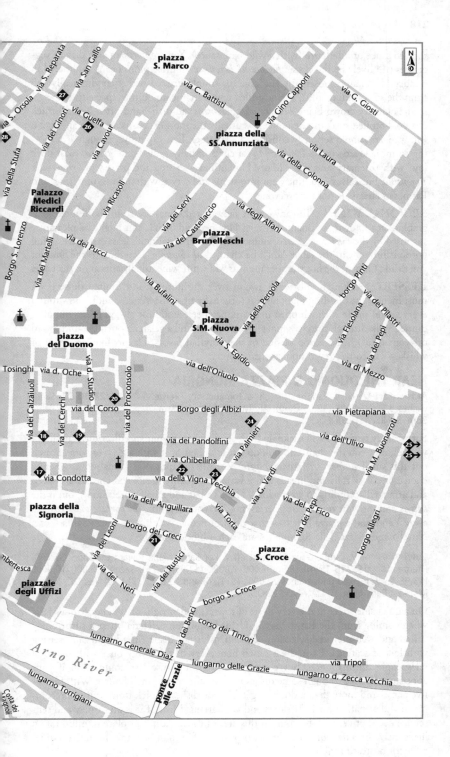

217

tomato sauce or **alla lepre** (with a wild hare sauce). Your *contorno* or side dish of vegetables will likely be the classic *fagioli all' uccelletto,* humble pinto beans smothered in a sauce of tomatoes, rosemary, and sage (or simply dressed with rich virgin olive oil from the surrounding hills). Rustic grilled meats are the ubiquitous specialty, the jewel in the culinary crown being *bistecca alla fiorentina,* an inch- (and often 2-inch) thick charcoal-broiled steak on the bone: It is usually the most expensive item on any menu (meat lovers should seriously consider the splurge). Less expensive, though as tempting to meat lovers, is the *lombatina* veal chop, usually grilled and **arista,** roast pork loin with rosemary and sage. Many Florentines also sing the praises of *trippa alla fiorentina,* but calves' intestines, cut into strips and served with onions, tomatoes, and Parmesan cheese, is not for everyone.

REGIONAL WINES   Tuscany's most famous red wines are from the limited geographic area known as Chianti between Florence and Siena. You might be pleasantly surprised by the *vino della casa,* or house wine—your restaurant's least expensive. A full bottle is brought to the table: You'll be charged *al consumo,* according to the amount you drink. Only in the hot summer months will white wine usually appear on the table.

DESSERT   Although you won't swoon over the unfussy and limited desserts on most menus, the pudding-like tiramisu (originally from the Veneto, but by now found everywhere) made with whipped mascarpone cheese is almost always great. But after dinner, walk through the city's quiet streets till you find a gelateria open late and round off your meal with a scoop of one of their myriad favors. Flavors like *riso* (rice) or whiskey will convert even nonice-cream lovers.

NEAR THE DUOMO & PIAZZA SIGNORIA

Alimentari Orizi. V. Parione 19r (off V. Tornabuoni), Firenze. ☎ **055/21-40-67.** Sandwiches 3,500–6,000L ($2.05–3.50). AE, MC, V. Mon–Fri 8am–3pm and 5–8pm, Sat 8am–3pm. SANDWICHES/DELI.

Surprisingly few spots will make up fresh sandwiches to your specifications, and fewer yet will offer you the chance to pull up a seat and enjoy it with a glass of wine. Search out this small *alimentari* (grocery store) just off the tony Via Tornabuoni, where a choice of crusty rolls and breads and a variety of quality meats and cheeses are sliced and arranged according to your whim. There's a bar and a half-dozen stools, but if the sun is shining you might consider asking for your creation *da portare via* ("to take away") and find a piazza bench with a view for people watching—Piazza Santa Maria Novella and Piazza della Repubblica are each 4 blocks away.

Caffè Caruso. V. Lambertesca 16r (east off V. Por Santa Maria toward the Uffizi Gallery), Firenze. ☎ **055/28-19-40.** Primi 7,000–9,000L ($3.95–$5.25); secondi 8,000–10,000L ($3.95–$5.95). Fixed-price menus 20,000L ($11.76) and 25,000L ($14.70). AE, DC, MC, V. Mon–Sat 8am–6pm. ITALIAN FAST FOOD.

On a quiet side street in the very heart of town (the first right off Via Por Santa Maria when coming from the Ponte Vecchio), this family run cafeteria offers a surprisingly varied and well-prepared selection of inexpensive hot dishes in a bright, airy setting with lots of seating—I could eat lunch here every day. It's very busy with the local salespeople during lunch, but continuous hours promise less commotion if your appetite is flexible (though some dishes run out after peak lunch hours). With four or five pastas and more than a dozen vegetable side dishes to pick from, this is a recommended destination for light eaters and vegetarians. Most of it is on display and self-service keeps prices rock-bottom for this area of town. Keep this place in mind for an inexpensive breakfast or coffee break, or just an afternoon beer that promises a quiet table for postcard scribbling.

✪ **Osteria del Caffè Italiano.** V. Condotta 56r (off V. Calzaiuoli). ☎ **055/29-10-82.** Primi 6,000L ($3.95); secondi 10,000L ($5.90). No credit cards. Daily 12:30–3pm and 8–10pm (bar open winter 8am–1am, summer to 8pm). ITALIAN.

Umberto Montano, the young, entrepreneurial owner of this handsome cafe (whose restaurants, including the new Osteria del Caffè Italiano, are among the city's best; see Near Santa Croce category below), has created an inviting turn-of-the-century ambience near the center's Piazza della Signoria and offers a simple and delicious lunch at reasonable rates to standing-room-only crowds (come early!). A handful of first courses changes daily: Delicate but full-flavored soups and an unusual variety of mousse-like soufflés of Parmesan or broccoli might be among the choices. Skip your entree without raising any eyebrows—all the more room for dessert. Don't miss them: Made on the premises by the talented pastry chef, they go perfectly with the cafe's exclusive blend of coffee from Africa.

✪ **Cantinetta del Verrazzano.** V. d. Tavolini 18/20r (off V. Calzaiuoli). ☎ **055/26-85-90.** Focaccia sandwiches 5,000–8,000L ($2.95–)$4.70); wine 3,500–5,000L ($2.05–$2.95). AE, DC, MC, V. Winter months Mon–Sat 8am–9pm; summer 8am–3:30pm and 5:30–9pm. WINE BAR.

Florence once boasted more than 100 wine vendors, of which only a handful remain today (look for characteristic old-time holes-in-the-wall billed as *vinaio* or *fiaschetteria*). Although it looks like it has been here forever, this recently opened wood-paneled *cantinetta* (with a full-service bar/pasticceria and seating area) helped spawn a revival of stylish wine bars as convenient spots for fast-food breaks Italian-style. Flat focaccia bread, plain or studded with peas, rosemary, onions, or olives, is fresh from the wood-burning oven in the back; buy it hot by the slice or *farcite* ("filled" with prosciutto, rugola, cheese, tuna, as sandwiches). Platters of typical Tuscan cold cuts and aged cheeses are also available. Verrazzano is the location of the owners' *fattoria* farm (the same town that gave us Giovanni da Verrazzano, the first European explorer to sight New York harbor); their **Castello di Verrazzano** supplies the wine bar with most of its products. There are always half a dozen varieties of full-bodied Chianti wines to try by the glass; you're encouraged to linger once the lunch crowd has dispersed.

Trattoria Belle Donne. V. d. Belle Donne 16r (north off V. d. Vigna Nuova). ☎ **055/ 2382609.** Reservations not accepted. Primi 10,000L ($5.90); secondi 10,000–15,000L ($5.90–$8.80). MC, V. Mon–Fri 12:30–2:30pm and 7:15–10:30pm. Closed most of Aug. TUSCAN

Sign-free and tucked away on a narrow street (whose name refers to the women of the night who once worked this then-shady neighborhood) parallel to the exclusive Via Tornabuoni, this packed-to-the-gills lunch spot immediately drew the area's chic boutique owners and sales staff. It now tries to accommodate them and countless others who have caught on (in other words: no lingering over lunch here; dinner isn't as rushed). The local cuisine gets reinterpreted and updated by the young, talented chef who placates the local palate without alienating it: traditional dishes appear in the company of innovative alternatives such as cream of zucchini and chestnut soup or lemon-flavored chicken. The regulars seem inured to the occasional rush job (which I admit I've never experienced), so don't take it personally.

Trattoria Croce al Trebbio. V. d. Belle Donne 49r (west of V. Tornabuoni). ☎ **055/ 287089.** Reservations recommended only for groups over four. Primi 8,000–13,000L ($4.70–$7.65); secondi 14,000–25,000L ($8.25–$14.70). AE, DC, MC, V. Tues–Sun noon–2:30pm and 7–10:30pm; open daily Mar–Oct. Closed Aug. TUSCAN

Local workers head for their regular table near the kitchen where spirited conversation turns to politics, soccer, and how last year's wine was better (they say that every year).

The menu is straightforward and delicious. The wait staff is young and friendly. And overseeing it all is the affable Signor Riccardo who has run this casual trattoria for the last 20 years which, despite die-hard regulars who extol its high praises, has maintained a low profile with the tourist set. The well-priced *menu Toscano* (23,000L/ $13.50) provides a choice of six primi and seven secondi plus a side dish and dessert. Simplicity is paramount in dishes such as *pollo arrosto con potate*, tender free-range chicken, roasted with baby potatoes and spiced with rosemary and sage. It tastes better if you're seated at one of the few tables in the 15th-century terra-cotta wine cellar.

Trattoria del Pennello. V. Dante Alighieri 4r (west of V. d. Proconsolo). ☎ **055/294848.** Reservations suggested. Primi 10,000L ($5.90); secondi 12,000–22,000L ($9.85–$11.90); menù turistico 30,000L ($17.65). No credit cards accepted. Tues–Sat noon–3pm and 7pm– midnight, Sun noon–3pm. Closed Aug. ITALIAN.

Though his house was just around the corner, Dante never dined here. That was his loss. Often referred to as "da Dante" (Dante's) nonetheless, this is an attractive restaurant with a bright interior full of original art that does little to evoke its early 17th-century origins and fame as one of Florence's oldest restaurants. The well-known specialty here is a wide array of two dozen delicious *antipasti* (appetizers) on display. Prices vary with quantity and variety, but expect to spend about 10,000L ($6.55) for a healthy sampling. Continue your sampling and order the *tris di primi a piacere*, your choice of any three pastas for a minimum of two people (20,000L/$11.75 per person). More contained appetites might be just as happy with a simple pasta (a signature specialty is the piquant tomato sauced *spaghetti alla carettiera*) and perfectly grilled *lombatina* veal chop for approximately the same cost. Credit cards are no longer accepted here, so come prepared.

Trattoria Le Mossacce. V. d. Proconsolo 55r (1 block south of the Duomo). ☎ **055/ 29-43-61.** Reservations suggested for dinner. Primi 7,500–8,500L ($4.40–$5); secondi 9,000– 12,000L ($5.30–$7.05). AE, MC, V. Mon–Fri noon–2:30pm and 7–9:30pm. TUSCAN.

Don't be fooled by its unpretentious entrance or bright ordinary dining room. The food is anything but ordinary here. This is straightforward *cucina toscana*, deftly prepared and served in a lively and pleasant atmosphere. Long-enduring favorites on the menu are the thick **ribollita** (literally "twice boiled") soup or any of the daily changing pastas (one day made with a sauce of tomato and *melanzane* or eggplant, another with the slightly spicy *all'amatriciana* sauce typical of Rome). If the thought of a thick slab of steak is your idea of dinner in heaven, indulge here in the *bistecca alla fiorentina*, perfectly grilled and not much of a strain at approximately 22,000L ($12.95).

NEAR THE TRAIN STATION, THE MERCATO SAN LORENZO & SANTA MARIA NOVELLA

✪ **Il Latini.** V. Palchetti 6r (off V. d. Vigna Nuova). ☎ **055/21-09-16.** Reservations necessary. Primi 8,000–10,000L ($4.70–$5.90); secondi 15,000–20,000L ($8.80–$11.75); fixedprice meal 50,000L ($29.40). AE, MC, V. Tues–Sun noon–2:30pm and 7:30–10:30pm. Closed July 20–Aug 10. TUSCAN.

Family patriarch Narcisio Latini and his sons, Giovanni and Torello, operate one of the busiest tavernlike trattorias in town. There's always a line waiting for a cramped seat at one of the long wooden tables (this is an even longer affair if you haven't reserved) in one of many rooms. But the raucous, delicious Tuscan adventure is worth the wait. There is a written menu, though you probably won't see one: One of the brothers will explain the selection in a working version of English. Only gargantuan eaters should indulge in the *menù completo*—a hearty, meaty feast for 50,000L ($32.90) that begins with an antipasto of *prosciutto crudo* (ham) and homemade sausage, followed by a pasta or soup, a main course such as the *misto di carne alla griglia* (assortment of mixed grilled meats), a fresh vegetable in season, gelato, and *biscotti di Prato* (hard almond cookies). Oh, and all the wine and mineral water you can drink, which may explain why at least one table usually breaks out into song and diners linger on forever. More restrained appetites and wallets should just order à la carte.

Nerbone. In the covered Mercato Centrale, entrance on V. dell'Ariento, stand no. 292 (ground floor) is on your right. Sandwiches 4,000L ($2.35); primi 6,000L ($3.50); secondi 7,000L ($4.10). No credit cards. Mon–Sat 7am–3pm. ITALIAN.

One of the best basic eateries in Florence for those seeking good food and lots of local color, this simple red-and-green food stand inside Florence's covered turn-of-the-century meat-and-produce marketplace is best described as a hole-in-the-wall minus the wall. Packed with market-goers and local working-class types who stand around the marble bar eating, drinking, and discussing union issues and local politics, Nerbone offers only four small tables next to an adjacent meat counter. Daily specials include a limited choice of pastas such as penne or rotelli, soups, huge plates of cooked potatoes and other vegetables, and fresh, fresh sandwiches. Service is swift, and wine and beer are sold by the glass. If at first you can't find Nerbone, just ask any of the market vendors.

✪ **Trattoria Antellesi.** V. Faenza 9r (near the entrance to the Medici Chapels). ☎ **055/21-69-90.** Reservations needed. Primi 8,000–12,000L ($4.70–$7.05); secondi 15,000–25,000L ($8.80–$14.70). AE, DC, MC, V. Daily noon–2:30pm and 7–10:30pm.

This is an attractive, welcoming spot in a converted Renaissance palazzo almost within reach of the Medici Chapels. As their restaurant empire expands, the young Florentine-Arizona combination of chef Enrico and manager/sommelier Janice Verrecchia are around less these days, but their skilled staff guarantees a lovely Tuscan experience of wonderfully authentic dishes accompanied by a well thought out wine list. Knowledgeable, capable, and never without a smile, they'll talk you through a memorable dinner that should start with their signature antipasto of Pecorino cheese and pears. Then onto small, light crepes stuffed with ricotta cheese and spinach then baked (*crespelle alla fiorentina*) or *spaghetti alla Chiantigiana* with Chianti-marinated beef slowly simmered in a tomato sauce. This is another great spot to try the Tuscan cuisine's winning *bistecca alla fiorentina* and, while you're at it, some of the cantina's excellent moderately priced red wines (21,000 to 25,000L/$12.35 to $14.70).

Trattoria I Cafaggi. V. Guelfa 35r (west of V. d. Ginori). ☎ **055/294989.** Reservations suggested for dinner. Primi 12,000–13,000L ($7.05–$7.65); secondi 16,000–25,000L ($9.40–$14.70). AE, DC, MC, V. Wed–Mon noon–2:30pm and 7:30–10:30pm. Closed 2 weeks in late July or Aug. TUSCAN

When I recently took a consensus of my Florentine friends and asked them where they go for a reliably good—dare I ask for very good—inexpensive meal, I always met with the same answer: to their mother's. A consistent runner-up was Cafaggi's, a roomy, plain-Jane trattoria that looks like it has always been there. The simple old-fashioned decor with mustard-colored tablecloths is not worth describing, but the cooking is. Maybe not as good as Mom's, but this is a very satisfying second choice. In the same family for generations, it was long ago discovered by the tourist trade, but the mix of diners still lean toward Florentine fans who come for moderately priced meals and quality fish in a carnivorous town. Budget watchers should take a look at the fixed-price menus available at lunch and dinner; don't overlook the Napoleon-like *millefoglie* or any of the homemade desserts.

Trattoria I' Toscano. V. Guelfa 70r (west of V. d. Ginori). ☎ **055/215475.** Reservations suggested for dinner. Primi 10,000–14,000L ($5.90–$8.25); secondi 14,000–22,000L

($8.25–$12.95). Fixed-price lunch menu 27,000L ($15.90). AE, DC, MC, V. Wed–Mon noon–2:30pm and 7:30–10:30pm. Closed Aug 1–15. TUSCAN

A clean, flowered-filled somewhat formal (well, for Florence) space showcases enduring old-time Florentine recipes made to seem new again. For a delicious crash course on the time-tested attributes of *cucina fiorentina,* start with the delicious home-made ravioli, outshone only by the truffle-sauced gnocchi. Typical of Tuscany's meat-heavy specialties and dictated by the season, game (*cacciagione*) plays an important role the menu; those so inclined should sample wild boar, venison, rabbit, and pheasant. More predictable and my own personal favorite is the *arista di maiale con patate arroste* (rosemary-flavored roast pork loin with potatoes). Fresh fish, so very un-Florentine despite Tuscany's strip of nearby coastline, is especially prominent on Friday.

Trattoria Le Fonticine. V. Nazionale 79r (at V. dell'Ariento, north end of the Mercato San Lorenzo). ☎ **055/282106.** Reservations recommended. Primi 7,000–20,000L ($4.10–$11.75); secondi 14,000–25,000L ($8.25–$14.70). AE, DC, MC, V. Tues–Sat noon–3pm and 7–10pm. Closed Aug. TUSCAN/BOLOGNESE.

Bruna Grazia, the naturally talented Bologna-born chef and co-owner of this art-filled restaurant on the very edge of the Mercato San Lorenzo (look for the outdoor 16th-century wall fountain next door by Luca della Robbia from which the restaurant takes its name), serves as an unofficial guarantee that you will leave your table with a smile. Silvano Bruci, Bruna's Florentine-born husband (and the collector of the restaurant's modern art) sees that his hometown's cuisine doesn't get short shrift: Diners enjoy the best of both worlds. Tortellini are the traditional pasta of Bologna, and they are hand-made and -stuffed here daily, with a hearty *alla bolognese* sauce that overshadows the menu's admirable roster of competing primi (ask about the pasta sampler). If you're seated in the back room, you'll pass the open kitchen and be rewarded a glimpse of the action.

Trattoria Palle d'Oro. V. Sant'Antonio 43–45r (in the Mercato San Lorenzo area). ☎ **055/28-83-83.** Reservations suggested for dinner. Primi 7,000–8,000L ($4.10–$4.70); main courses 8,000–19,000L ($4.70–$11.20). AE, D, MC, V. Mon–Sat noon–2:30pm and 6:30–9:30pm. Closed Aug. ITALIAN.

This marketplace trattoria is forever full at lunch; most of the crowd fills the front area where a number of pastas, soups, and vegetable side dishes are available for a quick lunch standing at the bar. The prices aren't much lower than those quoted above for table service in the less-crowded back area, but in the front, it's acceptable to eat and run. Wherever you wind up, make sure you look for the house specialty, *penne della casa,* made with porcini mushrooms, prosciutto, and veal. For a cholesterol boost with a kick, try the homemade *gnocchi alla gorgonzola.*

✪ **Trattoria Sostanza (aka Il Troia).** V. Porcellana 25r (near B. Ognissanti). ☎ **055/212691.** Reservations strongly suggested. Primi 6,000–12,000L ($3.50–$7.05); secondi 12,000–28,000L ($7.05–$16.50). No credit cards. Mon–Fri noon–2:30pm and 7:30–9:30pm. Closed Aug. FLORENTINE

As long as I can remember, the inside choice for the best *bistecca alla fiorentina* in town was Sostanza. Nowadays there are a few more contenders worth considering on the scene, but Sostanza continues to guarantee a blue-ribbon Florentine beefsteak experience like few others. Popularly called Il Troia (the Hog, or in Tuscan dialect, a woman of easy virtue), this white-tiled former butcher shop puts hoi polloi and wide-eyed visitors elbow to elbow at rough-finished tables for a traditional, thoroughly enjoyable Tuscan evening. The *petti di pollo al burro* (plump chicken breasts lightly fried in butter) gives the bistecca a run for its money. The house's third specialty, tripe, under-standably finds favor mostly with the regular Florentine customers— who, by the way, after all these years still keep the place as crowded as the tourists. The mélange is always an interesting one, and the degree of conviviality always runs high.

Trattoria 13 Gobbi (Tredici Gobbi). V. Porcellana 9r (north of B. Ognissanti). ☎ **055/ 284015.** Reservations recommended for dinner. Primi 9,000–13,000L ($5.30–$7.65); secondi 18,000–25,000L ($10.60–$14.70). AE, DC, MC, V. Tues–Sun noon–2:30pm and 7–10:45pm; Mon 7–10:45pm. TUSCAN

La Fiorentina refers to both the charcoal-grilled Florentine beefsteak and the local soccer team—both cherished components of the local heritage, and both available here at the newly recharged and recently reopened "13 Hunchbacks." The best new place in town offers soccer habitues a handsome, relaxed atmosphere with exposed 15th-century beams and terra-cotta floors. Those who choose to dine alfresco can watch the neighbors' laundry billow overhead and catch a glimpse of the campanile of the Church of Ognissanti. Introduce yourself to the delicious Tuscan *pici*, a home-made spaghetti-like pasta rarely found outside country kitchens. Meat-lovers can go straight for the *Tagliata di Bistecca all' Acetto Balsamico*, tender steak that is grilled, sliced, then sautéed with balsamic vinegar and presented on a bed of arugula. The choice of wines is a winning one, with some of the best not appearing on the menu.

Trattoria Zà-Zà. Pz. Mercato Centrale 26r. ☎ **055/21-54-11.** Reservations recommended. Primi 7,000–11,000L ($4.10–$6.50); secondi 13,000–18,000L ($7.65–$10.60); menù turistico 20,000L ($11.75). AE, DC, MC, V. Mon–Sat noon–3pm and 7–11pm. Closed Aug. TUSCAN.

The walls are lined with Chianti bottles and photographs of old movie stars and not-so-famous patrons, while the long communal wooden tables overflow with an eclectic mix of tourists and local workers. Convenient to the open-air San Lorenzo market— and forever crowded despite the recent addition of outdoor tables—this typical Florentine eatery serves such long-enduring Tuscan favorites as *ribollita* and *crostini caldi misti* at reasonable prices. This is also a reliably good spot to try the fabled *bistecca fiorentina* without losing your shirt (the menu typically quotes price per ounce, so consult your waiter: The average steak costs approximately 25,000 to 30,000L/$14.70 to $17.65). Zà-Zà has just opened a lively and immediately popular wine bar next door at 27r under the curious name of **John Torta** (daily till 1am); but its serious competition can be found directly around the corner at the family run **Da Mario,** on V. Rosina 2 (also closed Sunday), whose simple trattoria decor, good food, and slightly less expensive prices make it a great (albeit equally crowded) alternative choice; it's open, unfortunately, for lunch only (come early).

NEAR SANTA CROCE

Il Che C'è, C'è. V. Magalotti 11r (off V. Proconsolo and B. dei Greci). ☎ **055/216589.** Reservations recommended. Primi 7,000–14,000L ($4.10–$8.25); secondi 14,000–30,000L ($8.25–$17.65). AE, MC, V. Tues–Sun noon–3pm and 7–11:30pm. Closed 3 weeks late Aug and early Sept. TUSCAN

First of all the name: a local expression that approximately translates to "What you see is what you get." You won't have to hope for more, and you certainly won't be settling for less, because what there is, is excellently prepared and disappoints no one. The irreverent name is compatible with the casual, family run atmosphere of the place, but the quality of the menu that is Tuscan in spirit hints of the chef/owner's formal training in the kitchens of London: He knows what he's doing. Everything is kept simple, but the ingredients are obviously the best and the results are full-flavored. Unlike many full-throttle Tuscan menus, fish is given its share of the limelight here. There are set-price menus for both the economically minded (20,000L/$11.75) and those curious to expand their culinary horizons without breaking the bank (50,000L/$29.40).

Il Pizzaiolo. V. de' Macci 113r (near Mercato Sant'Ambrogio), Firenze. ☎ **055/24-11-71.** Reservations necessary for dinner: two seatings only, 8 and 9:30pm. Pizza 7,000–12,000L ($4.10–$7.05); primi 8,500–10,000L ($5–$5.90); secondi 9,000–12,000L ($5.30–$7.05). No credit cards. Mon–Sat 12:30–3pm and 8pm–midnight. PIZZERIA/TRATTORIA.

Italy remains proudly and adamantly regionalistic about its food: No one prepares risotto like the Milanesi, and don't even think of eating pesto outside of Liguria. Pizza? You're looking for trouble unless your roots are in the south, home of this simple poor man's food. And so Florence was elated to welcome Carmine Calascione, who headed north after 30 years in Naples perfecting his art, bringing with him his expertise and such integral ingredients as garlic and oregano. The crowd waiting out on the sidewalk is confirmation that this new pizzeria guarantees the best pizza in town. There's a full menu here but no one seems to order anything other than pizza. The simple pizza Margherita (fresh tomato, mozzarella, and oregano) is perfect, as is the more endowed *pizza pazza,* a "crazy pizza" decorated with fresh tomato, artichokes, olives, mushrooms, and oregano.

✪ **Osteria del Caffe Italiano.** V. Isola d. Stinche 11/13r (2 blocks west of Piazza Santa Croce). ☎ **055/289368.** Reservations for restaurant (not wine bar) suggested. Wine bar primi 7,000L ($4.10); secondi 12,000L ($7.05). DC, MC, V. Tues–Sun noon–1am. WINE BAR/TUSCAN.

The front room of this newly opened wine bar/trattoria is warmed by burnished wood paneling, and made even more welcoming with prices and hours so attractive that people stop in all day long. Housed in the stalwart 13th-century landmark Palazzo Salviati, the informal Osteria is the new brain child of Umberto Montano (see Caffè Italiano) who proves he can do no wrong on the Florentine restaurant scene as long as he continues to think with his palate and heart. Beneath a magnificent wrought-iron chandelier hanging from the vaulted 20-foot ceiling, casual diners sample from the short and delicious lunch menu. Look for the added bonus of fresh-produced *mozzarella di bufala* specially delivered from a private supplier in Naples every Thursday, Friday, and Saturday (not available June to August). Stop by at nonmealtime hours for a by-the-glass introduction to Montano's renowned wine cellar and an assortment of Tuscan *salumi.* Or come back in the evening to dine in the more elegantly appointed back room and a chance to splurge with excellently prepared entrees from the grill and a more serious sampling of the Osteria's prodigious wine selection.

Pizzeria I Ghibellini. Pz. San Pier Maggiore 8–10r (at the end of B. degli Albizi east of V. d. Proconsolo). ☎ **055/21-44-24.** Reservations suggested for dinner. Pizza 6,000–12,000L ($3.50–$7.05); primi 6,000–8,000L ($3.50–$4.70); secondi 8,000–20,000L ($4.70–$11.75). AE, DC, MC, V. Thurs–Tues noon–4pm and 7pm–12:30am. ITALIAN/PIZZERIA

With its exposed brick walls and ceilings and curved archways inside and its white umbrellaed tables in the quiet, picturesque piazzetta outside, I Ghibellini is a good bet year-round. Pizza is the draw and there's a long list of possibilities to make your choice difficult: Go with the house specialty, *pizza alla Ghibellini* (prosciutto, mascarpone cheese, and pork sausage). The rest of the menu holds its own and deserves more merit, especially some of the pastas such as the *penne alla boccalona,* whose tomato sauce with garlic and a pinch of hot pepper is just spicy enough. Long hours and air-conditioning enhance this spot's popularity, blessed with a location in one of the city's most characterful corners. Stroll down Via delle Stinche for an après-pizza gelato at **Vivoli** (see Gelato, below), a Florentine institution.

✪ **Ristorante Acqua al Due.** V. d. Vigna Vecchia 40r (at V. dell' Acqua, behind the Bargello Museum). ☎ **055/28-41-70.** Reservations strongly suggested. Primi 8,000–10,000L ($4.70–$5.90); secondi 10,000–20,000L ($5.90–$11.75); assaggio di primi 13,000L ($7.65)

for pasta, assaggio di dolci 7,000L ($4.10) for dessert. AE, DC, MC, V. Daily 7pm–1am. ITALIAN.

Pasta lovers, take note: This is the perfect place to sample as much as you can at one sitting without breaking the bank or bursting your seams. The specialty of the house is the *assaggio di primi*, a sampling of five different types of pasta (with an occasional risotto alternative) in various sauces and shapes. These are not five full-size portions, but don't expect to have room (or feel obligated to find it) for an entree afterward either. There are also assaggi of salads (insalate) and sweets (dolci). There's no English menu, but all the waiters speak English since half the crowd (and there is always a crowd) is from foreign shores and everyone is in a very carbohydrate-happy mood. If you don't have a reservation, come back when you do. Low prices make this comfortable restaurant especially popular with an under-30 international crowd, while good quality guarantees a prevalent Florentine demographic who are fussy about their pasta sources.

Trattoria Cibreo. V. Andrea d. Verrocchio 4r (near the Mercato Sant'Ambrogio). ☎ **055/ 23-41-100.** Reservations not accepted. Primi 7,000L ($4.11); secondi 15,000L ($8.80). AE, DC, MC, V. Tues–Sat 1–2:30pm and 7:30–11pm. TUSCAN.

This is the casual, lesser-priced trattoria of celebrated chef/owner Fabio Picchi and his talented wife Benedetta; its limited menu comes from the same creative kitchen that put their premier 50-seat ristorante next door on the map, now considered one of Italy's best (peak at the menu for a future splurge: expect to spend approximately 80,000L/$47.05). A separate entrance around back leads you into the trattoria, where the ambience is rustic chic and the menu something of a revelation. Picchi takes his inspiration from traditional Tuscan recipes now quasi-extinct, but the first thing you'll notice is the absence of pasta (apparently a more recent arrival from more southern regions). After you taste the velvety yellow bell pepper soup, you won't care much. Stuffed roast duck demands the same admiration. Desserts, such as the bitter chocolate tart, are made to perfection by Fabio's wife, Benedetta. To complete the Cibreo experience, enjoy your after-dinner espresso at the handsome Caffè Cibreo across the way.

IN THE OLTRARNO

Bar Ricchi. Pz. Santo Spirito 9r. ☎ **055/21-58-64.** Reservations not accepted. Primi 7,000L ($4.10); secondi 10,000L ($5.90). AE, V, AE. Mon–Sat 12–2:30pm. Bar open winter 7am– 8:30pm. Summer 7am–1am. ITALIAN.

This much-beloved bar (especially so when spring arrives and tables appear outside in one of Florence's great piazze) has a great inexpensive menu for lunch—if only it were available at dinner. Four or five pastas are made up "espresso" upon order. As an alternative to the usual entrees (such as *arista*, a thick slice of roast pork seasoned with garlic and rosemary, or roast chicken), peruse the different "supersalads" (8,000L/$4.70), a brief nod to foreign influence. A table in the shady piazza (one of few green piazze in Florence) is ringside, but don't leave without taking a look at the cozy inside room whose walls are covered with 350 framed designs from an unofficial (and highly creative) 1980 contest to design the unfinished facade of Brunelleschi's Church of Santo Spirito.

Borgo Antico. Pz. Santo Spirito 6r. ☎ **055/21-04-37.** Reservations suggested for dinner. Pizza 10,000L ($5.90); primi 10,000L ($5.90); secondi 15,000–18,000L ($8.80–$11.60). AE, MC, V. Daily 12:45–2:30pm and 7:45–11pm (till midnight for pizza). ITALIAN/PIZZERIA.

In the spirit of the Oltrarno's "left bank" atmosphere and Santo Spirito, its favorite piazza, the Borgo Antico is a relaxed eating spot where you can order as little or as

⊕ Family-Friendly Restaurants

Gelateria delle Carrozze *(see p. 229)* The major advantage of this highly rec-ommended gelateria is its can't-miss location at the foot of the Ponte Vecchio (Old Bridge) and a windowed room full of tables to rest your feet.

✪ Il Latini *(see p. 220)* Family patriarch Narcisio Latini and his amiable sons, Giovanni and Torello, operate one of the busiest tavernlike trattorias in town where communal tables make for family friendliness with loved ones and strangers alike.

Pizzeria I Ghibellini *(see p. 224)* Dine under white umbrellaed tables in the quiet, outdoor, picturesque piazzetta. Pizza is the draw here and there's a long list of possibilities to make your children's choice difficult. Stroll down Via delle Stinche for an après-pizza gelato at Vivoli (see Gelaterie, below), a Florentine institution.

Ristorante Acqua al Due *(see p. 224)* Who doesn't love pasta? The specialty of the house is the *assaggio di primi,* a sampling of five different types of pasta (with an occasional risotto alternative) in various sauces and shapes. There are also assaggi of salads (insalate) and sweets (dolci). There's no English menu, but all the waiters speak English since half the crowd (and there is always a crowd) is from foreign shores.

Trattoria Casalinga *(see p. 228)* "Casalinga" refers to the home-style cooking that keeps this recently expanded, unpretentious place always full. The menu is straightforward classic Tuscan at extremely reasonable prices. You're just a 1-block walk east of Piazza Santo Spirito, so save your coffee and dessert for one of the indoor/outdoor cafes in one of Florence's most popular rendezvous spots.

Vivoli *(see p. 229)* This has been the much-beloved queen of the Florentine ice-cream scene. Grab any of their made-daily wonders, and find a stone bench at the Piazza Santa Croce for an impromptu soccer match among the neighbor-hood kids.

much as you want, and enjoy it in the interesting company of a mixed bag of tourists and Florentines. The scene inside is always buzzing (and bless the management for establishing a much needed no-smoking room), where an open kitchen and wood-burning pizza oven provide a show, but from April to September tables are set up out-side where the million-dollar view of Brunelleschi's church is thrown in for free. There are a dozen great pizzas to pick from and a number of combination "super salads," with mostly un-Italian ingredients such as corn, hearts of palm, and shrimp. Special-ties of the day get equally creative (as in "expensive"), but you'll most likely want to come here for the pizza-with-a-view.

Il Cantinone. V. Santo Spirito 6r (off Pz. Santa Trinita). ☎ **055/21-88-98.** Reservations rec-ommended for dinner. Crostoni 7,000–10,000L ($4.10–$5.90); primi 10,000–16,000L ($5.90–$9.40); secondi 20,000–28,000L ($11.75–$16.50). AE, MC, V. Tues–Sun. 2:30–11pm. WINE BAR/TUSCAN.

Appropriately set in the brick-vaulted cantina or wine cellar of a 16th-century palazzo, this well-known wine bar promises "a pinch of country Tuscan cooking, by candle-light, in the heart of Florence." You might consider it more jovial than romantic on nights when the wine gets flowing—there are five or six red wines available by the glass, but don't overlook a liter of the good house wine, a bargain at 13,000L ($8.55). Order a number of different appetizers and first courses and you'll understand

Tuscany's peasant food is called the food of kings. The specialty is *crostoni,* large slabs of home-baked bread covered with either prosciutto, *funghi* (mushrooms), tomatoes, or *salsiccia* (sausage). Primi might be a hearty *pappa al pomodoro* or thick *ribollita* soup, with a number of pastas (and large mixed salads for the American palate). All in all, it's delicious, basic fare to accompany a quintessentially Florentine evening.

Osteria del Cinghiale Bianco. B. San Jacopo 43r (off Pz. Santa Trinita). ☎ **055/ 21-57-06.** Reservations suggested for dinner. Primi 7,000–12,000L ($4.10–$7.05); secondi 13,000–22,000L ($7.65–$12.95). No credit cards. Thurs–Mon noon–2:30pm and 7–10:30pm. TUSCAN.

Set in a medieval tower, and with exposed stone walls setting the ambience, this friendly trattoria is dedicated to the *cinghiale,* the wild boar so ubiquitous in the Tuscan hills and traditional cuisine. Its presence is felt strongly during the autumn game season, but you'll usually see year-round dishes here such as pappardelle pasta with a cinghiale sauce or a wild boar sausage (*salsiccia*) antipasto to satisfy your curiosity. But most of the menu is cinghiale-free, such as the delicious *strozzapreti* (literally "priest stranglers"—don't ask), a baked pasta made with the ricotta-cheese-and-spinach mix usually found in ravioli, served with melted butter. Things are relaxed here during lunch, where the owners have even added an *insalata dello chef* (chef's salad), a concession to the light eating habits of American customers. A few small niches have been created for the romantically inclined, and it's a comfortable place to linger over dinner.

✪ **Trattoria Angiolino.** V. Santo Spirito 35r (west of Pz. S. Trinita). ☎ **055/2398976.** Reservations recommended. Primi 9,000–10,000L ($5.30–$5.90); secondi 15,000–20,000L ($8.80–$11.75). AE, DC, MC, V. Tues–Sun noon–2:30pm and 7:15–10:30pm. Closed Aug. FLORENTINE

Local noble families fill this Florentine classic on Sundays, while neighborhood artisans and antique store owners file in the rest of the week. It is hoped there will be room for you, and the chance to experience a perfect Florentine meal in a traditional rustic trattoria that looks lovingly unchanged for the last 100 years. From the first hint of the excellent quality extra virgin olive oil used in the house specialty of marinated fresh vegetables (eggplant, bell peppers, zucchini—whatever the season's bounty supplies) to the *penne all'Angiolino* (with a tomato and meat sauce flavored with Chianti wine), you'll appreciate the recent sensitive restoration that brightened up the place, but left the reliably great food and atmosphere of yesteryear in tact. An open kitchen provides between-the-bites entertainment while filling the place with the aroma of your next course.

Worth a Splurge

For an evening of splurge, you needn't go to Florence's white-glove restaurants and Michelin-starred choices. The more modestly priced trattorias that are listed above can bring you up to another level of spending—and enjoyment—when you leave restraint at the door and go for the sampling of antipasti to start, a choice of the more expensive grilled meats (and that fabled steak, *bistecca alla fiorentina*) and an extra fine bottle of Chianti classico. **Il Latini, Trattoria Antellesi, Trattoria Sostanza,** and ✪ **Osteria del Caffe Italiano** (all listed above) can effortlessly guarantee you that special evening for a few thousand lire more (usually just beyond the 50,000L/$29.40 mark). If you're a wine rookie, ask your waiter to help you choose from the best of the regional wines: Remember that the premier wines of the designated Chianti area are grown in Florence's backyard.

A Moveable Feast

Doing your own food shopping in Italy is an interesting and usually delightful (and sometimes frustrating) experience. To buy cold cuts, you'll have to look for a delicatessen-like *salumeria*. To pick up cheese or yogurt, you'll have to find a *latteria*. Vegetables and fruit can be found at a produce stand called *orto e vedura*. Most of the above can sometimes be found at a well-stocked *alimentari,* the closest thing Italy has to a grocery store, usually in miniature size. For bread to put all that between, wander into a *forno* or *panetteria*. That same *forno* might supply dessert. If not, a *pasticceria* will—and how. And for a bottle of wine to accompany it, search out a shop selling *vino e olio.* **Via dei Neri,** which begins at Via de' Benci near Piazza Santa Croce and stretches over toward Piazza della Signoria, is lined with an ever diminishing number of small specialty food shops and is a good area for purchasing food for an outing.

If you prefer to find all you need under one roof—or just for the photo-op of it all—visit the enormous, colorful **Mercato Centrale,** Florence's block-long two-story central marketplace, entrance at V. dell' Ariento 12, in the midst of the open-air San Lorenzo market that hawks tourist tchotchkes galore. In this area on V. Sant'Antonio 47r is the well-known **Fiaschetteria Zanobi** (off Via dell'Ariento), for the de rigueur bottle of excellent Chianti needed to accompany the quintessential Tuscan picnic.

If you're just as happy to have someone else make up your sandwiches for you, seek out **Forno Sartoni** on V. d. Cerchi 34r directly behind the large Coin department store on Via Calzaiuoli. This is something of an institution—the crowd in the back is waiting for fresh pizza straight out of the oven, sold by the slice and weighed by the ounce (the average slice costs 2,500L/$1.50). Fresh made-to-order sandwiches on freshly baked focaccia bread are available for

Trattoria Casalinga. V. Michelozzi 9r (between V. Maggio and Pz. Santo Spirito). ☎ **055/ 218-624.** Reservations recommended for dinner. Primi 5,500–7,000L ($3.25–$4.10); secondi 8,000–16,000L ($4.70–$9.40). AE, DC, MC, V. Mon–Sat noon–2:30pm and 7–10pm. TUSCAN.

"Casalinga" refers to the home-style cooking that keeps this recently expanded, unpretentious place always full. Along with the larger seating capacity came the frayed nerves of the help and a sometimes erratic performance from the kitchen. Or so I've heard, but I've never experienced anything but a smile and a good meal (well, OK, maybe just a good meal) in one of my favorite neighborhoods in Florence. The menu is straightforward classic Tuscan—try the hearty *ribollita* vegetable soup, or the less commonly found *ravioli al sugo di coniglio* in a wild rabbit-flavored sauce. You're just a 1-block walk east of Piazza Santo Spirito, so save room for coffee or dessert at one of the indoor/outdoor bars in one of Florence's most frequented after-dinner rendezvous spots.

GELATO (ICE CREAM)

Though gelato is generally considered a revered southern Italian institution, there are innumerable sources for this sweet treat around Florence. The following five are not only considered the best, they also have the largest selections, and are all centrally located. Ask for a *cono* or *coppa* (cup) ranging from 3,000 to 7,000L ($1.75 to $4.10) (none accept credit cards—point and ask for as many flavors as can be squeezed in.

approximately 3,500L ($2.05). **Alimentari Orizi,** on V. Parione 19r off Via Tornabuoni (see "Great Deals on Dining, p. 215 above), will also make up fresh sandwiches as ordered, with a greater selection of cold cuts, according to your specifications (ketchup and mustard are on hand for those peculiar American tastes). Ask for it *da portare via* (to go). My favorite is the chunky tuna (not masqueraded with mayonnaise in salad form) with plump red tomatoes on a crusty roll.

The **Boboli Gardens,** on the opposite side of the river Arno, is the best picnic spot in town (see "Exploring Florence," Palazzo Pitti and the Boboli Gardens). Within the garden is a grand amphitheater behind the Palazzo Pitti that provides historical (stone) seating and a lovely view of the palazzo and Florence beyond. But, it's worth the hike from there up to the top to the **Forte Belvedere** for the breathtaking view (and hence the fortress's name). For something less strenuous and more central: Park yourself on a park bench in the centro storico. A number of the city's most beautiful piazze have stone benches and open spaces: **Piazza Santa Croce** comes to mind for its proximity to Vivoli's (reason enough!) for a postlunch gelato. **Piazza Santa Maria Novella** offers stone benches and the only plot of grass in any of the city's squares (where sitting is not encouraged but done anyway). **Piazza Santissima Annunziata** is a wide Renaissance square with inviting steps for sun-basking on its west side (amid a like-minded number of students from the nearby university), and for convenience, you can't beat the central **Piazza della Repubblica** and its new circular planters-cum-seats. If Florence's summer heat has set in, look for the shady **Piazza Massimo d'Azeglio**, east of the Accademia near the Synagogue, and the lovely **Piazza Santo Spirito** in the Oltrarno—two of the very few green piazze in the city.

Gelateria often separate the gelati from the *semifreddi,* a concoction something akin to frozen mousse in a host of different flavors. A sign boasting *produzione propria* (homemade) is usually a good sign that you have happened upon a serious house of ice cream.

Of all the gelaterias in Florence, **Festival del Gelato** (V. d. Corso 75r; ☎ 055/23-94-386), closed Monday) has been the only serious contender to the premier Vivoli (listed below). Offering about 50 flavors along with pounding pop music and blinding neon, the gelateria is as much a scene as a substance. Both this and **Perche No!** (V. d. Tavolini 19r; ☎ 055/23-98-969; closed Tuesday in winter), are popular ice cream spots between the Piazza Signoria and Piazza Duomo; both are on side streets off the well-trod pedestrian Via Calzaiuoli. The major advantage of the always crowded **Gelateria delle Carrozze** (Pz. d. Pesce 3–5r; ☎ 055/23-96-810; closed Wednesday) is its can't-miss location at the foot of the Ponte Vecchio (Old Bridge). If you're coming off the Ponte Vecchio and about to head toward the Duomo, it is just to your right on a small alleyway that forks off the main street. It's just as wonderfully delicious as the best of them, maybe easier to find, and has quite a few tables inside for those who prefer to sit while savoring the moment or want a sandwich to complete the meal.

But the queen of the ice-cream scene has long remained ✪ **Vivoli,** on V. Isole d. Stinche 74 a block west of Piazza Santa Croce (closed Monday). It's world-famous, but recent taste tests have detractors wondering if it's now relying a bit too heavily on its

Avoiding the Lines

Beginning in late 1998 the new agency **Cooperative Opera** (aka Firenze Musei) was hired by the city of Florence to provide advance-purchase tickets. Each reservation request will cost 2,400L ($1.40) plus the standard cost of admission. Advance purchase tickets are possible for the following museums: **Galleria dell'Accademia, Galleria degli Uffizi, Galleria Palatina** (Palazzo Pitti) and the **Boboli Gardens, Cappelle Medicee** (Medici Chapels), **Museo San Marco,** the **Bargello,** and a handful of lesser visited museums. The special collections of **Contini Buonacossi** and the **Vasari Corridor** must be arranged as part of the Uffizi admission. To order tickets, contact Cooperativa Opera/Firenze Musei at ☎ **055/294882** or fax 055/264406. A Web site and e-mail address was expected by spring 1999. You can arrange the reservation through most hotels upon your arrival, but during the tourist season, you are encouraged to reserve in advance before your arrival. Credit cards were expected to be accepted by spring 1999 (MasterCard, Visa, and probably American Express and Diners Club). For the moment, all reserved tickets must be picked up at either the Uffizi or Palazzo Pitti. This, too, may change in the future.

reputation; I say it's still heaven. Exactly how renowned is this brightly lit gelateria? Taped to the wall is a postcard bearing only "Vivoli, Europa" for the address, yet it was successfully delivered to this world capital of ice cream.

A block south of the Accademia (pick up a cone after you've gazed upon David's glory), is **Carabé,** what local purists insist is Vivoli's only deserving contender to the throne as gelato king (V. Ricasoli 60r; ☎ **055/289476;** only open mid-February to mid-November). Offering genuine homemade Sicilian gelato in the heart of Florence, from fresh ingredients shipped in from Sicily by the hard-working Sicilian owners. Taste for yourself, and see if Florentines can hope to ever surpass such scrumptiousness direct from the island that first brought the concept of ice cream to Europe.

4 Exploring Florence

Seeing all of Florence in a short time requires organization. It's not just that there's so much to see in this great city; it's also that establishments (stores, churches, and so on) close for long lunch breaks and some museums close for the day at 2pm or sooner (remember that the last entrance is at least 30 minutes, sometimes 45 to 60 minutes, before closing). Many museums are closed on Monday. The first thing you should do stop by a tourist office (at the main train station or at V. Cavour 1r; ☎ 055/29-08-32) for an up-to-the-minute listing of museum hours or ask at your hotel. Beginning in 1996, the summer hours were extended more and more until, which saw many museums staying open until 11pm, though few people knew about it. Churches and the markets are good alternatives for afternoon touring time, since they usually remain open until 7pm. You won't waste precious hours if you plan in advance and purchase tickets to museums ahead of time (see "Avoiding the Lines," above, for advance-purchase information).

NEAR THE DUOMO & THE PIAZZA SIGNORIA

✪ **Duomo (Cathedral of Santa Maria del Fiore).** Pz. d. Duomo. ☎ **055/2302885.** Cathedral free; cupola ascent 10,000L ($5.90); excavations 4,000L ($2.35). Summer: Mon–Sat 10am–5pm, Sun 1–5pm (open Sun morning for services only; cupola and excavations closed Sun). Winter: Mon–Fri 10am–7pm, Sun 1–5pm (open Sun morning for services only; cupola and excavations closed Sun). Last entrance to ascend the cupola 40 minutes before closing.

The red-tiled dome of Florence's magnificent Duomo dominates the skyline today just as it did when it was constructed 5 centuries ago. When it was completed in 1434, it was the largest unsupported dome in the world, intended to dwarf the structures of ancient Greece and Rome. In Renaissance style, to be *"il piu bello che si puo"* (as beautiful as possible), it was and still is considered a major architectural feat and was the high point of architect Filippo Brunelleschi's illustrious career—it took 14 years to complete. The cathedral's tricolor marble exterior (also the color of the Italian flag) comes from Tuscan quarries: white stone from Carrara, red from Maremma, and green from Prato. This "modern" neo-Gothic facade, replacing the original, was only added in the late 19th century when Florence became the capital of the newly united Italy for a brief period (1861 to 1875). The polychromatic mosaic is an interesting contrast to the rather somber, sienna-colored medieval and fortresslike palazzi throughout the rest of the city.

Though much of the church's interior decoration has been moved to the Museo dell'Opera del Duomo (see below), the cavernous cathedral (the fourth largest church in Europe) still boasts three stained-glass windows on the entrance wall by Lorenzo Ghiberti (sculptor of the famous Baptistery doors) next to Paolo Uccello's giant *hora italica* clock (1443) using the heads of four prophets. In late 1996, an extensive and elaborate 15-year restoration was finally completed on the colorful 16th-century frescoes covering the inside of the cupola and depicting the world's largest painting of the Last Judgment. They were begun by the master Giorgio Vasari and finished by his far less talented student Federico Zuccari. When the restorers began their work, they discovered that a good portion of the work was executed not in "true fresco" but in tempera, which is much more delicate; when restored to its true, vibrant color palette most of Florence changed its mind about what had until then been considered a frivolous expense of city funds.

The most distinctive feature is ✪ **Brunelleschi's dome.** It was built double-walled and is strong enough to withstand the thousands of athletic tourists who climb the spiraling, dizzying 463 steps leading to the summit for its spectacular view of Florence (there's no elevator). Entrance to the staircase can be approached from the south facade door marked "Cupola di Brunelleschi," open Monday to Friday from 8:30am to 7pm, Saturday 8:30am to 5pm, and costs 10,000L ($5.90).

Beneath the Duomo's floor is the crypt (look for the Scavi della Cripta di Santa Reparata), the ruins of the Romanesque Santa Reparata Cathedral, believed to have been founded in the 5th century on this site; it was continuously enlarged until it was done away with in 1296 to accommodate the present structure that was being built around it. Brunelleschi's tomb is appropriately located here, discovered only in 1972, but generally there's not much to justify the admission price. The entrance to the excavations is through a stairway near the front of the cathedral, to the right as you enter.

✪ **Battistero (Baptistery).** Pz. di San Giovanni (adjacent to Piazza Duomo). ☎ **055/ 2302885.** Admission 5,000L ($2.95). Mon–Sat noon–6:30pm, Sun 8:30am–1:30pm.

In front of the Duomo is Florence's octagonal baptistery, dedicated to the city's beloved patron saint, San Giovanni or John the Baptist. The highlight of the Romanesque Baptistery, constructed in the 11th and 12th centuries (most likely on the site of an ancient Roman palazzo) and considered one of Florence's oldest buildings, is Lorenzo Ghiberti's bronze exterior doors known as the *Gates of Paradise,* on the side facing the Duomo (east)—look for the ever-present clump of tourists. Ten bronze panels depict various lifelike scenes from the Old Testament, including Adam and Eve in creation, in stunning three-dimensional low relief, considered some of the finest in Italian art. Ghiberti labored over his masterpiece from 1425 to 1452, dying three years later. Their name comes from Michelangelo who, when asked what he thought of

Florence Attractions

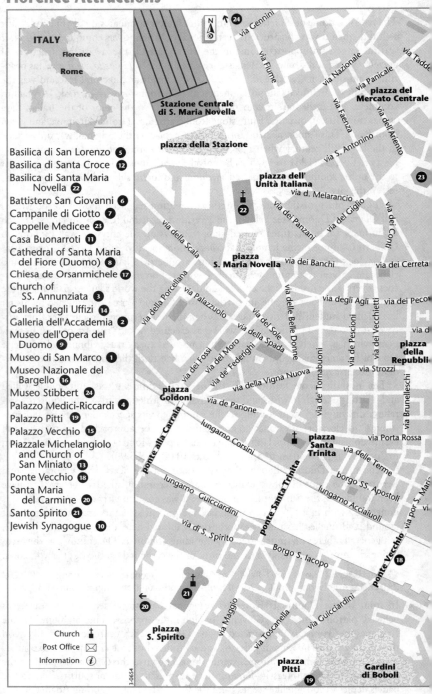

ITALY

Florence

Rome

Basilica di San Lorenzo ⑤
Basilica di Santa Croce ⑫
Basilica di Santa Maria
  Novella ㉒
Battistero San Giovanni ⑥
Campanile di Giotto ⑦
Cappelle Medicee ㉓
Casa Buonarroti ⑪
Cathedral of Santa Maria
  del Fiore (Duomo) ⑧
Chiesa de Orsanmichele ⑰
Church of
  SS. Annunziata ③
Galleria degli Uffizi ⑭
Galleria dell'Accademia ②
Museo dell'Opera del
  Duomo ⑨
Museo di San Marco ①
Museo Nazionale del
  Bargello ⑯
Museo Stibbert ㉔
Palazzo Medici-Riccardi ④
Palazzo Pitti ⑲
Palazzo Vecchio ⑮
Piazzale Michelangiolo
  and Church of
  San Miniato ⑬
Ponte Vecchio ⑱
Santa Maria
  del Carmine ⑳
Santo Spirito ㉑
Jewish Synagogue ⑩

Church ✝
Post Office ✉
Information ⓘ

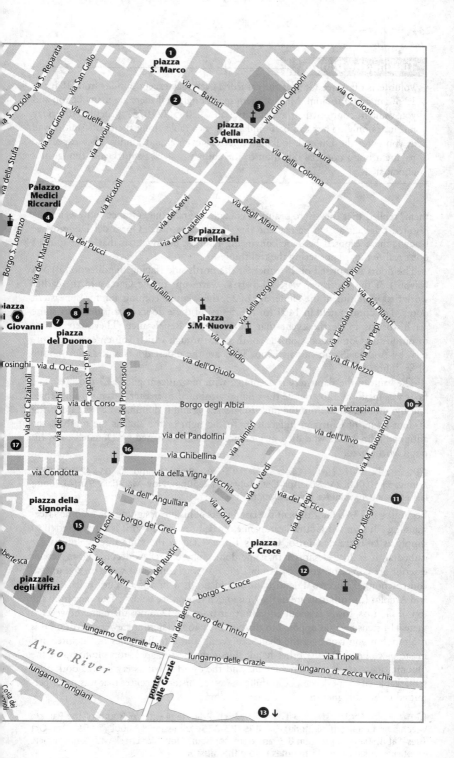

piazza
S. Marco ❶

via C. Battisti

via Gino Capponi

via G. Giosti

via S. Orsola · via S. Reparata

via San Gallo

❷

❸ †

piazza
della
SS.Annunziata

via dei Ginori

via Guelfa

via Cavour

via della Stufa

via Laura

via della Colonna

Palazzo
Medici
Riccardi ❹

via Ricasoli

via dei Servi

via degli Alfani

† Borgo S. Lorenzo

via dei Martelli

via dei Pucci

via del Castellaccio

piazza
Brunelleschi

via Bufalini

borgo Pinti

via dei Pilastri

iazza
i ❻
S. Giovanni

❺

❽ †

❼

❾

piazza
del Duomo

† piazza
S.M. Nuova

via della Pergola

via Fiesolana

via dei Pepi

osinghi

via d. Oche

via S. Egidio

via di Mezzo

via d. Studio

via dell'Oriuolo

via dei Calzaiuoli

via dei Cerchi

via del Corso

via del Proconsolo

Borgo degli Albizi

via Pietrapiana ❿→

via dei Pandolfini

via dell'Ulivo

via M. Buonarroti

❶❼

❶❻ †

via Ghibellina

via Palmieri

via Condotta

via della Vigna Vecchia

piazza della
Signoria

via dell' Anguillara

via G. Verdi

via del Pepi

via dei Fico

⓫

❶❺

borgo dei Greci

via Torta

piazza
S. Croce

borgo Allegri

❶❹

via dei Leoni

via dei Rustici

⓬ †

bertesca

via dei Neri

piazzale
degli Uffizi

borgo S. Croce

corso dei Tintori

via Tripoli

lungarno Generale Diaz

via dei Benci

ponte alle Grazie

lungarno delle Grazie

lungarno d. Zecca Vecchia

Arno River

lungarno Torrigiani

Costa dei nnoli

⓭ ↓

233

Touring the Duomo

Volunteers offer free tours of the cathedral every day except Sunday from 10am to 12:30pm and 3 to 5pm. Most of them speak English; if there are many of you and you want to confirm their availability, call ☎ **055/2710757** (Tuesday to Friday mornings only). They can be found sitting at a table along the right (south) wall as you enter the Duomo, looking rather professorial and kindly. They expect no payment but a nominal donation to the church is always appreciated though not anticipated.

them, replied that they were beautiful enough to grace the entrance to heaven. The restored originals are on permanent view in the Museo dell'Opera del Duomo (see below); those exposed here are convincing replicas. So much so that most tourists don't realize they're not seeing the real thing.

The doors comprised of 28 panels at the north side (facing the direction of Via Cavour) of the baptistery were Ghiberti's "warm-up" to the Gates and the earlier work that won him, at the tender age of 23, the eventual commission for the eastern doors. The contest held in 1401 for the design of these doors is considered by some art historians to be the event that launched the Renaissance. They were meant to outdo the Gothic doors on the south side, through which you enter the Baptistery, by Andrea Pisano cast in 1336. They are the oldest doors and depict the life of St. John.

The vault of the Baptistery is decorated with magnificent gilded ✪ **mosaics.** The floor was inlaid in 1209, while the ceiling, attributed to master artisans from Venice and Byzantium, dates from the mid- to late 1200s and is dominated by the imposing 26-foot figure of Christ in Judgement. To the right of the altar is the tomb of the antipope John XXIII who died in Florence of 1419, designed by Donatello and his pupil Michelozzo.

✪ **Campanile di Giotto (Giotto's Bell Tower).** Pz. d. Duomo. ☎ **055/23-02-885.** Admission 10,000L ($5.90). Apr–Oct, daily 9am–6:50pm; Nov–Mar, daily 9am–4:20pm; last entrance 40 minutes before closing.

Beginning in 1334, Giotto spent the last 3 years of his life designing the Duomo's freestanding "Tuscanized Gothic" campanile, or bell tower, and so it is often referred to simply as **la Torre di Giotto,** Giotto's Tower. Clad in the same three colors as the cathedral, it is 20 feet shorter than the dome. The bas-reliefs decorating its slender exterior are copies of works by Andrea Pisano (who continued work on the tower's construction), Francesco Talenti (who would finish it in 1359), Luca della Robbia, and Arnoldi (the originals are in the Museo dell'Opera, see below). The view from the top of Giotto's Tower is about equal to that from the Duomo; there are, however, a mere 414 steps here (as opposed to the Duomo's 463). There are fewer crowds on this rooftop, but you won't get the chance to get up and into Brunelleschi's architectural masterpiece here. On the other hand, this is the best flagpole-top photo-op of the Duomo, its terra-cotta covered cupola and the dwarfed baptistery below. Both offer remarkable cityscapes over a beautifully preserved historical center that was never permitted to build higher than the cathedral's dome.

✪ **Galleria degli Uffizi (Uffizi Galleries).** Pzle. degli Uffizi 6 (south of the Palazzo Vecchio and the Pz. d. Signoria). ☎ **055/23-885.** Admission 12,000L ($7.05). Apr–Oct Tues–Sat 8:30am–10pm, Sun 8:30am–8pm; for hours Nov–Mar check with tourist office. The ticket office closes 45 minutes before the museum.

The Uffizi is one of the most important art museums in the world and should be the first stop in Florence for anyone interested in the rich artistic heritage of the Renaissance. Six centuries of artistic development are housed in this impressive Renaissance palazzo, commissioned by Duke Cosimo de' Medici in 1560 and initiated by Giorgio Vasari to house the Duchy of Tuscany's administrative offices (*uffizi* means "offices"); from its onset, it was believed to be Vasari's greatest architectural work. The art collection, whose unmatched strong point is the Florentine Renaissance, but includes major works by Flemish and Venetian masters, was amassed by the Medici and bequeathed to the people of Florence in 1737 in perpetuity by Anna Maria Ludovica, the last of the Medici line who was determined to see that Florence's unrivaled patrimony not leave its home boundaries. If you have the time, try to see the collection in two half-day trips: Many rooms suffer the fate of being filled with nothing but masterpieces.

The gallery consists of 45 rooms where paintings are nicely grouped into schools in chronological order, from the 13th to the 18th century (don't overlook the details of the building itself, whose frescoed ceilings and tapestried corridors are overshadowed by the wealth of paintings). Vasari's monumental staircase leads upstairs to the superb collection that begins in **Room 2** in the east wing, with Giotto's incredible *Madonna* (1310), considered by most scholars the first painting to make the transition from Byzantine to Renaissance style. Look for the distinctive differences between Giotto's work and his teacher Cimabue's *Madonna in Maestà* (1280) on the opposite wall. Some of the museum's best-known and most visited rooms are dedicated to 15th-century Florentine painting, the eve of the Renaissance or the "First Renaissance." In **Room 7** the Renaissance starts shaping up as portrayed in the major works by Paolo Uccello, Masaccio, Fra Angelico, and the only work by Piero della Francesca to be found in Florence painted around 1465. As you proceed (**Room 8 and 9**), look for the elegant Madonnas of Filippo Lippi and Antonio Pollaiolo's delightful little panels that influenced Botticelli whose masterworks are next.

For many (and judging from the crowds), the Botticelli Rooms (**Room 10 to 14**) are some of the undisputed highlights of a museum whose every niche is hung with extraordinary art. Arguably the most stunning of the dozen or so are the restored *Primavera (The Allegory of Springtime)* whose three graces form the painting's principal focus and *The Birth of Venus* (commonly referred to as "Venus on the Half-Shell." Botticelli's *Adoration of the Magi* is interesting for the portraits he incorporated of his Medici sponsors, and his self-portrait, on the far right-hand side in a yellow robe and golden curls. Other notable works include Leonardo da Vinci's unfinished *Adoration of the Magi* and his famous *Annunciation* in **Room 15.**

And the collection goes on and on, with masterwork after famous masterwork. As you move through the works of the 16th century, follow the tour guides to Michelangelo's *Holy Family*, also called the **Doni Tondo** as it was a circular painting commissioned by the local Doni family in 1506; it is the only panel painting by the great painter better known for frescoes and sculpture.

Since the May 1993 car bombing that damaged 200 works (37 of them seriously) and killed five people including the museum's custodian and her family, the museum has staged an amazing recovery. Only four of those damaged were considered superior examples from the Italian Renaissance; two were destroyed beyond repair. Restorers, many of whom had recently spent decades working to undo the devastating effects of the 1966 floods, have again been working around the clock to repair the damage. In December 1998, Italy unveiled what it called the New Uffizi, a $15 million renovation that repaired all damaged rooms, added more than 20,000 square feet of new museum space, and displayed more than 100 works that had never been seen before.

It is part of a larger project to triple exhibition space by 2000. A handsome new book-and gift store on the ground floor and an elegant terraced cafe (on the top floor at the end of the west wing and overlooking the Piazza Signoria and Palazzo Vecchio) were part of the welcomed renovation. The **Corridoio Vasariano,** commissioned from Vasari by Cosimo I after the completion of the Uffizi, is an aboveground "tunnel" that runs along the rooftops of the Ponte Vecchio buildings and connects the Uffizi with Cosimo's then-new residence in the Pitti Palace on the other side of the Arno. The corridor is lined with portraits and self-portraits by a stellar list of international masters such as Bronzino, Reubens, Rembrandt, Ingres and others. When it is scheduled to re-open in Spring of 1999, finally repaired from damage incurred from the 1993 bombing, it will probably require special admission during morning hours only and an accompanying guide that can be arranged through the Uffizi; inquire at ticket window.

Piazza della Signoria, Palazzo Vecchio & Loggia dei Lanzi. Piazza della Signoria. ☎ **055/2768465.** Palazzo Vecchio (Appartamenti Monumentali): 10,000L ($5.90) Mon–Wed and Fri–Sat 9am–7pm, Sun 8am–1pm, Thurs 9am–2pm.

PIAZZA DELLA SIGNORIA   In Florence all roads lead to the spacious, elegant piazza—the cultural, political, and social heart of the city since the 14th century. Named after the **signoria** or oligarchy that ruled medieval Florence, it now serves as a picture-perfect outdoor sculpture gallery replete with pigeons, horse and buggies, groups of tourists, and outdoor cafes. It's one of Italy's most beautiful public squares.

PALAZZO VECCHIO (THE OLD PALACE)   The piazza is dominated by the imposing rough-hewn fortress architecture of this late 13th-century palace. Its severe Gothic style, complete with crenellations and battlements, is highlighted by a 308-foot campanile that was a supreme feat of engineering during its construction from 1299 to 1302 by master builder Arnolfo di Cambrio. It served as Florence's city hall for many years (a role it fulfills again today) and then was home to Duke Cosimo I de' Medici (that's Giambologna's late 16th-century bronze statue of him on horseback anchoring the middle of the piazza). He lived here for 10 years beginning in 1540, when much of the interior was remodeled to the elegant Renaissance style you see today, before moving to the Palazzo Pitti on the other side of the Arno. You'll enter through the stunning main courtyard of the palazzo, with its intricately carved columns and extraordinarily colorful 16th-century frescoes by Vasari; the central focus is the fountain of a Putto Holding a Dolphin, a copy of Verrochchio's original, which is displayed upstairs.

The highlight of the interior is the first-floor massive **Salone dei Cinquecento** (Hall of the Five Hundred) whose rich frescoes by Vassari depict Florence's history; formerly the city's council chambers where the 500-man assembly once gathered, it is still used for government and civic functions. The statue *The Genius of Victory* (1533–34) is by Michelangelo; originally commissioned for the tomb of Pope Julius, it was later acquired by the Medici. Upstairs, the richly decorated and frescoed salons, such as the private quarters of Cosimo's Spanish wife, Eleanora of Toledo, offer an intriguing glimpse into how the ruling class of Renaissance Florence lived.

Travel Tip

During the high season in 1998, evening hours at **Palazzo Vecchio** were extended to 11:30pm with free guided tours in English available. Check with the tourist office for expected repetitions in the future.

A small disk in the ground in front of Ammanati's enormous (and controversial—Michelangelo dismissed it as inferior) Neptune fountain (1576) marks the spot where Savonarola, fire-and-brimstone reformer and religious fundamentalist, was hanged and then burned at the stake for heresy in 1498. It was here that his successful Bonfire of the Vanities took place just years before. Flanking the life-size 19th-century copy of Michelangelo's *David* (the original that once stood here for centuries is now permanently on display in the Accademia) are copies of Donatello's *Judith Beheading Holofernes* (the original is in the Palazzo Vecchio) and his *Marzocco* (original in the Bargello) heraldic lion of Florence. Unfortunately placed next to David's anatomical perfection is Baccio Bandelli's **Heracles** (1534) that comes across looking like the "sack of melons" that Cellini described it to be when first placed here.

LOGGIA DEI LANZI This 14th-century outdoor sculpture gallery (also called Loggia della Signoria, or, after its designer, Loggia di Orcagna) sits on the south side of the Piazza Signoria. It underwent elaborate restoration for years, but the scaffolding is finally down and the loggia is open to visitors for the first time in decades. Benvenuto Cellini's rare work *Perseus* was moved to the Uffizi for a sorely needed restoration in late 1996 after standing here since 1545 and a copy will permanently take its place here sometime soon. Giambologna's important *Rape of the Sabine Women* is an original, a three-dimensional study in Mannerism, along side his *Hercules Slaying the Centaur* and *Duke Cosimo de' Medici*.

✪ **Museo Nazionale del Bargello (Bargello Museum).** V. d. Proconsolo 4 (at V. Ghibellina, near the Uffizi). ☎ **055/23-88-606.** Admission 8,000L ($4.70). Tues–Sun 8:30am–2pm (Tues and Sat open till 5pm). Open the 1st, 3rd, and 5th Sun of every month.

If a visit to the Accademia and a viewing of the fabled David has whetted your appetite for more fine Renaissance sculpture, then you'll be interested in this national museum's outstanding collection where the crowds, amazingly, are never bad. This stark, daunting 1255 Gothic building originated as the seat of the city's **Podestà** or chief magistrate and later served as the city's jail in Renaissance times. In the middle of the majestic courtyard, plastered with the coats of arms of the Podestà, is a tank where prisoners were once tortured and executed; some hangings took place out the windows for public viewing. Today, Il Bargello, named for the 16th-century police chief or Constable (Bargello) who ruled from here, houses three stories of treasures by Florentine Renaissance sculptors and a collection of Mannerist bronzes.

On the **ground floor** begin with a visit to Michelangelo's room, including his "other" *David,* originally called *Apollo* and sculpted 30 years after the original; the *Pitti Tondo* (1503–05) depicts the Madonna teaching Jesus and San Giovanni to read; and *Brutus* (1539). Take a look at his *Bacchus*—it was one of the young artist's first major works when he was 22 (1497), and effortlessly captures in marble the Roman god's drunken posture. Among the other important sculptures here are Ammanati's *Leda and the Swan,* his student Giambologna's significant *Winged Mercury* (1564), and several of Donatello's works, including his sexually ambiguous bronze *David* (1440–50), the first freestanding nude statue since classical times. In another room are the two original 1401 bronze plaques by Brunelleschi and Donatello's master, Ghiberti, depicting the **Sacrifice of Isaac** made for the competition to decide who should sculpt the second (eastern) set of doors for the Bapistery—of course, Ghiberti's won (the original doors are in the Museo dell'Opera; copies can be found on the Baptistery).

✪ **Ponte Vecchio.** At V. Por Santa Maria, north bank, and V. Guicciardini, south bank.

Linking the north and south banks of the Arno River at its narrowest point, the Ponte Vecchio has been as much a landmark symbol of the city as Michelangelo's *David* or

Brunelleschi's Duomo. It was destroyed and rebuilt many times before the construction of the 1345 bridge you see today, designed by Taddeo Gaddi, and has stood lined with these same goldsmith's shops for centuries. Many of the exclusive gold and jewelry stores today are owned by descendents of the 41 artisans set up on the bridge in the 16th century by Cosimo I de' Medici. No longer able to tolerate the smelly workshops of butchers and skin tanners on his daily trips to and from the new Medici residence in the Palazzo Pitti on the Oltrarno side of the river, he moved in the classier goldsmiths and upped the rent. Florentines tirelessly recount the story of how, in 1944, Hitler's retreating troops destroyed all the other bridges crossing the Arno (since reconstructed, often with the original material or at least according to archival designs) with the exception of the Ponte Vecchio. To compensate, they bombed both bridgeheads to block Allied access to the bridge, resulting in the 1950s look of those buildings in the otherwise medieval areas of Via Por Santa Maria and Via Guicciardini. The devastating flood of 1966 was less discriminating, and washed away most of the precious merchandise that filled the bridge's store windows; most, they say, is embedded for history in the muddy bottoms of the Arno.

Museo dell'Opera del Duomo (Cathedral Works Museum). Pz. d. Duomo 29. ☎ **055/23-98-796.** Admission 8,000L ($5.25) Mar–Oct, Mon–Sat 9am–7:30pm; Nov–Feb, Mon–Sat 9am–5:20pm; last entrance 60 minutes before closing.

Opened to the public in 1891 and ever since overlooked, this quiet, airy museum behind the cathedral was closed in late 1998 for renovations, with intentions to open sometime in 1999. It may result in a reshuffling of the order described below. The museum contains much of the art and furnishings that once embellished both the interior and exterior of the Duomo, subsequently brought here for protection from the elements. A bust of Brunelleschi at the entrance is a nod to the man who gave us the Duomo's magnificent cupola, and over the door hang two glazed della Robbia terra-cottas. In the second inner room to your left you'll find sculptures from the cathedral's old gothic facade (destroyed in 1587 to give way for a new facade that was completed until the late 1800s, the neo-Gothic one you see today), including work by the original architect, Arnolfo di Cambio (1245–1302), also responsible for the Palazzo Vecchio. Of the various statues, the most noteworthy is a weatherworn but noble *St. John* by Donatello and Nanni di Banco's intriguing *San Luca.*

The highlight of the **center room upstairs** is the enchanting twin white marble choirs lofts or *cantorie* dating from the 1430s by Donatello and Luca della Robbia that face each other, as well as two statues by Donatello: his haggard figure of *Mary Magdalene,* a late work in polychrome wood originally in the Baptistery (1453–55) and the most powerful of those he carved for the Campanile, that known as Pumpkin Head, *Zuccone.* In the next room, the **Sala delle Formelle** (Room of the Panels) are the original bas-reliefs that decorated the first two stories of the campanile's exterior. One of the museum's most important displays are ✪ **four of the original bronze panels** from Ghiberti's *Gates of Paradise* door of the Baptistery (the other six are eventually to appear as they are restored). A major attraction to the museum is Michelangelo's last, and unfinished, *Pietà.* Originally intended for his own tomb, and done when the sculptor was nearing 80 and partially blind, it is said that Nicodemus, holding Christ, is a self-portrait of the master sculptor. Historians believe that Mary was finished by a student and that the master was so frustrated and disillusioned with the work that he tried to destroy it. A 14th- to 15th-century silver-gilt altar front with scenes from the life of St. John, another priceless masterpiece, can be found in the last room on the second floor.

Chiesa di Orsanmichele. V. de' Calzaiuoli at V. Arte della Lana (north of Pz. Signoria). ☎ **055/284944.** Free admission. Daily 9am–noon and 4–6pm. Closed the first and last Mon of every month.

This 14th-century boxlike church is the last remnant of ornate gothic architecture in Florence and was originally built as a covered market with an upstairs granary, hence its appearance as a converted warehouse. The downstairs was eventually converted to an oratory, the open archways bricked up, and the outside's tabernacles decorated by donations from the city's powerful and wealthy *arti* or guilds, such as the tanners, silk weavers, bankers, furriers, goldsmiths; their patron saints fill the 14 niches surrounding the exterior of the church. Masters such as Ghiberti, Donatello and Giambologna were commissioned to cast the saints' images. They virtually comprise a history of Florentine sculpture from the 14th through the 16th centuries, though almost all of them have been relocated to the indoor museum on the second floor (see below) and slowly replaced with copies. In the dark candle-lit interior—among the vaulted Gothic arches, stained-glass windows, and 500-year-old frescoes—is the colorful, encrusted 14th-century Gothic tabernacle by Andrea Orcagna. It supports and protects the 1348 *Madonna and Child* painted by Giotto's student Bernardo Daddi. The entrance to the church's small museum (daily 9am–1:30, free admission though this may change in 1999) is located on the west side of the church in what once housed the powerful medieval Wool Guild. Upstairs, in the old granary rooms, eight of the original statues from the church's outside niches are here, returning from restoration one by one. The name Orsanmichele is a corruption of the Church of St. Michael's of the Garden, which occupied this site from the 8th to 13th centuries well before the granary was built.

NEAR SAN MARCO & PIAZZA SANTISSIMA ANNUNZIATA

✪ **Galleria dell'Accademia (Academy Museum).** V. Ricasoli 60 (between Pz. d. Duomo and Pz. San Marco). ☎ **055/23-885.** Admission 12,000L ($7.90). Tues–Sat 9am–7pm, Sun 9am–2pm; last entrance 30 minutes before closing.

Nowhere else in Europe do so many wait in line to see but one statue—albeit one of the world's most famous and magnificent. The wait can be up to an hour, so try getting there before the museum opens in the morning or around midday. The Accademia is home to Michelangelo's *David* (1501–04), generally considered his greatest work. Most remarkable is the fact that Michelangelo was just 29 years old, having established himself at 19 for his promising talents, namely the Pieta displayed in Rome's St. Peter's Basilica. Sculpted from a used, 17-foot column of white Carrara marble that had been discarded and abandoned (an endeavor poignantly described in Irving Stone's *The Agony and the Ecstasy*), the *David* looms in stark perfection beneath the rotunda of the main room built exclusively for its display in 1873 when it was moved here from the Piazza Signoria for safekeeping (a copy now stands in its place while a second copy lords over the Piazzale Michelangiolo). From its very beginning nicknamed "Il Gigante," or The Giant, the colossal statue stands on a 6-foot marble stand and has been protected by a high transparent Plexiglas shield since the 1991 attack that damaged its left foot (it was immediately and undetectably repaired).

So overpowering is this fabled sculpture, that after standing in awe before its magnificence, many visitors leave, drained, without seeing the museum's other Michelangelos. These include four never-finished *Prisoners* (or *Slaves*) struggling to free themselves, originally commissioned for the tomb of Julius II. Michelangelo believed he could sense their very presence inherent within the stone, and he worked to release their forms from within—on and off for more than 40 years while regularly being sidetracked by other papal projects. His Slaves never quite break through their prisons of stone and whether the master sculptor left them half-finished on purpose (or not) has been debated by art historians ad nauseam. The *Palestrina Pietà* is also here (while another *Pietà* is displayed in the Museo dell'Opera del Duomo), once attributed to Michelangelo but now thought to be the work of his students. The statue of *St. Matthew* (begun in 1504), is however, by the master. A number of 15th- to 16th-century Florentine artists are represented here, though overshadowed by the presence of the Giant. Search out the late 15th-century *Madonna del Mare* (*Madonna of the Sea*), attributed to Botticelli or his student Filippino Lippi.

⊙ **Museo di San Marco.** Pz. San Marco 1 (north of the Duomo on V. Cavour). ☎ **055/23-88-608.** Admission 8,000L ($4.70). Tues–Sun 8:30am–1:50pm. Also open the 1st, 3rd, and 5th Mon and the 2nd and 4th Sun of each month (same hours).

This small museum is a monument to the devotional work of Florentine-born friar/painter Fra Angelico, one of the early masters of the 15th-century Renaissance. He was the most celebrated of the friars who lived in this monastery first built in the 13th century and later enlarged by Michelozzo in 1437 as a new home for the Dominicans under the direction of Cosimo il Vecchio (Cosimo the Elder), founder of the Medici dynasty and grandfather of Lorenzo il Magnifico. He went on to establish here the first public library in Europe.

Directly to your right upon entering the museum and off a pretty cloister is the old pilgrims' hospice, **Ospizio dei Pellegrini**, a room containing the largest collection in Florence of Fra Angelico's painted panels and altarpieces. Signs point you to the Chapter House, the **Sala Capitolare**, home to his powerful *Crucifixion* fresco (1442). On the ground floor visit the Small Refectory (**Refettorio**), where Domenico Ghirlandaio (fresco master under whom a young Michelangelo apprenticed) painted his realistic *Cenacolo* or *Last Supper;* it is one of a half dozen Last Suppers in Florence of artistic importance (almost all of them found within monasteries). At the top of the stairs leading to the monks' cells on the second floor is Fra Angelico's solemn master-piece, *The Annunciation.* Most of the 44 small dormitory cells on this floor are deco-rated with simple frescoes from the life of Christ, painted either by Fra Angelico or by one of his assistants from 1439 to 1445 under the master's direction and intended to aid in contemplation and prayer. The frescoes in cells 1, 3, 6, and 9 are regarded as the most beautiful. Larger and more luxurious than the others, cells 38 and 39 were des-ignated for the occasional use of Cosimo il Vecchio himself.

At the end of the corridor is the cell of Girolamo Savonarola, which includes a stark portrait of the monastery's former prior by his convert and devout student, Fra Bar-tolomeo, as well as his sleeping chamber, notebook, and rosary, and remnants of the clothes worn at his execution. A reformer who crusaded against political and religious corruption, he led a revolt in 1494 that expelled the Medicis, and Florence was set up as a republic. Also a fundamentalist and fire-and-brimstone fanatic, he incited the people to participate in bonfires of their vanities (including the burning of priceless artwork and precious hand-illuminated books). His denunciations against the pope eventually led to his excommunication, arrest, and trial; he was hanged and then burned for heresy in Piazza Signoria in 1498.

Church of SS. Annunziata and the Piazza SS. Annunziata. Piazza SS. Annunziata. ☎ **055/2398034.** Free admission. Daily 8am–12:30pm and 4–6:30pm.

On the way to or from the obligatory visit to view Michelangelo's David, stop by the Piazza SS. Annunziata for a moment's respite in what historians-cum-urban developers called the most perfectly proportioned Renaissance square. It's surrounded by loggias on three sides, but at its center stands the equestrian statue of Grand Duke Ferdinando I de' Medici the last work of Giambologna, cast after his death by Tacca (who is also responsible for the twin fountains on either side). Facing south is the 13th-century **Church of Santissima Annunziata** (reconstructed during the Renaissance by Michelozzo) with a number of major works by Andrea del Sarto (who is also buried here, along with Cellini and Il Pontormo). In Florence, brides don't toss their bouquets: they bring them here for good luck to place them in front of a tabernacle designed by Michelozzo (to the left as you enter). It houses an allegedly miraculous portrait of the *Annunciation* (after whom the church was named) whose Madonna's face was said to have been painted by an angel. On the right as you enter the church is del Sarto's important *Birth of the Virgin* (1513); his *Madonna del Sacco* in an area off the cloisters is not always available for viewing.

As you exit the church on your left is the **Ospedale degli Innocenti,** the oldest foundling hospital in Europe. Its portico was designed in the years 1419 to 1426 by Brunelleschi, the area between its arches adorned with glazed terra-cotta reliefs of swaddled babies by Andrea della Robbia. It still functions as an orphanage in a limited capacity, but the small opening where Florentines could leave their unwanted infants in the dark of night, ring the bell, and run, is no longer in use.

NEAR THE TRAIN STATION, THE MERCATO SAN LORENZO & SANTA MARIA NOVELLA

Basilica di San Lorenzo and the ✪ Cappelle Medicee (Medici Chapels). Piazza Madonna degli Aldobrandini (at the end of B. San Lorenzo, north of the Duomo). San Lorenzo ☎ **055/26634.** San Lorenzo and the Biblioteca Laurenziana, free; Medici Chapels ☎ **055/2388602**; 10,000L ($5.90). Basilica, Mon–Sat 7:30am–12:30pm and Sun 3:30–5:30pm; Biblioteca Laurenziana ☎ **055/21-44-43**; Mon–Wed, Fri 8am–1:45pm; Thur, Sat 8am—5pm; Medici Chapels, Tues–Sat 8:30am–5pm. Open the 1st, 3rd, and 5th Sun of every month 8:30am–1:50pm. Open the 2nd and 4th Mon of every month 8:30am–1:50pm.

The San Lorenzo Basilica, whose unfinished brick facade looms semihidden behind dozens of market stalls hawking soccer banners and synthetic-silk scarves, was the Medici family's parish church as well as the final resting place for most of the clan. As the Medicis acquired wealth, they lavished much of it upon their church. Donatello's two pulpits, his final works, are worth a look, as is the second chapel on the right with the **Marriage of the Virgin** by Rosso Fiorentino. The Old Sacristy, off the left transept, designed by Brunelleschi and decorated by Donatello, contains several important works. Another key feature reached through the cloisters is the **Biblioteca Laurenziana,** a stunning bit of architecture by Michelangelo (1524) containing one of the largest and most valuable collections of manuscripts and codices in the world, amassed by the Medici. A curving **pietra serena** staircase designed by Michelangelo leads to it from the cloister. Although the Laurentian Library is closed at press time, it is scheduled to re-open sometime in 1999, possibly with new hours.

San Lorenzo is best known, however, for the **Medici Chapels.** These can only be entered by going around to the back of the church; you must walk through a side street chockablock with dozens of more stalls, before turning left where the church ends and a separate entrance is visible. Visitors first pass through the **Cappella dei Principi** (Chapel of the Princes), a baroque kaleidoscopic study of polychrome marble and semiprecious stones denounced through history for its opulence; it was added on in 1604 but not finished until 1962. Visually overwhelming, remember that the principal reason for your visit here is the far more serene ✪ **New Sacristy,** which contains the Michelangelo-designed tombs for Lorenzo II, duke of Urbino and grandson of Lorenzo il Magnifico (with the sculptor's well-known statues of female *Dawn* and male *Dusk*) on the left side as you enter. On the opposite wall is the tomb of Giuliano

---

Famous Scribbles

A large number of charcoal sketches, confirmed to be doodles by Michelangelo himself, were discovered by sheer chance in the 1980s in a room beneath the sacristy at the Medici Chapels. They are now available to the public for viewing for no additional admission but only upon special request: ask at the ticket booth upon arrival.

---

de' Medici, duke of Nemours (with the master sculptor's more famous statues of female *Night* and male *Day*); the two pairs are considered to be some of Michelangelo's greatest work (1521–34). One point never overlooked by tour guides is that *Dawn* and *Night* bring to focus the virility with which Michelangelo produced the female shape—only marginally less masculine and muscular than the male anatomy, but with breasts tacked on almost as if an afterthought. The New Sacristy was finished by Vasari in 1556.

Palazzo Medici-Riccardi and the ✪ Cappella dei Magi. V. Cavour 1 (north of the Piazza Duomo). ☎ **055/27-60-340.** Free admission. Cappella dei Magi 6,000L ($3.50). Mon–Tues and Thurs–Sat 9am–1pm and 3–6pm, Sun 9am–1pm.

Built for Cosimo il Vecchio (the Elder), founder of the Medici dynasty and grandfather of Lorenzo il Magnifico, by Brunelleschi's student Michelozzo, this austere palazzo was the private home of the Medici clan from 1460 to 1540 (before Cosimo I moved with his new Spanish wife, Eleanora de Toledo, to the Palazzo Vecchio and eventually the Palazzo Pitti on the other side of the Arno) and would be held as the prototype for subsequent residences of the nobility. Only two rooms are open to the public, but they make your trip worthwhile. A staircase to the right off the entrance courtyard leads to the ✪ **The Chapel of the Magi.** The jewel-box chapel takes its name from the gorgeously dense frescoes by Benozzo Gozzoli (completed in 1463), who worked several members of the Medici family into the tapestry as well as his master, Fra Angelico, and himself (on the right wall as you enter: Look for a young man on the far left wearing a red hat inscribed "Opus Benotii" who appears beneath the only man wearing a light blue hat. Or just ask the ever-present custodian who seems to enjoy pointing him out to the unknowing) into his beautiful depictions of the Wise Men's journey through the Tuscan countryside. The last Magi with the golden locks is a highly idealized version of a young Lorenzo il Magnifico. Upstairs is an elaborate 17th-century baroque gallery commissioned by the subsequent owners, the Riccardi; amid the gilt and stucco are Luca Giordano's frescoes, masterfully illustrating the Apotheosis of the Medici dynasty. The palazzo now houses government offices, though parts of it are frequently used for temporary and traveling exhibitions.

✪ **Basilica di Santa Maria Novella.** Piazza Santa Maria Novella (just south of the train station). ☎ **055/210113.** Basilica free; Cappella degli Spagnoli (Spanish Chapel), 5,000L ($2.95). Basilica, winter Mon–Sat 8–12:30am and 3–6:30pm, Sun 3–6pm; summer Mon–Sat 8am–6:30pm and Sun 3–6pm. Cappella degli Spagnoli (Spanish Chapel), Mon–Thurs and Sat 9am–2pm, Sun 8am–1pm.

Begun in 1246 and completed in 1360 (with a green-and-white marble facade, the top portion of which was not added until the 15th century), this cavernous Gothic church was built to accommodate the masses who would come to hear the word of God as delivered by the Dominicans (long known as a preaching order). To educate the illiterate, it was filled with cycles of frescoes that are today considered some of the most important art in Florence, a claim not to be taken lightly in this art-endowed city. In the **Cappella Maggiore** (Main Chapel or chancel) directly behind the main altar and its bronze crucifix by Giambologna, Domenico Ghirlandaio (Michelangelo's master) created an extensive fresco cycle supposedly depicting the lives of the Virgin and St. John the Baptist, when in fact what we see is a dazzling illustration of daily life in the golden days of Renaissance Florence. Sprinkled with local personalities and snapshot vignettes, a number of the faces belong to the local Tornabuoni family that commissioned the work. You'll find frescoes by Filippino Lippi (son of Filippo Lippi) to the right of this in the **Cappella di Filippo Strozzi.** To the extreme right is the **Cappella dei Bardi** covered with 14th-century frescoes; its lunette frescoes of the Madonna are much earlier and are believed to be by Cimabue, circa 1285.

Meanwhile, to the left of the Cappella Maggiore and central altar is the **Cappella Gondi** and the 15th-century crucifix by Brunelleschi, his only work in wood (for the historical anecdote about the crucifix contest, see the entry on Church of Santa Croce and Brunelleschi's friendly rivalry with Donatello). To the extreme left is the **Cappella Gaddi** and its important frescoes by Nardo di Cione (1357). The altarpiece is by Nardo's brother, Orcagna. The chapel awaits the return of Giotto's 13th-century Crucifix back from the restorer. Adjacent to this chapel is the church's sacristy, worth a peek for the delicate glazed terra-cotta lavabo by Giovanni della Robbia. In the left aisle near the main entrance is Masaccio's revolutionary *Trinity* (1428), the first painting to ever use perfect, linear mathematical perspective. Close by is Brunelleschi's 15th-century pulpit from which Galileo was denounced for his heretical theory that the earth revolved around the sun.

If you're not yet frescoed out, exit the church and turn right to visit the **Chiostro Verde** (Green Cloister) and its Cappellone degli Spagnoli (Spanish Chapel), whose important and captivating series of early Renaissance frescoes (recently restored) by Andrea de Bonaiuto glorify the history of the Dominican church. The chapel got its name from the nostalgic Eleanora de Toledo, wife of Cosimo I de' Medici, who permitted her fellow Spaniards to be buried here (the order was founded by the Spaniard, St. Domenico). The Green Cloister, on the other hand, took its name from the prevalent green tinge of Paolo Uccello's 15th-century fresco cycle, which, unfortunately, was heavily damaged in the 1966 floods.

Stibbert Museum. V. Stibbert 26 (off V. Vittorio Emanuele II, north of the train station). ☎ **055/475520.** Admission 8,000L ($4.70). Mon–Wed and Fri 10am–2pm, Sat–Sun 10am–6pm. By guided tour only, offered every 30 minutes. Sun free admission. Bus 4.

Anyone even remotely interested in armor and the historic days of chivalry should spend some time in the musty formerly private home of the fabulously wealthy Scotch-Italian collector, Frederick Stibbert. Opened to the public since shortly after his death in 1906, and considered one of the most important private collections in the world, Stibbert's house/museum is filled to the brim with—among countless other objects and antiques from the 16th through 19th centuries—thousands of pieces of armor from East and West (with Europe's largest collection of Japanese armor) and all the bellicose trappings: maces, pole-axes, crossbows, blunderbusses, and the like. **La Sala della Cavalcata** (The Hall of the Cavalcade) is the high point of the house with a dozen life-size models of knights on war horses dressed in full-body battle armor. In **Il Salone della Cupola** 50 men-at-arms wearing glistening suits of plate armor represent all parts of the world. Some of the historical armor is as striking as body sculptor, as decorative as body jewelry. The last few years (and the arrival of a new female European curator) have seen radical improvements in the museum's evolution, garnering the more appropriate attention it has long deserved.

NEAR SANTA CROCE

✪ **Basilica di Santa Croce and the Cappella Pazzi (Pazzi Chapel).** Piazza Santa Croce. ☎ **055/24-46-19.** Admission to Pazzi Chapel 5,000L ($2.95). Basilica, summer daily 8am–6:30pm, Sun 3–6pm. winter: daily 8–12:30pm and 3–6:30, Sun 3–6pm. Pazzi Chapel, summer Thurs–Tues 10am–12:30pm and 2:30–6:30pm; winter Thurs–Tues 10am–12:30pm and 3–5pm.

Begun in 1294 by Gothic master Arnolfo di Cambio, original architect of the Duomo and Palazzo Vecchio, the cavernous Church of Santa Croce was built to be the largest Franciscan church in the world, a gauntlet thrown to the Dominicans who were busy raising their own enormous Church of Santa Maria Novella across town. The church is a shrine to 14th-century frescoes. The humble presence of St. Francis is best felt in the two chapels located to the right of the main altar; entirely covered with faded early 14th-century frescoes by Giotto and his gifted student Taddeo Gaddi (and Gaddi's son Agnolo Gaddi), which depict the life of the saint and scenes from the Bible. Of these two, the Bardi Chapel immediately to the right of the main altar is the more famous of the two, if only as a setting for a scene in the film *Room with a View;* its deathbed scene of St. Francis is one of the church's most important frescoes. To the right of that is the Peruzzi Chapel—hard to believe, but in the fashion of the time, these frescoes were whitewashed over in the 17th century. They were uncovered in the mid 1800s and were so clumsily restored that they needed to be re-restored. To the left of the main altar is a wooden crucifix by Donatello, whose portrayal of Christ was considered way too provincial and unsophisticated by early 15th-century standards. A disapproving Brunelleschi told Dontello he had put a peasant on the cross and sculpted his own idea of an appropriate crucifix; his can be viewed in the Church of Santa Maria Novella.

Santa Croce is also the final resting place for many of the most renowned Renaissance figures: the Pantheon of Florence. More than 270 tombstones pave the floor of the church, but attention deservedly goes to monumental tombs such as that of Michelangelo, designed by Vasari, the first on the right as you enter the church; the three allegorical figures represent Painting, Architecture, and Sculpture. He died in Rome in 1564 at the ripe old age of 89; his body was smuggled here against the wishes of the pope, who wanted him buried in Rome. Dante's empty tomb is right next to him: He was exiled from Florence in 1302 for trumped-up political reasons and died in Ravenna in 1321. Ravenna has even since refused to give his remains back to the city who did not want him when he was alive; a statue of Dante stands as compensation just outside Santa Croce on your right as you exit. A wall monument honors Machiavelli, 16th-century statesman and author of the famous book *The Prince,* practical manual for all aspiring Renaissance rulers. Galileo, who died in 1642, was not allowed a Christian burial here until 1737, accused as he was of heresy for his insistence that the earth revolved around the sun (the pope finally lifted his excommunication in 1992). And finally we have Gioachino Rossini, who gave the world *The Barber of Seville* and *The William Tell Overture.*

You may have noticed signs for the Leather School (exit to the right of the main altar) set up here by the Franciscan fathers after World War II to train young men in a centuries-old craft (see "Shopping," in section 7).

The entrance to the tranquil **Pazzi Chapel** (marked "Museo dell'Opera di Santa Croce") is outside and to the left as you leave the church. Commissioned in 1443 by Andrea de' Pazzi, a key rival of the Medici family, and designed by master builder Filippo Brunelleschi, the chapel is a masterful example of early Renaissance architecture. The 12 glazed terra-cotta roundels of the apostles are the creation of Luca della Robbia finished in 1452. Next door, the 13th-century refectory today serves as the church's museum, housing many works from the 13th through the 17th century. The collection is highlighted by one of Cimabue's finest works, his enormous *Crucifixion*, one of myriad artistic works that suffered serious damage in the 1966 flood. Completely submerged when floodwaters rose to 3 feet within the church and 5 feet within the museum, it has now been restored and is displayed on an electric cable that will lift it out of reach of future harm, an expensive idea art authorities toyed with doing to many of the city's masterworks, but never made it past this one.

Museo della Casa Buonarroti. V. Ghibellina 70 (5 blocks east of the Bargello). ☎ **055/ 24-17-52.** Admission 12,000L ($7.05). Wed–Mon 9:30am–1:30pm. From Piazza Santa Croce, you'll find Casa Buonarroti at the top of V. d. Pinzochere, 2 blocks north of the piazza.

This graceful and modest house, which Michelangelo bought late in life for his nephew Lionardo, was turned into a museum by Lionardo's son, also named Michelangelo. It was he who would turn it into a virtual shrine to honor his great uncle, asking the finest painters of his day to adorn it with frescoes. There's not much to hold the interest of the mildly curious: Two of the master's most important early works are housed here, *Madonna alla Scala (Madonna on the Stairs)* done when he was approximately 16 and already under the patronage of the Medici family, and the later *Battaglia dei Centauri (Battle of the Centaurs)*, both sculpted when he was still working in bas-relief and before he would go on to create the *Pieta* (displayed in Rome's St. Peter's Basilica) at age 19 that would launch his fame and future. A crucifix found in Santo Spirito in 1963 is believed to be one of his early pieces but seems so removed from his distinctively robust style that not everyone buys its authenticity. The museum also houses a sizable collection of his drawings and scale models, particularly the one for the facade of San Lorenzo that was never realized. The small museum is commonly used for temporary exhibitions, not all of which have to do with the Renaissance period.

Jewish Synagogue (Tempio Isrealitico). V. Farini 4. ☎ **055/2346654.** Admission 6,000L ($3.50). Sun–Thurs 10am–1pm and 2–5pm, Fri 10am–1pm.

The 19th-century green copper-domed **Tempio Isrealitico** warrants a visit by those interested in architecture or the heritage of Florence's Jewish community. It's a 15-minute walk east of the Duomo (but closer to Santa Croce) in an area of Florence that sees little tourism (unless you're lucky enough to be staying at Florence's only Relais & Châteaux hotel, the Regency, in Piazza M. D'Azeglio). The neo-Moorish temple dates from the time when Florence's Old Market (Mercato Vecchio) and its bordering Jewish Ghetto were cleared away in the 1860s to make way for the Piazza della Repubblica when Florence was looking forward to its ever-so-brief stint as capital of the newly united Kingdom of Italy (the capital was moved to Rome in 1870). This oriental-inspired synagogue was begun in 1874 when its first stone arrived from Jerusalem. Heavily damaged by the Nazis in 1944, it was completely restored soon thereafter. A small museum houses a selection of Judaica dating back to the 17th century, and includes a number of photos of the ghetto before it was razed.

IN THE OLTRARNO (AND BEYOND)

✪ **Palazzo Pitti (Pitti Palace).** Piazza Pitti (south of the Ponte Vecchio in the Oltrarno, at end of V. Guicciardini). ☎ **055/2388614.** Galleria Palatina, 12,000L ($7.90); Galleria d'Arte Moderna (Modern Art Gallery), 4,000L ($2.65); Museo degli Argenti (Silver Museum), 8,000L ($5.25). Tues–Sun Palatina and Monumental Apartments 9am–7pm, all others 9am–2pm; last entrance 45 minutes before closing. Call to confirm hours.

It's ironic that this rugged golden palazzo, begun in 1458 (presumably by Brunelleschi) for the wealthy textile merchant and banker, Luca Pitti, in an attempt to keep up with the Medici, was bought by descendants of the Medici in 1549 when Pitti's heirs spiraled into bankruptcy. They used it as their official residence as rulers of Florence. The Medici, beginning with Cosimo I and his wife Eleanora di Toledo who moved here from the Palazzo Vecchio, tripled its size, elaborately embellished it, and graced it with the Boboli Gardens (see listing below) that still fan up the hill behind it, once the quarry from which the palazzo's *pietra dura* was taken. Today, it is home to seven museums, the largest collection of galleries in Florence under one roof.

✪ **GALLERIA PALATINA**   These 26 art-filled rooms in one first-floor of the palazzo, is the star attraction here. Home to one of the finest collections of Italian Renaissance and baroque masters in Europe, it's the most important collection in Florence after the Uffizi's. The art of the 16th century is the forte of the Palatina, in particular that of Raphael and Titian. Of the outstanding Raphaels displayed here, look for the prized and much beloved *Madonna of the Chair* (the best known of his many interpretations of the Madonna) and his second most famous, *La Fornarina* also known as *La Velata* (The Veiled Woman). A portrait of his baker's daughter and young mistress, if she looks particularly Madonna-like it is because she most likely posed for most of his Madonna commissions. The museum's treasures also include a large collection of works by Andrea del Sarto; Fra Bartolomeo's *San Marco* and his beautiful last work, *Descent from the Cross;* some superb works by Rubens, including *The Four Philosophers;* canvases by Tintoretto and Veronese. There are stunning portraits by Titian, including *Pope Julius II, The Man with the Gray Eyes,* and *The Music Concert*—his collection is regarded as some of the museum's most important, a hard call to make from such a cavalcade of superstars. Also represented are Caravaggio (namely, his *The Sleeping Cupid,* 1608), Pontormo, Van Dyck, and Botticelli.

After a tool past the jigsaw puzzle walls of the painting-lined Galleria Palatina, you may either want to rest your eyes with a stroll through the green Boboli Gardens (see below) or allow for a brief visit in the second-most visited museum within the Palazzo Pitti, the Appartamenti Monumentali, no less elaborate or extravagant than what you've just seen, but with a far less attention-riveting art collection.

APPARTAMENTI MONUMENTALI   These restored apartments are ornate, gilded, and chandeliered, and contain some paintings (look for Caravaggio's *Portrait of a Knigh of Malta*), tapestries, and over-the-top furnishings from the resplendent days of the Medici, and later the dukes of Lorraine.

GALLERIA D'ARTE MODERNA   You may not have come to Florence to view modern art, but those with any concentration left should head upstairs to this gallery; although closed at press time, it is expected to reopen in 1999. It houses an interesting array of 19th-century Italian impressionists (known as the *Macchiaioli* school after the *macchie* or "spots" used in their Impressionist style); the leader of the movement, Giovanni Fattori, is represented here, as is Lega, Signorini and early 20th-century predecessors.

OTHER MUSEUMS OF INTEREST   Among the least visited of the Pitti's panoply of small museums is the **Museo degli Argenti (Silver Museum),** on the ground floor, 16 rooms filled with the priceless, private treasure of the Medici family. Other small museums that follow their own drum when it comes to hours and closures include the **Museo della Porcellana** (Porcelain), currently open, the **Coach and Carriage Museum** (closed indefinitely), and the **Galleria del Costume** (closed for renovation but expected to reopen in 1999). The latter concentrates on costumes from the 18th to the 20th centuries with some earlier exceptions.

Boboli Gardens. Directly behind the Pitti Palace. Daily from 9am to 5:30pm (earlier in winter months). Closed the first and last Mon of every month; fortress hours vary with exhibitions.

Admission to the gardens 4,000L ($2.35); admission to fortress grounds free, but exhibition admission varies. Enter the gardens via the rear exit to the Pitti Palace after visiting the Galleria Palatina or through the entrance to the left when facing the palazzo.

The expansive Giardini Boboli begin directly behind the Pitti Palace and fan upward to the star-shaped Fortezza Belvedere, which crowns the hill behind it. The green gardens were originally laid out in the 16th century by the great landscape artist Tribolo. They are filled with graveled walkways, grottoes, and antique and Renaissance statuary and are the best spot in Florence for a picnic lunch (which you'll have to bring with you). The view from the hilltop **Forte Belvedere** (built 1590–95) is stunning, but there's not much to see inside unless there's a special exhibition; ask at the tourist office or look for posters around town. The view of Florence and the Duomo's cupola from a slight hill just behind the palazzo is an alternative (and less cardio-taxing) photo-op that is similarly, if not less dramatically, striking.

Church of Santa Maria del Carmine and the ✪ Cappella Bancacci. Piazza Santa Maria del Carmine (west of Piazza Santo Spirito and the Palazzo Pitti). ☎ **055/ 23-82-195.** Admission to Cappella Brancacci 5,000L ($2.95). Mon, Wed–Sat 10am–5pm, Sun 1–5pm.

This baroque church dates from the 18th century when a fire ravaged the original 13th-century structure built for the Carmelite nuns; smoke damage was major but the fire left the Brancacci Chapel miraculously intact. This was a miracle indeed, as the frescoes begun by Masolino in 1425 and continued by his young and brilliant student Masaccio (who quickly outshone his maestro but died at an early age) were a watershed in the history of art—seminally crucial to the development of early Renaissance painting. The frescoes were painstakingly restored in the 1980s, removing not only the dirt and grime but also the prudish fig leaves trailing across Adam and Eve's private parts. The painters' unprecedented expression of emotion as well as their pioneering use of perspective and chiaroscuro, is now more clearly evident. Massacio's *Expulsion of Adam and Eve* (extreme upper left-hand corner) best illustrates emotions of anguish and shame hitherto unknown in painting, while *The Tribute Money* (just to its right) is a significant study in perspective. The bulk of the frescoes depict the *Life of St. Peter* (who appears in a golden-orange mantle). The lower panels were finished by Filippino Lippi (son of the great painter Filippo Lippi) in 1480, 50 years after the very premature death of Masaccio at 27, who faithfully imitated the young master's style and technique. Even later masters like Leonardo da Vinci and Michelangelo came to see what they could learn from this seminal mastery of unprecedented perspective, light, colors, and realism.

Church of San Miniato and the Piazzale Michelangiolo. V. d. Monte alle Croci 34 (south, past Piazzale Michelangelo, a 10-minute walk). Admission free. Mon–Sat 8am–7pm. Bus: 12, 13.

No trip up to the green lofty heights of Piazzale Michelangiolo for sunset is complete without a visit first to San Miniato, an outstanding example of Florentine Romanesque architecture and the oldest religious building in Florence after the Duomo's baptistery. Lured here by a glimpse of its multicolored facade and glimmering 13th-century fresco that can be seen from the Ponte Vecchio and points down below, it's worth the trip if only for the breathtaking view of the city from the steps of the church. Construction of the present building began in 1013 (with the marble facade of geometrical design added later that century) on the site where St. Minias, a 3rd-century martyr, was said to have carried his severed head from the city below before collapsing at this precise spot, dead. The dark interior appears more mystical because of its undulating 13th-century oriental-carpetlike pavement mosaic with signs of the zodiac. In the center of the nave is a chapel by Michelozzo (1447) whose glazed terra-cotta ceiling is by Luca della Robbia. A visit to the 11th-century crypt with later frescoes by Taddeo Gaddi (architect of the Ponte Vecchio) and with fine columns and original capitals is evocative of the church's early days. Stay for the daily vespers sung in Gregorian chant at 4:30pm (followed by mass) by the handful of monks who live here for complete immersion in other times. You can imagine why Florentine nobility prefers to attend Christmas mass here and every bride dreams of being married here. The adjacent cemetery is interesting for a meander in search of the gravestone of Tuscan-born Carlo Lorenzini, also known as Carlo Colladi, author of Pinocchio. Now, stroll on over to the Piazzale Michelangiolo to catch sunset over Florence, take a photo of the second copy of Michelangelo's David, and enjoy the view you've seen on 1,000 postcards.

ESPECIALLY FOR KIDS

While children may feel like this museum-rich city is filled with stuff way too old for them to relate to, Florence's biggest plus for parents is the city's accessibility and compact layout in relatively traffic-free streets. Much of your visit will be spent strolling the ancient streets of a city that is, in fact, one big open-air museum. Young legs that can sustain a 400-plus step workout should head up to either Brunelleschi's cupola (see the Duomo) or the top of Giotto's campanile for an awesome view of the city and swarms of ant-sized tourists. Batteries can be recharged during picnic lunches in the green Boboli Gardens or, higher yet, on the grounds of the Forte Belvedere above. Kids will enjoy a leisurely (albeit expensive) horse-drawn cab ride through the cobblestone streets of the *centro storico* (establish your price before taking off). Carriages gather in the Piazza Signoria. If you're visiting in **June,** try to catch one of the four processions and games of the **Calcio Storico** (see "Special & Free Events," below) with their historical costumes and armored knights on steeds. The Florentine substitute for incentive is a guaranteed pleaser regardless of age or background—don't miss tasting your way through the many excellent **gelaterie,** or ice-cream parlors, whose variety (they can squeeze four or five flavors into some of those cups!) and quality makes Baskin Robbins look ho-hum. As Florentine authorities encourage residents to take up bicycle riding as the historical center's pedestrian zone grows, bicycle stands become more frequently found: If your child can handle a two-wheeler well, you have the blessing of tooling around a flat city (Florence is no hill town) in a generally traffic-free zone (but the cobblestones can do you in). The Stibbert Museum's unusually extensive collection of armor (see listing above) is also a guaranteed pleaser. And don't even think about leaving town without rubbing the nose of the famous bronze statue of the **porcellino** (wild boar) on the south side of the Straw Market (aka the Mercato Nuovo or New Market), ensuring good luck and a return to Florence.

5 Special & Free Events

The **Maggio Musicale,** or "Musical May," is Italy's oldest music festival and one of Europe's most prestigious. Events take place at various indoor and outdoor locations throughout Florence, including Piazza della Signoria and the courtyard of the Pitti Palace. Maestro Zubin Mehta is the honorary director, often conducting Florence's own Maggio Musicale Orchestra, and guest conductors and orchestras appear throughout the festival, which, despite its moniker, runs from **late April into early July.** For schedules and ticket information, inquire at one of the tourist offices.

From **June to August,** the Roman theater in nearby Fiesole comes alive with dance, music, and theater for the **Estate Fiesolana,** or "Summer in Fiesole." A.T.A.F. bus no. 7 travels to Fiesole from the train station and Piazza del Duomo.

The highlight of **June 24,** the feast day of Florence's patron saint, San Giovanni (St. John the Baptist), is the **Calcio Storico,** a rough-and-tumble no-holds-barred game, a cross between rugby, soccer, and wrestling, played with a ball and few (if any) rules (its origins date from the Renaissance, though many argue that its roots are medieval, or even reach back to ancient Roman). Teams representing the four original parishes of Florence, identified by their colors and clad in 16th-century costume, square off against one another in consecutive playoffs in the dirt-covered piazza Santa Croce. They compete vigorously for that year's bragging rights and the prize, a cow. The final *partita* is most worth seeing (it often falls on June 24 itself). Later on, fireworks light up the night sky, best viewed from along the north banks of the Arno River east of the Ponte Vecchio. See the tourist office for ticket information about numbered seats in the bleachers lining the piazza. No tickets are needed to view the equally dazzling procession in full historical regalia that wends its way through the cobblestone streets and piazze of Florence before each match.

The **month of July** sees the annual **Florence Dance Festival** held in the beautiful amphitheater in the Cascine Park. A wide range of dance is performed, varying from classic to modern, with an emphasis on the latter. The American-born longtime Florentine resident Keith Ferrone, is one of its leading exponents. Again, check with the tourist office for details.

At the biannual **International Antiques Show** held in mid-September for 2 weeks in uneven years only, more than 100 internationally noted dealers hawk their choicest and most exquisite pieces—the crowd is as interesting as the wares. It is not unlike visiting the royal apartments at the Palazzo Pitti, but imagine every piece with a price tag. The historically potent setting of the massive Renaissance Palazzo Strozzi could not be more appropriate, but check for a possible change of venue. Two to three weeks beginning mid-September, admission should be approximately 15,000L ($8.80). For information see the tourist information office.

6 Organized Tours

Both **C.I.T.,** at the corner of Piazza della Stazione and Piazza dell'Unità Italiana (☎ 055/21-09-64), and **SITA,** V. Santa Caterina da Siena 17r (☎ **055/214721**), offer two separate half-day guided-bus tours of the city, including visits to the Uffizi Galleries, the Medici Chapels, and the breathtaking Piazzale Michelangiolo overlooking the city; separate tours include secondary sites. Each tour costs 55,000L ($32.35). Both C.I.T. and SITA also offer organized tours to Pisa, Siena/San Gimignano, and the Chianti region for approximately 60,000 to 75,000L ($35.30 to $44.10) each. You can book the same tours through American Express (See "Fast Facts," above) and many other travel agencies throughout town or through your hotel.

The official city-recognized organization of private guides, **Ufficio Guide Turistiche** can be booked by the hour and according to your personal requests, at 242,000L ($142.35) for a minimum of 3 hours up to six people (☎ 055/2392283).

Walking tours have become popular in the last few years. Least expensive is the Thomas Cook-affiliated **Enjoy Florence** 3-hour tour by foot every day except Sunday at 10am (for information and to reserve, call toll-free from anywhere within Italy, ☎ 167-274819). Cost is 30,000L ($17.65) for those over 26, or 25,000L ($14.70) for those under 26. Also recommended is **Walking Tours of Florence** (☎ 055/ 2346225; www.artviva.com; e-mail: arcoiris@dada.it.), which offers 2-hour tours every Tuesday, Thursday, and Saturday at 10am for 35,000L ($20.60) (accompanied children free). Private guides and custom requests are also available. These tours explore the *centro storico* and follow the history of the city from its period of medieval

Cheap Thrills: What to See & Do in Florence for Free (or Almost)

- **Window-shop.** In what was traditionally one of Europe's great reasonably priced shopping meccas, prices aren't what they used to be but the window shopping still is. Every display is a showcase homage to the timeless made-in-Italy phenomenon that still flourishes, centuries after the Medici gave free reign to their artisans to create, embellish, and raise their crafts to an unprecedented level of artistry. Gold, leather goods, embroidery, fashion—maybe you can talk yourself into at least one instant heirloom. You can salivate your way along the temples of the high priests of fashion: Global names like Versace, Gucci, and Armani are concentrated along **Via Tornabuoni** and **Via della Vigna Nuova.** Other pipe-dreams can be sought out along the gold-laden **Ponte Vecchio** and its dozens of jewelry stores. Less extremely priced retail stores line the **Via Por Santa Maria**, **Via Roma** and, connecting the Piazza della Signoria with the Piazza Duomo, the **Via Calzaiuoli** (to name just a few).

- **Peruse the Florentine mercatos.** Little in Italy compares to the sprawling outdoor **Mercato San Lorenzo** surrounding the Church of San Lorenzo and the covered turn-of-this-century **Mercato Centrale.** The latter is a vast marketplace whose street-level stalls are occupied by butchers, fish vendors, cheesemongers and saturated with local color galore; the upstairs is mostly given over to the fertile region's heady bounty of produce, fruit, and flowers—you'll never again see so many different varieties of salad greens, pyramids of artichokes and plump tomatoes, porcini mushrooms as wide as Frisbees, and pearl-sized wild strawberries. The outdoor market is comprised of hundreds of canvas-awninged stalls that hawk tourist stuff, a lot of which is worth a walk-through for the guaranteed (and not infrequent) finds. Souvenir shop here first before hitting the city's countless tourist retail stores whose overhead hikes their prices.

- **Bike the streets.** It's not yet Amsterdam, but local authorities are encouraging the two-wheeler as transportation within the centro storico as traffic is clearly but slowly being forbidden within the *zona blu.* Florence is generally flat, so track down the half dozen stands around town that offer free bikes for the day (see the tourist office for locations, or "Getting Around by Bicycle," p. 199).

- **Take free tours.** Church volunteers await you within the **Duomo** for free guided tours of this early Renaissance wonder in English ("Exploring Florence"). For the first time in summer 1998, free guided tours were also being offered in some of the museums and churches, such as the **Palazzo Vecchio,** the **Church of Santa Maria Novella,** and the **Brancacci Chapel** in the Carmine Church, during specially extended evening hours that lasted at times

prominence through the glory days of the Renaissance, visiting the landmark sites. Call for starting points. Full-day walking or biking tours in (and outside of) Florence and cooking classes are among the multiple-interest specialties of the flexible **Accidental Tourist** (aka **Turista Per Caso**) who work with small groups or special requests for approximately 100,000L ($58.80) per person. Call for details (☎ **055/699376;** fax 055/699048; e-mail: info@accidentaltourist.com).

until 11:30pm. Check with tourist office for repetition of similar programs in the future.

- **Enjoy free museums and extended hours.** Not many museums in town offer free admission, except for the **Stibbert Museum,** which opens its doors on Sundays, free of charge. But check with the tourist office for other museums that may follow suit, and don't forget to request a listing of extended hours. In 1998, it was decided at the last minute that many museums would stay open until 8pm or later, but little was done to put the word out and the museums were empty of the anticipated crowds. You'll have to pay the standard admission ticket, but you'll pretty much have the place to yourselves unless the museums do a better job of disseminating the information in the future. **Church visits,** for the moment, remain free of charge, except for special admission fees to fresco-rich chapels such as the Brancacci (Church of the Carmine) or the Chiostro Verde (Santa Maria Novella).

- **Catch the daily vespers.** Florence's most beautiful Romanesque church (and one of its oldest), **San Miniato,** is the only venue for late afternoon vespers. A handful of monks sing their timeless Gregorian chant that will transport you back to the nascent days of the hilltop church's 11th-century origin.

- **Watch a postcard-perfect sunset.** For the Technicolor sunset over the Duomo amidst the **centro storico**'s terra-cotta rooftops seen on a million different postcards, hike on up to the Oltrarno's **Piazzale Michelangiolo.** Here is Michelangelo's second larger-than-life copy of the fabled *David* (the other is in the Piazza della Signoria), that stands vigil over Florence. Daytime sees the piazze transformed into a parking lot for tour-group buses; nighttime feels like a locals' lovers-lane-meets-the-looking-for-excitement-after-hours crowd. Dusk is no less popular, with a truly magnificent *spettacolo* over the Arno trellised by its many bridges and offset by the hills of Fiesole rising up behind; since time immemorial it has acted as a magnet that attracts roadsters and oldsters, local and foreign alike.

- **Listen to the Piazza della Repubblica.** The historical **Café Paszkowski** has been the site of alfresco evening music in this central square for generations. The recent transformation of parking lot to dignified piazza of old was a welcomed return to the way things were, including the addition of the occasional planters-cum-seats from which to enjoy the crowd-gathering live music until the wee hours without having to pay the steep cover charges imposed by the cafes. Paszkowski's elegant next door neighbor, **Gilli's,** is the traditional favorite cafe of choice, where you can nurse a Campari for hours for less than 12,000L ($7.05) while eavesdropping on the classic, pop, and light jazz tunes that fill the piazza.

If you want to escape Florence and spend a day walking, **I Bike Italy** (☎ 055/23-42-371; www.ibikeitaly.com) offers country walks in Tuscany (year-round), as well as 1-day bike rides (March through November). Guided walks are 80,000L ($47.05) and guided bike-rides (21-speed bikes supplied) are 90,000L ($59.95); shuttle to outskirts of town and hearty picnic lunch are included. Unless you plan to travel in Tuscany (see chapter 6), you should try to get at least an all-too-brief 1-day glimpse of the incomparable Tuscan countryside that has inspired Florence's master artists for centuries. There's no storefront, because everything is arranged by phone.

7 Shopping

In terms of good-value shopping, Florence is easy to categorize: It's paradise. This onetime capitalist capital, where modern banking and commerce first flourished, has something for every taste and price range. Whether you can afford little more than a bargain-priced wool sweater in the open-air market or are interested in investing in a butter-soft leather jacket that will burst your budget, Florence is for you. With a history of commercial and mercantile trade behind them, Florentine merchants are not the born histrionic negotiators of the south or yesteryear, and few will encourage bargaining. Only if you're buying with travelers checks and buying a number of items you should even broach the subject, and only in the most civilized manner. Good luck.

All stores follow the same general business hours; see "Fast Facts," above.

BEST BUYS "Alta moda" fashion in Florence is alive and well and living on **Via Tornabuoni** and its elegant offshoot **Via della Vigna Nuova,** where some of the high priests of Italian and international design and fashion share space with the occasional bank (which you may have to rob in order to afford any of their goods). But it makes for great window-shopping.

Between the Duomo and the river are the pedestrian-only **Via Roma** (which becomes **Via Por Santa Maria** before reaching the Ponte Vecchio) and the parallel **Via Calzaiuoli;** lined with fashionable jewelry and clothing stores (and the city's two largest and nicest department stores, **La Rinascente** and **Coin**), they are the city's main shopping streets. Stores here were traditionally only slightly less high fashion and less high priced than those on the gilded Via Tornabuoni—but there has been a recent trend to head down market. A gelato stop at any of the area's **gelaterie** is a guaranteed spirit-lifter for the nonshoppers among you.

Via del Corso and its extension east of Via del Proconsolo, **Borgo degli Albizi,** is another recommended shopping street, boasting historical palazzi as well as less pretentious and more approachable boutiques though fewer in number.

Unless you have a Medici-size fortune and hope to leave with a Renaissance trinket, window-shop (only) the stores with museum-quality antiques on **Borgo Ognissanti** near the Arno and the perpendicular **Via dei Fossi. Lungarno Corsini** and **Lungarno Acciaiuoli** run along the river, where you'll find merchants offering fine paintings and sculpture, objets d'art, and antiques and miscellany. But perhaps the most impressive antique row is **Via Maggio** in the Oltrarno neighborhood and, to a far lesser degree, its perpendicular offshoot, the **Via Santo Spirito.**

Florence is probably most famous for its ✪ **leather.** Many travelers are happily, albeit mistakenly, convinced that they can buy a leather coat for a song. For quality and selection, no European city can hold a candle to Florentine quality, but prices are higher than all those rumors you heard quoting dirt-cheap prices not seen since the 1970s. Expect to spend $200 to $300 for a leather jacket with moderate workmanship, detail, and skin quality. The shops around **Piazza Santa Croce** are the best places for leather and are not much more expensive than the pushcarts at the San Lorenzo Market. Leather apparel may be beyond your budget, but consider the possibilities of small leather goods, from wallets and eyeglass cases to fashion accessories such as shoes, belts, and bags.

Florence has been known for its gold for centuries, and jewelry shops of all price levels still abound. Dozens of exclusive gold stores line both sides of the pedestrian **Ponte Vecchio.** Gold is almost always 18 karat (ask them to point out the teensy stamp), beautifully (machine-) crafted and, though not a bargain, reasonably priced—think instant heirlooms.

MARKETS   There's nothing in Italy, and indeed perhaps nothing in Europe, to compare with Florence's bustling, sprawling, open-air **Mercato San Lorenzo.** Hundreds of awninged pushcarts crowd together along the streets around the San Lorenzo Church and the Mercato Centrale, offering countless varieties of hand-knit wool and mohair sweaters, leather jackets, handbags, wallets, and gloves—not to mention the standard array of souvenir T-shirts and sweatshirts, wool and silk scarves, and other souvenirs (if you remember the place being filled with Gucci and Fendi knock-offs, you'll be disappointed that the police have done away with them almost entirely. The follow-up act is the easy availability of Prada and Moschino bags sold by Senagalese sidewalk vendors around town and on the Ponte Vecchio after store hours).

The market stretches for blocks between Piazza San Lorenzo behind the Medici Chapel to Via Nazionale, along Via Canto de' Nelli and Via dell' Ariento, with stalls also set up along various side streets in between. The market operates daily from 9am to 7pm from mid-March through October (closed Sunday and Monday the rest of the year) though extremely slow periods (or during heat waves and inclement weather) may result in many or all of the vendors staying home. Many vendors accept credit and charge cards and some have been known to bargain, a dying art these days, unless you're buying a leather jacket or a multitude of smaller items. These hundreds of tchotchke vendors buzz around the turn-of-the-century **Mercato Centrale** (entrance on Via dell'Ariento) food market, a riotous two-floor feast for all senses, whether you breeze through looking for picnic goodies or photo-ops. It will leave you breathless, and hungry.

Much smaller, but still worth a look, is the outdoor **Mercato del Porcellino,** once known as the Straw Market and today more commonly known as the **Mercato Nuovo** or New Market, where a couple of dozen stalls crowd together beneath an open-sided arcade 2 blocks south of the Piazza della Repubblica. Vendors here offer mostly handbags, scarves, embroidered tablecloths, and miscellaneous souvenirs. The market is named for the bronze boar (*porcellino*) on the river side of the arcade, whose snout has been worn smooth by the countless Florentines who have touched it for good luck. Hours here are generally 9am to 6pm, daily from mid-March through November 3 and Tuesday to Saturday the rest of the year.

Mercato delle Pulci in the small Piazza Ciompi (follow the Via Oriuolo east out of Piazza Duomo) is Florence's rather unimpressive, permanent flea market that doubles in size the last Sunday of every month when a look-see can be fun. Tuesday to Saturday 8:30am to 1pm and 3:30 to 7pm. **Mercato delle Cascine** takes place every Tuesday in the grassy riverside park west of the Teatro Comunale from 8am to 2pm. This is where the locals shop, one of the reasons you'll want to go, but don't expect traditional tourist merchandise; do expect more contained prices on household goods and everyday clothes. Serious flea-market goers should check out Tuscany's major flea market held in Arezzo (accessible by bus or direct train in 1 hour) the first weekend of every month.

SHOPPING A TO Z
BOOKSTORES

The **BM Libreria Book Shop,** B. Ognissanti 4r (☎ **055/29-45-75**), at Piazza Goldoni west of Via Tornabuoni, is the best place in town for top-quality American and British books from both large and small publishing houses. **Paperback Exchange** (V. Fiesolana 31r; ☎ **055/24-78-154**) is east of the Duomo and offers a large selection of new and used titles, as well as the chance to trade in your used books. It also serves as a kind of multipurpose center for the Anglo-American expatriate community in Florence.

The oldest and most beautiful bookstore in town, **Libreria Internazionale Seeber,** V. Tornabuoni 68r (☎ **055/21-56-97**), sells a quality collection of guidebooks, novels, and Italian art, history, cuisine, and antiques books, a good number of them in English. The biggest and one of the newest bookstores is the very central **Libreria Feltrinelli,** V. Cerretani 30/32r (☎ **055/23-82-652**). It sells everything imaginable with a sizeable foreign language division. The best travel bookstore in town is the **Libreria Il Viaggio,** B. degli Albizi 41r (☎ **055/24-04-89**), sells guides and maps for every imaginable destination, including Florence and all of Italy, many in English.

CERAMICS

Sbigoli on V. Sant'Egidio 4r (☎ **055/24-79-713**) east of the Duomo has a large and lovely selection of hand-painted Tuscan ceramics, particularly 16th- to 17th-century reproductions. Products of skilled craftsmanship are never cheap (and shipping, which this store offers, is bound to double your expense), but here you'll find colorful terra-cotta mugs, ashtrays, and other small items that are easy to carry and reasonable in price. Short-term classes are available in the store's studio. **La Botteghina,** north of the Mercato San Lorenzo on V. Guelfa 5r (☎ **055/287367;** www.alba.fi.it/botteghina), specializes in a more discerning selection from the ceramics capitals of Deruta and Montelupo. This is better quality, but small carriable items can be found for 25,000 to 35,000L ($14.70 to $20.60). Around the corner from the Medici Chapels is another favorite, **Ceramiche Ricceri,** on V. d. Conti 14r (☎ **055/291296**), with typically Tuscan platters and dishes but occasionally small items that are less intimidating in price.

DEPARTMENT STORES

Standa, V. d. Panzani 31r (☎ **055/23-98-963**), is the last of the mid- to low-end department stores where you can come up with the occasional find in accessories, household goods, and miscellaneous items—a kind of upscale K-mart. Clothes are classic and either poor quality or nice quality, but expensive. Also a good spot to pick up needed toiletries on the ground floor.

Coin, on V. d. Calzaiuoli 56r (☎ **055/28-05-31**), is as close to Macy's as you'll get in Florence: four floors of made-in-Italy apparel and accessories for men, women, and children. There are moderately priced items mixed in with the high-end merchandise, and it all makes for enjoyable browsing even for those not buying. Check out the sales amid the January and July crowds. The newest arrival on the scene is the six-story local branch of the national chain of **La Rinascente** right in Pz. d. Repubblica 1 (☎ **055219113**). Often compared to Bloomingdale's, it's the nicest (and largest) to represent the best of made-in-Italy merchandising.

DESIGN & HOUSEHOLD ITEMS

Stop by on your way to or from a visit to see *David* at the Accademia to see the chock-ablock collection for sale at **Vice Versa** on V. Ricasoli 53r (☎ **055/23-98-281**), the design emporium that showcases the most interesting items from the creative studios of Milan. Much of this looks like it belongs in the Museum of Modern Art, with a number of small items that embody the latest in Italian design and make great souvenirs for yourself or design-conscious friends. You can spend a fortune, or you can concentrate on bottle openers, key rings, ashtrays, pens, and hot plates all for under 25,000L ($14.70). For a balanced mix of the cutting edge in design and traditional, time-tested kitchenware and household goods Italian style, **La Men agere,** near the Mercato San Lorenzo at V. d. Ginori 8r (☎**055/213875**), is a fun foray.

DISCOUNT FASHION

All those zeroes in the price tags of high fashion clothing disappoint every tourist who arrives with the 1970s fantasy that *la moda italiana* is actually affordable. Two good discount houses for men and women, offering sportswear, outerwear, and accessories are **Grandi Ferme** right off Via Tornabuoni on V. d. Trebbio 10r (☎ **055/2381527**) and **Il Guardaroba** on V. Verdi 28r (☎ **055/2478250**). There are a number of small branch locations for each of these chains, and the selections at both are erratic though thoughtfully displayed. These are no throw-away items at bargain-basement discounts and, although the name recognition is not of the Armani level, the quality if good to very good, the labels left in, and the clothes often from this season and rarely damaged.

HERBS & SPICES

Just a palazzo or two removed from the Piazza Signoria is the **Erboristeria Palazzo Vecchio** on V. Vacchereccia 9r (☎ **055/239-6055**), a tiny, old-world herbal store whose traditions and origins (and some of its recipes and formulas) go back centuries. There are natural pomades and elixirs for everything from dandruff to the blues, but you'll be most interested in the nicely packaged scented soaps, room scents, essences, candles, and sachets that will permeate your entire suitcase by the time you reach home. Packaged seasonings and spices used in the *cucina italiana* make nice gifts for Italophile friends. While this Erboristeria is affordable, the theatrical landmark **Farmacia Santa Maria Novella** at V. d. Scala 16r (☎ **055/216276**) is not. But this is some place to see, though browsing is limited and the help is notoriously unhelpful. The 16th-century setting alone is worth the trip, and you might be able to scrape up enough lire for some of their famous potpourri or beautifully packaged soaps and room scents.

GOLD

Gold in Italy hasn't been a bargain in decades. But the machine-made quality is the best and the selection unsettling. The Ponte Vecchio is a must-do for the ultimate in pipe-dreams window shopping, but for purchasing go to **C.O.I.** at V. Por Santa Maria 8r, second floor above Benetton (☎ **055/28-39-70**). There are no great discounts here (the weight per gram is government-regulated everywhere), but what you're guaranteed at this second-floor gold market is quality and quantity in a foreign-friendly atmosphere. There's an enormous selection of beautiful 18-karat jewelry, each piece carefully weighed before you, and a professional and patient English-speaking sales staff. Have some idea of what you want: a chain, hoop earrings, a child's bracelet, or a wedding band, and the sales help will return from the vault with rolls and rolls of every variation imaginable. (However, gold jewelry with precious and semiprecious stones is limited in selection.) The volume keeps prices down; the remarkable variety keeps customers coming back. The same centuries-old craftsmanship that's applied to the real thing can also be found in the nicest of the city's costume jewelry stores, **Bijoux Casio,** at the north end of the Ponte Vecchio on V. Por Santa Maria 1r (☎ **055/2382851**). You can choose between faux jewelry that looks remarkably like the real thing, or decidedly fake, but gorgeously so.

LEATHER, ACCESSORIES & SHOES

The city is awash in leather stores of all quality ranges. The low end of the gamut is a departure point worth considering: the outdoor Mercato San Lorenzo (see "Markets," above). A good 80% of the leather jackets are too cheaply made for the serious shopper, but a fair number of them are passable to decent, sometimes even very good. The problem is in finding them—you'll have to wade through a ton of mediocre stuff and once you've found the size, style, and price range you want, engage in haggling. For large and more expensive items such as outerwear, bargaining is a must. Check seams and lining and suppleness of leather. Don't bank on alterations once you get home: Few tailors do leather and those that do will charge dearly.

LEATHER If you're not of the market mentality and want to know what the price really is without having to banter and bargain, try the respectable (it's located in a church, after all) **Leather School** in the Church of Santa Croce, Piazza Santa Croce (☎ 055/244533). The fine quality of the varied selection of leather goods from wallets and key chains to bags and attaché cases is not cheap, but it's not overpriced either. The same goes for the selection at the established **Madova Gloves** on the south side of the Ponte Vecchio on V. Guicciardini 1r (☎ 055/2396526), whose quality and choice of colors and skins is the alternative for shoppers who aren't content with the middle-of-the-road merchandise (and prices) at the market. A reasonable alternative to the pricey designer labels of Via Tornabuoni, is **Anna** in Pz. Pitti 38-41r (☎ 055/283787), which provides fine quality and a professional staff who know their stuff. Apparel is classic to fashionable, and the price point is high but reasonable considering the goods. Alterations can be done by seasoned tailors in 24 hours.

ACCESSORIES Silk and pseudosilk scarves and 100% wool mufflers and shawls are some of the best-bet buys at Mercato San Lorenzo. Those wanting to graduate to the label-conscious level and price point of designer ties and labeled scarves of world-known designers will thrill at the selection in the small shop called **Mr. Aramis** on the easy-to-find V. Condotta 4r (☎ 055/282881). It's one-stop shopping for men and women, conservative to fashion forward. If you don't see what you want, ask about their second, nearby location.

SHOES Quality shoe stores abound, from the exquisite Florentine institutions of Via Tornabuoni to the fun and ultracheap. For the latter try **Eusebio,** V. d. Cor. 1 (at Via Proconsolo) (☎ 055/29-29-17), the cheapest shoe store in town, with large rooms chockablock with medium-quality knockoffs of yesterday's and some of tomorrow's runway fashions. Men's and women's shoes are arranged according to size, with styles ranging from out-of-date to the up-to-date, priced from 29,000 to 39,000L ($17.05 to $22.95).

PAPER GOODS

Marbleized paper and the myriad items it covers (agendas, albums, boxes, diaries, pencils, and pencil holders) is a centuries-old craft that has experienced a popular resurgence. Paper-covered goods are a lire a dozen these days. For the unknowning, little-deserving, or innocent child awaiting their souvenirs back home, the low-quality photocopy quality of what is sold at the Mercato San Lorenzo will suffice. But for all else, the best value for your money that I can find is at **Il Torchio** on V. de' Bardi 17 (☎ 055/23-42-862), whose artisans take great pride in the quality of their hand-printed papers and the carefully crafted items they cover (they'll also consider custom work). Its easy-to-reach Oltrarno location east of the Ponte Vecchio keeps prices lower than those in the high-rent Duomo neighborhood. Also recommended, because it is more central with five locations in Florence, is **Il Papiro,** whose largest branch is at V. Tavolini 13r (☎ 055/213823).

8 Florence After Dark

The best source for entertainment and happenings is the Italian-language monthly *Firenze Spettacolo* (3,000L/$1.75), offering comprehensive listings of dance, theater, and music events in the city. The magazine is available at most newsstands.

THE PERFORMING ARTS

One-stop shopping for most of the important venues in town is the ticket agency **Box Office** (☎ 055/264321 or 055/210084). Centrally located at V. Faenza 139r, this service became even more attractive when it recently introduced door-to-door hotel delivery in central Florence for 6,000L ($3.50) for one or more tickets. Your hotel can help you place the order by phone, though there are some English-speaking staff members. In addition to tickets for year-round events of all genres, Box Office also handles the summertime **Calcio in Costume** and the **Maggio Musicale** (see "Special & Free Events," above).

One of Italy's busiest stages, Florence's principal contemporary theater—**Teatro Comunale,** Cor. Italia 16 (☎ 055/21-11-58; fax 055/2779410)—offers everything from symphonies to ballet to plays, opera, and music concerts. The large main theater, on the western edge of town in the direction of the Cascine Park, is best known as the seat of the Maggio Musicale music and dance festival and the annual opera, symphony, and ballet seasons. Its orchestra rows are topped by horseshoe-shaped first and second galleries. The smaller **Piccolo Teatro** (part of the Teatro Comunale) is rectangular, offering good sight lines from most any seat. Tickets begin at 15,000 to 45,000L ($8.80 to $26.50), depending on the production (major performances of Maggio Musicale can approach 200,000L ($117.65)).

Teatro della Pergola, V. d. Pergola 12 (☎ 055/247-9651), is Florence's major playhouse, venue for classical and classic plays from Shakespeare to modern Italian playwrights—all performed in Italian. During the Maggio Musicale, it is sometimes used for concerts and dance performances. The excellent, centrally located and recently renovated **Teatro Verdi,** V. Ghibellina 101 (☎ 055/21-23-20), schedules regular dance and classical music events, often top-name foreign performers, troupes, and orchestras, and the occasional European pop star. Tickets vary greatly according to concert schedule; expect to pay approximately 10,000 to 35,000L ($5.90 to $20.60).

Stop by the tourist office for a list of the season's concerts that take place in the city's churches and theaters. For the important music festivals, **Maggio Musicale** and the **Estate Fiesolana,** see "Special & Free Events," above.

CLUBS & DISCOS

Nightlife is not Florence's strong suit (except for those clubs that come and go, attracting the disparate university student population), but it has improved considerably over the last few years. **Chiodo Fisso,** V. Dante Alighieri 16r (between Via dei Calzaiuoli and Via del Proconsolo, just west of the new American Express building; ☎ 055/23-81-290), is a cozy and intimate wine cavern, the only place to listen to live acoustic and folk music in Florence. There's no admission charge for this self-proclaimed "guitar club," this there is a nominal 2,000L ($1.75) cover charge for first-timers that buys an annual pass, plus the cost of drinks. There are small plates of finger foods and a bottle of Chianti—the only wine served—will set you back 25,000L ($14.70); a minicarafe (basically, two glasses), 6,000L ($3.50). It's closed for 2 weeks in August.

Of the numerous Irish-style pubs, the **Fiddler's Elbow,** Pz. Santa Maria Novella 7r (about 3 blocks from the train station; ☎ 055/21-50-56), is the best, always abuzz with young international travelers and assorted locals. It's one of the few places in town where you can get an authentic pint of Guinness on tap for 8,000L ($4.70). For a more sedate evening, there's **Full-Up,** V. d. Vigna Vecchia 25r, (☎ 055/29-30-06). Cover (includes one drink) is 15,000 to 25,000L ($8.80 to $14.70). Located in the city center, near Santa Croce, this long-enduring and upscale (no kick-back attire here) disco/piano bar is one of the top (though more restrained) dance spaces in Florence with some of the best-known DJs. There are plenty of theme evenings (revival, samba, punk), so call to find out what's on. You'll find the same older crowd at **Il Barretto,** V. d. Parione 50 (off Via Tornabuoni; ☎ 055/2394122), a small, lovely piano bar with an intimate ambiance with a limited but good traditional Tuscan menu to boot.

At **Space Electronic Disco,** V. Palazzuolo 37 (☎ **055/29-30-82; cover 25,000L** ($14.70), which includes the first drink; there's a 5,000L ($2.95) discount for bearers of this book), students and teenage revelers will find a balanced combination of tourists and Italians at this wildly decorated disco/karaoke bar. Its motley collection of artifacts and electronics includes two enormous carnival faces plucked right from an American boardwalk, an open parachute that hangs from the ceiling, an imitation space capsule that sails back and forth across the dance floor, and of course the requisite video screens and lasers. A publike area offers a wide selection of international and draft beer. The other popular cavern-size disco with a young American/Florentine crowd in the Piazzale della Cascine, bordering Cascine Park, is **Meccanò,** V. degli Olmi 1 (☎ **055/33-13-371**), with similar cover, prices and a wide range of music possibilities. One of the better arrivals on the nighttime scene is **Dolce Zucchero,** V. d. Pandolfini 38r (☎ **055/2477894**). There's a small dance floor and live DJ (with occasional live music) downstairs, and an older set approaching 40-something types upstairs. The setting is classic but contemporary, one that has already proven it has staying power beyond the average club's 15-minute life span.

Italy's oldest gay dance club is still Florence's most popular: **Tabasco,** Pz. Santa Cecilia 3 (☎ **055/21-30-00**). Cover ranges from 15,000 to 30,000L ($8.80 to $17.65). Open to both men and women of a 20- and 30-something demographic within a stone's throw of Piazza Signoria and Michelangelo's *David,* god of anatomical perfection. The dance floor is downstairs, while a small video room and piano bar is up top. There are occasional cabaret shows and karaoke.

CAFE & WINE BAR SOCIETY

While the above are most frequented by the members of the dozens of American university programs in Florence, and the golden Florentine boys looking for a socially inclined semester themselves, the following cafes are more enjoyable, less ear-taxing environments in which to while away a nocturnal hour or two for those beyond collegiate endeavors. For the classy historical landmark cafes, check out those in the Piazza della Repubblica, particularly **Gilli's** (no. 39r) or the beloved turn-of-the-century ✪ **Caffe Rivoire** in Piazza della Signoria (no. 5r) with a view of the Palazzo Vecchio and Micehlangelo's *David.* Among the trendy locales, drop by the **Cabiria Cafe,** Pz. Santo Spirito 4r. (☎ **055/21-57-32**). Once a haven for drug abusers, the shady piazza Santo Spirito has cleaned up its act, but still has enough edginess to be an authentic hangout for the young "alternative" crowd. There's some seating area inside but outdoor tables overlook the simple facade of the Brunelleschi-designed Santo Spirito Church. There's a variety of reasonably priced fresh dishes all day (approximately 6,000L/$3.50 each), but this place fills with those who come to hang out before and after dinner hours (closed Tuesday). Food is not the draw at the **Caffe degli Artisti/Art Bar,** V. d. Moro 4r. (☎ **055/28-76-61**). Also known as Caffe del Moro because of its street location (north of Ponte alla Carraia), this longtime favorite watering hole draws an interesting crowd that comes to mingle and talk (though music can get loud) and sample the long list of "cocktails" and mixed drinks (well, maybe it's the people who get loud), uncommon in this wine-imbibing society. The atmosphere is upscale, and a downstairs room with wooden tables attracts groups of friends who linger for hours (closed Sunday). More upscale is the **Caffé Cibreo,** V. Andrea d. Verrochio 5r (☎ **055/23-45-853**). From the clever and entrepreneurial Midas who gave Florence the restaurant and Trattoria Cibreo, this handsome bar across the street first became known for its informal and inexpensive lunch and dinner menus, many of whose dishes came from the acclaimed kitchen across the way. But this is also a lovely and quiet spot for an attractive, older crowd who take their hot chocolate, tea blends, or coffee roasts seriously or who want to people-watch before or after dining at the Trattoria Cibreo or the popular Il Pizzaiolo, also across the street (see "Great Deals on Dining," above).

For evening-time wine-bar choices, the traditional hole-in-the-wall *fiaschetterie* are not where you want to go: They're usually open during daytime hours for neighborhood regulars, and there's no place to sit. This wine tradition has spawned a number of new arrivals that offer longer hours and a seating area to socialize and linger with a reliably impressive selection of wines by the glass and good, simple food to accompany self-paced wine tastings, or just a leisurely after-dinner hour. See "Great Deals on Dining" for **Cantinetta del Verrazzano** (open only until 9pm) and ✪ **Osteria del Caffé Italiano** (open till 1am). Another that will be of great interest to the wine enthusiasts among you is the **Enoteca FuoriPorta,** whose name refers to its location just outside the 14th-century city gate and ramparts in the Oltrarno neighborhood on V. Monte alle Croci 10r (☎ **055/2342483**) on the way up to Piazzale Michelangiolo. The simple menu continues to expand, but centers around the characteristically Tuscan open-faced *crostini* that goes perfectly with the extensive wine list (one of the best in town, mostly Tuscan reds), many available by the glass (or bottle). It's closed on Sunday. More intimate and more accessible in its tiny hidden piazza just off the Ponte Vecchio in the Oltrarno is the refined wine bar **Le Volpi e L'Uva,** on Piazza de' Rossi behind Piazza Santa Felicità off the Via Guicciardini (☎ **055/2398132**). Here you can sample little known wines from Tuscany's small, unsung wine producers, while snacking on sandwiches or plates of regional cheeses or *salumi* indoors and out (closed Sunday).

9 Day Trip to Fiesole

For a more extensive choice of full day trips from Florence, take a look at the Tuscany chapter and the nearby towns of Lucca, San Gimignano, and Siena. For a quickie, consider Fiesole, an independent *comune* easily accessible by public bus, where Florentines take to the hills to escape the crowds and heat of the valley-locked city below.

Situated 5 miles to the north of town on a green hill rising above Florence, **Fiesole** is an important archaeological site, once a pre-Roman Etruscan settlement, and later a prominent Roman town. In more recent centuries, families of means have fled the city's summer heat, history's rash of plagues, family feuds, and urban ennui by taking to the cool cypress-studded environs above. It has long been known for its magnificent ancestral villas and million-dollar views. Many of the historical villas are now

Riding Through Tuscany

For a listing of rural farms or ranches that are within a 1-hour's drive of Florence, where riding can be arranged by the hour, see the box "Riding in Italy" in chapter 3. These rides should be booked in advance and are not a day-trip consideration for those without cars. Accommodations are available for those who want to extend their stay.

> ## Travel Tip
>
> Most sites in Fiesole are open in winter, Wednesday to Monday from 9am to 6pm; and in summer, Wednesday to Monday from 9am to 7pm.

associated with the dozens of American university programs, such as that of the famous art historian and critic Bernard Berenson, who left his Villa I Tatti to his alma mater Harvard University (today, it is a postdoctorate center for studies of Renaissance topics), or the Rockefellers' Villa Le Balze, bequeathed to Georgetown University.

Fiesole's private villas are not on view to the public, though other historical sites are, and most visitors come for the change of air, gorgeous views looking south over Florence and a piazza-side aperitif, light meal, or evening performance at the amphitheater.

GETTING HERE   Fiesole is an easy half-day excursion, accessible by public bus, so you may find yourself surrounded by fellow tourists. It can be reached in 30 minutes with bus no. 7 (costing the standard 1,500L/90¢) from the Piazza Stazione or Piazza San Marco to the end of the line.

EXPLORING THE AREA   Ancient Faesule was set up here by the pre-Roman Etruscans centuries before the Romans established a riverside trading base on the banks of the Arno circa 59 B.C. Their presence is still felt in the **Zona Archeologico** (☎ 055/59477), an enclosure of 2,000-year-old Etruscan and Roman ruins, highlighted by the restored 3,000-seat amphitheater that is used for the annual **Estate Fiesolana** festival of music, dance, and theater under the stars (a film festival may not interest non–Italian-speaking tourists); it takes place late June through August—check with Fiesole's tourist office in Pz. Mino 36 (☎ 055/598720) or Florence's offices back in town. The skeletal remains of the ancient baths circa the 1st century B.C. can also been seen. Next to it is an early 20th-century temple that houses the **Museo Civico** or the Museo Faesulanum, which contains many interesting finds from the excavations.

The town center evolves around the large piazza dedicated to the sculptor Mino da Fiesole (around 1430–84). Fronting the square is the Romanesque **Cattedrale di San Romolo,** dating from 1000, and much altered during the Renaissance. The Salutati Chapel contains important sculptures by Mino da Fiesole. Also on the piazza is the 17th-century **Bishop's Palace** and the **St. Maria Primerana Church.**

No one should leave without a look at the splendid heart-stopping (in every sense of the word) panorama of Florence and its encircling countryside below, but first you'll have to hike up the very steep pedestrian-only **Via di San Francesco**—go west (left) out of the main square—to the **Convento di San Francesco.** You can visit the Franciscan church and monastery, one time home of St. Bernardino of Siena, built in the Gothic style in the early 1400s. Inside are a number of paintings by Renaissance painters of the early 16th century. In the basement is an ethnological museum containing artifacts from the friars during their missionary travels in China and Egypt as well as an Etruscan-Roman collection. But a visit here is all about the views, so awesome that you'll see why this was the practical choice to build the ancient acropolis here in Fiesole's early days as an Etruscan stronghold.

Fiesole's restaurants, bars, and cafes are abundant, but principally work as tourist traps. Sip a Campari or order a gelato, but don't plan on eating a full meal here—restaurant choices are better back in town.

Tuscany & Umbria 6

by Patricia Schultz

Tuscany and Umbria share much of the same cultural and artistic heritage, a history that dates from the pre-Roman Etruscans, a cuisine, and to some degree a similarity in landscape. However, it'll behoove you to never to mention these two regions in the same breath to a Tuscan or Umbrian. Like two first cousins, Tuscany and Umbria are just as often fiercely individualistic in characteristics and traditions they have preserved and nurtured over the centuries.

Italians are rarely modest about their unabashed love for the region they call home. But nowhere is this emotion-packed loyalty of *provincia* so deservedly heartfelt as in Tuscany, one of the country's most visited (and deservedly so) rural destinations. Richly endowed with a wide variety of topography, from the Apennine Mountains in the northwestern corner to the open rolling plains of the Maremma area in the south, Tuscany is also endowed with a coastal riviera (admittedly less alluring than Liguria's, but with the benefit of wide sandy beaches) and a number of idyllic islands in the Ligurian Sea of which Elba, Napoléon's exile retreat, is the largest and most renowned.

Almost three-quarters of Tuscany is comprised of gentle hills, terraced by farmers over time to prevent erosion while providing more room for crops. It is not hard for the average visitor to recapture the magical beauty of a Merchant-Ivory movie: Hollywood would never think of filming on location elsewhere. Tuscans are only half-joking when they tell you that God may be responsible for the beauty that is Tuscany's, but the local genius Michelangelo drew up the plans.

The Umbrian cities featured in this chapter have not changed much since the Middle Ages, but you will never mistake them for museum cities: They are very much alive, fueled by their cultural interests and thriving economies only partially sustained by tourism. Two of Italy's most important summer festivals take place here, the Umbrian Jazz Festival in Perugia and Spoleto's Festival of Two Worlds.

A TASTE OF TUSCANY & UMBRIA The Tuscan and Umbrian *cucina* draws heavily from the grains, beans, and ingredients of the farmer's simple pantry and the woods and forests that cover its hills. Nouvelle cuisine it's not. Rustic sausage antipasti (*salsicce*), game (*cacciagione*), and tender quality meats roasted or *alla griglia* are the highlight of every meal—the *bistecca alla fiorentina* being the fabled (and bill boosting) entree you'll want to try at least once. The unquestioned prominence of olive oil makes an appearance from the acclaimed groves of Lucca and Spoleto, the Tuscan and Umbrian suppliers of

Tuscany & Umbria

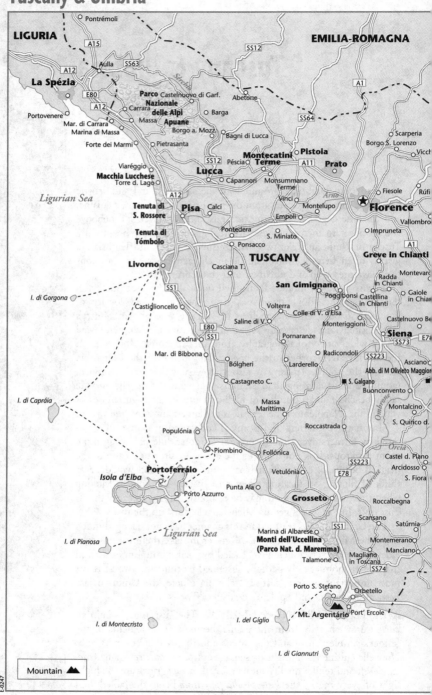

Mountain ▲▲

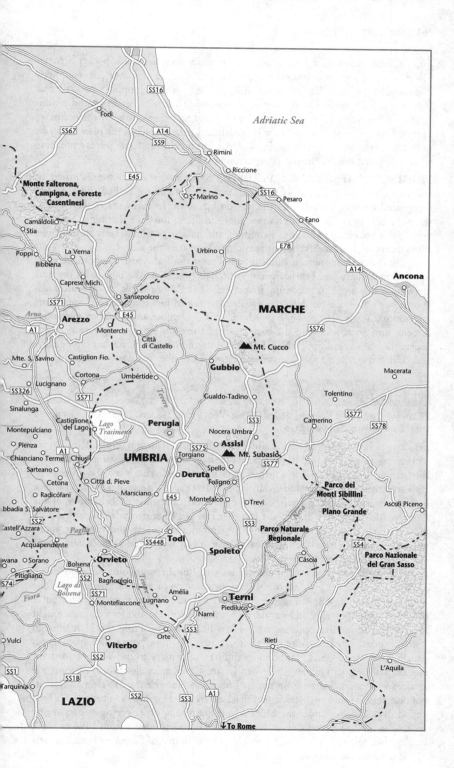

Europe's best *olio di oliva.* Renowned Chianti wines from the scenic pocket between Florence and Siena, and distinctive Orvieto whites make this area an oenophile's dream—and you most likely won't be disappointed with the humble *vino della casa* (house wine). Umbria's touted claim to gastronomic fame is the underground tartufo (truffle) from Norcia. Preciously grated over pastas and pizzas, it is expensive but its acquired taste is considered sublime by gourmand palates. This is the place to try it: not only for the local expertise and abundance but for the moderate prices (moderate when compared to over-the-top American ones).

FINDING AN AFFORDABLE PLACE TO STAY Most of the tourist offices in the towns and cities can supply you with lists of *affittacamere,* or bed-and-breakfast accommodations that often offer the best deal in town. In many places there is also the possibility of *agriturismo* accommodations in the countryside that range from the very basic to working farms with swimming and horseback riding. Lists are available, though they do little to describe or recommend one over the next.

Towns that rely on tourism (such as San Gimignano and Assisi) pretty much close up shop in January and February. Easter through June is usually busy, with the heat arriving in July and things coming to a standstill in August (look for off-season discounts but watch out for sleepless, nonair-conditioned nights and closed restaurants and shops). You'll need to book in advance for September and October, everyone's favorite time to tool around the back roads of these wine-producing regions; don't expect the brilliant colors of a New England autumn however. November can be rainy and cold and except for the Christmas holidays, December is a dead month.

1 Pisa

77 km (48.5 mi.) W of Florence, 21 km (13 mi.) W of Lucca, 335 km (211 mi.) N of Rome, 98 km (62 mi.) NW of San Gimignano

Legions of visitors descend on Pisa from every imaginable nation on the planet to see its Leaning Tower. Few buildings in the world have captured imaginations as much as the Leaning Tower of Pisa. Most surprising is the realization that it is one of three principle structures that occupy the vividly green piazza called Campo dei Miracoli and is, in fact, the free-standing (well, barely) cylindrical campanile or bell tower of the Duomo. Also surprising may be the fact that Pisa is a large riverside city with a population of close to 100,000—vibrant, contemporary, bustling and relatively indifferent to its leaning icon—something that may or may not appeal to those who expect a quaint and quiet Tuscan town.

Pisa is one of the great ancient cities of Italy, its Roman roots going back more than 1,000 years before the building of that curiously leaning campanile. The mouth of the Arno River has long since silted up, placing Pisa inland 7 miles from the coast, but it was once a vital port city and naval base for imperial Rome and for centuries fought to keep the Tyrrhenian coastline free of invading Saracens. From the 11th through 13th centuries, it had grown to rival the three other maritime powers of Italy—Genoa, Amalfi, and Venice—and gloried in its military supremacy in the Western Mediterranean. This was its Golden Age, when its artistic splendor flourished. But internal rivalries and external strife from nearby Lucca and Florence were to chip away at its political stability and in 1406 it was defeated by the Florentines. There was a brief period of well-being under the Medicis and flourishing of its prestigious university (established in 1343), and an even briefer period of independence from 1494 to 1509. But for the most part, Pisa's history would meld with that of Florence's from the early 1500s until Italian unification in the 1860s.

Travel Tip

Pisa's points of interest are attention deserving but limited, making it the perfect whistle-stop day trip from Florence or for those based in Lucca. Few visitors stay for more than 1 night. Others stay for the day alone, returning to Lucca, Florence or their rented countryside villa for the night.

FESTIVALS & MARKETS On your walk from the train station to the Campo dei Miracoli, stroll through Pisa's old-fashioned **food market,** located west off the arcaded shopping street of Borgo Stretto on the north side of the Arno. Its center is the small, picturesque 16th-century Piazza delle Vettovaglie, though it spills over to neighboring side streets (Monday to Saturday, 8am to 1:30pm). On the second weekend of every month (except in July and August), an **antiques fair** fills the side streets on both sides of the Ponte di Mezzo, with many stores in the area staying open on Sunday as well.

The most important holiday of the year is the that of the local patron, San Ranieri, celebrated **June 16 and 17** when the banks of the Arno are illuminated with torches (the **Luminaria**) on June 16 followed by a regatta the following day. It also means the arrival of the annual **Gioco del Ponte** (The Bridge Game), celebrated the last Sunday of June. Taking place on Ponte di Mezzo, teams from the north and south banks of the Arno River dress in Renaissance costume, and reenact a reverse tug-of-war trying to run each other over with a 7-ton decorated cart. An extravagant *corteo* procession of 600 people in historical costume precedes the "battle."

ESSENTIALS

GETTING HERE **By Train** Pisa-Florence is linked by trains leaving approximately every half hour throughout the day, making the trip in 1 to 1½ hours, and costing 7,500L ($4.40). A number of trains originating in Florence are heading for **Pisa Aeroporto** and not **Pisa Centrale** (☎ 050/41252): Make sure you're on the right train and get off at the latter in the center of town. More than 20 trains depart Lucca daily for the 25-minute trip for 3,500L ($2.05). The Campo dei Miracoli is due north of the train station, across the Ponte di Mezzo bridge, a 20-minute walk, or take the bus no. 1 from outside the train station.

By Bus **Lazzi** runs buses from Florence or Lucca to Pisa. Make sure the bus is a direct service and not local (☎ 050/46288). Buses arrive just north of the train station in the Piazza Vittorio Emanuele II, only marginally closer to the Campo dei Miracoli. Prices are similar to the train rates.

By Car The convenient **A12** autostrada connects Florence to Pisa (also called Firenze-Mare it continues west to its coastal destinations), travel time of 1 to 1½ hours is determined by the time it takes to get in and out of the cities. A car will be of no use within Pisa. As soon as you arrive, follow the signs for Campo dei Miracoli and large "P" parking lots immediately west of the piazza.

By Plane Many flights from the United States connect in European cities such as London, Paris, and Frankfurt for Pisa's international **Galileo Galilei Airport** (☎ 050/50-07-07) (domestic flights from within Italy arrive here as well), just 3 kilometers (2 mi.) south of Pisa. It is an easy 10-minute bus ride on the no. 7 to downtown Pisa's train station (a taxi costs about 15,000L/$8.80).

VISITOR INFORMATION The principal **tourist office** has a new location, at V. Cammeo 2 (☎ 050/560464) just outside the city walls, 2 minutes west of the Campo dei Miracoli. Hours are Monday to Saturday 9:30am to 1pm and 3 to 7pm. In the

same space, **Consorzio Turistico di Pisa** (☎ 050/560464; www.traveleurope.it/Pisa.
htm; e-mail: pisa.turismo@traveleurope.it) can help you with reservations and information regarding hotels, restaurants and tour guides. There's a small tourist office in
the train station (exit front doors and to your left); it's open Monday to Saturday,
9:30am to 1pm and 3 to 6:30pm (☎ 050/42291). Hours for both offices may be cut
back during winter months.

WHAT TO SEE & DO

The aptly named **Campo dei Miracoli** (Field of Dreams) by the Italian poet
D'Annunzio, more parochially known as **Piazza Duomo,** sits within the northwestern
stretch of Pisa's ancient city walls. The trio of elegant buildings in the piazza bear testimony to the importance of the Pisan Republic during the first 2 centuries of the last
millennium: this would be forever Pisa's legacy and the first such grandiose under-
taking since the times of ancient Rome. Once surrounded by farmlands, it still sits
within its own emerald green lawn, a paean to spatial geometry and visual brilliance—
the vivid green of the grass, the white marble icons against an intense blue sky—this
is undoubtedly one of the world's most memorable squares.

You must pay admission to the Duomo separately. The other sites in the Campo dei
Miracoli are linked together with a joint admission ticket. You may choose two of the
four remaining sites (excluding the Duomo) listed below for 10,000L ($5.90), or
15,000L ($8.80) for all four. The Leaning Tower can only be viewed from outside;
there has been no access to climb it since 1990, with little chance of this changing
during the life span of this book.

✪ **Duomo.** Piazza Duomo. ☎ **050/560547.** Winter Mon–Sat 10am–12:45 and 3–4:45;
Sun 3–4:45pm. Spring through autumn 10am–7:40pm; Sun 3–7:40pm. Admission 2,000L
($1.20) Mar–Oct; free rest of year.

The duomo was begun in 1064 and finished by the end of the 13th century. It is the
first construction to borrow from the Moorish architecture of Andalusia, the hori-
zontal stripe (known as banding) of black and white marble, with a facade of inlaid
colored-marble design (intarsia) and four graceful open-air galleries of mismatched
columns that diminish in size as they ascend. This would be the archetype of Pisan
Romanesque architecture and would go on to be much imitated (as your visits to
Lucca, Siena, and elsewhere will attest). The three sets of massive bronze doors facing
the Baptistery are from the 16th century, replacing originals lost in a fire, but the
highly stylized ✪ **Romanesque door of St. Ranieri** (the patron saint of Pisa) facing
the tower is by Bonanno Pisano and dates from 1180, completed 7 years after he had
begun work on the bell tower. The cathedral's interior is cavernous, close to 400 feet
long and interrupted by 68 columns. Giovanni Pisano's intricately carved ✪ **pulpit**
(1301–11) is the church's greatest treasure, destroyed in that same disastrous fire,
warehoused for centuries and later rebuilt with pieces of the original when it was rediscovered in 1926. It is similar (and, some believe, superior) to an earlier one in the Baptistery by Giovanni's father Nicola. Opposite the pulpit hangs the 16th-century
bronze **Galileo Lamp.** Pisa's most illustrious son, Galileo Galilei (1564–1642)
allegedly came up with his theory of pendulum movement by studying the swinging
of the lamp set in motion by a sympathetic sacristan though historians say the theory
was established by the local astronomer and physicist years before the lamp was cast.
Having survived the great fire is the apse's magnificent 13th-century mosaic **Christ
Pantocrator,** finished in 1302 by Cimabue.

Battistero (Baptistery). Piazza Duomo. ☎ **050/560547.** Winter 9am–4:40pm. Spring
and autumn 9am–5:40pm. Summer 8am–7:40pm. Admission, see above.

The lovely Gothic Baptistery sits west of the Duomo, best known for the beautifully carved hexagonal pulpit by Nicola Pisano in 1260, a half a century before the one in the Duomo created by his son Giovanni. The largest of its kind in Italy (348 feet in circumference), the Baptistery was begun in 1152 but not finished until the end of the 14th century. The vast interior is noted for its plainness and for its remarkable acoustics; tour guides usually illustrate the quality of echoes for their groups from the center of the building. If not, track down the custodian and ask him to do the same (and reward him for his trouble).

✪ **Campanile (Leaning Tower).** Indefinitely closed to the public.

The last of the campo's three structures to be built, the eight-story cylindrical belfry was begun in 1174. It wasn't until the architects completed the third floor in 1185 that the building began to list (at that point, only 3.8 centimeters) and construction was suspended for a century. Building was resumed in 1275 and completed in 1372. Countless millions had climbed its 294 steps until the tourism authorities finally closed it in a solemn ceremony on January 7, 1990, both for the safety of the public and the well being of their beloved **Torre Pendente.** In 1993, even its seven bells were silenced to avoid unnecessary vibrations that might aggravate its condition. Few give any credence to the romantic notion that the architect purposely intended it to lean to demonstrate his clever talents: the general consensus has always been that shifting subsoil foundation caused it to slowly list over the centuries—it is now close to 14 to 17 feet (accounts vary) off the perpendicular; Galileo exploited its overhanging in one of his famous experiments by dropping balls of different weights from the top floor to illustrate his theory of the constancy of gravity. From certain angles you'll wonder what all the hubbub is about; from other angles, the visible gravity of the listing is alarming. The same sandy subsoil is said to have resulted in less dramatic shifts in the Baptistery and Duomo as well, though you might go cross-eyed looking too hard for imaginary tilts. If it stood straight the tower would be approximately 185 feet tall. For years, word has circulated that by the year 2000 the tower would be open again, but don't count on it.

Camposanto. Piazza Duomo. ☎ **050/560547.** Same hours as Baptistery. Admission, see above.

The vast walled Camposanto, said to be the most beautiful cemetery in the world, is on the northern side of the Campo dei Miracoli. It was begun in 1278, legend goes, to hold the earth brought back from the Holy Land by the Fourth Crusade in 1203 so that important Pisans could be buried in sacred dirt. It is said to be the earth from Calvary where Jesus Christ was crucified. The magnificent frescoes by 14th-and-15th century Renaissance painters that once covered the Camposanto were destroyed by a 1944 air attack by Allied forces when Pisa was in the hands of the Nazis. When what remained of the frescoes was removed to be restored, the workers discovered the artists' preparatory sketches called *sinopie* beneath (they are now housed in the especially built Museo delle Sinopie, see below). Of the few frescoes that escaped damage are **The Drunkenness of Noah** by Renaissance painter Benozzo Gozzoli and the earlier, more important trio of the 14th-century **Triumph of Death, Last Judgement,** and **The Inferno,** whose authorship is disputed.

Museo del Duomo. Piazza Arcivescovado (adjacent to the Piazza Duomo). ☎ **050/560547.** Same hours as Baptistery. Admission, see above.

This is the city's most important collection, housed in a recently restored palazzo that dates from the 13th century. Used as both the Duomo's Chapter House and later as a Capuchin monastery, it is now divided into 19 rooms that are home to a wealth of works of arts from the different buildings of the Campo dei Miracoli. Sculptures by the various members of the Pisano family and their students are the highpoints of the museum. From Giovanni Pisano, whose pulpit is the focal point of the Duomo's interior, is his important statuette of **Madonna and Child** (1300), whose figures lean in to the natural curve of the ivory tusk from which it is carved; it originally was found on the Duomo's main altar. Another highpoint is the precious Pisan cross that led the local contingent off to the First Crusade in 1099. A 12th-century bronze **griffin,** a masterpiece of Islamic art, was picked up as war booty from the Saracens and was placed in the cathedral before being relocated here. The Islamic influence felt in many of the pieces on display is testimony to Pisa's history as a powerful maritime republic in the Mediterranean; examples of the inlaid marble intarsia of Moorish-influenced designs once decorating the Duomo's facade are now displayed here. The last few rooms are filled with a small Roman and Etruscan archaeological collection from the Camposanto. Most important are the 19th-century etchings of its Renaissance frescoes (being restored at that time) which are the only remaining record of the artwork that went up in flames when the Camposanto was bombed in 1944.

Museo delle Sinopie. Piazza Duomo. ☎ **050/560547.** Same hours as Baptistery. Admission, see above.

Of limited interest except to those particularly intrigued by the story of the Camposanto and its frescoes, this well-arranged museum is the newest of the Campo dei Miracoli's additions. Created exclusively in a 13th-century hospice to display the preliminary fresco sketches found beneath those destroyed in 1944 during an Allied bomb attack (when Pisa was still in the hands of the Nazis), the museum is dedicated to the **sinopie** or reddish-brown sketches made from Sinope clay. They are all that remains of the majority of the Camposanto's frescoes by leading early Renaissance masters that went up in flames. There is also an explanation of how frescoes were created in those days.

MORE PISAN SIGHTS

It's an easy 10-minute stroll down Via Santa Maria from the Piazza Duomo with a left on to Via dei Mille before you find yourself in Pisa's **Piazza Cavalieri.** There would be a lot more tourist hype about its architectural attributes if it didn't have the Campo dei Miracoli to vie with all these years. The Square of the Knights was built on the site of the old Roman Forum and takes its name from the Order of St. Stephen, a military and religious order founded in 1561 by the Medici whose cause was to protect the Mediterranean from the Turkish infidels. Next to the 16th-century church designed by Vasari is the fabulously (and recently restored) graffiti-covered Palazzo dei Cavalieri, once used to train the knights until Napoléon took over and founded the Scuola Normale Superiore in 1810. It is the Medici and not Napoléon represented by the statue that still stands outside: it is Grand Duke Cosimo I (1519–74). The third-most important building in the square is the **Palazzo dell'Orologio** (Clock Tower), two medieval towers joined together by Vasari. It today houses the library for the Scuola Normale Superiore.

Museo Nazionale di San Matteo. Lungarno Mediceo (near Ponte Fortezza). ☎ **050/ 541865.** Admission: 8,000L ($4.70). Tues–Sat 9am–7pm; Sun 9am–2pm. Bus: 5, 7, or 13.

Most of the major paintings from Pisa's churches are now gathered and on display here around the 15th-century cloister of the convent of San Matteo. Fourteenth-century religious works, from Pisa's final period of prosperity, make up the bulk of the collection that spans the period from the 12th to the 17th centuries.

WHERE TO STAY

Pisa is the quintessential day trip, and the selection of hotels is limited, with very reasonable prices. All the buses you see disgorging their passengers at the leaning tower will return them to their hotels in Florence at the end of the day. Should you have a problem with availability, the **Consorzio Turistico** (they share space with the Tourist Office at Via C. Cammeo, see above) will reserve a hotel for you at no cost. If the Royal Vicotoria hotel (below) is full, try the family-run **Villa Kinzica** at Pz. Arcivescovado 2, 56126 (just off Piazza Duomo; ☎ 050/560419, fax 050/551204), where doubles with a view of the Leaning Tower cost 150,000L ($88.25).

○ **Royal Victoria Hotel.** Lungarno Pacinotti 12, 56126 Pisa (west of the Ponte di Mezzo). ☎ **050/940111.** Fax 050/940180. www.csinfo.it/royalvictoriahotel. E-mail: rvh@info.it. 48 units, 40 with bathroom. TV TEL. 85,000L ($50) single without bathroom, 135,000L ($79.40) single with bathroom; 105,000L ($61.75) double without bathroom, 165,000L ($97.05) double with bathroom; 180,000L ($105.90) triple with bathroom; 190,000L ($111.75) quad with bathroom. Reduced rates for more than 4-night stay. Rates include breakfast. AE, DC, MC, V. Parking 30,000L ($17.65). Bus: 2, 3.

"I fully endorse the above," wrote Teddy Roosevelt of this history-steeped place in one of the yellowed guest books, and what was good enough for Teddy is good enough for most. Built in 1839 by the great-grandfather of the two present-day owners, this is by far Pisa's oldest and only hostelry full of character, charm and, during Sunday and Thursday lessons, the strains of tango music. Linking several medieval structures (room nos. 101, 201, 301, and 401 are found within a tower dating from the 10th century) facing the Arno River, it has done much to keep its old-world atmosphere with original pavements, etched glass swinging doors, antique furniture, and reproductions and frescoed ceilings and walls in many of the rooms. The Piegaja brothers undertake regular renovations to keep the years at bay—new firm mattresses one year, dozens of tastefully arranged silk-flowers another—but it is the very presence of 160 years of history within the same genteel family and their loyal staff that keeps guests, as Ruskin once wrote, "very comfortable in this inn." To get a better picture of this hotel, flip to the back cover of this book.

WHERE TO DINE

Even if you're one of Pisa's countless day-trippers, try to arrange your day around a nice lunch at any of the following informal places. Pisa has become a city for food lovers, and the new wave of young restaurant owners have brought it up a gastronomic notch in the last few years. Sharing the spotlight with La Grotta (see below) is Pisa's other favorite trattoria, **Da Bruno,** one of the few open on Sunday (closed on Tuesday; ☎ 050/560818). Located just north of the Campo dei Miracoli on V. Luigi Bianchi 12 outside the Porta Lucca, its prices are marginally higher, sucessfully specializing over the years in tried and true Pisan specialties.

✪ **La Mescita.** V. Cavalca 2 (steps off the market square Piazza Vettovaglie). ☎ **050/544294.** Reservations recommended. Primi 13,000L ($7.65); secondi 20,000L ($11.75). AE, MC, V. Tues–Sun 1–3pm and 8–11pm. Closed last 3 weeks of Aug. Bus: 2, 3, 4, 7. PISAN/ENOTECA

This small wine bar/trattoria's marketplace location means its clientele is a colorful one, and its ingredients are the best and freshest available. In a friendly atmosphere that serves as an enoteca wine bar in its late hours, the *cucina* is both local pisana and nontraditional, but always simple, interesting and delicious in an atmosphere that is upbeat and fun. Often found on the menu are soufflélike *sformati* based on fresh seasonal vegetables such as *melanzane* (eggplant) or *zucca* (pumpkin or squash). A more regional standby is the excellent *baccalà* (salt cod fish) made with chickpeas and potatoes. At similar prices and just a block away within the marketplace neighborhood is another equally favorite spot, the family owned ✪ **Trattoria S. Omobono**, in Pz. S. Omobono 6 (☎ **050/540847**). Prices and menu choices are similar for a delicious casual meal in the company of locals, university professors and market shoppers. It's closed Sunday, as most of Pisa's restaurants are.

La Grotta. V. San Francesco 103 (at corner of V. Case Dipinte). ☎ **050/578105.** Reservations recommended. Primi 10,000L ($5.90); secondi 15,000–22,000L ($8.80–$12.95). No credit cards. Mon–Sat 12:30–2:30pm and 8–11pm. Closed Aug. Bus: 2, 3, 4, 7. TUSCAN/ITALIAN.

Centrally located just east of the store-lined Borgo Stretto that runs from the river to the Campo dei Miracoli is this charming archetypal trattoria always full, always serving up great regional specialties to very happy-looking Pisan natives. There's an old-fashioned warmth between staff and local families who have frequented this faux-grotto for generations, as much for the traditional Tuscan specialties as for the unpretentious service. You can't go wrong with any of the roasted and grilled meats with herb-crusted potatoes, or the much requested *coniglio ripieno alle castagne* (rabbit stuffed and roasted with chestnuts). The dining room is small, so be ready to reserve in advance or arrive early—or join those who patiently wait, knowing it's worth the effort.

2 Lucca

72 km (45 mi.) W of Florence, 21 km (13 mi.) E of Pisa, 336 km (209 mi.) N of Rome, 96 km (60 mi.) NW of San Gimignano

You will hear first about and remember always the great walls of this unspoiled (albeit no longer undiscovered) Tuscan town. Brick ramparts rebuilt most recently in the 16th and 17th centuries encircle this elegant and graceful city in their Renaissance swath. Although it has a population of 90,000, only a marginal percentage lives within the ancient walls where a thriving small-town atmosphere prevails. The city preserves much of its tangible past: a flourishing colony of Rome in 180 B.C., its ancient legacy is still evident in the grid pattern of its streets. Today they are still lined with handsomely preserved medieval towered palazzi redolent of Lucca's wealth in past centuries. A sophisticated silk and textile trade reinterpreting the luxurious silks that arrived from the Orient made this small town famous throughout Europe in the Middle Ages and early Renaissance. But its wealth and power slowly dissipated and, having tenaciously kept its independence from neighboring Pisa and Florence for so many centuries, it finally fell to Napoléon, who handed it over to his sister Elisa Baciocchi as a principality in 1805, and in 1815 it was absorbed into the Tuscan Grand Duchy.

Today's quiet streets—where 25,000 workers once kept 3,000 hand looms operating—open onto small squares full of character, each anchored by a marble-faced church built during the city's golden heyday. Medieval highlights are the Duomo and the elaborate San Michele, both exquisite examples of Pisan-Lucchese architecture.

Proximity to Pisa airport makes this an excellent first or last stop in Tuscany, recommended more than the far larger city of Pisa itself, despite its legendary leaning tower (stay here with a day trip to Pisa). The lack of traffic enhances Lucca's low-profile, unhurried air where moneyed matriarchs, whose noble family histories have survived the centuries, do their daily shopping around town on battered bicycles. The hotel situation does not bode well for the budget traveler, but once you find a place to settle down, the general lack of mass tourism is the city's, and your, greatest blessing.

FESTIVALS & MARKETS   An **Antiques Fair** takes place the third Sunday of every month and the Saturday that precedes it. About 200 vendors converge upon the area around Piazza Antelminelli and Piazza Giusto. Reserve (in advance) for lunch at Da Giulio or Da Leo to complete the Lucchese experience. The opera season takes place at the **Teatro Comunale del Giglio** (Piazza del Giglio) in **September or October**, and usually features at least one opera by the hometown hero Puccini. For ticket information, call the **Lucca Informa** special tourist hot line for information on any events happening in Lucca (☎ **0583/419689**) or contact the tourist office. Those on the Puccini Trail will want to take in a performance at the annual **Puccini Festival** in nearby Torre del Lago where Lucca-born Puccini kept a summer villa and where he and his family are buried. Outdoor performances are usually held last week of July and first 2 weeks of August (☎ **0584/359322;** fax 0584/350277). In the United States contact Edwards & Edwards for advance purchase tickets (☎ **212/332-2435**). The annual **Settembre Lucchese** fills the month of September with a lively combination of music, dance, and celebrations. The town's centuries-old highlight is the **Volto Santo** feast day on September 13–14 (see the Duomo under "What to See and Do," below). Summer musical events are sometimes scheduled in the gardens of the historical villas in the surrounding countryside; ask for details at the tourist office.

ESSENTIALS

GETTING HERE   By Train   Lucca is on the Florence-Viareggio line. Trains from Florence are not infrequent but they are usually locals, taking 70 to 90 minutes (7,000L/$4.10); bus transportation is more direct and recommended. Trains to Pisa Centrale take approximately 20 to 30 minutes and some go the extra 10 minutes directly to Pisa Aeroporto (Pisa's airport).

Lucca's station (☎ **0583/48360**) is south of the city walls near Porta San Pietro; it is an easy walk only if you're unencumbered with luggage (there's the bus no. 16 and others into town and taxi service into the center of town).

By Bus   LAZZI buses (☎ **0583/58-48-77**) connect Lucca with Florence and other principal cities (from Lucca to Pisa's airport; 30 min.) while **CLAP** (☎ **0583/58-78-97**) services most outlying Tuscan towns. Quasi-hourly LAZZI buses leave to or from Florence from 6am to 8pm Monday to Saturday (every 2 hours Sunday), and cost 10,000L ($5.90) each way for the 1¼-hour ride (avoid the lengthy route of local buses). The buses let you off on the west side of town in the area of Piazzale Verdi within the walls, just across the piazza from the tourist office. A small **taxi stand** means a few taxis are usually waiting about; if not call ☎ **0583/581305.**

By Car   You'll have to leave your car in a parking facility (the largest, in Piazza Napoleone, fills up fast), as almost all of Lucca's historical core is closed to traffic. The effortless Autostrada del Sole (**A11**, direction west) connects Florence to Lucca in just over one hour; it splits here continuing either southward to Pisa, or west and northwest to the "direzione mare" (the popular seaside resorts of Viareggio and Forte dei Marmi). While a car enables you to explore the idyllic countryside outside Lucca, getting here to and from Florence or Pisa and visiting the town itself is easily done by public transportation and on foot.

By Plane   Many flights from the United States connect in European cities such as London, Paris, and Frankfurt for Pisa's international **Galileo Galilei Airport** (☎ **050/50-07-07**), an easy 20- to 30-minute bus ride from Lucca. Florence's newly expanded **Amerigo Vespucci Airport** (☎ **055/37-34-98**) is another option. If you're heading directly to Lucca upon landing, take the city bus from the Florence airport to the central bus station in town and change for a LAZZI bus to Lucca (see "By Bus," above).

VISITOR INFORMATION   **Tourist Information** is available at Vecchia Porta San Donato at Piazzale Verdi (☎ **0583/41-96-89;** fax 0583/419689; e-mail: aptlucca.info@lunet.it). It's open summer (April through November), daily 9:30am to 6:30pm, winter 9:30am to 3:30pm.

CITY LAYOUT   Lucca is an easy place to get your bearings. The historical center is entirely contained within its 16th-century walls; the modern city outside them holds little of interest to the visitor. **Piazza San Michele** has been the center of town since Roman times, and a climb to the top of the tower of the **Palazzo Guinigi** will give you an awesome view of the city and the mountains beyond.

GETTING AROUND   There's nothing of interest that you can't easily cover by foot. Lucca is not a hill town; in fact it's rather flat. This, plus the fact that it is quasi devoid of car traffic, makes it perfect for bike touring. You can rent one from outside the tourist office in Piazzale Verdi (April through October) at 4,000L ($2.35) per hour (☎ **0583/44293536**). Two rental shops open year-round for similar rates are **Barbetti Cicli,** V. Anfiteatro 23 (☎ **0583954444**), and **Poli Antonio Biciclette** in Pz. Santa Maria 42 (☎ **0583/493787**). Bikes are also a great way to experience the tree-lined promenade atop the Renaissance walls that encircle the city.

WHAT TO SEE & DO

The aerial photograph of Lucca's **Anfiteatro Romano** (located between Via Fillungo and Via Mordini) on local postcards is remarkable, showing the perfect elliptical shape of the ancient theater built here in the second century A.D.; the buildings from varying eras you see today were built on its ancient foundations, and many incorporated its arches into their walls. The most recent structures date to the 19th century when Napoléon's sister, Elisa, as city governor attempted to clean up the medieval jumble. The amphitheater, which once could seat 10,000, testifies to Lucca's early importance as a Roman city; the city's neat grid pattern of streets further reflects its origin as a Roman outpost.

You can succumb to the leisurely pace of this human-scale city, and stroll or bike the shady 4-kilometer (2.5-mi.) path atop its perfectly intact walls. Here you can enjoy a view of the city's architecture within the walls and the lovely countryside that unfolds without. These are the city's third set of walls, an enormous feat of engineering and considered the best-preserved of Renaissance defense ramparts in Europe. They were begun in the 16th century long after centuries of feuds and strife, apparently from the belief that good fences make good neighbors. They measure 115 feet at the base and 40 feet high with a double avenue of 19th-century trees lining their 60-foot width. The emerald-green lawns that stretch out beyond them were not planted until the last century. You can access the tree-lined promenade at any of the 11 bastions (there are six gates), such as behind the tourist office in **Piazzale Verdi** (which is where, during the summer, you can rent a bike; see "Getting Around," above).

A full circuit of the walls takes approximately one hour by foot and 20 minutes by bike.

✪ **Duomo (Cattedrale di San Martino).** Piazza San Martino. Admission to church free; sacristy 3,000L ($1.75). Summer Mon–Sat 9:30am–5:30pm, Sun 1–5:30pm. Winter Mon–Sat 9:30am–4:30, Sun 1–4:30pm.

Started in 1060 and completed 2 centuries later, the Duomo has a much admired asymmetrical facade (to accommodate the adjoining bell tower from a former building on this site) of three galleries of slender, unmatched twisting columns, and early 13th-century bas-reliefs that are some of the finest sculptures in the city. It is one of the finest examples of exuberant Pisan-Romanesque architecture for which this area of

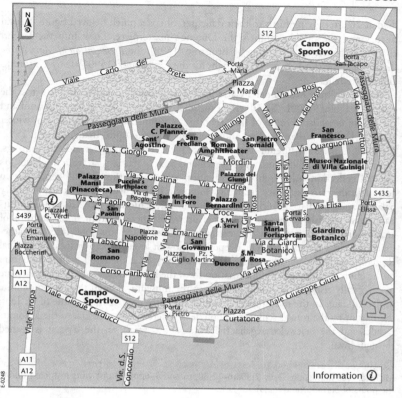

Tuscany is known (Pisa's Duomo is usually held as the supreme archetype). The main protagonist of the church's interior and Lucca's most precious relic is the robed figure of Jesus on the cross: The hauntingly beautiful wooden **Volto Santo** (the Holy Face) is enshrined in its own elaborate 15th-century **Tempietto** or marble chapel by Lucchese sculptor Matteo Civitali. The darkened crucifix is said to be carved by Nicodemus, a fervent follower of Christ who helped lower him from the cross, and is therefore believed to be a true image of Jesus (art historians attribute the work to 12th-century Eastern origin). Set adrift at sea, it was miraculously transported from the Holy Land across the Mediterranean and washed up on Tuscany's shores near La Spezia; the bishop of Lucca transported it here in 782. Local merchants spread the word throughout Europe and Lucca became famous for its portrait of Christ throughout the Middle Ages and became a point of pilgrimage for those on their way to Rome. Every September 13 and 14 the whole town turns out in a very special and evocative procession to carry the venerated statue dressed up in kingly jewel-encrusted robes through the streets illuminated by candlelight.

Competing for historical importance is the recently restored ✪ **Tomb of Ilaria del Carretto Guinigi,** now located in the former sacristy (admission fee) along with the superb *Madonna and Saints* altarpiece by Domenico Ghirlandaio (1494), the young Michelangelo's fresco master. Sculpted with her beloved dog at her feet (representing fidelity) by the Sienese master Jacopo della Quercia (1408) who breathed softness into the silklike folds of her dress, Ilaria was the young wife of a prominent lord of Lucca, in a politically arranged marriage that became a true union of love. She died at 26 after giving birth to their daughter. She is a much beloved figure in local history and the marble tomb is the Duomo's masterpiece. Look into the second chapel on the left for a painting by Bronzino (1598), the *Presentation of Mary at the Temple*, and the third chapel on the right for the *Last Supper* (1590–91) by Tintoretto and his students.

You can visit the **Museo della Cattedrale (Cathedral Museum),** directly across the street, on a joint 7,000L ($4.10) ticket together with the Chiesa di San Giovanni and the Duomo's sacristy (Tomb of Ilaria); hours are summer daily 10am to 6pm, winter Monday to Friday 10am to 2pm and weekends 10am to 6pm. Inaugurated in 1992, the small Cathedral Museum displays choice pieces of religious art such as paintings, silver chalices and reliquaries, and wooden and marble statuary, all from the Duomo's original collection. Although the restoration was severe, there is still much left to admire in the museum space created by joining a 13th-century tower, a 14th-century palazzo, and an adjacent 16th-century church. The **Chiesa di San Giovanni** and its baptistery, recently reopened after years of work where stratum upon stratum of archaeological foundations was unearthed, provides a one-stop look into the cathedral's and city's distant past. The deepest and lowest level you can visit is the original Roman foundation that dates from the 1st century B.C., the latest is the foundation of the church's most recent reincarnation from the late Middle Ages. Future plans are to eventually relocate the Tomb of Ilaria to the museum, though there is no definite projected date. In the meantime, don't miss the early 15th-century statue of St. John the Baptist by the tomb's sculptor Jacopo della Quercia that once graced the Duomo's facade, and the bejeweled regalia the Volto Santo wears on the days it is carried through town.

✪ **Chiesa di San Michele in Foro (Church of St. Michael in the Forum).** Pz. di San Michele. Free admission. Daily 7:30am–12:30pm and 3–6pm (tourist visits restricted during the hours of Sun morning mass).

San Michele is considered the social and geographic, if not the religious, center of town, built on the original site of the ancient Roman Forum and hence its name. Understandably mistaken by visitors as the Duomo, it is one of the dozens of churches that populate this small city, and is second only to the Duomo in importance. Begun in 1143, it is dedicated to the huge winged archangel Michael who crowns its remarkable facade (flanked by two angels), and is a wonderful example of the elaborate Pisan-Lucchese architecture influenced by the cathedral in nearby Pisa. The exquisite Romanesque facade begins with ground-level arches, above which four tiers of twisted, patterned columns of every variety, size, and thickness are displayed; the ornate facade soars considerably higher than the church itself. A number of national patriots were added during a heavy 19th-century restoration, such as Cavour and Garibaldi. The impressive campanile is the city's highest. Things are decidedly less exuberant inside since money ran out after completion of the facade's extravaganza, but there is a beautifully framed painting of several saints by Filippino Lippi, student of Botticelli; among the most important of his works, it can be found on the far wall in the right transept. A glazed terra-cotta bas-relief by Andrea della Robbia (some say it was his uncle Luca) is inset on the first altar on the right. Take a minute to stroll past the buildings that line the piazza; some of them date back to the 13th century, while others are as recent as the 15th and 16th centuries. Giacomo Puccini was born in 1858 just a block from here on V. di Poggio 30. Both his father and his grandfather were organists here, and young Giacomo sang in the choir.

San Frediano. Piazza San Frediano. Free admission. Mon–Sat 7:30am–noon and 3–6pm, Sun 3–6pm.

A restored, colorful 13th-century **Christ in Majesty** fresco on the stark white facade of San Frediano sets it apart from the city's countless other churches, one reason it figures on the short list (together with the Duomo and San Michele) of Lucca's most visited. Also typical of the local Pisan-Lucchese style, but minus the open loggias full of ornate columns, it is dedicated to the 6th-century Irish Bishop St. Frigidian who is said to have brought Christianity to Lucca (the first town in Tuscany to embrace it) and is buried under its high altar. Upon entering, you'll happen upon one of the church's highlights, a huge, elaborately carved 13th-century baptismal font. Beyond the font and high on the wall is the glazed terra-cotta *Annunciation* by Andrea della Robbia. Behind the font is the chapel of St. Zita, the patron saint of domestics and ladies-in-waiting. Her feast day is April 26, when the Piazza San Frediano is carpeted with flowers and her lace-enwrapped body is carried out to be glorified by the local residents.

If you have visited the Duomo (see above), you will have seen the Tomb of Ilaria Caretto by the master Sienese sculptor Jacopo della Quercia, whose marble reliefs on an altar and a pair of tombstones (1422) can be found here in the Capella Trenta, the fourth chapel on the left. Nearby, in the second chapel you can find the 16th-century *Arrival of the Volto Santo* by Amico Aspertini, Lucca's finest frescoes (the yearly procession of the holy relic begins at the Duomo and ends here). His recently restored frescoes about the life of San Frediano can also be found here.

As you leave the church, head around the left side of the church to Via Battisti to the 17th-century **Palazzo Pfanner** whose sumptuous walled gardens were used as location shots for the 1996 film *Portrait of a Lady*. If you tool around the city's ramparts you can look down into the gardens, as the palazzo has been closed to the public for a number of years.

Pinacoteca Nazionale e Museo di Palazzo Mansi (National Picture Gallery). V. Galli Tassi 43. ☎ **0593/55-570.** Admission 8,000L ($4.70). Tues–Sat 9am–7pm; Sun 9am–2pm. (From Pz. San Michele, head down V. San Paolino, and take a right on V. Galli Tassi.)

This small-scale museum is both impressive and appropriate for a city of this size and historical background. This was the town dwelling of the Mansi, a wealthy local family that still lives in the family country villa outside of town. The 16th to 19th century palazzo is now used as a picture gallery for works by Guido Reni, Bronzino, Pontormo, and others, though not their most important. Don't leave without seeing the *Camera degli Sposi* (Bridal Chamber), an elaborate 17th-century Versailles-like alcove of decorative gold leaf, putti, and columns, where trembling Mansi brides awaited their conjugal duties amidst the sumptuous Luccan silks and heavy brocades.

WHERE TO STAY

The hotel situation in Lucca continues to be disheartening. Most of the one- and two-star hotels are in the newer, less interesting section of town outside the walls. In high season, be sure to make a hotel reservation in advance, or you may have to stay in Florence, nearby Pisa, or (if you have a car) one of the seaside resorts. If there is no vacancy within the walls, don't think twice about staying in the charming B&B operated by the Favilla family at their **Villa Romantica,** a tree-shaded Liberty villa with six comfortable doubles with private facilities; it's a 5-minute walk to the walls, 10 minutes into the center of town. It's at 246 Via N. Barbantini (☎ **0583/496872;** fax 0583/957600; www.lunet.it/aziende/vromantica; e-mail: villaromantica@lunet.it). Rates are 120,000L ($70.60) for a single, 150,000L ($88.25) for a double. Breakfast is not included. All credit cards are accepted.

Hotel Diana. V. d. Molinetto 11 (just off the Piazza Duomo), 55100 Lucca. ☎ **0583/ 49-22-02.** Fax 0583/467795. www.onenet.it/LU/Diana. E-mail: aldiana@tin.it. 9 units, 7 with bathroom. TV TEL. 50,000L ($29.40) single without bathroom; 80,000L ($47.05) double without bathroom, 98,000L ($57.65) double with bathroom; 133,000L ($78.25) triple with bathroom. Breakfast 5,000L ($2.95) served in guest rooms. AE, MC, V.

This is one of the nicest of the town's two-star hotels and, at just one block west of the Duomo, it has the best location. A 17th-century palazzo houses contemporary rooms with appreciated amenities such as telephones, color TV, hair dryers, and cool marble floors. Quiet rooms overlook a next-door neighbor's garden. There is no breakfast rooms so breakfast is served in your room. An annex around the corner was scheduled to be completed by the 1999 summer season, offering six new rooms with private bathroom and similar amenities, plus air-conditioning and CNN; two of them will be handicap accessible. Ask for the *dipendenza* when booking if these new rooms are your preference. Prices are expected to be slightly higher, at approximately 110,000L ($64.70) per double with bathroom.

Hotel La Luna. V. Fillungo (in Cor. Compagni) 12, 55100 Lucca. ☎ **0583/49-36-34.** Fax 0583/49-00-21. 30 units, all with bathroom. A/C TV TEL. 100,000L ($58.80) single; 140,000L ($82.35) double; 200,000L ($117.65) suite. Breakfast buffet 15,000L ($8.80). AE, DC, MC, V. Limited parking (reserve in advance; 20,000L/$11.75 a day). Closed Jan 6–31.

Set off in a small courtyard a block from the amphitheater (and near the Church of San Frediano) and quietly functioning as a hotel for more than 2 centuries, this efficient choice may have a little less charm than the small Piccolo Puccini but offers better availability during the high season. Rooms are well thought out and decorated in a fresh and contemporary vein—although those who splurge on the suites (sleeping two to four people) will find more spacious and characteristic quarters with turn-of-the-century ceiling frescoes, original fireplaces, and large sitting areas. Late risers with big appetites can tuck into the well-supplied breakfast buffet table and later skip lunch without feeling it—though that would be a shame given Lucca's choice of eating establishments. A convenient alternative to the pricey breakfast is the lobby bar, where a coffee and croissant keep costs more contained.

Hotel Universo. Pz. d. Giglio 1, 55100 Lucca. ☎ **0583/49-36-78.** Fax 0583/95-48-54. www.lunet.it/aziende/hoteluniverso. E-mail: hotel.universo@telcen.lunet.it. 72 units, all with bathroom. MINIBAR TV TEL. 120,000–195,000L ($70.60–$115.70) single; 160,000–220,000L ($94.10–$129.40) double; 185,000–260,000L ($108.80–$152.95). Continental breakfast 12,000L ($7.05). MC, V. Nearby parking 7,000L ($4.10).

This hotel-with-an-attitude aspires to be the grandest of Lucca's limited hotel roster; a gradual ongoing renovation of all guest rooms is resuscitating some to their former 19th-century charm. Ask for any of the refurbished rooms that overlook the small Piazza del Giglio and its Teatro Comunale, the town's opera house (others overlook the Piazza Napoleone, an impressive name for the local parking facility). They vary greatly in decor from contemporary to period, with chintz or damask bedspreads and the occasional added treats of molded ceilings, antiques, and hand-painted tiles in the bathrooms. Some rooms are air-conditioned (specify when booking). If you've biked around town and are too tired to make it to Giulio's, check out the hotel's well-known restaurant: a fixed-price menu offers five first courses and as many entrees to choose from for 30,000L ($17.65); closed Thursday.

○ **Piccolo Hotel Puccini.** V. di Poggio 9, 55100 Lucca. ☎ **0583/55-421.** Fax 0583/ 53-487. www.onenet.it/lu/hotel_Puccini. E-mail: hotelpuccinilu@onenet.it. 14 units, all with bathroom. TV TEL. 90,000L ($52.95) single; 125,000L ($73.50) double. Ask about off-season discounts. Breakfast 8,000L ($4.70). AE, DC, DISC, MC, V. Nearby parking 7,000L ($4.10) daily.

This charming three-star hotel is in a 15th-century palazzo that sits just in front of the building where Puccini was born. Some of the hotel rooms overlook the small piazza and its bronze statue of Puccini that borders the far side. Paolo and Raffaella, the young and enthusiastic couple that has recently taken over the management, have brightened up the place with a new marble-tiled lobby, flower arrangements in the public areas, and an extremely helpful and friendly attitude. A perfect choice for those who appreciate tasteful attention and discrete professionalism. Breakfast is optional, so head for any of the cafes in the Piazza San Michele, one of Lucca's loveliest squares, two steps away. Book early to make sure you find room at this inn: Word is out.

WHERE TO DINE

Da Guido. V. Battisti 28 (at V. degli Angeli near Pz. Sant'Agostino), Lucca. ☎ **0583/47219.** Reservations not necessary. Primi 5,000–7,000L ($2.95–$4.10); secondi 9,000L ($5.30). 3-course menù turistico 19,000L ($11.20). AE. Mon–Sat noon–2:30pm and 7:30–10pm. TUSCAN.

The amiable proprietor Guido welcomes local cronies and hungry out-of-towners with the same warm smile and filling meals that keep 'em all happy. The bar in the front and the TV locked into the sports channel create a laid-back atmosphere that will make you want to linger; the fresh tortellini made on the premises and the simplicity of roast rabbit (coniglio) or veal (vitello) will wipe out any conflicting inclinations to do otherwise. This is a cut below the price and quality level of Giulio's (see below), but you're guaranteed a good home-cooked meal here in a no-frills, family run trattoria.

Da Leo. V. Tegrimi 1 (off Pz. San Michele), Lucca. ☎ **0583/49-22-36.** Reservations suggested for dinner. Primi 9,000L ($5.30); secondi 12,000–15,000L ($7.05–$8.80). No credit cards. Mon–Sat noon–2:30pm and 7:30–10:30pm; open for lunch the 3rd Sun of every month for Antique Fair as well as Sun lunch in Aug and Dec. TUSCAN.

There's usually an English menu floating around somewhere—the good-natured waiters are used to dealing with foreigners who have discovered one of the best and most authentic *lucchese* eating spots in town, run by the amiable Buralli family. This is not as much a bare-bones tavern as Guido's, but not quite as polished an operation as the well-regarded Giulio's, but as beloved by a devoted local following nonetheless. Its location, two steps from the central Piazza San Michele, draws strolling tourists who happen by, lured into the cozy peach-colored rooms by the aroma of roasting meats and the scent of rosemary. The ubiquitous *farro* soup made from elmer (a kind of barley) followed by the simple but delicious *pollo fritto con patate arroste* (perfectly fried chicken with roast potatoes) with the good house wine is my stock order. My friend from Lucca told me that if he won the lottery, this is where he would eat every day.

✪ **Da Giulio.** V. d. Conce 45 (north of the Porta San Donato), Lucca. ☎ and fax **0583/55-948.** Reservations highly recommended. Primi 10,000L ($5.90); secondi 12,500–15,000L ($7.35–$8.80). AE, DC, MC, V. Tues–Sat 12:30–2:30pm and 7–11pm, open for lunch the third Sun of each month for Antique Fair. Closed 2 weeks in Aug. TUSCAN/LUCCHESE.

Delighted foreigners and locals of uncompromising allegiance agree that this big, airy, and forever busy trattoria is one of Tuscany's undisputed stars. Although casual, this is not the place to occupy a much-coveted table for just a pasta and salad. Save up your appetite and come for a full-blown home-style Tuscan feast, trying all of Giulio's traditional rustic specialties. Begin with the thick *farro* soup made with a local barleylike grain or the fresh *maccheroni tortellati* pasta stuffed with fresh ricotta and spinach, both made to perfection. Meats, stewed for hours, are delicious. Perfect also are the grilled and roast meats such as an *arrosti misti* of beef and turkey or *pollo al mattone,* chicken breast flattened and roasted under the weight of heated bricks. Waiters know not to recommend certain local favorites to non-Italian diners, unless you look like the tripe, *tartara di cavallo* (horse meat tartare) or veal snout type. Fixed-price menus come and go at approximately 30,000L ($17.65).

SIDE TRIPS FROM LUCCA

Surrounding Lucca is the fertile **Lucchesia** corner of Tuscany, one of Italy's richest agricultural areas renowned worldwide for its deep green virgin olive oil and other produce. The remote hills and valleys of the Serchio River directly north of Lucca make up the **Garfagnana** area, providing a heavily wooded area, mountain towns locked in time warps, and lovely hiking trails. If you don't have your own car, the area is serviced by daily CLAP buses (see "Getting Here," above). The tourist office in Lucca has information in English and maps of suggested itineraries and hikes. The Garfagnana's most important town, **Bagni di Lucca,** famous in the 19th century as a spa resort, has a tourist office at Vle. Umberto I no. 139 (☎ **0583/805508;** fax 0583/807877). To get here, take the main **SS12 road north** as it diverges east up the Lima Valley.

A number of villas of historical importance are within biking distance of Lucca's historical center, notably the **Villa Reale** (once home to Napoleon's sister Elisa Baciocchi) in Marlia and the **Villa Torrigiani** in Camigliano (visit the tourist board for a map and a listing of occasional summertime concerts that take place in their gardens). Lucca is also convenient to **Pisa,** where you can spend half a day seeing the famous tower and its Duomo and baptistery (see Pisa p. 264 for details). On the Tuscan coastline to the northwest in the direction of Liguria and the Italian Riviera (follow green autostrada signs that say DIREZIONE MARE on the A11/12 northwest) lie the seaside resort towns of **Viareggio** (25 kilometers/15.8 mi.) and the tonier, less developed and more picturesque **Forte dei Marmi** (34 kilometers/21.4 mi.) beyond. In the summer season, CLAP and LAZZI buses leave frequently from Lucca's Piazzale Verdi bus station (see "Getting Here," above). Avoid the coastal towns in the dismal winter months when little remains open except, to some degree, on weekends. Inland from Forte dei Marmi, in the direction of the Appenine mountains that still supply untold cemeteries and Arabian palaces, are the celebrated marble quarries of **Carrara**—already famous for centuries when frequented by the master sculptor Michelangelo from nearby Florence—and the artist- and sculptor-magnet destination of **Pietrasanta.** Both are most easily visited by those with cars, for a pleasant afternoon of peeking into shops, galleries, and workshops: Some of the marble world's principal artwork is still created here and a small international artist community works and vacations here during summer months.

3 San Gimignano

57 km (35 mi.) SW of Florence, 65 km (40 mi.) SE of Lucca, 90 km (56.7 mi.) SE of Pisa, 42 km (26 mi.) NW of Siena, 100 km (62 mi.) SE of Lucca

San Gimignano has arrested the traveler's imagination as the quintessential Tuscan hill town for centuries. Its stunning skyline bristles with medieval towers (there remain 14 of an estimated 70) whose construction dates from the 12th and 13th centuries when they were built as much for defense purposes as for the prestige of outdoing the neighbors. Located on the ancient Francigena road that transported medieval trade and pilgrims from northern Europe to Rome (imagine the impressive sight it was to those approaching from afar, with its 70-some-odd towers still intact, heralding the town's prominence), San Gimignano was considered quite the wealthy agricultural town in its 14th-century heyday and could therefore afford handsome palazzi and impressively frescoed churches. It has held on to its rugged, rustic good looks, and tourist authorities fancy its sobriquet of "the Medieval Manhattan" and much is written about its distinctive profile and its towers being the archetypes for today's skyscrapers (some of the remaining towers are over 150 feet high). Considered by many to be the poster child for Italian hill towns everywhere, it boasts the perfect combination of a rural small-town atmosphere, stunning views, a crop of great eating establishments, and enough history and museums to occupy the curious and impressive the discerning.

SPECIAL EVENTS & MARKETS   San Gimignano has two patron saints, San Gimignano himself (a 4th-century bishop from Modena), whose feast day is celebrated **January 31,** and Santa Fina (who died in 1253 at the age of 15), whose feast day is on **March 12.** Both are celebrated with a High Mass in the Duomo and an all-day outdoor fair in the main square. San Gimignano also boasts one of Tuscany's more animated *carnevali* held each of the four Sundays before Ash Wednesday. The third weekend of June is the **Fiera delle Messi,** when the town effortlessly resuscitates its medieval character during a weekend of outdoor markets, musical and theatrical events, and a jousting tournament of knights on horseback, all in medieval costume. Since 1924, mid-June throughout August has been dedicated to dance and music performances for the **Estate Sangimignese** festival, when you can look for art exhibits, outdoor classical concerts, alfresco opera, or ballet in the Piazza della Cisterna. See the tourist office for a schedule. Santa Fina shows up again for the first Sunday of August's **Festa di Ringraziamento;** the next day (Monday) a small fair takes place in the main square. The only market in town worth a look-see is the bustling biweekly produce market in the Piazza Duomo Thursday and Saturday mornings.

ESSENTIALS

GETTING HERE   By Train   There is no train station in San Gimignano; the nearest is in Poggibonsi, where you'll need to connect to bus service (20 min.). If you're traveling from Florence, bus service is more convenient, although not direct (with the obligatory change in Poggibonsi).

By Bus   All SITA or TRA.IN buses (☎ **0577/20-41-11**) that run between San Gimignano and both Florence (to the north) or Siena (to the south) change in the small Poggibonsi bus station. One-way bus fare from Florence to San Gimignano is 10,000L ($5.90); from Siena to San Gimignano is 8,600L ($5.40). The trip from Florence to Poggibonsi takes about an hour, from Siena to Poggibonsi about 45 minutes. Count on a layover in Poggibonsi of anywhere from 10 minutes to an hour (usually the former, but check at the bus station before deciding which bus to take) before you can catch a connection for the remaining 10- to 20-minute ride to San Gimignano. There are no direct buses from Pisa to either Poggibonsi or San Gimignano; you'll have to take a train from Pisa to Empoli and catch a connecting bus to San Gimignano.

The bus station for San Gimignano is nothing more than a covered stop with a posted schedule immediately outside the city walls, southwest of the Porta San Giovanni on the Piazza Montemaggio (you can also get a bus schedule and buy tickets from the tourist office in town).

By Car   If you're coming from Lucca, it's a 1½-hour drive (110 kilometers/68 mi.). It's most direct to backtrack to Florence on the **A11** autostrada, then head south on the Superstrada del Palio Firenze-Siena. Exit at Poggibonsi and follow signs west for S324 to San Gimignano. A slightly longer alternative bypassing Florence and avoiding the superhighways is to leave Lucca on the autostrada southwest for Pisa Aeroporto. Head east, in the direction of Ponte a Elsa, where you turn south for Certaldo. From here follow the signs to San Gimignano. These directions are similar for those coming from Pisa.

San Gimignano is entirely closed to traffic within the walls (except to drop off luggage at your hotel), so you'll need to park in any one of a number of small parking areas along the road that follows the outer rim of the walls.

VISITOR INFORMATION   Associazione Pro Loco is the local name for the **tourist office,** located in Pz. Duomo 1 (☎ **0577/940008;** fax 0577/940903; www. sangimignano.com; e-mail: prolocsg@tin.it). Summer hours are 9am to 1pm and 3 to 7pm (daily). Winter hours (November 1 through February 28) are 9am to 1pm and 2 to 6pm (daily). The office also acts as a currency exchange (*cambio*) and will help with hotel accommodations and restaurant recommendations.

CITY LAYOUT   The principal entrance points from outside the walls are **Porta San Matteo** in the northwest, and the more popular **Porta di San Giovanni** in the south, where most bus routes begin and end. Anchored by a 13th-century well, the central **Piazza della Cisterna** is lined with herringbone bricks and interlocks with the more austere Piazza Duomo just north of it. All roads radiate out from these squares, the most important being the store-lined **Via San Giovanni** to the south and the slightly less commercial **Via San Matteo** north of Piazza della Cisterna. The **Via del Castello** runs east out of the piazza. Any of the cobblestoned back streets offer the chance to escape the San Gimignano package-tour crush. You can walk across town in 15 minutes or take the whole day. The entire town is encircled by its medieval ramparts, beyond which a smattering of newer construction has taken place.

GETTING AROUND   The town's position atop one of the valley's many hills means gentle inclines in the streets leading to and from the main square. You'll have to get around by foot, as traffic is rigidly restricted within the walls, and public transportation does not exist.

WHAT TO SEE & DO

The *biglietto comulativo* (joint ticket) is no great deal at 16,000L ($9.40) and only offers savings to those with the time and inclination to see all the museums included: Museo Civico, Torre Grossa, Museo d'Arte Sacra/Museo Etrusco, Capella di Santa Finta (in the Duomo). It does not include the privately owned Museum of Medieval Criminology. At press time, the tourist office is reassessing the involvement of the different museums and whether the joint ticket should be continued for the 1999 season. It is probable that the Duomo will be requesting an admission fee for 1999, though the amount hasn't yet been determined and will probably be a joint fee for the Duomo and the Chapel of Santa Fina. Check at the tourist office for the 1999 update.

If it has reopened for the summer of 1999 as expected, spend a few minutes in the small **Museo d'Arte Sacra, Museo Etrusco** to the left of the Duomo (enter from the Piazza Pecori and arch to the left of the Duomo's entrance) for its medieval tombstones, wooden sculptures, and Etruscan artifacts that prove that the city's roots run deeper than the Middle Ages. It is expected to keep the same hours as the Museo Civico. Admission is 7,000L ($4.60).

✪ **Duomo (also called the Collegiata).** Pz. d. Duomo. Free admission to Duomo, but fee expected in the near future. Admission to the Cappella di Santa Fina 6,000L ($3.50). Apr–Oct Mon–Fri 9:30am–7:30pm, Sat 9:30am–5pm, Sun 1–5pm; Nov–Mar Mon–Sat 9:30am–5pm, Sun 1–5pm.

Because there is no longer a bishop of San Gimignano, the Duomo (cathedral) has been demoted to a Collegiata (though forever a "Duomo" in the locals' eyes) and is a prime example of not judging a 12th-century church by its facade. Never finished on the outside, its interior is heavily frescoed with scenes from the Bible, testimony to the city's prosperity in centuries past and one of Tuscany's, perhaps Italy's, most lavishly decorated churches. On the north wall are three levels comprised of 26 scenes from the Old Testament; on the south wall, scenes from the life of Christ and on the back wall are scenes from the Last Judgment, attributed to Lippo Memmi—brilliant colors set off by the typical arches of black and white striped marble of Pisan-Romanesque architecture. The tiny ✪ **Cappella di Santa Fina** in the southwest corner of the Duomo can't be missed for the important frescoes by Florentine Renaissance master Domenico Ghirlandaio (1475) recounting the life of a young local girl named Fina born in San Gimignano in 1238. The towers of San Gimignano appear in the background of the scene depicting her funeral. St. Fina spent most of her 15 short years in prayer and is the patron saint (although never officially canonized, but don't bring this up with any of the locals), together with San Gimignano, of the town. Make sure you find another of Ghirlandaio's superb works, ✪ *The Annunciation* (1482); it graces a loggiaed courtyard adjacent to the Baptistery.

Museo Civico (Civic Museum) and the ✪ **Torre Grossa (tower).** Palazzo del Popolo, Pz. d. Duomo 1. ☎ **0577/94-03-40.** Admission: Museo 7,000L ($4.10), tower 8,000L ($4.70); joint ticket 12,000L ($7.05). Mar 1–Oct 31 daily 9:30am–7:30pm; Nov 1–Feb 28 9:30am–1pm and 2:30–5pm.

Labor to the top of the Palazzo's 117-foot Torre Grossa (The Big Tower, 1311), the highest of San Gimignano's towers, and the only one in town you can climb. You'll feel like you're on top of a flagpole with heart-stopping views of the town, its towers, and the sweep of the Val d'Elsa beyond. It might just be the best tower-top view of its kind in Tuscany—and that says something. Once you've gotten that out of your system, backtrack to see some of the museum's collection, housed in the perfectly preserved 14th-century Palazzo del Popolo or Comune (town hall).

The first public room, the **Sala di Dante** is frescoed with hunting scenes and is the spot where the poet Dante, as ambassador from pro-pope (Guelph) Florence, came to pro-emperor (Ghibelline) San Gimignano in the year 1300 to plead for unity. Here you'll find the museum's—and the town's—masterpiece, the *Maestà (Enthroned Madonna)* by Sienese painter Lippo Mimmi (1317). The **pinacoteca** (picture gallery) on the second floor is composed mostly of 12th- to 15th-century paintings from the Sienese school, with highlights by Bennozzo Gozzoli, Pinturicchio, Filippino Lippi, and a late 14th-century painting of the 4th-century bishop, San Gimignano, himself, holding the town in his lap, by Taddeo di Bartolo. San Gimignano shouldn't have a problem recognizing the town today.

Museo di Criminologia Medioevale (Museum of Medieval Criminology). V. d. Castello 1. ☎ **0577/94-22-43.** Admission 15,000L ($8.80). Summer hours (daily) 10am–8pm. Winter hours Mon–Sat 10am–5:30pm, Sun 10am–7pm.

Is it karmic happenstance or a quirk of history that this peculiar museum of medieval torture is housed in the 13th-century Palazzo del Diavolo (The Devil's Palace)? Inarguably one of Tuscany's more unusual attractions, this surprisingly expansive chamber of horrors contains over 100 instruments of torture. Most of them are original pieces, and all of them are thoughtfully and impressively displayed and explained in both Italian and English. This is good, because items such as knuckle- and skull-crushers, and iron gags to stifle screams are not always immediately recognizable to the innocent. It's worth the admission just to see the cast-iron chastity belts. As unsettling as some of the original prints depicting the atrocities of the 15th-century Inquisition are many of the item descriptions, such as that accompanying the *garrote*—a punishment used in Spain until 1975 and still used in South America today.

Church of Sant'Agostino. Pz. Sant'Agostino. Free admission. Summer daily 7am–noon and 3–7pm; winter 7am–noon and 3–6pm.

If you're not all frescoed out after a visit to the Duomo, visit the large 13th-century church of Sant'Agostino in the north end of town by following the flagstone Via San

Guided Walks in God's Country

For those blessed with the opportunity of spending more than a rushed afternoon in San Gimignano, stop by the tourist office to inquire about guided excursions into the countryside. Gentle walks through the nearby hills include visits to an Etruscan necropolis, abandoned medieval castles, churches dating from the 1100s, and even a tipple or two at wine-producing estates. Bilingual guides take small groups for half-day (10,000L/$5.90) or full-day (20,000L/$11.75) excursions that technically must be booked a minimum of two days in advance, though last-minute queries are not encouraged but accommodated where possible. Call the **tourist office** at ☎ **0577/94-00-08** (fax 0577/94-09-03). For self-guided tours, pass by the office in Piazza Duomo to pick up a map of designated walking paths in the area.

Matteo through one of the town's less commercial corners. The church's simple Romanesque exterior contrasts with its rococo interior completed in the mid-1700s. The interior's highlight is the cycle of frescoes covering the choir behind the main altar and showing seventeen scenes from ✪ **The Life of St. Augustine** by Benozzo Gozzoli, a 15th-century Florentine painter. Hired after yet another plague passed through town in 1464, Gozzoli was commissioned to cover the walls floor to ceiling.

WHERE TO STAY

Ask the tourist office for a list of bed-and-breakfast or farm accommodations in the immediate countryside. They will provide a listing, but no description other than the price, and telephone contact. You can also seek out the **Ostello della Gioventù** (Youth Hostel) at V. d. Fonti 1, 53037 San Gimignano (☎ **0577/94-19-91;** fax 055/80-50-104; e-mail: franchostel@ftbcc.it), which has 75 beds in 9 rooms costing 21,000 to 25,000L ($12.35 to $14.70) per person. Breakfast is included.

Hotel Bel Soggiorno. V. San Giovanni 91, 53037 San Gimignano. ☎ **0577/94-03-75.** Fax 0577/943149. www.web.tin.it/san.gimignano. E-mail: pescille@iol.it. A/C TV TEL. 21 units, all with bathroom. 135,000L ($79.40) single; 160,000L ($94.10) double; 200,000L ($117.65) triple. Breakfast 15,000L ($8.80). AE, DC, MC, V. Often closed a few weeks in Jan or Feb. Nearby parking 20,000L ($11.75).

Located close to the San Giovanni city gate, and a gentle 5-minute walk uphill toward the main square, this well-known hostelry gets two thumbs up—one for the simply decorated rooms with large patios that command awesome views of the rolling hills of Tuscany's Val d'Elsa (add 15,000L/$8.80 to a double rate for the view), and one for the acclaimed restaurant, Bel Soggiorno, with-a-view downstairs (see "Where to Dine," below) where guests are encouraged though not obliged to have their meals (no great hardship here!). Half of the hotel's rooms are blessed with the priceless view, but only three share the large terra-cotta patio. If you have access to wheels and long for a more rural environment, ask at the desk about their country property, the **Hotel Le Pescille,** a nearby converted farmhouse/hotel with 50 rooms, boasting a lovely setting 2.5 miles out of town, with pool, tennis, and very reasonable rates comparable to those quoted above (☎ **0577/943165;** fax 0577/94-01-86; e-mail: pescille@iol.it). Open mid-March through October.

✪ **Hotel La Cisterna.** Pz. d. Cisterna 23, 53037 San Gimignano. ☎ **0577/94-03-28.** Fax 0577/94-20-80. www.web.tin.it/san_gimignano/alberghi/htm. E-mail: lacisterna@iol.it. TV TEL. 50 units, all with bathroom. 95,000–118,000L ($55.90–$69.40) single; 140,000–195,000L ($82.35–$114.70) double; 190,000–220,000L ($111.75–$129.40) suite. Rates include buffet breakfast. AE, DC, MC, V. Closed Jan 10–Mar 10 (dates vary). Nearby parking 20,000L ($11.75).

This is the town's nicest hotel in this price category. It's housed in one of the imposing palazzi flanking the central Piazza della Cisterna and run by the Salvestrini family since 1919. Like the Bel Soggiorno, the hotel includes one of San Gimignano's better restaurants, Le Terrazze (open Monday, Tuesday, and Friday to Sunday for lunch and dinner; Wednesday for dinner only), which keeps the public areas busy during lunch hours. But repair upstairs to the serenity of your large room, many of which have balconies whose views are spellbinding. If Tuscany's hill towns are lovely to view from a distance, they are even more wonderful for the vantage points they offer and panoramas from windows such as these. If you saw the film *Where Angels Fear to Tread* (1991) with Helen Mirren and Helena Bonham-Carter, you'll recognize that some parts were filmed in this hotel. Here's the rub: Some rooms are small, some with no view at all, making them appear even smaller still.

Hotel Leon Bianco. Pz. d. Cisterna 8, 53037 San Gimignano. ☎ **0577/94-12-94.** Fax 0577/94-21-23. E-mail: leonbianco@see.it. A/C TV TEL. 20 units, all with bath. 104,000L ($61.20) single; 185,000–205,000L ($108.80–$120.60) double; 245,000L ($144.10) triple. Rates include buffet breakfast. AE, CB, DC, MC, V. Usually closed Nov 15–Dec 12 and Jan 15–Feb 15; dates vary. Parking next door 20,000L ($11.75).

Located directly across the main piazza from La Cisterna, this smaller hotel is housed in a beautifully restored medieval palazzo. The central part of the hotel is housed in a 12th-century patrician home that was eventually expanded in the next century with the addition of a medieval tower on either side, parts of which are incorporated into the hotel. Modernized rooms are historically offset with exposed brick walls, vaulted ceilings, archways, and terra-cotta floors and are priced according to size and view: Five overlook the main piazza, nine have views of the countryside, and all others overlook an enclosed courtyard. The brick courtyard is the lovely setting for breakfast from May through September and there's a sunny roof terrace for postcard writing. There's no restaurant on the premises, but stroll across the lovely piazza to La Cisterna's restaurant Le Terrazze or to the Bel Soggiorno down the street.

WINING & DINING IN CHIANTI'S BACKYARD

A stroll up **Via San Giovanni** will impress you with the number of wine shops whose windows are stocked floor-to-ceiling with the fruits of the surrounding Chianti vineyards. The gently rolling hills of Tuscany supply Italy's finest red wines, while San Gimignano itself is well known for its celebrated *vernaccia,* a distinctive white wine unique to this corner of Italy old enough to have been mentioned in Dante's **Divine Comedy.** The curious and the *appassionati* should make a beeline for **Da Gustavo,** a small, old-time wine bar run by the Becucci family since 1946 (☎ **0577/94-00-57;** V. San Matteo 29; summer daily 8am to midnight; winter Saturday to Thursday 8am to 8pm). You can orchestrate an informal wine tasting from over 20 types of Tuscan and Italian white and red wines by the glass (generally 3,000 to 5,000L/$1.75 to $2.95 per glass). There's no place to sit, but there are fresh, delicious panini sandwiches made to order; you can choose from a delicious selection of the region's top-quality cheeses and salamis. Take your picnic and head west of here (behind the Duomo) to the **Rocca,** the remains of the 14th-century fortress atop the ramparts, now a public park with wonderful views.

A more expensive alternative with a view is the lovely, sit-down **Bar Enoteca il Castello** (☎ **0577/94-08-78),** V. d. Castello 20; open Thursday to Tuesday 9am to 11:30pm, where you can stop by for a glass of wine (from 3,500L/$2.05), perhaps a simple plate of crusty bread and Tuscan salami and cheese, and a memorable view of the hills in the soft, late afternoon light. Full or light meals with fixed-price tourist menus cost about 30,000L ($17.65).

Le Vecchie Mura. V. Piandornella 15 (1st right off V. San Giovanni coming from Porta San Giovanni). ☎ **0577/94-02-70.** Reservations recommended. Primi 10,000L ($5.90); secondi 12,000–20,000L ($7.05–$11.75). AE, DC, MC, V. Wed–Mon 12:30–2:30pm and 6–10pm. Closed mid-Dec–mid-Jan. TUSCAN.

The first thing you must do is see if either of the two comfortable bedrooms with bathrooms upstairs are available (70,000L/$41.20 for a double). If not, console yourself with a marvelous meal downstairs in the cool, brick-vaulted trattoria in what once served as a patrician family's stables in the 1700s. The thick *ribollita* cabbage-based soup and homemade *tagliatelle al cinghiale* (pasta with wild-boar sauce) are deservedly the house specialties. The regional specialty of wild boar shows up again a favorite entree, marinated in the local Vernaccia white wine then grilled. Scheduled to be ready in 1999 is a small alfresco terrace directly across the narrow graveled road, whose gorgeous views out over the ancient city walls and valley beyond may make concentrating on your meal difficult.

✪ **Ristorante Bel Soggiorno.** Via San Giovanni 41 (near Porta San Giovanni). ☎ **0577/ 94-31-49.** Reservations recommended. Antipasti and primi 10,000–15,000L ($5.90–$8.80); secondi 18,000–25,000L ($10.60–$14.70); menù turistico, minimum 40,000L ($23.50). AE, DC, MC, V. Thurs–Tues 12:30–2:30pm and 7:30–10pm. TUSCAN.

This rustic and spacious restaurant boasts a menu that shares the spotlight with the area's glorious countryside framed by oversized windows. Tuscan bigwigs who work in the area's wine industry entertain their important buyers here, assured of the *bella figura* they'll make with a meal that is both casual but of the utmost Tuscan quality, showcasing the area's gastronomic bounty. Many of the kitchen's limited-production ingredients are from the owners' private estate: olive oil, honey, grappa, and wines labeled AZIENDA AGRICOLA PESCILLE. Thick-crusted bread and wide *pappardelle* noodles are made fresh daily—if it's autumn, look for the latter traditionally prepared with a tomato sauce flavored with either hare (*alla lepre*) or wild boar (*al cinghiale*). The specialty of meats simply prepared on the grill is ultra-Tuscan; ultradelicious is the homemade *crostata di ficchi* dessert, a delicate fig tart that proves you can measure happiness by the slice. Want to stay forever? You can stay at the family's country inn or in their guest rooms just upstairs; see "Where to Stay," above.

Trattoria Chiribiri. Pz. d. Madonna (off V. San Giovanni near Porta San Giovanni). ☎ **0577/94-19-48.** Reservations not accepted. Primi 10,000L ($5.90); secondi 12,000L ($7.05). No credit cards. Thurs–Tues noon–10pm. TUSCAN.

If you arrive at the perfect moment, the bells of the tiny Chiesa della Madonna will be pealing your arrival. This cozy trattoria (with just 10 tables) is situated off the principal pedestrian Via San Giovanni on a tiny piazzetta it shares with the church. Its highly unusual "no-stop" hours afford you the chance to procure one of those coveted tables if you come before or after the crush of conventional dining hours, when you can get away with a simple plate of homemade pasta and salad. But with such reasonable prices and impressive talent in the kitchen, this is also the right spot to indulge in a multicourse meal of the unpretentious *cucina toscana* and discover the delights of the region's poor-man's cuisine.

4 Siena

34 km (21 mi.) S of Florence, 100 km (63 mi.) SE of Pisa, 42 km (26 mi.) SE of San Gimignano, 230 km (143 mi.) NE of Rome, 107 km (66 mi.) NW of Perugia

Siena "the Beloved" is often bypassed by the mad rush of visitors traveling the Rome-Florence autostrada. Others allot it minimum time to revel in its perfectly preserved medieval charm. You will see nothing of the baroque so prevalent in Rome nor the

Renaissance character of nearby Florence. Founded as **Sena** by the Etruscans and colonized by ancient Rome as **Saena Julia,** Siena flourished as a republic in the Middle Ages from the wool and textile trade and early, pre-Medici banking. It was considered one of the major cities of Europe in its day and became a principal center of art and culture as well. The Piazza del Campo, the city's imposing palazzi, the Duomo, and churches that you see today were the result of a building boom that flourished in those years, an unrivalled urban development. Its noted university dates back to that period, founded in 1240. But prosperity was aborted after devastating and recurring bouts with the bubonic plague beginning in 1348 that diminished the city's population from 100,000 to 30,000. Today's population is over 60,000, one still proud of its rich medieval heritage.

Forever locking horns over the centuries with its powerful neighbor Florence, and never having fully stabilized after its brush with the Black Death, it finally succumbed to Florence after an 18-month siege in 1554–55, became part of the Grand Duchy of Tuscany under Medici rule, and was reduced to a small provincial town of little consequence with a population that once dipped as low as 8,000. Florence's disinterest in Siena during the golden years of the Renaissance is today's tourist's great fortune: seemingly frozen in time, it is one of the country's best preserved medieval cities. Because of its golden days when coffers overflowed, it boasts one of the most beautiful Gothic duomos, town halls, and main squares—the Piazza del Campo—in all of Italy.

The Monte dei Paschi Bank in the postcard-perfect Piazza Salimbeni was founded in 1472; it is Europe's (many say the world's) oldest bank and still one of Italy's most solvent. It has long played a large role in sponsoring much of the city's cultural life. But while Siena's architectural expansion may have never progressed beyond the early years of the Renaissance, Siena today is still a very vital city, as you can witness during the early evening passeggiata hour when the city's folk take to strolling the Via di Città and the Via Banchi di Sotto and Via Banchi di Sopra. Proud, handsome, fashionably turned out, and more welcoming than the ultrareserved Florentines, the Sienese people still stand by the famous inscription found at the ancient gate of Porta Camolia: "Siena opens up its heart to you more than any other."

Siena is an ideal gateway for central and southern Tuscany for those with and without rental cars. From here, you can meander off to experience the various hill towns and hamlets in the Siena orbit of patchwork farmland and vine-draped estates. While the rest of Tuscany sleeps, return here for its artistic riches and marginal dash of cosmopolitan cultural life, and a number of dining choices. Best of all, finish your day with that after-dinner gelato in any of the cafes that ring the Piazza del Campo, arguably the most beautiful piazza in all of Italy, the best place around to sit and take in your extreme good luck.

FESTIVALS & MARKETS   Though travel material would have you believe otherwise, there is more to see here than just the twice-annual Palio horse race. A two-week **Antiques Fair** takes place in February of even years. A **Wine Week (Settimana dei Vini)** takes place the first week of June at the Enoteca Nazionale. The **Settimana Musicale Sienese,** a noteworthy weeklong classical musical festival, takes place in July or August, attracting world-class names and usually culminating in the beginning of August. Contact the tourist office for a schedule or call the **Accademia Musicale Chigiana** (☎ **0577/46-152;** fax 0577/288124), the city's prestigious music conservatory that organizes the festival. The weekly market is a large affair, and takes place on Wednesday (8am to 1pm) near the Fortezza Medicea and La Lizza Park. Vendors hawk everything from tube socks to CDs and fresh cut flowers and tripe sandwiches.

Foremost of the year's events is the legendary ✪ **Palio,** held July 2 (7:30pm) and August 16 (7pm); the latter is the more important of the two. Tickets in the bleachers are exorbitant, usually costing at least 200,000L ($117.60) and can only be purchased directly from the piazza's 30-some-odd stores and cafes who own the rights for ticket sales in the bleachers put up outside their businesses. Some of them have faxes; a list of names and contacts can be had from the tourist office. Tickets for either of the two Palios usually are sold out by January (and hotels by February); a last-minute appeal directly to a store or cafe owner might turn up a cancellation. The whole scenario is pretty much a frustrating and often useless venture unless you know the mayor. The alternative is to join the crowd, estimated anywhere from 50,000 to 100,000 strong, that stands in the inner piazza (the later in the day you show up, the farther from the outer rail you'll find free space); remember this all happens during the peak summer heat, vision is limited, and emotions run high. But hey, it's free. A remarkable procession, the **corteo storico,** unfolds where each of the 17 *contrade* (wards, to which the Sienese have a long historical allegiance, with names like Giraffe, She-Wolf, Wave, and Tower) are represented by dozens of pages, drummers, and banner-bearers dressed in the contrada's colors and elaborate historical costumes. A highlight of the parade is the synchronized flag-throwing that Sienese youths practice yearlong from their earliest days.

You can also attend two *prove,* or trial races, run the night before each Palio, though these tickets are also hard to come by (the trial races held 2 nights before the race offer the best chance to find tickets). If the crowd scene is too insane and the bleacher seats too expensive—and you're not related to the pope—seek out any of the contrada's neighborhoods the evening before or, much better yet, the winning contrada's neighborhood the evening of or after the Palio for guaranteed celebration that will go on well into the next day, if not much of the subsequent week.

ESSENTIALS

GETTING HERE   By Train   If you're arriving from either Florence or Pisa, the train is less convenient than the bus. Siena is not on a principal line, so it is likely that you'll have to change trains and wait (probably in Empoli), and departures are not half as frequent as the bus. Additionally, Siena's **train station** (☎ **0577/28-01-15**) is located 2 kilometers (1 mi.) north of town, so you'll have to catch a bus or taxi into the town center. Florence/Siena one-way is 10,000L ($5.90), from Pisa rates are similar. From Siena's train station, buses (1,200L/75¢) will bring you as far as Piazza Matteotti or call a taxi (☎ **0577/49222**).

By Bus   SITA and **TRA.IN** buses leave Florence for Siena about every 30 minutes from the SITA bus station at V. Santa Caterina da Siena 15r, Florence (☎ **055/ 48-36-51**), located near the train station. The 75-minute *corsa rapida* journey follows a lovely route for the most part and costs about 11,000L ($6.50) each way; avoid the local buses that can take up to two hours. In Siena, buses will leave you off in Piazza San Domenico (☎ **0577/20-42-45**) (the bus company's headquarters), an easy (if you have no luggage) 15-minute walk uphill to the Piazza del Campo.

By Car   From Florence take the Florence-Siena autostrada (it has no number; just follow the green autostrada signs) or, alternatively, the **S222** (the ✪ **Chiantigiana**), which takes a more winding, panoramic route through the Chianti countryside (see "Side Trips," below) as does the old Via Cassia **SS2.** From Pisa, take the autostrada toward Florence and at Empoli, exit onto the **SS429** heading south to Siena. If you're coming from San Gimignano, follow the signs for Poggibonsi. Avoid picking up the Florence-Siena autostrada, but instead follow the signs for the secondary "panoramic" road to Staggia, Monteriggioni, Badesse, Uopini, and Siena.

The entire historical center of Siena is closed tight to traffic. The majority of car parks are located around the stadium near the Fortezza Medicea (signs also read the

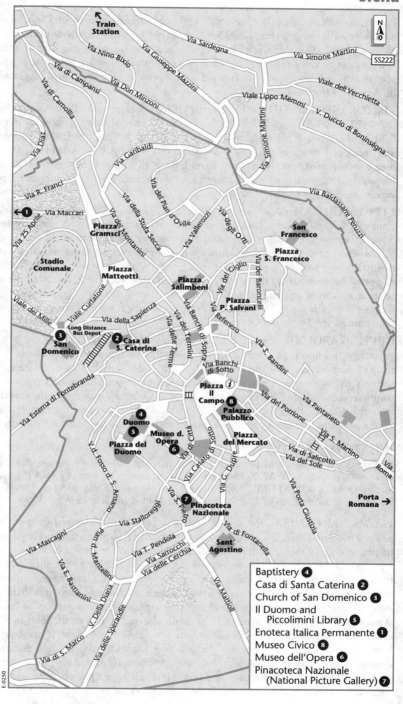

Siena

Train Station

Via Sardegna

Via Nino Bixio

Via Giuseppe Mazzini

Via Simone Martini

SS222

Via di Campansi

Via Don Minzoni

Viale dell'Vecchietta

Via di Camollia

Viale Lippo Memmi

V. Duccio di Boninsegna

Via Diaz

Via Garibaldi

Via Simone Martini

Via R. Franci

Via Maccari

Via Baldassarre Peruzzi

Via 25 Aprile

Via del Pian d'Ovile

Via della Stufa Secca

Via Vallerozzi

Via degli Orti

Piazza Gramsci

San Francesco

Stadio Comunale

Via dei Montanini

Via del Giglio

Via dei Baroncelli

Piazza S. Francesco

Piazza Matteotti

Piazza Salimbeni

Viale Curtatone

Via della Sapienza

Via Banchi di Sopra

Piazza P. Salvani

Viale dei Mille

Via Refenero

Via delle Terme

Via dei Termini

Long Distance Bus Depot

③ San Domenico

② Casa di S. Caterina

Via S. Bandini

Via Esterna di Fontebranda

Via Banchi di Sotto

Piazza il Campo ⓘ

Via del Porrione

Via S. Martini

Via Pantaneto

④ Duomo

⑤

Museo d. Opera ⑥

Piazza del Duomo

V. di Fosso d. S. Ansano

Via di Città

Via di Casato di Sotto

⑧ Palazzo Pubblico

Piazza del Mercato

Via di Salicotto

Via del Sole

Via Roma

V. di Casato di Sotto

Via C. Dupre

⑦ Pinacoteca Nazionale

Via Porta Giustizia

Porta Romana →

Via Stalloreggi

Via S. Pietro

P. del Mantellini

Via T. Pendola

Via di Fontanella

Via Mascagni

Via E. Bastianini

Via Sarrocchi

Sant' Agostino

Via delle Cerchia

Via di S. Marco

Della Diana

Via delle Sperandie

Via Mattioli

Baptistery	④
Casa di Santa Caterina	②
Church of San Domenico	③
Il Duomo and Piccolimini Library	⑤
Enoteca Italica Permanente	①
Museo Civico	⑧
Museo dell'Opera	⑥
Pinacoteca Nazionale (National Picture Gallery)	⑦

E-0250

287

Fortezza Santa Barbara), a 10-minute walk to the church and piazza of San Domenico, where signs will point you into town. Some of the hotels listed will provide paid, more convenient parking within a few blocks of their property; ask when reserving a room. You may not be able to use your car while in Siena, but it is invaluable to have if you plan to explore Chianti's wine estates and small towns, or other hill towns suggested in "Side Trips from Siena," below.

VISITOR INFORMATION The **Tourist Office** is located in the Pz. d. Campo 56 (☎ **0577/28-05-51;** fax 0577/270676), open in summer Monday to Saturday from 8:30am to 7:30pm, in winter Monday to Friday 8:30am to 1pm and 3:30 to 6:30pm and Saturday 8:30am to 1pm only. The main office, the **A.P.T. (Azienda di Promozione Turismo)** (mainly administrative) is on V. di Città 43 (☎ **0577/42-209**). It's primarily administrative and has much less information. For help with hotel reservations, see "Where to Stay," below.

CITY LAYOUT The city is laid out around the fan-shaped **Piazza il Campo** (or simply "il Campo")—some fascinated (and dare I say unadventurous) visitors never make it beyond the outdoor cafe tables that ring this unique piazza. Its principal palazzo-lined streets are also the address for the most interesting stores and bars: **Via di Città** (which will lead you to and from il Campo to the Duomo) and **Via Banchi di Sotto.** Perpendicular to the latter is **Via Banchi di Sopra.** The best vantage point to see it all is from atop the **Torre del Mangia** next to the Palazzo Comunale in the Campo; it's worth the 505 steps. A runner-up is the view from the Facciatone, accessible through the Museo del Duomo.

GETTING AROUND Siena is built on three hills. Some of the alleyways can be so steep they turn into steps. There is no real public transportation system (a number of small minibuses called **pollicini** are of only marginal interest to the sites worth seeing); the only real way to see the town is by foot. How much you'll discover depends on your tolerance and time. Because of the wide-open spaces, it's easy to lose the crowds around il Campo, the Palazzo Pubblico, and the Duomo. Even in the heat of the summer months, the narrow streets are shaded and cool, but the hills don't go away.

WHAT TO SEE & DO

✪ **Piazza del Campo and the Palazzo Pubblico aka Palazzo Comunale (Museo Civico).** Pz. d. Campo. ☎ **0577/29-22-63.** Admission to Torre del Mangia 7,000L ($4.10); Museo Civico 8,000L ($4.70). Torre (Tower) and Museo Civico: summer Mon–Sat 9:30am–6:30, Sun 9:30am–1:30pm; winter Mon–Sat 10am–5pm, Sun 9:30am–1:30pm.

PIAZZA DEL CAMPO You will see posters and postcards with aerial shots of the unusual fan-shaped Piazza (commonly and simply called il Campo), though they don't prepare you for its sheer breadth or monumental beauty. All roads and events, all visitors and residents gravitate toward it; you can catch a glimpse of its sunlit expanse from a dozen narrow alleys that lead down and empty into it. Built at the point where the city's three hills converge and the site of the ancient Roman forum, it is divided into nine marble-trimmed strips representing the city's ancient Government of Nine **(Governo dei Nove),** established in 1290, but is also said to imitate the folds in the cloak of the Virgin Mary, protector of the city since time immemorial. It has always been the city's center stage—the one-time site of executions, bullfights, and demonstrations—and is today lined with handsomely restored 13th- and 14th-century palazzi and their ground-floor cafes and stores. It is still a great place to hang out for residents and visitors alike, like the Rambla in Barcelona or the Spanish Steps in Rome. Locals meet, gossip, shop, cross it at every angle, young university-goers loiter about, and senior citizens congregate against this backdrop of matchless harmony. At

Visiting Hours

When visiting the Duomo in Siena, beware. The Duomo itself, the Library Piccolomini, the Baptistery, and the Museo dell'Opera all have different schedules.

Duomo:

January 1 to March 14	daily 7:30am to 1:30pm and 2:30 to 5pm
March 15 to October 31	daily 9am to 7:30pm
November 1 to December 31	daily 7:30am to 1:30pm and 2:30–5pm

Libreria Piccolomini:

January 1 to March 14	daily 10am to 1pm and 2:30 to 5pm
March 15 to October 31	daily 9am to 7:30pm
November 1 to December 31	daily 10am to 1pm and 2:30 to 5pm

Baptistery:

January 1 to March 14	daily 10am to 1pm and 2:30 to 5pm
March 15 to September 30	daily 9am to 7:30pm
October 1 to October 31	daily 9am to 6pm
November 1 to December 31	daily 10am to 1pm and 2:30 to 5pm

Museo dell'Opera:

January 1 to March 14	daily 9am to 1:30pm
March 15 to September 30	daily 9am to 7:30pm
October 1 to October 31	daily 9am to 6pm
November 1 to December 31	daily 9am to 1:30pm

its highest point is the piazza's famous **Fonte Gaia,** dedicated to the ancient mythological goddess of the seas (though many sources say its name translates as gay and carefree). It is a poor 19th-century copy of the original early 15th-century fountain by local master Jacopo della Quercia (original marble reliefs can be found in the Palazzo Pubblico's Museo Civico) and is fed by a 15-mile aqueduct that has supplied the city with fresh water since the 14th century.

PALAZZO PUBBLICO   Also known at the Palazzo Comunale, this palazzo, with its sky-scraping 320-foot bell tower, the **Torre del Mangia,** takes up virtually the entire south side of the piazza. A stunning and perfectly preserved symbol of civic pride, and still the site of the Town Hall, the elegant Gothic facade of the Palazzo Pubblico, completed in 1310 and expanded in the 17th century, is slightly curved in keeping with the unusual parameter of the Piazza del Campo. The adjacent brick bell tower crowned with marble, the highest medieval tower in Italy after that of Cremona, was added to punctuate its significance. The tower is named after its first bell ringer, who was nicknamed "mangiagaudagni" (literally profit-eater) because of his notorious idleness. Its bells were used to announce the opening and closing of the city gates, threat of attack, and special events such as the arrival of a pope. Its 505 steps will provide you with vertigo-inducing views over il Campo, the three hills of Siena's centro storico, and the Tuscan countryside that picks up where the modern city sprawl beyond the city walls diminishes (the other heart-stopping view in town is from atop the Facciatone, adjacent to the Duomo; see below). At the base of the tower is the Cappella di Piazza (1352–76, erected by the grateful Sienese people in thanksgiving for the passing of the Black Death in 1348. It is not open to the public).

MUSEO CIVICO   Within the Palazzo Pubblico, this museum houses some of the Sienese school of art's most significant works. One of the two important rooms is the

Sala del Mappamondo (the Globe Room named after a long lost map of the world) frescoed in 1315 with two important works by the prominent local artist Simone Martini, a student of Duccio. On the left is his splendidly restored ✪ *Maestà (Madonna Enthroned)* (1315) and on the opposite wall ✪ *Guidoriccio da Folignano* (1328), a captain of the Sienese army in full battle regalia; both were meant to protect the city from harm and pestilence (the latter fresco had always been attributed to Martini until recent controversy that keeps historians divided). The next room, the **Sala di Pace** (Hall of Peace), was the meeting place for the medieval Government of Nine and today contains the two famous allegorical frescoes by local master Ambrogio Lorenzetti ✪ *The Effect of Good and Bad Government on Town and Country* (1337–39). You won't have a hard time determining which is which. They are some of the earliest and most important secular artworks to survive from medieval Europe. Lorenzetti is believed to have died from the plague not long after completing the fresco cycle.

✪ **Duomo.** Piazza Duomo. Admission free to Duomo; 2,000L ($1.20) to Libreria Piccolomini; 3,000L ($1.75) to Baptistery; 6,000L ($3.50) to Museo dell'Opera.

Begun in 1196, this black-and-white marble striped cathedral dedicated to Santa Maria dell'Assunta (Our Lady of the Assumption) sits atop Siena's highest hill, and is one of the most beautiful and ambitious Gothic churches in all of Italy. If you arrive by bus in Piazza San Domenico, look for its postcard-perfect view from afar. Much of what you see today was completed within the 13th century. The unfinished, free-standing construction to the right of the Duomo is what the Sienese call the *Facciatone* (Big Facade). Begun in 1339 (when Siena was reaching its medieval zenith and in response to its old-time rival Florence's construction of its own enormous Duomo), plans were launched to build an even greater duomo that would incorporate the extant structure as the transept and thus become Christendom's largest church outside of Rome. Work was abandoned forever when money ran short, the bubonic plague of 1348 altered local history, and the economy fell apart.

Local attention turned back to the original church, whose extravagant zebra-striped marble bands borrowed from Pisan-Lucchese architecture are reflected in the interior. Entry can be visually startling, with your focus soon being drawn to the priceless ✪ **pavement of masterful mosaics,** 56 etched and inlaid marble panels created by more than 40 artisans between the mid-14th through the 16th centuries, with some finished as late as the 19th century. They are partially roped off and many are covered by protective cardboard for protection, but all are uncovered for a few weeks before and after the August 15 feast day of the Assumption (and sometimes into September).

Located beneath the central vault is the octagonal pulpit, whose famous upper panels depicting the life of Christ were carved by master Tuscan sculptor Nicola Pisano in 1265, assisted by his son Giovanni (who would be responsible for designing the Duomo's lower facade in 1284) and Arnolfo di Cambio. It is considered his masterpiece, even greater and more elaborate than his then-recent work in Pisa's baptistery, and is one of the Duomo's (and city's) most important artistic treasures. Within the Duomo at an entrance in the north (left) aisle is the lavish Libreria Piccolomini, built in the late 15th century by Cardinal Francesco Piccolomini (the future Pius III—for all of 18 days in office before he died) to house the important illuminated book collection of his uncle, Pope Pius II, the quintessential Renaissance man and humanist, both from an important local family. The elder pontiff's life is the subject of 10 giant, brilliantly colored frescoes, together the acknowledged masterpiece of Umbrian artist Pinturicchio (1509); he was assisted by his students who included, history goes, a talented young painter called Raphael. One of the most famous frescoes depict the canonization of the Siena-born St. Catherine, the third fresco on the left as you enter. An ancient Roman copy of a Greek-inspired statue of the *Three Graces* stands in the center. As you leave the library, on your right you will see the late 15th-century Piccolomini altar adorned with four statues attributed to a very young Michelangelo; although commissioned to do 15, he left early for Florence to create his *David*.

BAPTISTERY OF ST. JOHN   Due to its separate entrance and obscure placement down the stairs and around the back right flank of the Duomo, few people visit this baptistery. Look for the ✪ **15th-century hexagonal baptismal font** by local son Jacopo della Quercia, adorned with gilded bronze bas-reliefs panels by Donatello and Ghiberti. If you have visited Lucca, you will have seen his important Tomb of Ilaria in the sacristy of the local Duomo.

MUSEO DELL'OPERA METROPOLITANA   Located in the "new" part of the Duomo that was never finished, with the above-mentioned adjoining Facciatone, this museum houses much of the sculpture and artwork that formerly graced the cathedral inside and out. Most interesting is the first-floor's collection of weather-worn Gothic facade statuary by Giovanni Pisano with a single, important contribution by Donatello, a marble tondo of the Madonna and Child. Upstairs in a room by itself is the ✪ *Maestà* (*Madonna Enthroned*) (1311) the museum's most celebrated work, once the Duomo's altarpiece; it is a complex work by Duccio di Buoninsegna, a student of Cimabue and a native son of Siena and has long been considered one of the most important late medieval paintings. Follow signs for access to the top of the Facciatone (there is no elevator) for an ✪ **inspiring view over Siena,** arguably better than the view from the Campo's Torre di Mangia. During peak months when hours allow, try to make it for sunset.

✪ **Pinacoteca Nazionale (National Picture Gallery).** Palazzo Buonsignori, V. San Pietro 29. Admission 8,000L ($4.70). Tues–Sat 9am–7pm, Sun 8am–1pm, Mon 8:30am–1:30pm; hours may be shorter in winter months.

If you have visited the Duomo Museum or the Museo Civico in the Palazzo Pubblico, you will recognize some of the names and styles of the Sienese school of painters, whose works are displayed here in the elegant Gothic Palazzo Buonsignori, a typical 14th-century construction redolent of the city's golden period of wealth and power. Though it cannot hold a candle to what was transpiring simultaneously in nearby Florence, this sliver of local art history is fascinating.

The ground floor is usually bypassed on the way to the second floor's principal treasures, highlighted by the works of Duccio di Buoninsegna, simply known as Duccio. He was considered the last great painter of antiquity and the most acclaimed of Siena's movement; artistic advancements in composition, perspective, and expression can be followed in his work. His student Simone Martini is also represented, as are the Lorenzetti brothers, Pietro and Ambrogio, and others. The predictable use of gold hangs on longer in the Sienese school than the Florentine, perhaps a preference of the patrons who commissioned these paintings to have their works shine in the gloomy medieval chapels. Florence was already onto more advanced developments, while Siena was slow to break with its religious compositions.

✪ **Enoteca Italica Permanente.** Fortezza Medicea (beyond Stadium, NW corner of town). ☎ **0577/28-84-97.** Free admission. Glass of wine 3,000–6,000L ($1.75–$3.50). Daily noon–1am. AE, MC, V.

There could be no better setting to showcase Italy's timeless wine culture, making this a unique and obligatory destination for both serious connoisseurs and casual oenophiles alike. Set within the massive military fortress built by Cosimo dei Medici in 1560 after Siena had fallen to Florence, this wine-tasting bar provides a wide selection of wines to be enjoyed both inside and out, where tables are set up on a sunny terrace. It's most popular in the late afternoon or early evening when local wine devotees and a young crowd drop in for an *aperitivo,* choosing from dozens of wines sold by the glass (wines can also be purchased by the bottle). The emphasis is on Tuscan wines—many made in Siena's backyard—but this enoteca is a national concern owned and operated by the government to support the Italian wine tradition. Its 750-label collection is representative of the country's various regions and generally considered to be one of the most prodigious and discerning selections of its kind in Italy, Italy's official state-mandated **museo del vino** since 1950.

Casa di Santa Caterina (Sanctuary and House of St. Catherine of Siena). Costa di Sant'Antonio (between V. d. Spaienza and V. S. Caterina). Free admission. Summer daily 9am–12:30pm and 2:30–6pm; winter 9am–12:30pm and 3:30–6pm.

This is the 14th-century birthplace and home of St. Catherine of Siena, patron saint of Italy (together with St. Francis of Assisi) and one of the first women ever elevated to Doctor of the Church. If you have arrived at a time when there is a tour group or crowd of people, wait until they leave to fully absorb the quiet serenity of this simple and reflective place. After you cross through a brick-lined courtyard, the points of interest are the small chapel on your right where a painted 13th-century crucifix is said to be the crucifix in front of which she received the stigmata in 1375, and an oratory to the left built on the spot of the family home, with wide steps leading down to her cell below (and a gift shop where you can find material about her life). St. Catherine died at 33 in 1380, the year that St. Bernard of Siena was born (d. 1444). Their mysticism exerted a deeply felt grip on the age, a time of heightened spirituality during an onslaught of draughts, bubonic plagues, and declining economies. The eloquent St. Catherine is perhaps most remembered for her instrumental involvement in persuading the pope, Gregory XI, to return the seat of the papacy to Rome from Avignon in France after a 67-year exile. She was canonized in 1464, and her home transformed into this pilgrimage site not long thereafter.

Church of San Domenico. Pz. San Domenico. Free admission. Summer 7am–1pm and 3–6:30pm; winter 9am–1pm and 3–6pm.

This monastic church has always been closely linked with the city's beloved St. Catherine, who had taken the Dominican veil in 1355 after her first vision of Christ. This barnlike 13th-century church juts above a high position affording beautiful views of the Gothic Duomo and Siena's rooftops. But it is most visited for the special ✪ **Chapel of St. Catherine** halfway along the nave on the right wall added in 1460 to house the saint's severed head in a gilded tabernacle. All except the right wall were frescoed by Sodoma in 1526 with scenes from the saint's life. Catherine experienced most of her trances and visions of Christ in this church, and received her stigmata in the raised Cappella delle Volte in the west end of the church (on your right as you enter). Over the chapel's altar, a contemporary portrait of her by one of her friends Andrea Vanni (c. 1380) is said to be the only authentic depiction of her.

SHOPPING

Siena puts up a noble effort in keeping up with its centuries-old rival Florence as a shopping destination but it pales, alas, in comparison. It is, however, far better in variety and quantity than any of the other cities in this chapter, with Perugia the only close contender, or Deruta (a side trip from Perugia) for those interested in ceramics alone.

The pride and elegance exuded by Siena's residents is obvious in its cluster of stores along the principle streets noted in the city layout. There are the predictable designer and accessories boutiques of world-recognized names, but visitors will be more drawn to its cache of ceramics stores and shops selling artisanal crafts or *prodotti toscani* (gourmet items). The chock-full ceramics store **Zina Provvedi,** V. di Città 96 (☎ **0577/286068**), has one of the best selections with the nicest of quality, and will ship. Within this same block alone, there are at least five other friendly ceramics competitors selling everything from spoon rests to turkey-sized platters, simply decorated (less expensive) or elaborately covered (very expensive). Also nearby is **Il Papiro** on V. di Città 37 (☎ **0577/284241**), whose attractive paper goods you may have seen in its hometown of Florence, but in this retail outpost you'll also find a handsome series of postcards and note cards of water-color vignettes depicting Siena's loveliest medieval palazzi.

If you've meandered about, you may have happened upon any of the five Nannini bars or pasticcerie. A sacred local institution, the Nannini name is known beyond the confines of Siena, if not for its famous packaged sweets than for the famous pop-singer Gianna Nannini (a cross between Madonna and a Streisand wannabe). Their largest and oldest bar/cafe is on Via Banchi di Sopra near the Piazza del Campo (☎ **0577/ 41591**). Although the fruit-and-nut cake *panforte* and the cookielike *ricciarelli* sweets made of almond paste are typically associated with Siena and Nannini's, food connoisseurs will guide you to the city's best one-stop-shop for gourmet products, **Enoteca San Domenico,** ultraconvenient to those leaving or arriving by bus (V. d. Paradiso 56 just off the Piazza San Domenico; ☎ **0577/271181**). Here the just-sweet-enough *ricciarelli* are the best I've ever tasted (9,900L/$5.80), and the selection of regional wines, oils, dried herbs, and other handsomely packaged gourmet goods will cover every hard-to-shop-for person on your list, yourself included.

WHERE TO STAY

There are no youth hostels directly in town; ask at the tourist information office about the two located a few miles outside of town (one in a lovely corner of Chianti). Both are under the same management as the hostel in San Gimignano (see San Gimignano, "Where to Stay," p. 282). If all the hotels listed below are full, try the English-speaking **Prenotazioni Alberghiere** (hotel reservations) stand (☎ **0577/28-80-84;** fax 0577/ 280290) in the Piazza San Domenico—convenient for those arriving by bus—where you'll pay 3,000 to 8,000L ($1.75 to $5.25) per reservation according to the category of hotel. Hours in summer are Monday to Saturday 9am to 8pm; winter Monday to Saturday 9am to 7pm.

For **long stays,** Siena's fabled Piccolomini family has opened one of their Renaissance palazzi as furnished rentals by the week or month. Close to the Piazza del Campo, top-floor apartments with a view sleep two to three people and rent for $1,200 per week, much less for longer periods. In New York contact Manfredi Piccolomini (☎ **212/932-3480;** fax 212/932-9039; www.idt.net/~manpico/; e-mail: manpico@idt.net). In Florence, call ☎ **055/244456** (fax 055/2345552).

Hotel Antica Torre. V. Fieravecchia 7 (off V. Banchi di Sotto), 53100 Siena. ☎ and fax **0577/222255.** 8 units, all with bathroom. TEL. 130,000L ($76.50) single; 160,000L ($94.10) double; 180,000L ($105.90) triple. Ask about off-season discounts. Breakfast 11,000L ($6.50). AE, MC, V.

There are just eight cozy—some might call them small —guest rooms in this unusual and charming tower hotel. Installed in a 16th-century tower (one of Siena's more recent constructions) with a time-worn travertine stairwell, the higher floors offer rooms slightly larger and with lovely views over Siena's rooftops and rolling green hills. Most rooms have cool terra-cotta pavements, exposed-beamed ceilings, white-lace curtains, and beds with wrought-iron headboards; bathrooms are compact and brand new. Although the hotel is located on a quiet side street in a relatively residential niche of town near the Porta Romana, it's still a convenient 10-minute walk to the Piazza del Campo. You could even have breakfast there in one of the expensive outdoor cafes for less than what you'd pay at the hotel. The breakfast room, a 14th-century potter's bottega on top of which the tower was built, is a charming spot full of character, but definitely not for claustrophobes—especially before morning coffee. TVs are available upon request.

Hotel Chiusarelli. V. Curtatone 15 (near Pz. San Domenico), 53100 Siena. ☎ **0577/ 28-05-62.** Fax 0577/27-11-77. 49 units, all with bathroom. TV TEL. 112,000L ($65.90) single; 165,000L ($97.05) double; 227,000L ($133.50) triple. Rates include breakfast. AE, MC, V. Nearby parking 30.000L ($17.65).

Two regal palms (not entirely surprising flora for Tuscany) stand guard before the columned facade of this neoclassical 19th-century villa-turned-hotel. On the outskirts of the historical center, it's an easy 1-block walk from the bus station for those with light luggage, and yet also an easy walk uphill to the central piazza once you've unpacked and are ready to sightsee. This is one of the larger hotels we're listing, so availability is slightly better here during prime months if you book in advance. Plain, modernized rooms are prettied up with rose chenille or flowered bedspreads—light sleepers should request a room overlooking the green stadium behind, not terribly picturesque but quieter (except during Sunday matches) than those on the trafficked Via Curatone. This is a "proper" hotel (that has yet to install air-conditioning) replete with bar, breakfast terrace, brick-vaulted restaurant (to be passed by on your way to one of our suggestions below), and, alas, tour groups that come and go.

✪ **Hotel Piccolo Etruria.** V. Donzelle 3 (off V. Banchi di Sotto), 53100 Siena. ☎ **0577/ 28-80-88.** Fax 0577/28-84-61. E-mail: hetruria@sienaet.it. 13 units, all with bathroom. TV TEL. 70,000L ($41.20) single; 110,000L ($64.70) double; 145,000L ($85.30) triple. Breakfast 8,000L ($4.70). Ask about low-season rates. AE, DC, MC, V. Nearby parking 10,000–15,000L ($5.90–$8.80).

This recently refurbished hotel is lovely enough to be your base in Tuscany—it's too great a find to be used as a mere 1-night stop. The proud Fattorini family oversaw every painstaking detail in its recent renovation, and the taste and quality level is something one usually finds in hotels at thrice the cost. Rooms are simple but very thoughtfully decorated and charming; the use of terra-cotta pavements and blond oak wood is ubiquitous; and housekeeping is impeccable. Rooms are divided between the main building and a *dipendenza* directly across the narrow, traffic-free street; some guests prefer the privacy of the latter, others seek out the friendly presence of the Fattorini family in the former. The many appreciated touches include fresh floral bedspreads, sheer ultrawhite curtains, and hair dryers in the brand-new, white-tiled bathrooms. The Fattorinis are hoping for a summer 1999 opening of their small, inhouse restaurant specializing in home-style cuisine. In high season book well in advance—this secret is out.

CHIANTI HIDEAWAYS

✪ **Borgo Argenina.** Localiatà Argenina (near San Marcellino Monti), 53013 Gaiole in Chianti. ☎ and fax **0577/747117.** 5 units, all with bathroom, 2 apts. TV. Ask about single and triple rates; 220,000L ($129.40) double. 250,000L ($147.05) apt. Off-season discounts. Rates include country breakfast. No credit cards.

You'll need your own transportation to get to this little slice of the Tuscan dream 15 kilometers (9.5 mi.) north of Siena. From the flagstoned terrace of Elena Nappa's newly opened hilltop bed-and-breakfast (she bought the whole medieval hamlet), you can see the farmhouse where Bertolucci filmed his cinematographically gorgeous *Stealing Beauty* in 1996 (required viewing for those planning a visit to Tuscany). Against remarkable odds (she'll regale you with the anecdotes), doting hostess Elena has created the rural retreat of her dreams. It doesn't get any better than this. Her innate design talents and keen attention to charm and detail is the stuff of country design magazines. This is the untrammeled corner of vine-covered Chianti you've been looking for, but it's not easy to find. English-speaking Elena will fax you directions when you reserve.

Hotel Residence San Sano. Localiatà San Sano, 53010 Lecchi in Chianti. ☎ **0577/ 746130.** Fax 0577/746146. www.chiantinet.it. E-mail: hotelsansano@chiantinet.it. 14 units, all with bathroom. A/C. 190,000L ($111.75) single; 190,000–250,000L ($111.75–$147.05) double; 280,000L ($164.70) triple. Rates include buffet breakfast. AE, MC, V. Closed Dec–Feb.

Giancarlo Matarazzo and his German wife, Heidi, traded in their jobs as school-teachers in Germany for this idyllic niche of Chianti and opened a very special rural hideaway. There are no hardships here: The purposeful lack of TVs in the rooms is meant to enhance the utter tranquillity found here. The medieval jumble of stone buildings dating from the 13th century boasts a beautifully sited pool nestled amid the vineyards. The hosts will help map out a number of different day trips over scenic back roads to wine-producing estates and hilltop towns (Radda and Gaiole are both about 10 kilometers/6.3 mi. away; see "Side Trips from Siena," below) and the chance to sample local trattorias—but most guests wind up gravitating back to the Matarazzo's cozy country kitchen for optional dinners of simple *cucina toscana* and animated dinner talk they offer to road weary hotel guests. Decor is rustic, simple, and perfect. So are the views. And Siena is a lovely 20-kilometer drive (12.6-mi.) away.

WHERE TO DINE

✪ **Antica Trattoria Papei.** Pz. d. Mercato 6 (southeast of Pz. d. Campo), Siena. ☎ **0577/ 28-08-94.** Reservations suggested. Primi 10,000–12,000L ($5.90–$7.05); secondi 10,000–15,000L ($5.90–$8.80). MC, V. Tues–Sun noon–3pm and 7–10:30pm. TUSCAN.

It's rather ambitious, in a city whose origins date from the ancient Roman Empire, for a restaurant to call itself the "Old Trattoria" when its been around for a mere 50 years. But three generations of the proud Papei family have put this wonderful restaurant on the map from day one. You'll understand why its future is secure when the homemade *papparedelle alla cinghiale* (flat noodles in a wild-boar–flavored tomato sauce) arrive at your outdoor table in one of the city's oldest and most popular piazzas. The quintessential Tuscan theme continues with *coniglio all'arrabiata*, rabbit marinated in white wine then simmered with sage and a pinch of hot pepperoncino. Too gamy? Homemade *pici*, a hand-rolled egg pasta that looks like fat spaghetti and simply prepared here with a full-flavored fresh tomato sauce, is one of myriad possibilities for the non-hunters among us. Discovered by foreigners, locals rigorously hang on, though they seem to avoid the modern room to the right as you enter. So should you.

Da Roberto. V. Calzoleria 26 (near Pz. Salimbeni). ☎ **0577/28-50-80.** Reservations suggested. Pizza 8,000–12,000L ($4.70–$7.05); primi 9,000L ($5.30); secondi 9,000–14,000L ($5.30–$8.25). Four-course menù turistico 25,000L ($14.70). No credit cards. Wed–Mon 12:30–2:30pm and 7:30–11:30pm. TUSCAN/PIZZERIA.

The delicious pizza indubitably overshadows the full restaurant menu here. But during my last visit I broke away from my love story with Roberto's special *pizza alla fattoressa* (smothered with tomato, mozzarella, and thinly-sliced potatoes sprinkled with fresh rosemary) long enough to order from the other half of the menu. I bravely ordered homemade *pici alla pettitosa*, a hard-to-find spaghetti-like pasta with a faintly spicy tomato sauce, followed by *cosce di maiale*, roast leg of pork fragrant with rosemary. The most demanding Sienese diner would have been won over: This was *cucina toscana* as you can only hope to find at these prices. But I'm still going back for the pizza— maybe it's the wood-burning oven.

○ **Osteria le Logge.** V. d. Porrione 33 (just off the Campo). (☎ **0577/48013.** Reservations required. Primi 12,000–15,000L ($7.05–$8.80), secondi 25,000–28,000L ($14.70–$16.50). AE, DC, MC, V. Mon–Sat noon–3pm amd 8–10pm. Closed last 3 weeks in Nov and 10 days in June. Bus: B, N, A. SIENESE/TUSCAN.

Owner Gianni Brunelli is *appasionato* about what he does, and it shows. So are his devotees and they are legion. This is one of those rare, highly recommended Sienese eateries where you'd do well to call ahead before arriving in town, rather than risk the sad-sack scenario of having to settle for buying one of Gianni's cookbooks when the standing-room-only scenario turns you away. There's always a fresh homemade pasta to launch a memorable meal, followed by entrees that are all about the simple perfection of grilled meats, though I've seen vegans looking mighty content, too. The excellent choice of extra-virgin olive oil is enough to confirm the owner's seriousness, seconded by a small but discerning wine list that is topped by his own limited production of Rosso and Brunello di Montepulciano. You won't understand how exceptional this atmospheric locale is (a cabinet-lined former pharmacy) until you've eaten elsewhere in Siena.

Pizzeria da Carlo e Franca. V. di Pantaneto 138 (near V. d. Pispini). ☎ **0577/22-04-85.** Pizza 5,500–6,500L ($3.25–$3.80). Thurs–Tues noon–3pm and 5pm–midnight. No credit cards. PIZZERIA.

It's always crowded at this unpretentious pizzeria—the pizza's too good and the prices too moderate to expect otherwise. Plain wooden tables with paper place mats can't accommodate the lines, so the more impatient patrons know to grab a *pizza al taglio* (by the slice) and eat it on the run. But if you come a little early you can sit, order an appetizer of *bruschetta* (small slabs of toasted bread brushed with garlic and drizzled with olive oil) and peruse at leisure the 30 different types of pizza and calzone. Most ultimately opt for the house specialty: *pizza alla boscaiola* with tomatoes, sausage, mushrooms, mozzarella, and garlic.

SIDE TRIPS FROM SIENA

If you have access to wheels, equip yourself with a map of *Siena provincia* supplied by the tourist office and take to the hills. The fabled ○ **Chianti region** stretches between here and Florence along the **S222** (La Chiantigiana), where you'll want to make stops in the small towns within a half-hour's drive: Northeast of Siena you'll find **Radda** in Chianti Pro Loco (tourist information) Pz. Ferrucci 1 (☎ and fax **0577/738494**); **Gaiole** in Chianti Pro Loco (tourist information) V. Ricasoli 50 (☎ **0577/749411;** fax 0577/749375); and **Castellina** in Chianti (Tourist Office, Pz. d. Comune 1; ☎ **0577/740201;** fax 0577/740625)—the three picturesque rural towns that made up the ancient Chianti League. You can also take-in the quiet town of **Monteriggioni,** northwest of Siena, sitting atop a hill within perfectly preserved 13th-century walls. Farther afield and closer to Florence is **Greve** in Chianti (tourist information) Via Luca Cini (☎ and fax **055/8545243**), a small town with an ancient marketplace in the central piazza that's worth poking around by foot, and host of the annual September wine fair. The adjacent village of **Montefioralle** has a medieval castle and the ornately decorated Church of San Stefano.

Along the way look for the signs DEGUSTAZIONE or VENDITA DIRETTA, advising that these are wine operations that offer tastings and sales direct to the public. The signs AZIENDA AGRICOLA, TENUTA, or FATTORIA indicate the wine-producing operations—some multimillion-dollar affairs, others unsung and family run. Each will offer its own unique experience.

The wine-producing towns of southern Tuscany are still relatively unknown compared to those found in the popular Florence-to-Siena stretch, being just a mile too

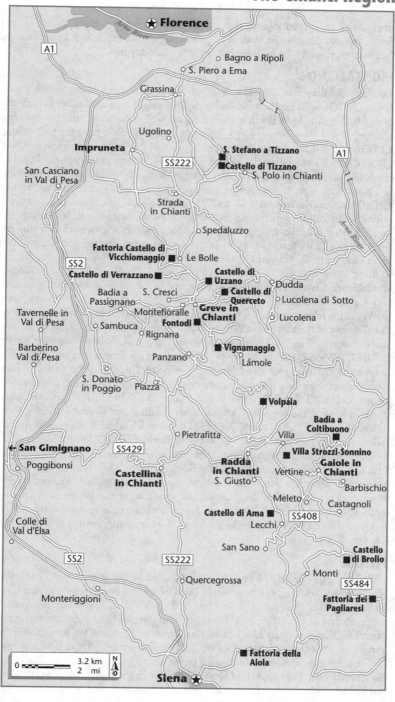

The Chianti Region

★ **Florence**

Arno River

A1

○ Bagno a Ripoli
○ S. Piero a Ema

Grassina

Ugolino

Impruneta ○

SS222

San Casciano
in Val di Pesa

■ **S. Stefano a Tizzano**
■ **Castello di Tizzano**
○ S. Polo in Chianti

A1

Arno River

Strada
in Chianti

○ Spedaluzzo

**Fattoria Castello di
Vicchiomaggio** ■ ○ Le Bolle

SS2

Castello di Verrazzano ■

Badia a
Passignano ○

**Castello di
Uzzano** ■

○ Dudda

S. Cresci ○

■ **Castello di
Querceto**

○ Lucolena di Sotto

Tavernelle in
Val di Pesa ○

Montefioralle ○

**Greve in
Chianti**

○ Lucolena

○ Sambuca

Fontodi ■

Barberino
Val di Pesa

Rignana ○

■ **Vignamaggio**

Panzano ○

○ Lámole

S. Donato
in Poggio ○

Piazza ○

■ **Volpáia**

**Badia a
Coltibuono** ■

○ Pietrafitta

○ Villa

← **San Gimignano**

SS429

Villa Strozzi-Sonnino ■

Poggibonsi ○

**Radda
in Chianti**

**Gaiole in
Chianti**

**Castellina
in Chianti**

Vertine ○

S. Giusto ○

○ Barbischio

Meleto ○

○ Castagnoli

Colle di
Val d'Elsa ○

Castello di Ama ■

SS408

Lecchi ○

○ San Sano

**Castello
di Brolio** ■

SS2

SS222

○ Quercegrossa

○ Monti

SS484

Monteriggioni ○

**Fattoria dei
Pagliaresi** ■

0 ━━━ 3.2 km
    2 mi

N

**Fattoria della
Aiola** ■

Siena ★

E-0251

297

many away for Florence-based day trippers. They are more easily accessible from Siena, and can generally be reached by public transportation, though a rental car will facilitate enormously the logistics and flexibility of a day trip.

MONTALCINO

Located 43 kilometers (27 mi.) south of Siena, this is the home of the power-house ✪ **DOCG Brunello wine,** and its lighter-weight cousin Rosso di Montalcino. Sleepy and small, Montalcino is nonetheless a well-to-do town that has remained unchanged since the 16th century with lovely vistas, especially from the 14th-century ✪ **Fortezza,** which also moonlights as its enoteca. Wines by-the-glass begin at 3,000L ($1.75), but go right for the Brunello at 7,000L ($4.10) and a savory plate of the local cheeses or salami, 7,000L ($4.10) each, for Montalcino's perfect meal. The other perfect place in town for wine tasting is in the palazzo-rimmed Pz. d. Popolo no. 6, at the **Caffè/Fiaschetteria Italiana** (☎ **0577/849043**) closed Thursday, open 7:30am to midnight. In a 19th-century ambience or at a few choice tables outside, you can revel in a self-styled Brunello-tasting, with three or four varieties to choose from by the glass for 8,000 to 12,000L ($4.70 to $7.05). Brunello's most revered producer, Biondi-Santi had two stellar years in 1993 and 1990. You can buy a bottle at the Fiaschetteria to bring home with you, if you want to part with 100,000L ($58.80). Montalcino's small **Museo Civico** just moved to its collection of Sienese paintings dating from the 1400s to the Renaissance to their new home in 1997, the handsomely restored former St. Augustine monastery on Via Ricasoli 31 (☎ **0577/846014**). Admission is 8,000L ($4.70). Two of the area's most alluring experiences can be found outside of the town walls, however. The 12th-century Cistercian abbey of **Abbazia di Sant'Antimo** (☎ **0577/835659**) rests in its own pocket-sized vale amid olive trees and cypresses 10 kilometers (6.3 mi.) south of Montalcino. One of Tuscany's most perfectly intact Romanesque churches, the abbey is especially worth visiting during the Gregorian chants performed daily by a handful of monks who still live there. Check the tourist office in Montalcino for hours, and all other information: Tourist Office, V. Costa d. Municipio 8 (☎ and fax **0577/849331**), closed Monday. While at Sant'Antimo, follow the signs for the nearby ✪ **Fattoria Barbi** (☎ **0577/848277**; fax 0577/849356), one of the area's most respected wine producers of the full-bodied Brunello, in the same family since the 16th century. Wine tastings are available Monday to Saturday, but so are excellent country meals (closed Wednesday) with most products direct from the estate's farm. Rustic accommodations at the inn will tempt you to stay on indefinitely. **From Siena,** Montalcino is relatively easy to reach. A dozen or so TRA.IN buses make the 60-to 90-minute trip, costing 6,000L ($3.50) one way.

PIENZA

This Renaissance jewel (24 km/15 mi. from Montalcino and 52 km/33 mi. from Siena), is easy to reach from Montalcino (west of here, or from Montepulciano east of Pienza) by public bus. But with just two or three bus departures from Siena and no trains, a rental car will make your life easier. Film director Franco Zefferelli found the perfect backdrop awaiting him here to film *Romeo and Juliet* in 1968, bypassing "fair Verona" as the obvious choice. Despite its theatrical set depicting a medieval town, Pienza is more noteworthy as testament to the ambitions and ego of a quintessential Renaissance man. Pope Pius II (of Siena's illustrious Piccolomini family) was born here in 1405 when it was called Corsignano, and in 1459 (a year after he was elected pope) commissioned Florentine architect Bernardo Rossellino to level the medieval core of town and create the first stage of what would be the model High Renaissance city (and renamed it Pienza, in his own honor). The grand scheme didn't get very far (the pope died in 1464), but what has remained, remains perfectly preserved (and protected as a UNESCO site) as can be seen in the graceful ✪ **Piazza Pio II.** Visit the piazza's Palazzo Piccolomini (the pope's private residence, lived in by descendents of the Piccolomini family until 1968) and the Duomo; walk behind the Duomo for sweeping views of the dormant Mt. Amiata and the wide Val d'Orcia. The piazza is also the location for the tourist office (☎ and fax **0578/749071**). Ask about free guided tours of the town during the summer months.

You can see most of the town, with a population of 2,500, in just half a day. It will take only 5 minutes to cover Pienza's main drag, **Corso Rossellino**, whose food stores specialize in the gourmet products from this bountiful corner of Tuscany, namely wines, honey and its famous ✪ **pecorino cheese** (also known as **cacio**). Cheese-tasting is more popular than wine tasting here, and stores offer their varieties of *fresco* (fresh), *semistagionato* (partially aged), *pepperocinato* (dusted with hot peppers), or *tartufi* (truffles). Taste as much cheese as you will, but by all means save room for lunch at the town's well-known and reasonably priced **Dal Falco,** in Pz. Dante Alighieri 7 (☎ **0578/48551**), closed Friday. A meal of homemade *pici* pasta and a delicious grilled meat will cost around 30,000L ($17.65). There are six simple doubles with private bathrooms upstairs for 90,000L ($59.95).

MONTEPULCIANO

Perched some 2,000 feet above sea level, the steeply graded city gives new height to the expression hill town. Built along a narrow limestone ridge, and compared to a ship by Henry James, it is also known as "The Pearl of the 16th Century" for its architecture (the result of a particularly prosperous period of political affiliation with Florence and the Medicis) and its premier red wine. Generally held as a runner-up to the ne plus ultra Brunello di Montalcino, its DOCG ruby red ✪ **Vino Nobile di Montepulciano** has put this highest of hilltowns on the map for centuries. Full-bodied, elegant, and world-esteemed, this red wine has imbued this Renaissance town with a sense of distinction and pride, and a certain city air prevails despite its small-town size. A long winding street called il Corso runs up to its civic and historic heart, the monumental **Piazza Grande,** the highest point in town. The spacious piazza is overseen by the unfinished facade of the 16th-17th century **Duomo** and, upon exiting, the severe 13th-century Gothic **Palazzo Comunale** (Town Hall) on the left. Purposefully reminiscent of Florence's Palazzo Vecchio, with a similar square tower that provides a **fantastic view** of the graceful Tuscan countryside for those who can tolerate the narrow, steep stairs. They say that on a clear day, you can see as far as Siena, 65 kilometers (41 mi.) away. And don't leave town without a visit to the small **church of San Biagio**, the gem of 16th-century High Renaissance architecture by Sangallo the Elder. Built of golden travertine, it sits alone in an open field, overlooking the valley, a one-mile walk from the Piazza Grande, west of the Palazzo Comunale. From here you can look up to Montepulciano that looms above you, and contemplate the hike back up.

Directly across the piazza is the **Palazzo Contucci,** begun by Florentine architect Sangallo the Elder in 1519, as was the **Palazzo Nobili-Tarugi** facing the Duomo. It is still the august home of the Contucci family, the only noble family left in Montepulciano, and one of the principle producers of the Vino Nobile di Montepulciano. Their retail outlet offers *degustazione* daily, as does their friendly long-time competitor, the award-winning **Poliziano** enoteca in the same building. Depending upon vintages, expect to pay 19,000 to 36,000L ($11.20 to $21.20) for a bottle of Vino Nobile, half that for the Rosso di Montepulciano. Both producers and their enoteche are open daily, always have a few different bottles open for tasting and, for serious shoppers, will arrange for shipping. And where there is good wine, there is good food. From the number of highly recommended restaurants, locals favor the noisy but friendly **Trattoria Diva,** where a dinner of homemade unpretentious fare should cost about 30,000L ($17.65). It's located just inside the old city gate on V. Gracciano d. Cor. 92 (☎ 0578/716951). It's closed Tuesday, and no credit cards are accepted.

One block south of the piazza is the attractive **Albergo Duomo,** recently restored and with 13 comfortable rooms with telephone, television, and new bathrooms; doubles are 150,000L ($88.20). It's at V. San Donato 14 (☎ and fax 0578/757473). On the other side of the square on V. Ricci 9 is the A.P.T./Tourist Office (☎ 0578/758687). **From Siena,** about five TRA.IN buses make the 90-minute run daily to Montepulciano, stopping in Pienza. There are a handful of trains from Perugia or Siena to Montepulciano, but instead of getting off at the Montepulciano Stazione stop: Get off at **Chiusi,** where the local bus connections up to the hill town are better (a taxi ride of 30,000L/$17.65 awaits those who get off at Montepulciano Stazione and find no buses waiting).

AREZZO

Only 74 kilometers (47 mi.) east of Siena and an easy 1-hour train trip from Florence (81 km/51 mi.), Arezzo is worth a day's stay for a meander through its medieval centro storico and a visit to see the stunning fresco cycle of the ✪ **Legend of the True Cross** (La Leggenda della Vera Croce) (1452–66) by Piero della Francesca. For a peek, head to the 14th-century **Church of San Francesco** in Piazza San Francesco, which has kept the frescoes under wraps since 1985. A 1999/2000 completion looks good but not guaranteed, but visitors can at least see the left-hand half that was unveiled in 1997. Nearby is the lopsided, wonderfully charming ✪ **Piazza Grande**, recognizable to those who saw Roberto Benigni's 1998 Oscar-winning film *La Vita E Bella* (*Life is Beautiful!*). Arezzo is transported back to the Dark Ages with its much-felt historical ✪ **Giostra del Saracino** (Jousting Tournament) held in this off-kilter piazza the last Sunday in August and the first Sunday in September; for tickets contact the local **tourist information office** in Pz. d. Repubblica 22 just outside the train station (☎ 575/37-76-78; fax 575/20-839). If you can't get tickets for the joust itself, go for the elaborate *corteo* procession that wends through the narrow cobblestone streets beforehand—the rich costumes and authentic armor (on knights and horses alike) are the result of meticulous archival research and the theatrical know-how of Tuscan-born Franco Zefferelli. If you can time it right, the sprawling **antiques fair** the first weekend of every month fills the hill-top Piazza Duomo; it is considered Italy's largest.

Should you arrive in town and nothing much is happening, go for lunch or dinner at the centrally located **Osteria L'Agania** (on the popular V. Mazzini no. 10, 2 blocks from the Church of S. Francesco), everyone's favorite trattoria in town (☎ 0575/25381; closed Monday; credit cards accepted). If it's full, you'll be happy next door at the Trattoria del Saracino (no. 6) for a similarly casual ambience. Arezzo's finest restaurant, the **Buca di San Francesco** is housed in the frescoed cellar of a 14th-century palazzo next door to the Church of San Francesco on V. S. Francesco 1 (☎ 0575/23271). It's a bit more expensive (average dinner is 40,000L/$23.50 without wine), a lot more dramatic, and the traditional Tuscan menu is delicious. Closed Monday for dinner and all day Tuesday; credit cards accepted.

To get to Arezzo From Florence **by car**: take the **A1 autostrada** that links Florence to Rome (exit for Arezzo); from Florence **by train**, dozens of direct trains daily, 60 to 90 minutes; from Florence **by bus**, not as convenient, CAT buses, take 80 minutes to 2 hours. From **Siena** to Arezzo by car, take **S326** east out of Siena to pick up **A1 autostrada** north to Arezzo exit; a few LFI buses leave Siena daily (trip time: 1 hour, 30 minutes—because it makes local stops).

5 Perugia

80 km (50 mi.) SE of Arezzo, 188 km (117 mi.) NE of Rome, 154 km (96 mi.) SE of Florence, 26 km (16 mi.) NW of Assisi, 75 km (47.3 mi.) NE of Orvieto, 110 km (69 mi.) SE of Siena

From Tuscany's Siena, we cross over into the region of Umbria, the "green heart of Italy," and head toward its commercial and economic capital. Close your eyes to the charmless modern-day sprawl that you pass through on your way into the elegant heart of ancient Perugia. Principally known today for its celebrated university and as home to Biuttoni and Perugina chocolate (now part of Nestlé), Perugia is a prosperous city dressed in medieval hill town clothing. It is a good home base for travelers with and without cars who would like to visit Umbria's many characteristic hill towns such as Assisi, Gubbio, and Spoleto and the shopping mecca ceramics, Deruta. Even Orvieto is a feasible day trip (approximately 50 mi.) for those who have wheels. Perugia's historical center's cosmopolitan and urban bustle is a vibrant contrast to the rustic sleepiness of Umbria's hinterland for those inclined to venture afield.

As the easternmost satellite of the 12 Etruscan League cities, Perugia's strategic position later made it a Roman stronghold in the 3rd century B.C. and lasting for 8 centuries. But Perugia would assert itself as a strong and progressive city, an independent self-contained *comune* with the griffin as its emblem; trade and the arts flourished, and its still prominent university was established in 1270. This was Perugia's heyday and much civic architecture was constructed upon the Roman foundations, which were, in turn, built upon Etruscan foundations. The city's Arco Etrusco (Etruscan Arch) is the city's oldest testimony: Elaborated upon by the Romans who rebaptized it Arch of Augustus, it would later be topped by a Renaissance balcony. You can peel away the epochs and follow the story of Perugia's legendary past, and count the appearances of the griffin that can still be sighted around town. Centuries later it was still capturing the imagination of tourists such as Henry James who called it "the city of the infinite view."

If everyone you see seems to be 21 (and playing hooky), it's because, in addition to the ancient state university, which is one of Italy's largest, there is also a Università per Stranieri, the country's most prestigious school teaching the Italian language and culture to foreigners. Set up by Mussolini to improve the image of Italy abroad, it now enrolls more than 5,000 students representing more than 110 countries. This explains the proliferation of concerts, pizzerias, music stores, and an air of energy and vitality that crescendos during the annual Umbria Jazz Festival, since 1973 one of Europe's foremost music events, that is all but absent in many of Italy's provincial or historical cities.

FESTIVALS & MARKETS   Undoubtedly the highlight of Perugia's yearly events is the important **Umbria Jazz,** Italy's foremost jazz event, which takes place over a 10-day period in early or mid-July (musicians such as Wynton Marsalis and Herbie Hancock set the tone for this much-respected event). For ticket sales see either "Visitor Information," below, or call ☎ **075/57-32-432;** fax 075/57-22-656; www.umbriajazz.com; e-mail: umbriajazz@tin.it. A more dispersed **Jazz Fest** is held throughout the region of

Hitting the Books in Perugia

Perugia's University for Foreigners is Italy's oldest and largest. Programs of 1-, 2-, 3-, and 6-month duration are offered year-round and feature studies of the Italian language and culture. Prices range from 200,000 to 350,000L ($117.65 to $205.90) per month for each basic course; to 500,000L ($294.10) per month for each intensive course. Contact the Office of Administration (☎ **075/5746215;** fax 075/5732014; www.unistrapg.it; e-mail: diramm@unistrapg.it).

Umbria February through April and a jazz minifestival is held in Orvieto every New Year's Eve weekend for 5 days; contact the tourist information office. The world-class **Sagra Musicale Umbra (Umbrian Festival of Sacred Music)** has been held the last 2 weeks of September since 1937. It has attracted such major maestros as Van Karajan and Riccardo Muti (☎ **075/57-21-374;** fax 075/57-27-614). A secondary **Festival of Sacred Music** is held annually just before Easter (same contact as above). For 10 days at the end of October and the beginning of November a large **international antique fair** is held in the Rocca Paolina (☎ **075/57-31-322;** fax 075/5724725).

The **Eurochocolate Festival** is held annually for 1 week mid-to late October. Pick up a list of hour-by-hour festivities held throughout town, staged by chocolate manufacturers from all over the world. You can witness a chocolate-carving contest, when the scraps of 1,000-kilo chocolate blocks are yours for the sampling, and entire multiple-course menus are created around the chocolate theme. Half-day lessons from visiting chefs are also available. Contact Eurochocolate Organization, V. D'Andreotto 19, 06124 Perugia (☎ **075/5732670;** fax 075/5731100; www.chocolate.perugia.it; e-mail: cpc@chocolate.perugia.it).

For picnic provisions, the daily market (Monday to Saturday mornings only) takes place in the **Mercato Coperto** (Covered Market) east of the Palazzo dei Prior; entrance is from Piazza Matteotti. The much larger weekly market takes place every Saturday morning near the Stadium (behind the train station) in Piazza Umbria Jazz. An unusual organic food market, **Umbria Terraviva,** takes place the first Sunday of every month; check with the tourist office for new location.

ESSENTIALS

GETTING HERE   By Train   Almost all trains from Rome connect in Foligno for an approximately 3-hour trip total if you make an immediate connection (the wait can be from 10 to 40 min.). There are occasional direct trains. All trains cost 18,000L ($10.60), but the IC direct requires an additional 10,000L ($5.90) supplement. There are four direct trains from Florence, though most make the same easy connection in Terontola. Direct IC trains from Florence take 2¼ hours, and trains that stop in Terontola are an additional 20 to 30 minutes longer if the connection is immediate. All trains cost 14,000L ($8.25), but the IC direct requires an 8,500L ($5) supplement.

Perugia's **train station** (☎ **1478/88088** toll free within Italy) is inconveniently located far below the town's center in Piazza Vittorio Veneto. Take bus 20, 26, 27, 28, or 29 to Piazza Italia, the city's public transportation bus hub, which is as far as they can go into the *centro storico*.

By Bus   There are five buses daily servicing Perugia to and from downtown Rome (2½ hours; 20,000L/$11.75 one way), some continuing onto Rome's airport (3¼ hours; 29,000L/$17.05 one way). One bus daily makes the 2-hour trip to and from Florence for 19,000L ($11.20) one way. Call **SULGA** (☎ **075/50-09-641**) for information. Different regional lines service the towns of day-trip interest to most visitors, such as Assisi, Deruta, Gubbio, and Spoleto (☎ **167/512141** toll-free, or 075/5731707). All long-distance buses depart from Piazza Partigiani.

By Car   From Florence or Rome use the **Austostrada del Sole A1** as far as the junction for Perugia, then head due east. From Siena, take the scenic **S73,** which will connect with the autostrada east to Perugia. Cars are not allowed within Perugia's centro storico and you might have to request a pass from the traffic police to drop your luggage off at the hotel before returning your car to a pay parking lot on the outskirts.

VISITOR INFORMATION   The **A.P.T. (Azienda Promozione Turistica) or tourist information office** has relocated to the very central Pz. IV Novembre no. 3 (next to the steps of the Palazzo dei Priori; ☎ **075/57-36-458**). It is open daily 9am

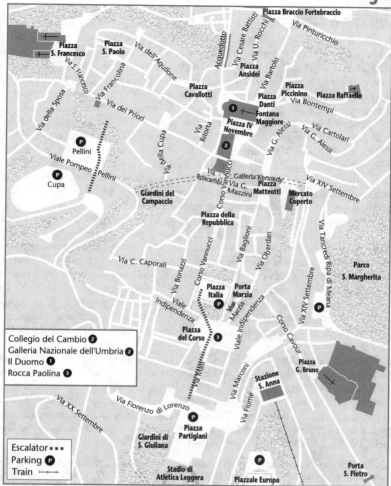

Collegio del Cambio ❷
Galleria Nazionale dell'Umbria ❷
Il Duomo ❶
Rocca Paolina ❸

Escalator ▪▪▪
Parking Ⓟ
Train ┼───┼

to noon and 3 to 7:30pm; closed Sunday afternoons. The Web site for all of Umbria is www.regione.umbria.it/turismo. Pick up a copy of *Perugia: What When and Where* to find out what's going on around town and details on upcoming events.

CITY LAYOUT   The main artery and pedestrian thoroughfare is **Corso Vannucci,** Perugia's medieval Main Street. It is anchored on the north by **Fontana Maggiore,** the city's social hub, with the Duomo just beyond it and on the south by the adjacent **Piazza della Repubblica** and **Piazza Italia,** home to the shaded Giardini Carducci park, with benches and a beautiful view over the Tiber Valley. Beneath the gardens are the foundations of the 16th-century *Rocca Paolina* fortress and the *scala mobile* network of escalators that bring you down through the ruins of the fortress to the town's lower level and long-distance bus station at Piazza Partigiani. **Corso Vannucci,** lined with historical cafes, bars, and the city's best stores, is the city's highest point and social and commercial center. Connecting Piazza Italia in the south to Piazza IV Novembre in the north, it is a wide palazzo-lined pedestrian thoroughfare with narrow, vaulted streets branching off west and east and invariably lead down, often with steps built into them. Corso Vanucci will often seem to be the only level strip in town.

WHAT TO SEE & DO

If ever there was a venue to see and be seen, the **Corso Vannucci,** the city's north-south pedestrian strip and nerve center, is it. Small clumps of the young and beautiful stand here and there, tables are set up to collect signatures supporting human rights, local politicians, or the cause of the moment, matrons with their dogs, pensioners with their cronies discussing soccer and union dues increases, cafe tables set out to capture the sun (or shade)—and that's just on an a slow moment. Siena's major strip was named after Pietro Vannucci, aka Perugino (1445–1523), Perugia's most celebrated local painter whose works can be seen in the National Gallery in the Palazzo dei Priori.

The ✪ **Fontana Maggiore** (The Great Fountain) is the elaborately decorated centerpiece of the wonderfully picturesque Piazza IV Novembre. It is justifiably held to be one of Italy's most charming and historically rich piazzas. The two-tiered fountain is scheduled to resurface in 1999 from the glass-domed bubble that protected it during a lengthy 5-year renovation that promises to have it once again appear as the city's greatest artistic treasure that it was meant to be. Designed and engineered in 1278 by a local monk and architect, Fra Bevignate (known in his time for his involvement in the construction of Orvieto's Duomo) to commemorate the completion of the town's aqueduct, it was then decorated with a lower tier of 50 bas-relief panels by Gothic master sculptor Nicolò Pisano of Pisa. Already known for the pulpits commissioned for Siena's duomo and his hometown's baptistery, this would be his last major work. The panels of the Fontana Maggiore depict everything from Aesop's fables and signs of the zodiac to episodes from Genesis and the origin of ancient Rome. The upper tier of 24 statuettes and panels is attributed to Nicolò's son, Giovanni.

The plain-faced cathedral to the north of the fountain was built after the fountain's completion. It was begun in 1347 and its external walls have been left in their uncompleted state. There are a number of 15th- and 16th-century paintings decorating the baroque interior, but the most curious item on display is the alleged wedding band of the Virgin Mary, displayed (though hidden within 15 boxes that graduate in size, each locked by a key kept under safekeeping with a different church official) in the **Cappella del Sant'Anello** (The Chapel of the Holy Ring), the first chapel on the left.

✪ **Palazzo dei Priori & the Galleria Nazionale dell'Umbria (National Gallery).** Cor. Vannucci 19 (at Piazza IV Novembre), Perugia. ☎ **075/57-41-247.** www.sbaaas.umbria.it. Admission 8,000L ($4.70). Mon–Sat 9am–7pm; Sun 9am–1pm. (Check for probable extension of evening hours in summer months).

The bulk of the impressive Palazzo dei Priori (the Priors' Palace) lines the west side of the Corso Vannucci, but its oldest facade presides over the Piazza IV Novembre. Dating to the 13th century, the pink-tinged facade is distinguished by a grand staircase (always used by tired visitors and students enjoying a social moment between classes), and bronze copies of the 13th-century griffin (the city symbol) and the Guelph (papal) lion that hold the massive, ancient chains that were once used to close the city gates of Siena, taken from the town after a Perugian victory in 1358. It is crowned by a row of bristling crenellations above rows of Gothic windows. Used as the town hall for hundreds of years, the Palazzo dei Priori is one of the greatest extant examples of secular architecture from its period.

On the Corso Vanucci side of the palazzo you'll find an entrance to the Collegio del Cambio (see below) and a separate entrance for the fourth-floor **Galleria Nazionale dell'Umbria,** the region's most important museum of Umbrian art. It has just undergone an extensive refurbishment and reorganization that once again secures its former status as one of central Italy's richest art collections. The 33-room gallery, expanding by an additional eight rooms in early 1999, is a showcase of Umbrian art that traces its chronology from the 13th to the 18th centuries and the schools that influenced it. Rooms dedicated to Tuscan masters include works by Duccio, Fra Angelico, and Piero della Francesca that just about steal the show. But a dozen or so paintings by local celebrity Pietro Vannucci, alias Perugino, native son and Umbrian master artist, are the museum's treasure, particularly his *Pietà* and the *Adoration of the Magi* from the late 15th century. Known for his gentle landscapes and as being the teacher of Raphael, he is regarded as one of the principal figures of the Italian Renaissance, certainly the most illustrious of the Umbrian school of painting. Others may contend that the gentle landscapes and deep colors of Pinturicchio—another of Perugino's students, occasional collaborator, and the one responsible for the Piccolomini Library in Siena's Duomo—demand their fair share of attention.

Other than very minor damage done to the Duomo, the Palazzo dei Priori absorbed the brunt of the 1997 serial earthquakes that shook Umbria and were felt marginally in Perugia (see "Assisi," p. 309). The scaffolding is down, but the fissures in the ancient facade of the Palazzo dei Priori remain, with massive steel bolts securely holding the facade together, visible from both the outside and inside.

✪ Collegio del Cambio and the Collegio della Mercanzia. Cor. Vannucci no. 25 and 15 (both within the Palazzo dei Priori). (☎ **075/57285999**. Admission to Collegio del Cambio 5,000L ($2.95); admission to Collegio della Mercanzia 2,000L ($1.20); joint admission 6,000L ($3.50). Mar–Oct and Dec 20–Jan 6 Mon–Sat 9am–12:30pm and 2:30–5:30pm, Sun 9am–12:30pm. Nov 1–Dec 19 and Jan 7–Feb 28 Tues–Sat 8am–2pm, Sun 9am–12:30pm.

The work of Perugino is the highlight of the small 15th-century Collegio del Cambio, the precursor of Perugia's commodities exchange. This was the seat of the Exchange Guild, whose wealthy and affluent members chose Perugino, the finest Renaissance artist of the time to fresco their offices between 1496 and 1500. These vibrant frescoes are held to be his masterpiece, including scenes from the bible, the prophets and female figures representing the virtues—and quite a vivid depiction of late 15th-century fashion. Perugino did not overlook including his own self-portrait enframed on a trompe l'oeil column on the left wall as you enter. Both Pinturicchio and a 17-year-old apprentice Raphael were said to have collaborated with him.

PERUGINA CHOCOLATE

The Perugina chocolate industry is a local success story. Founded in 1907 by two local families, it grew from strength to strength, heightened by the creation of the **bacio** candy in 1922. They currently produce 200 million baci a year, to be found in stores worldwide. A popular runner-up in popularity is the gaily wrapped Easter eggs that are as much a tradition as the holiday itself. Opened in 1997 for the 90th anniversary of the Perugina manufacturer, the Perugina Museum explores the long history of the Perugina trademark. You can also visit the factory itself at Località San Sisto, Nestlé Italiana (☎ **075/5276796**). It's open Monday to Friday 9am to 12:30pm and 2:30 to 5pm; Saturday and Sunday by arrangement; admission is free. The rest of the year, tourists can buy Perugina goodies in just about any bar/cafe, although there is no Perugina outlet per se. A well-stocked choice is always the **Caffe del Cambio** (see "Where to Dine," below), any of the other bar/cafes on Corso Vanucci or the Perugina store on the east side of the Piazza Italia.

WHERE TO STAY

Agrilife Turismo Rurale (☎ **075/35746**) and **Viaggiatori, Viandanti e Sognatori** (☎ **075/5722645;** fax 075/5722974) are two independent agencies that can book you at any of 30 Umbrian farms that rent rooms of varying costs (request their catalogue). The tourist office can supply a less descriptive list of these rural accommodations, as well as a list of half a dozen religious institutions that offer inexpensive lodgings in town. For info about the city's youth hostel call ☎ and fax **75/5722880. Promhotel Umbria** is a local travel agency that can book you into one of more than 80 hotels in Perugia and throughout Umbria (☎**0678/62-033** toll-free within Italy, or 075/50-02-788; fax 075/50-02-789; e-mail: promhotelumbria@krenet.it). Also note that the **Hotel Eden** at V. Cesare Caporali 9 (west off the Pz. Italia), 06123 Perugia (☎ **075/57-28-102;** fax 075/57-20-342), offers well-located, contemporary rooms with bathroom for 60,000L ($35.30) single; 90,000L ($52.95) double; 120,000L ($70.60) triple; 150,000L ($88.25) quadruple.

✪ **Hotel Fortuna Perugia.** V. Bonazzi 19 (west of Pz. Italia), 06123 Perugia. ☎ **075/57-22-845.** Fax 075/57-35-040. 34 units, all with bathroom. MINIBAR TV TEL. 137,000L ($80.60) single; 188,000L ($110.60) double. Rates include breakfast. AE, DC, V.

The Fortuna is recommended for its four-star accommodations at three-star rates. Beveled and leaded glass doors welcome you to this charming hotel where thoughtful service and details such as silk and dried-flower arrangements and white-lace doilies hint more of a provincial inn. That same cozy charm continues in most of the guest rooms where a contemporary character prevails despite the floral bedspreads and upholstery and matching blond-wood headboards and tables. New management arrived in 1998, and work is being done here and there, including the likelihood of air-conditioning in all rooms by 1999 (inquire when booking). Rooms have rooftop views over the historical center or out over the Umbrian Valley. In warm weather breakfast is served on a fifth-floor roof-garden/terrace with stunning vistas; your cappuccino will never taste this good again.

Hotel La Rosetta. Pz. Italia 19 (at southern end of Corso Vanucci), 06121 Perugia. ☎ and fax **075/57-20-841.** 96 units, all with bathroom. MINIBAR TV TEL. 165,000L ($97.05) single; 199,000L ($117.05) double; 269,000L ($158.25) triple. Rates include breakfast. AE, DC. Parking 30,000L ($17.65).

This favorite of the international music crowd that descends during the Umbria Jazz festival began as a small inn in 1927 and has gradually expanded piecemeal, explaining its almost labyrinthine layout and variety in the quality and decor of the rooms. Some are quite grand with parquet floors and frescoed ceilings, others more modest with floor-to-floor carpeting and more contemporary furnishings. But they are all peaceful, clean, and well maintained—this is a four-star hotel with rates that are comfortably low. An accommodating staff and perfect location augment its appeal, with an excellent restaurant that is very well known, though on the expensive side, with primi averaging 25,000L ($14.70) (open daily, lunch and dinner; same telephone as hotel). You'll see a lot of celebrated performing artists chowing down here during the days of the festival.

Hotel Priori. V. d. Priori (west off the Cor. Vannucci), 06123 Perugia. ☎ **075/57-23-378.** Fax 075/57-23-213. 51 units, all with bathroom. TEL. 90,000L ($52.95) single; 130,000L ($76.50) double; 170,000L ($100) triple; 200,000L ($117.65) quad. Rates include buffet breakfast. Ask about discounts for stays of 2 nights and longer (not available during holidays or Jazz Festival). MC, V. Parking 15,000L ($8.80).

Well positioned 3 short blocks down the principal Via dei Priori and directly behind the Palazzo dei Priori, this modernized hotel still enjoys the fruits of a 1995 renovation. Half the spacious rooms with terra-cotta floors overlook the Chiesa di San Filippo Neri, the lucky ones overlook the hotel terrace and the valley beyond. The terrace is surprisingly spacious, given the typical hill-town problems of limited space. When weather permits, begin your day here, when breakfast is served beneath white canvas umbrellas and yours is the terra-cotta roofscape and gentle countryside that inspired Umbria's painters. TVs are available upon request for 5,000L ($2.95) a day, and a new annex in an adjoining historical palazzo means six new rooms with air-conditioning at 20,000L ($11.75) per day extra (request upon booking).

WHERE TO DINE

In addition to the restaurants below, try **Caffè Sandri,** Cor. Vanucci 32, **Caffè Ferrari,** Cor. Vanucci 43, or **Caffè del Cambio,** Cor. Vanucci 29. They're all central and reasonably priced spots for a light lunch, offering sandwiches and even primi for 5,000 to 11,000L ($2.95 to $6.50) at the bar, or at tables indoors and out. Caffè Sandri is the local favorite, small but rich with atmosphere, its wood-paneled 19th-century interior cramped but cozy. It quadruples in seating capacity when warm weather permits it to set up outdoor tables in the very middle of the corso's pedestrian catwalk. The new meeting spot in town, the **Caffè di Perugia** (off the Corso Vanucci on V. Mazzini 10/14) is elegantly housed within a medieval palazzo, comfortably looking like it has always been there. Fixed-price lunches include a primi plus vegetable side dish (16,000L/$9.40), or spend half that at the busy bar for a sandwich and drink. Food fans should make sure at least one casual meal is had at the **Enoteca Provinciale** on V. Ulisse Rocchi no. 18, where platters of salads or regional cheeses and salami (8,000L/$4.70) are just a savory side; the draw here is the 5 to 10 red and white regional wines available by the glass in a beautifully restored 13th-century palazzo (3,000 to 10,000L/$1.75 to $5.90).

✪ **Cesarino.** Pz. IV Novembre 4/5 (west of fountain), Perugia. ☎ **075/57-28-974.** Reservations recommended. Primi 10,000–15,000L ($5.90–$8.80); secondi 14,000–22,000L ($8.20–$12.95). AE, MC, V. Thurs–Tues 12:30–2:30pm and 7:30–11pm. UMBRIAN.

Cesarino's new location is easy to find directly on the piazza anchored by the Fontana Maggiore, with preferred outdoor tables offering a view of this most characteristic corner of time-locked Perugia. The cooking is a hats-off salute to the bounty and wonder of a simple, home-style cooking—traditional *cucina umbra* at its best. Whatever today's special pasta is, order it. If you eat indoors, you'll be privy to free cooking lessons if seated near the open kitchen where white-capped *signoras* roll out fresh pasta made daily while a white-aproned man tends to the open hearth and its crackling and sizzling meats on a spit.

La Taverna. V. d. Streghe 8 (off the Cor. Vanucci), Perugia. ☎ **075/57-24-128.** Reservations recommended. Primi 10,000–20,000L ($5.90–$11.75); secondi 16,000–25,000L ($9.40–$14.70). AE, MC, V. Tues–Sun 12:30–2:30pm and 7:30–11:30pm. UMBRIAN.

The location of this well-known eatery in the cantina of a 14th-century palazzo reached by a dark, stepped alleyway curiously called The Street of the Witches is too much to resist. Surprisingly the space is bright and welcoming, even elegant with waiters in jacket and white ankle-length aprons hovering over candlelit tables set with linen clothes beneath high brick barrel-vaulted ceilings. The menu is as traditional as it is innovative, the latter half hinting of the Umbrian chef's experience abroad—in Florida, no less. The trappings of La Taverna may strike you as a splurge choice, but unless you let loose with any of the discerning wine list's better options and overindulge in the justifiably well-known desert cart, the cost of a lovely and romantic dinner here needn't set you back.

Pizzeria il Cantinone. V. Ritorta 6 (west of the Fontana Maggiore), Perugia. ☎ **075/57-34-430.** Reservations suggested. Pizza and primi 8,000–12,000L ($4.70–$7.05); secondi 9,000–20,000L ($5.30–$11.75). AE. Wed–Mon noon–3pm and 7pm–midnight. PIZZERIA/UMBRIAN.

If you're in search of something casual and inexpensive in the area of Corso Vannucci or Piazza IV Novembre, wander down the narrow street west of the Fontana Maggiore and, where the pedestrian traffic flows right onto Via Ulisse Rocchi, look to the left instead, where you'll find this popular pizzeria in a cool brick-vaulted medieval setting. Despite its central location, prices are kept moderate while the lure of their pizzas keeps the place full. There's a full menu of local specialties as well, though the steady patrons are pizza devotees who return for the *pizza alla gorgonzola e porcini* (made with heady Gorgonzola cheese and mushrooms) or any one of the dozens of others.

✪ **Ristorante Vecchia Perusia.** V. Ulisse Rocchi 9 (north of Pz. IV Novembre), Perugia. ☎ **075/57-25-900.** Reservations suggested. Primi 8,000–13,000L ($4.70–$4.65); secondi 11,000–16,000L ($6.50–$9.50). No credit cards. Mon–Sat 12:30–2:30 and 7–11pm. UMBRIAN.

There are just 10 tables in this small, homey trattoria where the aroma from the open kitchen is enough to have you order one of everything. If you don't have an Umbrian grandmother, come here for the genuine *cucina umbra* that you've been missing. Every day a new "pasta fresca" appears (look out for *tagliatelle con porcini freschi,* made with fresh mushrooms), but happy habitués all seem to go with the *crepe alla perusia:* homemade crepes spread with four cheeses and ham, then rolled, smothered with a mushroom-and-cream sauce, and baked. There's the menu's traditional Umbrian game (*faraona*/pheasant, *coniglio*/rabbit) to choose from, or the simplicity of a pork or veal chop simply prepared on the grill.

SIDE TRIPS FROM PERUGIA

This is the countryside that inspired the monastic communities of Saints Francis and Clare of Assisi, and modern-day gastronomes who visit for Orvieto's distinctive white wine and the region's unrivaled contribution to the gourmet world: black truffles from the area east of here around Norcia. Visit **Gubbio** (1 hr. northeast of Perugia; take the S298; see p. 319), hyped as the Umbrian Siena, though I find it more like an Umbrian San Gimignano minus the towers. Ten miles to Perugia's southeast lies the small town of **Torgiano,** whose unique wine museum (and wonderful retail **enoteca** next door) is a must-do pilgrimage for serious wine lovers. It's on Cor. Vittorio Emanuele 11 in the Palazzo Baglioni (☎ **075/9880200**). Admission is 5,000L ($2.95); it's open Monday through Sunday 9am to 1pm and 3 to 7pm (in winter until 6pm). With 20 well-organized, well-lit rooms that trace every aspect of viticulture, this is the only museum of its kind in Italy. The owners, the well-known wine-producing Lungarotti family, have become Umbria's most noted and celebrated in the Italian wine scene.

Known since the Middle Ages as a ceramic center, the tiny town of **Deruta** lies farther south (20 kilometers/12.6 mi.) of Perugia (by car, take the S3 bus; there are a few daily 30-minute buses (but no train service)—check the tourist office for schedule and make sure not to miss the last bus back). Awash with store after store, particularly along the Via Tiberina, Deruta's embarrassment of choices can be mind boggling. Making ceramics since the 15th century (the city's history of ceramic production is recorded as far back as the 12th century), the family of Ubaldo Grazia guarantees one of the best selections of original Deruta patterns, some dating back to the 16th century, some refreshingly modern and most unusual. And yes, you probably did see his wares in Saks or Neiman Marcus. Credit cards aren't accepted, but personal checks and travelers checks are okay. The store is at V. Tiberina 16 (☎ **075/9710201;** fax 075/972018). The Regional Museum of Ceramics houses a precious collection of Deruta ceramics of various periods from the Middle Ages to the 1930s (Largo San Francesco; ☎ **075/9711000;** Wednesday to Monday 10am to 1pm and 3:30 to 7pm; check for shorter hours off-season). Admission is 5,000L ($2.95).

GETTING AROUND The smaller towns of Umbria are serviced by frequent buses (☎ **075/57-31-707** for information or check at the Tourist Office). Trip times and one-way prices are as follows: **Deruta** (30 min.; 3,800L/$2.25); **Gubbio** (70 min.; 8,000L/$4.70); Todi (75 min.; 10,000L/$5.90); **Torgiano** (20 min.; 3,500L/$2.05). Almost all buses leave from the Piazza dei Partigiana, down the *scala mobile* (escalator) and through the Rocca Paolina from Piazza Italia. Before leaving Perugia, check on return times, careful of weekday versus weekend schedules.

6 Assisi

190 km (120 mi.) SE of Florence, 26 km (16 mi.) SE of Perugia, 177 km (111.5 mi.) NE of Rome, 48 km (30 mi.) N of Spoleto

More than 700 years—and countless hundreds of millions of pilgrims and tourists—have passed since St. Francis lived and died here in this small hill town of muted-pink stone that sits on the wooded slopes of Mount Subasio. It's Umbria's most visited city and yet, despite the mania of stores and shops that sell St. Francis everything—from ashtrays and pot holders to embroidered tea towels and glow-in-the-dark rosary beads—the spirit of the young barefoot monk who forsook these very material goods to preach poverty, chastity, and obedience lives on. His spirit may seem diminished at times when unparalleled crowds and heat reach their peak, but it is easy to find it again, in a quiet moment at the saint's crypt below the Lower Basilica or during a delightful walk to the shaded serenity of the unspoiled hermitage outside the city's medieval walls. The universality of his humanity and love for nature and the animal kingdom transcend all nationalities and religions, and Francis is often held as a medieval flower child, an environmentalist of the Middle Ages who would write the first poems in the Italian language. If the Church had to create a figure that would endure the last millennium and go forward bravely into the next and be so embraced by so many, it could not have outdone this disarmingly simple character who lived to love God and all those who inhabited this planet—a welcomed departure from the doom-and-gloom strictures of the Dark Ages.

Born in 1182 to a local well-to-do family of textile merchants, Francis renounced his social status and youthful carousing only after a number of apparitions and visions. He traveled on foot through Italy, Spain, and Egypt, a revolutionary spirit who took the Roman Catholic Church back to the basics when the papacy was rotten with corruption. Dante compared him to John the Baptist; his fame grew quickly beyond the confines of Umbria and even Italy. In 1210, he founded an order of mendicant monks that would become known thereafter as the Franciscans. Within 15 years there was a growing community of 5,000 who followed the barefoot asceticism of *il Poverello* (the Poor One) and he enjoyed great veneration and acceptance within his lifetime. He was the first to ever receive the "stigmata" wounds in his hands, feet, and side in 1224 at a hilltop retreat in Tuscany called La Verna—mirroring the same wounds inflicted upon Jesus Christ during his Crucifixion. His friendship with the lovely *Chiara* (Clare), a local girl of a minor noble and wealthy family who followed him, would soon follow by her founding the Second Order of St. Francis, the nuns known as **le Sorelle Clarisse,** the Poor Sisters of St. Clare (more simply known as the Poor Clares), in 1212 when she was just 17; together they pushed this sleepy Umbrian town unto the Church's center stage, where it has remained ever since. Today it is the largest of all Catholic orders and St. Francis, made patron saint of all of Italy in 1939, is the most beloved and well known of Christendom's galaxy of saints.

St. Francis's spirit somehow survives the unashamed commercialization of the town. The unprecedented numbers of pilgrims expected for the Jubilee Year 2000 may prove otherwise. Young groups of Italian and European students who come for seminars, and pilgrims from the earth's four corners who come to pay homage to one of

---

THE EARTHQUAKES

On September 26, 1997, serial earthquakes (5.7 and 5.6 on the Richter scale) with the epicenter located just outside of Assisi violently shook much of this otherwise serene corner of Umbria. More than 13,000 Umbrians were left homeless, and the structure that sustained the most damage was Assisi's crown jewel, the Basilica of San Francesco. Two monks and two inspectors were killed by the two tons of debris that crashed from the vaulted ceiling, and entire sections of priceless frescoes—some of the art world's most important—may be permanently beyond repair. Pope John Paul visited in January 1998, encouraging the area's residents to bear up "in a Franciscan spirit," and heal the wounds of their hearts and of their homeland. Work began immediately, and much of the scaffolding is already down from repair work that has been completed on all but the most damaged sites (you'll continue to see scaffolded buildings throughout Umbria's cities and towns in the years to come). The future of the Upper Basilica has not yet been determined, despite sophisticated technology, impressive budgets of repair funds allocated by the government, the Vatican and individuals around the world, and the conviction of the local people to recreate Assisi's priceless treasures. At press time, 80,000 fragments of frescoes no larger than a thumbnail are still to be sorted through, a Herculean attempt to put the world's largest jigsaw puzzle back together again. Similar earthquakes that hit Umbria in 1984, damaged many of Assisi's baroque edifices but left medieval structures intact, and were not half as devastating as this.

Despite the eventual outcome of the Basilica's future, atheists, agnostics, and devouts alike will continue to visit Assisi as a site of pilgrimage, artistic appreciation, and cultural curiosity; during peak months, numbers are legion. Moderate-priced accommodations are very good (and the restaurants serving Umbrian specialties even better) and numerous, but booking ahead during busy months is almost obligatory. Things quiet down in the evening—the majority of pilgrims and religious groups usually lodge outside of town in the larger roadside hotels—but you still might want to move on after the day or two spent seeing the sites.

And if the countless numbers show for the Holy Year that the Vatican has predicted, be prepared if Assisi takes on something of a circus attitude.

---

the holiest men to have walked this planet, find in these narrow back streets something of the town as it was in the saint's own time. As a former Roman stronghold, Assisi reached its medieval zenith in the years surrounding the lives of Francis and Clare. Much of what you see today is true to its 13th-century origins, and the city, with its patrician palazzi made of a local pink-tinged stone, is handsomely preserved.

FESTIVALS & MARKETS   The **Settimana Santa (Holy Week)** that precedes Easter is understandably commemorated with numerous processions between churches, including evocative nighttime processions by torchlight. The feast day of the ✪ **Calendimaggio** is the year's largest event and is celebrated during a 3-day period the first week of May (starting the first Thursday after May 1) when the entire town is thrown back to its medieval glory. Reenacting the rivalry between two upper and lower factions of town that can be traced back to the 1300s, there are competitions of concerts, crossbows, and flag-throwing, to name a few, and the entire town turns out in elaborate medieval costume. Oddly, San Rufino (after whom the Duomo is named) and not St. Francis is the patron saint of Assisi, and his **feast day** is celebrated August 11 with a procession and crossbow contest in medieval costume. It is followed by the feast day of Santa Chiara (St. Clare) August 12. On October 3 and 4 **Festa di San Francesco** commemorates the saint's death; as patron saint of Italy, he is duly honored with great pageantry. The yearly **Assisi Antiquariato** antiques fair is held for 2 weeks in the end of April and the beginning of May in the suburb of Bastia. A weekly market fills Piazza Matteotti every Saturday morning.

ESSENTIALS

GETTING HERE   By Train   Like rail travel to all hill towns, the inconvenience is in connecting to bus service to bring you from the train station down below to the hilltop site. Buses run every 20 to 30 minutes, and almost all that stop in front of the small Assisi train station near Santa Maria degli Angeli (☎ **075/8040272**) are headed up to Assisi's Piazza Matteotti, your ultimate destination. Trains make the trip from Perugia in under 30 minutes and leave every 30 to 45 minutes (3,500L/$2.05 one way). Ten trains daily leave from Florence, half of them direct to Assisi, half connecting in Terontola (20,000L/$11.75 one way for the 2½-hr. trip); a dozen trains daily make the trip from Rome in 2 to 3 hours, some direct, some with a transfer in Foligno (18,000L/$10.60 one way).

By Bus   Most buses leave Assisi from Piazza Matteotti, northeast of Piazza del Comune. At least 10 buses daily service Perugia (1 hr.; 5,000L/$2.95). There are two buses daily to Rome (3 hr.; 30,000L/$17.65) and two daily to Florence (2½ hr.; 25,000L/$14.70). For bus information call Sulga at ☎ **075/5009641.**

By Car   From Perugia, head southeast on **SS3**; at the junction of Route 147 follow signs east for Assisi. It's a half-hour drive. The entire historical center is closed to traffic, but traffic police will let you drop off your bags at a hotel; check with hotel for special agreements they may have with nearest municipal parking lot.

VISITOR INFORMATION   The new location for the **Ufficio Informazioni or tourist information office** (☎ 075/81-25-34; fax 075/81-37-27; e-mail: aptas@krenet.it) is in the main square, Piazza del Comune, adjacent to the columned Temple of Minerva. Hours are Monday to Friday 8am to 2pm and 3 to 6:30pm; Saturday 9am to 1pm and 3:30 to 6:30pm; Sunday 9am to 1pm.

CITY LAYOUT   The city is long and narrow, running west to east, and even the farthest sites such as the Convent of San Damiamo and the Eremo delle Carceri can be reached by foot for those in good shape (you can taxi it back). The **Basilica di San Francesco** is at the westernmost end, while the center of town is the main square, Piazza del Comune. Northeast of this is Piazza Rufini, site of the Duomo, and beyond this the Piazza San Matteotti, last stop for all long-distance buses. Pick up a map from the Tourist Office upon your arrival.

GETTING AROUND   Your feet are all you need to get you around. Unlike some other small hill towns, taxis are on standby about town, but can only be found at a few designated places (the Basilica di San Francesco, Piazza del Comune).

GUIDED TOURS   For guided walking tours contact the Tourist Office or the **Assoc. Guide Turistiche** (☎ 075/815228; fax 075/815229) for their list of certified English-speaking guides (110,000L/$64.70 for 3 hr., groups of 5 or less). American-born Anne Robichaud (☎ **075/802334**; fax 075/8042630; e-mail: arobichaud@tecnonet.it) is a local personality who will make your stay in town or visiting Umbrian sites an exceptional one ($225/half day for up to 4 people). The Franciscan community affiliated with the Basilica offers free guided tours by English-speaking friars: Stop by the office just left of the entrance to the Lower Basilica in Piazza Inferiore, Monday to Saturday 9am to noon and 2 to 5:30pm (to 4:30pm in winter), Sunday afternoons only (☎ **075/8190084;** fax 075/8190035; e-mail: chiu@krenet.it). Tours do not go into the basilica itself to avoid disrupting visitors, but visit other sites and explore the life and tenants of St. Francis and today's religious community.

WHAT TO SEE & DO

Mt. Subasio is a protected regional park and offers an extensive network of footpaths that attracts do-it-yourself trekkers and mountain bikers. A map called *Sentieri di Mt. Subasio* (Footpaths of Mt. Subasio) is sometimes available at the tourist office. If it is out of stock, look for two alternatives maps that are usually on sale in local shops: the map put out by **C.A.I.** (Club Alpino Italiano) for 8,500L ($5) or **Kompass** 10,000L ($5.90). Half-hearted walkers who are happy with a brisk amble but nothing more taxing should consider the **Eremo delle Carceri** (see below).

The **Piazza del Comune** is the very heart of Assisi, and much of what you see dates to the 12th to 14th centuries and the very days of economic prosperity that Francis and Clare eschewed. Its most ancient component is the white ✪ **Tempio della Minerva,** the majestic Corinthian-columned temple on its north side that dates as far back as the 1st century B.C.; so perfect in classical design and proportion, "one could never stop looking at its facade," wrote an enthralled Goethe during his 18th-century Italian journey. Its most recent reincarnation is that of a Baroque church that provides, at most, a pew and a cool moment for reflection. Adjoining the former pagan temple to your right as you exit is the new (and possibly temporary) home of the tourism office, housed on the ground floor of the tall 13th-century **Torre del Popolo.** Facing the temple and dominating the south side of the piazza is the **Pinacoteca** (admission 6,000L/$3.50; closed Monday), the town's unremarkable picture gallery, housed in the 14th-century Palazzo dei Priori, closed more frequently than it is open. Check the piazza's tourist office for regularly changing hours.

Beneath the flagstoned piazza and unbeknownst to the flocks of tourists that fill it sit the remains of the ancient Roman Forum. Glimpses of its ongoing renovation are part of the draw of the small, generally overlooked **Museo Civico e Foro Romano** (entrance on Via Portica off western edge of Piazza del Comune), and its collection of Etruscan and Roman artifacts (☎ 075/813053; admission 4,000L/$2.35; summer hours daily 10am to 1pm and 3 to 7pm; winter hours reduced).

✪ **Basilica di San Francesco (Basilica of St. Francis). Pz. di San Francesco.** ☎ **075/ 81-90-01.** Admission to basilica free. Apr–Oct, daily dawn–dusk. Sun morning visits allowed only for those attending services. Check on following winter hours: Nov–Mar, daily 6:30am– noon and 2–6pm. Basilica Treasury (Tesoro della Basilica) and the Perkins Collection (Collezione Perkins) 3,000L ($1.75), check on following hours: Apr–Oct 9:30am–noon and 2–6pm; closed in winter.

Shored up and extending from the western end of town, the upper and lower levels of the Basilica of St. Francis is the first thing you see upon approaching this pink-hued hill town. It was a massive architectural feat and is still considered one of the engineering marvels and most outstanding monuments to art and faith of the medieval period in the Western world. If you haven't pinpointed what it is that bothers you, it most likely is what has bothered the Franciscan religious community for centuries: The commanding figure cut by the imposing two-tiered basilica has little if nothing to do with the vows of utter poverty and humility and stark asceticism that were the very tenets of St. Francis's back-to-basics life. While this may hardly be the lavish display of extravagance one tries to come to terms with at the Vatican, it is nevertheless disheartening to know that Brother Elias of Cortona, one of Francis's earliest disciples and the controversial monk who would be firmly in control in the years following Francis's death in 1226 (he was canonized almost immediately in 1228), cashed in on the saint's popularity by selling indulgences across Europe (Brother Leone, who sym-

Assisi

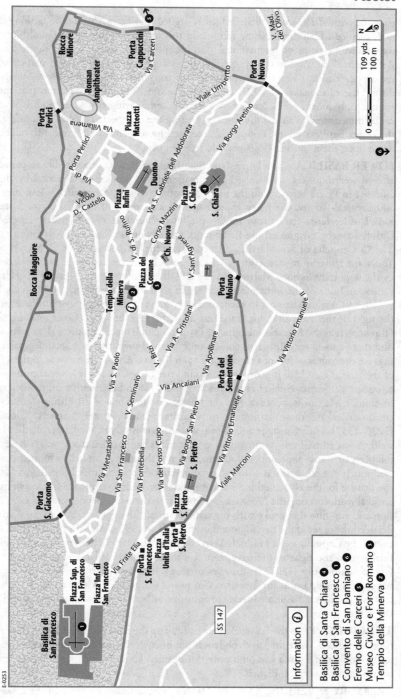

Information ℹ

- Basilica di Santa Chiara ❹
- Basilica di San Francesco ❶
- Convento di San Damiano ❻
- Eremo delle Carceri ❺
- Museo Civico e Foro Romano ❸
- Tempio della Minerva ❷

SS 147

Map labels:

Basilica di San Francesco
Plazza Sup. di San Francesco
Plazza Inf. di San Francesco ❶
Porta S. Giacomo
Rocca Maggiore ❷
Rocca Minore
Roman Amphitheater
Porta Cappuccini
Via Carceri
Porta Nuova
V. Mad. del Olivo
Porta Perlici
Via di Porta Perlici
Via Villamena
Piazza Matteotti
Viale Umberto
Via Borgo Aretino
Duomo
Vicolo D. Castello
Piazza Rufini
V. di S. Rufino
Via S. Gabriele dell'Addolorata
Piazza S. Chiara
S. Chiara ❹
Tempio della Minerva ❷
Corso Mazzini
Piazza del Comune ❸
Ch. Nuova
V. Sant'Agnese
Porta Molano
Via A. Cristofani
Via Apollinare
Via Vittorio Emanuele II
Via S. Paolo
V. Brizi
V. Seminario
Via Ancaiani
Porta del Sementone
Via Metastasio
Via San Francesco
Via Fontebella
Via del Fosso Cupo
Via Borgo San Pietro
S. Pietro
Viale Marconi
Via Vittorio Emanuele II
Via Frate Elia
Porta S. Francesco
Plazza Unità d'Italia
Porta S. Pietro
Plazza S. Pietro

0 109 yds
0 100 m
N

E-0253

313

pathized with *il Poverello*'s beliefs, futilely argued that Francis would be nothing if not horrified). Elias' fund-raising resulted in this impious monument to wealth and importance, a point of international Catholic pilgrimage seconded by Rome and Bethlehem alone. And so it was especially devastating that the Basilica (in particular, the Upper Basilica) was the region's one structure that suffered the most damage during the earthquakes of 1997, and that it would be within the church that the region's only four deaths occurred: two friars accompanying two local officials who came immediately to survey the damage. During the unexpected second earthquake, the Upper Basilica's vaulted ceilings collapsed and more than two tons of debris rained down upon them, priceless 700-year-old frescos included.

LOWER BASILICA   The Lower (and slightly older) Basilica was speedily reopened after the earthquakes, its damages only marginal by comparison. Reached by the entrance in Piazza Inferiore on the south side of the church, the basilica is low, dark, and mystical—if you are lucky enough to find a moment of calm in between the arrival of fender-to-fender tour buses—the lower church is almost entirely covered with frescoes by the greatest pre-Renaissance painters of the 13th and 14th centuries. The ✪ **Cappella di San Martino** (first chapel on the left), dedicated to St. Martin of Tours, the father of monasticism in 4th-century A.D. France, is covered with frescoes by the important Simone Martini of Siena and date from the early 14th century. The earliest and one of the most prominent artists to work in the church was Cimabue (1240–1302) whose frescoes in the transept are some of the most important here. To the right of the main altar, his faded but masterful ✪ *Madonna, Child and Angels* (also known as the **Maestà**) includes St. Francis looking on, the popular depiction of him that you will see duplicated endless times around town. Below Cimabue's paintings are the tombs of five of Francis's original followers. Across the transept to the left of the altar is a cycle of frescoes that surround the *Deposition of the Cross,* considered to be one of the masterpieces of the Tuscan painter Pietro Lorenzetti, a contemporary of Simone Martini from Siena. But the frescoes creating one of art history's greatest controversies are those attributed to Cimabue's most famous student, Giotto (1226–1337) (both Cimabue and Giotto worked extensively in the Upper Basilica as well). At the turn of this century, most art historians had decided that it was nameless followers or fellow apprentices of Giotto, and not the master himself, who had covered much of both basilicas with cycles of frescoes. His work, they believed, was far too mature for the 20-something student rookie who hadn't yet proven himself in his epochal work covering the Arena Chapel in Perugia; these frescoes depicted an expression and emotion that broke with the static icons of the rigid Byzantine School and heralded the onset of the Renaissance movement. The 1995 completion of the restoration of the **Cappella della Maddalena** or Chapel of St. Mary Magdalen (the third and final one to the right of the nave close to the altar), provided the confirmation of Giotto's authorship (1307) in the eyes of many Italian scholars. To keep everyone happy, authorship is still attributed to "Giotto and workshop." Vespers are sung by the friars in the Lower Basilica Monday to Saturday, at 5pm in the summer and 6pm in the winter.

THE CRYPT   From the Lower Basilica halfway up the nave you can reach the Crypt (free admission) where the saint's body was not discovered until 1818; a new and typically simple stone tomb was built early this century. Four of his closest followers are buried together with St. Francis.

TREASURY & PERKINS COLLECTION   From another entrance in the Lower Basilica (behind the main altar to the right) you can reach this collection, where glass cases display the likes of chalices and silver objects, but of most note are the saint's original gray patchwork sackcloth (the brown tunic was adopted by the order much later), the white tunic worn during the last year of his life, a knotted rope belt and worn slippers. On a more somber note is the stone upon which he rested his head in his coffin and the suede cloth used to cover his stigmata. The Perkins Collection is a small but rich collection bequeathed by an American philanthropist with some surprisingly important Tuscan Renaissance artworks.

UPPER BASILICA   Let's hope that the Upper Basilica has reopened as projected in late 1999: From the south transept of the Lower Basilica the stairs lead to the Upper Basilica (1230–53), built upon the Romanesque framework of the lower church. Where the lower spaces encouraged awe, contemplation, and meditation, the upper reaches of the airy, Gothic basilica are another experience entirely: Tall, bathed in light (unless the interior scaffolding remains, blocking the natural light from the stain glass windows), it was created, it would seem, as the blank canvas on which Giotto was to create the masterpiece frescoes depicting the ✪ *The Life of St. Francis* (1296–1304). These are the highlight of the basilica and generally escaped the earthquakes' wrath intact, 28 scenes (the last four not attributed to Giotto) that unfold left to right beginning in the transept; one of the most famous and charming of panels is the *Sermon to the Birds* found on the entrance wall, underlining the saint's tenet that all nature is the reflection of God. In many of the narrations you will see medieval Assisi illustrated much as you see it now, starting with the very first panel's *Homage in Piazza del Comune*. Upon reopening of the Upper Basilica, officials hope that this cycle of frescoes will be on view, even if a good portion of the church is still be under wraps.

Giotto was believed to be just 29 when he began this cycle of frescoes, already a longtime lay follower of St. Francis. He seemed to particularly embrace the message of St. Francis, whose love of man and warmth of expression is reflected in Giotto's radical break from the lifeless images of the Byzantines' icons. The single undivided nave was meant to accommodate the masses while Giotto's extensive pictorial narrations were meant to educate them about Assisi's native son while attempting to express his love for nature and humanity. Francis broke with the traditional excesses of the medieval papacy as Giotto would revolutionize the art world with his break from the lifeless Byzantine order. Other highlights include the 15th-century choir, made of 105 inlaid stalls. The choir's central "throne" was reserved for the pope, the only papal throne outside of St. Peter's. The reopening of the upper church and the Pope's plans to celebrate Christmas Eve mass here in December 1999 to launch the Holy Year are pending the progress of the repair work feverishly being done to beat the clock. Located behind and above in the left transept is a cycle of time- (and not earthquake-) damaged cycles by Cimabue dominated by his dramatic ✪ *Crucifixion*.

✪ **Eremo delle Carceri (Prisons' Hermitage).** V. Eremo d. Carceri. No phone. Donations appreciated. 8am–dusk. About 4 kilometers (2½ mi.) east outside of town.

St. Francis and his followers spiritually "imprisoned" themselves in prayer at this peacefully isolated retreat on the ilex- and oak-wooded slope of Monte Subasio. They lived in tiny *carceri* or cells naturally carved out of the stone centuries before the extant friary was built. A time-worn holm oak, thought to be at least 1,000 years old, still stands supported by metal crutches near the saint's cave where he meditated and prayed. The gnarled tree is said to have shaded Francis and the birds that gathered to listen to his sermons; they once flew off in the four cardinal directions, symbolizing how the Franciscans would one day leave Assisi to bring the word of Francis to all corners of the world.

Leave behind the crowds in the basilica and the town's ticky-tacky tourist shops; it's an easy 1-hour walk from the town's eastern gate, the Porta Cappuccini (leaving from the Rocca Minore north of the Porta is not recommended as the pathway is not as clearly marked) on a signposted paved road past cypresses and with wide-open views used by both pedestrians and cars (taxis should charge 20,000 to 25,000L/$11.75 to $14.70 one way). A handful of friars still live at the retreat established by St. Bernard of Siena (who lived here after Francis from 1438 to 1440) and act as guides; a donation of any size is appreciated—the friars live by alms alone. A visit here better conveys the spirit and serenity of St. Francis than the cavernous basilica built by his followers.

Basilica di Santa Chiara. Pz. di Santa Chiara (southwest of Pz. d. Comune). Free admission (donations for earthquake repair appreciated). 10am–noon and 3–5pm.

St. Clare died surrounded by her nascent following of nuns in the Convent of San Damiano down below on August 12, 1253; just 12 years later this pink-and-white basilica made from local marble was dedicated to her and became the home of the Poor Clares (the small community is currently living in Perugia until earthquake repairs are finished). The interior is Spartan, due to the 17th-century obliteration of elaborate frescoes that were whitewashed over by orders of a German bishop who attempted to discourage tourism and the temptations it would supply the nuns. The Oratorio del Crocifisso houses a few relics of the saint and the 12th-century Crucifix of San Damiano that spoke to a young St. Francis in 1209, informing him of his calling. It is indefinitely closed to the public while earthquake repairs continue. The crypt containing the remains of St. Clare is open. An anonymous crucifix older than the church itself hangs over the main altar. The small, adjacent Church of San Giorgio predates the basilica; it was the site of Francis's early schooling and where his remains awaited the completion of the Basilica of St. Francis upon his death. On the Basilica's terracelike piazza, lovely views of the surrounding countryside and Umbrian plains draw locals and visitors at any hour of the day, particularly during sunset hours.

Convento di San Damiano. 1½ miles from Porta Nuova. No phone. Free admission. 9am–noon and 2pm–dusk. Transportation by foot, car, or taxi.

Standing alone amid the olive groves and wildflowers, in the serenity of the Spoleto Valley, this quiet spot easily evokes the time and atmosphere of a young Francis who came here (the church dates from the 11th century) to escape the wrath of his father. It was in this church in 1209 that a wooden crucifix told a restless world-weary 27-year-old Francis to go and "repair the Church (*Vade, et repara domum meam*)," referring to the decadent papacy and corrupt monastic orders (the crucifix is now housed in the Basilica of St. Clare). Francis took the orders literally, however, and sold his father's textile stock and offered the money to St. Damian's priest, who threw the money pouch back at him. In 1210, he would find the approval of Pope Innocent III to create his own order of mendicant monks and, in 1212, a second order for women. St. Clare would later live here at San Damiano as abbess, her Order of Poor Clares moving up to the newly constructed Basilica of St. Clare after her death; you can visit the simple 13th-century convent's dormitory where a cross marks the spot of the saint's death in 1226. The cloisters and refectory still have the original tables and benches where the nuns shared their meager meals. St. Francis visited just once during Clare's stay here and is said to have composed his famous *Canticle of the Creatures* here. **To get here:** From the Piazza Santa Chiara or the Basilica di Santa Chiara, take Via Borgo Aretino and at Porta Nuova (the eastern gate to the city) take a right and head south down a steep road to the Convent of San Damiano following the signs. It's 20 to 30 minutes downhill; a road for vehicle traffic runs parallel to a pedestrian road. Taxis that have dropped passengers off are usually lingering about to take you back uphill for 20,000 to 25,000L ($11.75 to $14.70) one way.

WHERE TO STAY

Promising to be Italy's most visited city after Rome by religious tourism during the holy Jubilee Year, advance hotel reservations are a must. If the following places are full and you need help finding a room, call the **Consorzio Albergatori,** Viale Marconi (☎ **075/81-35-99;** fax 075/812315; e-mail: caa@krenet.it), a kind of clearinghouse for local hotels that will help you stick to your budget by booking a hotel category you request with no fee involved. Unless you have no choice or it's all the same to you, make sure you insist on being in the historical center of town and not the satellite town of Santa Maria degli Angeli (which always tries to pass itself off as *Assisi centro* to unwitting tourists) down near the train station or, worse yet, the town of Bastia where tour buses usually put up their groups 4 kilometers (2.5 mi.) outside of town. If the town is full (or closed—a number of hotels and restaurants close up shop in January and February), don't overlook using Perugia as your base.

SMALL TWO-STAR DELIGHTS   A number of small hotels in the historical center of town offer limited accommodations only slightly more expensive than the religious institutions. With an average of seven rooms with bathrooms at approximately 85,000 to 110,000L ($50 to $64.70) each, they fill up fast and are often closed in the winter months. Try the following: **Hotel La Fortezza,** Vc. d. Fortezza 19b (☎ **075/81-24-18;** fax 075/8198035; www.assind.perugia.it/hotel/fortezza; e-mail: fortezza@krenet.it); see "Where to Dine," below; **Hotel Lieto Soggiorno,** Via A. Fortini (☎ **075/81-61-91**); **Hotel Palotta,** V. San Rufino 6 (☎ and fax **075/81-23-07**); **Hotel Properzio,** V. San Francesco 38 (☎ **075/81-31-88;** fax 075/81-52-01).

RELIGIOUS INSTITUTIONS   The tourist information office has a list of *Case Religiose di Ospitalità,* 17 local religious convents, monasteries, and religious-run hostelries that offer accommodations; a double with bathroom ranges from 50,000 to 80,000L ($29.40 to $47.05) and many close for the low season mid-November through mid-March. **Sisters of the Atonement** (Suore dell'Atonement) at V. Galeazzo Alessi 10 (northeast of the Piazza del Comune), 06081 Assisi (☎ **075/81-25-42;** fax 075/813723), is the only American religious order, though almost all others are English-speaking to some degree. Prices range from 50,000 ($29.40) for a single to 80,000L ($47.05) for a double and 120,000L ($70.58) for a triple (no credit cards).

Hotel dei Priori. Cor. Mazzini 15 (1 block east of the Pz. d. Comune), 06081 Assisi. ☎ **075/81-22-37.** Fax 075/81-68-04. www.assind.perugia.it/hotel/dpriori. E-mail: hpriori@edisons.it. 34 units, all with bathroom. A/C TV TEL. 135,000L ($79.40) single; 188,000–248,000L ($110.60–$145.90) double, standard and superior; triple and quad upon request. Rates include breakfast. AE, DC, MC, V. Parking nearby 18,000L ($10.60).

A stay in this seigniorial 16th-century palazzo of grand proportions and stained-glass windows will take you back in time when local families made their fortunes in trade and textiles and lived like royalty, as can you—for a price. Royal rates are something this book avoids, but I find the lovely rooms in this hotel housed in a landmark building to be more than reasonable; spend the extra lire and book one of the 10 superior *camere dei Priori* replete with 19th-century frescoed ceilings. Persian runners and valuable antiques and handsome prints decorate both the public rooms and the guest rooms, all of which have been refreshened by a 1998 renovation. This is the type of character and history you would never be able to afford in a similar hotel in Rome or Florence. Ask for off-season discounts (including July and winter months).

Hotel Giotto. V. Fontebella 41 (just east of Pz. San Francesco), 06082 Assisi. ☎ **075/81-22-09.** Fax 075/81-64-79. www.htlgiotto.tin.it. 70 units, all with bathroom. MINIBAR TV TEL. 150,000L ($88.25) single; 220,000L ($129.40) double; 300,000L ($176.50). Rates include special discount for Frommer's readers. Rates include breakfast. AE, DC, MC, V. Free parking.

This stately hotel, Assisi's largest, is located in the western part of town not far from the Basilica of St. Francis. It has five floors built into the side of the hill with wonderful views from almost all of its rooms. If you ask when booking, the staff will do its best to hold one of the five rooms that share a large terra-cotta terrace. A wonderful outdoor breakfast terrace comes equipped with the same expansive view that includes the Romanesque church of San Pietro below. The rooms are nice in an old-fashioned kind of way, with brass headboards and bathrooms that will soon need a facelift but are fine for the moment. Gracious aspects of its public areas—open landings of patterned gray-and-white marble tiles, wrought-iron handrails, and Persian runners on the wide marble steps—are reminiscent of better days. With so many rooms, you'll likely find availability—and the tour groups that fill them.

Hotel Sole. Cor. Mazzini 35 (2 blocks east of Pz. d. Comune), 06081 Assisi. ☎ 075/ 81-23-73. Fax 075/81-37-06. E-mail: sole@tecnonet.it. 35 units, all with bathroom. TV TEL. 80,000L ($47.05) single; 100,000L ($58.80) double; 130,000L ($76.50) triple. Breakfast 10,000L ($5.90). Ask about low-season rates in winter and July. AE, DC, MC, V. Nearby parking 10,000L ($6.60).

This is one of the loveliest family run hotels for these prices that I have seen in Umbria. Its excellent location is enhanced by the charm of the freshly redone rooms on the top two floors and those across the street in the annex (even those not yet refurbished are nice enough). There's an elevator in the annex, though not in the principal building, yet I prefer the latter whose spacious rooms have generally been done with more charm. Furnishings range from contemporary to antique (and antique-inspired) wrought-iron painted beds and thoughtfully chosen framed prints. Beige chenille bedspreads and light terra-cotta tiles keep things cool, while exposed stone walls and wide marble staircases hint of the building's antiquity. The family's restaurant, Hostaria Ceppo della Catena, is set in theatrically stone-vaulted rooms in a 15th-century palazzo adjacent to the restaurant, where half-board can be arranged (85,000L/$50 per person, double-occupancy basis); open March through October.

✪ **Hotel Umbra.** V. degli Archi 6 (off southwest corner of Pz. d. Comune), 06081 Assisi. ☎ 075/81-22-40. Fax 075/81-36-53. E-mail: humbra@mail.caribusiness.it. 25 units, all with bathroom. A/C MINIBAR TV TEL. 125,000L ($73.50) single; 170,000–200,000L ($100–$117.65) double. Rates include buffet breakfast. AE, DC, MC, V. Closed mid-Jan–Feb. Nearby parking 15,000L ($8.80).

The majority of this three-star hotel dates from the 15th century, but the basement's laundry and kitchen area boast ancient Roman foundations. Three generations of a local family have proudly run this excellently situated hotel, known for its well-respected alfresco restaurant (fixed-price 35,000L/$23); closed all day Sunday and Wednesday at lunch. Patrons dine in a shaded garden patio where birdsong easily reminds you that St. Francis was born just blocks away and lamp-lit dinners are no less romantic, despite the lack of view. Most rooms are highlighted with well-worn 18th- and 19th-century antiques. When booking, ask for one of the rooms that overlook the Umbrian Valley; a few are double blessed with a balcony. I recommend springing for the view. The main square is just paces away, but it is easy to feel removed from the pilgrimage jostle.

WHERE TO DINE

✪ **La Fortezza.** V. d. Fortezza 2b (north of the Pz. Comune), Assisi. ☎ **075/81-24-18.** Fax 075/8198035. E-mail: fortezza@krenet.it. Reservations suggested. Primi 8,000–15,000L ($4.70–$8.80); secondi 11,000–17,000L ($6.50–$10). AE, DC, MC, V. Mon–Wed, Fri–Sun 12:30–2:30pm and 7–10:30pm. Closed in Feb. UMBRIAN.

Up a stepped alleyway from the central Piazza Comune and considered by many to be the best place in town, this lovely and very centrally located restaurant has been family run for 40 years and is prized for its high quality and very reasonable prices. An exposed ancient Roman wall to the right of the restaurant's entrance immediately establishes the antiquity of this handsomely refurbished palazzo with brick-vaulted ceilings, the rest of which dates from the 13th century. The delicious homemade pastas are prepared with sauces that follow the season's fresh offerings, while the roster of meats skewered or roasted on the grill (*alla brace*) range from veal and lamb to duck. The ubiquitous *tartufo nero* (black truffle) is available here, yet contained prices can guarantee you one of your most enjoyable meals in Umbria for approximately 30,000L ($19.75)—house wine included! La Fortezza also rents seven rooms upstairs; see "Small Two-Star Delights," above.

Pizzeria Duomo. V. Porta Perlici 11 (north of Pz. San Rufino), Assisi. ☎ **075/81-63-26.** Reservations not necessary. Pizza 7,000–10,000L ($4.10–$5.90); primi 8,000–11,000L ($4.70–$6.50). AE, DC, MC, V. Daily noon–2pm and 5pm–midnight; closed Wed in winter. PIZZERIA.

Just enough beyond the Piazza Comune–Piazza San Rufino route to discourage the masses, this is a casual and reliable place frequented by locals. With three spacious rooms in medieval surroundings and the modern-day luxury of air-conditioning, you can always find a cool respite here despite the wood-burning oven, which produces a stream of delicious, bubbling pizzas. There are more than 30 from which to pick, but it looks like the simple *pizza alla margherita* (with tomato, oregano, and mozzarella) and the *pizza con funghi porcini* (with fresh porcini mushrooms) contend for first place. The region's famous Norcia truffles show up on the *pizza al tartufo*, a delicious "white pizza" (no tomato sauce) of mozzarella and black truffles. Pastas, fresh vegetables, and salads are also available.

Trattoria Pozzo della Mensa. V. Pozzo d. Mensa 11 (off V. San Rufino east of Pz. d. Comune), Assisi. ☎ **075/81-62-47.** Pastas 8,500–16,000L ($5–$9.40); secondi 9,000–20,000L ($5.30–$11.75). AE, DC, MC, V. Daily noon–2:30pm and 7–9:30pm. Closed Wed in winter and 3 weeks late Jan/early Feb. UMBRIAN.

This bustling spot, which sits on a hidden alleyway off the street that connects Piazza Comune and Piazza San Rufino, provides inexpensive, delicious Umbrian meals— that is, if you don't surrender to the temptation of tartufo-flavored dishes. On the other hand, even the prices for truffle dishes are very reasonable, so if you want to see what all the fuss is about, sample the homemade *strengozzi al tartufo*, a typical Umbrian pasta, or ravioli al tartufo, filled with cheese—both are flavored with the potent black tubular fungus that put Umbria on the culinary map. Among the entrees are regional specialties such as *coniglio* (rabbit) and *agnello* (lamb) or, if your first course has you hooked, the specialty *tornedo del Pozzo*, a tender beef sirloin marinated in red wine and flavored with, you guessed it, black truffles.

7 Gubbio

39 km (24.5 mi.) NE of Perugia, 170 km (107 mi.) SE of Florence, 200 km (126 mi.) N of Rome; 90 km (57 mi.) SE of Arezzo, 54 km (34 mi.) N of Assisi

An austere, proud, mountain outpost, the tiny no-nonsense stone town of ✪ **Gubbio** hangs on to its medieval charm and wonderful flavor of authenticity despite its growing popularity with off-the-beaten-trackers looking for a picturesque hill town minus masses of tourists. Untrammeled it is not, but compared to, say, San Gimignano, the overly popular Tuscan town of towers, one can comfortably consider

Gubbio downright quiet, undiscovered, and cocooned within the middle of nowhere. The last five years have shown a commendable growth in the accommodations scene, with renovations and a handsome new hotel in an enviably located historical palazzo opening up.

Set into the rugged steep slope of forest-clad Mt. Ingino, Gubbio was a modestly prosperous Roman settlement, Iguvium, whose Roman amphitheater dating from the time of Augustus still sits at the foot of today's town. Like its Umbrian neighbor Spoleto, south of here, it flourished from its strategic location on the heavily trafficked Via Flaminia, linking ancient Rome and the imperial capital of Ravenna on the Adriatic. Today's visitor can easily evoke the Eugubium of the Dark Ages, a busy little market center, when its most important local personality, the sage Bishop Ubaldo Baldassini (today, Gubbio's beloved patron saint) sidestepped destruction by the fierce hand of Barbarossa (Red Beard) in 1155. Its second-most celebrated resident was the ferocious Wolf of St. Francis–related fame. The 13th-century saint, from the nearby Umbrian town of Assisi, strove to save the life of the hungry animal, which had been attacking flocks and terrorizing residents. After an alleged heart-to-heart, the saint convinced the wolf to change its ways and accepted its paw in peace. The townfolk agreed to feed it regularly and a pact was sealed. This simple tale of **The Taming of the Wolf of Gubbio** has survived more than 7 centuries though the part about the repenting wolf bursting into tears after striking the deal with St. Francis may be discounted as historical embellishment.

Much of the Gubbio welcoming visitors today was built in the early part of the 14th century, when local master architect Matteo Gattapone, responsible for the famous arched bridge of Spoleto, constructed the Palazzo dei Consoli during Gubbio's most florid period in the much-photographed central square, the Piazza Grande. From 1387 to 1508, the Montefeltro counts of Urbino oversaw a long, if not brilliant, period of rule. It was during this time, as happened with its Umbrian neighbor Deruta, that Gubbio became widely known as a center for the high-quality glazed ceramics and majolica that came from its workshops; many are still operating today, but don't expect the quantity of choice you'll find in Deruta. Maestro Giorgio Andreoli (1465–1552), one of the world's greatest masters of the craft, developed a particularly intense ruby red glaze that was never discovered by neighboring towns. He is the city's most famous resident after St. Ubaldo and that pesky wolf.

FESTIVALS & MARKETS   The end-all festival in town is the ✪ **Corso dei Ceri** on May 15, the eve of the **Festa di Sant'Ubaldo,** Gubbio's patron saint. Three massive 16-foot-high wooden "candles" (*ceri*) weighing 400 kilos each (880 lbs.) crowned with small statues of Saints Ubaldo, George, and Anthony are vertically raced through town to the hilltop Basilica of St. Ubaldo. Oddly, St. Ubaldo always wins, but that doesn't diminish the excitement level—or the number of folks who show up to follow all the events that take place before, during, and after the race. To keep May a merry month, the last Sunday is dedicated to the **Palio della Balestra,** a crossbow competition against its ancient rival Sansepolcro in medieval costume that is also held in mid-September. An internal competition between four local teams is held August 14. Two weeks of **classical music concerts** take place in the end of July through the beginning of August, with performances held in the evocative venue of the ancient Roman Amphitheater and an illuminated Gubbio as dramatic backdrop. **Spettacoli Classici** (Classical Plays) in Italian take place in the Roman Amphitheater mid-July to mid-August. Umbria's town of Nocera may be famous for its black truffle, but Gubbio's rare albino rendition is the reason for the annual **Mercato del Tartufo Bianco** during last weekend of October: Expect to pay at least 300,000L ($176.50) per 100 grams.

ESSENTIALS

GETTING HERE   By Train   The nearest train station to Gubbio is 19 kilometers (12 mi.) away in Fossato di Vico (see or contact Gubbio's Tourist Office for schedules); a number of trains arrive from Rome on the Rome-Ancona line, a minimum of 3 hours. Connecting bus service to Gubbio is 30 minutes. Bus service is preferable.

By Bus   At least 10 **A.P.M. buses** leave Perugia daily for Gubbio, making the trip in 70 minutes. Four make the trip on Sunday (7,400L/$4.35). Some connect with ongoing service to Assisi (☎ **075/506781**). One daily **Sulga bus** runs to Rome (25,000L/$14.70) in 3½ hours (☎ **075/5009641**). Only one bus to Perugia (A.P.M.) makes the connection to Florence (Sulga). Check at Gubbio's tourist office for schedules.

All buses arriving in Gubbio arrive in the Piazza 40 Martiri, within walking distance of the main square Piazza Grande and other sites.

By Car   Follow the SS298 through the mountainous northern corner of Umbria. Easiest parking is in the Piazza 40 Martiri at the foot of the town.

VISITOR INFORMATION   The local tourist information office is located in the teensy Pz. Oderisi 6 (on Corso Garibaldi; ☎ **075/9220693;** fax 075/9273409). It's open Monday to Friday 8am to 2pm and 3 to 6pm (6:30 in summer months); Saturday 9am to 1pm and 3 to 6pm (6:30pm in summer); Sunday 9:30am to 12:30pm. A small private company **Easy Gubbio** can help you with general information or hotel reservations. It's located 1 block from Piazza 40 Martiri on V. d. Repubblica 11 (☎ **075/9220066;** fax 075/0220548.)

SHOPPING

You can't miss the fact that Gubbio is still famous for ceramics after all these years. The two main shopping strips are **Via dei Consoli** that heads west out of the Piazza Grande and **Via XX Settembre** that heads east from the piazza, though small shops selling the town's artisanal crafts can be found along its secondary streets as well. You'll find everything from items of amateur quality to those appropriate for serious collectors, the latter represented by the well situated **La Mastro Giorgio di Valentino Biagioli** in the Piazza Grande 3 (☎ **075/9271574**). Another excellent retail outlet-cum-workshop is **Rampini Ceramiche d'Arte,** V. Leonardo da Vinci 94 (☎ **075/9272963**), where traditional patterns influence contemporary and modern designs.

Copies of medieval *balestre* (crossbows) are but a sampling of the exquisite wrought-iron craftsmanship (*ferro battuto*) handed down over the centuries. The best store/laboratory in town is **Artigianato Ferro Artistico,** V. Baldassini 22 (☎ **075/9273079**). Handsomely crafted leather goods are the reason to search out the stores/workshops of **Mastri Librai** on V. d. Consoli 48 (☎ **075/9277425**) and **Officina Libris** on V. Baldassini 16 (☎ **075/9276650**).

WHAT TO SEE & DO

The wide open expanse of the brick-paved ✪ **Piazza Grande** is the center stage of the **Città Alta** (The High City). A good chunk of the old medieval town was razed and leveled to make way for this square and the crenellated **Palazzo dei Consoli** and its slender campanile that dominates it. Meant to represent the power and pride of a small medieval *comune* in the golden age of its 14th-century political and economic might, it does just that. Behind the nondescript blank facade is the palazzo's cavernous municipal council chamber, the Salone dell'Arengo (from which the word *harangue* is believed to be derived), the **Pinocoteca** picture gallery and **Museo Civico,** whose **Eugubine Tablets** (Tavole Eugubine) are by far the museum's most interesting highlight. The seven bronze tablets discovered by a shepherd in 1444 are held to be Umbria's most important archaeological find. The only extant example of the ancient written Umbrian language, they may date back as far as the 3rd to 1st centuries B.C. The museum also houses the city's only work of ceramics (1527) by Gubbio's master artisan Mastro Giorgio (d. 1552); with none to their name, the city bought it at Sotheby's for an undisclosed sum in 1992 and returned it to its rightful home. Admission to the Palazzo dei Consoli, Pinacoteca, and Museo (☎ **075/9274298**) is 7,000L/$4.10. Open daily April to September 10am to 1pm and 3 to 6pm; October to March 10am to 1pm and 2 to 5pm.)

From here head up the Via Ducale following signs for the Palazzo Ducale and the Duomo. The **Palazzo Ducale** was built in the 1470s as a scaled down version of the ruling Duke Federico di Montefeltro's more lavish palace in Urbino. Most of the lordly trappings and furnishings are gone, but its worth a visit for some of the original frescoes, a smattering of baroque paintings and the hanging gardens with a view that are open in the summer months (Via Federico da Montefeltro; ☎ **075/9275872**). Admission is 6,000L/$3.50; it's open Monday to Saturday from 9am to 1:30pm and 2:30 to 7pm; Sunday 9am to 1pm.

If you weren't blown away by the Palazzo Ducale, you might want to save yourself a visit to the 12th-century Duomo across the way, a Gothic pile that pales when compared to some of those in the region you've likely seen in Spoleto, Orvieto, or Assisi (no phone; free admission; open daily 9am to noon and 3:30 to 8:30pm). From behind the Duomo, follow the signs for one of Gubbio's two popular treks for the sturdy of knee; the least taxing is the paved road to the **Basilica of St. Ubaldo,** on the hillside above town at 2,690 feet. The walk up steep Via Sant Ubaldo is 2 kilometers (1.3 mi.) along a consistent incline—most Eugubines drive it, reaching the Basilica for their Sunday afternoon stroll. During warm weather months, an open **funivia** cable car departs from the Porta Romana (a remaining 13th-century tower that permitted access to town), east of the Piazza Grande, up to the Basilica (it is tentatively scheduled to reopen summer 1999 following work (closed Wednesday off-season, otherwise open daily; admission 6,000L/$3.50). Check with the tourist office for a new schedule. The quiet 16th-century Basilica holds the remains of the city's 12th-century patron saint in a glass casket, and the three massive wooden *ceri* that turn the town upside down every May 15 when they are raced through town in a folkloric feast second only to Siena's Palio in terms of local hysteria (see "Festivals & Markets," above). Got your second breath? You can continue by foot (the way is signposted) from the Basilica another 15 minutes or so to the remains of the 12th-century military fortress **La Rocca,** on the 3,000-foot pinnacle of Monte Igino, for ✪ **one-of-a-kind views** of the wild Appenine Mountains and the Umbrian plains.

WHERE TO STAY

Off-season rates are also offered by some hotels in the winter months, as well as the slow months of June and July (considered high season in other towns).

Hotel Bosone Palace. V. XX Settembre (near Pz. Grande). ☎ **075/9220688.** Fax 075/9220552. 32 units, all with bathroom. MINIBAR TV TEL. 110,000L ($64.70) single; 140,000L ($82.35) double; 170,000L ($100) triple; 295,000L ($173.50) suite for four. Buffet breakfast 10,000L ($5.90). Off-season discounts offered. AE, MC, V. Closed 3 weeks in Jan or Feb.

Until the Relais Ducale opened, the Bosone was the city's most atmospheric and historically important hotel. Built in the 1300s and enlarged during the Renaissance, it's steps from the city's architectural heart, the Piazza Grande, and allows guests to enjoy that same suspension of time and a return to lifestyles of the rich and famous of other centuries. Owned by the local patrician Raffaelli clan, this formerly private residence once hosted an exiled Dante Alighieri (persona non grata in his hometown of Florence for trumped-up political charges). Its lobby's monumental marble staircase leads to standard rooms that are comfortable, simple, and spacious, and whose bathrooms are mostly new (so much for time travel). Ask for one of the three with small terraces and big, big views. For the remarkable, book one of the two dramatic Renaissance suites with stuccoed ceilings elaborately frescoed in the 17th century and reproduction period furnishings.

Hotel Gattapone. V. Ansidei 6. ☎ **075/9272489.** Fax 075/9272417. www.gubbio.com/hotelgattapone. 18 units, all with bathroom. MINIBAR TV TEL. 110,000L ($64.70) single; 140,000L ($82.35) double; 170,000L ($100) triple. Off-season discounts offered. AE, MC, V. Closed Jan 8–Feb 1.

After reopening in 1997 following a complete refurbishment, the long loved Gattapone deservedly graduated to three-star status, but with prices that are more than reasonable given the quality and style. It's housed in a medieval building on a stepped alleyway down from the Piazza Grande; many rooms overlook the Romanesque church and bell tower of San Giovanni. The redesigned guest rooms, however, reflect little of the hotel's ancient roots, with the exception of an occasional wood-beamed ceiling left intact. The tiles in the brand-new bathrooms pick up the color scheme of each room. It's not far from the Piazza 40 Martiri but if you call upon arrival, the hotel will send its van to collect you and your luggage. This is a sister hotel of the Bosone, a more imposing and historically rich palazzo but not yet slated for a facelift.

✪ **Hotel Relais Ducale.** V. Ducale 2 (overlooking Pz. Grande). ☎ **075/9220157.** Fax 075/9220159. 32 units, all with bathroom. MINIBAR, TV, TEL. 180,000L ($105.90) single; 280,000L ($164.70) double; 320,000L ($188.25) triple. 360,000L ($211.75) suites. Breakfast included. Off-season discounts. AE, MC, V. Open year-round.

Housed in the aristocratic guest quarters of the ruling Dukes of Urbino, nestled between their Palazzo Ducale (above) and the central Piazza Grande (below), this new hotel offers a combination of historical importance and unrivaled panoramic location you're not likely to stumble upon elsewhere. Hanging gardens shaded by regal palms and scented by jasmine offer views over the medieval city's windswept square, monumental palazzi and a breathtaking panorama that unfolds beyond. The timeless view that must have bedazzled the privileged guests of the ruling Montefeltro Dukes is the same one enjoyed by today's guests lingering over breakfast in the hotel's carefully groomed gardens, or from many of the elegantly appointed rooms. Rich parquet floors, damask bedspreads and matching curtains, and the occasional historical touch (stone vaulted ceilings) or modern luxury (Jacuzzi baths) make this Gubbio's unrivaled premier hotel, and for affordable prices during its nascent years when it irons out the wrinkles of being a spanking new four-star operation. If you're not staying here, stop by the hotel's Caffe Ducale in the Piazza Grande no. 5 (the hotel rises above the cafe, carved into many different levels and medieval structures), the most refined and best situated of the city's watering holes.

WHERE TO DINE

Taverna del Buchetto. V. Dante 30 (near Porta Romana). ☎ **075/9277034.** Reservations suggested. Primi 6,000–15,000L ($3.50–$8.80); secondi 12,000–22,000L ($7.05–$12.95). Fixed-price menu 23,000L ($13.50) and 30,000L ($17.64). AE, MC, V. Tues–Sun noon–3pm and 7–11pm.

Simple, straightforward, and a real pleasure describes both the menu and ambience of this neighborhood trattoria/tavern where, amid the enjoyable hubbub of family like regulars, pretensions and cares are left at the door. Since it's in the general area of the funicular that heads up to the Basilica in an atmospheric 13th-century warehouse, this is a great place to come for lunch before heading up for a late afternoon or sunset moment at the Basilica. The taverna's menu is testimony to the pleasures of Umbria's peasant fare: delicious homemade *pappardelle* noodles are a quasi-constant on the menu. It is hoped you'll find them prepared with a wild hare–flavored tomato sauce. The homemade gnocchi are best regardless of their changing sauce. Things are kept simple and delicious with a number of different meats (or, when in season, plate-sized porcini mushrooms) sizzled *alla griglia.* Two fixed-price menus including house wine are a good value for your money for those with a substantial appetite.

✪ **Taverna del Lupo.** V. Ansidei 21 (at corner of V. Repubblica). ☎ **075/9274368.** Reservations recommended. Primi 15,000–30,000L ($8.80–$17.65); secondi 18,000–30,000L ($10.60–$17.65); fixed-price menu 35,000L ($20.60). AE, MC, V. Tues–Sun noon–10pm.

The local Mencarelli empire that today includes the hotels listed above started here 30 years ago in what continues to be Gubbio's culinary landmark. The family run restaurant is large, but divided up into vaulted and brick-walled rooms that are handsomely appointed with Umbrian ceramics and prints. The atmosphere is one of elegant coziness despite the buzz that comes from a well-oiled machine and professional kitchen that rarely goes wrong with the regional specialties and well-chosen wine list. Flexible hours accommodate those trying to see the sites and sample local gastronomy on a limited day-trip schedule. The fixed-price menu is always interesting enough, but I always opt for anything *tartufo* (truffle) enhanced, (beginning with the full-flavored sauce used for their special homemade *tagliatelle* pasta), as the kitchen seems to know just how to do it. It's worth the extra lire.

8 Spoleto

129 km (80 mi.) N of Rome, 209 km (130 mi.) S of Florence, 48 km (30 mi.) SE of Assisi, 64 km (40 mi.) SE of Perugia

The world-famous ✪ **Spoleto Festival** (until recently known as the Festival of Two Worlds) put Spoleto back on the map after centuries of historical obscurity. However, it was the obscurity that is responsible for the town's untouched medieval preservation that makes it worth visiting, even when the world-class arts festival is not turning it on its ear. Established by Italian American composer and maestro Gian Carlo Menotti in 1957, the celebrated arts festival brings together performers from all over the world for 3 weeks of dance, concerts, art, and drama known for their diversity and quality.

Much is made of the city's Roman past. As Spoletium, it was one of the empire's most important outposts. Strategically situated on the well-trafficked Via Flaminia linking Rome and the late imperial capital of Ravenna it flourished for centuries, and proudly held out when fiercely attacked by Hannibal in the 3rd century A.D. It became the capital of the important Lombard Duchy of Spoleto from the 6th to the 8th centuries. The arrival of the emperor Barbarossa in 1155 saw widespread destruction, after which the city only partially recovered before falling into the hands of the Church and the stifling Papal States. The 15th-century Pope Alexander VI presented the town to his teenage daughter Lucrezia Borgia and appointed her governor. And that was pretty much the cap on excitement until Maestro Menotti arrived in 1957. Spoleto was far enough away from the epicenter of Umbria's 1997 earthquakes to have escaped with little to no damage.

There's no traipsing through countless museums and dimly lit churches in Spoleto. The much-used adjectives "quaint" and "charming" are put to excellent use here where, after a visit to the city's Duomo—whose lovely, sloping piazza passes for one of the country's most evocative outdoor venues during the festival's closing night concert—

your time will be spent wandering the vaulted back streets and poking around small antique shops and gourmet-stocked stores, and always winding up in its ancient Piazza del Mercato, a perfect reminder of the city's ancient roots as a market town during its day in the Dark Ages.

FESTIVALS & MARKETS   For 3 weeks every year beginning in the last week of June, Spoleto turns its attention to ✪ **The Spoleto Festival,** the American-Italian arts and music festival. World-class symphonies and music ensembles, dance and drama troupes come from all over the world, culminating in the final evening's standing-room-only symphonic performance in the picturesque ✪ **Piazza del Duomo.** There are often 5 to 10 events happening daily at different indoor/outdoor venues about town. Tickets usually go on sale mid-April. Edinburgh-type "fringe" and "alternative" performances are finding their way into the program to resuscitate some of the cutting-edge energy of the festival's early years, and tickets can often be found at the last moment. For general program information and instructions for ticket purchase after mid-April, contact **Associazione Spoleto Festival** (☎ **167/565600** toll-free within Italy, or 0743/220320; www.spoletofestival.net; e-mail: spoletofestival@krenet.it).

To keep the cultural activity level at a consistent high, the relatively new **Spoletoestate** (Spoleto Summer) arts festival picks up where its big-sister festival leaves off, organizing performances around town from July until September. See the tourist office for listings.

A daily morning produce and flower market (except Sunday) takes over the ancient Piazza del Mercato, originally the site of the ancient Roman Forum, in fragrant and organized chaos. The second Sunday of every month a **Mercato delle Briciole** takes place here and in neighboring piazzas (pick up information at the tourist office), where merchants hawk collectibles and choice antiques together with junky stuff.

ESSENTIALS

GETTING HERE   By Train   Spoleto is on the popular Rome-Ancona line; **Rome** is 1 hour, 40 minutes away (13,000L/$7.65 one way). There are numerous trains to/from **Assisi,** ½ hour (4,700L/$2.75); these trains continue onto **Perugia,** 1 hour away (5,900L/$4.50). **Orvieto** requires a half-hour connection in Orte (10,000L/$5.90). A number of public buses run from the train station in the Lower Town to the Upper Town's Piazza della Libertà. The tourist office has schedules posted. The first thing to catch your eye upon exiting the train station is the 66-foot-high statue by American artist Alexander Calder (1962).

By Bus   There are two buses daily to/from **Perugia** (1½ hr.; 10,000L/$5.90) and Assisi (7,400L/$4.35), and one bus daily to/from **Rome** (1 hr., 50 min.; 10,000L/$5.90). The tourist information office has schedules posted or call the **Societa Spoletina Trasporti (S.S.T.)** at ☎ **0743/212211.**

By Car   From Perugia or Assisi, head south on S3 to Spoleto, an easy 30-minute drive from Assisi. Once you arrive in Spoleto, it is best to leave your car parked in the Upper Town, preferably at your hotel or close to it. Ask about parking arrangements when making your reservations.

VISITOR INFORMATION   The **tourist information office** or newly renamed S.T.T. (Servizio Turistico Territoriale) is located in the central Pz. d. Libertà 7 (☎ **0743/22-03-11;** fax 0743/46-241; e-mail: info@iat.spoleto.pg.it). Summer hours are Monday to Friday, 9am to 1pm and 4:30 to 7:30pm, Saturday to Sunday 10am to 1pm and 4:30 to 7:30pm (all hours are slightly extended during the Spoleto Festival; winter hours are Monday to Friday, 9am to 1pm and 3:30 to 6:30pm, Saturday 10am to 1pm and 3:30 to 6:30pm, and Sunday 10am to 1pm; closed Sunday in January and February).

WHAT TO SEE & DO

With the exception of the Duomo, there isn't much to see here. But a walk through town will illustrate the antiquity of a city that is still very much alive, and that does not live for tourism's sake alone. Begin your visit at the **S.S.T. office** (tourist information) in the Piazza della Libertà, which will supply you with a map and any other information you might need. Just west of here is the ancient **Teatro Romano** that dates from the 1st century A.D., when Spoleto was a thriving Roman city. It has recently been restored and is a popular venue for festival performances (admission 4,000L/$2.35; Monday to Saturday 9am to 7pm; Sunday 9am to 1pm).

From the Piazza della Libertà, take a right on Via Brignone and a left on Via Arco di Druso, which leads into the **Piazza del Mercato,** a window to centuries past. Stores around its periphery sell the gourmet products of Umbria, including the prized black truffles from nearby Norcia. Outdoor cafes such as the **Bar Primavera** (excellent gelato) set up tables outside as alfresco command posts for taking in the piazza life (Pz. d. Mercato no. 8). Explore the vaulted alleyways and hidden corners just off the piazza, or follow the characteristic **Via dei Duchi** north out of the Piazza del Mercato to window-shop on one of the city's most pleasant streets. At its end, turn left onto Via del Mercato or right onto Via Fontesecca for more streets evocative of the city's medieval past, now inhabited by tasteful shops, antique stores, and boutiques.

It's a short walk east to the ✪ **Duomo,** a 12th-century building (on the site of a 7th-century church) whose simple but elegant facade is graced by five rose windows and crowned with a mosaic by Solsterno (1207). The most illustrious (recently restored and mercifully untouched by the earthquakes of 1997) pictorial masterpiece of the city is found in the domed apse—the last works done by the Florentine painter Filippo Lippo (1467–69). From left to right they are the *Annunciation,* the *Passage of the Virgin Mary,* and the *Nativity;* the *Coronation* fills the space above. In the scene of the Virgin's death you'll find self-portraits of the painter and his son Filippino to the right. His premature death, rumor goes, came from poisoning when he was found to have seduced the nubile daughter of a well-heeled noble family. It was bad enough that, as a monk, he had taken up with Lucrezia Buti, a nun who posed as the Madonna in many of his works. Filippino, the son of Filippo and Lucrezia, designed his father's tomb found in a chapel in the right transept, funded by Florence's Lorenzo de' Medici, the master's patron; the body mysteriously disappeared for a brief period two centuries later, stolen, they say, by descendants of the compromised girl. The other work of note is the fresco cycle in the **Erioli Chapel,** at the beginning of the right nave. The author was a 17-year-old Pinturicchio, not yet famous for his future work in the Piccolomini Library in Siena's Duomo. The Duomo is open from 8am to 1pm and 3 to 6:30pm (closing at 5:30pm in winter). Down the steps on the west side of the Piazza Duomo are the shaded, hanging gardens of the **Piazza della Signoria,** whose benches and postcard views of the valley make this the city's most idyllic picnic spot (buy your provisions at the open-air market before vendors pack up at 1pm).

The decade-long renovation of the towered and crenellated papal **Rocca fortress** is rumored to be near completion for the summer of 1999 (even if it's not, it's usually open to poke your nose around during peak-season months). Built by the Gubbio-born architect Gattapone from 1359 to 1363 for the tireless papal envoy Cardinal Albornoz (also responsible for the Rocca fortress that sits above Assisi), it was temporary home to the Lucrezia Borgia, teenage daughter of the 15th-century Pope Alexander VI. It was recently used as a prison, most recently having housed Pope John Paul II's would-be assassin Ali Agha for a brief period and is rumored to be used in the future as a museum. Take a walk up, if only for the town's best picture-perfect views and a visit to the 14th-century **Ponte delle Torri** (Bridge of the Towers). Initially begun upon the foundation of an ancient Roman aqueduct, Gattapone later incorporated into the city's defenses. Its 10 Gothic arches span a 760-foot-wide chasm 240 feet above a torrent and to this day, it is held as an awe-inspiring engineering endeavor for that period. A favorite summertime hike is to the rural retreat and **monastery of Monteluco,** once favored by St. Francis and St. Bernardino of Siena who came to live here after him (open daily 9am to noon and 3 to 6pm). If the footbridge is closed, as it often is, you can catch a bus from Piazza della Libertà (2,600L/$1.50) for the 5-mile ride. The tourist office can supply you with maps of walking paths to Monteluco and other sites of interest in the immediate countryside.

WHERE TO STAY

Rates are usually discounted November through March (low season). If you plan to visit during the festival, book 2 to 3 months in advance (last-minute cancellations are rare); you might also consider commuting by car or bus from Perugia or the neighboring towns during the festival when the town is at zero vacancy. Note that prices during the 3-week festival may be higher than those quoted below: Hoteliers charge whatever they believe the demand will support.

Hotel Aurora. V. Apollinare 3 (on Pz. d. Libertà), 06049 Spoleto. ☎ **0743/22-03-15.** Fax 0743/22-18-85. 15 units, all with bathroom. MINIBAR TV TEL. 80,000L ($47.05) single; 120,000L ($70.60) double; 175,000L ($102.95.50) triple. Continental breakfast 8,000L ($4.70). AE, DC, MC, V. Free parking.

Directly off the principal Piazza della Libertà in a small courtyard that ensures a central location but quiet nights, this popular hotel is especially recommended if you can procure any of the renovated guest rooms (*camere nuove*)—ask when booking. Rather stylish for these rates, the new rooms boast a warm, coordinated decor of wall-to-wall carpeting, discreetly patterned wallpaper, and rich, heavy curtains of deep mauve. The other rooms—with bathrooms that hark back to the 1970s—have been kept up but are due for a facelift. Within the hotel but of an independent management is the acclaimed Ristorante Apollinare, one of the city's more upscale dining spots with a menu offering regional Umbrian specialties prepared with a light, and at times creative, hand.

Hotel Charleston. Pz. Collicola 10 (northwest of Pz. d. Libertà), 06049 Spoleto. ☎ **0743/22-00-52.** Fax 0743/22-12-44. A/ MINIBAR TV TEL. 18 units, all with bathroom. 117,000L ($68.80) single; 160,000L ($94.10) double; 210,000L ($123.50) triple. Buffet breakfast 12,500L ($7.35). AE, DC, MC, V. Garage parking 15,000L ($8.80).

Much of the hotel's centuries-old character survived a recent renovation by new management with open fireplaces, chestnut-beamed ceilings, and terra-cotta pavements admirably intact. Within such a historical context, the mix of contemporary furnishings and artwork is a seamless and tasteful one. Despite its small size, the Charleston is run with an efficient air, offers amenities such as a sauna (at 25,000L/$14.70 per person, per visit), and organizes walking tours and bicycle outings in the immediate area.

Hotel il Panciolle. V. d. Duomo 3–5 (2 blocks west of the Pz. d. Signoria), 06049 Spoleto. ☎ **0743/45-677.** 7 units, all with bathroom. TEL. 60,000L ($35.30) single; 90,000L ($52.95) double; 120,000L ($70.60) triple. Breakfast 8,500L ($5). Rates discounted 20%–25% low season. AE, V.

You can't beat this inexpensive family run place for new, clean, and nicely decorated accommodations so close to the Duomo. Newly painted white walls offset the guest rooms' matching sets of oak headboard, armoire, and bedside table; bathrooms are smallish but were recently redone and are as nice as you could hope for at these rates.

In warm weather breakfast can be enjoyed on the restaurant's flagstone terrace, also a wonderfully pleasant setting for a home-style dinner (see "Where to Dine," below).

✪ **Hotel Nuovo Clitunno.** Pz. Sordini 6 (just west of Pz. d. Libertà), 06049 Spoleto. ☎ **0743/22-33-40.** Fax 0743/22-26-63. www.spoletol.com/hotelclitunno.html. E-mail: hotel-clitunno@spoletol.com. 45 units, all with bathroom. TV TEL. 105,000L ($61.75) single; 170,000L ($100) double; 221,000L ($130) triple. Rates include buffet breakfast. Rates discounted off-season. AE, DC, MC, V. Closed Feb. Free parking available. Bus from station A, B, C.

Little is left from the time when this 19th-century palazzo was a firehouse. But the Tomassoni family's welcome augments the comfort and warmth of the public area's fireplace, beamed ceilings, and gold-plastered walls. To accommodate disparate tastes, the guest rooms have recently been refitted in two distinct styles. Request "old style" and you'll have reserved one of 18 lovely rooms with terra-cotta floors, antique iron beds, armoires, and rough-hewn ceiling beams. The majority of rooms are decorated in a "standard" style (nominally less expensive than the old-style rooms), with stylish contemporary furnishings in warm pastel colors. All have new bathrooms but only 15 of the standard-style rooms offer a handsome view over the Vale Spoletino. Not all rooms have air-conditioning; it is available at no extra cost, but should be requested when booking. The Tomassonis try to accommodate wherever possible— and then some.

WHERE TO DINE

✪ **Enoteca Provinciale.** V. A. Saffi 7 (between Pz. d. Duomo and Pz. d. Mercato), Spoleto. ☎ **0743/22-04-84.** Antipasti 3,000–6,000L ($1.75–$3.50); primi 6,500–14,000L ($3.80–$8.25); secondi 6,000–19,000L ($3.50–$11.20). Wines and liqueurs by the glass 2,500–4,000L ($1.65–$2.65). AE, DC, MC, V. Summer Wed–Mon 10:30am–3:30pm and 7pm–midnight; winter closing at 10pm. UMBRIAN/WINE BAR.

Make at least one of your lunches, light dinners, or snacks in the converted livestock stalls of this medieval tower where casual meals are accompanied by self-organized wine tastings. Meals consist of the region's simplest, and in this case the most delicious, offerings. The toasted *bruschetta all'olio di Spoleto* showcases the local olive oil; home-made *strangozzi al tartufo* pasta is just an excuse to revel in its unrivaled truffle sauce; *polenta alla spoletina* is made with a barleylike flour (not the usual cornmeal) and heaped with sausage and lentils. You can a sample a cross section of more than 30 red and white Umbrian wines by the glass, but toast the night with the very unusual *amaro di tartufo*, a bitter liqueur made from the ubiquitous truffle. Eat and drink as little or as much as you want; the atmosphere is relaxed and jovial and you'll be wel-comed into the fold the longer you stay and the more you imbibe.

Il Panciolle. V. d. Duomo 3–5 (W of Pz. d. Signoria and the Duomo), Spoleto. ☎ **0743/45-598.** Reservations suggested. Primi 9,000–16,000L ($4.30–$9.40); secondi 11,000–18,000L ($6.50–$10.60). AE, MC, V. Thurs–Tues 12:30–2:30pm and 7:30–11:30pm. Closed first half of Aug. UMBRIAN.

This family run restaurant, popular with performers during the festival, offers two wonderfully distinctive eating experiences: a wintertime evening in the cantina's stone-walled room with beamed ceilings and an open fireplace, where the aroma of roasting meat teases your appetite before you're even seated; and in the warm weather a dinner on the open flagstoned terrace, shaded by a huge pine and enhanced by an open view of the Spoleto Valley. What remains invariable is the *cucina umbra casalinga*, the home cooking Umbria-style that is the kitchen's specialty. Homemade *strangozzi* pasta can be enjoyed simply prepared with *aglio e olio* (garlic and olive oil) or dressed up royally with *funghi e tartufi* (truffles and mushrooms). The meats *alla brace* (grilled over an open fire) are delicious, but also sample the grilled mozzarella or the smoke-cured cheese *scamorza alla brace,* a peasant's dish you could serve to a king. For the restaurant's charming rooms, see "Where to Stay," above.

✪ **La Barcaccia.** Pz. Fratelli Bandiera (north of Pz. d. Mercato), Spoleto. ☎ **0743/ 22-11-71.** Reservations suggested. Primi 8,000–12,000L ($4.70–$7.05); entrees 16,000–25,000L ($9.40–$14.70). Menù turistico 28,000L ($16.50). AE, DC, MC, V. Wed–Mon 12:30–2:30pm and 7:30–11pm. UMBRIAN.

This is one of Spoleto's finer restaurants, where you can have a modestly priced dinner if you resist, alas, the allure of its otherwise highly recommended truffle dishes. A safe way to dine is with the well-priced menù turistico that includes a choice of truffle-free pasta, a meat entree, fresh vegetable, fruit, and service—everything except a glass of the local Umbrian vintage. A covered terrace extends the length of the restaurant in front, though the small piazza's use as a parking lot does little to romanticize the view. Truffle-deprived and -innocent diners should employ the carpe diem approach to dining in Umbria and try any of the truffle-sprinkled first courses: risotto, tagliatelle, and strangozzi dishes all cost a reasonable 18,000L ($10.60). An entree of mixed roast meats (*grigliata alla brace*) is the house's deservedly promoted specialty.

Pizzeria Arco di Druso. V. Arco di Druso 25 (off Pz. d. Mercato), Spoleto. ☎ **0743/ 22-16-95.** Reservations suggested. Primi and pizzas 7,000–13,000L ($4.11–$7.65); secondi 10,000–20,000L ($5.90–$11.75). Menù turistico 25,000L ($14.70). MC, V. Tues–Sun 12:30–2:30pm and 7–11pm. PIZZERIA/UMBRIAN.

With a location practically within the lively daily market, there's little doubt that what winds up on your plate was a farmer's freshly picked special this morning. The wood-burning stove turns out a stellar *pizza al tartufo* and *pizza con funghi porcini* with mushrooms. Ceilings alternate between vaulted brick and exposed wooden beams, redolent of the palazzo's origins in the 1400s as horse stables. Humans now chow down in two busy rooms with murals and pink linen tablecloths, a fancy setting for such simple offerings as the delicious *polenta con funghi porcini.* Any of the season's changing pastas are good; ask which is the day's *pasta fatta a casa* (homemade specialty).

9 Orvieto

45 km (28.3 mi.) W of Todi, 87 km (55 mi.) W of Spoleto, 86 km (54 mi.) SW of Perugia; 152 km (95.8 mi.) S of Florence, 121 km (75.6 mi.) N of Rome

One of the most dramatically sited hill towns in Italy, Orvieto is perfectly situated between Florence and Rome, atop a volcanic plateau over 1,000 feet above a wide valley. It is an amazing sight, one visible from miles away, when the setting sun is reflecting off the glittering mosaic facade of the Duomo, which, by the way, is considered by many to be one of Italy's most outstanding cathedrals.

Orvieto was of Etruscan origin—one of the original League of twelve important satellite cities and possibly its religious center—and later destroyed in 264 B.C. by the Romans who would transform it into their own stronghold. As the Etruscans before them, they sculpted the porous tufa butte into a labyrinth of tunnels, storage caves, wells, and living space (much of the underground can be visited daily with an English-speaking guide, 10,000L/$5.90; contact the tourist office). The Middle Ages saw a thriving period as an influential *comune,* enjoying its golden days in the 13th and 14th centuries, when many of today's palazzi and churches were built. Orvieto was also prominent papal seat: As many as 33 pontiffs had their summer residence here. The proximity to the Vatican was a plus, as was the high-altitude tabletop setting that made it a natural fortress while guaranteeing cool weather during Rome's infernal summers.

Those intending to stay overnight and longer may have to fend off not the day trippers, but the possible disappointment of its limited sites. Those with cars, however, will enjoy using Orvieto as a base for visiting the area's prominent vineyards and other charming hilltowns such as Todi and Spoleto.

FESTIVALS & MARKETS   Seven weeks after Easter, **Pentecost Sunday** (usually falling in June) is festively celebrated in Orvieto. On this day, **La Palombella** commemorates the descent of the Holy Spirit on the Apostles amidst much fanfare. Nine weeks after Easter, **Corpus Christi** (usually the first half of June) reenacts an event in 1264 in the time of Pope Urban IV (see Il Duomo listing, below). Since 1950, the precious, ancient relic (the Holy Corporal) kept in the Duomo is carried through the streets, accompanied by a *corteo* of 400 people in costume, evoking the period when Orvieto was a prominent papal seat. For 5 days surrounding New Year's Eve (and ending January 3rd) **Umbria Jazz Winter,** the relatively new mini jazz festival has been catching on.

Every Thursday and Saturday, a morning market fills the **Piazza del Popolo** with fresh produce and fruits, as well as an interesting smattering of stalls hawking clothing, ceramics, and miscellaneous items.

ESSENTIALS
GETTING HERE   By Train   The Orvieto train station is actually located in the valley below in Orvieto Scalo; the no. 1 bus makes the twisting 3-kilometer (2-mi.) drive up to the old center. The alternative is the modern, small-scale funicular operating daily from directly outside the train station and departing every 15 minutes or so. Cost one way is 1,500L (88¢). This ticket allows you to make an immediate connection with a minibus above (Piazza Cahen) that brings you right into the Piazza Duomo.

From **Rome,** there are at least a dozen daily trains making the direct trip in about 75 minutes (12,000L/$7.05). From **Perugia,** all trains make a direct connection in Terontola, making the trip in 2 hours ($5.90). **Assisi** follows the same schedule as Perugia (12,100L/$7.10). From **Florence,** a dozen daily trains make the direct trip in 2 hours (16,000L/$9.40). Trains from **Spoleto** change in Orte, a local train making a short trip into a 2-hour ordeal (10,100L/$5.95).

By Bus   Train transportation to any of the above destinations is generally preferred to the extremely limited bus service to and from Orvieto. For bus information call ☎ 0763/301234 or visit the tourist information office.

By Car   Coming south from Florence (2 hr.) or heading north from Rome (about 90 min.), exit the **A1** autostrada at Orvieto Scalo. From Perugia, head down the **SS3bis** to Todi, then head west on the **SS448** (from Todi the longer but more picturesque SS79bis).

VISITOR INFORMATION   The **Tourist Office** is in Pz. Duomo 24 (☎ 0763/341772; fax 0763/344433). It's open Monday to Friday 8am to 2pm and 4 to 7pm, Saturday 10am to 1pm and 4 to 7pm, Sunday 10am to noon and 4 to 6pm.

CRAFTS & WINE
The shopping scene is limited but varied, representing Orvieto's tradition of centuries-old crafts: lace and embroidery work, woodwork (carved objects, inlays, and veneers), ceramics, and wine (with the local DOC white wine Orvieto Classico holding out as everyone's purchase). Shops are concentrated around the area of the Duomo and along the pedestrian shopping strips west of the Duomo, namely Via Duomo and Via Cavour. Visit **Michelangeli** (V. Gualtiero Michelangeli 3; ☎ 0763/342660) for the

most creative woodwork and inlays in town. One of the very few lace workers left in town is the gracious **Maria Moretti** (V. Maurizio 1; ☎ **0763/341714**). Ceramics are the easiest to come by with a number of artisan shops along the pedestrian strips mentioned above. Wine lovers should give some time and attention to the city's many *cantine* and *enoteche* open to the public: **Enoteca Barberani** (V. Michelangeli 14; ☎ **0763/341532**) sells excellent wines and oils from its own estate, as well as a sampling of other food products such as truffles, preserves, and liqueurs (they can arrange to have you visit their wine-growing estate approximately 16 km/10 mi. east outside of town); **Cantina Foresi** (Pz. Duomo 2; ☎ **0763/341611**) represents a number of different local wine producers, as does **La Bottega del Buon Vino** (V. d. Cava 26, closed Tuesday), which sits above ancient Etruscan excavations (ask the friendly shopkeeper if you can take a peek; consider hanging around for lunch as well, at the enoteca's popular trattoria). The tourist information office has a brochure and map called *Andar per Vigne* (*Visiting the Vineyards*), with information about a dozen major producers in the region within a 5- to 20-kilometer (3- to 13-mi.) radius of Orvieto and their visiting hours. The **Castello di Sala** of the storied Antinori family probably wins out as the most picturesque, replete with medieval castle, ideal setting, and important vintages.

WHAT TO SEE & DO

✪ **Il Duomo.** Pz. d. Duomo. ☎ **0763/341167.** Free admission to Duomo. 3,000L ($1.75) to Cappella S. Brizio. Nov–Feb daily 7:30am–12:45pm and 2:30–5:15pm; Mar and Oct 6:15pm–closing. Apr–Sept 7:15pm–closing. Check tourist office for hours for Cappella S. Brizio.

This city's singular draw is its spacious Piazza del Duomo and its unmissable 13th-century **Duomo,** one of Italy's treasures. It is noted for its breathtaking facade influenced by dozens of architects and artists; inside, the Duomo contains one of the greatest fresco cycles of the Renaissance in the ✪ **Chapel of San Brizio,** recently reopened after a lengthy period of restoration. The cycle, begun by Fra Angelico and completed by Luca Signorelli, depicts in vivid detail the Last Judgment, one that was said to have influenced Michelangelo and his own interpretation in the Sistine Chapel. Leonardo da Vinci wouldn't give it the time of day.

The Duomo was built to shelter the relic of the Miracle of Bolsena, an incident that happened in 1263 just a few miles south of Orvieto and has since been celebrated by the Catholic Church as the feast of the Corpus Christi. A doubting priest who questioned the sacrament of the Transfiguration (one of the Church's most sacred mysteries: that the consecrated communion Host contains the incarnation—the actual body and blood—of Christ), witnessed that the bleeding host had stained the linen altar cloth. This precious relic is now protected in a gold-and-enamel reliquary (1339) that mimics the facade of the cathedral in the **Cappella del Corporale,** a chapel to the left of the main altar, and paraded through town once a year to major fanfare (see "Festivals & Markets," above). It spawned what would become the construction of Orvieto's cathedral, one of the most important in Italy (and that's saying something).

Much attention is given to the glittering mosaics of the elaborate facade, but in fact they were not added until the 17th and 18th centuries and are not held to be major works. Work continued as recently as this century: The Duomo's controversial (mainly because they're contemporary) central bronze doors were made in 1964 by Sicilian sculptor Emilio Greco. Some of the earliest work are the bas reliefs on the lower parts of the pillars (protected by Plexiglas due to threats of vandalism in the 1960s)—the work of the Sienese master Lorenzo Maittani, one of the original architects involved in the cathedral's early years until his death in 1330. The facade's delicate rose window was the work of Florentine Andrea Orcagna from the mid–14th century. If you're still in town at sunset, join the small knot of savvy visitors who know to be nowhere else when the moment and lighting is something unforgettable.

The Duomo's pièce de résistance is the interior's famous ✪ **Cappella Nuova** or **Cappella di San Brizio,** begun by Fra Angelico in 1447 (see his work over the chapel's altar) with the help of Benozzo Gozzoli, but resumed and finished in 1499 to 1503 by Luca Signorelli (the last chapel to the right of the main altar; admission) of Cortona.

WHERE TO STAY

Orvieto Promotion, associated with the local travel agency Effe & G Viaggi (☎ 0763/344666; fax 0763/343943; e-mail: effegi@etorvienet.it), will help with hotel reservations free of charge if the following hotels are full. Specify the category or price range you're interested in. You should also check out the **Hotel Duomo** (☎ 0763/341887; fax 0763/341105) at Vc. Maurizio 7, which at press time was undergoing renovations. Located 1 block from the Duomo, the hotel is planning to offer large gracious rooms, which will run from 43,000L ($25.30) for a single without a bathroom to 120,000L ($70.60) for a double with bathroom (triples also available).

✪ **Hotel La Badia.** Località La Badia, Orvieto 05019. ☎ **0763/301959.** Fax 0763/305396. 26 units, all with bathroom. A/C MINIBAR TV TEL. 211,000L ($124.10) single; 284,000L ($167.05) double. Breakfast 18,000L ($10.58). AE, MC, V. Closed Jan–Feb. Free parking. Located 3 mi. east of town center.

"La Badia" (the Abbey) is an ecclesiastical enclave of golden-stone buildings dating as far back as the 8th century (and then enlarged as a Benedictine monastery in the 12th). Located outside of Orvieto proper, it's gorgeously sited amid the quiet and bird-song in the idyllic green countryside. The rural hotel lends itself to seminars, wedding receptions, and group tours, and the remote other-worldliness the monks once knew can get lost amid the one-night traffic. But it remains a highly unique and historically rich hotel made more attractive when rates are discounted (doubles cost 254,000L/ $149.40) off-season (March through May and October 15 through December). The hotel likes to encourage half-board (the stone-vaulted dining hall and open hearth is high on drama) although if you insist, it's not mandatory. Country club amenities such as tennis courts and a pool make this a good spot to settle in for a few days R&R, but inconvenient for those without cars. The size of the rooms varies greatly, and the whole place is aging, but it carries its age well. Ten rooms have views of Orvieto, some overlook the Abbey's 12th-century, 12-sided bell tower, said to be the only one of its kind in the world. If you don't have car, you can take a taxi here from the train station for about 17,000L ($10.00).

Hotel Palazzo Piccolomini. Pz. Ranieri 36, 05018 Orvieto. ☎ **0763/341734.** Fax 0763/ 391046. E-mail: piccolomini.hotel@orvienet.it. 32 units, all with bathroom. A/C MINIBAR TV TEL. 140,000L ($82.35) single; 160,000–180,000L ($94.10–$105.90) double; 180,000L ($105.90) triple; 250,000L ($147.05) suite, double occupancy. Breakfast 12,000L ($7.05). AE, DC, MC, V.

The recent 1998 opening of this converted Renaissance palazzo is the sole reason behind the suspiciously low prices. Pray they stay this low through 2000, but know that their days are numbered and act now. Looking very pretty in pink, this 16th-century palazzo was the Orvieto home of the illustrious Tuscan family that gave us two popes. It is quietly back in operation following a complete top-to-toe refurbishment that has kept the historical shell and its grand dimensions of vaulted ceilings and wide halls, while creating an uncluttered ambience that is quasi-minimalist with cool terra-cotta floors and white slip-covered furniture. If the unusual concept of modernized

Renaissance strikes your fancy, hang your hat here while the promotional rates make this an exceptionally interesting value for your money.

WHERE TO DINE

If you're in between meals, or just looking for a nibble, consider **Enoteca Barberani** (see "Crafts & Wine," above); **Bar/Caffe Montanucci** (Cor. Cavour 21, closed Wednesday) for the best coffee in town, or shop for delicious picnic ingredients at either of the two best delicatessens: **Dai Fratelli** (V. d. Duomo 10, closed Wednesday) or **Antonia Carraro** (V. Cavour 101, closed Wednesday). The Piazza Duomo is ground zero for tourist spots, but its also the location for the **Cantina Foresi** (no. 2, closed Tuesday in winter), perfect for a tasty sandwich and a glass of local wine, or the **Gelateria del Duomo** (no. 14, open daily), for the best ice cream in town.

Antica Trattoria dell'Orso. V. d. Misericordia 18 (immediately north off the Pz. d. Repubblica). ☎ **0763/341642**. Reservations recommended. Primi 7,500–15,000L ($4.40–$8.80); secondi 9,000–15,000L ($5.30–$8.80). AE, DC, MC, V. Wed–Sun noon–2:30pm and 7:30–10pm; Mon noon–2:30pm only. Closed mid-Jan to mid-Feb. UMBRIAN.

The ubiquitous *umbrichelli* (the homemade spaghetti-like specialty of Umbria) is best here *alla campagnola* ("country style" with zucchini, eggplant, and onions). Any of the fresh pastas, in fact, are must-trys at this unprepossessing trattoria full of locals, somewhat free of tourists because of its location one step too far off the beaten path (it's a 10-min. stroll from the Duomo). The ingredients of fresh market offerings and home-grown herbs help confirm the impression of a day in the country. The simplest of dishes—an omelettelike frittata of asparagus or potatoes—is a wonderful surprise, full of the season's flavor and the masterful touch of chef Gabriele di Giandomenico, who seems to be able to do no wrong.

✪ **Tipica Trattoria Etrusca.** V. L Maitani 10 (1 block west of Duomo). ☎ **0763/344016.** Reservations recommended. Primi 9,500–15,000L ($5.60–$8.80); secondi 9,000–20,000L ($5.30–$11.75). Fixed-price menu 35,000L ($20.60, without wine). AE, DC, MC, V. Tues–Sun noon–2:30pm and 7:30–10pm. Closed Jan 7 to early Feb. UMBRIAN.

Precede or cap off a visit to Orvieto's Duomo with a meal here and you will have orchestrated the perfect day with next to no effort, at moderate cost and immense personal pleasure. The Etrusca offers a cool respite during a hot Umbrian afternoon, on the ground level of a 15th-century palazzo whose roots (like much of Orvieto) are lost in Etruscan times. A much requested primo is the regional homemade pasta *umbrichelli*, an almost chewy flour-and-water spaghetti served here *alla orvietana* (a slightly spicy tomato sauce with bacon). To complete a meal typical of this game-rich region, try the tried-and-true Umbrian specialty of rabbit, *coniglio all'Etrusca* in a savory sauce of herbs and spices. Stay close to home with fresh ricotta cheese from a local supplier, dusted with sugar and covered with fresh berries for a light dessert. A thoughtful selection of Umbrian and Tuscan wines fills the restaurant's wine cellars, carved into the ancient Etruscan foundations below.

TODI: SIDE TRIP FROM ORVIETO

With so little to see or do in Todi, it is always surprising that this medieval hill town is on everyone's itineraries these days. Smack-dab between Orvieto to the west and Spoleto to the east (each approximately 45 kilometers/28 mi.), Todi also makes the perfect day's jaunt from those setting up base in Perugia, equidistant to the north (unless you're based in Perugia, bus service is not good; you'll need your own wheels). The twisting, winding back roads that lead you there are some of the loveliest through southern Umbria's less trammeled corners.

What you do once you arrive is up to you. For 10 days at the end of August and the beginning of September, the classy **Festival di Todi** aspires to be a small version of the world-famous festival in Spoleto, and comes close to succeeding. Todi's growing popularity with Rome's arts and media set, and as the preferred summer-retreat of choice of an Anglo-American artist community (as an alternative destination to the always more "crowded" Tuscany) is the result of the camera crews and on-location film crews that have "discovered" the fairy-tale medievalism of this town and spread the word. There is no discounting its small-town charm, just don't expect your days to be chockablock with sightseeing; strolling and snacking, yes.

The ✪ **Piazza del Popolo** has long been described as one of medieval Italy's loveliest compendium of secular and religious palazzi, generally from the 13th-century period when Todi was a thriving commercial *comune.* Here also is **Umbria** (☎ 075/8942737 or 075/8942390; closed Tuesday) at V. S. Bonaventura 13 (off the Piazza del Popolo), Todi's finest restaurant, with special views from its terrace tables as well as regional cuisine with a nod to Roman specialties. Average meal for one without wine is 35,000L ($20.60); all credit cards accepted. **Enoteca dell'Academia dei Convivianti,** Todi's best enoteca wine store, is next door.

The second most important site in town is the **Church of San Fortunato** in the Piazza della Repubblica; its size alone is testimony to Todi's medieval might. It was begun in 1291 but not finished until 1459, so the initial Gothic style is mingled with that of the Renaissance. Finishing off the triumvirate of sites is **Santa Maria della Consolazione,** a late Renaissance work 99 years in the making. Inspired by plans by Bramante, architect of Rome's St. Peters, it is often written about as a Renaissance masterwork and, by the time it was finished in 1607, had been collaborated upon by a series of architects including Sangallo the Younger and Vignola. The **tourist information office** (also called S.T.T.) is located under the arches in the Piazza del Popolo (☎ 075/8942686; fax 075/8942406).

Bologna & Emilia-Romagna

7

by Stephen Brewer

Emilia-Romagna comprises two ancient lands: Emilia, named for the Roman road that bisects its plains and art cities, and Romagna, named for its prominence in the Roman Empire. History has left its mark here on some of Italy's most beautiful cities—**Ravenna,** last capital of the empire and later the stronghold of the Byzantines and the Visigoths; **Ferrara,** center of art and culture for much of the Renaissance; **Parma,** one of the most powerful duchies in Europe under the Farnese family; **Modena,** famous for vinegar and opera stars; **Bologna,** a university center since the Middle Ages and Italy's most youthful and exuberant city.

Many travelers speed through Emilia-Romagna on high-speed trains and autostradas en route to and from Florence, Milan, Venice, or Rome. Not only are they bypassing some of Italy's finest art and architecture, but also the opportunity to experience a way of life that has been largely unaffected by those two great demons of the 20th century: mass tourism and massive industrialization.

REGIONAL CUISINE With such a collection of exquisite cities at hand, the pleasures of the region are primarily urban. No small part of the delight of visiting these cities is to partake of the bounty of the rich farmland that lies between them and comes to the tables of the region's simple but excellent restaurants—prosciutto, parmigiano cheese, fruits and vegetables, salamis, the cream and butter used in the rich sauces that top tortellini and other pastas, and from the nearby Adriatic, a bounty of seafood. This is a wealthy province, and the food tends to be rich: *Alla Bolognese* means served with a thick meat sauce; lasagna *verde,* made with spinach noodles, contains layer upon layer of meat, béchamel sauce and parmigiano. Meat dishes are plentiful, and it's indicative of culinary preferences here that most restaurants serve a good *bollito misto,* a selection of boiled beef, tongue, pig's foot, capon, pork sausages, and maybe oxtail (the selection varies) that's rolled to the table on a cart and topped with a *salsa verde* (herbs and capers).

1 Bologna

105 km (63 mi.) N of Florence, 210 km (126 mi.) SE of Milan, 210 km (126 mi.) S of Venice, 380 km (220 mi.) N of Rome

Bologna is known the world over as the home of the oldest university in Europe, and this venerable institution accounts for much of what

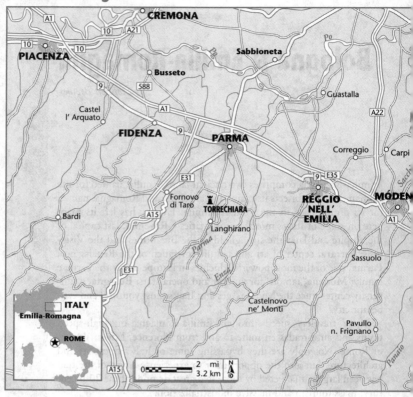

you'll see of the city's past and present. By the 13th century, scholars had begun descending upon the city in droves, and the city took shape to accommodate them. The city's famous loggias, 21 miles in length, covered sidewalks and gave students the opportunity to stroll and discourse in any kind of weather; palazzi and churches were built by the burgeoning community, and artists came from throughout Italy to decorate them. These treasures remain, amid a handsome cityscape of ocher-colored buildings, red-tile rooftops, and the occasional tower constructed by powerful medieval families to display their wealth and power. The students remain a vibrant presence in Bologna, giving the city a youthful exuberance.

FESTIVALS & MARKETS   If you're in Bologna in July and August, you can spend your evenings at the jazz concerts and other free events that are part of the **Bologna Sogna festival** and are held in church cloisters and other scenic settings throughout the city center. A much less tame event is the **Made in Bo** festival, a series of late-night outdoor disco events held in July and August in Parco Nord (bus no. 25 or 91a serves the area from the train station; free buses from Piazza Maggiore are provided for some events). Ask the tourist office for details on both these festivals, as well as the many other concerts, dance and theater performances and other events the city stages throughout the year.

ESSENTIALS

GETTING HERE   **By Plane**   European flights land at Aeroporto G. Marconi (☎ **051/312-336**), 4 miles north of the city and connected to the train station by

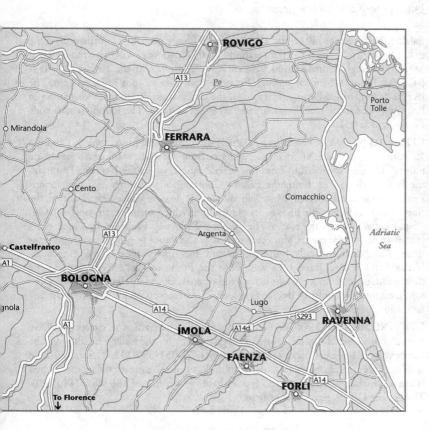

Aerobus, which runs every 20 minutes; the trip takes half an hour and service runs from 6am to midnight and costs 6,000L ($3.35) each way.

By Train Trains arrive from and depart for the following major Italian cities almost hourly: **Florence** (1 hr.; 8,200L/$4.80), **Rome** (4 hr.; 34,000L/$20; or 2.5 hr. via Eurostar Italia high-speed service, 52,000L/$30), **Milan** (3 hr.; 18,000L/$10.60; or 1.5 hr. via high-speed service, 28,000L/$16.50), and **Venice** (2.5 hr.; 14,000L/$8.25). Buses 25 and 30 make the run from the station to Piazza Maggiore in the center of the city, which is within comfortable walking distance of about 15 minutes down Via Indipendenza, Bologna's major avenue.

By Bus Bologna relies more on trains than it does on buses for service to other cities. But **ATC buses** serve suburban towns from a terminal just outside the train station (☎ 051/248-374); a bus that may be of interest to travelers is the hourly one to Ferrara (1 hr.; 6,000L/$3.55).

By Car Bologna lies directly on the A1 autostrada, which runs up the center of the peninsula and connects Rome and Milan. Using this high-speed corridor, Bologna is only an hour from Florence and 2 hours from Milan. Bologna is also linked by the A13 autostrada to Venice (about 2 hr.) and by the A14 to Rimini (a little over an hour) and the other Adriatic cities.

VISITOR INFORMATION The main **IAT tourist office** is in the Palazzo Communale, on Piazza Maggiore (☎ 051/239-660; www.comune.bologna.it), open Monday to Saturday from 9am to 7pm, Sunday from 9am to 2pm. The English-speaking staff is extremely helpful and dispenses a library's worth of information on the city. The branch office in the train station (☎ **051/246-541**) will book rooms; open Monday through Saturday from 9am to 7pm. The office at the airport (☎ **051/647-2036**) is open Monday through Saturday from 9am to 1pm and 2 to 4pm. The IAT has also installed terminals all around the city that display tourist information in English; look for the machines marked TUTTO BOLOGNA. The telephone area code for Bologna is **051.**

CITY LAYOUT The center of Bologna is the **Piazza Maggiore,** which is about a 10-minute walk down Via dell'Indipendenza from the train station. All sights are more or less on a short radius from this central square, where the Neptune Fountain, the Basilica di San Petronio, the Palazzo Communale and other sights of monumental Bologna are located. Since old Bologna is densely concentrated within the ring roads that follow the lines of its old walls, anything of interest is only a 10- to 15-minute walk from the piazza. For instance: Following **Via Rizzoli,** which skirts the north end of the piazza, you come to Bologna's famous leaning towers, and from there **Via Zamboni** leads northeast toward the university and the Pinacoteca Nazionale; **Via Ugo Bassi** runs west from the Piazza to Via del Pratello and the surrounding area, with its antique shops and osterias; and **Via della Orefici** takes you southeast into the midst of Bologna's colorful food markets and toward the San Stefano church complex.

GETTING AROUND With its covered sidewalks and traffic-free streets (cars have been all but banned from the center), Bologna is a joy for the walker. In addition, the excellent ACT bus network serves all of Bologna; ☎ **051/350-111.** Tickets, available at tobacco shops and newsstands, cost 1,500L (90¢) and you must validate them when boarding the bus—failure to do so is punishable with a fine of 180,000L ($105.90). The Tourist Offices provides bus maps.

FAST FACTS: Bologna

Bookstore Feltrinelli International, V. Zamboni 7 (☎ **051/268-070**), sells a large selection of English-language titles. You're best bets for finding English-language newspapers and magazines are at the newsstands on Via Indipendenza and at the train station.

Crime Bologna reportedly has a low incidence of purse snatching and other crimes against tourists; however, beware of pickpockets in and around the train station. In recent years there has been an alarming and highly visible increase in the number of intravenous drug users, especially in the streets off Via Indipendenza.

Currency Exchange The **Banca di Sicilia** operates the most conveniently located exchange counters—one at V. Indipendenza 7 (Monday through Friday, 8:20am to 1:20pm and 2:45 to 3:45pm) and in the train station (daily 7:15am to 8pm). ATMs are plentiful throughout Bologna.

Drugstores The pharmacy at Pz. Maggiore 6 (☎ **051/238-509**), is open 24 hours.

Emergencies As in all of Italy, the general emergency number is ☎ **113;** to report a fire, call ☎ **115;** for medical emergencies, call ☎ **333333.** The Carabinieri, Italy's military-trained state police corps, can be reached at ☎ **112.** The central station for municipal police is at Pz. Maggiore 6 (☎ **051/582-307**).

Hospitals   Hospitals in and near the city center are Ospedale Santa Orsola, V. Massarenti 9 (☎ **051/636-3111**), and Ospedale Maggiore, V. 1 Nigrisoli 2 (☎ **051/647-8111**).

Laundry   **Ondablu Lavanderia** has two handy self-service laundries in central Bologna, one at V. San Donato 4/B-C, and another at V. Saragozza 34/A-B; open 8am to 10pm 7 days a week.

Lost Property   **The Lost Property Office of the Communale,** at V. Mirasole 4, handles all lost property that has been turned over to the police, the carabinieri, and the railway police. For articles left in taxis, contact the offices of Radiotaxi (☎ **051/582-307**).

Luggage Storage   Luggage storage is available at the train station. The office is open 24 hours a day, 7 days a week; the fee is 5,000L ($2.95) per bag for each 12-hour period.

Post Office   The main Post Office is in Piazza Minghetti, which is a few blocks southeast of Piazza Maggiore, off Via Farini; ☎ **051/223-598.** It is open Monday through Friday 8:15am to 6:30pm and Saturday 8:15am to 12:20pm. The postal code for central Bologna is 40100.

Taxis   Il Taxi provides 24-hour radio taxi service; ☎ **051/372-727.** You can find taxis at taxi stands throughout the city, often in major piazzas. In the city center, you will find taxi stands on Via dell' Indipendenza and on Via Rizzoli near Piazza Maggiore.

Telephones   There are **Telecom Italia** offices, equipped with long banks of pay phones, at Piazza VIII Agosto, off Via Indipendenza several blocks south of the train station, and a smaller one just north of Piazza Maggiore on Via Fossalta; both are open from 8am to 10pm. The phones, like most public phones in Bologna, require phone cards, which are dispensed from machines on the premises and are also available at newsstands.

Travel Services   The English-speaking staff at **Bigtours,** just off Piazza Maggiore at V. Indipendenza 12 (☎ **051/239-950),** makes plane, boat, and train reservations (including those for couchettes and sleeping cars) and can also reserve hotel rooms and sightseeing tours. For budget travel options, contact **Centro Turistico Studentesco,** off Via Zamboni at Largo Respighi 2F (☎ **051/ 261-802**); open Monday through Friday, 9am to 12:30pm and 2:30 to 6pm. Visitors to Bologna's many fairs can use the free services of **Centro Servizi Per I Turisti** (CST) (☎ **1678-56065** toll-free, or 051/648-7607)**.** Among other services, CST makes theater bookings, arranges for parking, and offers discounts in

Driving in Bologna

Much of central Bologna is closed to cars without special permits from 7am to 8pm daily (including Sundays and holidays). When booking a room, be prepared to present your car registration number, which the hotel will then provide to the police to ensure you are not fined for driving in restricted areas. Also ask about parking facilities (many hotels provide them at an extra fee) as well as the most efficient routes to take to reach the hotel, since many streets in central Bologna are permanently closed to traffic. A permit is required to park in the center; hotel guests can obtain one through their hotel for 8,000L ($4.70) a day; ask for details when you book.

some restaurants. Check with the tourist office for more information and a CST discount booklet.

WHAT TO SEE & DO

PIAZZA MAGGIORE & FONTANA DEL NETTUNO Bologna's central square and heart of the city is flanked by the city's finest buildings: the medieval **Palazzo di Rei Enzo,** named for Enzo, king of Sardinia, who died here in 1272 after languishing in captivity for 23 years until his death; the Romanesque **Palazzo del Podesta;** and the **Palazzo Communale,** seat of the local government. The square is dominated, though, by a relative newcomer: an immodestly virile, 16th-century bronze statue of **Neptune,** who presides over an ornate fountain inhabited by sensual sirens.

ZONA UNIVERSITA (UNIVERSITY DISTRICT) Bologna's university is Europe's oldest, rooted in a Roman law school dating from A.D. 425 and officially founded in the 10th century. By the 13th century, more than 10,000 students from all over Europe were descending upon this center of learning, and their scholarly numbers have included Thomas à Becket, Copernicus, Dante, Petrarch, and, much more recently, Federico Fellini. Always forward-thinking, even in the unenlightened Middle Ages the university employed female professors, and the political leanings of today's student body are displayed in leftist slogans that emblazon the 15th- to 19th-century buildings.

You may visit one of the old buildings, the **Palazzo di Archiginnasio,** near the university district, south of Piazza Maggiore, just behind the duomo at Pz. Galvani 1. This large, baroque palazzo houses an anatomical theater where ancient wooden benches surround a much-used marble slab and eerily humanlike pillars support the lectern. It's open Monday to Saturday from 9am to 1pm; admission is free.

Basilica di San Petronio. Pz. Maggiore. ☎ **051/225-442.** Free admission. Apr–Sept daily 7:15am–12:55 and 2:30–6:30pm, Oct–Mar daily 7:15am–1pm and 2–6pm. Bus: 11, 17, 25.

Massive as this church is, it's not nearly as big as its 14th-century architects intended it to be. Rome got wind of the Bolognese scheme to build a church bigger than Saint Peter's and cut off the funds. Even so, the structure that was erected over the next three centuries is impressively grand, fronted by a facade that is partially striped in white and red, the city's heraldic colors, and punctuated by one of the great works of the Italian Renaissance: a marble doorway surrounded by reliefs depicting the Madonna and Child and scenes from the Bible, carved by Jacopo della Quercia and now sadly weather worn. The cavernous interior beyond (where Charles V was crowned Holy Roman Emperor in 1530) is richly decorated with frescoes, the best of which are in the chapels to the left as you enter. One contains Lorenzo Costa's Madonna and Child, and the other, the so- called Bolognini Chapel, is enlivened with colorful depictions of heaven and hell. Embedded in the floor is an enchanting curiosity—Italy's largest sundial, an astronomical clock that the astronomer Cassini installed in 1655.

Basilica di Santo Stefano. V. Santa Stefano 24. ☎ **051/223-256.** Free admission. Daily 9am–1pm and 3:30–5:30pm. Bus: 11, 17, 25.

This remarkable assemblage of hallowed buildings incorporates four churches, dating from the 4th to the 13th centuries. A walk through the complex provides a remarkable overview of the history of Bologna. The first church you enter is **Crocifisso,** begun in the 11th century (as you enter, notice the altar built into the facade). San Petronio, Bologna's patron saint, lies in the church to the left, the most charming in the group, the 12th-century **Chiesa del San Sepolcro,** a polygon modeled after the church of the Holy Sepulchre in Jerusalem. According to legend, the basin in the

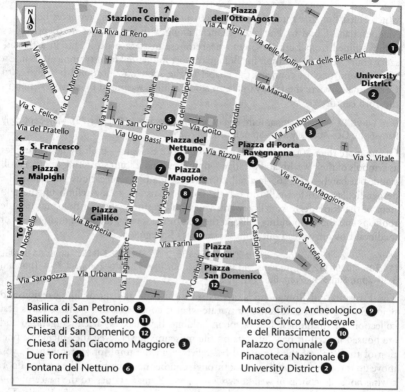

Basilica di San Petronio **8**
Basilica di Santo Stefano **11**
Chiesa di San Domenico **12**
Chiesa di San Giacomo Maggiore **3**
Due Torri **4**
Fontana del Nettuno **6**

Museo Civico Archeologico **9**
Museo Civico Medioevale
  e del Rinascimento **10**
Palazzo Comunale **7**
Pinacoteca Nazionale **1**
University District **2**

courtyard is the one in which Pontius Pilate absolved himself after condemning Christ to death (in truth, it's a Lombard piece from the 8th century). The oldest church here is the 5th-century **Santi Vitale e Agricola,** incorporating fragments of a Roman temple to Isis; Charlemagne allegedly worshipped here in the 8th century. Just beyond is the 13th-century **Trinita** and the complex's 11th-century cloisters, where plaques honor Bologna's war dead.

Chiesa di San Domenico. Pz. San Domenico 13. ☎ **051/640-0411.** Free admission. Daily 7am–1pm and 2:15–7pm. Bus: 17, 30.

Here, in the sixth chapel on the right, is one of the great treasures of Bologna, the beautifully crafted tomb of St. Dominic, founder of the teaching order that bears his name. These saints and angels are a joint effort of Michelangelo, Pisano, and, most notably, Nicolo di Bari, who was so proud of his work on the cover of the tomb (arca) that he dropped his last name and is better known as Nicolo dell' Arca. A plan near the entrance to the chapel tells you who carved what, and an English-speaking guide will give you a highly informative lecture about the tomb and the saint, who died in Bologna in 1221.

Chiesa di San Giacomo Maggiore. Pz. Rossini. ☎ **051/225-970.** Free admission. Daily 8am–noon and 3:30–6pm. Bus: 11, 17.

The masterpiece in this 13th-century church, which took on its Gothic appearance in subsequent centuries, is the chapel-cum-burial chamber of the Bentivoglio family, which ruled Bologna through the 15th century. Among the masterpieces here are a Madonna and Child by Francesco Erancia, along with the frescoes the Bentivoglios commissioned from Lorenzo Costa, the Ferrarese master, to depict life in a Renaissance court, an apt decoration for Bologna's most influential (and tyrannical) clan. An underground passage connects the chapel to the spot, now occupied by the Teatro Communale, where the family's palazzo stood until it was razed by an angry mob in the 16th century.

Due Torri. Pz. Porte Ravegna. Torre degli Asinelli, admission 3,000L ($1.75). May–Sept daily 9am–6pm, Oct–Apr daily 9am–5pm. Bus: 11, 17, 25.

Of the more than 200 towers that once rose above Bologna—built by noble families as symbols of their wealth and prestige—only these and a scant scattering of others still stand, but barely—the 165-feet-tall Torre Garisenda tilts a precarious 10 feet off the perpendicular; 320-feet-tall Torre degli Asinelli leans 7½ feet. A climb up the 500 steps of the Torre degli Asinelli rewards you with a stunning view of Bologna's red-tile rooftops and the surrounding hills. At the base of the towers, the seven main streets of medieval Bologna spread out from Piazza Porta Ravegna.

Museo Civico Archeologico. V. dell'Archiginnasio, 2. ☎ **051/233-849.** Admission 8,000L ($4.70), 4,000L ($2.35) students and seniors over 60. Tues–Fri 9am–2pm, Sat 9am–1pm and 3:30–7pm, Sun 3:30–7pm. Bus: 11, 17, 25.

The Etruscan and Roman finds at this museum from the surrounding region and many fine Egyptian antiquities constitute what is considered to be one of Italy's best collections of antiquities. The Egyptian holdings have recently been reorganized and are housed in well-lit new quarters on the museum's lower level; they include a portion of the Book of the Dead and bas-reliefs from the tomb of Horemheb. As you move up through the building, walk through another new exhibit on the ground floor, a wing housing replicas of well known Greek and Roman statues, to the peaceful central courtyard, which is evocatively littered with milestones from the Via Emilia. The next floor is filled with the museum's impressive Etruscan collection, which includes many remnants from Bologna's own beginnings as the Etruscan outpost Felsina. Among the burial items and other artifacts is a bronze urn from the 5th century B.C., the Situla di Certosa, decorated with a depiction of a ceremonial procession.

Museo Civico Medioevale e del Rinascimento. V. Manzoni 4. ☎ **051/228-912.** Admission 8,000L ($4.70), 4,000L ($2.35) children 17 and under and seniors over 60. Mon–Fri 9am–2pm, Sat–Sun 9am–1pm and 3:30–7pm. Bus: 11, 17, 25.

Though a Roman wall runs through the courtyard, the collection here is determinedly devoted to depicting life in medieval Bologna. At that time, the city revolved around its university, and the most enchanting treasures are the sepulchers of professors, surrounded for eternity by carvings of dozing and mocking students. Also on view are some fascinating cooking utensils from daily life in medieval Bologna, along with a sizeable collection of armor.

Pinacoteca Nazionale. V. d. Belle Arti 56. ☎ **051/243-222.** Admission 8,000L ($4.40) adults, 4,000L ($2.20) children 17 and under. Tues–Sat 9am–2pm, Sun 9am–1pm. Closed holidays. Bus: 32, 33, 37.

Many of these second-floor galleries, which are badly in need of better lighting and signage, are devoted to Bolognese painters or painters from elsewhere who worked in Bologna. The galleries house, for instance, Italy's largest repository of the painting of Bologna's most illustrious artist, Guido Reni (1575–1642). Perhaps his best-known work, *Ritratto della Madre*, a portrait of his mother, is here, and in the same room hang many of his other works, including *Samson the Victorious*. More striking, however, is a work by an earlier Bolognese artist, the 14th-century *St. George and the Dragon* by Vitale da Bologna. The museum's most sought out work is not by a native son, but by Raphael, whose *Ecstasy of St. Celia* is considered to be one of the great achievements of Renaissance painting.

WHERE TO STAY

Hotel prices in Bologna tend to vary from season to season, reaching their height during periods when the city is hosting one of its trade fairs and their lows during the summer—especially in August, when Bolognese tend to flee the city for cooler realms. Do not be shy about bargaining for a better rate during the low period; hotel keepers eager to fill their empty rooms will often offer them at rates that are substantially lower than the ones they publish.

Albergo Accademia. V. Belle Arti 6, 40124 Bologna. ☎ **051/232-318.** Fax 051/263-590. 28 units, all with bathroom. TV. 115,000L ($67.65) single; 170,000L ($100) double. No credit cards.

If you are looking for a high level of comfort and service, don't even consider staying here. On the other hand, the location, on a lively street near the university, is superb, and the surroundings are full of character. Accommodations are spread across several floors of a centuries-old palazzo, and the lobby and entrance, with well-worn stone flooring and vaulted ceilings, are deceivingly grand, as is the sweeping staircase that leads to the guest quarters (no elevator). The prices are fare for the bright and no-thrills but comfortable rooms, which have recently been refurbished with bland contemporary-style armoires, desks, and headboards. Unfortunately, bathrooms do not seem to have been updated for a couple of decades, so fixtures and tiles are worn and the half-size bathtubs can pose a bit of a challenge.

Albergo Apollo. V. Drapperie 5, 40124 Bologna. ☎ **051/239-55.** Fax 051/238-732. 14 units, 10 with bathroom or shower. TEL. 55,000L ($32.35) single without bathroom; 90,000L ($52.95) double without bathroom, 120,000L ($70.60) double with bathroom; 140,000L ($82.35) triple with bathroom. AE, MC, V.

We like staying here simply for the pleasure of walking in and out of the front door, since this pleasant pensione is set amid Bologna's lively market area, where an incredible array of food shops spill their wares onto the pedestrian streets. While the miniscule lobby and hallways are floored with parquet and show other signs of the days of grandeur, *modest* is the operative word here. The guest rooms are basic but large, and they have been brought up to date with crisp modern furnishings; bathrooms are adequate though miniscule, with shower arrangements that are guaranteed to soak everything in range (some of the singles use the spotless facilities in the hallways).

Albergo Centrale. V. d. Zecca 2, 40121 Bologna. ☎ **05I/225-114.** Fax 051/235-162. 20 units, 17 with bathroom or shower. A/C TV TEL. 80,000L ($47) single without bathroom; 100,000L ($58.80) single with bathroom; 135,000L ($79.40) double with bathroom; 180,000L ($105.90) triple with bathroom; 220,000L ($129.40) quad with bathroom. AE, MC, V.

This attractive pensione offers one of Bologna's best lodging values. An ancient cage elevator deposits you at the door on the third floor of an old apartment house a few blocks off the Piazza Maggiore. Once inside you'll find yourself in the amiable company of the English-speaking owner and an interesting mix of travelers from all over the world. A nicely appointed bar, breakfast room, sitting room, and several of the guest rooms are located on this floor, while others are reached via an internal staircase to the floor above. Oriental runners and crystal chandeliers lend an air of elegance to the hallways, and the charm extends to the dapper, white-tile-floored guest rooms. All have recently been redone with crisp modern furnishings and pleasant pastel fabrics.

Bathrooms are small but newly tiled in gleaming white and nicely fitted out with large sinks and commodious stall showers. Several of the rooms have three and four beds, making this an especially affordable stopover for families.

Albergo Panorama. V. Livraghi 1, 40121 Bologna. ☎ **051/221-802.** Fax 051/266-360. 9 units, 3 (triples & quads) with bathroom. TV. 65,000L ($38.25) single; 90,000L ($52.95) double; 115,000L ($67.65) triple; 135,000L ($79.40) quad; 150,000L ($150) quint. No credit cards.

We're delighted to know that charming old-fashioned pensiones like this are still in business—in fact, if you don't mind rooms without bathrooms or air-conditioning, you may want to consider staying here even if your budget allows for more luxurious accommodation. The location near the Piazza Maggiore is excellent, and the women who own and manage the hotel, which occupies one of the upper floors of an old apartment house, like to make guests feel like they're one of the family. Rooms are very large and high ceilinged, and most look over a pleasant courtyard garden through large windows. Furnishings are functional, but include enough wooden armoires and other homey touches to render them cozy; some rooms sleep four and five. The premises are kept spanking clean and showers and toilets are ample; one of the bathrooms houses a washing machine in which the management will do a load of wash for you for 15,000L ($8.80).

Albergo Rossini. V. Bibiena 11, 40121 Bologna. ☎ **051/237-716.** Fax 051/268-035. 19 units, 12 with bathroom. TEL. 65,000L ($38.25) single without bathroom, 95,000L ($55.90) single with bathroom; 100,000L ($58.80) double without bathroom, 150,000 ($88.25) double with bathroom. AE, MC, V.

Its location in the heart of the university district is what draws many guests to this plain but comfortable hotel, which is often filled with visiting academics. If you prefer basic comfort at a good price over luxury and fancy amenities, the Rossini will certainly fill the bill, if not thrill. Rooms are not much more than functional, right down to the no-nonsense small bathrooms (about a third of the rooms share clean but Spartan facilities in the hallways). They tend to be large, however, and the bland modern furnishings include well lit desks and, a real luxury in Italian hotels in this price range, reading lights over the beds. The bar in the lobby is a fun place to sit around sipping a glass of wine and listening to some intellectual chatter.

Hotel Orologio. V. IV Novembre 10, 40123 Bologna. ☎ **051/231-253.** Fax 051/260-552. www.venere.com/hotelm/4781.html. 29 units, all with bathroom. A/C TV TEL. 150,000–190,000L ($88.25–$111.20) single; 210,000–350,000L ($123.55–$205.90) double. Rates include breakfast. AE, MC, V. Parking 30,000L ($17.65)

A loyal cadre of travelers have come to love this recently renovated small hotel, which looks across a small pedestrian street adjacent to Piazza Maggiore toward the clock tower (hence the name) of the Bologna Communale. Aside from this wonderful location, one of the attractions is the bright second-floor lounge, with its comfy couches and armchairs, as well as the adjacent breakfast room, where a generous buffet is served every morning. Another is the welcome afforded by the English-speaking staff and members of the Orsi family, who own this and other hotels in central Bologna and whose welcome extends to the loan of a bicycle for a spin around town. Guest rooms are small but nicely done with sponge-washed wall coverings and old photos of Bologna and handsome contemporary furnishings, and they have well-equipped modern bathrooms with lighted mirrors and hair dryers.

✪ **Hotel Roma.** V. D'Azeglio 9, 40123 Bologna. ☎ **051/226-322.** Fax 051/239-909. 86 units, all with bathroom. A/C TV TEL. 170,000L ($100) single; 230,000L ($135.30) double. Rates include breakfast. AE, DC, MC, V. Parking 25,000L ($14.70).

This old-fashioned and gracious hotel enjoys a marvelous location only steps away from the Piazza Maggiore and offers many of the amenities you would expect to find only in larger hotels—including a cozy bar off the lobby, an adequate though not outstanding in-house restaurant, an efficient, English-speaking staff at the front desk, porters to carry your bags, and an in-house garage. What really makes this hotel worth seeking out, though, are its unusually commodious and comfortable guest rooms. Most have foyers between the bathrooms and bedrooms that have closets at one end, so they double as dressing rooms. Bedrooms are large and bright, with attractive brass beds that are often king sized, roomy armchairs, and long tables where you can spread out belongings without being messy. (For those who prefer neutral decor, one drawback may be the profusion of tastefully matching floral patterns that dominates the wallpaper, draperies, and comforters). The tiled bathrooms were redone several years ago and tend to be huge, with bidets, long vanities flanking the sinks, and luxuriously deep tubs. You may want to ask for one of the rooms on the top floor with a terrace, which do not cost extra.

Hotel Touring. V. de' Mattuiani 1/2, 40124 Bologna. ☎ **051/584-305.** Fax 051/334-763. 31 units, all with bathroom. TV TEL. 150,000L ($88.25) single in older rooms, 180,000L ($105.90) in newer rooms; 190,000L ($111.20) double in older rooms, 250,000L (147.05) in newer rooms. Rates include breakfast. AE, DC, MC, V. Parking 30,000L ($17.65)

You have your choice of two kinds of rooms at this quiet hotel on the edge of the centro storico near the Chiesa San Domenico—those on the first floor, which have not been renovated and are not air-conditioned, and the more stylish accommodations on the floors above, which do have air-conditioning. While drab 1970s-era draperies and furnishings are the hallmark of the less expensive rooms, they are large and quite comfortable, with serviceable bathrooms. You may, though, want to spend the extra money for one of the newly renovated rooms, which have been nicely fitted out with shiny hardwood or marble floors and sleek contemporary furnishings accented by brass wall lamps, silk wall coverings, and attractive fabrics. The bathrooms are striking, with stylish gilt frame mirrors on the white tile walls, deep sinks (there are double sinks in a few of the rooms), roomy stall showers, and such amenities as hair dryers and scales. The roof terrace affords wonderful views over Bologna's tiled rooftops and landmarks around the Piazza Maggiore, which is only about 10 minutes away by foot.

WORTH A SPLURGE

✪ **Hotel Dei Commercianti.** V. Pignattari 11, 40123 Bologna. ☎ **051/233-052.** Fax 051/224-733. www.italyhotel.com/hotelm/4769.html. 31 units, all with bathroom or shower. A/C MINIBAR TV TEL. 200,000L ($117.65) single; 300,000L ($176.50) double. Rates include breakfast. AE, MC, V. Parking 20,000L ($11.75).

Historic is not quite the word for this lovely building, which faces the flanks of the Chiesa di San Petronius and was built in the 12th century as the city's first seat of government. A recent renovation takes full advantage of this provenance, even to the point of showing off some of the original beams and flooring in cutaway views through protective glass. There are lovely antique pieces and Oriental carpets in the lobby and vaulting and columns in the lower level breakfast room (where a nice morning buffet is served). The polished woodwork and rustic tiles extend down the twisting hallways into the stunning guest rooms, which have been carved out of the centuries-old structure and vary widely in size and shape. Even the smallest, though, are welcoming; most of the beds are canopied, the fabrics are richly hued in tasteful shades of red, gold, and blue, and many of the ceilings beamed. The bathrooms, meanwhile, are modern and nicely equipped with hair dryers, deep sinks, and glass-enclosed showers. Some of the rooms have small, nicely planted terraces.

WHERE TO DINE

There's good reason it's called "Bologna the Fat." Chubby tortellini are filled with cheese and meat and topped with cream sauces. Heaping platters of grilled meats are served without a care for cholesterol. Not surprisingly, you can eat very well in Bologna—what is surprising is that you need not spend a fortune doing so.

L'Osteria del Montesino. V. d. Pratello 74/6. ☎ **051/523-426.** Primi 5,000–9,000L ($2.95–$5.30); secondi 7,000–12,000L ($4.10–$7.05). No credit cards. Thurs–Tues 8am–1am. BOLOGNESE.

Of the many osterias that line Via del Pratello, this would be our choice for a light meal. There's a huge selection of *crostini,* and you can taste all of them when you order a heaping platter of *crostini misti* (about 11,000L/$6.50). The salads (14,000L/$8.25) are excellent, too, and many are hearty concoctions heaped high with such substantial ingredients as roast chicken or shrimp. The interior rooms are quite plain, so you will not be missing out on the ambience if you choose to sit on the covered terrace out front, which is usually open except in the chilliest midwinter months.

✪ **Olindo Facccioli** V. Altabella 15/B. ☎ **051/223-171.** Primi 7,000L ($4.10); secondi 9,000–12,000L ($5.30–$7.05). No credit cards. Mon–Sat 6pm–2am. Closed Aug. BOLOGNESE.

Wander into this inconspicuous little place near the Due Torri for a glass of wine and you may end up spending the entire evening. Nine tables are wedged into two tiny, handsome rooms that are lined high with the more than 400 vintages the proprietor serves. While this selection and the ambience is reason enough to linger, you'll probably want to stay for a meal and sample the limited but delicious offerings from the kitchen (there's no menu but the daily offerings are posted on a blackboard). If you want to eat, try to arrive before nine to ensure that you'll get a table before the rooms fill with patrons who linger over wine into the late evening. A carpaccio of tuna or selection of bruschetti or *crostini misti* (toasted breads with various toppings) are perfect openers, and can be followed with the few specials that change each evening but lean toward lighter, vegetarian fare—zucchini flowers stuffed with mozzarella or *crespellini* (cheese-filled little crepes) are delicious, as is a light and fresh *tagliatelle con pesto* (flat noodles topped with homemade pesto). While 2am is the official closing hour, Carlo, the owner, often chooses to stay open later, and he stays open in August if he decides he doesn't want to take a vacation.

Ristorante dal Duttour Balanzon. V. Fossalta 3. ☎ **051/232-098.** Primi 10,000–18,000L ($5.90–$10.60); secondi 15,000–25,000L ($8.80–$14.70). AE, MC, V. Wed–Mon noon–3pm and 7:30–10:30pm. Closed Tues. BOLOGNESE.

No one is going to mention this old eatery just off Piazza Maggiore in the same breath as the nearby Ristorante al Montegrappa da Nello (see below). But while Duttour Balanzon is not as distinguished in culinary achievements, it is every bit as much a Bologna institution, and you can dine well if you stay with one of the basic Bolognese offerings—rich *tortellini alla panna* (the city's signature pasta, filled with pork and topped with a light cream sauce), or excellent lasagna, maybe followed by a simple scaloppini with lemon. The ambience is delightful: Old wooden booths line two walls of an enormous room, and are occupied by businesspeople, families out for a special meal, and tourists who wander in from the nearby hotels; a cadre of aging waiters who have worked here for decades provide attentive service and are happy to recommend the best offerings of the day.

Trattoria Anna Maria. V. Belle Arti 17/A. ☎ **051/266-894.** Reservations recommended. Primi from 8,000L ($4.70); secondi 10,000–20,000L ($5.90–$11.75). AE, MC, V. Tues–Sun noon–3:00pm and 7:30pm–midnight. Closed July 27–Aug 27. EMILIA-ROMANGNOLA.

Anna Maria, the friendly proprietor, always seems to be on hand at this popular and animated spot, and she and her staff serve some of the finest trattoria food in Bologna in a big room adorned with old photos of opera stars who have performed at the nearby Teatro Communale. All of the pasta is freshly made and appears in some unusual variations, such as *quadrettini*, four different shapes of ricotta-stuffed pasta floating in chicken broth, and a wonderful tortellini al gorgonzola. While any of these pasta dishes constitute a meal in themselves, you may be tempted to continue on and try one of the substantial second courses, most of which are simple, deliciously prepared dishes from the region and include the likes of *trippa con fagioli* (tripe and beans)and *fegato con cipolli* (liver and onions).

Trattoria Belfiore. V. Marsala 11a. ☎ **051/226-641.** Primi 7,000–10,000L ($4.10–$5.90); secondi 8,000–15,000L ($4.70–$8.80). MC, V. Mon–Wed and Fri–Sun noon–3pm and 7:30pm–midnight. BOLOGNESE.

This series of narrow high-ceiling rooms is located on one of the old streets that run between the Via dell' Indipendenza and the university area, and as a result it attracts an incongruous group of students and businesspeople who chatter noisily as overworked waiters run back and forth from the kitchen. This is not the place for a romantic conversation or a foray into haute cuisine, and simple really is the rule here. Dishes don't get much more elaborate than a platter of *salsiccia al ferri* (grilled sausages) or a *pollo arrosto* (roast chicken), but like much of the fare, including the pizzas, they are prepared over an open fire and, as this eclectic clientele has long ago discovered, is delicious and very fairly priced.

Trattoria Da Danio. V. San Felice 50. ☎ **051/555-202.** Primi 7,000–9,000L ($4.10–$5.30); secondi 8,000–15,000L ($4.70–$8.80); menù turistico 18,000L ($10.60). AE, MC, V. Mon–Sat noon–2:30pm and 7:30pm–10pm. BOLOGNESE.

This simple restaurant, which consists of one brightly lit tiled room, is family run, and likewise is usually filled with the clamor of families that live in this old neighborhood just east of the Piazza Maggiore (follow the Via Ugo Bassi its length to Via San Felice). The kitchen sends out good, substantial servings of traditional Bolognese fare: heaping bowls of tortellini topped with Bolognese sauce, delicious gnocchi stuffed with spinach and ricotta, homey chicken and pork dishes, and the like. The menù turistico (pasta, main course, and glass of wine) is a great deal.

Trattoria Fantoni. V. del Pratello 11/A. ☎ **051/236-358.** Primi 7,000–9,000L ($4.10–$5.30); secondi 7,000–14,000L ($4.10–$8.25). No credit cards. noon–2:45pm and 7:45–10:15pm. Closed Sat–Sun. BOLOGNESE.

Of all the casual and extremely popular eateries along the via del Pratello, this down-to-earth restaurant is probably our favorite. The two simple dining rooms are almost always jammed with people who work in the neighborhood (which is why the management closes on weekends), and the menu reflects their culinary tastes. You can venture into the horse meat that appears on many traditional Bolognese menus, including *bistecca cavallo* and *cavallo alla tartara* (horse steak and horse meat tartare), or try some of the nicely prepared versions of more familiar fare, such as *salsiccia or tacchino alla griglia* (grilled sausage or turkey breast). The vegetable dishes are also especially good—the *melanzane al forno* (baked eggplant) and *finocchi lessi* (boiled fennel) constitute meals in themselves. The food is so good and the prices so low that you can expect to wait for a table just about any evening.

Trattoria-Pizzeria Belle Arte. V. Belle Arti 14. ☎ **051/225-581.** Primi from 9,000L ($5.30); secondi from 15,000–25,000L ($8.80–$14.40); menù turistico 22,000L ($12.95); pizzas from 9,000L ($5.30). AE, MC, V. Mon–Tues and Thurs–Sun noon–2:30pm and 7pm–midnight. Closed part of Jan and Aug. PIZZERIA/ITALIAN.

Why do theater-goers flock here after performances at the nearby Teatro Communale? Because the food is excellent and the kitchen keeps later hours than most Bologna restaurants. Even on weeknights you may have to wait to get a table in the handsome brick- and panel-walled dining room, but once the *tortellini alla panna* (homemade tortellini in cream sauce) or *tagliattelli con funghi porcini* (flat noodles with wild mushrooms) start arriving at the table, you'll be glad you waited. You might want to sample this fare on the menu turistico, which includes your choice of first and second courses, wine, and dessert. Or choose from a stupendous selection of pizzas that emerge from a wood-burning oven. At lunch, a menu of *piatti unici* (single plates)—a nice selection of salads, cheese plates and other light dishes—is available for 14,000L ($8.25).

WORTH A SPLURGE

Ristorante al Montegrappa da Nello. V. Montegrappa 2. ☎ **051/236-331.** Reservations recommended for dinner. Primi 10,000–20,000L ($5.90–$12.95); secondi 15,000–40,000L ($8.80–$23.55). AE, DC, MC, V. Tues–Sun noon–3pm and 7:30–11:30pm. Closed Aug. BOLOGNESE.

Just watching the whirl in the clamorous, cavernous dining rooms is part of the experience at this venerable Bologna institution. You can get by with a simple and relatively inexpensive meal here, but you'll probably want to spend the extra lire and sample this excellently prepared fare, which relies on the fresh ingredients of the season, without fiscal constraint. Truffles and funghi porcini are hallmarks of the house, and they appear in salads, atop rich pastas, and accompanying grilled meats, which range into wild boar and venison in season. There's a menu, but since the chef only prepares what's fresh at the market that day, it's best just to let the waiters tell you what they're serving; in fact, you can get a preview of the daily offerings in appetizing displays near the entrance.

SNACKS & GELATO

First off, many Bolognese claim that **Gelateria Creperia Gianna** at V. Montegrappa 11, a short walk from Piazza Maggiore, serves the city's best gelato. ✪ **Bar Giuseppe** at Pz. Maggiore 1 is a popular and long-established watering hole that stretches for at least a block beneath arcades facing the Piazza Maggiore. It's the perfect spot to linger over a glass of wine or one of the many cocktails on the bar menu and watch the human comedy that transpires endlessly in this grand space. Giuseppe is also known for its homemade **gelato,** which comes in at least 40 flavors and can be enjoyed in a cone (from 3,000L/$1.75) or in elaborate concoctions with fruit, chocolate, whipped cream, and other toppings.

The dark paneled **Bar Roberto** at V. Orefici 9/A is near Bologna's central market. It's probably the only smoke-free place that you are likely to find in Italy. The ban of smoking, according to Roberto, is to ensure the purity of the delicious, homemade pastries (which attract a loyal breakfast clientele who can be seen waiting at the door when the bar opens at 8am). There's something refreshingly staid at the **Gran Bar** at V.M. D'Azeglio 8. Maybe it's the long mahogany bar beneath a ceiling of stained glass. Since it's just a few steps off Piazza Maggiore, this is a handy spot to enjoy a glass of wine or a light snack. You'll find the attractive **Il Caffé Della Corte** if you follow the newly renovated shopping arcade that connects Strada Maggiore with one of Bologna's favorite landmarks, the Chiesa di San Stefano; in fact, this is an excellent place to relax after touring that lovely church complex. There's some tempting antipasto type fare

A Moveable Feast

At **Enoteca Italiana,** V. Marsala 2/B (☎ 051/235-989), an inviting and aromatic shop-cum-wine bar on a side street just north of Piazza Maggiore, you can stand at the bar and sip on a local wine while enjoying a sandwich. For a moveable feast, you can also stock up on a wide selection of ham, salamis, and cheese at the deli counter, and enjoy a picnic near the gurgles of the Neptune fountain. It's open daily from 10:30am to 3pm and 6 to 9:30pm.

On a stroll through the **Pescherie Vecchie,** the city's market area near the Due Torri, you can assemble a meal. Along the Via Drapperie and adjoining streets, salumerias, cheese shops, bakeries, and vegetable markets are heaped high with attractive displays. The stalls of Bologna's other food market, the **Mercato delle Erbe,** V. Ugo Bassi 2, are open Monday to Wednesday and Friday and Saturday, 7:15am to 1pm, and Monday to Wednesday from 5 to 7pm.

here such as Prosciutto et melone. The pastries are also excellent.

BOLOGNA AFTER DARK

THE PERFORMING ARTS   The **Teatro Communale,** V. Lgo. Respighi 1 (☎ 051/529-999), hosts Bologna's lively opera, orchestra, and ballet seasons. The box office is open Monday through Friday, 3:30pm to 7pm and on Saturday, 9:30am to 12:30pm and 3:30 to 7pm. A good way to keep up with performances here and elsewhere in Bologna—whether it's a poetry reading in the back of a bar or a pop concert at the Stadio Communale—is to scan the posters that are plastered on walls around the university. The tourist office also distributes updates on cultural events. *Il Bo* is a weekly that covers local events and has many listings; it's in Italian but is sprinkled liberally with English and distributed for free around the city.

BARS   Given its young and restless student population, Bologna stays up later than most Italian cities. The **Via del Pratello** and, near the university, **Via Zamboni and Via delle Belle Arte** and their surrounding areas are the usual haunts of night owls. You can usually find a place for a drink, shot of espresso, or a light meal as late as 2am.

Head to the **Cabala American Bar** at S. Maggiore 10 (☎ 051/265-445) to hear a piano player who plays nightly and favors American classics and show tunes. You'll want to retire at 10:30pm to the cellars of a 16th-century palazzo near the university **at Cantina Bentivoglio** at V. Mascarella 4b (☎ 051/265-416). That's when you'll hear some of the best jazz in Bologna. This is also a popular spot for filmgoers, who stop in after catching one of the first-run movies at the Odeon 2 across the street. **Cassero** at Pz. Porta Saragozza 2 (☎ 051/644-6902b) is Bologna's most popular gay bar (Thursday is woman's night), with a noisy discolike atmosphere and floor shows. The biggest attraction here, though, is the setting—the club occupies one of Bologna's medieval gates, the top of which serves as a roof garden and open-air dance floor in good weather. There's Guinness and Harp on tap and an attendant Anglophone following at the **Irish Times Pub** at V. Paradiso 1 (☎ 051/261-648), though a well-dressed but not always so well-behaved young Italian crowd predominates in the noisy, smoky publike rooms. **Osteria de Poeti** at V. Poeti 1 (☎ 051/236-166) is Bologna's oldest osteria and has been in operation since the 16th century—the brick-vaulted ceilings, stone walls, and ancient wine barrels provide just the sort of ambience you would expect to find in such a historic establishment. Stop in to enjoy the live jazz and folk music that is on tap most weeknights and on weekends. **Piccolo Bar** at Pz. Giuseppe Verdi 4 (☎ 051/227-147) is the closest Bologna comes to a counterculture bar, though it's pretty tame compared to what you'd find in London or New York. Most of the purple-haired youths who hang out here all the day long are cutting classes from the nearby university.

2 Ferrara

45 km (27 mi.) N of Bologna, 110 km (66 mi.) S of Venice, 250 km (150 mi.) SE of Milan, 425 km (250 mi.) N of Rome

One family, the Estes, accounts for much of what you will find in this enchanting city on the plains of Romagna. From 1200 to 1600, the Estes ruled and ranted from their imposing palazzo-cum-fortress that is still the centerpiece of the city. They endowed the city with palaces, gardens, and avenues, as well as intrigues, including those of their most famous duchess, Lucrezia Borgia. After the Estes left (when Rome refused to recognize the last heir of the clan as duke) Ferrara fell victim to neglect and finally, during World War II, to bombs. Despite the bombing, much of the Renaissance city remains and has been restored. In fact, this city of rose-colored brick is one of the most beautiful in Italy, and shrouded in a gentle mist from the surrounding plains as it often is, one of the most romantic.

FESTIVALS & MARKETS Though not quite as dramatic as its counterpart in Siena, Ferrara's **Palio di San Giorgio** is a much-attended event held in the Piazza Ariostea the last Sunday of May. Two legged creatures run first, in separate races for young men and young women. They are followed by donkeys, and finally, in the main event, bare-backed horses mounted by jockeys representing Ferrara's eight traditional districts.

During summer, the streets of Ferrara seem like one great theater. Some excellent jazz and classical concerts are the main events of **Estate a Ferrara,** an outdoor festival that begins in early July and runs until late August, when the festivities are augmented by street musicians, mimes, and orators who partake in the **Busker's Festival**.

ESSENTIALS

GETTING HERE **By Train** Trains arrive from and depart for **Bologna** (45 min.) about every half hour between 6:30am and 11pm (3,900L/$2.30). There is also frequent, 24-hour service to and from **Venice** (about 2 hr.), with trains running about every half hour (10,000L/$5.90) during peak times. **Ravenna** is 1 hour away by train, with service about every hour between 7:30am and 8pm (7,500L/$4.40). The train station (☎ 053/770-340) is a 15-minute walk from the center; just follow Viale Costituzione through the small park in front of the station to Viale Cavour, which leads directly into the center of town. City buses 1, 2, and 9 stop in front of the station and go to the center; buy your ticket (1,500L/$.90) at the newsstand and validate it when you board the bus. You can rent a bike from the lot just to the left as you leave the main entrance; it's open from 8am to 7:30pm and rentals are 1,500L ($.90) an hour, 4,000L ($2.35) for 4 hours. Luggage storage is available in the station; the office is open from 8 to 10am and 11am to 7pm and the fee is 5,000L ($2.95) a bag for each 12-hour period.

By Bus Ferrara's main bus terminal is south of the center near the city walls on Rampari San Paolo; however, most buses also stop in front of the more conveniently located train station (☎ 053/240-679). Hourly bus service to Ferrara from **Bologna** runs from 6:30am to 8pm; the trip takes 1 hour and costs 6,000L ($3.55). Buses also link Ferrara with **Modena,** running every 45 minutes from 7am to 5pm; the 1½-hour trip costs 9,000L ($5.30).

Museum Madness

A cost-efficient way to tour Ferrara's many museums is to purchase a *biglietto cumulativo* for 20,000L ($11.75); it is valid for 1 week and is good for admission to the Palazzo Schifanoia, the Palazzo Massari, the Palazzina di Marfisa d'Este, and other municipal museums; you can purchase it at the ticket offices of any of the participating museums.

By Car   Ferrara is about half an hour north of Bologna on A13 and about a little more than a hour south of Venice, which is reached via A13 to Padua and from there A4.

VISITOR INFORMATION   The extremely helpful **tourist office** is located in new quarters in Castello Estense (☎ **053/209-370**). It's open Monday to Saturday from 9am to 1pm and 3 to 7pm, and Sunday from 9am to 1pm. (Note that much of the literature the office distributes still lists the old address on Corso Giovecca.) The telephone area code for Ferrara is 0532.

WHAT TO SEE & DO

Casa Romei. V. Praisolo and V. Savonarola. ☎ **0532/240-341.** Admission 4,000L ($2.35). Tues–Sat 8:30am–7pm, Sun 8am–2pm.

The most famous visitor to this airy villa, built by 15th-century merchant Giovanni Romei, was Lucrezia Borgia, who retreated here from the rigors and intrigues of court life at the castello. (Wife of Duke Alfonso I D'Este, her reputation for murders, poisonings, and intrigues has been shown by history to be largely unwarranted.) The lovely rooms, connected by loggias that wrap around two peaceful courtyards, are partially filled with frescoes and statues rescued from Ferrara's deconsecrated churches and convents, but it is the elegant architecture of the house that will win you over.

Castello Estense. V. Cavour and Cor. Ercole I d'Este. ☎ **0532/299-233.** Admission 8,000L ($4.70) adults, children 10 and under free. Tues–Sun 9:30am–5:30pm.

This imposing, moat-encircled castle dominates the city center and much of Ferrara's Renaissance history. It was here in 1435 that Nicolo III d'Este, with a contrivance of window mirrors, caught his young wife Parisina Maletesta in *flagrante delicto* with his son Ugo and had them beheaded in the dank dungeons below. Robert Browning recounted the deed in his poem "My Last Duchess," and today's visitors clamber down a dark staircase to visit the damp cells where the lovers and others who fell out of favor with the Este clan once languished. Not to be overlooked is the fact that the Estes also made Ferrara a center of art and learning, and the infamous (and unjustly maligned) Lucrezia Borgia entertained poets and artists beneath the fragrant bowers of the orangerie. Most of the palace is used as offices for the province, but you can still catch a glimpse of the Este's enlightenment in what remains of their grand salons—the Sala dell'Aurora and Sala dei Giochi (Game Room), both ornately festooned with frescoes. Another remnant of court life is the marble chapel built for Renta di Francia, the daughter of Louis XII.

Cimitero di Certosa and Cimitero Erbacio (Jewish Cemetery). Both near the walls off the Cor. Porta Mare. Certosa: daily 8am–8pm; Cimitero Erbacio: guided tours (in Italian) Tues–Fri 10am, 11am and noon.

The centerpiece of the Certosa is the Church of San Cristoforo, a graceful sweep of a building by architect Biagio Rossetti. The Jewish cemetery, with its ancient tumble of

Good Walls Make Good Biking

The preferred mode of transportation in Ferrara is pedal-powered; beware of octogenarian cyclists whizzing by you with shopping bags flapping in the wind. Ferrara's medieval walls, massive enough to be topped by trees and lawns, encircle the city with an aerie of greenery. The wide paths are ideal for ✪ **bicycling,** jogging and walking and provide wonderful views of the city and surrounding farmland.

Many hotels offer guests free use of bicycles, or you can rent them from the lot outside the train station.

The walls and Ferrara's other green spaces are ideal for a picnic. Buy what you need on the **Via Cortevecchia,** a narrow brick street near the cathedral where locals come to food-shop. It is lined with salumerias, cheese shops, and bakeries. The nearby **Mercato Communale,** at the corner of Via Santo Stefano and Via del Mercato, is crowded with food stalls and open until 1pm Monday through Saturday, and 3:30 to 7:30pm on Friday. At **Negozio Moccia,** V. degli Spadari 9, you can indulge in a chunk of *pampeteto*, Ferrara's hallmark chocolate-covered fruit cake.

overgrown tombstones, is the most haunting place in Ferrara. A monument to the Ferrarese murdered at Auschwitz is a reminder of the fate of the city's once sizable Jewish community, whose last days are recounted in the film *Garden of the Finzi-Continis*, evocatively set in the gardens and palaces of Ferrara and required viewing for anyone planning to visit the city.

Duomo. Cor. Liberta and Pz. Cattedrale. ☎ **0532/207-449.** Church Mon–Sat 7:30am–noon and 3–6:30pm, Sun 7:30am–1pm and 4–7:30pm. Museum (donation requested) Apr–Sept Tues–Sun 10am–noon and 3–5pm, Oct–Dec Tues–Sat 10am–noon and 4–5pm. Closed Jan–Feb.

With its pink-marble facade emblazoned with layers of arches, this handsome 12th-century cathedral reflects a heady mix of the Gothic and the Romanesque. The glory of the otherwise austere structure is its marble porch, where carvings by an unknown artist depict a fearsome scene of the Last Judgement. An 18th-century renovation relegated many of the paintings, sculptures, and other works that noble families commissioned for the cathedral over the centuries to the **Museo della Cattedrale,** reached by the stairs on the left as you enter. The pride of the collection is a heady rendering of St. George slaying the dragon by Cosme Tura, Ferrara's 15th-century master. Another masterpiece here is Jacopo della Quercia's *Madonna of the Pomegranate,* in which Mary seems to balance the fruit in one hand and the Christ Child in the other. A nearby relief showing the 12 months of the year once graced the exterior of the cathedral, where it served prosaically as a calendar for the largely illiterate citizenry. **The Loggia of the Merchants,** flanking one side of the church, is still the scene of active secular trade, as it has been since the 18th century, and the surrounding streets and piazzas are filled with lively cafes.

Palazzo dei Diamanti. Cor. Ercole I D'Este 21. ☎ **0532/205-844.** Admission 12,000L ($7.05), 8,000L ($4.70) children 17 and under. Daily 9am–7pm.

You will have no problem figuring out where this palazzo gets its name: 9,000 pointed marble blocks cover the facade. Less interesting are the collections in the cluster of museums housed within. The most deserving of a visit is the **Pinacoteca Nazionale,** containing some notable works by Cosme Tura and other painters of the Ferrara school, as well as Carpaccio's *Passing of the Virgin;* by and large, though, the holdings are not as stellar as the works to be seen elsewhere in Ferrara. The ground-floor galleries often house temporary exhibitions and charge separate admission; check with the ticket office here or the tourist office to see what is on view.

Palazzo Ludovico il Moro. V. XX Settembre. Tues–Sun 9am–6pm. Admission 8,000L ($4.70).

Ludovico il Moro, duke of Milan who married Beatrice D'Este, commissioned this lovely little palazzo as a place to retire from his courtly duties. Beatrice died young and the duke spent his last years as a prisoner of the French, but their 15th-century palace, built around a lovely rose garden, contains their furniture and paintings and provides a lovely view of life in Ferrara during its Renaissance heyday. Part of the palazzo houses the small but fascinating collections of the **Museo Archeologico.** The bulk of the treasures are Etruscan and Greek finds unearthed near Ferrara at Spina.

Palazzina di Marfissa d'Este. Cor. d. Giovecca 170. Admission 3,000L ($1.75), 2,000L ($1.20) students, free 2nd Sun and Mon of each month. Daily 9am–12:30pm and 3–6pm.

A recent restoration has returned the 16th-century home of this ardent patron of the arts to its former splendor. Period furniture and ceiling frescoes bespeak the heyday of the Este dynasty, and the little theater in the garden is a reminder that drama, on stage as well as off, was one of the family's great passions.

Palazzo Massari. Cor. Porto Mare 9. ☎ **0532/206-914.** Admission 6,000L ($3.55). Daily 9:30am–1pm and 3:30–7pm.

The complex of museums housed in this exquisite palace contain Ferrara's modern art holdings, most notably the works of Giorgio de Chirico and other 20th-century painters in the **Museo Documentario della Metafisica.** Also here are the **Museo Giovanni Boldini,** with works by the 19th-century Italian painter, and the **Museo Civico d'Arte Moderna,** largely devoted to works by contemporary regional artists.

Palazzo Schifanoia and Museo Civico d'Arte Antica (Civic Museum of Ancient Art). V. Scandiana 23. ☎ **0532/641-78.** Admission 6,000L ($3.55) adults, 3,000L ($1.75) students, children 17 and under free. Daily 9am–7pm. Closed major holidays.

Borso D'Este, who made Ferrara one of the Renaissance's leading centers of art, commissioned the frescoes you'll find here in the Salon of the Months: a fascinating cycle of the months that is both a Renaissance wall calendar and a rich portrayal of life and leisure at the 15th-century Este court. Each of the 12 sections shows Ferrara's aristocrats going about their daily business; looming above them in each, though, is a different god from classical mythology. The work is a composite of the genius of Ferarra's heyday—Francesco del Cossa painted the March, April, and May scenes, Ercole de'Roberti and other court painters executed the rest, and Cosme Tura, the official painter of the Este court, oversaw the project. Also here is small collection of coins, bronzes and other artifacts unearthed from the plains around Ferrara, as well some medieval ceramics.

WHERE TO STAY

Rates at the high end of the ranges below apply in the summer tourist season.

Albergo San Paolo. V. Baluardi 9, 44100 Ferrara. ☎ **0532/762-040.** Fax 0532/768-333. 20 units, all with bathroom. 80,000L ($47) single; 110,000L ($64.70) double. AE, MC, V.

Our favorite budget choice in Ferrara is on the edge of the old Jewish ghetto, with its warren of lanes and small shops, and faces the old city walls. Add to this atmospheric location the attentive service of the proprietors, who rent bikes, dispense advice on sightseeing and restaurants, and serve coffee from the little lobby bar. Rooms, on the other hand, are a little bland, but they are tidy and comfortable and decorated in inoffensive contemporary blonde furnishings, and all but a few have small but functional bathrooms. Note that an additional 20 rooms are under construction, with completion expected in mid-1999, and the rest of the premises are slated for renovation (including the installation of air-conditioning). The hotel will remain open during the work, but we are told that rates may jump with the added amenities.

☻ B&B Locanda Borgonuovo. V. Cairoli 29, 44100 Ferrara. ☎ **0532/211-100.** Fax 0532/248-000. www.4net.com/business/borgonuovo. 4 units, all with bathroom. A/C MINIBAR TV TEL. 95,000L ($55.90) single, 140,000–160,000L ($82.35–$94.10) double. Rates include breakfast. AE, MC, V.

This elegant bed-and-breakfast near the Este palace is the most charming hostelry in Ferrara. The gracious owner, Signora Adele Orlandini, has spruced up an old apartment, which once housed her father's law offices and is located in a medieval palazzo on a pedestrian street just around the corner from the Castello d'Estense. She accommodates her guests in large and very stylish rooms filled with a tasteful mix of country-style and art-deco antiques and equipped with posh new bathrooms (one large double also has a kitchenette). She also provides a hearty breakfast (served in the lovely rear garden, weather permitting), bicycles, discount coupons for museums and nearby shops, and plenty of advice on how to enjoy her native Ferrara. Book well in advance, since Signora's rooms and hospitality are much in demand; fortunately, she's planning to expand her domain to three or four more rooms in a church complex down the street.

Casa degli Artisti. V. Vittoria 66, 44100 Ferrara. ☎ **0532/761-038.** 27 units, 5 with bathroom. 30,000L ($17.65) single without bathroom; 54,000L (31.75) double without bathroom, 70,000L ($41.20) double with bathroom. No credit cards.

Though the surroundings are utilitarian, this old and basic budget hotel is very reasonably priced, and it is not without charm. It's nicely located in the atmospheric medieval quarter; the simple rooms are big, bright, and clean; the heavy 1950s-era pieces are a nice change from the banal furnishings you find in most hotels in this price range; and the shared bathroom facilities are plentiful and clean. Plus, there are some pleasant and unusual amenities here—guests have use of kitchen facilities at the end of the hallway on each floor, and there's a nice terrace on the roof.

Hotel Europa. Cor. d. Giovecca 49, 44100 Ferrara. ☎ **0532/205-456.** Fax 0532/212-120. 40 units, all with bathroom. A/C MINIBAR TV TEL. 120,000L ($70.60) single; 185,000L ($108.80) double; 220,000L ($129.40) suite. Rates include breakfast. AE, DC, MC, V. Parking 12,000L ($7.05).

Built in the 17th century, this elegant palazzo across from the Castello d'Estense has served as a hotel since 1880. Many subsequent renovations have left the hotel with a somewhat contemporary look, though enough of the original architecture remains to render the premises atmospheric and charming. The ground floor sitting rooms and bar area are furnished in 19th-century antiques, as are several enormous guest rooms on the floor above that have been converted from grand salons and have frescoed ceilings. While the other rooms are less grand, they are gracious and large, with a nice mix of contemporary furnishings and reproduction Venetian antiques, and all have gleaming new bathrooms.

Hotel Santo Stefano. V. Boccacanale d. San Stefano 21, 44100 Ferrara. ☎ **0532/ 206-924.** Fax 0532/210-261. 27 units, 18 with bathroom. TEL. 30,000–48,00L ($17.65–$28.25) single without bathroom; 50,000–85,000 ($29.40–$50) double without bathroom, 70,000–110,000L ($41.20–$64.70) double with bathroom. MC, V.

A wonderful location on a quiet street a few blocks south of the Este palace and the duomo makes this hotel an excellent budget choice. Be advised, however, that the decormatches the very reasonable rates. The surroundings are rather staid and more functional than charming, and the furnishings in the lobby and guest rooms are standard hotel issue from the 1970s; room furnishings don't get much more elaborate than a steel framed bed with a plain spread and a Formica-veneered armoire. Even so, singles and doubles are very large and bright, and the premises (including communal bathrooms in the hallways) are spotless.

WORTH A SPLURGE

✪ **Ripagrande Hotel.** V. Ripagrande 21, 44100 Ferrara. ☎ **0532/765-250.** Fax 0532/764-377. www.4net.com/business/ripa. 40 units, all with bathroom. A/C MINIBAR TV TEL. 150,000–200,000L ($88.25–$117.65) single; 180,000–260,000L ($105.90–$141.15 double; 330,000L ($194.10) junior suite. Rates include breakfast. AE, DC, MC, V. Parking 20,000L ($11.75).

Occupying a converted Renaissance palazzo near the center of town, this enchanting hotel provides the perfect atmosphere for a stay in this elegant city. The cavernous entrance foyer and public rooms are walled in rose-colored brick and have tall vaulted ceilings, and are built around two cloisterlike courtyards and a rear garden. Upstairs, the guest rooms are large and distinctive, furnished in a carefully chosen mix of reproduction antiques and contemporary furnishings. Many are trilevel, with a bathroom and dressing room connected by a short staircase to a sitting room, and with a loftlike bedroom above; top-floor rooms, some with balcony bedrooms above a sitting room, open onto large terraces overlooking red-tile rooftops. The price of a room includes a buffet breakfast, use of bicycles, and gracious service.

WHERE TO DINE

✪ **Al Brindisi.** V. d. Adelardi 11. ☎ **0532/209-142.** Sandwiches from 4,000L ($2.35); other dishes from 9,000L($5.30); menù turistico 30,000 ($17.65). MC, V. Tues–Sun 1pm–midnight. Closed July 10–Aug 20. WINE BAR/OSTERIA.

What claims to be the oldest wine bar in the world (since 1435) serves a staggering selection of wines by the glass (from 3,000L/$1.75) and a wonderful selection of panini and other light fare. In fact, you may want to come here to sample the offerings of the kitchen as well as those of the cellar. The *torta rustica,* a selection of little pies filled with an assortment of vegetables, is perfect as a starter or a light meal; the *tortelli di zucca* (pumpkin ravioli) is sublime here, as is a substantial combination of sausage and potatoes. This excellent food and drink is served in the convivial confines of two timbered rooms stacked to the ceiling with wine bottles or, weather permitting, at booth-like tables on a little lane facing a flank of the duomo. The tourist menu is quite a bargain and includes a feast of appetizers, a special main course of the day, dessert, and a carafe of wine.

Antica Osteria Al Postiglione. V. d. Teatro 4. ☎ **0532/204-937.** Sandwiches, pastas, and other dishes 7,000–10,000L ($4.40–$5.90). AE, MC, V. Mon–Sat 9:30am–3:30pm and 5pm–1am. Closed Sun. WINE BAR.

Dozens of kinds of beer and an extensive selection of local wines are available at this cozy wine bar and osteria on a narrow lane near the Teatro Communale and Piazza Castello. You can also eat very well here, and the family members who cook and wait tables pride themselves on such simple home-cooked dishes as grilled *salsiccia* (sweet sausages), mozzarella alle forno (baked mozzarella), and pasta e fagioli, a substantial soup of beans and pasta. Desserts, including a delicious *zuppa inglesi* (the Italian version of the English, or *Ingelisi,* trifle, a homily decadent concoction of pound cake soaked in rum and smothered in sweet custard cream), are made fresh daily.

Buca San Domenico. Pz. Sacrati 22b. ☎ **0532/209-152.** Pizza from 8,000L ($5.25); primi 8,000–11,000 ($5.25–$6.50); secondi 10,000–16,000L ($5.90–$9.40). AE, MC, V. Sat–Thurs noon–2:30pm and 7:30–11:00pm. Closed Aug. PIZZA/PASTA.

This local institution on a charming square just a couple of blocks from the castello is almost always booked solid on Saturday and Sunday evenings. The main dining room is cozy and rustic, with wooden booths and the fragrant odor of baking pizzas and wood smoke wafting from the large ovens in the rear. (Unfortunately, the adjoining dining room used to accommodate overflow is modern and garishly lit.) You can dine very well and inexpensively here are on what many locals consider to be the best pizza in town, or venture into the simple menu. The best choices are the homemade soups, including a delicious tortellini in brodo, and pastas—the *tortelli di zucca* (pumpkin ravioli) is excellent.

Grotta Azzurra. Pz. Sacrati 43. ☎ **0532/209-152.** Reservations recommended. Primi 8,000–12,000L ($4.70–$7.05); secondi 13,000–25,000L ($7.65–$14.70). AE, DC, MC, V. Mon–Tues and Thurs–Sun 12:30–2:30pm and 7:30–9:30pm. Closed part of Aug, and Jan. SEAFOOD/FERRARESE.

The name evokes easygoing southern climes, but the pink dining room glowing beneath crystal chandeliers is somewhat fussy and formal. The bow-tied serving staff is friendly, though, and supervised by burly, outgoing manager Giovanni, who sits behind a desk at one end of the dining room. Tables are usually filled with a devoted and animated local clientele that comes here to enjoy a menu that, true to the restaurant's aquatic name, leans toward seafood, including a wonderful platter of grilled Adriatic fish. The kitchen also prepares many excellent meat dishes, including grilled game with polenta, and salama da sugo, a round sausage that looks like a matzo ball and is served in a broth of its own juices.

♦ La Provvidenza. Cor. Ercole I d'Este 92. ☎ **0532/205-187.** Reservations required. Primi 12,000–20,000L ($7.05–$11.75); secondi 18,000–30,000L ($10.60–$17.65). AE, DC, MC, V. Tues–Sun noon–2:30pm and 8–10:30pm. Closed part of Aug. FERRARESE/ITALIAN.

One of the pleasures of dining at this charming restaurant a few steps from the town walls on the northern edge of old Ferrara is to walk here along a stone-paved road that leads past the Palazzo dei Diamanti and many of the city's most lovely old mansions and gardens. Once inside the dining room, with its cream colored walls and attractively rustic furnishings, you'll feel you're in the country; there's even a garden for outdoor dining in good weather. If you want to eat a full meal, begin with grilled vegetables, salamis, and other selections from the antipasto buffet. The pastas are excellent and include *crespellini,* tiny crepes filled with parmigiano, tortellini stuffed with Gorgonzola and walnuts, and tagliatelli topped with *funghi porcini* (wild mushrooms); you can order a sampling of several. The *petto d'anatra all acceto balsamico* (duck breast in balsamic vinegar*), filletto barolo* (a thick fillet in Barolo wine) and *a fritto misto di carne* (mixed grill) are our favorites among the wonderful meat dishes. The dessert of choice (all pastries are made in house) is a Ferrarese specialty, *torta di tagliatelle.*

Orsucci dal 1949 Pizzeria. V. Garibaldi 76. ☎ **0532/205-391.** Pizza from 8,000L ($5.25). Daily noon–11pm. No credit cards. PIZZA.

One of the newer entries on Ferrara's casual dining scene, this charming, beamed-ceiling room has a cozy bar up front and a pretty dining area in the rear with large windows opening to a courtyard. The focal point is the wood-burning oven, from which a delicious array of individual-size pizzas emerge, served with frosty glasses of beer and salads; pasta dishes and sandwiches are also available.

SNACKS & GELATO

The outdoor terrace and large interior room of the **Duca d'Este** (at Pz. Castello 22; ☎ **0532/207-688;** one of several cafes that surround the Castello) are almost always full of locals who stop by at all times of day and evening for coffee or stronger libations and snacks. A nice selection of sandwiches and salads is served, as is a daily selection of pasta dishes. The main draws here, though, seem to be the gelato, available in 40 flavors, and fresh pastries that can be accompanied by excellent coffee and make this a mandatory stop in the morning.

3 Ravenna

75 km (45 mi.) SE of Bologna, 75 km (45 mi.) SE of Ferrara, 135 km (81 mi.) NE of Florence

Few cities in Europe are so firmly entrenched in so distant a past. The last days of ancient Western Civilization waned in this flat little city on the edge of the marshes that creep inland from the Adriatic. Though Ravenna has been an off-the-beaten-track backwater since the 6th century, it continues to dazzle its visitors with its mosaics and other artistic vestiges of the Romans, the Byzantines, and the Visigoths. Aside from its horde of treasures, Ravenna is also a fine place to pass the time in sun-drenched piazzas and pleasant cafes.

FESTIVALS & MARKETS   Ravenna takes advantage of its lovely piazzas to stage concerts and other performances throughout the summer. The **Ravenna Festival International** in July and August has become world renowned, drawing a top list of classical musicians and stars of the opera. The tourist office provides information, or call ☎ **0544/213-895;** tickets begin at 25,000L ($14.70). **Ravenna Teatro** is a less glitzy but more accessible affair, offering free concerts (most of them outdoor) throughout the summer. The **Dante Festival,** sponsored by the church of San Francesco the second week of September, honors Ravenna's adopted son with readings and exhibits; check with the tourist office or call ☎ **0544/213-895.**

A walk through Ravenna's lively food market, the **Mercato Coperto,** will introduce you to the bounty of land; it's near the center on Piazza Andrea Costa and is open Monday through Saturday from 7am to 2pm, and on Friday from 4:30 to 7:30pm.

ESSENTIALS

GETTING HERE   By Train   Twelve trains travel daily from **Ferrara** to Ravenna between 6:30am and 9:30pm (about 1hr.); the one-way fare is 6,700L ($3.95). Ferrara is the connection point for trains to **Venice,** another 2 hours. **Bologna** is a little more than an hour away, with trains every 2 hours from 5am to 11pm; the one-way fare is 7,500L ($4.40). **Rimini** is 40 minutes away, with as many as three trains an hour between 5:30am and 9:30pm. The train station is only about a 10-minute-walk down Viale Farini (which becomes Via Diaz) from the Piazza del Popolo. The lot near the front of the station rents bikes, the preferred mode of transport in this quiet, flat city (open Monday through Saturday, 6:30am to 8pm; rates are 2,000L ($1.20) an hour, 15,000L ($8.80) for the day. Luggage storage is available at the station for 5,000L ($2.95) a bag each 12-hour period; the office is open daily from 9am to 5:45pm.

By Bus   While trains link Ravenna with many other cities in Emilia-Romagna, local **ATM buses** connect Ravenna with a number of nearby towns, including some nearby beach resorts (see below). Buses leave from the front of the train station, where you'll also find a ticket office that's open Monday through Saturday 6:30am to

8:30pm (7:30pm in winter) and Sunday 7am to 8pm (7:30am to 7:30pm in winter); ☎ **0544/ 352-88.** At other times you can buy tickets from a newsstand inside the station.

By Car Ravenna is about an hour southeast of Bologna on A14 and A13 and a little more than an hour southeast of Ferarra on the slower S309.

VISITOR INFORMATION The **tourist office,** an essential stop for the maps that will guide you to the mosaics, is just off the Piazza Popolo at V. Salara 8; ☎ **0544/ 354-04;** open Monday to Saturday from 8:30am to 6pm, and Sunday from 9am to noon and 3pm to 6pm. The telephone area code for Ravenna is 0544.

EXPLORING RAVENNA

Most of Ravenna's stunning mosaics adorn buildings that are in and near the city center, most within a 5-minute walk of **Piazza del Popolo.** The exception is **Sant' Apollinare in Classe,** which is 10 minutes away by bus no. 4 or 44 from the train station or, closer to the center, **Piazza Caduti.**

Basilica di Sant'Apollinare Nuovo. V. Carducci. ☎ **0544/473-004.** Admission 6,000L ($3.55). Apr–Sept, daily 9am–noon; Oct–Mar, daily 9am–4:30pm.

The famous mosaics in this 6th-century church, punctuated by Greek columns taken from a temple, are clearly delineated by gender. On one side of the church, the side traditionally reserved for women, a procession of 22 crown-carrying virgins make their way toward the Madonna; on the other side, the men's side, 26 male martyrs march toward Christ. The mosaics near the door provide a fascinating look at the 6th-century city and its environs—one on the right shows the monuments of the city, including Emperor Theodoric's royal palace, and one on the left shows the port city of Classe.

Basilica di San Vitale. V. San Vitale 17. ☎ **0544/344-24.** Admission 6,000L ($3.55), includes admission to the mausoleum of Gallo Placidia. Daily 9am–6:30pm.

Ravenna's most dazzling display of mosaics adorn the dome of this 6th-century octagonal basilica that is not by accident exotically Byzantine in its design—the emperor Justinian commissioned the church to impose the power of Byzantine Christianity over Ravenna. The emperor and his court appear in splendidly detailed mosaics of deep greens and golds on one side of the church; Theodora, his empress (a courtesan born into the circus whose ambition, intelligence, and beauty brought her to these lofty heights) and her ladies-in-waiting appear on the other; and above and between them looms Christ, clean-shaven in this early representation.

Battistero Neoniano. V. Battistero. Admission 5,000L ($2.95). Apr–Oct daily 9:30am–6:30pm, Nov–Apr daily 9:30am–4:30pm. Closed Christmas and New Year's Day.

This enchanting 4th-century octagon was built as the baptistery of a cathedral that no longer stands; it is now behind Ravenna's banal, present-day duomo, built in the 19th

---

One-Stop Shopping

Your first stop in Ravenna should be the tourist office, where the helpful staff will equip you with a map and a money-saving comprehensive ticket that costs 10,000L ($5.90) and is valid for admission to: **Basilica di San Vitale, Basilica di Sant' Apollinare Nuovo,** the **Mausoleum of Galla Placidia,** the **Battistero Neoniano,** the **Museo Arcivescovile,** and the **Basilica dello Spirito Santo.**

A Day at the Beach

Just 20 minutes from Ravenna by bus, the Adriatic washes up to white-sand beaches backed by pine forests. Well, it's not all that paradisiacal: The strands are lined with beach clubs and gelato shops and are usually packed sardine-style in the summer. But a trip out here can be a refreshing respite from the rigors of gazing at mosaics. From Piazza Farini in front of the train station, hop onto bus no. 70 to Punta Marina and Marina di Ravenna or Punta Marina and Lido Adriano. Tickets are 1,700L ($1) each way and can be purchased at tabacchi and newsstands.

century. Fittingly for the structure's purpose, the blue and gold mosaics on the dome depict the baptism of Christ by John the Baptist, surrounded by the Twelve Apostles. Entrance to the baptistery includes, and is included in, admission to the nearby Museo Arcivescovile.

Museo Arcivescovile e Capella di San Andrea (Archepiscopal Museum and Chapel of San Andrea). In the Archbishop's Palace, Piazza Arcivescovado. ☎ **0544/391-96.** Admission 5,000L ($2.95). Tues–Sat 9am–7pm (to 4:30pm Nov–Apr).

The highlight of this small museum, housed in the 6th-century Archbishop's Palace and in itself a remarkable monument, is another 6th-century treasure—the ivory throne of Emperor Maximilian. Adjoining the museum is a small chapel built in the shape of a cross and dedicated to St. Andrea, every inch of which is emblazoned with dazzling mosaics. Of the early Christian imagery that confronts you here, the most remarkable scene is of a warlike Christ, wearing armor and stepping on a serpent.

Mausoleum of Gallo Placidia. V. San Vitale, behind the Basilica di San Vitale. ☎ **0544/342-66.** Admission 6,000L ($3.55), includes admission to Basilica of San Vitale. Apr–Sept, daily 9am–7pm; Oct–Mar, daily 9am–4:30pm.

Perhaps the most striking of all Ravenna's monuments is this small and simple tomb of Galla Placidia, lit only by small alabaster windows. The life of this early Christian was not without drama. She was the sister of Honorius, last emperor of Rome and wife of Ataulf, king of the Visigoths. Upon his death she became regent to her 6-year-old son, Valentinian III, and, in effect, ruler of the Western world. The three sarcophagi beneath a canopy of blue and gold mosaics—a firmament of deep blue lit by hundreds of bright gold stars—are meant to contain Galla Placidia's remains and those of her son and husband, but it is more likely that she lies unadorned in Rome, where she died in A.D. 450.

Sant'Apollinare in Classe. V. Romeo Sud, Classe. ☎ **0544/527-004.** Free admission. Daily 8:30am–noon and 2–5:30pm. Bus: 4 or 44 from Pz. Farini in front of the train station (every 20 min.).

This long and high early Christian basilica and its campanile have loomed amid the pine woods near the old Roman port, long ago silted up, since the 6th century. The plain exterior belies the splendor that lies within. At the end of the long, sparse nave, punctuated by Greek columns, you come to the apse, the dome of which is covered with lustrous gold mosaics—made so by the application of gold leaf that suggests a heavenly light; imagine how transporting the effect was when the floor, too, was tiled in gold mosaic. The dominating figure depicted here, flanked by 12 lambs representing the apostles, is St. Apollinare, the bishop of Ravenna to whom the basilica is dedicated.

Tomba di Dante. V. Dante Alighieri. Basilica and tomb free, museum 4,000L ($2.65). Daily 9am–noon and 2–5pm.

In exile from Florence, the poet Dante Alighieri made Ravenna his home, and it was here that he died in 1321. Despite efforts by the Florentines to reclaim their famous son's remains, he resides here for eternity, next to the Basilica di San Franceso, beneath an inscription, "Here in this corner lies Dante, exiled from his native land, born to Florence, an unloving mother." To pay further tribute to the poet, step into the adjoining **Museo Dantesco** for a look at some Dante memorabilia, including a manuscript of the *Divine Comedy.*

WHERE TO STAY

Albergo Al Giaciglio. V. R Brancaleone 42, 48100 Ravenna. ☎ **0544/39-403.** 16 units, 9 with bathroom or shower. 35,000L ($20.60) single without bathroom, 45,000L ($26.50) single with bathroom; 52,000L ($30.60) double without bathroom, 60,000L ($35.30) double with bathroom. Half-board, 50,000L ($29.40) without bathroom, 60,000L ($35.30) with bathroom; full-board, 80,000L ($47) a person without bathroom, 90,000L with bathroom. AE, MC, V.

If your needs don't extend beyond having the basic comforts, don't look any further than this family-run hotel/restaurant—you're not going to find better lodgings for the price in Ravenna. The rooms are no-frills but bright, clean, and quite comfortable, with a homey array of mismatched-furniture, and more than half the rooms have tidy, functional bathrooms; shared facilities are plentiful and spotless. There's a good restaurant downstairs (Al Giaciglio, see below) where you can opt to take meals on a half- or full- pensione plan, and the location, 5 minutes from the center and near the train station and Ravenna's medieval castle and its surrounding park, is excellent. Given the prices and these appealing features, you'd be wise to reserve.

✪ **Albergo Cappello.** V. IV Novembre 41, 48100 Ravenna. ☎ **0544/219-813.** Fax 0544/ 219-814. 7 units, all with bathroom. A/C MINIBAR TV TEL. 140,000–160,000L ($82.35–($94.10) single, 160,000–200,000L ($94.10–$117.65) double. Rates include breakfast. AE, MC, V.

Ravenna now has a hotel that is truly exciting—and remarkably affordable given the luxuries and amenities it provides. Opened in 1998, the Cappello occupies an old and beautifully restored palazzo in the center of the city. Four rooms (those at the upper end of the price ranges above) have been carved out of the grand salons and are enormous, while other rooms are smaller and occupy less grand but no less stylish quarters of the old palazzo. Frescoes, murals, terra-cotta floors, and other architectural features have been restored when possible, and what's new is tasteful. Handsome striped silk patterns cover the walls and furnishings are either reproduction antique or classic contemporary designs. The sumptuous bathrooms are clad in marble or highly polished hardwoods, fitted out with luxurious stall showers and tubs, and, like the bedrooms, lit with Venetian glass fixtures. Some of the suites have pullout couches to accommodate extra guests. Since the Cappello is operated as an annex of the Hotel Diana (see below), services are minimal—the front desk is staffed only during the day—but there are two restaurants on the premises (see below). Reserve well in advance.

Albergo Ravenna. V. Maroncelli 12, 48100 Ravenna. ☎ **0544/212-204.** Fax 0544/ 212-077. 26 units, 24 with bathroom or shower. TV. 50,000–60,000L ($29.40–$35.30) single without bathroom, 70,000–L80,000L ($41.20–$47) single with bathroom; 80,000L ($347)–100,000L ($58.80) double with bathroom; 135,000L (79.40) three-bed room; 160,000L (94.10) four-bed room. The lower rates apply in winter. No credit cards. Free parking.

Right across from the train station, this small, pleasant hotel is handy for late arrivals and early departures but is also only a 10-minute walk to the sights in the town center. You will find many more amenities here than you would expect from a hotel in this price range. There is ample free parking in the hotel's own lot, an elevator has recently been installed, and, for a pleasant, welcoming touch, the hallways and public spaces are attractively enlivened with paintings. The rooms, fitted out with standard hotel-issue modern furnishings, are immaculately kept and large (some very large rooms have been equipped with extra beds for families) and most are far enough from the street to be extremely quiet. Bathrooms are up to date but tiny, and since the showers are not enclosed, you will have to keep your wits about you if you want to keep towels and toiletries dry during your ablutions. The two rooms without bathrooms ensuite have their own facilities in the hallway.

Hotel Centrale Byron. V. IV Novembre 14, 48100 Ravenna. ☎ **0544/212-225.** Fax 0544/34-114. 54 units, all with bathroom or shower. A/C TV TEL. 80,000L ($47) single, 115,000L ($67.65) double. Rates include breakfast. AE, MC, V. Parking 20,000L ($11.75).

True to its name, this hotel couldn't be more central, right off the Piazza del Popolo. The second part of the name is a tribute to Lord Byron, who shared a nearby palazzo with his mistress and her husband. Despite these colorful associations (and a sleek, elegant marble lobby), this hotel is no nonsense and serviceable. Once upstairs, the narrow hallways are harshly lit and the run-of-the-mill modern style furnishings in the tile-floored (and immaculate) rooms are showing signs of wear and tear. Single travelers make out well with unusually large and sunny single accommodations, many of which are equipped with so-called "French beds," wider than a single bed but a little narrower than a standard double.

Hotel Diana. V. G. Rossi 47, 48100 Ravenna. ☎ **0544/391-64,** 0544/391-19, or 0544/390-09. Fax 0544/300-01. 33 units, all with bathroom. A/C TV TEL. 125,000L ($73.50) single, 174,000L ($102.35) double, 211,000L ($124.10) triple, 248,000L ($145.90) quad. Rates include breakfast. AE, D, MC, V.

Though this stylish hotel occupies an old palazzo just north of the city center, it has the feel of a pleasant country hotel. The surrounding streets are residential and quiet, and the bright, airy lobby, breakfast room, and bar open onto a lovely garden. The rooms, no two of which are the same, are handsomely decorated with an innovative flair—pretty striped wallpapers, brass lamps, and mahogany headboards and armories. Those on the top floor are the most charming, with sloping ceilings and large skylights. All the bathrooms have recently been redone with care, and have glass-enclosed tub and shower arrangements, heated towel racks, and hair dryers.

WHERE TO DINE

The slick-looking **Sorbetteria Degli Esarchi** (V. IV Novembre 11; ☎ **0544/363-14**), located off the Piazza del Popolo, seems to supply its offerings to every visitor who sets foot in Ravenna. Esarchi is popular with locals, too, because it uses only the freshest ingredients and follows secret recipes that unfailingly deliver delicious results. The eponymous sorbets are especially notable and come in a dozen or so flavors, depending on what fresh fruit is available. Creamier gelatos are also available and, like the sorbets, made on the premises several times a day.

Al Giaciglio. V. Rocca Brancaleone 42. ☎ **0544/394-03.** Primi 8,000L9–9,000L ($4.70–$5.30); secondi 10,000–15,000L ($5.90–$8.80); pizza from 6,000L ($3.55). AE, DC, MC, V. Daily noon–2:30pm and 7–9:30pm. PIZZERIA/PASTA.

This comfortable, friendly restaurant comprises a large, paneled room on the ground floor of the pensione of the same name (see above). The no-nonsense food is delicious, with a nice selection of basics such as *pasta e fagiole* (a hearty souplike concoction of pasta and beans), spaghetti Bolognese, and *scaloppini al funghi*. When the family that owns this restaurant fires up the wood-burning oven in the evenings, an appreciative crowd of locals packs the place to enjoy what many consider to be the best pizzas in Ravenna.

Ca de Ven. V. C. Ricci 24. ☎ **0544/301-63.** Light meals from 5,000L ($2.95). AE, MC, V. Tues–Sun 11am–2:30pm and 6–10:30pm. Closed Mon. RAVENNESE.

The most atmospheric osteria in Ravenna is tucked away on the ground floor of a 16th-century building next to Dante's tomb. In fact, Dante is said to have lived here when the premises served as lodging house. The ornate shelves that line most of the walls come from a later reincarnation and were installed to outfit a 19th-century spice shop; they now display hundreds of varieties of Emilia-Romagna wines, many of which are available by the glass to accompany a light meal (from 3,000L/$1.75 a glass). *Piadine,* the local flat bread, is a specialty here, topped with cheeses and vegetables, or served plain as a perfect accompaniment to cheese and assorted salamis.

Cantina Cappello. V. IV Novembre 41. ☎ **0544/219-813.** Light meals 10,000–12,000L ($5.90–$7.05). AE, MC, V. Mon 7–11pm, Tues–Sat 11am–2:30pm and 7–11pm. WINE BAR.

The high-shuttered windows, timbered ceiling, and ocher-colored walls render this room on the ground floor of the stylish albergo of the same name (see above) both chic and inviting. In fact, with these attractive surroundings, friendly service, excellent choices of drink and food, and a handy location just off the Piazza del Popolo, this is our first choice for a light meal in Ravenna. You can order just about any wine from Emilia-Romagna here, and the house choices are available either by the glass (from 3,000L/$1.75) or carafe (from 10,000L/$5.90). The food, however, is not to be overlooked. You can order *crostini,* slices of bread covered with vegetables, salamis, or other toppings, or choose from the four or five special selections of the day, which often include substantial omelettes of prosciutto and fresh vegetables. The daily menu also usually includes a pasta dish or two—when available, try the tortelli with walnut sauce. Don't leave without ordering a coffee, which is delicious here.

La Gardela. V. Ponte Marino 3. ☎ **0544/217-147.** Reservations recommended. Primi 8,000–9,000L ($4.70–$5.30); secondi 9,000–19,000L ($5.30–$11.20). AE, MC, V. Wed–Tue noon–3:30pm and 7–10pm. Closed Feb 10–20 and Aug 10–20. RAVENNESE/SEAFOOD.

Nicely located in the heart of the old city, this fine old establishment is a good place to satisfy your appetite after wandering through the food stalls of the **Mercato Coperto,** which is across the street. Decor in the two dining rooms (one on a balcony overhanging the main room) is plain but elegant, the service is pleasant and attentive, and the kitchen sends out delicious renditions of local specialties. These include a wonderful array of starters, such as a *carpaccio alla rucola e grana* (thin slices of beef topped with fresh arugula and aged parmigiano cheese), *zucchini e pinoli* (oven-roasted zucchini stuffed with pine nuts), or locally cured prosciutto served with fresh figs. Daily specials often include seafood from the nearby Adriatic, and the pasta and meat dishes are excellent—the tortellini alla burro e salvia (freshmade tortellini in a light sauce of butter and sage) proves just how memorable a simple dish can be.

Osteria del Vicolo. Vicolo Gabbiani. ☎ **0544/212-443.** Primi 7,000–8,000L ($4.10–$4.70); secondi 10,000–14,000L ($5.90–$8.25); menù turistico 20,000L ($11.75). AE, MC, V. Thurs–Tue noon–3pm and 7pm–1:30am. RAVENNESE.

Open into the wee hours, this charming osteria on a back street near one of the city's leaning towers is one of the few places in Ravenna where you can dine in the late evening. Don't come too late, though, because you'll be tempted to linger here for a long evening amid the attractive, rustic decor while enjoying the excellent trattoria fare. Many diners choose to make do with one of the many pasta dishes on the menu—the *tortelli di zucca* (a large tortellini stuffed with pumpkin) is a local specialty and done very nicely here, as is the tagliatelle with wild porcini mushrooms. You can follow up with a succulent *porchetta con carcioffe* (roast pork served with a sauce of its own juices and artichoke hearts) or one of the other substantial meat dishes.

Renato-Guidarello. V. Mentana 33. ☎ **0544/213-684.** Primi 7,500–9,000L ($4.40–$5.30); secondi 9,000–16,000L ($5.30–$9.40); menù turistico 22,000L ($12.95). MC, V. Daily 12:15–2:30pm and 7:30–9:30pm. ITALIAN.

The cavernous rooms seem to extend forever, and even at that there never seem to be enough tables to accommodate locals and tourists alike who come here to enjoy pizzas and hearty trattoria fare. Roast meats seem to dominate the menu and include several turkey preparations, including a simply prepared *paillard di tacchino* (grilled turkey breast). Given the proximity of the Adriatic, daily specials also often include fresh fish. If there's not a table to be had (which is often the case), try **Ristorante Renato Galleria** around the corner at V. R. Gessi 9—same management, same food, same prices, same boisterous atmosphere, same hours, but closed Sunday.

Silvano. Pz. Einaudi 7. ☎ **0544/212-432**. Light meals 6,000–12,000L ($3.55–$7.05). MC, V. Mon–Sat 7am–3am. BAR/CAFE.

Although you can settle into one of the tables here and order only a coffee, Silvano is also an excellent choice for lunch or an unfussy dinner. The menu of casual fare is unusually extensive. There's a huge selection of sandwiches and *piadine*, a delicious flat bread topped with cheese, vegetables, and numerous other toppings (from 6,000L/$3.55), and a nice array of large salads that serve as a meal in themselves (from 10,000L/$5.90). Pizza, baked in a wood-burning oven, is served in the evening (from 9,000L/$5.30), and the evening menu also includes some excellent daily specials—the *vitello tonato* (cold veal with a sauce of tuna and capers) is quite good. The large terrace overlooking the piazza is the best place to sit, and it's open in all but the chilliest midwinter months.

FAENZA: A DAY TRIP FROM RAVENNA

In the 16th century, the local artisans brought fame to this little city by applying new firing techniques to the production of majolica-style pottery and creating faience ware that became the international rage. The tradition, which involves giving a ceramic piece a white glaze then applying designs in yellow and blue tones, lives on.

GETTING HERE   Faenza is only half an hour from Ravenna by train, but you will have to time your trip carefully. The seven daily trains from Ravenna to Faenza leave very early in the morning (at **6:30 and 7:35am** and not again until **11:34am**), and from then roughly every 2 hours. Likewise, the return trains leave mainly in the afternoon, though the last train is not until 7:50pm, allowing plenty of time to linger in the museum. One-way fare is 3,300L ($1.75). From **Bologna,** 15 trains a day run almost hourly and make the trip in 1 hour and 20 minutes; the one-way fare is 6,200L ($3.65). **By car,** it is a quick trip of less than half an hour via S253 from Ravenna to Faenza and from Bologna the trip down A14 takes about 45 minutes.

WHERE THE ART IS

Faenza is very much an artisan's center, with a major institute for ceramics study, **Instituto d'Arte per la Ceramica,** and many workshops where you can buy the wares of artisans (**Associate Ente Ceramica** at Voltone Molinella 2, ☎ **0546/251-110,** provides a list of workshops with sales rooms).

Almost as soon as you set foot in town you should pay a visit to the **Museo Internazionale delle Ceramiche,** at V. Campidoro 2 (☎ **0546/21-240**). You'll get an overview of the town's famous craft, as well as a firm grounding in ceramics from the Etruscans to pre-Columbian Peruvians to Chinese masters. The most popular works are those by modern masters not usually associated with ceramics—a platter by Picasso incorporates his famous dove of peace design, and there are works by Matisse, Chagall, and Léger as well.

The museum is open from June through September, Tuesday through Saturday from 9am to 7pm and Sunday from 9:30am to 1pm and 3 to 7pm; from October through May, hours are Tuesday through Friday from 9:30am to 1:30pm, Saturday 3 to 6pm, and Sunday 9:30am to 1pm and 3 to 7pm; closed New Year's Day, May Day, August 15, and Christmas Day. Admission is 10,000L ($5.90), 4,000L($2.35) for children 17 and under.

DINING

Enoteca Astorre. ☎ **0546/681-407.** Light meals, 6,000–12,000L ($3.55–$7.05). AE, MC, V. Tues–Sat 12:30–3pm and 6–11:30pm. Closed Sun lunch. WINE BAR.

Located next to the unfinished duomo, this handsome wine bar seems to be the hub of Faenza's social life. Many local artisans relax here, and like them you can enjoy a huge selection of wines from throughout Italy and lunch lightly on bruschetta, sandwiches, salads, or one of the special pasta dishes served daily.

4 Modena

40 km (25 mi.) NW of Bologna, 56 km (34 mi.) SE of Parma, 400 km (250 mi.) N of Rome

The Via Emilia has run through the center of Modena since the city was founded as a Roman colony in 183 B.C., and this prominent location seems to have brought nothing but prosperity. Modena is, after all, known the world over for the balsamic vinegar and the Ferrari and Maserati automobiles it produces, for its prosciutto, lambrusco wines, and culinary achievements of its chefs, and for the operatic voices of citizens Luciano Pavorotti and Mirella Freni. Modena is a treat for the eye, too. Visitors will be delighted to find an elegant city of palaces, churches, piazzas, and artworks, most of which can be attributed to the Este family. Forced to leave Ferrara at the end of the 16th century, the Estes came to Ferrara and soon began building suitable quarters, the Palazzo Ducale (which now houses the military academy), and clearing away cramped medieval lanes to create elegant avenues and piazzas. You can easily visit Modena on a day trip from Bologna or Parma, but there is enough to see and do to warrant a stopover of at least 1 night; in fact, given Modena's proximity to Bologna and that city's tendency to fill up during its trade fairs, Modena is a pleasant alternative.

FESTIVALS & MARKETS In July and August, Modena stages **Sipario in Piazza,** a program of opera and other musical performances; many events are held next to the duomo in the Piazza Grande, and the great Pavarotti himself has been known to grace the stage. The Tourist Office provides schedules, but for tickets (from 15,000 to 50,000L/$8.80 to $29.40) go to the **Sipario office** in the Palazzo Communale in Piazza Grande (☎ 059/206-460; Monday to Saturday 10am to 12:30pm and 4 to 7pm). All of Modena seems to be a stage during 1 week each year at the end of June or beginning of July, when vendors, artists, mimes, and other performers take to the streets for the **Settimana Estense;** festivities culminate in a parade in which the town turns out in Renaissance attire.

Fiera d'Antiquariato is a monthly event, held the fourth weekend, in which vendors sell antiques, junk, crafts, and ordinary household supplies; there are musical performances and food stalls as well. The fair is held just outside the city center at **Ex Ippodromo exhibition park** (take bus no. 7); the tourist office can provide further details.

ESSENTIALS

GETTING HERE   By Train   Trains arrive from and leave for **Bologna** (20 min.) every half hour; one-way fare is 3,400L ($2). There is also service to and from Parma (30 min.) on the half hour; one-way fare is 5,100L ($3). The train station is a 10-minute walk from the center; follow Corso Vittorio Emanuele and Via Farini to Piazza Grande. Bus no. 7 also runs from the station to the piazza (1,300L/75¢). You can rent a bike from the lot in front of the main entrance to the station for 2,000L ($1.20) for 2 hours, 500L (30¢) an hour after that, 4,000L ($2.35) a day; the lot is open from 6:30am to 8pm. Luggage storage is available at the station for 5,000L ($2.95) a bag for each 12-hour period; the office is open 6:30 to 11:30am and 2 to 8pm.

By Bus   Buses, leaving from the station just to the right of the train station off Viale Monte Kosica, serve the surrounding region. Buses also link Modena with Ferrara, running every 45 minutes from 7am to 5pm; the 1½-hour trip costs 9,000L ($5.30).

By Car   Modena is conveniently located on A1, halfway between Bologna to the south and Parma to the north and only about half an hour from either.

VISITOR INFORMATION   The **tourist office** is in the historic center, at Pz. Grande 17 (☎ **059/20-66-60**). It's open Monday to Saturday from 8:30am to 1pm and 3pm to 7pm (closed Wednesday afternoon) and Sunday from 2:30 to 5:30pm. The telephone area code for Modena is **059**.

WHAT TO SEE & DO

Il Duomo. Piazza Grande. ☎ **059/216-078.** Daily 6:30am–12:30pm (noon July–Aug) and 3:30–7pm.

Built in the 12th century and one of the glories of the European Romanesque, the arched and carved facade. Many of these intricate reliefs are the work of the sculptor Wiligemus and depict scenes from the Old Testament; others—including the lions that surround the main portal and the scenes from the life of Modena's patron saint, Geminiano, that decorate the south entrance—are by Viligelmo. Rising from the rear of the edifice is the Ghirlandina, a 12th- to 14th-century campanile. You may want to retire to one of the cafes facing the Piazza Grande to admire this remarkable assemblage before venturing inside, where polychrome reliefs depicting the New Testament, a huge painted crucifix, and more sculpted lions lend a Byzantine air to the vast space. Saint Geminiano is entombed near the choir in a stone coffin, though his arm is encased in silver on the altar—and carried through the streets on his feast day, January 31.

Biblioteca Estense. Palazzo dei Musei, Largo Sant'Agostino 48 (off the northwestern end of V. Emilia). ☎ **059/222-248.** Admission free. Mon–Sat 9am–1pm.

One of Europe's most extensive historic libraries contains more than half a million books and some 15,000 incunabula, codices, and other rare manuscripts. While most of the collection is open only to scholars, the gems are displayed in one large room. Among the medieval maps and letters is the most treasured illustrated manuscript of Renaissance Italy: the *Bibbia di Borso d'Este,* a magnificently illustrated 1,200-page bible.

Galleria Estense. Palazzo dei Musei, Lgo. Sant'Agostino 48 (off the northwestern end of V. Emilia). ☎ **059/222-145.** Admission 8,000L ($4.70); children 17 and under and seniors 60 and over free. Tues and Fri–Sat 9am–7pm, Wed–Thurs 9am–2pm, Sun 9am–1pm.

A 5-minute walk up Via Emilia from Piazza Grande brings you to another treasure of Modena, the sizeable art collection that the Este family brought with it from Ferrara and continued to gather during its tenure here. Shown off to their best advantage in newly renovated galleries, the works are staggering in their magnitude and array—a portrait of Duke Franceso I by Velazquez as well as bust of him by Bernini, along with canvases by Tintoretto, Corregggio, Guido Reni, and Emilian artist Cosimo Tura. It's a sign of the Este's wide-ranging tastes that the collection also includes an El Greco and canvases by Flemish masters.

Galleria Ferrari. V. Dino Ferrari 43, Maranello. ☎ **0536/943-204.** (About 10 min. south of the center via no. 2 bus from the bus station, near the train station off Vle. Monte Kosica). Admission 15,000L ($8.80). Tues–Sun 9:30am–12:30pm and 3–6pm.

For those whose taste extends beyond vinegar to Modena's other famous product, a visit to the Ferrari showroom and museum, part of the famed automaker's factory, is a must. Racing enthusiasts will find the many trophies that the Ferrari team has won in international competitions over the years, but pride of place belongs to the gorgeous automobiles the company has produced over the years.

WHERE TO STAY

Albergo Centrale. V. Rismondo 55, 41100 Modena. ☎ **059/21-88-08.** Fax 059/23-82-01. 41 units, 39 with bathroom. A/C TV TEL. 60,000L ($35.30) single without bathroom, 110,000L ($64.70) single with bathroom; 160,000L ($94.10) double. Rates include breakfast. AE, DC, MC, V. Parking 15,000L ($8.80).

The Centrale is indeed in the center of things, wonderfully situated on a charming old street just a few steps from the duomo. Besides the great location, there's an inviting, sky-lit breakfast room and bar area downstairs, and unusually large guest rooms upstairs. Furnishings are contemporary and spanking new, and the bathrooms are small but equipped with efficient stall showers. Most rooms have nice views over the surrounding palazzi of old Modena, and two of them have tiny antechambers with a single bed, making them ideal for families.

WORTH A SPLURGE

✪ **Canalgrande Hotel.** Cor. Canalgrande 6, 41100 Modena. ☎ **059/217-160.** Fax 059/221-6-4. www.hotelinfoplus.com/modena/canalgrande.htm. 66 units, all with bathroom. A/C MINIBAR TV TEL. 189,000L ($111.20) single, 275,000L ($161.75) double, from 432,000 ($254.10) suite. Rates include breakfast. AE, DC, MC, V. Parking 15,000L ($8.80).

Chances are, you will not regret exceeding your budget on this exquisite hotel, which provides just the sort of ambience you would expect to find in a city as atmospheric and elegant as Modena. The ground floor public rooms of this 17th-century villa retain splendid terra-cotta floors and elaborate plasterwork and frescoes, and are decorated in a pleasing blend of Victorian and traditional furnishings. French doors open to a large, beautifully planted garden (you should ask for a room facing this side of the building). Upstairs, ongoing renovations are bringing the guest rooms up to date in perfect style—the silk pastel-colored draperies and bed coverings, linen sheets, and contemporary furnishing, mixed with a smattering of Venetian-style antique reproductions, provide handsome and soothing surroundings. The new, marble-clad bathrooms are sumptuous and equipped with such amenities as massaging shower heads and hair dryers. Service is both efficient and friendly, and there's an osteria-style restaurant in the cellars, **La Secchia Rapita.**

WHERE TO DINE

Degustazione Caligari. Pz. Grande 38. ☎ **059/230-090.** Sandwiches and other light fare from 4,000L ($2.35). AE, D, MC, V. Mon–Sat 8am–9:30pm. CAFE.

Caligari is an excellent food shop, where travelers can stock up on many different kinds of balsamic vinegars and local wines. The management also takes advantage of a scenic location facing the duomo and Piazza Grande with a lovely terrace and an airy interior room where sandwiches, coffee and wine, and pastries are served throughout the day.

Giusti. Vc. Squallore 46. ☎ and fax **059/22-25-33.** Reservations required. Primi from 8,000–20,000L ($4.70–$11.75); secondi 20,000–26,000L ($11.75–$15.30). AE, MC, V. Tues–Sat noon–3pm (lunch only). Closed July 20–Aug 31 and Dec. MODENESE.

We hesitate to mention this five-table eatery only because it can be so hard to procure a table—you must phone or fax for a reservation at least a month before you plan to be in Modena, but the experience of lunching here is well worth the effort. You enter through a shop fragrant with balsamic vinegars and parmigiano, and put yourself in the hands of Nano Morandi and Laura Galli, the husband and wife proprietors who take delight in serving their creations. You will want to try the capon in two forms— a capon broth with tortellini (which, like all the pastas, is made on the premises) and a crunchy capon salad dribbled with aged balsamic vinegar. A stinco (roast joint) of veal or pork is the perfect dish with which to proceed, and even if you feel you can't, do indulge in one of the delicious homemade cakes.

Ristorante Oreste. Piazza Roma. ☎ **059/24-33-24.** Reservations recommended. Primi 8,000–20,000L ($4.70–$11.75); secondi 20,000–26,000L ($11.75–$15.30). AE, D, MC, V. Thurs–Tues noon–3pm and 7:30–10:30pm. Closed Sun evening and July 10–31. MODENESE.

Oreste was last redecorated in 1959, and the glass globe lamps, blonde paneling, and Danish-modern furnishings suggest a timelessness that is reflected in the flawless service and an excellent menu of traditional Modenese favorites. You can sample a wonderful assortment of antipasti (including prosciutto supplied directly from a nearby producer and vegetables delivered fresh daily to the kitchen door) at the self-service buffet (8,000L/$4.70 for a half portion, 16,000/$9.40 for a full portion). Many vegetarian pastas are available (including a risotto with wild mushrooms and tortelloni stuffed with ricotta and spinach), but Oreste is justifiably well known for its flawlessly prepared meat dishes. You would be hard pressed to find a richer osso buco or more succulent roast of veal or pork (served with heavenly rosemary infused potatoes). The attentive staff is happy to help you with the extensive wine list, which includes many local vintages.

WORTH A SPLURGE

Fini. Rua Frati Minori 54. ☎ **059/223-314.** Reservations required. Primi 15,000–30,000L ($8.80–$17.65); secondi 20,000–50,000L ($11.75–$29.40). AE, D, MC, V. Wed–Sun noon–3pm and 8–10:30pm. Closed July 23–Aug 26 and Dec 24–Jan 3. MODENESE.

Fini was founded as an annex to a salumeria in 1912 and since then has been one of Italy's most noted restaurants, and it lives up to its far-flung reputation without fail. The surroundings are vaguely art deco and surprisingly relaxed, service is impeccable without being stuffy, and the kitchen sends out meals that are sure to be memorable. An unusual and delectable starter is the pâté of chicken and prosciutto, and carnivores

Living Off the Fat of the Land

Modena's well-deserved reputation for culinary excellence is not confined to the city's elegant restaurants. To equip yourself for a picnic, pick your way through the food stalls of the outdoor market on **Via Albinelli,** open weekdays from 6:30am–2pm and Saturday afternoons in summer from 5 to 7:30pm. Purists may want to procure local hams during tastings at the **Consorzio del Prosciutto di Modena,** Vle. Corassori 72 (☎ **059/343-464**), and accompany them with wines from the Consorzio Tutela del Lambrusco di Modena, V. Schedoni 41 (☎ **059/235-005**).

More readily available are the balsamic vinegars, prosciutto, and other food-stuffs sold at several gourmet shops throughout the city. Two of these emporia are connected with well-known restaurants (see "Where to Dine," above): **Salumeria Giuseppe Giusti,** V. Farini 75 (☎ **059/441-203**), and **Fini**, Piazza San Francesco (☎ **059/223-314**).

should move on to the house's famous *bollito misto-zampone* (stuffed pig's feet), wild fowl and other meats are rolled to your table on a cart and served with an accompaniment of sauces, including *mostarda de Cremona* (fruits preserved in mustard sauce) and *peperonata* (diced peppers). The fare doesn't get too much lighter than fried sweetbreads or kidneys topped with truffle shavings; however, vegetarians will be satisfied with many of the pasta dishes, which change daily and are nicely infused with funghi porcini and other fresh ingredients in season. The wine list includes many Lambruscos from Fini's own vineyards.

5 Parma

95 km (57 mi.) NW of Bologna, 122 km (75 mi.) SE of Milan

Its hams and cheeses are justly famous, as they have been since Roman times, but the pleasures of this exquisite little city extend far beyond the gastronomic. The Farneses, who made their duchy one of the art centers of the Renaissance, were succeeded by Marie-Louise, a Hapsburg and wife of Emperor Napoléon. Her interest in everything cultural ensured that Parma never languished as a once-glorious backwater, as was the case with nearby Ferrara and Ravenna. As a result, today's residents of Parma live in one of Italy's most prosperous cities and are surrounded by palaces, churches, and artworks—all of which, of course, can also be enjoyed by travelers who choose to spend some time here.

FESTIVALS & MARKETS   Parma celebrates its musical traditions in July and August with **Concerti Nei Chiostri,** when classical concerts are performed in churches, cloisters and piazzas around the city. Admission is 23,000L ($13.50) per event, children 17 and under 18,000L ($10.60); the tourist office provides a list of times and locations as does the festival office (☎ **0521/283-224**).

To partake of Parma's preoccupation with food, take a walk through the **food market** in Piazza Ghiaia, near the Palazzo della Pilotta. It's open Monday to Saturday from 8am to 1pm and 3 to 7pm.

ESSENTIALS

GETTING HERE   **By Train**   Since Parma is on the busy north-south rail lines, connections are excellent. There are 34 daily trains to and from Bologna, running about every half hour between 6am and 11pm (1 hr.; 7,200L/$4.25); most also stop in Modena (30 min.; 5,100L/$3). Milan is 1½ hours away, with 20 trains a day providing almost hourly service (11,700L/$6.90). Seven direct trains a day connect Parma and Florence (3 hr.; 15,500L/$9.10). The Parma–La Spezia line is handy for travelers who want to come to Emilia-Romagna from Liguria and the Tuscan coast; there are 10 trains a day and the 2-hour trip costs 14,200L ($8.35). The train station is about a 20-minute walk from the center; from the front of the station follow Viale Bottego east for 1 block to Via Garibaldi, which leads to Piazza Duomo. Luggage storage is available at the station for 5,000L ($2.95) per bag for each 12-hour period; the office is open daily from 6:30am to 10pm.

By Bus   The bus station, next to the train station on Piazzale Carlo Alberto della Chiesa, serves surrounding towns.

By Car   The A1 autostrada connects Parma with Bologna in less than an hour and with Milan in a little over an hour. Modena, also on the A1, is about half way between Parma and Bologna.

VISITOR INFORMATION   The **tourist office,** V. Melloni 1B (☎ 0521/ 218-889), is open Monday to Saturday from 9am to 7pm, Saturday and Sunday from 9am to 1pm. The English-speaking staff is extremely helpful. The telephone area code for Parma is 0521.

WHAT TO SEE & DO

✪ **Batissero.** Pz. Duomo. ☎ **0521/23-58-86.** Admission 3,000L ($1.75) adults, 1,000L ($.60) students. 9am–12:30pm and 3–6pm.

This stunning octagon, begun in 1196 and clad in pink marble, is a tribute to the work of Benedetto Antelami, one of the most important sculptors of the Italian Romanesque. His friezes of allegorical animals encircle the base of the structure, which rises in five graceful tiers. Inside is his famous 14-statue cycle depicting the 12 months and winter and spring, set against 13th-century frescoes by an unknown artist that portray the lives of the apostles in a stunning display of visual storytelling and color.

Camera di San Paolo. V. Melloni 3 (just off Pz. Pilotta). Admission 4,000L ($2.35). Daily 9am–1:45pm.

When the abbess of this convent sought to commission an artist to fresco her dining room, she went to Correggio, one of masters of the Italian High Renaissance who lived and worked in Parma in the early 16th century. He rose to the occasion with magnificent, highly colored re-creations of mythological scenes that include a portrait of the abbess as Diana, goddess of love. These intimate rooms are an excellent place to begin a tour of Parma—you'll encounter Correggio again in the city's churches and it's museum, but nowhere else are you able to observe his work so closely.

Casa Natale e Museo di Arturo Toscanini (Arthur Toscanini Birthplace and Museum). Palazzo d. Pilotta, Pz. d. Palce. ☎ **0521/233-718.** Admission 3,000L ($1.75). Tues–Sat 10am–6pm, Sun 10am–1pm.

Arturo Toscanini, one of the greatest conductors of the early 20th century was born in Parma in 1867, and though he traveled the world he often returned to Parma to conduct at the Teatro Regio. He is remembered in the house of his birth with memorabilia that includes some original furnishings, programs, photos, and a copy of every recording he ever made.

Chiesa di San Giovanni Evangelista. Pzle. San Giovanni (just behind the Duomo). ☎ **0521/235-592.** Admission to church and cloisters free, pharmacy 4,000L ($2.35). 6:30am–noon and 3:30–8pm.

Behind the baroque facade of this church just to the east of the duomo are works by the two masters of Parma, Corregio and Il Parmigiano. Corregio's dome painting here, the *Vision of San Giovanni,* is considered to be one of the great achievements of the High Renaissance; his fresco of the saint writing down his vision is next to the main altar. Il Parmagianino frescoed two of the side chapels. Off one of the cloisters in the adjoining monastery is the pharmacy from which the good monks supplied Parma with potions and poultices for nearly 600 years, up until the late 19th century. An array of medieval-looking mortars and jars continue to line the shelves.

✪ **Duomo.** Pz. d. Duomo. ☎ **0521/235-886.** Free admission. 7am–12:30pm and 3–7pm.

Parma's Duomo, made of soft pink marble and embellished with three rows of loggias and flanked by a graceful campanile, was built in the 12th century and is one of the great achievements of Italian Romanesque architecture. Once inside, all eyes are lifted to celestial realms: What is considered to be Corregio's great masterpiece, his dramatic *Assumption of the Virgin,* adorns the octagonal cupola. The Virgin and her entourage of *putti* seem to be floating right through the roof into an Easter egg-blue heaven, and Corregio captured them in what seems to be three-dimensional depth—long before this technique became prominent during the baroque. Even before Corregio added his crowning embellishment, between 1522 and 1534, the Duomo shone with another masterpiece—bas-relief of *The Deposition from the Cross* by the 12th-century sculptor Antelami. Look for it in the right transept.

Galleria Nazionale. Palazzo d. Pilotta, Pz. d. Palce. ☎ **0521/233-309.** Admission 12,000L ($7.05); theater only, 5,000L ($2.95). National Gallery open daily 9am–1:45pm; theater open daily, June–July 9am–1:45pm, Sept–May 9am–7:30pm.

This massive and grim-looking complex, which the Farneses put up near the banks of the river Parma in 1603, would be an empty shell if it weren't for Marie-Louise, the Hapsburg wife of Emperor Napoléon and niece of Marie-Antoinette, who ruled the duchy in the early 19th century. Marie-Louise shared her aunt's passion for art, and under her guidance paintings from throughout her domain were brought here to fill the rooms the Farneses had left empty when Isabella Farnese assumed the throne of Spain in the 18th century and the clan left Parma for good. Though Allied bombings came close to flattening the palace, much of it has been rebuilt. Visitors enter the museum **Teatro Farnese,** a wooden jewel box of a theater that Giambattista Aleotti, a student of Palladio, built for the Farneses in 1618, modeling it after the master's Palladian theater in Vicenza (see chapter 9); this was the first theater in Europe to accommodate moving scenery, and its elegant proportions provide a warm, intimate atmosphere. A tour of the museum's outstanding collections continues along a series of raised metal walkways through otherwise bare salons, with the effect of bringing you dramatically face to face with some of Europe's great masterpieces. The works of Parma's great masters are here, including Corregio's *St. Jerome with Madonna and the Child* and Il Parmigianino's *Marriage of St. Catherine.* Another prize of the collection is a sketch by Leonardo da Vinci, *La Scapigliata.* However, some of the most striking treasures are by non-Italians, reflecting Maria Louisa's worldly tastes—one of Frans Holbein's most famous portraits, of Erasmus, is here, and there is a small collection of other works by northern Europeans as well, including canvases by Peter Brueghel and Van Dyck.

Parks in Parma

The gravel paths, wide lawns, and splashing fountains of the **Parco Ducale,** another Farnese creation across the river from the Palazzo Pilotta, provide a nice retreat from Parma's busier quarters. It's open May through August daily from 6am to midnight; September through April, daily from 7am to 6pm.

Museo Archeologico Nazionale. Palazzo d. Pilotta, Pz. d. Palce. ☎ **0521/233-718.** Admission 4,000L ($2.35), children 17 and under and seniors over 60 free. Tues–Sun 9am–6pm.

This small collection spans antiquity, with a nicely displayed collection of Egyptian sarcophagi, Etruscan vases and Greek statues. Pride of place, though, belongs to a local treasure, an engraved Roman tablet excavated near Piacenza at Velleia.

WHERE TO STAY

Albergo Brenta. V. G. B. Borghesi 12, 43100 Parma. ☎ **0521/208-093.** Fax 0521/208-094. 15 units, all with bathroom. TEL. 85,000L ($50) single; 125,000L ($73.50) double. Continental breakfast 8,000L ($4.70). AE, DC, MC, V.

One of the nicer hotels near the train station, this is a perfectly decent fallback if the more atmospheric places in town are full. The dark-paneled lobby is a little drab, but don't let that put you off. The English-speaking management is very helpful and eager to point visitors to sights and nearby restaurants, and surroundings brighten considerably as you go upstairs. Guest rooms are large and quite up to date, with functional modern furniture and new bathrooms with stall showers. Most face side streets and are extremely quiet. One convenience the hotel doesn't have is an elevator.

Astoria Executive. V. Trento 9, 43100 Parma. ☎ **0521/272-717.** Fax 0521/272-724. 80 units, all with bathroom. A/C MINIBAR TV TEL. 112,000L ($65.90) single, 174,000L ($102.35) double. In annex, 50,000L ($29.40) single, 70,000L ($41.20) double. Rates include breakfast. AE, DC, MC, V. Parking 15,000L ($8.80).

No-nonsense and *businesslike* are the terms that come to mind at this modern hotel only steps away from the train station. The facade is sheeted in blue-tinted glass, and the lobby, breakfast, and bar area and guest rooms sport sleek, contemporary decor. This doesn't mean the Astoria isn't welcoming—if you don't mind the complete absence of old-world charm, it's an excellent choice, and certainly convenient for late-night arrivals or early morning departures by train. Guest rooms are compact but tidily furnished with wood-veneer cabinetry and firm, low-slung beds and have smallish but efficient bathrooms. Double-glazed windows ensure a good-night's sleep. Several Spartan, tile-floored rooms with very basic furnishings (right down to cotlike beds) are located in an old building around the corner. They have none of the amenities of the rooms in the main building (including air-conditioning) and are a bit grim, but they're priced accordingly.

Hotel Button. Bgo. Salina 7, 43100 Parma. ☎ **0521/208-039.** Fax 0521/238-783. 41 units, all with bathroom. TV TEL. 130,000L ($76.50) single, 165,000L ($97.05) double. Continental breakfast 15,000L ($8.80). Closed July 5–31.

Just off the Piazza Garibaldi, this pleasant small hotel, which is usually filled with European tourists, enjoys a central location, but since the surrounding warren of little streets and squares don't see much traffic, it's also surprisingly serene. The rooms are large and serviceable though a little somber, with dark floral wallpaper and Spartan modern furnishings, and baths are nicely tiled and have stall showers. Single travelers enjoy quarters that are much large than the ones to which they are unusually relegated, with "French beds" that are quite a bit wider than standard single beds, and a few of the doubles have small balconies overlooking a piazzetta behind the hotel. The Cortesis, who run the place, are most accommodating, and you are always welcome to join them in the lobby lounge to watch a soccer match.

Hotel Torino. V. A. Mazza 7, 43100 Parma. ☎ **0521/281-046.** Fax 0521/230-725. 33 units, all with bathroom. A/C TV TEL. 110,000L ($64.70) single, 160,000L ($94.10) double. AE, DC, MC, V. Parking 15,000L ($8.80). Closed Aug 1–22.

At our top choice for moderately priced accommodations in Parma, the location in the pedestrian zone near the Duomo is only half the allure; it's also wonderful because the elegant proprietor has fitted out her modern hotel with a careful eye to style and comfort. There are fresh-cut flowers and a collection of antique porcelains in the pretty lobby. The charming breakfast room and bar area are graced with antiques. Breakfast is something of an occasion, served on china and including fresh pastries from Parma's top bakers, excellent coffee, and a selection of teas and juices. Guest rooms are comfortably modern with many natty grace notes, including dramatic head-boards emblazoned with reproductions of Corregio frescoes. The bathrooms are sparkling and fitted out with hand-milled soaps and other toiletries.

Locanda Lazzaro. Bgo. XX Marzo 14, 43100 Parma. ☎ **0521/20-89-44.** 8 units, 4 with bathroom. 42,000L ($24.70) single without bathroom, 65,000L ($38.25) double with bathroom. AE, MC, V.

The main business here is the lively ground-floor restaurant (see Ristorante Lazzaro below), but the eight simple rooms upstairs are quite comfortable (provided you're not looking for an in-room phone or any other amenity) and a real bargain. With their tall windows and high-beamed ceilings they have character, and are furnished in helter-skelter but cozy fashion with old armoires and cane chairs. In single rooms you'll have to use a bathroom down the hall, but you'll be sharing it with only one other room. There's no sign indicating the hotel entrance, so go into the restaurant and ask about the rooms; don't show up without a reservation on Sunday because the restaurant, and hence the informal check-in system, is closed.

Park Hotel Toscanini. Vle. Toscanini 4, 43100 Parma. ☎ **0521/289-141.** Fax 0521/283-143. 48 units, all with bathroom. A/C MINIBAR TV TEL. 190,000L ($111.20) single, 240,000L ($141.20) double. AE, DC, MC, V. Parking 15,000L ($8.80).

A hotel named after Parma's famous native composer would have to meet high standards, and the Park Toscanini, nicely located near the center along Parma's lovely river-front, does so admirably. Service is notably gracious, and the English-speaking staff at the reception desk is more than happy to make restaurant reservations and lend bicycles. Rooms are large and soothingly contemporary, with pastel shaded carpeting and matching draperies; this somewhat nondescript decor is enlivened with reproductions of works by the city's masters. Ask for a room in front to enjoy the river views (double-glazed windows keep noise from the busy riverfront avenue to a minimum). Since the hotel caters mostly to businesspeople, the management is usually willing to lower rates considerably during August and other slow periods.

WHERE TO DINE

One of the great pleasures of being in Parma is dipping into the wonderful local bounty, most notably ham (prosciutto di Parma) and cheese (Parmigiano Reggiano). The favored pastas on Parma tables are tagliatelli and tortellini, often stuffed with pumpkin or squash, and they come to the table with some wonderfully creative sauces. Main courses lean heavily toward meat, including the *filletto di cavallo* (fillet of horse meat) that is a staple on most menus. Parma's hallmark wine is Lambrusco, a sparking red that is not to everyone's taste.

Croce di Malta. Bgo. Palmia 8. ☎ **0521/235-643.** Reservations recommended. Primi 8,000–12,000L ($4.70–$7.05); secondi 12,000–25,000L ($7.05–$14.70). AE, DC, MC, V. Mon–Sat 12:30–2:30pm and 7:30–11pm. PARMIGIANA.

Weather permitting, the place to dine here is on the pretty terrace in front, facing the adjoining church. Inside this former convent, and later an inn, the turn-of-the-century decor is a bit stuffy and out of sync with the friendly, informal service and down-to-earth, traditional Parmigiana fare at which the kitchen excels. Most diners begin with a huge platter of assorted salamis and follow it with one of many variations of tagliatelli, tortelli, and tortellini—including a substantial dish of tortelli stuffed with potatoes and topped with a sauce of wild mushrooms. Those with fortitude continue with one of the meat courses, which include such favorites as trippa alla Parmigiana (veal tripe served with feathery shavings of Parmigiano).

Enoteca Fontana. Via Farina 24/a. ☎ **0521/286-037.** Daily 9am–noon and 3–9:45pm. Sandwiches from 3,000L ($1.75), pasta from 8,000L ($4.70). WINE BAR.

In this atmospheric wine bar and shop, you can stand at the ancient old bar or take a seat at one of the long communal tables and sample your choice of hundreds of wines from Emilia-Romgana, many of them from the immediate region (from 3,000L/$1.75 a glass); all but a few of the cask wines are available by the bottle. You may decide to dine here as well and accompany your tasting with a light meal from the short menu of panini, platters of ham, salami, and cheese, and a few pasta dishes.

Gallo Doro. Bgo. d. Saline 3. ☎ **0521/208-846.** Primi 8,000–10,000L ($4.70–$5.90); secondi 10,000–20,000L ($5.90–$11.75). AE, DC, MC, V. Mon–Sat 12:30–3pm and 7pm–midnight. Closed Tues. PARMIGIANA.

Diners are wedged in among an odd assortment of antique toys, movie posters, and casks of the wonderful house Lambrusco in this lively, yellow-walled trattoria near Piazza Garibaldi. The kitchen keeps longer hours than most places in town, and the huge platters of prosciutto di Parma and assorted salamis make a satisfying late-night supper. The homemade tortellini di zucca (stuffed with pumpkin) is sublime), and the innovative main courses include a thick chicken breast rolled with prosciutto and parmigiano and served in white wine sauce.

Pizzeria La Duchessa. Pz. Garibaldi 1. ☎ **0521/235-962.** Primi 9,000L ($5.30); secondi 10,000–15,00L ($5.90–$8.80); pizza from 7,000L ($4.10). MC, V. Tues–Sun 10:30am–2:30pm and 7pm–1am. Closed Mon. PIZZA/PASTA.

The most popular pizzeria in Parma is open late and almost always crowded. You'll probably have to wait for a table, especially if you want one outdoors, but there's a lot of activity to watch in the piazza while you're waiting. Although you can eat a full meal here, you're best off with the exquisite pizzas and meal-in-themselves plates of pasta, washed down with a carafe of Lambrusco.

Ristorante Lazzaro. V. XX Marzo 14. ☎ **0521/208-944.** Primi 8,000–12,000 ($4.70–$7.05); secondi 10,000–20,000L ($5.90–$11.80). AE, V. Mon–Sat 11:30am–3:30pm; also, Fri–Sat 7:30–10:30pm. PARMIGIANA.

This white-walled, boisterous trattoria caters to mostly business clientele at lunchtime, and it opens on weekend evenings to serve families for whom a meal here is a favorite outing. The menu focuses on meat dishes, beginning with a tray of prosciutto, and the best of main courses are the grilled veal and lamb chops; horse meat is presented in many different variations as well. The homemade pastas are wonderful, too, and are served in copious portions; in fact, even herbivores can dine very well here on one of the vegetarian dishes, such as tagliatelle topped with wild mushrooms (the vegetarian menu includes any number of such pasta dishes, as well as salads and grilled vegetables).

Trattoria l' Oca Nera. V. G. B. Borghesi 3. ☎ **0521/233-126.** Primi 7,000–9,000L ($4.40–$5.30); secondi 10,000–16,000L ($5.90–$9.40). No credit cards. Wed–Mon, noon–2:30pm and 6:30–10:30pm. PARMIGIANA.

Formerly the Trattoria Madonna, this storefront establishment was prized by residents of this neighborhood between the center and the train station for its excellent home-style cooking. Now under new ownership, the restaurant continues to meet these expectations. There's no menu, and the five tables would be right in the kitchen if the tiny room weren't divided by a low counter. Often, there's a wonderful lasagna in the oven, and many variations of freshly made tortellini, tortelli, and tagliatelle (topped with fresh wild mushrooms in season) are served as well. Main courses often include a savory rabbit stew or a veal chop that has been flattened and grilled and topped with arugula and tomatoes.

WORTH A SPLURGE

⭕ **La Greppia.** Strada Garibaldi 39A. ☎ **0521/233-686.** Reservations required. Primi 12,000–25,000L ($7.05–$14.70); secondi 25,000–40,000L ($14.70–$23.55). AE, DC, MC, V. Wed–Sun 12:30–3:30pm and 7:30–10:30pm. Closed July. PARMIGIANA.

Our choice for a memorable meal in one of Parma's serious temples of gastronomy manages to be unpretentious while making diners feel they are experiencing a meal of a lifetime. This is due to the presence of wife and husband owners Paola Cavassini and Maurizio Rossi, who preside over the plain dining room with grace and ease. While you can enjoy many traditional Parmigiana favorites here (the *stracotto,* braised beef, is considered to be the city's best), the menu ventures into dozens of exciting dishes that rely not only on Parma's famous hams and cheeses but also its vegetables. Fresh asparagus lightly topped with prosciutto and tortelli stuffed with fresh herbs are a per-fect pair of starters. Our favorite main course is veal kidneys served with truffle shav-ings, though a very close second is the veal scaloppini with lemon and a sauce of white wine and herbs that is so light it nearly floats from the plate to your mouth. The dessert chef prepares many different kinds of fruit tarts, including one made with green tomatoes, and a chocolate cake that will convince you that you have indeed enjoyed the meal of a lifetime.

SNACKS & GELATO

The lively **Cluny Bar** in Piazza Garibaldi has a prime location on the city's main square, which can be nicely enjoyed from one of the outdoor tables. In warm weather, it's the house gelato that draws the crowds. The **Miss Pym Sala de Te** at Bgo. Parmiginao is a refuge for footsore shoppers laden with bags from the chic shops between Piazza Garibaldi and the Duomo. **Pasticerria Torino** at V. Garibaldi is an ele-gant, century-old shop-cum-coffeehouse, where you can enjoy Parma violets—a prissy delicacy of violets coated in sugar that you've probably encountered affixed to wedding cakes, plain or topping an assortment of cakes and tarts (they make a great gift for pastry-chef friends back home).

PARMA AFTER DARK

THE PERFORMING ARTS   Parma's opera house, the **Teatro di Regio,** is not too far down the scale of high regard from Milan's La Scala. After all, Verdi was born nearby (see below) and Arturo Toscanini, who often conducted at the theater, is a

Hamming It Up in Parma

For a true taste of Parma, in addition to visiting the outdoor food market at Piazza Ghiaia (see "Festivals & Markets," above), you should also sniff out **Salumeria Specialita di Parma,** V. Farini 9C (☎ **0521/235-606**), for a huge selection of prosciutto and other meats, and **Formaggio Del Re,** V. Garibaldi 46E, which is piled ceiling-high with wheels of Parmigiano. Aficionados can tour the factories of the **Consorzio del Parmigiano Reggiano,** V. Gramsci 26 (☎ **0521/292-7000**), and **Consorzio del Prosciutto di Parma,** V. Dell'Arpe 8B (☎ **0521/243-987**).

native son. Tickets can be hard to come by, since they're swallowed up for the entire October though March season well in advance by opera buffs from all over Emilia-Romagna. However, the tourist office sometimes sells standing-room tickets, and you should also check out the box office (☎ **0521/218-910**) on Via Garibaldi near Piazza della Pace for last-minute cancellations.

The nearby Teatro Due is home to the **Colletivo di Parma,** a world-renowned theater troop. Their performances, as well as other theatrical events, are staged from October through June; ask the tourist office or box office (☎ **0521/230-242**) for details.

BARS & CLUBS   Parma does not have a lively nightlife. The prime night spots are the cafes and bars in and around Piazza Garibaldi; see some of our choices above. Parma's top dance clubs are **Dadaumpa,** Via Emilio Este (☎ **0521/483-802**), and **Astrolabio,** V. Zarotta 86A (☎**0521/460-538**).

DAY TRIPS FROM PARMA

TORRECHIARA   The fertile plains that surround Parma are dotted with castles. One of the most dramatic is the 15th-century Farnese fortress of Torrechiara, near the village of Langhirano, whose gloomy, massive walls and crenellated towers top a bluff above the river Parma. Aside from the thrill of stepping back in time, the main attraction here is the **camera d'oro,** a room adorned with frescoes and wall tiles by Benedetto Bembo. You can top off your outing with a pizza at **Taverna del Castello,** housed in what were once the castle dungeons; a table on the terrace comes with a view over the valley below. Admission is 5,000L ($2.95), children 17 and under and seniors 60 and over free. The castle is open Tuesday to Sunday from 9am to 1pm and 3 to 7pm; ☎ **0521/355-255.**

Getting Here   The castle is 11 miles south of Parma. A bus makes the 40-minute trip hourly (5,000L/$2.95), but be sure to check the time of the last return bus (usually about 5:30pm). Tell the driver where you want to get off.

BUSSETO   All of Busseto seems to be a shrine to the beloved composer Giuseppe Verdi, who was born nearby in the little village of Roncole Verdi. The modest home of his youth is now a museum filled with scores, personal effects, and some of the original furnishings; ☎ **0524/922-339;** 4,000L ($2.35). The composer returned to the region in 1849 and built, just outside Busseto, the **Villa Verdi di Sant'Agata.** He shared his retreat with a companion, the soprano Giuseppina Strepponi, who later (and after much local gossip) became his wife. Their villa is filled with the couple's mementos and, touchingly, houses a reconstruction of the hotel room in Milan where the composer died. The villa (☎ **0523/830-210**) is open April through October

Tuesday through Sunday from 9 to 11:40am and 3 to 6:40pm. Admission is 8,000L ($4.70).

Shops all over town sell Verdiana—scores, recordings, prints, postcards, and just about all manner of objects, many of them quite tacky, upon which the composer's visage can be imprinted. If you're lucky, you may stumble into town on one of the rare occasions when a Verdi work is being performed in the **Teatro Verdi,** a little opera house in the castle.

Getting Here   Busseto is about 18 miles northwest of Parma via route S9, or, really speedily, via the autostrada A15 from Parma to Soragana and from there a few miles farther northwest to Busseto. There are eight buses a day from Parma (6,000L/$3.55).

Venice 8

by Patricia Schultz

Certainly, the tourists are inescapable. And prices can be double what they are elsewhere in Italy. But this is Venice, **La Serenissima**—the Serene Republic, what Lord Byron described as "a fairy city of the heart." Visitors flock to this canaled wonder for a very good reason: Venice is extraordinary, it is magical, and it is worth every lira. It shouldn't exist and yet it does, and underneath its otherworldly beauty and sometimes-stifling tourism, Venice is a living, breathing, singular city that seems almost too exquisite to be genuine, too fragile to survive the never-ending stream of visitors that began well over 1,000 years ago.

Venice was at the crossroads of the Byzantine and Roman worlds for centuries, a fact that lends to its unique heritage of art, architecture, and culture. And although traders and merchants no longer pass through "La Repubblica Serena" as they once did, it nonetheless continues to find itself at a crossroads: an intersection in time between the uncontested period of maritime power that built it and the modern world that keeps it ever-so-gingerly afloat.

It is a great disservice to allot Venice the average stay of 2 nights and 3 days (it will take you 1 day just to find your hotel). If you have no choice, do it, and know that your brief introduction will have you promising to come back time and time again. But if you can, stay at least 3 nights and preferably more—it will most likely be the highlight of your travels through Italy. Venice is a city too special and unique on this globe to be rushed. And leave your heels and excess luggage at home.

SPECIAL VENICE DISCOUNTS Anyone between 16 and 29 is eligible for a **Rolling Venice pass,** entitling the holder to discounts in museums, restaurants, stores, language courses, hotels, and bars across the city. The *tessera* (membership card) is valid for 1 year, it costs 5,000L ($2.95) (for twice that, you can get a booklet listing the hundreds of participating discounters around town). It can be picked up at a special Rolling Venice booth at the train station from July 1 through September 30, or year-round at the Assessorato alla Gioventù, Corte Contarina 1529 (off the Frezzeria west of St. Mark's Square) (☎ 041/27-47-650).

The 17,000L ($10) *biglietto cumulativo* ticket includes admission to the Palazzo Ducale and the Museo Correr (purchasing your ticket at either box office of the Palazzo Ducale).

Some hotels offer up to 50% discounts in the winter months (while many just shut down entirely). Look for discounts in the slow months of July and August as well.

Check with a tourist office for free tours being offered (erratically and usually during high season) in some of the churches, particularly the Basilica di San Marco and occasionally the Frari Church.

1 Arriving

BY PLANE You can fly into Venice from North America via Rome or Milan with Alitalia, or by connecting through a major European city with a number of European carriers. All flights land at the **Aeroporto Marco Polo,** 7 kilometers (4.5 mi.) due north of the city on the mainland (☎ **041/26-06-111**).

Airport Transfers The most fashionable, convenient and traditional way to arrive in **Piazza San Marco** is by boat. The **Cooperative San Marco** (also called **Alilaguna**) (☎ **041/52-22-303**) keeps that tradition alive, operating a large *motoscafo* (shuttle-boat) service between the airport, with limited stops at Murano, the Lido, and the Piazza San Marco, where it arrives after approximately 1 hour; the cost is 17,000L ($10) each way. Call for the daily schedule of the dozen or so round-trips from approximately 6am to midnight, which changes with the season and is coordinated with the arrival and departure schedules of principal airlines (most hotels will have the monthly schedule posted). If your hotel is not in the immediate Piazza San Marco area, you will have to make a connection with the vaporetto launches (your hotel can help you with the specifics if you have booked before leaving home). A private water taxi (20 to 30 minutes) into town is quicker and twice as convenient but costly, about 130,000L ($76.50) for the first two passengers, which includes luggage. It is worth considering if you have an exceptionally early flight, a lot of cumbersome luggage (a Venice no-no), or are traveling with one or more people. It may be able to drop you off at the front door of your hotel, or as close as it can maneuver given its location (check with your hotel before arriving). Your taxi captain should be able to tell you before boarding just how close he can get you.

By land, there are two bus alternatives to the **Piazzale Roma** area. The special airport shuttle bus, run by the **Azienda Trasporti Veneto Orientale (ATVO)** (☎ **041/52-05-530**), connects the airport with Piazzale Roma, not far (southwest) from Venice's Santa Lucia train station area and the closest point to Venice's attractions accessible by land. Buses leave to and from the airport roughly every hour, cost 5,000L ($2.95), and make the trip in about 30 minutes. Public transportation offers the less expensive alternative, the local **ACTV** bus no. 5 (☎ **041/78-01-11**), at 1,500L (90¢) per person. These buses leave to and from the airport and Piazzale Roma twice/hourly and can take up to 1 hour with all the stops. For either of the two bus alternatives, you will have to walk from the Piazzale Roma bus drop-off to the nearby vaporetto stop for your hotel or final destination—your first, and not last, realization that luggage in Venice is bad news. A land taxi from the airport to the Piazzale Roma to pick up your vaporetto will run approximately 50,000L ($29.40).

BY TRAIN Trains from all over Europe arrive at the **Stazione Venezia—Santa Lucia** (☎ **147/888-0888** toll free from anywhere in Italy). To get there, all trains must pass through (though not necessarily stop at) a station marked VENEZIA-MESTRE. Don't be confused: Mestre is a charmless industrial city and the last stop on the mainland. Occasionally trains end at Mestre, in which case you'll have to catch any of the frequent 10-minute shuttle trains that connect Mestre with Venice; so when booking your ticket, confirm that the train's final destination is Stazione Venezia—

Santa Lucia. Travel time from **Rome** is about 5½ hours, 3½ from **Milan**, 4 from **Florence**, and 2 from **Bologna.** The high-speed ES (Eurostar) trains shave about 1 hour off of each of these destinations, something not really justified by the considerable increase in cost.

At the far end as you come off the tracks at the Santa Lucia train station is the luggage depot or *deposito bagagli* (near the head of track 8). You'll do well to pack a bag of essentials to take to Venice and leave your heavy or excess gear here during your stay, especially if you're planning to look around for accommodations. The depot charges 10,000L ($5.90) per piece/per day and is open 24 hours daily. For security reasons, no open bags (such as shopping bags) are accepted. There's an **Albergo Diurno** (day hotel) at the far right side of the station as you face the tracks; it's open daily from 7am to 8pm and charges 8,000L ($4.70) for a shower. The rest room (WC) is alongside track 1; an *Oggetti Rivenuti* (lost and found office), is at track 14.

The official city tourist board, **Azienda Autonoma di Soggiorno e Turismo** (☎ **041/71-52-88**), operates an understaffed (and resultantly surly) information office between the station's large front doors. Lines can be discouraging. It's open daily from 8am to 7pm in the summer; closed Sunday in the winter.

The **train information** office, marked with a lowercase "**i**," is also located in the station's main hall. It's staffed daily from 8am to 8pm. Two banks for **currency exchange** (*cambio*) keep long hours (usually until 9pm) and compete with each other for business. Compare their rates and commission charge (often in fine print) before exchanging money. There is an **ATM** near the bank of doors on the right when exiting the station.

Finally, on exiting the station you'll find the Grand Canal immediately in front of you, making a heart-stopping first impression. The landing stages for vaporetto lines (the public motor launches or "water buses") are both to your right and left with different stops listed for each line. The ticket vendors speak a cornucopia of languages and will help getting you on the right line.

BY BUS   Although Venice is serviced by long-distance buses from all over mainland Italy and the occasional foreign city, rail travel is more convenient and commonplace. For schedules call **ACTV** (☎ **041/528-7886**). Final bus destination is the Piazzale Roma, where you'll need to pick up a vaporetto launch to connect with stops in the heart of Venice.

BY CAR   The only wheels you'll see in Venice are those attached to luggage and the occasional skateboard. Arriving for a stay by car can be problematic and expensive—and downright exasperating if it's high season and the limited parking facilities are full (a good percentage booked yearly by Venice's residents), a not uncommon situation.

When arriving from the mainland, follow signs for Venice that invariably lead you to **S11,** the Ponte della Libertà, that connects terra firma with Venice. The man-made Tronchetto island appears to your right where the bridge comes to an end.

There are three parking garages in Venice with differing rates, the **Tronchetto,** touted as Europe's largest parking lot, being the least expensive: the **Venice Terminal** designated by a "**P**" (☎ **041/52-07-555**), charging an average of 30,000L ($17.65) per day. If your hotel is a member of the Venetian Hoteliers Association, it may be able to supply you with a discount voucher for a special daily rate of 20,000L ($11.75) to submit upon departure when payment is due; make sure you ask while making your hotel reservation and before your arrival in Venice so you can pick your garage accordingly. From the Tronchetto Garage, take the convenient vaporetto 17 or 82, not any of the private boats that are notorious for cheating befuddled and tired tourists, and insisting they are the only way to get you to your destination (sometimes declaring that there is a daylong *sciopero* or strike).

The alternative to the Tronchetto lies just beyond, the Piazzale Roma—no hotel-affiliated discounts here!—where you'll find the **Garage Comunale** (☎ 041/52-22-308), charging 35,000L ($20.60) per day for an average-size car. Here you'll also find Venice's most expensive, the privately owned **Garage San Marco** (☎ 041/523-22-13) that charges about 50,000L ($32.90) per day for an average-size car. Vaporetto service lines 1, 82, or 52 are available. Lots are guarded, but leave your personal effects in your locked car or trunk at your own risk. If you're staying in Venice long, calculate your costs and consider dropping off your rental car at the rental agency at Piazzale Roma, and then rearranging for a new car upon your departure.

2 Orientation

VISITOR INFORMATION

In addition to the **tourist office** inside the train station (see above), there's a tourist office at the Palazzetto Selva, also called the Palazzina del Santi (☎ 041/52-26-356), located in between the Giardini (or Giardinetti) Reali, the small green park on the Grand Canal west of Piazza San Marco, and the famous Harry's Bar. This is a new location for the tourist office; in 1998 its longtime standby reopened in the southwest corner of Piazza San Marco (its official address is C. dell'Ascensione 71; ☎ 041/52-98-727). Hours are Monday through Saturday from 9:30am to 3:30pm in winter, daily 9:30am to 6:30pm in summer. The staff is as unwelcoming as their train station colleagues (make sure your questions are specific and don't expect any welcome-to-Venice smiles). Look for the ubiquitous posters around town with exhibition and concert schedules that are far more helpful or hope your hotel staff can help. Ask the tourist offices for a schedule of the month's special events and an updated listing of museum and church hours, as these can change erratically (watch for extended nighttime hours during summer months). During peak season months, a small information booth with erratic hours operates in the Arrivals Hall at the Marco Polo airport.

Street Maps   The free map offered by the tourist office and most hotels has good intentions, but it doesn't even show, much less name or index, all the **calli** and pathways of Venice. For that, pick up a more detailed map (ask for a *pianta della città*) for sale in any of a number of bookstores or newsstands. The best (and most expensive) available is the easy-to-read, spiral-ringed, highly detailed **Touring Club** edition (16,000L/$9.40). The recognizable red, white, and black map put out by Nicola Vincitorio Pub. (6,000L/$3.50) is just as handy. The newspaper and magazine stand at the train station carries a number of alternatives to the poorly detailed tourist-office freebie. Apparently word got out centuries ago that maps in Venice are a useless thing. If you're lost, you're better off just asking a local Venetian to point you in the right direction.

CITY LAYOUT

Keep in mind as you wander seemingly hopelessly among the *calli* (streets) and *campi* (squares) of Venice that the city was not built to make sense (or appear impressive) to those on foot but rather to those plying its myriad canals. No matter how good your map and sense of direction, time after time you'll get wonderfully lost and happen upon Venice's most intriguing corners and vignettes.

Venice lies 2½ miles from terra firma, connected to mainland Mestre by the Ponte

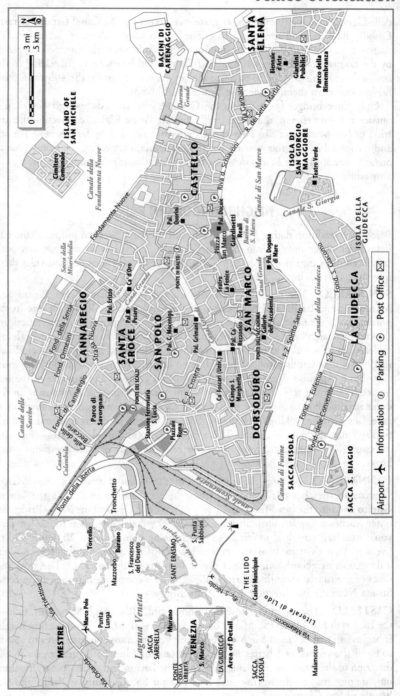

Venice Orientation

ISLAND OF SAN MICHELE

Cimitero Comunale

Canale della Fondamenta Nuove

BACINI DI CARENAGGIO

SANTA ELENA

SAN

Darsena Grande

Biennale d'arte

Giardini Pubblici

Parco della Rimembranza

Sacca della Misericordia

Fondamenta Nuove

CASTELLO

Via Garibaldi

R. dei Sette Martiri

R. del Schiavoni

Canale di San Marco

ISOLA DI SAN GIORGIO MAGGIORE

Teatro Verde

Canale S. Giorgio

Canale della Giudecca

Fond. della Sensa

Fond. Ormesini

CANNAREGIO

Strada Nuova

Pal. Erizzo

Ca' d'Oro

Canal Grande

Pal. Querini

Pal. Ducale

Giardinetti Reali

Piazza San Marco

Pal. Dogana di Mare

Bacino di S. Marco

Canal Grande

ISOLA DELLA GIUDECCA

Canale S. Giacomo

LA GIUDECCA

Fond. S. Giacomo

Fond. delle Convertite

Fond. S. Eufemia

SANTA CROCE

SAN POLO

Pal. Pesaro

Pal. C. Corner

Pal. C. Mocenigo

Pal. Grimani

Teatro La Fenice

SAN MARCO

Pal. Ca' Rezzonico

Gallerie dell'Accademia

DORSODURO

F.ta S. Spirito-Santo

Canale della Giudecca

Fond. di Cannaregio

Canale delle Sacche

Calle delle Beccarie

Canale Colombola

Parco di Savorgnan

S. Croce

Ca' Foscari (Univ.)

Campo S. Margherita

S. P. Croce

Ponte di Rialto

Ponte degli Scalzi

Stazione Ferroviaria S. Lucia

Piazzale Roma

Ponte della Libertà

Tronchetto

SACCA FISOLA

Canale di Fusine

SACCA S. BIAGIO

Canale Scomenzera

Lower inset map

Laguna Veneta

MESTRE

Via Orlanda

Via Triestina

Marco Polo

Punta Lunga

Torcello

Burano

Mazzorbo

S. Francesco del Deserto

SANT'ERASMO

Canale di Tessera

S. Punta Sabbioni

SACCA SARENELLA

Murano

SACCA SESSOLA

PONTE DELLA LIBERTÀ

VENEZIA

S. Marco

LA GIUDECCA

Area of Detail

Riva S. Nicolò

THE LIDO

Casinò Municipale

Litorale di Lido

Via Malamocco

Malamocco

Legend

Airport ✈   Information ℹ   Parking Ⓟ   Post Office ☒

N

.3 mi

.5 km

della Libertà. Snaking through the city like an inverted S is the **Canal Grande (Grand Canal)**, the wide main artery of Venice. The "streets filled with water" are in fact 177 narrow canals that cut through the interior of the two halves of the city, flowing gently by the doorsteps of centuries-old palazzi. They would be endlessly frustrating to the landlubbing tourists trying to navigate the city on foot if not for the 400 small foot-bridges that cross them, connecting Venice's 118 islands.

Only three bridges (*ponti*) cross the Grand Canal: the **Ponte degli Scalzi,** just outside the train station; the elegant white marble **Ponte Rialto,** connecting the districts of San Marco and San Polo at the center of town and by far the most famous and recognizable; and the wooden **Ponte Accademia,** connecting the Campo Santo Stefano area of the San Marco district with the Accademia museum across the way in Dorsoduro.

NEIGHBORHOODS IN BRIEF

Based on a tradition dating from the 12th century, for tax-related purposes, the city has officially been divided into six *sestieri* (literally "sixths," or wards) that have basically been the same since 1711. The "Canalazzo" or Grand Canal neatly divides them into three on each bank.

SAN MARCO   The central sestiere is anchored by the magnificent **Piazza San Marco** and the **Basilica di San Marco** to the south and the **Rialto Bridge** to the north. This is the most visited (and resultantly the most expensive) of the sestieri. It's the commercial, religious, and political heart of the city and has been for more than a millennium (it was also its musical heart until a fire destroyed La Fenice Opera House in 1996; it now stands a hollow shell). It is no surprise, then, that it is the city's most visited and expensive district. Although you'll find glimpses and snippets of the real Venice, ever rising rents have nudged resident Venetians to look for housing in the outer neighborhoods: You'll be hard-pressed to find a grocery store or dry cleaners here. But if you're looking for Murano glass trinkets and mediocre restaurants, you'll find an embarrassment of choices. This area is a mecca for first class hotels—but, with direction from Frommer's, you can stay here in the heart of Venice without going broke.

CANNAREGIO   Sharing the same side of the Grand Canal with San Marco, Cannaregio stretches north and east from the train station to include the **Jewish Ghetto** and into the canal-hugging vicinity of the Ca' d'Oro and the Rialto Bridge. Its outer reaches are quiet, unspoiled and residential (what high-season tourist crowds? you'll wonder); one-third of Venice's ever-shrinking population of 20,000 is said to live here. Venice's majority of one-star hotels are clustered about the train station—not a dangerous neighborhood, but not one known for its charm either. The gloss and dross of the tourist-shop-lined **Lista di Spagna** strip continues as it morphs into the **Strada Nuova** in the direction of the Rialto Bridge.

CASTELLO   This quarter, whose tony "boulevard," **Riva degli Schiavoni,** follows the Bacino di San Marco (St. Mark's Basin), is lined with first-class and deluxe hotels. It begins just east of Piazza San Marco, skirting Venice's most congested area to absorb some of the crowds and better hotels and restaurants. But head further east in the direction of the **Arsenale** or inland away from the Bacino and the people traffic thins out, despite major visit-worthy sites like **Campo SS. Giovanni e Paolo** and the **Scuola di San Giorgio.**

SAN POLO   This mixed-bag sestiere of residential corners and tourist sites stretches northwest of the Rialto Bridge to the principal church of **Santa Maria dei Frari** and the Scuola di San Rocco. The hub of activity at the foot of the bridge is greatly due to the **Rialto market** that has taken place here for centuries—some of the city's best restaurants have flourished here for generations, alongside some of its worst tourist-traps. The spacious **Campo San Polo** is the main piazza of Venice's smallest sestiere.

SANTA CROCE   North and northwest of the San Polo district and across the Grand Canal from the train station, Santa Croce stretches all the way to Piazzale Roma. Its eastern section is generally one of the least visited sections of Venice—making it all the more desirable for curious visitors. Less lively than San Polo, it is as authentic, seemingly light-years away from San Marco. The quiet and lovely **Campo San Giacomo dell'Orio** is considered to be its heart.

DORSODURO   You'll find the residential area of Dorsoduro on the opposite side of the Accademia Bridge from San Marco. Known for the **Accademia** and **Peggy Guggenheim museums,** it is the largest of the sestieri and has been known as something of an artists' haven (hence the tireless comparison with New York's Greenwich village—a far cry) until recent escalations of rents forced much of the community to relocate elsewhere. Good neighborhood restaurants, a charming gondola boatyard, the lively **Campo Santa Margherita** and the sunny quay called **le Zattere** (a favorite promenade and gelato stop) all add to the character and color that make this one of the city's most visited areas.

LA GIUDECCA   Venice shares its lagoon with several other islands. Located opposite the Piazza San Marco and Dorsoduro, **la Giudecca** is a tranquil working-class residential area where you'll find the youth hostel and a handful of hotels (including the deluxe Cipriani, one of Europe's finest).

LIDO DI VENEZIA   This slim, 7-mile-long area is the city's beach; separating the lagoon from the open sea and permitting car traffic, it is a popular summer destination because of its concentration of seasonal hotels (its landmark hotels serving as home base for the annual **Venice Film Festival**) but is also quite residential.

MESTRE   This dreary gateway to Venice is located on the mainland and has nothing to explore. In a pinch, its host of inexpensive hotels are worth consideration when Venice's hotels are full, but that's about it.

MURANO, BURANO & TORCELLO   These three areas, which are located northeast of the city and easily accessible by public transportation, are popular tourist destinations. Since the 13th-century Murano has exported its glass products worldwide; it's an interesting day trip if you have the time (or a burning interest to visit a *fornace* or glass-blowing factory, or the noteworthy glass museum), but shoppers can do just as well in Venice's myriad glass stores. Burano was and still is famous for its lace, an art now practiced by so few that prices are generally unaffordable. Torcello is the most remote and the least populated. The 40-minute boat ride is worthwhile for history and art buffs who will be awestruck by the incredible Byzantine mosaics of the cathedral, some of the finest outside of Ravenna.

SAN MICHELE   This cemetery island is the final resting place of celebrities such as Stravinsky and Diaghilev.

FINDING AN ADDRESS

Not confused enough yet? Each sestiere is divided further into an indeterminate number of small *parrochie,* literally parishes or neighborhoods. These indications don't appear on maps and are of little or no use to the navigating tourist, although the piazzas (called *campi* in Venice) within each parrochia are frequently reference points and social hubs. There are hundreds of campi (or "fields"—they were unpaved for centuries) throughout Venice, but only one piazza: San Marco.

The Ride of Your Life

As much a symbol of Venice as the winged lion, the **gondola,** one of the city's great traditions, is as romantic as it looks (all those detractors who write it off as too touristy and silly have most likely never tried it). Though you may be quoted higher prices in peak season, the "official" rate is 120,000L ($70.60) for up to 50 minutes, for up to six passengers per vessel, and 60,000L ($35.30) for every additional 25 minutes. There's a 30,000L ($17.65) surcharge after dark, but aim for late afternoon before sundown when the light does its magic on the canal reflections (and bring along a bottle of prosecco and two glasses). If the price is too high, ask around at your hotel or seek out other tourists lingering about at the gondola stations and inquire if they'd like to share the cost (and dilute the romance). Establish cost, time (some gondolieri may offer fewer minutes for fewer lire if they're having a slow day but don't count on it; you'll also find that the 50-minute hour can get even further foreshortened to 40 minutes), and route (any of the quiet back canals are preferable to the trafficked and often choppy waters of the Grand Canal) before setting off in your 36-foot-long black wonder. And what about the accompanying musicians and serenading gondolieri immortalized in film? A musical ensemble of accordion player and tenor is so expensive it is shared among several gondolas traveling together. A number of travel agents around town book the evening serenades for approximately 50,000L ($29.40) per person (ask at the American Express office). The number of gondolieri willing to brave the winter cold and rain are minimal, though some come out of their wintertime hibernation for the Carnevale period.

There are 12 gondola stations spread throughout Venice, including **Piazzale Roma,** the **train station,** the **Rialto Bridge,** and **Piazza San Marco.** A number of smaller stations can be found about town, with gondoliers standing alongside their shiny black boats. They all speak enough English to communicate the necessary details.

To tourists, gondolas mean romance, but to Venetians they're a basic form of transportation. With just three bridges that cross the Grand Canal, a number of two-manned *traghetto* gondolas ferry the general public back and forth at seven other points along the Grand Canal, expertly dodging what at times can look like rush-hour traffic of ✪ **vaporetti,** delivery boats, water taxis, and private boats. You'll find on your map or during your meandering a traghetto gondola station at the end of any calle with the name "Traghetto." There's one, for instance, right alongside the San Tomà vaporetto station, or next to the Ca' d'Oro or Ca' Rezzonico museums. The ride is short and Venetians **always** stand (leaving the tourists to scramble for the very few seats available), but at only 1,000L (58¢) each way (handed directly to the gondoliere; no tickets necessary), it's priced for the local citizenry, not the wealthy tourists.

Within each sestiere is an ancient and most original (read: discombobulating) system of numbering the palazzi or buildings, using one continuous string of 6,000 or so building numbers (faded into thin air on most buildings), which wind their way among the canals and calli in a fashion known to no living person except perhaps the postman. When looking for an address, always find out first the name of the sestiere, then ask for a campo as a reference point and locate it on a map. The format for addresses in this chapter is the official mailing address: the name of the sestiere followed by the building number within that district, followed by parenthesis with the name of the street or campo on which you'll find that address: For example, a store may be listed as San Marco 1471 (Salizzada San Moisé), 30121 Venezia. Don't be surprised to find it listed elsewhere as Salizzada San Moisé 1471 (San Marco), the alternative system commonly found. By the way that place in San Marco 1471 may be right across the alleyway from San Marco 1953. Happy hunting!

GETTING AROUND

To be a successful tourist in Venice, there are two time-tested rules of thumb: First, pack light enough so you can get yourself and your luggage to your hotel door without despairing at the common absence of a (costly) *portabagagli* (porter) just when you need him (20,000L/$11.75 for one piece, 30,000L/$17.65 for two). Second, always imagine yourself to be like a child's miniature battery-operated toy car that, when driven into a wall or other obstacle, instantly turns and continues on its way. Time and again, you'll think you know exactly where you're going, only to wind up at the end of a dead-end street or at a canal with no bridge to the other side. Just remind yourself that the city's physical complexity—that is, getting lost— is an integral part of its charm and a memorable experience that Venice guarantees every visitor.

Note: With its countless stepped footbridges and with almost no elevators in any of the buildings, Venice is one of the worst cities in the world for the physically disabled.

BY BOAT   A comprehensive vaporetto system of about a dozen lines is operated by the **Azienda del Consorzio Trasporti Veneziano (ACTV),** C. Fuseri 1810, off the Frezzeria in San Marco (☎ **041/52-87-886**). Transit maps are available at the tourist offices and at some ACTV stations (be aware that vaporetto stops and lines were changed and renumbered in 1994 and 1996—a number of old maps may still be in circulation). Contrary to what you may think, it's easy to get around Venice by foot. But don't avoid the public transportation all together: Few cities in the world can brag about their buses being as romantic as Venice's ✪ **vaporetti,** or motor launches. Together with the city's fleets of **motoscafi,** these "water buses" principally service the Grand Canal (and can be horribly crowded in the summer months; watch your valuables), as well as the outskirts and outer islands. The crisscross network of small and considerably narrower canals is the province of delivery vessels, gondolas, and private boats.

The average flat-rate fare on most lines is 5,000L ($2.95); they run daily every 10 to 15 minutes from 7am to midnight, then hourly until morning; most ticket booths have timetables posted. Note, however, that not all stations sell tickets after dark; if you haven't purchased a block of 10 tickets (called a *carnet* or *blochetto,* 50,000L/$29.50), you'll have to settle up with the conductor on board (you'll have to find him, he won't come looking for you) for an extra 1,000L (60¢) per ticket, or gamble on a 40,000L ($23.50) fine, with no excuses accepted.

Although the city, no larger than New York's Central Park, is extremely easy to navigate on foot, boat lovers might want to consider the 18,000L ($10.60) **Biglietto 24 Ore** that entitles the bearer to 24 hours of unlimited travel on any ACTV vessel. The **Biglietto 3 Giorni,** covering three full days of unlimited travel, doesn't seem like much of a savings at 35,000L ($20.60); holders of the Rolling Venice membership get a 10,000L ($5.90) discount. Even less impressive is the **Biglietto 7 Giorni** for 7 days at 60,000L ($35.30), unless you really intend to use the system. The **Biglietto Isole,** a ticket valid for unlimited 1-day travel in one direction on line 12 (which services the islands of Murano, Mazzorbo, Burano, and Torcello) costs 5,000L ($2.95).

Venetian Dialect: What Would Dante Say?

If, after a few days in Rome and Florence, you were just getting the hang of correlating your map to the reality of your new surroundings, you can put aside any short-term success upon your arrival in Venezia. Even the Italians (non-Venetian ones) look befuddled when trying to decipher street names and signs (given that you can ever find any). Venice's colorful thousand-year history as a once-powerful maritime republic has everything to do with its local dialect, which absorbed nuances and vocabulary from far-flung outposts in the East and from the flourishing communities of foreign merchants who, for centuries, lived and traded in Venice. A linguist could gleefully spend a lifetime trying to make some sense of it all.

But for the Venice-bound traveler just trying to make sense of Venetian addresses, the following should give you the basics. (And don't even try to follow a conversation between two gondolieri!)

ca'   The abbreviated use of the word "casa" is used for the noble palazzi, once private residences and now museums, lining the Grand Canal: Ca' d'Oro, Ca' Pesaro, and Ca' Rezzonico. There is only one palazzo, and it is the Palazzo Ducale, the former doge's residence. However, as time went on some great houses gradually began to be called "palazzi," so today you'll encounter the Palazzo Grassi or the Palazzo Labia.

calle   Taken from the Spanish (though pronounced as if Italian, i.e., *ca*-lay), this is the most commonplace word for street, known as "via" or "strada" elsewhere in

---

Line 1, ironically called the *accellerato* when it in fact is the slowest, is the most important (and most used) for the average visitor, making all stops along the Grand Canal from the Piazzale Roma to Piazza San Marco before continuing on to the Lido. **Line 82,** a *diretto,* also travels the Grand Canal, though it makes limited stops such as Piazza San Marco, the Accademia Bridge, the Rialto Bridge, and the Ferrovia (train station) among others before circling Dorsoduro and crossing the lagoon to the Lido. Check before getting on. **Line 52,** the *circolare,* is another major line, circling the perimeter of the city and crossing the lagoon to Murano on one side and the Lido on the other. **Line 12** runs hourly, also crossing the waves to Murano, continuing on to Burano and Torcello.

Since there are just three bridges spanning the Grand Canal, to fill in the gaps, ***traghetti*** **gondolas** cross the canal at seven or so intermediate points. You'll find a traghetto station at the end of any street named "Calle del Traghetto" on your map and indicated by a yellow sign with the black symbol of a gondola. The fare, regulated by the local government, is 1,000L (58¢) which you hand to the gondoliere when boarding. Most Venetians cross standing up, it's the foreigners who scramble for the few seats. For the experience, try the crossing that connects the Ca' d'Oro and the Pescheria fish market, opposite each other on the Grand Canal just north of the Rialto Bridge—the gondoliers expertly dodge water traffic at this point of the canal where it is the busiest and most heart-stopping.

BY WATER TAXI   *Taxi acquei* (water taxis) prices are high and not for the average visitor watching his lire. For (unlikely) journeys up to 7 minutes, the rate is 27,000L ($15.90); click off 500L (30¢) for each additional 15 seconds. There's an 8,500L ($5) supplement for night service (10pm to 7am), and a 9,000L ($5.30) surcharge on

Italy. There are numerous variations. "Ruga" from the French word "rue" once meant a calle flanked with stores, a designation no longer valid. A "ramo" (literally "branch") is the offshoot of a street, and is often used interchangeably with "calle." "Salizzada" once meant a paved street, implying that all other less important "calles" were once just dirt-packed alleyways. A "stretto" is a narrow passageway.

campo   Elsewhere in Italy it's "piazza." In Venice the only piazza is the Piazza San Marco (and its two bordering "piazzette"); all other squares are "campi" or the diminutive, "campielli." Translated as "field" or "meadow," these were once small, unpaved grazing spots for the odd chicken or cow. Almost every one of Venice's campi carries the name of the church that dominates it (or once did) and most have wells, no longer used, in the center.

canale   There are three wide, principal canals: the Canal Grande (affectionately called "il Canalazzo," the Canal), the Canale della Giudecca, and the Canale di Cannaregio. Each of the other 160-odd smaller canals is called a "rio". A "rio terrà" is a filled-in canal—wide and straight—now used as a street. A "piscina" is a filled-in basin, now acting as a campo or piazza.

fondamenta   Referring to the foundations of the houses lining a canal, this is a walkway along the side of a rio. Promenades along the Grand Canal near the Piazza San Marco and the Rialto are called "riva" as in the Riva del Vin or Riva del Carbon, where cargo such as wine and coal were once unloaded.

Sunday and holidays; note that these two supplements cannot be applied simultaneously. If you call for one to pick you up, tack on another 8,000L ($5). You'll be charged an extra 2,200L ($1.30) for each large piece of luggage.

There are six **water-taxi stations** serving various key points in the city: the Ferrovia (train station) (☎ **041/71-62-86**), Piazzale Roma (☎ **041/71-69-22**), the Rialto Bridge (☎ **041/52-30-575**), Piazza San Marco (☎ **041/52-29-750**), the Lido (☎ **041/52-60-059**), and Marco Polo Airport (☎ **041/54-15-084**). **Radio Taxi** (☎ **041/522-23-03**) will come pick you up any place in the city, for a surcharge, of course.

BY GONDOLA   To come all the way to Venice and not indulge in a gondola ride could be one of your biggest regrets. Yes, it's touristy and yes, it's expensive (see box on gondolas, p. 384), but only those with a heart of stone will be unmoved by the quintessential Venetian experience. Do not initiate your trip, however, until you have agreed upon a price and synchronized watches. Oh, and don't ask them to sing.

ON FOOT   You can get a map and spend your day trying to make some sense out of it. Or then again, you can jettison that map and just wander. Look for the ubiquitous yellow signs that direct travelers toward five major landmarks: **Ferrovia** (the train station), **Piazzale Roma,** the **Rialto** (Bridge), (Piazza) **San Marco,** and the **Accademia** (Bridge). Sometimes it's enough just to follow the human stream of traffic (this doesn't mean the solitary old woman with her bulging shopping bags—you'll probably wind up following her home). To truly experience the city, just walk and walk and walk. Take a break in a neighborhood *bacaro* wine bar, then walk some more. You'll be exhausted but elated at the end of the day.

FAST FACTS: Venice

Acqua Alta The notorious acqua alta floods, a peculiarity related as much to the tides and winds as to rainfall, can start as early as October (even late September), usually taking place from November to March. As many of 50 a year have been recorded since they first started in the late 1700s. If an extreme acqua alta is expected, a warning will be sounded 1 hour before its crest so people can get home, and the city puts out boardwalks (*passarelle*) along the major routes. Acqua alta generally lasts only about 2 or 3 hours at a time and first hits the lowest points in the city, such as Piazza San Marco. The better hotels even keep a storeroom full of galoshes for hotel guests.

American Express See "Currency Exchange," below.

Baby-Sitters There are no baby-sitting agencies in Venice per se. Your best bet is to make arrangements through the hotel, although this is a service usually not provided by the small hotels listed in this book. They may by able to help, however, by calling on a family member or friend but try to give them ample notice.

Banks Banks are normally open Monday to Friday from 8:30am to 1:30pm and 2:35 to 3:35pm or 3 to 4pm; some banks are open on Saturday year-round (others in July or August only) and follow an 8:30 to 11:30am schedule. ATMs are relatively recent, though their numbers are rapidly growing and are no longer found at banks alone.

Bookstores Two centrally located bookstores that carry a line of softcover and hardcover books in English are the **Libreria Sansovino** in the Bacino Orseolo 84 immediately north of the Piazza San Marco (☎ **041/52-22-623**) and the **Libreria San Giorgio,** C. Larga XXII Marzo 2087 (☎ **041/52-38-451**), beyond the American Express Office toward Campo S. Stefano. Both carry a selection of books about Venetian art, history, and literature.

Business Hours Standard hours for shops are 9am to 12:30pm and 3 to 7:30pm Monday to Saturday. In winter, shops are closed on Monday morning, while in summer it's usually Saturday afternoon. Most grocers are closed on Wednesday afternoon throughout the year. In Venice just about everything is closed on Sunday, though tourist shops in the tourist areas such as San Marco area are permitted to stay open during high season. Restaurants are required to close at least 1 day per week (*il giorno di riposo*), though the particular day varies from one trattoria to another. Many are open for Sunday lunch but close for Sunday dinner. Many restaurants specializing in fish and seafood also close Monday when the fish market is closed. Restaurants will close for holidays (*chiuso per ferie*) sometime in July or August, frequently over Christmas, and sometime in January before the Carnevale rush.

Climate May, June, and September and early October are the best months with respect to weather to visit (and the most crowded). July and August are hot—at times unbearably so. April or late October/early November are hit or miss; it can either be glorious, or cool, rainy, and damp and only marginally less crowded. Also see "Acqua Alta," above.

Consulates The Consulate of the **United Kingdom** is at Dorsoduro 1051 (☎ **041/52-27-207**), just west of the Accademia Bridge in the Palazzo Querini; it's open Monday through Friday from 9am to noon and 2 to 4pm. The **United States** has a consulate in Milan (☎ **02/29-03-51**) as do **Canada** and **Australia.**

Crime Be aware of petty crime such as pickpocketing on the crowded vaporetti, particularly the tourist routes where passengers are more intent on the passing scenery than watching their bags. Venice's deserted back streets used to be virtually crime-free; the occasional tale of theft is beginning to circulate.

Currency Exchange Both exchange offices (*cambio*) at the train station are open 7 days a week. The **American Express** office, San Marco 1471, on Salizzada San Moisé (☎ **041/52-00-844**), exchanges traveler's checks and cash commission-free. To find it: With your back to the Basilica di San Marco, exit the piazza by way of the arcade at the far left (western) end; you'll see a mosaic sign in the pavement pointing the way straight ahead. The office is open in summer for banking Monday to Saturday from 8am to 8pm (all other services 9am to 5:30pm); in winter, Monday to Friday from 9am to 5:30pm and Saturday from 9am to 12:30pm . Be careful of the privately owned cambio around town whose boards boast good rates but whose commonly high commissions (based on the amount changed) appear at the bottom in small print. They follow the same schedule as retail shops, not banks, but often staying open during lunch or after shops close and on Sundays during peak season.

Dentists/Doctors For a shortlist, check with the consulate of the United Kingdom, the American Express office, or your hotel.

Drugstores Pharmacies take turns staying open all night. To find out which one is on call in your area, ask at your hotel or dial ☎ **041/52-30-573.**

Emergencies Dial ☎ **113** to reach the police. Some Italians will recommend that you try the military-trained Carabinieri (phone ☎ **112**), in the opinion of some a better police force. For an ambulance, phone ☎ 041/52-30-000. To report a fire, dial ☎ **115.**

Fax From both the main post office and its Piazza San Marco branch (see "Mail," below) you can send faxes to almost any destination with the odd exception of the United States. For service to the United States, most hotels will agree to do it for either a per-page or estimated-per-minute cost. Or look for SERVIZIO FAX signs in the windows of *cartolerie* (stationery stores).

Holidays Venice's patron saint, San Marco or St. Mark, is honored on April 25.

Laundry The self-service laundry most convenient to the train station is the **Lavaget** at Cannaregio 1269, to the left as you cross the Ponte alle Guglie from Lista di Spagna, open Monday to Friday from 8:30am to 12:30pm and 3 to 7pm; the rate is about 16,000L ($9.40) for up to 4.5 kilos (10 lbs.).

Lost & Found The central Ufficio Oggetti Rinvenuti (☎ **041/78-82-25**) is in the annex to the City Hall (Municipio), at San Marco 4134, on Calle Piscopia o Loredan, just off riva del Carbon on the Grand Canal, near the Rialto Bridge (on the same side of the canal as the Rialto vaporetto station). Look for scala (stairway) "C"; the lost-and-found office is in the "Economato" section on the "mezzanino" level, one flight up. The office is ostensibly open only on Monday, Wednesday, and Friday from 9:30am to 12:30pm, but there's usually someone available weekdays from 9:30am until the building closes at 1:30pm.

There's also an Ufficio Oggetti Smarriti at the airport (☎ **041/26-06-436**), and an Ufficio Oggetti Rinvenuti at the train station (☎ **041/78-52-38**), right at the head of Track 14; open Monday to Friday from 8am to 4pm.

Luggage Storage See "By Train" under "Arriving" above for a safe place to check your luggage.

Mail   Venice's main Posta Centrale is at San Marco 5554, on Salizzada Fontego dei Tedeschi (☎ **041/271-7111**), just off Campo San Bartolomeo, in the area of the Rialto Bridge on the San Marco side of the Grand Canal. This office is usually open Monday to Saturday from 8:15am to 7pm. Stamps are sold at Window 12.

If you're at Piazza San Marco and need postal services, walk through Sottoportego San Geminian, the center portal at the opposite (western) end of the piazza from the basilica on Calle Larga dell'Ascensione. This branch is open Monday to Friday from 8:15am to 1:30pm and Saturday from 8:15am to 12:10pm.

Remember that you can buy stamps (*francobolli*) at any tabacchi with no additional service charge; postcards differ according to destination (to the United States 1,300L/75¢), letters according to weight. The limited mailboxes seen around town are red.

Porters   When you can find them at the principal vaporetto stops (San Marco, Piazzale Roma, and so on), they will charge 20,000L ($11.75) for your first piece of luggage, 10,000L ($5.90) for each additional piece. Leaving from your hotel to the vaporetto stop is less problematic, as the hotel will call and have a porter come to pick you up.

Rest Rooms   For the cost of an espresso or mineral water you can use the rest rooms in any bar (*signori* means men, *signore,* ladies). Museums and galleries will also have facilities. Public "WCs" can be found at the train station; near the Giardinetti Reali park next to the Tourist Information office (Palazzetto Selva aka Palazzina del Santi); on the west side (Dorsoduro) of the Accademia Bridge; next to the post office branch just west of the Piazza San Marco on Calle Larga dell'Ascensione; and off Campo San Bartolomeo.

Shoe Repair   Try the one at Dorsoduro 871 on Calle Nuova Sant'Agnese, on the main route between the Accademia and the Peggy Guggenheim Collection.

Time   Dial ☎ **161** for exact time recorded in Italian only.

Travel Agencies   See "Currency Exchange" above. Also centrally located are **Intras City Service** in Pz. San Marco 146 (near Clock Tower) (☎ **041/522-48-70; fax 041/528-63-47); Kele e Teo** on the Mercerie 4930 (☎ **041/520-87-22; fax 041/520-89-13).

Weather   Dial ☎ **191** for weather forecast recorded in Italian only.

3 Accommodations You Can Afford

Hotels, like just about everything else in Venice, are more expensive than in any other city in Italy, surpassing even Florence and Rome. Whatever you've been spending in other parts of the country, you can plan on spending more (at times a good deal more) here with no apparent upgrade in amenities. If single rooms are small elsewhere, they can be downright tiny in Venice, where space everywhere is a premium and even the

Travel Tip

As Italy gears up for unprecedented numbers of tourists during the Holy Year 2000, 1999 remains a testing ground. Traditionally, in summertime when reservations drop, hotels, restaurants, and stores close up. But, if tourism remains constant in 1999, these places probably will probably stay open year-round. The best advice for this situation is to call and reserve in advance whenever possible.

deluxe Danieli's rooms could hardly be called spacious. At worst, inexpensive hotels are clean (well, at least the ones we vouch for) and functional; at best they are charming and thoroughly enjoyable. Some may even provide you with your best stay in Europe. Elevators can be an engineering impossibility in this most unique city: if stairs are a problem for you, confirm the existence (or not) of an elevator and the location of your room. And don't expect sweeping hill-town views. If you're lucky, you'll overlook a charming narrow canal or small **campo.** If you're not, you'll overlook another wall. And if the absence of traffic makes you think any room will ensure quiet, remember that low floors make you privy to every pedestrian's conversation and every deliveryman's shout (and those romantic canal-side rooms can carry noise as well as serenades).

We strongly suggest that you book in advance once your itinerary is planned, regardless of the period. In June and the September/October period and during special events year-round, it can seem that there is not a budget (or any) lodging to be had in Venice, especially if you arrive after noon. If you haven't booked, arrive as early as you can, for time literally is money. The tourist office in the train station will book rooms for you, but the lines are long and (understandably) the staff's patience is sometimes thin. If you're holding a **Rolling Venice card** (see "Special Venice Discounts," above) the small office in the Santa Lucia train station will help with reservations free of charge. Those not holding the card can also take advantage of a summertime **Hotel Reservations** booth in the train station. For 1,000L (60¢) they will try to find you a hotel of the price range of your choice; upon confirmation from the hotel, they will accept the deposit from you by credit card, issue you a voucher, and you pay the balance upon your arrival at the hotel. Another alternative for reserving the same day as your arrival can be done through the **A.V.A. (Venetian Hoteliers Association)**, toll free by phone within Italy (☎ **1678-43006**); simply state the price range you want to book and they will confirm a hotel while you wait. Neither of the two booking possibilities does much to help you understand the quality or location of the hotel.

SEASONAL CONSIDERATIONS   Finally, keep in mind that most hotels usually observe high- and low-season rates, though they are gradually adopting a single year-round rate. Be sure to ask when you book, or upon arrival at a hotel, whether off-season prices are in effect. High season in Venice runs from March 15 through November 5, with a lull during the hot and muggy months of July and August when you'd do well to insist on a hotel with air-conditioning and hope for a low season discount. Some hotels close altogether (sometimes without notice if bookings are slow) from November or December until Carnevale, opening for about 2 weeks around Christmas and New Year's at high-season rates.

IN SAN MARCO

✪ **Albergo al Gambero.** San Marco 4687 (on C. d. Fabbri), 30124 Venezia. ☎ **041/ 52-24-384** or 52-01-420. Fax 041/52-00-431. E-mail: hotelgambero@tin.it. MINIBAR TV TEL. 26 units, 14 with bathroom. 85,000L ($50) single without bathroom, 165,000L ($97.05) single with bathroom; 140,000L ($82.35) double without bathroom, 210,000L ($123.50) double with bathroom; 189,000L ($111.20) triple without bathroom, 283,000L ($166.50) triple with bathroom; 238,000L ($140,000) quad without bathroom, 357,000L ($210), quad with bathroom. Rates include continental breakfast. MC, V. Vaporetto: Rialto. At the vaporetto stop, turn right along the canal, cross the small footbridge, turn left onto C. Bembo, which becomes C. d. Fabbri; the hotel is about 5 blocks ahead, on your left.

One of Venice's former budget hotels, which occupies an enviable location midway on a main strip connecting Piazza San Marco and the Rialto bridge, just underwent a laborious Cinderella makeover in 1998 (the paint was still drying during my last stay). Enthralled with the beautifully tiled and marbled bathrooms (by 2000, all rooms should have such new private bathrooms), and handsome striped damasklike

Venice Accommodations & Dining

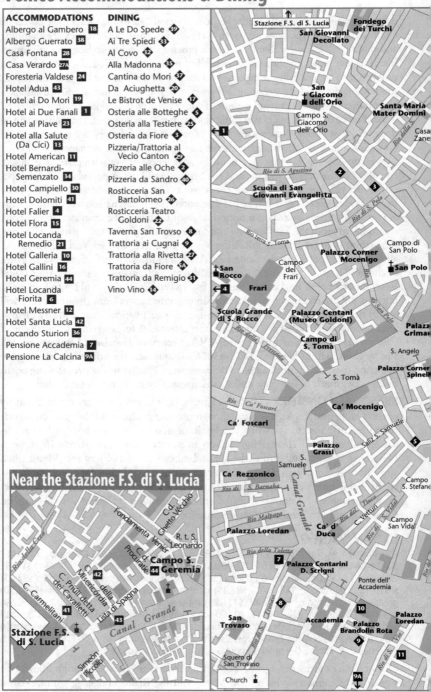

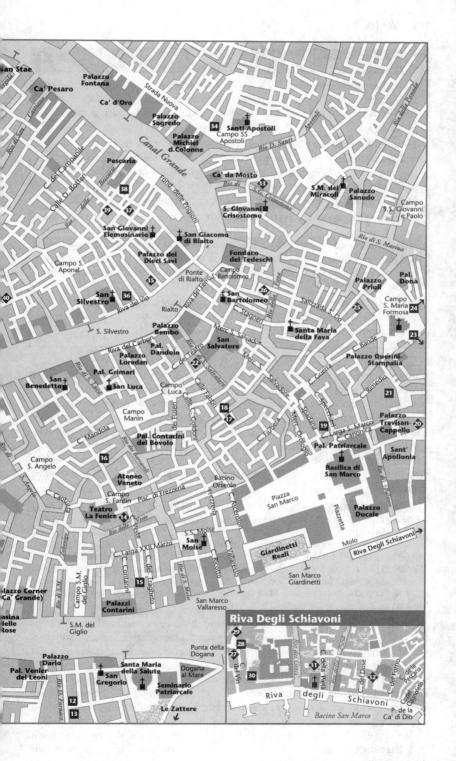

San Stae

Palazzo Fontana

Ca' Pesaro

Ca' d'Oro

Palazzo Sagredo

Palazzo Michiel d.Colonne

Strada Nuova

Canal Grande

Pescaria

C. del Campanile

Calle D. Botteri

38

39

37

San Giovanni Elemosinario

Palazzo dei Dieci Savi

San Silvestro

36

40

S. Silvestro

Rialto

35

Ponte di Rialto

Campo S. Aponal

San Giacomo di Rialto

S. Giovanni Crisostomo

Ca' da Mosto

33

Rio di S.G. Crisostomo

S.M. dei Miracoli

Palazzo Sanudo

Campo S.S. Giovanni e Paolo

Rio di S. Marina

Fondaco dei Tedeschi

Campo S. Bartolomeo

San Bartolomeo

26

Riva del Ferro

C. Stagner

Merc S. Salvador

Santa Maria della Fava

Palazzo Priuli

Pal. Donà

Campo S. Maria Formosa

25

24

23

Palazzo Querini-Stampalia

Palazzo Bembo

Pal. Dandolo

Palazzo Loredan

Riva del Carbon

Pal. Grimani

San Benedetto

San Luca

San Salvatore

22

Merc. S.

Salvadore

Campo S. Luca

Calle Fabbri

Calle Coldoni

del Fuseri

18

17

Campo Manin

Pal. Contarini del Bovolo

16

C. Mandola

Campo S. Angelo

C. Caotorta

Ateneo Veneto

Teatro La Fenice

14

Campo S. Fantin

Pisc. di Frezzeria

Rio delle Veste

Larga XXII Marzo

S.S. Moise

San Moise

C. Vallaresso

Bacino Orseolo

Piazza San Marco

Basilica di San Marco

Pal. Patriarcale

19

Sant' Apollonia

Palazzo Trevisan-Cappello

20

21

Rio di S. Marco

Piazzetta

Palazzo Ducale

Giardinetti Reali

Molo

Riva Degli Schiavoni

Palazzo Corner (Ca' Grande)

Casina delle Rose

Campo S.M. del Giglio

S.M. del Giglio

15

Palazzi Contarini

San Marco Vallaresso

San Marco Giardinetti

Palazzo Dario

Pal. Venier dei Leoni

San Gregorio

Santa Maria della Salute

Rio D. Fornace

12

13

Punta della Dogana

Dogana al Mare

Seminario Patriarcale

Le Zattere

Riva Degli Schiavoni

29

28

27

30

C. del Vin

31

Rio dei Greci

C. della Pietà

C. de Dose

32

C. del Forno

Riva   degli   Schiavoni

P. de la Ca' di Dio

Bacino San Marco

34

Santi Apostoli

Campo SS Apostoli

Rio D. Santi

393

ⓗ Family-Friendly Hotels

Hotel Bernardi-Semenzato (*see p. 396*)   Owner Maria Teresa moonlights as an English teacher on the side. As a mother of three herself, she's the perfect host for families who will appreciate the renovated rooms that easily pass as triples or quads.

Locanda Sturion (*see p. 403*)   Scottish-born Helen or her daughter Nicolette will settle you into any of the spacious rooms, two of which will guarantee the special thrill of a Grand Canal view within sight of the famous Rialto Bridge. Make sure the 69-step hike to the lobby is not a deterrent for the little ones or for those who haven't mastered the art of traveling lightly.

Albergo Guerrato (*see p. 403*)   Young lire-conscious families will enjoy the inexpensive rates of this former convent where an informal and casual atmosphere is nurtured by the upbeat brothers-in-law that run it as if it were their home. Kids should get a kick out of being in the middle of the market's hubbub right on the Grand Canal and within steps of the Rialto Bridge. Spacious rooms are an added plus.

Hotel Ai Do Mori (*see p. 391*)   Good news for weary legs: The larger family-oriented rooms are on the lower floors in this elevator-challenged hotel. Can-do English speaking Antonella has a solution for every problem.

---

bedspreads matching the generously draped curtains, I slumbered in one of the many canal-side rooms within earshot of the serenades of the passing gondoliers. High ceilings (and no elevator) make rooms on the first two floors preferable for some. Air-conditioning is only in rooms with private bathrooms. By Venice standards, the one-star (for the moment) Gambero has all the appreciated trappings of a three-star hotel at two-star prices. Book it while you can: the above-quoted 1999 prices are likely to increase in 2000. Guests receive a 10% discount in the lively and always popular ground-floor Le Bistrot de Venise (see "Great Deals on Dining," below), co-owned by the hotel.

✪ **Hotel ai do Mori.** San Marco 658 (on C. Larga San Marco), 30124 Venezia. ☎ **041/ 52-04-817** or 52-89-293. Fax 041/52-05-328. 11 units, 7 with bathroom. A/C TV TEL. 70,000L ($41.20) single without bathroom; 130,000L ($76.50) double without bathroom, 160,000L ($94.10) double with bathroom; 160,000L ($94.10) triple without bathroom, 210,000L ($123.50) triple with bathroom; 200,000L ($117.65) quad without bathroom, 280,000 ($164.70) quad with bathroom. Ask about off-season rates. MC, V. Vaporetto: San Marco. Exit the Piazza San Marco underneath the Torre d. l'Orologio (Clock Tower); turn right at the first opportunity (at the Max Mara store) and you'll find the hotel on the left, just before McDonalds.

Antonella, the *simpatica* 30-something owner of this supercentral hotel just two steps from the Clock Tower, creates a professionally run yet comfortable ambience with special care given to Frommer's readers. The more accessible lower floors (there is no elevator and the hotel begins on the second floor with most rooms above) are slightly larger and offer interesting rooftop views, but the somewhat smaller top-floor rooms boast wonderful views that embrace San Marco's many domes and the nearby Torre dell'Orologio (Clock Tower), whose two bronze Moors ring the bells every hour. All rooms are sunny and pleasant, enhanced by the ambitious improvement-minded owner/manager. You can't top these prices for the location and the amenities you'll find: large double-paned windows to ensure quiet, brand-new bathrooms (with hair dryers), air-conditioning, and wonderfully firm mattresses for tourist-weary bodies.

Hotel Gallini. San Marco 3673 (C. d. Verona), 30124 Venezia. ☎ **041/52-04-515.**
Fax 041/52-09-103. TEL. 50 units, 40 with bathroom. 100,000L ($58.80) single without bath-
room, 145,000L ($85.30) single with bathroom; 150,000L ($88.25) double without bath-
room, 205,000L ($120.60) double with bathroom; 270,000L ($158.80) triple with bathroom.
Off-season rates are approximately 10% lower. Rates include continental breakfast. AE, MC, V.
Closed Nov 15–Carnevale. Vaporetto: Sant'Angelo. Follow the zigzag road southward toward
Campo Sant'Angelo. Exit the campo at northeast end by taking the store-lined C. de la Mandola. Take a right at the "Ottica" optometrist onto C. d. Assasini, which becomes C. d. Verona.

The Gallini is a good-value, spotlessly maintained family run choice and large enough
to offer more availability during peak periods. The amiable Ceciliati brothers, Adriano
and Gabriele, have been at the helm since 1952, so you can be assured that things run
without a glitch. Though the fire that destroyed the neighboring La Fenice opera
house in 1997 temporarily cast a pall on this area, life is back to normal and goes on
in the nearby Campo Sant'Angelo and its adjacent Campo San Stefano. Four floors
(but no elevator!) of bright, spacious rooms simply furnished and big modern bathrooms are kept clean as a whistle by a smiling housekeeping staff. Rich-looking marble
floors in green, red, or speckled black alternate with intricate parquet floors to lend an
old-world air of stateliness. Gondoliers' tunes waft up to the 10 rooms overlooking the
narrow Rio d. Verona. A few rooms are equipped with air-conditioning for a daily supplement of 10,000L ($5.90).

Hotel Locanda Fiorita. San Marco 3457 (Campiello Novo off Cam. S. Stefano), 30124
Venezia. ☎ **041/52-34-754.** Fax 041/52-28-043. E-mail: locafior@tin.it. 13 units, 10 with
bathroom. TV TEL. 95,000L ($55.90) single without bathroom, 120,000L ($70.60) single with
bathroom; 150,000L ($88.25) double without bathroom, 170,000L ($100.00) double with
bathroom. Extra person 30% of room rate. Rates include continental breakfast. AE, DC, MC, V.
Vaporetto: Accademia. Cross the Accademia Bridge and continue north to the large Campo San
Stefano. Cross the campo and at the far northern end after the church, take a left at a flower
stand. Go up three steps to reach the raised campiello, where you'll find the villalike hotel.

New owners have created a charming hostelry in this striking *rosso veneziano* (Venetian
red) hotel, parts of which date from the 1400s, with a voluminous wisteria vine that
partially covers its facade (usually blooming in May or June). An excellent choice year-
round, whether for its simple rooms and new bathrooms—both recently renovated—
or its enviable location on a tiny picture-perfect campiello off the far grander Campo
San Stefano, one of the city's most beloved. Two lucky rooms (no. 1 and 10) have their
own little terraces beneath the lush wisteria pergola and overlook the campiello—
inquire upon arrival. Legend goes that the city's handful of small raised campielli such
as this one were once used as burial grounds (particularly during times of pestilence),
hence the elevated pavement. (For centuries, however, the city has used the island of
San Michele as the official cemetery.) Air-conditioning is optional in most rooms at
20,000L ($11.75) daily. In 1998, an annex was renovated in a lovely but less archi-
tecturally interesting palazzo just 1 block away, with a second independant annex
scheduled to open sometime in 1999. Some of the first annex's eight rooms overlook
a tiny canal: at 220,000L ($129.40) they are slightly more elegant in decor with
amenities such as air-conditioning (included) and newer bathrooms, but I would still
opt for a room in the main building if available.

Hotel Locanda Remedio. San Marco 4412 (on C. d. Remedio), 30122 Venezia. ☎ **041/
52-06-232.** Fax 041/52-10-485. 13 units, all with bathroom. A/C MINIBAR TV TEL. 120,000L
($70.60) single; 200,000L ($117) double; 250,000L ($147) triple. Rates include breakfast.
Rates reflect special discounts for readers of this book. MC, V. Vaporetto: San Marco. Exit Pz.
San Marco under the Torre del'Orologio Clock Tower, turn right at the Max Mara store onto
C. Larga San Marco; at the Ristorante All'Angelo turn left onto C. va al Ponte del'Angelo, and
take the 1st right onto Ramo dell' Anzolo. Cross the small footbridge onto the C. d. Remedio;
the hotel will be on your right.

Renato is another of the new breed of Venice's young hotel owner/managers, striving to create quality and charming lodgings at moderate rates—something relatively nonexistent in this tourist town until recently. By Venetian standards, the Remedio offers unusually large double rooms in an ancient palazzo in a surprisingly quiet neighborhood just steps from the tourist-dense Piazza San Marco area and its teaming side streets. Many of the larger rooms are located on the second floor (one even has lovely ceiling frescoes and a number have enlarged and modernized bathrooms) off a ballroom-size corridor/salon naturally lit by oversized leaded windows.

WORTH A SPLURGE

✪ **Hotel Flora.** San Marco 2283 (off C. Larga XXII Marzo, near Cam. San Moisè), 44 units, all with bathroom. ☎ **041/520-58-44.** Fax 041/522-82-17. www.hotelflora.it. E-mail: info@hotelflora.it. A/C MINIBAR TV TEL. 260,000L ($152.95) single; 340,000L ($200) double. Extra person 85,000L ($50). Rates include continental breakfast. AE, DC, MC, V. Slow season discounts of approximately 15%. Vaporetto: San Marco. Walk down C. Valleresso and turn left on to the V. XXII Marzo. After crossing the San Moisè Bridge and passing the Deutsche Bank, you'll see a sign on left side of street for the hotel, located down a narrow passageway off the V. XXII Marzo.

Utter the expression "small hotel of great charm" and my mind drifts to images of the refined Flora. Its simple name refers to its greatest attribute, a jewel-like patio garden immediately visible beyond the welcoming lobby. A delightful place to have breakfast, afternoon tea, or an aperitif, it is enclosed by climbing vines and ivy-covered walls, with an antique well, potted flowers, and blooming plants that create a cool green enclave, one of the hotel's many pleasant places to retreat and sit with your thoughts or a companion. Seamlessly run by two generations of the highly professional Romanelli family and their friendly staff, the Flora has long been one of Venice's favorite spots and is ideally located just west of the American Express office on a tony shopping street. Despite rooms that can vary greatly (from small to standard in size, and rather plain to the nicest ones overlooking the garden), and small bathrooms that could do with a facelift, it is forever full of loyal devotees and romance-seekers. On the top-floor, room no. 47 looks onto the alleged Desdemona's palazzo (of Shakespeare's tragedy *Othello*), with the dome of La Salute Church beyond.

IN CANNAREGIO

Expect most (but not all) of these least expensive suggestion to be in or near the train station neighborhood, one full of trinket shops and budget hotels. This area is comparatively charmless (though safe), and in the high-season months is wall-to-wall with tourists who window-shop their way to Piazza San Marco, an easy half-hour to 45-minute stroll away. Vaporetto connections from the train station are convenient.

Hotel Adua. Cannaregio 233a (on Lista di Spagna), 30121 Venezia. ☎ **041/71-61-84.** Fax 041/24-40-162. 13 units, 9 with bathroom. TV TEL. 80,000L ($47) single without bathroom; 125,000L ($73.50) single with bathroom; 95,000L ($55.90) double without bathroom, 160,000L ($94.10) double with bathroom; 128,000L ($75.30) triple without bathroom, 216,000L ($127.05) triple with bathroom. Breakfast 10,000L ($5.90). DC, MC, V. Vaporetto: Ferrovia. Exit the train station and turn left onto the Lista di Spagna. The hotel is relatively close by on your right.

The Adua family, in the low-end hotel business more than 30 years, has closed its small enterprise for a makeover that was scheduled to be finished by spring 1999. The good news is that this longtime favorite stands to be reborn as an upscale and more attractive operation, the bad news is I didn't get to witness the reincarnation firsthand. I continue to include it, however, as the rooms were on the largish side even in their 1970s prerefurbishment days—and with the owners' many years in the hotel world,

I'm banking on the hope that the improvement can only be a most favorable one. An independent palazzo across the street with nine refurbished rooms are part of the upgrade and expansion. Proximity to the generally charm-challenged train station area keeps even the raised rates reasonable.

☻ Hotel Bernardi-Semenzato. Cannaregio 4366 (on C. de l'Oca), 30121 Venezia. ☎ **041/52-27-257.** Fax 041/52-22-424. Main house: 18 units, 10 with bathroom. Annex: 8 units, 5 with bathroom. A/C MINIBAR TV TEL. 63,000L ($37.05) single without bathroom, 84,000L ($49.40) single with bathroom; 85,000L ($50) double without bathroom, 130,000L ($76.50) double with bathroom; 120,000L ($70.60) triple without bathroom, 145,000L ($85.30) triple with bathroom. Rates include continental breakfast. Inquire about off-season rates. AE, MC, V. Vaporetto: Ca D'Oro. From the vaporetto stop, walk a short distance straight ahead to S. Nova, turn right in the direction of Cam. SS. Apostoli, and look for Cannaregio 4309, a stationery/toy store on your left; turn left on this narrow side street, the C. Duca, then take the first right onto C. de l'Oca.

From outside, this weather-worn palazzo just north of the Rialto Bridge area doesn't begin to hint of the recent top-to-toe renovation, one that has left hand-hewn ceiling beams exposed, rooms outfitted with tastefully coordinated headboard/bedspread sets, and bathrooms newly modernized and brightly retiled. The young and enthusiastic English-speaking owners, Maria Teresa and Leonardo Pepoli, aspire to three-star style, and may eventually aim at a two-star category, but are content to offer one-star rates (prices get even more interesting when off-season rates apply). The addition of a newly refurbished annex 3 blocks away offers you the chance to feel like you've rented your own aristocratic apartment, with large rooms boasting brand-new bathrooms (all annex rooms are expected to have private bathrooms by the end of 1999; inquire when booking), intricate parquet floors, and Murano chandeliers—room no. 6 overlooks a narrow canal, no. 5 the lovely garden of a palazzo next door.

Hotel Dolomiti. Cannaregio 72–74 (on C. Priuli), 30121 Venezia. ☎ **041/71-51-13.** Fax 041/71-66-35. 50 units, 20 with bathroom. TEL. 90,000L ($52.95) single without bathroom, 135,000L ($79.40) single with bathroom; 110,000–130,000L ($64.70–$76.50) double without bathroom; 165,000–190,000L ($97.05–$111.75) double with bathroom; 162,000L ($95.30) triple without bathroom, 225,000L ($132.35) triple with bathroom; 192,000L ($112.95) quad without bathroom, 260,000L ($152.95) quad with bathroom. Rates include breakfast. MC, V. Closed Nov 15–Jan 31. Vaporetto: Ferrovia. As you exit train station turn left onto the Lista di Spagna and take the first left onto C. Priuli.

Late arrivals or early departures are the only reason to stay in the vicinity of the train station. To make the best of an extratouristy neighborhood, here is an old-fashioned, comfortable, and reliable choice. With 50 large (many comfortable for families of four), clean, but ordinary rooms spread over four floors (and no elevator!), you have a better chance of finding available accommodations at this family-owned hotel than at some of the smaller ones we suggest. Sergio and Lorenzo, the efficient polylingual front-desk staff in the old-world lobby, supply weather forecasts, umbrellas, restaurant suggestions, and a big smile after your long day meandering about this remarkable city.

☻ Hotel Geremia. Cannaregio 290/A (Cam. San Geremia), 30121 Venezia. ☎ **041/ 71-62-45.** Fax 041/52-42-342. 20 units, 14 with bathroom. TV TEL. 125,000L ($73.50) double without bathroom, 190,000L ($111.75) double with bathroom; inquire about rates and availability of singles, triples, and quads. Rates reflect special discounts for readers of this book. 20% discounts in off-season. Rates include continental breakfast. AE, MC, V. Vaporetto: Ferrovia. From the train station, turn left (east) onto Lista di Spagna and follow it until arriving in the Cam. San Geremia. Hotel is on left.

Show your Frommer's book upon check-in, and mention it when booking and the management will offer you the special rates above. If this renovated two-star hotel had an elevator and was located in the high-rent San Marco neighborhood, you'd pay twice the price. Work wasn't yet finished during my last visit, but you can expect tastefully renovated rooms—ideally one of the eight that overlook the small campo (better yet, one of two top-floor rooms with a small private terrace for guests who relish a Stairmaster-type workout). All rooms were previously outfitted with either blond wood paneling or deep green or burnished rattan headboards and matching chairs, a look that should survive the renovation. Top-of-the-line bathrooms offer three-star amenities such as hair dryers and heated towel racks. English-speaking owner/manager Claudio will regale you with helpful tips as well as free passes to the winter Casino, just 10 minutes by foot. It's also 5 to 10 minutes by foot east of the train station (pack light!).

Hotel Santa Lucia. Cannaregio 358 (on C. d. Misericordia), 30121 Venezia. ☎ and fax **041/71-51-80.** 18 units, 7 with bathroom. 80,000L ($47.05) single without bathroom; 130,000L ($76.50) double without bathroom, 150,000L ($88.25) double with bathroom; 140,000L ($82.35) triple without bathroom, 180,000L ($105.90) triple with bathroom; 220,000L ($129.40) quad with bathroom. Rates include continental breakfast. AE, DC, MC, V. Erratic winter closing, generally Jan 7–Feb 10. Vaporetto: Ferrovia. Exiting the train station, turn left onto Lista di Spagna and take the second left on C. d. Misericordia.

This rather contemporary building and its sunny flagstone terrace bordered by roses, oleander, and ivy create a quiet oasis in the hubbub of the train-station neighborhood. White patio furniture lures hotel guests to linger over breakfast on the terrace (April until October), served in an old-fashioned way, with coffee and tea brought in sterling-silver pots (guests are also welcome to brown-bag their lunch and enjoy it here). Friendly owner Emilia Gonzato oversees her operation with pride. The large rooms are simple but bright and clean—it takes little to overlook the low-watt bulbs and soft mattresses (something I've found in deluxe hotels at four times these rates). She doesn't speak much English (though it rarely seems to get in the way), but her son, Gianangelo, does.

IN CASTELLO

Casa Fontana. Castello 4701 (Cam. San Provolo), 30122. ☎ **041/522-05-79.** Fax 041/ 523-10-40. www.hotelfontana.it. E-mail: hplcasa@gpnet.it. 16 units, all with bathroom. TV TEL. 150,000L ($88.25) single; 250,000L ($147.05) double; 300,000L ($176.50) triple; 330,000L ($194.10) quad. AE, DC, MC, V. Vaporetto: San Zaccaria. From the Riva Schiavoni, take any narrow street north to the Campiello SS. Filippo e Giacomo. Exit this small campo from the east side (in the direction of Cam. San Zaccaria) until you come to the small Cam. San Provolo.

The warmth and coziness of the Stainer family's Casa Fontana literally beams out of the lobby's leaded glass windows—it drew me in. I found myself attracted to the homeyness of its old-fashioned ambience, a commodity increasingly more difficult to find in Italy's tourist cities and modernized hotels. The charm is in no small part due to the three generations of Stainers behind the front desk since 1967 (for centuries before that the Casa Fontana was a convent for Austrian nuns) and still involved in the hotel's day-to-day affairs. Situated on the main strip heading east of the Basilica San Marco (an easy stroll away) that connects the piazza with the Church of San Zaccaria, the four-story hotel offers a pensione-like family atmosphere coupled with a crisp professional operation of well-kept-up comfortable rooms (two on higher floors have private terraces) and well-lit bathrooms. There's no elevator, but those not weak of knee who request the higher floors are compensated by views of San Zaccaria's handsome 15th-century facade. The Fontana's prices are on the high side, but I include it here nonetheless, given its central location that justifies the price, and because it is more compatible with the hotels of this category than if placed with the fancier choices of the worth-a-splurge category below.

Frommer's Discounts

Reading Frommer's has its privileges. Many hotels recognize the name and will give readers a Frommer's discount. Just show the book when you check in. A lot of the prices listed in the book apply only to the likes of you and me—people who use this book.

○ **Casa Verardo.** Castello 4765 (at the foot of Ponte Storto), 30122 Venezia. ☎ **041/ 52-86-127.** Fax 041/52-32-765. 10 units, 9 with bathroom. 80,000L ($47.05) single without bathroom; 120,000L ($70.58) single with bathroom; 140,000L ($82.35) double without bathroom, 160,000L ($94.10) double with bathroom, 200,000L ($117.65) triple without bathroom, 240,000L ($141.20) triple with bathroom. MC, V. Vaporetto: San Zaccaria. From vaporetto stop, walk straight ahead on the C. d. Rasse to Cam. SS. Filippo e Giacomo; cross the small campo to take the C. Rippeto la Sacrestia, which begins at Bar Europa. Cross the first small bridge, the Ponte Storto, and you'll find the hotel immediately on your right.

Hats off to the amiable Massimo and Sandra for the no-corners-cut metamorphosis of this quaint hotel. From the moment you step inside the wood-paneled lobby anchored by an ancient stone well, to your morning enjoyed on the small but lovely open-air breakfast terrace with terra-cotta pavement and blooming geraniums, you'll feel welcomed and relaxed. Thought and care are everywhere evident in the top-to-toe renovation undertaken by the young and enthusiastic new owners of what was once a run-down but ever popular pensione in an area a stone's throw from Piazza San Marco. The good stuff mercifully got salvaged—time-warped mosaic floors, Murano-glass chandeliers, imposing armoires—but everything else got tossed and replaced by new wiring, new mattresses, fresh wallpapering and—voilà! A guaranteed future Frommer's favorite was born. By the end of 1998, the last of the bathrooms were scheduled to have been renovated, making this work-in-progress a completed showcase of this young couples' style and graciousness.

Foresteria Valdese (Palazzo Cavagnis). Castello 5170 (at the end of C. Lunga Santa Maria Formosa), 30122 Venezia. ☎ **041/528-67-97.** Fax 041/241-62-38. www.doge.it/ valdesi/01.htm. E-mail: valdesi@doge.it. 6 units with bathroom and TV (2–4 beds), 3 dorms (8, 11, and 16 beds), none with bathroom. 2 mini-apts. (sleeping 4 and 5, minimum stay often required) with kitchen and bathroom. 29,000L ($17.05) dorm bed; 60,000L ($35.30) per person double or triple with bathroom; 40,000L ($23.50) per person quad with bathroom; 170,000–180,000L ($100–$105.88) apt. sleeping 4 or 5. Rates include breakfast except in apts. Closed 2 weeks in Nov. MC, V. Vaporetto: Rialto. Head southeast to the Cam. Santa Maria Formosa; look for the Bar all'Orologio, just where C. Lunga Santa Maria Formosa begins. The campo is just about equidistant from Pz. San Marco and the Rialto Bridge.

Those lucky enough to get a place at this weathered, albeit elegant, 16th-century palazzo will find simple accommodations in a charming *foresteria*, the name given to religious institutions that traditionally provided lodging for pilgrims and guests. Affiliated with Italy's Waldesian and Methodist Church, the large dormitory-style rooms are often booked with visiting church groups, though everyone is warmly welcomed and you'll find an international and inter-religious mix here. Each of the plainly furnished rooms in this once-noble residence opens onto a balcony overlooking a quiet canal. The frescoes that grace the high ceilings in the doubles and two of the dorms are by the same artist who decorated the Correr Museum. The two apartments complete with kitchen facilities, are the best budget choice in town for traveling families of four or five. A complete five-year renovation, which began in 1995 (with minimal inconvenience to guests) is nearing its completion. The reception is open Monday to Saturday from 9am to 1pm and 6 to 8pm and Sunday 9am to 1pm.

○ **Hotel Al Piave.** Castello 4838/40 (Ruga Giuffa), 30122 Venezia. ☎ **041/52-85-174.** Fax 041/52-38-512. www.elmoro.com/alpiave. E-mail: hotel.alpiav@iol.it. 13 units, 11 with bathroom. A/C TV TEL. Special rates for Frommer's readers: 160,000L ($94.10) single with bathroom; 150,000L ($88.25) double without bathroom, 220,000L ($129.40) double with bathroom; 280,000L ($164.70) triple suite with bathroom; 350,000L ($205.90) quad suite with bathroom. 400,000L ($235.30) apt. sleeping 5 (lower rates for fewer guests). Rates include continental breakfast. Closed Jan 7 until Carnival time. AE, DC, DISC, MC, V. Vaporetto: San Zaccaria. Walk straight ahead on the C. d. Rasse to the small Cam. SS. Filippo e Giacomo. Exit the campo right (east) and continue to the next small Cam. San Provolo. Here take a left (north), cross the first small footbridge and follow the zigzag calle, which becomes Ruga Giuffa, a popular store-lined strip.

The Puppin family's small and ultra tasteful hotel is a steal at these prices: This level of attention coupled with the sophisticated *buon gusto* in decor and spirit is a rare find in Venice's two-star price category: orthopedic mattresses, immaculate white lace curtains, stain glass windows, spanking new bathrooms—I'd give this place two stars if I could (the end of 1999 may see all rooms with private baths). A discerning, savvy international clientele has ferreted out this classy spot, so you'll need to reserve far in advance. Located on a busy store-lined calle a convenient and pleasant 10-minute walk northeast of Piazza San Marco, you may have a hard time finding it the first time around, but it's definitely worth the search: so pack light and just ask any Venetian to point you in the direction of the well-trammeled Ruga Giuffa.

WORTH A SPLURGE

Hotel Campiello. Castello 4647 (Campiello d. Vin), 30122 Venezia. ☎ **041/52-05-764.** Fax 041/52-05-798. www.hcampiello.it. E-mail: campiello@hcampiello.it. 16 units, all with bathroom. A/C TV TEL. 170,000L ($100) single; 260,000L ($152.95) double; 325,000L ($191.20) triple. Rates are about 30% lower in off-season. Rates include continental breakfast. AE, DC, MC, V. Vaporetto: San Zaccaria. Facing the well-known waterfront Savoia e Jolanda Hotel, take the narrow alleyway on its left, which leads to the small Campiello d. Vin; the hotel is on your right.

This gem of a family-run hotel, located within easy striking distance of the Piazza San Marco, is nestled on a tiny quiet campiello just off the prestigious Riva degli Schiavoni (and the canal-front location of the legendary Danieli Hotel and other pricey five-star contenders). These prices are hardly considered a splurge in Venice. The atmosphere here is airy and bright, largely due to the seamless and smiling management of the always-present Bianchini sisters, Monica and Nicoletta; third-generation hoteliers at the helm, they are as attractive and charming as they are efficient and professional. A 1998 refurbishment transformed much of the guest rooms' contemporary style into a more traditional decor, with most done up in authentic art nouveau furnishings. The Campiello offers comfortable, relaxed hospitality and good-quality service that far surpasses its two-star status. The hotel's original 15th-century marble-mosaic pavement is still evident, a vestige of the days when this was a convent under the patronage of the nearby Church of San Zaccaria; you'll catch a glimpse of it in the lounge area, which opens onto a pleasant breakfast room where the buffet is an attractive and abundant affair.

IN DORSODURO

Hotel Alla Salute ("Da Cici"). Dorsoduro 222 (on Fond. Ca' Balà), 30123 Venezia. ☎ **041/52-35-404.** Fax 041/52-22-271. 58 units, 22 with bathroom, 12 with shower only/no toilet. TEL. 110,000L ($64.70) single without bathroom, 150,000L ($88.25) single with shower only; 140,000L ($82.35) double without bathroom, 200,000L ($117.65) double with bathroom; 210,000L ($123.50) triple without bathroom, 270,000L ($158.80) triple with bathroom. Rates include continental breakfast. No credit cards. Closed for most of the period Nov 15–Feb 1, but usually open for Christmas. Vaporetto: Salute. Facing La Salute Church, turn right and head to the first small bridge. Cross it and walk as straight ahead as you can to the next narrow canal, where you'll turn left (before crossing the bridge) onto Fond. Ca' Balà.

An airy lobby with beamed ceilings and marble floors, a small but lovely terrace garden where breakfast is served in warm weather, and cozy cocktail bar occupy the ground level of this converted 17th-century private palazzo on the picturesque Rio della Fornace. Upstairs, the comfortable guest rooms have high ceilings and huge windows (10 with canal view and four facing the garden), many of them large enough to accommodate families of four or even five at 50,000L ($29.40) per person above the triple-room rates. The Salute is in a secluded residential neighborhood just off the main strip leading to the Guggenheim Collection, behind La Salute church.

Hotel Falier. Dorsoduro 130 (Salizzada San Pantalon) 30135. ☎ **041/71-08-82.** Fax 041/71-10-05. www.hotelfalier.com. E-mail: falier@tin.it. 19 rooms, all with bathroom, TV TEL. 200,000L ($117.65) single; 240,000L ($141.20) double. Rates discounted 50% during low season. Rates include continental breakfast. AE, MC, V. Vaporetto: Ferrovia. If you've packed lightly, the walk from the train station is easy, easier yet from the Piazzale Roma. From the train station, cross the Scalzi Bridge, turn right along the Grand Canal for 150 feet, then left toward the Tolentini Church. Continue along the Salizzada San Pantalon in the general direction of Cam. Santa Margherita.

Owned by the same fellow who put the lovely Hotel American (see below) on Venice's three-star map, the Falier is his savvy interpretation of less expensive lodging, particularly worth booking when half-price low season rates apply. Renovated in the early 1990s, it is a reliably good-value at this price range with standard-size rooms (and modern bathrooms) attractively decorated with white lace curtains, flowered bedspreads, and some with wood-beamed ceilings. The old-world lobby sets your first impression with potted ferns and Doric columns and triangled, marble floors. The neighborhood needs mentioning, as detractors may feel the need to be closer to Piazza San Marco, when the truth is the Falier is much closer to the real Venice, in a lively area lined with stores and bars. It is situated between the large Campo Santa Margherita, one of the city's most characterful piazzas, and the much visited Frari Church.

Hotel Galleria. Dorsoduro 878a (at the foot of the Accademia Bridge), 30123 Venezia. ☎ **041/52-32-489.** Fax 041/52-04-172. E-mail: galleria@tin.it. 10 units, 8 with bathroom. 95,000L ($55.90) single without bathroom; 135,000–145,000L ($79.40–$85.30) double without bathroom; 165,000–195,000L ($97.05–$114.70) double with bathroom; 250,000L ($147.05) triple with bathroom. Rates include continental breakfast. AE, DC, MC, V; personal checks from U.S. banks. Vaporetto: Accademia. With the Accademia Bridge behind you, the hotel is just to your left next to the Totem Il Canale art gallery.

Location, location, location! If you're stuck on a room with a view, step through this 17th-century palazzo's leaded-glass doors and ascend the narrow spiral staircase to the Galleria, renovated in 1997 by the new owners Luciano Benedetti and Stefano Franceshini with red velvet wallpaper (potentially jarring to the non-Venetian eye, but traditionally Venetian) and oriental carpets. What puts this charming one-floor hotel just next to the Accademia Bridge on the map are the six rooms commanding views of the Grand Canal—the same awesome views without the usual awesome rates of Venice's grandes dames hotels. Even the rooms not lucky enough to overlook Venice's aquatic main street will still provide you with a sense of the palazzo's history and a convenient base in the shadow of the Galleria dell'Accademia, the city's most important museum. Not yet open at the time of this printing (opening Carnival 1999), but likely to be as appealing a choice as the Galleria, the owners have created the **Locanda Leone Bianco,** housed in a converted 13th-century palazzo on the Rio degli Apostoli across the Grand Canal from the Rialto Market (☎ and fax **041/523-35-72;** e-mail: leonebi@tin.it). Of the eight spacious rooms with bathroom, three overlook the Grand Canal northeast of the Rialto Bridge (200,000 to 250,000L ($117.65 to $147.05 double) in the sestiere of Cannaregio.

Hotel Messner. Dorsoduro 216/237 (on Fond. Ca' Balà), 30123 Venezia. ☎ **041/52-27-443.** Fax 041/52-27-266. E-mail: a.nardi@lashnet.it. Main House: 11 units, all with bathroom. Annex: 20 units, all with bathroom. A/C TEL (main house only). Main House: 136,500L ($80.30) single; 200,000L ($117.65) double; 252,000L ($148.25) triple; 284,000L ($167.05) quad. Room rates for Main House only reflect special discounts for readers of this book. Annex: 121,000L ($71.20) single; 168,000L ($93.35) double; 221,000L ($130) triple; 160,000L ($105.25) quad, 242,000L ($142.35) quad. Rates include continental breakfast. AE, DC, MC, V. Closed mid-Nov–mid-Dec. Vaporetto: Salute. Follow the small canal immediately to the right of La Salute Church. Turn right onto third bridge and walk straight ahead until you see the white awning of the hotel just before reaching the Rio d. Fornace canal.

This two-part hotel consists of the *Casa Principale* (Main House), where you'll find a handsome beamed-ceiling lobby and 11 rooms in a stately 14th-century palazzo, and the quasi-adjacent 15th-century annex, with 20 rooms, just 20 meters away. With three rooms overlooking the picturesque Rio della Fornace, and the close attention to detail in decor, the **Main House** is usually preferred, but other guests opt for the independence and slightly lower rates of the **Annex** (where groups and students are more likely to be accommodated). The similarly priced Hotel Alla Salute next door (see above) is a convenient alternative when the Messner is full. Both are good canal-side choices for this pleasant residential neighborhood close to La Salute Church and the Guggenheim Collection.

Pensione La Calcina. Dorsoduro 780 (Zattere al Gesuati) 30123. ☎ **041/520-64-66.** Fax 041/522-70-45. 29 units, all with bathroom. A/C TEL. 120,000–150,000L ($70.60–$88.25) single; 170,000L ($100) double; 240,000–280,000L ($141.20–$164.70) double with canal view. Rates include continental breakfast. AE, D, MC, V. Vaporetto: Zattere. Follow le Zattere east; hotel is on the water before the first bridge.

British author John Ruskin holed up here in 1876 when penning *The Stones of Venice* (you can still request his room, no. 2, but good luck), one reason perhaps it has remained to this day a quasi-sacred preference of writers, artists, and those of a Bohemian bent. You can imagine their horror when word of a recent overhaul was announced—one that was executed so sensitively (and successfully) that the third-generation owners refused to update the rooms with TVs (don't even ask about where to plug in your laptop) nor raise rates, keeping them at an all-time low for such lovely waterfront accommodations. On the sunny Zattere in the southern untrampled Dorsoduro district of Venice, half of the unfussy but luminous and comfortable rooms overlook the wide Giudecca Canal in the direction of Palladio's 16th-century Redentore church. Alternate between the hotel's outdoor floating terrace or rooftop terrace, each a glorious way to begin or end any day.

WORTH A SPLURGE

Hotel American. Dorsoduro 628 (on Fond. Bragadin), 30123 Venezia. ☎ **041/52-04-733.** Fax 041/52-04-048. www.hotelamerican.com. E-mail: hotameri@tin.it. 29 units, all with bathroom. A/C MINIBAR TV TEL. 230,000L ($135.30) single; 340,000L ($200) double; 370,000L ($217.65) double with canal view. Rates include buffet breakfast. Extra person 85,000L ($50). AE, MC, V. Vaporetto: Accademia. Veer left around the Galleria dell'Accademia museum, taking the first left turn and walk straight ahead until you cross the first small footbridge. Turn right to follow the Fondamenta Bragadin that runs alongside the Rio di San Vio canal. The hotel is on your left.

Despite its potentially unromantic name (did you travel transatlantic for this?), the Hotel American is a splurge recommendation for both its style and its substance, one of the nicest of Venice's three-star hotels. The perfect combination of old-fashioned charm and utility, this three-story hotel located near the Peggy Guggenheim Collection offers a dignified lobby and breakfast room liberally dressed with lovely oriental carpets and marble flooring, polished woods, and leaded-glass windows and French doors. The best choices here are the larger corner rooms and the nine overlooking a quiet canal; some even have small terraces overlooking the canal. Every room is outfitted with traditional Venetian-style furnishings that usually include hand-painted furniture and Murano glass chandeliers. If it's late spring, don't miss a drink on the second-floor terrace beneath a wisteria arbor dripping with plump violet blossoms.

✪ **Pensione Accademia.** Dorsoduro 1058 (Fondamenta Bollani west of the Accademia Bridge), 30123. ☎ **041/521-05-78.** Fax 041/523-91-52. 27 units, all with bathroom. A/C TV TEL. 185,000L ($108.80) single; 285,000–345,000L ($167.65–$202.95) double; 360,000–410,000L ($211.75–$241.20) triple. Off-season discounts available. AE, DC, V. Vaporetto: Accademia. Facing the Accademia Gallery, follow the narrow street to the right that leads to the Rio San Trovaso. Cross the small bridge and turn right, back toward the Grand Canal until you come to the wrought-iron gates of the villa/hotel.

Katherine Hepburn fans will remember this romantically sited canal-side villa as her fictional residence in her classic film *Summertime* (1955) with Rossano Brazzi. Formally and appropriately called the Villa Maravege (Villa of Wonders), it was built as a patrician villa in the 1600s and used as the Russian Consulate until the 1930s. Its outdoor landscaping (the Venetian rarities of a flowering patio on the small Rio San Trovaso that spills into the Grand Canal and the grassy formal rose garden behind) and interior details (original pavement, wood-beamed and decoratively painted ceilings) still create the impression of being a privileged guest in an aristocratic Venetian home from another era. The nicely decorated garden- or canal-view rooms vary, each tastefully done with a Venetian touch. Vicinity to the Gallerie dell'Accademia and a fiercely loyal clientele make availability here impossible unless you call months in advance (make that a year for Carnival time).

IN SAN POLO

Albergo Guerrato. San Polo 240/a (C. Drio la Scimia near the Rialto Market), 30125 Venice. ☎ **041/522-71-31.** Fax 041/528-59-27. E-mail: hguerrat@tin.it. 14 units, 9 with bathroom. 130,000L ($76.50) double without bathroom, 180,000L ($105.90) double with bathroom; 160,000L ($94.10) triple without bathroom, 210,000L ($123.50) triple with bathroom; 270,000L ($158.80) quad with bathroom. Rates include buffet breakfast. MC, V. Closed Dec 20–27, Jan 12–Feb 1. Vaporetto: Rialto. From north side of Rialto Bridge, walk straight ahead through stalls and market vendors. At corner location of Banca di Roma, turn right. Hotel at end of narrow street on right.

Funky, fun, and central, the Guerrato is as good, reliable, clean, and recommended a one-star hotel choice as you're likely to find at these rates. Piero and Roberto, the two young upbeat brothers-in-law who own and run this former pensione in a 13th-century convent, are responsible for much of the popularity that keeps this well-maintained favorite always full (mostly with Americans). Firm mattresses, good modern-ish bathrooms, and discerningly chosen flea-market finds (hand-carved art deco headboards and matching armoires) demonstrate their determination to run an inexpensive unpretentious hotel in overpriced Venice. Suffused with old-world charm (Maria Callas is a favorite CD choice) and good quality (they exaggerate not when describing their buffet breakfast as *buonissimo*), a lack of the usual amenities (no telephones or TVs in the rooms) keeps rates contained. Smack in the heart of the lively Rialto market, think of 7am wake-up noise before requesting one of six rooms that overlook the colorful (read: boisterous) marketplace.

WORTH A SPLURGE

Locanda Sturion. San Polo 679 (on Calle dello Sturion), 30125 Venezia. ☎ **041/52-36-243.** Fax 041/52-28-378. E-mail: sturion@tin.it. www.sayville.com\locanda-sturion. 11 rms, all with bath. A/C MINIBAR TV TEL. 171,000L ($100.58) single; 310,000L ($182.35) double without Grand Canal views, 360,000L ($211.75) double with Grand Canal view;

405,000L ($238.25) without Grand Canal view, 455,000L ($267.65) triples with Grand Canal View. Quads available. Special rates will be made for families. Rates include buffet breakfast. AE, MC, V. Vaporetto: Rialto. From the Rialto stop, cross the bridge, turn left at the other side, and walk along the Grand Canal; C. d. Sturion will be the 4th narrow alleyway on the right, just before San Polo 740.

Though there's been a pensione on this site since 1290, a recent gutting and rebuilding has made the Sturion into a tastefully reincarnated three-star hotel managed by the charming Scottish-born Helen and co-owner Flavia. The hotel's reception area is perched four flights (and 69 challenging steps) above the Grand Canal (and, depending on the location of your room, there could be even more stairs involved). Unfortunately, only two in-demand rooms offer canal views of the Rialto Bridge (as does the delightful breakfast room—is there a better way to start your day?) and command higher rates; they are spacious enough to accommodate families or groups of three, even four. The other rooms have charming views over the Rialto area rooftops. Throughout, the hotel is tastefully decorated with 18th-century inspired Venetian furniture, parquet floors, red carpeting, and rich damask-like wallpaper.

IN SANTA CROCE

۞ Hotel Ai Due Fanali. Santa Croce 946 (Cam. San Simeone Profeta), 30125. ☎ **041/ 71-84-90.** Fax 041/71-83-44. E-mail: request@aiduefanali.com. 17 units, all with bathroom. A/C MINIBAR TV TEL. 260,000L ($152.95) single; 330,000L ($194.10) double; 400,000L ($235.30) triple. Rates include continental breakfast. Off-season discounts of 40%. AE, MC, V. Vaporetto: a 10-min. walk from the train station or get off at the Riva di Biasio stop. Closed most of Jan.

Checking in at the Ai Due Fanali's 16th-century altar-turned-reception-desk is your first clue that this is the hotel of choice for lovers of aesthetics and impeccable taste. The hotel is located on a quiet square in the residential Santa Croce area, a 10-minute walk across the Grand Canal from the train station but a good 20 minute stroll from the Rialto Bridge. Signora Marina Stea and her daughter Stefania have beautifully restored a part of the 14th-century Scuola of the Church of San Simeon Grando with their innate "buon gusto." It is wall-to-wall evident from the lobby furnished with period pieces, to the third-floor breakfast terrace with a glimpse of the Grand Canal. Guest rooms boast headboards painted by local artisans, high-quality bed linens, chrome and gold bathroom fixtures, and good, fluffy towels. Prices drop considerably November 8 through March 30 with exception of Christmas week and Carnival. Ask about the four equally classy waterfront apartments with a view (and kitchenette) near Vivaldi's Church (La Pietà) east of Piazza San Marco sleeping 4 to 5 people at similar rates per person.

4 Great Deals on Dining

Eating cheaply in Venice is not easy, though by no means impossible. So plan well and don't rely on the serendipity that may serve you in other cities. If you've qualified for a **Rolling Venice card,** ask for the discount guide listing dozens of restaurants offering 10% to 30% discounts for cardholders. When budgeting for a meal, don't forget to calculate nominal charges for *servizio* (service) and a salad or *contorno* (vegetable side dish). And bear in mind that Venice is a city of early meals compared to Rome and other points south: you should be seated by 7:30 to 8:30pm. Most kitchens close at 10 or 10:30pm, even though the restaurant may stay open till 11:30pm or midnight.

BUDGET DINING   Pizza is the fuel of Naples and bruschetta and *crostini* (small, open-face sandwiches) the rustic soul food of Florence. In Venice it's *tramezzini*— small, triangular white-bread half-sandwiches filled with everything from thinly sliced meats and tuna salad to cheeses, and vegetables; and *cicchetti* (tapaslike finger foods

Fishy Business

If you order fresh fish or seafood, know it will hike the price of an average meal. And don't forget, the price indicated on the menu commonly refers to *l'etto* (per 100 grams), a fraction of the full cost (have the waiter estimate the full cost before ordering); larger fish are intended to feed two. Eating a meal based on the day's catch (restaurants are legally bound to print on the menu when the fish is frozen) will be enjoyable but never inexpensive, so avoid splurging on fish or seafood on Mondays when the Fish Market (and most self-respecting fish-serving restaurants) are closed.

such as calamari rings, speared fried olives, potato croquettes, or grilled polenta squares), traditionally washed down with a small glass of wine called an **ombra** (shadow). Venice offers countless neighborhood bars called *bacari* and cafes where you can stand or sit with a tramezzino, a selection of cicchetti, a *panino* (sandwich on a roll), or a *toast* (grilled ham and cheese sandwich). All of the above will cost approximately 1,500 to 2,500L (90¢ to $1.50) if you stand at the bar, as much as double when seated. Bar food is displayed countertop or in glass counters and usually sells out by late afternoon, so don't rely on it for a light dinner, though light lunches are a delight. A concentration of popular, well-stocked bars can be found along the Mercerie shopping strip that connects Piazza San Marco with the Rialto Bridge, the always lively Campo San Luca (look for **Bar Torino**, **Bar Black Jack**, or the characterful **Leon Bianco wine bar**) and **Campo Santa** Margherita. Avoid the tired-looking pizza (revitalized only marginally by microwaves) you'll find in most bars; informal sit-down neighborhood pizzerias everywhere offer savory and far fresher renditions for a minimum of 6,000L ($3.50), plus your drink and cover charge—the perfect lunch or light dinner.

CULINARY DELIGHTS   Venice has a distinguished culinary history, much of it based on its geographical position on the sea and, to a lesser degree, its historical ties with the Orient. You'll see things on Venetian menus you won't see elsewhere, together with local versions of time-tested Italian favorites. For first courses, both pasta and risotto (more liquidy in the Veneto than usual) are commonly prepared with fish or seafood: risotto *alla sepie* or *alla seppioline* (tinted black by the ink of cuttlefish, also called *risotto nero* or black risotto) or *spaghetti alle vongole* or *alle vorace* (with clams; clams without their shells are not a good sign!) are two commonly found specialties. Both appear with *frutti di mare,* "fruit of the sea," which can be a little bit of whatever looked good at this morning's fish market. *Bigoli,* homemade pasta of whole wheat, is not commonly found elsewhere, while creamy **polenta,** often served with *gamberetti* (small shrimp) or tiny shrimp called *schie,* or as an accompaniment to *fegato alla veneziana* (calf's liver with onions Venetian style) is a staple of the Veneto. Fish and seafood to look out for are *branzino* (a kind of sea bass), *rombo* (turbot or brill), *moeche* (small soft-shelled crab) or *granseola* (crab) and *sarde in saor,* sardines in a sauce of onion, vinegar, pine nuts, and raisins.

From a host of good local wines, try the dry white **Tocai** and **Pinot** from the Friuli region and the light, Champagne-like **Prosecco** that Venetians consume almost like a soft-drink (it is the base of Venice's famous **Bellini** drink made with white peach puree). Popular red wines include **Merlot**, **Cabernet**, **Raboso,** and **Refosco.** The quintessentially **Italian Bardolino**, **Valpolicella,** and **Soave** are from the nearby Veneto area. *Grappa,* the local firewater, is an acquired taste and is often offered in a dozen variations. Neighborhood *bacari* wine bars provide the chance to taste the fruits of leading wine producers in the grape-rich regions of the Veneto and neighboring Friuli.

Where the Restaurants Are

All the Venice restaurants discussed in this section are on the "Venice Accommodations & Dining" map on p. 392.

IN SAN MARCO

✪ **Le Bistrot de Venise.** San Marco 4685 (on C. d. Fabbri). ☎ **041/523-66-51.** www.bistrotdevenise.com. E-mail: bistrot@tin.it. Reservations not necessary. Appetizers and crepes 8,000–14,000L ($4.70–$8.25); primi 13,000–15,000L ($7.65–$8.80); pizza 8,000–13,000L ($4.70–$7.65); secondi 19,000–30,000L ($11.20–$17.65). MC, V. Daily 9am–1am. Vaporetto: Rialto. From the Rialto Bridge vaporetto stop, turn right, walk along the Grand Canal, cross the small footbridge, then turn left onto C. Bembi, which becomes C. d. Fabbri; Le Bistrot is about 5 blocks ahead, on your left. VENETIAN/CONTINENTAL.

I've grown to love this comfortable, relaxed, visitor-friendly spot—and one that's open late—with indoor (it's air-conditioned and there's even a no-smoking section) and outdoor seating areas, young *simpatici* English-speaking waiters, and a varied, eclectic menu. It's a popular meeting spot for Venetians and artists, where you're welcome to sit and write postcards over a steaming cappuccino, enjoy a simple lunch such as risotto and salad, or dine when most of Venice is shutting down. Here, you can linger over an elaborate meal that might include timeless dishes from 15th-century Venetian archival recipes, or you can opt for a large combination salad. Create your own pizza, mixing and matching more than 30 ingredients, or choose from a dozen entree or dessert crepes. The small back room is Venice's best venue of scheduled cultural events—check their Web site—such as poetry readings, live music, and art exhibits. It has become the hot spot in town for well organized and widely varying cultural and cabaret events that recall Paris in the old days.

Osteria alle Botteghe. San Marco 3454 (C. d. Botteghe off Cam. Santo Stefano). ☎ **041/52-28-181.** Reservations not accepted. Pizza 7,000–14,000L ($4.10–$8.25); primi 8,000L ($4.70); secondi 14,000L ($8.25). DC, MC, V. Mon–Sat 11am–4pm and 7–10pm. Vaporetto: Accademia or Sant'Angelo. Find your way to the principal Cam. Santo Stefano (follow the stream of people or ask), take the narrow C. d. Botteghe at the Gelateria Paolin across from the church of Santo Stefano; the osteria is on the right. PIZZERIA/ITALIAN.

Casual, easy on the palate, easy on the wallet, and even easy to find (given that you've made it to the bigger-than-life Campo Santo Stefano), this is a great, centrally located choice for a pizza, light snack, or elaborate meal. Stand-up hors d'oeuvres (*cicchetti*) and fresh sandwiches can be had at the bar or window-side counter, while more serious diners can choose from the dozen pizzas, pasta dishes, or *tavola calda* (a buffet of prepared dishes such as eggplant parmigiana, lasagna, and fresh, cooked vegetables in season, reheated when you order) and repair to tables in the back. Vegetarians will be happy with a simple pizza margherita, the classic can't-miss favorite, made with tomato sauce and mozzarella cheese, and a side dish or two of spinach, grilled peppers, or zucchini, enhanced with a drizzle of virgin olive oil.

Rosticceria San Bartolomeo. San Marco 5424 (on C. d. Bissa off Cam. San Bartolomeo). ☎ **041/52-23-569.** Reservations not accepted. Menù turistico 15,000–26,000L ($8.80–$15.30) in the ground-floor dining room, or 32,000–42,000L ($18.80–$24.70) upstairs; pizza and primi 7,000–8,000L ($4.10–$4.70) in the ground-floor dining room, about 30% more upstairs; secondi 15,000–23,000L ($8.80–$13.50) in the ground-floor dining room, about 20% more upstairs. AE, MC, V. Summer changes yearly but usually daily 9am–9:30pm; winter Tues–Sun 9am–2:30pm and 4:30–8:40pm. Vaporetto: Rialto. With the bridge at your back on the San Marco side of Canal, walk straight ahead to the Cam. San Bartolomeo. Take the underpass slightly to your left marked Sottoportego d. Bissa; you'll come across the rosticceria at the first corner. Look for Gislon (its old name) above the entrance. ITALIAN/TAVOLA CALDA.

⊕ Family-Friendly Restaurants

Rosticceria San Bartolomeo (*see p. 406*)   There's not much that isn't served at this big, efficient, and bustling fast food emporio in the Rialto Bridge area. Much -of it is displayed in glass cases to pique the fussy appetite, and you won't raise any eyebrows if you eat too little, too much, or at hours when the natives have either finished or haven't yet started.

Alla Madonna (*see p. 412*)   For the proper evening out in an enjoyable trattoria atmosphere, you can absorb the bustle of this long-beloved institution where patient English-speaking waiters are accustomed to dealing with patrons of all ages and nationalities. Afterwards, retreat to the waterside walkway and watch the lights of nighttime boat traffic where the Rialto Bridge looms across the Grand Canal.

With a dozen pasta dishes, and as many fish, seafood, or meat entrees, this old favorite (and newly refreshed) *tavola calda* (literally "hot table") can satisfy any combination of cravings for the cost conscious. The ready-made food displayed under the long glass counter eliminates any language barriers. There's no *coperto* if you take your meal standing up or seated at the stools in the aroma-filled (and always busy) ground-floor eating area. There is a bar in the back with tramezzini sandwiches and cicchetti bar food. For those who prefer to linger, head to the dining hall upstairs (though for a sit-down meal, you can do much better than this unremarkable setting). This appears to be the most popular rosticceria in Venice (and for good reason), so the continuous turnover guarantees fresh food and a considerable selection.

Rosticceria Teatro Goldoni. San Marco 4747 (on the corner of C. d. Fabbri between the Rialto and Cam. San Luca) ☎ **041/52-22-446.** Reservations not accepted. Menù turistico 23,000L ($13.50); pizza and primi 8,000–14,000L ($4.70–$8.25); secondi 8,000–14,000L ($4.70–$8.25). AE, DC, V. Daily 8am–10pm (closed Wed Nov–Dec). Vaporetto: Rialto. From the Cam. San Bartolomeo head southwest in the direction of Cam. San Luca; the snack bar is on your left before reaching the Teatro Goldoni. ITALIAN/INTERNATIONAL/FAST FOOD.

So this won't be your most memorable culinary experience in Venice. But as far as location, value, variety, and pleasant atmosphere go at this Venetian showcase of fast food, you won't be disappointed—nor go berserk trying to locate it when starved. Bright and modern—though it has been here for more than 50 years—this bar/cafe/rosticceria/tavola calda (ground floor) and pizzeria (upstairs) offers seating areas and continuous hours. A variety of sandwiches and pastries are displayed in a glass counter, alongside another filled with prepared foods such as lasagna, eggplant parmigiana, or roast chicken. A selection of large mixed salads is a concession to the American set, though much of the crowd is composed of the area's merchants and vendors.

Trattoria da Fiore. San Marco 3561 (C. d. Botteghe off Cam. Santo Stefano). ☎ **041/ 52-35-310.** Reservations suggested in high season. Primi 9,000–14,000L ($5.30–$8.25); secondi 18,000–26,000L ($10.60–$15.30). AE, MC, V. Wed–Mon noon–3pm and 7–10pm. Vaporetto: Accademia. Cross the Accademia Bridge to the San Marco side and walk straight ahead to the wide expanse of the Cam. Santo Stefano. At the northern end of the campo, exit left at the Bar/Gelateria Paolin onto the C. d. Botteghe. The trattoria is on your right. VENETIAN/ITALIAN.

Don't confuse this authentic neighborhood trattoria with the famous and far more expensive Osteria da Fiore (see below). The food may not be as remarkable, but neither is the bill. Start with the house specialty, *pennette alla Fiore* (prepared with olive oil, garlic, and seven different in-season vegetables), and you may be happy to call it a night. Or skip right to another popular specialty, *frittura mista,* comprised of more than a dozen different varieties of fresh fish and seafood. At prices ranging from 20,000 to 25,000L ($11.75 to $14.70) depending upon the day's catch, it's a bargain. The *zuppa di pesce alla chef,* a delicious bouillabaisse-like soup, is stocked with mussels, crab, clams, shrimp, and tuna. At only 25,000L ($14.70), it doesn't get any better and is a meal in itself. This is a good neighborhood place for an afternoon snack or light lunch at the Bar Fiore next door (10:30am to 10:30pm).

✪ **Vino Vino.** San Marco 2007 (on Ponte d. Veste near La Fenice Opera House). ☎ **041/ 52-37-027.** www.anticomartini.com/vinovino.htm. Primi 8,000L ($4.70); secondi 8,000–15,000L ($4.70–$8.80). AE, DC, MC, V. Wed–Mon 10am–midnight. With your back to the Basilica di San Marco, exit the Pz. San Marco through the arcade on the far left (west) side; keep walking straight, pass the American Express office, cross over the canal, turn right onto C. d. Veste just before the street jags left, and Vino Vino is just ahead, after a small bridge, and on your left. If you reach the burned-out shell of La Fenice Opera House, you've gone too far. WINE BAR/ITALIAN.

Detractors say it ain't the same, but someone is keeping this Venetian institution always abuzz. A local wine-bar archetype offering honest, well-prepared food, Vino Vino's biggest pull is its consistently impressive selection of Italian and European wines (check out the Web site) sold by the bottle or glass. Daily changing Venetian specialties are written on a chalkboard, but are also usually displayed at the glass counter so you can see what you're ordering. After placing your order, settle into one of a dozen or so wooden tables squeezed into two simple storefront-style rooms. The high quality of this ever-popular locale is attributable to the owner—the eminent Antico Martini, a few doors down, with whom it shares a kitchen. It's also a great spot for a leisurely self-styled wine tasting (1,500 to 3,000L/90¢ to $1.75 per glass) with great *cicchetti* bar food, the Venetian habit that visitors find addicting. If you've come for dinner, the food often runs out around 10:30pm, so don't come too late.

IN CANNAREGIO

Ai Tre Spiedi. Cannaregio 5906 (Salizzada San Cazian). ☎ **041/52-08-035.** Reservations recommended in high season. Menù turistico: with meat secondo/entree 22,000L ($12.95) or with fresh fish secondo/entree, 30,000L ($17.65). Primi 6,000–8,000L ($3.50–$4.70); secondi 16,000–26,000L ($9.40–$15.30). AE, MC, V. Tues–Sun noon–3pm and 7–10pm. Vaporetto: Rialto. On the San Marco side of the bridge: exit the Cam. San Bartolomeo to the northeast, following the stream of people past the post office, Coin department store, and Church of San Crisostomo on your right. Cross the first bridge after the church and turn right at the toy store onto Salizzada S. Cazian. The restaurant is on your right. VENETIAN/SEAFOOD

Venetians bring their visiting friends here to make a *bella figura* (good impression) without breaking the bank, then swear them to secrecy. The setting is homey and pleasant in this small, casual trattoria that still manages to be refined and elegant with exposed beam ceilings and some of Venice's most reasonably priced fresh-fish dining. If you order à la carte, ask the English-speaking waiters to estimate the cost of your fish entree, since it may appear priced by *l'etto* (100 grams) on the menu. This restaurant, Alla Madonna, and the Trattoria da Fiore (see above) are three of our most reasonable choices for a genuine Venetian dinner that won't send your budget into tilt. The more opportunities you have to dine around town, the more you'll understand what finds they indeed are.

IN CASTELLO

Da Aciughetta. Castello 4357 (in Cam. SS Filippo e Giacomo east of Pz. San Marco) ☎ **041/52-24-292.** Reservations suggested on weekends. Pizzas and primi 7,000–14,000L ($4.10–$8.25). AE, MC, V. Daily 8am–midnight. Closed Wed Nov–Mar. Vaporetto: San Zaccaria. Walk north on the C. d. Rasse to the small Cam. SS Filippo e Giacomo. The awninged restaurant is on the north side of campo. VENETIAN/WINE BAR/PIZZERIA.

After you enjoy the obligatory aperitif in the theater-set lobby of the fabled Hotel Danieli (vowing to be reincarnated as a Rockefeller next time around), walk a short block north to the small campiello behind the waterfront deluxe hotels to the area's best wine bar. Its name refers to the toothpick-speared marinated anchovies that join other pick-me-up cicchetti lining the bar of this friendly bacaro, where an excellent wine selection can be enjoyed by the glass at any hour of the day. The owners have successfully created the unusual combination of pizzeria/wine bar with additional trattoria-like selections of primi and secondi. Perhaps due to the jovial wine tasting happening in the SRO bar area (often four deep during the busiest hours before and after meals), the staff is relaxed about those not ordering full multiple-course meals— a pasta and glass of wine will keep everyone very happy.

Pizzeria/Trattoria al Vecio Canton. Castello 4738a (at the corner of Ruga Giuffa). ☎ **041/52-85-176.** Reservations not accepted. Pizza 7,000–12,000L ($4.60–$6.60); primi 8,000–14,000L ($4.60–$7.90); secondi 14,000–22,000L ($9.20–$14.50). AE, CB, DC, MC. Wed 7–10:30pm, Thurs–Mon noon–2:30pm and 7–10:30pm. Vaporetto: San Zaccaria. From the Riva degli Schiavoni waterfront, walk straight ahead to Cam. SS. Filippo e Giacomo then turn right and continue east to the small Cam. San Provolo. Take a left heading north on the Salizzada San Provolo, cross the first footbridge and you'll find the pizzeria on the first corner on the left. ITALIAN/PIZZA.

Good pizza is hard to find in Venice, and I mean that in the literal sense. Tucked away in a northeast corner behind Piazza San Marco on a well-trafficked route connecting it with Campo Santa Maria Formosa, the Canton's wood-paneled taverna-like atmosphere and great pizzas are worth the time you'll spend looking for the place. There is a full trattoria menu as well, with a number of pasta and side dishes (*contorni*) of vegetables providing a palatable alternative. New ownership in 1998 didn't sit well with neighborhood residents who don't relish change: The local jury is still out, divided between those who pine for the old days and those who feel the change has made for many improvements. Keep posted.

Trattoria alla Rivetta. Castello 4625 (on Salizzada San Provolo east of Pz. San Marco). ☎ **041/52-87-302.** Reservations recommended. Primi 8,000–14,000L ($4.70–$8.25); fish secondi 12,000–26,000L ($7.05–$15.30); other secondi 12,000–15,000L ($7.05–$8.80). AE, MC, V. Tues–Sun noon–2:30pm and 7–10pm. Closed last week of July and first 3 weeks in Aug. Vaporetto: San Zaccaria. With your back to the water and facing the Savoia e Jolanda Hotel, walk straight ahead (north) to the Cam. SS. Filippo e Giacomo; the canal-side trattoria is literally tucked away next to (and almost under) a bridge just off the east (right) side of the campo in the direction of Cam. San Zaccaria. SEAFOOD/VENETIAN.

It's lively, frequented by gondoliers, neighboring merchants, and tourists who are drawn to its bustling popularity (the latter usually seated in the back room—less congested but not as much fun), and it's one of the safer bets for Venetian cuisine and company in the San Marco area, an easy 10-minute walk east of the piazza. All sorts of fresh fish—the specialty—decorate the window of this plain, brightly lit place, where there's usually a short wait, even in the off-peak season. Not to worry, as the front part of the restaurant is a small bar area where a fresh array of delicious finger-foods (*cicchetti*) and toothpicks are put out to keep you busy and happily sustained. Once seated, be sure to try the *antipasto di pesce* and whatever is penciled in as the daily special (often priced by *l'etto* or per 100 grams).

✪ **Trattoria da Remigio.** Castello 3416 (C. Bosello near San Giorgio d. Greci). ☎ **041/ 52-30-089.** Reservations recommended especially on weekends or high season. Primi 7,000–10,000L ($4.11–$5.88); secondi 10,000–20,000L ($5.88–$11.75). AE, DC, MC, V. Mon

1–3pm, Wed–Sun 1–3pm and 7–11pm. Vaporetto: San Zaccaria. Follow the Riva degli Schiavoni east until you come to the white Chiesa della Pietà. Turn left onto the C. d. Pietà, which jags left into C. Bosello. The restaurant is about 3 blocks ahead on your left. ITALIAN/VENETIAN.

Famous for its straightforward renditions of Adriatic classics, Remigio is the kind of place where you can order something as simple as *gnocchi alla pescatora* (homemade gnocchi in a tomato-based sauce of seafood) and know it will be memorable. English-speaking headwaiter Pino will talk you through the day's fresh fish dishes (John Dory, sea bass, sole, monk fish, cuttlefish); commonly sold by weight. You can expect freshness and perfect preparation here; the same goes for any antipasto. There are a dozen or so delicious meat possibilities, quite a concession in this fish-crazed town, but that's not what Remigio's (or this town) is about. Locals still predominate in the two pleasant but smallish dining rooms here; even late on a winter weekday you can expect a possible wait unless you've reserved. Remigio's is quite well known, although not easy to find, so just ask.

WORTH A SPLURGE

✪ **Al Covo.** Castello 3968 (Campiello d. Pescheria, east of Chiesa d. Pietà in the Arsenale neighborhood). ☎ **041/52-23-812.** Reservations suggested. Primi 22,000L ($12.95); secondi 34,000L ($20). 3-course fixed-price lunch 50,000L ($29.40). No credit cards accepted. Fri–Tues 12:30–3pm and 7–10:30pm. Closed Dec 15–Jan 15 and 2 weeks in Aug. Vaporetto: Arsenale. Walk a short way back in the direction of Pz. San Marco, turning right at the Bar/cafe il Gabbiano. The restaurant is on your left. Otherwise it is an enjoyable 20 minute stroll along the waterfront Riva degli Schiavoni from Pz. San Marco, past the Chiesa d. Pietà (Vivaldi's Church) and the Metropole Hotel. VENETIAN/SEAFOOD

For years this lovely restaurant has been consistently (and deservingly) popular with American food writers, putting it on the short list of every food-loving American tourist. There are nights when it seems you hear nothing but English spoken. But this has never served to compromise the incredible dining at this warm and welcoming spot, where the preparation of superfresh fish and an excellent selection of moderately priced wines is as commendable today—perhaps more so—as in its nascent days of pretrendiness. Much of its tourist-friendly atmosphere is due to the naturally hospitable Diane Rankin, the co-owner and dessert whiz who hales from Texas. She will eagerly talk you through a wondrous fish-studded menu that can otherwise seem like Greek to non-Venetians. Her husband, Cesare Benelli, is known for his infallible talent in the kitchen. Together they share an admirable dedication to their charming gem of a restaurant—the quality of an evening at Al Covo is tough to top in this town.

Osteria Alle Testiere. Castello 5801 (on C. d. Mondo Novo off Salizzada San Lio). ☎ **041/ 52-27-220.** Reservations required for each of two seatings. Primi 18,000L ($10.58); secondi 24,000–30,000L ($14.10–$17.65). MC, V. Mon–Sat two seatings: 7 and 9:15pm. Vaporetto: equidistant from either the Rialto or San Marco stops. Find the store-lined Salizzada San Lio (west of the Cam. Santa Maria Formosa) and from there ask where to turn off on the C. d. Mondo Novo. VENETIAN/ITALIAN.

The limited seating for just 24 savvy (and lucky) patrons at butcher-paper covered tables, the relaxed young staff and upbeat tavernlike atmosphere belie the seriousness of this informal newcomer. Already proving it will persist far beyond the average 15 minutes, this is your guaranteed choice if you are of the foodie genre, curious to experience the increasingly interesting Venetian culinary scene without going broke. Start with the carefully chosen wine list, most of whose 90 labels can be ordered by the half bottle (average cost 30,000/$17.65). The delicious homemade *gnocchetti ai calamaretti* (with baby squid) makes a frequent appearance, as does the traditional "secondo" specialty *scampi alla busara*, in a "secret" recipe some of whose identifiable ingredients include tomato, cinnamon, and a dash of hot pepper. Cheese is a rarity in these parts, except for Alle Testiere's exceptional choice of a half dozen winners.

IN DORSODURO

Taverna San Trovaso. Dorsoduro 1016 (on Fondamenta Priuli west of Accademia Bridge).
☎ **041/52-03-703.** Reservations recommended. Menù turistico 26,000L ($15.30); pizza
and primi 7,000–15,000L ($4.10–$8.80); secondi 12,000–27,000L ($7.05–$15.90). AE, MC,
V. Tues–Sun noon–2:45pm and 7–9:45pm. Vaporetto: Rialto. Walk to the right around the Galleria dell'Accademia, taking an immediate right onto C. Gambara. When this street ends at the
small canal Rio di San Trovaso, turn left onto the Fondamenta Priuli; the taverna is on your left
just before the small bridge. ITALIAN/VENETIAN.

Wine bottles line wood-paneled walls, and vaulted brick ceilings augment the sense of
character in this enjoyable neighborhood tavern near the Accademia, always packed
with an interesting mix of locals and first-timers alike. The menù turistico includes
wine, an ample *frittura mista* (assortment of lightly fried seafood), and dessert. Order
à la carte from a wide variety of primi selections (the homemade gnocchi is great), or
secondi (from a variety of pizzas to the local specialty of *fegato alla veneziana*) or
simply grilled fish, the taverna's claim to fame. While in the neighborhood, stroll along
the Rio San Trovaso toward the Canale della Giudecca: On your right you'll see the
Squero di San Trovaso, one of the very few working boatyards in Venice that still
makes and repairs the traditional gondolas.

Trattoria Ai Cugnai. Dorsoduro 857 (C. Nuova Sant'Agnese east of the Galleria dell'Accademia). ☎ **041/52-89-238.** Reservations suggested on weekends. Primi 10,000–12,000L
($5.90–$7.05); secondi 18,000–22,000L ($10.60–$12.95). AE, MC, V. Tues–Sun 12:30–3pm
and 7–10:30pm. Vaporetto: Accademia. Head east of the bridge and museum in the direction
of the Guggenheim Collection; on the straight street connecting the two museums, the
restaurant in on your right (south side). VENETIAN

Unless you're looking for it (and you should be), the unassuming storefront of this
long-time favorite does little to announce that herein lies some of the neighborhood's
best dining. The name refers to the brothers-in-law of the three women chefs, all sisters, who serve classic *cucina veneziana,* such as the reliably good *spaghetti alle verace*
(with clams). Their homemade gnocchi and lasagna would meet any Italian grandmother's approval (you won't go wrong with any of the menu's *fatta a casa* choices of
daily homemade specialties). Equidistant from the diverse Accademia Gallery and the
Peggy Guggenheim Collection, Ai Cugnai is the perfectly convenient destination to
recharge after art overload.

IN SAN POLO

✪ **A Le Do Spade.** San Polo 860 (Sottoportego Do Spade near the Pescheria Market).
☎ **041/52-10-574.** Reservations not accepted. Primi 8,000–12,000L ($4.70–$7.05); secondi 15,000–18,000L ($8.80–$10.60). AE, MC, V. Mon–Wed, Fri–Sat 9am–3pm and 5–11pm,
Thurs 9am–3pm. Vaporetto: Rialto or San Silvestro. At the San Polo side of the Rialto Bridge,
walk away from the bridge and through the Rialto open-air market until you see the covered
Pescheria (fish market) on your right. Take a left here and then take the second right onto the
Sottoportego Do Spade. Walk 2 blocks; the wine bar is on your left. WINE BAR/VENETIAN.

Since 1415, workers, fishmongers, and shoppers from the nearby Mercato della
Pescheria (fish market) flock to this historical *bacaro* wine bar (it was already 300 years
old when Casanova was a regular). There's color and bonhomie galore amid the locals,
here for their daily *ombra* ("shadow" or glass of wine) affably administered by owner
and bartender Giorgio "Sommelier." A large number of excellent Veneto and Friuli
wines are available by the glass (1,500 to 3,000L/90¢ to $1.75), accompanied by a
counter full of cicchetti. Unlike most bacari, and a great stroke of luck for the touring
footsore, this quintessentially Venetian cantina has recently added a number of tables
and introduced a sit-down menu to include a dozen daily changing pastas, and local
(mostly fish-based) specialties, including the ubiquitous *fegato alla veneziana,* liver and
onions. You won't be disappointed here.

✪ **Alla Madonna.** San Polo 594 (C. d. Madonna) ☎ **041/52-23-824.** Reservations not accepted. Primi 12,000–14,000L ($7.05–$8.25); secondi 17,000–24,000L ($10–$14.10). AE, MC, V. Thurs–Tues noon–3pm and 7–10pm. Closed 2 weeks in Aug and most of Jan. Vaporetto: Rialto. From the foot of the Rialto Bridge on the San Polo side of the Grand Canal, turn left and follow the Riva d. Vin along the Grand Canal; C. d. Madonna (also called Sotto-portego d. Madonna) will be the second calle on your right (look for the big yellow sign). The restaurant is on your left. ITALIAN/VENETIAN.

This bright and busy trattoria is a classic, and has been packing them in for more than 50 years. This authentic Venetian institution has it all: a convenient location near the Rialto Bridge, five large dining rooms to accommodate the demand, an encouraging mix of loyal local regulars and foreign patrons, a characteristic decor of high-beamed ceilings and walls frame-to-frame with local artists' work, and—most important—a competent and professional kitchen that prepares a menu of irreproachably fresh fish and seafood to perfection. With all of this, and (by Venetian standards) moderate prices to boot, it's no surprise this place is always jumping (and what a disappointment you can't reserve, though some hotels manage to secure a confirmation—give it a try!). So don't expect the waiter to smile if you linger too long over dessert. Most of the first courses are prepared with seafood, such as the spaghetti or risotto with *frutti di mare* (seafood) or pasta with *sepie* (cuttlefish), blackened from its own natural ink. Most of the day's special fish selections are best simply and deliciously prepared *alla griglia* (grilled).

✪ **Cantina do Mori.** San Polo 401 (entrances on C. Galiazza and C. Do Mori near the Pescheria Market). ☎ **041/52-25-401.** Reservations not accepted. Sandwiches and cic-chetti, each 1,000–3,000L (60¢–$1.75). No credit cards. Mon–Sat 8:30am–9:30pm. Vaporetto: Rialto. Cross the Rialto Bridge to the San Polo side, walk to the end of the market stalls, turn left, then immediately right, and look for the small wooden cantina sign hanging on the left side of the street. WINE BAR/SANDWICHES.

Venetians stop to nibble and socialize at this characterful *bacaro* before and after meals, but if you don't mind standing (there are no tables) and are in the market for a snack or light lunch (a thought that would horrify Venetians who see cicchetti grazing as a constitutional interlude but never as a substitute for a full meal), this is one of the best and most famous spots in Venice, and an ideal window for a close-up look at the real Venice. Do Mori, often associated with Le Do Spade, another venerable old-time bacaro nearby (albeit one with seating and a new trattoria-like menu; see above) extended their hours and selection of regional and Italian wines by the glass—just about the best news I got during my most recent visit to Venice.

Pizzeria da Sandro. San Polo 1473 (off the Campiello d. Meloni near Cam. San Polo). ☎ **041/52-34-894.** Reservations not accepted. Pizza 7,500–14,000L ($4.40–$8.25); primi 8,000–15,000L ($4.70–$8.80); secondi 12,000–25,000L ($7.05–$14.70). AE, DC, MC, V. Sat–Thurs 11:30am–11:30pm. Vaporetto: San Silvestro. From the vaporetto stop, with your back to the Grand Canal, walk straight ahead to the store-lined Ruga Vecchia San Giovanni and take a left. Follow the stream of people heading toward the Cam. San Polo until you come upon the small Campiello d. Meloni; the pizzeria is just beyond on your right. ITALIAN/PIZZA.

Like most pizzerias/trattorias, Sandro offers a dozen varieties of pizza (his specialty) as well as a full trattoria menu of pastas and entrees. But if you're looking for a simple 10,000L ($5.90) pizza-and-beer meal, this is a reliably good spot on the main drag linking the Rialto to Campo San Polo (if you find yourself in Campo San Polo—and you should, but not right now—you've gone too far). There's communal seating at a few wooden picnic tables placed outdoors (the passing parade of pedestrians makes for great mealtime people watching), with eight small tables inside where the squeeze is tight but amiable. An unusual "no-stop" schedule means you'll find Sandro's open if a pizza craving hits you off-hours.

WORTH A SPLURGE

✪ **Osteria da Fiore.** San Polo 2202 (on C. d. Scaleter north of Cam. San Polo). ☎ **041/ 72-13-08.** Fax 041/72-13-43. Reservations required, fax in advance. Primi 22,000–26,000L ($12.95–$15.30); secondi 38,000–42,000L ($22.35–$24.70). AE, MC, V. Tues–Sat noon–3pm and 7–10pm. Closed 3 weeks following Jan 10, and 3 weeks in Aug. Vaporetto: San Tomà or San Stae. The neighborhood's principal reference point is the expansive and easy to find Cam. San Polo. Exit the campo from the northeast corner along the Rio Terà S. Antonio, which becomes the C. Bernardo da Ca', and then the C. d. Scaleter. ITALIAN/SEAFOOD.

Here's il Grande Splurge, worth every half-lire for its all around excellence and the probable hardship of having to fax weeks in advance for a coveted table. Despite its revered (and justified) hype as Venice's best, Da Fiore's quiet elegance is welcoming and unpretentious. With sophisticated food that is simple and nearing perfection, you'll eat remarkably well for the only borderline-extravagant prices. The whole seamless operation is a 20-year labor of love of the gracious owners, chef Mara Zanetti Martin and her husband and host, Maurizio, whose family of impeccably professional (and wonderfully friendly) English-speaking waitstaff will help you orchestrate your best meal in Venice. Fresh fish is the natural draw of the daily and seasonally changing menu, but discerning vegetarians and carnivores can also have their own unprecedented field day. And no one should leave without tasting Mara's sublime homemade dessert, her *sorbetto di limone*, the grand finale.

IN SANTA CROCE

Pizzeria alle Oche. Santa Croce 1552 (on C. d. Tintor south of Cam. San Giacomo dell'Orio). ☎ **041/52-41-161.** Reservations recommended for weekends. Pizza 6,500–14,000L ($3.80–$8.25). MC, V. Tues–Sun noon–midnight (in summer open daily). Vaporetto: equidistant from Rio San Biasio and San Stae. You can walk here in 10 min. from the nearby train station; otherwise from the vaporetto station find your way to the Cam. S. Giacomo dell'Orio and exit the campo south on to the well-trammeled C. d. Tintor. PIZZERIA.

When I have a hankering for carbohydrate overload, and what better country to find yourself in when the mood strikes, I head for the Baskin-Robbins of Venice's pizzerias. Italians are zealously unapologetic about tucking into a good-size pizza and a pint of beer (with more than 20 here from which to choose); the walk to and from this slightly peripherally located hangout (with outside eating during warm weather) allays thoughts of calorie counts. Count 'em: 85 varieties of imaginative pizza fill the menu (could Mae West possibly have eaten here when she said too much of a good thing is wonderful?), a dozen being of the tomato sauce-free "white" variety (*pizza bianca*). The clientele is a mixed bag of young and old, students and not, Venetian and visitors—most happily putting away the classically wonderful margherita version (6,500L/$3.80). Simplicity is everything. When I asked for the second-most favored selection, I got hooked for life: Try the **Campagnola** (no. 59; 11,000L/$6.50), a symphony of tomato, mozzarella, mushrooms, brie cheese, speck, arugula, and oregano, and see if your reaction isn't the same.

PICNICKING

You don't have to eat in a fancy restaurant to have a good time in Venice. Prepare a picnic, and while you eat alfresco, you can observe the life of the city's few open piazzas or the aquatic parade on its main thoroughfare, the Grand Canal. And you can still indulge in a late dinner *alla veneziana*. Plus, doing your own shopping for food can be an interesting experience since there are very few supermarkets as we know them and small *alimentari* (food shops) in the highly visited neighborhoods (where few Venetians live) are scarce.

MERCATO RIALTO   Venice's principal open-air market is a sight to see, even for nonshoppers. It has two parts, beginning with the **produce section,** whose many stalls, alternating with souvenir vendors, unfold north on the San Polo side of the Rialto Bridge (behind these stalls are a few permanent food stores whose delicious cheese, cold cuts, and bread selections make the perfect lunch). The vendors are here Monday to Saturday from 7am to 1pm, with a number who stay on in the afternoon.

At the market's farthest point, you'll find the covered **fresh-fish market,** with its carnival atmosphere, picturesquely located on the Grand Canal opposite the magnificent Ca' d'Oro and still redolent of the days when it was one of the Mediterranean's great fish markets. The area is filled with a number of small *bacari* bars frequented by market vendors and shoppers where you can join in and ask for your morning's first glass of prosecco with a *cicchetto* pick-me-up. The fish merchants take Monday off (which explains why so many restaurants are closed on Monday; those that are open are selling Saturday's goods—beware!) and work mornings only.

CAMPO SANTA MARGHERITA   On this spacious campo, on Tuesday through Saturday from 8:30am to 1 or 2pm, a number of open-air stalls set up shop, selling fresh fruit and vegetables. You should have no trouble filling out your picnic spread with the fixings available at the various shops lining the sides of the campo, including an exceptional *panetteria* (bakery), **Rizzo Pane,** at no. 2772, a fine *salumeria* (deli) at no. 2844, and a good shop for wine, sweets, and other picnic accessories next door. There's even a conventional supermarket, **Merlini,** just off the campo in the direction of the quasi-adjacent campo San Barnabà at no. 3019. This is also the area where you'll find Venice's heavily photographed floating market operating from a boat moored just off campo San Barnabà at the ponte dei Pugni. This market is open daily from 8am to 1pm and 3:30 to 7:30pm, except Wednesday afternoon and Sunday. You're almost better off just buying a few freshly prepared sandwiches (*panini* when made with rolls, *tramezzini* when made with white bread).

THE BEST PICNIC SPOTS   Alas, to stay behind and picnic in Venice means you won't have much in the way of green space (it's not worth the boat ride to the Giardini Publici past the Arsenale, Venice's only green park). An enjoyable alternative is to find some of the larger piazzas or campi that have park benches, and in some cases even a tree or two to shade them, such as **Campo S. Giacomo dell'Orio** (in the quiet sestiere of Santa Croce). The two most central are **Campo Santa Margherita** (sestiere of Dorsoduro) and **Campo San Polo** (sestiere of San Polo). For a picnic with a view, scout out the **Punta della Dogana** (Customs House) area near La Salute Church for a prime viewing site at the mouth of the Grand Canal. It's located directly across from the Piazza San Marco and the Palazzo Ducale—pull up a piece of the embankment here and watch the flutter of water activity against a canvaslike backdrop deserving of the Accademia Museum. In this same area, the small **Campo San Vio** near the Guggenheim is directly on the Grand Canal (not many campi are) and even boasts a bench or two.

If you want to create a real Venice picnic, you'll have to take the no. 12 boat out to the near-deserted island of Torcello, with a hamper full of bread, cheese, wine, and reenact the romantic scene of Katherine Hepburn and Rossano Brazzi from the 1950s film *Summertime.*

But perhaps the best picnic site of all is in a patch of sun on the marble steps leading down to the water of the Grand Canal, at the foot of the Rialto Bridge on the San Polo side. What a ringside seat for the Canalazzo's passing parade, and it's always free when I show up. Is it possible no one knows about it—until now?

5 Exploring Venice

Venice is notorious for changing and extending the opening hours of its museums and, to a lesser degree, its churches. Before you begin your exploration of Venice's sights, ask at the tourist office for the season's list of museum and church hours. During the peak months, you can enjoy extended museum hours—some places stay open until 7 or even 10pm. Unfortunately, these hours are not released until approximately Easter of every year. Even then, little is done to publicize the information, so you'll have to do your own research.

IN THE PIAZZA SAN MARCO

✪ **Basilica di San Marco.** San Marco, Piazza San Marco. ☎ **041/52-25-205.** Basilica free; Museo Marciano (St. Mark's Museum, also indicated as la Galleria) (includes Loggia dei Cavalli), 3,000L ($1.75) adults, 1,500L (90¢) students; Pala d'Oro 3,000L ($1.75) adults, 1,500L (90¢) students; Tesoro 4,000L ($2.35), adults, 2,000L ($1.20) students. Summer Mon–Sat 9:00am–5:30pm, Sun 2–5:30pm; winter Mon–Sat 9:30am–4:30pm, Sun 1:30–4:30pm. Last entrance 30 min. before closing time. Vaporetto: San Marco.

Venice for centuries was Europe's principal gateway between the Orient and the West, so it should come as no surprise that the architectural style for the sumptuously Byzantine Basilica di San Marco, replete with five mosquelike bulbed domes, was borrowed from Constantinople. Legend has it that in 828 two enterprising Venetian merchants conspired to smuggle the remains of St. Mark the Evangelist from Alexandria in Egypt by packing them in pickled pork to bypass the scrutiny of Muslim guards. Thus St. Mark replaced the Greek St. Theodore as Venice's patron saint and a small chapel was built on this spot in his honor. Through the subsequent centuries (much of what you see was constructed in the 11th century), wealthy Venetian merchants and politicians alike vied with one another in donating gifts to expand and embellish this church, the saint's final resting place and, with the adjacent Palazzo Ducale, a symbol of Venetian wealth and power. Exotic and mysterious, it is unlike any other Roman Catholic church you will visit.

And so it is that the Basilica di San Marco earned its name as the Chiesa d'Oro (Golden Church), with a cavernous interior exquisitely gilded with Byzantine mosaics added over some 7 centuries (the earliest date from the 11th century) and covering every inch of both ceiling and pavements. For a up-close look at many of the most remarkable ceiling mosaics and for a better view of the oriental carpetlike patterns of the intricate undulating pavement mosaics, pay the museum admission to go upstairs to the **Galleria** (the entrance to this and the Museo Marciano is in the atrium at the principal entrance); this was originally the women's gallery or *matroneum*. It is also the only way to access the outside Loggia dei Cavalli (see below). More important, it's here where you can mingle with the celebrated *Triumphal Quadriga* of four tethered, gilded bronze horses (dating from the 2nd or 3rd century A.D.) brought to Venice from Constantinople (although probably cast in Imperial Rome) in 1204 together with the Lion of St. Mark (the patron saint's and the former republic's mascot) and other booty from the Crusades; they were a symbol of the unrivaled Serene Republic and are the only quadriga to have survived from the classical era. The recently restored originals have been moved inside to the small museum.

A visit to the outdoor **Loggia dei Cavalli** is an unexpected highlight, providing an excellent view of the piazza and what Napoléon called "the most beautiful salon in the world" upon his arrival in Venice in 1797 (he would later cart the quadriga off to Paris, but they were returned after the fall of the French Empire). The 500-year-old Torre

A St. Mark's Warning

The basilica is open Sunday morning for those wishing to attend mass; all others are strongly discouraged from entering (see hours above). At all times, guards stand at the entrance and are serious about forbidding entry to anyone in inappropriate attire or shorts.

dell'Orologio (Clock Tower) stands to your right; to your left is the Campanile (Bell Tower) and beyond, the glistening waters of the open lagoon and Palladio's Chiesa di San Giorgio on its own island. It is a photographer's dream.

The church's greatest treasure is the magnificent altarpiece known as the **Pala d'Oro** (Golden Alterpiece), a Gothic masterpiece encrusted with close to 2,000 precious gems and 255 enameled panels. It was created as early as the 10th century, and embellished by master Venetian and Byzantine artisans between the 12th and 14th centuries. It is located behind the main altar, whose green marble canopy on alabaster columns covers the tomb of St. Mark. Also worth a visit is the **Tesoro** (Treasury), to the far right of the main altar, with a collection of the Crusaders' plunder from Constantinople and other icons and relics amassed by the church over the years. Much of the Venetian booty has been incorporated into the interior and exterior of the basilica in the form of marble, columns, capitals, and statuary. Second to the Pala d'Oro in importance is the 10th-century *Madonna di Nicopeia,* a bejeweled icon absconded from Constantinople and exhibited in its own chapel to the left of the main altar. She is held as one of present-day Venice's most protective patrons.

TOURS & ADMISSION   Admission to the basilica is free but restricted and there is often a line to get in during peak months, but don't leave Venice without visiting its candlelit, mysterious, and glittering interior. In July and August (and with much less certainty the rest of the year) there are free tours Monday through Saturday given by church-affiliated volunteers. They leave a few times daily (although which days will vary from year to year) usually beginning at 11am; groups gather in the atrium. Check the atrium for posters with changing schedules or ask at the tourist office: Not every tour is offered in English.

✪ **Palazzo Ducale and Ponte dei Sospiri (Ducal Palace and the Bridge of Sighs).** San Marco, Piazza San Marco. ☎ **041/5224951.** Joint admission (includes entrance to Correr Museum) 17,000L ($10) adults, 10,000L ($5.90) students. Daily 9am–7pm (winter hours may vary). Last entrance 1 hr. before closing. Vaporetto: San Marco.

The pink-and-white marble Gothic-Renaissance Palazzo Ducale, residence and government center of the *doges* ("dukes," elected for life) who ruled Venice for more than 1,000 years, stands between the Basilica di San Marco and St. Mark's Basin. A symbol of prosperity and power, it was destroyed from a succession of fires and was built and rebuilt in 1340 and 1424 in its present form, escaping the Renaissance fever that was in the air at the time. Forever being expanded, it was slowly grew to be one of Italy's greatest civic structures. A 15th-century Porta della Carta (Paper Gate, the entrance adjacent to the basilica where the doges' official proclamations and decrees were posted) opens onto a splendid inner courtyard with a double row of Renaissance arches. Ahead you'll see Jacopo Sansovino's enormous **Scala dei Giganti staircase** (Stairway of the Giants, scene of the doges' lavish inaugurations and never used by mere mortals), that leads to the wood-paneled courts and elaborate meeting rooms of the interior. The walls and ceilings of the principal rooms were richly decorated by the Venetian masters, including Veronese, Titian, Carpaccio, and Tintoretto, to illustrate the history of the puissant Venetian Republic while impressing visiting diplomats and

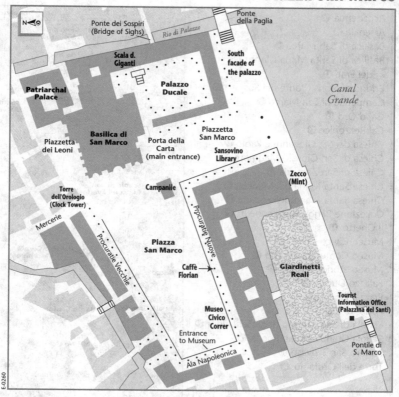

emissaries from the far-flung corners of the maritime republic with the uncontested prosperity and power it had attained.

If you want to understand something of this magnificent palace, the fascinating history of the 1,000-year-old Maritime Republic and the intrigue of the government that ruled it, search out the infrared **audio guide** or audio tour (at entrance: 7,000L/ $4.10). Unless you can tag along with an English-speaking tour group, you may otherwise miss out on the importance of much of what you're seeing.

The first room you'll come to is the spacious **Sala delle Quattro Porte** (Hall of the Four Doors), whose ceiling is by Tintoretto. The **Sala del Anti-Collegio** (adjacent to the College Chamber whose ceiling is decorated by Tintoretto), the next main room, is where foreign ambassadors waited to be received (and thus the rich embellishment of its canvases that served as self-aggrandizement) by this committee of 25 members: It is richly decorated with Tintorettos and Veronese's *Rape of Europe*, considered one of the palazzo's finest. It steals some of the thunder of Tintoretto's *Three Graces*, and *Bacchus and Ariadne*—the latter considered one of his best by some critics. A right turn from this room leads into one of the most impressive of the spectacular interior rooms, the richly adorned **Sala del Senato** (Senate Chamber), with Tintoretto's ceiling painting, *The Triumph of Venice*. Here laws were passed by the Senate, a select group of 200 chosen from the Great Council. The latter was originally an elected body but from the 13th century and onward, it was an aristocratic stronghold that could number as many as 1,700. After passing again through the Sala delle Quattro Porte, you'll come to the Veronese-decorated **Stanza del Consiglio dei Dieci** (Room of the

Venice Attractions

3-0689

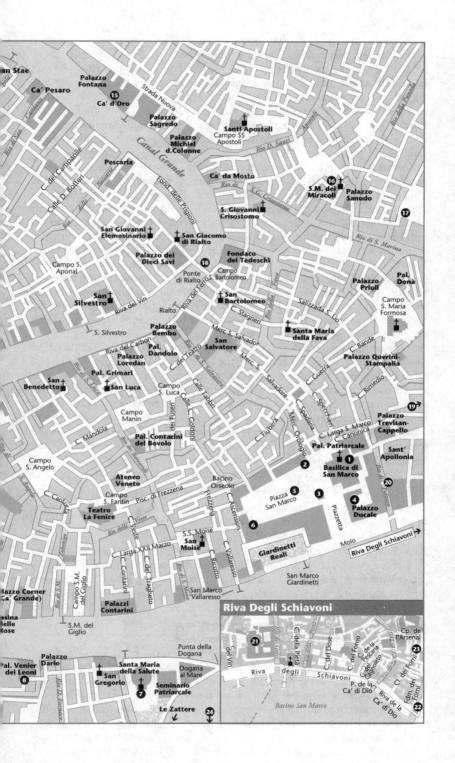

an Stae

Ca' Pesaro

Palazzo Fontana

15 **Ca' d'Oro**

Palazzo Sagredo

Strada Nuova

Palazzo Michiel d.Colonne

Santi Apostoli
Campo SS Apostoli

Rio D. Santi

Canal Grande

Pescaria

C. dei Campanile

Calle D. Boteri

Fond. delle Prigioni

Ca' da Mosto

Rio di

S.M. dei **16** **Palazzo**
Miracoli **Sanudo**

Apostoli

Rio della Panada

17

S. Giovanni Crisostomo

San Giovanni Elemosinario

† **San Giacomo di Rialto**

Palazzo dei Dieci Savi

18

Ponte di Rialto

Fondaco dei Tedeschi

Campo S. Bartolomeo

Rio di S. Marina

Campo S. Aponal

Rialto

Riva del Vin

†**San Silvestro**

S. Silvestro

Palazzo Bembo

Riva del Carbon

Pal. Dandolo

Palazzo Loredan

Pal. Grimari

San †
Benedetto

† **San Luca**

Campo S. Luca

Calle Fabbri

Calle C. Goldoni

Campo Manin

C. Mandola

Pal. Contarini del Bovolo

Ateneo Veneto

Campo S. Angelo

C. Caotorta

Campo S. Fantin

Teatro La Fenice

Pisc. di Frezzeria

Palazzi Contarini

Campo S.M. del Giglio

C. Larga XXII Marzo

C. del Traghetto

S.M. del Giglio

lazzo Corner (Ca' Grande)

asina elle tose

Pal. Venier dei Leoni

8

Palazzo Dario

Santa Maria della Salute

San Gregorio

7

Punta della Dogana

Dogana al Mare

Seminario Patriarcale

Le Zattere

24

†**San Bartolomeo**

C. Stagnen

C. della Fava

† **Santa Maria della Fava**

Merc S. Salvador

San Salvatore

Merc. S.

Salvadore

Salizzada S. Lio

Palazzo Priuli

Pal. Dona

Campo S. Maria Formosa

C. Bande

Palazzo Querini-Stampalia

C. Rimedio

C. Guerra

C. Specchieri

19

Palazzo Trevisan-Cappello

C. Larga S. Marco

C. Canonica

Sant' Apollonia

Pal. Patriarcale

2

1

Basilica di San Marco

20

Piazza San Marco

5

3

Piazzetta

4 **Palazzo Ducale**

6

Bacino Orseolo

Frezzeria

C. Ascension

C. Vallaresso

C. Ricoto

S.S. Moise

San Moise

Giardinetti Reali

Molo

Riva Degli Schiavoni →

San Marco Vallaresso

San Marco Giardinetti

Riva Degli Schiavoni

21

C. della Pietà

C. del Dose

C. del Forno

C. del Forno

Cp. de l'Arsenal

23

Riva   degli   Schiavoni

P. de la Ca' di Dio

Riva de la Ca' di Dio

C. del Forni

Fdm. dei Forni

22

Bacino San Marco

Council of Ten, the republic's dreaded security police), which is of particular historical interest as in this room justice was dispensed (and decapitations ordered). Formed in the 14th century to deal with emergency situations, the Ten were frequently considered more powerful than the Senate, and feared by all. Just outside the adjacent chamber, the **Sala della Bussola** (The Compass Chamber), notice the **Bocca dei Leoni** ("lion's mouth"), a slit in the wall into which secret denunciations and accusations of alleged enemies of the state were placed for quick action by the much feared Council.

The main sight on the next level down—indeed in the entire palace—is the **Sala del Maggior Consiglio** (Great Council Hall). This enormous space is made special by Tintoretto's huge *Paradiso* at the far end of the hall above the doge's seat (he was in his 70s when he undertook the project with the help of his son and would die 6 years later). Measuring 23 by 75 feet, it is said to be the world's largest oil painting; together with Veronese's gorgeous *Il Trionfo di Venezia (The Triumph of Venice)* in the oval panel on the ceiling, it affirms the power emanating from the Council sessions held here. Tintoretto also did the portraits of the 76 doges encircling the top of this chamber; note that the picture of the Doge Marin Falier, who was convicted of treason and beheaded in 1355, has been blacked out. Venice has never forgiven him. Although elected for life since sometime in the 7th century, over time *il doge* became nothing but a figurehead (they were never allowed to meet with foreign ambassadors alone); the power rested in the Great Council. Exit the Great Council Hall via the tiny doorway on the opposite side of Tintoretto's *Paradiso* to find the enclosed **Ponte dei Sospiri** (Bridge of Sighs), which connects the Ducal Palace with the grim Palazzo delle Prigioni (Prisons). The bridge took its current name only in the 19th century, when visiting northern European poets romantically envisioned the prisoners' final breath of resignation upon viewing the outside world one last time before being locked in their fetid cells awaiting the quick justice of the Terrible Ten. Some attribute the name to Casanova who, following his arrest in 1755 (he was accused of being a Freemason and spreading antireligious propaganda), crossed this very bridge. He was one of the rare few to escape 15 months after his imprisonment, alive, returning to Venice 20 years later. Some of the stone cells still have the original graffiti of past prisoners, many of them locked up interminably for petty crimes.

Campanile di San Marco (Bell Tower). San Marco, Piazza San Marco. ☎ **041/ 52-24-064.** Admission 8,000L ($4.70) adults, 4,000L ($2.35) students. June–Aug, daily 9am–7pm; Sept–May, daily 10am–4pm. Vaporetto: San Marco.

It's an easy elevator ride up to the top of this 324-foot bell tower for a breathtaking view of the cupolas of St. Mark's. It is the highest structure in the city, offering a pigeon's-eye view that includes the lagoon, its neighboring islands, and the red rooftops and church domes and bell towers of Venice—and, oddly, not a single canal.

An Insider's Look at the Palazzo Ducale

The **Itinerari Segreti del Palazzo Ducal** (Secret Trails of the Palazzo Ducale) are guided tours of otherwise restricted quarters and hidden passageways of this enormous palace, such as the doge's private chambers and the torture chambers where prisoners were interrogated. These tours have become so popular that they were recently introduced in English—they're given daily at 10:30am (you must reserve in advance at the ticket-buyers' entrance or by calling the number above), The tour, which cost 24,000L ($14.10) is also offered in Italian daily at 10am and noon for those with a smattering of the language when the English tour is sold out.

On a clear day you may even see the outline of the distant snow-capped Dolomite Mountains. Originally built in the 9th century, then rebuilt in the 12th, 14th, and 16th centuries when the pretty marble loggia at its base added by Jacopo Sansovino. It collapsed unexpectedly in 1902, miraculously hurting no one except a cat. It was rebuilt exactly as before, using most of the same materials, even rescuing one of the five historical bells that is still uses today (each bell was rung for a different purpose, such as war, the death of a doge, religious holidays, and so on).

Torre dell'Orologio (Clock Tower). San Marco, Piazza San Marco. No phone. Scheduled to reopen in 1999/2000. Vaporetto: San Marco.

Unfortunately the Clock Tower has been closed for a number of years despite original plans to open it in time for the 500-year anniversary of its construction. As you enter the magnificent Piazza San Marco, it is one of the first things you see, standing on the north side, next to and towering above the Procuratie Vecchie (the ancient administration buildings for the Republic). The Renaissance tower was built in 1496 and the clock mechanism of that same period still keeps perfect time but is getting a cleaning up by Piaget, the sponsor of the renovation, in time (hopefully) to ring in the Jubilee Year 2000. The two bronze figures, known as "Moors" because of the dark color of the bronze, pivot to strike the hour. The base of the tower has always been a favorite **punto di incontro** for Venetians ("meet me at the tower"), and is the entrance way to the ancient Mercerie (from the word for merchandise), the principal souklike retail street of both high-end boutiques and trinket shops that zigzags its way to the Rialto Bridge. Visits to the top, stopped in the late 1980s, will resume upon the tower's reopening.

Museo Civico Correr (Correr Museum). San Marco, Piazza San Marco. ☎ **041/ 52-25-625.** Joint admission with Palazzo Ducale (Ducal Palace) 17,000L ($10) adults, 10,000L ($5.90) students. Summer daily 9am–7pm; winter 9am–5pm. Last entrance is 45 minutes before closing time. Vaporetto: San Marco.

This museum, which you enter through an arcade at the west end of Piazza San Marco opposite the Basilica, is no match for the Accademia but does include some interesting paintings of Venetian life, and a fine collection of artifacts, such as coins, costumes, the doges' ceremonial robes and hats, and an incredible pair of 15-inch platform shoes, that gives an interesting feel for aspects of the day-to-day life in La Serenissima in the heyday of its glory. Bequeathed to the city by the aristocratic Correr family in 1830, the museum is divided into three sections: the Painting Section, the History Section, and the Museum of the Risorgimento (1797–1866). The latter two aren't worth much mention. Of the painting collection from the 13th to 18th centuries, Vittorio Carpaccio's *Le Cortigiane (The Courtesans)*, in room 15 on the upper floor, is one of the museum's most famous paintings (are they courtesans or the respected elite?), as are the star-attraction paintings by the Bellini family, father Jacopo and sons Gentile and Giovanni. For a lesson in just how little this city has changed in the last several hundred years, head to room 22 and its anonymous 17th-century bird's-eye view of Venice. Most of the rooms have a sign with a few paragraphs in English explaining the significance of the contents.

TOP ATTRACTIONS BEYOND SAN MARCO

✪ **Gallerie dell'Accademia (Accademia Gallery).** Dorsoduro, at the foot of the Accademia Bridge. ☎ **041/52-22-247.** Admission 12,000L ($7.05). Daily 9am–7pm in winter; summer hours expected to be extended to 8pm Tues–Sat; 2pm closing on Mon. Vaporetto: Accademia. Museum is at the foot of the Accademia Bridge.

The glory that was Venice lives on in the Accademia, the definitive treasure house of Venetian painting and one of Europe's great museums. Exhibited chronologically from the 13th through the 18th centuries, there is said to be no one hallmark masterpiece in this collection; rather, this is an outstanding and comprehensive showcase of works by all the great master painters of Venice, the largest such collection in the world. It includes Paolo and Lorenzo Veneziano from the 14th century; Gentile and Giovanni Bellini (and Giovanni's brother-in-law Andrea Mantegna from Padua) and Vittore Carpaccio from the 15th century; Giorgione (whose *Tempest* is one the gallery's most famous highlights), Tintoretto, Veronese, and Titian from the 16th century (works by Tintoretto and Veronese are found frequently in Venice's churches and scuolas but the bulk of Titian's work is found here; exceptions are those found in La Salute Church and the Frari Church); and from the 17th and 18th centuries, Canaletto, Piazzetta, Longhi, and Tiepolo, among others. Most of all, though, the works open a window onto the Venice of 500 years ago. Indeed, you'll see in the canvases how little Venice, perhaps least of any city in Europe, has changed over the centuries. Housed in a deconsecrated church its adjoining scuola, the church's confraternity hall, it is Venice's principal picture gallery, and one of the most important in Italy. Admission is limited, due to fire regulations, and lines can be daunting (but check for extended evening hours in the peak months), but put up with the wait and don't miss it.

✪ **Collezione Peggy Guggenheim.** Dorsoduro 701 (on C. San Cristoforo east of the Accademia Bridge). ☎ **041/52-06-288.** Admission 12,000L ($7.05) adults, 8,000L ($4.70) students. Wed–Mon 11am–6pm (winter hours may vary). Vaporeto: Accademia. Walk around the left side of the Accademia Gallery and take the first left. Walk straight, following the signs—you'll cross one canal, then walk alongside another, until turning left when necessary.

Considered to be one of the most comprehensive and important collections of modern art in the world and one of the most visited attractions in Venice, this collection of painting and sculpture was assembled by eccentric and eclectic American expatriate Peggy Guggenheim. She did an excellent job of it with particular strengths in Cubism, European Abstraction, Surrealism, and Abstract Expressionism since about 1910. Max Ernst was one of her early favorites (she even married him), as was Jackson Pollock.

Among the major works are Magritte's *Empire of Light*, Picasso's *La Baignade*, Kandinsky's *Landscape with Church (with Red Spot)*, Metzinger's *The Racing Cyclist*, and Pollock's *Alchemy*. The museum is also home to several haunting canvases by Ernst, Giacometti's unique figures, Brancusi's fluid sculptures, and numerous works by Braque, Dalí, Léger, Mondrian, Chagall, and Miró.

Directly on the Grand Canal, the elegant 18th-century Palazzo Venier dei Leoni, never finished and thus its unusual one-story structure, was purchased by Peggy Guggenheim in 1949 and became her home in Venice until her death in 1979. The year 1998 was marked by special exhibits to celebrate the centennial of her birth. The graves of her canine companions share the lovely interior garden with several prominent works of the Nasher Sculpture Garden, while the canal-side patio watched over by Marino Marini's *Angel of the Citadel* is one of the best spots to simply linger and watch the canal life. A new and interesting book and gift shop and cafe/bistro (recommended but not inexpensive) has opened in a separate wing across the inside courtyard where temporary exhibits are often housed.

Check the tourist office for an update on museum hours; it is often open when many others are closed and sometimes offers a few hours a week of free admission. Don't be shy about speaking English with the young staff working here on internship; most of them are American.

✪ **Scuola Grande di San Rocco (Confraternity of St. Roch).** San Polo 3058 (on Cam. San Rocco, adjacent to Cam. d. Frari and the Frari Church). ☎ **041/52-34-864.** Admission 8,000L ($4.70), students 6,000L ($3.50). Apr–Oct, daily 9am–5:30pm; Nov–Mar, daily 10am–4pm. Vaporetto: San Tomà. Walk straight ahead on C. d. Traghetto and turn right and

---

Cheap Thrills: What to See & Do in Venice for Free (or Almost)

- **Tour the Basilica di San Marco.** Straddling East and West, the ancient Basilica is unlike any other Roman Catholic church in the Western world. Try for one of the free guided tours given by church-affiliated volunteers; check with the tourist office for days and times.

- **Linger in Piazza San Marco.** The small three- and four-piece orchestras that play at the historic cafes lining the magnificent Piazza San Marco will make your cappuccino a worthwhile one. Take in the scenario for free by sitting on the steps on the south and west side of the piazza with a friend or your thoughts. The moon-illuminated mosaic-facade of the basilica is magic.

- **Drink in the scene.** For a dollar or two, hang out at the bar of one of Venice's countless neighborhood *bacari* wine bars. Regional wines by the glass and the tasty finger foods that accompany them are a draw, but not half as interesting as the experience itself. What language barrier?

- **Eat ice cream.** *Gelato* is commonplace the further south you venture, but Venice has two wonderful gelaterias, **Paolin** and **Nico** (see "Clubs, Bars *(Birrerie)* & Gelaterie," p. 438), that would pass muster with any Roman or Neapolitan. To go or to stay, it will only augment the day's enjoyment.

- **Cruise the Grand Canal.** It might be easier and faster to get there by foot, but if you board the **vaporetto** no. 1 (ticket 5,000L/$2.95) and ply the full length of the 2-mile Grand Canal (the world's most celebrated boulevard), you'll get a front row look at the aquatic palazzo-lined thoroughfare whose buildings never moved beyond the 18th century.

- **Enjoy the views.** Buy a crusty panino, or just some fresh fruit and cheese and pull up a piece of the embankment at **La Dogana** (Customs House) at the mouth of the Grand Canal (and east of La Salute Church), directly across from the Palazzo Ducale and the Piazza San Marco. This is the same heart-stopping first glimpse of the Serene Republic as glimpsed by visiting diplomats and foreign merchants who arrived during the glorious thousand year period when Venice held sway.

---

then immediately left across campo San Tomà. Walk as straight ahead as you can, on Ramo Mandoler, C. Larga Prima, and finally Salizzada San Rocco, which leads into the campo of the same name—look for the crimson sign behind the Frari Church.

This museum is a dazzling monument to the work of **Tintoretto**—the largest collection of his work anywhere. The series of the more than 50 dark and dramatic works took him more than 20 years to complete, making this the richest of the many confraternity guilds or *scuole* that once flourished in Venice.

Jacopo Robusti (1518–94), called Tintoretto because his father was a dyer, was a devout, unworldy man who only traveled once beyond Venice. His epic canvasses are filled with phantasmagoric light and intense, mystical spirituality.

Begin upstairs in the **Sala dell'Albergo**, where the most notable of the enormous, powerful canvases is the moving *La Crocifissione (The Crucifixion)*. In the center of the gilt ceiling of the Great Hall, also upstairs, is *Il Serpente di Bronzo (The Bronze Snake)*. Among the eight huge, sweeping paintings downstairs, each depicting a scene from the New Testament, *La Strage degli Innocenti (The Slaughter of the Innocents)* is the most noteworthy, so full of dramatic urgency and energy that the figures seem almost to tumble out of the frame. As you enter the room, it's on the opposite wall and at the far end of the room.

There's a useful guide to the paintings inside posted on the wall just before the entrance to the museum. There are a few Tiepolos among the paintings, as well as a solitary work by Titian. Note that the works on or near the staircase are not by Tintoretto.

Venice's second most important and richly decorated scuola or confraternity is that of **San Giorgio degli Schiavoni** (also called San Giorgio dei Greci); see below.

✪ **Canal Grande (Grand Canal).** Two most popular stations located at Piazzale Roma/Ferrovia (Train Station); and at Piazza San Marco. Vaporetto 1, ticket 5,000L ($2.95).

A leisurely cruise along the "Canalazzo" from Piazza San Marco to the Ferrovia (train station), or the reverse, is one of Venice's (and life's) must-do experiences. Hop on the no. 1 vaporetto in the late afternoon (try to get one of the coveted outdoor seats in the prow), when the weather-worn colors of the former homes of Venice's merchant elite are warmed by the soft light and reflected in the canal's rippling waters, and the busy traffic of delivery boats, vaporetti and gondolas that fills the city's main thoroughfare has eased somewhat. The sheer number and opulence of the 200-odd palazzi, churches, and imposing republican buildings dating from the 14th to the 18th centuries is enough to make any boat-going visitor's head swim. Many of the largest are now converted into imposing international banks, government or university buildings, art galleries and dignified consulates. They unfold along this singular 2-mile ribbon of water that loops through the city like an inverted S, crossed by only three bridges (the Rialto spans it at midpoint) and dividing the city into three **sestieri** neighborhoods to the left, three to the right. Some of the waterfront palazzi have been converted into condominiums whose lower water-lapped floors are now deserted, but the higher floors are still the coveted domain of the city's titled families, who have inhabited these glorious residences for centuries; others have become the summertime dream homes of privileged expatriates, drawn here as irresistibly as the romantic Venetians-by-adoption who preceded them—Richard Wagner, Robert Browning, Lord Byron, and, more recently, Woody Allen.

IN SAN POLO

Basilica di Santa Maria Gloriosa dei Frari (Church of the Frari). San Polo 3072 (Cam. dei Frari). ☎ **041/52-22-637.** Admission 3,000L ($1.75). Mon–Sat 10am–5:30pm, Sun 3–5:30pm. Vaporetto: San Tomà. Walk straight ahead on C. d. Traghetto, turn right and then immediately left across Cam. San Tomà. Walk as straight ahead as you can, on Ramo Mandoler, then C. Larga Prima, and turn right when you reach the beginning of Salizzada San Rocco.

Known simply as "i Frari", this immense 13th- to 14th-century Gothic church is easily found around the corner from the Scuola Grande di San Rocco—make sure you visit both when in this area. Built by the Franciscans ("frari" is a dialectal distortion of "frati" or brothers), it is the largest church in Venice after the Basilica of San Marco together with the cavernous Dominican Church of Santi Giovanni e Paolo in Castello northeast of Piazza San Marco. The Frari has long been considered something of a memorial to the ancient glories of Venice. Since St. Francis and the order he founded emphasized prayer and poverty, it is not surprising that the church is austere both inside and out. Yet it houses a number of important works including two of Titian's masterpieces (you may have noticed the scarcity of Titian's works in Venice outside of the Accademia and La Salute Church), the more striking being the *Assumption of the Virgin,* over the main altar, painted when the artist was only in his late 20s. His *Virgin of the Pesaro Family* is in the left nave; Titian's wife posed for the figure of Mary (then died soon afterward in childbirth) for this work commissioned by one of Venice's most powerful families. The church's other masterwork is Giovanni Bellini's important triptych on wood, the *Madonna and Child,* displayed in the Sacristy (take the door on the right as you face the altar); it is one of his finest portraits of the Madonna. There is also an almost primitive-looking wood carving by Donatello of St. John the Baptist. The grandiose tombs of two famous Venetians are also here: Canova (d. 1822), the Italian sculptor who led the revival of classicism and Titian who died in 1576 during a deadly plague.

   Note: Free tours in English are sometimes offered by church volunteers during the high season months; check at the church.

IN CASTELLO

Chiesa dei SS. Giovanni e Paolo (Church of Saints John and Paul). Castello 6363, Cam. Santi Giovanni e Paolo. ☎ **041/52-35-913.** Free admission. Mon–Sat 8am–12:30pm and 3–6pm; Sun 3–5:30pm (open Sun morning for those attending services only). Vaporetto: Rialto.

This massive Gothic church was built by the Dominican order during the 13th to 15th centuries and, together with the Frari Church in San Polo, is second in size only to the Basilica di San Marco. An unofficial Pantheon where 25 doges are buried (a number of tombs are part of the unfinished facade), the church, commonly known as Zanipolo in Venetian dialect, is also home to a number of artistic treasures. Visit the **Cappella del Rosario** through a glass door off the left transept to see the three recently restored ceiling canvases by Paolo Veronese, particularly *The Assumption of the Madonna.* Also recently restored is the brilliantly colored *Polyptych of St. Vincent Ferrer* (circa 1465) attributed to a young Giovanni Bellini, in the right aisle. You'll also see the foot of St. Catherine of Siena encased in glass. Adjacent to the church is the old Scuola di San Marco, an old confraternity-like association now run as a civic hospital, most noteworthy for its beautiful 15th-century Renaissance facade.

   Anchoring the large and impressive campo, a popular crossroads for this area of Castello, is the ✪ **statue of Bartolomeo Colleoni,** the Renaissance *condottiere* who defended Venice's interests at the height of its power and until his death in 1475. The 15th-century work is by the Florentine Andrea Verrocchio; it is considered one of the world's great equestrian monuments and Verrocchio's best.

Chiesa di San Zaccaria (Church of St. Zacchary). Castello, Cam. San Zaccaria. ☎ **041/52-21-257.** Free admission. Daily 10am–noon and 4–6pm. Vaporetto: San Zaccaria.

Behind (east of) St. Mark's Basilica is a 9th-century Gothic church with its original 13th-century campanile and a splendid Renaissance facade designed by Venetian architect Mario Codussi in the late 15th century. Of the interior's many artworks is the important *Madonna Enthroned with Four Saints* by Giovanni Bellini in 1505 and recently restored, above the second altar in the left aisle; art historians have long held this as one of his finer Madonnas. Apply to the sacristan to see the **Sisters' Choir,** with works by Tintoretto, Titian, Il Vecchio, Anthony van Dyck, and Bassano. The paintings aren't labeled, but the sacristan will point out the names of the artists. In the fan vaults of the Chapel of San Tarasio are the faded ceiling frescoes of the Florentine-born artist Andrea del Castagno, who was the first to bring the spirit of the Renaissance to Venice.

Museo Storico Navale and Arsenale (Naval History Museum and the Arsenal). Castello 2148 (Cam. San Biasio). ☎ **041/52-00-276.** Admission 2,000L ($1.20). Mon–Sat 9am–1:30pm. Thurs 2:30–5pm. Vaporetto: Arsenale.

The Naval History Museum's most fascinating exhibit is its collection of model ships. It was once common practice for vessels to be built, not from blueprints, but from the precise scale models that you see here. The prize of the collection is a model of the legendary **Bucintoro,** the lavish ceremonial barge of the doges. Another section of the museum contains an array of historic vessels. Walk along the canal as it branches off from the museum to the **Ships' Pavilion,** where the historic vessels are displayed.

To reach the Arsenal from the museum, walk up the Arsenale Canal and cross the wooden bridge to the Campo del'Arsenale, where you will soon reach the land gate of the **Arsenale,** not open to the public. The marble-columned Renaissance gate with the republic's winged lion above is flanked by four ancient lions, booty brought at various times from Greece and points further east. It was founded in 1104, and at the height of Venice's power in the 15th century it employed 16,000 workers who turned out merchant and wartime galley after galley on an early version of massive assembly lines at speeds and in volume unknown until modern times. Occupying one-fifth of the city's total acreage, the Arsenal was once the very source of the republic's maritime power. It is now used as a military zone and is as closed as Fort Knox to the curious.

Scuola di San Giorgio degli Schiavoni. Castello 3259, C. Furlani. ☎ **041/52-28-828.** Admission 5,000L ($2.95). Tues–Sat 9:30am–12:30pm and 3:30–6:30pm, Sun 9:30am–12:30pm. Vaporetto: San Zaccaria.

At the St. Antonino Bridge (Fondamenta dei Furlani) is the second most important guild house to visit in Venice. The Schiavoni were an important and wealthy trading colony of Dalmatian merchants who built their own scuola or confraternity (the coast of Dalmatia—the former Yugoslavia—was once ruled by the Greeks and therefore the scuola's alternative name of San Giorgio dei Greci). Between 1502 and 1509, Vittore Carpaccio (himself of Dalmatian descent) painted a pictorial cycle of nine masterpieces illustrating episodes from the lives of St. George (patron saint of the scuola) and St. Jerome, the Dalmatian patron saints. These appealing pictures freeze in time moments in the lives of the saints: St. George charges his ferocious dragon on a field littered with half-eaten bodies and skulls (a horror story with a happy ending); St. Jerome leads his lion into a monastery, frightening the friars; St. Augustine has just taken up his pen to reply to a letter from St. Jerome when he and his little dog are transfixed by a miraculous light, and a voice telling them of St. Jerome's death.

IN GUIDECCA & SAN GIORGIO

Chiesa di San Giorgio Maggiore. On the island of San Giorgio Maggiore, across St. Mark's Basin from Piazzetta San Marco. ☎ **041/52-27-827.** Free admission. Apr–Oct Mon–Sat 9:30am–12:30pm and 2:30–6:30pm; Nov–Mar 10am–12:30pm and 2:30–4:40pm. Sun afternoons only (open Sun morning to those attending services). Transportation: Take the Giudecca-bound vaporetto (no. 82) on Riva degli Schiavoni and get off at the first stop, the island of S. Giorgio Maggiore.

This church sits on the little island of San Giorgio Maggiore. It is one of the masterpieces of Andrea Palladio, the great Renaissance architect from nearby Vicenza. Most known for his country villas built for Venice's wealthy merchant families, Palladio was commissioned to build two churches (the other is the Redentore on the neighboring island of Giudecca), beginning with San Giorgio, designed in 1565 and completed in 1610. To impose a classical facade on the traditional church structure, Palladio designed two interlocking facades, with repeating triangles, rectangles, and columns that are carefully and harmoniously proportioned. Founded as early as the 10th century, the interior of the church was reinterpreted by Palladio with whitewashed surfaces, stark but majestic, and unadorned but harmonious space. The main altar is flanked by two epic paintings by an elderly Tintoretto, *The Fall of Manna* to the left and the more noteworthy *Last Supper* to the right, famous for its chiaroscuro. Through the doorway to the right of the choir leading to the **Cappella dei Morti** (Chapel of the Dead) you will find Tintoretto's *Deposition.*

FOR A CHURCH WITH A VIEW   To the left of the choir is an elevator that you can take to the top of the campanile, for a charge of 3,000L ($1.75), to experience an unforgettable view of the island itself, the lagoon, and the Palazzo Ducale and Piazza San Marco across the way.

A handful of remaining Benedictine monks gather for Sunday mass at 11am, sung in Gregorian chant.

IN DORSODURO

Ca' Rezzonico (Museo del '700 Veneziano; Museum of 18th-c Venice). Dorsoduro (on the Grand Canal on Fondamenta Rezzonico). ☎ **041/24-18-506.** Admission 12,000L ($7.05) adults, 8,000L ($4.70) students. Summer Sat–Thurs 10am–5pm; winter Sat–Thurs 10am–4pm. (These are hours predicted for 1999 opening; call in advance.) Vaporetto: Ca' Rezzonico. Walk straight ahead to Cam. San Barnabà, turn right at the piazza and go over one bridge, then take an immediate right for the museum entrance.

This museum was expected to reopen in 1999. A complete restoration is currently winding down on this handsome palazzo on the Grand Canal, offering an intriguing look into what living in a grand Venetian home was like in the final years of the Venetian Republic. Begun by Baldassare Longhena, 18th-century architect of La Salute Church, the Rezzonico home is a sumptuous backdrop for this collection of period paintings (most important, works by Venetian artists Tiepolo, Guardi, and a special room dedicated to the dozens of works by Longhi), furniture, tapestries, and artifacts. This museum is one of the best windows into the sometimes frivolous life of Venice of 200 years ago, as seen through the tastes and fashions of the wealthy Rezzonico family of merchants—the lavishly frescoed ballroom alone will evoke the lifestyle of the idle Venetian rich. The English poet Robert Browning, after the death of his wife Elizabeth Barrett Browning, made this his last home; he died here in 1889.

Chiesa di Santa Maria della Salute (Church of the Virgin Mary of Good Health). Dorsoduro, Cam. d. Salute. ☎ **041/52-25-558.** Free admission to church; sacristy 2,000L ($1.20). Daily 9am–noon and 3–5:30pm. Vaporetto: Salute.

Generally referred to as "La Salute," this crown jewel of 17th-century baroque architecture proudly reigns at a commercially and aesthetically important point, almost directly across from the Piazza San Marco, where the Grand Canal empties into the lagoon. The first stone was laid in 1631 after the Senate decided to honor the Virgin Mary of Good Health for delivering Venice from a plague (and after the completion of the neighboring Chiesa di San Giorgio: together with the Piazza San Marco, city elders were looking to create an ensemble of awe-inspiring structures to impress those arriving in Venice for the first time). They accepted the revolutionary plans of a young, relatively unknown architect, Baldassare Longhena (who would go on to design, among other projects, the Ca' Rezzonico). He dedicated the next 50 years of his life overseeing its progress (he would die 1 year after its inauguration but 5 years before its completion). The only great baroque monument built in Italy outside of Rome, the octagonal Salute is recognized for its exuberant exterior of volutes, scrolls, and more than 125 statues and rather sober interior, though one highlighted by a small gallery of important works in the Sacristy (you have to pay to enter and the entrance is through a small door to the left of the main altar). A number of ceiling paintings and portraits of the Evangelists and church doctors are all by **Titian** (few paintings of his can be found in Venice outside of the Accademia and the Church of I Frari). On the right wall is Tintoretto's *Marriage at Cana,* often considered one of his best.

Squero San Trovaso. Dorsoduro 1097 (on the Rio San Trovaso, southwest of the Accademia Gallery). No phone. Free admission.

Just north of the Zattere (the wide sunny walkway that runs alongside the Giudecca Canal in Dorsoduro), the squero (boatyard) is next to the Church of San Trovaso on the narrow Rio San Trovaso (not far from the Accademia Bridge).

One of the most interesting (and photographed) sights you'll see in Venice is this small boatyard, which first opened in the 17th century. It is surrounded by Tyrolian-looking wooden structures (a true rarity in this stone city built on water) that are home to the multiple-generational owners and original workshops for the traditional boats. Putting together one of the sleek black boats is a fascinatingly exact science that is still done in the revered traditional manner. The boats have been painted black since a 16th-century sumptuary law—one of many passed by the local legislators as excess and extravagance spiraled out of control. Whether regarding boats or baubles, laws were passed to restrict the gaudy outlandishness that, at the time, was commonly used to outdo the Joneses. Propelled by the strength of a single *gondoliere,* these boats unique to Venice have no modern equipment and rarely move at any great speed but with unrivaled grace. The right side of the gondola is lower since the gondoliere always stands in the back of the boat on the left. Although this squero, or boatyard, is the city's oldest and one of only three remaining (the other two are immeasurably more difficult to find), it works predominantly on maintenance and repair. Occasionally they build a new one (which takes some 40 to 45 working days), carefully crafting the gondola from the seven types of wood—mahogany, cherry, fir, walnut, oak, elm, and lime—necessary to give the shallow and asymmetrical boat its various characteristics. After they put all the pieces together, the painting, the *ferro* (the iron symbol of the city affixed to the bow), and the wood carving that secures the oar are commissioned out to various local artisans. While there were reportedly 10,000 of these elegant boats plying Venice's canals in the 16th century, today there are but 350 and the job of gondoliere is still a coveted profession, passed down from father to son over the centuries.

Aware they have become a tourist site, they don't mind if you watch them at work from across the narrow Rio di San Trovaso but don't try to invite yourself in. It's the perfect midway photo-op after a visit to the Gallerie dell'Accamdemia and a trip to the well-known gelateria, **Da Nico** (Zattere 922) whose chocolate *gianduiotto* is not to be missed.

IN CANNAREGGIO

Ca' d'Oro (Galleria Giorgio Franchetti). Cannaregio 3934 (on the Grand Canal, on the narrow C. Ca' d'Oro north of the Rialto Bridge). ☎ **041/52-38-790.** Admission 6,000L ($3.50). Daily 9am–7pm (experimental hours; check with tourist office). Vaporetto: Ca' d'Oro. Museum entrance is 50 yards away. Or it's an easy 15-min. walk northwest of the Rialto Bridge.

The 15th-century Ca' d'Oro is one of the best-preserved and most impressive of the hundreds of patrician palazzi lining the Grand Canal. After the Palazzo Ducale, it is said to be the finest example of Venetian gothic architecture in the city. A laborious restoration of its delicate pink-and-white marble facade (its name, the Golden Palace, refers to a gilt-covered facade that faded away long ago) was only completed in 1995. Inside, the ornate beamed ceilings and palatial trappings provide an attention-grabbing backdrop for the private collection of the former owner, Baron Franchetti, who bequeathed his palazzo and artwork to the city during World War I. The core collection, expanded over the years, now includes sculptures, furniture, tapestries, an impressive bronze and iron collection (12th to 16th centuries), and an art gallery whose two most important canvases include Andrea Mantegna's gripping and haunting *San Sebastiano,* immediately as you enter, and Titian's *Venus at the Mirror,* on the top floor, as well as lesser paintings by Tintoretto, Carpaccio, van Dyck, Giorgione, and others. For a delightful break, step out onto the palazzo's loggia, overlooking the Grand Canal for a view up and down the aquatic waterway and across to the covered Pescheria (fish market), a timeless vignette of an unchanged city.

Chiesa Santa Maria dei Miracoli. Cannareggio, Rio d. Miracoli. No phone. Admission 2,000 ($1.20). Mon–Sat 10am–5:30pm, Sun 3–5:30pm. Vaporetto: Rialto. Located midway between the Rialto Bridge and the Cam. SS. Giovanni e Paolo.

At a charming canal-crossing hidden in a quiet corner of the residential section of Canareggio northeast of the Rialto Bridge, the small 15th-century "Miracoli" is once again open to the public after a laborious 10-year renovation. It is one of the most attractive religious buildings in Europe, with one side of the precious polychrome-marbled facade running along side a canal, creating colorful and shimmering reflections. The architect, Pietro Lombardo (a local artisan whose background in monuments and tombs is obvious) would go on to become one of the founding fathers of the Venetian Renaissance. The less romantic are inclined to compare it to a large tomb with a dome, but the untold couples who have made this perfectly proportioned jewel-like church their choice for weddings will dispel such insensitivity. The small square in front is the perfect place for gondolas to drop off and pick up the newly betrothed. The inside is intricately decorated with early Renaissance marble reliefs, its pastel palette of pink, gray, and white marbles making an appropriately elegant venue for all those weddings. In the 1470s, an image of the Virgin Mary was responsible for a series of miracles (including bringing back to life someone that spent half an hour at the bottom of Giudecca Canal) that led pilgrims to leave gifts and, eventually, enough donations to have this church built. Look for the icon now displayed over the main altar.

Il Ghetto (the Jewish Ghetto). Cannaregio (Cam. d. Ghetto Nuovo). Vaporetto: Guglie or San Marcuola. From either of the two vaporetto stops, or if walking from the train station area, locate the Ponte delle Guglie. Walking away from the Grand Canal along the Fondamenta di Cannaregio, look for a doorway on your right with Hebrew etched across the threshold. This is the entrance to the C. d. Ghetto Vecchio that leads to the Cam. d. Ghetto Nuovo.

Venice's relationship with her longtime Jewish community fluctuated over time from acceptance to borderline tolerance, attitudes often influenced by the fear that Jewish moneylenders and merchants would infiltrate other sectors of the Republic's commerce under a government that thrived on secrecy and control. In 1516, 700 Jews were forced to move to this then-remote northwestern corner of Venice, to an abandoned site of a 14th-century foundry (*ghetto* is old Venetian dialect for foundry, a word that would soon be used throughout Europe and the world to depict isolated minority groups). As was commonplace with most of the hundreds of islands that make up Venice, this too was totally surrounded by water. Its two access points were controlled at night and early morning by heavy gates manned by Christian guards (paid for by the Jews), both protecting and segregating its inhabitants. Within one century, the community grew to more than 5,000 representing many languages and cultures. Although the original Ghetto Nuovo (New Ghetto) was expanded to include the Ghetto Vecchio, and later the Ghetto Nuovissimo (Newest Ghetto), land was limited and quarters always cramped. A very small, ever-diminishing community of Jewish families continues to live here today: Some 2,000 are said to live in all of Venice and Mestre.

Museo Communità Ebraica. Cam. d. Ghetto Nuovo 2902. ☎ **041/71-53-59.** Summer 10am–7pm; winter 10am–4:30pm; closed Sat. Tours hourly 10:30am–3:30pm; 12,000L ($7.05) includes admission to museum. Vaporetto: Guglie or San Marcuola.

The only way to visit any of the area's five 16th-century synagogues is through one of the Museo Communità Ebraica's frequent organized tours conducted in English. Your guide will elaborate on the commercial and political climate of those times, the unique "skyscraper" architecture (overcrowding resulted in many buildings having as many as seven low-ceilinged stories with no elevators), and the daily lifestyle of the Jewish community until the arrival of Napoléon in 1797, who declared the Jews free citizens. Venice's first kosher restaurant, **Gam Gam,** recently opened on Fond. di Cannaregio 1122 (☎ **041/715284**) near the entrance to the Ghetto and nearby the Guglie vaporetto stop. Owned and run by Orthodox Jews from New York, it serves lunch and dinner every day except Saturday, with an early Friday closing after lunch.

ESPECIALLY FOR KIDS

It goes without saying that a **gondola ride** will be the thrill of a lifetime for any child or adult. If that's too expensive, consider the convenient and far less expensive alternative: the ✪ **no. 1 vaporetto.** They offer two entirely different experiences, that of seeing Venice through the back door (and a ride past **Marco Polo's house**), and a tool down its aquatic Main Street, the Grand Canal, respectively. Look for the ambulance boat, the garbage boat, the firefighters boat, the funeral boat, the garbage boat, even the Coca Cola delivery boat. Best sightings are the special gondolas filled with flowers and rowed by gondolieri in livery taking the happy bride and groom to the church.

Judging from the squeals of delight, **feeding the pigeons in Piazza San Marco** (purchase a bag of corn and you'll be draped in pigeons in a nanosecond; these birds have radar) could be the epitome of your child's visit to Venice, and it's the optimal photo op. Be sure your child won't be startled by the all the fluttering and flapping.

A jaunt to the neighboring island of **Murano** can be as educational as recreational—follow the signs to any *fornace* where a glass-blowing performance of the island's thousand-year-old art is free entertainment. But be ready for the almost guaranteed sales pitch that follows.

Before you leave town, take the elevator to the top of the **Campanile di San Marco** (the highest structure in the city) for a pigeon's-eye view of Venice's rooftops and church cupolas, or get close up and personal to the four bronze horses on the facade of the **Basilica San Marco.** Its **outdoor loggia with a view** holds the copies of the famous **quadriga** (you can see the real ones in the Basilica's Museo Marciano), but the view from here is something hard for you or your children to forget.

Children enjoy the **Museo Navale & Arsenale** with its ship models and old vessels, and the many historic artifacts in the **Correr Museum** that are a vestige of when Venice was a world unto itself.

The **winged lion,** said to have been a kind of good-luck mascot to St. Mark, patron saint of Venice, was the very symbol of the Serene Republic and to this day appears on everything from cafe napkins to T-shirts. Who can spot the most flying lions? They appear on facades, atop columns, over doorways, as pavement mosaics, government stamps, and on the local flag. You'll spot more here than on a safari in Botswana.

6 Organized Tours

Most of the centrally located travel agencies will have posters in their windows advertising half-day and full-day walking tours of the city's sites. Most of these tours are piggy-backed onto those organized by **American Express** (see "Fast Facts" in the

"Orientation" section earlier in this chapter), known for the best quality and value for the money. The half day should cost the same as the American Express tours, approximately 40,000 to 45,000L ($23.50 to $26.50). The alternative of a personal guide (a list of qualified polylingual guides is available from the tourist office) is available for 3-hour tours at 169,000L ($99.40) for up to 30 people—a consideration if there is a fair number of you traveling together. You can also cover most of the major sights of Venice by taking your own self-guided tours with the guide *Frommer's Walking Tours: Venice.* Introduced in 1998 and a welcomed newcomer is the **Enjoy Venice** walking tour offered by Thomas Cook: 30,000L ($17.65) or for those under 26 years 25,000L ($14.70). Just show up Monday through Saturday for the 10am departure at the Thomas Cook office off the Rialto (Castello 5144) or call toll-free from anywhere in Italy ☎ 167-274819.

Free organized tours of the Basilica and some of the other principal churches can be erratic, as they are given by volunteers. Ask at the tourist office and check the monthly publication *Ospite a Venezia (Guest in Venice)* for "Talks and Guided Tours." This can be one of many incidents that demonstrate how poorly organized the city's fractious agencies can be in these matters.

Organized 3- and 4-hour tours visit the **Islands of the Venetian Lagoon,** and include a brief visit to Murano, Burano, and Torcello for approximately 25,000 to 40,000L ($14.70 to $23.50). The tours leave from different booths on the Riva degli Schiavoni and from in front of La Zecca near the tourist office in Palazzetto Selvi (aka Palazzina del Santi) just west of the Palazzo Ducale. But buy a special 1-day excursion ticket (round-trip) on the no. 12 vaporetto for 10,000L ($5.90) and you can do a tour yourself, but check on the connecting interisland boats and the infrequent return departures from the outer islands to Venice. The islands are small and easy to navigate. See "Exploring Venice's Islands," below.

7 Festivals & Special Events

During the wintertime **Carnevale,** countless musical and cultural events (many of them outdoors despite the weather and free of charge) fill the calendar for 2 or 3 weeks leading up to Ash Wednesday, the beginning of Lent. Things come to a climax the night of *martedì grasso,* "Fat Tuesday" or Mardi Gras, with a grand finale fireworks display and some kind of big extravaganza (no tickets needed) in Piazza San Marco. Contact the tourist office for full details on all festivities. Good luck: Nothing really gets organized with printed material until a few weeks beforehand. Hotels should be booked months ahead, especially for the two weekends prior to Shrove Tuesday. Your booked hotel will sometimes offer to fax you listings of events—if and when they can get a hold of them themselves. You're better off just showing up, with a secure hotel reservation, and going with the flow. There's always something fun going on, much of it spontaneous. Since so much of Carnevale happens in the street, make sure to dress warmly; go to see and be seen but be ready for inclement weather—this isn't Rio! And don't forget your costume—or just buy a mask and silly hat upon your arrival. Even staunch non-exhibitionists get sucked into the revelry.

The **Voga Longa** (literally "long row"), a 30-km (18-mile) rowing "race" from San Marco to Burano and back again, has been enthusiastically embraced since its inception in 1975, following the city's effort to keep alive the centuries-old heritage of the regatta. It takes place on a Sunday in mid-May; for exact dates, consult the tourist office. The event itself is colorful, and every local seems to have a relative or next-door neighbor competing; it's a great excuse for a party.

Carnevale a Venezia

Venetians once more are taking to the open piazzas and streets for the pre-Lenten holiday of ✪ **Carnevale.** The festival traditionally marked the unbridled celebration that preceded Lent, the period of penitence and abstinence prior to Easter, and its name is derived from the Latin *carnem levare,* meaning "to take meat away."

Although lasting no more than 5 to 10 days today (and really culminating in the Friday to Tuesday before Ash Wednesday), in the 18th-century heyday of Carnevale in La Serenissima Republic, well-heeled revelers came from all over Europe to take part in festivities that began months ahead, gaining crescendo until their raucous culmination at midnight on Shrove Tuesday. As the Venetian economy declined, and its colonies and trading posts fell to other powers, the Republic of Venice in its swan song turned to fantasy and escapism. The faster its decline, the longer, and more unlicensed, became its anything-goes merrymaking. Masks became ubiquitous, affording anonymity and pardoning 1,000 sins. They permitted the fishmonger to attend the ball and dance with the baroness, the properly married to carry on as if they were not. The doges condemned it and the popes denounced it, but nothing could dampen the Venetian Carnevale spirit until Napoléon arrived in 1797 and put an end to the festivities.

Resuscitated in 1980 by local tourism powers to fill the empty winter months when tourism came to a screeching halt, Carnevale is calmer nowadays, though just barely. The born-again festival got off to a shaky start, met at first with indifference and skepticism, but in the years since then, it has grown from strength to strength. In the 1980s Carnevale attracted an onslaught of what was seemingly the entire student population of Europe, backpacking young people who slept in the piazzas and train station. Politicians and city officials adopted a middle-of-the-road policy that helped establish Carnevale's image as neither a backpacker's free-for-all outdoor party nor a continuation of the exclusive private balls in the Grand Canal palazzi available to a very few.

Carnevale is at its dazzling best as it approaches its 20th anniversary, a harlequin patchwork of musical and cultural events, many of them free of charge, that

Stupendous fireworks fill the night sky during the **Festa del Redentore,** on the third Saturday night and Sunday in July. The celebration, which marks the July 1578 lifting of a plague that had gripped the city, is centered around the Palladio-designed Chiesa del Redentore (Church of the Redeemer) on the island of Giudecca, which was built by way of thanksgiving. A bridge of boats across the Giudecca Canal links the church with the banks of le Zattere in Dorsoduro for the occasion, and hundreds of boats of every vintage and size fill the Giudecca Canal. It's one big floating **festa** until night descends and an awesome half-hour spettacolo of fireworks fills the sky.

The **Venice International Film Festival,** held in late August and early September, is considered the finest summer celebration of celluloid in Europe after Cannes. Films from all over the world are shown in the Palazzo del Cinema on the Lido as well as various venues across the city—and occasionally outside in some of the campi. Ticket prices vary but are usually modest; some outdoor screenings are free. Check with the tourist office for listings. Star gazers might spot Uma, Tom, Bruce and Sean, depending upon the year's hot releases. Hotels and the tourist office can help you try to get your hands on the limited number of tickets available to the public.

appeal to all ages, tastes, nationalities, and budgets. At any given moment, musical events are staged in any of the city's dozens of piazzas—from reggae and zydeco to jazz to baroque and chamber music—and special art exhibits are mounted at numerous museums and galleries. The recent involvement of international corporate commercial sponsors has met with a mixed reception, although it seems to be the direction of the future.

Carnevale is not for those who dislike crowds. The crowds are what it's all about. All of life becomes a stage, and everyone is on it. Whether you spend months creating an extravagant costume, or grab one ad hoc from the countless stands set up about the town, Carnevale is about giving in to the spontaneity of magic and surprise around every corner, the mystery behind every mask. Masks and costumes are everywhere, though you won't see anything along the line of Teletubbies or Zorro. Emphasis is on the historical, for Venice's Carnevale is the chance to relive the glory days of the 1700s when Venetian life was at its most extravagant. Groups travel in coordinated getups that range from a contemporary passel of Felliniesque clowns to the court of the Sun King in all its wigged-out, over-the-top drag-queen best. There are the three musketeers riding the vaporetto; your waiter appears dressed as a nun; sitting alone on the church steps is a Romeo waiting for his Juliet; late at night crossing a small, deserted campo a young, laughing couple appear out of a gray mist in a cloud of crinoline and sparkles, and then disappear down a small alley. The places to be seen in costume (only appropriate costumes need apply) are the historical cafes lining the Piazza San Marco, the **Florian** being the unquestioned Command Post. Don't expect to be seated in full view at a window seat unless your costume is straight off the stage of the local opera house.

The city is the quintessential set, the perfect venue; Hollywood could not create a more evocative location. This is a celebration about history, art, theater, and drama, as one would expect to find in Italy, the land that gave us the Renaissance and Zefferelli—and Venice, an ancient and wealthy republic that gave us Casanova and Vivaldi. Venice and Carnevale were made for each other.

Venice hosts the latest in modern and contemporary painting and sculpture from dozens of countries during the prestigious **Biennale d'Arte,** an international modern-art show that fills the pavilions of the public gardens at the east end of Castello from late May through October of every uneven-numbered year (1995 marked its 100th anniversary; beginning in the year 2000 it may revert back to its usual even-numbered year). Many great modern artists have been "discovered" at this world-famous show. Note that the Giardini Pubblici gardens are marked **Esposizione Internazionale d'Art Moderna** on most maps; take vaporetto 1 or 52 to the Giardini stop.

The **Regata Storica** (Historical Regatta), which takes place on the Grand Canal on the first Sunday in September, is first an extravagant seagoing parade in historical costume as well as a genuine regatta. Just about every seaworthy gondola in Venice, richly decorated for the occasion and piloted by gondolieri in colorful period livery that recall the halcyon days of the Serene Republic, participates in this maritime cavalcade. The aquatic parade is followed by three individual regattas that are wildly cheered on as they proceed along the Grand Canal. Grandstand tickets can be purchased through the tourist office; or come early and pull up a piece of embankment near the Rialto Bridge for the best seats in town.

Other notable events include November 21st's **Festa della Salute,** when a pontoon bridge is erected across the Grand Canal to connect the churches of La Salute and Santa Maria del Giglio, commemorating another delivery from a plague in 1630 that wiped out a third of the lagoon's population; it is the only day the Salute Church opens its massive front doors (a secondary entrance is otherwise used). The **Festa della Sensa,** on the Sunday following Ascension Day in May, reenacts the ancient ceremony when the doge would wed Venice to the sea. **April 25** is a local holiday, the feast day of Saint Mark, beloved patron saint of Venice and of the ancient Republic. A special high mass is celebrated in the Basilica of San Marco and Venetians exchange roses with those they love.

Finally, the ultimate anomaly: Venice's annual **October Maratona (Marathon),** starting at Villa Pisani on the mainland and ending up along the Zattere for a finish at the Basilica di Santa Maria della Salute on the tip of Dorsoduro; it's usually held the last Sunday of October.

8 Shopping

Scores of trinket stores and middle-market to upscale boutiques line the narrow zigzagging **Mercerie,** the centuries-old retail axis that runs north–south between the Piazza San Marco and the Rialto Bridge. More expensive clothing and gift boutiques make for great window-shopping on the **Calle Larga XXII Marzo,** the wide street that begins west of Piazza San Marco and wends its way to the expansive Campo Santo Stefano in the area of the Accademia museum. The narrow, crowded, store-lined **Frezzeria,** also west of Piazza San Marco, offers a grab bag of bars, souvenir shops, and tony clothing stores.

In a city that for centuries has thrived almost exclusively on tourism, remember this: Where you buy cheap you get cheap. The hotel and restaurant prices are some of the highest in Italy: Retail stores hold no exceptions. There are few bargains to be had and there is nothing to compare with Florence's outdoor San Lorenzo market; the **Rialto Market** is as good as it gets. Here you'll find cheap T-shirts, plastic gondolas that glow in the dark, and tawdry glass trinkets. This is the tourist-clogged area found immediately upon descending the Rialto Bridge on its west (San Polo) side. Keep heading straight ahead (away from the bridge) and on the right side you'll find the covered, canal-side **Pescheria** fish market—now, this is a true *spettacolo* not to be missed! (See the section on picnicking above for more information.) Venetians, centuries-old merchants, are not known for bargaining. You'll stand a better chance for a discount when paying in cash, buying more than one, and when buying costly items such as glassware.

Venice is famous for several ancient local crafts hard to come by elsewhere: ✪ **glass** from the island of Murano, delicate **lace** from Burano, and the *carta pesca* (papier-mâché) masks you find in endless botteghe or mask shops around town, where you can watch artisans paint amid their wares. Now, here's the bad news regarding each of these local arts: There is such an overwhelming sea of cheap glass gewgaws, that it becomes something of a turnoff (shipping and insurance costs make most things unaffordable); there are so few women left in Burano willing to spend countless and tedious hours keeping alive the dying art of lace making that the few pieces you'll see *not* produced by machine in Hong Kong are sold at stratospheric prices; masks are mass-produced with little attention to quality or finish.

ANTIQUES

The interesting **Mercatino dell'Antiquariato** (Antiques Fair) takes place three times yearly in the charming Campo San Maurizio between Piazza San Marco and Campo

Venice Shopping Strategies

There are two rules of thumb for shopping in Venice: If you have the good fortune of continuing on to Florence or Rome, then wait to shop for clothing, leather goods, or accessories when you get there. However, if you happen upon something that strikes you, consider it twice on the spot (and not back at your hotel), then buy it. Don't plan on returning: In this web of alleyways, you'll waste precious time trying to find that shop again.

Santo Stefano. Dates change yearly for the 3-day weekend market but generally fall the first weekend of April, mid-September, and the weekend before Christmas. More than 100 vendors sell everything from the sublime piece of Murano glass to quirky dust collectors. Early birds might find reasonably priced finds such as Murano candy dishes from the '50s, Venetian-pearl glass beads older still, old Italian posters advertising Campari-sponsored regattas, or antique postcards of Venice that could be from the 1930s or the 1830s—things change so little. Those for whom price is less an issue might pick up antique lace by the yard, or a singular museum-quality piece of hand-blown glass from a local master.

CRAFTS

The **Murano Art Shop** at San Marco 1232 (on the store-lined Frezzeria, parallel to the western border of, and close to, the Piazza San Marco; ☎ 041/52-33-851) is a cultural experience. At this small, precious shop, every inch of wall space is draped with the whimsical crafts of the city's most creative artisans. Fusing the timeless with the contemporary and whimsical—with a nod to the magic and romance of Venice past—the results are a dramatic and ever-evolving collection of masks, puppets, music boxes, marionettes, costume jewelry, and the like. It's all expensive, but this rivals a visit to the Doge's Palace.

When it seems as if every gift-store window is awash with collectible bisque-faced dolls in elaborate pinafores and headdresses, head to **Bambole di Trilly** at Castello 4974 (Fondamenta dell'Osmarin, off the Cam. San Provolo on your way east out of Piazza San Marco in the direction of the Church of San Zaccaria; ☎ 041/52-12-579), where the hand-sewn wardrobes of rich Venetian fabrics and painstakingly painted faces are particularly exquisite; the perfect souvenir starts at 35,000L ($20.60) in this well-stocked work space east of Piazza San Marco and north of Campo San Zaccaria.

EMBROIDERED LINENS

A doge's ransom will buy you an elaborately worked tablecloth at **Jesurum** at San Marco 4857 (on the very busy Mercerie shopping strip that zigzags from Piazza San Marco to the Rialto Bridge; ☎ 041/52-06-177), but some of the small items make gorgeous affordable gifts for discerning friends for under 20,000L ($11.75): small, drawstring pouches for your baubles, hand-embroidered linen cocktail napkins in different colors, or hand-finished doilies and linen coasters.

FOODSTUFFS

Food lovers will find the perfect, charmingly packaged food products for themselves or friends at the well-known past manufacturer **Giacamo Rizzo** near the major Coin department store (but on the opposite side of the narrow street) northeast of the Rialto Bridge at Cannaregio 5778 at Calle S. Giovanni Grisostomo (☎ 041/52-22-824).

Pasta made in the shape of gondolas, colorful carnival hats and dozens of other imaginatively shaped possibilities (colored and flavored with squash, beet, spinach) cost 7,000 to 11,000L ($4.10 to $6.50) per package. Those with a sweet tooth should head in the opposite direction, to **Pasticceria Marchini** just before Campo Santo Stefano (San Marco 2769 at Ponte San Maurizio; ☎ 041/52-29-109). A selection of traditional cookies are beautifully prepackaged for traveling—the delicate *baicoli,* cornmeal raisin *zaleti,* and the s-shaped *buranelli.*

GLASS

Cut to the chase and visit the spacious emporium of quality glass items at **Marco Polo** (San Marco 1644, ☎ 041/52-29-295) just west of the Piazza San Marco. The front half of the first floor offers a variety of small gift ideas (candy dishes, glass-topped medicine boxes, paperweights). Cheap they are not, but no one else has such a lovely representation of ✪ **handblown Murano glassware.** Consider a pair of lovely Murano drinking glasses or flutes to toast in the year 2000. Glass beads are called "Venetian Pearls," and an abundance of exquisite antique and reproduced baubles are the draw at **Anticlea** at Castello 4719 (on the Cam. San Provolo in the direction of the Church of San Zaccaria, ☎ 041/52-86-946). Once used for trading in Venice's far-flung colonies, they now fill the coffers of this small shop east of Piazza San Marco, sold singly or already strung. The open-air stall of **Susie and Andrea** (Rv. degli Schiavoni, near Pensione Wildner; just ask) has handcrafted beads that are new, well made and strung, and moderately priced. The stall operates from February through November.

LEATHER

One usually thinks of Florence when thinking of Italian leather goods. But the plethora of mediocre-to-refined shoe stores in Venice is testimony to the tradition of small shoe factories along the nearby Brenta canal that supplies most of Italy and much of the world with its made-in-Italy footwear. If you're not going on to Florence and are in the market for a handbag or small leather goods, the two-storied **Marforio** shop very near the Rialto Bridge (on the Merceria Due Aprile 5033; ☎ 41/25734) stocks small leather goods and accessories on the street level, and bags according to color and style (evening, casual, shoulder-strapped, back-pack style) on the floors above. Not a good place just to browse, but a great place if you know what your looking for. There are some designer labels, but less expensive lines are abundant and the selection is probably the largest in Venice.

MASKS

A shortage of mask bottegas in Venice is not your problem; the challenge is ferreting out the few exceptionally talented artists producing one-of-a-kind theatrical pieces. Only the quality-conscious should shop at **La Bottega dei Mascareri** (San Polo 80—at northern end of the Rialto Bridge amid the tourist booths, ☎ 041/52-23-857), where the charming Boldrin brothers' least elaborate masks begin under 25,000L ($14.70). Anyone who thinks a mask is a mask is a mask should come here first for a look-see.

MUSIC

If you attended any of the many marvelous concerts in Venice's churches and scuole, you'll want to bring some of the musical magic home with you. **Nalesso** (San Marco 2765, on your left just before Campo Santo Stefano if you're arriving from the Piazza San Marco area; ☎ 041/52-03-329) specializes in classical musical recording, particularly the entire works of Vivaldi and 18th-century Venetian music. You can also pick up tickets here to most of the concerts around town.

9 Venice After Dark

Whatever time of year you're visiting Venice, be sure to go to one of the tourist information centers for current English-language schedules of the month's special events
(up-to-date entertainment listings are posted in the tourist offices, in hotels and
around town, but ask for a printed copy). The monthly tourist-oriented magazine
Ospite de Venezia is distributed free of charge and is extremely helpful, but is usually
only available in the more expensive hotels.

If you're looking for nocturnal action, you're in the wrong town. You're best bet is
to sit in the moonlit Piazza San Marco and listen to the cafes' outdoor orchestras, with
the illuminated Basilica before you—the perfect opera set. It's magic. And a seat on
the steps lining the southern side of the piazza gets you in for free.

THE PERFORMING ARTS

Venice has a vigorous and rich tradition of classical music. Several Venetian churches
and scuole regularly host classical-music concerts (with an emphasis on the baroque
music that once flourished here, primarily that of Vivaldi and his contemporaries) by
local and international artists.

The city stood still in shock as the famous **Teatro la Fenice** went up in flames
during a devastating fire in January 1996. For centuries it was the city's principal stage
for world-class opera, music, theater, and ballet. A concert here was always a cultural
experience, set in a gilt and red-velvet jewel box—nothing remained after the fire. Car-
penters and artisans were on standby to work around the clock to create a replica of
the old Teatro Fenice of 1836 according to archival designs; the money flowed in from
around the world—and nothing happened. Locked in bidding wars, local authorities
are now promising to begin work in spring 1999. In the meantime the **Orchestra
della Fenice** and **Coro della Fenice** attempt to re-create the magic for the 1999
season in substitute venues around town; a year-round tentlike structure, the
PalaFenice is located in the unlikely area of the Tronchetto parking facilities near the
Piazzale Roma (☎ 147/88-22-11 toll free within Italy). Ticket costs should remain
the same, starting at approximately 30,000 to 150,000L ($17.65 to $88.35). Information about the status of future performances is available at the tourist office. La
Fenice is located at San Marco 1965, on Campo San Fantin (☎ 041/78-65-62 for
information).

Chiesa di Vivaldi, known officially as the Chiesa della Pietà, is the most popular
venue for the music of Vivaldi and his contemporaries. It was here that the "red priest"
was choral director, and the church offers some of the highest quality ensembles. If
you're lucky, they'll be performing *Le Quattro Staggioni (The Four Seasons)*. Tickets are
sold at the church's box office in the church (☎ 041/52-31-096), on Riva degli Schiavoni, or at the front desk of the well-known Metropole Hotel just next door; they
usually cost 40,000L ($23.50), students 25,000L ($14.70). Music lovers: Go for the
splurge—it will be one of the highlights of your stay. Information and schedules are
available from the tourist office; tickets for most concerts can be bought at many of
the principal hotels or travel agencies in town. A number of other churches such as
Santo Stefano, San Stae, and the Scuola Grande of San Rocco and the (less magnificent) Scuola di San Giovanni also host concerts year round.

CAFES

Venice is a quiet town in the evening and offers very little in the way of nightlife. For
tourists and locals alike, Venetian nightlife mainly centers around the many cafe/bars
in one of the world's most remarkable piazzas: Piazza San Marco; even Napoléon

called it the most beautiful drawing room of the world. It is also the most expensive and touristed place to linger over a Campari or cappuccino, but a splurge that should not be dismissed too readily.

The nostalgic 18th-century ✪ **Caffè Florian,** at San Marco 56a–59a, on the south side of the piazza (closest to the water), is the most famous (closed Wednesday) and has the most theatrical interior for winter interludes. It's also extremely expensive— have a Bellini at the back bar (with just four seats) and spend half what you'd pay at a table. It's said that when Casanova escaped from the prisons in the Doge's Palace, he stopped here for a coffee before fleeing Venice.

On the opposite (north) side of the square at San Marco 133–34 are the old-world **Café Lavena** (closed Tuesday) and **Cafe Quadri** (closed Monday) at no. 120. At any of these spots, a cappuccino, tea, or Coca-Cola at a table will set you back about 10,000L ($5.90), but no one will rush you, and if the weather is good and the late afternoon/evening orchestras are playing, the outdoor tables are the best ticket in town. Around the corner (no. 11) and smack in front of the magnificent pink-and-white marble Palazzo Ducale with the lagoon sparkling in the moonlight on your right is the lesser known, slightly less expensive—and in my book, the best deal—✪ **Cafe Chioggia** (closed Sunday). Come here at midnight and watch the Moors strike the hour atop the Clock Tower from your outside table, while the quartet or pianist plays everything from quality jazz to pop till the wee hours (and without taking a break every 6 minutes; they also take requests). You won't hear "New York, New York" or "Moon River" here.

If the weather is chilly or inclement, or for no reason other than to revel in the history and drama of Venice's grand dame hotel, dress up, look confident and stroll into the hotel **Danieli's** landmark lobby's **Bar Dandolo** (Castello 4196 on Riva degli Schiavoni east of Piazza San Marco). Tea or coffee will only set you back 8,000L ($4.70) and you can sit forever, taking in what once was the former residential palazzo of a 15th-century doge. A pianist plays from 7 to 9pm and from 10pm to 12:30am. Drinks are far more expensive; ask to see the price list before ordering.

CLUBS, BARS (BIRRERIE) & GELATERIE

Although Venice boasts an old and prominent university, clubs and discos barely enjoy their 15 minutes of popularity before changing hands or closing down (some are only open in the summer months). Young Venetians tend to go to the Lido or mainland Mestre.

For just plain hanging out in the late afternoon and early evening, popular squares that serve as meeting points include **Campo San Bartolomeo,** at the foot of the Rialto Bridge, and nearby **Campo San Luca;** you'll see Venetians of all ages milling about engaged in animated conversation, particularly from 5pm till dinnertime. In late-night hours, for low prices and a low level of pretension, I'm fond of the **Campo Santa Margherita,** a huge open campo about halfway between the train station and Ca' Rezzonico. Look for the popular **Green Pub** (no. 3053, closed Thursday), **Bareto Rosso** (no. 2963, closed Sunday) and **Bar Salus** (no. 3112). **Campo Santo Stefano** is also worth a visit, namely to sit and sample the goods at the **Bar/Gelateria Paolin** (no. 2962, closed Friday) one of the city's best ice-cream sources. Its runner-up, **Gelateria Nico,** is on the Zattere in Dorsoduro 922, south of the Gallerie dell'Accademia. For occasional evenings of live music, cabaret or just a relaxed late-night hangout for a drink and a bite, consider the ever popular **Le Bistrot de Venise** (see "Great Deals on Dining," above).

Note: Most bars are open Monday to Saturday from 8pm to midnight.

Piccolo Mondo at Dorsoduro 1056 (near Accademia; ☎ **041/52-00-371**), wears many hats to survive. Self-billed as a "disco-pub," it serves sandwiches and pizzas during lunchtime to the tune of America's latest disco music, and offers a Happy Hour late afternoon. But the only reason you'd want to come is if you're in the market for a disco night (summer only). It's frequented mostly by curious foreigners and some young Venetians who seek them out.

Devil's Forest Pub at San Marco 5185 (Calle Stagneri; ☎ **041/520-06-23**), and El Moro Pub (see below) are the latest in the city's trend to imitate British *birrerie*—something you wouldn't anticipate seeking out in Italy. But both pubs offer the out-sider an authentic chance to take in the convivial atmosphere and find out just where the local Venetians hang out. The Devil's Forest has all the basic elements right: carved-wood bar, interior stained glass, and a good selection of draft beers, including Guinness Stout. A pint of beer costs 7,000L ($4.10), while a variety of simple pasta dishes and sandwiches run 6,000 to 8,000L ($3.50 to $4.70). To **get here** note that Calle Stagneri begins at the right (southeast) end of Campo San Bartolomeo, which is at the foot of the Rialto Bridge on the San Marco side of the Grand Canal (with your back to the bridge, look for the Banca Commerciale Italiana on the corner).

With a half-dozen beers on tap (a pint will cost 8,000L/$4.70), **El Moro Pub** at Castello 4531 (Calle delle Rasse; ☎ **041/52-82-573**), is the biggest draw in town. The crowd can be a bit older here, where postuniversity types congregate at the bar. TVs sometimes transmit national soccer or tennis matches and the management wel-comes those who linger, but sensitive nonsmokers won't want to.

Come to **Paradiso Perduto** at Cannaregio 2540 (Fondamenta della Misericordia; Vaporetto: Ferrovia; ☎ **041/72-05-81**), for the live jazz performed on a small stage several nights a week. It's popular with American and other foreigners living in Venice, all of whom have managed to find this place and pass the word, this bar was once devoid of tourists, primarily because it's hard to find and off the beaten path. But the word is out and now there's even a good selection of well-prepared pizzas and pastas for under 10,000L ($5.90); arrive early for a table. Beer runs 6,000L ($3.50). To **get here** from the train station, walk along Lista di Spagna, past Campo S. Geremia, and across the first bridge onto Rio Terrà San Leonardo; turn left onto Rio Terrà Farsetti, cross the bridge, turn right onto Fondamenta della Misericordia, and the bar will be straight ahead on your left.

THE CASINO

From May to October, **Casino Municipale di Venezia** located at Palazzo Vendramin Calergi, Cannaregio 2400 (Fondamenta Vendramin; Vaporetto: Marcuola; ☎ **041/52-97-111**), moves to its nondescript summer location on the Lido, where a visit is not as strongly recommended as during the winter months when it is housed in this handsome 15th-century palazzo on the Grand Canal. Venice's tradition of gambling goes back to its glory days of the republic, and they live on here in this august Renais-sance palace built by Mauro Codussi. Though not of the caliber of Monte Carlo, and on a midweek winter's night, occasionally slow, this is one of only four casinos on Italian territory—and what a remarkable stage setting it is! Richard Wagner lived and died in a wing of this palazzo in 1883.

Check with your hotel before setting forth; some offer free passes for their guests. Otherwise, if you're not a gambler or curiosity seeker, it may not be worth the admis-sion cost of 18,000L ($10.60). *Note:* A passport is required and the casino is open daily 3pm to 3am.

10 Exploring Venice's Islands

Venice shares its lagoon with three other principal islands, which are only an easy and convenient visit away. Vaporetto line 52 goes to all the islands; in addition, line 13 goes to Murano; line 12 services Murano, Burano, and Torcello; and lines 1, 6, and 82 make the journey to the Lido. Check the vaporetto schedules so you don't waste most of your day waiting.

Guided tours of Murano, Burano, and Torcello are operated by the **Serenissima Company,** with departures from a dock between Piazza San Marco and the Hotel Danieli, right next to the wharf for the *motonave* to the Lido (☎ **041/52-28-538**). The 3- and 4-hour tours cost 25,000 to 40,000L ($14.70 to $23.50); tours leave daily at 9:30am and 2:30pm. See also "Organized Tours," above.

MURANO

Murano is famous throughout the world for the products of its glass factories. Glass has been Venice's most important export since the early Middle Ages, when all glass furnaces were moved to the island of Murano both to protect the city from the possibility of mass conflagration and to make foreign industrial spying more difficult. Glass production virtually stopped after Napoléon's conquest in 1797, but was revived again in the 19th century and flourishes today.

As you stroll through Murano, you'll find the factory owners are only too glad to have you come in and watch their process. However, you'll have to be firm to resist the sales pitch that will invariably go along with the demonstration.

The **Museo Vetrario (Museum of Glass Art),** Fond. Giustinian 8 (☎ **041/ 73-95-86**), is housed in a Renaissance palazzo, and contains a spectacular collection of Roman, early Venetian, and 19th-century revival glass. The museum is open 10am to 5pm; closed Wednesday. Admission is 8,000L ($4.70).

BURANO

Lace is the claim to fame of Burano, an art now practiced by so few island women that prices are generally exorbitant. However, it's still worth a trip if you have time to stroll in the island's opera-set of back streets, whose canals are lined with the simple, brightly colored homes of the *buranesi* fisherman. Visit the school and lace museum, **Scuola di Merletti** (School of Lace Making), Piazza Galuppi (☎ **041/73-00-34**). If you go up to the second floor, you can see the lace makers, mostly young women, at work. It's open Wednesday to Monday from 10am to 5pm. Admission is 8,000L ($4.70).

TORCELLO

Nearby Torcello is perhaps the most charming of the islands. It was the first of the lagoon islands to be called home by the mainland population fleeing persecution (from here they moved to the area around the Rialto Bridge). It is home to the oldest Venetian monument in existence, the **Cattedrale di Torcello (Santa Maria Assunta),** whose foundation dates from the 7th century; it was later reconstructed in 1008 upon the existing structure. It is famous for its outstanding Byzantine mosaics, particularly the 13th-century Madonna and Child in the apse, which rival those at Ravenna and in St. Mark's Basilica. The cathedral is open from 10:30am to 6pm. Admission is 4,000L ($2.35).

Also of interest is the adjacent church dedicated to St. Fosca and a small archaeological museum, open from 10:30am to 12:30pm and 2 to 4pm; closed Monday. Admission is 4,000L ($2.35).

THE LIDO

Although a convenient 15-minute vaporetto ride away from San Marco, Venice's Lido **beaches** are not much to write home about. The Adriatic waters have had pollution problems in recent years, and for bathing and sun-worshipping there are much nicer beaches in Italy. But the parade of wealthy Italian and foreign tourists (plus a good number of Venetian families with children) who frequent this *litorale* throughout summer is an interesting sight indeed, though you'll find many of them at the elitist beaches affiliated with such deluxe hotels as the legendary Excelsior and the Des Bains.

There are two beach areas at the Lido. **Bucintoro** is at the opposite end of Gran Viale Santa Maria Elisabetta (referred to as the Gran Viale) from the vaporetto station Santa Elisabetta. It's a 10-minute walk; walk straight ahead along Gran Viale to reach the beach. **San Nicolò,** a mile away, can be reached by bus B. You'll have to pay 20,000L ($11.75) per person (standard procedure at Italy's beaches) for use of the cabins (you can't change on the beach) and umbrella rental. Alternatively, you can patronize the more crowded and noisier **public beach,** Zona A at the end of Gran Viale. If you stay at any of the hotels on the Lido, most of them have some kind of agreement with the different beach establishments or *bagni.*

The Lido's limited sports amenities, such as golf and tennis, are affiliated with its deluxe five-star hotels. Although there is car traffic, the Lido's wide, shaded boulevards are your best bet for jogging while you're visiting Venice. A number of bike-rental places along the Gran Viale rent bicycles for 5,000 to 6,000L ($2.95 to $3.50) an hour. Vaporetto lines 1, 6, 52, and 82 cross the lagoon to the Lido from the San Zaccaria–Danieli stop near San Marco.

9 The Veneto

For centuries the Venetian Republic ruled most of the northeastern region called the Veneto, turning its attentions inland once its maritime power was well established throughout the Mediterranean and eastward. Many of the inland cities of the Veneto had been around for centuries when the city of Venice was officially founded with the election of its first doge in A.D. 726. As ancient Roman strongholds, these cities had already lived through a glorious period—Verona's wealth of Roman sites and its magnificent ancient amphitheater has garnered it the name "Little Rome." Columns topped by the winged-lion mascot of St. Mark and representing the Most Serene Republic—a symbol of those distant often glorious times—still stand in the main squares of Padua, Vicenza, and Verona. Venetian Renaissance palazzi, frescoed churches, and basilicas still stand proudly today, making a tour through the Veneto a rewarding and often fascinating trip. Shakespeare may have never stepped foot in these parts, but he chose to place many of his best works in "fair Verona" and the surrounding area that fascinated from afar.

Until the arrival of Napoléon in 1797, the Veneto, sharing the bounty of the Serene Republic was built up and embellished. Many of the Palladian villas that dot the hills of the Veneto were the extravagant summertime legacy of wealthy Venetian merchants whose urban palazzi-cum-warehouses lined Venice's Grand Canal. The Veneto also boasts churches and municipal buildings that show the Byzantine-Oriental influence so prominent in Venice's Gothic architecture, some adorned with the frescoes of Giotto, and later of the Venetian masters Tiepolo, Veronese, Titian, and Tintoretto.

The Veneto is a region of great diversity. The northeastern boundaries of the region reach up to the pale, pink-tinged mountain range of the regal Dolomites that separate Italy from the Tyrol. Farther south, the alluvial plains surrounding the mighty Po River are unrelentlessly flat, though punctuated with the Berici Mountains south of Vicenza and the Euganean Hills near Padua. In addition to the Po, the Adige, Brenta, Piave, and other rivers make fertile the hills that are rich with the vineyards, fruit orchards, and lucrative small-scale farms that together create the agricultural wealth that has been the Veneto's sustenance.

Padua, Vicenza, and Verona not only hold the most historical and artistic interest in the Veneto, but they are extremely accessible by public transportation. Trains between these cities are inexpensive,

frequent, and user-friendly, all being major stops on the west/east Milano/Venice route. In fact, the distances between them are so small that you could very well stay put in Venice and tool into Verona—the most distant of the three—for an easy day trip. But this would be a great shame, indeed, as each of them warrants the time it takes to explore them slowly. Enjoy them in the late afternoon and early evening hours when the day-trippers have gone and the cities are left to their own—an aperitivo, a leisurely *passeggiata,* window-shopping along streets lined with tony boutiques that represent the well-to-do status of the *veneti.* End your day with a moderately priced meal of home-cooked regional specialties in a characteristic wine tavern amid much bonhomie and brio, followed by a good night's rest in a small and friendly hotel located just off the postcard-perfect main square. These three towns also offer a host of day excursions into the real countryside, where you'll need a car or the slightest sense of adventure to jump on a local bus and enjoy the back roads and backwaters of the Veneto.

REGIONAL CUISINE   The Veneto's food products are as diverse as its geography. From the mountains and their foothills come a proliferation of mushrooms and game. Much of the cuisine is based on the rice and corn grown here; the appearance of polenta on most menus is frequent, sauced with a hearty game stew with hints of Austrian influence. Rice is commonly served as risotto, a first course along with the season's vegetables or, more characteristically, offerings from the Adriatic on the east. The ubiquitous olive oil of Tuscany's cuisine is used here only minimally—it is not unusual to sense the use of butter, so commonly associated with Emilian food. But above all it is the Adriatic that dictates even the landlocked cuisines of the Veneto. The proliferation of desserts is a throwback to the two times in history that Veneto was ceded to Austria—sweet remnants are still evident in many pastry shops. The now universal favorite of **tiramisu** is said to have originated in the Veneto and remains a ubiquitous favorite finale.

The Veneto—and Verona especially—play an all-important role in the production and exportation of wines: Soave, Bordolino, and Valpolicello are world-recognized labels that originate in these acclaimed vineyards. No other region in Italy produces as many DOC (*Denominazione di Origine Controllata*, zones of controlled name and origin) red wines as the Veneto. The rich volcanic earth of the Colli Euganei produces a good number of these while a light and *frizzante* Prosecco hails from the hills around Asolo. Wine is an integral element in any meal; it is no compromise to limit yourself to the local regional wines that are some of Europe's finest.

1 Padua

42 km (26 mi.) W of Venice, 81 km (50 mi.) E of Verona, 32 km (20 mi.) E of Vicenza, 234 km (147 mi.) E of Milan

The University of Bologna had already grown to 10,000 students by the time Padua founded its university in 1222. Padua was long the academic heartbeat of the powerful Venetian Republic—and far before that, an Ancient Roman stronghold—and for this reason, one of the most important medieval and Renaissance cities in Italy. Dante and Copernicus studied here, Petrarch and Galileo taught here. And when you wander the narrow, cobbled, arcaded side streets in the timeless neighborhoods surrounding the "Bo" (named after a 15th-century inn that once stood on the present-day site of the university), you will be transported back to those earlier times.

Padua is a vital city, with a young university population that gets about by bicycle and keeps the city's piazzas and cafes alive. The historical hub of town is still very evocative of the days when the city and its university flourished in the late Middle Ages and Renaissance as a center of learning and art.

Pilgrims of another ilk secure Padua's place on the map: For more than 700 years, the enormous **Basilica di Sant'Antonio** has drawn millions from around the world. A mendicant Franciscan monk born in Lisbon, Antonio spent his last years in Padua. He died here in 1231, was canonized almost immediately and the basilica—a fantastic mingling of Romanesque, Byzantine, and Gothic—was begun within a year. St. Anthony is one of the Roman Catholic Church's most beloved saints, universally known, perhaps, for his powers to locate the lost. Countless handwritten messages left on his tomb within the great domed church call upon this power to help find everything from lost love to lost limbs. Both the church and the miracle worker are simply referred to as "il Santo," and the church warrants a visit for its artistic treasures and architectural importance as well as religious significance; for centuries it has been one of Europe's principal destinations of pilgrimage.

Most visitors bypass Padua in their rush to get to nearby Venice. During peak season some even stay here when Venice's hotels are full, but see nothing outside the train station. You can spend a few hours or a few days in Padua, depending on your schedule. Its most important sites for those with limited time are Giotto's magnificent, not-to-be-missed frescoes in the **Scrovegni Chapel** and the revered pilgrimage site of the eight-domed Basilica of Sant'Antonio di Padova, whose important equestrian statue by Donatello stands in the piazza before it.

FESTIVALS & MARKETS The beloved **Sant'Antonio** celebrates his feast day June 13, when his relics are carried about town in an elaborate procession joined in by the thousands of pilgrims who come from all over the world.

The outdoor markets (Monday through Saturday) in the twin **Piazza delle Erbe** (for fresh produce) and **Piazza della Frutta** (dry goods) that flank the enormous Palazzo della Ragione are some of Italy's best. The third Sunday of every month sees the area of the **Prato delle Valle** inundated by more than 200 antique and collectibles dealers, one of the largest **antique fairs** in the region. Only early birds will beat the large number of local dealers to the worm. Antique lovers with a car might want to visit Italy's second-largest **Mercato dell'Antiquariato** at the 18th-century Villa Contarini (in Piazzola sul Brenta, a lovely 30-minute drive that can combined with visiting some of the other Palladian and Palladian-inspired country villas along the Brenta Canal; see "Day Trips from Padua," below), held the last Sunday of every month. An estimated 350 vendors hawk their wares; the villa is open for visits during those hours.

Less important, but far more frequent, is the weekly **Saturday outdoor market** of nonantique goods (clothes, pet food, household goods—nothing fascinating, but an interesting peek into local life and a good place to pick up kitchen items to recreate the **cucina italiana** back home) also held in the **Prato della Valle.** Its large number of (inexpensive) shoe stands is due to the many shoe factories for which the nearby Brenta Canal area has long been renowned; you might get lucky. At worst, both the monthly market listed above and this weekly market will give you a reason to visit the 18th-century Prato della Valle, said to be one of the largest piazzas in Europe. Located just southwest of the Basilica di Sant'Antonio, it is ringed by a canal, peopled with more than 80 statues.

ESSENTIALS

GETTING HERE   By Train   The main train station is at Piazza Stazione (☎ 049/ 87-51-800), in the northern part of town, just outside the 16th-century walls. Padua is well connected by frequent train service to points directly west and east: **Padua to Verona** (1 hr.) costs 8,500L ($5), add an InterCity supplement of 5,400L ($3.20); **Padua to Venice** (30 min.) is 4,500L ($2.65), add 3,800L InterCity supplement ($2.25); **Padua to Vicenza** (25 min.) is 4,200L ($2.50), add 3,500L InterCity supplement ($2.05); **Padua to Milano** (2½ hr.) is 19,000L ($11.20), add InterCity supplement of 10,000L ($5.90).

By Bus   The main **ATAP bus station** is located behind (east of) the Scrovegni Chapel and Arena Gardens area on V. Trieste 40 (near Piazza Boschetti) (☎ 049/ 82-06-844). Frequent bus service to Venice and Verona costs approximately the same as train tickets, though tourists and locals alike seem to use this station principally for the smaller outlying cities such as Bassano del Grappa (6,000L/$3.50).

By Car   Padua is located directly on the principal **A4** autostrada that links Venice with Milan. All the points of interest listed below are located within the city's historical center, which is closed to traffic. When booking at your hotel, ask about the closest parking lot. Hotels usually have an agreement with their neighborhood parking lot and pass those savings along to hotel guests.

VISITOR INFORMATION   The city's one **I.A.T. tourist information office** is at the train station (☎ 049/875-20-77; fax 049/87-55-008), open Monday to Saturday from 9am to 7pm, Sunday from 9am to noon (fewer hours in winter months).

GUIDED TOURS   Few guided group tours of the city are available. Every Friday at 3pm and Monday at 9am, guided tours of the city are offered by Xanadu Viaggi (☎ 049/664255; fax 049/656021; 38,000L/$22.35 per person). Contact the I.A.T. office (see "Visitor Information," above) for a listing of all accredited individual tour guides, or you can all or fax directly **Sindicato Guide Turistiche** (☎ 049/82-09-711; fax 049/82-09-726).

GETTING AROUND Hotels, restaurants, and points of interest all fall within the historical center and can be reached on foot. Public **ACAP** buses service much of the center's streets otherwise limited to traffic (pick up a bus map from the tourist office), although a 1-day pass of 5,000L ($2.95) is probably not worth your while (single tickets cost 1,500L/90¢).

WHAT TO SEE & DO

Pick up a map from the tourist office and plan your attack. The **train station** marks the city's northernmost point, and the **Prato delle Valle** and **Basilica di Sant'Antonio** mark the southernmost. The following sites of interest can be organized into three clusters and are all within walking distance of each other: the **Cappella degli Scrovegni** (also called the Arena Chapel) and the adjacent **Museo Civico** are across a small piazza from the **Eremitani Church;** the **Caffe Pedrocchi** can be found near the **Palazzo della Raggione** in the Piazza Cavour area (the **Piazza della Frutta** sits to the north and **Piazza delle Erbe** just to the south of the palazzo, with the **Piazza degli Signori** bringing up the west); and the **Basilica di Sant'Antonio** caps the southern end of town with the enormous **Piazza Prato delle Valle** just beyond. Sites below are in geographical order.

✪ **Cappella degli Scrovegni (Scrovegni Chapel or the Arena Chapel).** Pz. Ermitani 8 (off Cor. Garibaldi). ☎ **049/82-04-550.** Fax 049/82-04-566. E-mail (for reservations): musei.comune@padovanet.it Admission (joint ticket with the Museo Eremitani) 10,000L ($5.90). Feb–Oct, daily 9am–7pm; Nov–Jan, daily 9am–6pm. Entrance through the Museo Eremitani. Bus: 3, 8, 10, 12, 32, 42.

This is the one uncontested must-see during your stay in Padua, so be prepared for high-season lines, a wait made even longer by the small numbers of controlled groups allowed to enter the chapel at any one time (limits of 20-minute visits are often imposed during peak periods; check when buying your ticket so you can plan your visit accordingly). Once inside, art lovers armed with binoculars behold the scene in awe—the recently renovated cycle of vibrant frescoes by Giotto that revolutionized 14th-century painting is still held to be some of the most important early Renaissance art. A brilliant cobalt blue is the dominant color, in illustrations that are easy to understand in typical medieval comic-strip format; here they take on an unprecedented degree of realism and emotion. Together with the cycle of frescoes that Giotto would later paint in Assisi's St. Francis's Basilica (some of them feared to be irreparably damaged by the 1997 earthquakes), these are the largest and best preserved. Giotto worked from 1303 to 1306 to completely cover the ceiling and walls with 38 scenes illustrating the lives of Mary and Christ from floor to ceiling. With your back to the front door, the three bands that cover the walls are: top right, *Life of Joachim;* top left, *Life of the Virgin;* right center, *The Childhood of Christ;* left center, *Christ's Public Life;* right bottom, *The Passion of Christ* (the third panel of Judas kissing Christ is perhaps the best known of the entire cycle); left bottom, *Christ's Death and Resurrection.* Above the entrance is the fresco of the *Last Judgment:* Christ, as judge, sits in the center, surrounded by the angels and apostles. Below him, to the right, are the blessed, while to the left, Giotto created a terrible hell in which devils and humans are condemned to eternal punishment.

The area around the Ancient Roman Arena where the chapel now stands (and hence the chapel's alternative name) was purchased in 1300 by a wealthy Paduan, Enrico Scrovegni. He built an extravagant palazzo (destroyed in 1820), and the family chapel, which stands next to it, whose exterior remains simple and unadorned. Dedicated to his father, an unethical usurer so notorious in his time that he was refused a Christian burial, the son hoped to atone for his father's ways and commissioned

Tuscan-born Giotto, whose work he had seen in the Basilica di Sant'Antonio. Giotto felt obligated to include the father in the portrait of the *Last Judgment's* blessed souls. Dante felt otherwise, immortalizing him by placing him amid the userers condemned to hell in his epic *Inferno*.

Museo Civico Eremitani. Piazza Ermitani 8 (off Cor. Garibaldi and adjacent to the Cappella Scrovegni). ☎ **049/82-04-550.** Admission (joint ticket with the Cappella degli Scrovegni) 10,000L ($5.90). Feb–Oct, Tues–Sun 9am–7pm; Nov–Jan, Tues–Sun 9am–6pm. Bus: 3, 8, 10, 12, 32, 42.

The centuries-old cloisters that were once home to the monks (*eremitani* means hermits) who officiated in the adjacent Scrovegni Chapel (officially part of the museum complex) have been handsomely renovated to provide an airy display space as the city's new civic museum. Its prodigious collection begins on the ground floor with the Archeological Museum's division of Egyptian, Roman, and Etruscan artifacts and antiquities. The upstairs collection represents an impressive panorama of minor Venetian works from major Venetian artists from the early 15th century to the 19th century. You'll find works by Titian, Tiepolo, and Tintoretto, whose *Crucifixion* is the museum's finest work. Special mention is given to Giotto's unusual wooden crucifix and Bellini's *Portrait of a Young Senator.*

Chiesa degli Eremitani (Church of the Hermits). Pz. Eremitani (off Cor. Garibaldi). ☎ **049/87-56-410.** Free admission. Daily 8:30am–12:30pm and 4:30–7pm. Bus: 3, 8, 10, 12, 32, 42.

Padua's worst tragedy was the complete destruction of this church by Nazi bombings in 1944; some art historians consider it the country's greatest artistic wartime loss. It has been remarkably restored to its original early 13th-century Romanesque style, but the magnificent cycles of frescoes by the 23-year-old Andrea Mantegna could not be salvaged, except for a corner of the Ovetari Chapel on the right of the chancel. Here you'll find enough fragments found in the rubble of the frescoes he painted from 1454 to 1457, to understand the loss of what was considered one of the great artistic treasures of Italy. Mantegna was born in Padua (1431–1506) and studied under the Florentine master Donatello, who lived here while completing his commissions for the Basilica di Sant'Antonio as well as the famous equestrian statue that now stands in the piazza before it. Look for classical music concerts occasionally held in the church.

✪ **Caffè Pedrocchi.** V. VIII Febbraio 15 (at Pz. Cavour). ☎ **049/82-05-007.** Tues–Sun 9:30am–12:30pm and 3:30–8pm (for historical salons upstairs). Bar open daily 7am–midnight.

The Pedrocchi is a historic landmark, as beloved by the Paduans as "their" own St. Anthony (who actually hailed from Lisbon). When it first opened in 1831 it was the largest cafe in Europe—who were they expecting? Famous are the literary and political characters and local luminaries who made this their command post—French-born Henri Beyle, aka Stendhal, had it in mind when he wrote: "The best Italian cafe is almost as good as the Parisian ones." Countless others were less reserved, calling it arguably the most beautiful coffeehouse in the world. Heavily damaged during World War II, it was completely rebuilt in its original neoclassical 19th-century stage-set splendor and, after a laborious renovation and heralded December 1998 reopening that was, for Padua, the social event of the year, it is again the social heartbeat for university students and ladies of a certain age alike. It has the nicest rest rooms in town, for the use of cafe patrons. They're worth the cost of a coffee. In warm weather Pedrocchi opens wide its doors (and hence its curious description as a "doorless cafe") onto the pedestrian piazza; sit here for a while to absorb the Paduan spirit. As is always the case, drinks cost less when you're standing at the bar, but then you will have missed the *dolce far niente* (sweetness of doing nothing) experience for which Pedrocchi has always been known. A cappuccino, tea, beer, or glass of white *prosecco* wine will cost 5,000L ($2.95) at your table (half that at the bar), and hunger can be held at bay with a plate of dainty teatime pastries or a grilled ham-and-cheese *toast*, each 5,000L ($2.95).

Bo (Università Palazzo Centrale). V. VIII Febbraio (south of Pz. Cavour). ☎ **049/ 827-51-11.** Admission 7,000L ($4.10). By guided tour, some in English. Ask at tourist office for status of renovation.

Galileo's battered desk and podium where he taught from 1592 to 1610 is still on display in Italy's second oldest university after Bologna. His name joins a legendary honor roll of students and professors—Petrarch, Dante, the poet Tasso, Copernicus—who came here from all over Europe. The University of Padua was founded in 1222 and grew to become one of the most famous and ambitious learning centers in Europe reaching its zenith in the 16th and 17th centuries. Today, a number of buildings are spread about town, but the **Palazzo del Bo** (named after the "Bo" or Ox Inn—a favorite student hangout that stood on this spot in the 15th century) is the university's main seat. Ongoing restoration keeps most of it off-limits, but the perfectly **preserved Teatro Anatomico** is one of the few sites open for a visit in 1999. Built in 1594, it was here that William Harvey most probably developed his theory of the circulation of blood when taking his degree in 1602.

Palazzo della Ragione (Law Courts) and the surrounding twin markets of ✪ **Piazza delle Erbe and Piazza della Frutta.** ☎ **049/82-05-006.** Admission to palazzo 7,000L ($4.10). Tues–Sun 9am–6pm. Bus: 8.

Located just south of the historic Caffè Perocchi, and a necessary and inevitable destination for those meandering about the historic center of town, the picturesque open-air markets of Piazza delle Erbe (Square of the Herbs) and Piazza della Frutta (Square of Fruit) frame the massive 13th-century palazzo at their center; together they have stood as the town's political and commercial nucleus for centuries. Before being distracted by the color, smells, and cacophony of the sprawling outdoor fruit and vegetable market stalls, turn your attention to the magnificent Palazzo della Ragione, whose interior is as impressive as its exterior. Food shops by the dozen fill its ground floor, and stand-up bars and outdoor cafes make this lunchtime central. The two-story loggia-lined "Palace of Reason" is topped with a distinctive sloped roof that resembles the inverted hull of a ship, the largest of its kind in the world. It was built in 1219 as the seat of Padua's parliament and was used as an assembly hall, courthouse, and administrative center to celebrate Padua's newly won independence as a republican city. Considered a masterpiece of civil medieval architecture, it was heavily damaged by a fire in 1420 that destroyed, among other things, an elaborate cycle of frescoes by Giotto and his students that adorned the **il Salone** (the Great Hall). The Hall, 270 feet long, was almost immediately rebuilt and is today the prime draw, both for its floor-to-ceiling 15th-century frescoes immediately commissioned after the fire, similar in style and astrological theme to those that had been painted by Giotto (and one of the very few complete zodiac cycles to survive until modern times), and a large wooden sculpture of a horse attributed to Donatello (although many art historians don't agree). Museum-quality exhibitions are often held here, an impressive venue and twice the reason to visit.

On the far (west) side of the adjoining piazzes' canvas-topped stalls, flanking the Palazzo della Ragione, is the **Piazza dei Signori,** most noteworthy for the 15th-century clock tower that dominates it, the first of its kind in Italy.

✪ **Basilica di Sant'Antonio.** Pz. d. Santo (east of Prato d. Valle). ☎ **049/878-97-32.** Free admission. Summer daily 7am–7:45pm; winter daily 7am–7pm. Bus: 8, 12 or 18.

When Venice Overflows

Padua is convenient to both Venice and Verona. There isn't a wide choice of desirable hotels in the *centro storico,* but you'll pay close to half the rates of comparable accommodations in Venice and find the commute, just 19 miles, an easy and inexpensive one (and often a necessary one when Venice is booked full).

Standing out amid the smattering of stalls across the large piazza in front of the basilica selling St. Anthony-emblazoned everything, is Donatello's famous *Gattamelata* equestrian statue. The first of its size to be cast in Italy since Roman antiquity, it is important for its detail, proportion, and powerful contrast between rider (the inconsequential Venetian *condottiere* Erasmo da Narni, nicknamed the "Spotted Cat") and horse. It would have a seminal effect on Renaissance sculpture and casting and restore the lost art of the equestrian statue. Inside, the enormous basilica houses the body of Padua's patron St. Anthony (Sant'Antonio), simply and commonly referred to as "il Santo," who was born in Lisbon in 1195 and died just outside of Padua in 1231. Work began on the church almost immediately but was not completed until 1307. Its eight domes bring to mind the Byzantine influence found in Venice's St. Mark's Basilica that predates Padua's Romanesque-Gothic construction by more than 2 centuries. A pair of octagonal, minaret-like bell towers enhance its Eastern appearance.

The imposing interior is richly frescoed and decorated, filled with a number of tombs, works of art, and inlaid checkerboard marble flooring. Of most importance is the tomb holding the saint's body. In the direction of the main altar, it is found off the left aisle and up three steps in its own **Cappella del Santo;** it is always covered with flowers, photographs, and handwritten personal petitions left by devout pilgrims from every corner of the globe whose numbers have remained constant over the centuries. The saint is the patron of lost or mislaid objects, and the faithful who flock here look for everything from lost love to lost health. The series of nine bronze bas-reliefs of scenes from the saint's life are some of the finest works by 16th-century northern-Italian sculptors. The seven bronze statues and towering central *Crucifixion* that adorn the main altar are by Donatello (1444–48) and are the basilica's artistic highlight.

In his lifetime, St. Anthony was known for his eloquent preaching, so interpret as you will the saint's perfectly (some say miraculously) preserved tongue, vocal chords, and jawbone on display in the **Cappella del Tesoro** in the back of the church directly behind the main altar. These treasured relics are carried through town in a traditional procession every June 13 to celebrate the feast day of "il Santo." You'll also see one of the original tattered tunics of il Santo dating from 1231.

WHERE TO STAY

When making reservations, note that low season is usually considered December and January, and July and August. Inquire about discounts if you'll be in Padua at this time of year.

Hotel al Fagiano. V. Locatelli 45 (west of Pz. d. Santo), 35122 Padua. ☎ **049/87-50-073.** Fax 049/87-53-396. 32 units, 29 with bathroom. A/C TV TEL. 50,000L ($29.40) single without bathroom, 90,000L ($52.95) single with bathroom; 70,000L ($41.20) double without bathroom, 120,000L ($70.60) double with bathroom; 140,000L ($82.35) triple with bathroom. Breakfast 10,000L ($5.90). Rates slightly discounted off-season. AE, DC, MC, V. From train station: bus no. 8, 12, 18 or 32.

Although small and family run, this newly renovated and well-located hotel is a great value-for-your-money deal for the budget-minded. It doesn't exactly ooze coziness and charm, but given the less than encouraging hotel situation in town, the Fagiano's bright, modern, and clean rooms are still a standout choice. Bathrooms have also been freshly redone and include niceties such as hair dryers and bright lighting. conditioning and television at these rates. Located just a few steps off the expansive Piazza del Santo (its most appealing asset), don't confuse this Fagiano with the recently renamed Hotel Buenos Aires, formerly known as the Fagiano and just a block away.

Leon Bianco. Piazzetta Pedrocchi 12 (at V. Cavour), 35122 Padua. ☎ **049/87-50-814.** Fax 049/87-56-184. E-mail: leonbianco@writeme.com. 22 units, all with bathroom. A/C MINIBAR TV TEL. 130,000L ($76.50) single; 156,000L ($95.30) double. Buffet breakfast 7,500L ($4.40). AE, DC, MC, V. Nearby parking available 25,000L ($14.70). From train station: bus no. 3, 8, or 18.

This is the three-star sister of the four-star Majestic Toscanelli listed below, and the most centrally located of its competitors. In fact, it's the best in terms of location regardless of category: The heartbeat of town—the landmark Caffè Pedrocchi and the open-air marketplace—is just outside your front door. The 100-year-old palazzo is done up in an uninspired once-contemporary theme in need of a facelift with an art collection hung in the public areas. A top floor al fresco terrace redeems things considerably: Linger with your breakfast cappuccino or an afternoon aperitif under white canvas umbrellas with views over the lumbering Palazzo della Raggione and the city center's medieval rooftops. Some of the simply furnished rooms are noteworthy for their parquet floors strewn with Persian rugs or their more than ample size, a good choice for families of three or four. Although the decor hasn't aged well, housekeeping is attentive, the service very good, and the place well maintained with an excellent location that keeps it always in demand.

WORTH A SPLURGE

✪ **Hotel Majestic Toscanelli.** V. dell'Arco 2 (2 blocks west of V. Roma and south of the Pz. d. Erbe), 35122 Padua. ☎ **049/66-32-44.** Fax 049/87-60-025. E-mail: majestic@writeme. com. 32 units, all with bathroom. A/C MINIBAR TV TEL. 169,000L ($99.40) single; 240,000L ($141.20) double; 280,000L ($164.70) triple. Rates include buffet breakfast. Rates discounted mid-July 14–Aug 31. AE, DC, MC, V. Valet parking 25,000L ($14.70).

A four-star hotel this nice would cost a great deal more in nearby Venice, which is why the Toscanelli often finds itself with guests who make this their home base while visiting neighboring cities and the surrounding area. A 1992 redo has kept the hotel's old-world charm fresh and handsome, with rooms tastefully done in classic decor with coordinated pastel themes, burnished cherry-wood furniture, and large bathrooms bright with white ceramic and marble tiles. Work in early 1999 will freshen up the lobby, transforming it with highlights of gold leaf that hint of the Venetian rococo era. Off the lobby a bright and attractive breakfast room serves a good buffet breakfast. This quiet, historic neighborhood is entirely closed to traffic, with porticoed alleyways lined with antique shops and wine bars. From here it's an easy walk to the Via Roma and the Piazza delle Erbe.

WHERE TO DINE

Brek. Pz. Cavour 20. ☎ **049/87-53-788.** No reservations accepted. Primi and pizza 6,000–10,000L ($3.50–$5.90); secondi 7,000–13,000L ($4.10–$7.65). Sat–Thurs 11:30am–3pm and 6–10pm. No credit cards; AE and V expected by 1999. ITALIAN.

Both proud and embarrassed, I admit that with the exception of a brief dalliance in Rome's McDonald's many years ago, I made my first acquaintance with Italian fast food only recently. It was in Padua's Brek (as in "Let's take a *brek* . . . ") self-service *all'italiana*. Put your language problems and calorie counting aside as you help yourself to pastas that are made up fresh while you wait and point to the sauce of your choice. There's a counter just for omelets made express, another for entrees and pizza.

The dessert cart virtually groans with a copious array of cheeses, fresh fruits, fruit salads, and fruit-topped tarts and cobblers. Join the thoroughly local eat-on-the-run lunch crowd from the university and surrounding shops, and save your day's budget for dinner.

✪ **Enoteca Leonardi.** V. Pietro d'Abano 1 (on a side street just north of the Pz. d. Frutta). ☎ **049/87-50-083.** Reservations suggested. Primi 10,000–25,000L ($5.90–$14.70); secondi 20,000–25,000L ($11.75–$14.70). Sun noon–2:30pm, Tues–Sat noon–2:30pm and 7pm–12:30am. Closed 1 week in Aug. AE, CB, DC, V. WINE BAR/PADUAN.

After a heady wander through the sights, sounds, and smells of Padua's open-air marketplace, one of Italy's most colorful and authentic, head for a moment's respite at this new enoteca. Your head need spin no longer, despite the 700 labels with which it stocks its well-respected wine cellar (at least 30 are available to sample by the glass at 3,000 to 5,000L/$1.75 to $2.95). A stylishly minimal decor in the cool moss-green interior is attractive, but the outdoor courtyard where centuries-old horse stables have been converted for modern-day grazers is the warm-weather draw. An interesting number of antipasti is as sophisticated as the setting: Look for the *mousse di fegato grasso d'oca tartufato,* a lighter-than-air foie gras heightened by the hint of truffles, or a platter of various Italian cheeses or *salumi,* each a perfect complement to Leonardi's very impressive selection of wines, with some interlopers from the Napa Valley. This is a favorite lunch place, or a contemporary spot to sit and sip amid a fashionable clientele. But for dinner (and a comparable level of quality wine tasting), book at La Vecchia Enoteca (see "Worth a Splurge," below).

✪ **Osteria Dei Fabbri.** V. d. Fabbri 13 (on a side street south of Pz. d. Erbe), ☎ **049/ 65-03-36.** Reservations suggested. Primi 8,000–10,000L ($4.70–$5.90); secondi 15,000–17,000L ($8.80–$10). Mon–Sat noon–3:30pm and 5:30pm–1am. AE, CB, DC, MC, V. PADUAN.

Simple, well-prepared food is the great equalizer. This rustic old-fashioned tavern or osteria is a lively spot where intellectual types share tables with Zegna-suited bankers, and students stop by for a tipple or to find a quiet corner in which to pore over the newspaper (a pastime not encouraged during hours when meals are served). Some of the day's specials are displayed on the heavy oak bar—antipasti of grilled vegetables, rosemary potatoes, seafood salads—while hot dishes pour out of the kitchen. There's always at least one homemade pasta choice to start with, and osso buco, the specialty of the house, is especially memorable when accompanied by any of the local (and excellent) Venetian wines available by the bottle or glass. Stop by at least for the *dopo cena* (after-dinner drink) to top off your day in Padua. If this restaurant is full, head 2 blocks over to the reliable **Osteria L'Anfora** at V. d. Soncin 13 (east of Piazza Duomo; ☎ **049/65-66-29**) for inexpensive wine and good food.

WORTH A SPLURGE

✪ **La Vecchia Enoteca.** V. S. Martino e Solferino 32 (just south of Pz. d. Erbe). ☎ **049/ 875-28-56.** Reservations recommended. Primi 10,000–15,000L ($5.90–$8.80); secondi 22,000–25,000L ($12.95–$14.70). Mon 7–10:30pm, Tues–Sat noon–2:15pm and 7:30–11:30pm. Closed 2 weeks mid-Aug. MC, V. PADUAN.

The sophistication of the Veneto's prodigious viticulture is shown off here in an appropriately refined venue that could easily fit into a less expensive category. Cozy, in a rustic and elegant kind of way, La Vecchia Enoteca is for that special evening of white linen and smooth service when you'd like the full-blown experience of Paduan cuisine and award-deserving wines (and hence its placement in our splurge department). Prices are unintimidating and contained enough to encourage diners to leave caution at the door and indulge in a delicious menu and commendable selection of regional and Italian wines. The menu showcases the bounty-rich Veneto: The traditional polenta and risotto change with the season, as does the light, homemade gnocchi. Meat possibilities are numerous and tempting, while the influence of the Adriatic appears in entrees such as the favored *branzino in crosta di patate,* sea bass roasted in a light crust of potatoes.

PADUA AFTER DARK

The classical music season usually runs from October to April at different venues around town. The historic **Teatro Verdi** at V. d. Livello 32 (☎ **049/876-03-39**) is the most impressive venue. Programs are available at the tourist office. Look for posters advertising performances by the world-class **Solisti Veneti,** who are Paduans but spend most of the year, alas, traveling abroad.

As a university city, Padua's student population makes itself visually present at all times—everyone looks 22 and in search of themselves. You can network with the student crowd at any of the popular cafes along Via Cavour, or the **osterie,** wine bars and beer dives in the porticoed medieval side streets encircling the Palazzo della Ragione (the area around the Bo) and its bookend Piazza delle Erbe and Piazza della Frutta.

DAY TRIPS FROM PADUA

The **Euganean Hills** (*Colli Euganei*) are the center of the small but renowned wine industry of the Veneto, located southwest of Padua. A "Strada dei Vini" wine route map can be had from the tourist office (when in stock!). It also leads you to the small city of **Terme di Abano** (12 kilometers/7.5 miles from Padua) famous as a center for radioactive springs and mud treatments unique to this volcanic range.

THE FORGOTTEN RIVIERA The navigable Brenta Canal links Padua with Venice in the east. Ambitiously called "The Forgotten Riviera," because of the dozens of historic summertime villas built here by Venice's aristocracy and wealthy merchants, it can be visited by car or by boat. Some of the villas are far more outstanding than others. A few are designed by 16th-century master architect Palladio, others are Palladian-inspired (see "Vicenza," below, for background on Palladio and how to visit his villas). Many of the privately owned villas are open only to those arriving on organized tours. Try **Il Burchiello** boat (New Siamic Express; ☎ **049/66-09-44;** fax 049/ 66-28-30; e-mail: siamic@tin.it). Modern launches leave from Padua Wednesday, Friday, and Sunday, March 21 through October (cost 114,000L/$67.05, lunch optional 40,000L/$23.50). More than 30 villas can be viewed from the boat (some only partially or at a great distance), but only three are visited: the important 18th-century **Villa Pisani** in Stra, commissioned by the family of a Venetian doge and famous for its ballroom frescos by Tiepolo; the 18th-century **Villa Valmarana** in Mira (the largest concentration of country villas can be found between Stra and Mira if you're thinking of doing this on your own), dramatically set amid weeping willows; and the **Villa Foscari** (also known as Villa Malcontenta, "The Unhappy Woman"), one of Palladio's finest examples. The boat arrives in Venice at approximately 6pm; transfers by bus or train to Padua are not included but the connections are easy, frequent, and inexpensive (see "Getting Here," above). Alternatively, you can stay on in Venice; ask the Burchiello representative about bringing your luggage with you. If you want to do the tour yourself, note that the secondary road S11 runs alongside some of the canal; at certain points it departs from the canal but remains the best of any extant roadways for viewing the villas. A do-it-yourself tour needs some planning, as visiting hours and days differ from villa to villa and season to season. See the tourist office about a map; but be careful about difficult, erratic visiting hours and public bus connections that make this close to impossible for those without their own wheels.

✪ VILLA BARBARO   This villa (☎ **0423/92-30-01** or 0423/92-30-04) is one of Palladio's most celebrated. It is in Maser, a 30-minute car ride due north of Padua (and just outside of Asolo; see directions below from Padua north to Bassano di Grappa, then travel east to Asolo). Probably the most famous of the Palladian villas after Vicenza's Villa Rotonda and one of the most beautiful, the Barbaro is a standout for its frescoes by Veronese (which La Rotonda lacks). It's privately owned by some very, very lucky folks and is open year-round, but with extremely limited hours and not daily (and only weekends during winter months). Don't expect to just pop in: Call for current schedule.

ASOLO   Known as the "Town of a Hundred Horizons" because of its panoramic views, Asolo was the Renaissance-era home of Caterina Cornari of Venice, who was awarded the realm of Asolo for her help in (unsuccessfully) keeping the Turks out of Cyprus. Much of the 15th-century charm you see today is due to her 12-year presence and patronage in the town. Other VIP residents were the English poet Robert Browning and Italy's grande dame of the stage, Eleonora Duse. Cornari's beautifully sited 18th-century villa is now the deluxe home of the Hotel Villa Cipriani (☎ **0423/ 952-166**). The $250 rooms may be a bit steep for your pockets, but you can still enjoy the same breathtaking views from the lovely terrace bar for the cost of an iced tea (10,000L/$5.90). To get here **by car** from Padua, take **SS47** north to Bassano di Grappa, then drive east to Asolo on **SS248** (48km/30 mi.). From Asolo it's an easy and enjoyable 11-mile segue to the small city of **Bassano del Grappa** (26 mi. north of Padua). But since it's officially located in the province of Vicenza, see "Day Trips from Vicenza," below, for more information.

2 Vicenza

32 km (20 mi.) W of Padua, 74 km (46 mi.) W of Venice, 51 km (32 mi.) E of Verona, 204 km (128.5 mi.) E of Milan

Vicenza pays heartfelt homage to Andrea di Pietro della Gondola (born in Padua in 1508, died in Maser in 1580). He came to Vicenza at the age of 16, and lived out his life and dreams here under the name Palladio at a time when Vicenza was under the sway of Venice's still powerful republic. Although not highly innovative, he was the most important architect of the High Renaissance, one whose living monuments inspired and influenced architecture in the Western world over the centuries up to this very day. Vicenza and its surroundings are a mecca for the architecture lover, a living museum of Palladian and Palladian-inspired architectural monuments and consequently one designated a protected UNESCO World Heritage Site in 1994. However, an evening stroll through illuminated piazzas and along boutique-lined streets is just as enjoyable for those of you who have never heard of Palladio—though you'll leave a rookie architecture buff once you've been here: A day in Vicenza is worth a semester back in school.

Vicenza today is one of the wealthiest cities in Italy, thanks in part to the recent burgeoning of the local computer-component industry (Federico Faggin, inventor of the silicon chip, was born here). It is also the traditional center of the country's gold manufacturing industry (one-third of Italy's gold is made here and each year three prestigious international gold fairs make finding a hotel in these parts impossible) and as one of Europe's largest producers of textiles. The average Vicentino is well off and it shows; join the entire town for the daily passeggiata and pick up on the palpable attitude.

FESTIVALS   The well-established summertime series of **Concerti in Villa** takes place in June and July; a few concerts are held outdoors at Vicenza's famed Villa la

Rotonda, for others you will need a car. The tourist office will have the schedule and availability of seats; tickets usually cost around 30,000L ($17.65).

ESSENTIALS

GETTING HERE   By Train   Most visitors arrive by train from Venice (50 min.). The train station is in Piazza Stazione, also called Campo Marzio (☎ 0444/ 32-50-46), at the southern end of Viale Roma. Expect to pay the following one-way fares: **from Venice** 6,000L ($3.50), add 4,000L InterCity supplement ($2.35); **25-minute ride from Padua** 4,200L ($2.50), add 3,500L InterCity supplement ($2.05); a **30-minute ride from Verona** 5,500L ($3.25), add InterCity supplement of 4,200L ($2.50).

By Bus   The FTV bus station (the Stazione Pullman) is located on Viale Milano (☎ 0444/22-31-15), just to the west (left) of the train station. Buses leave frequently for all the major cities in the Veneto and to Milano; prices are comparable to train travel.

By Car   Vicenza is on the **A4 autostrada** that links Venice to the east with Milano to the west. Coming from Venice (about 1 hr.), you'll bypass Padua before arriving in Vicenza.

VISITOR INFORMATION   The **tourist information office** is in the Pz. Matteotti 12 (☎ and fax **0444/32-08-54** or fax 0444/32-70-72; www.comune.vicenza.it), next to the Teatro Olimpico. Hours are Monday to Saturday from 9am to 1pm and 2:30 to 6pm, Sunday from 9am to 1pm. In low season (mid-October through mid-March), closing time is 5:30pm. During summer months, an office opens at the train station, Monday to Saturday 9am to 2pm only, and Sunday 1 to 6pm.

CITY LAYOUT   The city's layout is quite straightforward and easy to navigate on foot. The **train station** lies at its southernmost point. From here head straight ahead on **Viale Roma;** it ends at a turnabout with gated gardens beyond. Head right (east) into the centro storico, marked by the Piazza Castello, from which the main thoroughfare starts, the **Corso Palladio.** Lined with shops, offices and banks, the arrow-straight Corso cuts through town, running southwest (from Piazza Castello) to northeast (Piazza Matteotti), site of the Teatro Olimpico. Along the Corso you'll find urban palazzi by Palladio and his students; midway, the **Piazza dei Signori** (and it s Basilica Palladiana) will be found on your right (south). Perpendicular to the Corso is the important **Contrà Porti,** a lovely palazzo-studded street, on your left (north).

GETTING AROUND   There is limited traffic (for taxis, buses, and residents) once you enter the Piazza del Castello and the centro storico. Everything of interest can be easily reached on foot; pick up a map at the tourist office. Even the two villas just outside town (see "Villas & a Basilica Nearby," below) can be reached by foot (not suggested in the heat of high season) or bike as well as by bus or car.

EXPLORING THE PALLADIAN HERITAGE

A *biglietto cumulativo* for joint entrances to the Teatro Olimpico and the Museo Civico costs 9,000L ($5.30)—a small savings—is available at either one of the museums.

PIAZZA DEI SIGNORI

South of Corso Palladio on the site of the ancient Roman Forum and still the town hub, this central square should be your first introduction to the city and Palladio, its local boy wonder.

The magnificent bigger-than-life ✪ **Basilica Palladiana** is not a church at all and was only partially designed by Palladio. Beneath it stood a Gothic-style Palazzo della Ragione (Law Courts and Assembly Hall) that Palladio was commissioned to convert to a High Renaissance style befitting a flourishing late 16th-century city under Venice's benevolent patronage. It was his first public work and secured his favor and reputation with the local authorities. He created two superimposed galleries, the lower with Doric pillars, the upper with Ionic. The roof was destroyed by World War II bombing, but has since been rebuilt in its original style. It's open April to September Tuesday to Saturday from 9:30am to noon and from 2 to 7pm; Sunday from 9:30am to 12:30pm and from 2 to 7pm. Off-season, it's closed Sunday afternoon; free admission.

The towering 12th-century **Torre Bissara** (or Torre di Piazza) bell tower belonged to the original church and stands near two columns in the piazza's east end (the Piazza Blade), one topped by the winged lion of Venice's Serene Republic, the other by the *Redentore* (Redeemer). Of note elsewhere in the piazza are the **Loggia del Capitaniato** (1570), begun but never finished according to plans by Palladio except for the four massive redbrick columns (on north side of piazza alongside the well-known Gran Caffè Garibaldi). Behind the Basilica (to the south) is the **Piazza delle Erbe,** site of the daily produce market.

Corso Andrea Palladio

This is Vicenza's main street, and what a grand one it is, lined with the magnificent palazzi of Palladio and his students (and their students who, centuries later, were still influenced by the mastery of Palladio's work), today converted into cafes, swank shops and imposing banks. The first one of note, starting from its southwest cap near the Piazza Castello, is the **Piazza Valamarana** at no. 16, begun by Palladio in 1566. On the right (behind which stands the Piazza dei Signori and the Basilica Palladiana) is the **Palazzo del Comunale,** the Town Hall built in 1592 by Scamozzi (1552–1616), a native of Vicenza and Palladio's protégé and star pupil. This is said to be Scamozzi's greatest work.

From the Corso Palladio and heading northeast, take a left onto the **Contrà Porti,** the second most important street for its Palladian and Gothic palazzi. The two designed by Palladio are the **Palazzo Barbarano Porto** at no. 11, and (opposite) **Palazzo Thiene** at 12 (now the headquarters of a bank); Gothic palazzi of particular note can be found at no. 6 to 10, 14, 16, 17, and 19. Parallel, on Corso Fogazzaro, look for no. 16, **Palazzo Valmarana,** perhaps the most eccentric of Palladio's works.

Returning to Corso Palladio, look for no. 145/147, the pre-Palladian **Ca d'Oro** (Golden Palace), named for the gold leaf used in the frescoes that once covered its facade. It was bombed in 1944 and rebuilt in 1950. The simple 16th-century palazzo at no. 163 was Palladio's home.

Before reaching the Piazza Matteotti and the end of the Corso Palladio you'll see signs for the **Church of Santa Corona,** set back on the left on the V. Santa Corona 2 (open daily from 8:30am to noon and 2:30 to 6pm). An unremarkable 13th-century Gothic church, it shelters two masterpieces (and Vicenza's most important church paintings) that make this worth a visit: Giovanni Bellini's *Baptism of Christ* (fifth altar on left) and Veronese's *Adoration of the Magi* (third chapel on right). This is Vicenza's most interesting church, far more so than the cavernous Duomo southwest of the Piazza dei Signori, but worth seeking out only if you've got the extra time. At the end of the Corso Palladio at its northeastern end is Palladio's world-renowned Teatro Olimpico and, across the street, the Museo Civico in the Palazzo Chiericati.

⊙ **Teatro Olimpico and Museo Civico.** Pz. Matteotti (at Cor. Palladio). ☎ **0444/ 32-37-81.** Admission for each is 5,000L ($2.95); joint ticket for entrance to both is 9,000L ($5.30). Apr–Sept, 9am–12:30pm and 2:15–5pm; Sun 9:30am–12:30 and 2–7pm. Oct–Mar, 9am–12:30pm and 2:15–5pm; Sun 9:30am–12:30pm.

The splendid Teatro Olimpico was Palladio's greatest urban work, and one of his last. He began the project in 1580, the year of his death at the age of 72; it would be completed 5 years later by his student Vicenzo Scamozzi. It was the first covered theater in Europe, inspired by the theaters of antiquity. The seating area, in the shape of a half-moon as in the old arenas, seats 1,000. The stage seems profoundly deeper than its actual 14 feet, thanks to the permanent stage "curtain" and Scamozzi's clever use of trompe l'oeil added after Palladio's death. The stage scene represents the ancient streets of Thebes, while the faux clouds and sky covering the dome further the impression of being in an outdoor Roman amphitheater. Drama, music, and dance performances are still held here year-round; check with the tourist office.

Across the Piazza Matteotti is another Palladian opus, the Palazzo Chiericati, which houses the Museo Civico (Municipal Museum). Looking more like one of the country villas for which Palladio was equally famous, this major work is considered one of his finest and is visited as much for its two-tiered, statue-topped facade as for the collection of Venetian paintings it houses on the first floor. Venetian masters you'll recognize include Tiepolo, Tintoretto, and Veronese, while the lesser known include works from the Vicenzan (founded by Bartolomeo Montagna) and Bassano schools of painting.

VILLAS & A BASILICA NEARBY

To reach the two important villas in the immediate environs of Vicenza, southeast of the train station, you can walk, bike, or take the no. 8 bus. First stop by the tourist office for a map, and check on visiting hours, which tend to change from year to year. The following two villas are generally open from mid-March to early November.

The ⊙ **Villa Rotonda** (☎ **0444/32-17-93;** fax 0444/8791380), alternatively referred to as Villa Capra Valmarana after its owners, is considered one of the most perfect buildings ever constructed and has been added to the World Heritage List by UNESCO; it is a particularly important must-do excursion for students and lovers of architecture. Most authorities refer to it as Palladio's finest. Obviously inspired by ancient Greek and Roman designs, Palladio began this perfectly proportioned square building topped by a dome in 1567; it was completed by Scamozzi after Palladio's death, between 1580 and 1592. You will perhaps recognize it, for it is the model that inspired Jefferson's home in Monticello, the Chiswick House near London, myriad plantation homes in America's Deep South, and countless other noble homes and government buildings in the United States and Europe. It is worth a visit if only to view it from the outside. Admission for outside viewing is 5,000L ($2.95); admission for visits to the lavishly decorated interior is 10,000L ($5.90). Check for hours.

From here it is only a 10-minute walk to the **Villa Valmarana** (☎ **0444/ 54-39-76**), also called "ai Nani" ("dwarves") after the statues that line the garden wall. Built in the 17th century by Mattoni, an admirer and follower of Palladio, it is an almost commonplace villa whose reason to visit is an interior covered with remarkable 18th-century frescoes by Giambattista Tiepolo and his son Giandomenico. Admission is 8,000L ($4.70). Check with the tourist office for changing hours.

Also in this area is the Basilica or **Santuario di Monte Berico** built in 1668 by a Bolognese architect and, if you've already visited the Villa Rotonda, you will understand where he got his inspiration. The interior's most important work is in a chapel to the right of the main altar, a *Lamentation* by Bortolomeo Montagna (1500), founder of the local school of painting and one of the Veneto's most famous. The terrace in front of the church affords beautiful views of Vicenza, the Monti Berici, and the distinct outline of the nearby Alps. The basilica is open in summer months Monday to Saturday from 6am to 12:30pm and 2:30 to 7:30pm, Sunday 6am to 8pm; earlier closing in winter months; free admission.

ORGANIZED TOURS

The success of each summer's guided tours never seems enough to bring them back the following year. Something usually appears, however, in a new incarnation, often free of charge, with the arrival of each tourist season (approximately April through mid-October). In 1998, free walking tours were offered every Saturday alternatively at 10am and 3pm. Free evening tours, also every Saturday, concentrated on some of Palladio's lesser known palazzi. Check with the tourist office upon your arrival in town, or in advance by visiting its Web site (see "Visitor Information," above). Die-hard architect buffs may want to splurge for the services of any of the accredited polylingual tour guides through their association Guide Turistiche Autorizzate (☎ 0444/ 324123; fax 0444/541244). Rates are 169,000L ($99.40) for half day, up to 30 people.

WHERE TO STAY

Unlike Padua, which gets the overflow when Venice is full, or the tourism-magnet Verona, Vicenza can be very quiet in high season, August, or winter months when trade fairs are not in town; some hotels close without notice for a few weeks if there's little demand. Make sure you call in advance; the city's number of hotels is limited.

Cristina. Cor. San Felice 32 (west of Salvi Gardens), 36100 Vicenza. ☎ **0444/32-37-51.** Fax 0444/54-36-56. E-mail: hotel.cristina@keycomm.it. A/C MINIBAR TV TEL. 33 units, all with bathroom. 150,000L ($88.25) single; 200,000L ($117.65) double; triples and quads available. Rates include buffet breakfast. Discounts possible in low season. AE, DC, MC, V. Parking available.

Located west of the Piazza Castello and the green Giardino Salvi, this recently refurbished hotel is still within easy walking distance of the historic center's principal sites. It's a perfect choice for those with wheels and a few extra dollars. A contemporary approach with occasional exposed beams and marble and parquet flooring results in a handsome, well-maintained lodging and makes this one of Vicenza's preferred three-star properties. An internal courtyard provides welcome parking space for a nominal fee and guests have access to bicycles for touring the traffic-free center of town as well as the nearby villas just southeast of the train station. After all that cycling, coast back to the hotel and into its recently added Finnish sauna.

Due Mori. V. Do Rode 26 (1 block west of Pz. d. Signori), 36100 Vicenza. ☎ **0444/ 32-18-86.** Fax 0444/32-61-27. 26 units, 23 with bathroom. TEL. 65,000L ($38.25) single with bathroom; 75,000L ($44.10) double without bathroom, 100,000L ($58.80) double with bathroom; 87,000L ($51.20) triple without bathroom, 112,000L ($65.90) triple with bathroom. Breakfast 10,000L ($5.90). AE, MC, V.

A full renovation in 1996 has resulted in this fresh, bright, inexpensive hotel choice. Add that to the Due Mori's family-run hotel's history as the oldest in Vicenza and its convenient location on a quiet side street just west of the sprawling Piazza dei Signori, and you have the deservedly most popular spot in town for the budget sensitive. All of this to say: Book early. In a modernized shell of a centuries-old palazzo, tasteful and authentic 19th-century pieces distinguish otherwise plain rooms whose amenities are kept at a minimum (though 1999 may see the arrival of hair dryers), but so are the prices. This is as good as it gets in the very center of Palladio's home town.

Palladio. V. Oratorio d. Servi 25 (east of the Pz. d. Signori), 36100 Vicenza ☎ **0444/ 32-10-72.** Fax 0444/54-73-28. 24 units, 15 with bathroom. TEL TV. 60,000L ($35.30) single without bathroom, 95,000L ($55.90) single with bathroom; 100,000L ($58.80) double without bathroom, 120,000L ($70.60) double with bathroom; 150,000L ($88.25) triple with bathroom. Breakfast 10,000L ($5.90). AE, MC, DC, V. Bus from station: 1, 5, 7, 2.

A popular two-star choice, the Palladio is the friendliest of the city's few hotels worth mentioning. Just a two-minute walk from the Piazza dei Signori (and equidistant from the Piazza Matteotti and the Teatro Olimpico), this family run hotel offers small, no-frills but efficient rooms in a quiet neighborhood. Parking can be arranged, as can daily bicycle rentals (10,000L/$5.90 per day).

WHERE TO DINE

Antica Casa d.la Malvasia. Contrà d. Morette 5 (off Cor. Palladio). ☎ **0444/54-37-04.** Reservations suggested during high season. Primi 6,500L ($3.80); secondi 10,000–14,000L ($5.90–$8.25). V, AE. Tues–Sun noon–3pm and 7pm–midnight (sometimes later). VICENTINO.

This ever lively, taverna-like osteria sits on a quiet, characteristic side street that links the principal Corso Palladio with the Piazza dei Signori. Service is with a smile and informal, the cooking homemade and regional (there's usually one waiter or more whose English will help eliminate the guessing game). The food is reliably good, but it's just an excuse to accompany the selection of wines (80), whiskies (100), grappas (150), and teas (over 150). No wonder this place always buzzes. Even if you don't eat here, stop in at least for a late-night toddy, *vicentino*-style—it's a favorite spot for locals and visitors alike and there's often live music on Tuesday and Thursday evenings.

Gran Caffè Garibaldi. Pz. d. Signori 5. ☎ **0444/54-41-74.** No credit cards. Thurs–Tues 8am–midnight. CAFE

If it's a lovely day, set up camp here in the shade of a table with an umbrella that over-looks Vicenza's grand piazza. The most historically significant cafe in Palladio's city is as stage-set impressive inside as you would imagine. The upstairs restaurant is too expensive for what it offers, but the outside terrace gives you the chance to sit and gaze upon the wonders of the whale-sized Basilica, yet another Palladian masterpiece. A chef's salad like Insalata Garibaldi for 12,000L ($7.05) makes a great lunch, as do any of the sandwiches and panini at 5,000L ($2.95) or less. Or just nurse a cappuccino or aperitivo for the same lire at your outside table; prices are slightly less at the bar, but go for the front-row seats and the theater-in-the-round that the city's beautiful Piazza dei Signori offers.

Righetti. Pz. Duomo 3/4. ☎ **0444/54-31-35.** Primi 5,000L ($2.95); secondi 10,000L ($5.90). No credit cards. Mon–Fri noon–2:30pm and 7–10pm. VICENTINO/ITALIAN.

For a self-service operation, this place is a triple surprise: The diners are all local (and loyal); the food is reliably good—of the home-cooked generous portions kind; and indoors is rustic, welcoming, and pleasant considering its inexpensive profile. But it's the opportunity to sit outdoors in the quiet, traffic-free Piazza Duomo that first drew me here. There are three or four first courses to choose from (Tuesday and Friday are risotto days) and as many entrees. Evenings offer the added option of grilled meats (which makes eating indoors in the cold winter months more enjoyable), though this is the perfect relaxed place to revel in a simple lunch of pasta and side vegetable, opting for a more special dinner venue.

WORTH A SPLURGE

✪ **Trattoria Tre Visi.** Cor. Palladio 25 (near Pz. Castello). ☎ **0444/32-48-68.** Reservations suggested. Primi 12,000L ($7.05); secondi 20,000–30,000L ($11.75–$17.65). Tues–Sun

12:30–2:30pm; Tues–Sat 7:30–10pm. AE, MC, DC, V. Closed Sun dinner and Mon. VICENTINO/ITALIAN.

Operating since the early 1600s around the corner until a 1997 change of address, this Vicentino institution is now located on this important palazzo-studded street in a setting somewhat less dramatic than the previous 15th-century palazzo (though here there is an al fresco courtyard). The menu has stayed unchanged, however, and this is good: Ignore items that concede to foreign requests and concentrate on the regional dishes they know how to prepare best. Almost all the pasta is made fresh daily, including the house specialty, *bigoli con anitra,* a fat spaghetti-like pasta served with duck ragout. The region's signature dish, *baccalà alla vicentina* (a poor man's dish that, when prepared properly, is delicious) is a tender salt codfish simmered in a stew of onions, herbs, anchovies, garlic, and parmigiano for 8 hours before arriving at your table in perfection. Ask your kind waiter for help in selecting from of Veneto's wide spectrum of very fine wines: It will enhance your bill as well as the memories you'll bring home with you.

DAY TRIPS FROM VICENZA

In addition to the two villas located in the immediate outskirts of Vicenza, a tour of the dozens of country *ville venete* farther afield is the most compelling outing from Vicenza. Check at the tourist office to see availability of organized tours, something that has been on-again (and more frequently), off-again for the last few years. You most probably will have to do it yourself (this means having access to wheels). The tourist office will arm you with reams of information to help with the problem of erratic hours for visiting the villas (not all can be visited, others permit only visits to the grounds but not the interiors), many of which are still privately owned and inhabited. The tourist office also has maps, and a host of varied itineraries outlining the most important villas (not all of which are 16th-century Palladian designs), of which many are UNESCO protected sites. Public transportation for these visits is close to nonexistent. If you do have access to a car, ask about the summer concert series in June and July, **Concerti in Villa** (see "Festivals" above), which has drawn some first-class talent in the classical music world.

Bassano di Grappa, about 22 miles north of Vicenza, can be incorporated into a tour of the villas. Renowned for both its centuries-old production of ceramics and grappa, it is a picturesque town located on the Brenta River. Its covered wooden bridge built by Palladio in 1568 is a highlight of the small centro storico. The city's arcaded homes whose facades are painted in the traditional manner, and small squares make this a lovely break from the art-laden larger towns in this chapter. Bassano's yearly **Opera Estate Festival** takes place from early July through August, with alfresco performances of opera, concerts and dance. For information, call the A.P.T. (tourist office) (☎ **0424/52-43-51;** fax 0424/52-53-01). To **get here** from Vicenza, you can take one of a dozen daily buses that make the 1-hour trip (frequent buses from Padua to Bassano take half the time, making fewer stops); one-way tickets from both cost 6,000L ($3.50). In Vicenza, buses leave from the FTV bus station on Viale Milano to the left of the train station upon exiting (☎ **0424/30850**).

The delightful medieval walled town of **Marostica,** 17 miles north of Vicenza (and 7km/4.4 miles west of Bassano), comes alive à la Brigadoon every other summer, in even years only, when the entire town dresses up to commemorate a true centuries-old chess game between two enamored knights for the hand of Lionora. (Are you surprised? This is the region that gave us Romeo and Juliet.) The chivalric **Partita a Scacchi** is re-enacted on the main piazza with human figures in full elaborate Renaissance costume, preceded by a flag-throwing procession with everyone in town taking part, and the evocative torch-lit nighttime setting is gorgeous. The next performance is the second Sunday of September, 2000, and tickets must be purchased months in advance; for information, call ☎ **0424/72-127** (fax 0424/72-800; www.telemar.it/ ,arostica.htm; e-mail proloco@telemar.it. Marostica's engaging **Sagra del Ciliege** (Cherry Festival) takes place in June. You can **get here** on the buses that from Vicenza to Marostica (change in Bassano). Dozens of local buses daily do the short run from Bassano to Marostica (it's only 7km/4.4 mi.). **By car,** you can get to Marostica from Bassano by going west on **S248** (7km/4.4 mi.).

3 Verona

114 km (71 mi.) W of Venice, 80 km (50 mi.) W of Padua, 61 km (38 mi.) W of Vicenza, 157 km (99 mi.) E of Milan

Suspend all disbelief regarding the real-life existence of Romeo and Juliet, and your stay in Verona will be extraspecial, even magical. After Venice, this is the Veneto's (and one of Italy's) most visited city. Verona reached a cultural and artistic peak during the 13th and 14th-centuries under the puissant and often cruel and sometimes quirky della Scala or Scalageri dynasty that took up rule in the late 1200s. In 1405, it surrendered to Venice, which remained in charge until the invasion of Napoléon in 1797. During the time of Venetian rule, Verona became a prestigious urban capital and controlled much of the Veneto and as far south as Tuscany. You'll see the emblem of the *scala* (ladder) around town, heraldic symbol of the della Scala or Scaligeri dynasty. The city retains its locked-in-time character that recalls its medieval and Renaissance heyday, and the magnificent medieval palazzi, towers, churches, and stagelike piazzas you see today are picture-perfect testimony to its centuries-old influence and wealth.

And what about Romeo and Juliet? Did they really exist? Originally a Sienese legend, first put into novella form in 1476, this story was subsequently retold in 1524 by Veneto-born Luigi da Porto. He chose Verona in the years 1302–04 during the reign of the della Scalas, and renamed the young couple Romeo and Juliet. The popular **storia d'amore** was translated into English and became the source and inspiration of Shakespeare's tale (no one ever said it was original, although the engaging 1998 film *Shakespeare in Love*, a highly enjoyable fictionalized tale, will have you believe it is the Bard's own). Translated into dozens of languages and performed endlessly around the world (just look at the number of Asian and Eastern European tourists that flock to Juliet's House), this tale of pure love in the tempestuous days of a medieval city whose streets were stained with the blood and hatred between feuding families. The tale is universal and timeless in its content and no other city is so naturally and authentically stagelike (although Zefferelli chose to film his classic 1968 interpretation in the tiny Tuscan town of Pienza, south of Siena).

Visitors spend remarkably little time in this beautiful medieval city. While it has a short list of attractions, it is a handsome town to spend time in at a leisurely pace. Statistics clock most tourists stopping for a mere overnight stay (or less)—try for at least 2 nights.

FESTIVALS & MARKETS   The **Teatro Romano** is known for its **Festival Shakespeariano** (Shakespeare Festival) from June through August, which celebrated its 50th anniversary in 1998 with a week of English-language performances by the Royal Shakespeare Company, intended to be repeated in 1999 and 2000. Festival performances begin in late May and June with jazz concerts. In July and August there are a number of ballets (such as Prokofiev's *Romeo and Juliet*) and modern dance performances. Check for schedule (☎ **045/80-77-111** or with the tourist office).

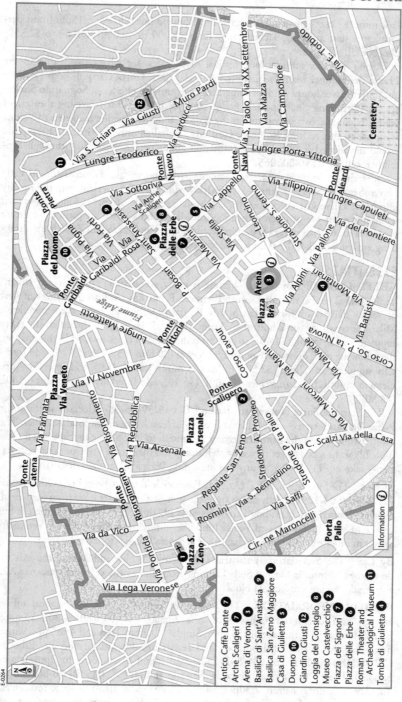

Verona

Cemetery

Via E. Torbido
Via S. Paolo Via XX Settembre
Via Mazza
Via Campofiore
Muro Pardi
Via Giusti
Via S. Chiara
Lungre Teodorico
Via Carducci
Lungre Porta Vittoria
Via Filippini
Lungre Capuleti
Via del Pontiere
Ponte Aleardi
Via Sottoriva
Via Cappello
Via Arche Scaligeri
Sant'Anastasia
Via Pigna
Via Forti
Via Garibaldi
P. Bosari
Via Mazzini
Via Stella
L. Leoncino
Stradone S. Fermo
Via Pallone
Via Montanari
Via Alpini
Via Battisti
Ponte Pietra
Ponte Nuovo
Ponte Navi

Piazza del Duomo
Piazza delle Erbe
Piazza Brà
Arena

Ponte Garibaldi
Ponte Vittoria
Fiume Adige
Lungre Matteotti

Via IV Novembre
Piazza Veneto
Via Farinata
Via Risorgimento
Via le Repubblica
Via Arsenale
Piazza Arsenale
Ponte Scaligero
Coso Cavour
Via Manin
Via Valverde
Corso So. p.ta Nuova
Via G. Marconi
Via C. Scalzi Via della Casa

Ponte Catena
Ponte Risorgimento
Via da Vico
Via Pontida
Regaste San Zeno
Via S. Bernardino P.ta Palio
Stradone A. Provolo
Via Rosmini
Via Saffi
Cir. ne Maroncelli
Porta Palio

Piazza S. Zeno
Via Lega Veronese

Information

Antico Caffè Dante **7**
Arche Scaligeri **7**
Arena di Verona **3**
Basilica di Sant'Anastasia **9**
Basilica San Zeno Maggiore **1**
Casa di Giulietta **5**
Duomo **10**
Giardino Giusti **12**
Loggia del Consiglio **8**
Museo Castelvecchio **2**
Piazza dei Signori **7**
Piazza delle Erbe **6**
Roman Theater and
Archaeological Museum **11**
Tomba di Giulietta **4**

461

Last-minute tickets go on sale at the Teatro Romano box office at 8:15pm (most performances start at 9pm). Tickets range from 15,000 to 40,000L ($8.80 to $23.50) plus booking charges.

During Verona's summer-long festival of the arts, see what's happening in the **Piazza dei Signori** where frequent free concerts (jazz, tango, classical) keep everyone out until the wee hours. And for something truly unique, check out **Sognando Shakespeare** (Dreaming Shakespeare): Follow this *teatro itinerante* (traveling theater) of young, talented actors in costume as the wander about the medieval corners of Verona from site to site, reciting **Romeo e Guilietta** (in Italian only) **in situ,** as Shakespeare would have loved it to be. For information about performances July through September, call ☎ 045/8000065.

Other important events are the famous 4-day horse fair, *Fieracavalli,* in early November and the important 5-day **VinItaly** wine fair (that overlaps with the equally important **Olive Oil Fair**) mid-April. (Verona's schedule of fairs is long and varied; while not many are of interest to those outside the trade, their frequency can create problems for tourists in regard to hotel availability.) The **Piazza San Zeno** hosts a traveling antiques market the third Saturday of every month; come early.

ESSENTIALS

GETTING HERE   By Train   Verona is easily accessed on the west-east Milan-Venice line as well as the north-south Brennero-Rome line. At least 30 trains run west of Venice daily (look for the fast hourly IC trains, a 90-min. trip); even more leave Milan westward for the 2-hour trip). From Milan, 12,100L ($7.05), add an InterCity supplement of 7,500L ($4.40). To and from the Veneto's cities covered in this chapter, the following costs quoted are one way: Vicenza (30 min.), 5,500L ($3.25), add InterCity supplement 4,200L ($2.50); Padua (55 min.) 8,500L ($5.), add InterCity supplement 5,400L ($3.20); Venice 10,400L ($6.10), add InterCity supplement 6,500L ($3.80).

The Stazione **Porta Nuova rail station** (☎ 045/59-06-88) is located south of the Piazza Brà (and Arena) area and is serviced by at least half a dozen local bus lines. The bus network within the historical center is limited, so if you have luggage you'll most probably want a taxi to get to your hotel. But if you insist on a bus from the train station—take no. 11, 12, 13, or any bus indicating Piazza Brà as final destination

By Bus   The bus station, A.P.T. (Azienda Provinciale Trasporti) is at Piazza XXV Aprile (☎ 045/80-04-129) directly across from the train station. Buses leave from here for all regional destinations, including Largo di Garda (9,800L/$5.75). Although there is bus service to Vicenza, Padua, and Venice (only the summertime departures for Venice are direct; in other months there's a change), it is generally easier to travel by train.

By Car   The **Serenissima autostrada (A4)** links Venice and Milan; the exit for downtown Verona is Verona Sud. Coming from the north or south, use the A22 autostrada, taking exit Verona Nord.

VISITOR INFORMATION   The two most central tourist information offices are on V. Leoncini 61 (adjacent to the Arena) (☎ 045/8068680), summer hours Monday to Saturday 9am to 8pm, Sunday 10am to 1pm and 4 to 7pm; winter hours usually mean closed Sundays and less hours other days; and Pz. Erbe 38 (☎ 045/80-00-065; fax 045/8010682), year-round hours 8am to 2pm (closed Sunday). There's also a small office at the train station (☎ 045/80-00-861), open Tuesday to Saturday 8am to 7:30pm, Sunday and Monday 10am to 4pm. You can get more information by logging on to the town's Web site at **www.verona-apt.net**; e-mail: veronapt@mbox.vol.it.

Will the Fat Lady Sing?

The well-known opera season that takes place every July (usually beginning the last few days of June) and August in Verona's ancient amphitheater began in 1913 with a staging of *Aïda* to commemorate the 100th anniversary of Verdi's birth. *Aïda* in all of its extravagant glory has been performed yearly ever since; expect to see other Verdi works such as *Un Ballo in Maschera, Nabucco,* and *Rigoletto.* Those seated on the least expensive, unreserved stone steps costing 42,000L ($24.70) enjoy fresh air, excellent acoustics, and a view over the arena's top to the city and surrounding hills beyond. The rub is that Jose Carreras will only appear to be 1 inch high. Numbered seats below cost from 180,000L ($105.90) to 290,000L ($170.60); all tickets are subject to an advance booking fee of 5,000 to 38,000L ($2.95 to $22.35). These are weekend prices: Weekday prices are slightly less, opening night tickets slightly higher. The box office is located on V. Dietro Anfiteatro 6/B; credit card purchase (AE, DC, V) accepted by phone (☎ 045/80-05-151; fax 045/80-13-287; e-mail: ticket@www.arena.it); tickets are picked up the night of the performance. Bank drafts can be sent to the above address, but it's better to call or fax. If you hope to find tickets upon arrival, remember that *Aïda* is everyone's most requested performance; weekend performances are usually sold out. As a last-minute resort, be nice to your hotel manager or concierge—everyone has a connection, or a relative with a connection. An extraspecial schedule was expected for the 2000 season (with works by Verdi and others) with more performances than usual, visit the Web site at www.arena.it.

Guided Tours   An air-conditioned "**bus turistico**" departs thrice daily for a 1½-hour Giro Turistico tour of the city's historical center every day except Monday from June 30 until September 6. The cost is 20,000L ($11.75) for a recorded spiel in four languages. It leaves from the Gran Guardia in the Piazza Brà. The Saturday afternoon tour leaves at 3:30pm with a real live tour guide that ups the cost to 35,000 ($20.60).

You can ask for a listing of accredited polylingual tour guides recognized by the Associazione Guide Turistiche (Association of Tourist Guides) at any of the tourist offices or call them directly at ☎ 045/8278959; fax 045/8278966. A 2-hour tour for any group up to 30 people is 185,000L ($108.85)

CITY LAYOUT   The city lies alongside the banks of the S-shaped Adige River. As far as the average visitor is considered, everything of interest—with the exception of the Teatro Romano—is found in the centro storico on the south side of the river's loop; there's no site that cannot be easily and enjoyably reached by foot. The massive and impressive ancient Roman amphitheater, **the Arena,** sits at the southern end of the city's hub in the airy cafe-ringed **Piazza Brà.** The piazza is linked by the popular **Via Mazzini** pedestrian thoroughfare to the **Piazza delle Erbe** and its adjacent **Piazza dei Signori.** The grid of pedestrian-only streets between are lined with handsome shops and cafes and make up the principal strolling and window-shopping destination in town. Slightly out of this loop (though still an easy walk) is the **Basilica di San Zeno,** west of the Arena, and **Juliet's tomb,** southeast of the Arena (only diehard Juliet fans will appreciate the trek here). Both the train station and the Fiera di Verona conference center are located in the southern part of town beyond the Porta Nuova.

GETTING AROUND   Verona lends itself to walking and strolling and most sites are concentrated within a few history-steeped blocks of each other. Venture off the store-lined treadmill and seek out the narrow, cobblestoned side streets that are evocative of eras past. Little to no traffic is permitted in town, so upon arrival stash your car in a parking area suggested by your hotel (where they'll most likely have a special arrangement), and let your feet do the transporting.

WHAT TO SEE & DO

If you're in town the **first Sunday of any month,** check if entrance is still free for the following sites (projected but not confirmed at time of printing): Castelvecchio Museum, the Roman Theater, and Juliet's Tomb.

Since there are so many churches in Verona, a recent admission charge has been imposed (a recent, unprecedented trend in Italy's churches) in an attempt to cover custodian charges and offer longer hours. An expensive *biglietto cumulativo* (joint ticket) of 10,000L ($5.90) is worthwhile only if you intend to visit all five churches involved: San Zeno, the Duomo, and Sant'Anastasia; San Fermo and San Lorenzo. Of these, we have included the first three (and most visit-worthy) below.

TOP ATTRACTIONS

✪ **Arena di Verona.** Pz. Brà ☎ **045/800-32-04.** Admission 6,000L ($3.50). Tues–Sun 9am–6pm. During the July–Aug summer opera season 8am–3:30pm.

The best preserved Roman amphitheater in the world and the best known in Italy after Rome's Colosseum, the elliptical Arena was built in a slightly pinkish marble around the year A.D. 100 and stands in the very middle of town with the Piazza Brà on its southern flank. Built to accommodate more than 20,000 people (outdone by Rome's contender that could seat more than twice that), it is in remarkable shape today (despite a 12th-century earthquake that left only four arches of the outer ring standing), beloved testimony to the pride and wealth of Verona and its populace. Its perfect acoustics have survived the millennia and make it one of the wonders of the ancient world and one of the most fascinating venues for live performances today (which are conducted without microphones). If you're in town during the summer opera performances in July and August, do everything possible to procure a ticket (see "Will the Fat Lady Sing?," above) for any of the outdoor evening performances (for last-minute tickets or the popular weekend performances, try the front desk at your hotel). Even opera-challenged audience members will take home the memory of a lifetime. The cluster of outdoor cafes and trattorias/pizzerias on the western side of the Piazza Brà line a wide marble esplanade called Il Liston; they stay open long after the opera performances end and some serious after-opera people-watching goes on here.

✪ **Piazza Delle Erbe.** Between V. Mazzini and Cor. Porta Borsari. Open-air produce and flower market Mon–Sat 8am to 7pm.

This bustling marketplace—the palazzi-flanked Square of the Herbs—sits on the former site of the Roman Forum where chariot races once took place. The herbs, spices, coffee beans, and bolts of silks and damasks that came through Verona after landing in Venice from faraway Cathay have given way to the fresh and aromatic produce of one of Italy's wealthiest agricultural regions—offset by the inevitable ever-growing presence of T-shirt and french-fry vendors, as the piazza has become something of a tourist trap. But the perfume of fennel and vegetables fresh from the earth still assaults your senses in the early morning, mixing with the cacophony of vendors touting their plump tomatoes, dozens of different variations of salad greens, and picture-perfect fruits that can't possibly taste as good as they look, but do. Add to this the canary lady, the farmer's son who has brought in a half a dozen puppies to unload, and the furtive pickpocket who can spot a tourist at 50 paces—and you have one of Italy's loveliest and, before the first tour group arrives (9 or 10am), most authentic outdoor markets. A ground-zero rest-stop is one of the steps leading up to the small, 14th-century fountain in the piazza's center and a Roman statue dubbed *The Virgin of Verona*.

✪ Piazza Dei Signori (Piazza Dante).

To reach the Piazza dei Signori from the Piazza delle Erbe, exit under the Arco della Costa (the Arch of the Rib), which you'll be able to spot by the enormous whalebone hanging overhead. It was placed here 1,000 years ago when it was said to have been unearthed during excavations on this spot, indicating this area was once underwater. Local legend goes that the rib will fall on the first person to pass beneath it who has never told a lie—thus explaining the nonchalance with which every Veronese passes under it. The perfect antidote to the color and bustle of the Piazza delle Erbe, the serene and elegant Piazza dei Signori is a slightly sober square, one of Verona's innermost chambers of calm. Its center is anchored by a large 19th-century statue of the "divine poet" Dante, who found political exile from Florence in Verona as a guest of Cangrande I and the Scaligeri family (in appreciation Dante wrote of his patron in his poem "Paradiso"). If entering from the Archway, you'll be facing the Scaligeri's 13th-century crenellated residence before it was taken over by the governing Venetians. Left of that, behind Dante's back, is the **Loggia del Consiglio** (Portico of the Counsel), a 15th-century masterpiece of Venetian Renaissance style. Opposite that and facing Dante is the 12th-century Romanesque **Palazzo della Ragione,** whose courtyard and fine Gothic staircase should be visited. This piazza is Verona's finest microcosm, a balanced and refined assemblage of historical architecture. Secure an outdoor table at the square's legendary command-post, the **Antico Caffè Dante,** and take it all in over a late-afternoon Campari and soda.

✪ Museo Castelvecchio. Cor. Castelvecchio 2 (at V. Roma, on the Adige River). ☎ 045/59-47-34. Admission 6,000L ($3.30). Free 1st Sun of each month. Tues–Sun 9am–7:15pm.

A 5-minute walk west of the Arena amphitheater on the Via Roma and nestled on the banks of the swift-flowing Adige River, the "Old Castle" is a crenellated fairy-tale pile of brick towers and turrets, protecting the bridge behind it. It was commissioned in 1354 by the della Scala warlord Cangrande II to serve the dual role of residential palace and military stronghold. It survived centuries of occupation by the Visconti family, the Serene Republic of Venice, and then Napoléon, only to be destroyed by the Germans during World War II bombing. Its painstaking restoration was initiated in 1958 by the acclaimed Venetian architect Carlos Scarpa and re-opened in 1964, now a fascinating home to some 400 works of art. The ground-floor rooms, displaying statues and carvings of the Middle Ages, lead to alleyways, vaulted halls, multileveled floors, and stairs, all as architecturally arresting as the Venetian masterworks from the 14th to 18th centuries it offsets—notably those by Tintoretto, Tiepolo, Veronese, Bellini, and the Verona-born Pisanello—that you'll find throughout. Don't miss the large courtyard with the equestrian statue of the warlord Cangrande I (a copy can be seen at the family cemetery at the Arche Scaligeri) with a peculiar dragon's head affixed to his back (it appears to be his armor's helmet removed from his head and resting behind him). A stroll across the pedestrian bridge behind the castle affords you a fine view of the castle, the Ponte Scaligeri (built in 1355 and also destroyed during World War II; it was reconstructed using the original materials) and the river's banks.

☼ **Casa di Giulietta (Juliet's House).** V. Cappello 23 (southeast of Pz. d. Erbe). ☎ **045/ 80-34-303.** Admission 6,000L ($3.50). Tues–Sun 9am–7:15pm.

There is no proof that a Capuleti (Capulet) family ever lived here (or if they did, that a young girl called Juliet ever existed), and it wasn't until 1905 that the city bought what was an abandoned, overgrown garden and decided its future. So powerful is the legend of Juliet that millions of tourists flock here every year to visit the simple court-yard and home (admission to latter only) that are considerably less affluent-looking than the sumptuous Franco Zefferelli version as you may remember it (the movie was filmed in Tuscany). Myriad are those who leave behind layer upon layer of graffiti such as "Gianni, ti amo, T" or who engage in the peculiar tradition (whose origin no one can seem to explain) of rubbing the right breast (now buffed to a bright gold) of the 20th-century bronze statue of a forever nubile Juliet. The curious might want to fork over the entrance fee to see the spartan interior of the 13th-century home, restored in 1996. Ceramics and furniture on display are authentic of the era but did not belong to Juliet's family—if there was a Juliet at all. Stop by just before closing time, when the courtyard is relatively empty of tourists and it is easiest to imagine Romeo uttering, "But Soft! What light through yonder window breaks? It is the east, and Juliet is the sun!" No one would confirm to me (or not) that the balcony was added to the palazzo as recently as the 1920s.

La Tomba di Giulietta (Juliet's Tomb) is about a 15-minute walk south of here (near the Adige River on V. d. Pontiere 5, admission 5,000L/$2.95, free 1st Sunday of each month; Tuesday to Sunday 9am to 7pm). The would-be site of the star-crossed lovers' suicide is found within the graceful medieval cloisters of the Capuchin monastery of San Francesco al Corso; die-hard romantics may find it more evocative than the crowded scene at Juliet's House and worth the trip. Others will find it over-rated and shouldn't bother. The adjacent church is where their secret marriage was said to have taken place. There is a small museum of frescoes adjacent.

MORE ATTRACTIONS

Arche Scaligeri (Scaligeri Tombs). Corner of V. d. Arche Scaligeri, northeast of Pz. d. Sig-nori. No entry; viewed from outside only.

Exit the Piazza dei Signori opposite the Arch of the Rib and immediately on your right, at the corner of Via delle Arche Scaligeri, are some of the most elaborate Gothic funerary monuments in Italy—the raised outdoor tombs of the della Scala or Scaligeri family (seen behind the original decorative grillwork), powerful and often ruthless rulers of Verona. The most important are those by the peculiar names of Mastino I (founder of the dynasty, date of death unknown), Mastino II (Mastiff the Second, d. 1351), and Cansignorio (Head Dog, d. 1375). The most interesting is found over the side door of the family's private chapel Santa Maria Antica—the tomb of Cangrande I (Big Dog, d. 1329), with dogs (*cani*) holding up a ladder (*scala*), both elements that figure in the Scaligeri coat of arms. That's Cangrande I—patron of the arts and pro-tector of Dante—and his steed you see above (the original can be seen in the Museo Castelvecchio). Recently restored, these tombs are considered one of the country's greatest medieval monuments.

Around the corner on V. d. Arche Scaligeri 2 is the alleged 13th-century home of Juliet's significant other, Romeo Montecchi, which incorporates the popular Osteria dal Duca (See "Where to Dine," below).

Basilica San Zeno Maggiore. Pz. San Zeno. ☎ **045/80-06-120.** Single admission 3,000L ($1.75). Mar–Oct, Tues–Sat 8:30am–6pm; Sun 1–6pm. Nov–Feb, Tues–Sat 10am–4pm; Sun 1–4pm.

This is one of the finest examples of Romanesque architecture in northern Italy, built between the 9th and 12th centuries. Slightly out of the old city's hub but still easily reached by foot, San Zeno, dedicated to the city's patron saint, is Verona's most visited church. Spend a moment outside to appreciate the fine, sober facade, highlighted by the immense 12th-century rose window, the "Ruota della Fortuna" (the Wheel of Fortune!). This pales in importance compared to the entrance below—two pillars supported by marble lions and massive doors whose 48 bronze panels were sculpted from the 9th to the 11th centuries and are believed to have been some of the first castings in bronze since Roman antiquity. They are one of the city's most cherished artistic treasures and are worth the trip here even if the church is closed. Not yet as sophisticated as those that would adorn the Baptistery doors of Florence's Duomo in the centuries to come, these are like a naive illustration from a child's book and were meant to educate the illiterate masses with scenes from the Old and New Testaments and the life of San Zeno. They are complemented by the stone bas-reliefs found on either side of the doors, the 12th-century work of Niccolo who was also responsible for the Duomo's portal. The 14th-century tower on the left belonged to the former abbey while the freestanding slender campanile on the right was begun in 1045. The massive interior is filled with 12th- to 14th-century frescoes and crowned by the nave's ceiling, designed as a wooden ship's keel. But the interior's singular highlight is the famous triptych of the *Madonna and Child Enthroned with Saints* by Andrea Mantegna (1459), behind the main altar. Absconded by Napoléon, the beautiful centerpiece—a showcase for the Padua-born Mantegna's sophisticated sense of perspective and architectural detail—was eventually returned to Verona, although two side panels stayed behind in the Louvre and in Tours. Look for the colored marble statue of a smiling San Zeno, much loved by the local Veronesi, in an act of blessing; it can be found in a small apse to the left of the altar.

Basilica di Sant'Anastasia. Pz. Anastasia at Cor. Anastasia. ☎ **045/59-28-13.** Single admission 3,000L ($1.76). Mar–Oct, Tues–Sat 9:30am–6pm; Sun 1–6pm. Nov–Feb, Tues–Sat 10am–4pm; Sun 1–4pm.

Built between 1290 and 1481, this is Verona's largest church, considered the city's finest example of Gothic architecture, even though the facade remains unfinished. A lovely 14th-century campanile bell tower is adorned with frescoes and sculptures. The church's interior is typically Gothic in design, highlighted by two famous *gobbi* (hunchbacks) who support the holy-water fonts, an impressive patterned pavement, and 16 side chapels containing a number of noteworthy paintings and frescoes from the 15th to the 16th centuries. Most important is Verona-born Pisanello's *St. George Freeing the Princess of Trebisonda* (1433) in the Giusti Chapel in the left transept; it is considered one of his best paintings and is of the armed-knight-and-damsel-in-distress genre—with the large white rump of St. George's steed as one of its focal points. Also worth scouting out are the earlier 14th-century frescoes by the Giotto-inspired Altichiero in the Cavalli Chapel.

Teatro Romano (Roman Theater) and the Museo Archeologico (Archeoligal Museum). V. Rigaste Redentore (over the Ponte Pietra bridge behind the Duomo, on the north banks of the river Adige). ☎ **045/80-00-360.** Admission 5,000L ($2.95); free 1st Sun of each month. Tues–Sun 9am–7pm; during theater season 9am–3pm.

The oldest extant Roman monument in Verona dates from the time of Augustus when the Arena was built and Verona was a strong Roman outpost at the crossroads of the Empire's ancient north/south, east/west highways. There is something almost surreal about attending an open-air performance of Shakespeare's *Two Gentlemen of Verona* or *Romeo and Juliet* here—even if you can't understand a word (See box "Will the Fat Lady Sing?" above). Classical concerts and ballet and jazz performances are also given here, with evocative views of the city beyond. A small Archeological Museum housed above in an old monastery is included in the admission ticket.

The Duomo. Pz. Duomo (at V. d. Duomo). ☎ **045/59-28-13**. Single admission 3,000L ($1.76). Mar–Oct, Mon–Sat 9:30am–6pm; Sun 1–6pm. Nov–Feb, Mon–Sat 10am–4pm; Sun 1:30–4pm.

Begun in the 12th century and not finished until the 17th, the city's most important church still boasts its original main doors and portal, magnificently covered with low reliefs in the Lombard Romanesque style that are attributed to Niccolo, whose work can be seen at the Basilica of San Zeno Maggiore. The church was built upon the ruins of an even more ancient paleochristian church dating to the late Roman Empire. Visit the **Cappella Nichesola,** the first chapel on the left, where Titian's serene but boldly colorful *Assumption of the Virgin* is the cathedral's principal treasure, with an architectural frame by Sansovino (who also designed the choir). Also of interest is the semicircular screen that separates the altar from the rest of the church, attributed to Sanmicheli. Don't leave the area without walking behind the Duomo to the river: Here you'll find the 13th-century **Torre di Alberto della Scala tower** and nearby **Ponte della Pietra bridge,** the oldest Roman monument in Verona (2nd-century B.C.; rebuilt 14th century). There has been a crossing at this point of the river since Verona's days as a 1st-century Roman stronghold when the Teatro Romano was built on the river's northern banks and the Arena at its hub.

VIEWS & GARDENS

The view of Verona from the Roman Theater is beautiful any time of day, but particularly during the evening performances—the ancient Romans knew a thing or two about drama. For other views, you can take a rickety elevator to the 10th-century **Church of Santa Libera** above the theater, or to the former **monastery and cloisters of San Girolamo,** which now houses a small archaeological museum. Above this is the **Castel San Pietro,** whose foundations go back to the times of the Romans and whose terraces offer the best view in town.

Nearby are the well-known, multitiered **Giardino Giusti,** gardens whose formal 16th-century layout and geometrical designs of terraces, fountains, statuary, and staircases inspired, among many, Mozart and Goethe. The gardens are open daily from 9am to dusk; admission is 7,000L ($4.10).

SHOPPING

Unlike Venice, all these people walking the boutique-lined pedestrian streets are locals not tourists. Come to Verona to spend some time doing what the locals do, shopping-and-stopping in any of the myriad cafes and *pasticcerie*. Despite Verona's acknowledgement of the tourism that supplements its economy (unlike Venice, Verona does not live for tourism alone and it shows), there is only the predictable souvenirs to be found in the tourist trinket market. Shopping is mostly for the Veronesi, and upscale clothing and accessories boutiques line the two most fashionable shopping streets, **Via Mazzini** (connecting the Arena and the Piazza delle Erbe) and **Via Cappello,** heading southeast from the piazza and past Juliet's House. There's also Corso Borsari to check out, and Corso S. Anastasia (heading west and east, respectively, out of the Piazza delle Erbe), the latter with a concentration of interesting antique stores.

WHERE TO STAY

Although the following prices reflect peak season rates, expect inflated prices during the July/August opera season (when Venice is offering low season discounts) or when one of the major trade fairs are in town. With these exceptions, **low season** is November through mid-March. The **C.A.V. (Cooperativa Albergatori Veronesi)** is an organization of dozens of two-to five-star hotels that will help you with bookings for a fee determined by your choice of hotel category (☎ **045/80-09-844;** fax 045/80-09-372).

Hotel Aurora. Pz. d. Erbe 2 (southwest side of piazza), 37121 Verona. ☎ **045/59-47-17.** Fax 045/80-10-860. 19 units, 17 with bathroom. A/C TV TEL. 80,000–115,000L ($47.05–$67.65) single without bathroom; 160,000–190,000L ($94.10–$111.75) double with bathroom. Rates include buffet breakfast. Prices discounted 10% off-season. AE, DC, MC, V. Parking 20,000L ($11.75). Bus: 72 or 73 to Pz. d. Erbe.

Until now it was location, location, location that had loyal guests return to the Aurora. As of a 1996 refurbishing of all guest rooms and en suite bathrooms, it is the updated decor as well. Six doubles are blessed with views of one of the world's great squares, the Piazza delle Erbe, and its white-umbrella stalls that make up the daily marketplace. Consider yourself blessed if you snag the top-floor double (there is an elevator!) with a small balcony. There's another terrace overlooking the **mercato** for the guests' use on the second floor, just above the breakfast room where the hotel's daily ample buffet is worth a mention here.

✪ **Hotel Torcolo.** Vc. Lisone 3 (just 1 block off the Pz. Brà), 37121 Verona. ☎ **045/80-07-512.** Fax 045/80-04-058. 19 units, all with bathroom. A/C MINIBAR TV TEL. 133,000L ($78.25) single; 190,000L ($111.75) double; 248,000L ($145.88) triple. Rates include optional breakfast (deduct 18,000L/$10.60 per person if not taken). Above rates are in effect during the peak July/Aug opera season. Inquire about other rates during regular and low season. V. Closed Jan 5–31. Parking nearby 16,000–20,000L ($9.41–$11.75). From train station: all buses to Pz. Brà.

Lifelong friends Signoras Silvia and Diana are much of the reason behind the deserving success of this small, comfortable hotel just 1 peaceful block off the lively Piazza Brà. Bright and homey, it is inviting for its unfussy but tasteful decor found throughout. Each guest room is individually done, one lovely for its wrought-iron bed, another for the intricate parquet floor. No. 31 is a sunny top-floor room (the hotel has an elevator) with exposed ceiling beams, while no. 34 is done with original furnishings from the art nouveau period known in Italy as Liberty. The recently redone bathrooms have welcomed amenities such as hair dryers. You can deduct the rather expensive breakfast from your room rate, but consider enjoying it outdoors on the hotel's small patio if the weather is pleasant.

Locanda Catullo. V. Catullo 1 (just north of the V. Mazzini; entrance from the alleyway Vc. Catullo), 37121 Verona. ☎ **045/80-02-786.** 21 units, 4 with bathroom; 60,000L ($35.30) single without bathroom; 80,000L ($47.05) double without bathroom; 100,000L ($58.80) double with bathroom; 115,000L ($67.65) triple without bathroom; 145,000L ($85.30) triple with bathroom; 190,000L ($111.75) quad suite with bathroom. No credit cards. Parking 18,000L ($10.60). From train station: any bus going to Pz. Brà.

It's a three-floor hike to this homey pensione-like place that has been run by the affable Pollini family for more than 25 years, but it's ultracentral and the rooms are spacious and clean, the bathrooms nice and bright. The prices attract the 20- and 30-something lire-counters who make up the majority of the hotel's clientele. With impressive details and touches such as decorative plaster molding, French doors, and marble or parquet floors, the superfluous hanging tapestries and dried flower arrangements become too much. Single rooms are large and come equipped with a sink; solo travelers feel comfortable in the family atmosphere that prevails. There's no breakfast service available, but the bar downstairs couldn't be more convenient.

WORTH A SPLURGE

✪ **Hotel Giulietta & Romeo.** Vc. Tre Marchetti 3 (south of V. Mazzini, 1 block E of the Arena), 37121 Verona ☎ **045/80-03-554.** Fax 045/80-10-862. www2.easynet.it/gr. E-mail: giuliettaeromeo@easyl.easynet.it. 30 units, all with bathroom. A/C MINIBAR TV TEL. 180,000L ($105.90) single; 260,000L ($152.95) double; 320,000L ($188.25); 340,000L ($200) quad. Rates include buffet breakfast. Mention Frommer's when booking and show book upon arrival for a 10% discount. Add approximately 30% to all above rates during the opera season and major trade fairs. AE, DC, MC, V. Parking nearby 20,000–30,000L ($11.75–17.65). From train station: all buses going to Pz. Brà.

In the shade of the Arena is this handsomely refurbished palazzo-hotel recommended for its upscale ambience, cordial can-do staff, and its location in the very heart of the centro storico. Brightly lit guest rooms are warmed by burnished cherry wood furnishings, and the large marble-tiled baths are those you imagine finding in tony first-class hotels at less reasonable rates. The hotel takes its name seriously; sure enough, there are two small marble balconies à la Juliet, but their view is unremarkable (and, lo!, no Romeo). The hotel is located on a narrow side street that is quiet and convenient to everything, but you might want to just luxuriate in your room a little longer.

WHERE TO DINE

✪ **Bottega del Vino.** V. Scudo di Francia 3 (off V. Mazzini), Verona. ☎ **045/80-04-535.** www.ifinet.it/bottega. E-mail: Bottega.Vino@ifinet.it. Reservations necessary for dinner. Primi 10,000–15,000L ($5.90–8.80); secondi 22,000–30,000L ($12.95–$17.65). Restaurant Wed–Mon noon–3pm (bar 10:30am–3pm) and 7pm–12am (bar 6pm–12am). AE, DC, MC, V. VERONESE/WINE BAR.

Oenophiles can push an evening's meal here into the stratosphere if they succumb to the wine cellar's unmatched 80,000-bottle selection, the largest in Verona. This atmospheric bottega first opened in 1890 and the old-timers who spend hours in animated conversation seem to have been here since then. The atmosphere and conviviality are reason enough to come by for a tipple at the well-known bar, where five dozen good-to-excellent wines are for sale by the glass (1,800 to 25,000L/$1.05 to $14.70). There's no mistaking Verona's prominence in the wine industry here. At mealtimes the regulars head home, and the next shift arrives: Journalists and local merchants fill the few wooden tables ordering simple but excellent dishes where the Veneto's wines have infiltrated the kitchen, such as the *risotto al Amarone,* sauced with Verona's most dignified red.

Brek. Pz. Brà 20. ☎ **045/80-04-561.** No reservations accepted. Primi and pizzas 6000–10,000L ($3.50–$5.90); secondi 7,000–15,000L ($4.10–$8.80). AE, V. Daily 11:30am–3pm and 6:30–10pm. PIZZERIA/TRATTORIA.

The Veronesi (and Italians in general; Brek is part of a north-Italian restaurant chain) are forever dismissing this place as a mediocre tourist spot, but who are all these Italian-speaking, local-looking patrons with their trays piled high, cutting in front of me in line at the pizza station and clamoring for all the best tables outside with a brilliant view of the sun-kissed Arena? This strip of the Piazza Brà is lined with pleasant al fresco alternatives such as the more serious Olivo and Tre Corone, but Brek is an informal, inexpensive preference of mine for a casual lunch where I can splurge (a lot) and walk away satisfied and solvent. Yes, this is fast food *alla veronese*—but do the Italians ever really go wrong in the culinary department? Inside it's a food fest, with various pastas and fresh vegetables made up as you wait, and some self-service where fruit salads and mixed green salads are displayed.

✪ **Osteria dal Duca.** V. Arche Scaligeri 2 (east of Pz. d. Signori). ☎ **045/59-44-74.** Reservations not accepted. Primi 10,000L ($5.90); secondi 15,000L ($8.80). Menù turistico 21,000L ($12.35). MC, V. Mon–Sat 12:30–2:30pm and 7–10:30pm. VERONESE.

There are no written records to confirm that this 13th-century palazzo was once owned by the Montecchi (Montagues) family and, thankfully, the discreet management never considered calling this place the "Ristorante Romeo". But here you are, nonetheless, dining in what is believed to be Romeo's house, a characteristic medieval palazzo, and enjoying one of the nicest meals in town in a spirited and friendly neighborhood ambience. You might find penne with *pomodoro e melanzane* (fresh tomato sauce with eggplant) or a perfectly grilled chop or fillet with rosemary-roasted potatoes. It will be simple, it will be delicious, you'll probably make friends with the people sitting next to you, and you will always remember your meal at Romeo's Restaurant. If you don't fancy yourself an adventurous palate, avoid anything on the menu that has *cavallo* in it, unless you want to sample horse meat, a local specialty.

Pizzeria Impero. Pz. d. Signori 8. ☎ **045/80-30-160.** No reservations accepted. Primi and pizzas 7000–14,000L ($4.10–$8.25); secondi 16,000–22,000L ($9.40–$12.95). D, MC, V. Summer daily noon–2am. Winter Thurs–Tues noon–3:30pm and 7pm–midnight. PIZZERIA/TRATTORIA.

Location is not everything, but to sit with a pleasant lunch or moonlit dinner in this most elegant of piazze will be one of those Verona memories that stays with you. Impero makes a perfectly respectable pizza (with a full trattoria menu to boot), and any of the dozen or so varieties will taste pretty heavenly if you're sharing an outdoor table with your Romeo or Juliet. If Impero is full and the Arena/Piazza Brà location is more convenient to your day's itinerary, try the well-known and always busy **Pizzeria Liston,** V. Dietro Listone 19 (closed Wednesday) that also serves a full trattoria menu (all credit cards accepted); its pizzas are said to be better, but its side-street setting doesn't match Impero.

CAFES, PASTRIES & WINE BARS

When all is said and done in Verona, one of the most important things is to consider where you'll stop to sip, recharge, socialize, nibble, and revel in this handsome and affluent town.

CAFES & PASTRIES   Verona's grande dame of the local cafe society is the ✪ **Antico Caffè Dante** in the beautiful Piazza dei Signori (☎ **045/59-52-49**). Verona's oldest cafe, it is rather formal indoors (read: expensive) where meals are served. But it's most recommended for those who want to soak up the million-dollar view of one of Verona's loveliest ancient squares from the outdoor tables smack in the midst of it all. During the Arena summer season, this is the traditional après-opera spot to complete—and contemplate—the evening's experience. It's open from 9am to 4am.

The oldest of the cafe/bars lining Verona's market square is **Caffè Filippini** at Pz. d. Erbe 26. (☎ **045/80-04-549**). Repeated renovations have left little of yesteryear's character or charm but centuries-old habits die hard: It's still the command-post of choice whether indoors or out (preferably out), a lovely spot to take in the cacophony and colorful chaos of the market. It's open daily in summer months; Thursday to Tuesday 8am to 1am in winter.

An old-world temple of caffeine, **Caffè Tubino** (Cor. Porta Borsari 15/d, 1 block west of the Piazza delle Erbe; ☎ **045/80-32-296**) is stocked with packaged blends of Tubino-brand teas and coffees displayed on racks lining parallel walls in a small space made even smaller by the imposing crystal chandelier. The brand is well known, nicely packaged, and makes a great gift. It's open daily from 7am to 11pm. On the same street is **Pasticceria Bar Flego** (Cor. Porta Borsari 9; ☎ 045/80-32-471), a beloved institution with eight tiny tables-for-two. Accompany a frothy cappuccino with an unbridled sampling of their deservedly famous bite-size pastries by the piece at 1,000 to 2,000L (60¢ to $1.20) each. A regional specialty are the *zaletti*, traditional cookies made with corn flour, raisins, and pine nuts—much better tried than described! It's closed on Monday.

One of Verona's oldest and most patronized pasticcerias is **Cordioli,** a moment's stroll from Juliet's house on V. Cappello 39 (☎ 045/80-03-055). There are no tables and it's often three-deep at the bar, but with coffee this good and pastries this fresh (made on the premises), it's obvious why. Verona's perfect souvenir? How about home-made *baci di Guilietta* (vanilla meringues called Juliet's kisses) and *sospiri di Romeo* (Romeo's sighs, chocolate hazelnut cookies)? It's closed Sunday afternoon and Wednesday.

WINE BARS   Verona is the epicenter of the region's important viticulture (Veneto produces more DOC wine than any other region in Italy), but the old time wine bars are decreasing in number and atmosphere. Recapture the spirit of yesteryear at **Carro Armato,** in a 14th-century palazzo at Vc. Gatto 2A at Viccolo San Piero Martire (1 block south of Piazza Sant'Anastasia; ☎ 045/80-30-175), a great choice for after-hours or any hour when you want to sit and sample some of 30 or so regional wines by the glass (2,000 to 5,000L/$1.20 to $2.95) and make an informal meal out of fresh and inexpensive bar food. Oldsters linger during the day playing cards or reading the paper at long wooden tables, while a younger crowd fills the place in the evening. A small but good selection of cheeses and cold cuts or sausages might be enough to take the edge off, but there is always an entree or two and a fresh vegetable side dish. It's open Monday to Friday from 10am to 2pm and 5pm to 2am; Saturday and Sunday nonstop hours.

The wonderfully characteristic old wine bar, **Enoteca dal Zovo,** on Vc. San Marco in Foro 7/5 (off Corso Porta Borsari near the above-mentioned Caffe Tubino; ☎ 045/80-34-369) is run by Oreste, who knows everyone in town, and they all stop by for his excellent selection of Veneto wines averaging 2,000L ($1.20) a glass, or you can go for broke and start with the very best at 4,000L ($2.35). Oreste's *simpatica* American-born wife, Beverly, can give you a crash course. Salami, olives, and finger foods will help keep you vertical, since the few stools are always occupied by senior gentlemen who are as much a part of the fixtures as the hundreds of dusty bottles of wines and grappas that line the walls. Open Tuesday to Sunday from 8am to 1pm and 2 to 8pm.

SIDE TRIPS FROM VERONA

The ancient Greeks called Italy "Enotria"—the land of wines. It produces more wine than any other country in the world, so the annual ✪ **VinItaly wine fair** held every April in Verona is an understandably prestigious event. The Veneto produces more DOC (Denominazione di Origine Controllata, zones of controlled name and origin) than anywhere else in Italy, particularly the Veronese trio of bardolino and valpolicella (reds) and soave (white). The costly, dry Valpolicello wine known as Amarone comes from the vineyards outside of Verona. ✪ **Masi** is one of the most respected producers, one of many in the Verona hills, whose *cantine* are open to the public for wine tasting visits Visit Verona's tourist information office for a listing of wine estates open to the public. No organized tours are available and you'll need your own wheels, but oeno-logically-minded visitors will want to taste some of Italy's finest wines at the point of their origin.

The Dolomites & South Tyrol

10

by Stephen Brewer

Mountains—the Alps and the Dolomites—dominate much of this region that stretches north from Lombardy and the Veneto. Here you'll discover a different Italy; in fact, you'll discover an Italy that often doesn't seem very Italian at all. Most of the Dolomites and South Tyrol—which encompasses the Trentino and Alto Adige regions—belonged to Austria until it was handed over to Italy at the end of World War I, and many residents (especially in and around Bolzano) still prefer the ways of the north to those of the south. They speak German, eat Austrian food, and go about life with Teutonic crispness. And they live amid mountain landscapes that are more suggestive of Austria than of Italy. The eastern Alps that cut into the region are gentle and beautiful; a little farther to the east rise the Dolomites—dramatically craggy peaks that are really coral formations that only relatively recently reared up from ancient seabeds. Throughout Trentino-Alto Adige, soaring peaks, highland meadows, and lush valleys provide a paradise for hikers, skiers, and rock climbers, and set amid these natural spectacles are pretty and interesting towns to explore.

REGIONAL CUISINE   The cuisine of the Alto Adige is more or less Austrian, with a few Italian touches. *Canederli* (dumplings) often replace pasta or polenta and are found floating in rich broths infused with liver; *speck* (smoked ham) replaces prosciutto; and *Wiener schnitzel grostl* (a combination of potatoes, onions, and veal—the local version of corned beef hash), and pork roasts are among preferred secondi. As you move east into Friuli-Venezia Giulia, the cuisine continues to be firmly of the mountain variety, with some exotic and hard-to-pronounce variations belying the region's mixed cultural heritage. Among these are *cvapcici,* Trieste's signature meatball dish, and *brovada,* a secondo that combines turnips, grape skins, and pork sausage (a farmer's supper if ever there was one). San Daniele, probably the best prosciutto in all of Italy (no small claim), comes frm this region. The preferred spirit is *grappa*—made from grape skins—heady, and sure to take the chill out of the night.

1 Trento (Trent)

230 km (143 mi.) NW of Milan, 101 km (63 mi.) N of Verona, 57 km (35 mi.) S of Bolzano

Surrounded by mountains, this beautiful little city on the banks of the Adige River definitely has an Alpine flair. Yet unlike other towns up here

The Dolomites

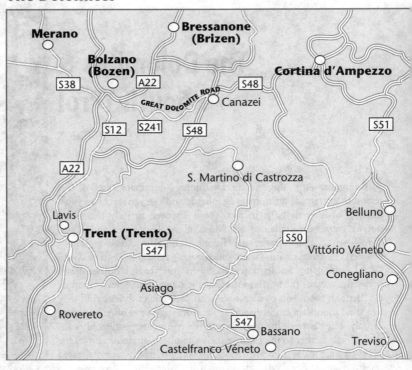

Merano

Bressanone
(Brizen)

Bolzano
(Bozen)

S38   A22

Cortina d'Ampezzo

GREAT DOLOMITE ROAD

S48

Canazei

S12   S241   S48

S51

A22

S. Martino di Castrozza

Belluno

Lavis

Trent (Trento)

S50

Vittório Véneto

S47

Conegliano

Asiago

Rovereto

S47

Bassano

Castelfranco Véneto

Treviso

in the far north, which tend to lean heavily on their Austrian heritage, Trento is still essentially Italian. The piazze are broad and sunny, the palaces are ocher-colored and tile-roofed, Italian is the lingua franca, and pasta is still a staple on menus. With its pleasant streets and the remnants of its most famous event, the 16th-century Council of Trent, Trento is a nice place to stay for a night or to visit en route to Bolzano (see section 2 below) and other places in the Trentino-Alto Adige.

FESTIVALS & MARKETS   In May and June, churches around the city are the evocative settings of performances of the **Festivale di Musica Sacra** (Festival of Sacred Music). Its final performances coincide with **Festive Vigiliane,** a medieval pageant for which townspeople turn up in the Piazza del Duomo appropriately decked out. An ambitious program aptly named **Superfestival** stages musical performances, historic dramas, and reenactments of medieval and Renaissance legends in castles surrounding Trento; it runs from late June through September.

A small daily food market covers the paving stones of **Piazza Alessandro Vittorio** every morning from 8am to 1pm. A larger market, this one with clothing, crafts and bric-a-brac as well, is held Thursday from 8am to 1pm in **Piazza Arogno** near the Duomo, and this same piazza hosts a flea market the third Sunday of every month.

ESSENTIALS

GETTING HERE   By Train   Strategically located on a main north-south rail line between Italy and Austria, Trento is served by some 30 trains a day to and from Verona, a major transfer point for trains to Milan, Florence, Rome, and other points south; the **Verona-Trento** trip takes 1 hour and costs 8,200L ($4.85). Trento is linked to **Bolzano,** about 40 minutes away, by 40 trains a day; the fare is 5,100L ($3).

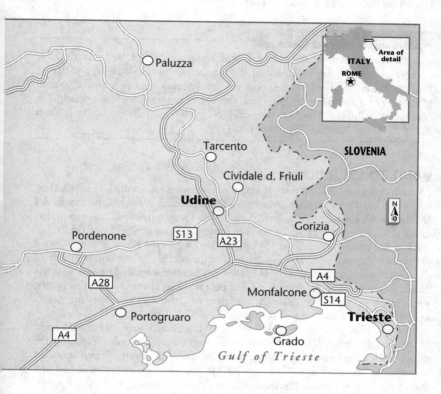

Luggage storage is available at the station; the office is open daily almost around the clock, except from 4 to 5:30am, and the charge is 5,000L ($2.95) a bag for each 12-hour period.

By Bus Buses, which leave from a terminal next to the train station, are the major links to outlying mountain towns. One long-distance route that may be of interest to travelers is the hourly service to and from **Riva del Garda** on Lago di Garda, making it easy to adjoin Trento and its region to a tour of the Lakes; the trip take 1¼ hours and costs 5,200L ($3.05). For more information, contact Atesina at ☎ **0461/821-000.**

By Car The **A22 autostrada** connects Trento with Verona in about an hour; from Verona you can connect with the **A4** for Milan (total trip time between Milan and Trento is about 2½ hr.) and with **A22** to Modena and from there **A1** for Florence and Rome (Trento is a drive of about 3½ hr. from Florence and about 6½ hr. from Rome). A22 also runs north to Bolzano, a little over half an hour away; the slower **S12** also connects Trento and Bolzano, and from it you can get on the scenic **Strada di Vino.**

VISITOR INFORMATION The **local tourist office,** near the train station at V. Alferi 4 (☎ **0461/983-880**), is open July through August, Monday to Saturday from 9am to noon and 3 to 6pm, Sunday from 9am until noon; September through June, Monday to Friday from 9am to 1pm and 3 to 6pm and Saturday 9am to noon. The **APT tourist office,** with information on the entire Trentino region, is near the castello at V. Romagnosi 3 (☎ **0461/839-000**), open Monday to Saturday from 8:30am to 12:30pm and 2:30 to 6pm.

Getting a Lift Out of Town

For a breezy view of Trento and a heart-thumping aerial ride as well, take the cable car from Ponte di San Lorenzo near the train station up to Sardagna, a village on one of the mountainsides that enclose the city. You may want to provision yourself at the market and enjoy an alpine picnic on one of the grassy meadows nearby. The cable car (☎ **0461/910-332**) runs daily, every 30 minutes from 7am to 6:30pm and the fare is 1,300L (75¢) round-trip.

WHAT TO SEE & DO

To reach the center of town from the train station, where you will also find parking, follow the Via Pozzo through several name changes until it reaches the **Piazza del Duomo** as Via Cavour. As you amble around this lovely town, you'll soon learn that much of what's notable about Trento is in some way connected with the Council of Trent, called by the Vatican from 1545 to 1563 to counter the effects of the new wave of Protestantism that was sweeping down from the north. The outcomes of many of the council sessions were announced in the 13th- to 16th-century **Duomo,** which is delightfully situated on the wide expanse of the cafe-filled Piazza Duomo; this square, with a statue of Neptune at its center, is referred to as the city's *salotto* (sitting room), so popular is it as a place to pass the time.

More specifically, the decrees that came out of the Council were read in the Chapel of the Crucifix, beneath an enormous 15th-century cross. Beneath the altar of the main church is the fascinating **Basilica Palecristiana,** a 6th-century church later used as a crypt for the city's powerful prince-bishops. You can visit the crypt as part of a tour of the Duomo's **Museo Diocesano Tridentino,** which is housed in the adjoining, heavily fortified palace of these bishops. The museum displays some fascinating paintings of Council sessions that serve almost as news photos of the proceedings (one provides a seating plan for delegates), as well a collection of 16th-century tapestries and statuary and other objects from the Duomo's treasury. The Duomo is open daily from 6:30am to noon and 2:30 to 7:30pm; the Museo Diocesano (☎ **0461/234-419**) is open Monday through Saturday 9:30am to 12:30pm and 2:30 to 6pm; admission to the museum is 5,000L ($2.95).

Many Council sessions were held in the **Castello di Buonconsiglio,** which you can reach by walking north from the Duomo along Via Belenzani, then east on Via Roma—both, especially the former, are lined with the palaces, many with faded frescoes on their facades, built to house the church officials who came to Trento to attend the council sessions. The mazelike castello incorporates the 13th-century Castelvecchio, surrounded by medieval fortifications, and the elegant Magno Palazzo, a palace built for a prince-bishop in the 15th century. Within the vast complex is the **Museo Provincale d'Arte,** where the pride of the collection is the 15th-century *Cico dei Mesi* (Cycle of the Months) housed in the Torre dell'Aquila (Eagle's Tower). It's an enchanting fresco cycle that presents a detailed look at life at court and in the countryside, showing amusements among the lords and ladies and much hard work among the peasants.

You can also visit the cell where native son Cesare Battiste was held in 1916 for his part in the Ireedentist movement, which sought to return Trento and other parts of the region to Italy—which indeed came to pass with the Treaty of Versailles in 1919, but not before Battiste was shot in the moat that surrounds the Castelvecchio. From May through September the complex is open Tuesday through Sunday from 9am to 6pm and from October through April it is open from 9am to 12:15pm and 2 to

5:15pm. Admission is 10,000L ($5.90) from July through October and 7,000L ($4.10) from November through June.

WHERE TO STAY

Al Cavallino Bianco. V. Cavour 29, 38100 Trento. ☎ **0461/23-15-42.** 24 units, 3 with bathroom. 42,000L ($24.70) single without bathroom, 60,000L ($35.30) single with bathroom; 65,000L ($38.25) double without bathroom, 88,000L ($51.75) double with bathroom; 120,000L ($70.60) triple with bathroom. AE, MC, V. Closed June 16–26 and Dec 16–26.

The surrounding neighborhood near the Duomo is charming, but this hostelry is basic—you should come here only if the Venezia is booked. However, these prices and the privacy that the spacious rooms afford make this a good base from which to explore the expensive region. The lobby is actually quite amusing—with AstroTurf, picnic tables, and a photo-realistic mural of alpine meadows. The guest rooms don't have much more than a bed and a chair, and most don't have bathrooms—but they do have in-chamber showers and sinks.

Hotel Aquila D'Oro. V. Belezani 76, 38100 Trento. ☎ **0461/98-62-82.** 20 units, all with bathroom. MINIBAR TV TEL. 100,000L ($58.80) single, 140,000L ($82.35) double. Rates include breakfast. AE, DC, MC, V.

A recent renovation of an older hotel that in turn occupied a centuries-old palazzo has created some of the nicest rooms in Trento, with a wonderful location right around the corner from the Piazza Duomo. Decor throughout is stylishly contemporary, with a nice smattering of oriental carpets, vaulted ceilings, and other interesting and cozy architectural touches in public rooms. The guest rooms are a little plainer, but have glossy, streamlined new furnishings and gleaming tile bathrooms.

Hotel Venezia. V. Belenzani 70, 38100 Trento. ☎ **0461/234-111.** 47 units, 20 with bathroom. 42,000L ($24.70) single without bathroom, 60,000L ($$35.30) single with bathroom; 65,000L ($38.25) double without bathroom, 85,000L ($50) double with bathroom. MC, V.

This old hotel has much more charm than the Cavallino Bianco, above. Marked by 1950s-style furnishings, the simple, high-ceiling rooms are a bit dowdy but offer solid, old-fashioned comfort (unfortunately, some beds still bear the sags left by travelers generations removed from now). Plus, those in the front come with stunning views over the Piazza Duomo. Some of the younger members of the family who run the hotel speak English and are more than happy to dispense advice on what to see and do in town and the surrounding area.

WHERE TO DINE

It's almost a requirement to stroll down Trento's renaissance streets with a gelato from **Torre-Verde-Gelateria Zanella** on V. Suffragio 6 (☎ **0461/232-039**). Many flavors, are made from fresh, local fruits in season, while others make no such attempt at wholesomeness and incorporate the richest chocolate and cream.

Birreria Pedavena. Pz. Fera 13, 38100 Trento. ☎ **0461/986-255.** Wed–Mon 8:30am–midnight. Primi 5,000–9,000L ($2.95–$5.30); secondi 7,000–15,000L ($4.10–$8.80); pizza from 6,000L ($3.55). MC, V. CAFETERIA/PIZZERIA.

It seems as if this dark cavernous beer hall–style cafeteria can feed all of Trento, and it just might. It draws a big crowd for coffee and pastries in the morning and keeps serving a huge mix of pastas, wurst, schnitzel, and pizza all day. You will probably be happiest if you order simply, maybe a plate of wurst (essentially, hot dogs) or *speck* (cured mountain ham) or one of the excellent pizzas. Pedavena keeps some of the latest hours in town, making this something of a late evening spot in a town where the nightlife is scarce.

La Cantinota. V. San Marco 24. ☎ **0461/238-527.** Reservations recommended. Fri–Wed noon–3pm and 7–11pm (piano bar, 10:30pm–2:30am). Primi 7,000–10,000 ($4.10–$5.90); secondi 9,000–25,000L ($5.30–$14.70). ITALIAN/TYROLEAN.

With its white tablecloths, excellent service, and reasonably priced menu, La Cantinota could be the most popular restaurant in Trento. The color red is used with abandon and a goose wanders among the tables in the atrium garden. The fare includes Italian and Tyrolean dishes and is truly inspired, making use of fresh local ingredients: wonderful homemade gnocchi, rich risottos with wild mushrooms (fungi porcini), grilled sausages with polenta, and veal with a rich red wine sauce (*vitello barolo*). The adjoining piano bar is popular with local talent who tend to intersperse Frank Sinatra renditions with yodeling.

Pizzeria Duomo. Pz. Duomo 22. ☎ **0461/98-42-86.** Sun–Fri, 11:30am–2:30pm and 5–11:30pm. Primi 7,000–9,000L ($4.10–$5.30); secondi 9,000–16,000L ($5.30–$9.40); pizza from 7,000L ($4.10). MC, V. PIZZERIA/ITALIAN.

This pleasant eatery facing the Duomo has a no-frills, tile-floor and white-walled dining room, but offers much more romantic dining on its terrace overlooking the church and its square. While it's possible to eat a full meal of the standard pasta and veal variety here, the pizzas are the big draw—topped with everything from tomatoes to wurst. Be prepared to wait in line on Friday and Sunday nights.

VISITING NEARBY ROVERETO

There are several reasons to visit this noble, medieval town 24 kilometers (15 mi.) south of Trento. One is simply to stroll through its winding streets and elegant, quiet piazze that seem to hover in the shadow of the 15th-century **Castello di Rovereto.** The other is to pay homage to the thousands of mostly Italian and Austrian soldiers who died in the surrounding hills during some of the fiercest fighting of World War I. They are commemorated by the nightly ringing of the *Campana dei Caduti* (Bell of the Fallen) and in the **Museo della Guerra,** which occupies part of the castle and displays photographs, weaponry, and other memorabilia associated with this and other battles; the museum is open from April through November from 8:30am to 12:30pm and 2 to 6pm; admission is 5,000L ($2.95). The fascinating **Museo Depero** is devoted to the designs that the futurist artist Fortunato Depero executed for Campari and other commercial clients, as well as his paintings. The museum, at V. d. Terra 53 (☎ 0464/434-393), is open Tuesday through Sunday from 9am to 12:30pm and 2:30pm to 6pm; admission is 5,000L ($2.95).

The third reason to come to Rovereto is to attend one of its much-heralded cultural events: the **Rovereto Festival** in early September features dance performances and a major exhibition of contemporary art (☎ 0464/452-159 for more information) and **Festival Internazionale Mozart** features world-renowned performances of the composer's work (☎ 0464/452-159). Rovereto is less than half an hour south from Trento via A22. **Several buses** a day make the trip; contact **Atesina** (☎ 0461/821-000) for more information.

EN ROUTE TO BOLZANO: THE STRADA DI VINO

Some of Italy's finest wines are produced on the vines that cloak the hillsides between Trento and Bolzano. (These local wines include many Pinot Grigios and Pinot Noirs among whites, and Vernatsch, the most common red of the region.) If you are traveling by car between the two cities you can make the trip on the well-marked **Strada di Vino (Weinstrasse)**. Leave Trento on S12; 2 kilometers north (a little more than a mile) you will come to the village of Lavis, and from here easy-to-follow yellow signs will lead you along a series of twisting roads through seemingly endless vineyards and around Lago di Caldaro to Bolzano. Many of the vineyards have tasting rooms open to the public and sometimes offer cheese, sandwiches, and other refreshment as well. If you don't have your own wheels, the tourist offices in Trento and Bolzano can provide lists of local tour companies that lead wine tours.

2 Bolzano

154 km (92 mi.) N of Verona, 118 km (73 mi.) S of Innsbruck, 57 km (35 mi.) NE of Trento

Without even crossing a border, you'll find yourself in a place that doesn't resemble Italy at all. During its long history, this pretty town at the confluence of the Talvera and Isarco Rivers has been ruled by the bishops of Trent, the counts of Tirol, and the Hapsburgs, to name but some of the empires to which it has belonged. Bolzano has been part of Italy since the end of World War I, but as you explore the narrow streets and broad piazze and stroll through the parks that line the town's two rivers you get the sense that, with its high gabled, Tyrolean-style houses and preference for the German tongue, the city is still more Nordic than Italian.

FESTIVALS & MARKETS   Bolzano celebrates spring with weekend concerts throughout **April and May** in Piazza Walther, and adds a flower show, with more music, around the first of May. The city's most serious musical event is the **Concorso Internazionale Piantistico F. Busoni,** an international piano competition held in **August.** The **Festival del Teatro di Strada** draws wandering musicians, mimes, puppeteers, and other performers to the streets of the old city in **October.** One of the more colorful events in the region is the **Bartolomeo Horse Fair,** which brings together the region's most beautiful equines on the Renon plateau, which can be reached by funicular (see "Funiculars" below).

One of the most enjoyable walks in the old city takes you through the stalls of the fruit and vegetable market in **Piazza delle Erbe,** which operates Monday through Saturday from 8am to 7pm. From **November 28 to December 23** the city hosts a much-attended **Mercatino di Natale (Christkindlmarkt),** in which handmade ornaments, wooden toys, and other seasonal crafts, along with Christmas pastries and mulled wine, are sold from booths in a festively decorated Piazza Walther. A flea market fills the **Passegiata del Talvera** along the River Talvera (follow Via Museo from the center of town) the first Saturday of every month, opening at 8am and closing at 4pm.

ESSENTIALS

GETTING HERE   By Train   Bolzano is on the north-south rail line that links Verona with Innsbruck, Austria, via the Brenner Pass. It's 1½ to 2 hours north of **Verona,** with almost 30 daily trains; and less than an hour north of **Trento,** with about 40 trains daily. The fare between Verona and Bolzano is 12,100L ($7.10), and between Trento and Bolzano it's 5,100L ($2.30). Hourly train service links Bolzano with **Merano,** a trip of about 45 minutes; the fare is 2,800L ($1.65). Luggage storage is available at the station; the office is open daily almost around the clock, except from 4am to 5:30am, and the charge is 5,000L ($2.95) a bag for each 12-hour period.

By Bus   Bolzano is the hub of the excellent **SAD bus network,** serving even the most remote mountain villages (☎ **0471/450-111**). There are buses to and from Merano every hour, with the first bus leaving Bolzano at 6:45am and the last one at 11:35pm; the one-way fare is 4,000L ($2.35). Four buses a day make the trip to and from **Cortina** (about 3½ hr., often with a change in Dobbiaco) and the fare is 12,000L ($7.05). Buses to and from **Trento** run almost hourly, and the fare is 5,000L ($2.95). The extremely helpful staff at the bus station, next to the train station, will help you make sense of the routing.

By Car The **A22 autostrada** connects Bolzano with **Trento** in a little over half and hour and with **Verona** (where you can connect with the A4 for Milan and Rome) in a little over an hour; and, farther south, **Modena** (where you can connect with the A1 for Florence and Rome); A22 runs north to Innsbruck.

VISITOR INFORMATION Two tourist offices, both near the Duomo, dispense a wealth of information on Bolzano and the South Tyrol. The **APT city tourist office,** Pz. Walther 8 (☎ **0471/975-656**), provides lists of accommodations, restaurants, and activities in and around Bolzano; it's open from Monday to Friday from 8:30am to 6pm and on Saturday from 9am to 12:30pm. The **APT provincial tourist office,** just off Piazza Walther at Pz. Parrochia 22 (☎ **0471/993-808**) provides information on hiking, skiing, sightseeing, and other activities throughout the region.

WHAT TO SEE & DO

With its two rivers, surrounding hills, expansive greens, and medieval center, Bolzano is an extremely appealing city that seems effortlessly to meld urban sophistication with an appreciation for nature. The compact medieval old city is still the heart of town, and at its center is **Piazza Walther** honoring a 12th-century wandering minstrel. The piazza seems to capture the mood of its lighthearted historical associations with a fringe of cafe tables to one side and the brightly tiled roof and lacy spire of the **Duomo** on the other. The interior of this 12th- to 14th-century edifice is far plainer, enlivened somewhat by some much-faded frescoes and an intricately carved pulpit (☎ **0471/ 973-734;** open Monday to Friday from 9:45am to noon and 2 to 5pm and Saturday from 9:45 to noon; Sunday for services only).

A far more enticing church is the **Chiesa dei Domenicani,** just a few steps west of the Duomo. Inside this 13th-century church are two sets of frescoes that comprise the city's greatest artistic treasures. One from the 15th century, on the walls of the cloisters, depicts court life; the other, in the Capella di San Giovanni, is a 14th-century religious cycle attributed to the school of Giotto, including the Triumph of Death; already in these rich frescoes you can a heady dose of realism and can see the beginnings of the use of such elements as perspective and foreshortening, suggesting the influence of the early Renaissance (☎ **0471/973-133;** open Monday through Saturday from 9:30am to 6pm; Sunday for services only).

There is one more church to see in Bolzano, but before you reach it, you will be distracted by the considerable worldly pleasures this city offers. If you walk north from Piazza Walther you will soon come to the lively clamor of **Piazza dell'Erbe,** actually one long street that winds past a statue of Neptune through the old town and is so called because it has hosted Bolzano's fruit and produce market for centuries. The so-called piazza is lined with shops selling bread, cheese, strudel, wine and other comestibles, which spill into stalls along the pavement to create a cheerful, open-air supermarket. At the north end is Bolzano's atmospheric main shopping street, **Via dei Portici,** also closed to traffic and lined with 15th-century houses whose porticoes overhang the sidewalk to create a cozy effect that is definitely more northern European than Italian in its appeal.

The aforementioned church, **Chiesa dei Francescani,** is across Via dei Portici on Via Francescani. Inside its warm stone interior there's a sumptuously carved altar from 1500, one of the Gothic masterpieces of the Trentino-Alto Adige. The 14th-century cloisters are charming—intimate, frescoed on one side, gracefully vaulted and beautifully planted (☎ **0471/977-293;** open Monday through Saturday from 10am to noon and 2:30 to 6pm; Sunday for services only).

A walk across the River Talvera (follow Via Museo west across the Ponte Tavera) brings you into the newer "Italian" section of Bolzano, constructed in the 1920s when the Mussolini government encouraged workers from other parts of Italy to settle here in the newly won territory. Those who bid the call were either inspired or intimidated by the imposing Fascist-era structures put up along Corso Libertá (including the Monumento della Vittoria, a triumphal arch that is frequently the target of attacks by German-speaking groups that want the region to revert to Austrian rule). In a few blocks, though, the Corso brings you into the pleasant confines of **Gries,** once an outlying village and now a quaint, leafy neighborhood built around the **Abbazia dei Benedettini di Gries,** a Benedictine abbey (not usually open to the public) prettily surrounded by vineyards and gardens. Just beyond is the **Vecchia Parrochiale di Gries,** the village's parish church, whose treasures include a 12th-century crucifix and an elaborately carved 15th-century altar (☎ **0471/260-485;** open Monday through Friday, 10:30am to noon and 2:30 to 4pm; closed November through March). If you wish to continue walking, Gries is the terminus of the **Passeggiata del Guncina,** a beautiful maintained, 8-kilometer- (5-mi.) long trail that leads through parklike forests planted with many botanical specimens to a belvedere.

CASTLES   Of the many castles that surround Bolzano, the closest to the center is the **Castel Mareccio,** just a short walk along the River Talvera (from the Piazza delle Erbe, follow the Via Museo west to the Ponte Tavera and from there the Lungo Talvera Bolzano north for less than half a kilometer/a quarter of a mile). Though it is now used as a convention center and its five towers rise from a residential neighborhood of recent vintage, this 13th-century fortress is a stunning sight, all the more so since it is surrounded by a generous swath of vineyards that have been saved from urban encroachment and backed by forested hills. You can step inside for a glimpse at the stone-walled medieval interior and enjoy a beverage at the bar; the castle is open to the public Wednesday through Monday, 9am to 6pm (hours vary when conferences are in session; ☎ **0471/976-615**).

A longer walk of about 2 kilometers (a little over a mile) leads out of town north to the 13th-century **Castel Roncolo,** beautifully ensconced high above the town and beneath a massive, foreboding cliff face; from the Chiesa dei Francescani follow the Via Castel Roncolo north; you will pass one side of the Castel Mareccio, at which point sign posts will lead you along Via Beatro Arrigo and Via San Antonio for a gradual uphill climb to Castel Roncolo. The interior is decorated with faded but fascinating frescoes from the 14th and 15th centuries that depict secular scenes from the story of Tristan and Isolde and other tales of romantic love and chivalry. These painted scenes are remarkably moving in their almost primitive craftsmanship that nonetheless reveals a certain worldliness. Admission is 7,000L ($4.10); the castle is open Tuesday to Saturday from 10am to 4pm.

FUNICULARS   Several cable cars will whisk you right from the center of Bolzano into the surrounding mountains. The most dramatic ride takes you 3,000 feet up to the **Altopiano del Renon,** a pasture-covered plateau that provides dizzingly views down to Bolzano and up to higher Dolomite peaks. The funicular deposits you in **Soprabolzano** (Oberbozen), where you can sip a beer and enjoy the view, then venture farther by footpath or an electric tram into a bizarre landscape of spindly rock spires, worn needle thin by erosion and each seeming to balance a boulder on the top, that surrounds the village of Collabo. The cable car (☎ **0471/978-479**) makes the ascent in 15 minutes and operates daily from a terminus 500 meters (about 1,500 ft.) east of the train station on Via Renon; it operates hourly from 7am to 8pm; the round-trip, 15 minutes each way, costs 9,400L ($5.55) and includes tram fare between Soprabolzano and Collabo.

The **Funivia di San Genesio** whisks you up a forested hillside to the pretty village of San Genesio Atesino, surrounded by woods and mountain peaks. Cable cars

(☎ 0471/978-436) leave hourly from 7am to 7pm (from 8am on Sunday) from a terminus on Via Sarentino on the northern outskirts of Bolzano; the trip takes 15 minutes and the round-trip fare is 6,500L ($3.85).

WHERE TO STAY

Hotel Feichter. V. Grappoli 15, 39100 Bolzano. ☎ **0471/978-768.** Fax 0471/978-471. 30 units, all with bathroom. TV, TEL. 85,000L ($50) single, 130,000L ($76.45) double. Rates include breakfast. MC, V.

This charming little inn is one of the few hotels in the old city and, for the location and atmosphere it provides, is one of the city's better lodging values. On the main floor there's a Tyrolean-style lobby and a bar and self-service restaurant that resemble a weinstube. The rooms may not be full of mountain ambience, but they have serviceable, modern furnishings that are comfortable; the firm beds are equipped with that wonderful local luxury: thick down quilts.

Hotel Regina. A. V. Renon 1, 39100 Bolzano. ☎ **0471/972-195.** Fax 0471/972-195. 30 units, all with bathroom. TV TEL. 65,000L ($38.25) single, 120,000L ($70.60) double, 135,000L ($79.40) triple. Rates include breakfast. MC, V.

For pleasant and affordable lodgings in Bolzano, you need look no further than this modern hotel across the street from the train station. Though it's administered by the Catholic Church, the Regina is open to all and you won't encounter many hints of its religious associations. The bright rooms are unusually large and, while quite plain, are very nicely decorated with streamlined Scandinavian furnishings, and all offer a level of comfort and have amenities you would expect in a much more expensive hotel—including large bathrooms nicely equipped with stall showers.

Stadt Hotel Citta. Pz. Walther 21, 39100 Bolzano. ☎ **0471/975-221.** Fax 0471/976-688. 100 units, 88 with bathroom. TEL. 105,000L ($61.75) single without bathroom, 115,000L ($67.65) single, 180,000L ($105.90) double, 207,000L ($121.75) triple. Rates include breakfast. AE, DC, MC, V. Parking 15,000L ($8.80).

This serviceable old-fashioned hotel, with an attractive arcaded façade typical of this city's distinctive architecture, commands a sunny corner of Bolzano's main piazza. The ground floor bar and cafe that opens to the square is a popular gathering spot, and the handsome paneled and terra-cotta-tiled lobby is also a much-used meeting place. Upstairs are large and bright guest rooms, many with small terraces. Some retain the slightly frayed elegance of bygone eras, with comfy upholstered furniture, big bedsteads, and oriental carpets. The best rooms overlook the square and the Duomo. Mussolini stayed in one of them (no. 303), a suite with a corner balcony.

WHERE TO DINE

Some of the least expensive meals in towns are supplied by the vendors who dispense a wide assortment of wurstel from carts in the Kornplatz and Piazza dell'Erbe.

Batzenhasuel. V. Andreas Hofer/Andreas Hoferstrasse 30. ☎ **0471/976-183.** Primi 8,000–10,000L ($4.70–$5.90); secondi 10,000–25,000L ($5.90–$14.70). No credit cards. Wed–Mon 6:30pm–2am. TYROLEAN.

The two floors of dining rooms are charming and cozy, with dark carved Tyrolean benches, hardwood floors, and heavily beamed ceilings; downstairs is primarily a weinstube, a tavernlike room where you are welcome to linger over a beer and a plate of cheese. On both floors you can also order from a menu that, like those in many other restaurants in town, is typically Tyrolean, which means mostly Austrian with some Italian touches. While an excellent minestrone is sometimes available, this is also the place to sample *leberknodelsuppe*, a thick broth with a liver dumpling floating in it. Pork loin, roast beef with potatoes, and other heavy northern fare dominate the entree choices.

Cavallino Bianco. V. d. Bottai/Bindergasse 6. ☎ **0471/97-32-67.** Primi 7,000–9,000L ($4.10–$5.30); secondi 9,000–20,000L ($5.30–$11.75). No credit cards. Mon–Fri 7am–3pm and 7pm–midnight, Sat 7am–3pm. TYROLEAN.

This atmospheric *stube* (beer hall) near the Piazza dell'Erbe is darkly paneled and decorated with carved wooden furniture to create a cozy, typically Tyrolean atmosphere. The restaurant opens early to operate as a cafe, dispensing coffee and pastry for breakfast, and remains opens well into the night, sending out hearty lunches and dinners of local fare with only a slight Italian influence. Fried Camembert, herrings, and assorted salamis are among the dozens of appetizers, while a pasta dish (and there are many to choose from) is likely to be followed by a main course of Wiener schnitzel or wurstel.

Ristorante Hostaria Argentieri. V. Argentieri 14. ☎ **0471/981-718.** Reservations recommended. Primi 12,000–15,000L ($7.05–$8.80); secondi 18,000–25,000L ($10.60–$14.70). MC, V. Mon–Sat noon–2:30pm and 7 to 10:30pm. ITALIAN.

You'll feel like you've come back to Italy when you step into this attractive cream-colored, tile-floored room. There are several risottos on the menu, including one with fresh wild mushrooms (fungi porcini), as well as lovely gnocchi with ricotta and some other simple pasta preparations with tomato sauces (not a common ingredient in this region). Main courses, again, are a little lighter than most regional fare and include *scaloppine di vitello,* simply sauced with lemon or Borolo wine, and an *arrosto di vitello* (a roast veal shank). In good weather there is dining on a tiny terrace in front of the restaurant, facing an attractive cobblestone street that is indeed Tyrolean in character.

Vogele. V. Goethe 3. ☎ **0471/973-938.** Primi 12,000–16,000L ($7.05–$9.40); secondi 17,000–25,000L ($10–$14.70). V. Mon–Fri 9am–midnight, Sat 9am–3pm. TYROLEAN.

If you ask someone in Bolzano where to eat, there's a very good chance you will be sent to this attractive, always busy weinstube and restaurant in the center of the old city just off Piazza Erbe. Like many such places in Bolzano, it is open continuously all day and evening, and some of the patrons seem to stop by for every meal and for coffee and a beer in between. One half of the vaulted rooms is set up as a cafe, and the other side as a more formal dining room. Both have traditional, woody Tyrolean furnishings, and wherever you sit you can order lightly, or relatively so, if you wish from the long appetizer menu, maybe a platter of speck or smoked meats (*piatto affumicate*). First and second courses alike include many traditional favorites; a wonderful *zuppa di vino* (a soup with a white wine and cream base) or different kinds of *canederli* (dumplings that here are laced with liver, bacon or ham) are the ways to begin, followed by a *stinco di miale* (roast pork shank) or other roast meat dish.

BARS & CAFES

To sample the local wines (from 2,000L/$1.20 a glass), step into this tiny little stand-up bar at **Etti's Thekki** at Pz. Erbe 11 (☎ 0471/971-705). The chic **Exil** at Kornplatz 2A (☎ 0471/971-814) is filled with a young crowd night and day and for whom it probably provides a welcome alternative to the many weinstubes around town. Exil has the ambience of coffeehouse (excellent coffee, pastries, and sandwiches are served) and a bar as well, with many kinds of bars from Italy and north of the Alps on tap. On weekend evenings, the elegant Park Hotel Lauren on V. Lauren 4 (☎ 0471/980-500) turns its art nouveau decorated lobby—a sumptuous room overlooking the hotel's private park—into a jazz club. An enthusiastic crowd turns out, making this one of the most popular places in town to be.

You won't find a more distinctive locale in Bolzano than **Fishbanke** at V. d. Streiter 26A (☎ **0471/971-714**) in which to bend your elbow; in fact, a stop at this outdoor wine bar is mandatory if your visit coincides with one of its seasonal openings. Wine, beer and a few snacks (cheese and bruschetta) are served on the well-worn stone slabs of Bolzano's centuries-old former fish market, an unusual experience that attracts a friendly crowd of regulars who, along with the animated proprietor, are always pleased to welcome strangers into their midst.

3 Merano

86 km (53 mi.) N of Trento, 28 km (17 mi.) NW of Bolzano

This well-heeled resort, tucked into a valley half an hour west of Bolzano, sports Europe's northernmost palm trees—the product of a mild microclimate that ensures that summers are never too hot or humid and that winter temperatures remain above freezing, even though the surrounding slopes fill with snow. With its handsome, shop-lined streets, riverside promenades, and easy access to mountainous wilderness, Merano is a nice place to visit for a day or two of relaxation or hiking.

FESTIVALS & MARKETS   The **Piazza del Duomo** is the scene of Merano's civic life. A morning fruit and produce market is held here from 8am to 1pm Monday through Saturday, and from late November through Christmas it fills with stalls selling carved ornaments and other seasonal paraphernalia during the town's Christkindl-markt. On the **second Sunday of October,** enthusiasts of the grape take over the square for a festival, with tastings, honoring the wines and grape juice yielded by local vineyards.

ESSENTIALS

GETTING HERE   **By Train**   Hourly train service links Merano with **Bolzano,** a trip of about 45 minutes; the fare is 2,800L ($1.65).

By Bus   **SAD buses** arrive and depart from the train station and stop in the center of town, connecting Merano with Bolzano hourly and with villages throughout the region; the one-way fare is 4,000L ($2.35).

By Car   Route **S38,** a pretty road that cuts through vineyards and mountain meadows, links Merano and Bolzano in less than half an hour.

VISITOR INFORMATION   The tourist office on Freiheistrasse 35 (☎ **0473/ 235-223**), is open March through September, Monday to Friday from 9am to 12:30pm and 2 to 6:30pm and Saturday from 9am to 12:30pm; October through February, it is open Monday through Saturday from 9am to 6:30pm and Sunday from 9:30am to 12:30pm. The English-speaking staff can provide a list of accommodations and restaurants, help you with bus schedules, and equip you with maps and informa-tion on hiking and skiing in the area. Another good source of information on hiking the region is the local office of the Club Alpino Italiano at Freiheistrasse 188, ☎ **0473/448-944.** It is open Monday to Friday from 6:30 to 8:30pm.

WHAT TO SEE & DO

Austrian nobility and in their wake bourgeois vacationers from all over the Continent have been descending on Merano since the 19th century. But the town flourished long before that. In fact, the counts of Venosta were lords of all of what would become Aus-tria from here through much of the 13th and 14th centuries; the name "Tyrol" came from the Castel Tirolo, just above Merano, from which they ruled. The capital of the vast territories that passed from the house of Vernosta to the Hapsburgs wasn't moved from Merano to Innsbruck until 1420.

Taking the Cure

With its mild climate and mineral-rich springs bubbling up from beneath the town, Merano has long enjoyed a reputation as a spa town. To this day, one of Merano's most popular pastimes is taking the cure. You can take a complete treatment (mud bathroom, mineral rap, hydrotherapy) at the Terme di Merano in the center of town, or just take a dip in the pool of mineral-rich water (15,000L/$8.80). A poor man's version of an elaborate spa regimen—but one you can follow only when grapes from the vineyards surrounding the town ripen in late September and early October—is Merano's famous *cura delle uva* (grape cure). One drastic form of the grape cure, which is allegedly beneficial for digestive disorders, requires eating two pounds of grapes a day. A more palatable approach calls for drinking several glasses a day of the delicious fresh grape juice, *spermuta di uva fresca,* that appears in cafes in the fall.

The charming old town that is a vestige of this noble past clusters around the **Piazza del Duomo,** where the namesake 14th-century cathedral has a crenellated facade and heavy buttresses that make it look almost like a castle. There is a castle nearby, just to the west on Via Galilei—**Castello Principesco,** built by the counts of Tyrol in 1470 and still filled with the austere furnishings they installed, along with a collection of armor and musical instruments; the castle (☎ **0473/237-834**) is open Tuesday through Saturday from 10am to 5pm and Saturday; admission is 2,700L ($1.60).

Merano's picturesque main shopping street, **Via Portici** (leading west from Piazza del Duomo) is lined with Tyrolean-style houses whose porticoes extend over the sidewalk. The preferred places to stroll in Merano, though, are along any number of scenic promenades. Two follow the banks of the river Passer: the **Passeggiata d'Inverno** (Winter Walk, which faces south) and **Passegiata d'Estate** (Summer Walk, which faces north). The delightful **Passeggiata** ½ mi.) into a very well-tended, parklike mountain wilderness.

The top of the Passeggiata is just below Castel Tirolo, which you can also reach by car or by walking along **Via Monte San Zeno** for 5 kilometers (3 mi.) from Merano. Here, amid stony splendor, you can see the throne room from which the Counts of Tyrol ruled much of present-day Austria and northern Italy (and also enjoy a magnificent view that hasn't changed much since then) and a beautifully frescoed Romanesque chapel. The castle (☎ **0473/220-221**) is open from mid-March through the beginning of November, Tuesday through Sunday from 10am to 5pm; admission is 7,000L ($4.10).

THE NATIONAL PARKS

For more strenuous excursions, Merano is the gateway to two national parks. The tourist office in town provides information on them, as does the **Club Alpo Italiano,** Cor. Liberta 188 (☎ **0473/48-944;**); both parks also have their own visitor centers within their boundaries.

PARCO NAZIONALE DELLA STELVIO   In this vast 1.3 million-acre wilderness east of Merano, elk and chamois roam the mountainsides and craggy snowcapped peaks pierce the sky. A network of trails crisscross some almost virgin wilderness, and some of Europe's largest glaciers provide year-round skiing. The park can be entered at Silandro, and there is a park office at V. d. Cappuccini 2 (☎ **0473/704-43**). It dispenses maps, lists of hiking trails, and *rifugi* (huts where hikers can overnight) within the park as well as other information; there are several buses a day from Merano to Silandro, which is about 30 kilometers (18 mi.) east via route S38.

PARCO NAZIONALE DI TESSA　This Alpine wonderland surrounds Merano with a pleasant terrain of meadows and gentle, forest-clad slopes. A relatively easy path, the southern route of the **Meraner Hohenweg,** allows even the most inexperienced hikers to cross the park effortlessly (in 2 days if you wish to follow the entire route) and is conveniently interspersed with restaurants and farmhouses offering rooms. The northern route is much more isolated, difficult, and scenic, with snack-bar equipped rifugi conveniently placed every few hours or so along the route. The park office in Naturno, about 15 kilometers (9 mi.) north on Route S44, provides a wealth of information on hiking trails, meals, and accommodations. Hourly buses run between Merano and Naturno; the half-hour trip costs 2,500L ($1.50).

WHERE TO STAY

April, August through October, and the Christmas holidays constitute high season in Merano, when rates are highest and rooms are scarce.

Garni Domus Mea. V. Piave 8, 39012 Merano. ☎ **0473/236-777.** Fax 0473/23-02-21. 10 units, all with bathroom. TEL. 80,000L ($47) single, 96,000L ($56.50) double. Rates include breakfast.

Simple little bed-and-breakfasts are just about the only alternative to Merano's high priced lodging, and this pleasant house is one of the nicer of them. It is well located, on a major street about a 10-minute walk on the other side of Ponte Teatro from the center of town. The friendly proprietor keeps the premises immaculate and welcoming, with fresh flowers and freshly waxed floors. The rooms are basically but nicely furnished with hints of a Tyrolean look added by wood dressers and armoires, and some have balconies overlooking the peaks. Places like this tend to fill up very quickly, so be sure to reserve.

Hotel Europa Splendid. Cor. Liberta 178, 39012 Merano. ☎ **0473/23-23-76.** Fax 0473/23-02-21. 55 units, all with bathroom. MINIBAR TV TEL. 78,000–100,000L ($45.90–$58.85) single, 126,000–160,000L ($74.10–$94.10) double. Rates vary with season and include breakfast. Half-board 83,000–108,000L ($48.80–$63.55) per person; full board 99,000–128,000L ($58.25–$75.30) per person, depending on season. AE, MC, V.

Conveniently located in the center of town a block off the river Passer, the Europa is an old-fashioned hotel that caters to guests who return year after year. The decor is charmingly faded, with an elegant, regency-style salon and Tyrolean-style bar downstairs. The large, bright guest rooms upstairs haven't been redecorated since the 1960s, but are bright and very comfortable, with handsome, sturdy furnishings and old but well maintained bathrooms. Many of the rooms have small, flower-filled balconies, and a large, sun-filled hotel terrace is on the first floor.

WORTH A SPLURGE

Castel Schloss Labers. V. Labers 25, Merano 39012. ☎ **0473/234-484.** Fax 0473/234-146. 30 units, all with bathroom. TEL. Half-board 120,000–175,000L ($70.60–$102.95) per person, depending on season and type of accommodation. Bed-and-breakfast–only rates are available on request. AE, DC, MC, V. Closed Nov until 2 weeks before Easter.

The Stapf-Neubert family turned its pitch-roofed castle into a hotel decades ago, and in so doing has provided a remarkable place to stay. The library, salons, and billiard and dining rooms of the former residence have been converted seamlessly to guestrooms. Upper floors house distinctive and gracious accommodations, no two of which are alike—in some, cozy conversation nooks are tucked into towers; others are luxurious garretlike arrangements under the eaves, and some are simply commodious, high-ceilinged and elegantly appointed. The grounds wander down a hillside toward the surrounding hillside and contain a swimming pool, tennis courts, and a pleasant terrace overlooking the valley below and the peaks that hem it in.

WHERE TO DINE

Bolzoner Tor. V. Haller 4. ☎ **0473/232-318.** Primi 8,000–9,000L ($4.70–$5.30); secondi 18,000–22,000L ($10.60–$12.95). No credit cards. Mon–Fri 11:30am–2:30pm and 6–9pm, Sat 11:30am–2:30pm. ITALIAN/TYROLEAN.

This friendly beer hall and trattoria near the Duomo is decidedly Tyrolean, with alpine-style furnishings gracing the vaulted and paneled dining room. Tyrolean dishes such as *Schlutzkrapfen* (ravioli filled with sauerkraut) and *herrengrostl* (a hearty stew of beef, potatoes, and herbs) are served, but many dishes are typical of regions to the south: the risottos are excellent, especially the one with *fungi porcini* (wild mushrooms) when available, and there is often a fish special or two.

Café Darling. Passeggiata d'Inverno 5–9. ☎ **0473/237-221.** Pastries from 2,000L ($1.20), sandwiches from 4,000L ($2.40). MC, V. Thurs–Tues 7:30am–1am. CAFE.

The so called "Winter Walk" along the banks of the River Passer is lined with cafes, and this one is especially pleasant. There's a covered terrace out front, as well a small riverfront terrace where the tables practically hang over the river, and the comfortable interior room has a casual ambience that's not too common in this staid, refined resort. You'll probably feel comfortable passing some time reading a book here while sipping a beer or a glass of the house grape juice. Pastries and light sandwiches are also available.

Kavalier. V. Carducci 29. ☎ **0473/236-561.** Primi 8,000–11,000L ($4.70–$6.50); secondi 19,000–23,000L ($11.20–$13.55). MC, V. Thurs–Tues 11:30am–2:30pm and 5:30–9pm. ITALIAN/TYROLEAN.

Just a few steps off the river near Piazza Teatro, this informal cafe-style restaurant, with a pleasant terrace to one side, is a handy stop and can accommodate whatever level of hunger you happen to be experiencing. A full menu of mostly Tyrolean fare is served, featuring heaping platters of *speck,* a hearty beef goulash and an amazingly filling pasta dish, *gnocchetti alla spinachi con prosciutto e panna* (little spinach gnocchi filled with ham in a cream sauce). However, you can also dine lightly, on salads and omelettes, or just stop by for a frosty glass of Forst, a rich and slightly bitter beer that is brewed in Merano.

Rothaler Weinstube. V. Portici 41. ☎ **0473/369-13.** Cheese and meat plates about 6,000L ($3.55). No credit cards. Mon–Sat 8am–midnight. WEINSTUBE.

If you want a big dose of the Tyrol, you need only step into this cozy tavern on Merano's arcaded main street. There's a simple, contemporary bar up front where many shoppers and workers stop by for a glass of wine or beer, but to get the full experience you must step into the back room, which is half-paneled, heavily frescoed with images of grapes and vineyards, and lit by a collection of rustic lanterns that have been electrified. The offerings seem to vary by the hour, but typically include a wheel of Parmesan or other cheese, *speck* (the region's cured and aged ham), and *carre di miale affumiata* (smoked pork loin).

4 Bressanone (Brixen)

40 km (24 mi.) N of Bolzano, 68 km (41 mi.) E of Merano

Tucked neatly in the Val d'Isarco between the Eisack and Rienz Rivers and surrounded by orchards and vineyards that climb the lower flanks of the surrounding peaks, ✪ **Bressanone** is a gem of a Tyrolean town with a hefty past that today's quaint, small town atmosphere belies. From 1027 to 1803, Bressanone was the center of a large ecclesiastical principality, and its bishop-princes ruled over much of the South Tyrol. Their impressive monuments arise amid the town's heavily gabled, pastel-colored houses and narrow cobblestone streets.

FESTIVALS & MARKETS With its cozy, twisting medieval lanes and snug Tyrolean-style houses, Bressanone is especially well suited to Christmas celebrations. The main holiday event is a **Christkindlmarkt** (Christmas market) from late November to Christmas Eve; stalls on and around Piazza Duomo sell hand carved ornaments, other crafts, holiday pastries, and other seasonal merchandize. A fruit and vegetable market enlivens Piazza Parrocchia near the duomo Monday through Saturday, from 8am to noon and 3 to about 6pm.

ESSENTIALS

GETTING HERE **By Train** Bressanone lies on the same north-south rail line as Bolzano and Verona, making connections between those cities extremely easy, with more than 30 trains a day. The trip between Bolzano and Bressanone takes 35 minutes and costs 3,500L ($2.05).

By Bus SAD buses leave from the front of the train station and connect Bressanone and Bolzano, making the 50-minute trip every hour for a fare of 5,000L ($2.95). Buses also connect Bressanone with outlying villages, including Sant'Andrea, a good base for hiking and skiing (see below); several buses a day make the 20-minute trip and the fare is 3,000L ($1.75); buses run every half hour during ski season and service is augmented by a ski bus that is free for pass holders.

By Car Bressanone is about a half-hour drive north of Bolzano on **A22.**

VISITOR INFORMATION The tourist office, near the train station at V. Stazione 9 (☎ 0472/836-401), is open from Monday to Friday from 8:30am to 12:30pm and 2:30 to 6pm and on Saturday from 9am to 12:30pm. The telephone area code for Bressanone is 0472.

WHAT TO SEE & DO

It's easy to get around Bressanone by foot—it's compact many of its streets are closed to cars. If you arrive by car, you will probably use the large parking lot on the south of the city on Via Dante (you will pass it as you drive into the city from the autostrada); the center is 5 minutes away up the Via Roma. From the train station follow Viale Stazione for about 10 minutes to the center.

The center of town is the **Piazza Duomo,** a long, rectangular tree-shaded square with cafes on one side and the white facade of the duomo on the other. A baroque renovation to the tall exterior, flanked by two bell towers, has masked much of the cathedral's original 13th-century architecture, which you'll see more of in the interior and in the crypt. The heavily frescoed cloisters are especially charming, even though the view of Judgement Day they portray is gloomy. Open daily 8am to noon and 3 to 7pm (hours vary); there are guided tours (in Italian and German) Monday through Saturday at 10:30am and 3pm.

Just south of the Piazza del Duomo, on the adjoining Piazza Vescovile, stands the palace of the prince-bishops, whose power over the region—and the fragility of that power—is made clear by the surrounding moat and fortifying walls. The massive 14th-century palace now houses the **Museo Diocesano,** where more than 70 rooms display wooden statuary, many somewhat unremarkable Renaissance paintings by local artists, and what is considered to be the museum's treasure and the objects most likely to capture your attention—an extensive and enchanting collection of antique nativity scenes, filling eight rooms and one of the largest such assemblages anywhere.

Hitting the Slopes

Bressanone's major playground is **Monte Plose,** and the gateway to ski slopes and hiking trails alike is the outlying village of **Sant'Andrea** (see "Getting Here by Bus," above). Skiing here is not as glamorous as it is in better-known resorts like Cortina, but it is excellent and much less expensive. A ski pass is about 40,000L ($23.50) a day and can be purchased at one of the outlets near the Sant'Andrea funicular, which costs 4,500L ($2.65) and runs from July through mid-September and from December through May (winter schedules vary considerably with snow conditions; a summer ascent will take you to a network of alpine trails near the stop at Valcroce). The tourist board in Bressanone provides maps, information on skiing, mountain refuges, and other details you need to know to enjoy this mountain wilderness.

The museum (☎ 0472/830-505) is open March 15 to October 31, Tuesday through Sunday from 10am to 5pm; the nativity-scene galleries only open again from December 15 through February 10, Tuesday through Sunday from 2 to 5pm (closed December 24 and 25); admission to the complete museum collection is 7,000L ($4.10), to the nativity scene exhibit only is 3,000L ($1.75).

WHERE TO STAY

Albergo Cremona. V. Vittorio Veneto 8, 39042 Bressanone. ☎ 0472/835-602. 12 units, 10 with bathroom. 65,000L ($38.25) single without bathroom, 100,000L ($58.80) double with bathroom. No credit cards.

Like many of the other well-heeled resorts in this part of the world, Bressanone doesn't offer many inexpensive beds. That's why this small, plain hotel near the train station and about a 10-minute walk to the center of town is a good find. The neighborhood is not as quaint as much of the rest of Bressanone but it's safe, and the tiny reception area and rooms are more functional than charming. All but the two bathroomless singles are large, the beds are firm and covered with the feather quilts that are standard issue in this part of the world.

Hotel Goldene Krone/Corona d'Oro. V. Fienili 4, 39042 Bressanone. ☎ 0472/835-154. Fax 0472/835-014. 31 units, all with bathroom. MINIBAR TV TEL. 70,000–80,000L ($41.20–$47) single, 160,000–200,000L ($94.10–$117.65) double. Rates include breakfast. Half-board 90,000–115,000L ($52.95–$67.65) per person; full board 110,000–135,000L ($64.70–$79.40) per person. AE, MC, V. Parking 10,000L ($5.90). Closed Jan 6–Feb 1.

Everything about this amiable hotel at the edge of the old city suggests solid comfort, from the homey, wood-paneled lounge to the weinstube-style bar to the breakfast room and restaurant, where boothlike tables are lit by pretty shaded lamps. There are two categories of guest rooms, and hence the range of prices. Those in the lower range are pleasant enough, with streamlined modern furnishings, and many have terraces. The more expensive rooms are really quite special, though, and well worth the extra expense. They're actually suites, with separate sitting and sleeping areas, equipped respectively with roomy couches and armchairs and king-sized beds. The bathrooms are grand, with double sinks and large tubs equipped with Jacuzzis.

WORTH A SPLURGE

Hotel Elefante. V. Rio Bianco 4. 39042 Bressanone. ☎ 0472/832-750. Fax 0472/836-579. 44 units, all with bathroom. TV TEL. 150,000 ($88.25) single, 232,000L ($136.50) double. Breakfast 24,000L ($14.10). Half-board 194,000L($114.10) per person; full board 230,000L ($135.30) per person (minimum 3 days). AE, MC, V. Parking 11,000L ($6.50). Closed Jan 10–Feb 28.

One of Italy's oldest and most famous inns is named for a 16th-century guest—an elephant accompanying Archduke Maximilian of Austria on the long trek from Genoa to Vienna, where the beast was to become part of the royal menagerie. During its 2-week stay the pachyderm attracted onlookers from miles around, and the innkeeper renamed his establishment and commissioned a delightful elephant-themed fresco that still graces the front of the building. Today's hotel matches its provenance with excellent service and extraordinary environs that include dark paneled hallways and grand staircases. The distinctive old rooms are full of nooks and crannies and furnished with heavy old Tyrolean antiques and some tasteful modern pieces, include wonderfully solid beds. A generous buffet breakfast emphasizes delicious Austrian pastries, and many guests also choose to take their other meals in the justly famous restaurant. One the hotels nicest assets is a large garden and pleasant swimming pool.

WHERE TO DINE

Caffè Duomo. Pz. Parocchia 3. ☎ **0472/838-277.** Sandwiches, snacks from 5,000L ($2.95). Tues–Sun 7am–10pm. CAFE.

These minimalist, white-walled, chicly lit environs provide a contemporary version of the woody taverns that prevail in this part of the world (there are still little nooks off to one side for intimate conversation). There is no attempt at serious cuisine here, but there is a nice selection of panini (sandwiches), made with local hams and mountain cheeses, as well as some sumptuous cakes and pastries. The coffee is excellent, and the wine and beer list extensive.

Fink. V. Portici Minori 4. ☎ **0472/834-883.** Primi 8,000–12,000L ($4.70–$7.05); secondi 10,000–24,000L ($5.90–$14.10). AE, DC, MC, V. Thurs–Tues noon–2:30pm and 7–10pm. Closed Tues evening Oct–June and July 1–14. TYROLEAN.

It only seems right that Bressanone's charmingly arcaded main street should have a restaurant like this, with paneling hung with antlers and oil paintings, while dishing out excellent local cuisine. There are many mountain-style dishes that you are likely to encounter only within a close radius of Bressanone, including a *piatto alla Val d'Isarco,* a platter of locally cured hams and salamis, and a *zuppa di vino,* a traditional Tyrolean soup made with white wine that here includes crusty pieces of cinnamon toast. The *miale gratinato,* a pork roast topped with a cheese sauce, is surprisingly light and absolutely delicious, as are the local cheeses served for dessert. If in doubt about what to order, just ask—the English-speaking staff is extremely gracious.

Finsterwirt. Vc. Duomo 3. ☎ **0472/835-343.** Salads and light meals from 13,000L ($7.65). AE, DC, MC, V. Tues–Sun 10am–midnight. Closed Sun evening and Jan 10–Feb 2 and June 15–30. WINE BAR.

Occupying the same quarters as Oste Scuro restaurant (see below) and run by the same family, this ground-floor tavern near the cathedral has the same dark paneling, leaded window ambience. The fare and service, however, are much more casual, though excellent, and you are welcome to settle into one of the nooklike tables for as long as you'd like to enjoy a beer or glass of local wine (from 2,000L/$1.20) and a plate of fresh goat cheese or a platter of speck and salami. A lovely rear garden, candlelit at night, is open throughout the summer and well into chillier days when people from more southerly climes wouldn't think of sitting outdoors.

Oste Scuro. Vc. Duomo 3. ☎ **0472/835-342.** Reservations recommended. Primi 10,000–15,000L ($5.90–$8.80); secondi 13,000–24,000L ($7.65–$14.10). AE, DC, MC, V. Tues–Sun 11:30–2pm and 6:30–9pm. Closed Sun evening and Jan 10–Feb 2 and June 15–30. TYROLEAN.

What may be Bressanone's temple of gastronomy (Fink, above, is a close contender) occupies a welcoming series of intimate candlelit rooms above the Finsterwirt wein-stube (see above). The first of these rooms contains a standup bar where patrons stop by just to order one of the excellent wines by the glass. It would be a shame not to dine here, though, because the kitchen excels at simple but innovative preparations of the freshest local ingredients. A *tartina di ricotta* is a concoction of creamy cheese atop a bed of lightly sauteed spinach; even if you have been finding the region's steady diet of *canederli* (dumplings) heavy, try them here because they are light and infused with fresh wild mushrooms. The kitchen excels at meat dishes, included an herb-infused veal roast. Fresh berries top off a meal in season, and the strudels are perfection.

EN ROUTE TO CORTINA: THE STRADA DI DOLIMITI

The Great Dolomite Road, the scenic route between Bolzano and Cortina going east, **SS241** and **SS48,** is 110 kilometers (66 mi.) of stunning views. The road curves around some of the highest peaks in the Dolomites, including 10,000-foot-tall Mar-molda, and goes through a scattering of mountain villages and ski resorts before drop-ping out of a high pass into Cortina. Some tour buses follow this route (the tourist offices in Bolzano and Cortina can provide a list of tour operators; check with the bus station in Bolzano), as do two daily buses of the **SAD** network from July through Sep-tember (check with the bus station in Bolzano or call ☎ **0471/450-111**). However, you may want to rent a car if only for a day to make the spectacular round trip, one of Europe's most scenic drives (allow at least 2½ hr. each way over the twists and turns of the passes). Keep in mind, though, that the Strada di Dolomiti is often closed to vehicles because of heavy snow in the winter months, and you will often need to put chains on your tires between November and April.

5 Cortina d'Ampezzo

133 km (82 mi.) E of Bolzano, 166 km (100 mi.) N of Venice

Italy's best-known mountain resort, put on the international map when it hosted the 1956 Winter Olympics, is usually associated with wealth and sophistication. Long before the Olympics, though, Cortina was attracting European alpine enthusiasts, who began coming here for stays in the town's first hotels as early as the 1860s. In 1902, Cortina hosted its first ski competitions, and in 1909, the completion of the first road in and out of the town, the magnificent Strada di Dolomiti (built by the Austro-Hungarian military), opened the slopes to more skiers.

Even without its 90 miles of ski runs and 50 cable cars and chair lifts that make the slopes easily accessible, Cortina would be one of Europe's most appealing alpine towns. The surrounding Dolomite peaks are simply stunning. Eighteen of them rise more than 10,000 feet, ringing Cortina in an amphitheater of craggy stone. In full light the peaks are a soft bluish gray, and when they catch the rising and setting sun they take on a welcoming rosy glow.

True to its reputation for glamour, Cortina can be expensive (especially in August and the high ski season months of January through March). Many well-to-do Italians have houses here, and a sense of privilege prevails. What's often forgotten, though, is that for all the town's fame, strict zoning has put the damper on development, and, as a result, Cortina is still a mountain town of white timbered houses, built aside a rushing stream and surrounded by forests, meadows and, of course, the stunning Dolomite peaks.

FESTIVALS & MARKETS The Piazza Italia near the bus station doubles as Cortina's marketplace. Stalls sell produce, mountain cheeses, clothing, housewares, and other items on Tuesday and Friday mornings from 8:30am to 1pm. While chic Cortina concerns itself mostly with secular pursuits, the town turns out for a solemn religious procession down the main street, Corso Italia, on Good Friday.

ESSENTIALS

GETTING HERE   **By Bus**   Frequent **SAD bus service** provides the only public transportation in and out of Cortina; (☎ **167/846-047** toll free, or 0436/867-921). If you are coming from **Bolzano** on one of four daily buses, it is usually necessary to change at Dobbiaco, 32 kilometers (19½ mi.) to the north (6,000L/$3.55 each way). There is also one daily bus to and from **Venice** (a 3-hr. trip) and a daily bus to and from **Milan** (6½ hr.). The bus station in Cortina is located in the former train station on Via Marconi.

By Train   The closest train station to Cortina is the one at **Calalzo di Cadore,** 30 kilometers (19 mi.) south. There are nine trains a day to and from Calalzo and **Venice** (the trip often requires connections and takes 3 to 4 hours; fare is 14,000L/$8.25 each way); from Calalzo, 10 daily buses, 4,000L ($2.35) each way, connect with Cortina. For information and schedules, call ☎ **0436/867-921.**

By Car   The spectacularly scenic **Strada di Dolomiti** (see above) links Bolzano and Cortina, while **S51** heads south toward Venice, connecting south of Belluno to Autostrada A27, for a total trip time of about 3 hours between Cortina and Venice. Much of the center of Cortina is off limits to cars, and as you approach the town you will be funneled onto an extremely well designed and scenic network of circumference roads. You are allowed to drive into the town only if you are staying at one of the hotels, which are clearly marked from the circumference road; otherwise you will be directed into one of the outlying parking lots.

VISITOR INFORMATION   The **APT tourist office,** Pzta. San Francesco 8 (☎ **0436/32-31**), is open Monday to Friday from 9am to 12:30pm and 4 to 7pm, Saturday from 10am to 12:30pm and 4 to 7pm, and Sunday from 10am to 12:30pm. In addition to a list of accommodations, the English-speaking staff will also provide a wealth of information on ski slopes, hiking trails, and bus schedules. The telephone area code for Cortina is 0436.

WHAT TO SEE & DO

The main in-town activity in Cortina appears to be walking up and down the main street, the pedestrian-only **Corso Italia,** in the most fashionable skiwear money can buy. Most of the buildings are new, but pleasingly low scale and alpine in design, and at the town center is the pretty 18th-century church of Santi Filippo e Giacomo, with a charming bell tower eclipsed in height only by the majestic peaks. It is on these peaks that most visitors set their sights, enjoying an amazing array of outdoor activities on the slopes.

EXPLORING PEAKS   Skiers and nonskiers alike will enjoy the eye-popping scenery on a trip up the surrounding mountainsides on the funicular systems that leave right from town. The most spectacular trip is the ascent on the **Freccia nel Cielo** (Arrow of the Sky), which departs from a terminus near the Stadio Olimpico del Ghiacchio (Olympic Ice Skating Stadium), about a 10-minute walk north and west of the town center. The top station is at Tafano di Mezzo, at 10,543 feet; the round-trip is 45,000L ($26.45). It is less expensive (30,000L/$17.65), and just as satisfying if mountain scenery and not high-alpine skiing is your quest, to make the trip only as far as Ra Valles, at 8,500 feet. The views over glaciers and the stony peaks are magnificent, and a bar serves sandwiches and other refreshments on an outdoor terrace. The funicular runs from mid-July to late September and mid-December through May 1, with departures every 20 minutes from 9am to 4 or 5pm, depending on the time of sunset; ☎ **0436/5052** for information.

The **Funivia Faloria** arrives and departs from a terminus on the other side of town, about a 10-minute walk southeast of the town center. The ride is a little less dramatic than the one on the longer Freccia nel Cielo. Even so, the ascent over forests and meadows then up a sheer cliff to the 7,000-foot-high ski station at Faloria is not without thrills, and the view from the terrace bar at Faloria, down to Cortina and to the curtain of high peaks to the north, is one you won't soon forget. Like the Freccia nel Cielo, the Funivia Faloria runs from mid July to late-September and mid-December through May 1, with departures every 20 minutes from 9am to 4 or 5pm, depending on time of sunset; round-trip fare is 23,000L ($13.55), 18,000L ($10.60) one way; ☎ **0436/2517** for information.

Another trip for funivia enthusiasts is the one from the top of **Passo Falzarego,** 25 kilometers (15 mi.) west of Cortina, to **Lagazoul,** a little skiing and hiking station at the 8,500-foot level. In summer, you can follow a network of trails at the top and scamper for miles across the dramatic, rocky terrain. The ride is a nearly vertical ascent up the rocky face of the mountain, and as an eerie alternative to the funicular you can make the climb up or down through a series of tunnels dug into the cliff during World War I fighting. Falzarego is the last pass through which you descend if you follow the Strada di Dolimiti into Cortina, so you may want to stop and board the funicular for a scenery-filled introduction to the region. If you are not driving, five buses a day make the 35-minute trip between Cortina and the funicular stop at the top of the Passo Falzarego; the fare is 2,500L ($1.45) each way (☎ **0436/867-921** for information). The funivia runs from mid-July to late September and mid-December through May 1, with departures every 30 minutes; round-trip fare is 18,000L ($10.60), 13,000L ($7.65) one way; ☎ **0436/867-301** for information.

DOWNHILL SKIING Cortina is Italy's leading ski resort, and it lives up to this reputation with eight exceptional ski areas that are easily accessible from town. Two of the best, **Tofana-Promedes** and **Faloria-Tondi,** are accessible by funiculars that lift off from the edges of town (see "Exploring Peaks" above), as are the novice slopes at Mietres. You can enjoy these facilities fairly economically with one of the comprehensive **Dolomiti Superski** passes that provide unlimited skiing (including all chairlift and funicular fees, as well as free shuttle bus service to and from Cortina and the ski areas) at all eight of Cortina's ski areas and those at 10 outlying resorts. The cost during high season, December 24 to January 6 and January 31 to March 15, is 59,000L ($34.70) for 1 day, 166,000L ($97.65) for 3 days, and 309,000L ($181.75) for 7 days. For more information, contact the tourist office or Consorzio Esercenti Impianti a Fune, V. d. Castello 33, 32043 Cortina (☎ **0436/862 171;** fax 0473/868-069; www.DolomitiSuperski.com). For lessons, contact either the **Scuola di Sci Azzurra,** V. Ria de Zeto 8 (☎ **0436/2694**), or **Scuola di Sci Cortina,** Corso Italia (☎ **0436/2911**). Both offer 6 consecutive days of group lessons, about 4 hours a day, for a cost of approximately 700,000L ($411.75) in high season. You can rent skis at many outlets throughout town, including stands at the lower and upper stations of the Freccia nel Cielo cable car and other funiculars; rentals average 15,000L to 25,000L (48.80 to $14.70).

HIKING & ROCK CLIMBING In this mountainous terrain, these two activities are often synonymous. The tourist office can provide maps of hiking trails throughout the surrounding region. For high-altitude hiking, canyoning, and rock climbing, you may want to join one of the excursions led by **Gruppo Guide Alpine Cortina,** Cor. Italia 69/a (☎ **0463-868-505),** open 8am to noon and 4 to 8pm.

HORSEBACK RIDING   Fattoria Memguto, in outlying Fraina (☎ **0463-860-441),** offers group and individual riding through the lovely valleys surrounding Cortina; the stables are open from late spring through late fall from 9am to noon and 3 to 7pm and rides cost 15,000L ($8.85) for 30 minutes and 30,000L ($17.65) for an hour.

ICE SKATING   At the **Stadio Olimpico del Ghiacchio,** just to the northwest of the town center on Via del Stadio (☎ **0436/2661),** you can practice turns on the two recently refurbished rinks where Olympians tried for the gold in the 1956 games. Admission is 5,000L ($2.95), skate rental another 5,000L ($2.95).

MOUNTAIN BIKING   The roads and tracks leading into the peaks provide arduous biking terrain; many cyclists from all over the world come to Cortina to practice for events. If you want to test your mettle, you can rent a bike from the **Mountain Bike Center,** Cor. Italia 294 (☎ **0436/0336).** Rentals are 20,000L ($11.75) for 2 hours, 40,000L ($23.50) for 4 hours, and 60,000L ($35.30) for a day. The English-speaking staff will point you in the direction of routes that match your abilities.

RELAXING   Unwind after any of these activities in the indoor swimming pool at the **Piscina Coperta Comunale,** just north of town in outlying Guargne. It is open daily from 3 to 7pm, until 10pm on Tuesday and Thursday; admission is 12,000L ($7.05). You will find relief for sore muscles at **La Sauna di Cortina,** V. Stazione 18 (☎ **0463-866-784);** it's open daily from 9am to 9pm and use of the facilities, which include Finnish saunas and Turkish baths, and costs 40,000L ($23.55).

WHERE TO STAY

Cortina is booked solid during the high season: August, Christmas, and late January through March. You should reserve well in advance. Rates are lowest in late spring and early fall. Keep in mind that many innkeepers prefer to give rooms to guests who will stay several days or longer and who will take meals at the hotel. Given the scarcity of reasonably priced restaurants in town, you will probably be happy settling for a half- or full-board plan. The tourist board provides a list of private homes that take in guests, a way to keep costs down while enjoying the local hospitality, which is considerable.

Hotel Bellaria. Cor. Italia 266, 32043 Cortina d'Ampezzo. ☎ **0436/25-05.** Fax 0436/57-55. 22 units, all with bathroom. TV TEL. 80,000–160,000L ($47–$94.10) single, 120,000–260,000L ($70.60–$152.95) double. Rates include breakfast. Full board 100,000–200,000L ($58.80–$117.65) a person. AC, MC, V.

The Mujoni family, which owns this pleasant hotel a short walk from the center on the northern edge of town, did a complete refurbishing recently, and they chose to keep prices down for the benefit of the patrons who come here season after season. As a result, they still provide some of Cortina's most reasonably priced accommodations, and they house their guests in handsome, sunny rooms that overlook the mountains and have fresh alpine-style pine furnishings, firm new beds, and crisp fabrics. All of the bathrooms have been redone and fitted out with roomy stall showers. Downstairs, there's a lovely paneled lounge, a dining room, and a pleasant terrace in front of the house.

✪ **Hotel Montana.** Cor. Italia 94, 32043 Cortina d'Ampezzo. ☎ **0436/862-126.** Fax 0436/868-211. 30 units, all with bathroom. TV TEL. 73,000–104,000L ($42.95–$61.20) single, 106,000–196,000L ($62.35–$115.30) double. Rates include breakfast. AE, MC, V.

Right in the center of town, this hotel occupies a tall, pretty alpine-style house and is run by the amiable Adriano and Roberta Lorenzi, who provide some of the resort's nicest lodgings for the price. Guest rooms are pleasant and cozy, with old-style armoires, hardwood floors, and down quilts on the beds, and many open to balconies overlooking the peaks. Most of the doubles are quite large, and many are beautifully paneled and have separate sitting areas. Half the rooms here are singles, making this an ideal spot for solo travelers or cranky twosomes who need to get away from each other. There is no restaurant, but breakfast is served in a pleasant room where guests tend to linger through much of the morning.

Villa Nevada. V. Ronco 94, 32043 Cortina d'Ampezzo. ☎ **0436/4778.** Fax 0436/4853. 10 units, all with bathroom. TV TEL. 65,000–150,000L ($38.25–$88.25) single, 120,000–210,000L ($70.60–$123.55) double. Rates include breakfast. AE, MC, V.

On a grassy hillside overlooking the town, valley and mountains, the Villa Nevada is a low-slung alpine building that has the appearance of a private home. The same ambience prevails inside, where an attractive, paneled lounge is grouped around a hearth and opens to a sunny terrace, inviting guests to linger as they might in a living room. The guest rooms are large and bright, and afford wonderful views over the alpine landscape; they are nicely furnished with pine pieces and thickly carpeted, and they have large bathrooms. Located on the road to the outlying settlement of Ronco, this is probably a better option for those with a car than for those without—the center of Cortina is a pleasant 20-minute walk downhill, but it could be a long uphill trek home in bad weather or late at night.

WORTH A SPLURGE

Hotel Menardi. V. Majon 110, 32043 Cortina d'Ampezzo. ☎ **0436/24-00.** Fax 0436/862-183. www.sunrise.it/cortina/alberghi/menardi. 51 units, all with bathroom. TV TEL. 125,000–245,000 ($73.55–$144.10) single, 145,000–345,000L ($85.30–$202.95) double. Rates include breakfast. Half-board 105,000–270,000L ($61.75–$158.85) per person, depending on season. AE, MC, V. Closed Apr 10–June 20 and Sept 20–Dec 20. Parking 15,000L ($8.85).

One of the oldest and most charming hostelries in Cortina successfully combines the luxury and service of a fine hotel with the homelike comfort of a mountain inn. The Menardi family, which converted its farmhouse into a guest house in the 1920s, has over the years beautifully appointed the public rooms with antiques and comfortable furnishings, and done up the high-ceilinged, wood-floored guest rooms simply but tastefully with painted armoires and bedsteads, down quilts, and attractive floral fabrics. Rooms in the rear of the house are especially quiet and pleasant, looking across the hotel's spacious lawns to the forests and peaks; some newer rooms are located in an annex next door. Most guests take half-board to avail themselves of the excellent meals, but it is also possible to make bed-and-breakfast arrangements when the hotel is not fully booked.

WHERE TO DINE

Inexpensive meals are hard to come by in Cortina—even pizzerias are few and far between. For a low-cost meal, you might want to equip yourself for a picnic at **La Piazzetta,** Cor. Italia 53, with a mouth-watering assortment of salamis, cheeses, breads, and other fare. Another source of supplies is **La Cooperativa,** Cor. Italia 40, the largest, best-stocked supermarket for miles around.

Al Camin. V. Alvera 90. ☎ **0436/862-010.** Reservations recommended. Primi 8,000–18,000L ($4.70–$10.60); secondi 14,000–25,000L ($8.25–$14.70). MC, V. Tues–Sun, noon–3pm and 7–11:30pm. ALPINE.

If you follow the Via Alvera along the Ru Bigontina, a rushing mountain stream, about 10 minutes east from the center of town, you'll come to this charming, rustic restaurant. The tables in the wood-paneled dining room are grouped around a large stone fireplace, and the menu includes many local favorites. Your meal may include what is known in this part of the region as *kenederli* (these dumplings flavored with liver are known as *canederli* outside of the immediate vicinity of Cortina), as well as some dishes, many of them seasonal, that you may not encounter elsewhere—these include *radicchio di prato,* a mountain green that appears in early spring and is served dressed with hot lard, and in winter, *formaggio fuso con funghi e polenta,* a lush combination of creamy melted mountain cheese and wild mushrooms served over polenta.

Café Royal. Cor. Italia. ☎ **0436/867-045.** Sandwiches and other snacks from about 4,000L ($2.35). Wed–Mon 8am–10pm. MC, V.

The Corso Italia, Cortina's pedestrians-only main street, is the center of the town's social life. This cafe is one of several that occupy the ground floor of large hotels along the street, and it is one of the more pleasant. As soon as it's even remotely possible to sit outdoors, tables are set out front on a sunny terrace. At other times patrons are welcome to sit for hours over coffee, pastries, or light fare such as sandwiches in a pleasant room off the lobby of this hotel of the same name.

La Tavernetta. V. d. Stadio 27 a/b. ☎ **0436/867-494.** Reservations recommended. Primi 12,000–20,000L ($7.05–$11.75); secondi 15,000–30,000L ($8.80–$17.65). AE, MC, V. Thurs–Tues noon–2:30pm and 7:30–11pm. ALPINE.

A former barn, just steps from the Olympic ice-skating stadium, has been delightfully converted to a very stylish yet reasonably priced restaurant, with handsome paneled walls, timbered ceilings, and tile floors. The menu relies on local ingredients and typical dishes of the Alto Adige, and the rustic environs may inspire you to eat heartily. You might want to begin with a dish of polenta delicately infused with *asparagi selvatici* (the tips of fresh wild asparagus) or *gnocchi di spinachi* (filled with spinach and topped with a rich wild game sauce), then move on to a robust *stinco di vitello con patate* (veal shank served with creamy potato) or *cervo ai mirtilli* (venison with a sauce of myrtle berries).

Ospitale. Locale Ospitale. ☎ **0436/4585.** Primi 10,000–12,000L ($5.90–$7.05); secondi 15,000–22,000L ($8.80–$12.95). AE, MC. Tues–Sun noon–2:30pm and 7–10pm. ALPINE.

A trip out to this roomy restaurant in a high-gabled house (about 5 miles north of Cortina on the road to the village and lake of Dobbiaco) is a favorite outing for residents of Cortina. Many members of the Alvera family are on hand in the series of comfortable, wood-floored dining rooms and in the kitchen, preparing and serving local specialties as well as traditional Italian dishes. In season, fresh vegetables appear in such pasta dishes as *pappardelle ai porcini* (flat noodles with porcini mushrooms) and *casunziei rossi,* a short, local pasta mixed with beets, or *gnocchi di zucca con ricotta* (gnocchi made from squash and stuffed with ricotta). The *goulash con polenta* is one of any number of substantial main courses. If you don't have a car, you can take one of the hourly buses out here from the bus station in Cortina, but that is only an option at lunch.

6 Udine

71 km (43 mi.) NW of Trieste, 127 km (78 mi.) N of Venice

Surrounded by the green, rolling plains of the Friuli, Udine is a delightful small city with a vibrant air, wonderful piazze and Gothic and Renaissance monuments, and some stunning artworks by the rococo painter Tiepolo. A possession of the Venetian Republic from the 14th century, Udine has enjoyed great prosperity as a major trading center and a crossroads for trade across the Alps, just to the north. The late 18th century saw an Austrian takeover, the 19th century saw unification with Italy, the 20th century brought intense World War II bombings. Through it all, the city's landmarks and distinct character (which reflects Italian, Nordic, and central European influences) have remained intact.

FESTIVALS & MARKETS   Udine d'Estate is the city's major festival, running from July into mid-September with concerts and theatrical performances in churches and in Udine's beautiful piazze. An outdoor food market fills the atmospheric Piazza Matteotti daily, from 8am to 1pm.

ESSENTIALS

GETTING HERE   By Train   From its train station on Viale Europa Unità, ☎ **0432/503-656,** Udine is extremely well-connected with Venice and Trieste; there are two trains an hour throughout and the day and night to and from each. **Venice** is 2 hours away and the fare is 12,100L ($7.10); **Trieste** is 1½ hours away and the fare is 7,400L ($4.35). Luggage storage is available at the station; the office is open daily from 7:30am to 10:30pm and the fee is 5,000L ($2.95) a bag for each 12-hour period.

By Bus   The bus station is 1 block east of the train station on Viale Europa Unità. Aside from one-a-day service to and from **Venice** (2 hr.; 11,000L/$6.50) there is extensive service to other cities and towns in Friuli-Venezia-Giulia with service provided by **Autolinea Ferrari,** ☎ **0432/504-012.** Hourly buses (more frequent between 7 and 9am and 4 and 7pm) make the hourly trip to and from **Trieste** for 7,000L ($4.10).

By Car   Udine is an easy 2-hour drive north and west of Venice on autostrada **A4** east to **A23** and north on that. From **Trieste** it's a trip of a little under an hour west on A4 then north on A23. If you are driving **from Cortina d'Ampezzo** or other Dolomite resorts, you will drop down from the mountains into Belluno on **S51** as if you were going to Venice, but head east on **S13** at Conegliano. Allow about 3 hours for the drive.

VISITOR INFORMATION   The **APT tourist office** is at Pz. 1 Maggio 7 (the other side of the castello from Piazza della Libertà; ☎ **0432/295-972**), and is open Monday through Saturday from 9am to 1pm and 3 to 6pm. The telephone area code for Udine is 0432.

CITY LAYOUT   Much of the center of Udine is closed to traffic and surrounded by ring roads. The train and bus stations are at the southern end of this ring network, on Viale Europa Unità. From them it is about a 15-minute walk into the center, following **Via Aquilea** and its continuation, **Via Veneto,** to **Piazza della Libertà.** Buses 1, 3, and 8 make the trip from the train station to the center (1,400L/80¢).

WHAT TO SEE & DO

In the center of Udine, handsome streets sometimes cross little streams and open every few blocks or so into another stunning piazza. The effect is like walking from one stage set to another. The heart of the city is the elegant **Piazza della Libertà,** which bears the telltale marks of Venetian presence in the city: On one side is the **Loggia del Lionello,** the town hall, built in the mid–15th century in Venetian style with a pink and white striped facade. Across the piazza is the Renaissance **Porticato di San Giovanni,** with a long portico supported by slender columns and, rising above it, a clock tower emblazoned with the Venetian lion and topped with two Moors who routinely strike the hours.

The great Renaissance architect Palladio designed the **Arco Bollani,** to one side of the clock tower. Pass through it and make the short climb through verdant gardens to the sober 16th-century **castello,** which rises above the Piazza della Libertà on a hillock. Many Udinese come up here just to admire the view over the town and countryside, but you can also venture into the castle and visit the **Museo Civico.** While many of the galleries house an eclectic collection that includes coins and old photographs of Udine, the treasures are in the **Galleria d'Arte Antica.** You'll get a taste here of the work of Giambattista Tiepolo, who came to Udine from Venice in 1726, when he was 30 and already regarded as a master of a rococo style that was the last great burst of Italian painting. His *Consilium in Arena* is pure Tiepolo, a swirl of lush skies and plump putti. The museum (☎ 0432/501-824) is open Tuesday through Saturday from 9:30am to 12:30pm and 3 to 6pm, Sunday 9:30am to 12:30pm; admission is 4,000L ($2.35), 2,000L ($1.20) for students.

Many visitors come to Udine just to enjoy the Tiepolos that grace many of its buildings. To follow in their footsteps, descend again to Piazza della Libertà and follow Via Veneto south for a block or so to Piazza Duomo. The church (open Monday through Saturday, 7:30am to 12:30pm and 3 to 7pm) dominates the square with its 14th-century Gothic facade, but the interior is theatrically baroque. The first, second, and fourth altars in the right nave are adorned with Tiepolo frescoes; in the fourth chapel, his airy version of Christ's Ascension imparts lightness and a sense of exhilaration at leaving earth.

Tiepolo also frescoed the **Oratorio della Purità** (across the piazza). In the *Fall of the Angels,* the plummeting cherubs look like children who have just been scolded. An Assumption, appropriately adorning the ceiling, is so light that it seems to draw the viewer right off the floor. To enter, you must ring the bell (only between 9am and 1pm Monday through Saturday) and wait for a sacristan to let you in; he'll expect a tip, which should be at least 5,000L ($2.95) per person.

Udine's largest collection of the artist's works adorn the **Palazzo Patriarcale,** just north of the duomo on Piazza Patriarcato. This palace was once home to Udine's bishops, and one of them brought the artist here to Udine to paint these airy frescoes depicting Old Testament scenes (note, however, that the familiar Biblical characters wear clothing that looks disarmingly worldly, like those fashionable in 18th-century Europe, in fact). The palazzo (☎ 0432/250-03) is open Wednesday to Sunday from 10am to noon and 3:30 to 6:30pm, and admission is 4,000L ($2.35). One more museum deserves a visit, and that is the **Museo d'Arte Moderno,** on the other side of the city on Piazza Diacono (from Piazza della Libertà follow Via Mazzini and Via Anton Morro north to the edge of the old center). Here you will be shaken out of the reverie induced by Tiepolo's airy views of miracles and the afterlife—the galleries are filled, surprising in a small provincial city, with the works of 20th-century powerhouses such as Picasso and Giogio De Chirico, as well as 1970s works by Americans Lichtenstein and de Kooning.

WHERE TO STAY

Al Vecchio Tram. V. Brenari 32, 33100 Udine. ☎ **0432/502-516**. 10 units, 2 with bathroom. 35,000L ($20.60) single without bathroom; 55,000L ($32.35) double without bathroom; 65,000L ($38.25) double with bathroom. No credit cards.

What's best about this old hotel is its location—it's one of the few hotels in the city center, and one of the few lower-cost hostelries you'll be able to reach from the train station without taking a bus or taxi. Just about the only amenity is a friendly neighborhood bar on the ground floor, convenient for breakfast or a glass of wine in the evening. Upstairs, the rooms are large and very clean, though very basically furnished, and with creaky beds. Most of the rooms are bathroom-less, but all are only a few steps away from the ample and clean facilities in the hallways.

Hotel Europa. Vle. Europa Unità 37, 33100 Udine. ☎ **0432/294-446**. Fax 0432/512-654. 50 units, all with bathroom. MINIBAR TV TEL. 80,000L ($47) single, 120,000L ($70.60) double. Breakfast 12,000L ($7.05). AE, DC, V.

The blocks in front of Udine's train station are a pleasant residential neighborhood and many of the city's hotels are clustered here. The Europa is one of the nicest, with a new renovation that, instead of rendering the premises banally modern, has combined style and comfort. A lot of old-world charm remains in the ground-floor lobby and breakfast areas, while the guest rooms are handsomely outfitted with sleek wood cabinetry and headboards, thick carpeting, and some nice touches that include brass wall lamps and framed reproductions. All of the bathrooms are new and equipped with generous basins and stall showers. The quietest rooms are those in the back, facing a sunny courtyard, but double glazing on the windows keeps noise in the front rooms to a minimum, too.

WHERE TO DINE

Caffè Bistrot. Pz. Matteotti. ☎ **0432/506-341.** Sandwiches and snacks from 4,000L ($2.35). Tues–Fri 7:45am–2am and Sat–Sun 9am–2am. MC, V. CAFE.

This welcoming cafe faces Udine's oldest square, which is surrounded by tall old houses with porticos and where a colorful morning produce market is held. You can take in these atmospheric surroundings from a table on the terrace, though the interior rooms, which spread across two floors, are inviting. Students, businesspeople, and neighborhood residents alike sit for hours chatting and reading over a cup of coffee or one of the excellent local wines served by the glass (from 1,500L/90¢). The delicious homemade pastries make this a popular breakfast spot, and a large assortment of gelato (from 2,000L/$1.20 for a single scoop) is dispensed late into the night. Sandwiches and a few other dishes, including an *insalata caprese* (with mozzarella, basil, and tomato) and crepes filled with ham and cheese, are also served throughout the day and night.

Osteria Florio. Vc. d. Banca. ☎ **0432/501-524.** Primi 8,000–10,000L ($4.70–$5.90); secondi 12,000–18,000L ($7.05–$10.60). AE, MC, V. Mon–Sat noon–3pm and 7:30–11pm.

One of the streams that lace Udine rushes past one side of this osteria. In good weather you can enjoy a waterside table on a pleasant terrace. At other times, dining is in a large room that is simply but elegantly furnished, with sepia prints of Old Udine adorning the walls. The menu provides an excellent way to sample the local cuisine, which tends to be hearty. A *zuppa d'orzo e fagioli* (soup with barely and beans) or *orecchiette al radichio* (ear-shaped pastas in a sauce of this pungent red-colored green, lightly grilled) are excellent starters, while *gulyas* (the local spelling of goulash) or *salame con polenta* (salami sautéed with vinegar and served on a bed of polenta) are typical regional main courses and are excellent here.

Ristorante-Pizzeria Al Portici. V. Veneto 8. ☎ **0432/508-975.** Primi 7,000–15,000L ($4.10–$8.80); secondi 8,000–20,000L ($4.70–$11.75). Pizzas from 6,000L ($3.55). MC, V. Wed–Mon 9am–1am. PIZZERIA/UDINESE.

Udine has a large and energetic population of students, and they seem to spend much of their time in this large trattoria with red-checked tablecloths. The pizza oven turns out the most popular fare, but you can also dip into some of the city's simple, casual cuisine here, such as *cialzons*, as gnocchi are called here and often stuffed with smoked ricotta cheese, and *brovada* (a poor man's dish of turnips and pork sausage). Given the establishment's long opening hours, you can stop by any time during the day for a coffee or beer, or a glass of some of the excellent Friuli wines.

7 Trieste

158 km (98 mi.) E of Venice, 68 km (40 mi.) SE of Udine, 408 km (245 mi.) E of Milan

On a map, Trieste faces west, toward the rest of Italy, to which it is appended by a long, narrow sliver of coast that juts into what is now Slovenia. For many of its traditions, though, from the Slavic dialects you are likely to hear in the streets to the addition of goulash and Viennese pastries to its menus, this handsome city of medieval, neoclassical, and modern buildings turns to other parts of Europe. Mostly, though, Trieste turns to the Adriatic for inspiration and for a sense of its past. Already a thriving port by the time it was absorbed into the Roman Empire at the second century A.D., Trieste competed with Venice for control of the seas from the 9th through the 15th centuries. For several centuries it thrived under the Hapsburgs; in the late 18th century, Maria Theresa, and later her heirs and successors, gave the city its grandiose neoclassical look. The city was the chief seaport of the Austro-Hungarian Empire until the end of World War I, when the Friuli was reunited with Italy. That changed again during World War II, when Trieste fell to the Nazis in 1943, went to Yugoslavia at the end of the war, then rejoined Italy in 1954. Politics continue to shape this city—today you're likely to notice the influx of refuges from war torn parts of the former Yugoslavia. You're also likely to notice that Trieste is a seagoing city. The traditional passeggiata here means a stroll along the waterfront to enjoy a sea breeze and watch the sun set over the Adriatic.

In the city's remaining cafes (thinner on the ground now than they were before World War I), you can experience its history as one of Europe's intellectual centers. James Joyce arrived in 1904 and stayed for more than a decade, teaching English and writing *Portrait of an Artist* and at least part of *Ulysses;* the poet Rainer Maria Rilke lived nearby; and the city was home to Italo Svevo, one of Italy's greatest 20th-century novelists, and to Umberto Saba, one of its greatest 20th-century poets.

FESTIVALS & MARKETS   The city celebrates summer with a series of concerts and films, many free and held in the outdoor theater in the **Castello di San Giusto.** If you are going to be in Trieste at this time, ask the tourist office for a copy of *Eventi Luglio-Agosto.* Trieste's two food markets provide colorful surroundings and a chance to eye the makings of the local cuisine. The covered market, at the corner of Via Carducci and Via della Majolica, is open Monday from 8am to 2pm and Tuesday through Saturday from 8am to 7pm. The open-air market is on Ponte Ponterosso, alongside the canal that cuts into the center of the city from the harbor, and it operates Tuesday through Saturday from 8am to 5:30pm.

ESSENTIALS

GETTING HERE   By Train   Trains arrive at and depart from Stazione Centrale on Piazza della Liberta (☎ 040/418-207), northwest of the historic center. There are on average two trains an hour to and from **Venice,** 2½ hours away; 14,000L/$8 (from there you can make connections to Milan and other Italian cities). There are also frequent, twice-hourly connections to and from **Udine,** 1½ hours away (4,600L/$2.70) Two trains a day connect Trieste and **Budapest,** an 11-hour trip; 87,000L ($51.20).

By Bus   The bus station is on Corso Cavour, just across Piazza della Liberta from the train station (☎ 040/336 0300). Frequent buses (28 a day) link Trieste and **Udine** (1½ hours away; 6,900L/$4), and many other towns throughout the region.

By Car   Trieste is a 2-hour trip from Venice along the Autostrada **A4.**

VISITOR INFORMATION   There are two main tourist offices in Trieste where English is spoken and cultural information is dispensed. One is in Stazione Centrale (☎ 040/420-182), and is open Monday through Saturday from 9am to 7pm and Sunday from 10am to 1pm and 4 to 7pm. The other is closer to the center, at V. San Nicolo 20 (☎ 040/679-611). It is open Monday through Friday from 8:30am to 7pm and on Saturday from 8:30am to 1pm.

CITY LAYOUT   The center of Trieste, which is snuggled between the hills and the sea, is compact and easy to get around on foot. The bus and train stations are at the northern end of the center, on the Piazza della Libertà. From there, follow the harbor south for about 10 minutes along **Corso Cavour** (you'll soon cross Trieste's Canal Grande, a pale imitation of its Venetian counterpart) and its continuation, **Riva III Novembre,** to the **Piazza dell'Unità d'Italia.** This dramatic space—with Hapsburg-commissioned, neoclassical buildings on three sides, open to the sea on one side, and a fountain in its center—is the heart of old Trieste and the present-day city as well. **Via Carducci,** Trieste's main shopping street, cuts through the center of the orderly 19th-century city. It begins in Piazza Oberdan (a few blocks east of the train station on Via Ghega) and cuts a straight swath south to Piazza Goldoni; from there, the Corso Italia leads west to Piazza dell'Unità d'Italia and the sea.

GETTING AROUND   Central Trieste is easily navigable on foot, but the footsore can use the extensive network of ACT buses and trams (☎ **040/779-51**) that run throughout the city. You can purchase tickets at any *tabacchi* for 1,200L (70¢). One foot-saving route is the no. 24 line from the train station to the hilltop Castello San Giusto and its adjoining cluster of remarkable buildings (see below).

WHAT TO SEE & DO

The oldest part of Trieste climbs the **Colle Capitolino** (Capitoline Hill), just behind the grandiose Piazza dell'Unità d'Italia and is where many of the city's most interesting museums and monuments (including Roman remains) are located. A good way to approach the hill is to leave the southeastern end of Piazza dell'Unità d'Italia and step into Piazza Cavana. In contrast to the assemblage of 18th- and 19th-century buildings on the main piazza, this part of Trieste is medieval, a warren of tiny streets climbing the hillside away from the sea. From Piazza Cavana follow Via Felice Veneziano to Via Cattedrale, and follow that for about 10 minutes up the flanks of the Colle Capitolino to the church of San Giusto (see below); just above that is the Castello di San Giusto (see below), from which Trieste and the Adriatic will unfold in an unforgettable view at your feet. For a quicker descent you can take the 265-step **Scala dei Giganti** (Steps of the Giants) back down the hill to Piazza Goldoni and Via Carducci, Trieste's main shopping street.

Cattedrale di San Giusto. Pz. Cattedrale, Colle Capitolino. ☎ **040/302-874.** Free admission. Daily 8:30am–noon and 4–7pm.

This hilltop basilica is one of several remarkable buildings atop the Colle Capitollino (Capitoline Hill), which is littered with the Roman ruins that are evidence of the city's long history as an important port. In fact, the cathedral's squat, 14th-century campanile rises from the ruins of a first-century A.D. Roman temple. Pleasingly asymmetrical and unornamented except for a large rose window, the cathedral is dedicated to Saint Just, Trieste's patron saint. It incorporates two 5th-century Romanesque basilicas, one also dedicated to San Giusto and the other to Santa Maria Assunta. You'll see what remains of both as you step inside: The two right-hand naves belong to the original San Giusto, the two left-hand naves to Santa Maria Assunta, and in the center is the 14th-century nave that was added to bring them together.

Castello di San Giusto. Pz. Cattedrale, Colle Capitolino. ☎ **040/309-362.** Castle 2,000L ($1.20), Civico Museo del Castello 3,000L ($1.75). Daily 9am–sunset, museum Tues–Sat 9am–1pm.

The tall walls of this bastion, built between 1470 and 1630, rise just behind the cathedral. Within the walls are an open-air theater, the **Cortile delle Milizie,** where a summer film and concert festival is held (see "Festivals & Markets" above) and the

Civico Museo, but the walls themselves steal the show. A walk along them affords amazing views over Trieste and the Adriatic, making this a popular spot just before its sunset closing time. The museum provides an interesting if not profound experience—a series of period rooms includes a "Venetian chamber" that is filled with antique chests, 17th-century Flemish tapestries and other furnishings, as is the **Appartamento del Capitano,** the residence of the castle's 18th-century commander. A collection of antique weaponry is housed in the rooms of the castle watch.

Museo di Storia e Arte. V. Cattedrale 15. ☎ **040/310-500.** Admission 2,000L ($1.20), 1,000L (60¢) students. Daily 9am–1pm.

The Via Cattedrale is on one of the old streets leading down the to the seafront, and this excellent small collection warrants a stop en route. This is Trieste's archeological collection, and it includes prehistoric finds, exquisite Greek pieces (including some fine vases) and remnants of the city's Roman past. The bulk of Roman architectural fragments, though, are scattered about the **Orto Lapidario** (Lapidary Garden), to one side of the museum (and included in the admission price). A few rooms of the museum house a growing Egyptian collection, which includes a female mummy. Two other remnants of Roman Trieste are near the bottom of the Colle Capitolino. If you descend on Via Cattedrale you'll come to the **Arco di Riccardo,** one of the gates of the Roman city built by Octavian in A.D. 33. The arch is near the foot of Via Teatro Romano, which you can follow for a few blocks for a look at the Teatro Romano (Roman Theater), built in the second century A.D. Only partially unearthed, you can glimpse the ruins through a fence, and let your imagination take you to the days when 6,000 spectators packed in for gladiatorial contests.

NEARBY SIGHTS

Castello di Miramare. V. Miramare, Grignano. ☎ **040/224-143.** Castle 8,000L ($4.70), children under 19 and seniors over 60 free, English-language tours available for 22,000L ($12.95); grounds free. Castle Apr–Sept daily 9am–6pm; Oct–Mar daily 9am–1pm. Grounds Apr–Sept daily 9am–7pm; Oct–Mar daily 9am–5pm. Bus: 36 (catch it at train station).

This vision of gleaming white turrets looms over the coast north of the city, 4½ miles from the center. Archduke Maximilian, brother of Austrian Emperor Franz Joseph, built this castle in the 1850s when he was assigned to Trieste to command the Austrian Navy. The interior reflects the somewhat insipid royal taste of the day, with room after room of gilt and velvet. Far more romantic are the adjoining gardens, where oaks, firs, and cypresses sway in sea breezes. Alluring, too, is the belief that those who sleep in the castle will meet a violent end, and history has put some credence to the legend—the same Maximilian went to Mexico in 1864 to assume the brief role of emperor and was shot there in 1867; Archduke Ferdinand spent the night here before journeying to Sarajevo, where he was assassinated on the eve of World War I; and a later owner, Duke Amadeo of Austria, was also assassinated in 1938.

For sheer theatrics in such a theatrical setting, you can attend one of the campy sound-and-light shows in July and August; they depict Maximilian's final days in Mexico and are staged Tuesday, Thursday, and Sunday at 9:30 and 10:45pm; tickets begin at 15,000L ($8.80).

Grotto Gigante. Opicina. ☎ **040/327-312.** Admission 13,000L ($7.65), 9,000L ($5.30) children 6 to 14. Mar and Oct, Tues–Sun 9am–noon and 2–5pm, tours every 30 min.; Apr–Sept 9am–noon and 2–7pm, tours every 30 min.; Nov–Feb 10am–noon and 2:30–4:30pm, tours every hour. Bus: 45.

The "Gigantic Cave" lives up to its name: 380 feet high, the single-chamber cave is said to be the world's largest underground cavern that can be visited. You can do so on guided tours (in Italian) only, during which you ascend and descend on a series of staircases. The cave is about 9 miles north of the city near the community of Opicina. An exciting way to get to the cave is via the rickety tram that climbs into the hills from Place Oberdan (just west of the train station) and ends at Opicina, where you can catch the no. 45 bus to the cave. The tram runs every 20 minutes from 7:30am to 8pm, and the fare is 2,000L ($1.20).

WHERE TO STAY

Albergo Milano. V. Ghega 17, 34132 Trieste. ☎ **040/369-680**. Fax 040/369-727. 44 units, all with bathroom. A/C TV TEL. 130,000L ($76.45) single, 180,000L ($105.90) double. Rates include breakfast. AE, DC, MC, V. Parking 20,000L ($11.75).

Quiet and geared to business travelers as well as foreigners, this modern hotel is near the train station but within an easy walk to most of the sights in the city center. There's a spacious lounge and bar on the ground floor, as well as a breakfast room where a generous buffet, the only meal served, is laid out in the morning. The bright, cheerful guest rooms are decorated in contemporary style with wood-veneer furnishings to provide a comfortable ambience. The small bathrooms are completely up-to-date.

Hotel al Teatro. Capo di Pz. G. Bartoli 1, 34132 Trieste. ☎ **040/366-220**. Fax 040/366-050. 45 units, 35 with bathroom. TV TEL. 75,000L ($44.10) single without bathroom, 100,000L ($58.80) single with bathroom; 115,000L ($67.65) double without bathroom, 150,000L ($88.25) double with bathroom. Rates include breakfast. AE, MC, V. Parking 32,000L ($18.85).

Not only does this old hotel enjoy a wonderful location steps away from the Piazza dell'Unita d'Italia, it also provides a lot of character along with its old-fashioned comforts. Occupying a late 18th-century building, the hotel takes its name from the nearby Roman theater, although it has long been the preferred hostelry for performers appearing at the Teatro Verdi. The large, parquet-floored rooms are very comfortable, and the 1970s-style furnishings complement the bohemian ambience. The bathrooms are perfectly adequate though a few could do with an overhaul to replace worn fixtures.

Locanda Centro. V. Roma 13, 34100 Trieste. ☎ **040/634-408**. 16 units, none with bathroom. 55,000L ($32.35) single, 65,000L ($38.25) double. No credit cards.

If securing an inexpensive bed in a central location is your only lodging requirement, this simple pensione is a good choice; if you desire more than that, you'll probably be happier elsewhere. The centro occupies a floor of a large building about midway between the train station and the Piazza dell'Unità d'Italia, and it is less than a 10-minute walk to either. Though amenities here are few and far between, the management is extremely friendly and keeps the premises, including down-the-hall facilities, in tiptop shape. The smallish rooms are furnished with not much more than cotlike beds and an armoire, but most guests prefer to relax in a lounge off the tiny reception area.

WHERE TO EAT

Al Bagatto. V. F. Venezian 2. ☎ **040/301-771**. Reservations required. Primi 10,000–20,000L ($5.90–$11.75); secondi 15,000–35,000L ($8.80–$20.60). AE, MC, V. Mon–Sat noon–3pm and 7:30–10pm. Closed Aug 15–30 and Dec 15–31. SEAFOOD

The best fish restaurant in Trieste occupies simply decorated quarters, overseen by a staff that seems to have been working the perpetually crowed dining room for decades. The emphasis is clearly on the freshest fish in simple but tasty preparations. *Risotto ai frutti di mare* is laden with tiny shrimp and squid from the Gulf of Trieste, and they also find their way into the *zuppa di pesce*. It would be a shame, though, to come this far and not join most of the other diners in the house's *frittura mista,* a delicately fried sampling of the sea creatures that are fresh at the market that morning. You'll push the bill up to the splurge-meal range in doing so, but chances are you won't regret it.

Buffet da Pepi. V. Cassa di Risparimo 3. ☎ **040/366-858.** Fixed-price menu 15,000L ($8.80). No credit cards. Mon–Sat 9am–9pm. Closed July 15–Aug 7. TRIESTINO

Trieste has many such self-service *tavola caldi* like this, though none compare to century-old Pepi, a much-beloved institution and one of the most popular eateries in the city. You work your way down a line and pile a plate with the offerings for a set price (15,000L/$8.80), but this is where the similarities to an American all-you-can eat buffet end. There are many varieties of pork dishes, the house specialty: spicy *cotechini* (pork sausages), *porchetta* (roast pork), *bolito di maiale* (a Trieste dish of boiled pork), and prosciutto, served with *crauti* (sauerkraut) and other vegetables.

La Piola. V. San Nicolò 1/b. ☎ **040/366-354.** Primi 8,000–15,000L ($4.70–$8.80); secondi 10,000–18,000L ($5.90–$10.60). Fixed-price menu 20,000L ($11.75) at lunch. AE, MC, V. Mon–Sat noon–3pm and 7:30–10pm. Closed July 15–Aug 7. TRIESTINO

This animated trattoria in the center of town near Trieste's Greek Orthodox church of San Nicolò dei Greci is popular with workers from the surrounding offices. The *jota*, a soup of beans and cabbage, *cvapcci* (Trieste's special meatballs, with their unique spelling), and *gnocchi di patate* (potato gnocchi filled with cheese) and many other fresh pastas are excellent, especially those topped with fresh porcini mushrooms. Main courses concentrate on meat, including a *bistecche di cavallo* (horsemeat steak) or *costine di miale* (roast pork ribs), though fresh Adriatic fish, served grilled, is often available.

COFFEE & GELATO

Coffee is one of Trieste's most important products—**Illy** and many other major Italian brands are located here. More to the point for travelers, coffee-drinking is a local pastime, and the city's exquisite blends can be enjoyed in any number of august cafes. **Caffe degli Specchi** at Pz. dell'Unità d'Italia 7 (☎ **040/605-33**) enjoys a marvelous position on the city's main, seafront piazza, making its terrace a prime spot to linger. In bad weather, a series of elegant rooms fill with shoppers and business people. The pastries are excellent, as is the coffee. James Joyce spent much of his 12 years in Trieste at **Caffè-Pasticceria Pirona** on Lgo. Barriera Vecchia 12 (☎ **040/630-46**). It was here that he allegedly wrote part of *Ulysses.* With its photographs of old Trieste and gilded mirrors, the premises bear the mark of one of Europe's great remaining literary cafes. **Caffè San Marco** at V. Battisti 18 (☎ **040/371-373**) is one of Trieste's most elegant cafes; it dates from 1914, with a Liberty-style (as art nouveau is called in Italy) interior. A pianist puts the final touches on the ultimate cafe experience.

Gelateria Zampolli at V. Ghega 10 (☎ **040/364-868**) is reputed to be the best gelateria in Trieste. It's located near Stazione Centrale and the city center, serving more than 50 flavors, made on the premises daily. Another Zampolli, owned by a different member of the same family, is located on Pz. Cavana 6, just south of Piazza dell'Unità d'Italia.

Milan, Lombardy & the Lakes

by Stephen Brewer

There is a lot more to Italy's most prosperous province than the factories that fuel its economy. Many of the attractions here are urban—in addition to Milan, a string of Renaissance cities dots the Lombardian plains, from Pavia to Mantua. To the north the region bumps up against craggy mountains and romantic lakes and to the south Lombardy spreads out in fertile farmlands fed by the Po and other rivers. The Lombardians, who over the centuries have been ruled by feudal dynasties, the Spanish, the Austrians, and the French, are a little more continental than their neighbors to the south, faster talking, and a little more fast-paced as well. They even dine a little differently, tending to eschew olive oil for butter and often forgoing pasta for polenta and risotto.

Among the region's greatest treasures (aside from some notable works of art and architecture, of course) are lakes—*the Italian lakes,* admired over the centuries by poets and writers from Catullus to Ernest Hemingway. Backed by the Alps and ringed by lush gardens and verdant forests, each has its own charms and, accordingly, its own enthusiasts. Not least among these charms are their easy accessibility to many Italian cities, making them ideal for short retreats: **Lago Maggiore** and **Lago di Como** are both less than an hour's distance from Milan, and **Lago di Garda** is tantalizingly close to Venice, Verona, and Mantua.

REGIONAL CUISINE Polenta or risotto—a meal in Lombardy will probably start with one or the other, and both are served in variations that can sometimes stand in for an entire meal. *Polenta alla Bergamasca,* for one, is cooked with tomatoes, sausage and cheese, and creamy risottos are often embellished with fish (in Mantua, perhaps with pike-like *luccio*) or any other ingredients an innovative chef might find at hand; one of the simplest and ever so common preparations here is *risotto alla milanese,* infused with saffron. In Mantua, you have a third choice of pasta—*tortelli,* little envelopes that are folded over and stuffed most commonly with zucca, or pumpkin. Meat dishes tend to be plain and hearty. Best known and most typical of the region are *ossobuco,* slowly braised veal shank served with *gremolada,* a sauce of lemon and parsley) and *cotoletta all milanese,* a veal cutlet that is breaded, dipped in egg and sautéed in butter—not what would be considered a healthy dish, but so delicious it warrants a departure from a diet at least once during a stay in the region.

1 Milan (Milano)

552 km (343 mi.) NW of Rome, 288 km (179 mi.) NW of Florence, 257 km (160 mi.) W of Venice, 140 km (87 mi.) NE of Turin, 142 km (88 mi.) N of Genoa

True, Italy's financial center, business hub, fashion capital, and one of the most industrialized major cities is crowded, noisy, hot in the summer and damp and foggy in the winter, less easy-going and more expensive than other Italian places—in short, not as immediately appealing a stopover as Venice, Florence, or Rome. Milan, though, reveals its long and event-filled history in a pride of monuments, museums, and churches, sets one of the finest tables in Italy, and supports a cultural scene that embraces La Scala, fashion shows, and nightlife. With its dazzling shop windows and sophisticated ways, Milan is a pleasure to get to know—and, despite all that's been said about the city's exorbitant prices, you needn't empty the bank account to do so.

FESTIVALS & MARKETS   Though it's overshadowed by the goings-on in Venice, Milan's pre-Lenten Carnevale is becoming increasingly popular, with costumed parades and an easygoing good time, much of it focusing around Piazza del Duomo beginning a week or so before Ash Wednesday. Just before the city shuts down in August, the city council stages a series of June and July dance, theater, and music events in theaters and open-air venues around the city; call ☎ 02/8646-4094 for more information.

In a city as well dressed as Milan, it only stands to reason that some great-looking castoffs are bound to turn up at street markets. **Milan's largest street market** is the one held on Via Papiniano in the Ticinese/Navigli district on Tuesday mornings from 8am to 1pm and on Saturdays from 9am to 7:30pm; many of the stalls sell designer's seconds as well as barely used high-fashion ware (Metro: Sant'Agostino). There's an **antique market** on Via Fiori Chiari in the Brera district the third Saturday of each month, from 9am to about 7:30pm, but not in August (Metro: Moscova) and another the last Sunday of each month on the quays along the Canale Grande in the Navigli district the last Sunday of each month, from 9am to about 7:30pm (☎ 02/8940-9971; Metro: Sant'Agostino). Every Sunday morning there's a large **flea market,** with everything from books to clothing to appliances, at the San Donato metro stop. A fascinating array of handicrafts, from different regions of Italy and around the world, is on sale at the market around Viale Tunisia, Tuesday through Sunday from 9:30am to 1pm and 3 to 7:30pm (☎ 02/2940-8057; Metro: Porta Venezia). The city's largest **food market** is the one at Piazza Wagner, just outside the city center due west of the church of Santa Maria delle Grazie (follow Corso Magenta and its extension, Corso Vercelli to Piazza Piemonte; the market is 1 block north; it's held Tuesday through Saturday from 8am to 1pm and 4pm to 7:30pm and Monday from 8am to 1pm; the displays of mouthwatering foodstuffs fill an indoor market space and stalls that surround it (Metro: Piazza Wagner).

ESSENTIALS

GETTING HERE   By Train   Milan is one of Europe's busiest rail hubs, with connections to all major cities on the Continent. Trains arrive and depart about every half hour to and from **Venice** (3 hours, 36,000L/$21.50), and hourly to and from **Rome** (5 hours, 68,000L/$40), and hourly to and from **Florence** (3 hours, 38,000L/$22.35). **Stazione Centrale,** a vast structure of Facist-era design, is about a half-hour walk northeast of the center, with easy connections to Piazza del Duomo by metro, tram, and bus. The station stop on the metro is **Centrale F.S.**; it is only 10 minutes (and 1,500L/88¢) away from the Duomo stop, in the heart of the city. If you want to see something of the city en route, take the no. 60 bus from the station to

Lombardy & The Lake District

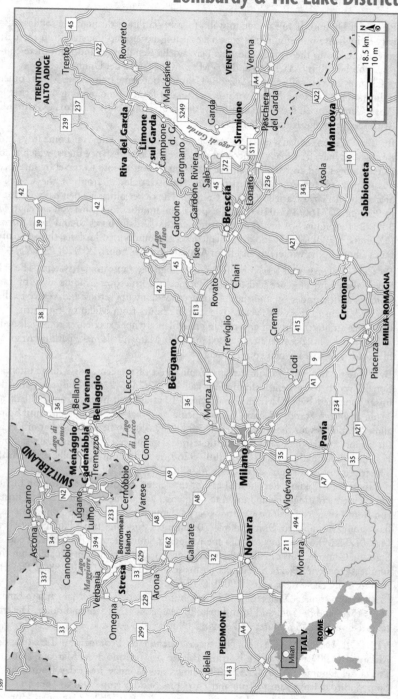

Piazza del Duomo. If you decide to walk, follow Via Pisani through the soulless district of high-rise office buildings that have sprung up around the station in the past several decades to the equally cheerless Piazza della Repubblica, and from there continue south on busy Via Turati and Via Manzoni to Piazza del Duomo.

Chances are you will arrive at Stazione Centrale, but some trains serve Milan's other train stations: **Stazione Nord** (with service to and from Como, among other cities), **Porta Genova** (with service to and from Alessandria and Asti), and **Porta Garibaldi** (with service to and from Lecco).

By Bus Given Milan's excellent rail links with other cities in Lombardy and throughout Italy, it's usually unnecessary to travel by long-distance buses, which tend to take longer and cost more than the trains do. If you choose to travel by intercity bus, expect to arrive at and depart from **Autostradale,** in front of the Castello Sforzesco on Piazza Castello (Metro: Cairoli). The ticket office is open daily 6:30am to 9:30pm, ☎ **166/845-010** (this is a special toll number for which you are charged 500L/29¢ a minute). A few common runs are the 12 daily buses to and from **Turin** (2½ hours, 5,700L/$3.35) and, for Milanese ski and outdoor enthusiasts, the two daily buses (more in the winter) to and from **Aosta** (allow 3½ hours, 20,000L/$11.75).

By Car Milan is well served by Italy's superhighway (autostrada) system. The **A1** links Milan with Florence and Rome (Florence is a little over 3 hours away by car, Rome is a little under 6), and the A4 connects Milan with Verona and Venice to the east and Turin to the west (Venice is about 2½ hours from Milan by car, Turin is a little over an hour). Driving and parking in Milan are not experiences to be relished; in fact, much of the central city is closed to traffic. Many hotels make parking arrangements for guests; ask when you reserve a room.

By Plane Malpensa, 45 kilometers (27 mi.) west of the center, is Milan's international airport; for general information, call ☎ **02/7485-2200. Malpensa shuttle buses,** operated by STAM, run to Stazione Centrale half-hourly from 5:30am to 11pm and from Stazione Centrale to Malpensa every half-hour from 5am until 8pm; allow 50 minutes for the trip. Tickets (13,000L/$7.65) can be purchased at offices at the airport and at the Malpensa Shuttle terminal at the east end of the train station. For more information, call ☎ **02/4009-9260** (recorded info, partially in English). The trip into town by taxi costs about 90,000L ($52.95).

Linate, only 7 kilometers (4 mi.) east of the center, handles some European flights (which are increasingly being moved to Malpensa) and domestic flights. **STAM buses** run from Linate to Stazione Centrale every 20 minutes from 7am to 7pm and every half hour from 7 to 9pm; allow 20 minutes for the trip. Purchase tickets (4,500L/$2.65) on the bus or from the Malpensa Shuttle terminal at the east end of Stazione Centrale. You can also take a city bus, no. 73, to and from Linate, from the southeast corner of Piazza San Babila, just east of the Duomo (1,500L/88¢). The trip into town by taxi costs about 30,000L ($17.65).

Buses also connect Malpensa and Linate, but irregularly—from Malpensa to Linate at 10:45am and 3:45pm and from Linate to Malpensa at 9:15am and noon. The trip takes 1 hour and 15 minutes and costs 18,000L ($10.60).

VISITOR INFORMATION The main **Azienda di Promozione Turistica del Milanese (APT)** tourist office is in the Palazzo del Turismo at V. Marconi 1 on the Piazza del Duomo, ☎ **02/7252-4300;** hours are Monday to Friday from 8am to 8pm, Saturday from 9am to 1pm and 2 to 7pm, Sunday from 9am to 1pm and 2 to 5pm. There is also an office in Stazione Centrale, ☎ **02/7252-4360;** open Monday to Friday 8am to 7pm, Saturday 9am to 6pm and Sunday 9am to 12:30pm and 1:30 to 6pm. These offices issue maps, museum guides, hotel and restaurant listings, and a wealth of other useful information. Some helpful literature you can pick up for free are the periodicals *Milano: Where, When, How; Milano Mese;* and *Hello Milano,* all with extensive listings of museum exhibitions, performances and other events. Throughout the year, the APT leads sightseeing tours in English of the city's monuments and museums. They cost from 20,000 to 25,000L ($11.75 to $14.70) and include tours of the Duomo, the Galleria and La Scala; the Poldi-Pezzoli museum; the Pinacoteca Ambrosia; and the Pinacoteca Brera.

CITY LAYOUT   Think of Milan as a series of concentric circles radiating from the Piazza del Duomo at the center. Within the inner circle, once enclosed by the city walls, are many of the churches, museums, and shops that will consume your visiting hours. For a general overview of the lay of the land, obtain one of the serviceable maps, with indices, that the tourist offices provide for free.

GETTING AROUND   An extensive and efficient subway system (Metropolitana Milanese), trams, and buses make it very easy to move around Milan. The metro closes at midnight, though buses and trams run all night. Tickets good for one metro ride (or 75 minutes of surface transportation) cost 1,500 lire (88¢). You can also purchase a ticket good for unlimited travel for one day (5,000L/$2.95) or two days (9,000L/$5.30), and you can purchase a block of 10 tickets for 14,000L ($8.25). Tickets are available at metro stations and at newsstands. It's obligatory to stamp your ticket when you board a bus or tram—you can be slapped with a fine of 135,000L ($79.40) if you don't. For information about Milan public transportation, visit the ATM information office in the Duomo metro stop, open Monday through Saturday 7:45am to 7:15pm; ☎ **02/675-001.**

FAST FACTS: Milan

American Express   The office is just north of La Scala and near the Pinocoteca di Brera at V. Brera 3 (☎ **02/7200-3693**, and is open Monday to Thursday from 9am to 5:30pm, Saturday from 9am to 5pm (Metro: Cairoli). Card members can arrange cash advances, receive mail (the postal code is 20121), and wire money.

Bookstores   The American Bookstore, between the Duomo and Castello Sforzesco at V. Camperio 16 (off Via Dante) ☎ **02/878-920,** offers a large selection of English-language books, including many new titles from American publishers; it's open Monday from 2 to 7:30pm, Tuesday through Friday from 10am to 7pm and Saturday from 10am to 1pm and 2:30 to 7pm (Metro: Cardusio). **Rizzoli,** the glamorous outlet of one of Italy's leading publishers in the Galleria Vittorio Emanuele, ☎ **02/8646-1071,** also has some English-language titles, as well as a sumptuous collection of art and photo books; open daily 8am to 8pm. For English-language newspapers and magazines, check out the newsstands in Stazione Centrale and around Piazza del Duomo.

Consulates   Americans will find their consulate at V. Principe Amadeo 2/10, ☎ **02/290-35141;** it's open Monday through Friday from 9 to 11am and 2 to 4pm (Metro: Turati). The **Canadian Consulate** is at V. Pisani 19, ☎ **02/675-81,** open Monday to Thursday 8:30am to 12:30pm and 1:15 to 5:30pm (Metro: F.S. Centrale or Repubblica); the **British Consulate** is V. San Paolo 7, ☎ **02/230-01,** open Monday to Friday from 9:15am to 12:15am and 2:30 to 4:30pm (Metro: Duomo); the **Australian consulate** is at V. Borgogna 2, ☎ **02/777-041,** open Monday to Thursday 9am to noon and 2 to 4pm (Metro: San Babila); and the **New Zealand Consulate** is at V. Arezzo 6, ☎ **02/4801-2544,** open Monday to Friday from 9am to 11am (Metro: Pagano).

Crime   For Police emergencies dial ☎ **113;** you can reach the English-speaking staff at the tourist police at ☎ **02/863-701.** There is a police station in Stazione Centrale and the main station, the Questura, is just west of the Giardini Pubblici at V. Fatebenefratelli 11, ☎ **02/622-61** (Metro: Turati). Milan is generally safe, with some notable exceptions, especially at night, including the public gardens, Parco Sempione, and the area to the west of Stazione Centrale. The train station is notorious for pickpockets, whose favorite victims seems to be distracted passengers lining up for the airport buses at the east side of the building. You should likewise be vigilant for pickpockets on all public transportation and at street markets.

Currency Exchange   The Banca Cesare Ponti, Pz. d. Duomo 19, ☎ **02/ 88211,** is one of many banks on and around this central square offering currency exchange (look for the "CAMBIO" sign); banks are generally open Monday through Friday from 8:30am to 1:30pm and 2:45 to 3:45pm. The currency exchange at Stazione Centrale is open Monday through Saturday from 8:30am to 1pm and 2 to 7:30pm, and currency exchanges at the airports are generally open daily from 7:30am to 9pm or later—all of these, however, charge higher commissions than do banks in the central city. ATMs, from which you can withdraw funds in lire against your bank account at home, are located throughout Milan; they are especially plentiful in and around Piazza del Duomo.

Drugstores   Pharmacies rotate 24-hour shifts; dial ☎ **192** to find pharmacies that are open around the clock on a given day or look for sign posted in most pharmacies announcing which shop is keeping a 24-hour schedule. The **Farmacia Stazione Centrale** (☎ **02/669-0735**), in the main train station, is open 24 hours daily and some of the staff speaks English.

Emergencies   The general number for emergencies is ☎ **113.** For the police, call ☎ **112;** for first aid or an ambulance, dial ☎ **118.**

Hospitals   The Ospedale Maggiore Policlinico, ☎ **02/556-812,** is centrally located a 5-minute walk southeast of the Duomo at V. Francesco Sforza 35 (Metro: Duomo or Missori). Some of the medical personnel speaks English.

Laundry   A handy place to have your clothes laundered is **Minola,** south of the Duomo at V. San Vito 5 (follow Via Torino south from the Piazza del Duomo for about 5 blocks where it intersects with Via San Vito, ☎ **02/5811-1271** (Metro: Missori). The staff will do your laundry (wash and dry) for 17,000L ($10) per 5 kilograms (11 lb.) and dry-cleaning for 20,000L ($11.76) per 5 kilos (11 lb.). Open Monday to Friday from 8am to 6pm and Saturday from 8am to noon.

Lost Property   The lost baggage number for Aeroporto della Malpensa is ☎ **02/7485-4215;** for Aeroporto Linate the number is ☎ **02/7010-2094.** The English-speaking staffs at these offices handle luggage that has gone astray on most airlines serving the airports, though a few airlines maintain their own lost baggage services. The lost and found at Stazione Centrale (located in the same office as the luggage storage) is open daily from 7am to 1pm and 2 to 8pm, ☎ **6371-2667.** The city-run lost-and-found office is just south of Piazza del Duomo at Via Friuli 30, ☎ **02/551 6141,** and is open Monday to Friday 8:30am to 12:45pm and 2:15 to 5pm (Metro: Duomo or Missori).

Luggage Storage   The luggage storage office in Stazione Central is open daily from 5am to 4am; the fee is 5000L ($2.95) per piece of baggage for each 12-hour period.

Milan

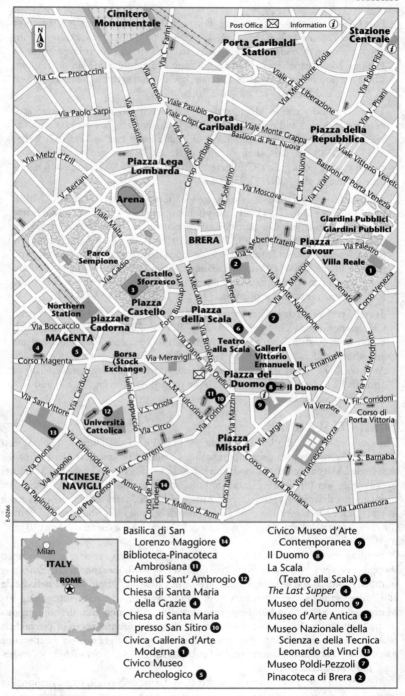

511

Post Office   The main post office, Poste e Telecommunicazioni, is just west of Piazza del Duomo at V. Cordusio 4, ☎ 02/805-6812 (Metro: Cardusio). Windows are open Monday to Friday 8am to 7:40pm and Saturday 8:30am to 1:50pm. Most branch offices are open Monday to Saturday 8:30am to 1:50pm. There is a post office in Stazione Centrale, open Monday through Friday 8:15am to 7:30pm and Saturday 8:15am to 3:30pm.

Taxis   To find a taxi in Milan, walk to the nearest taxi stand, usually located near major piazzas and major Metro stops. In the center, there are taxi stands at Piazza Duomo and Piazza della Scala. Or, call a radio taxi at ☎ **6767, 8585, 5353, or 8388** (the desk staff at many hotels will be happy to do this for you, even if you are not a guest). Cab meters start at 6,000L ($3.55), and add a nighttime surcharge of 5,000L ($2.95).

Telephones   You'll find Italy's orange public telephones throughout Milan. Local calls cost 200L (11¢), and the phones accept coins or phone cards (*carta telefonica*), which you can purchase at tobacco shops in increments of 5,000L ($2.95), 10,000L ($5.90) or 15,000L ($8.80). You can also make calls from the **SIP/Telecom office** in Stazione Centrale, open daily from 8am to 9:30pm, and the one in the Galleria Vittorio Emanuele, open daily from 8am to 7:30pm. Some phones in these offices also accept major credit cards, and you can buy Italian phone cards on the premises. The area code for Milan is ☎ **02.**

Travel Services   For budget travel options, including low-cost flights, contact CIS, in the Galleria Vittorio Emanuele, ☎ **02/863-701;** open Monday through Friday from 9am to 7pm, Saturday from 9am to 1pm and 2 to 6pm. Students and those under 25 should try CTS (Centro Turistico Studentesco), V. S. Antonio 2, ☎ **02/5830-4121,** open Monday through Friday from 9:30am to 1pm and 2 to 6pm (no lunchtime closing from June through August) and Saturday from 9:30am to noon.

WHAT TO SEE & DO

The city's major neighborhoods encircle the hub, Piazza del Duomo. Looking east from the Duomo, you can see the imposing **Castello Sforzesco,** at one end of the well-heeled Magenta neighborhood. You can walk to the Castello in about 15 minutes by following Via Orefici to Piazza Cordusio and from there Via Dante. The other major tourist draw in Magenta is the **Church of Santa Maria delle Grazie;** to reach it, you'll leave Via Dante at Via Meravigli, which becomes Via Magenta and leads to the church (total walking time from Piazza del Duomo to the church is about 20 minutes).

Heading north from the Piazza del Duomo, walk through the city's glass-enclosed shopping center (the world's first), the **Galleria Vittorio Emanuelle II.** Emerging from the northern end of the Galleria you'll be just steps away from **Piazza della Scala** and Milan's famous opera house. A walk northeast of about five minutes along Via Manzoni takes you to **Via Montenapoleone** and the city's high-fashion shopping district, the epicenter of Italian design. A walk of about 10 minutes north of Piazza della Scala along Via Brera brings you into the atmospheric neighborhood of the same name, where cobblestone streets and old palazzos surround the city's major art collection, **the Pinacoteca di Brera.**

Another neighborhood to set your sights on is **Ticinese/Navigli,** usually referred to by the last word in that combination, which translates as "canals." Beyond the central city and due south of Piazza del Duomo, the Navigli's old quays follow what remains of an elaborate canal system, designed in part by Leonardo da Vinci, that once laced

Milan in a Day

For an excellent overview of the city, hop aboard tram no. 20 bus, distinguished by "Ciao Milano" emblazoned on its sides, for a tour with commentary in English and five other languages. The 1 hour and 45-minute tours run daily at 11am, 1pm and 3pm and start at Piazza Castello (Metro: Cairoli); the cost is 30,000L ($17.65). For more information, call ☎ 02/805-5323.

through the city. The moody charm of these waterways is not lost on prosperous young Milanese who are converting old lofts and moving into former quarters of the working classes. The attendant bars and shops have appeared to serve their needs. You can walk to the Navigli in about 30 minutes from Piazza del Duomo by following Via Torino south to Corso Porta Ticinese, but a metro ride to Porta Genova will get you there more quickly.

Despite Milan's size and sprawl, many of its museums, churches, and other sights are within easy walking distance of one another in the vicinity of the Duomo and Castello Sforzesco.

Castello Sforzesco. Pz. Castello. ☎ **02/6208-3940.** Free admission. Tues–Sun, 9:30am–1pm and 2–5:30pm. Metro: Cairoli, Cadorna, or Lanza.

Though it's been clumsily restored many times, most recently at the end of the 19th century, this fortresslike castle continues to evoke Milan's two most powerful medieval and Renaissance families, the Viscontis and the Sforzas. The Viscontis built the castle in the 14th century and the Sforzas, who married into the Visconti clan and eclipsed them in power, reconstructed it in 1450. The most influential residents were Ludovico il Moro and Beatrice d'Este (he of the Sforzas and she of the famous Este family of Ferrara). After ill-advisedly calling the French into Italy at the end of the 15th century, Ludovico died in the dungeons of a château in the Loire valley—but not before the couple made the Castello and Milan one of Italy's great centers of the Renaissance. It was they who commissioned the works by Bramante and Leonardo da Vinci, and these splendors can be viewed on a tour of the miles of salons that surround the Castello's enormous courtyard. The salons house a series of small city-administered museums known collectively as the **Civici Musei Castello Sforzesco.** They include a pinacoteca with works by Bellini, Correggio and Magenta, and the extensive holdings of the Museo d'Arte Antica, filled with Egyptian funerary objects, prehistoric finds from Lombardy and the last work of 90-year-old Michelangelo, his unfinished *Pietà Rondanini.*

Chiesa di San Lorenzo Maggiore. Cor. di Porta Ticinese. Free admission. Mon–Sat 8am–noon and 3–6pm, Sun 10:30–11:15am and 3–5:30pm. Metro: Missori.

The oldest church in Milan attests to the days when the city was the capital of the Western Roman Empire. The 4th-century early Christian structure has been rebuilt and altered many times over the centuries (it's dome, the highest in Milan, is a 16th-century embellishment) but it still retains the flavor of its roots in its octagonal floor plan and a few surviving remnants. These include fifth-century mosaics (one depicting a beardless Christ) in the *Cappella di Sant'Aquilino,* which you enter from the atrium. A sarcophagus in the chapel is said to enshrine the remains of Galla Placidia, sister of Honorius, last emperor of Rome and wife of Ataulf, king of the Visigoths; ironically, her mausoleum is one of the mosaic masterworks of Ravenna, and it is most likely she is buried in Rome, where she died. You'll be rewarded with a glimpse at even earlier history if you follow the stairs from behind the altar to a cryptlike room that contains what remains of a Roman amphitheater.

Chiesa di Santa Maria delle Grazie. Pz. Santa Maria delle Grazie. ☎ **02/498-7588.** Admission to *Last Supper* 12,000L ($7.05), church free. *Last Supper* Tues–Sun 8am–1:45pm, church only Mon–Sat 7:30am–noon and 3–7pm, Sun 3:30–6:30pm. Metro: Cardona or Conciliazione.

What draws so many visitors here is the *Cenacolo Vinciano (Last Supper)*. From 1495 to 1497 Leonardo da Vinci painted this poignant portrayal of confusion and betrayal for the far wall of the refectory when this was a Dominican convent. Aldous Huxley called this fresco the "saddest work of art in the world," a comment in part on the deterioration that set in even before the paint had dried on the moisture-ridden walls. The fresco was completely repainted in the 18th and 19th centuries, and a recent restoration has done away with these centuries of overpainting, along with clumsy patching and damage inflicted when Napoléon's troops used the wall for target practice and Allied bombing during World War II left the fresco exposed to the elements for three years. Even so, the *Last Supper* is still, quite literally, a mere shadow of the work the artist intended it to be—only an outline and a few ghostly streaks of color remain, but the work, which captures the moment when Christ told his apostles that one of them would betray him, is amazingly powerful and emotional nonetheless. Only 25 people are allowed to view the fresco at one time, and they must pass through a series of devices that remove pollutants from clothing. Accordingly, lines are long.

Often overlooked are the other great treasures of this late 15th-century church, foremost among them the fine dome and other architectural innovations by the one of the great architects of the high Renaissance, Donato Bramante, who was also one of the first architects of St. Peter's in Rome. To one side of the apse, decorated in marble and terracotta, is a lovely cloister.

Chiesa di Sant'Ambrogio. Pz. Sant'Ambrogio 15. ☎ **02/8645-0895.** Church free; museum, 3,000L ($1.75). Church, Mon–Sat 9:30am–noon and 2:30pm–6:30pm; museum, Mon, Wed–Fri 10am–noon and 3–5pm, Sat–Sun 3–5pm, Tues 10am–noon. Metro: Sant'Ambrogio.

From the basilica that he constructed on this site in the 4th century A.D.—when he was bishop of Milan and the city, in turn, was briefly capital of the Western Roman Empire—Saint Ambrose had a profound effect on the development of the early church. Little remains of Ambrose's church, but the 11th-century structure built in its place, and renovated many times since, is remarkable. It has a striking atrium, lined with columned porticos and opening on side to the brick façade, with two ranks of loggias and, on either side, a bell tower. Look carefully at the door on the left, where you'll see a relief of Saint Ambrose. Note the overall effect of this architectural assemblage, because the church of Sant'Ambrogio set a standard for Lomard Romanesque architecture that you'll see imitated many times on your travels through Lombardy.

On your wanderings through the three-aisled nave you'll come upon a gold altar from Charlemagne's days in Milan, and, in the right aisle, the all-too-scant remains of a Tiepolo fresco cycle, most of it blown into oblivion by World War II bombs. The little that remains of the original church is the Sacello di San Vittore in Ciel d'Oro, a little chapel in which the cupola glows with fifth-century mosaics of saints (enter from the right aisle). The skeletal remains of Ambrose himself are on view in the crypt. One of the "later" additions as you leave the main church from the left aisle is another work of the great architect Bramante—his Portico dell Canonica, lined with elegant columns, some of which are sculpted to resemble tree trunks. The adjoining Museo di Sant'Ambrogio houses a small but riveting collection of treasures connected with the church, including some fragments of 5th-century mosaics.

Chiesa Santa Maria Presso di San Satiro. V. Torino (at V. Speronari). Free admission. Daily 9am–noon and 2:30–6pm. Metro: Duomo or Missori.

What makes this beautiful church, just south of Piazza del Duomo, so exquisite is what it doesn't have—space. Stymied by not being able to expand the T-shaped apse to classical Renaissance, cross-shaped proportions, the architect Bramante created a marvelous relief behind the high altar. The effect of the trompe-l'oeil columns and arches is not entirely convincing but nonetheless magical. Another gem lies to the rear of the left transept: the Cappella della Pietà, so called for the 15th-century terracotta pietà it now houses but built in the 9th century to honor Saint Satiro, the brother of Saint Ambrose. The namesake statue is not the most alluring adornment in this charming little structure; it's the lovely Byzantine frescoes and Romanesque columns that will catch your eye. While this little-visited complex is now eclipsed by other, more famous Milan churches, it was an important pilgrimage site in the 13th and 14th centuries, after news spread through Christendom that an image of the Madonna here shed real blood when stabbed.

Civica Galleria d'Arte Moderna (Civic Gallery of Modern Art). In the Villa Reale. V. Palestro 16. ☎ **02/7600-2819.** Free admission. Tues–Sun 9am–5pm. Metro: Porta Venezia.

The sumptuous palazzo, where Napoléon and his stepson Eugene de Beauharnais lived, houses a collection that is "modern" in the true 19th-century sense. The salons are filled with works by Lombardians and other Italian painters who embraced trends from France. You'll probably be more familiar with the works by Cézanne, Gauguin, and other non-Italian modernists also included in the galleries (in a section housing the noted Grassi Collection), but it's fascinating to see the same dreamy landscapes and the flight from creeping industrialism reflected in the works of lesser known Italian artists. The upper-floors of the museum house the equestrian works of 20th-century sculptor Marino Marini.

Civico Museo Archeologico. Cor. Magenta 15. ☎ **02/8645-0665.** Free admission. Tues–Sun, 9:30am–5:30pm. Metro: Cadorna.

The most fascinating finds in this sizable repository of civilizations past are the everyday items—tools, eating utensils, and jewelry from Roman Milan. The exhibits, which seem to fill every corner of the 16th-century monastery in which the museum is housed, also include Greek, Etruscan, and Roman pieces from throughout Italy; there's also a section devoted to ancient remains from Ghandara, India. You can get a glimpse of Roman architecture in the garden, where two Roman towers and a section of a road, part of the walls enclosing the settlement of Mediolanum, once capital of the Western Roman Empire, remain in situ. This lovely patch of greenery, incidentally, is an evocative place to rest from the rigors of museum going.

✪ **Duomo.** Pz. d. Duomo. ☎ **02/8646-3456.** Duomo free; admission to roof 6,000L ($3.55), 8,000L ($4.70) with elevator; crypt 2,000L ($1.20); baptistery 3,000L ($1.75); Duomo Museum 10,000L ($5.90) adults, 8,000L ($4.70) children under 18 and seniors 60 and older. Duomo, daily 7:15am–6:45pm. Roof, daily 9am–4:30pm. Crypt, daily 9am–noon and 2:30–6pm. Baptistery, Tues–Sun 10am–noon and 3–5pm. Duomo Museum, Tues–Sun 9:30am–12:30pm and 3–6pm. Metro: Duomo.

When Milanese think something is taking too long, they refer to it as *la fabbrica del duomo*—the making of the Duomo, a reference to the 5 centuries it took to complete the magnificent gothic cathedral that rises from the center of the city. The last of Italy's great gothic structures—begun by the ruling Visconti family in 1386—is the third largest church in the world (after St. Peter's in Rome and the Seville cathedral), with 135 marble spires, a stunning triangular facade, and 2,000-some statues flanking the massive but airy, almost fanciful exterior. The cavernous interior, lit by brilliant stained-glass windows, seats 40,000 but is unusually Spartan and serene, divided into five aisles by a sea of 52 columns. The poet Shelley used to sit and read Dante amid monuments that include a gruesomely graphic statue of *St. Bartholomew Flayed* and the tombs of Giacomo de Medici, two Viscontis, and many cardinals and archbishops. Another British visitor, Alfred, Lord Tennyson, rhapsodized about the view of the Alps from the roof, and on a clear day you may well do the same. You are joined high above Milan by a gold statue of *Madonnina* (the little Madonna), the city's beloved protectress.

Back on terra firma, the crypt contains the remains of San Carlo Borromeo, one of the early cardinals of Milan. A far more interesting descent is the one down the staircase to the right of the main entrance to the Battistero Paleocristiano, the ruins of a 4th-century church believed to be where Saint Ambrose baptized Saint Augustine.

The Duomo houses many of its treasures across the piazza in the Palazzo Reale, where the **Museo del Duomo** (☎ 02/860-358) adjoins the **Museo Civico d'Arte Contemporanea** (with works by living artists and such masters as De Chirico and Modigliani). Among the legions of statuary saints is a gem of a painting by Jacopo Tintoretto, *Christ at the Temple,* and some riveting displays chronicling the construction of the cathedral.

Galleria Vittorio Emanuele II. Just off Pz. d. Duomo and Pz. d. Scala. Metro: Duomo.

Milan's late 19th-century version of a piazza is this wonderful steel-and-glass–covered, cross-shaped arcade. More to the point, the elegant Galleria is the prototype of the enclosed shopping malls that were to become the hallmark of 20th-century consumerism. It's safe to say that none of the imitators have come close to matching the Galleria for style and flair. The designer of this urban marvel, Giuseppe Mengoni, didn't live to see the Milanese embrace his creation: He tripped and fell from a girder a few days before the Galleria opened in 1878. His shopping mall par excellence provides a lovely route between the Duomo and La Scala and is a fine locale for watching the flocks of well-dressed Milanese—you'll understand why the Galleria is called *Il Salotto di Milano* (the drawing room of Milan).

Museo Nazionale della Scienza e delle Tecnica Leonardo da Vinci. V. San Vittore 21. ☎ **02/4801-0040.** Admission 10,000L ($5.90), 6,000L ($3.55) children 18 and under and seniors 60 and over, 10,000L (5.90) for two people on Sat–Sun. Tues–Fri, 9:30am–5pm, Sat–Sun 9:30am–6:30pm. Metro: Sant'Ambrogio.

The heart and soul of this engaging museum are the reconstructions and models of Leonardo's submarines, airplanes, and other engineering feats (each exhibit includes a reproduction of the master's drawings and a model of his creations). This former Benedictine monastery and its beautiful cloisters are also filled with planes, trains, carriages, sewing machines, typewriters, optical devices, and other exhibits, including some enchanting recreations of workshops, that comprise one of the world's leading collections of mechanical and scientific wizardry.

Museo Poldi-Pezzoli. V. Manzoni 12. ☎ **02/794-889.** Admission 10,000L ($5.90). Tues–Fri 9:30am–12:30pm and 2:30–6pm; Sat 9:30am–12:30pm and 2:30–7:30pm, Sun 9:30am–12:30pm; closed Sun afternoons Apr–Sept. Metro: Duomo or Montenapoleone.

The pleasant effect of seeing the Bellinis, Bottecellis, and Tiepolos amid these salons is reminiscent of a visit to other private collections, such as the Frick Collection in New York City and the Isabella Stewart Gardner Museum in Boston. This stunning treasure trove leans a bit toward Venetian painters (Francesco Guardi's elegantly moody *Grey Lagoon* is here, for instance), but also ventures widely throughout Italian painting and into the northern and Flemish schools. It was amassed by 19th-century collector Giacomo Poldi-Pezzoli, who donated his villa and its treasures to the city in 1881. Antonio Pollaiuolo's *Portrait of a Young Woman* is the Italian equivalent of the Mona Lisa, in that it is a haunting image you will recognize immediately upon seeing it. The collections also include porcelain, watches, jewels and many of the palazzo's original furnishings.

Pinacoteca Ambrosiana. Pz. Pio XI, 2. Admission 12,000L ($7.05). Tues–Sun 10am–5:30pm. Metro: Cardusio.

Much to the appreciation of art lovers who waited through the late 1990s for the museum to reopen, this exquisite collection is housed in newly restored galleries. The collection focuses on treasures from the 15th through 17th centuries: *An Adoration* by Titian, Raphael's cartoon for his *School of Athens* in the Vatican, Bottecelli's *Madonna and Angels*, Caravaggio's *Basket of Fruit* (his only still life), and other stunning works hang in a series of intimate rooms. Notable (or infamous) among the paintings is *Portrait of a Musician*, attributed to Leonardo but, according to many scholars, of dubious provenance; if it is indeed a Leonardo, the haunting painting is the only portrait of his to hang in an Italian museum. The adjoining Biblioteca Ambrosiana, open to scholars only except for special exhibitions, houses a wealth of Renaissance literaria, including the letters of Lucrezia Borgia and a strand of her hair. The most notable holdings, though, are Leonardo's *Codice Atlantico*, 1,750 drawings and jottings the master did between 1478 and 1519. These and the library's other volumes, including a rich collection of medieval manuscripts, are frequently put on view to the public; at these times, an entrance fee of 18,000L ($10.60) allows entrance to both the library and the art gallery.

Pinacoteca di Brera. V. Brea 28. ☎ **02/722-631.** Admission 8,000L ($4.70), free for citizens of EU countries under 18 and over 60. Tues–Sat, 9am–5:30pm, Sun, 9am–12:30pm. Metro: Lanza or Montenapoleone.

This 17th-century palazzo houses one of Italy's finest collections of Medieval and Renaissance art; it's inarguably the world's finest collection of Northern Italian painting. The concentration of so many masterpieces here is the work of Napoléon, who used the palazzo as the repository for the art he confiscated from public and private holdings throughout northern Italy; fittingly, a bronze likeness of the emperor greets you upon entering the courtyard. Just as a sampling of what you'll encounter in these 40 or so rooms, three of Italy's greatest masterpieces hang here: Andrea Mantegna's *Dead Christ*, Raphael's *Betrothal of the Virgin*, and Piero della Francesa's *Madonna with Saints (the Montefeltro Altarpiece)*. It is an indication of this museum's ability to overwhelm visitors that the last two masterpieces hang near each other in one room dedicated to works by Tuscan and Umbrian painters.

Paintings are continually being rearranged, but in the wake of a recently completed renovation, in the first rooms you will not encounter Napoleonic bounty but the museum's sizeable collection of 20th-century paintings. From there you enter several galleries of sumptuous Venetian works, including Jacopo Tintoretto's *Finding of the Body of St. Mark*, in which the dead saint eerily confronts appropriately startled grave robbers who come upon his corpse. Caravaggio (*Supper at Emmaus* is his masterpiece here) is surrounded by works of his followers, and just beyond is a room devoted to works by foreigners; among them Rembrandt's *Portrait of a Young Woman*. Given Napoléon's fondness for the Venetian schools, it is only just that the final rooms are again filled with works from that city, including Canaletto's *View of the Grand Canal*.

Teatro alla Scala. Pz. d. Scala. ☎ **02/8053-418.** Admission to Museo Teatrale 5,000L ($2.95), 4,000L ($2.35) students. Mon–Sat, 9am–12:30pm and 2–5:30pm, Sun (May–Oct only), 9:30am–12:30pm and 2:30–6pm. Metro: Duomo.

Built in the late 18th century on the site of a church of the same name, La Scala is hallowed ground to lovers of Giuseppe Verdi, Maria Callas, and legions of other composers and singers who have hit the high notes of fame in the world's most revered opera house.

La Scala is set for an overhaul again, to begin sometime early in the 21st century. A whiff of nostalgia for days gone by pervades the **Museo Teatrale alla Scala,** where you'll find Toscanini's baton, a strand of Mozart's hair, and a fine array of Callas postcards.

SHOPPING

The best fashion gazing is to be done along four adjoining streets north of the Duomo known collectively as the **Quadrilatero d'Oro** (Golden Quadrilateral): Via Monte-napoleone, Via Spiga, Via Borgospesso and Via Sant'Andrea, lined with Milan's most expensive high-fashion emporia. (To enter this hallowed precinct, follow Via Manzoni a few blocks north from Piazza della Scala; San Babila is the closest metro stop.) If your fashion sense is greater than your credit line, don't despair: Even the most expensive clothing of the Armani ilk is usually less expensive in Italy than it is abroad, and city wide *saldi* (sales) run from early January into early February and again in late June and July.

Or, inspired by the window displays in the Quadrilatero, you can scour the racks of shops elsewhere for designer seconds, last year's fashions, imitations, and other bargains. (Unless otherwise indicated, most of these discount shops are open Monday, 3:30 to 7:30pm and Tuesday through Saturday from 9am to 1pm and 3:30 to 7:30pm, and take credit cards). The place to begin is **Il Salvagente,** several blocks east of the Quadrilatero off Corso XXII Marzo at Via Bronzetti 16 (☎ 02/7611-0328), where you can browse through an enormous collection of designer clothing for men, women and children at wholesale prices (Metro: San Babila). Another haven for bargain hunters (women only in this case) is **Eliogabaldo,** in the Navigli neighborhood at Pz. Sant'Eustorgio 2 (☎ 02/837-8293), where some of the offerings may be second-hand, but only in the sense that a model donned them briefly for a show or shoot (Metro: San Agostino). Also in the Navvigli, **Biffi,** Cor. Genova 6 (☎ 02/837-5170), attracts fashion-conscious hordes of both sexes in search of designer labels and the store's own designs (Metro: San Agostino or San Agostino). One more Navigli stop, and again well stocked with designer ware for men and women, is nearby **Floretta Coen Musil,** V. San Calocero 3 (☎ 02/5811-1708), open Monday through Saturday, afternoons only from 3:30 to 7:30pm; no credit cards (Metro: San Agostino or San Agostino).

The other hunting ground for discount fashions is **Corso Buenos Aires,** northeast of the center and just east of Stazione Centrale (follow Via Vitruvio from Piazza Duca d'Aosta in front of the station; Metro stops Lima and Loreto are the gateways to this bargain stretch). If you're a man, you will want to stop at **Darsena,** Cor. Buenos Aires 16 (☎ 02/2952-1535), where you just might find an Armani suit or jacket at a rock-bottom price. **Il Drug Store,** Cor. Buenos Aires 28 (☎ 02/2951-5592), keeps Milanese of both sexes attired, affordably so, in chic clothing best worn by the young and the thin. **Calzaturificio di Parabiago,** Cor. Buenos Aires 52 (☎ 02/2940-6851), shods men and women fashionably at reasonable prices, with an enormous selection and a helpful staff.

For Milanese design with which to dress the bed and table and not the body, visit **Frette,** Via Visconti di Modrone (☎ 02/777-091). The high-fashion linen house offers some, but certainly not all, of its tablecloths, towels, robes and bedding at substantial discounts (Metro: San Babila). To complete the tabletop, make a stop **Richard-Ginori,** the renowned Florentine purveyor of fine china, at Cor. Buenos Aires 1 (☎ 02/2951-6611); the house's fine porcelain and crystal, as well as offerings from other manufacturers, is often available at discounted prices (Metro: Lima or Loreto). **Spacci Bassetti,** V. Procaccini 32 (☎ 02/3450-125), is a discount outlet of the august Bassetti line of high-quality linen, and the huge spaces offers the luxurious towels and sheets at excellent prices; the shop is open Monday through Saturday from 9:30am to 7:30pm (no midday closing and no credit cards).

ACCOMMODATIONS YOU CAN AFFORD

While you can pay more for a hotel room in Milan than you would almost anywhere else in Europe, there are also some decent accommodations at reasonable prices in good locations. It's difficult to find rooms in any price category when fashion shows and trade fairs are in full swing (often in October and March). Many hotels raise their prices at these times, too. August is low season, and hotels are often willing to bring prices down considerably, as they will sometimes on slow weekends. Rule of thumb: Always ask for the lowest possible rate when booking and be prepared to bargain.

NEAR THE DUOMO

Hotel Cesare Correnti. V. Cesare Correnti 14, 20123 Milano. ☎ **02/805-7609.** Fax 02/7201-0715. 9 units, none with bathroom. TV. 50,000L ($29.40) single; 70,000L (41.20) double; 90,000L ($52.95) triple. Breakfast 6,000L ($3.55). No credit cards. Metro: Duomo. Tram: 8, 19.

You expect to find a sign saying ABANDON ALL HOPE YE WHO ENTER HERE on the dark stairway leading up from a courtyard to this third-floor pensione in an old building between the Duomo and the church of San Lorenzo. Press on, though, because the family run establishment is sparkling clean and very welcoming. The rooms are basically furnished but attractive, with tall old-fashioned windows overlooking the courtyard, and all have TVs. Guests share ample bathrooms in the hallway, which is lined with comfortable chairs and lamps to serve as a lounge. The family that runs the place will do a load of wash for you for 6,000L ($3.95).

Hotel Santa Marta. V. Santa Marta 4, 20124 Milano. ☎ **02/8645-2661.** Fax 02/8645-2661. 15 units, all with bathroom. A/C TV TEL. 130,000–170,000L ($76.45–$100) single; 180,000–250,000L ($105.90–$147.05) double. AE, MC, V. Metro: Cordusio or Duomo.

The narrow Via Santa Marta is a slice of old Milan, cobblestoned and lined with charming old buildings. The Santa Marta is in one of these buildings. It's also across the street from one of the city's most atmospheric restaurants (the Milanese), and a short walk from the Duomo and other sights. Recent modernizations have left this small hotel with its old-fashioned ambience, while adding such modern comforts as air-conditioning. The tile-floored guest rooms are large and comfortable and decorated with a matter-of-fact fashion sense.

Hotel Ullrich. Cor. Italia 6, 21023 Milano. ☎ **02/8645-0156.** 7 units, none with bathroom. TV. 50,000L ($29.40) single; 70,000L ($41.20) double; 90,000L ($52.95) triple. No credit cards. Metro: Duomo. Tram: 12, 24.

A 10-minute walk from the Duomo, this attractive pensione offers a lot of comfort and amenities in addition to its prime location. The friendly management is related to the family that runs the Cesare Correnti (see above) and they must share tips about how to run a good pensione. Rooms are furnished in a pleasant mixture of old armoires and a smattering of modern pieces (including good beds); each has a TV and a tiny washroom with sink and bidet but no toilet; large, spanking-clean bathrooms are in the hallway. Rooms on the street side open to small balconies. One of the bathrooms is equipped with a washing machine, and guests can do a load for 8,000L ($4.70). The Ulrich books up quickly, so be sure to call ahead.

IN MAGENTA & BRERA

Hotel Giulio Cesare. V. Rovello 10, 20121 Milano. ☎ **02/7200-3915.** Fax 02/7200-2179. 25 units, all with bathroom. A/C TV TEL. 110,000–130,000L ($64.70–$76.45) single;

180,000–220,000L ($105.90–$129.40) double. Breakfast 10,000L ($5.90). MC, V. Metro: Cordusio.

A recent renovation has brought this old establishment thoroughly up to date, with a grandiose marble lobby and a handsome lounge and bar area with deep couches and a stunning terracotta floor. Upstairs, the attempt at contemporary chic renders the rooms rather antiseptic—they reflect the building's centuries-old heritage with their tall windows and high ceilings, and some are quirkily shaped, but the white tile floors and minimalist furnishings are starkly modern. The new bathrooms gleam and they are equipped with roomy stall showers. This is one of several similarly priced hotels in the immediate area off Via Dante, tucked away between the Duomo and La Scala in one direction and the Castello in the other. (see the London and Rovello listings).

Hotel Rovello. V. Rovello 18, 20121 Milano. ☎ **02/8646-4654.** Fax 02/7202-3656. 10 units, all with bathroom or shower. TV TEL. 150,000L ($88.25) single; 180,000L ($105.90) double. Rates include breakfast. AE, MC, V. Metro: Cordusio.

The Rovello is one of three hotels we recommend on this quiet street between the Duomo and the Castello and, like its neighbor the Giulio Cesare, it has recently emerged from a thorough renovation, with striking results. The large guest rooms occupy the second and third floors of a centuries-old building and incorporate many of the original architectural details, including exposed timbers and beamed ceilings. Handsome contemporary Italian furnishings are set off by gleaming hardwood floors, the tall casement windows are covered with attractive fabrics, and walls are painted in soothing gold tones. Many of the rooms have dressing areas in addition to the large new bathrooms. A breakfast of rolls and coffee is served in a sunny room off the lobby.

London Hotel. V. Rovello 3, 20121 Milano. ☎ **02/7202-0166.** Fax 02/8057-037. 29 units, all with bathroom. A/C TV TEL. 130,000–150,000L ($76.45–$88.25) single; 180,000–220,000L ($105.90–$129.40) double. MC, V. Parking 35,000L ($20.60). Metro: Cordusio.

Unlike its neighbor the Giulio Cesare, the London sticks to its old-fashioned ways. The big fireplace and cozy green velvet furniture in the lobby say a lot about the comfort level and friendly atmosphere that bring many guests back time after time. Just beyond the lobby, there's a bar where beverages are available almost around the clock; guests can purchase cappuccino or a continental breakfast in the morning. Upstairs, the rooms look like they haven't been redecorated in a number of decades, but they're roomy and bright, and the heavy old furnishings lend a charm very much in keeping with the ambience of the hotel. Guests receive a 10% discount at the trattoria next door, the Opera Prima.

Worth A Splurge

✪ **Antica Locanda Solderino.** V. Castelfidardo 2, 20121 Milano. ☎ **02/657-0129.** Fax 02/657-1361. 10 units, all with bathroom. TV TEL. 200,000–250,000L ($117–$147.05) single or double. Rates include breakfast. AE, DC, MC, V. Parking 25,000–30,000L ($14.70–$17.65) nearby. Metro: Moscova or Repubblica.

If this charming old hotel in the arty Brera neighborhood hadn't been discovered long ago by members of the fashion world and film stars (this was Marcello Mastroianni's preferred Milan hostelry) you would consider it a find. The rooms have more character than they do modern comforts but, to the loyal guests, the eclectic smattering of country antiques and art nouveau pieces more than compensate for the absence air-conditioning and frigo bars. Nor do the repeat customers seem to mind that some of the bathrooms are miniscule (though modern), there is no lobby or breakfast room (coffee and rolls are delivered to your room), and the desk staff is casual (the lone attendant may be around the corner enjoying a coffee in one the neighborhoods cafes). So be it—this is a delightful place to stay in one of Milan's most enticing neighborhoods.

Ariosto Hotel. V. Ariosto 22, 20145 Milano. ☎ **02/4817-844.** Fax 02/4980-516. 53 units, all with bathroom. A/C MINIBAR TV TEL. 140,000–175,000L ($82.35–$102.95) single; 210,000–260,000L ($123.55–$152.95) double. Rates include breakfast. AE, MC, V. Metro: Conciliazione.

Tucked away in a residential neighborhood of apartment houses and old villas near the Santa Maria della Grazie church, the Ariosto is a refreshingly quiet retreat—all the more so because many of the newly refurbished rooms face a private garden, and some open onto balconies overlooking it. In keeping with this peaceful ambience, all the rooms are decorated with soothing blue fabrics and handsome white-wood contemporary furnishings. As a result, you may be overcome with the relaxing impression that you're near the seashore; in fact, the skinny single accommodations are reminiscent of ship's cabins. Many of the doubles have separate dressing areas off the bathrooms, which are equipped with hair dryers and complimentary toiletries.

EAST OF THE DUOMO

America. Cor. XXII Marzo 32, Milano. ☎ **02/738-1865.** Fax 02/738-1490. 10 units, 3 with bathroom. TV TEL. 50,000L ($29.40) single without bathroom; 80,000L ($47) double without bathroom, 90,000L ($52.95) double with bathroom; 115,000L ($67.65) triple with bathroom. AE. Tram: 27 from the station; 12 from Duomo.

Though this establishment is a bit off the beaten track in a middle-class neighborhood due east of Piazza del Duomo, the young owner and his family work overtime to make this pensione one of the best lower-priced lodgings in Milan. The newly refurbished rooms occupy the fourth floor of an apartment house. Several have private bathrooms, and all are bright and nicely decorated with streamlined, wood-veneer modern furnishings. Guests are welcome to join the resident innkeepers in the living room and watch TV. The Rolling Stone music club, a venerable fixture on the Milan nightlife scene, is on the ground floor of the building, a good reason to ask for a room facing the quieter courtyard. For more conventional sightseeing, the Duomo is about 20 minutes away by foot or 10 minutes by tram.

Hotel Pavone. V. Dandolo 2, 20122 Milano. ☎ **02/5519-2133.** Fax 02/5519-2421. 24 units, all with bathroom. TV TEL. 130,000L ($76.45) single; 190,000L ($111.75) double; 230,000L ($135.30) triple. AE, MC, V. Tram: 12.

Just off the Corso di Porta Vittoria, around the corner from the Palace of Justice and about a 15-minute walk east of the Duomo, the Pavone is a no-frills establishment geared to business travelers (Linate, Milan's domestic airport, is only 10 minutes away by bus from nearby Piazza San Babila). Likewise, the surrounding neighborhood is more geared to business than to the tourist trade, but the friendly desk staff is eager to point out nearby restaurants and other conveniences, which are plentiful. Rooms are a bit sparse, with gray tile floors and no-nonsense Scandinavian-style furniture, but unusually large and quiet. Many are outfitted as triples and are large enough to accommodate an extra bed, making this a fine choice for families.

NEAR STAZIONE CENTRALE & CORSO BUENOS AIRES

Hotel Kennedy. Vle. Tunisia 6 (6th floor), 20124 Milano.☎ **02/2940-0934.** Fax 02/2940-1253. 12 units, 3 with shower, 2 with bathroom. 50,000–70,000L ($29.40–$41.20) single without bathroom; 70,000–90,000L ($41.20–$52.95) double without bathroom; 120,000–140,000L ($70.60–$82.35) double with bathroom. Breakfast 6,000L ($3.55). MC, V. Metro: Porta Venezia.

The name reflects the English-speaking management's fondness for the late president, and the husband and wife team is genuinely welcoming to the many Americans who find their way to their pensione about midway between the station and Corso Buenos Aires. Their homey establishment on the sixth floor of an office-and-apartment building (there's an elevator) is sparkling clean and offers basic accommodations in large, tile-floored rooms. Amenities include a bar in the reception area, where coffee and soft drinks are available, as is a light breakfast of brioche and coffee that doesn't cost much more than it would in a cafe.

Hotel Paganini. V. Paganini 6, 20131 Milano. ☎ **02/204-7443.** 8 units, 1 with bathroom. 70,000L ($41.20) single without bathroom, 90,000L ($52.95) double without bathroom; 120,000L ($70.60) double with bathroom. AE, DC, MC, V. Metro: Loreto.

Occupying an old house on a quiet residential street off the Corso Buenos Aires, the Paganini has minimal public areas (except for a brightly lit reception area with a self-serve espresso machine), but the guest rooms are large, bright, and embellished with parquet floors, high ceilings and elaborate moldings. Furnishings, however, are new and, if a little more banal than the woodwork and other architectural elements, include solid beds. The shared facilities are modern and kept spanking clean by the young, enthusiastic staff, who are happy to point their guests to restaurants and sights. The best rooms are in the rear, overlooking a private garden. There is much to be said for this location: The station is only a 10-minute walk way down Via Pergolsi, and if shopping is on your agenda, the nearby Corso Buenos Aires is one of the city's bargain fashion meccas.

✪ **Hotel Promessi Sposi.** Pz. Oberdan 12, 20129 Milano. ☎ **02/2951-3661.** Fax 02/2940-4182. 40 units, all with bathroom. TV. 110,000–140,000L ($64.70–$82.35) single; 160,000–220,000L ($94.10–$129.40) double; 190,000–280,000L ($111.75–$164.70) triple. AE, MC, V. Metro: Porto Venezia.

Travelers often find their way to this rambling hotel on the recommendation of former guests, many of them in the fashion world, who tend to rave about the friendly service, unusually pleasant accommodations and the excellent value. Downstairs, there's a cheerful lobby and bar area, overlooking Piazza Oberdan and the public gardens through large windows and furnished with multicolored couches; a buffet breakfast, included in the rates, is served in an adjoining breakfast room. Upstairs, the spacious rooms are airily decorated in soothing whites and pastels and furnished with comfortable rattan furniture; bathrooms are spacious and nicely maintained. The name, which translates as "the Fiancée," is a reference to the 19th-century masterpiece by the Lombardian novelist Alessandro Manzoni.

Worth A Splurge

Doriagrande Hotel. Vle. Andrea Doria 22, 20124 Milano. ☎ **02/669-6696.** Fax 02/669-6669. 112 units, all with bathroom. A/C MINIBAR TV TEL. Special rate (see below) 190,000L ($111.75) single; 230,000L ($135.30) double. Rates include breakfast. AE, DC, MC, V. Metro: Loreto or Stazione Centrale.

This luxury hotel offers a special price that applies on weekends (Friday and Saturday nights), most of August, and the Christmas/New Year holiday (check for exact dates before booking). For an especially comfortable stay in Milan, you may well want to plan your visit to coincide with one of these periods when the hotel offers the special rate above, which are about half the normal tariff. The Doriagrande is one of the large newer hotels that cluster around the station and is far more comfortable and stylish than most hotels in its luxury class. The oversized guest rooms are exquisitely appointed with handsome wood and marble furniture and fabric wall coverings and draperies in soothing neutral tones, and beautiful marble bathrooms, and they come with such amenities as linen sheets and complimentary bedroom slippers and bathrobes. The beautiful marble bathrooms are equipped with generous sized tubs and vanities, as well as with hair dryers and a generous selection of toiletries. A sumptuous buffet breakfast is served in a stylishly decorated room on a level beneath the lobby.

GREAT DEALS ON DINING

Geared to business as the city is, Milanese are more willing than Italians elsewhere to break the sit-down-meal tradition and grab a sandwich or other light fare on the run. And with so many students and young professionals underfoot, Milan has no shortage of pizzerias and other low-cost eateries.

NEAR STAZIONE CENTRALE & CORSO BUENOS AIRES

Brek. V. Lepetit, 20. ☎ **02/670-5149.** Primi 5,000–8,000L ($2.95–$4.70), secondi 7,000–10,000L ($4.10–$5.90). AE, MC, V. Mon–Sat 11:30am–3pm and 6:30–10:30pm. Metro: Stazione Centrale. CAFETERIA.

This outlet of Italy's popular cafeteria chain is not to be dismissed too quickly. Brek takes food, and its presentation, seriously. Pastas and risotto are made fresh; pork, veal, and chicken are roasted to order; the large selection of cheeses would put many a formal restaurant to shame. Excellent wines and many kinds of beer are also available. Behind-the-counter service is friendly and helpful, and the country-style decor is quite attractive.

Da Abele. V. Temperanza 5. ☎ **02/261-3855.** Primi 8,000–15,000L ($4.70–$8.80), secondi 14,000– 22,000L ($8.25–$12.95). MC, V. Tues–Sun 7–10:30pm. Closed July 15–Sept 1. Metro: Loreto. MILANESE

Once you get away from the sights and shops of the city center, you'll find yourself in some middle-class neighborhoods. Da Abele is in one of them, a pleasant enclave of shops and apartment houses east of Stazione Centrale and north of Corso Buenos Aires shopping strip. This pleasant, plain trattoria caters to local residents (hence it's evening-only hours) and serves a nice selection of soups (including a hearty *zuppa di pesce*) and many kinds of risotto, including one with a selection of fresh seafood (*frutti di mare*) and others with fresh mushrooms in season (*funghi porcini*). The amiable staff doesn't mind if you venture no further into the menu, but if you do, there is a nice selection of roast meats.

Isola del Panino. V. Felice Casati 2. ☎ **02/2951-4925.** Sandwiches from 4,500L ($2.65). No credit cards. Tues–Sun 8am–midnight. Metro: Lima. SANDWICHES

This cafelike sandwich shop, in the midst of the bustle of the Corso Buenos Aires discount shops, sells some 50 different kinds of *panini.* You needn't feel you are forgoing an Italian experience in enjoying one of these sandwiches. In Milan, a *panino* is a very popular snack or lunch choice and is usually served warm; bread is stuffed with seafood, cheese, salami, vegetables, whatever, then grilled. You can eat the delicious creations here on the premises in an airy, chrome-and-tile dining area, or take them with you, perhaps for a picnic on the nearby public gardens.

Ristorante Versilia. Vle. Andrea Doria 44. ☎ **02/670-4187.** Primi 8,000–14,000L ($4.70–$8.25), secondi 9,000–16,000L ($5.30–$9.40). MC, V. Mon–Sat, noon–2:30pm and 7–10pm. Closed Sat evening and Sun. Metro: Loreto. NORTHERN ITALIAN.

The white tiles and high-tech lighting suggest that this single room between the station and Corso Buenos Aires has more pretensions than it does. The modern environs are the result of a recent renovation to this friendly, family run eatery that serves the surrounding neighborhood with excellent food and attentive service. The risottos are superb, including *alla pilota*, with sausage. While the menu includes a costoletta alla milanese and other meat dishes, daily specials often include a wide selection of the freshest seafood.

Worth a Splurge

Joia. V. P. Castaldi 18. ☎ **02/295-22124.** Reservations required. Primi 15,000–30,000L ($8.80–$17.65), secondi 18,000–35,000L ($10.60–$20.60). Tasting menus 55,000L ($32.35),

65,000L ($38.25) and 75,000L ($44.10); fish menu 95,000L ($55.90). AE, DC, MC, V. Mon–Fri 12:30–3pm and 7–10:30pm. Closed Aug. Metro: Repubblica. VEGETARIAN.

Milanese, who tend to be carnivorous, have embraced this vegetarian restaurant just north of the public gardens with great enthusiasm. Travelers may welcome the respite from northern Italy's orientation to red meat; those who have become accustomed to smoke-free environments back home will enjoy the *non fumare* section of Joia's blonde-wood, neutral-toned dining room. The innovative vegetarian creations of Swiss chef Pietro Lemman incorporate the freshest vegetables and herbs, which appear in many traditional pasta dishes, such as *lasagne con zucchine pomodoro* (layered with zucchini and fresh tomatoes and served at room temperature), *ravioli di melanzana* (stuffed with eggplant), or tagliolini with a simple tomato sauce. Any of these first courses can be ordered as a main course, and many of the main courses can be ordered as starters. These *secondi* include some excellent fish choices, as well as elaborate vegetables-only creations such as *melanzani viola al vapore con finferli* (steamed eggplant with chanterelle mushrooms). There's a wonderful assortment of cheeses and, likewise, a large wine menu.

NEAR THE DUOMO

La Crêperie. V. C. Corenti 24. ☎ 02/837-5708. Crepes from 4,500L ($2.65). Daily 11am–1am. Metro: Sant'Ambrogio. CREPERIE.

About a 10-minute walk southeast of Piazza Duomo (Via C. Corenti is an extension of Via Torino, one of the major avenues fanning out from the square), this busy creperie is an ideal stop for a light lunch or a snack while visiting the nearby church of Sant'Ambrogio or Museo Nazionale di Scienza e di Tecnica. At lunch you can sample the far-ranging offerings with a special that includes two crepes: one with such protein options as *prosciutto e formaggio* (ham and cheese) and another of the dessert variety (the Nutella, with the creamy chocolate spread, is highly recommended).

Luini. V. Santa Radegonda 16. ☎ **02/806-918.** Panzerotto 4,000L ($2.35). No credit cards. Tues–Sat, 9am–6pm. Metro: Duomo. SNACKS.

At this stand-up counter near the Galleria, you'll have to elbow your way through a throng of well-dressed people to purchase the house specialty: *panzerotto*, a pocket of pizza crust stuffed with cheese and tomato. You'll also find many different kinds of panini here.

MAGENTA & BRERA

Latteria. V. San Marco 42. ☎ **02/659-7653.** Primi 5,000–7,000L ($2.95–$4.10), secondi 7,000–12,000L ($4.10–$7.05). No credit cards. Mon–Sat, 11:30am–3:30pm and 7–10:30pm. Metro: Moscova. MILANESE.

The main business here was at one time dispensing milk and eggs to a press of neighborhood shoppers, but now the emphasis is on serving the La Brera neighborhood delicious, homemade fare in a rooms decorated with paintings and photographs of roses. The minestrone and other vegetable soups are delicious, as are the many variations of risotto, including some otherwise hard to find variations such as *riso al salto*, a delicious dish of leftover risotto alla milanese that is fried with butter. The menu changes daily, and the friendly staff, including owners Arturo and Maria, won't mind explaining what the different dishes are or allowing you to take a look in the kitchen.

Worth a Splurge

✪ **La Milanese.** V. Santa Maria 11. ☎ **02/864-51991.** Reservations required. Primi 15,000–30,000L ($8.80–$17.65), secondi 18,000–35,000L ($10.60–$20.60). AE, DC, MC, V. Wed–Mon 7pm–1am. Metro: Cardusio. MILANESE.

Giuseppe and Antonella Villa preside over the centuries-old premises, tucked into a narrow lane in one of the oldest sections of Milan, just west of the Duomo, with a watchful eye. In the three-beamed dining room, Milanese families and other patrons share the long, crowded tables. Giuseppe, in the kitchen, prepares what many patrons consider to be some of the city's best traditional fare. The risotto alla milanese, with saffron and beef marrow, not surprisingly, is excellent, as is a minestrone that's served hot in the summer and at room temperature in the summer. The costoletta alla milanese, breaded and fried in butter, is all the better here because only the choicest veal chops are used and it's served with the bone in, and the osso buco is cooked to perfection. Polenta, with rich Gorgonzola cheese is one of the few nonmeat second courses. The attentive staff will help you choose an appropriate wine.

Peck. V. Victor Hugo 4. ☎ **02/876-774.** Primi 7,000–12,000L ($4.10–$7.05), secondi 18,000–22,000L ($10.60–$12.95). AE, DC, MC, V. Mon–Sat, 7:30am–9pm. Closed Jan 1–10 and July 1–20. Metro: Duomo. DELI.

Milan's most famous food emporium offers a wonderful selection of roast veal, risottos, porchetta, salads, aspics, cheeses, pastries, and other fare from its exquisite larder in this natty snack bar adjoining its shop. If you choose to eat here, you will do so at a stand-up bar where, especially around lunchtime, it can be hard to find elbow room. This shouldn't discourage you, though, because the pleasure of having access to such a cornucopia of delicacies at a reasonable price will be a gourmand's vision of paradise. Of course, you can also wander through Peck's food halls to equip yourself amply for a picnic or hotel-room dinner.

Pizzeria Grand'Italia. V. Palermo 5. ☎ **02/877-759.** Pizza from 6,000L ($3.55), salads from 10,000L ($5.90). No credit cards. Wed–Mon, 12:15pm–2:45pm and 7pm–1:15am. Closed Tues (except in Aug). Metro: Moscova. PIZZA/PASTA.

One of Milan's most popular pizzerias serves a huge assortment of salads, pizzas, pastas, and *focacce farcite* (focaccia bread stuffed with cheese, mushrooms, and other fillings). The late hours make this a prime night spot, and part of the fun is watching the chic, young Milanese stopping buy for a snack as they make the rounds of the nearby La Brera district bars and clubs.

EAST OF THE DUOMO

Trattoria da Bruno. V. Bronzetti 1. ☎ **02/730-029.** Primi 7,000–10,000L ($4.10–$5.90), secondi 9,000–15,000L ($5.30–$8.80). No credit cards. Mon–Sat, noon–2pm and 7–11pm. Tram: 60. MILANESE.

Strolling Through Milan

The prime spot for a *passeggiata* (stroll) is the Piazza Duomo and the adjoining Galleria, but many of the neighborhoods that fan out from the center are ideal for wandering and looking into the life of the Milanese. The **Golden Quadrilateral** (the city's center for high fashion), just north of the Piazza Duomo on and around Via Montenapoleone, is known for window shopping; **Magenta** is an old residential quarter, filled with some of the city's most venerable churches, west of Piazza Duomo (follow Via Orifici and it's extension, Via Dante, toward the Castello Sforzesco); the **Brera,** a parcel of old Milan clustered around the Pinacoteca Brera (follow Via Brera from the Teatro alla Scala); and the trendy **Navigli** neighborhood, at the southern edge of the center city along the remaining *navigli* (canals) that once laced the city (take the metro to Sant'Agostino). A stroll in Milan almost always includes a stop at a cafe or gelateria (see below).

It's well worth the trek out to this attractive, family run place, just off the Corso Indipendenza about a 15-minute walk east of the Duomo. The soups here are delicious and fortifying and can be followed by *costoletta alla Milanese* and other straightforward main courses, which often include a selection of fresh fish. Bruno usually offers a fixed-priced menu consisting of the freshest ingredients he has in the kitchen that day, at a price that rarely edges over the 20,000L ($11.75) mark.

CAFES & GELATO

Caffè Miami (in the Galleria; ☎ **02/8646-4435**; Metro: Duomo) is best known by its original name, "the Camparino." It's the most attractive and popular of the many bars in the Galleria, which introduced Italy to Campari, the country's ubiquitous red cordial. You can linger at the tables set up in the Galleria or in one of the Art Nouveau rooms inside. You can find organic gelato at the **Gelateria Ecologica** (Cor. di Porta Ticinese 40; ☎ **02/5810-1872**; Metro: Sant'Ambrogio or Missori) in the Ticinese/Navigli neighborhood. It's so popular, there's no need for a sign out front. Strollers in the atmospheric Brera neighborhood sooner or later stumble upon **Gelateria Toldo** (V. Ponte Vetero 11; ☎ **02/8646-0863**; Metro: Cordusio or Lanza), where the gelato is wonderfully creamy and many of the sorbetto selections are so fruity and fresh that they seem healthy. **Passerini** (V. Hugo 4. ☎ **02/8646-4995**; Metro: Cordusio) is more than the typical stand-up counter. This elegant ice cream parlor a few blocks west of the Duomo upholds its 80-year tradition gallantly, serving several dozen variations of the creamy concoctions—including a *cioccolato gianduia* (chocolate hazelnut topped with whipped cream) that bring chocolate lovers back time and again.

The **Pasticceria Confetteria Cova** (V. Montenapoleone 8; ☎ **02/600-0578**; Montenapoleone) is nearing its 200th year in refined surroundings near the similarly atmospheric Museo Poldi-Pezzoli. It's usually filled with shoppers making the rounds in this high-fashion district. You can enjoy a quick coffee and a brioche at the long bar, or take a seat in one of the elegant adjoining rooms. **Pasticceria Marchesi** (V. Santa Maria alla Porta 13; ☎ **02/862-770**; metro: Cardusio) is a distinguished pastry shop, with an adjoining wood-paneled tearoom. Since it's only steps from the church of Santa Maria delle Grazie, you can enjoy the old-world ambience and a cup of excellent coffee (or one of the many teas and herbal infusions) as you dash off postcards of the *Last Supper*. Of course, you'll want to accompany your beverage with one of the elegant pastries, perhaps a slice of the *panettone* (the cake laden with raisins and candied citron) that is a hallmark of Milan. No one prepares it better than they do at Marchesi.

MILAN AFTER DARK

On Wednesdays and Thursdays Milan's newspapers tend to devote a lot of ink to club schedules and cultural events. If you don't trust your command of Italian to plan your nightlife, check out the tourist office in Piazza Duomo—there are usually piles of fliers announcing upcoming events lying about. The tourist office also keeps visitors up to date with *Milano: Where, When, How,* a periodical it distributes for free with schedules of events, as well as listings of bars, clubs and restaurants.

THE PERFORMING ARTS   The ✪ **Teatro alla Scala** (Pz. d. Scala; ☎ **02/860-787** box office; **02/7200-3744** information line), will be closing sometime soon for renovation, but it the meantime it's opera as usual (opera season here runs from December 7 into July). Although tickets sell out well in advance, it's worth checking with the box office for one of the less-desirable (and more likely to be available) seats at the top of the house. The box office is open daily noon to 6pm. In addition, 200

Nightlife Tip

The **Navigli/Ticinese** neighborhood is currently on the ascent as Milan's prime night turf, though **Brera** retains its pull with night owls as well.

standing room places go on sale on the day of performance. (See above also, under "What to See & Do.") For schedules and to purchase tickets on the Internet, visit La Scala's Web site at **www.lascala.milano.it**. Tickets run from 30,000 to 60,000L ($17.65 to $35.30) at the **Conservatorio Giuseppe Verdi** (V. d. Conservatorio 12; ☎ **02/7621-101;** metro: San Babila), Milan's major venue for classical music. The year-round schedule brings the world's finest musicians and orchestras to the city.

MOVIES   In Italy, English-language films are almost always dubbed into Italian, providing English speakers with an opportunity to bone up on their Italian but taking some of the fun out of a night at the movies. Milan, fortunately, breaks the rule with several cinemas that screen English-language films in the original version one night a week: **Anteo**, V. Milazzo 9, ☎ **02/659-7732,** on Monday (Metro: Moscova); **Arcobaleno,** Vle. Tunisia 11, ☎ **02/2940-6054,** on Tuesday (Metro: Porta Venzia); and **Mexico,** V. Savona 57, ☎ **02/4895-1802,** on Thursday (Metro: Porta Genova). Admission is 8,000L ($4.70).

BARS   A publike atmosphere, induced in part by Guinness on tap (6,000L/$3.55), prevails at **Bar Magenta,** in the neighborhood for which it takes its name at V. Carducci 13 (☎ **02/805-3808**), open Tuesday through Sunday (Metro: Sant'Ambrogio). One of the more popular La Brera hangouts, with a young following, is **El Timbin de San Marc,** which despite its name is an English-pub style bar at V. San Marco 25 (☎ **02/659-0833**); open Monday through Saturday. If you're not quite young and up to partying with those who are, a pleasant alternative to Milan's youth-oriented venues is **Bar Margherita,** where there's jazz on the sound system (and sometimes live on stage) and a nice selection of wines and grappa from about 4,000L ($2.35); it's in La Brera at V. Moscova 25 (☎ **02/659-0833**); open Monday through Saturday (Metro: Moscova). Among the Navigli night spots (growing in number all the time) is **El Brelin,** an intimate, canal-side piano bar on Vicolo della Lavandaia, off Alzaia Naviglio Grande (☎ **02/5810-1351**), open Monday through Saturday (Metro: Genova FS).

JAZZ CLUBS   Milan's best-known jazz club is **Capolinea,** in the Navigli at V. Lodovico il Moro 119 (☎ **02/8912-2024**); some of the performers are big names and the cover is 15,000L ($8.80), which includes one drink (it's higher with bigger names); open Tuesday through Sunday (Metro: Porta Genova). The other contender on the jazz club scene is **Le Scimmie,** which is smaller and funkier in both surroundings and musical leanings (the cover is about the same, though); it's in the same vicinity, at V. Ascanio Sforza 49 (☎ **02/8940-2874**), and operates Wednesday through Monday (Metro: Porta Genova).

MUSIC & DANCE CLUBS   The dance scene changes all the time in Milan, but at whatever club is popular (or in business) at the moment, expect to pay a cover of 20,000L ($11.75). Models and the attendant fashion set favor **Hollywood,** which is small, chic and centrally located in La Brera at Cor. Como 15 (☎ **02/659-8996**); the 25,000L ($14.70) cover includes one drink (Metro: Moscova). **Grand Café Fashion,** Corso di Porta Ticinese at Via Vetere (☎ **02/8940-0709**), brings a beautiful crowd to the Navigli neighborhood, where they dance the night away nightly (at least from 10pm to 4am) to classic disco music (Metro: Porta Genova). Milan's most venerable music club is **Rolling Stone,** Cor. XXII Marzo 32 (☎ **02/733-172**), in business since the 1950s. Most of the performers these days are of a hard-rock bent, and the club is as immensely popular as ever. Cover runs from 12,000 to 25,000L ($7.05 to $14.70), depending on who's performing, less expensive for women than for men, and more expensive on weekends than on weekdays (Tram: 12).

GAY CLUBS   Milan's largest gay clubs is **Nuovo Idea,** V. de Castilla 30 (☎ **02/6900-78-59**); it attracts a mostly male crowd of all ages and offers everything from disco to polkas, in a huge techno room. The 15,000L ($8.80) cover includes one drink; open Thursday to Sunday (Metro: Gioia). **Recycle,** V. Calabria 5, ☎ **02/376-1531,** is a women-only club, open Thursday to Sunday from 9pm to 2am, sometimes later.

DAY TRIPS FROM MILAN
PAVIA & THE CERTOSA

At one time the quiet and remarkably well-preserved little city of Pavia, 22 miles south of Milan, was more powerful than Milan. It was the capital of Lombardy in the 7th and 8th centuries, and by the early Renaissance, the Viscontis and later the Sforzas, the two families who so influenced the history of Milan and all of Lombardy, were wielding their power here. It was the Viscontis who built the city's imposing Castello, made Pavia one of Europe's great centers of learning (when they founded the university) in 1361, began construction on the Duomo (with the third largest dome in Italy) in 1488, and founded the city's most important monument and the one that brings most visitors to Pavia, the Certosa.

The Certosa is 8 kilometers (5 mi.) north of Pavia. One of the most unusual buildings in Lombardy, if not in Italy, this religious compound was commissioned by Gian Galeazzo Visconti in 1396 as a Carthusian monastery and a burial chapel for his family. The facade of colored marbles, the frescoed interior, and the riot of funerary sculpture is evidence that this brood of often tyrannical despots were also dedicated builders with grand schemes and large coffers. The finest and most acclaimed statuary monument here, that of Ludivico il Moro and Beatrice d'Este, sits in the massive church, beneath frescoes by Perugino. Its presence here is a twist of fate—the monks at Milan's Chiesa di Santa Maria della Grazie (which houses the *Last Supper*) sold the tomb to the Certosa to raise funds. To the right of the church is an enormous cloister, lined with the monk's cells, each of which is actually a two-story cottage with its own garden plot; most are inhabited by the small community that continues to live at the Certosa. It is possible to visit their refectory and an adjoining shop, where they sell their Chartreuse liqueur and herbal soaps and scents. Admission to the Certosa (☎ **0382-925-613**) is free; it's open Tuesday to Sunday, 9:30am to 11:30am and 2:30 to 6pm (until 4:30pm November to February and 5:30pm September, October, March and April). To reach the Certosa from Pavia, take one of the half-hourly buses from the Autocorriere station (next to the train station); the trip takes about 15 minutes and costs 1,900L ($1.10). Trains from Milan usually stop at the station near the Certosa, just before the main Pavia station. They run every half hour and the 35-minute trip costs 3,500L ($2.05). **By car,** the Certosa is about half an hour south of Milan Via **autostrada A7** (follow exit signs). The APT tourist office is near the train station at V. Fabio Filzi 2 (☎ **0382/22-156**); it's open Monday to Saturday, 8:30am to 12:30pm and 2pm to 6pm.

CREMONA

Violins have been drawing visitors to this little city on the river Po, 57 miles southeast of Milan, since the 17th century, when fine string instruments began emerging from the workshops of Nicolo Amati and his more-famous protégé, Antonio Stradivari. The tradition continues: Cremona's **Scuola di Luteria** (Violin School) is world renowned.

Cremona's charms extend far beyond the musical. Its central Piazza del Commune is one of the largest and most beautiful town squares in Italy, fronted by remarkable structures. Among these is the 12th-century Duomo, clad in pink marble and over-shadowed by Italy's tallest campanile; inside, it is covered with 16th-century frescoes (admission is free and hours are Monday to Saturday from 7am until noon and 3 to 7pm, Sunday from 7am to 1pm and 3:30 to 7pm). The Palazzo del Commune rises gracefully above a Gothic arcade and is embellished with terra-cotta panels. Its **Saletta dei Violini** displays a small collection of 17th-century furnishings and violins (☎ **0372/4071-31971**); admission is 6,000L ($3.55) and includes admission to the Museo Stradivariano, below; hours are Tuesday to Saturday from 8:30am to 6pm, Sunday from 9:15am to 12:15pm and 3 to 6pm. The **Museo Stradivariano,** V. Palestro 17 (☎ **0372/461-886**), displays the finest violins ever made, including those by Amatis, Stradivari, and Guaneri. The admission of 6,000L ($3.55) includes entrance to the Palazzo Communale and other museums around town. The **APT tourist office** is near the Duomo at Pz. d. Commune 5 (☎ **0372/23-233**); Monday to Saturday from 9:30am to 12:30pm and 3 to 6pm, Sunday from 9:45am to 12:15pm.

GETTING HERE Trains arrive almost hourly from Milan (1¼ hours; 8,200L/$4.85). Hourly trains to Brescia (¾ hour; 5,400L/$3.20) also make it possible to combine an excursion from Milan to Cremona and Brescia (see below). Four daily buses travel between Milan and Cremona; the trip of 1½ hours costs 9,300L ($5.45). If you are traveling by car, you can make the trip to Cremona by following A1 from Milan to Piacenza and A21 from Piacenza to Cremona.

BRESCIA

Ringed by industrialized suburbs, Brescia does not readily beckon travelers to stop. Those who do, however, have the pleasure of wandering through a centuries-old town center where Roman ruins, not one but two duomos, and medieval palazzi line winding streets and gracious piazzas.

The center of Brescia is the Piazza Duomo, named for the two duomos—the 17th-to 19th-century **Duomo Nuovo** and the much more charming 11th- to 12th-century **Duomo Vecchio** (also called Rotonda, for its shape). The New Duomo is open daily from 8am to noon and 4 to 7:30pm; the Old Duomo April through September, Thursday to Tuesday from 9am to noon and 3 to 7pm. Brescia's Roman past emerges if you leave the piazza on Via dei Musei and follow it to the **Capitolino**, a temple erected in A.D. 73; columns and other artifacts, including the famous first-century bronze Victory of Brescia (also known as Winged Victory), are on display at the adjoining **Museo Romano,** V. d. Musei 7 (☎ **030/46-031**). Admission is 5,000L ($3.30); hours are Tuesday to Friday from 9am to 12:30pm and 3 to 5pm, Sunday 10am to noon and 3 to 6pm.

A few steps down the street and through the centuries bring you to the **Monasterio di San Salvatore e Santa Giulia**, where Charlemagne's ex-wife Ermengarde spent her last days; the monastery incorporates several churches, and together they house a repository of medieval religious objects. The monasterio is at V. d. Musei 81 (☎ **030/44-327**); admission 5,000L ($2.95), hours are Tuesday to Saturday from 9am to 12:30pm and 3 to 5pm (until 6pm June to September), Sunday 10am to noon and 3 to 6pm.

If you leave Piazza del Duomo from the other direction, through the archways into Piazza Loggia, you come upon Brescia's most enchanting building, its medieval town hall, the **Broletto.** The **Torre dell'Orlogio**, on the opposite side of the square, resembles the campanile on Piazza San Marco in Venice, bespeaking the days when Brescia was a Venetian stronghold. Brescia's excellent painting collection, the **Pinacoteca Tosio-Matinengo,** is at Pz. Moretto 4, ☎ **030/377-4999.** (From Piazza Loggia walk south into the ugly, Facist-era Piazza Vittorio and follow that south into Piazza dei Mercati; from there Corso Zanardelli and Corso Magenta lead west to Via Crispi, which leads south to the museum.) Works by Moretto, Foppa, and other painters of the school of Brescia hang alongside Raphaels and Tintorettos in an old palazzo. Admission is 5,000L ($2.95), children 15 and under and seniors over 65 free, and it's open Tuesday to Friday from 10am to 12:30pm and 3 to 6pm, Saturday and Sunday from 10am to 12:30pm and 3 to 7pm. The **APT tourist office** is at Cor. Zanardelli 34 (☎ **030/43-418**); it's open Monday to Friday from 9am to 12:30pm and 3 to 6pm, Saturday from 9am to 12:30pm.

GETTING HERE   Trains arrive from Milan about every half hour; the trip takes one hour and costs 7,200L ($4.25). Brescia is linked to Milan by the A4 autostrada, which continues east to Verona and Venice; the trip from Milan to Brescia takes a little less than an hour.

2 Bergamo

47 km (28 mi.) NE of Milan, 52 km (31 mi.) NW of Brescia

Bergamo is two cities. **Bergamo Bassa,** the lower, mostly 19th- and 20th-century city, concerns itself with everyday business. **Bergamo Alta,** a beautiful medieval and Renaissance town perched on a green hill, concerns itself these days with entertaining the visitors who come to admire its piazzas, palazzos and churches, enjoy the lovely vistas from its belvederes, and soak in a hushed beauty that inspired the Italian poet Gabriel d'Annunzio to call old Bergamo "a city of muteness." The distinct characters of the two parts of this city go back to its founding as a Roman settlement, when the *civitas* was on the hill and farms and suburban villas dotted the plains below.

FESTIVALS & MARKETS   Bergamo is a cultured city, and its celebrations include the May-through-June **Festivale Piantistico,** one of the world's major piano competitions that draws pianists from around the world. In September, the city celebrates its native composer Gaetano Donizetti with performances of his works, most of them at the Teatro Donizetti in the Citta Bassa (see below).

ESSENTIALS

GETTING HERE   By Train   Trains arrive from and depart for **Milan** hourly; the trip takes 1 hour and costs 5,100L ($2.95); service to and from **Brescia** is even more frequent, with half-hourly service during peak early morning and early evening travel times; the trip takes 45 minutes and costs 4,300L ($2.55). (Given the frequency of train service, you can easily make a daylong sightseeing loop from Milan, arriving in Bergamo in the morning, moving on to Brescia in the afternoon, and returning to Milan from there.) If you're coming from or going on to nearby Lake Como, there is hourly service between Bergamo and **Lecco,** on the southeast end of the lake; the trip takes 40 minutes and costs 7,400L ($4.35). Luggage storage is available at the station; the office is open daily from 7am to 9pm and charges 5,000L ($2.95) per piece of luggage for each 12-hour period.

By Bus   An extensive bus network links Bergamo with many other towns in Lombardy. There are nine buses a day to and from **Como** (1 hour, 8,000L/$4.70) and eight a day to and from **Brescia** (45 minutes, 6,500L/$3.85). Service to and from **Milan** runs every half hour from 5:30am to 11pm, and the hour-long trips costs 7,200L

($4.30). The bus station is next to the train station on Piazza Marconi; for information, call ☎ **035/248-150.**

By Car   Bergamo is linked directly to Milan via the **A4 autostrada,** which continues east to **Brescia, Verona,** and **Venice.** The trip between Milan and Bergamo takes a little over half an hour. Parking in or near the Città Alta, most of which is closed to traffic, can be difficult; there is a lot on the northern end of the Città Alta near Porta Garibaldi (about 2,000L/$1.20 an hour) and street parking along Viale delle Mura, which loops around the outer flanks of the walls of the Città Alta.

VISITOR INFORMATION   The APT tourist office is near the train station at Papa Giovanni XXIII 106 (☎ 035/242-226), open daily from 9am to 12:30pm and 3 to 5:30pm. There is a branch in the Città Alta near the Piazza Vecchia at Vc. Aquila Nera 2 (☎ 035/232-730), open daily the same hours.

CITY LAYOUT   The Piazza Vecchia, Colleoni Chapel, and most of the other sights that bring visitors to Bergamo are in the Città Alta—the exception is the Accademia Carrara, which is in the Città Bassa but on the flanks of the hillside, so within easy walking distance of the upper town sights. **Via Colleoni** cuts a swath through the medieval heart of the Città Alta, beginning at Piazza Vecchia. To reach this lovely square from the funicular station at Piazza Mercato delle Scarpi, walk along Via Gombito for about five minutes. Most of the Città Alta is closed to traffic, but it is compact and easy to navigate on foot.

Down below, the main square known as the **Sentierone** is the center of the Città Bassa. It's about a 5-minute walk from the train station north along Viale Papa Giovanni XXIII.

GETTING AROUND   Bergamo has an extensive bus system that runs through the Città Bassa and to points outside the walls of the Città Alta; tickets are (1,500L/90¢) and are available from newsstands and tobacco shops. With the exception of the trip from the train or bus stations up to the Città Alta, you probably won't have much need of public transit, since most of the sights are within an easy walk of one another. To reach the Città Alta from the train station, take bus no. 1 or 3 (1,500L/90¢) and make the free transfer to the **Funicolare Bergamo Alta,** which connects the upper and lower cities and runs every 7 minutes from 6:30am to 12:30am. You can make the walk to the funicular easily in about 15 minutes (and see something of the pleasant new city en route) by following Viale Papa Giovanni XXIII and its continuations Viale Roma and Viale Vittorio Emanuele II straight through town to the funicular station. If you're feeling hearty, a footpath next to the funicular winds up to Città Alta; the steep climb up (made easier by intermittent staircases) takes about 20 minutes.

EXPLORING THE CITTÀ BASSA

Most visitors scurry through Bergamo's lower, newer town on their way to the Città Alta, but you might want to pause long enough to enjoy a coffee in the **Sentierone,** the piazza at the center of town. This spacious square graciously combines a mishmash of architectural styles (including 16th-century porticos on one side, the Mussolini-era Palazzo di Giusttizia and two imitation Doric temples on another). Locals sit in its gardens, lounge in its cafes, and attend classical concerts at the **Teatro Donizetti.** This 19th-century theater is the center of Bergamo's lively culture scene, with a fall opera season and a winter-through-spring season of dramatic performances; check with the tourist office or call the theater, ☎ **035/249-631,** for more information.

The main draw for most visitors down here, though, is the **Accademia Carrara.** The painting gallery is about a 10-minute walk from the Sentierone—from the east end of the square, take a left on Largo Belloti, then a right on Via Giuseppe Verdi and follow that for several blocks to Via Pignolo and turn left to Via Tomaso, which takes you to Piazza Carrara and the Accademia (the route is well signposted).

The **Galleria dell'Accademia Carrara** (☎ 035/399-643), the city's exquisite art gallery, one of the finest in Italy, was founded in 1795, when Napoléon's troops were busy rounding up the art treasures of their newly occupied northern Italian states. Many of these works ended up in Bergamo under the stewardship of Count Giacomo Carrara. The collection came into its own in the Post World War I years, when a young Bernard Berenson, the 20th century's most noted connoisseur of art, wandered through the galleries taking stock of what was here and classifying the immense holdings, making sure "every Lotto is a Lotto." Lorenzo Lotto (1480 to 1556) was a Venetian who fled the stupefying society of his native city and spent 12 years in Bergamo, from 1513 to 1525, perfecting his highly emotive, intimate portraits. Many of his works from the Accademia recently toured the United States, and they are now back in place, hanging in the salons of a neoclassical palace alongside a staggering inventory that includes paintings by Bellini, Canaletto, Carpaccio, Guardi, Mantegna, and Tiepolo. Most of these masterworks are in the 17 third-floor galleries.

It's easy to become overwhelmed in the midst of this surplus, but among the paintings you might want to view first is **Lotto's portrait of Lucina Brembrati,** in which you will see the immense sensitivity with which the artist was able to imbue his subjects (also look carefully at the moon in the upper-lefthand corner, which has the letters "ci" painted into it—a playful anagram for the sitter's first name, "luna" plus "ci"). Bottocelli's much reproduced **portrait of Giuliano de Medici** hangs nearby, as does Raphael's sensual *Saint Sebastian.* You can easily visit the Accademia on foot from the Città Alta by following the Via Porta Dipinta halfway down the hill to Porto Sant'Agostino, and from there a terraced, ramplike staircase to the doors of the museum at Pz. Carrara 82a. Admission is 5,000L ($2.95), children 17 and under and seniors 60 and over free, free for all ages on Sunday. It's open Wednesday to Monday 9:30am to 12:30pm and 2:30 to 5:30pm.

EXPLORING THE CITTÀ ALTA

The higher, older part of Bergamo owes its hefty stone palazzos, proud monuments and what remains of its extensive fortified walls to more than 3 centuries of Venetian rule, beginning in 1428 when soldiers of the Republic wrestled control of the city out of the hands of the Milan-based Visconti family. The Venetians left their mark elegantly in the town's theatrically adjoining squares, the Piazza Vecchia and the Piazza del Duomo, which together create one of the most beautiful outdoor assemblages in Italy—actually, the French writer Stendahl went so far as to call this heart of old Bergamo the "most beautiful place on earth."

On Piazza Vecchia, you'll see traces of the Venetian presence in the 12th-century **Palazzo della Ragione** (Courts of Justice), which has been embellished with a graceful arcade on the ground floor and, the Lion of San Mark's, symbol of the Venetian Republic, above a 16th-century balcony reached by a covered staircase, (the bells atop its adjoining tower, the Torre Civico, sound the hours sonorously); across the piazza, the Bibliotheca Civica is modeled after the Sansovino Library in Venice.

The **Piazza del Duomo,** reached through one of the archways of the Palazzo della Ragione, is filled with an overpowering collection of religious structures that include the Duomo and the much more enticing **Capella Colleoni,** baptistery and the basilica of Santa Maria Maggiore (see below).

Colleoni has lent his name to the upper town's delightful main street, cobblestoned and so narrow you can just about touch the buildings on either side when standing in the center. If you follow it to its far western end you will emerge into **Largo Colle**

Aperto, refreshingly green and open to the Città Bassa and valleys below. For better views and a short excursion into the countryside, board the Funicolare San Vigilo for the ascent up the **San Vigilo hill;** the funicular (2,500L/$1.45) runs daily every 30 minutes between 7am and midnight. The strategic importance of these heights was not lost on Bergamo's medieval residents, who erected a summit-top castello, now mostly in ruin; its keep, still surrounded by the old walls, is a park in which every bench affords a far-reaching view; it's open daily, from 10am to 8pm April to September, 10am to 6pm in October and March, and 10am to 4pm November to February.

The **Castello** is a good place to begin a trek around the flanks of the Città Alta—first back down the San Vigilo hill (or take the funicular), then back into the Città Alta through the Porta San Alessandro. For a look at the old walls and some more good views, instead of following Via Colleoni back into the center of the town turn left on Via della Mura and follow the 16th-century bastions for about half a mile to **Porta Sant'Agostino** on the other side of the town.

Capella Colleoni. Pz. Duomo. ☎ **035/210-061.** Free admission. Apr–Sept, Tue–Sun, 9am–noon and 2:30–5:30pm; Oct–Mar, Tues–Sun, 9am–noon and 2:30–4:30pm.

Bartolomeo Colleoni was a Bergamese *condottiere* who fought for Venice to maintain the Venetian stronghold on the city. In return for his labors, the much-honored soldier was given Bergamo to rule for the Venetian republic. If you have visited Venice, you may have encountered Signore Colleoni astride the famous Verrocchio equestrian bronze in Campo Santi Giovanni e Paolo. He rests for eternity in this elegant and elaborate funerary chapel designed by Amadeo, the great sculptor from nearby Pavia (where he completed his most famous work, the Certosa; see page 528). The pink and white marble exterior, laced with finely sculpted columns and loggias, is airy and almost whimsical; inside, the soldier and his favorite daughter, Medea, lie beneath a ceiling frescoed by Tiepolo and surrounded by reliefs and statuary; Colleoni appears on horseback again atop his marble tomb.

Basilica di Santa Maria Maggiore. Pz. d. Duomo. Free admission. May–Sept 8am–12:30pm and 3–7pm, Oct–Apr 8am–noon and 3–6pm.

Behind the plain marble facade and a portico whose columns rise out of the backs of lions, lies an overly Baroque interior covered with gilt and hung with Renaissance tapestries. Gaetano Donizetti, the wildly popular composer of frothy operas who was born in Bergamo in 1797 (see below) and returned here to die in 1848, is entombed in a marble sarcophagus that is as excessive as the rest of the church's decor. The finest works here are the choir stalls, with rich wood inlays depicting landscapes and Biblical scenes; they are the creation of Lorenzo Lotto, the Venetian who worked in Bergamo in the early 16th century and whose work you will encounter at the Accademia Carrara and elsewhere around the city. The stalls are usually kept under cloth to protect the sensitive hardwoods from light and pollutants, but they are unveiled for Lent and briefly on guided tours (in Italian only) throughout the rest of the year Monday through Friday at 6pm and Saturday and Sunday at 4:30pm, 5pm, 5:30pm, and 6pm. (8,000L/$4.70). The octagonal baptistery in the piazza outside the church was originally inside, but removed, reconstructed and much embellished in the 19th century.

Museo Donizettiano. V. Arena 4. ☎ **035/399-269.** Free admission. Mon–Sat, 9am–noon and 2:30–5pm.

This charming little museum commemorates Gaetano Donizetti, who was born in Bergamo in 1797 and—little wonder given the romance of his boyhood surroundings—became one of Italy's most acclaimed composers of opera. Fans can swoon over his sheet music, piano, and other memorabilia, and see the deathbed where he succumbed to syphilis in 1848. Thus inspired, you can make the pilgrimage to the humble house where he claimed to have been born in a cellar, the **Casa Nateledi Gaetano Donizetti,** at V. B. Canale 14, a rural street that descends the hillside from Porta Sant'Alessandro on the western edge of the city (☎ **035/399-432**); it's open on weekends only from 11am to 6:30pm (donations requested).

WHERE TO STAY

The charms of staying in the Città Alta are no secret. Rooms tend to fill up quickly, especially in summer and on weekends. Reserve well in advance.

Agnello d'Oro. V. Gombito 22, 24100 Bergamo. ☎ **035/249-883.** Fax 035/235-612. 20 units, all with bathroom. TV TEL. 75,000L ($44.10) single; 125,000L ($73.50) double. AE, DC, MC, V.

In keeping with its location a few steps from the Piazza Vecchia, the Agnello d'Oro looks like it's right out of an old tourist brochure extolling the quaint charms of Italy. The tall, narrow ocher-colored building, with flower boxes at each of its tall windows, overlooks a small piazzetta where a fountain splashes next to potted greenery. The cozy wood-paneled lounge and intimate dining room add to the charm quotient, which declines somewhat as you ascend in a tiny elevator to the guest rooms. These lean more toward serviceable comfort than luxury, though warm color schemes and old prints help compensate for the lack of space and amenities; the bathrooms are roomy and have been modernized. Rooms in front (the ones to request) have narrow balconies overlooking the piazza. This is the most popular hostelry in the Città Alta, so reservations are mandatory.

Albergo San Lorenzo. Pz. Mascheroni 9A, 24129 Bergamo. ☎ **035/237-383.** Fax 035/237-958. 25 units, all with bathroom. A/C MINIBAR TV TEL. 138,000L ($81.20) single; 198,000L ($116.50) double. Rates include breakfast. AE, DC, MC, V. Free parking available.

Bergamo Alta was blessed with some much needed additional hotel rooms when this stylish hotel opened in 1998, in a former convent building of the church of Santa Agata. The centuries-old setting is tailor-made for the unusually pleasant inn that this is—most of the rooms face a courtyard and open through French doors to a balcony that wraps around it; though the hotel is right in town, just a few steps off Via Colleoni, its hillside location provides views over the green slopes flowing down to the valley below. The guest rooms are small but comfortable, with striped silk draperies and bed coverings, brass wall lamps, and cane-backed lounge chairs; each of the marble bathrooms is equipped with make-up lights around the mirrors, hand held shower massager, hair dryer, and a basket of complimentary toiletries. A sumptuous breakfast is served buffet style in a lower-level breakfast room. The discovery of Roman ruins put the brakes on construction of an underground parking facilities, though the hotel provides a permit that allows you to park for free in the adjoining square.

Hotel Gourmet. V. San Vigilo, 24129 Bergamo. ☎ and fax **035/437-3004.** 11 units, all with bathroom. TV TEL. 100,000L ($58.80) single; 140,000L ($82.35) double. AE, MC, V.

This pleasant hotel offers the best of both worlds—it's only steps away from the Città Alta (it's just outside the Port Sant'Agostino on the road leading up to the Castello) but on a rural hillside, giving it the air of a country retreat. The villa-style building is set behind walls in a lush garden and enjoys wonderful views. A wide terrace on two sides of the building make the most of these views. Many of the very large, bright guest rooms look across the hillside to the valley, too. They are tidily furnished in plain modern fashion geared more to solid comfort than to style, and the king-sized beds and ample countertops and built-in cabinets will tempt you to unpack, tuck the bags away, and relax. There's a highly reputed restaurant downstairs, hence the name, with indoor and outdoor tables, where guests are welcome to enjoy glass of wine or cup of coffee.

WHERE TO DINE

Your gambols through the Città Alta can be nicely interspersed with fortifying stops at the city's many pastry shops and stand up eateries. **Forno Tresoldi** at V. Colleoni 13, sells excellent pizzas and foccacia breads topped with cheese, salami and vegetables by the slice (from 3,000L/$1.75); it's open Tuesday to Sunday from 8am to 1:30pm and 4 to 10pm.

Al Donizetti. V. Gombito 17a. ☎ **035/242-661.** Primi 8,000–12,000L ($4.70–$7.05), secondi 10,000–18,000L ($5.90–$10.60). MC, V. Sat–Thurs, noon–3pm and 7:30–10:30pm. NORTHERN ITALIAN.

Bergamo's revered composer lends this name to this charming and unusual restaurant that faces the upper city's old covered market, which now serves no purpose other than to look medieval and romantic. In good weather tables are brought out under the market's arcaded loggia, and meals are also served in two small, vaulted-ceilinged dining rooms. Be it a primi or a secondi, order whatever you want from the menu (in whatever order). Many different kinds of salamis and hams are available, though many dishes rely on fresh vegetables—these offerings include a light zucchini flan, *raddichio con gorgonzola* (the bitter red greens are lightly grilled and the creamy cheese is added at the last minute), and a simple penne with pesto sauce. More than 300 wines are available (most by the glass, from 3,000L/$1.75) to accompany a meal, and the helpful staff will help you choose the right one.

Antica Hosteria del Vino Buono. V. Donizetti 25. ☎ **035/247-993.** Reservations recommended. Primi 10,000–12,000L ($5.90–$7.05), secondi 15,000–22,000L ($8.80–$12.95); tasting menus 50,000L ($29.40). MC, V. Thurs–Tue, noon–4pm and 7:30pm–midnight. NORTHERN ITALIAN.

At this cozy restaurant tucked into two smallish ground-floor rooms on a corner near the funicular station and Piazza Mercato della Scarpe, an enthusiastic young staff takes food and wine seriously. It's a pleasure to dine in the handsome surroundings of brick, tile work, and photos of old Bergamo. For an introduction to food from the region, try one of the several different tasting menus. Polenta figures prominently among the primi and is served *alla bergamese* (with wild mushrooms), and sometimes with olive paste folded into it). The main courses lean toward meat. A dish like roast quail or rabbit should be accompanied by a Valcalepio Rosso, a medium-strength red from local vineyards.

Vineria Cozzi. V. Colleoni 22. ☎ **035/238-836.** Sandwiches, from 6,000L ($3.55); primi 7,000–9,000L ($4.10–$5.30), secondi 8,000–15,000L ($4.70–$8.80). V. Thurs–Tues, 12:30–2:30pm and 7–10pm, closed Thurs. NORTHERN ITALIAN.

Cozzi isn't just a wine bar, but a Bergamo institution. Its cane chairs are well worn with use by Bergamese and visitors who can't resist stopping in for a glass of wine while walking down the Via Colleoni. Hundreds of bottles from throughout Italy line the walls and are served by the glass (from 3,000L/$1.75). Sandwiches are always available, as are several kinds of cheese, but the changing daily offerings also usually include several pasta dishes and polenta with rich cheese folded into it, perhaps a torta stuffed with fresh vegetables and a main course or two—if the duck breast stuffed with cabbage is available, order it.

CAFES

Caffè del Tasso, Pz. Vecchia 3, is a prime piece of real estate on the main square of Città Alta. It began life as a tailor's shop 500 years ago, but it's been a bar since 1581. Legend has it that Garibaldi's Redshirts used to gather here (Bergamo was a stronghold of Italian independence, which explains why an edict from the 1850s on the wall of this cafe prohibits rebellion). While the location of **Caffè della Funicolare** in the Piazza Mercato delle Scarpe, in the upper terminal of the funicular that climbs the hill from Città Bassa to Città Alta, doesn't suggest a memorable dining experience, the station dates from 1887 and has enough belle epoque flourishes and curlicues to make the surroundings interesting. Plus, the dining room and terrace look straight down the hill to the town and valley, providing some the best tables with a view (accompanied by low-cost fare) in the upper town. Stop in for a coffee, one of the 50 kinds of beer on tap, a sandwich, or a salad.

3 Mantua (Mantova)

158 km (95 mi.) E of Milan, 62 km (37 mi.) N of Parma, 150 km (90 mi.) SW of Venice

One of Lombardy's finest cities is in the farthest reaches of the region, making it a logical addition to a trip to Venice or Parma as well as to Milan. Like its neighboring cities in Emilia-Romagna, Mantua owes its past greatness and its beautiful Renaissance monuments to one family, in this case the Gonzagas, who rose from peasant origins to conquer the city in 1328 and ruled benevolently until 1707. You'll encounter the Gonzagas—and, since they were avid collectors of art and ruled through the greatest centuries of Italian art, the treasures they collected—in the massive **Palazzo Ducale** that dominates much of the town center, in their refreshing suburban retreat, the **Palazzo Tei,** and in the churches and piazzas that grew up around their court. One of Mantua's greatest charms is its location—on a meandering river, the Mincio, which widens here to envelop Mantua in a necklace of moodily romantic lakes. Often shrouded in mist and surrounded by flat, lonely plains, Mantua can seem almost melancholy. Aldous Huxley wrote of the city, "I have seen great cities dead or in decay—but over none, it seemed to me, did there brood so profound a melancholy as over Mantua." Since his visit in the 1930s, though, the Palazzo Ducale and other monuments have been restored, and what will probably strike you more is what a remarkable gem of a city Mantua is.

FESTIVALS & MARKETS   Mantua enlivens its steamy summer with a July jazz festival. Year-round, **Piazza dell'Erbe** is the scene of a bustling food market Monday through Saturday from 8am to 1pm. On Thursdays, a bigger market, filled with clothing, housewares and more food, spills through Piazza Magenta and adjoining streets.

ESSENTIALS

GETTING HERE   By Train   Trains arrive from **Milan,** via Brescia, nine times a day (2 hours; 14,000L/$8.25) and from **Verona** (with connections to Venice) 11 times a day (40 minutes; 3,500L/$2.05).

By Car   The speediest connections from Milan are via the autostradas, the **A4** to Verona and the **A22** from Verona to Mantua; the trip takes less than 2 hours). From Mantua it is also an easy drive south to Parma and other cities in Emilia-Romagna, on **S420.**

VISITOR INFORMATION   The APT tourist office is at Pz. Mantegna 6 (☎ **0376/32-82-54**); open Monday to Saturday, 9am to noon and 3 to 6pm, Sunday, 9am to noon.

CITY LAYOUT   Mantua is tucked onto a point of land surrounded on three sides by the river Mincio, which widens here into a series of lakes, named prosaically Lago Superiore, Lago di Mezzo, and Lago Inferiore. Most of the sights are within an easy walk of one another within the compact center, which is only a 10-minute walk from the lakeside train station. Follow Via Solferino to Via Marangoni, turn right and follow that to Piazza Cavallotti, where a left turn on Corso Umberto I will bring you to the **Piazza delle Erbe,** the first of the gracious piazzas that flow through the city center to the palace of the Gonzogas. You can also make the trip on the no. 2 bus, which leaves from the front of the station; fare is 1,400L (82¢).

EXPLORING THE CITY

Mantua is flat and much of its center is closed to traffic, making it good biking terrain. You can join the city residents and get around on two wheels with a rental from **La Rigola**, on the lakeside on Lungolago dei Gonzaga, in front of Piazza Arche, ☎ **0376/366-677** (follow Via Accademia east to the lake from Piazza Sordello). The concession is open daily from 8am to 8pm, and rentals are 4,000L ($2.35) an hour Monday through Saturday, 5,000L ($2.95) on Sunday, 11,000L ($6.50) per day Monday through Saturday, 16,000L ($9.40) on Sunday.

As you wander around, you'll notice that Mantua's squares are handsomely proportioned spaces surrounded by medieval and Renaissance churches and palazzi. The piazze open one into another, creating for walkers in the city the wonderful illusion that they are strolling through a series of opera sets. The northernmost of these squares, and the place to begin your explorations, is **Piazza delle Erbe,** so named for the produce and food market that transpires in stalls to one side (see "Festivals & Markets," above). Mantua's civic might is clustered here in a series of late-medieval and early Renaissance structures that include the Palazzo della Ragione (Courts of Justice) and Palazzo del Podestà (Mayor's Palace), from the 12th and 13th centuries, and the Torre dell'Orlogio, topped with a 14th-century astrological clock. Mantua's earliest religious structure, the Rotunda di San Lorenzo, a miniature round church from the 11th century, is on this square (it's open 10:30am to 12:30pm and 2:30 to 4:30pm, though hours vary; admission free), and the city's Renaissance masterpiece, the church of Sant'Andrea (see below) is off to one side on Piazza Mantegna.

In the adjoining **Piazza Broletto** (just north as you work your way through the old city), the statue of Virgil commemorates the poet, who was born near here in 70 B.C. and celebrated Mantua's river Mincio in his Bucolics. The next square, **Piazza Sordello** is huge, rectangular and somberly medieval, lined with crenulated palazzos. Most notably, though, the massive hulk of the Palazzo Ducale (see below) forms one wall of the piazza. To enjoy Manuta's soulful lakeside vistas, follow **Via Accademia** through Piazza Arche and the Lungolago Gonzaga.

Before you pay for admission to one of the city's museums, ask at the ticket counter for a lire-saving **biglietto unico;** it costs 18,000L ($10.60) and is good for entry to the Palazzo Ducale, the Palazzo d'Arco and the Palazzo Te, as well as some of the city's other monuments.

Chiesa Sant'Andrea. Pz. Mantegna. Daily 7:30am–noon and 3:30–7:30pm.

One of the most graceful facades of the Renaissance period fronts this 15th-century church designed by Leon Battista Alberti. The clean simple arches seem to float beneath the classic pediment, and the unadorned elegance forms a sharp visual contrast to other Lombardy monuments such as the Duomo in Milan, the Cappella Colleoni in Bergamo, and the Certosa in Pavia. Inside, the vast, classically proportioned space is centered on a single aisle. Mantegna, the Gonzaga court painter, is buried here, and the crypt houses a reliquary containing the blood of Christ (allegedly brought here by Longinus, who obtained the relic by thrusting his spear into the body), which is carried through on March 18, the feast of Mantua's patron, Sant'Anselmo.

Palazzo d'Arco. Pz. d'Arco 1. ☎ **0376/322-242.** Admission 5,000L ($2.95). Mar–Oct, Tues–Fri 10am–12:30pm and 2:30–6pm, Sat–Sun 10am–6pm. Nov–Feb Sat–Sun 10am–12:30pm and 2–5pm, Sun 10am–5pm.

Mantua's aristocratic D'Arco family lived in this elegant Renaissance palazzo until the early 20th century, when the last member of the family donated it to the city. A highlight of the rooms is the Sala dello Zodiaco, which is brilliantly frescoed with astrological signs by Giovanni Falconetto in 1520. The adjoining gardens are nestled among surrounding palazzos.

Palazzo Ducale. Pz. Sordello. ☎ **0376/320-283.** Admission 12,000L ($7.05), by guided tour (in Italian only). Tues–Sat 9am–1pm and 2:30–6pm; Sun–Mon 9am–1pm.

Behind the walls of this massive, fortress-cum-palazzo lies the history of the Gonzagas, Mantua's most powerful family, and what remains of the treasure trove they amassed in a rule that began in 1328 and lasted into the early 18th century. Between their skills as warriors and their penchant for marrying into wealthier and more cultured houses, the Gonzagas managed to acquire power, money, and an artistic following that included Pisanello, Titian, and most notably, Andrea Mantegna, their court painter who spent most of his career working for his Mantua patrons. The most fortunate of these unions was that of Francesco Gonzaga to Isabelle d'Este in 1490. This well-bred daughter of Ferrara's Este clan commissioned many of the frescoed and art-filled apartments you see today, including the Camera degli Sposi in Isabella's apartments—the masterpiece, and only remaining fresco cycle of Mantegna. It took the artist 9 years to complete the cycle, and in it, he included many of the visitors to the court; as a result, it is a fascinating account of late 15th-century court life. Most of Mantegna's works for the palace, though, have been carted off to other collections; his famous *Parnassus,* which he painted for an intimate room known as the studiolo, is now in the Louvre, as are works that Perugino and Corregio painted for the same room (in one of the more compelling current stories from the art world, Mantua is demanding their return).

The Gonzagas expanded their palace by incorporating any structure that lay within reach, including Mantua's Duomo. As a result, it's now a small city of 500 rooms connected by a labyrinth of corridors, ramps, courtyards, and staircases. A guide leads groups of 20 through the Camera degli Sposi and the studiolo, the Sala del Pisanello, where frescoes painted by Pisanell painted from 1439 to 1444 were only discovered beneath layers of plaster in 1969, the Galleria degli Specchi (Hall of Mirrors), the low-ceiling Appartemento dei Nani (apartments of the dwarfs), where a replica of the Holy Staircase in the Vatican is built to miniature scale (in keeping with noble custom of the time, dwarfs were part of Isabella's court), the Galleria dei Mesi (the frescoed Hall of the Months), and some of the mostly delightful chambers in the vast complex, the Appartimento Estivale (Summer Apartments), which look over a courtyard where hanging gardens provide the greenery.

Palazzo Te. Vle. Te. ☎ **0376/323-266.** Admission 12,000L ($7.05), 10,000L ($5.90) children 17 and under and seniors 60 and over. Tues–Sun, 9am–6pm.

Frederico Gonzaga, the refined and pleasure-loving son of Isabella D'Este, built this splendid Mannerist palace as a retreat from court life. You will see that the purpose of this palace was to amuse as soon as you enter the courtyard—the keystone of the monumental archway is designed to look like it is falling out of place. Throughout the lovely, whimsical interior, sexually frank frescoes (by Giulio Romano, who left a scandal behind him in Rome that arose over his licentious engravings) depict Psyche and other erotically charged subject matter and make unsubtle reference to one of Frederico's favorite pastimes (horses and astrology, Frederico's other passions, also figure prominently). The greatest and most playful achievement here, though, has to do with power: In the Sala dei Giganti (Room of the Giants), Titan is overthrown by the gods in a dizzying play of architectural proportion that gives the illusion that the ceiling is falling. The palazzo is a 20-minute walk from the center of town along Via Mazzini. En route, devotees of Mantua's most famous painter may choose to stop for a look at the **Casa di Mantegna** at V. Acerbi 47; admission is free and it's open daily from 10am to 12:30pm and 3 to 6pm (hours vary).

WHERE TO STAY

If you're interested in the lowest-priced accommodations, the tourist office (Pz. Mantegna 6, ☎ **0376/32-82-54**) can provide information and make reservations for rooms at five hostel-like farmhouses in the surrounding countryside. Rates are low, about 20,000L ($11.75) a person. Since several of the properties are within a few kilometers of town, you can reach them without too much trouble by bike or combination bus ride and trek.

Hotel ABC Moderno. Pz. Don Leoni 25, 46100 Mantova. ☎ and fax **0376/325-002.** 27 units, all with bathroom. TV TEL. 85,000L ($50) single, 130,000L ($76.45) double. Rates include breakfast. MC, V.

The prices at this recently renovated hotel located across from the train station are remarkably low, considering the pleasant surroundings and the amenities. Downstairs, a pleasant lounge area and breakfast room open onto a sunny terrace. Upstairs, the renovated rooms have bright new tile floors, fresh plaster and paint, new furnishings, and new bathrooms; architectural details, such as stone walls and patches of old frescoes, have been uncovered to provide decorative touches. The management is extremely helpful, and their hospitality extends to bike rentals (10,000L/$5.90). If the Moderno is full, bypass the other nearby hotels, which tend to be dreary and overpriced.

Hotel Broletto. V. Accademia 1, 46100 Mantova. ☎ **0376/32-67-84.** Fax 0376/22-12-97. 16 units, all with bathroom. A/C MINIBAR TV TEL. 100,000L ($58.80) single; 150,000L ($88.25) double. Breakfast 12,000L ($7.05). AE, MC, V.

This atmospheric and pleasant old hotel is in the center of the old city, only a few steps from the lake and the castello, making it a fine base for a late-night stroll through the moonlit piazzas. The guest rooms have contemporary furnishings that are vaguely rustic in design; the most alluring feature of the decor, though, are massive beams on the ceilings and other architectural details.

Hotel Mantegna. V. Fabio Filzi 10, 46100 Mantova. ☎ **0376/328-019.** Fax 0376/368-564. 39 units, all with bathroom. A/C TV TEL. 95,000L ($55.90) single,;140,000L ($82.35) double. Breakfast 13,000L ($7.65). AE, MC, V.

On a quiet side street just a few steps south of the centro storico, the Mantegna offers solid comfort in surroundings that are thoroughly modern. The cozy narrow singles resemble ships' cabins, but the doubles are unusually roomy. All have been renovated within the past few years and have new bathrooms; many face a sunny and quiet courtyard. There's free parking behind the hotel.

WORTH A SPLURGE

Albergo San Lorenzo. Pz. Concordia 14, 46100 Mantova. ☎ **0376/220-500.** Fax 0376/327-194. 41 units, all with bathroom. A/C MINIBAR TV TEL. 135,000–270,000L ($79.40–$158.80) single; 160,000–370,000L ($94.10–$217.65) double. Rates include breakfast. AE, MC, V. Parking 20,000L ($11.75).

One of Italy's more noteworthy and gracious inns was fashioned out of a row of old houses just off the Piazza Dell'Erbe. Oil paintings and oriental carpets grace the marble-floored salons, and the guest rooms, no two of which are alike, are furnished with exquisite reproductions of 19th-century antiques and equipped with elegant bathrooms and all the other conveniences you would expect from a luxury hotel. A panoramic roof terrace overlooks the towers and rooftops of the centro storico, and a lavish buffet breakfast is served in an elegant breakfast room overlooking the rotunda.

WHERE TO DINE

Mantovian cuisine is quite refined—exquisite risotto dishes, an array of pastas stuffed with pumpkin and squash, and given the proximity of lakes and rivers, a fine selection of fish appears on menus.

Leoncino Rosso. V. Giustiziati 33. ☎ **0376/323-277.** Reservations recommended. Primi 7,000–10,0000L ($4.10–$5.90); secondi 8,000–12,000L ($4.70–$7.05). MC, V. Mon–Sat, noon–3pm and 7–10pm. Closed in Aug and 3 weeks in Jan. MANTOVIAN.

This fine old restaurant, just off the Piazza Broletto in the center of the old city, has been serving food since 1750. With an attractive, rustic dining rooms, this is a good place to sample Mantua's distinctive cuisine. Topping the list is *tortelli di zucca,* a large ravioli pillow stuffed with pumpkin. If you want to continue to eat as the Mantovese do, move on to *stracotto di asino* (stewed donkey); for more familiar fare from the barnyard, try the delicious *cotechino e fagioli* (pork sausage and beans).

Ochina Bianca. V. Finzi 2. ☎ **0376/323-700.** Reservations required. Primi 8,000–12,000L ($4.70–$7.05); secondi 10,000–18,000L ($5.90–$10.60). MC, V. Tues 7:30–10:30pm, Wed–Sun noon–3:30pm and 7:30–10:30pm. MANTOVIAN.

Gilberto and Marcella Venturini serve distinctive variations on the local cuisine in a simple and elegant sculpture-filled dining room a few blocks north of the center. Many of the dishes rely on fresh fish from the Mincio, which finds it way into such creations as *peperoni ripieni di pesce di fiume* (peppers filled with smoked fish and topped with a fresh tomato sauce) and many of the risottos. Grilled or sauteed freshwater fish is also often on the menu, as are many traditional meat specialties, including *coniglio alla porchetta* (a roasted rabbit with a pork stuffing). *Torta sabbiosa* is a local dessert, and the homemade gelato is delicious. The carefully chosen wine list is extensive.

Pescheria Lanfranchi. V. Pescherie. No listed phone. Fish specialties from 4,000L ($2.35). Mon–Sat, 8:30am–1pm and 4:30–7:30pm. Closed Mon afternoons and Sun. SEAFOOD.

There's no end to the creatures, most of them deep-fried, at this fish stall on wheels. It's parked south of the centro storico near the banks of a scenic canal. A plate of squid, octopus, or lake fish makes a fine light meal or snack.

Trattoria Due Cavallini. V. Salnitro 5. ☎ **0376/328-431.** Primi 5,000–9,000L ($2.95–$5.30), secondi 12,000–15,000L ($7.05–$8.80). AE, MC, V. Tues–Sun, noon–3pm and 7:15pm–midnight. MANTOVIAN.

Your reward for the 10-minute walk south of the center (follow Via Trieste and its continuation, Corso Garibaldi) is a meal at one of Mantua's favorite informal trattorias, where you can eat in a shady courtyard in good weather. The menu is typically Mantovian, with excellent tortelli di zucca and an aromatic stinco di miale (roasted pork joint, infused with fresh herbs). The *torta sbrisolona,* a traditional Mantovese cake of cornmeal, almonds, and butter, is served fresh from the oven.

A DAY TRIP TO SABBIONETA

Ever since the death of Duke Vespasiano Gonzaga in 1591, this tiny Renaissance city, about 20 miles southwest of Mantua, has been a backwater town. Along with the duke, died his dreams of grandeur for Sabbioneta, which he envisioned as the seat of his ducal court. He spent 15 years building the little city, a relatively short time for what he achieved in the design of what he considered to be the realization of the Renaissance ideal of an urban center, surrounded by star-shaped walls. A recent restoration has put some dazzle back into the Palazzo Ducale, the Teatro Olimpico, the Palazzo del Giardino (summer palace) and the other structures that Gonzaga commissioned. They can be visited on guided tours (in Italian, though in English on request and depending on the availability of an English-speaking guide) arranged through the tourist office; the cost is 10,000L ($5.90).

There are seven buses a day from Mantua; make sure to check the time of the last return bus before setting out. The 45-minute trip costs 5,600L ($3.30). By car, Sabbioneta is a half an hour ride from Mantua on **S420,** the main Mantua-Parma-Mantua road. The **tourist office,** V. Vespasiano Gonzaga 31 (☎ **0375/52-039**) is open April through September, Monday to Friday from 9am until noon and 2:30 to 6pm, Saturday and Sunday from 1:30 to 7pm; October through March, daily from 9am until noon and 2:30 to 5pm (until 6pm Saturday and Sunday).

4 Lago di Garda

Sirmione 127 km (76 mi.) E of Milan, 149 km (90 mi.) W of Venice, Riva del Garda 170 km (102 mi.) E of Milan, 199 km (120 mi.) NW of Venice, 43 km (26 mi.) S of Trent

Poets, composers, and mere mortals have been rhapsodizing about the Italian lakes for centuries—most vocally since the 18th century, when it became de rigueur for travelers on the Grand Tour to descend through the Alps and enjoy their first days on Italian soil on the shores of the lakes.

Lake Garda, the largest and easternmost of the lakes, laps against the flat plains of Lombardy and the Veneto at its southern extremes, and in the north becomes fjord-like and moody, its deep waters backed by Alpine peaks. All around the lake, Garda's shores are green and fragrant with flowery gardens, groves of olives and lemons, and forests of pines and cypress. This pleasing, vaguely exotic landscape has attracted the likes of poet Gabriele D'Annunzio, whose villa near Gardone is one of the lake's major attractions, and Benito Mussolini, whose Republic of Salo was headquartered here. Mussolini was also captured and executed on these shores. Long before them, the Romans discovered the hot springs that still gush forth at Sirmione, the famed resort on a spit of land at the lake's southern reaches. Today's visitors come to swim (Garda is the cleanest of the major lakes), windsurf (Riva del Garda, at the northern end of the lake, is Europe's windsurfing capital), and enjoy the easy-going ambience of Garda's many pleasant lakeside resorts.

SIRMIONE

Garda's most popular resort juts several miles into the southern waters of the lake on a narrow, cypress- and olive-grove–clad peninsula. Despite an onslaught of visitors, pretty Sirmione manages to retain its charm. Vehicular traffic is kept to a minimum (the few motorists allowed onto the marble streets of the old town are required to switch off their cars' engines at traffic lights), and the emphasis is on strolling, swimming in waters that are warmed in places by underwater hot springs, and relaxing on the sunny terraces of pleasant lakeside hotels. One caveat: You might find Sirmione to be less than charming in July and August, when the crowds descend in full force.

ESSENTIALS

GETTING HERE By Train Connections are via nearby Desenzano, which is on the Milan-Venice rail lines, with trains almost every half hour in either direction, stopping in Verona, Brescia, and other towns on the busy corridor. **Venice** is 2 hours away, and the fare is 14,000L ($8.25); **Milan** is 1½ hours away, and the fare is 10,100L ($5.95). From Desenzano, you can reach Sirmione in about 20 minutes by half hourly bus service; the fare is 2,100L ($1.25).

By Bus   Hourly bus service links Sirmione with **Brescia;** the 1-hour trip costs 5,400L ($3.20); for more information contact SAIA buses in Brescia, ☎ **030/223-761.**

By Boat   Hydrofoils and ferries ply the waters between Desenzano, Sirmione, and other towns on the lake; service is curtailed in the off-season months, October through April. Most boats are operated by Navigazione Lago di Garda (☎ **030/91-41-321**), headquartered on the dock in Desenzano.

By Car   Sirmione is just off the **A4** autostrada between Milan and Venice. From Bologna, Florence, Rome, and other points south, take the **A22** autostrada north from Modena to Verona, and from there the **A4** west to Sirmione. The trip from Venice takes about 1½ hours, and the trip from Milan a little over an hour. There is ample parking in the lakeside lots that line Viale Marconi, the broad avenue that runs down the peninsula to the entrance of the old town.

VISITOR INFORMATION   The **APT tourist office** is just outside the old town near the castle at Vle. Marconi 2 (☎ **030/916-245**). It's open April through October, daily from 9am to 12:30pm and 3 to 6pm; November through March, Monday to Friday from 9am to 12:30pm and 3 to 6pm, Saturday from 9am to 12:30pm. The helpful, English-speaking staff dispenses a wealth of information about Sirmione and other sights on the lake and will reserve a room for you.

EXPLORING THE TOWN

In addition to its attractive though tourist-shop–ridden old town, Sirmione has many lakeside promenades, pleasant beaches, and even some open countryside where olive trees sway in the breeze. Anything you'll want to see can be reached easily on foot, though an open-air tram (2,500L/$1.50) makes the short run out to the Roman ruins from the northern edge of the old town.

The moated and turreted **Castello Scaligero** marks the only land-side entrance to the old town. Built in the 13th century by the della Scala family, who ruled Verona and many of the lands surrounding the lake, the castle (☎ **030/91-61-48**) warrants a visit mainly for the views from its towers. It's open April through October daily from 9am to 6pm and October through March Tuesday through Sunday from 9am to 1pm. Admission 8,000L ($4.70). From the castle, Via Vittorio Emanuele leads through the center of the town and emerges after a few blocks into the greener, garden-lined lanes that wind through the tip of the peninsula to the **Grotte di Catullo** (☎ **030/ 91-61-57**). Whether or not these extensive ruins at the northern tip of the peninsula were really, as they are alleged to have been, the villa and baths of the pleasure-loving Roman poet Catullus is open to debate. Even so, their presence here, on a hilltop fragrant with wild rosemary and pines, demonstrates that Sirmione has been a deservedly popular retreat for millennia, and you can wander through the evocative remains while enjoying wonderful views of the lake. The ruins are open April through September from Tuesday through Sunday, 8:30am to 7pm and October through March from Monday through Saturday from 8:30am to 4:30pm and Sunday 9:30am to 4:30pm; admission is 8,000L ($4.70).

WATER SPORTS   If you want to enjoy the clean waters of the lake, the place to head is the small **Lido delle Bionde** near the castle off Via Dante. In summer, the beach concession rents lounge chairs with umbrellas for 10,000L ($5.90), as well as kayaks (8,000L/$4.70 an hour) and pedal boats (12,000L/$7.05 an hour).

WHERE TO STAY

Sirmione has many pleasant, moderately priced hotels, all of which book up quickly in the high-season months of July and August, when they also charge higher rates (reflected in the high end of the rates below). You are not allowed to drive into the old town until a guard at the entrance near the castle confirms that you have a hotel reservation.

Hotel Corte Regina. V. Antica Mura 11, 25019 Sirmione. ☎ and fax **030/916-147.** 10 units, all with bathroom. TV TEL. 90,000–120,000L ($52.95–$70.60) single; 120,000–150,000L ($70.60–$88.25) double. Rates include breakfast. AE, MC, V.

This older, attractive hotel is housed in a stone building on a narrow side street that leads to the lake and a beach. While it doesn't enjoy the same lakeside views as the Grifone (see below), the Corte Regina, with its pleasant accommodations and friendly ambience, is an excellent alternative if that hotel is full. Outside, there's a sunny terrace. Upstairs, a recent renovation provided the large, tile-floored rooms with contemporary furnishings and new bathrooms.

Hotel Eden. Pz. Carducci 17/18, 25019 Sirmione. ☎ **030/916-481.** Fax 030/916-483. 33 units, all with bathroom. A/C MINIBAR TV TEL. 132,000–157,000L ($77.65–$92.35) single; 180,000–225,000L ($105.90–$132.35) double. Rates include breakfast. AE, MC, V.

The American poet Ezra Pound once lived in this pink-stucco lakeside hotel, which is located on a quiet side street leading to the lake in the center of town. Despite its long history as a lakeside retreat, the Eden has recently been modernized with enormous taste and an eye to comfort. The lake can be seen from most of the bright, attractive rooms, which are decorated in handsome, contemporary furnishings, and pastel shades. The mirrored walls enhance the light and lake views. The large, gleaming bathrooms are new and many have large tubs. Downstairs, the marble lobby opens to a delightful, shaded terrace and a swimming pier that juts into the lake.

Hotel Grifone. V. Bocchio 5, 25019 Sirmione. ☎ **030/916-014.** Fax 030/916-548. 16 units, all with bathroom. TV TEL. 80,000L ($47) single; 104,000L ($61.20) double. No credit cards. Closed Nov–Easter.

One of Sirmione's best-value lodgings is also one of its most romantic hostelries—the stone, vine-clad building next to the castle enjoys a prime piece of property on the lake. Guests can enjoy this waterside setting from a shady patio off the lobby, from a small beach, or from any of the guest rooms with a view. Brother and sister team Nicola and Christina Marcolini oversee the hotel and adjoining restaurant with a great deal of graciousness, carrying on several generations of a family business. The guest rooms are simple but pleasant, with tile floors and plain but unobtrusive furnishings; the tidy bathrooms are equipped with stall showers. The Grifone books up quickly, often with return guests, so reserve well in advance.

Hotel Olivi. V. San Pietro 5, 25019 Sirmione. ☎ **030/9905-365.** Fax 030/916-472. 60 units, all with bathroom. A/C MINIBAR TV TEL. 140,000–160,000L ($82.35–$94.10) single; 180,000–240,000L ($105.90–$141.20) double. Rates include breakfast. AE, MC, V. Closed Dec 15–Jan 31.

This pleasant, modern hotel is not directly on the lake, which can be seen from most of the rooms and the sunny terrace, but commands a hilltop position near the Roman ruins in a countryside of pines and olive groves. Rooms are stunningly decorated in varying schemes of bold, handsome pastels and earth tones. They have separate dressing areas off the bathrooms, and most have balconies. There is a swimming pool in the garden and, to bring a lakeside feeling to the grounds, an artificial river that streams past the terrace and glass windows of the lobby and breakfast room.

Hotel Speranza. V. Castello 6, 25019 Sirmione. ☎ **030/916-116.** Fax 030/916-403. 13 units, all with bathroom. TV TEL. 65,000L ($38.25) single; 110,000L ($64.70) double. Rates include breakfast. MC, V.

This modest hotel occupies the upper floors of an old building that arches across Sirmione's main street, providing a prime location near the castle and only a few steps in either direction from the lake. The emphasis here is on clean efficiency rather than luxury: public rooms consist of a tiny lobby and breakfast room, and the bare-bones rooms are tidy and perfectly serviceable; in fact, the plain modern furnishings set against tile floors and stark white walls provide a fairly chic look.

WHERE TO DINE

La Roccia. V. Piana 2. ☎ **030/916-392.** Primi 7,000–10,000L ($4.10–$5.90), secondi 11,000–15,000L ($6.50–$8.80), pizza from 8,000L ($4.70). MC, V. Fri–Wed 12:30–3pm and 7–10:30pm.

This trattoria and pizza parlor caters to the flocks of tourists who stream through Sirmione, but does so with excellent food and unusually pleasant surroundings. In good weather the best seating is in the large garden to one side of the restaurant. The menu includes many kinds of salads, which can be ordered as a single-course meal, and excellent pizzas made in a wood-burning oven. Many traditional pastas (including excellent cheese tortellini) are also available. The fish and meat are excellent, and the best dishes are grilled over an open fire.

Ristorante Al Progresso. V. Vittorio Emanuele 18. ☎ **030/916-108.** Primi 7,000–10,000L ($4.10–$5.90), secondi 12,000–18,000L ($7.05–$10.60). MC, V. Fri–Wed noon–2:30pm and 6:30–10:30pm. SEAFOOD/ITALIAN.

This brightly lit room on the main street of the old town is appealingly plain. The pastas include some excellent tortellini variations, as well as some with shellfish not from the lake but from the not-too-distant Adriatic. Fresh grilled lake trout is often on the menu, as are some simple veal preparations, including a *vitello al limone,* made with fresh lemons that grow on the shores of the lake.

RIVA DEL GARDA

The northernmost town on the lake is not just a resort but a real place, too, with medieval towers, a nice smattering of Renaissance churches and palazzi, and narrow cobblestone streets where the everyday business of a prosperous Italian town proceeds in its alluring way.

FESTIVALS & MARKETS Riva becomes a cultural oasis in July, when the town hosts an international festival of classical music.

ESSENTIALS

GETTING HERE **By Bus** Six buses a day link Riva and **Desenzano** on the southern end of the lake, about a 2-hour trip (6,400L/$3.75). You can also travel between **Sirmione** and Riva by bus, a 2-hour trip, though you must transfer at Peschiera (8,300L/$4.90). Buses connect Riva and **Trento** (eight a day make the 1-hour trip, 5,200L/$3.05; see chapter 10 for train connections to that city) and from **Verona** (14 a day make the 2-hour trip, 9,300L/$5.45; see chapter 9 for train connections).

By Boat Navigarda boats (4 hours) and hydrofoils (2 hours) connect Riva and **Sirmione** and **Desenzano,** making stops at major towns along the lake. Fares are 12,900L ($7.60) to Sirmione and 15,400L ($9.05) to Desenzano, with a supplement of 1,800 to 5,000L ($1.05 to $2.95) for the hydrofoil, depending on the destination. Schedules vary with season, with very limited service in the winter.

By Car The fastest link between Riva and points north and south is via the **A22** autostrada, which shoots up the east side of the lake (exit at Mori, 13 kilometers/9 mi., east of Riva). A far more scenic drive is along the western shore, on the beautiful corniche between Riva and Salo that hugs cliffs and passes through mile after mile of tunnel. Depending on the route, by car Riva is about an hour from **Verona** and about 45 minutes from **Sirmione.**

VISITOR INFORMATION The tourist office, which supplies information on hotels, restaurants, and activities in the area, is near the lakefront Giardini di Porta Orientale 8 (☎ **0464/554-444**). It is open Easter through mid-September, Monday to Saturday from 9am to noon and 3 to 6:30pm; mid-September through Easter, Monday to Friday from 9am to noon and 2 to 7pm.

EXPLORING THE TOWN

Riva's old town is pleasant enough, though the only historic attractions of note are the 13th century Torre d'Apponale and, nearby, the moated lakeside castle, **La Rocca.** Part of the castle interior now houses a small and unassuming collection of local arts and crafts (☎ **0464/573-869**); it's open Tuesday through Sunday from 9:30am to 12:30pm and 2:30 to 5:30pm; admission is 4,000L ($2.35).

The main attraction, not surprisingly, is the lake, which Riva takes advantage of with a waterside promenade stretching for several miles past parks and pebbly beaches. The water is warm enough for swimming from May into October, and air currents fanned by the surrounding mountains make Garda a popular spot for windsurfing year-round.

WATER & LAND SPORTS A convenient point of embarkation for an easygoing outing on the lake is the beach next to the castle, where you can rent rowboats for 14,000L ($8.25) an hour; the concession is open daily March through October from 8am to 8pm. For a more adventurous outing, check out the Professional Windsurfing School, V. Roverto 100 (☎ **0464/556-077**), where you can rent equipment for 70,000L ($41.20) a day or 22,000L ($12.95) an hour; multiday and weekly packages, as well as lessons, are also available. You can rent mountain bikes (20,000L/$11.75 a day) and regular bicycles (10,000L/$5.90 a day) from Girelli, Vle. Damiano Chiesa 15 (☎ **0464/556-602**) and Giuliani, V. Bruno Galas 29a (☎ **0464/554-719**).

WHERE TO STAY

Albergo Vittoria. V. Dante 39, 38066 Riva del Garda. ☎ **0464/554-398.** Fax 0464/555-641. 15 units, all with bathroom. 60,000L ($35.30) single, 80,000L ($47) double. MC, V.

A short walk from the lake on one of the streets of the old town, this family run hotel is one of the few low-cost places around. Downstairs there's a muraled dining room and a cozy, Tyrolean-looking bar with a vaulted stone ceiling. Upstairs, the guest rooms are snug and comfortable, with streamlined modern furnishings and small, tidy bathrooms with showers.

Hotel Sole. Pz. Novembre 23, 38066 Riva del Garda. ☎ **0464/552-686.** Fax 0464/552-811. 53 units, all with bathroom. A/C MINIBAR TV TEL. 190,000–210,000L ($111.75–$123.55) single; 230,000–270,000L ($135.30–$158.80) double. AE, MC, V. Closed Nov, Feb to mid-Mar.

One of the finest hotels in town enjoys a wonderful location right on the lake off the main square. The attentive management lavishes a great deal of attention on the public rooms and guest rooms, and charges very fairly, given the amenities offered. The lobby is filled with rare Persian carpets and abstract art. The guest rooms reached via a sweeping circular staircase are warm and luxurious, with lush fabrics, tasteful blond furnishings, and marble bathrooms; the best rooms have balconies that hang out over the lake. Amenities include a formal restaurant, a casual cafe/bar that extends onto a lakeside terrace, a rooftop solarium with sauna, and a garage.

WHERE TO DINE

Birreria Spaten. V. Mafferi 7. ☎ **0464/553-670.** Primi 6,000–9,000L ($3.55–$5.30), secondi 7,000–12,000L ($4.10–$7.05). MC, V. Tues–Sun 10:30am–3pm and 5:30pm–midnight; closed Mon Oct–Apr. ITALIAN/TYROLEAN.

This large, noisy, indoor beer garden occupies the ground floor of an old palazzo and features a wide-ranging mix of food from the surrounding regions, so you can dine here on the cuisine of Trento or Lombardy or from the other side of the Alps. Many of the German and Austrian visitors who favor Riva opt for the wide range of the schnitzel-sauerkraut-sauerbraten fare, but you can also enjoy many pasta or a simply grilled lake trout.

STAYING & DINING NEARBY IN LIMONE SUL GARDA

Limone sul Garda is a pretty resort wedged between the lake and mountains just 10 kilometers (6 mi.) south of Riva on the lakeside corniche; in summer, ferries make the half-hour trip from Riva almost hourly (9,000L/$5.30). Despite an onslaught of tourists who come down through the mountains from Austria and Germany, it's a pleasant place to spend some time and has more moderately priced lakeside hotels than Riva does. The Romans planted lemon groves here and covered them with protective structures, the ruins of which are still visible on the hills around the town. Lemons continue to thrive on every available parcel of land.

Hotel Le Palme. V. Porto 30, 25010 Limone sul Garda. ☎ **0365/954-681.** Fax 0365/954-120. 28 units, all with bathroom. TV TEL. 140,000L ($82.35) single; 140,000–200,000L ($82.35–$117.65) double. AE, MC, V. Closed Nov–Mar.

This gracious hotel is one of the most pleasant places to stay on Garda. It's located on the lake at one end of Limone's narrow main street and surrounded by palm trees. Downstairs, a bar and restaurant flow onto a flowery lakeside terrace. Upstairs, the large, pleasant guest rooms are furnished in Venetian-style reproduction antiques, and all but a few face the lake; the best have small balconies that hang out over the water (if your room doesn't have a balcony, you can enjoy the lake from the downstairs terrace or rooftop solarium). There's a small beach just a few steps down the road, and the hotel also has a swimming pool nearby.

Ristorante Gemma. Pz. Garibaldi 11. ☎ **0365/940-145.** Primi 9,000 –12,000L ($5.30–$7.05), secondi 12,000–18,000L ($7.05–$10.60). MC, V. Thurs–Tues, 11:30am–2:30pm and 6:30–10pm. ITALIAN.

In a town where many eateries cater to tourists with fish-and-chips and bratwurst, Gemma remains an authentic, family style trattoria. It also enjoys a pretty lakeside location, and the waves lap right against a dining terrace. Gemma is the best place in town for grilled lake trout, which, like all entrees, can be accompanied by a fine spaghetti alla mare and other delicious pastas.

A DAY TRIP TO GARDONE

This little resort, 26 miles south of Riva on the western shore of the lake, has two interesting attractions worthy of an excursion, including the home of Gabriele D'Anunzio, Italy's most noted modern poet. Once Italy's most famous soldier/poet, D'Anunzio is today better remembered for his adventures and grand lifestyle at Il Vittorale, a hillside estate that is one of Lake Garda's major attractions, than for his lackluster verse. He bought the estate (it is also alleged that Mussolini presented it to the poet as a way to coerce his sympathies), in 1921 and died here in 1936. The claustrophobic rooms of his ornately and bizarrely decorated villa are filled with bric-a-brac and artifacts from his colorful life, including many mementos of his long-running affair with the actress Eleanora Duse. Elsewhere on the grounds, which cascade down a hillside in a series of luxuriant gardens, are the patrol boat D'Annunzio commanded in World War I, a museum containing his biplane and photos, and his pompous hilltop tomb.

Il Vittoriale (☎ **0365/20-130**) is on a hillside just above the lakeside resort. Admission is 8,000L ($4.70) to the grounds only, 8,000L ($4.70) additional for a tour of the villa, which can be visited only on a guided tour (in Italian). The estate is open April to September Tuesday to Sunday from 10am to 1pm and 2:30 to 6pm; October to March Tuesday to Friday 9am to 12:30pm and 2 to 5:30pm and Saturday and Sunday 9am to 12:30pm and 2 to 6pm.

Just down the hill on Via Roma is **Giardino Botanica Hruska,** a small but delightful bower planted a hundred years ago by the Swiss naturalist Arturo Hruska (a dentist whose clientele included European royalty). More than 2,000 species of exotic flora from around the world continue to thrive in the balmy microclimate around the lake. Admission is 7,000L ($4.10). The garden is open daily mid-March to mid-October from 9am to 6:30pm.

GETTING HERE   From **Riva,** most of the boats (2 hours, 11,300L/$6.65) and buses (1 hour, 5,600L/$3.30) that travel down the lake to Desenzano also stop at Gardone, about halfway between the two. Hourly buses also make the 1-hour trip to and from **Brescia** (4,800L/$2.85) and two buses a day make the 3-hour trip to and from **Milan** (15,100L/$8.90).

VISITOR INFORMATION   Gardone's **tourist office,** V. Repubblica 35 (☎ **0365/20-347**), is open April through October Monday to Saturday from 9am to 12:30pm and 4 to 7pm and November through March Monday through Wednesday 9am to 12:30pm and 3 to 6pm, Thursday 9am to 12:30pm and Friday 9am to 12:30pm and 3 to 6pm.

5 Lago di Como Bellagio & the Central Lake Region

78 km (47 mi.) NE of Milan, Menaggio 35 km (21 mi.) NE of Como and 85 km (51 mi.) N of Milan, Varenna 50 km (30 mi.) NE of Como and 80 km (48 mi.) NE of Milan

The first sight of this dramatic expanse of azure-hued water, ringed by gardens and forests and backed by the snowcapped Alps, is likely to evoke strong emotions. Romance, soulfulness, even gentle melancholy—these are the stirrings that over the centuries Como has inspired in poets (Lord Byron), novelists (Stendhal), composers (Verdi and Rossini), and plenty of other visitors, too—be they deposed queens, such as Caroline of Brunswick, whom George IV of England exiled here for her adulterous ways, or well-heeled modern travelers who glide up and down these waters in the ubiquitous lake steamers. In addition to its emotional effects, Como is also just an enjoyable place to spend time. Less than an hour from Milan by train or car, its deep waters and verdant shores provide a wonderful respite from modern life.

GETTING HERE

BY TRAIN   The closest train station to Bellagio and the other Central Lake towns is in **Como,** at the southern end of the lake (from there you can continue by bus or boat). Hourly trains to and from **Milan** arrive and depart from Como's Stazione San Giovanni on Piazzale San Gottardo; the trip takes about 1 hour and the fare is 7,800L ($4.60).

BY BOAT   Bellagio is 2 hours from Como by ferry (9,600L/$5.65) and 45 minutes by hydrofoil (15,000L/$8.80); many of the ferries carry cars for an additional fee. Schedules vary with season, but from Easter through September a ferry or hydrofoil makes the trip from Como to Bellagio and other towns along the lake at least hourly. For more information contact **Navigazione Lago di Como** (☎ 031/304-060); the office is on the lakefront in Como on Lungo Lario Trieste. Ferries also connect Bellagio with towns on the Centro Lago: among them, **Varenna** on the eastern shore and Cadenabbia and **Menaggio** on the western shore. One way tariff is 4,500L ($2.65) or you can purchase a daily pass for 12,000L ($7.05) that is good for unlimited travel within the Centro Lago region.

BY BUS   There are hourly SPT buses from Como to **Bellagio** and **Menaggio** (about an hour to each; 4,300L/$2.55); ☎ 031/304-744.

BY CAR   Bellagio is connected to Como by a picturesque lakeshore road, S 583, which can be very crowded in the summer. The A9 autostrada links Como with Milan in about an hour. To reach **Menaggio** from Como, follow route SS34 along the western shore of the lake. For **Varenna,** follow S342 to the industrial town at the far eastern end of the lake, and from there follow the eastern shore on S 36. All of these roads tend to be crowded, especially on weekends and during the summer, so allow at least an hour of traveling time.

BELLAGIO & THE CENTRAL LAKE REGION

By far the most lovely spot on the lake (and where travelers should definitely set their sights) is the section known as the **Centro Lago.** Three towns—Bellagio, Varenna, and Mennagio—sit across the water from one another on three different shorelines. ✪ **Bellagio** is at the tip of the peninsula at a point where the lake forks into three distinct basins: One long leg sweeps north into the Alps, Como is at the southern end of the western leg, and Lecco is at the southern end of the eastern leg. Boats from Bellagio make it easy to visit the nearby shores of the Centro Lago—not that you will be in a great hurry to leave this pretty old town, with its steep narrow streets, lakeside piazza, and beautiful gardens.

FESTIVALS & MARKETS   A pleasant way to spend a summer evening in Bellagio is at one of the concerts held in the Chiesa di Cappuccini on the grounds of the Rockefeller Foundation between **June and July.** Bellagio's outdoor market fills the waterfront every third Wednesday of the month.

VISITOR INFORMATION   The **tourist office** is at Pz. d. Chiesa 14 (☎ 031/950-204; hours are Monday, Wednesday, and Thursday from 8:30am to 12:15pm and 2:30 to 6pm.

EXPLORING THE TOWN

Bellagio is often called one of the most beautiful towns in Italy. Nestled amid cypress groves and verdant gardens, its earth-toned old buildings climb from the lakefront promenade along stepped and cobbled lanes. While Bellagio is a popular retreat for everyone from Milanese out for a day of relaxation to British and Americans who come to relax for a week or two, the town is for the most part unmarred by tourism.

One of Bellagio's famed gardens surrounds the **Villa Melzi,** built by Franceso Melzi, a friend of Napoléon and an official of his Italian Republic. The villa was later the retreat of Franz Liszt, and is now the home of a distinguished Lombardian family, which allows the public to stroll through their acres of manicured lawns and fountains and visit a pavilion where a collection of Egyptian sculpture is on display. It's open March to October, daily from 9am to 12:30pm and 2 to 4:30pm; admission is 5,000L ($2.95); ☎ 0344/950-318. Bellagio's other famous gardens are those of the **Villa**

Serbelloni, occupying land once owned by Pliny the Younger and now in the hands of the Rockefeller Foundation. The gardens can be visited on twice-daily guided tours, about 2 hours long, in Italian. From mid-April through mid-October, tours are Tuesday to Sunday at 10:30am and 4:30pm; the tour costs 5,000L ($2.95); for more information, call ☎ **0344/950-204.**

WHERE TO STAY

For a wider selection of moderately priced hotels, you'd do best to head across the lake from Bellagio to Mennagio or Varenna (see below).

Giardinetto. Pz. d. Chiesa, 22021 Bellagio. ☎ **031/950-168.** 14 units, all with bathroom. 45,000L ($26.50) single; 90,000L ($52.95) double. MC, V.

The best lodging deal in town is to be found at this charming little hotel at the top of town, reached from the lakefront by Bellagio's narrow, stepped streets. A snug lobby, grouped around a big fireplace, opens to a vine-covered terrace, where guests are welcome to bring their own food for an alfresco meal. Most of the rooms also overlook the terrace; they are quite large and airy and bright, with large windows (those on the upper floors provide nice views over the town and lake beyond) and they are comfortably furnished with old armoires, bedsteads and other solid furnishings.

Hotel Florence. Pz. Mazzini 45, 22021 Bellagio. ☎ **031/950-342.** 36 units, all with bathroom or shower. TV TEL. 170,000L ($100) single; 230,000L ($135.30) double. Rates include breakfast. AE, MC, V. Closed Nov–Mar.

This gracious old lakefront hotel, run by the Ketzlar family, is continually being renovated with a great deal of style. The public rooms (in part of the hotel that dates from 1720) with beamed ceilings, parquet floors and, in the main lounge, a welcoming marble hearth were made for relaxing. Each of the guest rooms is different, though all are large and stylishly decorated with attractive fabrics and handsome furnishings, many of them reproduction antiques. One of the nicest is the newly redone room 1, with a large terrace and an enormous, smartly tiled bathroom in which a claw-foot bathtub sits in the middle of the room. There's an excellent in-house dining room, as well as street-level bar (see below).

Worth A Splurge

Hotel du Lac. Pz. Mazzini 32, 22021 Bellagio. ☎ **031/950-320.** Fax 031/951-624. www.fromitaly.it/Bellagio/H3/DULAC. 48 units, all with bathroom or shower. A/C MINIBAR TV TEL. 172,000–212,000L ($101.20–$124.70) single; 228,000–298,000L ($134.10–$175.30) double. Rates include breakfast. AE, MC, V. Closed Nov–Mar.

The Leoni family ensures that an air of graciousness and old-fashioned comfort pervades its gracious, 150-year-old hotel overlooking the lake from Bellagio's main piazza. Downstairs, a bar spills onto the arcaded sidewalk in front and there are a series of pleasant sitting rooms. Meals are served in a nicely appointed dining room with panoramic views of the lake, and in the guest rooms, all of which are different, cushy armchairs and a nice smattering of antiques and reproductions lend a great amount of charm. Many of the rooms have balconies or terraces, and there is also a rooftop sun terrace with sweeping lake views.

Apartment Stays

Residenzia Ulivo (Grand Hotel Villa Serbelloni). 22021 Bellagio. ☎ **031/950-216.** Fax 031/951-529. 13 apartments, all with bathroom. 1,015,000–2,345,000L ($597.05–$1,379.40) a week. Rates are for two and vary with season and size of apartment. AE, MC, V.

The Villa Serbelloni is one of Italy's grandest hotels, surrounded by beautiful gardens and manicured lawns on a generous sweep of the lakeshore. For those looking for less grandiose and expensive accommodations than those the main hotel provides (while enjoying all the hotel's amenities, including its lovely lakeside swimming pool, private beach and fitness club), the hotel has recently added these stylish apartments in an outbuilding on a hill above the lake. All have sitting areas and either separate bedrooms or alcove sleeping areas, and are nicely decorated with terra-cotta floors and attractive rattan furniture to create a casual, pleasing ambience; all have kitchenettes. While rentals are by the week, shorter stays can be arranged when space is available.

WHERE TO DRINK & DINE

Bar Café Rossi. Pz. Mazzini 22/24. ☎ **031/950-196.** Fri–Wed 7:30am–midnight (open daily Apr–Oct). Sandwiches from 7,000L ($4.10). LIGHT FARE.

One of the nicest of Bellagio's pleasant lakefront cafes is tucked under the arcades of the town's main square. You can dine at one of the few outside tables or in the delightful art nouveau–style dining room, with intricate tile work and carved blonde wood. Wine and the excellent house coffee are available all day, but a nice selection of pastries and sandwiches makes this a good stop for breakfast or lunch.

Bar Florence. Pz. Mazzini 45, 22021 Bellagio. ☎ **031/950-342.** Daily 10am–1am, closed late Oct–Easter. Sandwiches and other fare from 7,000L ($4.10). LIGHT FARE.

This pleasant bar is as attractive as the rest of the Hotel Florence, of which it occupies one corner of the ground floor. There's some seating out front facing the lake, but the large interior is the preferred place to sit when there's live entertainment. Sunday nights are especially popular, because the bar hosts excellent jazz ensembles.

Ristorante Barchetta. Salita Mella 13. ☎ **031/951-389.** Reservations required. Primi 16,000–22,000L ($9.40–$12.95); secondi 30,000L ($17.65); fixed menus 60,000L ($35.30) and 75,000L ($44.10). AE, MC, V. Wed–Mon, noon–2:30pm and 6:30–10:30pm (open Sat only in Nov–Dec). SEAFOOD.

One of Bellagio's best restaurants specializes in fresh lake fish and other seafood. In all but the coldest weather, food is served on a delightful bamboo-enclosed, heated terrace. Most of the pastas do not use seafood but are innovative variations on traditional recipes, such as *ravioli caprino* (with goat's cheese topped with a pear sauce) and a savory risotto with hazelnuts and pistachios. For a main course, however, you should try one of the delicious preparations of local perch or angler fish; the meat entrees, including baby lamb chops with rosemary, are also excellent. You can enjoy a pasta dish, as well as a meat and a fish dish on one of the set menus.

La Grotta. Salita Cernaia 14. ☎ **031/951-152.** Primi 7,000–10,000L ($4.10–$5.90); secondi 12,000–18,000L ($7.05–$10.60); pizza from 6,000L ($3.55). AE, MC, V. Tues–Fri (daily Aug–Sept), noon–2:30pm and 7–10:30pm. ITALIAN/PIZZERIA.

Tucked away on a stepped street just off lakefront Piazza Manzini, this cozy, informal restaurant consists of a series of vaulted-ceiling dining rooms. The service is extremely friendly and the wide-ranging menu includes many pasta and meat dishes. Most of the regulars, though, come for the fish specials, including lake trout, or the delectable pizzas that are the best for miles around.

VARENNA

You can happily spend some time clamoring up and down the steep steps that substitute for streets in this charming village (on the eastern shore of the lake about 20 minutes by ferry from Bellagio) that until not too long ago made its living by fishing. The main attractions, though, are outside of town. The hilltop ruins of the **Castello di Vezio** are about a 20-minute walk above the town on a gradually ascending path; the main reason for a visit is to enjoy the stunning views of the lake, its shoreline villages, and the backdrop of mountains at the northern end. The castle (☎ 0341/831-000) is open March to September daily, 10am to 10pm; admission is 2,000L ($1.20).

The gardens of the **Villa Monastero** are more easily accessible at the southern edge of the town, and you can reach them by following the series of delightful lakeside promenades through the old town from the ferry landing. This villa and the terraced gardens that rise up from the lakeshore were once a not-so-Spartan monastery—until it was dissolved in the late 17th century, when the nuns in residence began bearing living proof that they were on too friendly terms with the priests across the way. If you find it hard to tear yourself from the bowers of citrus trees and rhododendrons that cling to terraces, you will find equally enchanting surroundings in the adjoining gardens of the **Villa Cipressi.**

Both gardens are open April through October, daily 10am to 12:30pm and 2:30 to 6pm and charge an admission of 3,000L ($1.75) to each garden or 5,000L ($2.95) for both; call ☎ 0341-830-172 for more information. In season, ferries make the 20-minute run between Bellagio and Varenna about every half hour (see above).

WHERE TO STAY & DINE

✪ **Albergo Milano.** V. XX Settembre 29, 22050 Varenna. ☎ and fax **0341/830-298.** 12 units, all with bathroom. TEL. 175,000L ($102.95) single or double. Rates include breakfast. AE, MC. V.

You'd have to look hard to find a more pleasant retreat by the lake. This family-run hotel occupies an old house hanging over Varenna's lakefront. Most of the simply furnished but comfortable rooms have views, and most have balconies; the two best rooms in the house are the ones on the first floor that open onto a wide terrace. The furnishings are a pleasant mix of old armoires as well as some unobtrusive modern pieces. The small bathrooms are equipped with good showers. Breakfast is served in a charming, antique-filled parlor on the main floor.

Vecchia Varenna. V. Scoscesa 10. ☎ **031/830-793.** Reservations required. Primi 15,000L ($8.80); secondi 18,000L ($10.60). AE, MC, V. Tues–Sun noon–2:30pm and 7–10:30pm. LOMBARD/SEAFOOD.

One of your most memorable experiences in the Lakes could well be a meal at this delightful and romantic restaurant at the water's edge in the oldest section of Varenna. Dining is in a beautiful stone floored room with white stone walls, or on a terrace right on the water. The kitchen makes the most of local herbs and vegetables and, of course, the bounty of the lake—for starters, *quadrucci* (pasta pockets) are stuffed with trout, and one of the best of the many risottos combines wild mushrooms and *lavarello* (a white fish from the lake). Grilled lake trout stuffed with mountain herbs is a sublime main course, though many other kinds of lake fish are also available.

Villa Cipressi. V. IV Novembre 18, 22050 Varenna. ☎ **0341/83-01-13.** Fax 0341/83-04-01. 21 units, all with bathroom. TV TEL. 115,000L ($67.65) single; 150,000–165,000L ($88.25–$97.05) double. Rates include breakfast. MC, V.

If you enjoyed your tour of Varenna's lush gardens (see above), there's no need to leave. The villa and several outbuildings have been converted to a hotel that's geared to conferences but takes other guests, space permitting. Though the rooms have been renovated without any attempt to retain the historic character of the building, they are extremely large and attractive. Many take advantage of the high ceilings and contain loft bedrooms, with sitting areas below, and all enjoy marvelous views over the gardens, which can also be enjoyed on a series of delightful terraces.

MENNAGIO

This pleasant, lively resort town hugs the western shore of the lake, across from Bellagio on its peninsula and Varenna on the distant shore. Hikers should stop in at the tourist office on Pz. Garibaldi 7, ☎ **0344/329-24,** open Monday to Saturday from 9am to noon and 3 to 6pm; the very helpful staff distributes an booklet, *Hiking in the Area around Mennagio,* with descriptions of more than a dozen walks, accompanied by maps and instructions on what buses to take to trail heads.

The major nearby attraction on this section of the lake is **Villa Carlotta,** a little over a mile south (you can take the C2 bus, 1,400L/82¢ from the lakeside bus stop near Piazza Garibaldi) or walk along the lake. Carlotta is the most famous villa on the lake and was begun in 1643 for the Marquis Giorgio Clerici, who made his fortune supplying Napóleon's troops with uniforms; he spent much of it on his neoclassical villa and gardens. After a succession of owners, including Prussian royalty who lavished their funds and attention on the gardens, Villa Carlotta is now in the hands of the Italian government. The villa is filled with romantic paintings and Empire furnishings, but the gardens are the main attraction here: azaleas, orchids, banana trees, cacti, and forests of ferns spread out in all directions. The nearest ferry landing is at Cadenabbia, just north of the gardens, though ferries run much more frequently to Menaggio. The villa and gardens (☎ **0344/40-405**) are open daily, March 15 to March 31 and October from 9 to 11:30am and 2 to 4:30pm and April to September 9am to 6pm. Admission is 8,000L ($4.70) adults and 5,000L ($2.95) for children 7 to 14; admission is free for children 6 and under.

WATER SPORTS   The lido, at the north end of town, has an excellent beach, as well as a swimming pool, and is open daily from late June to mid-September from 9am to 7pm. For information on waterskiing and other activities, contact Centro Lago Service, Via Castelli, ☎ **0344/320-03.** Also ask at the hostel (see below) about boat and bike rentals, which are available to nonguests during slow periods.

WHERE TO STAY & DINE

Albergo-Ristorante Il Vapore. Pz. Grossi 3, 22017 Menaggio. ☎ **0344/322-29.** Thurs–Tues noon–2:30pm and 6:30–9:30pm. Primi 7,000–9,000L ($4.10–$5.30); secondi 9,000–14,000L ($5.30–$8.25). Hotel: 10 units, all with bathroom. 45,000 single ($26.50); 75,000 double ($44.10). MC, V.

This very pleasant small restaurant and hotel faces a shady square just off the lakefront. Meals are served beneath a grape arbor or in an attractive pale-blue dining room decorated with paintings by local artists. The kitchen prepares many local specialties from the nearby mountain valleys, including *sciatt,* whole wheat pasta with fried cheese, and *strangolepreti,* a saladlike soup of bread, spinach, eggs, pine nuts, and raisins. The 10 guest rooms are comfortable, with plain modern furnishings; many have tall windows, which open onto partial lake views.

Bar Centrale. V. Mazzini 23. ☎ **0344/32194.** Sandwiches from 4,000L ($2.35). Daily 7am–midnight (closed Wed late Oct to Easter). CAFE

This lively bar just off the waterfront in the center of town is always busy, dispensing drinks and snacks on a large terrace from early spring well into the autumn. There's a good selection of panini for lunch, and many flavors of gelato.

Ostello La Prinula. V. IV Novembre 86. ☎ and fax **0344/323-56.** 17,000L ($10) per person bed-and-breakfast. Open mid-Mar to mid-Nov, office open 7:30–10am and 4–11pm.

This delightful hostel (it really is) is easily accessible from Bellagio and other towns on the Centro Lago by boat. Family suites with private bathrooms are available, and even the dorms are relatively cozy, with no more than four beds per room. Most of the rooms have a view of the lake, as does a large, sunny terrace. The dining room serves a 15,000L ($8.80) dinner that's so good, it even attracts locals. You can explore the surrounding countryside on one of the bikes that are available or get onto the lake in one of the kayaks (rentals for each are 17,000L/$10). The hostel offers special programs, such as two-week language classes, cooking courses, and organized bike trips and hikes.

COMO

The largest and southernmost town on the lake is not likely to charm you. Long a center of silk making, this city that traces its roots to the Gauls, and after them, the Romans, bustles with commerce and industry. You'll probably want to stay in one of the more peaceful settings farther up the lake, but Como amply rewards a day's visit with some fine Renaissance churches and palaces and a lovely lakefront promenade.

Part Renaissance and part gothic, Como's **Duomo** (in the center of town just off the lake; ☎ 031/265-244) is festooned with the same sort of exuberant masonry that adorns the Duomo in Milan. Statues of two of the town's famous native sons, Pliny the Elder and Pliny the Younger, flank the main entrance. Inside, beneath an 18th-century dome by Juavara—whom you might remember as the architect who designed much of Turin—is a lavish interior hung with paintings and tapestries (open daily 7am to noon and 3 to 7pm). The half-timbered, 13th-century **Broletto** (town hall) and adjoining **Torre del Commune** are on the other side of the Piazza del Duomo; and, as a study in contrasts, the starkly modernist and aptly named **Casa del Fascio,** built in 1936 as the seat of the region's fascist government, rises just behind the Duomo.

Como's main street, **Corso Vittorio Emanuele II,** cuts through the medieval quarter, where wood-beamed houses line narrow streets; and, just 2 blocks south of the duomo, the 12th-century, five-sided **Church of San Fedele** stands above a charming square of the same name; parts of the church, including the altar, date from the 6th century (open daily 7am to noon and 3 to 7pm). To see Como's most alluring church, though, it's necessary to venture into the dull, outlying neighborhood southwest of the center where, just off the Viale Roosevelt, you'll come to the five-aisle, heavily frescoed **Basilica of Sant'Abbondio,** a Romanesque masterpiece from the 11th century.

Lakeside life revolves around the Piazza Cavour and adjoining Giardini Publici, where the circular **Tempio Voltano** (☎ 031/574-705) houses memorabilia that will enlighten you about the life and experiments of native son and electricity pioneer Alessandro Volta. It's open April through September, Tuesday to Sunday from 10am to noon and 3 to 6pm; October through March, from 10am to noon and 2 to 4pm; admission is 4,000L ($2.35). For a quick retreat and some stunning views, take the funicular up to the top of **Brunate,** the forested hill that sits above the town (it leaves from the Lungo Lario Trieste every 15 minutes in summer and every half hour in winter; 4,000L/$2.35 one way, 7,100L/$4.15 round-trip).

VISITOR INFORMATION   The **tourist office** dispenses a wealth of information on hotels, restaurants, and campgrounds around the lake from its offices at Pz. Cavour 17 (☎ 031/269-712). It's open Monday to Saturday from 9am to 12:30pm and 2:30 to 6pm (Sunday 9am to 12:30pm in the summer).

A SNACK

Pasticceria Monti. Pz. Cavour 21. ☎ 031/304-833. Daily 7am–2am. Gelato from 1,500L (88¢) for a single scoop, pastries from 2,500L ($1.45), sandwiches from 4,000L ($2.35). MC, V. CAFE

Above all, the busy establishment on the main, lakefront piazza is one of Como's favorite place to gather and watch passersby. You can enjoy some of the excellent gelato or a coffee or cocktail, and excellent sandwiches and some other light fare, including some daily pasta dishes, are also served.

6 Lago Maggiore

Stresa 80 km (48 mi.) NW of Milan

Anyone who reads Hemingway will know this lake and its forested shores from *A Farewell to Arms.* That's just the sort of place Maggiore is—a pleasure ground that's steeped in associations with famous figures (Flaubert, Wagner, Goethe, and Europe's other great minds seem to have been inspired by the deep, moody waters, backed by the Alps) and not-so-famous wealthy visitors. Fortunately, you need not be famous or wealthy to enjoy Maggiore, which is on the Swiss border just a short dash east and north of Milan.

STRESA

The major town on the lake is a pretty, festive little place, with a long lakefront promenade, a lively and attractive commercial center, and a bevy of restaurants and hotels that range from the expensively splendid to the affordably comfortable.

FESTIVALS & MARKETS   Stresa draws visitors from around the world for its **Festival of Musical Weeks,** a major gathering of classical musicians in late August and early September.

ESSENTIALS

GETTING HERE   By Train   Stresa is linked with **Milan** (1 hour) by 20 trains a day, and by several a day to and from **Geneva** (2½ hours; 40,000L, $23.55). The fare between Milan and Stresa is 7,400L ($4.35).

By Boat   Boats arrive and depart from Piazza Marconi, connecting Stresa with the Isole Borromee and with many other lakeside spots; most boats on the lake are operated by **Navigazione Sul Lago Maggiore** (☎ **0322/242-352**).

By Car   Autostrada **A8** runs between Milan and Sesto, near the southern end of the lake; from there Route **S33** follows the western shore to Stresa. The trip takes a little over an hour.

VISITOR INFORMATION   The **tourist information office** is near the center of town at Principe Tomaso 70–72, ☎ **0323/30-150.** It's open May through September Monday through Saturday from 8:30am to 12:30pm and 3 to 6:15pm and Sunday 9am to noon and October through April Monday through Friday from 8:30am to 12:30pm and 3 to 6:15pm and Saturday 8:30am to 12:30pm. For hiking information, ask for the booklet *Lago Maggiore Trekking Per Tutti.*

EXPLORING THE TOWN

Strolling and relaxing seem to be the main activities in Stresa. The action is at the lakeside promenade, which runs from the center of town north past the grand lakeside hotels, including the Iles des Borromees, where Hemingway set *A Farewell to Arms.* Sooner or later, though, most visitors climb into a boat for the short ride to the famed islands themselves, the **Isole Borromee.** These three islands, named for the Borromeo family, which has owned them since the 12th century, float in the misty waters off Stresa and entice visitors with their stunning beauty. Public ferries leave for the islands every half hour from Piazza Marconi; a day pass (11,000L/$6.50) is the most economical way to visit all three. Private boats also make the trip out to the island; hucksters dressed as sailors will try to lure you aboard—especially for groups, the prices can be reasonable, but do your negotiating on the dock before you get on the boat.

Most of **Isola Superiore** (also known as Isola Pescatore) is a occupied by a not-so-quaint old fishing village—every one of the tall houses on this tiny strip of land seems to harbor a souvenir shop or pizza stand, and there are hordes of visitors to keep them busy. (It is 10 minutes from Stresa and the round-trip fare is 5,700L/$3.35).

Isola Bella (5 minutes from Stresa, 4,200L/$2.45) remains true to its name, with splendid 17th-century gardens that ascend from the shore in 10 luxuriantly planted terraces. The **Borromeo palazzo** provides a chance to explore opulently decorated rooms, including the one where Napoléon and Josephine once slept. It's open March through September, daily from 9am to noon and 1:30 to 5:30pm and October 9am to noon and 1:30 to 5:30pm; admission is 13,000L ($7.65); call ☎ **0323/30-556.**

The largest and most peaceful of the islands is **Isola Madre** (30 minutes from Stresa, 5,700L/$3.35), most of which is covered with the exquisite flora of the **Orto Botanico** (☎ **0323/31-261**). The botanical garden is open April through September, daily from 9am to noon and 1:30 to 5:30pm; admission is 13,000L ($7.65).

HIKING & BIKING   The forested slopes above Stresa are prime hiking and mountain biking terrain. To reach a network of trails, take the *funivia* from the near the lakefront at the north end of town up Monte Mottarone; the funivia (☎ **0323/302-95**) runs every 20 minutes between 9:15am and noon and 1:40 to 5pm and the fare is 10,000L ($5.90) each way; 5,000L ($2.95) for a bike. You can rent bikes at the station for 30,000L ($17.65). If you don't want to venture too far from the lake, there's a nice beach near the station.

WHERE TO STAY

Hotel Meeting. V. Bonghi 9, 28049 Stresa. ☎ **0323/32-741.** Fax 0323/33-458. 27 units, all with bathroom. MINIBAR TV TEL. 100,000L ($58.80) single; 130,000L ($76.45) double. Rates include breakfast. Parking 13,000L ($7.65). AE, MC, V.

The name comes from the proximity of Stresa's small conference center, where a much-attended music festival in held in late August and early September (see above). Although the lakefront is only a 5-minute walk away, the setting is quiet and leafy. The rooms, furnished in Scandinavian modern, are big and bright, and many have terraces. There's a cozy bar downstairs, as well as a casual dining room.

Hotel Mon Toc. V. Duchessa di Genova 67–69, 28049 Stresa. ☎ **0323/302-82.** Fax 0323/933-860. 18 units, all with bathroom. 60,000L ($35.30) single; 85,000L ($50) double.

Just uphill from the train station, this family run hotel surrounded by a big garden is convenient to the lake and town but far enough removed to provide an almost country-like atmosphere. With Oriental carpets and nice old furniture, the guest rooms are unusually pleasant for a hotel in this price range, and all have tidy bathrooms.

Hotel Primavera. V. Cavour 30, 28049 Stresa. ☎ **0323/31-286.** Fax 0323/33-458. 32 units, all with bathroom. MINIBAR TV TEL. 100,000L ($58.80) single; 155,000L ($91.20) double. Rates include breakfast.

For much of the spring and summer, the street in front of this hotel is closed to traffic and filled with flowering plants and cafe tables. This relaxed air prevails throughout this bright little hotel, just a block off the lake in the center of town. There's a lounge and bar downstairs. Upstairs, the airy, tile-floored rooms are furnished in walnut. Many have balconies overlooking the town or lake.

WORTH A SPLURGE

Hotel la Palma. Lungolago Umberto 133, 28049 Stresa. ☎ **0323/32-401.** Fax 0323/933-930. 128 units, all with bathroom. A/C MINIBAR TV TEL. From 170,000L ($100) single; 230,000–315,000L ($135–$185.30) double. Rates include buffet breakfast. AE, MC, V. Closed Dec–Feb.

The Palma is one of the nicest of Stresa's luxury hotels and, given the high-level comfort and the amenities offered, one of the most reasonably priced. Most of the guest rooms, recently redone in rich floral fabrics and light woods, open to balconies overlooking the lake, and many of the marble bathrooms are equipped with Jacuzzis. There is a rooftop sun terrace and fitness center, with steam room and sauna, but the most pleasant places to relax are in the flowery garden in front of the hotel and the terrace surrounding the lakeside swimming pool.

WHERE TO DINE

Hotel Ristorante Fiorentino. V. Bolongaro 9. ☎ **0323/30-254.** Primi 6,000–8,000L ($3.55–$4.70); secondi 8,000–18,000L ($4.70–$10.60). Fixed menu 21,000L ($12.35). MC, V. Mar–Oct daily 11am–3pm and 6–10pm. Closed Nov to mid-Mar. ITALIAN.

It's hard to find friendlier service or homier trattoria-type food in Stresa, especially at these prices. Everything that comes out of the family run kitchen is made fresh that day, including cannelloni and other pastas. You can dine in a big, cozy room or on a patio out back in good weather.

Ristorante Pescatore. Vc. d. Poncivo. ☎ **0323/31-986.** Reservations recommended. Primi 8,000–18,000L ($4.70–$10.60); secondi 13,000–25,000L ($7.65–$14.70). AE, MC. V. Fri–Wed, noon–3pm and 6–10pm. SEAFOOD.

This pleasant, small dining room in the center of town is where residents of Stresa come for a fish meal. The starters include a wonderful seafood salad, an appetizer of smoked salmon or tuna, or any number of pasta dishes served with clams or squid. The main courses include a paella worthy of southern Spain (the owners and some of the cooks and waiters are Spanish) as well as *zarzuela de pescada*, a rich fish stew. Lake or ocean fish are always fresh, and served grilled and topped with the simplest sauces.

Taverna del Pappagallo. V. Principessa Margherita 46. ☎ **0323/30-411.** Primi 7,000–12,000L ($4.10–$7.05); secondi 12,000–20,000L ($7.05–$11.75);pizza from 8,000L ($4.70). No credit cards. Thurs–Mon 11:30am–2:30pm and 6:30–10:30pm; daily during the summer. ITALIAN/PIZZERIA.

Most of Stresa seems to congregate in this pleasant restaurant for the most popular pizza in town. But just about all the fare, including the delectable homemade gnocchi and such dishes as grilled sausage that comes out of the family run kitchen, is delicious. Weather permitting, try to dine at one of the tables in the pleasant garden.

12

Piedmont & the Valle d'Aosta

by Stephen Brewer

Loosely translated, Piedmont, or *Piemonte* in Italian, means "at the foot of the mountains." Those mountains, of course, are the Alps, defining the region and part of Italy's northern and western borders. These dramatic peaks are visible in much of the province, most of which rises and rolls over fertile foothills that produce a bounty that is as rich as the region is green. This is a land of cheeses, truffles, plump fruit, and, of course, wines—among them some of Italy's most delicious reds, including Barbaresco and Barolo. Rising from the vineyards are medieval and Renaissance towns and villages, many of which are untrammeled by the 20th century.

Not that all of Piedmont is rural, of course. **Turin,** Italy's car town, is the region's capital, and within the ring of industrialized suburbs lies an elegant city of mannerly squares, baroque palaces, and stunning art collections. Turinese and their neighbors from other parts of Italy often retreat to the **Valle d'Aosta,** the smallest, northernmost, and most mountainous of Italian provinces.

REGIONAL CUISINE   Given such vast geographic diversity, it's not surprising that the region's cuisine varies according to the topography. In the southern stretches of Piedmont, the palate turns primarily to those magnificent red wines from the wine villages around Asti and Alba. Barbaresco, Barbera, Barolo, Dolcetto, Nebbiolo—the names are legendary, and they often appear on the table to accompany meat dishes stewed in red wine; one of the most favored of these is *brasato al barolo* (beef or veal braised in Barolo). The way to begin a meal here, but usually available in winter only, is with *bagna cauda,* literally, "hot bath," a plate of raw vegetables that are dipped into a steaming sauce of olive oil, garlic and anchovies. The Piedmontese pasta is *tarajin,* and it is often topped with sauces made with walnuts or, for a special occasion, what is perhaps the region's greatest contribution to Italian cuisine, white truffles. As the land climbs higher toward the Valle d'Aosta, mountain fare takes over—polenta is a popular primo, stews are thick with beef and red wine (*carbonada* is the most common stew like this), and buttery fontina is the preferred cheese.

1 Turin

669 km (401 mi.) NW of Rome, 140 km (84 mi.) E of Milan

It's often said that Turin is the most French city in Italy or the most Italian city in France. The reason is partly historical and partly architectural. From the late 13th century to Italy's unification in 1861 (when Turin served very briefly as capital), Turin was the capital of the House of Savoy. The Savoys were as French as they were Italian and whose holdings extended well into the present-day French regions of Savoy and the Côte d'Azur. The city's Francophile 17th- and 18th-century architects, inspired by the tastes of the French court, laid out broad avenues and airy piazzas and lined them with low-slung neoclassical buildings.

Most visitors come to Turin with business in mind (often at the Fiat and Pirelli works in the sprawling industrial suburbs). Those who take the time to look around the historic center, though, discover an elegant and sophisticated city that has changed little since more gracious centuries, with some stunning museum collections and the charm of a place that, for all its Francophile leanings, is quintessentially Italian.

FESTIVALS & MARKETS   Dance, opera, theater, and musical performances (most classical) are on the agenda in June and the first week of July, during the **Sere d'Estate festival;** companies come from around the world to perform. September is the month to enjoy more classical music—more than 60 classical concerts are held on stages around the city during the monthlong **Settembre Musica** festival.

Bric-a-brac of all kinds, be it household utensils, books or used clothing, fills the stalls of the **Mercato del Baton,** held every Saturday at Piazza della Republica. **Gran Baton** fills the piazza the second Sunday of every month and is a larger affair, with some genuine antiques and art works included in the mix. **Mercato della Crocetta** at Largo Cassini sells clothing at very low prices. For a look at the bounty of the surrounding farmlands, wander through the extensive outdoor food market at **Porta Palazzo,** Monday through Saturday from 6:30am to 1:30pm and from 3:30 to 7:30pm on Saturday.

ESSENTIALS
GETTING HERE   **By Plane**   Domestic and international flights land at the Caselle International Airport (☎ 011/567-6361), 9 miles north of Turin. Buses run between the airport and the city's main bus terminal on Corso Inghilterra and Porto Nuova train station; the trip takes 30 minutes and costs 6,000L ($3.55).

By Train   Turin's main train station is **Stazione Porta Nuova** (☎ 011/561-3333), just south of the center on Piazza Carlo Felice, which marks the intersection of Turin's two major thoroughfares, Corso Vittorio Emanuele and Via Roma. From this station, there are 18 trains a day to and from **Milan**—the trip takes 1¾ hours and costs 14,000L ($8.24) each way (many trains to and from Milan also stop at Stazione di Porta Susa); 12 trains a day to and from **Venice,** 4½ hours, 34,500L ($20.29); 16 trains a day to and from **Genoa,** 2 hours, 14,000L ($8.24); 9 trains a day to and from **Rome,** 10 hours away, 53,000L ($31.18). **Stazione di Porta Susa,** west of the center on Piazza XVIII Dicembre, connects Turin with many outlying Piedmont towns; it is also the terminus for TGV service to and from Paris, with three trains a day making the trip in about 6 hours (one-way fare is 160,000L/$94.10).

By Bus   Turin's main bus terminal is **Autostazione Terminal Bus,** Cor. Inghilterra 3 (near Stazione di Porta Sousa) (☎ 011/483-2525). The ticket office is open daily from 7am to noon and 3 to 7pm. Buses connect Turin and **Courameyeur** (4 hr.; 16,000L/$9.40), **Aosta** (3 hr.; 13,000L/$7.65), **Milan** (2 hr.; 17,200L/$10.10), **Chamonix** (3½ hr.; 37,000L/$21.75), and many smaller towns in Piedmont.

By Car   Turin is at the hub of an extensive network of autostradas. **A4** connects Turin with **Milan,** a little over an hour away; **A6** connects Turin with the **Ligurian coast** (and from there, with Genoa via A10, with a total travel time between the two cities of about 1½ hr.); **A5** connects Turin with **Aosta,** about an hour away; and **A21**

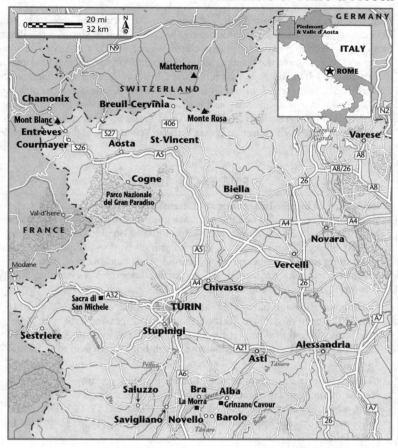

connects Turin with **Asti** and **Piacenza,** where you can connect with the **A1** for **Florence** (about 3½ hr. from Turin) and **Rome** (about 6½ hr. from Turin).

VISITOR INFORMATION APT **tourist offices** are located in the Porta Nuova train station (☎ **011/531-327**), open Monday through Saturday 9am to 7:30pm, and at V. Roma 226 (on Piazza San Carlo) (☎ **011/535-181**), open Monday through Friday from 9am to 7pm and Saturday 9am to noon and 1 to 6pm. Both offices will book rooms for you. A regional tourist office at Cor. Ferrucci 122 (☎ **011/352-440**) is a good place to stop for information to help plan forays into other parts of Piedmont; it's open Monday to Friday 9am to 7pm and Saturday 10am to 4pm.

GETTING AROUND It's easy to get around central Turin by foot. There is also a vast network of trams and buses. Tickets on public transportation are available at newsstands and cost 1,500L (88¢). It's obligatory to validate your ticket when you board a bus or tram—you can be slapped with a hefty fine if you don't.

CITY LAYOUT You will get a sense of Turin's refined air as soon as you step off a train into the mannerly 19th-century Stazione Porta Nuova. The stately arcaded **Via Roma,** lined with shops and cafes, proceeds from the front of the station through a series of piazzas toward the **Piazza Castello** and the center of the city, about a 15-minute walk. Directly in front of the station, the circular **Piazza Carlo Felice** is built around a garden surrounded by outdoor cafes that invite even business-minded Turinese to linger. A few steps farther along the street will lead you into the **Piazza San Carlo,** which is flanked by the twin churches of San Carlo and Santa Christina. At the end of Via Roma, the Piazza Castello is dominated by the Palazzo Madama, so named for its 17th-century inhabitant Marie-Christine. Just off the piazza is the **Palazzo Reale,** residence of the Savoys from 1646 to 1865, whose gardens now provide a pleasant respite from traffic and paving stones. A walk east toward the river along **Via Po** from here takes you through Turin's university district to one of Italy's largest squares, the much-elongated **Piazza Vittorio Veneto,** and at the end of this elegant expanse, the river.

FAST FACTS: Turin

Bookstore   **Libreria Internazionale Luxemborg,** between Piazza San Carlo and Piazza Castello at V. Accademia d. Scienze 3 (☎ **011/561-38-96**), has a large selection of British books and a helpful English-speaking staff; it is open Tuesday through Saturday 9am to 7:30pm and Monday 3 to 7:30pm. Turin has many stores specializing in rare books and old prints, and many of these shops sell their wares from the secondhand bookstalls along the Via Po, which runs between Piazza Castello and the river.

Consulates   British subjects will find their consulate at V. Saluzzo 60 (☎ **011/ 650-9202**), open Monday to Friday 9:15am to 12:15pm and 2:30 to 4:30pm. Americans will find their nearest consulate in Milan at V. Principe Amadeo 2/10 (☎ **02-290-35141**); it is open Monday through Friday from 9am to 11am and 2 to 4pm.

Crime   Turin is a relatively safe city, but use the same precautions you would exercise in any large city. Specifically, avoid the riverside streets along the Po at night, when they tend to be deserted. In an emergency call ☎ **113.** The central police station is near Stazione di Porta Susa at Cor. Vinzaglio, 10 (☎ **011/ 558-81-112**).

Currency Exchange   The exchange office in Stazione Porta Nuova is open daily 7:30am to 9pm. An exchange machine is located just outside the APT tourist office on Piazza San Carlo. Many of the banks along Via Roma have currency exchange windows and there are ATMs, from which you can withdraw currency in lire against your bank account back home, throughout the city.

Drugstores   A convenient late-night pharmacy is **Farmacia Boniscontro,** Cor. Vittorio Emanuele 66 (☎ **011/541-271**); it is open most of the day and night, closing only between noon and 3pm.

Emergencies   The general emergency number is ☎ **113;** for an ambulance dial ☎ **118.**

Lost Property   To report lost property, contact the Ufficio Oggetti Smarriti, ☎ **011/665-3315.**

Luggage Storage   Luggage storage is available at Porta Nuova train station; 5,000L ($2.95) per bag for each 12-hour period; the office is open daily from 4:30am to 2:30am.

Newspapers   Your best bet for English-language newspapers is at the newsstands in Porta Nuova station.

Turin

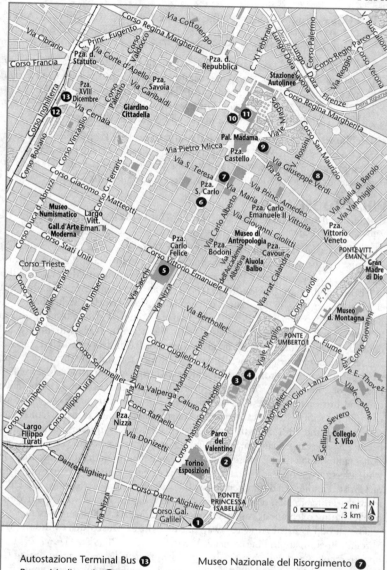

Autostazione Terminal Bus ⑬
Borgo Medioevale ②
Castello del Valentino ③
Cattedrale di San Giovanni
    (Shroud of Turin) ⑩
Mole Antonelliana ⑧
Museo dell Automobile ①
Museo Egizio
    and Galleria Sabauda ⑦

Museo Nazionale del Risorgimento ⑦
Palazzo Madama-Museo Civico
    de Arte Antica ⑨
Palazzo Reale (Royal Palace) ⑪
Parco del Valentino ④
Piazza San Carlo ⑥
Stazione Porta Nuova ⑤
Stazione di Porta Susa ⑫

Post Office   Turin's main post office is just west of Piazza San Carlo at V. Alfieri 10 (☎ **011/539-894**); it is open Monday through Friday from 8:15am to 5:30pm and Saturday from 8:15am to 1pm. The postal code for Turin is 10100.

Taxis   You can find taxis at cab stands; especially convenient in the central city are the stands in front of the train stations, around Piazza San Carlo and Piazza Castello. Dial ☎ **5737** for a radio taxi. The basic fare is 4,500L ($2.65) and 1,200L (71¢) for each kilometer. There is a 4,000L ($2.35) night surcharge and a 2,000L ($1.20) surcharge on Sundays and holidays.

Telephones   The main **Telecom Italia** office, near the Post Office and Piazza San Carolo at V. Arsenale 13, is open Monday through Friday from 8:30am to 12:30pm and 3 to 7pm. You can purchase telephone cards here, as well as at newsstands and tobacco shops. The telephone code for Turin is **011**.

WHAT TO SEE & DO

Cattedrale di San Giovanni. Pz. San Giovanni. ☎ **011/521-5960.** Free admission. Daily 9am–noon and 3–5pm.

The controversial **Shroud of Turin** (*Santissima Sindone*) and the chapel in which it is sometimes enshrined, Capella della Santa Sindone, hold pride of place in this otherwise uninteresting, pompous 15th-century church. Even without the presence of one of Christendom's most precious relics (and it is only rarely on view in the silver casket elevated on an altar in the center of the room), the chapel is well worth a visit. Recently restored after a fire in 1997, the chapel is somberly clad in black marble but, as if to suggest that better things await us in the heavens, ascends to an airy, light-flooded six-tiered dome, one of the masterpieces of Italian baroque architecture.

The shroud, of course, is allegedly the one in which the body of Christ was wrapped when taken from the cross—and to which his image was miraculously affixed. The image is of a man 5 feet 7 inches tall, wearing a crown of thorns and clearly showing cuts and bruises that suggest he was whipped, forced to carry a heavy burden like a cross, and crucified. Recent carbon dating suggests the shroud was manufactured sometime around the 13th or 14th centuries, but the mystery remains, at least in part, because no one can explain how the haunting image appeared on the cloth. Also, additional radio carbon dating has suggested that, since the shroud has been exposed to fire (thus affecting carbon readings), it could indeed date from around the time of the death of Christ. Despite scientific skepticism, the shroud continues to entice the faithful, more than three million of whom viewed the relic the last time it was exhibited to the public, during celebrations commemorating the cathedral's 500th anniversary.

The shroud is usually tucked away out of sight at **Museo della Sindone** (Holy Shroud Museum) around the corner at V. San Domenico 28 (☎ **011/464-799**), open only to scholars and church officials. It will be on view, however, again during Italy's millennium celebrations in 2000. Other times, you will have to content yourself with a series of dramatically backlit photos of the relic near the entrance to the Capella della Santa Sindone.

In front of the cathedral stand two landmarks of Roman Turin—the remains of a theater and the Porta Palatina, flanked by twin 16-sided towers.

Mole Antonelliana. V. Montebello 20. ☎ **011/817-049.** Free admission to exhibition space; observation platform 5,000L ($2.95). Tues–Fri 10am–4pm, weekends 9am–7pm.

Turin's most peculiar building—in fact, one of the strangest structures anywhere—is comprised of a squat brick base, a steep cone-like roof supporting several layers of Greek temples piled one atop the other, topped in turn by a needlelike spire, all of it rising 500 feet above the rooftops of the city center (a height that at one time made the Mole the world's tallest building). Begun in 1863 and designed as a synagogue, the Mole is now a monument to Italian unification and occasionally hosts temporary art exhibits. You can ascend to an observation platform at the top, an experience that affords two advantages—the view of Turin and the surrounding countryside, backed by the Alps, is stunning, and as Guy de Maupassant once said of the Eiffel Tower, this perch is the only place in Turin where you won't have to look at the damned thing.

Museo dell Automobile. Cor. Unita d'Italia 40. ☎ **011/677-666.** Admission 9,000L ($5.30). Tues–Sun 10am–6:30pm.

As befits a city that is responsible for 80% of Italian car manufacturing, this shiny collection of mostly Italian automobiles, housed in a purpose-built, light filled exhibition hall of classic 1960s design, draws car buffs from all over the world. Not too surprisingly, a century's worth of output from Fiat, which is headquartered in Turin, is well represented, and displays trace how the company has influenced the 20th-century history of the city. The collection includes most of the cars that have done Italy proud over the years, including Lancias, Isotta Frashinis and the Itala that came in first in the 1907 Peking to Paris rally. Some oddities include a roadster, emblazoned with the initials *ND*, that Gloria Swanson drove for her lead in *Sunset Boulevard*.

✪ **Museo Egizio and Galleria Sabauda.** V. Accademia d. Scienze 6. Museo Egizio. ☎ **011/561-7776.** Admission 12,000L ($7.05), children under 18 and adults over 60 free. Tues–Sat 9am–7pm, Sun 9am–2pm. Galleria Sabauda: ☎ 011/547-440. Admission 8,000L ($4.70). Tues, Thurs, Sat–Sun 9am–7pm, Wed and Fri 2:30pm–7:30pm. Closed Jan 1, May 1, Aug 15, and Dec 25.

Turin's magnificent Egyptian collection is one of the world's largest. This was in fact the world's first Egyptian museum, thanks to the fact that the Savoys ardently amassed artifacts through most of their reign and museum continued to mount collecting expeditions throughout the early 20th century. Of the 30,000 pieces on display, some of the more captivating exhibits are in the first rooms you'll enter on the ground floor. These include the Rock Temple of Ellessiya, from the 15th century B.C., which the Egyptian government presented to the museum in gratitude for Italian efforts to save monuments threatened by the Aswan dam. The two statuary rooms nearby are staggering in the size and drama of the objects they house, most notably two sphinxes and a massive, richly painted statue of Ramses II. Smaller objects—mummies, funerary objects, and a papyrus Book of the Dead—fill the galleries on the next floor; the most enchanting exhibit here is the everyday paraphernalia, including eating utensils and much-shriveled foodstuffs, from the tomb of the 14th-century B.C. architect Khaie and his wife.

The Savoy's other treasure trove, a magnificent collection of European painting, fills the salons of the Galleria Sabauda above the Egyptian collection. The Savoy's royal taste ran heavily to painters of the Flemish and Dutch schools, and the Van Dycks, Van Eycks, Rembrandts, and Van der Weydens, among others, comprise one of Italy's largest collections of northern European paintings. In fact, two of Europe's most prized Flemish masterpieces are here, Jan van Eyck's *Stigmata of St. Francis* and Hans Memling's *Passion of Christ*. Italian artists, including those from the Piedmont, are also well represented; one of the first canvases you come to upon entering the galleries is the work of a Tuscan, Fra Angelico's sublime *Virgin and Child*.

Museo Nazionale del Risorgimento. V. Accademia d. Scienze 5. ☎ **011/562-1147.** Admission 8,000L ($4.70). Tues–Sun 9am–7pm.

Much of modern Italian history has been played out in Turin, and much of it, fittingly, in this palazzo that was home to the first king of a unified Italy, Vittorio Emanuele II, and the seat of its first parliament, in 1861. While any self-respecting town in Italy has a museum of the risorgimento, the movement that launched Italian unification, this one is the best. Documents, paintings, and other paraphernalia recount the heady days when Vittorio Emanuele banded with Garibaldi and his Red Shirts to oust the Bourbons from Sicily and the Austrians from the north to create a unified Italy. The last room you come to houses a fascinating collection that chronicles resistance to Italian Fascism.

Palazzo Madama-Museo Civico di Arte Antica. Piazza Castello. ☎ **011/442-9911**. Admission 8,000L ($4.70). Tues–Sat 9am–7pm and Sun 10am–1pm and 2–7pm. Scheduled to reopen for Italy's millennium celebrations; check with the tourist board.

Do not settle for the baroque facade, added by the architect Filippo Juvarra in the 18th century: If you walk around the exterior of the palazzo (named for its most popular resident, Madama Reale, aka Marie Christine of France) you will discover that the massive structure incorporates a medieval castle, a Roman gate, and several Renaissance additions. Juvarra also added a monumental marble staircase to the interior, most of which is given over to the far reaching collections of the Museo Civico di Arte Antica. As this book went to press, the museum was scheduled to re-open after a decade-long restoration. The holdings focus on the medieval and Renaissance periods, shown off against the castle's unaltered, stony medieval interior. One of Italy's largest collections of ceramics is here, as too are some stunning canvases, including Anotello da Messina's *Portrait of a Man*.

Palazzo Reale (Royal Palace). Pz. Castello. ☎ **011/436-1455**. Admission 8,000L ($4.70). Tues–Sun 9am–7pm. Guided tours on Sun every 40 min.

The residence of the House of Savoy, begun in 1645 and designed by the Francophile count of Castellamonte, reflects the ornately baroque tastes of European ruling families of the time—a fact that will not be lost on you as you pass from one opulently decorated, heavily gilded room to the next. (The Savoys had a keener eye for painting than for decor, and most of the canvases they collected are in the nearby Galleria Sabauda). What's most notable here are some of the tapestries, including the Gobelins depicting the life of Don Quixote, in the **Sala delle Virtu** (Hall of Virtues), and the collection of Chinese and Japanese vases in the **Sala dell'Alcova.** One of the quirkier architectural innovations, an antidote to several monumental staircases, is a manually driven elevator from the 18th century.

One wing houses the **Armeria Reale** (Royal Armory), one of the most important collections of its kind in Europe (separate entrance on Piazza Castello; 8,000L/$4.70; open Tuesday and Thursday 2:30 to 7:30pm and Saturday 9am to 2pm). Behind the palace, and offering a refreshing change from its frippery, are the **Giardini Reali** (Royal Gardens), laid out by Andre Le Notre, more famous for the Tuileries and the gardens at Versailles.

PARKS & PIAZZAS

Piazza San Carlo, Turin's most beautiful square, is the city's outdoor living room, surrounded by arcaded sidewalks that house the terraces of the cafes for which Turin is famous (see below). In the center is an equestrian statue of Duke Emanuele Filiberto of Savoy and facing each other, at the northern end of the piazza, are a pair of 17th-century churches, San Carlo and Santa Cristina, and the overall effect is one of elegant harmony.

The **Parco del Valentino** (☎ 011/669-9372), a lush sweep of greenery along the Po south of Corso Vittorio Emanuele II, provides a wonderful retreat from Turin's well-mannered streets and piazzas. It is open daily 8am to 8pm. Aside from riverfront promenades and extensive lawns and gardens, inside the park, there's a collection of enchanting buildings. The **Borgo Medioevale,** built for Turin's 1884 world exposition, is a faithful reconstruction of a medieval village based on those in rural Piedmont and the Val d'Aosta, with shops, taverns, houses, churches, and even a castle (admission 5,000L/$2.95, open daily 9am to 7pm). The nearby **Castello del Valentino** is the real thing—a royal residence, begun in the 16th century but completed in the 17th century for Turin's beloved Maria Christine ("Madama Reale," wife of Savoy king Vittorio Amedeo) as a summer residence. It's a sign of Madama's Francophile leanings that, with its sloping roofs and forecourt, the castle resembles a French château. Since used as a school of veterinary medicine and a military barracks and currently as a university facility, the castello is continually undergoing renovations and much of it, including many frescoed salons, is open to the public only on special occasions.

NEARBY ATTRACTIONS

Basilica di Superga. About 4 mi. northeast of the town center in Parco Naturale d. Collina di Superga. ☎ **011/898-0083.** Free admission. Daily 9:30am–noon and 3–6pm. Reached by rack railway (4,000L/$2.35), with a terminus at Stazione Sassi on Pz. Gustavo Modena (follow Corso Casale on east side of the River Po). Tram: 15 from V. XX Settembre to Stazione Sassi.

As thanksgiving to the Virgin Mary for Turin's deliverance from the French siege of 1706, Vittorio Amedeo II commissioned Juvarra, the Sicilian architect who did his greatest work in Turin, to build this baroque basilica on a hill high above the city. The exterior, with a beautiful neoclassic porch and lofty drum dome, is far more interesting than the gloomy interior, a vast circular chamber beneath the dome with six side chapels. The church more or less serves as a pantheon for the House of Savoy, whose tombs are scattered about, many in the so-called Crypt of Kings beneath the main chapel. There's a fine view of the Alps from the terrace in front. The trip up to the basilica on a narrow railway through verdant parkland is a favorite Turinese outing.

Palazzina di Caccia di Stupinigi. Stupingi, 5 mi. southwest of the city center. ☎ **011/358-1220.** Admission 10,000L ($5.90). Tues–Sun 9:30am–11:50pm and 2–4:20pm. Bus: 4 from Porta Nouva train station to Pz. Caio Mario; change to bus 41.

The other great work of the architect Juvarra (see the Basilica di Superga, above) is this sumptuous, lavishly decorated hunting lodge that the Savoys commissioned in 1729. The main part of the lodge, to which the members of the House of Savoy retired for hunts in the royal forests that still surround it, is shaped like a Saint Andrew's cross, fanning out from a circular, domed pavilion that is topped with a large, gold-plated deer. Much of the lavish interior (and the only part open to the general public) is given over to the decorative collections of the **Museo d'Arte e Ammobiliamento** (Museum of Art and Furniture), a vast repository of furniture, paintings, and bric-a-brac assembled from the many Savoy residences. The museum is well worth visiting simply to stroll through the acres of excessively decorated apartments—an experience that will make it easy to understand why Napoléon chose this for his brief residency in the region. Outstanding among the many, many frescoes are the scenes of a deer hunt in the King's Apartment and the Triumph of Diana in the grand salon.

The elegant gardens and surrounding forests provide lovely terrain for a jaunt.

WHERE TO STAY

Hotel Bellavista. V. B. Galliari 15, 10125 Turin. ☎ **011/669-8139.** Fax 011/668-7989. 18 units, 7 with bathroom. TV TEL. 70,000L ($41.20) single; 95,000L ($55.90) double without bathroom, 120,000L ($70.60) double with bathroom; 145,000L ($85.30) triple with bathroom. AE, MC, V.

The neighborhood between the Porta Nuova railway station and Parco del Valentino is pleasant and residential, and this pensione occupies the sixth floor of an apartment house on a quiet street. What is likely to strike you immediately is just how pleasant the surroundings are—step off the elevator and you will find yourself in a sun-filled corridor that's a garden of houseplants and opens onto a wide terrace. There's also a pleasant bar area, where guests can buy rolls and coffee at breakfast. Rooms are airy and comfortable but a little less inspiring in decor, with banal, functional modern furnishings. Most, though, afford pleasant views over the surrounding rooftops—the best outlooks in the house are across the river toward the hills. What most rooms don't have is a private bathroom, though the several communal ones are well placed so most rooms are only a few steps away from a facility.

Hotel Bologna. Cor. Vittorio Emanuele II 60, 10121 Turin. ☎ **011/562-0290**. Fax 011/ 562-0193. 50 units, all with bathroom. TV TEL. 80,000L ($47) single, 100,000L ($58.80) double. Breakfast 6,000L ($3.55) for one, 10,000L ($5.90) for two. AE, MC, V.

This family run hotel just across the street from the Porta Nuova train station offers location, affordable comfort, and a very attentive, English-speaking staff. Each of the 50 rooms, spread over several floors of a gracious 18th-century apartment house, is different. Some are quite grand, incorporating frescoes, fireplaces, and other original details (of these, rooms 52 and 64 are the largest and most elegant). Other rooms have recently been renovated in sleek modern style, with laminated, built-in cabinetry and neutral carpeting; others fall in between, with a well-maintained 1970s style and linoleum flooring. Whatever the vintage, all of the rooms are spotlessly clean and nicely maintained.

Hotel Liberty. V. P. Micca 15, 10121 Turin. ☎ **011/562-8801.** Fax 011/562-8163. 35 units, all with bathroom. TV TEL. 90,000–130,000L ($52.95–$76.45) single, 150,000– 170,000L ($88.25–100) double. Breakfast 10,000L ($5.90). AE, DC, MC, V. Parking 20,000L ($11.75).

An excellent location a few blocks southeast of Piazza Castello puts the Liberty within easy walking distance of most of Turin's museums, other monuments and shops, and restaurants. What's most remarkable about this hotel, though, is its ambience. It occupies an early 20th century mansion built in the art-deco style, which in Italian is known as "Liberty." Many of the original features, such as ornately carved doorways and etched windows, remain, and the public rooms especially retain a great deal of grandeur with turn-of-the-century furnishings and polished parquet floors; there's a small bar and restaurant off the lobby. The guest rooms are large and nonfussily stylish, with some period pieces augmented by comfortable newer furnishings, including firm beds; the smallish bathrooms have been brought nicely up to date. These surroundings seem all the more pleasant with the attentive presence of the Anfossi family, which has run this charming hotel for decades.

Hotel Magenta. Cor. Vittorio Emanuele II 67, 10121 Turin. ☎ **011/54-26-49.** Fax 011/ 54-47-55. 18 units, 10 with bathroom. TV. 47,000L ($27.65) single without bathroom, 63,000L ($37.05) single with bathroom; 60,000L ($35.30) double without bathroom, 90,000L ($52.95) double with bathroom. Breakfast 7,000L ($4.10). AE, MC, V.

Unlike the areas around train stations in most large cities, the Porta Nuova neighborhood is stylish and safe, and many of the city's hotels are here. The Magenta is one of the least expensive, and it is handily located just west of the station along one of the arcaded sidewalks that follow busy Corso Vittorio Emanuele. The surroundings of this pleasant pension, which occupies a wing of the second floor of an apartment house, suggest that the premises have seen grander days. Ornate moldings and polished parquet floors and crystal chandeliers grace a long central hallway that is furnished with comfortable, upholstered easy chairs. With banal, standard-issue hotel furnishings, guest rooms are a bit less opulent, but they are spacious and high-ceilinged nonetheless and some have newly installed bathrooms. In the morning, you can enjoy an espresso and pastry at the little bar in the lobby.

WORTH A SPLURGE

Victoria Hotel. V. Nino Costa 4, 10123 Turin. ☎ **011/56-11-909.** Fax 011/56-11-806. 90 units, all with bathroom. A/C TV TEL. 170,000L ($100) single, 200,000L ($117.65) deluxe single; 240,000L ($141.10) double, 270,000L ($158.90) deluxe double. Rates include breakfast. AE, MC, V.

Step through the doors of this somewhat plain-looking building between the Via Roma and the river and you'll think you're in an English country house. That's the whole idea, and the Anglophile decor works splendidly. The lobby is decorated as a country house drawing room, with floral sofas, deep armchairs, and a view onto a garden; the room doubles as a bar and is an extremely pleasant place to enjoy a drink before setting out for one of the nearby restaurants. The glass-enclosed breakfast room, where a sumptuous buffet is served, resembles a conservatory. Accommodations are classified as deluxe or standard, depending on size and decor. Standard guest rooms are handsomely furnished in a chic style that soothingly combines contemporary and traditional styles, with mahogany bedsteads and writing desks, and rich fabric wall-coverings and draperies; deluxe accommodations, each with its own distinctive look, are oversized and furnished in carefully chosen antiques, with such flourishes as canopied beds and richly covered divans. All accommodations have sleek marble bathrooms that are nicely equipped with hair dryers, complimentary toiletries and have either roomy stall showers or full bathtubs.

WHERE TO DINE

One of the great pleasures of being in Piedmont is to sample the cuisine that is unique to this region. Two new pastas you will encounter on menus are *agnolotti* (a thick tube often stuffed with an infusion of cheese and meat) and *tajarin,* a flat egg noodle that is often topped with funghi porcini. While chilly, foggy evenings call for grilled meat and game, truffles abound in the moist soil and the farm gardens produce enough vegetables to make meatless meals a special occasion; one of the favorite preparations is *bagna cauda* (hot bath), in which raw vegetables are dipped into a heated preparation of oil, anchovies, and garlic. If you have a sweet tooth, you will soon discover that Turin and outlying towns can amply satisfying cravings for sweets. With wines as good as the ones Piedmont produces (see "Visiting the Wine Villages," below), even a carafe of the house red is likely to be excellent.

Da Mauro. V. Maria Vittoria 21. ☎ **011/839-7811.** Primi 8,000–12,000L ($4.70–$7.05), secondi 10,000–18,000L ($5.90–$10.60). No credit cards. Tues–Sun 12:30–3pm and 7–10pm. Closed July. ITALIAN.

This simple, tile-floored room is more relaxed than many Turinese restaurants, and if the informal ambience and the menu remind you of regions to the south, you are quite right. The family that owns and runs the restaurant emphasizes Tuscan dishes, though the range seems to run the gamut of Italian cooking. There are any number of spicy pasta dishes, including a deftly prepared cannelloni, and the meat courses are indeed similar to those you would find in Tuscany—steak, lamb, sausages, and game birds are simply grilled or roasted.

Dai Saletta. V. Belfiore 37. ☎ **011/668-7867.** Primi 8,000–15,000L($4.70–8.80); secondi 10,000–20,000L ($5.90–$11.75). AE, V. Mon–Sat 12:30–2:30pm and 7:30pm–1am. Closed Aug. PIEDMONTESE.

One of the few kitchens in Turin that remains open into the wee hours turns out a nice selection of homey trattoria fare, served in a tiny, cramped dining room near the train station. Homemade pasta dishes are delicious and you may want to order some of them, such as *tortelloni alla salsiccia* (a large pasta shell stuffed with sausage), or *peposelle* (a thick pasta tossed with Gorgonzola and walnuts) as a main course. If you want to venture on, it may well be with such traditional favorites as tripe.

Porto di Savano. Pz. Vittorio Veneto 2. ☎ **011/817-3500**. Primi 7,000–10,000L ($4.10–$5.90); secondi 9,000–15,000L ($5.30–$8.80). V. Tues 7:30–10:30pm, Wed–Sun 12:30–2:30pm and 7:30–10:30pm. Closed Aug 15–31. PIEDMONTESE.

What is probably the most popular trattoria in Turin is tucked under the arcades along the city's largest piazza. Seating is family style, at long tables that crowd a series of rooms beneath old photos and mementos, and the typically Piedmontese fare never fails to please (all the more so on Sunday, when many other restaurants in central Turin are closed). Several variations of gnocchi are usually made fresh daily, as is the Piedmontese flat noodle, *tajarin,* and *pasticcio,* a pasta casserole with meat and cream. Another way to start a meal is with some variation of funghi porcini, which are served in many different variations, perhaps best when simply sautéed. These starters can nicely be followed with one of the grilled meat dishes in which the house specializes.

WORTH A SPLURGE

C'era una Volta. Cor. Vittorio Emanuele II 42. ☎ **011/65-04-589**. Reservations recommended. Tasting menu 45,000L ($26). AE, MC, V. Mon–Sat 7–10:30pm. Closed Sun and Aug. TURINESE.

To enter Once Upon a Time, you must ring a bell at street level, then climb the stairs or take the elevator to a large, old-fashioned dining room filled with heavy old tables and chairs and dark credenzas. The food, delivered by a highly professional wait staff that has been here for years, is authentically Turinese and never seems to stop coming. A typical menu, which changes daily, might include crepes with ham and cheese, risotto with artichokes, a carrot flan, rabbit stew, a slice of beef with polenta, and any number of other wonderfully prepared dishes. You will want to accompany your meal with a Barolo or other regional wine.

CAFES & DELICACY SHOPS

Cafe sitting is a centuries-old tradition in sophisticated Turin. **Via Roma** and the piazze it widens into are lined with gracious salons that have been serving coffee to Turinese for decades, even centuries. Below are some of the city's classic cafes. While espresso and pastries are the mainstays of the menu at all of them, most also serve the chocolates—including the mixture of chocolate and hazelnuts known as *gianduiotti*—that are among the city's major contributions to culinary culture. Turin has a sizable sweet tooth, satisfied by any number of pastry and candy shops. Perhaps the best chocolatier north of Perugia is **Pfatisch,** at Cor. Vittorio Emanuele II 76 (☎ 011/568-3962), open Tuesday through Sunday from 10am to 1pm and 3 to 7:30pm. A wide variety of chocolates and other sweets, including sumptuous meringues, is dispensed at **Fratelli Stratta,** Pz. San Carlo 191 (☎ 011/541-567), open Tuesday through Sunday from 9:30am to 1pm and 3 to 7:30pm.

The surrounding region is known not only for its wines but also for vermouth—the famed Cinzano, for instance, is produced south of the city in the town of Santa Vittoria d'Alba. Come evening, a glass of vermouth is the preferred drink at many of the city's cafes. **Paissa,** at Pz. San Carlo 196 (☎ 011/562-8364), open Monday to Saturday from 9am to 1pm and 3:30 to 7:30pm, is an excellent place to purchase local vermouths by the bottle.

Caffè Confetteria al Bicerin. Pz. d. Consolata 5. ☎ **011/518-794.** Mon–Tues and Thurs–Fri 8:30am–19:30pm, Sat–Sun 8:30am–12:30pm and 3:30–7:30pm. AE, DC, MC, V. CAFE.

What claims to be Turin's oldest cafe in continuous operation (since 1763) is famous for its roster of illustrious clientele, which has included Nietszche, Dumas, and

Puccini, as well as its signature drink—the Bicerin (local dialect for "something delicious"). It's a heady combination of coffee, hot chocolate, and cream—to be accompanied by one the house's exquisite pastries.

Caffe-Pasticceria Baratti e Milano. Pz. Castello 29. ☎ **011/511-481**. Tues–Sun 8am–1am. CAFE.

No small part of the pleasure of sitting for a time in this stylish cafe, opened in 1875, is watching a clientele that includes auto executives, students from the nearby university, elegantly clad shoppers, and visitors to the nearby museums, all sipping espressos and munching on the delicious house pastries.

Caffè San Carlo. Pz. San Carlo 156. ☎ **011/515-317**. Tues–Fri 8am–1am, Sat 9:30am–2am, Sun 9:30am–1am. CAFE.

One of the essential stops on any tour of Turin is this classic cafe. The San Carlo opened its doors in 1837 and ever since has been accommodating patrons beneath a huge chandelier of Murano glass in a salon that is a remarkable assemblage of gilt, mirrors, and marble. An adjoining, frescoed tearoom is quieter and only a little less grand.

Caffè Torino. Pz. San Carlo 204. ☎ **011/545-118**. Mon–Sat 7am–1am. AE, DC, MC, V. CAFE.

Although some of the mirrored and frescoed salons here serve full meals, we suggest you dine at another restaurant and enjoy a light refreshment (one of the pastries or chocolates handsomely displayed in the main room) while soaking in the ambience of this classic, century-old cafe. Many mirrors, smoky oil paintings, and acres of carved wood create just the ambience you would expect to find in one the city's most beloved institutions.

TURIN AFTER DARK

Turin has a lively classical music and opera scene. Aside from the city's much attended summer festivals (see "Festivals & Markets," above) there are regular classical concerts at **Auditorium della RAI,** V. Rossini 15 (☎ **011/8800**). Other concerts, dance performances, and operas are staged at the city's venerable **Teatro Regio,** in the center of the city on Piazza Castello; the box office (☎ **011/881-5242**) is open Tuesday to Sunday from 10:30am to 6pm.

DAY TRIPS FROM TURIN

Sacra di San Michele. ☎ **011/939-130**. Donation requested. Apr–Sept daily 9am–noon and 2–7pm, Oct–Mar daily 9am–noon and 2pm–dusk.

Perched high atop Monte Pirchiriano (part of it projecting over the precipice on an elaborate support system that was one of the engineering feats of the Middle Ages), this dramatically situated abbey dedicated to Saint Michael provides views and an astonishing look at medieval religious life. It may well remind you of Mont Saint-Michel in France (both are laced with endless flights of stairs) or, with its dizzying views and scary drops, of the abbey in the film and novel *Name of the Rose.* Actually, Mont Saint-Michel was one of the 176 religious institutions that once fell under the jurisdiction of San Michele. Interestingly, author Umberto Ecco based his fictional abbey on this one. A vast staircase hewn out of rock and clinging to the abbey's buttresses (known as Scalone dei Morti, Stairs of Death, because corpses were once laid out here) leads to the massive carved doorway depicting the signs of the zodiac and the drafty Gothic and Romanesque church, decorated only with 16th-century frescoes by Secondo del Bosco. Another stairway leads down to three tiny chapels carved into the rock and containing tombs of some of the earliest members of the House of Savoy.

GETTING HERE Avigliana is connected by 15 trains a day with Turin, 2,700L ($1.60). That's the good news; the bad news is, buses no longer run up the mountain to the Sacra. You can walk (a not-too strenuous trek of about 2 hr.), or try to hitch a ride en route. By car, follow **E70** from the western edge of Turin; the trip to the abbey takes about an hour.

SAVIGLIANO & SALUZZO

Savigliano is one of those towns everyone dreams of stumbling upon in Italy—it's filled with Renaissance riches, but is still undiscovered. The town center is the broad expanse of the **Piazza Santa Rosa,** surrounded by arcades, overlooked by a medieval tower, and lined with many of the town's grand palaces, which once housed summering members of the Savoy clan. Unfortunately, these and another fine collection of palazzi along the **Via Jerusalem** are closed to the public, so you'll have to settle for a gander at their gorgeous facades.

The pride of Saluzzo is its sleepy upper town, huddled beneath its **Castello di Manta.** Along the warren of narrow lanes you'll find the 13th-century **Chiesa di San Giovanni** and the **Casa Cavassa,** which is worth a look, not for the musty civic museum it houses, but for its porticoed courtyard.

GETTING HERE Savigliano is 34 miles south of Turin, from which there are three daily trains (about a half-hour trip). From there, hourly trains make the 20-minute run to Saluzzo. Saluzzo is also connected with Turin by 15 buses a day. The most direct driving route to Savigliano from Turin follows the **A6 autostrada** for 21 miles south to the exit near Brà; from the exit, follow S231 west for 6 miles. Saluzzo is another 8 miles west on S231. If you are making the sweep through the wine country via Asti and Alba (see below), you can continue west from Alba for 21 miles on **S231** to Savigliano.

2 The Piedmont Wine Country

Asti is 60 km (36 mi.) SE of Turin, 127 km (78 mi.) SW of Milan; Alba is 60 km (32 mi.) S of Turin, 155 km (95 mi.) SW of Milan

South of Turin, the Po valley rises into the rolling Langhe and Roero hills, flanked by orchards and vineyards. You'll recognize the region's place names from the labels of its excellent wines, among them Asti Spumante, Barbaresco, and Barolo. Tasting these vintages at the source is one reason to visit the wine country, of course; another is to stroll through the medieval and Renaissance towns that rise from the vineyards and the picturesque villages that crown many a hilltop. And vines are not all that flourish in the fertile soil—truffles top the list of the region's gastronomic delights, which also include down-home country fare like rabbit and game dishes, excellent cheeses, and plump fruit.

ASTI

The Asti of sparkling-wine fame is a bustling city more concerned with everyday business than entertaining visitors, but there are many treasures to be found in the history-drenched old town—medieval towers (120 of them still stand), Renaissance palaces, and broad piazze provide the perfect setting in which to sample the town's famous product.

FESTIVALS & MARKETS In late June and early July, Asti stages **Asti Teatro,** a theater festival with performances that incorporate dance and music as well. September, though, is the town's busy cultural month, with townsfolk and horses alike donning medieval garb for its famous Palio on the third Sunday (see "Horses &

Horses & Donkeys

Asti and Alba, bitter rivals through much of the Middle Ages, each celebrate the autumnal harvest with equine celebrations that are horses of a very different color.

The **Palio,** Asti's annual horse race, is run the third Sunday of September. Like the similar but more famous horse race that the Tuscan city of Siena mounts, Asti's palio begins with a medieval pageant through the town and ends with a wild bareback ride around the Campo del Palio. The race coincides with Asti's other great revel, the **Douja d'Or,** a weeklong fair-cum-bacchanal celebrating the grape.

On the first Sunday of October Alba pulls a spoof on Asti with the **Palio degli Asini** (Race of the Asses). The event, which coincides with Alba's annual truffle fair, is not as speedy as Asti's slicker, horseback palio, but it's a lot more fun. Good-natured as the event is, though, it is rooted in some of the darkest days of Alba's history. In the 13th century Asti, then one of the most powerful republics of northern Italy, besieged Alba and burned the surrounding vineyards. Then, to add insult to injury, the victors held their palio in Alba, just to put the humbled citizenry further in its place. Alba then staged a palio with asses, a not so subtle hint of what they thought of their victors and their pompous pageantry.

Donkeys" box, above). Local wine producers converge on town the week or so before the Palio for the **Douja d'Or,** an exhibition of local vintages accompanied by tastings (from 4,000L/$2.35); this is an excellent way to sample the products of the many wineries in the hills surrounding Asti and nearby Alba. The second Sunday of September, surrounding villages mount feasts (almost always accompanied by a communal meal) known collectively as the **Pjasan.**

Agricultural center that it is, Asti has two food markets. The largest is held Wednesdays and Saturdays from 7:30am to 1pm in the **Campo del Palio,** with stalls selling every foodstuff imaginable—seeds, herbs, flowers, farm implements, and no end of other merchandise spilling over to two adjoining piazzas, the Piazza della Liberta and Piazza Alfieri. Meanwhile, Asti's covered food market, the **Mercato Coperto,** is also located in this vicinity, on Piazza della Liberta, and is open Monday through Wednesday and Friday and Saturday from 8am to 1pm and 3:30 to 7:30pm.

ESSENTIALS

GETTING HERE   By Train   Two trains an hour link Asti with Turin, only 45 minutes away; the fare is 5,100L ($3).

By Car   Asti, 73 kilometers (44 mi.) east of Turin, can be reached from Turin in less than an hour via the **A21 autostrada.**

VISITOR INFORMATION   The **APT tourist office** is near the train station at Pz. Alfieri 34 (☎ **0141/530-357**), open Monday to Friday from 9am to 12:30pm and 3 to 6pm, and Saturday from 9am to 12:30pm. Among the office's offerings is a *Carta del Vini,* an annotated map that will point you to surrounding vineyards that provide wine tastings.

EXPLORING THE TOWN

If you take the train to Asti, you will step right into the heart of the action, because the town's lively food markets occupy three adjoining piazze just to the north of the station (Campo del Palio, Piazza Liberta, and Piazza Alfieri). If you're driving into Asti, you're most likely to find parking in one of the lots in this area as well.

Walk through the piazze to **Corso Alfieri;** the town's Renaissance palaces are located on or just off this major thoroughfare, usually closed to traffic. This street and Asti's grandest piazza are named for the town's most famous native son, the 18th-century poet Vittorio Alfieri. His home, on the Corso at 375, houses a small, memento-filled museum.

Second to none in Asti is **San Secondo,** the town's patron saint. He was imprisoned in the Torre Rosse (at the western end of Corso Alfieri), one of many fine towers built by the town's powerful families, then beheaded on the spot just south of Corso Alfieri where the church erected in his honor, the **Collegiata di San Secondo,** now stands (open daily from 7am to noon and from 3:30 to 7pm). Not only does this Romanesque-Gothic structure have the honor of housing the saint's remains in its eerie crypt, but it is also the permanent home of the coveted **Palio Astigiano,** the banner awarded to the horseman who wins the town's annual Palio (see below; Secondo is the patron of this event).

Asti's "other" church is its 14th-century, redbrick **cattedrale,** which you can reach by walking through Piazza Cairoli, at the western end of Corso Alfieri, into the nearby Piazza Cattedrale. Every inch of this brick church's cavernous interior is festooned with frescoes by 16th- and 17th-century artists, including Gandolfino d'Asti; trompe l'oeil vines climb many of the columns. The cathedral is open daily from 7:30am to noon and 3 to 7pm. The most notable feature of the church of **San Pietro in Consavia,** at the eastern end of Corso Alfieri, is its round, 10th-century baptistery; the 15th-century interior and adjoining cloisters house a small archaeological collection (open Tuesday to Saturday from 9am to noon and 3 to 7pm, Sunday from 3 to 7pm).

WHERE TO STAY

Rainero. V. Cavour 85. ☎ **0141 353-866.** Fax 0141/594-985. 55 units, all with bathroom. 80,000–85,000L ($47–$50) single, 125,000–135,000 ($73.50–$79.40) double. Breakfast 12,000L ($7.05). AE, DC, MC, V. Parking 15,000L ($8.80). Closed first week of Jan.

Occupying a centuries-old house, the Raneiro enjoys a wonderful location near the Campo del Palio and the church of San Secondo. Not only is this setting convenient, but, since many of the surrounding streets are closed to traffic, the neighborhood is quiet. Despite the provenance of the structure, renovations are tasteful but lean toward a clean, modern look. As result the guest rooms are perfectly comfortable, though a little bland. However, the surrounding streets provide any character you might miss from the decor, and the attentive family management makes you feel right at home.

WHERE TO DINE

✪ Il Convivio. V. G. B. Giuliani 4/6. ☎ **0141/594-188.** Reservations recommended. Primi 7,000–10,000L ($4.10–$5.90); secondi 10,000–16,000L ($5.90–$9.40). AE, DC, MC, V. Mon–Sat, 1–2:30pm and 8–10:30pm. PIEDMONTESE

The decor of this double height, pastel colored dining room is straightforward, with a clean contemporary look. These no-nonsense surroundings reflect the fact that the main business here is to serve excellently prepared food and accompany it with the region's best, but not necessarily most expensive, wines (these are dispensed from an extensive *cave* that you are welcome to visit, and you can also purchase wine by the bottle or case on the premises). Only a few starters, pasta dishes, and main courses are prepared daily. They always include some wonderful fresh-made pastas, such as the lightest gnocchi in a sweet pepper sauce, a soup incorporating vegetables bought that morning from Asti's markets and some serious meat dishes, such as a masterful *ossibucho di vitello* or a *coniglio,* a rabbit that here is often sautéed with olives and white wine. Desserts, including a heavenly *pannacotta al cioccolato*, are as memorable as the rest of the dining experience.

Trattoria del Mercato. Cor. Einaudi 50 (at C. d. Palio). ☎ **0141/592-142.** Primi 5,000L ($2.95); secondi 8,000L ($4.70). No credit cards. Mon–Sat, noon–2:30pm and 7–10pm. PIEDMONTESE.

There's plenty of atmosphere here, but it is certainly not of the romantic candlelight variety. This plain old room, with worn blue and white ceramic tiles on the floor and heated by an ancient stove off to one side, has been welcoming patrons of Asti's nearby markets to its long communal tables for many decades. Signora Roasalba, who over-sees the kitchen and sees to the needs of her diners effortlessly, offers the few dishes she makes at any one meal—these usually are no more elaborate than a simple pasta pomodoro followed by *pollo alla cacciatora*. Good but inexpensive local wines are served by the glass or carafe.

ALBA

Lovely old Alba retains a medieval flavor that's as mellow as the wines it produces. It's a pleasure to walk along the **Via Vittorio Emanuele** and narrow streets of the old town, visit the 14th-century duomo, and peer into shop windows with lavish displays of Alba's wines, its other famous product, truffles, and its less noble but enticing *noc-ciola*, a decadent concoction of nuts and chocolate.

FESTIVALS & MARKETS   October is Alba's big month. Its **annual truffle festival** is held the first week, and this in turn climaxes in the **Palio degli Asini** (Race of the Asses), a humble version of neighboring Asti's equine palio. On Saturday and Sunday mornings from October through December, Alba hosts a truffle market where you may well be tempted to part with your hard-earned cash for one of the fragrant spec-imens (which could cost as much as $1,000 a pound).

ESSENTIALS

GETTING HERE   By Train   There are no direct trains between Turin and Alba; it's necessary to make the 1-hour trip to Brà, 9 miles west of Alba, on one of the hourly trains, and connect there for the 15-minute ride to Alba via hourly train service (5,900L/$3.50).

By Bus   Hourly buses make the trip between Alba and Turin in about 1½ hours (4,800L/$2.85).

By Car   The most direct way to reach Alba from Turin is to follow the **A6 autostrada** for 35 kilometers (21 mi.) south to the exit near Brà, and from the autostrada exit S231 east for 24 kilometers (14½ mi.) to Alba. If you want to work Alba into a trip to Asti, take A21 to Asti and from there follow S 231 southwest for 30 kilometers (18 mi.) to Alba.

VISITOR INFORMATION   The **APT tourist office** is on Piazza Medford, across from the bus station (☎ 0173/358-33), open Monday to Friday from 9am to 12:30pm and 2:30 to 6:30pm, and Saturday from 9am to 12:30pm.

EXPLORING THE TOWN

Alba's two major sights face the brick expanse of **Piazza Risogimento,** at the northern end of its major thoroughfare, Corso Vittorio Emanuele. The 14th-century duomo is flanked by a 13th-century bell tower and its stark cavernous interior is embellished with elaborately carved choir stalls. The town's two art treasures hang in the council chamber of the **Palazzo Communale** across the square—an early 16th-century por-trait of the Virgin by Alba's greatest painter, Macrino, and *Piccolo Concerto,* by Mattia

Preti, a follower of Caravaggio. From here, follow the Corso Vittorio a few blocks back into the quiet and traffic-free heart of the town.

WHERE TO STAY

Albergo Piemonte. Pz. Rossetti 6, 12051 Alba. ☎ and fax **0173/44-13-54.** 12 units, 10 with bathroom. 70,000L ($41.20) single; 100,000L ($58.80) double without bathroom, 120,000L ($70.60) double with bathroom. Rates include breakfast. MC, V.

This homey, old-fashioned hotel is nicely tucked away on a quiet piazza near the duomo and the Palazzo Communale, making it a fine base for strolls through Alba's medieval streets. The hotel occupies a centuries-old though much altered palazzo, and most of the pleasant rooms face a quiet courtyard. Even those facing the street are relatively quiet, because much of the central town is closed to traffic. The decor is modest and modern, but rooms have high-ceilings and are kept in sparkling, tiptop shape.

Cascina Reine. Altavilla 9, 12051 Alba. ☎ and fax **0173/440-112.** 9 units, 7 with bathroom. 110,000L ($64.70) double, 150,000L ($88) double with bathroom. No credit cards.

On a hillside outside Alba (about 2 miles from the center of town), this sprawling, ivy-covered villa, the home of the Pionzo family, is a pleasant and convenient retreat. Most of the public areas are outdoors and include a flower-filled patio and covered terrace overlooking the town and countryside; a breakfast of homemade cakes and jams, accompanied by cheeses from local farms, is served in a high-ceilinged dining room. You'll find an array of accommodations in the main house and outbuilding—some can be combined to provide family suites. All are furnished in a pleasant mix of old furnishings that have been passed down through the family and provide airy views over the countryside; some have terraces. **To get here,** from the Piazza Grassi in Alba follow signs to Barbareso, which will take you into the hills on Via Nizza-Acqui; there is a sign to the villa about a mile outside of Alba; turn left and follow the road to its end, where there is a gated drive into the property.

Hotel Savona. Pz. Savona 2, 12051 Alba. ☎ **0173/440-440.** Fax 0173/364-312. 98 units, all with bathroom. A/C MINIBAR TEL TV. 90,000L ($52.95) single; 130,000L ($76.45) double; 200,000L ($117.65) triple. Breakfast 15,000L ($8.80). AE, MC, V. Parking 10,000L ($5.90).

Recent renovations have added a slick, modern look to this old hotel facing a handsome brick piazza at the edge of the old town. In fact, the premises have more or less been denuded of character, but the hotel offers solid comfort and many more amenities than you would expect for the price. Downstairs there is a slick breakfast room and a bar that is also popular with patrons from the town. Upstairs, the guest rooms are pleasantly decorated in pastel shades and have contemporary furnishings and shiny new bathrooms (most with bathtubs and many with Jacuzzis); many open on to small terraces. The housekeeping staff seems to work overtime to keep the premises clean and running like clockwork.

WHERE TO DINE

✪ **Lalibera.** V. E. Pertinace 24/a. ☎ **0173/293-155.** Reservations recommended. Primi 8,000–10,000L ($4.70–$5.90); secondi 16,000–20,000L ($9.40–$11.75). AE, DC, MC, V. Mon–Sat noon–3pm and 7:30–10:30pm. Closed 2 weeks in Jan and 2 weeks in Aug. PIEDMONTESE

A careful eye to design permeates this stylish osteria in the center of town. The marble floors, blonde contemporary furnishings, and pale green walls provide a restful environment in which to enjoy the variations on traditional cuisine that the kitchen prepares. An *antipasta mista* (25,000L/$14.70) is a nice way to sample the daily specialties, which are often lighter than most of the regional cuisine—they might include *insaltina de tacchino* (a salad of fresh greens and roast turkey breast), a *vitello tonato* (the traditionally warm-weather Venetian dish of veal and tuna sauce) and *fiori di zucca* (zucchini flowers, which here are stuffed with a trout mouse). Pasta dishes are equally innovative, and many of them, such as *agnolotti* (a large tubular pasta) stuffed with cabbage and rice, often combine fresh vegetables.

Vineria dell'Umberto. Pz. Savona 4. ☎ **0173/441-397.** Primi 9,000L ($5.30); secondi 10,000–16,000L ($5.90–$9.40). MC, V. Tues–Sun 8pm–midnight. Closed Aug. PIEDMONTESE.

The premises are a little confusing: Upstairs is a busy cafe/bar that is one of Alba's few late-night scenes; downstairs is what the management calls the "Enoclub," a series of chic rooms with brick walls lined with bottles. The main business here is dispensing wines by the glass, from 2,000L ($1.20), making this a fine place to sample the produce of the local vineyards as well as wines from all over the world. Many patrons come here just to do just that, accompanying their selections with cheese or salamis; you can also order more substantial fare that includes a nice variety of rich pasta dishes, such as *tarajin* (Piedmont's answer to tagliatelle) topped with a rich lamb sauce.

VISITING THE WINE VILLAGES

Just to the south of Alba lie some of the region's, and Italy's, most enchanting wine villages. As you set out to explore the wine country, think of three words: *Rent a car.* While it's quite easy to reach some of the major towns by train or bus from Turin, setting out from those centers for smaller places can be difficult (there are some buses, but they tend to be few and far between). In Turin, contact **Avis,** Cor. Turati 15 (☎ **011/500-852**), or **Hertz,** Cor. Marconi 19 (☎ **011/470-528**). Before you head out on the labyrinth of small country roads, outfit yourself with a good map and list of vineyards from the tourist office in Alba or Asti.

While the wines of Chianti and other Tuscan regions are on the top of the list for many travelers of an enological bent, the wines of Piedmont are often less heralded among non-Italians, and unjustifiably so. Most are of exceptional quality, and usually made with grapes grown only in the Piedmont and usually on tiny family plots, making the region a lovely patchwork of vineyards and small farms. Some wines you are likely to encounter again and again as you explore the region are: **Barbesco,** refined, dry, and, with Barolo, one of the region's most exalted wines; **Barbera d'Alba,** smooth and rich, the product of many of the delightful villages south of Alba; **Barolo,** called the king of reds—hearty, rich, and the heartiest of the Piedmont wines, and the one most likely to accompany game or meat; **Dolcetto,** dry, fruity and mellow; **Nebbiolo d'Alba,** rich, full and dry (the Nebbiolo grape is also used in Barbarescos and Barolos); **Spumati,** the sparkling wine that has put Asti on the map for many travelers; and **Moscato d'Asti,** a floral dessert wine. You can taste and purchase these wines at cantinas and enotecas in almost all towns and villages throughout the region; several are noted below.

The central road through the region and running between Alba and Asti is **S231,** a heavily trafficked and unattractive highway that links many of the region's towns and cities; turn off this road whenever possible to explore the region's more rustic backwaters.

One of the loveliest drives takes you south of Alba to a string of wine villages in what are known as the **Langhe hills** (from Corso Europa, a ring road that encircles the old city in Alba, follow signs out of town for Barolo). After 8 kilometers (5 mi.) you'll come to the turnoff for **Grinzane di Cavour,** a hilltop village built around a castle housing an enoteca (open Wednesday to Monday from 9am to noon and from 2:30 to 6:30pm) where you can enjoy a fine sampling of local wines. Continuing south another 4 kilometers (2½ mi.) you'll come for the turnoff to **La Morra,** another hilltop village that affords stunning views over the rolling, vineyard-clad countryside and has several places to eat (see below) and taste the local wines. The **Enoteca Communale di La Morra,** on the Piazza del Municipo, represents local growers, selling and offering tastings of Barolos, Barbarescos, Dolcettos, and Nebbiolos. You can also procure a map of hikes in the local countryside, many of which take you through the vineyards to the doors of local growers.

✪ **Barolo,** a romantic-looking place dominated by its 12th-century castle (about 2 kilometers/1½ mi. from La Morra) is directly across the valley and enticingly in view from miles around (follow the signs from La Morra). Here, too, are a number of restaurants (see below) and shops selling the village's rich red wines. Among these outlets is the ✪ **Castello di Barolo** itself, which houses a wine museum and enoteca in its cavernous cellars; it's open Friday through Wednesday from 10am to 12:30pm and 3 to 6pm. Tiny ✪ **Novello** is a tiny hilltop village about 15 kilometers (9 mi.) south of Alba located about 3 kilometers (2 mi.) away from Barolo on well-signposted roads. It crowns the adjoining hilltop, offering some pleasant accommodations and yet more stunning views.

WHERE TO STAY

See "Visiting the Wine Villages," above, for information on how to get to the towns where the following hotels and restaurants are located.

✪ **Albergo Al Castello da Diego.** Pz. G. Marconi 4, 12060 Novello. ☎ **0173/744-011.** Fax 0173/73-12-50. 16 units, all with bathroom. TV TEL. 140,000L ($82.35) double, 200,000L ($117.65) suite. Rates include breakfast. MC, V.

Admittedly there is something forbidding about this spooky hilltop mansion, a brick Victorian built atop the ruins of a 12th-century castle. However, the welcome is friendly, the lodgings are unusual and delightful, and the views from the hillside perch are memorable. Guest rooms, reached by an endlessly winding staircase, are huge and filled with a pleasant mix of reproduction antiques and solid, oversized beds; many of the bathrooms are circular, tucked into turrets, and many rooms open to terraces. The enormous two-room suites occupy entire wings of the house, and are ornately furnished with late 19th-century furnishings that include draped beds and claw-footed divans. Several new suites have been fashioned out of the attics of an outbuilding and provide such luxuries as Jacuzzis. Breakfast is served in an intimate, paneled salon; there is a cavernous dining room that seats 1,000 and is a popular place for weddings and other fetes, but for more intimate meals you would do better to drive to nearby Barolo or La Morra.

Hotel Barbabuc. V. Giordano 35, 12060 Novello. ☎ and fax **0173/73-12-98.** 9 units, all with bathroom. A/C TV TEL. 160,000L ($94.10) double. Breakfast 15,000L ($8.80). MC, V. Closed in Jan.

This charming and intimate new hotel, which wraps around a garden, lies behind the centuries-old facade of a house near the village square. Walls of glass brick and open terraces ensure the premises are airy and filled with light. Guest rooms are placed on different levels of a central staircase, ensuring privacy, and are furnished with a tasteful mix of contemporary Italian pieces and country antiques; they have well-equipped bathrooms with large stall showers. Downstairs, there's a handsome bar area and sitting room opening to the garden, an enoteca where local wines can be tasted, and an intimate little dining room where a lavish buffet breakfast is served.

✪ **La Cascina del Monastero.** Frazione Annunziata 12064 La Morra. ☎ and fax **0173/509-245.** 5 units, all with bathroom. 120,000L ($70.60) double. No credit cards.

The main business at this delightful farm complex is bottling wine and harvesting fruit, but Giuseppe and Velda di Grasso have converted part of the oldest and most character-filled building into a bed and breakfast. Guests relax on a large covered terrace, furnished with wicker couches and arm chairs, or on the grassy shores of a pond. A sumptuous breakfast of fresh cakes, yogurt, cheese, and salamis is served in a vast brick-walled reception hall. The guest rooms, reached by a series of exterior brick staircases, have been smartly done with exposed timbers, golden hued tile floors, and attractive antique bureaus and armoires and brass beds. Bathrooms are sparkling new and quite luxurious, with state of the art stall showers and luxuriously beep basins. There are two kitchens in the guests quarters, which can closed off in such a way to provide one two-bedroom and one three-bedroom apartment.

WHERE TO DINE

L'Osteria del Vignaiolo. S. Maria 12, La Morra. ☎ **0173/503-35.** Reservations recommended. Primi 8,000–10,000L ($4.70–$5.90); secondi 15,000–20,000L ($8.80–$11.75). AE, DC, MC, V. Thurs 7:45–9:15pm, Fri–Tues 12:30–2pm and 7:45–9:15pm. PIEDMONTESE.

Halfway up the road to hilltop La Morra, this stylish countryside restaurant draws a clientele from many of the surrounding villages as well as from Alba, about 8 miles away. Pale gold walls, richly hued tiled floors, and handsome furnishings achieve a sophisticated rustic ambience, and the food, too, adds flare to local favorites. Duck breast appears in a salad of fresh picked greens; wild mushrooms are served in many variations, perhaps best when they are lightly fried and served with polenta. Veal appears thinly sliced in tagliatelle or more traditionally, infused with herbs and simply grilled. Wines, of course, are local, many from Barolo, the lights of which you can see twinkling across the valley.

La Cantinetta. V. Roma 33, Barolo. ☎ **0173/561-98.** Reservations recommended. Tasting menu 40,000L ($23.50). AE, V. Tues–Sun, noon–3pm and 7–10:30pm. PIEDMONTESE.

Two brothers, Maurilo and Paolo Chiappetto, do a fine job of introducing guests to the pleasures of the Piedmontese table (only a fixed-priced meal is served) in their cozy dining room grouped around an open hearth. A seemingly endless stream of servings, which change daily, emerge from the kitchen: a wonderful country pâté; *bagna cauda* (hot bath), in which raw vegetables are dipped into a heated preparation of oil, anchovies, and garlic; ravioli in a truffle sauce, risotto with wild mushrooms, a thick slab of roast veal; a tender cut of beef; and salad made with wild herbs. The wonderful house wines come from the vines that run right up to the door of this delightful restaurant.

Ristorante Belvedere. Pz. Castello 5, La Morra. ☎ **0173/501-90.** Reservations recommended. Primi 10,000L ($5.90); secondi 15,000–20,000L ($8.80–$11.75). AE, DC, MC, V. Tues–Sat noon–3pm and 7–10pm, Sun noon–3pm. Closed Jan–Feb. PIEDMONTESE.

The outlook from the baronial main room, built around a massive hearth and perched high above vineyards that roll away in all directions, is in itself a pleasure and draws many diners here. Many of these guests arrive on tour buses, and unfortunately, in the face of these onslaughts service can be brusque. But while the Belvedere is no longer the welcoming rustic retreat it once was, the kitchen maintains the high standards that have made it one of the region's most popular restaurants. A wonderful salad of truffles and Parmesan cheese, and homemade agnolotti in a mushroom sauce, are among the house specialties, which include many other pasta dishes and risottos. Main courses lean heavily to meat, including a rich *petto di anatra* (duck breast) and *vitello barolo*, a shank of veal braised with the local wine.

Vineria San Giorgio. V. Umberto I 1, La Morra. ☎ **0173/509-594.** Tues–Sun 11am–2am. Light meals 7,000–10,000L ($4.10–$5.90). MC, V. WINE BAR.

Not only is this friendly wine bar in the center of La Morra, but it also serves as the village social center, and the series of attractive rooms are filled with amiable chatter throughout the day and evening. Rough stones walls and vaulted brick ceilings provide just the right ambience in which to linger and enjoy the local wines (sold by the glass from 2,000L/$1.20) and such locally produced fare as salamis and cheeses, accompanied by homemade bread. Sandwiches are also available, as are three or four special dishes each day, usually including a delicious lasagna or other pasta dish.

3 Aosta & the Valle d'Aosta

Aosta is 113 km (68 mi.) NW of Turin, 184 km (111 mi.) NW of Milan; Courmayeur-Entrèves is 35 km (21 mi.) W of Aosta, 148 km (89 mi.) NW of Turin

Skiers, hikers, and fresh-air and scenery enthusiasts flock to this tiny, mountainous region less than 2 hours by train or car north of Turin, eager to enjoy one of Italy's favorite Alpine playgrounds. At its best, the Valle d'Aosta fulfills its promise. Snow-capped peaks, among them the Matterhorn and Mont Blanc, rise above the valley's verdant pastures and forests; waterfalls cascade into mountain streams; romantic castles cling to the hillsides.

Also plentiful in the Valle d'Aosta are crowds—especially in August, when the region welcomes hordes of vacationing Italians, and January through March, the height of the winter ski season—and one too many overdeveloped tourist center to accommodate them. You would be best off coming at one of the nonpeak times, when you can enjoy the valley's beauty in relative peace and quiet. Whenever you happen to find yourself in the Valle d'Aosta, two must-sees are the town of **Aosta** itself, with its Roman and medieval monuments set so dramatically against the backdrop of the Alps (and a fine place to begin a tour of the surrounding mountains and valleys), and the natural wonders of **Parco Nazionale de Gran Paradiso.** If you are looking for drama, add to the itinerary the thrill of a cable car ride over the shoulder of Mont Blanc to France. While much of the Valle d'Aosta is accessible by train or bus, you'll probably need a car to explore the quieter reaches of the region.

Of course, recreation, not sightseeing, is what draws many people to the Valle d'Aosta. Some of the best **downhill skiing,** accompanied by the best facilities, is on the runs at Courmayeur and Brevil Cervina, where you can expect to pay 35,000L ($20.60) and up for daily lift passes. **Cross-country skiing** is superb around Cogne in the Parco Nazionale del Gran Paradiso, where there are more than 30 miles of trails. The Valle d'Aosta is also excellent **hiking** terrain, especially in July and August. Some of the best trails are in the Parco Nazionale del Gran Paradiso and on the flanks of the Matterhorn around Cervina-Breuil.

FESTIVALS & MARKETS   Aosta celebrates it patron saint and warm winter days and nights with the **Fiera Sant'Orso** on the last 2 days of January. The festival fills the streets and involves a great deal of dancing, drinking vast quantities of mulled wine, and perusing the local craft pieces, such as lovely wood carvings and woven blankets, that vendors from throughout the Valle d'Aosta offer for sale. Aosta's other major event is the **Battaille des Reines,** the Battle of the Cows, in which these mainstays of the local economy lock horns—the main event is held the third Sunday in October and preliminary heats take place throughout the year. Aosta's weekly market day is Tuesday, when stalls selling food, clothes, crafts and household items fill the Piazza Cavalieri di Vittorio Veneto

AOSTA
GETTING HERE   By Train   Aosta is served by 13 trains a day to and from Turin; the trip takes 2 hours and the fare is 12,100L ($7.05); there are 10 trains a day to and from Milan; the trip takes a little more than 3 hours, requires a change in Chivasso, and costs 18,000L ($10.60).

By Bus Aosta's bus station, directly across the piazza from the train station, handles 10 buses to and from Turin daily; the 2-hour trip costs 12,500L ($7.35). Seven daily buses also connect Aosta and Milan; the trip takes 3½ hours and costs 20,500L ($12.05) each way. Buses also connect Aosta with other popular spots in the valley, among them **Courmayeur,** where you can connect with a shuttle bus to the Palud cable car (see below) and **Cogne,** a major gateway to the Parco Nazionale de Gran Paradiso (see below). For information, call ☎ **0165/262-027.**

By Car The **A5 autostrada** from Turin shoots up the length of the Valle d'Aosta en route to France and Switzerland via the Mont Blanc tunnel; there are numerous exits in the valley. The trip from Turin to Aosta normally takes about 1½ hours, but traffic can be heavy in the busy tourist months—especially in August and from January through March, the height of the ski season.

VISITOR INFORMATION The **tourist office** in Aosta, Pz. Chanoux 8 (☎ **0165/236-627**), dispenses a wealth of information on hotels, restaurants, and sights throughout the region, along with listings of campgrounds, maps of hiking trails, information about ski lift tickets and special discounted ski packages, outlets for bike rentals, and rafting trips. It's open Monday to Saturday from 9am to 1pm and 3 to 8pm, and Sunday from 9am to 1pm. The **office of the Club Alpino Italiano,** Piazza Chanoux 15 (☎ **0165/401-94**), can tell you about the best places to hike and climb; the office is open Monday, Wednesday and Thursday, 5 to 7pm, and Tuesday and Friday, 8 to 10pm. **Parco Nazionale del Gran Paradiso headquarters** are in Aosta at V. Losanna 5 (☎ **0165/44-126**); however, a better source for information on the park is the tourist office in Cogne (see below).

EXPLORING THE AREA

This mountain town, surrounded by snow-capped peaks, is not only pleasant but it has soul—the product of a history that goes back to Roman times. While you're not going to find much in the line of pristine Alpine quaintness here in the Valle d'Aosta's busy tourist and economic center, you can spend some enjoyable time strolling past Roman ruins and medieval bell towers while checking out the chic shops that sell everything from Armani suits to locally made Fontina cheese.

The Rome of the Alps sits majestically within its preserved walls, and the monuments of the Empire make it easy to envision the days when Aosta was one of Rome's most important trading and military outposts. Two Roman gates arch gracefully across the Via Anselmo, Aosta's main thoroughfare: The **Porta Pretoria,** the western entrance to the Roman town, and the **Arco di Augusto** (sometimes called Arco Romano), the eastern entrance built in A.D. 25 to commemorate a Roman victory of the Celts. A Roman bridge spans the river Buthier; just a few steps north of the Porta Pretoria you'll find the facade of the **Teatro Romano** and the ruins of the amphitheater, which once accommodated 20,000 spectators; the ruins of the forum are in an adjacent park. The theater and forum are open daily from 9:30am to 12:30pm and 2:30 to 5:30pm; admission is free. Architectural fragments from these monuments and a sizable collection of vessels and other objects unearthed during excavations are displayed in Aosta's **archeological museum** on Piazza Roncas (☎ **0165/364-1691**); it's open daily from 9:30am to 12:30pm and 2:30 to 5:30pm and admission is free.

Behind the banal 19th-century facade of Aosta's **Duomo,** on Piazza Giovanni XXIII, lie two remarkable treasures: an ivory diptych from A.D. 406 that depicts the Roman emperor Honorius and is housed along with other precious objects in the treasury, and a 12th-century mosaic in a side chapel. Heavy-handed restorations cloud the fact that the church actually dates from the 10th century. It's open Monday through Saturday 10am to noon and 3 to 6pm and Sunday 3 to 5:45pm.

Into the Great Outdoors

Recreation, of course, is what draws many people to the Valle d'Aosta. Some of the best **downhill skiing,** accompanied by the best facilities, is on the runs at Courmayeur, Brevil Cervina, and in the Valle di Cogne. At the first two, you can expect to pay 35,000L ($20.60) and up for daily lift passes. Weekly passes, providing access to lifts and slopes, run about 240,000L ($141.20); Cogne is a little less expensive, with daily passes running around 25,000L ($14.70), weekly passes around 170,000L ($100). A money-saving option is to take one of the **white-week packages** that include room and board and unlimited skiing and are available at resorts throughout the Valle d'Aosta. You can expect to pay at least 500,000L ($294.10) at Courmayeur, 350,000L ($205.90) at Cogne or one of the other less fashionable resorts. Contact the tourist board in Aosta for more information. **Cross-country skiing** is superb around Cogne in the Parco Nazionale del Gran Paradiso, where there are more than 30 miles of trails.

The Valle d'Aosta is also excellent **hiking** terrain, especially in July and August. For information about hiking in Parco Nazionale del Gran Paradiso, contact **Scoietà Guide Gran Paradiso** in the hamlet of Degioz, about 15 miles south of Aosta, to which it is connected by three daily buses (3,500L/$2.05); call ☎ **0165/955-74.**

The **Collegiata dei Santi Pietro e Orso,** at the eastern edge of the old city off V. San Anselmo 9 (☎ **0165/262-026**), is a hodgepodge from the 6th through the 18th centuries. An 11th-century church was built over the original 6th-century church, and that in turn has periodically been enhanced with architectural embellishments representing every stylistic period, from the Gothic through the baroque, since then. The 12th-century cloisters are a fascinating display of Romanesque storytelling—40 columns are capped with carved capitals depicting scenes from the Bible and the life of Aosta's own Saint Orso. In a room above the main church, a haunting, 11th-century fresco cycle recounts the life of Christ and the Apostles. It's open from April through September, Tuesday to Sunday from 9am to 7pm; October through March from 9:30am to noon and 2:30 to 5:30pm.

SIDE TRIPS FROM AOSTA

CASTLE OF FENIS   Built by the Challants, viscounts of Aosta throughout much of the Middle Ages, this castle near the town of Fenis is the most impressive and best preserved of the many castles perched on the hillsides above the Valle d'Aosta. You can scamper through ramparts, turrets, towers, and dungeons, and enjoy some fine views of the Alps and the valley below as well. One of the most appealing parts of a visit to Fenis is catching a glimpse into everyday life in a medieval castle—you can climb up to wooden loggias overlooking the courtyard and visit the cavernous kitchens.

Visitor Information   The castle (☎ **0165/764-263**) is 30 kilometers (18 mi.) east of Aosta on route S26; there are seven buses a day from Aosta, 1,700L ($1). Admission is 4,000L ($$2.35), and hours are April through September, Wednesday through Monday from 9:30am to 6pm, and October through March, Wednesday through Monday from 10am to 5pm.

CERVINA-BREUIL & THE MATTERHORN   You don't come to Cervina-Breuil to see the town, a banal collection of tourist facilities—the sight to see, and you can't miss it, is the ✪ **Matterhorn** (Monte Cervino in Italian). Its distinctive profile looms majestically above the valley, beckoning year-round skiers and those who simply want to savor a refreshing Alpine experience by ascending to its glaciers via cable car to the Plateau Rossa (about 42,000L/$24.70 round-trip). An excellent trail also ascends from Cervina-Breuil up the flank of the mountain. After about a moderately strenuous uphill trek of 90 minutes you come to gorgeous ✪ **Lac du Goillet,** and from there it's another 90 minutes to the ✪ **Colle Superiore delle Cime Bianche,** a plateau with heart-stopping views.

Visitor Information   The tourist office, V. Carrel 29 (☎ **0166-949-136**), can provide information on other hikes, ski packages, and serious ascents to the top of the Matterhorn. Cervina-Breuil is 30 miles northwest of Aosta via routes **A5** and **S406.** From Aosta, you can take one of the Turin-bound trains and get off at Chatillon (about 15 mi. down the line), and continue from there on of the six daily buses to Cervina-Breuil; combined fare is about 4,500L ($2.65).

PILA   It's well worth the trip up the winding road from Aosta to this mile-high resort, 10 miles south (follow Via Ponte Suaz—next to the train station—south out of town). The views are incredible. Aside from getting an eagle's-eye view of the valleys rolling away in all directions at your feet, you will also see Europe's two most spectacular peaks, Mont Blanc and the Matterhorn.

PARCO NAZIONALE DEL GRAN PARADISO   The little town of Cogne is the most convenient gateway to one of Europe's finest parcels of unspoiled nature, the former hunting grounds of King Vittorio Emanuele that now comprise this vast and lovely national park. The park encompasses five valleys and a total of 1,400 square miles of forests and pastureland where many Alpine beasts roam wild, including the ibex, a long-horned goat, and the chamois, a small antelope, both of which have hovered near extinction in the recent past.

Humans can roam these wilds via a vast network of well-marked trails. Among the few places where the hand of man intrudes ever so gently on nature is in a few scattered hamlets within the park borders, and in the **Giardino Alpino Paradiso,** a stunning collection of rare Alpine fauna near the village of Valnontey, just a mile south of Cogne (open June 10 through September 10, daily 9:30am to 12:30pm and 2:30 to 6:30pm. Admission is 3,000L/$1.75).

Visitor Information   Cogne also offers some downhill skiing, but it is better regarded for its many cross-country skiing trails. The tourist office in Cogne, Pz. Chanoux 34 (☎ **0165/740-40**), provides a wealth of information on hiking and skiing trails and other outdoor activities in the park and elsewhere in the region; it's open Monday through Saturday 9am to 12:30pm and 3 to 6pm and Sunday 3 to 6pm. Cogne is about 18 miles south of Aosta via S35 and S507; there are also six buses a day to and from Aosta; the 1-hour trip costs 3,200L ($1.90).

WHERE TO SAY

Many hotels in the Valle d'Aosta require that guests take their meals on the premises and stay 3 nights or more. However, outside of busy tourist times, hotels often have rooms to spare and are willing to be a little more liberal in their policies. Rates vary almost month by month; in general, expect to pay highest for a room in August, at Christmas and Easter, and the least for a room in the fall. For the best rates, check with the local tourist boards for information on **Settimane Bianche** (White Week) packages, all-inclusive deals that include room, board, and ski passes.

Belle Epoque. V. d'Avise 18, 11100 Aosta. ☎ **0165/262-26.** 12 units, 4 with bathroom. 35,000L ($20.60) single without bathroom, 45,000L ($23.50) single with bathroom; 65,000L ($38.25) double without bathroom, 75,000L ($44.10) double with bathroom. No credit cards.

The stucco exterior of this old building near the center of town has a cozy Alpine look to it, but the same can't be said of the somewhat stark interior. What is appealing about this hotel is the price, appreciated all the more in this often-expensive resort region. Rooms are Spartan, with the bare minimum of modern pieces scattered about, but are quite large and some have balconies and newly installed, tidy little bathrooms. An equally serviceable trattoria occupies most of the ground floor.

Bus. V. Malherbes 18, 11100 Aosta. ☎ **0165/436-45.** 40 units, all with bathroom. TV TEL. 70,000L ($41.20) single, 110,000L ($64.70) double; half-board 80,000–115,000 ($47–$67.65) per person. Breakfast 15,000L ($8.80). AE, MC, V.

One of the nicest things about this newer hotel is its location, on a pleasant side street just a short walk from the center of Aosta. The Roman ruins and other sights are within a 5-minute walk, yet this quiet neighborhood has an almost rural feel to it. Downstairs there is a contemporary-styled bar, restaurant, and breakfast area. Upstairs, the guest rooms are large and also comfortably furnished in a somewhat somber modern style that includes many wood veneer touches and thick carpeting. Since the hotel is taller than the surrounding houses, most of the rooms overlook meadows and the surrounding peaks. Except at some peak times, rooms are usually available without board.

Milleluci. Porossan Roppoz 15, 11100 Aosta. ☎ **0165/235-278.** Fax 0165/235-284. 12 units, all with bathroom. TV TEL. 100,000L ($58.80) single, 150,000L(88.25) double. Rates include breakfast. AE, V.

From its perch on a hillside just above the town, this homelike hotel, built to resemble a chalet and set in a garden, affords nice views and a pleasant retreat. The surroundings are a little more stylish than other hotels in this price range. Downstairs, a large, wood-beamed sitting area is grouped around an attractive hearth, and the guest rooms, some of which are tucked under the eaves, sport some nice touches like traditional wood furnishings and handsome prints on the walls; all have spacious bathrooms, most with tubs.

Roma. V. Torino 7, 11100 Aosta. ☎ **0165/41-000.** Fax 0165/324-04. 38 units, all with bathroom. TV TEL. 65,000–88,000L ($38.25–$51.75) single, 115,000–135,000L ($67.65–$79.40) double. Rates include breakfast. AE, DC, MC, V.

Tucked into a cul-de-sac near the center of town, the Roma is named for the monuments of the Empire that surround it. The paneled lobby and adjoining bar are pleasant places to relax, and with their plaid carpet and furnishings are a little cozier than the bright but crisply modern guest rooms upstairs. In good weather a generous breakfast is served on a covered, flower-bedecked terrace.

WHERE TO DINE

This is the land of mountain food—hams and salamis are laced with herbs from Alpine meadows, creamy cornmeal *polenta* accompanies meals, a rich beef stew, *carbonada*, warms winter nights, and buttery Fontina is the cheese of choice.

Caffè Nazionale. Pz. Lamoux 9. ☎ **0165/262-130.** Tues–Sun Pastries from 2,000L ($1.20). 8am–2am. No credit cards. CAFE.

This lovely fixture on Aosta's main square dates from 1886, and little has changed since then; for an almost sacred experience, try taking your coffee and pastry in the frescoed room that was once a chapel of the dukes of Aosta.

Grotta Azzurra. V. Croce di Citta 97. ☎ **0165/262-474.** Primi 7,000–12,000L ($4.10–$7.05); secondi 9,000–20,000L ($5.30–$11.75), pizza from 7,000L ($4.10). MC, V. Thurs–Tues, noon–2:30pm and 6–10:30pm. Closed July 10–27. PIZZA/SOUTHERN ITALIAN.

The best pizzeria in town also serves, as its name suggests, a bounty of fare from southern climes, along the lines of spaghetti with clam sauce. There is a wide selection of fresh fish, which makes this somewhat worn-looking trattoria popular with a local clientele. The pizzas emerge from a wood-burning oven and are often topped with Fontina and other rich local cheeses and salamis.

Taverna da Nando. V. de Tillier 41. ☎ **0165/444-55.** Primi 8,000–12,000L ($4.70–$7.05); secondi 10,000–22,000L ($5.90–$11.75). AE, DC, MC, V. Tues–Sun, noon–2:30pm and 7:15–9:30pm. VALDOSTAN.

On Aosta's main thoroughfare in the center of town, this popular eatery achieves a rustic ambience with vaulted ceilings, traditional mountain furnishings and very warm service. The kitchen, too, sticks to local traditions, serving such dishes as *fonduta* (a creamy mixture of Fontina, milk and eggs served atop polenta), *crepes la valdostana* (filled with ham and cheese), and *carbonada con polenta* (beef stew dished over polenta). There is also an excellent selection of grilled meats, and a wine list that includes many choices from the Valle d'Aosta's limited but productive vineyards and from the Piedmont.

Trattoria Praetoria. V. San Anselmo 9. ☎ **0165/443-56.** Primi 8,000–10,000L ($4.70–$5.90); secondi 10,000–18,000L ($5.90–$10.60). AE, MC, V. Fri–Wed, 12:15–2:30pm and 7:15–9:30pm. VALDOSTAN.

This small, woody trattoria, one of the friendliest and best-priced in Aosta, takes its name from the nearby Roman gate and its menu from the surrounding countryside. This is the place to throw concerns about cholesterol to the winds and introduce your palate to Valdostan cuisine. Begin with *fonduta* (melted Fontina cheese mixed with milk and eggs) and follow it with *boudin* (spicy sausages served with potatoes) or *carbonada* (a hearty beef stew).

COURMAYEUR-ENTRÈVES

The one-time mountain hamlet of **Courmayeur** is now the Valle d'Aosta's resort extraordinaire, a collection of pseudo-Alpine chalets and large hotels catering to a well-heeled international crowd of skiers. Even if you don't ski, you can happily while away the time sipping a grog while regarding the craggy bulk of **Mont Blanc** (Monte Bianco this side of the border), which looms over this end of the Valle d'Aosta and forms the snowy barrier between Italy and France. The Mont Blanc tunnel, the Italian terminus of which is just up the road from Courmayeur, now makes it possible to zip into France in just 20 minutes (43,000L/$25.30).

Entrèves, 2 miles north of Courmayeur, is the sort of place that the latter probably once was: a pleasant collection of wood houses and farm buildings surrounded by pastureland. Quaint as the village is in appearance, at its soul it is a worldly enclave with some nice hotels and restaurants catering to skiers and outdoor enthusiasts who prefer to spend time in the mountains in surroundings that are a little quieter than Courmayeur.

ESSENTIALS

GETTING HERE   By Bus   Eleven daily buses connect Courmayeur with Aosta; the trip takes an hour and costs 4,800L ($2.85) one way and 8,200L ($4.85) round-trip. Hourly buses run between Courmayeur and Entrèves, a 10-minute trip; the fare is 2,500L ($1.50).

By Car   The **A5 autostrada** from Turin to the Mont Blanc tunnel passes Courmayeur; the trip from Aosta to Courmayeur on this much-used route takes less than half an hour, and total travel time from Turin is less than 2 hours.

VISITOR INFORMATION The **tourist office** in Courmayeur, Pzlr. Monte Bianco 8 (☎ **0165/842-060**), provides information on hiking, skiing and other outdoor activities in the region, as well as hotel and restaurant listings.

ACROSS MONT BLANC BY CABLE CAR

One of the Valle d'Aosta's best experiences is the cable car trip from Palud, between Courmayeur and Entrèves, across Monte Blanc to several ski stations in Italy and down into Chamonix, in France. You make the trip in stages—first past two intermediate stops to the last aerie on Italian soil, **Punta Helbronner;** at 11,000 feet, this ice-clad lookout provides stunning views of the Mont Blanc glaciers and the Matterhorn and other peaks looming in the distance. (In summer, you may want to hop off before you get to Punta Helbronner at **Pavillion Frety** and tour a pleasant botanic garden, Giardino Alpino Saussurea; open daily July 15 to September 15.) For sheer drama, continue from Punta Helbronner to **Chamonix** to experience the dramatic sensation of dangling more than 2,000 feet in midair as you descend across glaciers. The end of the line is a viewing platform above Chamonix, to which you can descend on another cable car. Hours vary wildly, and service can be sporadic depending on weather conditions, but in general the cable car runs every 20 minutes from 7:30am 12:30pm and 2 to 5:30pm (closed November 2 to December 10); hourly buses (2,500L/$1.45) make the 10-minute run from Courmayeur to the cable car terminus at La Palud. The fare is 48,000L ($28.25) round-trip to and from Punta Helbronner; from there you will pay an additional 280 francs ($48) if you want to continue into France. Be sure to bring your passport if you want to descend on French soil.

A less expensive, albeit less dramatic way, to cross the flanks of Monte Bianco is on the **Courmayeur Monte Blanc Funivia,** which leaves from a terminus in Entrèves and ascends to the alpine Val Veny. The round-trip fare is 14,000L ($8.25). Cars depart every 30 minutes from 7:30am to 5:30pm; closed September to late December.

WHERE TO STAY

Eidelweiss. V. Marconi 42, 11013 Courmayeur. ☎ **0165/841-590.** Fax 0165/84-16-18. 30 units, all with bathroom. TV TEL. Room with half-board (required) 80,000–120,000L ($47–$70.60) per person. MC, V.

In winter, the pine-paneled salons and cozy rooms of this chalet-style hotel near the center of town attract a friendly international set of skiers, and in summer many Italian families spend a month or two at a time. The Roveyaz family extends a hearty welcome to all and provides large, modern accommodations; many open onto terraces overlooking the mountains. The nicest rooms are those on the top floor, tucked under the eaves. Basic, nonfussy meals are provided in the cheerful main-floor dining room, and breakfast and your choice of either lunch or dinner are included in the rates.

La Grange. C.P. 75, 11013 Courmayeur-Entrèves. ☎ **0165/869-733.** Fax 0165/869-744. 23 units, all with bathroom. MINIBAR TV TEL. 180,000–200,000L ($105.90–$117.65) double. Rates include breakfast. AE, DC, MC, V. Closed May–June and Oct–Nov.

What may well be the most charming hotel in the Valle d'Aosta occupies a converted barn in the bucolic village of Entrèves and is ably managed by Bruna Berthold Perri and her nephew Stefano. None of the rooms are the same, though all are decorated with a pleasing smattering of antiques and rustic furnishings; some have balconies overlooking Mont Blanc, which quite literally hovers over the property. The stucco-walled, stone-floored lobby is a fine place to relax, with couches built around a corner hearth and a little bar area. A lavish, buffet breakfast is served in a prettily paneled room off the lobby, and there is an exercise room and a much-used sauna.

Drinking with the Best of Them

The **Caffè della Posta,** at V. Roma 51, Courmayeur (☎ **0165/842-272**), is Courmayeur's most popular spot for an après ski grog. Since it opened 90 years ago, it has been welcoming the famous and not so famous into its series of cozy rooms, one of which is grouped around an open hearth.

WHERE TO DINE

Ristorante La Palud. S. la Palud, Courmayeur. ☎ **0165/89-169.** Primi 9,000–14,000 ($5.30–$8.25); secondi 10,000–25,000L ($5.90–$14.70). AE, MC, V. Thurs–Tues, noon–3pm and 7–10:30pm. SEAFOOD/VALDOSTAN.

Come to this cozy restaurant, in a little settlement just outside Courmayeur in the shadows of Mont Blanc, on Friday so that you can enjoy a wide selection of fresh fish brought up from Liguria. At any time, though, a table in front of the hearth is just the place to enjoy the specialties of the Valle d'Aosta: creamy mountain hams, *polenta concia* (with Fontina cheese and butter folded into it), and *cervo* (venison) in season. There is a selection of mountain cheeses for dessert, and the wine list borrows heavily from neighboring Piedmont but also includes some local vintages.

Worth A Splurge

Maison de Filippo. Courmayeur-Entrèves. ☎ **0165/869-797.** Reservations required. Fixed-price menu 50,000–60,000L ($29.40–$$35.30). MC, V. Wed–Mon 12:30–2:30pm and 7:30–10:30pm. Closed June and Nov–Dec 20. VALDOSTAN.

The atmosphere at this popular and cheerful restaurant in Entrèves is delightfully Alpine and the offerings so generous you may not want to eat again for a week. Daily menus vary, but often include an antipasto of mountain hams and salamis, a selection of pastas filled with wild mushrooms and topped with Fontina and other local cheeses, and a sampling of fresh trout and game in season. Service is casual and friendly, and in the summer you can choose between a table in the delightfully converted barnlike structure or on the flowery terrace.

13 | Liguria & the Italian Riviera

by Stephen Brewer

From the top of Tuscany to the French border, Italy follows a crescent-shape strip of seacoast and mountains that comprise the region of Liguria. The pleasures of this region are no secret. Ever since the 19th century, world-weary travelers have been heading for Liguria's resorts to enjoy balmy weather (ensured by the protective barrier of the Alps) and turquoise seas. Beyond the beach, the stones and tiles of proud old towns and cities bake in the sun, and hillsides are fragrant with the scent of bougainvillea and pines.

Liguria is really two coasts: the stretch east of Genoa is known as the **Riviera di Levante (Rising Sun)** and the stretch to the west of Genoa is known as the **Riviera di Ponente (Setting Sun).** Both are lined with fishing villages, including the remote hamlets of the Cinque Terre, and fashionable resorts, many of which, like San Remo, have seen their heydays fade but continue to entice visitors with palm-fringed promenades and gentle ways. **Genoa** itself, with its proud maritime history, is a world apart from the easygoing seaside places that surround it: brusque and clamorous, it is one of the most history filled, fascinating, and least visited cities in Italy.

REGIONAL CUISINE   Anywhere you travel in this region you will never be far from the sea. A truism, but a bit misleading because seafood is not as plentiful as you might assume here in the heavily fished north. What are plentiful are *acciughe* (anchovies), and once you try them fresh and *marinate* (marinated in lemon) as part of an antipasto, you will never underestimate the culinary merits of this little fish again. More noticeable than fish are the many fresh vegetables that are grown in patches clinging to the hillsides and find their way into tarts (the *torta pasqualina* is one of the most elaborate, with umpteen layers of pastry; some restaurants serve it year round), and sauces, none more typical of Liguria than pesto, a simple and simply delicious concoction of crushed basil. Ligurians are also adept at making fast food, and there's no better light lunch or snack than a piece of *focaccia*, flatbread that's often topped with herbs or olives, or a *farinata*, a chickpea crêpe that's offered by the wedges. Both are sold in bakeries and at small stands, making it easy to grab a bite then head out to enjoy the other delights of the region.

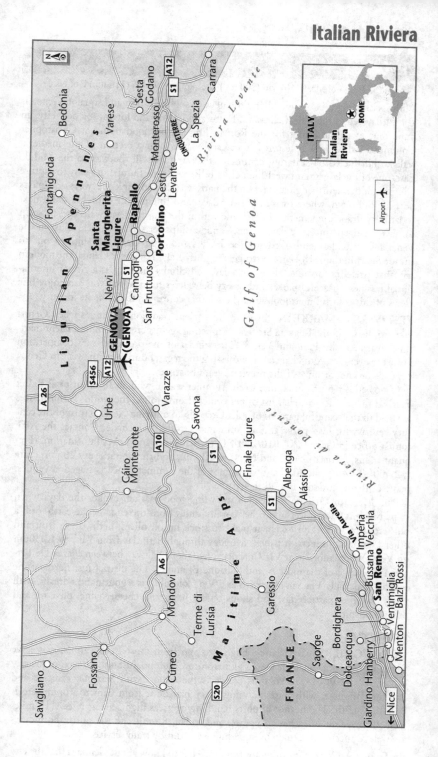

1 Genoa

142 km (85 mi.) S of Milan, 501 km (300 mi.) N of Rome, 194 km (116 mi.) E of Nice

With its dizzying mix of the old and the new, of sophistication and squalor, Genoa is as multilayered as the hills it clings to. It was and is, first and foremost a port city: an important maritime center for the Roman Empire, boyhood home of Christopher Columbus (whose much restored house still stands near a section of the medieval walls), and, fueled by seafaring commerce that stretched all the way to the Middle East, one of the largest and wealthiest cities of Renaissance Europe. It's easy to capture glimpses of these former glory days on the narrow lanes and dank alleyways of Genoa's portside old town, where treasure-filled palaces and fine marble churches stand next to laundry-draped tenements. In fact, life within the old medieval walls doesn't seem to have changed since the days when Genoese ships set sail to launch raids on the Venetians, crusaders embarked for the Holy Land, and Garibaldi shipped out to invade Sicily in the 19th-century struggle to unify Italy. The other Genoa, the modern city that stretches for miles along the coast and climbs the hills, is a city of international business, peaceful parks, and breezy belvederes from which you can enjoy fine views of this colorful metropolis and the sea that continues to define its identity.

FESTIVALS & MARKETS In **June,** an ancient tradition continues when Genoa takes to the sea in the **Regatta Storica,** competing against crews from its ancient maritime rivals, Amalfi, Pisa, and Venice. The winner of the previous year's competition hosts the event, so your chances of witnessing the regatta during a June visit to Genoa depends on the fortunes of the previous year's boatmen.

Genoa adds a touch of culture to the summer season with an **International Ballet Festival** that attracts a stellar list of performers from around the world. Performances are held in the beautiful gardens of Villa Gropallo in outlying Nervi, a turn of the century resort with lush parks and an animated seaside promenade. Contact the APT tourist office in Genoa (☎ **010/248-71**) for schedules and ticket information. (Frequent trains connect Genoa and Nervi in 10 min. and run about every 20 min.; fare is 2,400L/$1.40.) The APT also keeps tabs of the summer concerts staged at venues, many of them outdoor, around the city.

The **Mercato Orientale,** Genoa's sprawling food market, evokes the days when ships brought back spices and other commodities from the ends of the earth. Still a boisterous affair and an excellent place to stock up on olives, herbs, fresh fruit and other Ligurian products, it is held Monday through Saturday from 7am to 12:30pm on Via XX Settembre near Via Consolazione (about halfway between Piazza De Ferrari at the edge of the old city and Stazione Brignole). The district just north of the market (especially Via San Vincenzo and Via Colombo) is a gourmand's dream, with many bakeries, pasticcerias, and shops selling pasta and cheese, wine, olive oil and other foodstuffs.

ESSENTIALS

GETTING HERE **By Plane** Flights to and from most European capitals serve Aeroporto Internazionale de Genova Cristoforo Colombo, just 4 miles west of the city center; ☎ **010/601-51. Volabus** connects the airport with Stazione Principe and Stazione Brignole, with buses running every half hour from 6am to 10pm; fare is 8,000L ($4.70). The nearest airports handling overseas flights are at Nice, 116 miles west just over the border with France, and Milan, 85 miles to the north; both cities are well connected to Genoa by superhighways and by train service.

By Train An important thing for train travelers to know about Genoa is that the city has two major train stations, **Stazione Principe** (designated on timetables as Genova

P.P.), near the old city on Piazza Acqua Verde, and **Stazione Brignole** (designated on timetables as Genova BR.), in the modern city on Piazza Verdi. Many trains, especially those on long-distance lines, service both stations; however, many trains stop only at one, making it essential that you know the station at which your train is scheduled to arrive and from which it will depart. Trains connect the two stations in just 5 minutes and run about every 15 minutes (1,500L/88¢). City buses number 40 and 37 also run between the two train stations, leaving from the front of each station about every 10 minutes (1,500L/88¢); you must allow at least 20 minutes for the connection on Genoa's crowded streets.

Genoa is the hub for trains serving the Italian Riviera, with trains arriving and departing for **Ventimiglia** on the French border about every half hour and **La Spezia,** at the eastern edge of Liguria, even more frequently, as often as every 15 minutes during peak times between 7am and 7pm. Most of these trains make local stops at the coastal resorts. Sample travel times and fares are: **San Remo,** 3 hours, 12,000L ($7.05); **Santa Margherita Ligure,** 40 minutes, 2,800L ($1.65); and **Monterosso** (in the Cinque Terre), 2 hours, 7,200L ($4.25). Genoa is also well connected by train to other major Italian cities, including some 30 a day to and from **Milan** (1½ hr.; 12,100L/$7.10); some 30 a day to and from **Turin** (2 hr.; 14,000L/$8.25); and 14 a day to and from Rome (6 hr.; 38,000L/$22.35).

By Bus   An extensive bus network connects Genoa with other parts of Liguria, as well as other Italian and European cities, from the main bus station next to Stazione Principe. While it is easiest to reach seaside resorts by the trains that run up and down the coast, buses are the only link to many small towns in the region's hilly hinterlands. For tickets and information, contact **PESCI,** Pz. d. Vittoria 94/R (☎ **010/564-936**).

By Car   Genoa is linked to other parts of Italy and to France by a convenient network of superhighways. The **A10/A12** follows the coast and passes through dozens of tunnels to link Genoa with France to the west (Nice is less than 2 hr. away) and **Pisa,** about 1½ hours to the southeast. The **A7** links Genoa with Milan, a little over an hour to the north.

By Ferry   Port that it is, Genoa is linked to several other Mediterranean ports by ferry service. Most boats leave and depart from the **Stazione Marittima,** which is on a waterfront roadway, Via Marina D'Italia, about a 5-minute walk south of Stazione Principe. Check with **Tirrenia Navigazione,** Stazione Marittima (☎ **010/ 275-8041**), for a list of ports of call and schedules. Genoa is closer than ports in France to the French island of Corsica, reached by two daily ferries operated by **Corsica Ferries** (☎ **010/593-301**); the trip takes 6 hours and costs 47,000L ($27.65) each way.

VISITOR INFORMATION   The main tourist office, **Azienda di Promozione Turistica (APT),** is located near the aquarium on Via al Porto Antico (☎ **010/ 248-71**) and is open daily from 9am to 6:30pm. The agency also has branches at Stazione Principe (☎ **010/246-26-33**), open Monday through Saturday from 8am to 8pm and on Sunday from 9am to noon and at Cristoforo Colombo airport (☎ **010/ 241-5247**), open Monday through Saturday, 8am to 8pm. The office in Stazione Principe will book hotel rooms.

CITY LAYOUT   Genoa extends for miles along the coast, with neighborhoods and suburbs tucked into valleys and climbing the city's many hills. Most sights of interest are in the old town, a fascinating jumble of old palazzos, laundry-festooned tenements, cramped squares, and tiny lanes and alleyways clustered on the eastern side of the old port. The city's two train stations are located on either side of the old town, known as **Caruggi;** as confusing as Genoa's topography is, wherever you are in the old

Genoa Warning

Even locals are wary of back streets in the old city, especially after dark and in midafternoons and Sundays, when shops are closed and streets tend to be deserted. Purse snatching, jewelry theft, and armed robberies are all too common.

town you are only a short walk or bus or taxi ride from one of these two stations. **Stazione Principe** is the closest, just to the west; from Piazza Aquaverde in front of the station follow Via Balbi through Piazza della Nunziata to Via Caroli, which runs into Via Garibaldi (the walk will take about 15 min.). Palazzo-lined **Via Garibaldi** forms the northern flank of the old town and is the best place to begin your explorations. Many of the city's major museums and other major monuments are on and around this street, and from here you can descend into the warren of little lanes that lead through the cluttered heart of Caruggi down to the port.

From **Stazione Brignole,** follow **Via XX Settembre,** one of the city's major and more elegant avenues, due west for about 15 or 20 minutes to **Piazza De Ferrari,** which is on the eastern edge of the old town. From here, Via San Lorenzo will lead you past Genoa's cathedral and to the port, but if you want to use Via Garibaldi as your sightseeing base, continue north from the piazza on Via XXV Aprile to **Piazza delle Fontane Marose.** This busy square marks the eastern end of Via Garibaldi.

GETTING AROUND   Given Genoa's labyrinth of small streets (many of which can not be negotiated by taxi or bus), the only easy way to get around much of the city is on foot. This, however, can be a navigational feat that requires a good map. You can get a basic one for free at the tourist office, but it is woefully inadequate and lists only major arteries; purchase a more detailed map, preferably one with a good street index and a section showing the old city in detail, at a newsstand for about 3,000L ($1.75). Genoese are usually happy to direct visitors, but given the geography with which they are dealing, their instructions can be complicated. You should also be aware that Genoa's archaic street numbering system seems to have been designed to baffle tourists: Addresses in red (marked with an *r*) generally indicate a commercial establishment; those in black are offices or residences. So, two buildings on the same street can have the same number.

By Bus   Bus tickets (1,500L/88¢) are available at newsstands and at ticket booths at the train stations and at other locations throughout the city; look for the symbol **AMT** (for Azienda Mobilita' E Transporti). You must stamp your ticket when you board a bus. Bus tickets can also be used on most of the funiculars and public elevators that climb the city's hills. Upon presenting a passport, visitors can purchase a ticket valid for unlimited travel for 24 hours on city buses and local rail lines for 5,000L ($2.94); go to one of the AMT booths at the train stations and elsewhere throughout the city. If you are planning to spend some time in Genoa, you may want to purchase a carnet of 20 tickets for 26,000L ($15.30). The buses of most use to visitors are those that connect the train stations with museums and monuments around Via Garibaldi—**no. 20** to and from Stazione Principe and **no. 18, 39 and 40** to and from Stazione Brignole (on all these routes, get off at Piazza della Nunziata, at the end of Via Garibaldi); to reach Piazza De Ferrari, near Cattedrale San Lorenzo on the eastern edge of the old city, take bus **no. 19 and 41** from Stazione Principe and **no. 39 and 40** from Stazione Brignole. A special service, **Art Bus,** leaves from Stazione Principe every 25 minutes and makes a circuit of the city's museums and monuments. Fare is 1,500L (88¢) and tickets are available at newsstands and anywhere else bus tickets are sold; you are allowed to get on and off the bus at as many stops as you wish. Another AMT service worth investigating is the daily 3-hour bus tour of Genoa and its surroundings (including several belvederes affording wonderful views). The bus picks up passengers at central points beginning at 9am, including a pickup in Piazza Acquaverde in front of Stazione Principe at 9:25am. You can purchase tickets, 20,000L ($11.75), on the bus. For more information on all of these services, check with the tourist office, your hotel, or AMT, V. D'Annunzio 8/R (☎ 010/599-7414).

By Taxi   Metered taxis, which you can find at cab stands, are an especially convenient and safe way to get around Genoa at night—or by day, for that matter, if you are tired of navigating mazelike streets or trying to decipher the city's elaborate bus system. For instance, you may well want to consider taking a taxi from a restaurant in the old city to your hotel or to one of the train stations (especially Stazione Brignole, which is quite a bit farther). Cab stands at Piazza della Nunziata, Piazza Fontane Marose and Piazza De Ferrari are especially convenient to the old city; expect to pay about 12,000L ($7.05) from Piazza della Nunziata to Stazione Brignole.

FAST FACTS: Genoa

Bookstore   Genoa's best source for English-language books is **Bozzi,** V. Cairoli 4/R (☎ **010/298-742**), open Monday through Friday 8:30am to 7pm and Saturday 8:30am to 3:30pm.

Currency Exchange   You'll find exchanges at most of the banks clustered around **Piazza Corvetto,** which is just beyond Piazza Fontane Marose at the eastern end of Via Garibaldi. There are also exchange booths at both railroad stations, open daily 7am to 10pm. ATMs, dispensing currency in lire drawn against your bank account back home, are located throughout the city—however, given the city's well-warranted reputation for crime, be extremely cautious when using them and use only machines in well-lighted, well-trafficked areas.

Drugstores   Pharmacies keep extended hours on a rotating basis; dial ☎ **192** to learn which ones are open late in a particular week. Several that are usually open late are **Pescetto,** V. Balbi 185/R (☎ **010/246-2696**), across from Stazione Principe; **Ghersi,** Corte Lambruschini 16 (☎ **010/541-661**), and **Europa,** Cor. Europa 576 (☎ **010/380-239**).

Emergencies   The general emergency number is ☎ **113.** If you have automobile trouble call ACI, Soccorso Stradale ☎ **116.** If you require police assistance call ☎ **118.**

Hospitals   **Ospedale San Martino,** Vitale Benedetto XV 10 (☎ **010/55-51**), offers a variety of medical services.

Luggage Storage   You can store luggage at both train stations. The office at Stazione Principe is open daily 24 hours and the one at Stazione Brignole is open daily 6am to 10pm. The fee is 4,000L ($2.35) per bag for every 6 hours.

Post Office   Genoa's main post office is at Pz. Dante 4 (☎ **010/259-4687**). This office as well as those at the two train stations, the airport, and elsewhere around the city are open Monday through Saturday 8:10am to 7:40pm. The postal code for Genoa is 16100.

Telephones   There are public phone services at Stazione Brignole and Stazione Principe rail stations, open Monday through Saturday, 8am to 9:30pm. Italy's distinctive orange public phones are handily placed throughout Genoa. Local calls cost 200L (11¢), and the phones accept coins or phone cards (*carta telefonica*), which you can purchase at tobacco shops in increments of 5,000L

($2.95), 10,000L ($5.90), or 15,000L ($8.80). You can also make calls from the headquarters of **Telecom Italia,** V. San Vincenzo 2 (☎ **010/5971**), open Monday through Saturday 9am to 7pm; phone cards are dispensed from machines.

Travel Services CTS, V. San Vincenzo 117/R (☎ **010/564-366** or 010/532-748), specializes in budget travel. It's open Monday through Friday 9am to 1pm and 2:30 to 6pm.

WHAT TO SEE & DO

Before setting out to see the palaces, churches, and art hordes that remain from Genoa's many centuries of splendor, equip yourself with a copy of *Genoa: The Old City,* distributed for free at tourist offices, museums, and many hotels. This indispensable booklet takes you on two extensive walking tours through the labyrinth of lanes and hidden piazzas of old Genoa, pointing out the many sights of architectural and historical interest along the way. An excellent starting point for a tour of the old city is Via Garibaldi (see below).

Acquario di Genova. Ponte Spinola. ☎ **010/248-1205.** Admission 14,000L ($8.25). Mon–Fri 9:30am–6:30pm, Sat–Sun 9:30am–8pm. Bus: 12, 18, 19, and 34.

Europe's largest aquarium is one of Italy's biggest draws and a must-see for travelers with children. The structure itself is remarkable, resembling a ship and built alongside a pier in the old harbor (the aquarium is about a 15-min. walk from Stazione Principe and about 10 min. from Via Garibaldi). Inside, more than 50 aquatic displays realistically recreate red Sea coral reefs, pools in the tropical rain forests of the Amazon River basin, and other marine ecosystems. These environments provide a pleasant home for sharks, seals, and just about every other known kind of sea creature as well as a pleasant experience for visitors. Descriptions are in English.

Cattedrale San Lorenzo. Pz. San Lorenzo. ☎ **010/311-269.** Admission to cathedral free, treasury 8,000L ($4.70). Mon–Sat 8am–noon and 3–6:30pm, Sun noon–6:30pm. Bus: 19, 39, 40, and 41.

The austerity of this 12th-century, black-and-white striped structure is enlivened ever so slightly by the fanciful French Gothic carvings around the portal and the presence of two stone lions. A later addition is the campanile, completed in the 16th century and containing at one corner a beloved Genoa artifact—a sundial known as *L'Arrotino* (the knife grinder) for its utilitarian appearance. In the frescoed interior, chapels house two of Genoa's most notable curiosities: In the first chapel on the right there is a shell fired through the roof from a British ship offshore during World War II that (mirabile dictu) never exploded, and in the Cappella di San Giovani, a 13th-century crypt contains what crusaders returning from the Holy Land claimed to be relics of John the Baptist. Fabled tableware of doubtful provenance appears to be a quirk of the adjoining treasury: The plate upon which Saint John's head was supposedly served to Salome, a bowl allegedly used at the Last Supper, and a bowl thought at one time to be the Holy Grail. The less fabled but nonetheless magnificent gold and bejeweled objects here reflect Genoa's medieval prominence as a maritime power.

Museo di Architettura e Scultura Ligure di Sant'Agostino (Saint Augustine Museum of Ligurian Architecture and Sculpture). Pz. Sarzanno 35/R. ☎ **010/251-1263.** Admission 8,000L ($4.70). Tues–Sat 9am–7pm, Sun 9am–12:30. Bus: 39.

The cloisters of the 13th-century church and monastery of Sant'Agostino (most of which, save its two cloisters and a campanile, were destroyed in World War II bombings) are the evocative setting for an eclectic and fascinating collection of architectural

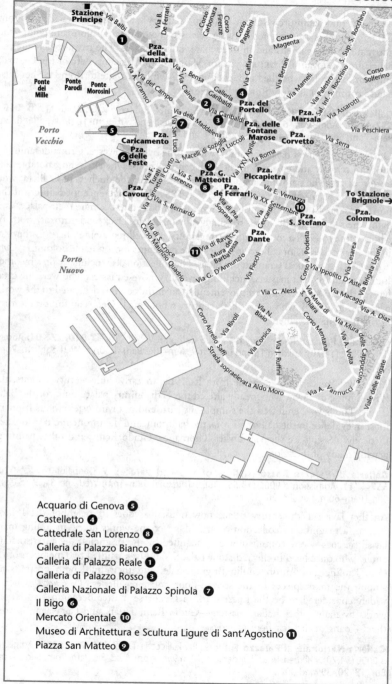

Genoa

fragments and sculpture. Roman columns, statuary, and architectural debris from Genoa's churches are scattered in what seems to be random fashion throughout the grassy monastery gardens and in a few bare interior spaces. The treasure here are the panels from Giovanni Pisano's crypt for Margherita of Brabant, wife of the German emperor Henry IV, who died in Genoa in 1312 while en route to Rome for her husband's coronation as Holy Roman Emperor.

Galleria di Palazzo Bianco (Gallery of the White Palace). V. Garibaldi 11. ☎ 010/557-3499. Admission 6,000L ($3.55). Tues, Thurs, and Fri 9am–1pm; Wed and Sat 9am–7pm; Sun 10am–6pm. Bus: 18, 20, 39, and 40.

One of Genoa's finest palaces, built of white stone by the powerful Grimaldi family in the 16th century and enlarged in the 18th century, houses the city's most notable collection of art. The paintings here reflect the fine eye of the duchess of Galliera, who donated the palace and her art to the city in 1884. Her preference for painters of the northern schools, whom the affluent Genovese imported to decorate their palaces and paint their portraits, becomes strikingly obvious. Van Dyck and Rubens, both of whom came to Genoa in the early 17th century, are well represented here, as they are in the city's other major collections; one of the museum's most notable holdings is *Portrait of A Lady* by Lucas Cranach the Elder. The collection also includes works by other European and Italian masters, including several Genovese masters who were the catalyst for the city's flourishing art movements—an entire room is dedicated to the works of Bernardo Strozzi, whose early 17th century school made Genoa an important force in the Baroque movement.

Galleria di Palazzo Reale (Royal Palace Gallery). V. Balbi 10. ☎ **010/271-01.** Admission 8,000L ($4.70); children 18 and under free. Sun–Tues 9am–1:30pm; Wed–Sat 9am–7pm. Bus: 20.

The Royal Palace takes its name from its 19th- to early 20th-century tenants, the Royal House of Savoy, who greatly altered the 17th-century palace built for the Balbi family. The Savoys endowed the sumptuous surroundings with ostentatious frippery, most in evidence in the hall of mirrors, the ballroom, and the throne room. More aesthetically pleasing are the Van Dykes, Giordanos, Guido Renis, and other paintings gracing many of the salons.

Galleria di Palazzo Rosso (Gallery of the Red Palace). V. Garibaldi 18. ☎ **010/557-4741.** Admission 6,000L ($3.55). Tues, Thurs, Fri 9am–1pm; Wed and Sat 9am–7pm; Sun 10am–6pm. Bus: 18, 20, 39, and 40.

Another lavish 17th-century palace now houses, as does its neighbor the Palazzo Bianco, a magnificent collection of art. Many of the works here—including many lavish frescoes—were commissioned or acquired by the Brignole-Sale, an aristocratic family who once lived in this red-stone palace. Van Dyck painted two members of the clan, Pauline and Anton Giulio Brignole-Sale, and their full-length portraits are among the masterpieces in the second-floor portrait galleries. *La Cuoca*, which is widely considered to be the finest work of Genovese master Bernardo Strozzi, and works by many other Italian masters—Gudio Reni, Titian, and Caravaggio among them—hang in the first-floor galleries.

Galleria Nazionale di Palazzo Spinola. Pz. Pellicceria 1. ☎ **010/270-5300.** Admission 8,000L ($4.70), children 17 and under free. Mon 9am–1pm, Tues–Sat 9am–7pm, Sun 2–7pm. Bus: 18, 20, 39, and 40.

Another prominent Genovese family, the Spinolas, donated their palace and magnificent art collection to the city only recently, in 1958. One of the pleasures of viewing these works is seeing them amid the splendor in which the city's merchant/banking families once lived. As you will in Genoa's other art collections, you will find master-works that range far beyond the city and the rest of Genoa. In facts, perhaps the most memorable painting here is *Ecce Homo,* by the Sicilian master Antonello da Messina. Guido Reni and Luca Giordano are also well represented, as are Van Dyck (including his *Young Boy*) and other painters of the Dutch and Flemish schools, whom Genoa's wealthy burghers were so fond of importing to paint their portraits.

HISTORIC SQUARES & STREETS

PIAZZA SAN MATTEO This beautiful little square is the domain of the city's most acclaimed family, the seagoing Dorias, who ruled Genoa until the end of the 18th century. The church they built on the piazza in the 12th century, San Matteo, contains the crypt of the Dorias' most illustrious son, Andrea, and the cloisters are lined with centuries-old plaques heralding the family's many accomplishments, which included drawing up Genoa's constitution in 1529. The church is open Monday through Saturday, 7:30am to noon and 4 to 6:30pm and Sunday 9am to noon and 4 to 6:30pm. The Doria palaces surround the church in a stunning array of loggias and black-and-white-striped marble facades denoting the homes of honored citizens—Andrea's at no. 17, Branca's at no. 14. To get there take bus no. 19, 39, 40 and 41.

VIA GARIBALDI Many of Genoa's museums and other sights are clustered on and around this street, one of the most beautiful in Italy, where Genoa's wealthy families built palaces in the 16th and 17th centuries. Aside from the art collections housed in the Palazzo Bianco and Palazzo Rosso (see above), the street contains a wealth of other treasures. The Palazzo Podesta, at no. 7, hides one of the city's most beautiful fountains in its courtyard, and the Palazzo Turisi, at no. 9, now housing the municipal offices, proudly displays artifacts of famous Genoans: letters written by Christopher Columbus and the violin of Nicolo Paganini (which is still played on special occasions). Visitors are allowed free entry to the building at times when the offices are open; Monday through Friday, 8:30am to noon and 1 to 4pm. To get there, take bus no. 18, 20, 39 and 40.

VIEWS & VISTAS

The no. 33 bus plies the scenic **Circonvallazione a Monte,** the corniche that hugs the hills and provides dizzying views over the city and the sea; you can board at Stazione Brignole or Stazione Principe. From Piazza Portello (at the eastern end of Via Garibaldi), a funicular climbs to the **Castelletto belvedere,** which offers stunning views and refreshing breezes and provides a handy break during sightseeing in the central city [600L/35¢], daily 6:40am–midnight). A similar, view-affording climb is the one on the **Granarolo funicular,** a cog railway that leaves from Piazza del Principe, just behind the railway station of the same name, and ascends 1,000 feet to Porto Granarolo, one of the gates in the city's 17th-century walls; there's a parklike belvedere in front (1,500L/88¢ each way or you can use a bus ticket; daily every 15 minutes from 6am to 11:45pm). An elevator lifts visitors to the top of **Il Brigo,** the modernistic, mastlike tower that is the new landmark of Genoa, built to commemorate the Columbus quincentennial celebrations in 1992; the observation platform provides an eagle's-eye view of one of Europe's busiest ports (5,000L/$2.95), 4,000L/$2.35 with aquarium ticket; open March to August, Tuesday to Saturday 11am to 1pm and 3 to 6pm, Sunday 11am to 1pm and 2:30 to 6:30pm; September to February, Tuesday to Friday 11am to 1pm and 2:30 to 4pm, and Sunday 11am to 1pm and 2:30 to 5pm.

Hour-long harbor cruises on one of the boats in the fleet of **Cooperativa Battel-lieri dei Porto di Genova** (☎ 010/265-712) provide a closer look at the bustle, along with close-up views of the **Lanterna,** the 360-foot-tall lighthouse built in 1544 at the height of Genoa's maritime might; boats embark daily from Stazione Marittima, on the a harbor, a short distance south of Stazione Principe (10,000L/$5.90 adults, 7,000L/$4.10 children under 10 and seniors over 59).

WHERE TO STAY

Genoa is geared more to business than to tourism, and as a result decent, inexpensive rooms are scarce. On the other hand, just about the only time the town is booked solid is during its annual boat show, the world's largest, in October. Except for the ones we include below, avoid hotels in the old city, especially around the harbor—most are unsafe and prefer to accommodate guests by the hour.

Albergo Barone. V. XX Settembre 2/23 (3rd floor), 16121 Genova. ☎ **010/587-578.** 12 units, 1 with bathroom, 1 with shower. 50,000L ($29.60) single; 70,000L ($42.75) double without shower; 75,000L ($46.05) double with shower; 85,000L ($52.65) double with bathroom; 100,000L ($58.80) triple with bathroom; 115,000L ($67.65) quad with bathroom. MC, V.

Nicely located near Stazione Brignole, this family run pensione occupies the large, high-ceilinged rooms of what was once a grand apartment. And, a rarity in Genoa, it offers unusually pleasant accommodations at very reasonable rates. Marco, the young proprietor, affords a gracious welcome, pointing guests to nearby restaurants, telling them what not to miss and joining them in the communal sitting room; self-service espresso is available around the clock. Accommodations are indeed baronial in size (some of the rooms here can be set up with extra beds for families and groups) and are reached by elegant hallways hung with gilt mirrors and paintings. While the eclectic furnishings are a bit less grand, beds are firm and comfortable, the linens are fresh, and the shared facilities are spotless.

Albergo Fiume. V. Fiume 9/R, 16121 Genova. ☎ **010/5916-91.** Fax 010/57-05-460. 20 units, 16 with bathroom or shower. 40,000L ($23.50) single without shower or bathroom, 55,000L ($32.55) single with shower; 65,000L ($38.25) double with shower, 95,000L ($55.88) double with bathroom. AE, MC, V.

Frankly, we don't include this choice as a recommendation for a memorable hotel experience. Rather, the Fiume is a serviceable budget option. It is clean, safe, and close to Stazione Brignole as well as to Genoa's intriguing food market, Mercato Orientale, and the profusion of food and wine shops that have sprung up around it. The desk staff in the brightly lit lobby can be brusquely efficient as they direct you to the rather Spartan guest rooms, where the furnishings consist of little more than cotlike beds, a table, and functional side chairs. Even so, the surroundings—including shared facilities in the halls—are immaculate, and the travelers from around the world who stay here provide good company.

✪ **Hotel Agnello D'Oro.** V. Monachette 6, 16126. ☎ **010/246-2084.** Fax 010/246-2327. 35 units, all with bathroom. TV TEL. 130,000L ($76.50) single; 160,000L ($94.10) double. Breakfast 15,000L ($8.80). AE, DC, MC, V.

This converted convent enjoys a wonderful location—it is only a few short blocks away from Stazione Principe, yet it is on the edge of the old city and a convenient base for sightseeing. Plus, the dead-end side street in front ensures peace and quiet. A few of the ground-floor rooms retain the building's original 16th-century character, with high vaulted ceilings. Those upstairs have been completely renovated in crisp modern style, with warm-hued tile floors and handsome wood furnishings; the tiled bathrooms are new and spotless. While all of the rooms are extremely comfortable, some of the ones on the top floor come with the added charm of balconies and views over the old town. The friendly proprietor dispenses wine and sightseeing tips in the cozy little bar off the lobby, where breakfast is also served.

Hotel Cairoli. V. Cairoli 14 int. 4, 16124 Genova. ☎ **010/246-1454.** Fax 010/246-1524. 12 units, all with bathroom. TV TEL. 90,000L ($52.95) single; 135,000L ($79.40) double. Breakfast 7,000L ($4.10). AE, DC, MC, V. Parking 25,000L ($14.70).

Location is a bonus at this pleasant, family run hotel on the third floor of an old building just south of Stazione Principe and near the port, the aquarium, and the sights of the old city. The small rooms are cozy and extremely pleasant, with tasteful modern furnishings and tidy little bathrooms outfitted with stall showers; double-paned glass keeps street noise to a minimum. The friendly management will do a load of laundry for you and serves a breakfast of rolls and coffee—in good weather, you can start the day this way or otherwise relax on a huge terrace affording views over the busy port.

Hotel Metropoli. Pz. Fontane Marose, 16123 Genova. ☎ **010/246-8888.** Fax 010/246-8686. 47 units, all with bathroom. A/C MINIBAR TV TEL. 155,000L ($91.20) single; 230,000L ($135.30) double. Rates include breakfast. AE, DC, V. Parking 32,000L ($18.80).

Facing a lovely historic square just around the corner from the Via Garibaldi, the Metropoli brings modern amenities, combined with a gracious ambience, to the old city. No small part of the appeal of staying here is that many of the surrounding streets are open only to pedestrians, so you can step out of the hotel and avoid the onrush of traffic that plagues much of central Genoa. Guest rooms have somewhat banal and businesslike contemporary furnishings, but with double-pane windows and pleasing pastel fabrics they provide an oasis of calm in this often unnerving city; the newly refurbished bathrooms are equipped with hair dryers and a nice selection of toiletries.

Hotel Rio. V. al Ponte Calvi 5, 16126 Genova. ☎ **010/246-1594.** Fax 010/290-554. 47 units, all with bathroom. TV TEL. 90,000L ($52.95) single; 135,000L ($79.40) double. Rates include breakfast. AE, DC, MC, V. Parking 25,000L ($14.70).

These airy, modern rooms are wonderfully located, amid the clamor and intrigue of the old city and just a few steps from the port. In fact, they're just about the only decent accommodations so close to the old harbor area. (You'll want to keep your wits about you, though, when coming and going late at night). The English-speaking reception staff is extremely helpful, and the guest rooms are large and nicely equipped with modern furnishings and pleasant bathrooms. Genoa's convention facilities are nearby, so reservations are essential at periods when the city hosts one of its trade fairs (many are held in October).

Ostello Per La Giovetti. V. Costanzi 10, 16136 Genova. ☎ and fax **010/242-2457.** 210 beds. 22,000L ($12.95) per person in dormitory accommodations, 23,000L ($13.50) per person in family accommodations. IYH card required, can be purchased at check-in for 30,000L ($17.65). Rates include breakfast. No credit cards. Closed from 9am–3:30pm and midnight–7am. Free luggage storage.

Even if you feel you've outgrown hosteling, the quality of the accommodations and the pleasant surroundings here may convince you to take another stab at the experience. This one is new and attractive, and affords some marvelous views over the city from its hillside near the terminal of the Righi funicular. Families make out especially well here, in four-bedded rooms with private bathrooms; other guests sleep four to eight in a room. There's a large terrace, a bar, a cafeteria where you can obtain a full meal for less than 10,000L ($5.90), TV room and a Laundromat (12,000L/$7.05 a load). Plus, though the hostel is in a safe area well above the hustle and bustle of the city, it's only about 20 minutes to Stazione Brignole on the no. 40 bus, which makes the run about every 10 minutes.

WHERE TO DINE

Da Genio. Salita San Leonardo 61/R. ☎ **010/588-463.** Reservations recommended. Primi 10,000–15,000L ($5.90–$8.80); secondi 12,000–22,000L ($7.05–$12.95). AE, D, MC, V. Mon–Sat 12:30–3pm and 7–10pm. Closed Aug.

One of Genoa's most beloved trattorias, handily situated near Piazza Dante in the old quarter, Da Genio is wonderfully animated, with rustically furnished dining rooms that almost always full of Genovese business people and families who have been coming here for years. The assorted antipasti provides a nice introduction to local cuisine, with such specialties as stuffed sardines and *torte di verdure* (vegetable pie). While the menu usually includes a nice selection of fresh fish and some meat dishes (including delicious tripe), you can also move on to some of the homey standbys the kitchen does so well, such as *spaghetti al sugo di pesce* (topped with a fish sauce) or an amazingly fresh *insalata di mare* (seafood salad). The wine list includes a nice selection from Ligurian vineyards.

Da Guglie. V. San Vincenzo 64/R. ☎ **010/565-765.** Primi 5,000–7,000L ($2.95–$4.10); secondi 8,000–10,000L ($5.30–$5.90). No credit cards. Daily noon–10pm. LIGURIAN.

The busy kitchen, with its open hearth, occupies a good part of this simple restaurant, which serves this neighborhood near Stazione Brignole with takeout fare from a counter and accommodates diners in a bare-bones little room off to one side. In fact, there's no attempt at all to provide a decorative ambience. The specials of the day (which often include octopus and other seafood) are displayed in the window; tell the cooks behind the counter what you want and they will bring it over to one of the oil-cloth-covered tables when it's ready. Don't be shy about asking for a sampling of the reasonably price dishes, because you can happily eat your way through Genoese cuisine here. *Farinata* (chick-pea crepes), focaccia with many different toppings, gnocchi with pesto, *riso di carciofi* (rice with artichokes), and other dishes are accompanied by Ligurian wines served by the glass or carafe.

Da Rivaro. V. d. Portello 16/R. ☎ **010/277-0054.** Reservations recommended. Primi 10,000–12,000L ($5.90–$7.05); secondi 12,000–18,000L ($7.05–$16). AE, DC, MC, V. Mon–Sat noon–3pm and 7–10pm. Closed Aug. LIGURIAN/ITALIAN.

Wonderfully located amid the Renaissance splendor of the nearby Via Garibaldi, this old institution does a brisk business with a loyal clientele from nearby banks and consulates, especially at lunch and in the early evening. The decor is pleasantly reminiscent of a ship's cabin, with inlaid wood panels and long wooden tables lit by brass lanterns; many of the attentive, white-jacketed waiters have worked here their entire careers. Ligurian classics such as *trenette al pesto con patate e fagiolini* (pasta with pesto, potatoes and beans) and a *zuppa da pesce* made with local fish emerge from the kitchen, but the menu also ventures far beyond Genoa to include a wide range of pastas from other regions (many with tomato and cream sauces) and grilled meats.

Trattoria da Maria. Vico Testadoro 14/R (just off V. XX Aprile). ☎ **010/581-080.** Primi 5,000–6,000L ($2.95–$3.55); secondi 7,000–9,000L ($4.10–$5.30); fixed-price menu 13,000L ($7.65). MC, V. Sun–Fri noon–2pm and 7–9pm, closed Mon evenings. LIGURIAN.

Maria Mante is something of a local legend and for decades has turned out delicious meals from her busy kitchen, attended by relatives young and old. Her cooking and the congenial ambience of the two-floor restaurant in the old city near Piazza delle Fontane Marose draw a crowd of neighborhood residents, students, businesspeople and tourists of all nationalities. This unlikely mix sits side by side at long tables covered with red-checked tablecloths and engage in animated conversation, while the staff hurries around them and shouts orders up and down the shaft of a dumb waiter. Daily

Fast Food, Genoa Style

Fast food is a Genoese specialty, and any number of storefronts all over the city disburse focaccia, the heavenly Ligurian flat bread often stuffed with cheese and topped with herbs, olives, onions, and other vegetables. A favorite place for focaccia, and so close to Stazione Principe that you can stop in for a taste of this aromatic delicacy as soon as you step off the train, is **La Focacceria di Teobaldo,** V. Balbi 115/R (☎ 010/246-2294), open daily 7:30am to 8pm; focaccia begins at 1,500L (88¢) a slice. Another Geonvese favorite is *farinata,* a cross between a ravioli and a crepe made from chick-pea flour that is stuffed with spinach and ricotta, lightly fried, and often topped with a cream and walnut sauce. Locals say this delicious concoction gets no better than it is at the two outlets of **Antica Sciamada,** V. Ravecca 19/R (☎ **010/280-843**) and V. San Giorgio 14/R, both open Monday through Saturday 9am to 7:30pm; from 3,500L ($2.05).

specials and the fixed-price menu of the day—which often include minestrone alla genovese and *zuppe da pesce* (a rich fish soup you must try if it's available) and such simple main courses as a fillet of fish sautéed in white wine or grilled sausages—are listed on sheets of paper posted to the shiny green walls. As befits a Genovese institution like this, the pasta with pesto sauce is especially delicious, as is *pansotti,* small ravioli covered with a walnut-cream sauce.

Trattoria Vegia Zena. Vico Serriglio 13–15/R. ☎ **010/299-891.** Primi 8,000–10,000L ($4.70–$5.90); secondi 10,000–20,000L ($6.60–$13.15). No credit cards. Tues–Sat noon–2:30pm and 7:30–10pm, Mon noon–2:30pm

In the *centro storico* near the old port, this lively, white-walled room lives up to its name (which is dialect for Old Genoa) with expertly prepared Genovese dishes, with a bow now and then, thanks to the origins of the chef, to Sardegna. Since the restaurant is very popular with Genovese from all over the city who consider this their favorite place to dine, you may well be asked to share one of the crowded tables with other diners. Pasta with pesto is excellent, followed by a fine selection of fresh seafood. The most popular dessert is *seadas,* fried, cheese-stuffed pasta topped with honey.

PASTRY & GELATO

✪ **Antica Pasticceria Gelateria Klainguti,** on Pz. Soziglia 98/R-100/R (☎ **010/ 247-4552**), is considered to be Genoa's best bakery, as well as its oldest—it was founded in 1828 by a Swiss family. One satisfied customer was the composer Giuseppe Verdi, who said the house's **Falstaff** (a sweet brioche) was better than his. This and a stupefying assortment of other pastries and chocolates, as well as light snacks (including panini), are served in a pretty Rococo style room or in the piazza out front. It's open daily 8am to 7pm. Add **Banarama** at V. San Vincenzo 65 (☎ **010/ 581-130**) to your explorations of the many food shops and markets in the neighborhood near Stazione Brignole. Is this the best gelato in Genoa? The jury is still out, but the creamy concoctions are indeed memorable. Just as good are the simple granites, shaved ice with fresh fruit flavorings. Open daily until 7:30pm. Just off the waterfront and near the fairgrounds, the simple, no-frills **Cremeria Augusto** at V. Nino Bixio 5 (☎ **010/591-884**) is almost a mandatory stop when taking a stroll through this part of the city. The house makes dozens of flavors of rich, delicious gelato fresh daily and it is marvelous, but the specialty is *crema,* a frozen egg custard. Open Sunday through Friday to 10pm.

GENOA AFTER DARK

The harbor area, much of which is unsafe even in broad daylight, is especially unseemly at night. You should confine late-hour prowls in the old city to the well-trafficked streets around **Piazza Fontane Marose** and **Piazza delle Erbe,** where many bars and clubs are located anyway.

PERFORMING ARTS

Genoa has two major venues for culture: **Teatro Carlo Felice,** Piazza de Ferrari (☎ 010/589-239), is home to Genoa's opera company and hosts visiting companies as well; the new **Teatro delle Corte** (☎ 010/570-2472), on Piazza Borgo Pila near Stazione Brignole, hosts concerts, dance events and other cultural programs.

BARS & CLUBS

Open all day, **Brittania** at Vico Casana (just off Piazza De Ferrari) serves pints to homesick travelers from morning to night, but caters to a largely Italian crowd at night.

New Yorkers will recognize the name and chic ambience from the branch of **I Tre Merli Antica Cantina** at Vico Dietro il Coro d. Maddalena 26/R. (☎ 010/247-4095), which does a brisk business in the SoHo section of their city. Here in Genoa, Tre Merli operates several enotecas, and this one, with a location on a narrow street just off Via Garibaldi that makes it a safe night spot in the old city, is delightful. A dark stone floor and walls of brick and stone provide a cozy setting, augmented by country style tables and chairs. You can sample the wide selection of wines from throughout Italy by the glass, and there is a full bar. Five or six dishes, usually including several pasta selections, salads, and a fish dish, are served as well, making this a good spot for a late-night meal. **Le Courbusier** at V. San Donato 36 (☎ 010/246-8652) opens early and closes late. This coffeehouse cum bar in the old quarter just west of Piazza delle Erbe is especially popular with students. The smoky room is perpetually busy, dispensing excellent coffee and sandwiches (from 4,000L/$2.35) as well as wine and spirits. Aficionados of jazz and blues should check out **M&M** at V. Salita Santa Caterina (off Piazza Fontane Marose, ☎ 010/586-787) after 10pm, when on many nights live musicians begin to play and continue until the small hours.

QUICK ESCAPES

Two seaside retreats within the city limits are Boccadasse and a little farther out, Nervi, both to the east of the city center and easily reached on public transportation. Take bus number 41 from Stazione Principe or Piazza De Ferrari to Boccadasse and bus no. 17 or one of the frequent trains from Stazione Brignole to Nervi (the train trip only takes 15 minutes).

Once a quaint fishing village, **Boccadasse** has long since given way to some urban development. Even so, this bustling seaside community is still a pleasant corner of the city. Fishing boats and nets litter the shore and the rocky seaside is lined with tall, colorful Ligurian houses, whose bottom floors now accommodate gelaterias, focaccerias, and simple restaurants with outdoor terraces.

Nervi was a fashionable resort a century ago, and it's still easy to see why. A mile-long seaside promenade affords stunning views of the sea, and elegant villas are surrounded by a lush profusion of flora. (Tempting as the waters are, you may want to refrain from a swim until you a little farther away from Genoa.) One of the most pleasant retreats in Genoa is Nervi's **Parco Villa Grimaldi,** where more than 2,000 varieties of roses bloom. Each July, Nervi hosts Genoa's International Ballet Festival (see "Festivals & Markets," above).

2 San Remo & the Riviera di Ponente

140 km (81 mi.) W of Genoa, 59 km (35 mi.) E of Nice

Gone are the days when Tchaikovsky and the Russian empress Maria Alexandranova joined a well-heeled mix of titled continentals and British gentry in strolling along San Remo's palm-lined avenues. They left behind an onion-domed Orthodox church, a few grand hotels, and a snooty casino, but San Remo is a different sort of town these days. It is still the most cosmopolitan stop on the Riviera di Ponente (Setting Sun), as the stretch of coast west of Genoa is called, catering mostly to sun-seeking Italian families in the summer and elderly Romans and Milanese who come to enjoy the balmy temperatures in the winter.

In addition to the gentle ambience of days gone by, San Remo offers its visitors a long stretch of beach and a hilltop old town known as **La Pigna.** For cosmopolitan pleasures, the casino attracts a well-attired clientele willing to try their luck.

San Remo is an excellent base from which to explore the rocky coast and Ligurian hills. So is **Bordighera,** a quieter resort just up the coast. With excellent train and bus connections, both are within easy reach of a full itinerary of fascinating stops that include the ghost town of **Bussana Vecchia; Giardino Hanbury,** one of Europe's most exquisite gardens; the fascinating prehistoric remains at **Balzi Rossi;** and ✪ **Docleacqua,** perhaps the most enticing of all the inland Ligurian villages (for more information on these places, see "Side Trips from San Remo and Bordighera," below).

FESTIVALS & MARKETS   **August 15,** the Feast of the Assumption, is celebrated with special flair in San Remo, with the festival of **Nostra Signora della Costa** (our Lady of the Coast). The Virgin Mary allegedly saved a local sailor from drowning, and she is honored with fireworks and a procession in medieval garb to her shrine on a hillside high above the town.

One of the most enjoyable things to do in San Remo is to wander through the stalls of the **Mercato di Fiori.** Horticulture is a major industry on this part of the Italian Riviera (as it is on the French Riviera) and, as the profusion of roses and other blooms attest, San Remo's flower market is one of the largest in Europe. The market is on Corso Garibaldi, just off Piazza Colombo, and operates daily from October through June, from 6 to 8am.

ESSENTIALS

GETTING HERE   **By Train**   There are trains almost hourly to and from **Genoa;** the trip takes about 2½ hours and costs 12,100L ($7.05). Trains from Genoa continue west for another 25 minutes to Ventimiglia on the French border; the fare from San Remo to Ventimiglia is 1,700L ($1). From Ventimiglia, you can continue across the border on one of the hourly trains to **Nice,** 40 minutes west; the fare is 11,000L ($6.50).

By Bus   Regular bus service (from a station behind the train station) connects San Remo with Bordighera and Ventimiglia, stopping at many of the coastal towns en route. The fare between San Remo and **Bordighera** is 2,000L($1.20) and between San Remo and Ventimiglia, 3,000L ($1.75); the ride takes 20 minutes.

By Car   The fastest driving route in and out of San Remo is the **A10 autostrada,** which follows the coast from the French border (20 min. away) to Genoa (about 45 min. away). The slower coast road, **S1,** cuts right through the center of town.

VISITOR INFORMATION   The **APT tourist board** is at Lgo. Nuvoloni 1 (☎ **0184/571-571**). It's open Monday to Saturday from 8am to 7pm, Sunday from

A Day at the Beach

Plunging into the Ligurian Sea in San Remo means spending some money. The pebbly beach below the Passaggiata dell'Imperatrice is lined with beach stations, where many visitors choose to spend their days: easy to do, since most provide showers, snack bars, and, of course, beach chairs, lounges, and umbrellas. Expect to spend at least 10,000L ($5.90) for a basic lounge, up to 25,000L ($14.70) for a more elaborate sun bed arrangement with umbrella.

9am to 1pm. In addition to a wealth of information on San Remo, the office also dispenses information on towns up and down the nearby coast, known as the Riviera dei Fiori. The telephone area code for San Remo is ☎ **0184.**

STROLLING AROUND TOWN

Though San Remo has a municipal bus system (fare is 1,500L/88¢), you should be able to get anywhere you want to go on foot. The train station is on the seaside and divides the commercial part of town from the resort and beach area. The tourist board is just in front of the station and just beyond that is the onion-domed **Chiesa Russa** (more formally the Chiesa di Cristo Salvatore), where the Russian nobility who once favored San Remo worshipped. You can step inside for a view of dark, icon-enriched interior; open daily 9:30am to 12:30pm and 3 to 6pm; admission 1,000L (59¢).

To the left as you leave the station is the beginning of the palm-lined promenade, the **Passaggiata dell'Imperatrice,** which skirts the narrow pebbly strand and any number of cramped beach stations. One of the more pleasant stops along the way is the **Giardini Communali Marsaglia,** a small but luxuriant hillside garden that bursts with exotic flora (open daily, dawn to dusk).

To the right of the station are the beginnings of Corso Roma and Corso Giacomo, San Remo's two main thoroughfares. **Corso Giacomo** will lead you past the casino and into the heart of the lively business district. Continue on that until it becomes **Via Matteotti,** which after a block runs into Piazza Colombo and the **flower market.** If you turn left (north) on Via Feraldi about midway down Corso Giacomo, you will find yourself in the charming older precincts of town. Continue through the Piazza degli Eroi Sanremesi to **Piazza Mercato,** where Via Monta leads into the old medieval quarter, **La Pigna.** The hill on which this fascinating district is located resembles a pine cone in its conical shape, hence the name. Aside from a few restaurants, La Pigna is today a residential quarter, with tall old houses that overshadow the narrow lanes that twist and turn up the hillside to the park-enclosed ruins of a castle at the top.

VISITING THE CASINO

Set intimidatingly atop a long flight of steps, San Remo's white palace of a casino not only lords over the center of town, it's also the hub of the local night life scene. You can't step foot inside without being properly attired (jacket and tie for gents), showing your passport, and unburdening yourself of 15,000L ($8.80)—and that's even before you hit the tables, which attract high rollers from the length of the Riviera. Gaming rooms are open daily, 2:30pm to 3am (to 4am on Sunday morning). Things are more relaxed in the rooms set aside for slot machines, where there is neither a dress code nor an entrance fee. Open Sunday through Friday 10am to 2:30am and Saturday 2:30pm to 3am.

Is Board Necessary?

Many hotels offer room and board rates that include breakfast and lunch and dinner (full board) or breakfast and one of these other two meals (half-board). Only in the busy late July, early August beach season do many *require* you take these meals, however. If you can procure a room without the meal plan, do so—San Remo has many excellent restaurants, and this is not a place where you have to spend a lot for a good meal.

WHERE TO STAY

Albergo Al Dom. Cor. Mombello 13, 18038 San Remo. ☎ **0184/501-460.** 12 units, all with bathroom. 40,000–50,000L ($23.50–$29.40) single; 60,000–90,000L ($35.30–$52.95) double. Breakfast 5,000L ($2.95). No credit cards.

This rambling, dark, old-fashioned pensione near the casino, city center and harbor occupies the second floor of a 19th-century apartment house. The rooms, basically furnished with a minimum of modern pieces, are carved out of former salons and tucked into the closed-off ends of ballroom-size hallways; tiny bathrooms (some of them modular units that resemble the public facilities you find in Paris and other cities) have been appended wherever they might fit. So, be prepared for the unexpected: You may well find yourself staring up at an ornately plastered ceiling from a metal-frame bed crammed next to a marble fireplace. In short, the surroundings may not be stylish, but they are memorable, and the family that runs the pensione is friendly and always on hand to see that guests are comfortable.

Hotel Paradiso. V. Roccasterone 12, 18038 San Remo. ☎ **0184/571-211.** Fax 0184/578-176. 41 units, all with bathroom. MINIBAR TV TEL. 85,000–160,00L ($50–$94.10) single; 100,000–195,000L ($58.80–$114.70) double. Half-board, 100,000 to 130,000L ($58.80 to $76.50) per person; full board 110,000–185,00L ($64.70–$108.80) per person. Breakfast 20,000L ($11.75). AE, DC, MC, V. Parking 20,000L ($11.75).

A former villa, set in a pretty garden above the seaside promenade, has been topped off with several extra floors of very pleasant guest rooms, many of which have flower-filled balconies overlooking the sea. An unfussy, understated elegance characterizes these relaxing surroundings. Guest rooms are extremely well maintained but retain the sort of old-fashioned comfort that brings a loyal clientele back year after year for their month by the sea. Furnishings are a homey collection of old armoires, armchairs, and upholstered headboards, and the tiled bathrooms, with large sinks and bathtubs, are luxuriously commodious. Cocktails are served in the comfortable, elegantly furnished salon in the evenings, or in the nicely planted garden in good weather, and guests can take meals in an airy dining room.

Hotel Riviera. Cor. Degli Inglesi 86, 18038 San Remo. ☎ **0184/502-215.** Fax 0184/502-216. 19 units, 15 with bathroom. TV TEL. 45,000–55,000L ($26.50–$32.35) single without bathroom, 60,000–90,000L ($35.30–$52.95) single with bathroom; 70,000–90,000L ($41.20–$52.95) double without bathroom, 90,000–130,000L ($52.95–$76.50) double with bathroom. Half-board 65,000–70,000L ($38.25–$41.20) per person in room without bathroom, 75,000–90,000L ($44.10–$52.95) per person in room with bathroom; full board 70,000–90,000L ($41.40–$52.95) per person in room without bathroom, 90,000–130,000L ($52.95–$76.50) in room with bathroom. Breakfast 7,000L ($4.10). AE, MC, V.

While convenient to the beach and other attractions, this family run pensione on one floor of a modern hillside apartment house is close to the center but just far enough off the beaten path to enjoy peace and quiet, and it often has rooms when other places in town fill up. Oriental runners, crystal chandeliers, and attractively slip-covered furniture lend an air of elegance to the public areas. The guest rooms, most of which overlook the sea and the old town, are spacious and modestly but attractively furnished in modern style with an eye to comfort—beds are firm, there are ample surfaces on which to spread out belongings, and the bathrooms are up to date, with stall showers; a few rooms share very well-kept facilities in the hallway.

✪ **Hotel Sole Mare.** V. Carli 23, 18038 San Remo. ☎ **0184/577-105.** Fax 0184/532-778. 21 units, all with bathroom. MINIBAR TV TEL. 25,000–50,000L ($14.70–$29.40) single without bathroom; 35,000–70,000L ($20.60–$41.20) single with bathroom; 65,000–110,000L ($38.25–$64.70) double with bathroom. Half-board 45,000–65,000L ($26.50–$38.25) per person in room without bathroom, 53,000–90,000L ($31.20–$52.95) per person in room with bathroom; full board 55,000–75,000L ($32.35–$44.10) per person in room without bathroom, 60,000–100,000L ($35.30–$58.80) in room with bathroom. Breakfast 9,000L ($5.30). AE, MC, V.

Don't let the location on a drab side street near the train station put you off. This cheerful pensione on the upper floors of an apartment house is a delight and offers its guests a friendly welcome along with some of the best-value lodgings in the resort area. A lounge, bar area, and dining room are flooded with light and, with gleaming white tile floors, blond-wood furniture and doors leading out to a terrace, are airy and spacious. The large guest rooms are also cheerful and are equipped with the trappings of much more expensive hotels—such as pleasant modern furnishings and soothing pastel fabrics, TVs and minibars, and small but modern and well-lit bathrooms; most rooms open to a wide terrace that looks out to the sea.

Hotel Villa Maria. Cor. Nuvoloni 30, 18038 San Remo. ☎ **0184/531-422.** Fax 0184/531-425. 38 units, all with bathroom. TEL. 80,000–110,000L ($47–$64.70) single; 120,000–200,000L ($70.60–$117.65) double. Rates include breakfast. Half-board, 88,000–150,000L ($51.76–$88.25) per person; full board 100,000–170,000L ($58.80–$100) per person. AE, DC, MC, V.

It's fairly easy to imagine San Remo's turn-of-the-century heyday in this charming hotel incorporating three villas on a flowery hillside above the casino. The promenade is only a short walk down hill, yet the hubbub of the resort seems miles away from this leafy residential district. A series of elegant salons and dining rooms with parquet floors, richly paneled ceilings and crystal chandeliers spread across the ground floor, and many of these public rooms open to a nicely planted terrace. The bedrooms, too, retain the grandeur of the original dwellings, with silk-covered armchairs and antique beds. All have modern bathrooms and many have balconies facing the sea. Since rooms vary considerably in size and decor, ask to look around before you settle on one that strikes your fancy.

WHERE TO DINE

✪ **Cantine Sanremese.** V. Palazzo 7. ☎ **0184/572-063.** Primi 6,000–9,000L ($3.55–$5.30); secondi 8,000–11,000L ($4.70–$6.50). AE, MC, V. Mon–Sat, 9am–9pm and 7–10:30pm. Closed July 1–15. LIGURIAN.

This cozy publike restaurant devoted to the local cuisine is firmly planted in the center of the modern town, as if to suggest that old San Remo traditions are not to be discarded. Patrons share tables as they enjoy the wide selections of wine by the glass (from 2,000L/$1.20) and sample the offerings that owner Renzo Morselli and his family prepare daily. The best way to dine here is not order a whole meal, but to sample all the dishes that tempt you. These may include *sardemaira*, the local foccacia-like bread, *torte verde* (a quiche of fresh green vegetables), and many kinds of soups, including a minestrone thick with fresh vegetables and garnished with pesto.

Ristorante L'Airone. Pz. Eroi Sanremesi 12. ☎ **0184/531-469.** Primi 9,000–13,000L ($5.30–$7.65); secondi 11,000–25,000L ($6.50–$14.70). Pizzas 8,500–13,000L ($5–$7.65). Menù turistico 24,000L ($14.10). MC, V. Fri–Wed, noon–2:30pm and 7:30–11:30pm. LIGURIAN.

With its pale gold walls and green-hued tables and chairs, this delightful, friendly restaurant in a pedestrian-only section of the city center looks like it's been transported over the border from Provence. The food, though, is definitely Ligurian, with a wide selection of fresh pastas, including gnocchi in pesto sauce, followed perhaps by a *grigliata mista* of fresh fish or grilled sole. For a more casual meal, light-crusted pizzas emerge from a tiled oven in the rear. In good weather, meals are served in small garden in the back of the dining room.

Trattoria Il Mulattiere. V. Palma 11. ☎ **0184/502-662.** Primi 7,000–10,000L ($4.10–$5.90); secondi 8,000–12,000L ($4.70–$7.05). No credit cards. Thurs–Tues, 12:30–2:30pm and 7:15–10pm. LIGURIAN.

Anyone who visits San Remo should plan to visit this family run trattoria in La Pigna, the oldest part of San Remo. Whether you come for lunch or dinner or just to enjoy a glass of wine you'll probably first want to stroll around the surrounding quarter, an amazing warren of steep lanes clinging to the side of a hill. This two-floor eatery is as rich in character as its surroundings—the tables, covered with red-checked cloths, are overshadowed by antique farm implements (Il Mulattiere means "Mule Driver") and other rural artifacts. The menu is simple, featuring Ligurian specialties that change daily and often include delicious *crostini all'acciughe* (toasted bread topped with fresh anchovies), *zuppa al pomodoro* (a spicy soup of fresh tomatoes) or minestrone, some form of fresh pasta topped with pesto, and grilled fish. For a light meal, you can choose from an antipasto table laden with fresh vegetables and olives, and accompany it with a bowl of pasta, for 15,000L ($8.80).

Trattoria Nuovo Piccolo Mondo. V. Piave 7. ☎ **0184/509-012.** Reservations recommended. Primi 9,000–11,000L ($5.30–$6.50); secondi 11,000–18,000L ($6.50–$10.60). No credit cards. Tues–Sat, noon–2:30pm and 7–10pm. LIGURIAN.

The attentive staff will make you feel comfortably at home the moment you step into the perpetually crowded rooms of this decades-old trattoria on a narrow side street near the waterfront in the commercial district. The clientele is local, and they come here in droves to enjoy the homey atmosphere (which includes the furnishings installed when the restaurant opened in the 1920s). But the true draw is the distinctly Ligurian fare—*verdura ripiena* (fresh vegetables stuffed with rice and seafood), fresh fish, and *polpo con patate* (octopus with potatoes). The menu changes daily to incorporate what is fresh in the markets, but also includes standards that include some excellent risottos and other pasta dishes, as well as several meat dishes. (The grilled veal chop topped with fresh mushrooms is delicious.)

THE CAFE & BAR SCENE

Bar Agora at Piazza San Siro (☎ **0184/533-06**), which faces San Remo's cathedral, makes no claim other than to be a comfortable watering hole, a function it performs very well. For footsore travelers the terrace out front, facing the pretty stone piazza and cathedral of San Siro, is a welcome oasis. Sandwiches and other light fare are served late into the night, when an after dinner crowd tend to make this one of the livelier spots in town. Any of your wanderings through the center of town should include a stop at the handsome wine bar **Enoteca Bacchus** (V. Roma 65; ☎ **0184/530-990**). This is where you can also stock up on olive oil and other Ligurian foodstuffs. Wine is served by the glass at a sit-down bar or one of the small tables, and you can accompany your libations with fresh focaccia, cheeses, vegetable tarts and even such substantial fare as *buridda*, a dish of salted cod, tomatoes, and other vegetables.

SIDE TRIPS FROM SAN REMO

For some interesting excursions near the French border, see "Side Trips from Bordighera", below. Closer to San Remo is the picturesque ghost town of **Bussana Vecchia,** in the hills about 5 miles east of town (follow **S1** east out of San Remo for about 2 mi., then follow the well-signposted road up to Bissana Vecchia). In 1877 an earthquake destroyed Bussana and inspired the surviving citizens to build a new town (now simply known as Bussana) down the hillside about a mile away. The collapsed church and other structures remain in evocative ruin, with trees growing from their midst. But Bussana is not the bona fide ghost town it appears to be—in the 1960s a few artisans began to take up residence in some of the buildings and the colony remains, engaging in a brisk trade selling art and crafts who wander through their unusual community.

3 Bordighera

155 km (93 mi.) W of Genoa, 15 km (9 mi.) W of San Remo, 45 km (27 mi.) E of Nice

Known throughout Italy for its palm trees, Bordighera lays claim to the legend that the seeds of date palms carried across the sea from Egypt first took root in European soil here. To this day Bordighera has the honor of supplying its ubiquitous fronds to the Vatican for Palm Sunday services. The palm trees create a verdant canopy that extend up the hillside from the Mediterranean and the cluster of modern seaside development to the charming old town. Bordighera's other claim to fame is its enormous popularity with elderly Italian and British pensioners (its reputation as a getaway for retirees similar to that of St. Petersburg in Florida). If you want glitter, you may be happier in San Remo; on the other hand, if you want to enjoy some peace and quiet and the same verdant vegetation that drew Claude Monet here, Bordighera may be just the stop for you.

FESTIVALS & MARKETS It's a sign of the pleasant nature of this resort that one of the major annual events is a humor festival, held in late July and August. Stand-up comics perform along the streets and seaside promenade, humorous films are shown, and other kinds of merriment is presented.

ESSENTIALS

GETTING HERE   By Train There are trains almost hourly to and from Genoa and San Remo; the trip to and from Genoa takes almost 3 hours and costs 12,100L ($7.10); the 15-minute run between San Remo and Bordighera costs 2,000L ($1.20).

By Bus Regular bus service, running about every 15 minutes, connects San Remo and Bordighera; the fare is 2,000L ($1.20). Buses also run between Bordighera and Ventimiglia; the fare is 2,000L ($1.20).

By Car You can take the **A10 autostrada** between Bordighera and San Remo, but the coast road, **S1,** is almost as fast. In fact, there is such a contiguous line of development along the route that you won't know where one town ends and the other begins.

VISITOR INFORMATION The tourist board is at V. Roberto 1 (☎ **0184/ 262-322**). It's open Monday to Saturday from 8am to 7pm, Sunday from 9am to 1pm (closed Sundays in winter).

STROLLING AROUND TOWN

Lungomare Argentina is Bordighera's seaside promenade, and it extends for a little more than a mile along a wide beach; the pebbly strand is public, so you can settle down anywhere you find a spot. If you want a more civilized beach experience, you can part with 10,000L ($5.90) for a lounge at any number of beach stations. The promenade remains lively well past the height of the day—since it faces west toward France's Côte d'Azur—it affords spectacular sunset views that most of the town turns out to witness. The modern town, which in parts is unattractively developed, clusters around the seafront, with many businesses lining coastal route S1. You need only head inland, though, to discover how lovely Bordighera is, with palm-fringed streets and pastel-colored villas hidden behind the walls of verdant gardens. The fortified old town, a picturesque cluster of ochre-colored stucco and red tile, is several hundred yards up the hillside from the sea. Aside from a few restaurants and a charming hotel (see below), there is not much in the old town to attract a visitor save for the beauty of centuries-old architecture, its charming ambience, and the stunning views from the gardens that skirt the centuries-old walls.

WHERE TO STAY

✪ **Hotel del Capo.** V. Al Capo 3, 18012 Bordighera. ☎ **0184/261-558.** Fax 0184/262-463. 14 units, 13 with bathroom. 45,000L ($26.50) single without bathroom, 50,000–70,000L ($29.40–$41.20) single with bathroom; 80,000–120,000L ($47–$70.60) double. Half-board 80,000–100,000L ($47–$58.80) per person. Breakfast 7,500L ($4.40). MC, V. Closed Nov.

The only hotel in the old city is a delightful pinkish structure surrounded by palm trees and an inviting terrace where many guest choose to spend most of their time. The hilltop location affords stunning views over the lower town and sea below, and there always seems to be a cooling breeze. Vaulted ceilings and colorful mallorca-tile floors lend almost a Moorish look to the lobby, sitting rooms and dining area, but once upstairs the decor becomes much utilitarian, though not unpleasing. Furnishings in the largish guest rooms are 1960s-style modern, but unobtrusive enough not to be offensive; baths have not been updated for awhile and tend to be small but are certainly adequate. The best features in the rooms are the shuttered doors that open to balconies and afford dazzling views up and down the coast.

Pensione Palme. V. Roma 5, 18012 Bordighera. ☎ **0184/261-273.** Fax 0184/251-977. 12 units, 9 with bathroom. 35,000–38,000L ($20.50–$22.35) single without bathroom, 38,000–40,000L ($22.35–$23.50) single with bathroom; 60,000–65,000L ($35.30–$38.30) double without bathroom, 65,000–70,000L ($38.25–$41.20) double with bathroom. Breakfast 5,000L ($2.95). No credit cards.

If you desire any degree of luxury, you would do well to look elsewhere. But if you want a decent and affordable place to lay your head, this simple pensione atop an apartment house directly across the street from the train station may fit the bill. The premises are a bit stark but the rooms are bright and sparkling clean, have old but well-maintained bathrooms, and are just steps from the beach. Add to these advantages the presence of the friendly proprietor who lived in New York for many years and enjoys speaking English.

Piccolo Lido. Lungomare Argentina 2, 18012 Bordighera. ☎ **0184/261-297.** Fax 0184/262-316. 33 units, all with bathroom. A/C MINIBAR TV TEL. 80,000–160,000L ($47–$94.10) single; 110,000–220,000L ($64.70–$129.40) double. Half-board 91,000–155,000L ($53.50–$91.15) per person, full board 100,000–170,000L ($58.80–$100) per person. Breakfast 10,000L ($5.90). AE, MC, V.

This pink, sun-filled villa is at the end of the seafront promenade, with direct access to the beach but far away enough away from the main seafront avenue and the center of things to afford a great deal of peace and quiet. The public rooms are airy and bright, opening to the terraces through large doors. Upstairs, the newly renovated rooms are bright and attractive, with white tile floors, pastel area rugs, and bright contemporary furnishings that include comfortable lounge chairs and some nice extras like round tables so you can dine in your room if you choose. Bathrooms are gleaming and modern, and nicely equipped with hair dryers and complimentary toiletries. The best rooms, of course, are those that open on to terraces overlooking the sea.

WHERE TO DINE

Giglio. V. Vittorio Emanuele 158. ☎ **0184/261-530.** Panini and snacks from 3,000L ($1.75). Daily 11am–2am, closed Mon in winter. CAFE.

The most popular cafe in Bordighera seems to suit patrons of all stripes, whether they be British pensioners who sit on the terrace and sip tea or teenagers who stop on their way to the beach for a gelato (in 30 flavors, 2,000L/$1.20 for a scoop) or night owls looking for a place to enjoy a glass of wine (not easy to do in this sleepy town). As a result, this is almost a mandatory stop for visitors interested in checking out the local scene. The more substantial fare includes sandwiches, salads, and crepes, and depending on the filling, are served either as a meal or as a dessert.

Magiarge. Pz. G. Viale. ☎ **0184/262-946.** Reservations recommended. Primi 10,000L ($5.90); secondi 12,000–15,000L ($7.05–$8.80). AE, DC, MC, V. Fri–Tues, 12:30–2:30pm and 7–10:30pm. LIGURIAN.

Only a half dozen or so tables occupy this attractive ochre colored room in the old city, and the rustic cabinets that line the walls also function as display cases for the Ligurian wines and olive oils for sale. These staples are shown to their best advantage in the delicious meals that emerge from the cramped kitchen. Only three or four pastas and main courses are prepared daily and are announced on a blackboard; invariably, pasta selections include *trenette* or another pasta with a rich pesto sauce and there is always a selection of fresh fish and one or two meat courses, often including a game hen cooked with local olives and fresh vegetables, a house specialty.

Piemontese. V. Roseto 8. ☎ **0184/262-946.** Primi 8,000L–10,000L ($4.70–$5.90); secondi 12,000–18,000L ($7.05–$10.60). AE, DC, MC, V. Wed–Mon, 12:30–2:30pm and 7–10pm. Closed Nov 15–Dec 15. PIEMONTESE/SEAFOOD.

Gino and Giuliana, the husband and wife proprietors, oversee things in the kitchen and simple adorned dining room a few blocks off the seafront, serving up the cuisine of the nearby Piedmonte region. While the menu includes such classic Piemontese dishes as risotto cooked with Barolo wine and a *torta alla ricotta* (a rich ricotta quiche), the offerings also suggest Liguria with their reliance on fresh seafood. Aside from simple but memorable grilled fish, there are also such memorable dishes as warm seafood salad and *tagliatelle al nero di seppia*, freshly made tagliatelle blackened with squid ink.

SIDE TRIPS FROM BORDIGHERA

Several interesting trips take you to the coast and hills surrounding **Ventimiglia,** a quiet and somewhat unremarkable Italian town on the border with France that is only minutes from Bordighera and San Remo by train, bus and car (see "Getting Here," above). While passing through Ventimiglia en route to the places below, you may want to pause long enough to view its splendidly preserved Roman theater, off Corso Genova to the east of town. **To get here,** take one of the hourly trains between Bordighera and Ventimiglia; the trip takes just 8 minutes and the fare is 1,500L (88¢).

Giardino Hanbury, on the coast 4 miles east of Ventimiglia, is one of Europe's largest and most noted botanical collections. British merchant Sir Thomas Hanbury planted the gardens, which descend on terraces to the sea, in 1867 to nurture exotic species from five continents. As immensely important as the gardens were to the 19th-century study of botany, today they are a pleasure dome, a stunningly beautiful bower with heart-stopping views of the sea around every corner. You can reach the gardens by **Riviera Transporti bus,** which leaves from Vzia Cavour, near the train station in Ventimiglia; fare is 2,000L ($1.20). The gardens are open daily March through mid-June 10am to 6pm, daily mid-June through September 9am to 7pm, and Thursday through Tuesday 10am to 5pm; admission is 8,500L ($5). For more information, call ☎ **0184/229-507.**

At **Balzi Rossi** (Red Rocks), right on the French border 1 mile farther east along the coast from Giardino Hanbury, one of prehistoric Europe's most advanced cultures lived in cliff-side caves more than 40,000 years ago. You can visit several of the caves, the most interesting of which is **Grotto del Cavglione,** named for a horse etched on one of the walls. Most of the finds—including weapons, fertility figures, and tools—are in the small Museo Prehistorcio. You can reach the caves by **Riviera Transporti bus,** which leaves from Via Cavour, near the train station in Ventimiglia; fare is 2,000L ($1.20) and the driver will let you off 10 minutes from the caves at Ponte San Luigi (be sure to tell the driver where you want to get off). The caves and museum are open Tuesday through Sunday, 9am to 6pm (to 7pm in summer); admission is 4,000L ($2.35), adults over 60 and children under 18 free. For more information, call ☎ **0184/381-13.**

Another excursion from Ventimiglia takes you inland for 6 miles up the Val Nervia to ✪ **Dolceacqua,** a stone village that is as sweetly picturesque as its name implies it will be. The ruins of a 16th-century castle crown the collection of houses that climb from the banks of the river, spanned here by a single-arched medieval bridge. If you stumble into town at certain times of the year you will find the locals engaged in strange revelries: On **January 20** (St. Sebastian's Day), a man carrying a tree hung with communion hosts leads a procession through the streets; on **August 15,** costumed dancers celebrate Ferragosto. Ten buses a day leave the train station in Ventimiglia for Dolceacqua; the fare is 2,000L ($1.20)

4 The Riviera Levante: Camogli, Santa Margherita Ligure, Portofino & Rapallo

Camogli 26 km (15 mi.) E of Genoa; Santa Margherita Ligure 31 km (19 mi.) E of Genoa; Portofino 38 km (25 mi.) E of Genoa; Rapallo 37 km (24 mi.) E of Genoa)

The coast east of Genoa, the Riviera Levante (Rising Sun), is more ruggedly beautiful than the Riviera Ponente, less developed, and hugged by mountains that plunge into the sea. Four of the coast's most appealing towns are within a few miles of one another, clinging to the shores of the Monte Portofino Promontory just east of Genoa: **Camogli, Santa Margherita Ligure, Rapallo,** and little **Portofino.**

CAMOGLI

Camogli (*Casa della Mogli*—House of the Wives) was named for the women who held down the fort while their husbands went to sea for years on end. The little town remains delightfully unspoiled, an authentic Ligurian fishing port with tall, ochre-painted houses fronting the harbor and a nice swath of beach. Given also its excellent accommodations and eateries, Camogli is a lovely place to base yourself while exploring the Riviera Levante.

FESTIVALS & MARKETS Camogli throws a much-attended annual party, the **Sagra del Pesce,** on the second Sunday of May. The town fries up thousands of sardines in a 12-foot-round pan and passes them around for free—a practice that is accompanied by an annual outcry in the press about health concerns and even accusations that frozen fish is used. Even so, the beloved event is much attended.

The first Sunday of August, Camogli stages the lovely **Festa della Stella Maris.** A procession of boats sails to Punta Chiappa, a point of land about a mile down the coast and releases 10,000 burning candles. Meanwhile, the same number of candles are set afloat from the Camogli beach. If currents are favorable, the burning candles will come together at sea, signifying a year of unity for couples who watch the spectacle.

ESSENTIALS

GETTING HERE By Train More than 30 trains a day connect Camogli with **Genoa,** only 20 minutes away; the fare is 2,000L ($1.20). **Santa Margherita** is only a train tunnel away (less than a 10-minute trip) and connected by two to three trains an hour; the fare is 1,500L (88¢). Many of the same trains, at least one an hour, continue on to the Cinque Terre and La Spezia; the trip takes a little over an hour and the fare is 5,900L ($3.50).

By Bus There is at least one bus an hour to **Santa Margherita,** leaving from Piazza Schiaffino; since the bus must go around and not under the Monte Portofino Promontory, the trip takes quite a bit longer, 30 minutes, and costs 2,000L ($1.20). For more information, call ☎ **0185/231-108.**

By Boat In summer, boats operated by **Golfo Paradiso** (☎ **0185/772-091**) sail from Camogli to **Portofino** (18,000L/$10.60 round-trip).

By Car The fastest route into the region is the **A12 autostrada** from Genoa; exit at Recco for Camogli (the trip takes less than half an hour. **Route S1** along the coast from Genoa is much slower but more scenic.

VISITOR INFORMATION The tourist office is across from the train station at V. XX Septembre 33 (☎ **0185/771-066**); from October through May, it's open Monday through Saturday from 8:30am to 12:30pm and 3:30 to 6pm, Sunday from 9:30am to 12:30pm; from June through September the office is open daily 9:30am to 12:30pm and 4 to 7pm. The telephone area code for Camogli is **0185.**

EXPLORING THE TOWN

Camogli is clustered around its delightful waterfront, from which the town ascends via steep, staired lanes to **Via XX Settembre,** one of the few streets in the town proper to accommodate cars (this is where the train station, tourist office, and many shops and other businesses are located). Adding to the charm of this setting is the fact that the oldest part of Camogli juts into the harbor on a little point where ancient houses cling to the 12th-century **Basilica di Santa Maria Assunta.** One of the nearby buildings, the Castello Dragone, houses the **Acquario Tirrenico,** a small but charming collection of local sea creatures. Admission is 4,000L ($2.35) and the museum is open May through September daily 10am to noon and 3 to 7pm; October through April it is open Friday through Sunday 10am to noon and 2:30 to 6pm and Tuesday through Thursday 10am to noon. Most visitors, though, seem drawn to the pleasant boardwalk that runs the length of the town. You can swim from the pebbly beach below, and should you feel your towel doesn't provide enough comfort, rent a lounge from one of the few beach stations for 10,000L ($5.90).

WHERE TO STAY

✪ **Albergo La Camogliese.** V. Garibaldi 55, 16032 Camogli. ☎ **0185/771-402.** 17 units, all with bathroom. TV TEL. 50,000–70,000L ($29.40–$41.20) single; 80,000–100,000L ($47–$58.80) double. Breakfast 10,000L ($5.90). AE, MC, V. Parking 20,000L ($11.75).

A lot of Genovese come out to spend the weekend in this friendly, attractive little hotel near the waterfront, and they appreciate it for the same simple charms that will appeal to travelers from farther afield. (In fact, given the hotel's popularity, it's always a good idea to reserve, and essential on weekends.) Proprietor Bruno and his family extend guests a warm welcome, and are happy to help them navigate the logistics of visiting the different towns on the nearby coast (which is especially easy to do from here, since the hotel is at the bottom of a staircase that leads to the train station). Rooms are large, bright, and airy, and decorated in modern furnishings that include comfortable beds; some have balconies and, while the house isn't on the waterfront, it faces a little river and is close enough to the beach that a slight twist of the head usually affords a view of the sea. Bathrooms are small but adequate. The family also runs the beachfront restaurant of the same name just down the road (see below).

Pension Augusta. V. Schiaffino 100, 16032 Camogli. ☎ **0185/77-05-92.** 18 units, all with bathroom. TV TEL. 55,000L ($32.35) single; 75,000L ($38.25) double. MC, V.

This is an acceptable alternative if the Camogliese (above) is full, and, more than a fall-back, it's pleasant and convenient, with a handy location a short walk from the station and up a steep staircase from the harbor. The elderly couple who runs the pension also operates the ground-floor trattoria, which serves as a sitting room for the guest rooms upstairs and makes it easy to enjoy a cup of coffee or glass of wine. The rooms are extremely plain, with functional furnishings and drab decor badly in need of sprucing up. But they are large and clean, and have good-sized bathrooms. Ask for a room in front—those in back face the train tracks.

Worth A Splurge

✪ **Cenobio del Dogi.** 16032 Camogli. ☎ **0185/7241.** Fax 0185/772-796. 107 units, all with bathroom. A/C MINIBAR TV TEL. 170,000–230,000L ($100–$135.30) single; 250,000–310,000L ($147.05–$182.35) double. Rates include breakfast. Half-board supplement 60,000L ($35.30) per person, full-board supplement 120,000L ($70.60). AE, DC, MC, V.

One of our favorite Ligurian getaways sits just above the sea at one end of town and against the forested flank of Monte Portofino. The oldest part of the hotel incorporates an aristocratic villa dating from 1565; a chapel, still occasionally used as such, dates from the 17th century. Converted to a hotel in 1956, the premises now include several wings that wrap graciously around a garden on one side and a series of terraces facing the sea on the other. There's a swimming pool and a private beach, and several airy salons, including a lovely bar/lounge area and a glass-enclosed breakfast room that hangs like a ship over the sea. The guest rooms vary considerably in size and shape, but all are furnished with a tasteful mix of contemporary pieces and period reproductions. Many overlook the sea and have balconies, and a few have terraces that drop directly into the swimming pool. In most rooms, the bathrooms have been redone with sumptuous amounts of marble and luxurious fixtures. One thing the hotel does not have is a train track running through its grounds, as do most properties on this coast; here in Camogli, the train follows a route far enough inland to ensure guests a good night's sleep. This is a restful retreat from which you can explore Genoa, which is only 20 minutes away.

WHERE TO DRINK & DINE

Bar Primula. V. Garibaldi 140. ☎ **0185/770-351.** Sandwiches and other light fare from 4,000L ($2.35); gelato from 1,500L (88¢) a small dish or cone. Daily 9am–midnight. AE, MC, V.

Camogli's most fashionable bar is on the waterfront, and it seems as if just about anything goes here. Drinking is taken seriously, as self-proclaimed "Capo Barman" Renato Montanari is well known in his trade. You can also enjoy a light meal (a pasta dish and seafood plate or two or usually available, along with sandwiches), but many regulars come in for a cup of the delicious house espresso and dessert, which presents a difficult choice between the delicious ice cream and pastries (if you're torn, try a sumptuous chocolate rumball-like concoction known as a "Comogliese").

Ristorante Il Faulo. V. Garibaldi 99. ☎ **0185/772-072.** Primi, 10,000–12,000L ($5.90–$7.05); secondi 15,000–25,000L ($8.80–$14.70). AE, MC, V. Daily, noon–midnight. LIGURIAN/SEAFOOD.

This extraordinary little restaurant on the seaside consists of a small exotic-looking room with low-slung tables and divanlike chairs. You would expect the food to be Moorish, but it is strictly Ligurian, and deliciously so, with an emphasis on local seafood—*calamari ripieni* (squid stuffed with baby shrimp and vegetables), *risotto al frutti di mare* (risotto with tiny clams and other seafood) and simply grilled scampi emerge from the tiny kitchen flawlessly prepared. You can begin a seafood meal with any number of vegetarian appetizers and pastas, including a heavenly *torta di carciofi* (artichoke tart) and several kinds of pasta topped with pesto made on the premises. In order that diners may enjoy their meals fully, smoking is not permitted. Although food is always available, you can also stop in between mealtimes for drinks.

Ristorante La Camogliese. V. Garibaldi 78. ☎ **0185/771-086.** Primi 7,000–12,000L ($4.10–$7.05); secondi 10,000–20,000L ($5.90–$11.75). AE, MC, V. Tue–Sun, noon–2:30pm and 7–10:30pm. SEAFOOD.

You probably won't be surprised to find that the menu at this bright, seaside spot, perched over the beach on stilts and one of the most popular and appealing restaurants in town, leans heavily to seafood. In fact, when the weather is pleasant and the windows that surround the dining room are open, you feel you are at sea. The hearty fish soup is a meal in itself, as are any number of pastas topped with clam and other seafood sauces, and there is always a tempting array of fresh fish entrees, caught that day, on hand as well.

AN EXCURSION TO SAN FRUTTUOSO

Much of the Monte Portofino Promontory can be approached only on foot or by boat, making it a prime destination for hikers. If you want to combine some excellent exercise with the pleasure of glimpsing magnificent views of the sea through a lush forest, arm yourself with a map from the tourist office in Camogli and set out for **Abbazia di San Francesco.** This medieval religious community, surrounded by a tiny six-house hamlet, is about 3 hours away by a not-too-strenuous hike. En route, you can clamor down well-posted paths that descend from the main path to visit **San Rocco, San Niccolo,** and **Punta Chiappa,** a string of fishing hamlets hugging the shore of the promontory.

Once you reach **San Fruttuoso,** you may well want to relax on the pebbly beach and enjoy a beverage or meal at one of the seaside bars. You can tour the stark interior of the abbey for 5,000L ($2.95); from May through October it is open Tuesday through Sunday from 10am to 1pm and 2 to 6pm, from November through January on weekends from 10am to 1pm and 2 to 4pm, and from March through April from

Tuesday through Sunday from 10am to 1pm and 2 to 4pm. Should you happen to have your Scuba gear along, you can take the plunge to visit Christ of the Depths, erected 50 feet beneath the surface to honor sailors lost at sea.

You can also visit San Fruttuoso by one of the boats that run almost every hour during the summer months from Camogli. The round trip fare is 12,000L ($7.05); for more information, call **Golfo Paradiso** at ☎ **0185/772-091.**

SANTA MARGHERITA LIGURE

Santa Margherita had one brief moment in the spotlight, at the beginning of this century when it was an internationally renowned retreat. Fortunately, the seaside town didn't let fame spoil its charm, and now that it's no longer as well known a destination as its glitzy neighbor Portofino, it might be the Mediterranean retreat of your dreams—a palm-lined harbor, a nice beach, and a friendly ambience make Santa Margherita a fine place to settle down for a few days of sun and relaxation.

FESTIVALS & MARKETS   Santa Margherita's winters are delightfully mild, but even so the town rushes to usher in spring with a **Festa di Primavera,** held on moveable dates in February. Like the **Sagra del Pesce** in neighboring Camogli, this festival also features food—in this case fritters are prepared on the beach and served around roaring bonfires.

One of the more interesting daily spectacles in town is the fish market on **Lungomare Marconi;** this colorful event transpires from 8am to 12:30pm. On Fridays, cars are banned from Corso Matteotti, Santa Margherita's major street for food shopping, turning the area into an open-air food market.

ESSENTIALS

GETTING HERE   By Train   More than 30 trains a day connect Santa Margherita and **Genoa;** the trip takes 35 minutes and the fare is 2,800L ($1.65). The same trains connect Santa Margherita with **Camogli** and **Rapallo,** each less than 10 minutes away; the trip between Santa Margherita and each of its neighbors costs 1,500L (88¢). Many of the same trains, at least one an hour, continue on to the **Cinque Terre** and **La Spezia;** the trip takes a little over an hour and the fare is 5,900L ($3.50).

By Bus   There is at least one bus an hour to **Camogli** (about half an hour) and to **Rapallo** (about 15 min.), leaving from Piazza Vittorio Veneto; the fare to each is 2,000L ($1.20). Buses also ply the stunningly beautiful coast road to **Portofino,** leaving every 20 minutes from the train station and Piazza Vittorio Veneto; fare is 1,700L ($1).

By Boat   **Tigullio ferries** (V. Palestro 8/1b; ☎ **0185/284-670**) make hourly trips to **Portofino** and **Rapallo** from 10am to 4pm (hours of service varies considerably with season; schedules are posted on the docks at P. Martiri della Liberta); the round-trip fare is 9,000L ($5.30).

By Car   The fastest route into the region is the **A12 autostrada** from Genoa; the trip takes about half an hour. **Route S1** along the coast from Genoa is much slower but more scenic.

VISITOR INFORMATION   The tourist office is near the harbor at V. XXV Aprile 2B (☎ **0185/287-485**), open Monday through Saturday from 9am to 12:30pm and 2:30 to 5:30pm, Sunday from 9am to 12:30pm. The helpful staff will give you a map pinpointing the location of hotels and steer you to those in your price range. The telephone area code is **0185.**

EXPLORING THE TOWN

Life in Santa Margherita centers around its palm-fringed waterfront, a pleasant string of marinas, docks for pleasure and fishing boats, and pebbly beaches. Landlubbers congregate in the cafes that spill out into the town's two seaside squares, **Piazza Martiri della Liberta** and **Piazza Vittorio Veneto.**

The station is on a hill above the waterfront, and a staircase in front of the entrance will lead you down into the heart of town. Santa Margherita's one landmark of note is its namesake **Basilica di Santa Margherita,** just off the seafront on Piazza Caprera. The church is open daily from 8am to noon and 3 to 7pm and is well worth a visit to view the extravagantly gilded interior.

WHERE TO STAY

Albergo Annabella. V. Costasecca 10, 16038 Santa Margherita Ligure. ☎ **0185/286-531.** 11 units, none with bathroom. 50,000–60,000L ($29.40–$35.30) single; 75,000–85,000L ($44.10–$50) double. Half-board 60,000–70,000L ($35.30–$41.20) per person, full board 70,000–75,000L ($41.20–$44.10) per person. No credit cards.

The nice proprietor manages to accommodate groups of just about any size in this old apartment that's been converted to an attractive pensione, with comfortable old furniture and handsome green walls covered with mirrors and paintings. Some of the rooms sleep up to four, and one family style arrangement includes a large room with a double bed and a tiny room outfitted with bunk beds for children. None of the rooms have private bathrooms, but the four shared facilities are ample and hot water is plentiful.

✪ Albergo Fasce. V. Luigi Bozzo 3, 16038 Santa Margherita Ligure. ☎ **0185/286-435.** 16 units, all with bathroom. 90,000L ($52.95) single; 160,000L ($94.10) double; 210,000L ($123.55) triple; 240,000L ($141.20) quad. Rates include breakfast. AE, DC, MC, V.

Aristide and Jane, the Italian/British couple that owns and operate this small hotel, take great efforts to make their guests feel comfortable, and as a result they provide some the most pleasant lodgings in Santa Margherita. Their hospitality includes the use of bicycles, laundry service (30,000L/$17.65 for a wash and dry), and free bus passes to get around town. The surroundings are lovely: A broad staircase leads into the flowery, courtyard like entryway, off which there's a pleasant lobby and breakfast area; a roof terrace affords lovely views of the sea and town. The guest rooms are large, bright, and modern in design, with cheerful white laminate furnishings and many thoughtful touches, such as copious amounts of storage space, shelves around the beds on which to place reading matter, and in-room safes. With these many amenities at such reasonable prices, it's a good idea to reserve.

Hotel Nuova Riviera. V. Belvedere 10–2, 16038 Santa Margherita Ligure. ☎ **0185/ 287-403.** 8 units, 1 with bathroom. 70,000–90,000L ($41.20–$52.95) single; 90,000–110,000L ($52.95–$64.70) double without bathroom; 100,000–130,000L ($58.80–$76.45) double with bathroom. Rates include breakfast. MC, V.

The Sabini family acts as if its sunny, turn-of-the-century villa in a quiet neighborhood behind the town center was a private home and guests were old friends. Every room is different, and though eclectically furnished with pieces that look like they may have passed through a couple of generations of the family, most retain the high-ceilinged elegance of days gone by and have a great deal more character than you're used to finding in rooms at this end of the budget scale; the best have expansive bay windows. There's a pretty garden out front and a homey, light-filled dining room where Signora Sabini serves breakfast with fresh-squeezed orange juice and a home-cooked, fixed-price dinner for 30,000L ($17.64), 15,000L ($8.80) for homemade pasta and salad.

WHERE TO DINE

Trattoria Baicin. V. Algeria 9. ☎ **0185/286-763.** Primi 6,500–20,000L ($3.80–$11.75); secondi 18,000–28,000L ($10.60–$16.45). Fixed-price menu 28,000L ($16.45). AE, DC, MC, V. Tue–Sun, noon–3pm and 7–10:30pm, closed Nov 1–Dec 15. LIGURIAN.

The husband-and-wife owners, Piero and Carmela, make everything fresh daily, from fish soup to gnocchi, and still manage to find time to greet diners at the door of their cheerful trattoria just a few steps off the harbor. You can get a glimpse of the sea if you choose to sit at one of the tables out front, and the owner/cooks are most happy preparing fish, which they buy fresh every morning at the market just around the corner; the sole, simply grilled, is especially good here, and the *fritto misto di pesce* constitutes a memorable feast. You must begin a meal with one of the pastas made that morning, especially if *trofie alla genovese* (a combination of gnocchi, potatoes, fresh vegetables and pesto) is available. By ordering the tourist menu, you can get a nice sampling of the expertly prepared dishes served here.

Trattoria da Prezzi. V. Cavour 21. ☎ **0185/285-303.** Primi 4,000–7,000L ($2.35–$4.10); secondi 6,000–11,000L ($3.55–$6.50). No credit cards. Daily noon–2:15pm and 7–9:15pm.

The atmosphere in this cozy little restaurant in the center of town near the market is pleasantly casual. Two white-washed, tile-floored rooms are usually filled with local workmen and businesspeople, who invite newcomers to share a table when no other place is available. Service is minimal—the chef puts what's he's prepared for the day on a table near the front door, you tell him what you want, and one of the staff will bring it to the table when it's ready. Focaccia, *farinata,* and other Genovese specialties are usually on hand, as are at least one kind of soup (the minestrone is excellent), a chicken dish and some variety of grilled fresh fish.

PORTOFINO

Portofino is almost too beautiful for its own good—in almost any season, you'll be rubbing elbows on Portofino's harborside quays with day-tripping mobs who join Italian industrialists, international celebrities, and a lot of rich but not so famous folks who consider this little town to be the epicenter of the good life. If you make an appearance in the late afternoon when the crowds have thinned out a bit, you are sure to experience what remains so appealing about this enchanting place—its untouchable beauty.

GETTING HERE   On a summer visit you may encounter crowds even before you get into town, since traffic on the shore hugging corniche from Santa Margherita, just a few miles down the coast of the promontory, can move at a snail's pace. You would do better to sail to Portofino on one of the **Golfo Paradiso ferries** (☎ **0185/772-091**) from Camogli (18,000L/$10.60 round-trip) or one of the Tigullio ferries (☎ **0185/284-670**) from **Santa Margherita** and **Rapallo** (9,000L/$5.30 round-trip). At less crowded periods, the **Tigullio bus** (☎ **0185/288-8334**) is an excellent way to reach Portofino. It leaves from the train station and Piazza Vittorio Veneto in Santa Margherita every 20 minutes and follows one of Italy's most beautiful coastal roads to Portofino; the trip takes about 25 minutes in light traffic and the fare is 1,700L ($1). In fact, given limited parking space in Portofino (visitors must pay to use a lot or the town garage) you would do well to leave your car in Santa Margherita and take the bus or boat.

VISITOR INFORMATION   Portofino's tourist office is at V. Roma 35 (☎ **0185/269-024**); in summer it's open daily from 9:30am to 1pm and 1:30 to 6:30pm and in the off-season it's open daily from 9:30am to 12:30pm and 2:30 to 5:30pm.

EXPLORING THE TOWN

The one thing that is free in Portofino is its scenery, which you can enjoy on an amble around the town. Begin with a stroll around the harbor, which—lined with expensive boutiques and eateries as it is—is stunningly beautiful, with colorful houses lining the quay and steep green hills rising behind them. One of the most scenic walks takes you uphill for about 10 minutes along a well signposted path from the west side of town just behind the harbor to the **Chiesa di San Giorgio,** built on the site of a sanctuary Roman soldiers dedicated to the Persian god Mithras. From there you'll want to continue uphill for a few minutes more to **Portofino's castle,** built to ward off invading Turks. You can step inside the walls to enjoy a lush garden and the views of the town and harbor below; the castle is open daily from 10am to 6pm (to 5pm from October through April) and admission is 3,000L ($1.75). For some of the best views on this stretch of coast, continue even higher up through lovely pine forests to the *faro* (lighthouse).

From Portofino you can also set out for a longer hike on the paths that cross the Monte Portofino Promontory to the **Abbazia di San Fruttuoso** (see the section on Camogli), about a 2-hour walk from Portofino. The tourist office provides maps.

DINING IN PORTOFINO

Portofino's charms come at a steep price. Its few hotels are expensive enough to put them in the "trip of a lifetime" category, and the harborside restaurants can take a serious chunk out of a vacation budget. We suggest you enjoy a light snack at a bar or one of the many shops selling focaccia and wait to dine in Santa Margherita or one of the other nearby towns.

La Gritta American Bar. Calata Marconi 20. ☎ **0185/269-126.** Salads and other light fare from about 15,000L ($8.80). Fri–Wed noon–3am.

James Jones called this snug little room the "nicest waterfront bar this side of Hong Kong." We're not sure your praise will go that far, but it is very attractive, very friendly, and far enough along the harborside quay to be a little less hectic than other establishments. Most patrons stop in for a cocktail, coffee, or other libation (the floating terrace out front is perfect for a drink at sunset), but light fare, such as omelettes and salads of tomatoes and mozzarella, are also available to provide a light and relatively affordable meal.

RAPALLO

Stepping out of Rapallo's busy train station you may be put off by the traffic, blocks of banal apartment houses, and runaway development that in some places has given the resort the look of any other busy town. Keep walking, though, because at its heart Rapallo remains a gracious old seaside playground and port, and it's easy to see what drew the likes of Ezra Pound, Max Beerbohm, and D. H. Lawrence to take up residence here. Most of the town follows the sweep of a pretty harbor guarded by a medieval castle, and the gracious seafront promenade is cheerfully busy day and night.

FESTIVALS & MARKETS Rapallo is at its most exuberant July 1 through 3, when it celebrates the **Madonna di Montallegro,** whose hilltop sanctuary crowns the town (see below). A famous icon of the Virgin is carried through the streets and a huge fireworks display culminates in the burning of the castle (a mock event, of course). **Piazza Venezia** is the site of a lively outdoor food market on Tuesday and Thursday mornings.

ESSENTIALS

GETTING HERE **By Train** More than 30 trains a day connect Rapallo and **Genoa;** the trip takes 45 minutes and the fare is 2,800L ($1.65). The same trains connect Rapallo with **Camogli,** about 20 minutes away, and with **Santa Margherita,** less than 10 minutes away; the trip between Rapallo and Santa Margherita is 1,500L (88¢); it's 2,000L ($1.20) between Rapallo and Camogli. Many of the same trains, at least one an hour, continue on to the **Cinque Terre** and **La Spezia;** the trip takes a little over an hour and the fare is 5,900L ($3.50).

By Bus   At least one bus an hour runs between Rapallo and **Santa Margherita** (about 15 min.); the fare is 2,000L ($1.20).

By Boat   Tigullio ferries (☎ **0185/284-670**) make hourly trips to Portofino via Santa Margherita from 10am to 4pm (hours of service varies considerably with season; schedules are posted on the docks); the round-trip fare is 9,000L ($5.30).

By Car   The **A12 autostrada** connects Rapallo with Genoa and takes about half an hour. **Route S1** along the coast from Genoa is much slower but more scenic.

VISITOR INFORMATION   The tourist office is at V. Diaz 9 (☎ **0185/230-346**) and is open Monday through Saturday from 9am to 12:30pm and 2:30 to 5:30pm and Sunday 9am to 12:30pm. The telephone area code is **0185.**

EXPLORING THE TOWN

From the train station, it's a walk of only about 5 minutes to the waterfront (follow Corso Italia to Piazza Canessa and the adjoining Piazza Cavour, and from there Via Cairoli to the harborside Piazza IV Novembre.) Dominating this perfect half-circle of a harbor is a castle built on a rocky outcropping reached by a causeway; it is open only for special exhibitions but the boulders around its base are usually teeming with sunbathers. Nearby, two other buildings reflect the fact that Rapallo enjoyed a long and prosperous existence before it became known as a retreat for pleasure seekers. The cathedral of Santi Gervasio e Protasio, on Via Mazzini, was founded in the 6th century, and the leper house of San Lorenzo across the street dates from the Middle Ages.

For striking views over the town and surrounding seacoast, make the ascent to the **Santuario di Montallegro.** You can take a bus from the train station (1,500L/88¢) or an aerial cableway (*funivia*) from Via Castagneto on the eastern side of town. The funivia operates March through October, every 30 minutes 8am to sunset; November through February, every 30 minutes 8:30am to 5pm; the trip takes seven minutes and costs 7,500L ($4.40) one way or 11,000L ($6.50) round trip; for more information, call ☎ **0185-273-444.** Inside this 16th-century church are some interesting frescoes and a curious Byzantine icon of the Virgin that allegedly flew here on its own from Dalmatia. The views over the sea and surrounding valleys are the main reason to come up here, though, and they are even more so from the summit of **Monte Rosa,** a short uphill hike away.

WHERE TO STAY

Hotel La Vela. V. Milite Ignoto 21/7, 16035 Rapallo. ☎ and fax **0185/50-551.** 13 units, 6 with bathroom. TEL. 35,000–45,000L ($20.60–$26.45) single without bathroom; 60,000–75,000L ($35.30–$44.10) single with bathroom; 60,000–75,000L ($35.30–$44.10) double without bathroom; 70,000–85,000L ($41.20–$50) double with bathroom. MC, V.

This friendly, family run pensione near the seaside promenade and the center of town is one of the better bargain choices in expensive Rapallo. The old-fashioned, high-ceilinged rooms are extremely comfortable and spacious, and they have excellent beds and some nice practical touches like writing desks and lounge chairs. About half of the rooms have large private bathrooms and those that don't share three commodious facilities in the hallway. Many of the rooms face a garden in the rear of the building, ensuring a good night's sleep, and in some rooms you can enjoy this quiet retreat from a large balcony. The hotel is connected with the excellent Ristorante Elite downstairs, where may well want to take most of your meals.

Hotel Riviera. Pz. IV Novembre 2, 16035 Rapallo. ☎ **0185/502-48.** Fax 0185/656-68. 20 units, all with bathroom. A/C MINIBAR TV TEL. 105,000–140,000L ($61.75–$82.35) single; 160,000–220,000L ($94.10–$129.40) double. Rates include breakfast. AE, MC, V.

The Gambero family has run this small hotel, which occupies an old villa on the waterfront, since 1939, and it is now in the capable hands of Claudio and Silvana. They have spent the past several years improving their property, with great attention to detail, especially in the guest rooms. New hardwood floors have been laid, and handsome wood desks and shelving units built to match; new double pane windows keep noise from the seaside avenue out front to a minimum and bathrooms have been redone with top-of-the-line fixtures. Many of the fine old touches remain—these include small balconies off many of the rooms, a sunny terrace overlooking the sea in front of the hotel and a breezy breakfast room where a generous buffet is served every morning.

WHERE TO DINE

O Bansin. V. Venezia 49. ☎ **0185/231-119.** Primi 6,000–8,000L ($3.55–$4.70); secondi 8,000–10,000L ($4.70–5.90). AE, DC, MC, V. Mon–Sat noon–2pm and 7:30–10pm; closed Mon evening and May. LIGURIAN.

This colorful and boisterous restaurant near the marketplace is an excellent place to sample the cuisine of Liguria. Minestrone, *trenette al pesto* (the local liguine-like pasta, served with pesto sauce) and *fitto misto di pesce* (a fresh, large platter of fried) are served without pomp and circumstance at communal tables in a character-rich interior hung with ship's clocks, nautical paintings, and old photos of Rapallo. The service is as warm and friendly as the environs.

Ristorante Elite. V. Milite Ignoto 19. ☎ **0185/50-551.** Primi 6,000–15,000L ($3.55–$8.80); secondi 14,000–30,000 ($8.25–$17.65); fixed-price menu 35,000L ($20.60). AE, MC, V. Thurs–Tues noon–2:30pm and 7:30–11pm. SEAFOOD.

This popular seafood restaurant is just up a busy avenue from the harbor, and the pleasant room, hung with nautical items and paintings of local scenes, is a little less formal than the many seafood restaurants on the waterfront. The kitchen long ago won the approval of locals, who come here for the fresh fish of the day, which can follow such starters as seafood salad, a *risotto gamberetti e asparagi* (risotto with small prawns and fresh asparagus) or a *zuppe di pesce* (a hearty fish soup). Fresh fish can also be enjoyed on the fixed-price menu, a veritable feast that also includes hot and cold seafood appetizers and a pasta course.

5 Cinque Terre

Monterosso, the northernmost town of the Cinque Terre, 93 km (56 mi.) E of Genoa

Olive groves and vineyards clinging to hillsides, proud villages perched above the sea, hidden coves nestled at the foot of dramatic cliffs—the Cinque Terre is about as beautiful a coastline as you're likely to find in Europe, or anywhere. What's best about the Cinque Terre (named for the five neighboring towns of Monterosso, Vernazza, Corniglia, Manarola, and Riomaggiore) is what's not here—automobiles, large-scale development or much else by way of 20th-century interference. The pastimes in the Cinque Terre don't get much more elaborate than ✪ **walking** from one lovely village to another along trails that afford spectacular vistas; plunging into the Mediterranean or basking in the sun on your own waterside boulder; and indulging in the tasty local food and wine.

Not too surprisingly, these charms have not gone unnoticed. On summer weekends especially, you are likely to find yourself in a long procession of like-minded trekkers making their way down the coast or elbow to elbow with day trippers on an excursion boat. Even so, the Cinque Terre still manages to escape the hubbub that afflicts so many coastlines, and even a short stay here is likely to reward you with one of the most memorable seaside visits of a lifetime.

ESSENTIALS

GETTING HERE   By Train   You can take one of the hourly trains from **Genoa** to **La Spezia** (1½ hr.; 10,100L/$5.95), south of the Cinque Terre, then backtrack from there (about one an hour) on trains that stop at each of the five towns. Some of the Genoa–La Spezia trains stop at Levanto, on the northern end of the Cinque Terre; change there for local service into each of the five towns. Local trains make frequent runs between the five towns; you can buy a day ticket (5,000L/$2.95) good for unlimited trips.

By Car   The fastest route is via **A12 autostrada** from Genoa, exiting at the Corrodano exit for Monterosso, where there is a huge car park. The trip from Genoa to Corrodano takes less than an hour, while the much shorter 15-mile trip from Corrodano to Monterosso (via Levanto) is made along a narrow road and can take about half that amount of time. A narrow, one-lane coast road hugs the mountainside above the towns, but all the centers are closed to cars and, unless you're a resident, parking outside them can be very difficult.

By Boat   From the port in Monterosso, **Navagazione Golfo dei Porto** (☎ **0187/ 967-676**) makes five trips a day to Manarola and Riomaggiore (9,000L/$5.30 one way) and five a day to Vernazza (4,000L/2.35 one way); Motobarca Vernazza makes hourly runs (more frequent in summer) to Vernazza; 4,000L ($2.35) one way.

VISITOR INFORMATION   The **APT tourist office** for the Cinque Terre is in Monterosso, at V. Fegina 38 (☎ **0187/817-506**). It's open April through October, Monday to Saturday, 10am to noon and 5 to 7:30pm; Sunday from 10am to noon.

EXPLORING THE AREA

Aside from swimming and soaking in the atmosphere of unspoiled fishing villages, the most popular activity in the Cinque Terre is hiking from one village to the next along centuries-old goat paths. Trails plunge through vineyards and groves of olive and lemon trees and hug seaside cliffs, affording heart-stopping views of the coast and the romantic little villages looming ahead in the distance. The well-signposted walks from village to village range in degree of difficulty and the length of time it takes to traverse them. Depending on your pace and how long you stop in each village for a fortifying glass of *sciacchetra,* the local sweet wine, you can make the trip between Monterosso, at the northern end of the Cinque Terre, to Riomaggiore, at the southern end, in about 5 hours.

The walk from **Monterosso to Vernazza** takes 1½ hours, on a trail that makes several steep ascents and descents (on the portion outside of Monterosso, you'll pass beneath funicular-like cars that transport grapes down the steep hillsides). The leg from the **Vernazza to Corniglia** takes the most time, 2 hours, and plunges into some dense forests and involves some lengthy ascents. Part of the path between **Corniglia and Manarola,** about 45 minutes apart, follows a level grade above a long stretch of beach, tempting you to break stride and take a dip. From **Manarola to Riomaggiore** it's easy going for about half an hour along a partially paved path known as the **Via dell'Amore,** so named for its romantic vistas.

Since all the villages are linked by rail, you can hike as many portions of the itinerary above as you wish and take the train to your next destination. Trails also cut through the forested, hilly terrain inland from the coast, much of which is protected as a nature preserve; the tourist office in Monterosso can provide maps.

BEACHES   The only sandy beach in the Cinque Terre is the crowded strand in Monterosso, on much of which you will be asked to pay 2,500L ($1.45) for a beach chair. **Guvano Beach** is a long, isolated pebbly strand that stretches just north of Corniglia and is popular with nudists. You can clamor down to it from the Vernazza-Corniglia path, but the drop is steep and treacherous. A weird alternative route takes you through a unused train tunnel that you enter near the north end of Corniglia's train station; you must ring the bell at the gated entrance and wait for a custodian to arrive to unburden you of 5,000L ($2.95), which is good for passage through the dank, dimly lit mile-long gallery that emerges onto the beach at the far end. There is also a long, rocky beach to the south of Corniglia, and it is easily accessible by some quick downhill scrambles from the Corniglia-Manrola path. Riomaggiore has a tiny, crescent shaped beach reached by a series of stone steps on the south side of the harbor.

MONTEROSSO

The Cinque Terre's largest village seems incredibly busy compared to its sleepier neighbors, but it's not without its charms. Monterosso is actually two towns—a bustling, character-filled old town built behind the harbor and, separated by a rocky promontory, a relaxed resort section that stretches along the Cinque Terre's only sand beach. The region's most famous art treasure is here: housed in the **Convento dei Cappuccini,** perched on a hillock in the center of town, is a crucifixion by Anthony Van Dyck, the Flemish master who worked for a time in nearby Genoa (you can visit the convent daily, 9am to noon and 4 to 7pm). While you will find the most conveniences in citified Monterosso, you'll have a more rustic experience if you stay in one of the other four villages.

SLEEPING, DRINKING & DINING

Albergo Amici. V. Buranco 36, 19016 Monterosso. ☎ **0187/817-544.** Fax 0187/817-424. 40 units, all with bathroom. TV TEL. Half-board 75,000–105,000L ($44.10–$61.75) per person, full board 86,000–118,000L ($50.60–$69.40). MC, V. Closed Nov 4–Dec 23.

The aptly named Amici is unpretentious but extremely pleasant, reached up a curving marble staircase lined with flowerpots and facing a delightful garden. While the hotel is not on the seafront, (which is only a few minutes away by foot), the garden and many of the rooms overlook the town and the sea beyond, and the location on a narrow street in the old town ensures quiet. The rooms are simply but tastefully furnished in blonde-wood contemporary pieces and open to balconies through French doors. Like most hotels in Monterosso, the Amici requires that guests choose either half-board (lunch or dinner) or full board (both meals); meals, served in a cavernous dining room, are adequate, but you would do well to opt for the half board plan so you can sample other restaurants throughout the region.

✪ **Enoteca Internazionale.** V. Roma 62. ☎ **0187/817-278.** Wine from 2,000L ($1.20) a glass. Wed–Mon 8:30am–8pm. WINE BAR.

All the towns in the Cinque Terre have little shops like this one, where you can taste and purchase the local wines by the bottle, or simply enjoy a glass on the premises. The selection here, in the bustling part of old Monterosso, also includes olive oil pressed just down the street and jars of homemade pesto.

Foccacerio Il Frontoio. V. Gioberti 1, Monterosso. No phone. Focaccia 3,000L ($1.75). No credit cards. Fri–Wed 9am–1:30pm and 4–8pm. SNACKS.

Many patrons say this bustling shop, with a takeout counter and a few tables where you can dine on the premises, serves some of the best focaccia in Ligure. That's quite a claim, but suffice it to say that the freshly baked bread (especially when topped with fresh vegetables) is heavenly and provides one of the best fast meals around.

Il Gigante. V. IV Novembre 9. ☎ **0187/817-401.** Reservations recommended. Primi 11,000–22,000 ($6.50–$12.95); secondi 14,000–32,000L ($8.25–$18.85). AE, DC, MC, V. Daily noon–3pm and 6:30–10pm. Closed Nov and Tues in winter. SEAFOOD.

This friendly, simple restaurant, a block off the waterfront in the newer part of town, serves some of the freshest and best prepared seafood in the region—which is why so many residents of Genoa and nearby towns drive to Monterosso just to eat in one of the attractive rooms here. There is no set menu but the offerings vary with the local catch. Staples, though, are the *zuppe di pesce*, which is almost legendary and starts off many a meal here, often followed by a huge platter of *fritto misto di pesce*.

VERNAZZA

It's hard not to fall in love with this pretty village. Tall houses cluster around a natural harbor (where you can swim among the fishing boats) and beneath a castle built high atop a rocky promontory that juts into the sea (open daily 9am to 8pm, admission free). The center of town is waterside **Piazza Marconi,** itself a sea of cafe tables.

SLEEPING & DINING

Albergo Barbara. P. Marconi 30, 19018 Vernazza. ☎ **0185/81-22-01.** 9 units, none with bathroom. 70,000–80,000L ($41.20–$47) single and double.

This pleasant pensione on the two upper floors of a tall old house on the waterfront is at the top of four flights of broad stone steps, and from there many of the rooms are reached by an additional climb up a ladderlike circular staircase. These efforts are rewarded, however, by an eagle's-eye view of Vernazza's harbor from almost every room. While the accommodations are basic, they are not without charm, with a pleasant smattering of homey furniture in the bathroom-less rooms, most of which have a sink; guests share three clean and nicely equipped bathrooms. If no one answers the buzzer, step across the square to Taverna del Capitano and ask about a room.

Gambero Rosso. P. Marconi 7. ☎ **0187/812-265.** Primi 12,000–22,000L ($7.05–$12.95); secondi 20,000–38,000L ($11.75–$22.35); tasting menu 55,000L ($32.35). AE, DC, MC, V. Daily 12:30–4pm and 7:15–10:30pm. Closed Mon in winter and Dec 15–Mar 1. SEAFOOD/ LIGURIAN.

It would be hard to find a more pleasant way to take in the scene on Vernazza's lively harborside square than to do so while enjoying the tasting menu on the terrace at this excellent restaurant. You will also be content ordering one or two choices from the a la carte menu—either way you can explore some hard to find dishes such as *acchiughe* (fresh anchovies) baked with onions and potatoes, *ravioli di pesci* (a delicate fish ravioli), and *muscoli ripieni* (muscoli is the Ligurian word for mussels, known as *cozze* elsewhere in Italy; here they are stuffed with fresh herbs). Another specialty, the grigliata mista of freshly caught fish, is excellent, and any meal should be followed by the house dessert, *sciachetra* (the local sweet wine) accompanied by homemade biscotti. The stone-walled, stone-floored, timbered-ceiling dining room is a pleasant alternative when the terrace is closed.

CORNIGLIA

The quietest village in the Cinque Terre is isolated by both its position midway down the coast and a hilltop position high above the open sea and its little harbor. Whether you arrive by boat or train, you'll have to climb more than 300 steps to reach the village proper, which is an enticing maze of little walkways overshadowed by tall houses. Once there, though, the views over the surrounding vineyards and up and down the coastline are stupendous—for the best outlook, walk to the end of the narrow main street to a belvedere that is perched between the sea and sky. More than these vistas, Corniglia is also the village most likely to offer you a glimpse into life in the Cinque Terre the way it was until a couple of decades ago.

SLEEPING, DRINKING & DINING

✪ **Albergo-Ristorante Da Cecio.** 19010 Corniglia. ☎ **0187/812-138.** 4 units, all with bathroom, 6 others in the village. 80,000L ($47) single and double. MC, V.

Proprietors Elia and Nunzio have converted the second floor of their old stone house in the countryside just 5 minutes outside Corniglia to what we consider one of the Cinque Terre's most pleasant inns. The four doubles are big and bright, with views over the sea, olive groves, and the hilltop town, and they all have modern bathrooms with good showers. The flowery terrace downstairs (which at mealtimes serves as an outdoor dining room for the excellent restaurant downstairs; see below) is the perfect place to idle away an afternoon. If a room is not available here, one of the proprietors will take you down to one of their six pleasant rooms in the village.

Bar Villagio Marino Europa. 19010 Corniglia. ☎ **0187/812-279.** Sandwiches and snacks from 1,500L (88¢). Mid-May–mid-Oct, daily 8am–midnight. Closed winter. BAR.

It would be hard to find a location more scenic than the one this simple outdoor bar enjoys, with stunning views up and down the coast from a hillside perch. Built to service guests at an attached bungalow village, the bar is also a welcome refuge for hikers on the Corniglia-Manarola path. The offerings don't get more elaborate than sodas and beer, panini and ice cream, but you will certainly want to stop here at least once on your treks up and the down the Cinque Terre to take in the view.

✪ **De Mananan.** V. Fieschi 117, Corniglia. ☎ **0187/821-166.** Reservations recommended. Primi 8,000–15,000L ($4.70–$8.80); secondi 16,000–20,000L ($9.40–$11.75). No credit cards. Wed–Mon 1–2:30pm and 8–10pm. LIGURIAN.

The pleasure of being in hilltop Corniglia is well worth the trek up to town, especially if the visit includes a meal at this tiny restaurant carved into the stone cellars of an ancient house. Agostino and Marianne, the husband and wife owners and chefs, draw on age-old local recipes and use only the freshest ingredients in their preparations, and the results, which are posted on a blackboard in the one handsome vaulted room furnished with granite tables, are wonderful. Fresh vegetables from gardens just outside the village are grilled and mixed with herbs and smoked mozzarella as a simple appetizer, which can be followed by any of the hand-rolled pasta topped with homemade pesto or *funghi porcini* (wild mushrooms). You can continue in this meatless vein with a plate of mussels, grilled fish, or fresh anchovies stuffed with herbs, but the few meat dishes on the daily menu are also excellent—especially the coniglio nostrano, rabbit roasted in a white sauce. Local wines accompany the meals.

Ristorante Cecio. Corniglia. ☎ **0187/812-138.** Primi 8,000–15,000L ($4.70–$8.80); secondi 15,000–22,000L ($8.80–$12.95). Daily in season noon–2:30pm and 7–10pm. MC, V. LIGURIAN.

Like the inn upstairs, the stone-walled, wood-beamed dining room and flower-filled terrace overlooking olive groves provide extremely pleasant surroundings. A nice selection of simple, homemade fare emerges from the family-run kitchen, including fresh pasta with a rich pesto or walnut sauce or alla scogliera, topped with fresh clams and mussels. Meat and fish are grilled over an open hearth. Outside of peak meals times, you can sit on the terrace and enjoy the view over a beer or glass of the house wine.

MANAROLA

Not as busy as nearby Riomaggiore or as quaint as its neighbor Corniglia, Manarola is a near-vertical cluster of tall houses that seem to rise piggyback style up the hills on either side of the harbor. In fact, in this region with no shortage of heart-stopping views, one of the most amazing sights is the one of Manarola as you descend into town down the path from Corniglia: From this perspective, the hill-climbing houses seem to merge into one another to form a row of skyscrapers. Despite these urban associations, Manarola is a delightfully rural village where fishing and wine making are big business. The region's major wine cooperative, **Cooperativa Agricoltura di Riomaggiore, Manarola, Corniglia, Vernazza e Monterosso**, is here; call ☎ **0187/920-435** for information about tours.

SLEEPING & DINING

Aristide. V. Discovolo 290. ☎ and fax **0187/920-000.** Primi 10,000–15,000L ($5.90–$8.80); secondi 16,000–30,000L ($9.40–$17.65). No credit cards. Tues–Sun noon–2:30 and 7–10pm. LIGURIAN.

In this old house up the hill from the harbor (just below the train station), diners are accommodated on a couple of levels of small rooms as well as on a covered terrace across the street. Many of these patrons live in the Cinque Terre or take the train here from nearby La Spezia, because this long-standing trattoria is known for its heaping platters of grilled fish, *gamberoni* (jumbo prawns), and *frittura di mare* (a selection of fried seafood). The *antipasta di mare* (seafood antipasta; 25,000L/$14.70) includes a nice selection of octopus, clams, sardines, and other local catches and serves well as a lighter meal. The house's white wine is from the hills above the town, and if the owner is in a good mood he may come around after your dinner proffering a complimentary glass of *sciachetra*, the local dessert wine.

Marina Piccola. V. Discovolo 38, 19010 Manarola. ☎ **0185/920-103.** Fax 0185/920-966. 9 units, all with bathroom. TEL. 100,000L ($58.80) single; 120,000L ($70.60) double. Half-board 130,000L ($76.45) single, 110,000L ($64.70) per person double; full board 150,000L ($88.25) single, 140,000L ($82.35) per person double. Breakfast 15,000L ($8.80). AE, MC, V.

This cozy inn on the harbor in Manarola is a favorite with many travelers to the Cinque Terre, and it's easy to see why. Part of the premises, including the glass enclosed seafood restaurant where you may be required to take half- or full board in the busy summer months, is right on the water, and many of the guest rooms in the tall house across the room have sea views as well. Decor is a cut above that of most inns in the region—the welcoming lobby doubles as a sitting room, with divans wrapping around a fireplace. Upstairs, old prints, brass lamps, and handsome headboards lend a great amount of charm to the small but serviceable rooms. The aforementioned meals are excellent, a cut above most room and board fare. Our only quibble with this otherwise pleasant hostelry is that on recent visits we've found the service to be somewhat unfriendly.

RIOMAGGIORE

Riomaggiore clings onto the vestiges of the Cinque Terre's rustic ways while making some concessions to the modern world. The old fishing quarter has expanded in recent years and Riomaggiore now has some sections of new houses and apartment blocks. This blend of the old and new works well—Riomaggiore is bustling and prosperous and makes the most of a lovely setting, with a tiny harbor and houses that cling to the hills that drop into the sea on either side of town. Many of the lanes end in seaside belvederes, and there's a pleasant little beach next to the harbor.

SLEEPING & DINING

Hotel Argentina. V. de Gaspari 187. 19017 Riomaggiore. ☎ **0187/920-213.** 15 units, all with bathroom. TV. 110,000–125,000L ($64.70–$73.50) single and double. Rates include breakfast. AE, DC, MC, V.

The only bona fide inn in Riomaggiore is in the newer section of town, on a hillside about a 5-minute walk from the center. This location affords astonishing views, which you can enjoy from most of the guest rooms, and provides a nice retreat from the tourist-crowded main street and harbor. A breezy terrace in front of the hotel and a plain bar area off the lobby are the places to relax, and while the tile-floored rooms upstairs will not overwhelm you with their character, they are large and pleasant, if blandly furnished.

La Lanterna. Riomaggiore. ☎ **0187/920-589.** Primi 7,000–15,000L ($4.10–$8.80); secondi 9,000–20,000L ($5.30–$11.75). MC, V. Daily in season noon–2:30pm and 7–10pm. SEAFOOD/LIGURIAN.

From a table on the terrace here, perched only a few feet above Riomaggiore's snug harbor, you can hear the waves lap against the rocks and watch the local fishermen mend their nets. Seafood, of course, dominates the menu, with many unusual Ligurian-style dishes. The antipasto of shrimp, smoked tuna, and grilled swordfish is excellent and can suffice as an entree; you should, however, make room for one of the house specialties, *chiche*—homemade gnocchi filled with seafood and topped with a spicy tomato sauce.

Luciano e Roberto Fazioli. V. Colombo 94. 19017 Riomaggiore. ☎ **0187/920-587.** Rooms and apts. from 40,000L ($26.30). No credit cards.

The brothers rent about a dozen rooms and apartments all over town out of a shop front on the main street. (One of them is likely to come out and greet you if you walk past the office carrying a bag). While the rooms vary considerably in size, views, and furnishings, most have newly installed bathrooms and cooking facilities. One of our favorite rooms is on the top of a house in the oldest part of town, and opens onto a private rooftop terrace with views over Riomaggiore to the sea. Another choice apartment is on the ground floor of a harborside house, with a chic new kitchen and bath and a sitting area from which you can hear the waves lapping against the rocks below.

14

Southern Italy: Campania & Apulia

By Reid Bramblett

The **Campania region** around Naples was the Hamptons of ancient Rome, where the rich built sumptuous summer villas and emperors went to retire. The province also boasts some of Italy's most gorgeous scenery, from the seductive island of **Capri** to the singularly beautiful **Amalfi Coast**, with its winding, white-knuckle Amalfi Drive road linking fishing villages, resort towns like Positano, and the ceramics center of Vietri. In **Naples**, you can delve into the 18th-century court of the Bourbons at their royal palace and theater, or pay homage to Caravaggio in one museum and ancient sculptors in another in between visiting baroque churches and sampling pizza in the very restaurant that invented it.

From a base in Naples or resorty **Sorrento**, you can day trip to visit one of the most destructive forces in western history, **Mt. Vesuvius.** A short train ride will take you to Pompeii and Herculaneum, two cities completely buried by the volcano's wrath in A.D. 79, frozen in time and offering an unparalleled glimpse into daily life almost 2,000 years ago. To cycle back even further in time, head to southern Campania, where you can wander amid the columns of some of the most intact Greek temples in the world in the forgotten 5th-century B.C. colony of **Paestum.**

Farther south, you'll encounter the heel of Italy's boot, peninsular **Apulia** (Puglia, *pool*-yah). It's the land of sunflowers and Santa Claus, olive oil and *orecchiette* pasta, Romanesque churches, and whitewashed villages. It's a cultural mélange unequaled in Italy, forming one of the country's most underrated, underexplored, and undiscovered regions. Nowhere else in Italy is there a more precise balance of east and west, Greek and Roman, Byzantine and Lombard, and Arab and Norman. You'll discover dozens of hand-rolled pasta shapes, loaves of bread almost two feet across in **Monte Sant'Angelo,** delicious mussels in **Taranto,** and some incredibly full, earthy, but little-known red wines like Salice Salentino, Primitivo, and Locorotondo. The craft industry also thrives in this area—specifically the papier-mâché statuettes of **Lecce** fashion. Overall, with 784 kilometers (470 mi.) of grotto- and beach-studded coastline, whitewashed cities, incredible seafood, archaeological museums, glittering caverns, and medieval castles, Apulia is a unique landscape just waiting for the outside world to discover it. The privately run Web site **www.inmedia.it/Puglia** contains a wealth of information on the entire region.

A TASTE OF CAMPANIA The world owes Naples a great debt if for no other reason than for the invention of the "plain" *pizza Margherita.* Naples had good stock to work with, as Campania is *the* center of mozzarella production in Italy, with fine **mozzarella di bufala,** or buffalo-milk mozzarella, served in restaurants across the province (actually, on pizza you'll more often find *fiordilatte* cheese, which is mozzarella made with cow's milk and holds up better to the heat of cooking). Mozzarella is a key ingredient in **gnocchi alla Sorrentina** (or any other pasta thusly named), a gooey mix of pasta, tomatoes, and cheese.

But since Campania is mainly coastal, some of its best cuisine is of a fishy nature. Any pasta or risotto **alla pescatora** (fisherman's style) or **ai frutti di mare** (literally "fruits of the sea") will be infused with a selection of seafood, generally some combination of **vongole** (clams), **cozze** (mussels), **ostriche** (oysters), **calamari** (squid), **polpo** (octopus), **gamberi/gamberoni/scampi** (shrimp), **ricci di mare** (sea urchin), **aragostini** (crawfish), **aragote** (lobster), or **granchio** (crab). Any pasta cooked **al cartoccio** is basically the same sort of seafood dish, only this time all the ingredients are tossed together, wrapped in foil, and baked. Naples's most typical dish is **spaghetti con le vongole,** spaghetti tossed with the tiny, delicious clams found in the city's bay. You may find your fresh fish cooked **all'acqua pazza,** in "crazy waters" with baby tomatoes, white wine, and spices (often including capers).

Of Campanian **wines,** some of the best include *Lacryma Christi,* "Christ's Tears," grown on the slopes of Vesuvius by monks, Ravello's juicy local white, and the dry *Greco di Tufo.* In shops on Capri and along the Amalfi Coast, you'll find bottles of **limoncello,** a liqueur made with lemon zest and lots of sugar (best when drunk ice-cold).

A TASTE OF APULIA Apulia's trinity of homemade pasta shapes are *orecchiette* ("little ears" shaped like tiny, thick Frisbees), *cavatelli* (orecchiette rolled into a short tube), and *troccoli* (fat, square spaghetti). Any pasta served with *cima di rape* comes with boiled turnip greens. After "little ears," the quintessential Pugliese dish is *purè di fave con cicoria* (broad beans pureed and sided or mixed with boiled chicory). Other popular dishes include *spaghetti ricci di mare* (with sea urchin), *polpette al sugo* (meatballs in tomato sauce), and *braciola* or *involtino* (veal rolled up and stewed for hours in tomato sauce). Fresh ewe's milk *ricotta* is often salt-cured to form a hard, gratable variety called *ricotta dura, ricotta forte,* or *cacioricotta*—when invoked in a pasta sauce (sometimes called *mantecati*) the hard ricotta is grated over a tomato puree.

1 Naples

202 km (125 mi.) SE of Rome, 207 km (162 mi.) W of Bari

Un gran cassino describes a great big teeming noisy mess. It also describes Naples perfectly, a seething cauldron of humanity showcasing the quicksilver southern Italian character at its warm, friendly best and its temperamental, bureaucratic worst. It's a city of unmissable (if a bit antiquated) art and archaeology museums showcasing a rich 2,500-year history. Naples is the birthplace of pizza, a city of lively markets and a lifestyle lived outside in the street and squares, surrounded by fabulous churches, cloisters, and vistas.

The original Greek colony of *Parthenope* was transformed into the *Neapolis* of the Romans, but little remains of the Greco-Roman epoch other than the overall street plan—plus a few, partially excavated walls sunken in city squares (which people seem to regard more as public trash bins) and in some church basements. And it's all run by a largely ineffectual, if earnest, municipal government that wages a continuous war against both its own Byzantine bureaucracy and the Camorra, the nastiest organized crime network this side of the Sicilian Mafia.

Bay of Naples & the Amalfi Coast

N

To Paestum

Baiano

Avellino

A30

A30

A16

San Vitaliano

Monte Somma

Vesuvio

A3

Ercolano (Herculaneum)

Torre del Greco

Torre Annunziata

18

Pompei (Archaeological Site)

Pompei

A3

Pagani

18

Salerno

Battipaglia

Vietri sul Mare

Ravello

Amalfi

Grotta d. Smeraldo

Praiano

Monti Lattari

366

Positano

Meta

Golfo di Salerno

Castellammare di Stabia

Sorrento

145

Termini

163

Massa Lubrense

Aversa

Frattamaggiore

Greater Naples

Napoli (Naples)

Nisida

▲ Solfatara

Pozzuoli

Baia

Miseno

Canale di Prócida

Prócida

I. DI PRÓCIDA

Cuma (Archaeological Site)

Castel Volturno

Golfo di Gaeta

Golfo di Napoli

ISLAND OF CAPRI

Anacapri

Capri

To Palermo

Lacco Ameno

Ischia Ponte

Ischia Porto

Forio

Barano

S. Angelo

I. DI ÍSCHIA

Ferry Route - - - - - -

3-0671

627

Naples is one of the most densely populated cities in Europe. Almost three million inhabitants live within less than 47 square miles—that's like taking the entire population of Oregon and squeezing it into San Francisco. The city suffers from one of Italy's highest crime rates and lowest standards of living, the bulk of citizens shoehorned into the tall tenements of the old city and *Quartiere degli Spagnoli* or the slapdash cement high-rises of the growing suburbs. Unemployment is high, and pickpocketing of tourists rampant. While one Neapolitan will hug you with genuine friendliness as he welcomes you to his city like a long-lost relative, the next is likely to reach into your pocket while he does so and relieve you of your wallet. But all of that describes Naples at its worst, and aside from the dinginess of Piazza Garibaldi outside the train station, you're unlikely to run into any of it. Just keep your wits about you as you navigate from the stupendous Archaeology Museum and Capodimonte painting gallery to the medieval, Renaissance, and baroque wonders of the churches, castles, and palaces downtown. And always keep one hand on your wallet.

ESSENTIALS

GETTING HERE **By Train** There are trains at least twice hourly **from Rome** (2 to 2.5 hr; 18,000L/$10.60). Get off at "Napoli-Stazione Mergellina" if you're staying at the Ausonia hotel below (or want to take the hydrofoil to Capri from the Mergellina docks), otherwise stay on until the "Napoli-Stazione Centrale/Piazza Garibaldi." For rail information call ☎ **081/553-4188.**

By Car Follow the A1 from Rome. For parking, see "Getting Around: By Car" below.

By Plane Naples airport is at Capodichino (☎ **081/789-6385**), north of the center. Alitalia's Naples number is ☎ **081/542-5333.** There's a CLP (☎ **081/531-1646**) shuttle bus downtown to Piazza Municipio every 50 minutes.

CITY LAYOUT Naples lies on the northern rim of the Bay of Naples. The heart of Naples is bounded by the bay to the south and hemmed in by low mountains all around (hilltops onto which the city has since spread). You'll arrive in the dingiest corner of the city, **Piazza Garibaldi,** on the eastern edge of the center. From here, wide **Corso Umberto I** runs diagonally across the center toward **Piazza Municipio** at the main port, **Molo Beverello.**

The historic **old center** of Naples is bounded by **Corso Umberto** on the south, **Piazza Cavour** on the north, **Via Duomo** on the east, and **Via Toledo** on the west. Though its heart runs **Spaccanapoli**, which translates loosely as "divide Naples in half" and refers both to this historic district as a whole and specifically to the arrow-straight street that runs down its middle going east–west and changes names from **Via S. Biagio dei Librai** to **Via Benedetto Croce** to **Via D. Capitelli** (it's actually the old Decumanus Maximus, or Main Street, of the Roman city).

Across Via Toledo to the west lies the checkerboard of the **Quartiere degli Spagnoli,** a grid of narrow streets laid out by the Spanish viceroys along the bottom slopes

---

Ticket to Ride

You only need one **ticket** for any intercity public transport: bus, metro, funicular, or the city portions of rail lines. This *giranapoli* ticket is available for 1,500L (90¢) at any *tabacchi,* most newsstands, and all metro stops, funicular stations, and train stations. It's valid for 90 minutes, during which time you can transfer between as many buses as you'd like, plus once only to each of the other public transport systems (metro, funicular). There's also a daily pass for 4,500L ($2.65).

of the Vomero hill. Its tall tenements are filled with lower income housing, and while you can see some of the most genuine Naples life in this area, be extra cautious; it is also one of the strongholds of the Camorra organized crime network. South of the Quartiere degli Spagnoli, Via Toledo spills into **Piazza Plebescito,** the heart of 18th-century Naples, with the royal palace and theater, and the docks just beyond.

West of the center are a trio of rather nicer, middle-class residential neighborhoods starting with the headland of **Santa Lucia** rising above Piazza Plebescito on the sea-ward slope of the Vomero. Beyond this is the long, wide harbor-side park of **Chiaia,** with a few blocks of buildings climbing behind it up a small ridge. At the end of Chiaia are the docks and train station of the workaday zone of **Mergellina.**

GETTING AROUND   By Metro, bus, and Funicular   Naples's **Metro** is really a commuter rail line, though it is handy for visitors to zip from Mergellina (where there are some fine hotels) into the center, or from the train station direct to Naples's top sight, the Archaeological Museum.

You'll more often be using the **bus/trolley** system. **Piazza Garibaldi,** in front of the central train station, is the terminus for almost every Neapolitan bus. The **E1 bus** circles endlessly around the heart of the historic center. **Tram 1** runs from the western edge of Piazza Garibaldi (the far side from the train station) direct to the Molo Beverello ferry docks. To get to the hilltop neighborhoods like the Vomero, has Naples built several *funiculari* (cog railways).

By Car   Only drive in Naples is you have a death wish or are practicing for the demolition derby. Neapolitan motorists drive twice as fast and three times as aggressively as your average Italian, and while red lights seem to be considered optional in the rest of Italy, here they're ignored entirely. No city in Europe (save perhaps Palermo or Athens) is more stressful, aggravating, confusing, and downright dangerous to drive in.

Do yourself a favor and **park** as soon as you arrive in town. If you want to explore the Amalfi Coast by rental car, pick it up the day you leave Naples (or, better yet, take the train to Sorrento and pick up your car there). There are garages just south of the central train station at V. Ferraris 40 (☎ **081/264-344**); near the center at V. Shelley 11 (between Via Toledo and Piazza Municipio; ☎ **081/551-3104**); near the Molo Beverello ferry docks at V. d. Gaspari 14 (☎ **081/552-5442**); and near Mergellina docks and Mergellina train station at Pz. Sannazaro 142 (☎ **081/681-437**).

By Taxi   Only use legitimate taxis, either from the following stands or by calling the Radiotaxi numbers below. There are taxi stands at **Piazza Garibaldi, Piazza Municipio, Piazza Trieste e Trento, Piazza dei Martiri, Piazza Vittoria, Via Partenope, Piazza S. Pasquale/Riviera di Chiaia,** and **Via Mergellina. Naples Radiotaxi** numbers are ☎ **081/556-4444,** 081/556-0202, 081/551-5151, and 081/570-7070.

There are occasional reports of unscrupulous drivers trying to pull one over on tourists, so know these official rates. Rides cost an initial 4,000L ($2.35), plus 100L (6¢) for every 100 meters. There are supplemental charges for Sundays (2,000L/ $1.20), rides between 10pm and 1am (3,000L/$1.75), luggage (500L/30¢ per bag), calling ahead for a radio taxi (1,500L/90¢), and travel to or from the airport (5,000L/$2.95).

Travel Tip

The Naples daily paper *Il Mattino* has a page near the back listing the **current transportation schedules** for the entire province, including the state and private rail lines, buses, and ferries.

VISITOR INFORMATION There's a tourist info desk in the train station (☎ **081/405-311**), the airport (☎ **081/780-5761**), in the Palazzo Reale at Piazza Plebescito (☎ **081/252-5711;** fax 081/418-619), Piazza del Gesù Nuovo (☎ **081-552-3328**), and at Pz. d. Martiri 58 (☎ **081-405-311**).

FAST FACTS: Naples

Books Feltrinelli (☎ **081/552-1436**) at V. Tommaso d'Aquino 70 (just off Via Torino) has travel books and novels in English (mainly Penguin classics) upstairs.

Consulates There's a **U.S. Consulate** on Piazza d. Repubblica (☎ **081/583-8111**); and a **U.K. Consulate** at V. F. Crispi 122 (☎ **081/663-511**).

Drugstores There are all-night pharmacies around the train station (in the station itself, at Pz. Garibaldi 11, Cor. Garibaldi 354); in the city center (at Pz. Municipio 54; Pz. Dante 71); in Chiaia (at Riviera di Chiaia 169, V. D. Morelli 22, V. Carducci 21); and on the Vomero (V. G. Merliani 27, V. Cliea 124).

Emergencies Call ☎ **113** for any emergency. For the Carabinieri police dial **112;** to report a fire call **115;** for an ambulance dial **081/752-0696;** for car breakdowns dial **116.**

Hospitals Anyone can head to the *pronto soccorso* (first aid) station of the nearest *ospedale* (hospital). Near the train station, the Ospedale Ascalesi is at Piazza Collenda/Via P. Colletta just off Cor. Umberto I (☎ **081/254-2111**); just south of the train station at the harbor is the Ospedale Loreto Mare on V. A. Vespucci (☎ **081/254-2111**); in the city center there is the Policlinico on Piazza Miraglia/Via del Sole just above Piazza S. Domenico (☎ **081/566-1111** or 081/746-1111); also in the center is the Ospedale Vecchio Pellegrini off Via Toledo on Via Porta Medina at the foot of the funicular up to the Vomero (☎ **081/254-2111**); and in Chiaia is the Ospedale Loreto Crispi where Via F. Crispi changes names to Via Schipa at Via A. Mirelli (☎ **081/254-7111**).

Lost/Stolen Objects The *uffico stranieri* (foreigner's office) of the police *questura* (headquarters) is at V. Medina 25 (☎ **081-794-1111**). The train station has an *oggetti rinvenuti* (lost and found) office (☎ **081/567-2366**).

Mail/Internet Access There are central post offices at Piazza Matteotti off Via Diaz (☎ **081/551-1456**), in the main train station, and in the Galleria Umberto I (☎ **081/552-3467**). All are open Monday to Friday 8:15am to 7:15pm, Saturday 8:15am to noon. The **Internetbar,** Pz. Bellini 74 (☎ **081/295-237**), allows you dial-up access for a one-time membership fee of 10,000L ($5.90), which includes the first hour of Internet time.

Safety/Crime Naples is more dangerous than Rome, Florence, or Venice, despite great strides in recent years toward cleaning up the city. The Camorra (Neapolitan Mafia) continues to control much of the city, and petty theft is rampant—though the rate of violent crime against visitors is, as in the rest of Italy, much lower than that of any U.S. city. Clutch your camera firmly (try to keep it out of view at all times), keep a hand on your wallet, and park in a garage. Pickpockets attempt to "bump" me at least 50% of the time as I exit the main train station onto Piazza Garibaldi. Be wary throughout the city center, especially around Piazza Garibaldi and in the Quartiere degli Spagnoli. The residential neighborhoods to the west—Santa Lucia, Chiaia, and Mergellina—are a bit safer, but not much so.

Naples

Parco di Capodimonte ①

CAPODIMONTE

OTTOCALLI

Albergo dei Poveri

ARENACCIA

Airport →

VASTO

PIAZZA CAVOUR

Piazza Garibaldi

Stazione Centrale

CENTRALE

MONTESANTO

FUNICULAR

Stazione Cumana

Piazza Bellini

Piazza S. Domenico

Piazza Dante

Università

Piazza del Mercato

Stazione Circumvesuviana

Via Marinella

FUNICULAR

Piazza Municipio

Stazione Marittima

Molo Beverello

Piazza Plebiscito

Piazza d. Martiri

← To Chiaia & Mergellina

Bacino del Piliero

Bacino Angiono

Golfo di Napoli

Castel dell'Ovo ⑱

Cappella San Severo	⑧
Castel dell' Ovo	⑱
Castel Nuovo	⑰
Catacombe di S. Gennaro	②
Certosa di S. Martino	⑬
Chiesa del Gesù Nuovo	⑪
Duomo	④
Galleria Umberto I	⑭
Museo Archeologico Nazionale	③
Museo Civico G. Filangeri	⑲
Museo e Gallerie Nazionali di Capodimonte	①
Orto Botanico	②
Palazzo Reale	⑯
S. Anna dei Lombardi	⑫
S. Chiara	⑩
S. Domenico Maggiore	⑨
S. Gregorio Armeno	⑦
S. Lorenzo Maggiore	⑤
Teatro San Carlo	⑮
Via S. Gregorio Armeno	⑥

Metro Ⓜ   Information ⓘ

Church ✝   Lighthouse ⚡

3-0670

Transportation Info For info on city buses, metro, and funicular, call ☎ **081/ 562-5222;** www.connect.it/napolipass. For further bus information, you can call ANM directly at ☎ **081/763-2177.**

SEE NAPLES & DIE
IN THE CENTER

✪ **Museo Archeologico.** Piazza Museo/Piazza Cavour (at the northern edge of the city). ☎ **081/440-166.** 12,000L ($7.05) adults, free under 18 and over 60. Mon, Wed–Sat 10am–10pm; Sun 9am–8pm. Bus: R1, R4, V10, 24, 42, 47, 110, and 137. Metro: Cavour.

This is one of the most significant archaeological collections in Europe (certainly southern Italy's best), the only absolutely required sight in Naples, and well worth 2 to 3 hours of your time. If you explore Pompeii without paying this museum a visit as well, you've missed out on half the riches. The best statues, mosaics, and wall paintings at Pompeii that could be carried off (and hadn't been already by looters) were long ago removed from the archaeological site to be preserved here, alongside finds from across southern Italy as well as many from Rome itself (including the important and impressive statuary collected by the Farnese family). The museum is poorly arranged and poorly labeled, but be sure to search out these highlights throughout the ill-lit rooms.

The **Doriforo**, or **Policleto's Spearman** (a Pompeiian Roman copy of a 440 B.C. Greek original) is the most accurate surviving copy of a masterpiece by Policletus of Argo, one of the geniuses of Greek Golden Age sculpture. It represents Policletus' embodiment of the ideal human form, carved with exacting mathematical proportions and a perfect figurative balance. The **Pozzuoli Sarcophagus** is a well-preserved A.D. 3rd-century Roman piece with a tumultuous high relief showing a seated, contemplative Prometheus creating Man surrounded by a swirl of gods and *putti* (cherubs).

The massively burly ✪ **Farnese Hercules** was excavated from Rome's Baths of Caracalla and is a fine example of the exaggerated A.D. 3rd-century Athenian style of the sculptor Glykon. Across the hall from it is the impressive ✪ **Farnese Bull,** the largest surviving sculpture (13 feet tall) from the ancient world. It shows four figures struggling with a bull while a boy, a dog, and various flora and fauna sculpted into the base look on—all carved from a single, gargantuan block of marble. This A.D. 2nd-century Hellenistic work copies a 1st-century B.C. original and tells the tale of Amphion and Zethos (the two nude men) avenging the maltreatment of their mother Antiope (standing at the back) by tying her tormentor Dirke (the woman about to get trampled) to the horns of a bull she was preparing to sacrifice.

On a mezzanine level between the ground and first floors (make sure you take the sweeping staircase on the left to gain access) is preserved the museum's most famous collection, the **mosaics and paintings from Pompeii,** including the slightly ruined but remarkably well-crafted ✪ **Battle of Alexander and Darius,** discovered in the House of the Faun at Pompeii. This scene, with a highly advanced use of color and minuscule mosaic chips to render the figures as well as any painting, depicts the Battle of Isse of 333 B.C., Alexander astride his horse (on the left) giving chase to Darius, who's retreating in his chariot. It's probably a Roman copy of an original that was crafted within a few decades of the actual battle.

Among the paintings here, be sure you don't miss the *portrait of a young woman* wearing a gold filigree hair net and pausing with her stylus to her lips as she collects her thoughts before returning to write in the wax volume she holds. This must have been a standard pose, for it appears again in the *portrait of Paquio Proculo and his wife,* a prosperous middle-class Pompeiian couple, probably bakers. This portrait was rather shocking when it was discovered, for it showed that interracial marriage was probably common (she appears to be European, he North African) in the ancient Empire. The portrayal of these women is also intriguing in that it implies ancient Pompeii enjoyed a great deal of sexual as well as racial equality: the first is probably writing poetry (an artist), the second possibly keeping the books for the couple's bakery (a businesswoman).

✪ **Santa Chiara.** Piazza Gesù Nuovo/Via Benedetto Croce. ☎ **081/552-6209,** or 081/797-1256 for museum. Admission to church and cloisters free; suggested museum donation 5,000L ($2.95). Daily 9:30am–12:30pm and 4–6pm (museum closes Sun afternoon and Wed). Bus: E1, R1, R3, R4, V10, 24.

Santa Chiara is the most rewarding of Naples's churches, built in 1328, half-destroyed by incendiary bombs in 1943, and restored as best as possible to its Gothic state in 1953. The light-filled interior is lined with chapels, each of which contains some left-over bit of sculpture or fresco from the medieval church, but the best three line the wall behind the High Altar. In the center is the towering, multilevel **tomb of Robert the Wise d'Angio,** sculpted by Giovanni and Pacio Bertini in 1343. To its right is Tino di Camaino's **tomb of Charles, duke of Calabria**; on the left is the 1399 **monument to Mary of Durazza.** In the choir behind the altar are more salvaged medieval remnants of frescoes and statuary including bits of a **Giotto** *Crucifixion.*

You have to exit the church and walk down its left flank to enter one of Naples's top sights—and the most relaxing retreat from the bustle of the city—the 14th-century ✪ **cloisters.** In 1742, Domenico Antonio Vaccaro took the courtyard of these flowering cloisters and lined the four paths to its center with arbors supported by columns, each of which is plated with colorfully painted majolica tiles, interspersed with majolica tiled benches. In the **museum** rooms off the cloisters are a scattering of Roman and medieval remains.

On the piazza outside is one of Naples's several baroque spires, the **guglia dell'Immacolata,** a tall pile of statues and reliefs sculpted in 1750.

✪ **Cappella Sansevero.** V. F. de Sanctis 19 (near Pz. S. Domenico Maggiore). ☎ **081/551-8470**. Admission 8,000L ($4.70) adults, 4,000L ($2.35) students. Wed–Sun 10am–6pm (5pm Nov–June). Bus: E1, R1, R3, R4, V10, 24, 42, 105, 105r.

If you want the best example of how baroque can be both ludicrously over-the-top, hauntingly beautiful, and technically brilliant all at once, search out the nondescript entrance to one of Italy's most fanciful chapels. This 1590 chapel is a festival of marbles, frescoes, and above all sculpture—in relief and in the round, masterfully showing off the considerable technical abilities and intricate visual storytelling of a few otherwise relatively unknown Neapolitan baroque masters. At the center is Giuseppe Sammartino's remarkable alabaster ✪ *Veiled Christ* (1753), one the most successful and convincing illusions of soft reality crafted from hard stone in the history of art, depicting the dead Christ lying on pillows under a transparent veil.

Three sculptures on the walls stand out as well, including Francesco Celebrano's 1762 relief of the *Deposition* behind the altar, Antonio Corradini's allegory of *Modesty* (a marble statue of a woman whose nudity is covered only by a decidedly immodest clinging, gauzy veil), and Francesco Queirolo's virtuoso allegory of *Disillusion,* represented by a man struggling with a rope net carved entirely of marble.

San Lorenzo Maggiore. Pz. S. Gaetano 316. ☎ **081/290-580** or 081/454-948 for scavi. Admission to church free; scavi 5,000L ($2.95) adults; 3,000L ($1.75) under 18 and over 60. Daily 9am–1pm and 4–6:30pm (scavi close Sun afternoon and Tues). Bus: E1, 42, 105, 105r.

The greatest of Naples's layered churches was built in 1265 for Charles I over a 6th-century basilica, which lay over many ancient remains. The interior is pure Gothic, with tall pointed arches and an apse off of which radiate nine chapels. This is where, in 1334, Boccaccio first caught sight of Robert of Anjou's daughter Maria, who became "Fiammetta" in his writings. Aside from some gorgeously baroque chapels of inlaid marbles, the highlight of the interior is Tino da Camaino's **canopy tomb of Catherine of Austria** (1323–25).

San Lorenzo preserves the best and most extensive (still rather paltry) **remains of the ancient Greek and Roman cities** currently open to the public. The foundations of the church are actually the walls of Neapolis' basilican law courts (this architectural type, the basilica, was adopted by the Paleochristians as a general blueprint for their first churches). In the cloisters are excavated bits of the Roman city's treasury and marketplace. In the crypt are the rough remains of a Roman-era shop-lined street, a Greek temple, and a medieval building.

Duomo (Cathedral). V. Duomo. ☎ **081/449-097.** Admission to church free; archaeological crypt and baptistery 5,000L ($2.95); baptistery only 2,000L ($1.20). Daily 9am–noon, 4:30–7pm (crypt and baptistery close Sun afternoon). Bus: E1, 42, 105, 105r.

The neo-Gothic facade of Naples's cathedral—built in the French Gothic style for Charles I in 1294 but rebuilt after a disastrous earthquake in 1456—was finished in 1905, but the central portal survives from the 1407 version. The 16 piers inside are made up of 110 antique columns of African and Asian granite removed from nearby pagan buildings.

The third chapel on the right is the sumptuous 17th-century **Cappella di San Gennaro,** elaborately frescoed by Domenichino and, later, Giovanni Lanfranco, who completed the concentric clouds of saints and angels spiraling up the airy dome. Also here is a painting of *San Gennaro Exiting Unharmed from the Furnace* by Giuseppe Ribera, showing a miracle by Benevento's persecuted bishop in A.D. 305, who survived both being thrown to lions and this roasting only to be done in by an ax to the neck. Among the silver reliquaries you'll see one of *St. Irene Protecting the City,* in which the saint holds a scale model of Naples circa 1733. The most venerable item in all of Naples, however, is the ears-poking-out and vaguely Asian-looking silver reliquary bust that preserves the head of the city patron, St. Gennaro, and two vials of his coagulated blood, also stored behind the chapel altar. The latter are taken out for the ✪ **Miracolo di San Gennaro** on the first Saturday of May and on September 19 and December 16 amid much religious pomp and ceremony, whereupon they miraculously boil and liquefy back into blood again (Gennaro, incidentally, is the patron saint of blood banks). The speed with which they do so is a prediction of Naples's prosperity for the coming months. When the miracle occurs, the faithful line up to kiss the vials.

To the right of the High Altar are two chapels with staccato remnants of 13th- and 14th-century frescoes and inlaid marble floor. The **Crypt of San Gennaro** (aka Cappella Carafa) beneath the High Altar is one of the greatest examples of Renaissance design in Naples, including the Cosmatesque-style tomb of Pope Innocent IV (1315). To the left of the High Altar is a chapel containing an *Assumption* by Umbrian master painter Perugino.

Off the left aisle is the entrance to the ancient **Basilica di Santa Restituta,** a pre-existing church built in the 4th century atop a Temple to Apollo, which is probably where the antique columns of the nave—rebuilt in the 14th century—come from. Luca Giordano's brush was active again here on the ceiling, but the highlight is the ✪ **baptistery** at the back. This domed cube of a room is the oldest building of its kind in Christian Europe, built in the 5th century and retaining impressive swatches of the original mosaics on the dome. From this little side church you can also descend to the basement where a few scraps of **Greek and Roman streets,** walls, and even mosaics remain.

ATTRACTIONS ON THE WATERFRONT

Teatro San Carlo. V. S. Carlo/Pz. Trieste e Trento. ☎ **081/797-2002.** Admission 5,000L ($2.95). Guided tours Sept 15–June 2pm–3:30pm, July 1–25 10am–noon. Bus: R2, R3, C25, V10, 24, 105, 105r, 140.

San Carlo is one of the oldest, largest, and most respected opera houses in Italy, built by Giovanni Medrano in 1737 under the auspices of Charles of Bourbon (who didn't particularly care for opera, but cared very much about his reputation as an enlightened patron of the arts). After a fire in 1816, the theater was rebuilt by Antonio Niccolini—who, it is said, filled the walls with terra-cotta vases to help give the performance space what is still widely regarded as the best acoustics in Europe—and San Carlo reopened under the musical direction of Gioacchino Rossini.

The glittering chandeliers and sumptuous red velvet and gold accouterments of the vast interior—seating 3,000 in six tiers of box seats—have seen the premiers of operas by Rossini, Bellini, and Donizetti. **Tickets for performances** run anywhere from 15,000 to 250,000L ($8.80 to $147.05), depending on the type of performance and where you sit.

Palazzo Reale. Pz. Plebescito. ☎ **081/580-8111.** Admission 8,000L ($4.70), free under 18 and over 60. Mon–Tues and Thurs–Sat 9:30am–10pm, Sun 9:30am–8pm. Bus: R2, R3, C25, V10, 24, 105, 105r, 140.

Naples's royal palace had to be restructured following Allied bomb damage in 1943, but retains some sumptuous royal apartments and, in niches along the 18th-century facade, statues of the greatest kings from the eight dynasties that have ruled Naples (Roger, Norman; Frederick II, Swabian; Charles I, Angevin; Alfonso, Aragonese; Charles V, Austrian; Charles III, Bourbon; Joachim Murat, French Napoleonic; and Vittorio Emanuele II, Savoy and ultimately Italian).

Construction on the palazzo was started by court engineer Domenico Fontana in 1599 under the viceroy Ruiz de Castro, who wished to create one of the most glorious palaces in the kingdom of Spain's King Philip III. The core was finished by 1616, but in 1759 Ferdinando Fuga was brought in by Ferdinand IV to amplify the palazzo with such lovely additions as the ornate **Teatro do Corte,** built on the occasion of the king's wedding to Maria Carolina of Hapsburg (Marie Antoinette's sister) and decorated with papier-mâché sculpture. Also here are preserved 15th-century bronze doors from the Castel Nuovo whose reliefs tell of Ferdinand of Aragon's feuds with the local barons (the cannonball jutting out of the bottom of one door is a testament to the battle waged by the French and Genoese navies in Naples's harbor). Sheets of paper describe each palatial room and its contents in English. Be sure not to miss the elaborate **Throne Room,** or Belsario Corenzio's ceiling frescoes in several chambers that depict the *Glories of the Spanish Monarchy.*

The expansive **Piazza Plebescito** in front of the royal palace is one of Naples's largest open spaces, laid out with a colonnaded hemicycle and equestrian statues of Charles III of Bourbon and Ferdinand IV in the early 18th century. The neoclassical church of **San Francesco di Paola** marking the center of the curve was modeled after

Rome's Pantheon in 1817 for Ferdinand IV, who ordered it built as an offering of thanks after he retook the city from Napoleonic troops.

Castel Nuovo (Maschio Angioino). Pz. Municipio. ☎ **081/795-2003.** Admission 10,000L ($5.90), 12,000L ($7.05) during some exhibitions. Mon–Sat 9am–7pm, Sun 9am–1pm. Bus: R2, R3, C25, C82, C82b, V10, 24, 105, 105r.

Though the core *Maschio Angioino*, or Angevin Dungeon, was built in the 13th century, the grand ✪ **entrance arch** wedged between two massive 15th-century bastions is pure Renaissance. This unique adaptation of a triumphal arch was grafted onto the castle to commemorate Alfonso I of Aragon's arrival in the city in 1443. The highlights inside are the statues and frescoes from the 14th and 15th century in the **Cappella Palatina;** a middling collection of paintings from the 15th to 20th centuries; and the huge **Sala dei Baroni,** the grand hall where Naples's City Council still meets.

ATTRACTIONS IN THE HILLS

✪ **Museo Capodimonte.** Parco di Capodimonte, V. Capodimonte. ☎ **081/744-1307.** Admission 8,000L ($4.70), free under 18 and over 60. Tues–Sat 10am–10pm, Sun 10am–8pm. Bus: 24, navetta, 137, 110.

Set in an 18th-century royal palace in the midst of shady, grassy Capodimonte park high above the city, this is by far the best painting gallery in all of southern Italy, particularly strong in works from Old Masters representing all phases of the Renaissance and baroque periods. The layout is currently being rearranged as the gallery integrates the original core Farnese collections with various canvases that belong to churches and other collections around town but were sent here for safekeeping.

Among the early Renaissance paintings is a simple and beautiful 1426 *Crucifixion* by Masaccio, and one of **Giovanni Bellini's** masterpieces, his ✪ *Transfiguration* (1478–79). From the great **Raphael** we have *Portrait of Cardinal Alessandro Farnese* (who became Pope Paul III; 1511), a cartoon of *Moses and the Burning Bush* (1514), and an *Eternal Father*. Representing the genius of **Michelangelo** is a cartoon of soldiers that he made as a study for his *Crucifixion of St. Peter* fresco in the Vatican.

There are High Renaissance pieces from Sebastiano del Piombo and **Correggio,** whose 1518 *Marriage of St. Catherine* is a finely studied classical work. **Titian** painted a whole gaggle of portraits of various Farnese cardinals in the 1540s, along with a provocative *Danäe* (1546) painted for Cardinal Alessandro Farnese (and probably using the cardinal's mistress as the goddess model), and the *Portrait of a Young Lady* (1546), which some scholars believe is actually a portrait of Titian's own daughter. **El Greco** contributes the haunting *El Soplón,* or *Youth Lighting a Candle with a Coal* (1575). There are many good **Mannerist** works from the brushes of Andrea del Sarto, Pontormo, Rosso Fiorentino, and Parmigianino.

After a breather of Flemish paintings—look especially for *The Misanthrope* and *The Blind Leading the Blind,* both 1568 works by **Peter Bruegel**—the baroque proper is rung in with a survey of the **Carracci** clan, including works by Agostino, Ludovico, and especially **Annibale Carracci,** who pokes fun at his arch-competitor Caravaggio by painting that artist's leering face on his rendition of a *Satyr.* **Caravaggio** got the last laugh, though, since art history books give but a paragraph to Carracci while filling pages with homage to Caravaggio's genius for composition and dramatic use of *chiaroscuro* (strongly contrasting light and dark areas), well evident in the ✪ *Flagellation of Christ* (1609) kept here.

A latter Caravaggesque master—and the early baroque's greatest (and virtually only) female artist—was **Artemisia Gentileschi,** whose rape as a teenager (and the subsequent highly public and sensational trial) may have later led her to turn her artistic lens often to the many examples throughout history, myth, and the Bible wherein women exact revenge upon men, as in this gallery's gory *Judith Beheading Holofernes.* **Luca Giordano** manages to give good compositional balance and use of light to baroque extravagance in his *Madonna del Baldacchino* (1686).

Pop into the small, excruciatingly elaborate Chinese-style **Salottino di Porcellana** for an excellent example of Italy's finest 18th-century porcelain, still being produced in a nearby factory (built in 1743) here on Capodimonte.

Catacombe di San Gennaro. V. Capodimonte 16 (enter around the left of the Basilica del Madre di Bonconsiglio and through the gate). ☎ **081/741-1071.** Admission 5,000L ($2.95), 3,000L ($1.75) under 15. Open by guided tour only, daily at 9:30am, 10:15am, 11am, and 11:45am (note: tours leave only if more than one person shows up). Bus: 24, 137, 110.

These wide tunnels lined with early Christian burial niches grew around the tomb of an important pagan family, but became a pilgrimage site when the bones of San Gennaro himself were transferred here in the 5th century. Along with several well-preserved 6th-century frescoes there is a depiction of San Gennaro from the A.D. 400s whose halo sports an alpha and omega, and a cross—symbols normally reserved exclusively for Christ's halo. The tour takes you through the upper level of tunnels, passing through several small early basilicas carved from the *tufa* rock. The cemetery remained active until the 11th century, but most of the bones have since been blessed and reinterred in ossuaries on the lower levels (closed to the public). The catacombs survived the centuries intact, but those precious antique frescoes suffered some damage when these tunnels served as an air raid shelter during World War II.

Certosa di San Martino. Lgo. S. Martino/V. T. Angelini (on the Vomero). ☎ **081/ 578-1769.** Admission 9,500L ($5.60), free under 18 and over 60. Tues–Sun 9am–2pm. Funicular: Montesanto, then Bus V1 (or walk).

This 14th-century Carthusian monastery was baroqued in the 17th century, and is today famous for its fine church, peaceful cloisters, great views, small painting gallery, and remarkable *presepio* collection of Christmas crèches. However, since many of the rooms are closed for the time being, that steep admission is a bit of a rip-off, but the ✪ **views** across the city below are still fantastic.

The marble-clad **church** has a ceiling painting of the *Ascension* by Lanfranco in the nave along with 12 *Prophets* by Giuseppe Ribera, who also did the *Institution of the Eucharist* on the left wall of the choir (Lanfranco painted the *Crucifixion* and Guido Reni the *Nativity* at the choir's back wall). In the church treasury is Luca Giordano's ceiling fresco of the *Triumph of Judith* (1704) and Ribera's masterful *Descent from the Cross.*

The vast ✪ **museum of presepi** houses dozens of Neapolitan Christmas crèches with an overall cast of thousands of peasant and holy figures that have come out of the workshops of Naples's greatest craftsmen over the past 4 centuries. The modest **painting and sculpture gallery** houses 15th- to 18th-century works, including a few by Bernini, Caracciolo, and Vaccaro.

Next door to the monastery is the star-shaped **Castel Sant'Elmo** (☎ **081/ 578-4030**), built in a strategic position above the city from 1329 to 1343 by the Angevins. It was enlarged in the 16th century and today offers a magnificent 360° panorama of Naples and its bay after a walk through the dark, echoey, medieval stone halls now used for conferences and exhibitions. Admission is 4,000L ($2.35).

WHERE TO STAY

Ausonia. V. Caracciolo 11 (at the Mergellina docks), 80122 Napoli. ☎ **081/664-536.** Fax 081/682-278. 20 units, 18 with bathroom. TV TEL. 80,000L ($47.05) single without bathroom, 110,000L ($64.70) single with bathroom; 100,000L ($58.80) double without bathroom, 160,000L ($94.10) double with bathroom. Rates include breakfast (request rates without breakfast and save 10,000L/$5.90 a head). AE, MC, V. Parking 25,000–30,000L ($14.70–$17.65). Metro: Mergellina. Bus: tram 1, R3, C16, C24, C21, 140 (to Mergellina).

Situated in the pleasant and safe neighborhood around the hydrofoil docks, the Ausonia is convenient for boats to Capri or Ischia, but you'll have to take a bus or metro to get to the city center. It's location at the back of a harbor front building, means you're cheated of an ocean view, but you're spared the traffic noise of the seaside boulevard. Instead, windows open onto the courtyard or a noisier back alley, and gauzy curtains graze the marble floors in the breeze. The nautical theme—porthole mirrors and ship's helm nightstands—is a bit silly, but accommodations are comfortable and relatively roomy, and the beds are soft but sleep well. Some bathrooms are tiny and the showers curtainless, but all are clean and modern.

Ideal. Pz. Garibaldi 99 (on the left side of the square as you exit the train station), 80142, Napoli. ☎ **081/269-237** or 081/202-223. Fax 081/285-942. 45 units, all with bathroom. TV TEL. 50,000–60,000L ($29.40–$35.30) single; 90,000–100,000L ($52.95–$58.80) double; 130,000L ($76.50) triple. These are special Frommer's rates, so be sure to flash this book. Rates include breakfast. AE, DC, MC, V. Parking 20,000L ($11.75). Metro: Napoli Centrale. Bus: tram 1, R2, 14, 14r, 42, 110 (to Pz. Garibaldi).

The name may be a bit of wishful thinking, but this large, clean budget standby is just 200 feet from the train station (and a 10-minute tram ride from the ferry docks) and indeed ideal if you plan on lots of day trips. It's also a haven of quality and security among many seedy hotels in an often squalid area. It's been family run for 50 years and a renovation in 1998 installed bathrooms in all rooms. Some of the tile floors are fantastically patterned, the walls decorated with simple stuccoes, and while most of the furniture is modular, some of the newest is quite stylish. Several rooms have terraces on the courtyard and are much quieter than those fronting traffic-choked Piazza Garibaldi. The student guidebooks are well aware of this place, so book in advance.

Le Fontane al Mare. Via Niccolú Tommaseo 14 (at V. Partenope), 80121 Napoli. ☎ and fax **081/764-3470.** 20 units, 7 with bathroom. Single without bathroom 67,000L ($39.40), single with bathroom 83,000L ($48.80); double without bathroom 83,000L ($48.80), double with bathroom 111,000L ($64.70); triple without bathroom 113,000L ($66.50), triple with bathroom 151,000L ($88.80). Breakfast 10,000–12,000L ($5.90–$7.05). AE, MC, V. Parking 25,000L ($14.70). Bus: tram 1, R1, R3, C12, C18, C19, C24, C25, C28, 140 (to Piazza Vittoria).

Naples's best bargain in water-view hotels occupies the top floors of a 17th-century palazzo. You trade some comfort for the vistas, price, and safe neighborhood. It's an old-fashioned pensione—few private bathrooms, but in-room sinks, aging tile floors, and high ceilings with crown molding. There are pleasantly incongruous Asian prints on the walls, an amalgam of solid old furnishings and flea-market cast-offs, and, of course, cot springs that are rapidly losing their battle with gravity. Only bathless rooms have sea views, which means plenty of cool breezes across your balcony—along with traffic noise from the boulevard below (one triple has both bathroom and vista). The public bathrooms are clean and large, while the private ones are holdovers from, yep, the sixties, the same era that thought the weird table lamps infesting most rooms were in good taste. The phones aren't direct-dial (the desk will ring you through), and be sure to carry 200L coins for the elevator—unless you relish a five-floor walk-up.

Rex. V. Palepoli 12 (between V. Nazario Sauro and V. Santa Lucia), 80123 Napoli. ☎ **081/764-9389.** Fax 081/764-9227. 38 units, all with bathroom. A/C TV TEL. 130,000L ($76.50) single; 170,000L ($100) double; 195,000L ($114.70) triple. Rates include breakfast. AE, DC, MC, V. Parking 25,000–30,000L ($14.70–$17.65) in hotel garage. Bus: tram 1, R3 (to the end of Galleria d. Vittoria tunnel); C25, 140 (to V. S. Lucia).

Set just off the noisy harbor road, the 1960s Rex is much more modernly comfortable than the nearby Fontane al Mare, making it another great bargain in Naples's toniest area (it's directly behind the top hotels in town). The modular pine furnishings, wicker chairs, hideous port-a-lamps, and brown or speckled-green floor tiles hint at the era in which it was built, but everything's been maintained immaculately, save the odd plumbing glitch. Prints on the walls and the occasional painted ceiling brighten the lackluster decor considerably, and in summer the air-conditioning can be a godsend. Most accommodations are amply sized without being large, and the beds are comfortable enough.

WHERE TO DINE

You can get all the **picnic fixings** you need in the string of little shops lining the first block of Salita S. Anna di Palazzo, off Via Chiaia.

Mimi alla Ferrovia. V. Alfonso d'Aragona 21 (off northwest corner of Pz. Garibaldi). ☎ **081/553-8525.** Reservations recommended. Primi 6,000–18,000L ($3.55–$10.60); secondi 12,000–20,000L ($7.05–$11.75). AE, MC, V. Mon–Sat noon–1am. Closed 1 week in Aug. Metro: Napoli Centrale. Bus: tram 1, R2, 14, 14r, 42, 110 (to Pz. Garibaldi). NEAPOLITAN.

Ceiling frescoes and photos of celebrity patrons give a refined air, almost elegant by Neapolitan standards, to this long-respected restaurant—certainly they help it to rise above the hookers, porn cinemas, and shifty eyes you have to wade through to get here. The few tourists who brave the surrounding streets join tables full of contented local regulars to dig into antipasti of *prosciutto e fichi* (prosciutto and fresh figs), or primi like *linguine alla Mimi* (noodles and scampi) and the rich pea-green *pasta e ceci* (flat pasta squares in a pasty chickpea mash). For secondo order a *bistecca di manzo ai ferri* (grilled steak) or the ever-popular *sogliole fresche mugnai* (sole meunière).

✪ **Osteria al Canterbury.** V. Ascensione 6 (just up from the Riviera Chiaia, down from Pz. Amadeo). ☎ **081/411-658.** Reservations recommended. Primi 7,000–9,000L ($4.10–$5.30); secondi 7,000–14,000L ($4.10–$8.25). AE, MC, V. Sun–Fri 1–4pm, 8pm–midnight; Sat 8pm–midnight. Closed Sun June–Aug and 15 days in Aug. Bus: tram 1, R3, C12, C18, C28, 140 (to Riviera di Chiaia). NEAPOLITAN.

During their courtship, the future Rino and Lilly Adamo had one of those singularly memorable meals in a tiny, friendly, old-fashioned osteria of a dozen wooden tables with high-back straw-seated chairs set on terra-cotta floors. They decided on the spot that one day, they'd open a place of their own just like it, and thus the Canterbury was born. Its name is apt, since it's cozy in a vaguely British manner: close tables set with flowers, a modest chandelier, dark wood cupboards, little curtains. Trust your waiter's advice implicitly. Perhaps he'll suggest starting with *paccheri con coccio* (wide pasta loops in a light sauce of baby tomatoes and local fish) or *maccheroni di casa Canterbury* (pasta with tomatoes, cheese, and eggplant). Move on to no-nonsense secondi like *agnello alla brace* (grilled lamb) or *petto di pollo in vino bianco* (chicken breast cooked in white wine), and definitely cap it all off with the homemade tiramisu.

Pizzeria Brandi. Salita S. Anna di Palazzo 1–2 (just off V. Chiaia, 2 blocks up from Pz. Trieste e Trento). ☎ **081/416-928.** www.brandi.it. Reservations highly recommended. Primi 9,000–17,000L ($5.30–$10); secondi 10,000–22,000L ($5.90–$12.95); pizza 7,000–13,000L ($4.10–$7.65). AE, DC, MC, V. Daily noon–3:30pm, 7:30pm–midnight. Closed Aug 14–16. Bus: R2, R3, V10, C22, C25, 24 (to V. S. Cairo/Pz. Trieste e Trento). PIZZA/NEAPOLITAN.

Naples's most famous and heavily touristed pizzeria is so proud of its traditions that rather than hide the kitchen, Brandi displays prominently the blue-and-white–tiled wood-fired oven and gleaming marble counters where skilled pizzaioli ply their craft. Popular legend holds that it was on this very spot in 1889 that, in honor of a visit by the first queen of a newly unified Italy, the pizzaiolo concocted a patriotic pizza modeled after the colors in the country's new flag: white *mozzarella di bufala*, red tomato sauce, and green basil. They named it after the queen herself, pizza Margherita. Book ahead for one of the six outside tables, or be contented with restaurant-style dining on cloth-covered tables inside. Although the hordes descend here just for the pizza (which is actually pretty good), Brandi does offer pasta dishes like linguine agli scampi, and some secondi as well, such as scaloppine al limone.

Pizzeria Port'Alba. V. Port'Alba 18 (between Pz. Bellini and Pz. Dante). ☎ **081/459-713.** Reservations not accepted. Primi 5,000–22,000L ($2.95–$12.95); secondi 6,000–20,000L ($3.55–$11.75); pizza 5,000–13,000L ($2.95–$7.65). AE, DC, MC, V. Thurs–Tues noon–2:30am. Closed 1 wk in Aug. Bus: E1, R1, R4, V10, 24, 137 (to Pz. Dante). PIZZA/NEAPOLITAN.

After a thorough and arduous survey of Naples's top pizzeria, I can honestly report that the Port'Alba, notwithstanding its touristy location and ability to accommodate bus groups, serves the tastiest pizza Margherita in Naples. On a pedestrian side street in the heart of old Naples—2 blocks from the archaeological museum or from Santa Chiara—the Port'Alba is said to be Naples's oldest pizzeria (est. 1738). You can dine on the alley under umbrellas or in the air-conditioned upstairs area. If that scrumptious margherita doesn't grab you—and you don't feel like going in for *pizza lasagna* (with ricotta) or *port'alba* (covered with shellfish) either—there's a wide menu that goes well beyond pizza that includes linguine al cartoccio as well as fresh fish or a nice veal scallop in Marsala wine.

Ristorante Umberto. V. Alabardieri 30–31 (2 blocks behind the Chiaia park at the Santa Lucia end, near Pz. d. Martiri). ☎ **081/418-555.** Reservations recommended. Primi 3,500–18,000L ($2.05–$10.60); secondi 8,500–21,000L ($5–$12.35); pizza 6,000–10,000L ($3.55–$5.90). AE, DC, MC, V. Tues–Sun noon–3:30pm, 7:30pm–midnight. Closed Aug 2–27. Bus: tram 1, R1, R3, C12, C18, C19, C24, C25, C28, 140 (to Pz. Vittoria). NEAPOLITAN/PIZZA.

The Umberto is a touch of class among Naples's minimalist eateries, a restaurant atmosphere at trattoria prices. Waistcoated waiters bring you tidbits to nibble while you choose between a pizza or a primo of *spaghetti alle vongole* or *pasta e lenticchie* (pasta with lentils). The walls are stark white, hung with antique mirrors and pictures. Cutting through the bustle and convivial chatter of satisfied diners are the folksy strains of a guitar player—no street busker but a restaurant fixture who belts out Neapolitan *bel canto* all evening long (it sounds touristy, but the clientele's largely Italian, and the locals even sing along sometimes). Among the hearty secondi are *impepata di cozze* (peppery mussel stew), fresh fish, or *involtini alla Umberto* (veal wrapped around prosciutto and provolone then stewed in a mushroom-and-pea sauce). There's a connected tromp l'oeiled pizzeria in back if you just want to pop in for a quick pie.

Vini e Cucina. Cor. V. Emanuele 762 (across the street and down a tad from the Mergellina train station). ☎ **081/660-302.** Reservations not accepted. Primi 5,000–10,000L ($2.95–$5.90); secondi 5,000–16,000L ($2.95–$9.40). No credit cards. Mon–Sat noon–4pm, 7pm–midnight. Closed Aug 10–30. Metro: Mergellina. Bus: tram 1, R3, C16, C24, C21, 140 (to Mergellina). NEAPOLITAN.

Michele's Mocci'a nine-table joint across from the Mergellina station is often crowded with locals, and the genial owner likes to take charge of your meal—sometimes even serving you what he thinks you should eat rather than what, in a strictly technical sense, you actually ordered. His basic spaghetti al pomodoro is okay, but much better are the *melanzane al parmigiana* (eggplant strips laden with tomatoes, mozzarella, and Parmesan), and his fresh fish secondi *alla brace* (grilled), including *pescespada* (a swordfish steak). It's a homey place; for dessert you can order the brownielike almond and chocolate cake made by Michele's mother.

CAFES

The grand dame of Neapolitan cafes is the 1860 ✪ **Gran Caffè Gambrinus,** Piazza Trieste e Trento (☎ **081/417-582**), where intellectuals and writers as diverse as Gabrielle d'Annunzio and Oscar Wilde have gathered since 1860 under the stuccoes, silks, and frescoes of the belle epoque interior. The ambience is a perfect background to enjoy an (albeit pricey) cappuccino and *sfogliatella* (Naples's premier pastry, a cream-stuffed horn made of flaky mille feuille dough). There's outdoor seating with an elegant view of the Teatro San Carlo, the Royal Palace, and Piazza Plebescito—but also plenty of noise and fumes from the cars that roar down Via Toledo to turnstile around the traffic circle at your back. It's closed Tuesdays and in August.

The pastry shop and bar **Scaturchio,** Pz. S. Domenico 19 (☎ **081/551-6944**), has also long been a favored spot to sample the rich bounty of Neapolitan pastry, though the setting is far less elegant (and prices a bit lower). You'll find the best gelato in town at **Gelateria della Scimmia,** Pz. Carità 4 (☎ **081/552-0272**), established in 1934; and the **Gran Bar Riviera,** Riviera di Chiaia 183 (no phone), which opened in 1860 and claims to have invented the tartufo ice cream ball.

A POMPEIIAN PRELUDE: HERCULANEUM

GETTING HERE   The private **Circumvesuviana rail** line (☎ **081/772-2444**) services Herculaneum (15 min; 2,200L/$1.30), Vesuvius (same stop), Pompeii, and Sorrento (the latter two are covered later in this chapter). It leaves from its own station in Naples on Corso Garibaldi, just south of Naples's central station, every 20 minutes (you can also catch Circumvesuviana trains underneath the main "Stazione Centrale" itself; follow the signs).

EXPLORING THE AREA   Pompeii gets all the press, but ✪ Herculaneum (☎ **081/739-0963**) is just as enthralling. Unlike workaday Pompeii, this ancient Roman city was a resort and retirement town for the rich, scenically set on the shore under the menacing bulk of Vesuvius. It suffered serious damage in the earthquake of A.D. 63, and was still rebuilding when the big one hit. In A.D. 79 Vesuvius blew its lid in the most famous eruption in human history, and Herculaneum was buried in a tidal wave of liquid mud that came thundering down the mountain to envelope the city with up to 82 feet of burning mud, sand, and rocks.

The archaeological site is considerably smaller than that of Pompeii. Herculaneum was around one-third the size, with about 5,000 inhabitants to Pompeii's 20,000, but the houses belonged to the wealthy and were much more elaborate, extensive, and sumptuously decorated—and more intact. Many still have their second stories. Floor mosaics, wall frescoes, ceiling stuccoes, and even wooden furnishings have all been preserved. Plenty of plebeian houses are mixed in as well, along with shops like the bakery with its stone grain grinders set up in the backyard.

For a long time, scholars believed that most of Herculaneum's inhabitants had time to escape, since only six bodies were found in the streets and houses (this compared to the 2,000 found at Pompeii). Then in 1982, while excavating around the docks at what was the shoreline in ancient times, a worker discovered hundreds upon hundreds of bodies, scorched by volcanic gasses right down to the bone, huddled in the dock houses. They had died waiting for the boats to carry them to safety.

Admission to Herculaneum is 12,000L ($7.05). It's open daily 9am to an hour before sunset.

Herculaneum

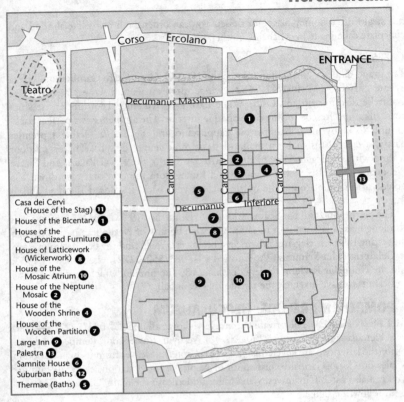

Casa dei Cervi
(House of the Stag) **11**
House of the Bicentary **1**
House of the
Carbonized Furniture **3**
House of Latticework
(Wickerwork) **8**
House of the
Mosaic Atrium **10**
House of the Neptune
Mosaic **2**
House of the
Wooden Shrine **4**
House of the
Wooden Partition **7**
Large Inn **9**
Palestra **13**
Samnite House **6**
Suburban Baths **12**
Thermae (Baths) **5**

2 Pompeii

20 km (12 mi.) SE of Naples, 15 km (9 mi.) SE of Herculaneum, 33 km (20 mi.) NE of Sorrento.

Though the ancient Oscan city of ✪ **Pompeii,** founded before the 6th century B.C., had its ups and downs, by A.D. 1st century it was a Roman colony of 20,000 and a thriving, bustling seaport. It occupied a prime stretch of coastline southeast of *Neapolis* (Naples), just on the other side of that huge mountain called Vesuvius. After 14 years of hard work, Pompeii was just getting back on its architectural feet following the massive earthquake of A.D. 63. The columns of the forum had been reerected, and villa owners had piled lime next to the last walls that needed replastering. They thought the worst was over.

At noon, August 24, A.D. 79, the peak of Mt. Vesuvius exploded, sending a mottled black-and-white mushroom cloud 12 miles into the air at twice the speed of sound, raining ash and light pumice down on the region. For 12 hours, the sheer force of the eruption kept that cloud aloft. Some Pompeiians fled. But more than 2,000 bodies have been uncovered at Pompeii—these souls probably thought the enormous cloud hanging over Vesuvius was just smoke, and saw no need to leave. When the cloud finally collapsed, the horror engulfed the city before anyone could run more than a few feet. Pompeii was buried by a pyroclastic flow, a superfast rush of hot ash and pumice with an undercurrent of rock and burning gasses, all of which came barreling down the mountain like a tidal wave, the force ripping the doors and roofs off houses, fusing metal house keys to skulls, and dismembering human bodies.

The Smoldering Mt. Vesuvius

Though one of the smallest and least regularly active volcanoes in the world, Vesuvius is one of the most famously destructive. The only active volcano on continental Europe, the 4,214-foot-high, broad cone of Mt. Vesuvius dominates the Bay of Naples from the northeastern shore. Its unexpected eruption in A.D. 79, buried the Roman cities of Herculaneum and Pompeii in ash and mud, but its activity has been sporadic ever since—the last time it even put on any mild fireworks was back in 1944.

To visit the surprisingly calm, rather plain gravel-filled depression that is Vesuvius' crater, take the Circumvesuviana train **from Naples or Sorrento** to the Ercolano stop, from which there's a special bus (☎ **081/739-2833**) five times daily up to the Colle Margherita parking lot (55 min.; 6,000L/$3.55). A guide (5,000L/$2.95) will walk you the 10 minutes from here to the crater's rim, a barren landscape with unparalleled views across Campania on clear days. The last return bus leaves Vesuvius at 5:30pm. You can also catch a "Trasporti Vesuviani" bus here five times daily **from Pompei,** down in the modern town's Piazza Anfiteatro, for 10,000L ($5.90) round-trip.

The 17-year-old Pliny the Younger was across the bay at the time, and he saw "a cloud of unusual size and appearance . . . like an umbrella pine." His uncle, the famed writer Pliny the Elder, fared worse. When he saw the volcano go, he took some boats to try to evacuate friends from a village on the shore below the mountain. The elder Pliny dictated his impressions to a scribe as they sailed, but the great author succumbed to the poisonous gasses while ashore and suffocated.

GETTING HERE   From Naples, take the half-hourly private Circumvesuviana train (☎ 081/772-2444) toward Sorrento and get off at POMPEII-VILLA DEI MISTERI (27 to 40 min; 3,100L/$1.80). En route, this train passes through **Ercolano** (20 min; 2,000L/$1.20). (**Note:** There are four Circumvesuviana lines and a bit of confusion: One of the two lines headed to Sarno diverges just before the site and also features a stop called "Pompei," but this is for the modern town, *not* the archaeological site.) This half-hourly Circumvesuviana train also runs **to or from Sorrento** (20 min; 2,200L/$1.30).

The bar in the train station will let you **leave your luggage** for 2,000L ($1.20) per bag until 6pm. Turn right out of the station, and the entrance to the site is just a few hundred feet down on your left. Continue down this road to enter modern Pompei after about ten minutes.

VISITOR INFORMATION   The ticket booth at the archaeological site will give you the free map and all you really need to explore Pompeii. There's also a tourist office in modern Pompei at V. Sacra 1 (☎ **081/850-7255;** fax 081/863-2401; www.uniplan.it/pompei/azienda), open Monday to Friday 9am to 2:30pm, Saturday and Sunday 9am to 2pm.

The "I's" Have It

No, you're not seeing things. "Pompeii" (with two *i's*) refers to the ancient city and archaeological site. "Pompei" (with one *i*) is the official name of the modern town just next door. Apparently, the second *i* got buried by Vesuvius along with everything else in A.D. 79.

HOURS & ADMISSION   Admission to Pompeii is 12,000L ($7.05); the site is open daily 9am to an hour before sunset (as early as 3:45pm in December, 8pm June to August).

EXPLORING THE ANCIENT CITY

Pompeii was not buried entirely; in fact the top floors of many houses poked above the new ground level. But between survivors returning to dig for personal belongings, the inevitable looters, and later farmers plowing their fields over the site, these building tops where shorn off. Within a few generations, incredibly, Pompeii was forgotten. In 1594, the architect Domenico Fontana was building an aqueduct through the area when he struck the ruins of Pompeii quite by accident. Most of the excavations have been carried out since the 18th century.

The ✪ **archaeological site** (☎ 081/861-0744; www.uniplan.it/ruins) is now enclosed, and takes a good, full day to explore. At the very least, it takes four hours to pop into the major sights. The roads are made of stone slabs, rutted deep with centuries' worth of wagon wheels. At most intersections are crosswalks of raised stepping stones—so citizens wouldn't have to step in the mucky, muddy streets. Besides the public buildings and mansions I'll highlight below, Pompeii is full of buildings that may be more pedestrian, but are just as fascinating for the insight they offer into daily life in an ancient Roman city. Poke around to find the shops with counters still in place and paintings describing the wares sold, bakeries with millstones and brick ovens in the backyard, even fast-food parlors with deep bowls set into the counters where prepared food was kept hot.

The ✪ **Forum,** the central square of any Roman city, sits a few blocks up from the entrance. Around the edges you'll see that there was once a two-story colonnade, its 470-foot length oriented so that, ironically, "scenic" Mt. Vesuvius serves as a natural backdrop. At the northern end of the eastern edge is a small room with a countertop embedded with bowl-shape depressions of increasing sizes. The Forum was also a central marketplace, and to forestall arguments between buyer and seller, these were used as the city's standards of measure.

Plaster casts of bodies are located just past the measuring table in an enclosed building. During the early excavations, archaeologists realized that the ash had packed around dying Pompeiians and hardened almost instantly. The bodies decayed, leaving just the skeletons lying in human-shaped air pockets under the ground. Holes were drilled down to a few and plaster was poured in, taking a rough cast of the moment of death. Some people writhe in agony. A dog, chained to a post, turns to bite desperately at his collar. One man sits on the ground, covering his face in grief.

Exit the Forum onto Via dell Abbondanza, detouring left down Via del Teatro to see the **Teatro Grande,** a 2nd-century B.C. theater that could seat 5,000. Under the stage lay a reservoir so that water would flood the area during mock naval battle scenes

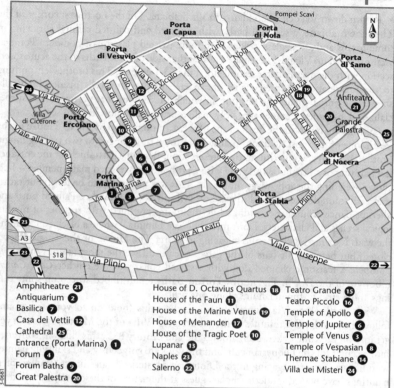

Pompei Scavi

Porta di Capua

Porta di Nola

Porta di Vesuvio

Porta di Samo

Anfiteatro

Villa di Cicerone

Porta Ercolano

Grande Palestra

Porta di Nocera

Porta Marina

Porta di Stabia

Viale Ai Teatri

Via Plinio

Viale Giuseppe

Amphitheatre 21	House of D. Octavius Quartus 18	Teatro Grande 15
Antiquarium 2	House of the Faun 11	Teatro Piccolo 16
Basilica 7	House of the Marine Venus 19	Temple of Apollo 5
Casa dei Vettii 12	House of Menander 17	Temple of Jupiter 6
Cathedral 25	House of the Tragic Poet 10	Temple of Venus 3
Entrance (Porta Marina) 1	Lupanar 13	Temple of Vespasian 8
Forum 4	Naples 23	Thermae Stabiane 14
Forum Baths 9	Salerno 22	Villa dei Misteri 24
Great Palestra 20		

(some suggest the water also helped amplify the acoustics during performances). Nearby on Via Stabiana is the **Odeon** or **Teatro Piccolo,** a much smaller theater (seating 1,000) used mainly for concerts. The **House of Menander** has painted scenes from the Trojan cycle in some rooms, and a floor mosaic of the Nile in the peristyle (members of the family that lived here were all found together, huddled in one room, killed when the roof caved in on them).

Past the intersection with Via Stabiana, long **Via dell Abbondanza** marks the site of the "New Excavations," undertaken since 1911. Many of the houses on both sides of this street retain their second stories. While those on the north/left side haven't been excavated much beyond the facades, those on the right have. And unlike in much of the older, more famous excavations (north of the Forum; we'll get there in a minute), many of the frescoes, mosaics, and statuary have been left in place rather than shipped off to a museum.

Among the houses along this street, be sure you pop into the **House of D. Octavius Quartius,** with lots of good frescoes and replanted gardens; and the **House of the Marine Venus,** with a large wall painting of the goddess stretched out on a clamshell. Near the end of the street, turn right to walk through the **Great Palestra**—a huge open space shaded by umbrella pines where the city's youths went to work out and play sports (many came here seeking shelter from the eruption; their skeletons were found huddled in the corner latrine)—to the **Amphitheater.** Built in 80 B.C., this is the oldest amphitheater in the world, and could hold 12,000 spectators who, according to the records, were just as wont to break into a brawl in the stands as watch the gladiators fighting on the field below.

Return down Via dell Abbondanza to Via Stabiana. On the northwest corner sit the **Thermae Stabiane,** a series of baths with stuccoed and painted ceilings surviving in some rooms and a few glass caskets with more twisted plaster cast bodies of Pompeii victims. Head up Vico del Lupanare on the other side of these baths to the acute intersection with the overhanging second story, the ✪ **Lupanar.** This brothel left nothing to the imagination. Painted scenes above each of the little cells inside graphically showed potential clients the position in which the lady of that particular room specialized. Until a few decades ago, only male tourists were allowed in to see it.

Continuing north to the heart of the Old Excavations, stop by the ✪ **House of the Vettii,** one of the most luxurious mansions in town (it belonged to two trading mogul brothers) and in a wonderful state of preservation. Behind a glass shield at the entrance is a painting of a priapus, a little guy with a grotesquely oversized male member—here shown weighing the appendage on a scale. This was not meant to be lewd, but rather was a common device believed to ward off evil spirits and thoughts. Painted putti and cherubs dance around the atrium while the rooms are filled with frescoes of mythological scenes and characters. Don't miss the "Sala Dipinta," where a black band around the walls is painted with cherubs engaging in sports. The **House of the Tragic Poet** is closed, but between the bars of the gate you can still see the most famous mosaic in Pompeii: a fearsome chained dog with a spiked collar and the epithet *Cave Canem* ("Beware of the Dog"). The nearby **Forum Baths** retain ribbed stucco on some ceilings and a strip of tiny telamons along one wall.

Walk north along Via Consolare to exit the ruins (hold on to your ticket) and follow the path for five minutes to the suburban ✪ **Villa of the Mysteries,** which you get into on the same ticket. Built around the 2nd century B.C., this villa was converted into a center for the Dionysian cult, and the walls are gorgeously and skillfully painted with life-size figures engaging in the Dionysian Mysteries of an initiate (though these paintings have helped modern scholars guess at the nature of these rites, we still don't know exactly what was involved). The scenes play out against a background of such deep, intense red that the color used is still called "Pompeiian red."

WHERE TO STAY & DINE

Motel Villa dei Misteri. V. Villa d. Misteri 11, 80045 Pompei (NA). ☎ **081/861-3593.** Fax 081/862-2983. ptn.pandora.it/hmisteri. 40 units, all with bathroom. 80,000L ($47.05) single or double. Breakfast 7,500L ($4.40). AE, DC, MC, V. Free parking. ¼ mile from site entrance and train station; turn left upon exiting station.

This remains the bland roadside inn of choice for die-hard archaeology buffs who want to sleep a stone's throw from the excavations (the entrance is a 2-minute walk downhill). Once you get past the cement bunker exterior, the amply sized rooms are pleasant enough, with balconies, shiny new tile floors, well-worn but serviceable furnishings, and recently overhauled bathrooms (although there's no place to hang the hand-held shower nozzles). The mattresses, however, still rest on lazy-springed cots. But the air-conditioning (available only in the 20 rooms of the main building for 15,000L/$8.80 per day) and statue-ringed pool (open late May to October) do wonders for its appeal. A walkway suspended above the pool leads to the decent but unmemorable restaurant, and there's a TV lounge with small bar area for mingling.

Zi Caterina. V. Roma 20. ☎ **081/850-7447** or 081/863-1263. Reservations recommended. Primi 10,000–15,000L ($5.90–$8.80); secondi 10,000–25,000L ($5.90–$14.70). AE, DC, MC, V. Wed–Mon noon–11pm. CAMPANIAN.

Among the countless glorified pizza joints with polyglot menus on modern Pompei's main drag, Zi Caterina stands out for its solid cooking and reasonable prices. The cavernous single room, antiqued with lots of wood, can get noisy as it fills up and the strolling troubadour starts strumming his guitar. The delicious risotto alla pescatora is heavily laden with shellfish, calamari, and shrimp, and the gnocchi alla sorrentina is also good. Secondi tend to be fishy as well, with a beach platter *sauté di frutti di mare* (clams, oysters, and mussels) or *baccalà* (dried salt cod), but landlubbers can always order *coniglio alla cacciatora* (rabbit stewed with tomatoes and mushrooms). If you're watching every lira, 10,000L ($5.90) will get you a pizza and soda.

3 Capri

4.8 km (3 mi.) off the tip of the Sorrentine peninsula

Capri is an island of seduction. It's 4 square miles of sharp lava blanketed with lush green foliage, white cube houses, and walls spilling over with bougainvillea. This Eden of oleander and jasmine is surrounded by sparkling deep blue and green waters and eerily lit sea grottoes. Capri's sheer physical beauty and dreamy laid-back lifestyle has attracted sun-seekers for millennia, from Roman emperors to latter-day hedonists. Homer certainly chose his spot well when he designated this island to be the home of the mythical Sirens, beautiful but monstrous flesh-eating women who lived on the off-shore rocks and sang an irresistible song to lure ancient sailors to their doom. Capri's allure today is still almost as strong, though the only doom you're likely to face these days is financial (case in point: the famed Blue Grotto has the highest admission of any sight in Italy).

Most visitors pop over on the ferry in the morning, fork over the lire for a quick row through the Blue Grotto, gawk at the obscene prices in Capri boutiques, or hike out to explore the ruins of Tiberius's Villa. Capri by day, especially in summer, experiences a tourist crush that veritably sucks the magic right out of the island. If at all possible, spend the night. As the day-trippers leave on the 5pm ferry, the cloying sounds and scents of Capri creep out of hiding along with the local population. They reclaim the island, restoring some of its Mediterranean mystery and a great deal of its charm and seductiveness. Take your extra day to visit the mountainside village of Anacapri, hike the undeveloped side of the island, or ride the chairlift up Monte Solaro for a panoramic sweep of the Bay.

ESSENTIALS

GETTING HERE   By Ferry or Hydrofoil   The *aliscafo* (hydrofoil) from Naples takes 40 minutes and costs 15,900L ($9.35). **Caremar** (☎ **081/837-0700;** caremar. gestelnet.it) and **NLG** (☎ **081/837-0819**) hydrofoils leave from Naples's Molo Beverello dock; **SNAV** (☎ **081/837-7577**) hydrofoils leave from Naples's Mergellina docks. *Traghetti* (**Ferries) from Naples's** Molo Beverello (1 hr. 15 min.; 8,800L/ $5.20) are run by Caremar.

The **LMV** (☎ **081/837-6995**) **hydrofoil from Sorrento** takes 20 minutes and costs 10,000L ($5.90). Both Caremar and LMV run 50-minute **ferries from Sorrento** for 7,000L ($4.10).

LUGGAGE STORAGE   There's a **luggage deposit** office in Capri Town, under the funicular station on the tunnel part of Via Acquaviva (follow signs for "*toilette*"); it costs 3,000L ($1.75) per bag per day. You can also drop off your luggage in Naples.

GETTING AROUND   You arrive on Capri at **Marina Grande,** the busy, touristy main port. A bus or funicular will take you up to Capri, the main town and home to most of the boutique shopping, posh hotels, chic nightlife, and Beautiful People (Tom Cruise, Nicole Kidman, and Julia Roberts all visited just while I was on the island researching this chapter). The center of Capri (the town) is **Piazza Umberto I,** called by everyone the **Piazzetta.** Out the other side of Capri is **Marina Piccola,** a smaller

---

This Boat's for You

When shopping for a boat out to Capri at Naples's Molo Beverello, there's no need to shop all the dock offices for the best price. **Ontano Tours** (☎ **081/580-0341**) is a central clearing house, located just to the left of the driveway leading into the dock area. This travel agency will book you on the next ferry or hydrofoil out, tell you which line it is, and sell you a voucher that you then carry to that line's dock office to trade in for a ticket—all at no extra cost.

---

yachting port consisting of several restaurant/beach establishments. Capri and the ports occupy the narrowest part of the island, from which a mountain rises in either direction. Halfway up the larger of these, Monte Solaro, sits the village of **Anacapri,** Capri town's historic rival but today the cooler, calmer, cheaper, and slightly less crowded and developed of the two towns—if any of village life survives on this touristy island, it's in Anacapri.

By Bus   Rides on Capri's miniature orange buses cost 1,500L (90¢)—when they bother collecting your money (to get on at Capri town's main depot, buy a ticket at the window; on any other ride you just pay the driver). When you arrive at Marina Grande and get to the base of the dock, straight ahead to the left is a funicular up to Capri (1,500L/90¢; every 15 min.). For buses to Capri (also every 15 min.) and Anacapri (at least once an hour), turn right at the dock's end and walk 200 feet up to the turnabout in the road. There are bus connections between Capri town's depot on Piazza Martiri d'Ungheria and: Anacapri (every 15 min.), Marina Grande, and Marina Piccola (every 30 min.). In Anacapri, the buses for Marina Grande (every 50 min.), Marina Piccola (at 10am and 11am), and Capri town leave from Piazza Caprile, passing through Piazza Vittoria. The depot for Anacapri's buses to the Blue Grotto and those to the Faro swimming hole (both every 20 min.) is on **Via de Tommaso.** For information on those last two bus routes, call ☎ **081/837-1544;** for all other bus routes and the funicular call ☎ **081/837-0420.**

On Foot   Capri has some gorgeous walks, but most have a significant grade to them. I wouldn't recommend the steep, uphill hike from Capri to Anacapri—although the reverse is doable in about half an hour, if you don't mind a little vertigo and walking primarily on the nonexistent shoulder of the main road (the Greek-era Scala Fenicia stairs connecting Marina Grande and Anacapri are in such bad repair they've been closed). From Capri, you can easily stroll down to Marina Grande in about 15 minutes, to Marina Piccola in 20 minutes. From Anacapri, you can reach the Faro in 20 minutes or the Blue Grotto in half an hour.

By Taxi   Taxis congregate wherever tourists do. You can often bargain, but to go anywhere usually costs about 25,000L ($14.70). There are stands in Capri on Piazza Martiri d'Ungheria, Anacapri on Piazza Vittoria, and at the docks of Marina Grande and Marina Piccola. You can also call for one in Capri at ☎ **081/837-0543;** in Anacapri at ☎ **081/837-1175.**

VISITOR INFORMATION   If you pop into the little tourist office along the right side of the ferry dock (☎ **081/837-0634**), there's no need to visit the similarly tiny offices in Capri, Pz. Umberto I 1, open Monday to Saturday 8:30am to 8:30pm, Sunday 9am to 1pm and 2:30 to 6pm (☎ **081/837-0686**); or Anacapri, V. G. Orlando 19a (just off Piazza Vittoria), open Monday to Saturday 9am to 3pm (☎ **081/837-1524**). The free map is fine, but if you plan on a lot of hiking and exploring, you'll want to by the more detailed version for 1,500L (90¢).

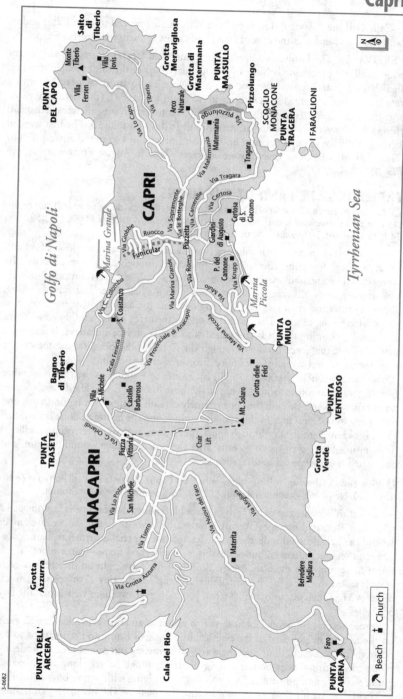

Golfo di Napoli

Tyrrhenian Sea

CAPRI

ANACAPRI

PUNTA DEL CAPO

PUNTA DELL' ARCERA

Grotta Azzurra

PUNTA TRASETE

PUNTA VENTROSO

Grotta Verde

PUNTA MULO

Cala del Rio

PUNTA CARENA

Faro

Belvedere Migliara

Materita

San Michele

Via Tuoro

Via Lo Pozzo

Via Grotta Azzurra

Via Nuova del Faro

Via Migliara

Piazza Vittoria

Chair Lift

Mt. Solaro

Grotta delle Felci

Villa S. Michele

Castello Barbarossa

Via G. Orlandi

Bagno di Tiberio

S. Coastanzo

Scala Fenicia

Via Provinciale di Anacapri

Via C. Colombo

Marina Grande

Ruocco

Funicular

Via Giobbe

Via Sopramonte

Via le Botteghe

Piazzetta

Via Roma

Via Marina Grande

Via Mulo

Via Marina Piccola

Marina Piccola

P. del Cannone

Giardini di Augusto

Via Krupp

Via Camerelle

Via Certosa

Certosa di S. Giacomo

Via Tragara

Via Matermania

Matermania

Tragara

Arco Naturale

Pizzolungo

Via Pizzolungo

Grotta di Matermania

Grotta Meravigliosa

PUNTA MASSULLO

SCOGLIO MONACONE

PUNTA TRAGERA

I FARAGLIONI

Monte Tiberio

Villa Jovis

Villa Fersen

Salto di Tiberio

Via Tiberio

Via Lo Capo

↗ Beach   ✝ Church

3-0682

649

CapriOnLine (www.capri.it) is the best Web site for general info on Capri and its businesses, and includes the official tourist office site (e-mail: touristoffice@capri.it).

FESTIVALS The festival of Capri's patron saint **San Costanzo** traditionally opens with an all-out procession behind a silver reliquary bust of the saint (people stand on their balconies and strew flower petals on the bust as it passes) on May 14, with a repeat procession from Marina Grande up to Capri on May 16 (this date may vary), and there are concerts and other community-sponsored events all week. Anacapri throws its own version to honor **St. Antonio di Padova** on June 13. The first week of January, **folklore groups** perform on the main piazzas of Capri and Anacapri. The Villa Axel Munthe hosts free **"sunset concerts"** June to August Fridays at 7:45pm (☎ 081/764-0737).

EXPLORING THE LAND OF THE SIRENS

✪ **Grotta Azzurra (Blue Grotto).** Boat from Marina Grande docks or walk (1 hr.) or bus (15 min.) from Anacapri to entrance. No phone. Admission Mon–Sat 23,000L ($13.50); Sun 24,500L ($14.40). Daily 9am–1 hr. before sunset.

Capri's biggest claim to fame is this long, low sea cavern whose water glows a brilliant, unearthly blue from the effect of light refracting through an entrance tunnel. **Be warned:** The scandalous wallet-gouging admission only gets you a quick 3-minute row through, the walls echoing unromantically with a half dozen boatfuls of oohing, ahhing tourists and their oarsmen spewing out facts (occasionally true ones) or, even worse, attempting to sing. That tunnel in one of the cave's walls that they often point out, usually claiming that it is connected with a villa of Tiberius above, is actually a natural fissure that leads nowhere (though the Roman villa above did use the cave as a nymphaeum, and several statues were discovered at the bottom).

You can save about 10,000L ($5.90) by busing or walking to the grotto entrance from Anacapri and just forking over for the boat into the caves. Hardy souls sometimes buddy up and swim in, but be extremely careful: There's a strong undertow and only a few feet of clearance in the entrance tunnel, and the boatmen don't leave much room between them to slip through (plus, they'll scream at you, pretending it's illegal to swim in). Don't even try to go until after the boatmen leave around 5:30pm, and only when the seas are extraordinarily placid.

✪ **Villa Jovis (Tiberius' Villa).** Follow signs from Capri's Piazzetta up V. di Botteghe (a 40-min. hike). No phone. Admission 4,000L ($2.35). Daily 9am to 1 hr. before sunset.

Set majestically at the top of a 977-foot sheer bluff above the sea, this is but one of 12 villas that Roman Emperor Tiberius built on his favorite island. You can clamber around the half-decayed walls that once defined the imperial apartments, baths complex, and servant's quarters, but none of it is in very good shape—come more for the romantic setting than the archaeology. Built into the ruins right on the cliff's edge at what is called the Salto di Tiberio ("Tiberius' Leap") is the tiny 17th-century church of Santa Maria del Soccorso, which treats you to a great sweeping view across the Bay of Naples.

Rome's second emperor, Tiberius, rose to power as an army general. After 12 years on the throne, he got tired of the political infighting of Rome and semiretired to his beloved Capri. A gruff, dour man, he was swift in meting out punishments, prudently modest in refusing most honors during his reign, tough to get along with, second guess, or bribe, and probably a little too fond of dallying with young boys and girls.

Tiberius spent his final 10 years throwing banquets on the island and communicating imperial decrees to the mainland by signaling with flashing lights. For centuries, we moderns have taken the famous ancient chronicler Suetonius's depiction of the emperor as gospel truth, which is why Tiberius has gone down in history as the man who, sitting in judgment at this cliff-top villa, ". . .ordered his victims, after prolonged and skillful torture, to be thrown into the sea before his very eyes. Below, a company of sailors beat them with boat hooks until the life was crushed from their bodies."

However, had Suetonius lived today, he probably would have been a reporter for *Hard Copy*. There is little doubt his reports were greatly exaggerated if not outright fabricated. The worst of Tiberius's crimes were letting the empire founder a bit while he was on his island retreat, and naming his certifiably deranged nephew Caligula as heir.

Villa San Michele (Villa Axel Munthe). V. Axel Munthe (a continuation of V. Capodimonte), Anacapri. ☎ **081/837-1401.** Admission 6,000L ($3.55). Nov–Feb 10:30am–3:30pm, Mar 9:30am–4:30pm, Apr and Oct 9:30am–5pm, May–Sept 9am–6pm.

The Swedish autobiographer, bird fancier, and selfless doctor Axel Munthe (1857–1949) had a love of Capri and an eye for stupendous, magical views. He built his classically inspired villa to capitalize on vistas and naturally frame the essences of Capri's beauty, whether it be crumbling walls overflowing with bougainvillea, arbored paths centered on copies of Greek bronzes, ancient columns supporting whitewashed Gothic arches, miniature temples hidden in lush gardens, or a bust-lined balustrade beyond which spill breathtaking panoramas of the island and azure waters. Inside, the villa is filled with archaeological knickknacks and memorabilia of the good doctor and his famous book, *The Story of San Michele.*

Chiesa di San Michele. Pz. S. Nicola, Anacapri. ☎ **081/837-2396.** Admission 2,000L ($1.20). Nov–Mar daily 10am–3pm, Apr–Oct daily 9am–7pm.

This 18th-century church is floored with a fantastical studied majolica representation of the *Garden of Eden* (1761), filled with remarkable detail and dozens of exotic plants and beasts. You can get an overall view from the choir loft.

Monte Solaro. *Seggovia* (chairlift) at V. Caposcuro 10 (of Pz. d. Vittoria). ☎ **081/837-1428.** Chairlift 7,500L ($4.40) round-trip. Wed–Mon Mar–Oct 9:30am–sunset, Nov–Feb 10:30am–3pm.

At 1945 feet, Monte Solaro is Capri's highest point, sporting a romantically ruined little 1806 British castle (built medieval-style) that offers dreamy island vistas and a ✪ **panorama of coastal Italy** that on clear days stretches as far as Calabria to the south and north almost to Rome. The ski liftlike *seggovia* takes 12 minutes to get up there; the steep walk takes an hour (the walk down, through the Valley of Santa Maria a Cetrella, is a pleasantly scenic workout). The chairlift was closed in 1998 for repairs, but it should be running again by the time this book hits the shelves.

SCENIC WALKS

Capri to the Arco Naturale/Matermania & Punta Tragara (90 min.)   Take Via Matermania out of Capri for a refreshing 20-minute walk to Le Grotelle restaurant. Here the path diverges left (1 min.) for the **Arco Naturale,** a high archway formed naturally by erosion in a spectacularly lush setting, or right (10 min.) for the steps down to the **Grotta di Matermania,** a cave adapted by the Romans to a temple for orgiastic rites in honor of the goddess Cybele (the Mater Magna, or Great Mother). You can turn around here, or continue for a less visited, less despoiled slice of Capri. The steps to Matermania continue down to a winding path that vertiginously skirts the Capri headland, passing the odd Villa di Malaparte (built for the writer in 1938), a Pompeiian red trapezoid accessible only by boat. Eventually, you rise again to the belvedere of Punta Tragara, with fantastic views of the Faraglioni and Marina Piccola. Via Tragara leads from here past posher and posher villas back into Capri Town.

Capri to the Giardini di Augusto (5 to 10 min.)   This is less of a walk than a visit to one of Capri's more fragrant spots, a small set of terraced and well-kept gardens (take Via V. Emanuele, which becomes Via F. Serena). Below these gardens to the left is the **Certosa di San Giacomo,** a vast mausoleum of a charter house built by the Carthusian monks in the 14th century, burned by pirates in the 16th century, and evicted by the Bonaparte dynasty in the 19th century. The cloisters are huge, bare, and relaxingly quiet after the tourist crush of Capri, but the meager collections (paintings, some crèche figurines) are barely worth poking around. Below the gardens to the right leads the **Via Krupp,** an almost comically switchbacked stone path that winds down (in 20 min.) to the sea and a Saracen tower at the edge of Marina Piccola (good swimming; see below).

Anacapri to La Migliera (20 to 30 min.)   This well-maintained path (**Via Migliera**) is one of Capri's flattest, easiest walks. It passes isolated houses and a very good restaurant (see below) to a lookout point. The vista casts over razor-sharp cliffs plunging 958 feet into the sea with the Faro lighthouse at the tip of the Punta Carena promontory.

FUN IN THE SUN & SHOPPING

BEACHES   Although Capri is a famous island resort, don't expect great beaches. Most of the island is sharp volcanic rock plunging into the azure waters—spectacular, but rough on tender hands and feet. Snorkeling, though, can be rewarding, and there are indeed a few places around the island where you can spread out your towel.

There's a scrap of pebbly beach just to the right of the ferry docks at **Marina Grande,** but it's crowded, a bit dirty, and really best only as a last resort "I need a swim" bathing spot. Capri's best beach for the past 2,000 years has been the **Bagni di Tiberio,** about a 20-minute walk west from Marina Grande. There's a pebble-and-sand shore, lots of sun worshippers and rocks to lie out on, and a crumbling wall to remind you that even Tiberius, capitalizing on the spot, built a small bath complex here.

Marina Piccola has several restaurant/bathing establishments right on the water—mostly rocks and piers with pools and decks for tanning. Even better, out either side of the little port are modest rocky beaches: to the east under a Saracen tower, to the west surrounding the stony spit known as **Scoglio delle Sirene**—according to legend the very rocks from which the flesh-eating Sirens sang irresistibly to lure sailors to their deaths (Homer's hero Odysseus prudently stuffed his crewmen's ears with wax and lashed himself to the mast as they passed so as not to be tempted—though when he heard their seductive song he fell under its spell and begged to be untied so he could rush to them; lucky for him, his crewmen refused).

A bus ride or 20-minute walk from Anacapri (down Via Nuovo del Faro, off Piazza Caprile) takes you to a secluded but lightly crowded swimming hole of **Punta Carena,** a rocky series of coves leeward of *il Faro* (the lighthouse). You can sun on the cement pier, or rent snorkel gear to get up close to the colorful schools of fish and small octopi; many of these rocks support colonies of spiky sea urchins, so watch where you set your feet underwater.

BOAT TRIPS   Check around Marina Grande for outfitters eager to show off the splendors of Capri's rocky perimeter and many sea-level grottoes (the Blue Grotto is just the most famous) in a cruise around the island. It'll last about 90 minutes and if you bargain well, cost around 20,000L ($11.75).

There's also a midget submarine, the *Tritone,* that, after a coastal boat ride, gives you a 40-minute, 150-foot-deep glimpse into the colorful coral and fish life around Capri for 50,000L ($29.40) adults, 36,000L ($21.20) kids. There's also a night dive.

SHOPPING   The most popular Capri purchase is ***limoncello,*** that wonderful, sugary lemon liqueur. Luckily, it can also be one of the cheapest buys. You pay more for the funky shape of the bottle than for the amount of booze inside, and can get sample-size gift bottles for as little as 3,000 to 5,000L ($1.75 to $2.95). For your own consumption, you may want to shell out 15,000 to 20,000L ($8.80 to $11.75) for ¾ liter. To buy the brand tossed back by Gorky, Krupp, and Axel Munthe, head to the shop run by their supplier's grandkids, **Limoncello di Capri**, V. Roma 79 (☎ 081/837-5561), in Anacapri at V. Capodimonte 27 (☎ **081/837-2927**). Limoncello's sugary lemon flavor stands out best when served close to freezing.

Staying on the aromatic end of shopping, Capri is a wonderfully scented island, and the **perfumes and colognes** sold here reflect it. You can find some good bargains at the popular **Carthusia,** V. Camerelle 10 in Capri; V. Capodimonte 26 in Anacapri (☎ **081/837-0368**). The store's Aria di Capri concoction of orange, lemon, mimosa, and peach was developed in the 17th century by the monks at the nearby certosa. You can also tour the store's tiny lab at V. G. Matteotti 2b.

Capri's other famous product is handmade strap **sandals**—but don't try to hike the island in them. The famous, bijoux-studded footwear pounded out by Angela at **Canfora,** V. Camerelle 3 in Capri (☎ **081/837-0487**), will run you a whopping 170,000L ($100). For the best bargains, head to **Vincenzo Faiella**'s shop on Capri's V. Vittorio Emanuele 49 (no phone), where cloth and rope shoes and slippers start at 26,000L ($15.30). My favorite cobbler is old Antonio Viva, who sits outside his Anacapri shop **L'Arte del Sandolo Caprese** at V. G. Orlandi 75 (☎ **081/837-3583**) and proclaims gently through his mustache "We make these shoes the artisan's way. We make them with heart." Antonio has the widest selection of handmade slippers on Capri, and his work goes for a modest 55,000 to 90,000L ($32.35 to $52.95).

WHERE TO STAY

High season usually runs mid-June to September, and unless otherwise noted that seasonal variance is what's reflected in the price ranges listed for hotels below.

IN CAPRI TOWN

La Tosca. V. D. Birago 5, 80073 Capri (NA). ☎ and fax **081/837-0989.** www.caprionline.it/latosca. E-mail: H.TOSCA@capri.it. 12 units, all with bathroom. TEL. 55,000–75,000L ($32.35–$44.10) single, 100,000–125,000L ($58.80–$73.50) double. Breakfast 12,000L ($7.05). MC, V. Closed late Oct–mid-Mar.

La Tosca is hidden on one of Capri's back alleys, surrounded by birdsong and seemingly a world away, yet only a 5-minute stroll, from the tourist crush of the Piazzetta. Ettore Castelli and his Connecticut-born wife have been improving La Tosca since taking over 3 years ago, and the investment is paying off. Most of the clean, sizable rooms have newish, functional furniture and high ceilings. While I was unimpressed with the creaky old bathrooms, Ettore promises they'll be replaced by 1999. Rooms 47 through 51 all have small terraces that look over the umbrella pines and nearby Certosa to the sea and *i Faraglioni* (but these rooms get smaller as they go up in number, and past no. 49 the trees block much of the view). You can take your breakfast on your own terrace or the public one out front near the TV lounge.

Pensione Belsito. V. Matermania 9–13, 80073 Capri (NA). ☎ **081/837-0969.** Fax 081/837-6622. E-mail: HBELSITO@mbox.caprinet.it. 13 units, all with bathroom. MINIBAR TEL. 80,000–100,000L ($47.05–$58.80) single, 120,000–180,000L ($70.60–$105.90) double. Half-pension of 30,000L ($17.65) required Sat–Sun, and daily in high season. Rates include breakfast. AE, DC, MC, V. Closed Nov.

This converted 18th-century house run as a hotel and restaurant by Mario and Liliana Tarantino is removed from the town bustle and very tranquil, yet still just 4 minutes from Capri's main piazza. The tile-or linoleum-floored rooms are small but bright, and the beds won't punish your spine. Rooms 22 to 27 have views over the arc of Capri, the sea, and the mass of Monte Solaro, while the balance of rooms do not have a view or indeed much light, but are cheaper. Everyone can enjoy the vistas from the roof terrace, however, and even if you don't take the half-pension deal, you still get a 10% discount at the attached and recommended restaurant/pizzeria.

Stella Maris. V. Roma 27, 80073 Capri (NA). ☎ and fax **081/837-0452.** 10 units, 7 with bathroom. TEL. 55,000–70,000L ($32.35–$41.20) single; 80,000–90,000L ($47.05–$52.95) double without bathroom, 100,000–110,000L ($58.80–$64.70) double with bathroom. Breakfast 20,000L ($11.75) required July–Aug. MC, V. Closed 12–15 days in late Jan/early Feb.

Capri's cheapest and certainly most central hotel overlooks the tiny bus stop piazza on the main road and has a bit of a worn, dingy air imparted by the troops of backpackers that book it solid through summer. Still, rooms are cozy without being cramped, the patterned tile floors and spanking white walls are clean, and the bathrooms and modular furnishings are in good repair. The beds, while on cots, are firm enough, and second-floor rooms get a bit better sea view over the shed where minibuses idle from 6am to midnight. Each bathless room has its own bathroom in the hall.

Worth A Splurge

✪ **Villa Krupp.** Vle. G. Matteoti 12, 80073 Capri (NA) (a long but pleasant path up from the main road). ☎ **081/837-0362.** Fax 081/837-6489. 12 units, all with bathroom. A/C TEL. 120,000L ($70.60) single; 170,000–230,000L ($100–$135.30) double. Rates include breakfast. MC, V. Closed Nov 6–Mar 1.

Villa Krupp is set like a crown jewel of old-world style atop the Giardini d'Augusto at the end of a path that winds up amid the umbrella pines. Its breezy back hill location is very quiet, but still convenient to Capri's shopping and restaurants and Marina Piccola's beach below. An old favorite of Russian intellectuals (Lenin lodged and Gorky lived here), the Krupp's rooms have period or antique-style furnishings on tile floors, brand-new bathrooms, and firm beds. The larger and more expensive nos. 18 to 21 are the best in the house, with high ceilings, small chandeliers, hair dryers, and killer terrace views over La Certosa and the wooded slopes of Monte Tuoro to *i Faraglioni* and the sea. Smaller, cheaper doubles look over the white-cube tumble of Capri's houses. Guests sit in the TV solarium to read and gaze out at the trees and bits of sea peeking through.

IN ANACAPRI

Biancamaria. V. G. Orlandi 54, 80071 Anacapri (NA). ☎ **081/837-1000.** Fax 081/837-2060. 25 units, all with bathroom. A/C TEL. 120,000–150,000L ($70.60–$88.25) single; 180,000–200,000L ($105.90–$117.65) double. Rates include breakfast. AE, MC, V. Closed Nov 1–Mar 31.

It's spare, dark, echoey, and right in the center of town. The family run Biancamaria has an old-fashioned attitude (they turn away scruffy backpackers) but ultramodern veneer furnishings in the rooms, along with sparkling new huge bathrooms featuring heated towel racks and hair dryers. Accommodations are generally very big, with contemporary tile floors, small easy chairs, and pale flowery prints on the bedspreads. Rooms with the Monte Solaro view have small terraces over the town's main drag, which gets quite late at night. For even more quiet, request a sea-view room with French doors opening onto a fantastic panorama of the Bay of Naples.

Il Girasole. V. Linciano 47, 80071 Anacapri (NA). ☎ **081/837-2351.** Fax 081/837-3880. www.ilgirasole.com. E-mail: ilgirasole@capri.it. 20 units, all with shower. 40,000–70,000L ($23.55–$41.20) single; 80,000–120,000L ($47.05–$70.60) double. Rates may rise in high season; bargain for longer stays. Breakfast 6,000–15,000L ($3.55–$8.80). AE, MC, V. A 5- to 10-min. walk from Anacapri. Call from Marina Grande and they'll come pick you up, or before your ferry leaves and they'll be waiting. Otherwise, ride Anacapri bus to end of line and follow signs.

Nestled amid vineyards and olives a 10-minute stroll from Anacapri, the family-run Girasole has changed dramatically from the student pensione of a few years ago. The room bunkers have become bungalows with summery accommodations of tile floors, new functional furnishings in wicker or wood, modern but teensy bathrooms, and good beds. The prices are still great, but it'll take a while before the replanted grapevine arbors grow back to their old scenic lushness. Nos. 8, 9, and 12 through 14 have the best views across the brick terraces and tumbling down the side of the island to the Bay of Naples. On lazy days, you can take a dip in the pool and nosh a gooey pizza in the informal restaurant. Groups should try to book the downscale minisuite. Internet access is available.

✪ **Villa Eva.** V. la Fabbrica 8, 80071 Capri (NA). ☎ **081/837-1549.** Fax 081/837-2040. www.caprionline.com/villaeva. 15 units, all with bathroom. 100,000–120,000L ($58.80–$70.60) double; 40,000–45,000L ($23.55–$26.50) per person in room for 5 or 6; 45,000–50,000L ($26.50–$29.40) per person in room for 3. Rates include breakfast. No credit cards. Closed mid-Nov–Feb 28. A 10- to 15-min. walk out the far end of Anacapri toward the Blue Grotto; call from Marina Grande for directions. If someone's free, they might come pick you up, or take the Blue Grotto bus from Anacapri and ask the driver to let you off for a 2-min. walk.

It's one of the island's best inns by a long shot, not only one of the cheapest but also the most exotic and tranquil—perfect for getting away from it all. Villa Eva is beloved by a host of regulars who book for weeks at a time, and by budget-seeking back-packers. Eva and Vincenzo's little corner of paradise is a series of small buildings nestled amid the birdsong of some of the lushest gardens on the island, scattered with secluded nooks and grottoes for relaxing with a book. Somewhere out there, there's a hidden bungalow bar/TV lounge and outdoor pool. Vincenzo himself built most of the comfy furnishings in the simple, rustic, idiosyncratic accommodations, and installed thoughtful touches like mosquito screens and firm beds. He also painted the art decorating the walls and personalized the structures with majolica tiles and architectural details like wood beams or tiny bifore windows leaning on stubby columns. Worth singling out is no. 5, Eva's childhood bedroom, with two rooms and a big terrace. Some second-floor rooms catch a bit of sea view over the trees, and guests get a discount at nearby Il Cucciolo restaurant (see below).

Worth A Splurge

✪ **Caesar Augustus.** V. G. Orlandi 4, 80071 Anacapri (NA). ☎ **081/837-1421.** Fax 081/837-1444. 58 units, 52 with bathroom. TEL. 120,000–250,000L ($70.60–$147.05) single; 200,000–350,000L ($117.65–$205.90) double with or without bathroom; 250,000–450,000L ($147.05–$238.25) suite. Discounts for longer stays, families, and when business is slow. Rates include breakfast. AE, MC, V. Closed Nov 1–Apr 19. At the final bend in the road up from Capri to Anacapri; ask the bus driver to let you off, or take the free hotel shuttle from Capri's Piazzetta.

Perched atop a sheer cliff 1,000 feet above the azure sea at Anacapri's edge, the island's most spectacularly sited hotel is surprisingly still within the upper reaches of budget (although rumor is an upscale is imminent). You'll understand the splurge rates when you see the rooms, a hodgepodge of mostly antiques in large, sun-drenched settings of soothingly pale colors brightened by fresh flowers and cool tile floors, some in festive patterns. You'll wonder why those rates aren't triple when you wander onto the wrap-around terrace (or, if you're lucky, just open your room window) for a panorama of the entire Bay of Naples, wrapping from Ischia past Vesuvius to the Sorrentina Peninsula. Room price here is tied directly to how good the view is. Besides peachy vistas, suites and "deluxe" rooms are classier and blessed with air-conditioning, TVs, and minibars. But the cliff is graced with a continual cool breeze, so you can live without the A/C in standard rooms (no. 215 is the best). The cozy bar and several lounge areas with TV all have picture windows for that panorama. A pool is going in amid the gardens that may be ready by 2000.

WHERE TO DINE

Island cuisine is mostly Campanian and very fishy, but one dish deserves to be singled out. Invented here in the 1950s for calorie-counting vacationers, the *insalata caprese*—often just called the *caprese* and now served in restaurants throughout Italy—is a salad of fresh tomato slices and mozzarella topped with torn basil and some cracked black pepper.

There's no lack of overpriced, poor-quality snack bars in Capri. For a good quick bite, your best bet is to pop into a local *alimentari* (grocery shop) and make your own panino or small picnic. For a treat, stop by **Sfizi di Pane,** a short stroll from the Piazzetta at V. Le Botteghe 4 (☎ 081/837-0160), to sample some of Ottavio Serena's outstanding pastries and breads, or a slice of passable pizza (closed Sunday afternoon).

AROUND CAPRI

Al Grottino. V. Longana 27. (Standing on the Piazzetta with your back to the Duomo, duck through the tunnel/alley in the center.) ☎ **081/837-0584.** Reservations highly recommended. Primi 11,000–17,000L ($6.50–$10); secondi 10,000–27,000L ($5.90–$15.90). Fixed-price lunch menu 40,000L ($23.55, no wine). AE, DC, MC, V. Daily noon–3pm and 7pm–midnight. Closed mid-Mar–mid-Nov and Tues in Oct. CAPRESE/ITALIAN.

The "Little Grotto" is one of our fanciest choices, the sort of place where the waiter prepares your fish for you and good Italian and French vintages supplement the local table wine. It has changed little since the days Ted Kennedy, the Gabor sisters, and Igor Stravinsky dined in the single room of tightly spaced tables under a stucco vaulted ceiling. Wine flasks, photos of famous patrons, and a rose on every table complete the decor, while a dozen tourist tongues (mixed with some local dialect) and the clamor of the adjacent kitchen set the tone. *Agnolotti al pomodoro caprese* (giant ravioli of cheese and ham topped with fresh baby tomatoes and torn basil) or *risotto alla pescatora* (rice infused with shellfish and tiny squid) make excellent first courses. For secondo, you can order *involtino alla Napoletana* (veal roll stewed in tomatoes) or *mozzarella in carrozza* (fresh mozzarella on toast fried to a golden brown). But Al Grottino's strong suit is fresh fish; try it cooked *all'acqua pazza* (with tomatoes, white wine, and spices).

Worth A Splurge

Da Luigi ai Faraglioni. V. Faraglioni 5. (Call ahead and they will pick you up at Marina Piccola for 10,000L/$5.90 a head; or walk the long stair/path to the Faraglioni in about 20–30 min.) ☎ **081/837-0591.** Reservations recommended. Primi 7,000–20,000L ($4.10–$11.75); secondi 13,000–38,000L ($7.65–$22.35). AE, MC, V. Daily noon–4pm (later June–Aug). Closed Oct–Easter. CAPRESE.

Da Luigi's is nothing if not well named: It truly is "at the Faraglioni," wedged into the rocks at sea level between the cliffs of Capri proper and the first of the sea stacks that rise dramatically from the waters. The boat ride here is spectacular, cutting between the Faraglioni themselves just as Odysseus did. Reserve a seat at the edge of the shaded terrace for an intimate study of the Sirens' stony home. The site is a natural wind tunnel—sometimes chilly in spring or fall, but welcome at the height of summer. Unfortunately, the food isn't nearly as remarkable as the setting. Best are the *spaghetti alla malafemmina* ("evil woman's" pasta, with baby tomatoes, capers, olives, basil, and hot peppers) and *ravioli alla caprese* (sauced with tomatoes and mozzarella). Afterward, try *pollo alla griglia*, a *fritto Italia* (mixed fry of julienned zucchini, ravioli, suppli rice balls, eggplant, and potato croquettes), or *zuppa di cozze* (mussel soup).

AROUND ANACAPRI

Al Nido d'Oro. V. de Tomasso 30–32. ☎ **081/837-2148.** Reservations not accepted. Primi 8,500–18,000L ($5–$10.60); secondi 9,000–17,000L ($5.30–$10); pizza 7,000–11,000L ($4.10–$6.50). No credit cards. Wed–Mon noon–3:30pm, 7:30pm–midnight. Closed 1 month in winter. CASARECCIA CAPRESE/PIZZA.

Make no mistake: This ain't fine dining, or a tourist restaurant with a view. This is one of the few places locals like to keep to themselves, with pizza take-out on one side and families crowding the eight tables of the other room in the early evening, giving way to couples and small groups after 9:30pm. Caprese dialect sets the tone while the busy woman in the kitchen whips up heaping plates of simple, filling, fragrant home cooking. The *trittico di ravioli* gets you pasta pockets stuffed variously with spinach, hazelnuts, or shrimp, while the *penne con crema di carciofi* is in a creamy artichoke sauce. Secondi are basic: *scaloppina al limone* or the overwhelmingly popular *frittura di calamari* (fried squid). You can also enjoy pizzas such as *pizza capricciosa* (topped with tomato, mozzarella, prosciutto, mushrooms, olives, capers, and Parmesan).

Da Gelsomina. V. Migliara 72. (A 20-min walk from Anacapri) ☎ **081/837-1499.** Reservations recommended. Primi 9,000–15,000L ($5.30–$8.80); secondi 11,000–20,000L ($6.50–$11.75). AE, DC, MC, V. Sept 22–Jan 31 and Mar–Apr, Wed–Mon noon–3:30pm; May–June 30, Wed–Mon noon–3:30pm, Sat–Sun noon–3:30pm, 8pm–midnight; June 21–Sept 21, daily noon–3:30pm, 8pm–midnight. Closed Feb. CAPRESE.

A long, but scenic, 20-minute walk from Anacapri brings you to this countryside hideaway of delicious food and sweeping vistas. You can dine on the shaded terrace or inside against the picture windows, where the view skips across vineyards and pines to the sea and Ischia in the distance. The classic ravioli *alla caprese* are stuffed fat with ricotta and gooey mozzarella, and the delicate cannelloni are thin sheets of homemade pasta wrapped around a blend of ricotta and meat, smothered in tomato sauce and Parmesan then baked till the ends are crispy. For secondo try the mixed seafood fry *frittura di pesce* (featuring squid, octopus, and shrimp) or veal scaloppini prepared however you'd like (but as this is Capri, make it a summery *al limone*). The ingredients are fresh—many of them homegrown—and their own label house white is perfect for lunch. To ensure your table has a view, reserve ahead.

Il Cucciolo. V. la Fabbrica 52 (take bus to Blue Grotto and ask to be let off for the restaurant; or a 20-min. walk from Anacapri). ☎ **081/837-1917.** Reservations recommended. Primi 10,000–18,000L ($5.90–$10.60); secondi 12,000–24,000L ($7.05–$14.10). AE, DC, MC, V. Wed–Mon noon–2:30pm, daily 7–11pm. Closed late Oct–Easter. CAPRESE.

Tucked away on a back road off the road to the Blue Grotto, Il Cucciolo offers abundant portions of quite excellent food on a terrace surrounded by lush greenery and views of the Bay of Naples below. The *caprese* salad is excellent, as are the *pennette alla contadina* (peasants' pasta quills in a savory sauce of onions, Parmesan, and lean pancetta), *ravioli cucciolo* (in a cream sauce studded with ham), or *farfalloni alla panna parmigiano* (bow ties in a creamy Parmesan sauce topped with cracked black pepper). For secondo try *pollo marinato alla griglia* (succulent marinated and grilled chicken— ask for the special "Argentina" sauce) or fresh *pesce alla griglia*.

Il Solitario. V. G. Orlandi 96 (on the main road in town). ☎ **081/837-1382.** Reservations recommended. Primi 8,000–15,000L ($4.70–$8.80); secondi 15,000–22,000L ($8.80– $12.95). Menù turistico 15,000L ($8.80, no wine). AE, DC, MC, V. Tues–Sun noon–3pm, 7:30–midnight. Open daily June 21–Sept 21; closed Nov–Mar. CAPRESE.

Reserve ahead in nice weather for the best seating out on the back terrace, where little tile-topped tables are shaded by the vines of a low hanging arbor. The clientele is likely to be half tourists and half regulars on a first-name basis with the chef/owner. The house dish is ravioli, stuffed with fresh cheeses and deservedly the most popular menu item. Also good are the *gnocchi alla sorrentina, tagliolini all'aragosta* (ribbons of egg pasta with tomatoes and baby lobsters), and *cannelloni caprese* (ricotta and spinach-stuffed paste tubes). For secondi, sample the simple omelette with mozzarella or *spiedini di carne mista* (shish kebabs of beef, sausage, and rabbit). For dessert, try the *tiramisu con le fragole* (covered with strawberries in season) or a lemon sorbet.

4 Sorrento

48 km (29 mi.) SE of Naples, 8 km (4.8 miles) NE of Capri, 17 km (10 mi.) W of Positano

The Greek (or perhaps Etruscan) city of *Sorrentum* on a bluff at the southern arms of the Bay of Naples was never terribly important in antiquity except as a middle-class resort for the Romans—and that status really hasn't changed for 2,000 years. Since the 19th century, English and German visitors especially have flocked here on package tours (still the town's chief source of income). Ibsen even found enough inspiration here to finish writing *Peer Gynt.* Sorrento is the launching pad for the buses down the Amalfi Coast, just 20 minutes by boat from Capri, and a quick train ride from Pompeii.

FESTIVALS   At Easter time, Sorrento throws a solemn, Byzantine religious procession in honor of **Good Friday.** In July and August, Sorrento hosts both a **classical music festival** in indoor and outdoor venues across town, and an **international film festival** that lacks the star quality of Cannes or Venice, but is starting to gain a certain following.

ESSENTIALS
GETTING HERE   By Train   The private Circumvesuviana rail line (☎ 081/536-8932 or 081/772-2444) leaves Naples for Sorrento twice an hour (52 to 67 min; 4,700L/$2.75).

By Car   From Naples, take route 18 to Castellammare di Stabia, where you transfer over to the SS145 to Sorrento.

By Ferry/Hydrofoil   There's an LMV (☎ 081/807-3024 or 081-878-1430) **hydrofoil from Naples's** Molo Beverello (30 min; 12,000L/$7.05). LMV also runs the **hydrofoil from Capri** (20 min; 10,000L/$5.90). Both Caremar (☎ 081/807-3077) and LMV run **ferries from Capri** (40 to 50 min; 7,000L/$4.10).

GETTING AROUND   By Bus   From the station, **Bus D** runs to Piazza Tasso (city center) and Corso Italia (the main drag). **Bus A** runs from Piazza Tasso out Via Capo (where you'll find lots of hotels). **Buses B and C** run from Piazza Tasso down to Marina Piccola (ferry dock) and back again. Tickets are 1,700L ($1).

By Rental Car   Since Sorrento makes such a good base, picking up a car or scooter here (rather than fighting the traffic in Naples) can make a lot of sense. The most reputable agencies, roughly in order from cheapest to most expensive, **De Martino (Auto Europe)**, Cor. Italia 253 (☎ 081/878-2801); **Sorrento Rent a Car,** Cor. Italia 210A (☎ 081/878-1386; www.tin.it/carservice); and **Hertz,** V. degli Aranci 9 (☎ 081/807-1646). All except Hertz also rent scooters—as does **Jolly Rent A Scooter,** V. Fuorimura 29 (☎ 081/878-1719)—for around 30,000 to 35,000L ($17.65 to $20.60) for 3 to 4 hours or 45,000 to 50,000L ($26.50 to $29.40) per day.

VISITOR INFORMATION   Sorrento's tourist info office is inside the Circolo dei Forestieri club just down from Piazza S. Antonio at V. L. de Maio 35 (☎ 081/807-4033; fax 081/877-3397). It's open Monday to Saturday 8:30am to 8pm (October to March it closes at 6:15pm).

STROLLING AROUND SORRENTO

Sorrento's sights consist of the 14th-century **cloisters of San Francesco** (now an art school) on Via V. Veneto, and the neighboring **Villa Comunale gardens** with views down to the marina and up the coastline. There is also a small museum at the east end of town, the **Museo Correale,** V. Correale 50 (☎ **081/878-1846**). The hodgepodge collections include lots of inlaid wood furnishings, majolica, porcelain figurines, Neapolitan baroque paintings (plus a Rubens), marvelous views over the gardens to the Bay of Sorrento, and crumbling bits of Roman statuary to remind you of the city's venerable, if little visible, heritage. Admission is a steep 8,000L ($4.70) adults, 5,000L ($2.95) under 12; it's open daily 9am to 2pm.

Luckily, although it lacks in sightseeing, Sorrento has some great **passeggiata** action along the streets of the old town, especially along modern Corso Italia and the parallel and cobbled Via S. Cesareo, the old *Decumanus Maximus* of the Roman town. While tourists and locals mill about the streets in the late afternoon, the town elders gather under the 15th-century loggia of the **Sedile Dominova** at the corner of Via S. Cesareo and Via P. R. Giuliano to play Italian cards games under the 18th-century frescoes (be sure you filter back amid the bar umbrellas on the tiny piazza out front to glimpse the Sedile's majolica dome growing weeds).

SWIMMING   Although it's a resort town, don't come to Sorrento expecting beaches. While the water's a bit cleaner than along most of the bay, swimming is mainly off piers jutting out over the rocks plus a few teensy pebble beaches—all of them private (read: pay) and an elevator's ride down from the town (look for these elevators along Via Marina Grande).

WHERE TO STAY

The budget dives lining the stretch of Corso Italia from the train station to the town center are just that: dives. Walk a bit farther, and you'll get significantly better quality almost as cheap. Don't forget about ever-developing **Via del Capo,** a clifftop road leading out the far end of town, which is host to a number of generally cheaper hotels.

Hotel del Corso Cor. Italia 134 (½ block beyond Pz. Tasso), 80067 Sorrento (NA). ☎ **081/ 807-3157.** Fax 081/807-1016. 21 units, 20 with bathroom. TEL. 90,000L ($52.95) single; 100,000L ($58.80) double with external bathroom, 110,000–140,000L ($64.70–$82.35) double with bathroom. In Aug, add 30,000L ($17.65) per person for obligatory half-pension. Rates include breakfast. AE, DC, MC, V. Parking 16,000–25,000L ($9.40–$14.70) in nearby garage or lot. Closed Dec–Jan.

The family-run Corso—the best bargain hotel along the car-trafficked main drag—is in the old section of town. Its biggest selling point is great people-watching from your window during passeggiata—either overlooking the busy Corso or from sought-after rooms 52 through 55, whose shoe-wide balconies hang over quiet, pedestrianized Via S. Cesareo. The plain accommodations feature exceedingly firm beds, lackluster modular furnishings, and a generous amount of elbow room, but the overall effect is a bit antiseptic. Corso rooms are noisy, as is the restaurant terrace that overlooks the street, so if you can't stand rumbling buses but can't score one of those ideal rooms, go for nos. 62 to 65 (no view, but still on the building's quieter back side).

✪ **Hotel Loreley et Londres.** V. Calfano 2, 80067 Sorrento (NA). ☎ and fax **081/ 807-3187.** 28 units, all with bathroom. Single or double 130,000L ($76.50); triple 180,000L ($105.90); quad 210,000L ($123.50). July 15–Sept 1 add 30,000L ($17.65) per person for obligatory half-pensione; 50,000L ($4.40) if you want full pension. Rates include breakfast. DC, MC, V. Parking free behind hotel. Closed Nov–Easter. It's a long walk from Pz. Tasso or the station; no bus makes the trip regularly, so head to the Museo Correale, around it the left, and down the road.

Sorrento

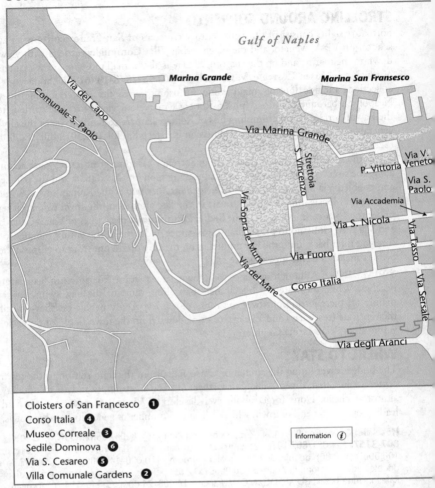

Cloisters of San Francesco **1**
Corso Italia **4**
Museo Correale **3**
Sedile Dominova **6**
Via S. Cesareo **5**
Villa Comunale Gardens **2**

Information *i*

This hospitable 100-year-old pensione is the most popular of Sorrento's budget hotels, despite the 10- to 15-minute walk from town and lack of phones or air-conditioning. It's well covered by the guidebook industry and word-of-mouth, so reserve ahead. Accommodations are very well worn, with mismatched functional furniture and a few near-antiques. They feature tile floors (some prettily painted), curtainless bathrooms and showers, cool breezes, and medium-soft beds. Most have at least a balcony—in some the terrace is almost larger than the room, as in no. 14 with a wraparound patio. Most rooms (the best are nos. 11 to 13) get at least part of the remarkable view sweeping from Sorrento and its marina around the bay to Vesuvius, but a few are on the road. Everyone enjoys the panorama from the bamboo mat–shaded terrace where you take meals in high season. There's an elevator down to a little bar and private swimming pier.

Hotel Villa di Sorrento. V. Fuorimura 6 (½ block north of Pz. Tasso.), 80067 Sorrento (NA). ☎ **081/878-1068.** Fax 081/807-2679. 21 units, all with bathroom. A/C TV TEL. 100,000–115,000L ($58.80–$67.65) single; 170,000–205,000L ($100–$120.60) double. Rates include breakfast (subtract 20,000L/$11.75 per person if you request rooms without breakfast). AE, DC, MC, V. Parking 20,000L ($11.75) in nearby lot. Open all year.

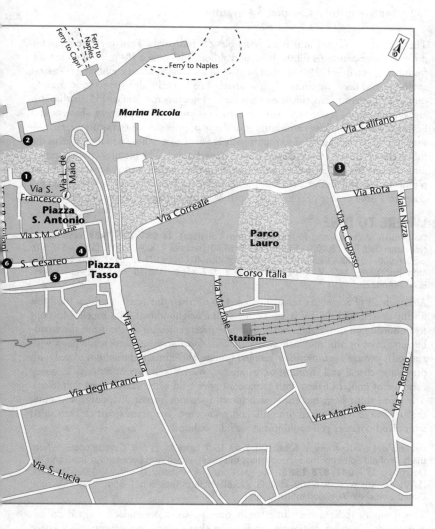

This is the rather more comfortable, climate-controlled hotel among our choices in Sorrento, with an excellent location just half a block up a tree-lined street from Piazza Tasso. As befits an upscale inn, the wood-framed beds are large and firm and the bathrooms are modern. Some rooms are smallish, but the air-conditioning and other amenities more than make up for it. Paintings or prints decorate the walls and a few near-antiques give most rooms a touch of class. No. 41 and 42 have terraces with the best views (over red-tiled roofs to greensward around town with even a sliver of sea below). If you splurge by opting for the breakfast—not bad, but not worth 20,000L either—you'll enjoy the vaulted dining room beyond a sofa scattered sitting room-cum-bar. The range in prices above reflects the season.

✪ **La Tonnarella.** V. Capo 31, 80067 Sorrento (NA). ☎ **081/878-1153**. Fax 081/ 878-2169. 21 units, all with bathroom. A/C TV TEL. 128,000–160,000L ($75.30–$94.10) single; 160–200,000L ($94.10–$117.65) double. Half-pension 120,000–130,000L ($70.60–$76.50); full pension 140,000–150,000L ($82.35–$88.25). Rates include breakfast. AE, MC, V. Parking free at hotel. Open all year. Bus: A.

The best of Via Capo's inns is the vista-blessed Tonnarella. Persian runners tumble down the stairs, antiques fill the halls, and although it's only a 10- to 15-minute walk from town, you'll feel like a tourism fugitive in a coastal hideaway, enjoying first-class amenities and decor at criminally low prices. The brightly tiled rooms sport an odd mix of 19th-century chairs and modern built-in headboards. Some of the bathrooms are getting on in years, but many are *modernissimo* with hyperspray showers and heated towel racks. There's a pleasing abundance of pine-shaded terra-cotta terraces— some public, others attached to rooms such as nos. 1 to 4, whose windows take in the full sweep of the bay (book ahead for a room with view). The picture-window restaurant, tucked with open balconies, could almost be recommended separately for its plump ravioli and fresh fish. There's an elevator (or stairs through a verdant gorge) down to a little private pebble beach, open May to September, with restaurant/bar.

WHERE TO DINE

Da Gigino. V. degli Aranci 15 (just down from Cor. Italia). ☎ **081/878-1927.** Reservations recommended. Primi 8,000–15,000L ($4.70–$8.80); secondi 9,000–28,000L ($5.30–$16.50); pizze 6,000–13,000L ($3.55–$7.65). Menù turistico 40,000L ($23.55, all seafood, hence the high price). AE, MC, V. Daily noon–3pm and 7–11pm. Closed Tues Sept–June. SORRENTINA/PIZZA.

Although all of Sorrento's restaurants cater to tourists, this one has a loyal local following as well, and the TV in the corner adds a neighborhood-joint touch. Most opt to sit outside on the cobbles of the tiny side street, enjoying a pizza from the wood-burning oven or a primo such as *scialatielli ai frutti di mare* (homemade pasta with seafood), *gnocchi verdi provola e gamberi* (potato-and-spinach dumplings tossed with provolone cheese and shrimp), or, as always, *gnocchi alla Sorrentina* (a rich, gooey casserole of gnocchi baked with tomatoes under a lid of mozzarella and Parmesan). The primi shine here, but the straightforward secondi doesn't disappoint, including the *grigliata di pesce* (mixed fish grill) and *pollo arrosto con patate* (roast chicken sided with bland potatoes you could just as well do without).

Osteria del Gatto Nero. V. S. Maria d. Pietà 36 (1 block north of V. Cavour; opposite from the bulk of old Sorrento; many people miss this street, which runs between Pz. Tasso and the Duomo). ☎ **081/878-1582.** Reservations recommended. Primi 5,000–10,000L ($2.95–$5.90); secondi 6,500–15,000L ($3.80–$8.80). Tues–Sun 1–3pm, 7pm–midnight. Closed 2 weeks in Aug. Sorrentina/Italian.

This is one of those perfect little family osterie—six tables under a vaulted ceiling, antipasti and homemade tiramisu chilling on glass shelves, the requisite black kitten curled up on a straw-bottomed chair, and great home cooking at decent prices. For primo try the *paglia e fieno* (a "hay and straw" mix of green and yellow fettuccine in a ham and cream sauce) or rigatoni all'amatriciana (perfectly al dente and in a tomato and pancetta bacon sauce that's just spicy enough). The simple, honest secondi include a *costa di maiale alla griglia* (grilled pork chop) or the lightly tangy *petto di pollo all'arancia* (chicken breast in an orange-based sauce).

Ristorante della Favorita O' Parrucchiano. Cor. Italia, 71–73. ☎ **081/878-1321.** Reservations recommended. Primi 6,500–14,000L ($3.80–$8.25); secondi 9,000–25,000L ($5.30–$14.70). MC, V. Thurs–Tues noon–4pm, 7–11:30pm. Open daily May–Nov 15. SORRENTINA.

At this restaurant, in a setting under a thicket of vines, lemons, and orange trees in botanical gardens with greenhouselike terraces and wraparound gardens, you won't even notice the tour groups dining beside you. Family managed for over 100 years, and boasting celebrities like Sophia Loren, Andy Warhol, and Vittorio de Sica as former patrons, O' Parrucchiano's vast popularity has not led it to raise prices unreasonably, nor to compromise quality. Most seafood dishes, since they change with daily availability, are printed on the "chef recommends" menu. Look for *scialatielli ai frutti di mare* (pasta with seafood) and *involtini di pesce spada* (swordfish roll-ups). Otherwise try *cannelloni "Favorita"* (pasta leaves wrapped around meat fillings and baked) or gnocchi followed by a *scaloppina di vitello alla Sorrentina* (veal scallops under tomato sauce and slices of mozzarella) or a *filetto al pepe rosa* (beef fillet with pink peppercorns).

Sant'Antonio. V. S. Maria d. Grazie 6 (off Pz. S. Antonio). ☎ **081/877-1200.** Reservations recommended. Primi 8,000–14,000L ($4.70–$8.25); secondi 9,000–14,500L ($5.30–$8.55); pizze 6,000–12,000L ($3.55–$7.05). Menù turistico: various versions 22,000–45,000L ($12.95–$26.50). AE, MC, V. Daily noon–3pm, 7–11pm. Closed Mon Sept–June. SORRENTINE/ITALIAN.

In fair weather the restaurant moves out onto a huge roof terrace—no views, just tables on an elevated shaded garden of orange trees, grape vines, and the occasional darting cat. Otherwise, it's inside with the rusticated rooms, high ceilings, and funky fireplace. The restaurant offers an impressive array of Italian and Campanian standbys, and all the specialties are showcased on the front of the menu. It's here you'll find *penne alla Francesina* (a rich and tasty ragout with cream and eggplant), *farfalle con zucchini* (bow ties in a cream of zucchini sauce), and *linguine in cartoccio* (homemade noodles mixed with seafood and baked in foil). For secondo sample *spiedini di carne mista* (mixed shish kebab of beef, sausage, pork, and chicken), or the *grigliata di pesce fresco* (a huge spread of cuttlefish, shrimp, swordfish, local fish, and shellfish) that could feed two.

5 Cruising Down the Amalfi Coast

17 km (10 mi.) E of Sorrento

The Amalfi Coast is one of Europe's great scenic wonders. High on the cliff side, the ✪ **Amalfi Drive road**, which dizzily winds along the coast, is a marvel of engineering and one of the world's best white-knuckle thrill rides outside of an amusement park. This 50-kilometer (30-mi.) stretch of crinkly coastline between Sorrento and Salerno offers breathtaking scenery as you make your tortuous, winding way from one gorgeous sea cove into the next, past craggy inlets so sheer and deep they almost qualify as minifjords. High, tree-swathed cliffs on your left plunge tumultuously into the azure waters below you on the right. The coastline's inlets and headlands are punctuated by scraps of beaches, terraced groves of giant lemons, and some of the most inviting, relaxing, and beautiful small towns in Italy.

The bougainvillea-crowned and jasmine-scented villages of the Amalfi Coast range from pricey resort town to old-fashioned fishing hamlet. Among the some dozen communities strung along the coast is a trinity of required stops: posh Positano, historic Amalfi, and garden-filled Ravello. In between you'll find everything from the Emerald Grotto sea cave to the ceramics of Vietri sul Mare. Many people on a daytrip take the bus from Sorrento to Amalfi then turn around to come back, but the most spectacular, least-developed sections of the coast lie east of Amalfi en route to Salerno. **Note:** Information on specific towns is detailed below.

GETTING AROUND   By Bus   The bus ride down the Amalfi Coast is one of the world's cheapest carnival rides, and by far the one with the most stunning scenery. The skilled drivers take on the stressful job of navigating the twists and turns, leaving you free to focus your camera and gasp in awe (and a bit of terror) as each bend brings vistas even more spectacular than the last into view and the side of the giant blue bus swings out over the edge of the cliff, giving you the sensation of dangling high above the sparkling waters.

Hardy SITA (☎ 081/552-2176) bus drivers make the drive down the Amalfi Coast from Sorrento to Amalfi. Buses leave about hourly from Piazza G. B. Curtis, in front of Sorrento's train station (buy your tickets at the station newsstand on Piazza G. B. Curtis). The Amalfi Drive itself skirts above **Positano** (35 min.), with the bus stopping twice (the second stop, "Sponda," is closer to the heart of town and the beach). The bus continues on to stop above **Praiano** (another 20 min.), **Conca dei Marini** (15 min. past Praiano), and end in the center of **Amalfi** at the port (10 min. from Conca, or 85 min. from Sorrento). It's a commuter, not a tourist, bus, so while you can hop on and off, you must buy a new ticket for each leg (about 2,200L/$1.30 between any two towns).

From Amalfi, hourly SITA buses run through Atrani up to **Ravello** and back (25 to 30 min.; 1,700L/$1), while other SITA buses run at least hourly through Atrani, Maiori, Minori, and **Vietri sul Mare** (1 hr. from Amalfi; 3,100L/$1.80), to end in **Salerno** (10 min. from Vietri, 1,700L/$1; or 70 min from Amalfi, 3,100L/$1.80).

By Car The bus is really the best, stress-free way to go. However, if you are determined to take your life into your own hands, you can drive yourself along the twisting, death-defying Amalfi Coast down the **SS163** from Sorrento to Salerno. Buses blare their horns when rounding blind, outside curves so you'll know they're coming. Be prepared to go into reverse and back up along with everybody else on the frequent occasions when the bus hasn't enough space and traffic going both ways has to ease back to make room.

By Boat There are **LMV** hydrofoils (☎ 089/871-483 in Amalfi, 089/875-092 in Positano; www.navlib.com) and **Travelmar** hydrofoils (☎ 089/873-190) from Positano to Amalfi (40 min.; 7,000L/$4.10) and from Amalfi to Salerno (30 min.; 5,000L/$2.95). There's also an LMV hydrofoil that leaves Capri at 4pm to bump down the coast stopping at Positano (4:50pm) and Amalfi (5:30pm) en route to Salerno (6pm).

6 Posh Positano

56 km (35 mi.) SE of Naples, 16.1 km (10 mi.) E of Sorrento, 266 km (165 mi.) SE of Rome

Trendy Positano is a fishing village-turned-tony-resort whose tumble of white and pastel buildings and fine beaches continue to serve as a Jet Set playground. Everyone from Picasso and Stravinsky to John Steinbeck, Liz Taylor, and Sir Laurence Olivier have vacationed here, and director Franco Zefferelli is among the many notables to keep a summer villa in town. Rudolf Nureyev even bought the **Li Galli** islets you'll see offshore on your way into town (once thought to be the home of Homer's Sirens). Positano's popularity among trend setters has meant it's seen several fashions introduced to the world, including the bikini (in 1959).

ARRIVAL & INFORMATION If riding the SITA bus, get off at **"Sponda,"** the second Positano stop, for the beach or center of town; the first stop, **"Chiesa Nuova,"** if you're staying at Hotel Casa Albertina or Casa Guadagno. A half-hourly "Interno

Positano" minibus will run you from "Chiesa Nuova" down the wide, looping Viale Pasitea to the heart of town (1,000L/$60, paid on the bus). If driving, head to **Russo parking** smack in the center at V. C. Colombo 2 (☎ **089/811-210**), which charges surprisingly competitive (for Positano) rates: 5,000 to 7,000L ($2.95 to $4.10) per hour, or 35,000 to 55,000L ($20.60 to $32.35) per day.

There's a small **visitor information** office at V. Saracino 4, in front of the church at the heart of town (☎ **089/875-067;** fax 089/875-760). It's open Monday to Friday 8:30am to 2pm, Saturday 8:30am to noon.

EXPLORING THE AREA

Once you've seen the baroque majolica-tiled dome of the 13th-century **Santa Maria Assunta** church, you've finished with the historical sights of Positano. But the real sightseeing here is wandering the twisting alleyways near the port, window shopping at the boutiques, and sipping aperitifs at the beachside bars while glancing around for celebrities.

BEACHES   About half of the **Spiaggia Grande** at the heart of town is free of charge (and full of boats waiting to be rented). For boatless sunbathing, you'll have to pony up 14,000L ($8.25) to one of the bathing establishments for a day with a beach chair and umbrella.

From the dock next to Spiaggia Grande, Via Positanesi d'America wraps around the headland to Positano's quieter half above **Fornillo Beach,** rather calmer and less trendy than Spiaggia Grande, but more pebbly with less sand. Again, the far right end is free, or fork over 10,000L ($5.90) for an umbrella and chair along the rest of the beach.

BOAT EXCURSIONS   You can rent boats from **Noleggio Barche Lucibello** (☎ **089/875-032**) right on the beach: rowboats and paddleboats cost 20,000L ($11.75) per hour, 80,000L ($47.05) per day; motorboats 40,000L ($23.55) per hour, 180,000L ($105.90) per day. This outfitter also runs an all-day **tour to Capri** (35,000L/$20.60 per person), a 2-hour tour to the **Emerald Grotto** (20,000L/ $11.75), and a half-day trip to the Emerald Grotto along with a swim at **Li Galli** islets (30,000L/$17.65). Entrance fees to the Emerald Grotto (or the Blue Grotto on Capri) are not included. Night excursions are also available.

WHERE TO STAY

High season in Positano lasts at least from June to September and Easter; some hotels extend it into May and October.

Albergo California. V. C. Colombo 141, 84017 Positano (SA). ☎ and fax **089/875-385.** 18 units, all with bathroom. TEL. 140,000–150,000L ($82.35–$88.25) single, 160,000– 170,000L ($94.10–$100) double. Rates include breakfast (ask for room without breakfast and save 10,000L/$5.90 per person). AE, DC, MC, V. Parking free. Closed mid-Nov–Feb.

The exceedingly friendly Mary runs the California, installed in a 1677 palazzo just five minutes from the beach. The 12 accommodations with a sea view sport balconies, and a precious four rooms have high, frescoed ceilings—although for fresher tile floors and bathrooms check into one of the rooms in the modern wing. Accommodations on the back have only small windows up high for light, so while you save some money you lose much atmosphere (the above prices are seasonal; bargain the back rooms down from there). There's a wide terrace with trailing vines out front where guests read and take their drinks in the cool breezes with a sweeping maritime vista. For now there's a common TV lounge, but Mary expects to have sets in the rooms by 1999.

Casa Guadagno. V. Fornillo 26, 84017 Positano (SA). ☎ **089/875-042.** Fax 089/811-407. 10 units, all with bathroom, plus 6 in nearby *dipendenza*. MINIBAR TEL. 70,000L ($41.20) single; 100,000–110,000L ($58.80–$64.70) double. Half-pension 30,000L ($17.65). Rates include breakfast. MC, V. Parking 25,000L ($14.70) in garage at top of hill. Amalfi Coast SITA bus to the first stop in Positano, then hop the Positano minibus and ask to get off *per Fornillo*.

Around Positano's headland to the west, in a quieter pocket of town that retains an echo of the old village feel, Casa Guadagno offers a comfortable stay in a friendly, family run establishment just five minutes up from the beach. Rooms are furnished with old marble-topped dressers, vases in arched niches, and very firm beds. Several have vaulted ceilings, painted tile floors, and small sea-view terraces. Some accommodations are miniapartments with an extra room, TV, sink, and midget fridge. The one complaint is that older bathrooms are still hanging on in some rooms, with nowhere to hang the shower head; however, these are slowly being replaced. Casa Guadagno offers decent dinners for 30,000 to 35,000L ($17.65 to $20.60) on an open-sided and cool terrace that's also used for breakfast. Rooms in the dipendenza nearby (same prices) are larger and furnished in an antique style.

○ **Villa Rosa.** V. C. Colombo 127, 84017 Positano (SA). ☎ and fax **089/811-955**. 12 units, all with bathroom. A/C. 100,000–120,000L ($58.80–$70.60) single; 150,000L ($88.25) double. Rates include breakfast. AE, DC, MC, V. Parking 20,000–25,000L ($11.75–$14.70) in garage. Closed Nov–Feb.

It's across the street from famous Hotel Le Sireneuse, with twice the view at one quarter the price. The large, square rooms are quiet and nos. 8 through 11 have large terraces shaded by vine-strewn arbors. The terraces offer postcard views of Positano's main village spur, as well as bits of the harbor and sea. The mattresses are orthopedic, tile floors painted prettily, furnishings peasant style, and bathrooms decidedly modest. All rooms have sea views and high vaulted ceilings (no. 11 even has frescoes). No. 13 has two rooms to sleep a family of four. This former *affittacamere* began its transformation into a hotel only in 1995, so slowly you'll find more amenities. When the hotel finally gets permission to install phones, TVs, and minibars sometime in 1999, prices may go up, but not astronomically. Breakfast is served on your own terrace.

WORTH A SPLURGE

Hotel Casa Albertina. V. Tavolozza 3 (a staircase tucked into a bend of Vle. Pasitea), 84017 Positano (SA). ☎ **089/875-143**. Fax 089/811-540. 19 units, all with bathroom. A/C MINIBAR TEL. 160,000–180,000L ($94.10–$105.90) standard single, 180,000–210,000L ($105.90–$123.50) superior single; 160,000–220,000L ($94.10–$129.40) standard double, 180,000–260,000L ($105.90–$152.95) superior double. Half-pension of 50,000L ($29.40) per person required in high season. Rates include breakfast. AE, DC, MC, V. Parking 30,000L ($17.65) with valet service. SITA coastal bus to first Positano stop, then walk down Viale Pasitea to the Hotel San Pietro—the white main hotel, not its yellow "residence" branch up the road—and take the stairs down just to the hotel's left; coming from Postiano's center, take the stairs up between Bar Ciro and Trattoria da Vincenzo.

Rather hard to find, but oh!—worth the splurge. Many of the rooms were recently renovated and, while small, have built-in closets and small terraces to make up for it. Most are done in Mediterranean blue and white, with padded headboards, marble-top sinks in the modern bathrooms, cool tile floors, and easy chairs beginning to show wear. But what you really come for are the perfect views over the Spiaggia Grande, majolica church dome, Positano's posh other half, and the stunning, undulating coastline beyond. No. 22 to 24 have the biggest terraces, and 24 has a Jacuzzi (but dusty-pink romantic no. 31 has a hot tub built for two in a bathroom-with-a-view). Avoid older rooms with the tiny balconies and aging furnishings, as well as nos. 25 to 27 with truncated vistas. Book early, by July the hotel's full until September. The drawback: a prodigious number of stairs down (and back up!) to the port; after dinner, you can head a few dozen steps down to Bar Ciro, with tables set on a panoramic curve of Viale Pasitea and often a guitar or mandolin player entertaining evening customers.

WHERE TO DINE

✪ **Donna Rosa.** V. Montepertuso 97–99 (a village in the hills above Positano). ☎ **089/811-806.** Reservations recommended. Primi 8,000–18,000L ($4.70–$10.60); secondi 7,000–35,000L ($4.10–$20.60). DC, MC, V. July–Sept daily 7:30–11pm or later and Wed–Sun 12:30–4:30pm; Oct–Nov 7, Dec 5–June Tues–Sun 12:30–4:30pm, 7:30–11pm or later. Closed Nov 8–Dec 4. Bus: bus to Montepertuso every 2 hr from V. Colombo; for lunch take the 10:20am or schoolchild-packed 12:20pm. If you reserve ahead, they might be able to pick you up in Positano. INVENTIVE CAMPANIAN.

The food at this countryside trattoria located high above Positano blows away the competition down in town. Attention to detail, from using the freshest of ingredients and making pastas and desserts by hand to a thoughtful presentation on your plate, is impeccable. Open with a *caprese* for a nest of tiny mozzarella balls amid a red sea of halved cherry tomatoes. To sample a variety of the kitchen's bounty, order a *trittico* for primo, a trio of pastas perhaps including *pappardelle funghi porcini e gamberi* (wide noodles with porcini mushrooms and shrimp), or *ravioli del Marchese* (stuffed with pumpkin in a sauce of fused butter, crisped sage, and Parmesan). Fresh fish is the order of the day for secondo, and the house white is perfectly refreshing. The kitchen is open to view—always a sign of honest cooking—and although it's almost deserted at lunch when everyone's down at the beach (but you can be up here in the cool breezes), nighttime packs it full until long after midnight, and one of the waitresses/daughters sings when the mood strikes. Definitely worth the journey up here.

Lo Guarracino. V. Positanesi d'America 12. ☎ **089/875-794.** Reservations recommended. Primi 9,000–18,000L ($5.30–$10.60); secondi 12,000–26,000L ($7.05–$15.30); pizza 9,000–15,000L ($5.30–$8.80). AE, MC, V. Wed–Mon noon–3pm, 7:30–11pm. Open Tues July–Aug. Closed Nov–Easter. POSITANO/PIZZA.

A cliff-hugging path from the Spiaggia Grande wraps around to this seaside trattoria/pizzeria in a scenic 5-minute stroll. Perhaps its being so hidden has kept prices low, despite the genuinely tasty food. Duck under the bougainvillea-shrouded entrance and find a table at the edge of the terrace to listen to the sea crash against Fornillo beach below and gaze at the Galli islets beyond ranks of floating fishing boats. The pizzas are quite good if you want something light and quick, or go local with linguine ai *ricci di mare* (sea urchin) or homemade gnocchi sorrentina. Unless you opt for something basic like a scaloppina al limone, the proximity of the sea guarantees you'll be following up with something fishy like *pesce spada* (grilled swordfish steak) or *zuppa di cozze* (mussel soup).

WORTH A SPLURGE

Buca di Bacco. V. Rampa Teglia 4. ☎ **089/875-699.** www.starnet.it/buca. Reservations required. Primi 12,000–30,000L ($7.05–$17.65); secondi 15,000–40,000L ($8.80–$23.55). AE, DC, MC, V. Daily 12:30–3pm, 8–11:30pm. Closed Nov–Easter. POSITANO/SEAFOOD.

Buca offers the best value among the see-and-be-seen splurge restaurants overlooking the beach at the center of town. Even if it's only to take a postbeach drink, definitely stop by to hobnob with the glitterati and occasional celebrity of Positano's summer set. For full meals—the kitchen has made great strides in recent years to rank it back among the top of the coast—head upstairs to the arbor-covered terrace and reserve well ahead of time for a table along the railing with the sea below. *Linguine all'astice* (noodles with prawns) is a popular primo, or try *spaghetti areganati* (with garlic, tomatoes, oregano, and a generous pinch of hot pepper). The best main courses are simple *gamberoni grigliati* (grilled giant prawns), *boccadero al limone* (red sea bream in a light, summery lemon sauce), or a *lombatina* (veal chop in butter and sage).

POSITANO AFTER DARK

At the far end of Spiaggia Grande is the dance club **Music on the Rocks** (☎ 089/875-874), carved into the cliff side and overlooking its own section of beach. The Beautiful People catch a boat to nearby Praiano and the hot club of the Coast, **Africana** (☎ 089/874-042), another sea-level grotto, this one with watery sinkholes in the dance floor (which fishermen sometimes come to dredge while the party's going on). You must book ahead at **Agenzia Viaggi Positour** (☎ 089/875-555) or **Music Station Quicksilver** (☎ 089/811-963); the boat (15,000L/$8.80) leaves at 11:30pm from the Pontile Lucibello dock at Spiaggia Grande, to return at 3am. Both clubs open nightly June to August, weekends in May and September, and close the rest of the year.

EN ROUTE TO AMALFI

About 3 kilometers (2 mi.) beyond Positano is its sister hamlet of **Praiano,** also a trendy resort (only much smaller and still little-known) with a majolica-domed church. Past the village of Furore the bus pops out of a tunnel to ride a bridge across one of the coast's most dramatic gorges, the **Vallone del Furore.** At kilometer marker 24, outside the fishing community of Conca dei Marini, are the stairs (or elevator) down to the **Grotta dello Smeraldo (Emerald Grotto).** This cavern was formed above sea level (you can tell since it has stalactites and stalagmites, which don't form in sea grottoes), then partially sunk below the water. The effect of light inside causes the water to glow an eerie green. Admission is 5,000L ($2.95); it's open daily 9:30am to 5pm (4pm in winter).

7 Historic Amalfi

61 km (38 mi.) SE of Naples, 18 km (11 mi.) E of Positanp, 34 km (21 mi.) W of Salerno, 272 km (169 mi.) SE of Rome

The whitewashed streets of the once-great maritime port of Amalfi are full of history, recalling a time in the Middle Ages when it rivaled Genoa, Pisa, and Venice as a trading behemoth. Amalfi's connections with the Orient led it to introduce to Europe such novelties as paper, coffee, carpet, and the compass—though Amalfi holds they themselves invented that last one, and have even erected a statue in the middle of the piazza at the port of hometown boy Flavio Gioia said to have fabricated the first compass. Amalfi also entered history when a local monk, backed by Amalfitani merchants, founded a hospital in Jerusalem along with a benevolent order that later became known as the Knights of Malta.

At its height, Amalfi had a population of 70,000 and lorded it over the Tyrrhenian Sea. But the Normans gave it a whooping in 1131, and soon after Pisa swept in to trounce its rival twice. The final blow came in 1343, when a one-two combination of tidal waves and earthquakes slumped much of the grand city into the sea. Amalfi is now a much reduced little resort town of 6,000 inhabitants, but left over from its glory days are a spectacular Duomo and the *Tavole Amalfitane,* the western world's first maritime code, a set of laws that continued to rule trade and the sea until 1570.

ARRIVING & INFORMATION   Amalfi Coast buses end their run at the main harbor front Piazza F. Gioia, where you can also pick up the bus up to Ravello, or the one to continue down the rest of the coast to Salerno. If you're driving, there's a public lot at the port that charges 3,000L ($1.75) per hour for **parking.** The **tourist info office** is hidden at the back left corner of a lovely little courtyard off Cor. Roma 19, along the harbor (☎ **089/871-107;** fax 089/872-619).

AMBLING THROUGH AMALFI

The star of Amalfi is the 13th-century ✪ **Duomo,** its magnificent Lombard-Norman facade of striped arches, Gothic tracery, interlocking arches forming blind arcades, and glittering mosaics rising majestically at the top of a mighty set of 62 stairs. Towering over it on the left is a bell tower of 1276 with a majolica drum at the top surrounded by four smaller drums. Simeon of Syria crafted the cathedral's massive bronze doors (whose panels feature crosses and saints inlaid with silver) in Constantinople in 1066. Like the other great maritime powers, Amalfi stole itself a venerable saint from the Holy Land in the 12th century, which is why the body of St. Andrew the Apostle lies under the altar. A separate entrance to the left of the main one gives access (for 3,000L/$1.75) to the **cloisters of paradise,** tiny Saracen-style cloisters from 1263 composed of interlocking and superimposed pointed arches forming a complex pattern above the colonnade.

Off Corso R. Marinare (the road east along the harbor), upstairs in the municipal buildings that surround a small piazza, is a tiny **Museo Civico** (free), which preserves those *Tavole Amalfitane* outlining the old maritime code.

HITTING THE BEACH & A BOAT EXCURSION   Amalfi's **beach,** right in the center of the port off Piazza F. Gioia, isn't much to write home about, but at least it's sandy and the section on the right is free. From the docks, boats leave hourly 9am to 4pm for an **excursion to the Grotta dello Smeraldo** (see above, in previous section) for 10,000L ($5.90) round-trip (not including the admission fee).

WHERE TO STAY

The higher price listed for any room below is for high season, which in Amalfi usually runs June through September.

Amalfi. V. d. Pastai 3 (about halfway up the main road in town, look for a sign pointing up a stair/street off to the left), 84011 Amalfi (SA). ☎ **089/872-440.** Fax 089/872-250. www.starnet.it/hamalfi. E-mail: hamalfi@starnet.it. 40 units, all with bathroom. TV TEL. 100,000–160,000L ($58.80–$94.10) single; 120,000–180,000L ($70.60–$105.90) double. Rates include breakfast (will go 10,000L/$5.90 less per person if ask for room without). AE, MC, V. Parking 20,000–25,000L ($11.75–$14.70) in hotel garage.

Run by seven siblings, the Amalfi sits in the casbah of whitewashed streets just off the main drag. It's a basic hotel, but clean and roomy, featuring broad tile floors, cots with little back support, and functional furnishings in light-tone wood lacquer. Some rooms overlook the gleaming white alleys surrounding the hotel, others the pretty gardens whose orange trees provide the fruit for your breakfast juice. There's also a roof terrace for dinners.

Residence. V. d. Reppubliche Marinare 9, 84011 Amalfi (SA). ☎ **089/872-229.** Fax 089-873-070. 27 units, all with bathroom. TV TEL. 100,000–140,000L ($58.80–$82.35) single; 160,000–180,000L ($94.10–$105.90) double. Rates include breakfast. AE, MC, V. Parking 25,000L ($14.70) in garage. Closed mid-Oct–Easter.

The faded, harbor-front facade is not promising, but once you get up to the guest quarters the Residence looks decidedly upscale—a large vaulted dining room whose shaded terrace overlooks the beach, statues in niches, a swirling central stair. The balconied rooms, too, are nicer than the price would suggest, many with patterned tile floors, new bath fixtures, oils on the walls, and pleasantly unobtrusive furniture mixed with some antiques. The beds could be firmer, and although rooms on the front are filled with the traffic sounds of the Amalfi Drive below by day (and Vespa-mounted teens by night), they also have a great view of the beach and port for people-watching. Some ceilings have fresco remnants, and the upper floors still get the sea view but less noise filtering up, while those in the flank look over the slightly quieter road leading into Piazza del Duomo.

WORTH A SPLURGE

Marina Riviera. V. P. Comite 9, 84011 Amalfi (SA). ☎ **089/871-104.** Fax 089/871-351. 22 units, all with bathroom. MINIBAR TV TEL. 190,000–220,000L ($111.75–$129.40) large single; 150,000–190,000L ($88.25–$111.75) tiny single; 230,000–260,000L ($135.30–$152.95) double. Rates include breakfast. AE, DC, MC, V. Parking 20,000L ($11.75) in garage with valet. Open all year.

Partly carved into the rock on an outward curve of the Amalfi Drive leading east out of Amalfi, the Marina Riviera overlooks Amalfi's beach side, with the Duomo just a 4-minute stroll away. It's run by the Gargano family, which knows how to treat guests—it also owns the Amalfi Coast's premier Hotel Santa Caterina—and although quieter than its third sister hotel, the Residence (see above), it's less central and lacks the quirky Old World elegance. All of the largish accommodations overlook the sea and are filled with light and cool breezes off the waters, enhanced by the whirring ceiling fans. Rooms are done with Mediterranean simplicity: whitewashed walls, clean tile floors, and firm beds. The spacious bathrooms were recently redone, and in summer, there's a breakfast terrace with water views.

WHERE TO DINE

✪ **Da Barraca.** Pz. degli Dogi (off the left of Pz. d. Duomo, duck under the arched street and bear right). ☎ **089/871-285.** Reservations recommended. Primi 7,000–11,000L ($4.10–$6.50); secondi 7,000–30,000L ($4.10–$17.65). Fixed-price menu 25,000L ($14.70, no wine). AE, MC, V. Thurs–Tues noon–3pm, 7pm–midnight. CAMPANIAN/SEAFOOD.

A real bargain gem, with tables on the only truly locals' piazza in Amalfi, surrounded by the fruit stands, butcher shops, and alimentari that ensure your food will be fresh. In cooler weather, you can sit under the fishing nets of the glassed-in veranda listening to records of Neapolitan guitar music. The meat-stuffed cannelloni are hearty, with cracked pepper for a spicy edge, while the perfectly cooked gnocchi alla sorrentina and *farfalle vongole e rughetta* (bow tie pasta with clams and rughetta) are also worthy. Secondi include scaloppine al marsala, an omelette alla mozzarella, or roasted fresh fish. The waiters are perennially harried, but give them time and while you wait for the bill enjoy a *profitterole al limone* (pastry stuffed with lemon cream) or *crostata di frutta* (fruit tart with a creamy lemon glaze).

Da Maria. V. Lorenzo di Amalfi (just off Pz. d. Duomo). ☎ **089/871-880.** Primi 15,000–18,000L ($8.80–$10.60); secondi 18,000–35,000L ($10.60–$20.60); pizza 5,000–15,000L ($2.95–$8.80). Menù turistico 30,000L ($17.65, no wine). DC, MC, V. Tues–Sun noon–2:30pm, 7:30–11pm. CAMPANIAN/SEAFOOD/PIZZA.

Da Maria is a standby on the main drag in the center of town, filling a cavernous pair of whitewashed rooms that are scattered with tables and look vaguely like an upscale cafeteria. The tasty, basic dishes such as risotto alla pescatore and *cubetti alle scogliere* (pasta with baby squid) are overpriced due to the prime location, but the excellent pizza has great crust and is the true bargain here—try the *colombina* with onions and pancetta.

Il Tarì. V. P. Capuano 9–11 (a continuation of V. Cavour, the main road into town). ☎ **089/871-832.** Reservations recommended. Primi 7,000–13,000L ($4.10–$7.65); secondi 13,000–27,000L ($7.65–$15.90); pizza 4,000–17,000L ($2.35–$10). Menù turistico 25,000L ($14.70; no wine). AE, MC, V. Tues–Sun 11:30am–3pm, 7–11pm. AMALFITANA/PIZZA.

Il Tarì's two packed rooms on Amalfi's main street are separated by duck-your-head arches that do nothing to ebb the flow of noisy babble in Italian and a half dozen tourist tongues. Its location and prices draw the crowds, but it has a cozier, friendlier atmosphere than the vast Da Maria down the block. The pizza has excellent crust—try it topped *à la Tarì*, with mozzarella, prosciutto, Parmesan shavings, and arugula. If you'd prefer pasta, dig into local specialty *scialatielli*, either *con frutti di mare* (seafood) or *con pomodoro, melanzane, e mozzarella* (a rich gooey mix of tomatoes, eggplant, and mozzarella). Secondi are less exciting, with a list of the same old *scaloppine* (veal cooked with herbs), *calamari in umido* (stewed octopus), or the somewhat more successful *pesce al cartoccio*.

WORTH A SPLURGE

✪ **La Caravella.** V. Matteo Camera 12 (under the tunnel on the main Amalfi Drive into the port). ☎ **089/871-029.** Reservations required. Primi 18,000–30,000L ($10.60–$17.65); secondi 20,000–32,000L ($11.75–$18.80). AE, MC, V. Wed–Mon noon–2:30pm, 7:30–11pm. Closed Nov. CAMPANIAN/SEAFOOD.

If you're feeling the heady dolce vita and want to splash out, head to this least chillingly priced of Amalfi's fine seafood restaurants. A refined setting for more than 30 years, Caravella's stuccoed rooms, discreet service, ample wine list, and subtly flavored dishes are steeped in Amalfitani tradition. Open with the house specialty *scialatelli alla caravella* (handmade pasta in a tomato-seafood sauce), *ovoletti di provola e rucola con pomodorini* (glorified ravioli stuffed with Parmesan), or *paccheri di gargano con cozze, patate, e rucola* (wide ribbons of pasta piled with mussels, arugula, and boiled potatoes in cream sauce). Popular dishes include fresh *pesce al forno con patate* (oven roasted fish) or *pescato del giorno all'acqua pazza* (fish of the day with tiny tomatoes) for secondo. Meat eaters will enjoy a *filetto di manzo al Barolo* (beef fillet in red wine). Save room for the renowned lemon soufflé (supposedly for two only, but they served it to me solo).

8 The Retreat of Ravello

275 km (171 mi.) SE of Rome, 66 km (41 mi.) SE of Naples, 29 km (18 mi.) W of Salerno

Hilltop ✪ **Ravello,** 6 kilometers (3.6 mi.) from Amalfi and 1,155 feet up in the hills, is a sweet-scented landscape bursting with color. It's a tiny town of profusely flowering vines and shrubs where discreet hotels share space with everyday houses, tumbled-down buildings planted with vegetable gardens, and crumbling villas whose grounds and lush pleasure gardens have become public parks. Almost every bend in the stony alleys and stairs opens upon a new eye-popping vista to the distant eastern stretch of the Amalfi Coast, or down into the Valle del Dragone (Valley of the Dragon) dropping below the western edge of town, a deep vale of green terraced with gardens and strewn with white houses and small hamlets.

Ravello and its excellent restaurants make a marvelous escape from the tourist crush of the sun-worshipping towns down on the coast, and has long been a favorite with writers and musicians looking for a quiet retreat. Gore Vidal maintains a villa up here, and D. H. Lawrence and Greta Garbo both spent time unwinding in Ravello, a lofty Garden of Eden along the already enchanting Amalfi Coast.

ARRIVING & INFORMATION   The bus lets you off just outside the tunnel-like gate into town. There's a **tourist info** office at Pz. Duomo 1, under the left side of the cathedral (☎ **089/857-096;** fax 089/857-977). It's open Monday to Saturday 8am to 8pm (7pm October to March).

WHAT TO SEE & DO

The gardens, villas, and churches of Ravello are perfect settings for the **series of chamber music,** orchestra, and soloist concerts that run throughout the year. In July especially, the music of Richard Wagner (another Ravellophile) is celebrated with performances by the likes of Placido Domingo conducted by Zubin Mehta and backed by world-class orchestras from Israel, London, Moscow, etc. Ask at the tourist office or contact the **Ravello Concert Society** (☎ **089/858-149;** www.rcs.amalficoast.it or www.agroa.stm.it/memo).

Duomo. Pz. Duomo. Admission to church free, museo 2,000L ($1.20). Daily 9:30am–1pm, 3–7pm.

Ravello's Romanesque cathedral was built in 1076. The central bronze doors were cast in 1099 at Constantinople and feature disarmingly simple low relief panels of archers, warriors, and Bible scenes. Inside are a pair of gorgeous 12th-century pulpits, carved of marble and carried on the backs of lions. The pulpits' panels are inlaid with mosaics of swirling designs, Christian symbols (look for the whale swallowing Jonah), and fantastic mythical beasts. The small museum displays Renaissance busts, late Imperial cinerary urns, and more medieval carvings and bits of mosaic.

✪ **Villa Rufolo.** Pz. Duomo. ☎ **089/857-657.** Admission 5,000L ($2.95) adults, 3,000L ($1.75) under 12 and over 65. Daily 9am to 9pm (some days it closes at 4pm).

The villa itself was started by the powerful Rufolo family in the 11th century and added to for generations in Saracen and Norman styles. The rooms of the restructured central villa are now used for art exhibits, and the surrounding grounds—filled with intimate flowering gardens set into the extensive villa ruins above a spectacular view down the eastern Amalfi Coast—are the backdrop for excellent outdoor concerts. This is only appropriate, since upon seeing this tropical paradise in 1880, composer Richard Wagner exclaimed, "The magical garden of Klingsor has been found!" and, inspired, went on to complete his *Parsifal.*

✪ **Villa Cimbrone.** At the end of V. S. Chiara (take V. S. Francesco out of Pz. Duomo). No phone. Admission 6,000L ($3.55) adults, 4,000L ($2.35) under 12. Daily 9am–sunset.

The parts of the 1904 villa you can explore are full of cryptlike nooks and cloistered crannies. The grounds are a huge playground of palms, magnificently spreading umbrella pines, ivy-clad walls, hidden flower gardens guarded by statues, panoramic terraces lined with busts, and vertigo-inducing cliff-top vistas from tiny templelike gazebos.

WHERE TO STAY

Toro. Vle. Wagner 3, 84010 Ravello (SA). ☎ and fax **089/857-211.** 9 units, 8 with bathroom. TEL. 70,000–80,000L ($41.20–$47.05) single; 110,000–120,000L ($64.70–$70.60) double with or without bathroom. Rates include breakfast. AE, DC, MC, V. Closed Nov–Easter.

Great location, great prices, good food, no sea view. That about sums it up for this small, friendly pensione across from the Duomo's left flank. Hey, if it was good enough for Greig, it should do us fine for a night. The firm beds rest on squeaky clean tile floors alongside functional furnishings and a comfy chair for snuggling down with a book. All but two rooms overlook vegetable gardens and the Valle del Dragone beyond. In summer, you can take inexpensive meals in an arbor-shaded garden.

Villa Amore. V. d. Fusco 5, 84010 Ravello (SA) ☎ and fax **089/857-135.** 16 units, all with bathroom. TEL. 55,000–65,000L ($32.35–$38.25) single; 100,000–110,000L ($58.80–$64.70) double. Rates include breakfast. MC, V. Take V. S. Francesco toward the Villa Cimbrone and veer left onto V. d. Fusco.

This little gem run by a pair of kindly ladies is quite a climb above the main piazza, but that only makes it feel more like a hidden retreat. The paisley-spread beds are a little soft and the phones aren't direct dial, but most baths are fairly new, the tile floors are scattered with rugs, it's heated in winter, and there are abundant breezes to part the curtains in summer. All rooms have small terraces to enjoy the views down the crinkly coast running east of Ravello; from upstairs rooms this vista is unobstructed, but downstairs you have to peek past a little flowering garden. The setting is quiet as can be, and breakfast is served on the panoramic terrace.

WORTH A SPLURGE

Villa Maria. V. S. Chiara 2 (follow V. S. Francesco toward the Villa Cimbrone), 84010 Ravello (SA). ☎ **089/857-255.** Fax 089/857-071. 16 units, 2 suites. A/C MINIBAR TV TEL. Oct–May 180,000L ($105.90) single; 220,000L ($129.40) double. June–Sept 260,000L ($152.95) single; 360,000L ($211.75) double with required half-board. AE, DC, MC, V. Rates include breakfast. Free parking.

Villa Maria, converted from a 1935 private home, offers a taste of the refined elegance that Ravello enjoyed in past centuries. The tone is set by an old-fashioned salon off the entrance, where a grand chandelier hangs over an antique silver tea setting. The rooms' floor tiles are richly patterned, the walls hung with quality prints and oils, and the period furnishings mixed with the odd futon couch. Firm mattresses rest on genuine box springs backed by wooden or brass headboards, and many of the ample bathrooms feature Jacuzzi tubs. Only nos. 6 and 7 have garden views rather than vistas down the Valle del Dragone to the sea. Guests can use the parking facilities and outdoor pool at the inn's nearby sister hotel, the Giordano. Villa Maria's garden restaurant, recommended below, is one of the town's best; for a pizza or light meal outdoors in summer, you can pop across the street to the owners' little Villa Eva park.

WHERE TO DINE

La Colonna. V. Roma 22. ☎ **089/857-411.** Reservations recommended. Primi 9,000–15,000L ($5.30–$8.80); secondi 12,000–25,000L ($7.05–$14.70); pizza 8,000–13,000L ($4.70–$7.65). AE, DC, MC, V. Easter–Oct daily noon–3pm, 7–midnight; Nov–Easter Wed–Mon noon–3pm. CAMPANIAN.

Call ahead for one of the few tables set in the flower-filled courtyard, or sit under the Gothic ceilings of the long main room that hint at the building's origins 800 years ago as stalls for the palazzo above. Ask after the fresh pasta of the day, which may be tagliatelle (thick, flat pasta ropes) with frutti di mare or in a creamy tomato sauce studded with eggplant, or perhaps you'd prefer *agnolotti* (like ravioli) stuffed with seafood in a zucchini sauce. In the secondi department, the restaurant's specialty is fish. If you're looking for something light, try the baked tomatoes stuffed with rice.

✪ **Cumpá Cosimo.** V. Roma 44–46. ☎ **089/857-156.** Reservations highly recommended. Primi 8,000–20,000L ($4.70–$11.75); secondi 15,000–30,000L ($8.80–$17.65); pizza 8,000–15,000L ($4.70–$8.80). AE, MC, V. Daily 12:15–3:30pm, 6:30pm–midnight. Closed Mon Nov–Dec 10 and Jan 8–Feb. CAMPANIAN.

Culinary matriarch Netta Buttone presides over these wood-beamed dining rooms, effusively displaying her joys of cooking and providing her guests with a memorable evening. Cumpá Cosimo has been a Ravello institution for more than 70 years—Bogie and Jackie O were once customers, and Gore Vidal is something of a regular. Ingredients come from the family farm, concocted into the likes of *gnocchi alla sorrentina*, marvelous *crespolini alla Cumpá Cosimo* (pasta crepes layered with prosciutto and cheese then rolled and baked), *fusilli al ragout*, and cheesy *maccheroni al forno.* The best way to sample the bounty is the *piatto misto della casa*, seven sampler-sized portions of Netta's primi, each better than the last. Secondi include *coniglio alla cacciatore* (rabbit with tomatoes and olives), *agnello scottaditto* (delicious lamb chops), and fresh fish. For dessert, try one of Netta's storied soufflés, or a peach or fig from the family orchards.

WORTH A SPLURGE

Villa Maria. V. S. Chiara 2. ☎ **089/857-255.** Reservations highly recommended. Primi 11,000–22,000L ($6.50–$12.95); secondi 13,000–28,000L ($7.65–$16.50). AE, DC, MC, V. Daily 12:30–3pm, 7:30–10:30pm. Closed Tues Oct–Easter. CAMPANIAN.

Save for Cumpá Cosimo, most of Ravello's great restaurants are, unusually, in its hotels. Villa Maria scores twice, with both the best splurge hotel and the finest restaurant in town. The dining terrace, which overlooks the hamlets of the Dragone Valley, is shaded by spreading tree branches and filled with the strains of classical music from hidden speakers. The waiter will suggest the specialties of the day, which may be fish-stuffed ravioli served with frutti di mare. If you can't decide between *crespolini* (flaky pasta wrapped around prosciutto and cheese), *raviolini* (stuffed with ricotta and meat under tomato sauce), or *soffratini* (pasta puffs filled with ricotta and spinach), sample all three in the *trittico*. Grilled fresh fish dominates the secondi, or you can fall back on *saltimbocca alla romana* (veal, sage, and prosciutto cooked in white wine). The tangy house white is of local vintage and perfect for lunch.

THE CERAMICS OF VIETRI

You'll pass though several more small villages as you make your way east on the Amalfi Coast toward Salerno, but the one most worth a stopover is at the tail end of the coast, **Vietri Sul Mare,** which is practically a suburb of Salerno. The bus lets you off right at the heart of the ceramics zone, so you can easily do a spot of shopping for these hand-painted plates and espresso sets before continuing on. Vietri is southern Italy's premier ceramics center, with dozens of *botteghe* plying a craft that's more than 500 years old, but has become a bit of a tourist industry. Among the gaggle of schlocky stores, seek out these quality workshops.

The best of those right on the main drag is **Avallone,** Cor. Umberto 122–124 (☎ **089-210-029**), with good price and quality control and some innovative patterns. My favorite shop is **V. Pinto,** Cor. Umberto 31 (☎ **089/210-271**). At 150 years, it's the oldest in town, and also one of the largest, as adept in creating new patterns as in following those of their display plates that date back to the early 1700s. **Francesco Raimondi,** one of their star artists, struck out on his own in 1998 with a little shop at V. Mazzini 3 (☎ **089/761-787**). In his highly symbolic and well-executed designs he practices both craft, by painting traditional patterns, and art by inventing his own. Don't leave town without checking out the funky, ceramic-studded building of **Solimene,** V. Madonna degli Angeli 7 (☎ **089/210-243**), an old ceramics school and factory now a bit dilapidated and serving as a vast showroom for the firm's output (good prices, but somewhat sloppy work).

SALERNO

Salerno—shipping port, anchor of the Amalfi Coast's eastern end, and gateway to southern Campania—ain't much to look at. It serves visitors mainly as a stopping point for those making connections to the Amalfi coast, Naples, and the Greek temples at Paestum.

ARRIVING & INFORMATION If arriving from the Amalfi Coast, stay on the bus until the end of the line, a block down and a few blocks over from the train station. For **SITA bus info** call ☎ **089/226-604;** for **train info** call the station at ☎ **089/252-020.** There's a tourist info office at Pz. Amendola 8 (☎ **089/224-744**) and a provincial office at V. Velia 15 (☎ **089/224-322**).

9 Paestum's Greek Temples

42 km (26 mi.) S of Salerno, 100 km (62 mi.) SE of Naples, 304 km (189 mi.) SE of Rome

Poseidonia, or the City of Poseidon, was founded in the 6th century B.C. by Greek colonists from Sybaris. It trucked along nicely as the Roman colony of Paestum after 273 B.C., and gained a small measure of fame for its enormous roses (which continue to bloom twice a year in gardens around the site). But malaria decimated the population, and in the 9th century the Saracens wiped it off the map and out of memory. It wasn't until the 18th century while building a road through the area that anyone other than farmers stumbled across the three incredible ✪ **Greek temples** jutting out the of landscape, surrounded by blue-gray mountains.

ESSENTIALS

GETTING HERE   By Train   Only local trains (*diretto* or *regionale*) stop at Paestum. **From Naples,** there are eight daily runs (87 min; 8,200L/$4.80). **From Salerno,** nine daily trains headed to "Paola" stop at Paestum (30 min; 4,700L/$2.75). The ticket office at Paestum's station is closed indefinitely, so when getting on here you can pay on the train with no penalty.

By Bus   SCAT buses (☎ **0974/838-415**) from **Salerno** (☎ **089/226-604**) are more frequent than trains (two or more per hour) and let you off right at the museum in front of the archaeological site (50 min; 4,700L/$2.75). They leave Salerno from Piazza d. Concordia at the waterfront, a few blocks down from the train station (and a few blocks over from where the Amalfi Coast SITA buses stop).

By Car   Take provincial road 175 south from Salerno.

GETTING AROUND   Paestum is in the middle of nowhere in mozzarella country, and the only signs of civilization are the postcard stands, hotels, and restaurants that a tourist site draws. From the train station, you can bargain with a taxi driver for the trip to your hotel (don't go over 15,000L/$8.80). Otherwise, head out of the station and continue straight under the arch at the intersection. After a 15-minute, 1-kilometer (.6-mi.) stroll, the road ends at the archaeological site and Albergo delle Rose. For the museum, main site entrance, and dinky tourist office, turn right. For the Hotel Helios, Nettuno restaurant, Porta della Giustizia site entrance (and, eventually, the beach): turn left, then right, for another 5-minute walk.

VISITOR INFORMATION   There's a tourist office near the museum at V. Magna Grecia 155 (☎ **0828/811-016;** fax 0828/722-322; www.fromitaly.it/Paestum). It's open Monday to Saturday 8am to 2pm.

EXPLORING ANCIENT GREECE IN CAMPANIA

Scavi (Archaeological Site). V. Magna Grecia. No phone. Admission 8,000L ($4.70). Daily 9am to 1 hour before sunset (as early as 3:30pm in late Nov, 7:30pm June–July).

Amid the grasses stained with poppies and crisscrossed by the low stone walls that outline the remains of the ancient city rise three mighty temples, all of which still go by their erroneous old names. The modestly sized **Basilica** was actually a **Temple of Hera,** built in 530 B.C. and the oldest temple at Paestum. Next door is the enormous and strikingly well-preserved ✪ **Temple of Neptune,** in reality probably dedicated to Apollo or Zeus, built in 450 B.C. and one of the three most complete Greek temples in the world. Its pediments and entablature are virtually intact atop 14, 30-foot-high fluted columns down each side, six each across the front and back, and a cella in the

---

Travel Tip

It take only 1 to 2 hours to explore the temples at Paestum; allow another hour to see the museum. You can easily see it all in one morning by taking an early train from Naples and lunching at the Nettuno restaurant on site before continuing on your way.

center divided by two more rows of smaller columns. Farther off in the site is the **Temple of Ceres,** more likely a temple to Athena, and the midget of the bunch, built around 500 B.C. and preserving, along with all 34 of its columns, some architrave and large chunks of its pediments. The Temples of Hera and Neptune were swathed in scaffolding throughout 1998 for restoration work, and there's no word as yet on when they'll be unveiled.

Museo Nazionale. V. Magna Grecia. ☎ **0828/811-023.** Admission 8,000L ($4.70). Daily 9am–6:30pm. Closed first and third Mon of every month.

Along with archaic Greek sculpture and vases, this museum preserves a great series of **metopes** (carved reliefs) from a nearby sanctuary of Hera, which depict scenes from Homeric myth and women dancing to honor the goddess. The museum's ✪ **Tomb of the Diver** paintings from 480 B.C., are the only surviving examples of ancient Greek painting in the world. Aside from their namesake image of a bronzed youth diving into a blue sea (a symbol of the journey to the afterlife), these paintings focus on a homoerotic banquet scene in which the revelers play at games and musical instruments (and at flirting) while reclining on couches.

WHERE TO STAY & DINE

True bargain hunters can head to Paestum's budgeteer crash pad of choice, the **Albergo delle Rose,** Via Magna Grecia (☎ **0828/811-070**). The small, plain, functional doubles upstairs go for 90,000L ($52.95) with bathroom and breakfast, and the restaurant downstairs serves tasty cheap pizze, an outstanding *caprese* salad, and other Campanian dishes.

Hotel Helios. V. P. di Piemonte, 84063 Paestum (SA). ☎ **0828/811-451.** Fax 0828/ 721-047. 30 units, 2 suites, all with bathroom. A/C MINIBAR TV TEL. 150,000L ($88.25) double; 350,000L ($205.90) suite. Rates include breakfast. AE, DC, MC, V. Parking free.

Nothing if not convenient, this contemporary hotel across from one of the archaeological site entrances has been completely overhauled in the past 2 years. Set in gardens around a pool and shaded terrace, a series of low, white buildings house the spacious whitewashed rooms. A bit bland in their functional modernity, the accommodations are quite comfortable, with long sofas, designer floor lamps, firm beds, and ultramodern bathrooms kitted out with Jacuzzi tubs. In the open spaces of the public rooms are a small bar and stylish restaurant with plate-glass views of the busy kitchen.

Ristorante Nettuno. V. P. di Piemonte. ☎ **0828/811-028.** Reservations recommended. Primi 6,000–13,000L ($3.55–$7.65); secondi 11,000–22,000L ($6.50–$12.95). AE, DC, MC, V. Tues–Sun 12:30–3pm. July–Aug sometimes open evenings and on Mon. ITALIAN.

Paestum's best, certainly most scenic, lunch remains this 18th-century country villa, converted to a restaurant in 1920s and often taken over by entire busloads of tourists. It's wedged between the parking lot and archaeological site entrance, with a glassed-in patio a scant 500 feet from the temples. Arrive early or book to get that prime view of the ruins, but if you find the crowds milling about the souvenir stands and into the site distracting, you can retreat to the grandly arched interior. The house dish is *crespolini* (baked pasta crepes wrapped around fresh mozzarella studded with prosciutto), or start with *stracciatella* (egg-drop soup with Parmesan) before sampling their *cotoletta alla milanese* (breaded veal cutlet) or *pollo al forno* (oven-roasted chicken).

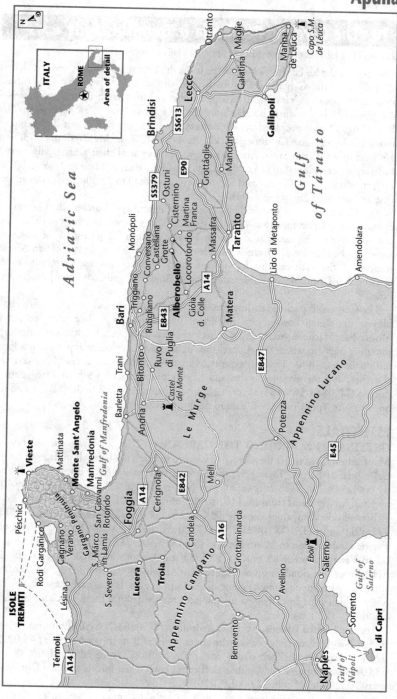

10 The Gargano Peninsula & Tremiti Islands

237 km (142 mi.) NE of Naples, 39 km (23.4 mi.) NE of Foggia

The spur on the heel of Italy's boot shape is the thickly forested, highly venerated, and eternally beautiful Gargano Peninsula. Ringed with fishing villages that have turned into resorts—such as **Vieste** with its long beaches and whitewashed medieval center— the peninsula is a favorite holiday spot among Italians (and a few Germans). The Bronze Age Daunia people of the 7th century BC called this 3,500-foot-high lump of limestone home. The ✪ **museum** (☎ **0884-587-838**) in **Manfredonia**'s 13th to 16th century Castello Svevo-Aragonese preserves several of their fantastically carved funerary steles. Admission is 4,000L ($2.35); its open daily 8:30am to 1pm and 3:30 to 7pm (summers also Friday and Saturday evenings 8:30 to 11:30pm). It's closed the first and last Monday of the month.

Aside from this and a few medieval castles and pilgrimage churches, the Gargano is mainly a destination for those seeking a secluded rocky lagoon in which to swim. You can also hike in the oak-shaded interior **Foresta Umbra** or retreat to the isolation found on the tiny **Tremiti Islands**—made up of the mini isle-mountain of **San Nicola** (capped by the 11th century, half-ruined abbey of Santa Maria a Mare) and pine-forested **San Domino**, where Roman Emperor Augustus' granddaughter Julia died in exile.

The Gargano is packed late July through August, and especially on any church holiday as the region hosts several important pilgrimage towns. The most famous is **Monte San Michele,** preserving a church cobbled together across the centuries surrounding a grotto where St. Michael the Archangel miraculously appeared to a local bishop in A.D. 490. This pretty mountain town also boasts a few 12th century churches, and the evocative ruins and stupendous views of a 9th to 15th century castello (☎ **0884-565-444**) to scramble around; admission is 3,000L ($1.75), and it's open 8am to 7pm in summer, 9am to noon in winter.

ESSENTIALS

GETTING TO & AROUND THE GARGANO   The gateway to the Gargano is **Manfredonia,** but to get there you'll have to go through the (fairly humdrum) provincial capital of Foggia. **To Foggia,** there are six daily trains from **Rome** (4 to 5 hrs.; 31,000L/$18.25); eight daily trains from **Naples** (100 to 175 min.; 16,000L/$9.40); and half-hourly trains from **Bari** (67 to 100 min.; 10,100L/$5.95).

Between the companies Ferrovie del Gargano (☎ **167/296-247** toll-free, or 0881/ 772-491) and SITA (☎ **0881/773-117**), there are 21 buses (three Sunday) **from Foggia**'s train station **to Manfredonia** (45 min.; 3,500L/$2.05). Six of them continue on **to Vieste** (another 85 min.; 8,500L/$5 total). From Manfredonia there are 18 SITA buses (five Sunday) up **to Monte Sant'Angelo** (40 to 60 min.; 3,500L/$2.05), three of which (none Sunday) come direct from Foggia. If you have a **car,** follow the SS89, which runs from Foggia to Manfredonia then skirts the ultrascenic Gargano coastline.

For the **Tremiti Islands,** Adriatica hydrofoils (☎ **0884/708-501**) run from Vieste to San Nicola three times daily in summer, daily at 9am in winter (1 hr.; 48,000L/ $28.25 round-trip). There's also one daily hydrofoil from Manfredonia (2 hr.; 68,000L/$40 round-trip). A public skiff runs between San Nicola and San Domenico every 10 minutes (5 min.; 2,000L/$1.20).

VISITOR INFORMATION   Manfredonia's tourist office, upstairs at Corso Manfredi 26 (☎ **0884/581-998**, fax 0884/583-295), has general Gargano information.

It's open Monday to Saturday 8:30am to 1:30pm. **Vieste**'s tourist office is on Piazza Kennedy, where Via Fazzini becomes Corso Italia (☎ 0884/708-806, fax 0884/707-495, www.viesteonline.it). It's open year-round Monday to Saturday 8am to 2pm; in summer also Monday to Saturday 4 to 9:30pm, Sunday 9am to 1pm. For information on the **Foresta Umbra**, contact Ecogargano, in a cabin located on the otherwise empty road through the center of the forest (☎ 0884/565-444 or 0884/565-579). The Gargano towns have banded together on the Internet at **www.gargano.it/citta** (in Italian).

WHERE TO STAY & DINE

Coppolarossa. V. d. Celestini 13 (off Cor. Manfredi 1 block from Pz. Marconi). ☎ 0884/582-522. Reservations recommended. Primi 8,000–12,000L ($4.70–$7.05); secondi 12,000–20,000L ($7.05–$11.75). No credit cards. Tues–Sun 12:30–3:30pm, 8–11pm. Closed 10 days in late June. PUGLIESE/SEAFOOD.

The "Red Cap" is a mix of youthful, casual atmosphere, a slightly old-fashioned decor, and decidedly traditional cooking. Service by the red-vested waiters in shorts or jeans can be pretty perfunctory and off-handed, which is odd since without a printed menu they have to recite the dishes of the day. Be sure to load up at the do-it-yourself antipasto spread laden with seafood and vegetable goodies. Sample the house dish *troccoli ai frutti di mare*, or the *orecchiette rucola e scampi* (with arugula and shrimp; they'll do it up with tomato sauce if you're all fished out). Secondi include a veal *bistecca* or a large *grigliata di pesce* (a grill of giant prawns, local fishes, and tiny squid).

Da Costanza. Cor. Garibaldi 67. ☎ 0884/561-313. Primi 7,000–8,000L ($4.10–$4.70); secondi 12,000–14,000L ($7.05–$8.25). Menù turistico 30,000L ($17.65; with wine). Daily noon–2pm, 7:30–9:30pm. Closed Fri Nov–June. PUGLIESE.

In business since 1916, this trattoria has a short menu—eight pastas, four meats—but each selection is excellent. The whitewashed, half-cylinder cellar rooms are plain but cool, and Donna Costanza displays her homemade pastas and grilled veggies at the table as you enter (that's her in the kitchen beyond, tasting the ragout sauce and adding just a bit more water). By all means try the orecchiette with that ragout, or orecchiette tipico—tossed the traditional way (before the advent of tomatoes) with rucola, pepperoncino, and anchovies. I can also recommend the *agnello alla brace* (grilled mutton) for a secondo or the massive tomato sauce–covered *involtino di vitello*. The fixed-price menu is an excellent value—you order what you like and it covers everything but coffee.

Hotel Gargano. Vle. Beccarini 2 (at the north end of town on the main shore drive), 71043 Manfredonia (FG). ☎ 0884/587-621. Fax 0884/586-021. 46 units, all with bathroom. A/C TV TEL. 115,000L ($67.65) single; 160,000L ($94.10) double. Breakfast 12,000L ($7.05). MC, V. Free parking.

It's your typical 1970s beach hotel, with Black Watch–plaid carpets but an otherwise white-and-blue Mediterranean color scheme and accommodations whose balconies overlook the round salt-water pool and across the palm-lined street to the sea. The hotel hasn't seen a renovation for almost 30 years, so the lacquer is chipping along the modular furnishings' edges. There are wide-open lobby spaces and lots of terrace-edge seating to sip drinks. It's a 10-minute seaside stroll from the castle and passeggiata on Corso Manfredi, and the hotel restaurant for once isn't half bad.

Hotel Seggio. V. Vieste 7/Pz. Seggio, 71019 Vieste d. Gargano (FG). ☎ 0884/708-123. Fax 0884/708-727. 28 units, all with bathroom. A/C TV TEL. Mar 28–June 26 and Sept 6–Oct 30, 95,000–125,000L ($55.90–$73.53) double. June 27–July 31 and Aug 23–Sept 5 150,000L ($88.24) double. Aug 1–22 265,000L ($155.90) double with required half-board. Rates include breakfast. AE, DC, MC, V. Closed Nov–Easter.

Vieste's 17th-century town hall, tucked halfway up the hill of the old quarter, is now home to the Hotel Seggio. Although rooms vary greatly, most have functional furnishings, and sadly sagging cots. Some are low ceilinged and poorly lit, but almost all accommodations are fairly large, and about half have water views. The choice room, no. 104, has windows on two sides, a high wooden ceiling, and a terrace overlooking both the sea and the postcard-size square below. The stone-walled restaurant has a medieval flair and Pugliese menu, there's a sofa-filled bar area for piano music after dinner some nights, and set into the cliffs below is a tiny pool and cement pier over the shallow, sandy waters.

Ristorante Al Dragone. V. Duomo 8 (under the cathedral). ☎ **0884/701-212.** Reservations recommended. Primi 6,000–12,000L ($3.55–$7.05); secondi 13,000–26,000L ($7.65–$15.30). AE, MC, V. Wed–Mon 12:30–2:30pm, 7–10:30pm. Open daily mid-June–Aug. Closed Oct 31–Mar 15. PUGLIESE/SEAFOOD.

Descending into this restaurant set into a low cavern carved from the living rock is indeed like walking into the dragon's lair—a dragon partial to candlelit, gold-clothed tables and contemporary metal sculptures. The dragon would also have to be something of a gourmand, as his kitchen turns out excellent *spaghetti ricci di mare, strasch'net al Dragone* (noodles in a sauce of fresh tomatoes and mussels), and the house specialty *troccoli basilico zucchine e caciocavallo* (homemade pasta tossed with grilled zucchini slices and covered with shredded basil and hard sheep's cheese). For a seafood secondo, try the *pescatrice con capperi e cipolla* (delicate, local, boneless fish in an onion/lemon sauce with capers). Otherwise, the *spiedino* (assorted meats grilled shish kebab-style with potatoes) isn't bad.

A CATHEDRAL & A CASTLE EN ROUTE TO BARI

TRANI   It's the towering Romanesque ✪ **Cathedral** that draws visitors to this busy fishing port. Begun in 1099 at the very tip of the harbor, it rises stark white and grandiose against the blue of the water beyond. You currently enter via the lower church around the right side while the central 12th-century **bronze doors** are being restored, but jog up the facade's stairs anyway to inspect those doors' reliefs and the intricately carved portal around them. Walk all around the exterior, decorated with carved doorways, blind arcading, and sculptures poking out everywhere. The tall bell tower dates from the 1300s, and there are three layers of lower churches and crypts beneath the airy, bright main church, all preserving ancient Roman columns with carved medieval capitals and some 14th-century sarcophagi, mosaics, and fresco remnants.

A train runs twice hourly **from Foggia** (50 min.; 7,400L/$4.35). There's a **tourist office** at V. Cavour 140 (☎ and fax **0883/588-825**), and an info office on Piazza d. Repubblica (☎ **0883/43-295**).

✪ **CASTEL DEL MONTE**   Frederick II was a poet and an architect in addition to being an all-around great leader. He built many castles that dominate the cities throughout his Italian kingdom, but his most ambitious and fantastic creation by far sits alone in the Pugliese countryside. The 1240 masterpiece of octagonal proportions, **Castel del Monte** (☎ **0883/569-848** or 0883/290-286), commands a 1780-foot hilltop, rising in the distance above wheat fields and olive groves like a vision, a geometric perfection of sharp lines and pale honey-gray stone with eight-sided towers at each corner. The virtually empty interior is constructed of high vaulted rooms angling off each other to surround an octagonal courtyard with mesmerizing sameness and precision. Admission is 4,000L ($2.35). It's open daily April to September 9am to 6:30pm, October to March 9am to 1:30pm.

The castle's on the **SS170bis** 20 kilometers (12 mi.) from the town of Andria (tourist info: ☎ **0883/592-283**). To Andria, take a twice hourly Ferrotranvia bus or train **from Bari** (60 to 90 min.; 6,000L/$3.55), or one of 23 (nine Sunday) SITA buses **from Trani** (25 min.; 2,500L/$1.45). Unfortunately, from Andria there are just a few buses, in summer only, to the castle (25 min.; 2,000L/$1.20); a taxi will run a whopping 50,000L ($29.40) round-trip.

11 Bari

138 km (83 mi.) SE of Foggia and the Gargano

Founded before the even the Greeks landed in Apulia, Bari, the second largest city in Southern Italy, is a busy port and oil refining city and the region's industrial powerhouse. It's also the home of Santa Claus—or rather, the bones of St. Nicholas, sheltered in Apulia's first grand Romanesque church. Beyond its vast industrial sprawl, Bari also retains a great Old City to wander (watch for pickpockets).

ESSENTIALS

GETTING HERE   By Train   Daily trains run twice an hour from **Foggia** (67 to 100 min.; 10,100L/$5.95) and pass through **Trani** (30 to 43 min.; 4,700L/$2.75). There are also six daily trains from **Rome** (4.5 hr.; 42,000L/$24.70).

The *Bari Centrale* station is on Piazza A. Moro at the south edge of town (☎ **080/524-0148**). This station is serviced by national FS trains plus several private lines, including the **Ferrovia Bari Nord** (ticket office on the left of Piazza A. Moro as you exit the main rail station; ☎ **080/521-3577**), which runs trains to Bitonto and Ruvo; and the **Ferrovia del Sud-Est** (☎ **080/546-2111**), which services Alberobello and the Valle D'Itria (see section 3 of this chapter).

By Bus   There are hourly SITA buses from **Barletta** (65 to 95 min.; 6,000L/$3.55) and **Trani** (60 to 90 min.; 5,000L/$2.95) and two early morning buses (none Sunday) from **Manfredonia** (2 hr. 15 min.; 12,000L/$7.05). In Bari, buses stop at Piazza A. Moro (the train station). The SITA office is at the edge of town, V. B. Buozzi 35 (☎ **080/521-3714** or 080/574-1800), but you can get tickets and info at the Marozzi office, Cor. Italia 3 (at the corner with Piazza A. Moro).

By Car   Bari's on the SS116 from Trani and Barletta and the A14 highway from Foggia. From Manfredonia, just follow the coastal road until it merges with the SS116.

VISITOR INFORMATION   The tourist information office is at Pz. A. Moro 32 (☎ **080/524-2244**), the right side of the square as you exit the train station. There's also an office inside the station (☎ **080/558-0817**) open Monday to Friday 8:30am to 7pm, Saturday 8:30am to noon. Youths should head directly to **Stop Over in Bari,** V. Nicolai 47 (☎ **080/521-4538**; www.inmedia.it/StopOver). Besides city info and a room-finding service (available to visitors of any age), the company offers (to those under 30) **free** city bus pass, bikes, camping, and weekly excursions. Coupons are available for shopping and restaurants. It's open Monday to Saturday 8:30am to 1:30pm and 4:30 to 8:30pm.

WHAT TO SEE & DO

✪ **San Nicola.** Pz. S. Nicola. ☎ **080-521-1205.** Admission free. Daily 7am–noon, 4:30–7pm.

Bari built the first great Norman Romanesque church in Apulia in 1087 to house the earthly remains of St. Nicholas, today mythologized as Santa Claus, but originally a

4th-century Turkish bishop renowned for his piety, kindness, and helpful miracles. The church's **central portal** is an especially fine marriage of Arab, Byzantine, and native styles, with carved decorations and a griffin-crowned gable whose columns are supported by two worn bulls. Inside the apse sits the **Bishop's throne,** crafted in 1098 with human telamones supporting the legs. In the **crypt** there's usually a service going on before St. Nick's tomb, but you can quietly circulate to examine the Byzantine and Romanesque capitals carved with lions, griffins, and peacocks.

Cattedrale (Cathedral). Pz. d. Odegitria. No phone. Admission free. Daily 7am–noon, 4:30–7pm.

Built about a century after the church of San Nicola, the cathedral is a striking Romanesque edifice, with a tall bell tower and an octagonal drum. The **facade** has some more recent embellishments, including baroque canopies over the doors and a modern rose window. The **pulpit** is a curious cobbling together of 13th-century fragments. Bits of **mosaic** flooring from an earlier, 8th-century church survive in the transept alongside some medieval **frescoes.**

Castello Svevo. Pz. Frederico II di Svevia. ☎ **080/5218-6111.** Admission 4,000L ($2.35). Tues–Sat 9am–1pm, 3:30–7pm; Sun 9am–1pm.

There are free guided tours of this massive fortress, started by Frederick II from 1233 to 1239 and expanded by the Aragonese in the 16th century. But for the next few years most of the castle will remain closed for refurbishment.

Pinacoteca Provinciale. V. Spalato 19 (off Lungomare N. Suaro). ☎ **080/541-2421.** Admission 5,000L ($2.95), 1,000L (60¢) students. Tues–Sat 9:30am–1pm, 4–7pm; Sun 9am–1pm.

This small collection is marked by some good pictures by medieval and baroque Pugliese painters, the Neapolitan school (including several by Luca Giordano), Venetian works by Bellini, Paolo Veronese, and Tintoretto, and some fine folk art (ceramics, presepio figurines) and canvases by local 19th-century artists.

WHERE TO STAY

Bari is a business town, and the hotel scene is pretty depressing. Stick to the choices below, since most other budget inns are dives. If you're having trouble lining up a room, stop by the folks at **Stop Over in Bari** (see above under "Visitor Information") or the train station **tourist office.**

Bristol. V. Califati 15, 70123 Bari. ☎ and fax **080/521-1503.** 17 units, all with bathroom. A/C MINIBAR TV TEL. 75,000–85,000L ($44.10–$50) single; 100,000–110,000L ($58.80–$64.70) double. No credit cards. Parking 25,000–30,000L ($14.70–$17.65).

In a pleasant older building that must have been stylish in its day, the Bristol offers clean, basic accommodations with rather unattractive furnishings, but there's elbow room to spare under the vaulted ceilings. The bathrooms are in good shape, but the beds are hard (not firm; hard, as in a lumpy mattress on an unforgiving wooden plank). I include the Bristol mainly for those who are looking for the amenities, but not the prices, of the Boston.

Moderno. V. Crisenzio 60, 70122 Bari. ☎ **080/521-3313.** Fax 080/521-4718. 34 apts, all with bathroom. A/C TV TEL. 60,000–70,000L ($35.30–$41.20) single; 95,000–115,000L ($55.90–$67.65) double. MC, V. Parking 18,000L ($10.60) overnight (extra charge for daytime).

This is more of a residence than a hotel—the rooms are cleaned twice a week rather than daily (plus, of course, before a new customer moves in)—and while nothing about it really merits a star rating, I can dub it the best value in Bari. Accommodations are all miniapartments featuring modern bathrooms and kitchenettes; even the singles are spacious. The furniture is all standardized, and beds predictably saggy. However, the prices are excellent for such comfort, and it's in a safe area convenient for day-tripping (the train station is just around the corner). The lower prices apply Friday to Sunday.

WOTH A SPLURGE

Boston. V. Piccinni 155, 70122 Bari. ☎ **080/521-6633.** Fax 080/524-6802. www.inmedia. it/boston. 69 units, all with bathroom. A/C MINIBAR TV TEL. 130,000–150,000L ($76.50–$88.25) single; 190,000–210,000L ($111.75–$123.50) double. Rates include breakfast. AE, DC, MC, V. Parking 25,000L ($14.70).

You pay for the level of comfort at this businessperson's hotel, but you're safely within the New City yet just a few short blocks from the castello and historic district. The well-built modular furnishings have suede accents, but the carpets are beginning to stain and scuff in places. Most rooms are cut to a modest size, and while windows are fairly soundproof, request a room on the back *cortile* to escape the bus and traffic noise. The lower rates are for weekends and August.

WHERE TO DINE

Da Margherita. Pz. Ferrarese 10–11. ☎ **080/523-5852.** Primi 7,000–9,000L ($4.10–$5.30); secondi 7,000–15,000L ($4.10–$8.80); pizza 5,000–8,000L ($2.95–$4.70). DC, MC, V. Thurs–Tues 11:30am–3pm, 7pm–1am. Closed Sept. BARESE/PIZZA.

Margherita's is a family affair where locals line up under stone vaulted ceilings for wood-oven pizza takeout or to enjoy full meals at sidewalk tables. The *cavatelli ai frutti di mare* (homemade pasta studded with seafood) is popular, but I prefer the *orecchiette alla Barese* (in a braciola sauce where a veal involtino is cooked in the tomato base for hours). Secondi are, of course, mainly fish—*speidino di seppioline* (cuttlefish grilled on a skewer, a Bari specialty), *scampi e gamberi arrosto* (roast scampi and giant shrimp), baked catch of the day—or try *scaloppine* (veal scallop) cooked in lemon or white wine.

Nuova Vecchia Bari. V. Dante Alghieri 47. ☎ **080/521-6496.** Reservations recommended. Primi 8,000–12,000L ($4.80–$7.05); secondi 17,000–25,000L ($10–$14.70). AE, DC, MC, V. Sat and Mon–Thurs 12:30–2:30pm, 7–10:30pm; Sun 12:30–2:30pm. Closed 20 days in Aug. BARESE.

It's expensive, but it's one of Bari's best, and you can still eat reasonably if you go without the overpriced secondi. In 1971, a couple of veteran Barese restaurateurs created this space of studied medievalism, with stone vaults, wines lining the walls, and niches filled with painted ceramic plates (each from a different restaurant in an national network of traditionalist eateries like this one). The seafood and veggie antipasti are famous; try the mix of greens, octopus, baby tomatoes, and scamorza baked in a ceramic crock. The chef conserves some of Bari's most traditional dishes, including *tortiera alla barese* (rice with potatoes, mussels, and zucchini) and *strascinate al ragù barese* (giant whole wheat orecchiette in a veal ragout). Under the same sauce come the veal *involtini*, or sample fresh fish or *agnello al forno con patate* (roast mutton with potatoes).

Taverna Verde. Lgo. Adua 19 (on Lungomare N. Sauro). ☎ **080/554-0870.** Reservations recommended. Primi 6,500–10,000L ($3.80–$5.90); secondi 8,000–16,000L ($4.70–$9.40); pizza 5,000–10,000L ($2.95–$5.90). AE, DC, MC, V. Mon–Sat noon–3pm, 7:30–midnight. Closed Aug 14–24. BARESE/PUGLIESE.

It pays to book ahead here since Bari families treat it as sort of a dining room away from home, filling the tables with three generations and lots of noisy chatter. Although there's a good selection of regional and national wines, a giant beer is the beverage of choice to accompany *papardelle alla taverna verde* (wide noodles with tomatoes, mushrooms, and prosciutto), *spaghetti alle cozze* (with mussels), or *orecchiette alla barese* (they claim it's a ragout, but I'm hard pressed to find any meat). As a nice change of pace, there are several light secondi such as an *omletta al prosciutto* or *crostino di mozzarella al prosciutto* (a log of alternating mozzarella and bread slices, toasted and topped with prosciutto). More substantial fare includes *filetto di manzo al pepe verde* (beef filet with green peppercorns) or the ever popular *frittura di calamari* (squid fry).

12 Alberobello & Capital of the Land of Trulli

63 km (38 mi.) SE of Bari

The lush, fertile Valle D'Itria is a fairytale landscape of grape vines and farmsteads where a goodly number of the locals still live in *trulli*, Italy's oddest example of idiosyncratic vernacular architecture. A *trullo* is a single-room, whitewashed cylindrical structure with a conical roof made of dark, flat rocks stacked in a spiral—all built without using mortar. No one is sure where trulli came from, though there are plenty of theories. One novel idea is that, during the Aragonese rule, the locals used them to avoid taxation; when they saw King Ferdinand's tax man coming, they'd just remove a stone from the trullo's roof, bringing it down and rendering the structure "unfinished," and hence untaxable.

✪ **Alberobello,** though not the largest town, is the de facto capital of the region for its two sizable neighborhoods composed of some 1,000 trulli—a cityscape so unique and well preserved that the entire town has been declared a national monument. You can also get good overviews of the valley by taking the train between the so-called "Balconies on the Valle D'Itria"—Locorotondo, Martina Franca, and Cisternino—high, whitewashed hill towns with panoramic vistas across this trulli landscape and some fantastic wines.

ESSENTIALS

GETTING HERE The **Ferrovia del Sud-Est** private rail line (☎ 080/546-2111) from **Bari** to Taranto services the valley, with 14 to 16 trains daily stopping at the Grotte di Castellana (1 hr.; 4,700L/$2.75), Alberobello (95 min.; 5,900L/$3.50), Locorotondo (104 min.; 6,700L/$3.95), and Martina Franca (110 min.; 6,700L/$3.95). A line runs from Martina Franca to Cisternino eight times daily (12 min.; 2,200L/$1.30).

VISITOR INFORMATION Alberobello's tourist office is in the *Casa d'Amore* trullo at Piazza Ferdinando IV (☎ 080/432-5171; fax 080/932-5706; www.traveleurope.it/trulli.htm). It's open Monday to Friday 9am to 1pm and 3 to 8pm, Saturday and Sunday 9am to 8pm (possibly shorter hours in winter).

WHAT TO SEE & DO

✪ **Alberobello** is rather touristy, but with two swatches of the townscape made almost entirely of trulli (and the rest of the town also simple and whitewashed), it is a sight to behold and a joy to wander. Alberobello is spread on two hills, and across from the main part of town is the slope known as **Rione Monti,** the larger of the two trullo zones with scrubbed clean stone pedestrian streets and loads of character. Most of Rione Monti's trulli are now souvenir or craft stands; if you want to see a more genuinely residential trullo zone, had behind Piazza XXVII Maggio through Piazza Plebescito for the **Aia Piccola** district.

The 18th-century **Trullo Sovrano,** on Piazza Sacramento, was the only trullo built with two stories. Originally a seminary, it was bought by a local family who returned from America with modest riches and set it up as a house. The admission of 2,500L ($1.50), 1,000L (60¢) under 12, includes a free guided tour through rooms decked out as they would have been two generations ago. It's open Monday to Friday 10am to 1pm and 3:30 to 8pm, Saturday and Sunday 9:30am to 1pm and 3 to 8:30pm.

A CAVERN EN ROUTE TO ALBEROBELLO

The **Grotte di Castellana** (☎ 080/496-5511; www.vol.it/castellanagrotte) is one of Italy's most spectacular cave systems, glittering with crystals and filled with weird and wondrous rock formations spread throughout a series of large caverns and long tunnels. The first great chamber is almost 200 feet deep, with a great oculus at the top open to the sunlight and rimmed with streamers of vegetation. Bring warm clothes for the 48°F temperature. The short, 1-hour, 1-kilometer (0.6-mi.) tour gives you a taste for this underworld, but it's worthwhile to take the 2-hour, 3-kilometer (1.8-mi.) tour that includes the caverns' most stunning sight, the fabulous "Grotta Bianca" where the calciferous water seeping through has so few impurities that the crystalline stalactites and stalagmites it has formed shine a brilliant white.

You'd think that for 25,000L ($14.70), 20,000L ($11.75) ages 6 to 14, they'd let you take photographs—or at the very least throw in the parking, which costs an extra 3,000L ($1.75). The caves are open daily 8:30am to 7pm. The longer tour (in English) currently leaves at 11am and 4pm; the shorter English-language tour—which costs 15,000L ($8.80) adults, 12,000L ($7.05) ages 6 to 14—leaves at 1pm and 6:30pm.

WHERE TO STAY & DINE

Hotel Lanzillotta/Cucina dei Trulli. Pz. Ferdinando IV 31 (off Pz. d. Popolo, across from the tourist office), 70011 Alberobello (BA). ☎ **080/432-1511.** Fax 080/432-1179. 27 units, all with bathroom. TV TEL. 60,000L ($35.30) single; 90,000L ($52.95) double. Rates include breakfast. AE, DC, MC, V.

Opened 100 years ago by the current owner's grandfather, the Lanzillotta is an old central favorite with a great restaurant (reviewed below). Although plans are underfoot to renovate, for now it remains an old-fashioned pensione. Rooms vary between the high vaulted ceilings of the original 19th-century palazzo (with bathrooms jerry-built into the corners) and the slightly larger accommodations of the top two floors tacked on in the 1960s. Furnishings are basic, beds comfy enough, bathrooms a little rickety, and while being around the corner from the main piazza is convenient, it can also stay noisy a bit too late for comfort. The attached **Cucina dei Trulli restaurant** (open to nonguests) serves exquisitely prepared Pugliese fare made of the freshest ingredients. The menù turistico is just 25,000L ($14.70; no wine). The restaurant closes Tuesdays and December 8 through 26 (but is open daily June through August).

Ristorante Trullo d'Oro. V. Felice Cavallotti 17. ☎ **080/721-821.** Reservations recommended. Primi 9,000–15,000L ($5.30–$8.80); secondi 15,000–30,000L ($8.80–$17.65). AE, DC, MC, V. Tues–Sun noon–3pm, 8–11pm. Closed Jan. PUGLIESE/ITALIAN.

Atmosphere it's got in spades—you dine in a complex of trulli—the food's good, and the portions huge. You can sample three of the most traditional primi with the *assaggini dello chef,* perhaps including *spaghetti al trullo* (with fresh tomatoes, arugula, and Parmesan), *orecchiette alberobellesi* (in ragout with savory bread balls on top), and *purè di fave con cicoria.* Secondi are less outstanding, but still done well. If the assaggini were almost too much, go easy with *melanzane ripiene* (stuffed eggplant). Otherwise dine on *capretto ai carboni* (kid cooked over coals), or the popular *arrosto misto* (mixed meat roast).

✪ **Trullidea.** V. Monte Nero 18, 70011 Alberobello (BA). ☎ and fax **080/432-3860.** 10 trulli apts (sleep 2–6 each), all with bathroom. 90,000L ($52.95) double, 110,000L ($64.70) in Aug. Lower weekly rates available. Rates include breakfast. No credit cards.

What can I say—here you have the chance to sleep in a bona fide trullo, most of them smack on the prettiest street of the historic district, for a reasonable price. Guido Antionetta's idea was simple but brilliant: help preserve the trulli zone by opening up uninhabited structures as miniapartments, and at the same time give visitors even greater incentive to make Alberobello their base for exploring the region. He's even revived the dying tradition of painting the roofs with magic symbols (Christian and pagan). The accommodations are terribly atmospheric, with their stone floors, wood beams crossing the inside of the conical roofs, sturdy peasant-style furnishings, firm beds, and kitchenettes. Trulli are naturally cool in summer and warm in winter—the space heaters and fireplaces help. There's no way this is staying a secret for long, so reserve ahead. By 1999 credit cards should be accepted.

13 Taranto

50 km (30 mi.) S of Alberobello, 87 km (52 mi.) SE of Bari, 68 km (41 mi.) W of Brindisi

The city of Taranto—half ancient fishing town, half steel and industrial power-house—is drawn out thin between two huge lagoons (one used to harvest mussels and oysters, the other Italy's second largest naval yard). The narrowest portion of the land between these two "seas" is sliced across with two canals to create the rectangular, central island where the Spartans founded the colony of Taras in 708 B.C., and where the medieval section of town survives.

ESSENTIALS

GETTING HERE   There's a daily **train** from **Naples** (4.5 hr.; 25,500L/$15); three daily from **Salerno** (4 hr.; 22,000L/$12.95); 19 to 21 daily from **Bari** (66 to 100 min.; 10,100L/$5.95); eight runs from **Martina Franca** (40 min.; 3,900L/$2.30); and 11 trains (six Sunday) from **Brindisi** (65–80 min.; 9,700L/$5.70). There are **11 daily FSE buses** (☎ 099/477-4627) from **Martina Franca** (40 min.; 3,300L/ $1.95); and six daily SITA buses (☎ 099/459-4089) from **Bari** (80 to 110 min.; 11,000L/$6.50).

If you're **driving** here, from **Alberobello,** take the SS172 to Locorotondo, where it runs south to head through Martina Franca to Taranto. **From Bari,** follow the A14 highway south until it end at the SS7, which leads in 17 kilometers (10 mi.) to Taranto.

VISITOR INFORMATION   The tourist office, Cor. Umberto 113 (☎ 099/ 453-2392; fax 099/453-2397), is open Monday to Friday 9am to 1pm and 5 to 7pm, Saturday 9am to noon. To get to it from the train station, hop bus 1/2, 3, or 8.

WHAT TO SEE & DO

The old city on its rectangular island is a confusing jumble of medieval churches, twisting Saracen streets, and the marvelous mayhem of the morning **fish market** at the island's northeast corner. At its center is a **Cathedral** raised in the 11th century but overhauled in the 16th, with a baroque facade of 1713 (some exterior Romanesque blind arcading survives around the sides and transepts). The capitals inside are Byzantine, a few carved with leafy forests and birds peeking out. The baroque *Cappella di S. Cataldo* (just right of the altar) is a fantasy of stuccoes, niched statues, expensive marbles, and a frescoed half-dome.

On the modern, mainland portion of Taranto you'll find the **Museo Archeologico Nazionale,** Cor. Umberto 41 (☎ 099/453-2112). It has the second largest archaeological collection in southern Italy (after Naples), including loads of exquisitely painted vases—especially of Corinthian and local manufacture—dating from the 8th century B.C., along with Roman floor mosaics of hunting and animal scenes and a superb collection of ancient gold and other jewelry (the diadems of intricately interwoven leaves and flowers are particularly noteworthy). The archaic bronze of Poseidon is probably tied to the legend that Taranto was founded by the sea god's son Taras, who came riding into the harbor on the back of a dolphin. Admission is 8,000L ($4.70); it's open daily, mid-June to August 8:30am to 1:30pm and 2:30 to 10pm, September to mid June 8:30am to 12:30pm. Take bus 1/2, 3, or 8.

WHERE TO STAY & DINE

Albergo Pisani. V. Cavour 43, 74100 Taranto. ☎ **099/453-4087.** Fax 099/470-7593. 20 units, 17 with bathroom. 40,000L ($23.55) single; 75,000–80,000L ($44.10–$47.05) double. Breakfast 3,000L ($1.75). No credit cards. Parking 25,000–35,000L ($14.70–$20.60).

This hotel's just half a block off the modern city's central Piazza Garibaldi and Via Duca d'Alba, scene of a lively passeggiata. As for the hotel, it ain't bad for budget; the rooms are clean and well lit, bathrooms older but in good order, and most accommodations overlook a quiet interior courtyard. If your modestly sized room starts feeling too cramped, you can join the laid-back management in the comfy downstairs TV lounge. Although Taranto does have some port city crime, the hotel is in a safe area of town, and the double gates are always locked.

✪ **Da Mimmo.** V. C. Giovinazzi 18. ☎ **099/459-3733.** Primi 6,000–9,000L ($3.55–$5.30); secondi 7,000–12,000L ($4.10–$7.05); pizza 5,000–8,000L ($2.95–$4.70). AE, MC, V. Thurs–Tues noon–2pm, 7–11:30pm. Closed 20 days in Aug. PUGLIESE/PIZZA.

The owner's name is Cosimo Mannarini, but everybody calls him Mimmo. Locals wait patiently up to 20 minutes to squeeze in at the outdoor tables with a bit of breeze, since the pizza oven keeps even the high stone vaults inside too warm for comfort in summer. The poet-cook is given to belting out Elvis ballads and Neapolitan folk songs, but that doesn't get in the way of his tossing excellent pizzas, which are small enough to leave you room for a secondo such as *involtino* or *popette al sugo*, or a *frittura di pesce fresco* (fry-up of the best catch from the docks that morning). If you'd rather not start with a pizza, among the primi you'll find the standby orecchiette al pomodoro, *pasta e fagioli* (pasta and beans), and *spaghetti alla cozze* (made with Taranto legendary mussels).

14 Brindisi

68 km (41 mi.) E of Taranto, 111 km (66.6 mi.) SE of Bari

Brindisi has always been a ferry port, from the days when the Romans built the Via Appia here from Rome, to medieval knights leaving for the Crusades, to modern sunseekers on their way to the Greek Isles. There are, however, a few low-key sights to pass the time while you await the evening departure of your ferry to Greece.

ESSENTIALS

GETTING HERE   By train, there are 11 daily runs from **Taranto** (65 to 80 min.; 9,700L/$5.70); twice hourly runs from **Bari** (80 to 90 min.; 10,100L/$5.95); and twice hourly runs from **Lecce** (25 to 45 min.; 3,900L/$2.30). There are also six daily trains from **Rome** (6 hr.; 49,000L/$28.80). Brindisi's **station** (☎ **0831/521-975**) is at the western edge of town on Piazza F. Crispi. If you're arriving **by bus,** FSE (☎ 080/542-6552 in Bari) runs three daily buses from **Bari** (105 min.; 11,000L/$6.50).

By Car   Take the SS7 from Taranto, the SS16 from Bari.

VISITOR INFORMATION   The main tourist office is 1 block down and to the left from the train station at V. C. Colombo 88 (☎ **0831/562-126;** fax 0831/562-149),

---

Ferries to Greece

It seems that almost every doorway in town that isn't a pizza joint is a travel agent. Trust none of them. A few are honest, but it's safest to go straight to the ferry lines themselves. There are plenty of shady ferry companies as well, but stick with the two biggies and you'll have no problems. **Adriatica** (☎ **0831/ 523-825**) is upstairs in the Stazione Marittima, Vle. Regina Margherita 13; **Hellenic Mediterranean Lines** (☎ **0831/528-531,** www.hml.it) is at Cor. Garibaldi 8.

Both run ferries every other day—daily June 26 to September 7—to Patras (where you can continue over land to Athens or Delphi, or by connecting ferry to the Greek islands), as well as regularly scheduled service to Corfu, Igoumenitsa, and Ithaca. Most ferries to Patras (a 19-hour trip) leave after 10pm, though some in summer leave at 7:30pm; present yourself at the ferry at least two hours before departure. One-way tickets to Patras run 35,000 to 95,000L ($20.60 to $55.90) depending on season, plus sleeping arrangements—free on the often quite chilly deck (or toss in a deck chair for 20,000L/$11.75) up to 30,000 to 155,000L ($17.65 to $91.20) per person for a cabin (depending on season and in-cabin facilities). Some rail passes like Eurail get you the travel free *but you must still reserve and pay for a cabin or deck chair.* Pick up *Frommer's Greece from $50 a Day* for more information on all these Greek destinations.

---

open Monday to Friday 8:30am to 1pm. There's an **information office** down at the port on Viale Regina Margherita (☎ **0831/523-072**), open Monday to Friday 7:30am to 2pm.

WHAT TO SEE & DO
On the Piazza del Duomo you'll find the 12th-century **Cathedral** (rebuilt in the 18th century, but with some original mosaics uncovered near the altar), the 15th-century **Portico dei Cavalieri Templari,** and the **Museo Archeologico Provinciale** (☎ **0831/221-401**). Inside are preserved Roman-era statues and trinkets like a pair of A.D. 1st-century dice, and some fine 4th-century B.C. bronzes fished out of the sea. Admission is free; it's open Monday to Friday 9:30am to 1:30pm (Tuesday also 3:30 to 6:30pm). The 11th-century Knights Templar church of **San Giovanni al Sepolcro** off Via S. Benedetto retains some worn but intriguing reliefs around the door and 13th-century frescoes inside (though it's usually locked).

Brindisi's one saving grace is a bus ride north of town, the A.D. 1322 Norman-Gothic church of ✪ **Santa Maria del Casale** (take bus 3d from the station and ask the driver to let you off), with a facade patterned in zigzags and chessboards of bluish-white and tan stones. Knights on their way to the Crusades would stop here to pray before boarding their boats, and the frescoes inside were meant to bolster their courage, reminding them what they were fighting for (on the right of the nave is a *Madonna Surrounded by Knights*) and what happened to eternal souls should faith fail (the gruesome *Last Judgment* filling the end wall).

WHERE TO STAY & DINE
Hotel Europa. Pz. Cairoli 5, 72100 Brindisi. ☎ **0831/528-546.** Fax 0831/568-351. 34 units, 14 with bathroom. TV TEL. 35,000L ($20.60) single without bathroom, 50,000–55,000L ($29.40–$32.35) single with bathroom; 60,000L ($35.30) double without bathroom, 80,000L ($47.05) double with bathroom. MC, V.

Signora Natalina is as welcoming to strangers at her spotless little hotel on the central piazza as to patrons who've been returning since their World War II days. Beaming wreathes of smiles around an ever-present cigarette, she'll chat your ear off while she struggles to check you in on the computer her English-speaking son insisted a modern hotel needs. At these prices you'll find the usual functional furniture and lazy-springed beds in the mostly huge rooms, but accommodations with bathrooms have rather nicer, newer built-in units and fabric-covered chairs that match the bedspreads. Strict budgeteers needn't worry—there is an ample number of, albeit cramped, hall bathrooms if you opt for the older, bathless rooms. Rooms are heated in winter, and five have air-conditioning.

Pantagruele. V. Salita di Ripalta 1–3 (near the port). ☎ **0831/560-605.** Reservations required. Primi 8,000–12,000L ($4.70–$7.05); secondi 12,000–25,000L ($7.05–$14.70). AE, DC, MC, V. Sept–June Tues–Sat 12:30–3pm, 7:30pm–midnight, Sun 12:30–3pm; July–Aug 6 Mon–Fri 12:30–3pm, 7:30pm–midnight, Sat 7:30pm–midnight. Closed Aug 7–31. Turn left off Cor. Garibaldi onto V. Amena, just past Adriatica's office. CREATIVE PUGLIESE.

The best of Brindisi's pricier restaurants—happily still at the low end of moderate—is hidden in the honeycomb of the port's back streets. The simple whitewashed rooms of wide-spaced tables enjoy a clientele of local cognoscenti and visiting foodies. Open with *trucioli con anelli di calamari* (homemade pasta in a cream sauce with squid rings, mussels, basil, and avocado), or *strossapreti con porcini, spek, e crema* (a hearty noodle dish with porcini mushrooms in a cream sauce with ham). If you're missing home, order their famous grilled Texas beefsteak for secondo, or go local with *tagliata di seppia* (cuttlefish fillets), adventurous with *fileto di struzzo alla miscela di pepe vari* (tender ostrich fillet in a sauce studded with peppercorns, sided with lightly fried potato slices), or traditional with the catch of the day. All the excellent desserts are homemade.

15 Lecce

143 km (86 mi.) SE of Bari, 85 km (51 mi.) E of Taranto

✪ Lecce's pedigree runs the gamut from a prehistoric and Greek settlement through the Romans, Byzantines, Normans, and Bourbons. It's been know both as the Apulian Athens for its scholarship (it's still home to one of Apulia's two universities), and the Florence of the Baroque for Lecce's unique, playful, and idiosyncratic take on the architectural style. Lecce's historic center is marked with a vibrant outdoor life of pastry cafes, street markets, and free summer concerts. Most sights have detailed explanatory plaques out front (in Italian and English), and many baroque facades are floodlit at night.

ESSENTIALS

GETTING HERE   There are twice-hourly **trains** from **Bari** (2 hr.; 12,100L/$7.10) that pass through **Brindisi** (23 to 43 min.; 3,900L/$2.30); five to eight runs from **Martina Franca** (110 min.; 10,100L/$5.95); and 11 runs (six Sunday) from **Taranto** (90 to 125 min.; 10,100L/$5.95). There are six daily trains from **Rome** (6 hr.; 53,000L/$31.20). **SITA** (☎ **0832/303-016**) runs four **buses** from **Brindisi** (30 min.; 10,000L/$5.90), and three from **Bari** (2.5 to 3 hr.; 17,000L/$10). If you're driving, Lecce's on the **SS613** from Brindisi.

VISITOR INFORMATION   The main tourist office is at V. Monte S. Michele 20 (☎ **0832/314-117;** fax 0832/314-814), but the central info office is near the Duomo on Via V. Emanuele, open Monday to Friday 9am to 1pm and 5 to 7pm, Saturday 9am to 1pm.

THE FLORENCE OF THE BAROQUE

Lecce's center is the broad **Piazza Sant'Oronzo,** which preserves the lower levels of a 1st-century B.C. **Roman amphitheater** in one corner, the **Sedile,** a surviving chunk of the 1592 town hall, and an **ancient Roman column** at the square's center (before lignting knocked it down and Lecce bought it, the pillar marked the end of the Appian Way in Brindisi).

The greatest of Lecce's baroque facades, **☼ Santa Croce,** was built between 1549 and 1679, a time span that explains the relative sobriety of the facade's lower half quickly giving over to Giuseppe Zimbalo's fantastic baroque exuberance above. The long interior has a coffered ceiling and some over-the-top side altars. Next door is the long, rather more subdued facade of the **Palazzo del Governo** (1659–95).

Hiding off Via V. Emanuele is one of Lecce's other gorgeous baroque corners, the enclosed, L-shaped **☼ Piazza del Duomo.** Giuseppe Zimbalo rebuilt the 12th-century **Duomo** in 1570, giving it a 225-foot bell tower and two facades: on the main entrance and around on the right transept, tucked into the other half of the piazza's "L" where it faces down the **Palazzo Vescovile** (1420–1632).

The **Museo Sigismundo Castromediano,** Viale Gallipoli at Viale F. Lo Re (☎ 0832-247-025), displays chipped Stone Age tools, a pair of prehistoric Earth-goddess "Venus" figurines, and the usual passel of terra-cottas and painted pottery. Admission is free; it's open Monday to Friday 8:30am to 1:30pm and 2 to 7pm.

SHOPPING　Lecce has been a *cartapesta* (papier-mâché) center since at least the 17th century. Perhaps the best artisan studio is that of **Claudio Riso** and his brothers at V. G. del Tufo 16 (off Via Federico d'Aragona; ☎ 0832/242-362). They produce remarkably detailed figures (starting at 60,000L/$35.30) from everyday, 18th-century Lecce life that have won them international prestige. One of my other favorite work-shops is the *bottega* of **Maurizio Ciafano,** V. Carlo Russi 10 (☎ 0360/740-906), where three young guys work hard in their tiny space to create peasant figures carrying bundles of twigs or wine jugs for 25,000 to 30,000L ($14.70 to $17.65). If you're looking for more variety, check out the **Mostra Permanente dell'Artigianato Salentino,** V. Rubichi 21 (☎ 0832/246-758), where you can peruse traditional crafts from across the province: small-town ceramics, cast iron, Lecce-made stone carving, and papier-mâché.

WHERE TO STAY & DINE

Cappello. V. Montegrappa 4, 73100 Lecce. ☎ **0832/308-881.** Fax 0832/301-535. www.thenet.it/hotelcappello. 32 units, all with bathroom. A/C MINIBAR TV TEL. 53,000L ($31.20) single; 85,000L ($50) double. AE, DC, MC, V. Parking 15,000L ($8.80). Leave the train station, turn left down V. Don Bosco, then left again onto V. Montegrappa.

The streets are quiet, but since the hotel abuts the train tracks, periodic noise is a problem, especially for rooms on the back. However, it's by far the best bargain in town. Rooms up on the first floor are the more attractive, although all are done in mis-matched functional pieces with squishy beds. Accommodations are pretty small, but there's a comfy air about them, and the high vaulted ceilings help as does the full array of in-room amenities.

☼ Cucina Casareccia. V. Costadura 19 (a road running north off the Villa Comunala gardens). ☎ **0832/245-178.** Reservations recommended. Fixed-price menu 30,000L ($17.65). MC, V. Tues–Sat 12:45–1pm, 7:30–10:30pm, Sun 12:45–1pm. Closed Aug 30–Sept 15, Dec 22–Jan 6. PUGLIESE HOME COOKING.

Concettina Cantoro makes coming to this spare, humble osteria like coming home for dinner. The place doesn't even have a name, just a sign that says "home cooking," but Concettina's culinary fame has spread—she's gone to Boston and New York to cook typical Pugliese dishes for top chefs. Concettina is a surrogate Leccese mamma to all her clients, from local regulars—some of whom are literally daily patrons—to the few lucky tourists who make it here. Let her take charge of your meal, offering a menu strong on local specialties such as puree of fava beans with wild chicory, lots of veggies, a potato-mussels-and-zucchini salad, *polpette* meatballs, and *sagna 'ncannulata* (tagliatelle rolled into rough spirals under a tomato and ricotta forte sauce).

Guido e Figli. V. XXV Luglio 14. ☎ **0832/305-868.** Reservations recommended. Primi 8,000–12,000L ($4.70–$7.05); secondi 7,000–8,000L ($4.10–$4.70); pizza 5,000–12,000L ($2.95–$7.05). AE, DC, MC, V. Tues–Sun noon–3pm, 7:30pm–1am. Open daily in Aug. Closed July 1–15. PUGLIESE/ITALIAN/PIZZA.

The low stone vaulting is atmospheric enough, but most patrons head straight back to sit under giant umbrellas on an untrafficked, pine-shaded piazza out back. The *orecchiette alla Guido* (Lecce's large whole wheat orecchiette in a tomato sauce with teensy meatballs, eggplant, and Parmesan) isn't bad, nor are the *fusili gran gusto* (pasta spirals with shrimp and salmon) or *parmigiana di melanzane* (a tomato, eggplant, and cheese casserole). Secondi include *polpette e messicane* (two types of meatballs, one stuffed with prosciutto and cheese, in a tomato and pepper sauce), *pollo al forno con patate* (oven-roasted chicken with roast potatoes), or *lumache* (snails) cooked however you like them (assuming you like them). Service is friendly, but can drag. Their popular **tavola calda** (a cafeteria sort of place) branch around the corner at V. S. Trinchese 10 (☎ 0832/300-802) also has outdoor tables on a pedestrian street off the main Piazza S. Oronzo. There's also prepared pastas (5,000L/$2.95), good meat dishes (8,000L/$4.70), and fine gelato.

Risorgimento. V. A. Imperiale 19, 73100 Lecce. ☎ **0832/242-125.** Fax 0832/245-571. 57 units, all with bathroom. A/C MINIBAR TV TEL. 97,000L ($57.05) single; 180,000L ($105.90) double. Rates include breakfast. AE, DC, MC, V. Parking 15,000L ($8.80).

It's a bit pricey, but by far Lecce's best bet—it simply couldn't be more central, half a block behind the main piazza and just a few minutes' walk from any of the city's baroque facades. Rooms are sizable, with patterned tile floors, fabric-covered walls, and antique-styled furnishings. Although beds are in good shape, the bathrooms show some wear, and the ancient air-conditioning units just don't cool the room at all. As a bonus, the hotel restaurant offers 25,000L ($14.70) set-price Pugliese meals

15

Sicily

by Reid Bramblett

Sicily is a triangle of tangled, rich history at the tip of Italy's boot, the largest island in the Mediterranean and only nominally considered part of Italy at all. It's a lush landscape of fertile valleys and imposing mountains, genteel resort towns and fantastic ancient ruins, glittering medieval mosaics and baroque cathedrals. Sicily is an endless spectacle of pagan festivals, puppet shows, and Mafia corruption, wine, volcanoes, and seafaring lore. No trip to Italy is complete without a visit to this island that sums up the best and the worst of Italy amid citrus groves, almond trees, and the hot Mediterranean sun.

Bronze Age Sikel and Sicani tribes lent the island their name, but it was the Greek colonies of Magna Graecia (8th to 4th century B.C.) that left the strongest ancient mark on the island. Here you'll find some of the most spectacularly sited and remarkably preserved Greek temples (at **Agrigento, Segesta,** and **Selinute**) and theaters (at **Siracusa, Taormina,** and **Segesta**) in the world. The Roman empire left Sicily the most extensive ancient mosaics in existence (at a villa outside Piazza Armerina), and Arabic Saracens founded the capital of Palermo in the 9th century.

The Normans came along in the early 11th century and set up a syncretic, highly advanced, and tolerant monarchy that incorporated the best of Greek, Arabic, Roman, and their own Celtic fashions. Under such enlightened rulers as Roger II and the Hohenstaufen emperor Frederick II, Sicilian literature came into its own a full 200 years before Dante. Frederick II was such a wise ruler and patron of the arts he earned the nickname *Stupor Mundi,* "wonder of the world." The Normans left the northern coast (Cefalù, Palermo, Monreale) scattered with Norman cathedrals and Arab-style palaces filled with some of the most gorgeous mosaic cycles in Europe.

In some respects, Sicily languished for more than 500 years under Spanish and Bourbon rule, mostly missing out on the Renaissance—though it did tune in for the baroque era, when native architects and sculptors developed the Sicilian baroque style to rebuild churches, palaces, and even entire cities after a series of devastating earthquakes. It wasn't until 1860 that Sicily joined Italy at all, and it wasn't until the 1980s and 1990s that the criminal organization we call the Mafia began to lose its dominance over corrupt local governments (see "Men of Honor" box).

Sicily's culture is one of the most enigmatic and difficult to fathom in Italy—Sicilian dialect is so far from common Italian that some

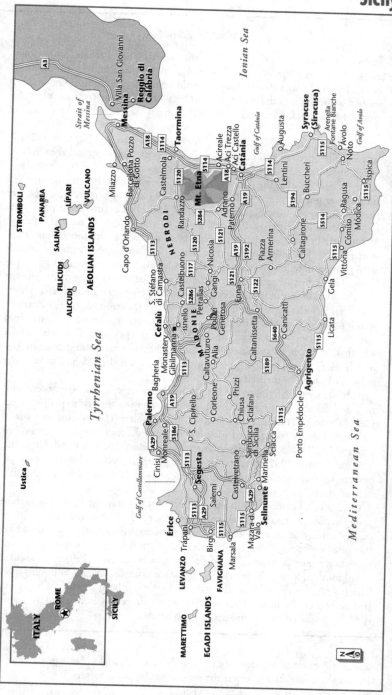

Men of Honor

In Sicily, they don't call it the Mafia (from the Arabic *mu'afah* or "protection"). They call it *Cosa Nostra,* literally "our thing," but more accurately "this thing we have." Its origins are debated, but the world's most famed criminal organization seemed to grow out of the convergence of local agricultural overseers working for absentee Bourbon landowners—hired thugs, from the peasant workers' point of view.

Members of the Sicilian Mafia—or "Men of Honor" as they like to be called—traditionally operated as a network of regional bosses who controlled individual towns by setting up puppet regimes of thoroughly corrupt officials. It was a sort of devil's bargain with the national Christian Democrat party, which controlled Italy's government from World War II until 1993 and, despite its law-and-order rhetoric, tacitly left Cosa Nostra alone so long as the bosses got out the party vote.

Men of honor trafficked in illegal goods, of course, but until the 1960s and 1970s their income was derived mostly from funneling state money into their own pockets, low-level protection rackets, and ensuring that public contracts were granted to fellow *mafiosi* (all reasons why Sicily has experienced grotesque unchecked industrialization and modern growth at the expense of its heritage and the good of its communities). But the younger generation of Mafia under-bosses got into the highly lucrative heroin and cocaine trades in the 1970s, transforming the Sicilian Mafia into a major world player on the international drug trafficking circuit—and raking in the dough. This ignited a clandestine Mafia war that, throughout the late 1970s and 1980s, generated lurid headlines of bloody Mafia hits. The new generation was wiping out the old, and turning the balance of power in their favor.

This situation gave rise to the first Mafia turncoats, disgruntled ex-bosses and rank-and-file stoolies who opened up and told their stories, first to police prefect Gen. Alberto Dalla Chiesa (assassinated 1982), and later to crusading magistrates Giovanni Falcone (slaughtered May 23, 1992) and Paolo Borsellino (murdered July 19, 1992), who staged the "maxitrails" of *mafiosi* that sent hundreds to jail. The magistrates' 1992 murders, especially, garnered public attention to—and, perhaps for the first time, true shame regarding—the *dis*honorable methods that defined the new Mafia.

On a much broader, and in many ways culturally important, scale it is these young *mafiosi,* without a moral center or check on their powers, that have driven many Sicilians to at least secretly break the unwritten code of *omertà,* which translates as "homage" but means "silence," when faced with harboring or even tolerating a man of honor. The Mafia still controls much of Palermo, the small towns south of it, and the provincial capitals of Catania, Trapani, and Agrigento. Throughout the rest of Sicily, though, its power has been slipping. The heroin trade is a far cry from construction schemes and protection money, and the Mafia is swiftly outliving its usefulness and its welcome.

consider it a distinct language—but this only serves to make the region one of the most fun to explore, and it secrets the most rewarding to discover.

A TASTE OF SICILY—The triad of Sicilian culinary staples is eggplant, pasta, and lots of fresh fish, with a heavy dose of native *limone* (lemon) and *mandorle* (almonds) thrown in for good measure. Some of the quintessential Sicilian dishes served all over the islands include *pasta all Norma* (short pasta, usually rigatoni, prepared in a casserole with cubed eggplant, fresh mozzarella, and tomatoes), *involtini di pesce spada* or *involtini di spada alle brace* (tiny swordfish roll-ups, usually breaded and grilled), *involtini di vitello* (like the swordfish, only made of veal), and *spaghetti ai ricci di mare* (spaghetti with sea urchins).

ESSENTIALS

GETTING HERE   By Train   If you buy a train ticket from a mainland city to anywhere in Sicily, the train will board the ferry for the crossing with you on it, so just sit tight.

By Car Ferry   The car ferry from Villa S. Giovanni in Calabria to Messina in Sicily runs like clockwork. When you exit the highway, just follow the lanes indicated by the pictogram of a boat with a car in it. When you see everyone parking haphazardly in an open lot to hop out and run into a little building, that's your cue to do the same to buy your ticket (take your car-rental form in with you; they'll need documentation of the license plate). The ferry runs every 20 minutes or so and costs 27,000 to 35,000L ($15.90 to $20.60), depending on the size of your car. The crossing takes 25 minutes. Foot passengers pay a mere 1,700L ($1).

VISITOR INFORMATION   The main tourist office in Palermo (see this chapter's section 3) has information on the entire island. Sicily's official Web site is **www.sicily.infcom.it.**

1 Messina

237 km (142 mi.) E of Palermo, 683 km (410 mi.) SE of Rome, 469 km (281 mi.) S of Naples

Sicily's primary port and third largest city doesn't offer many attractions aside from succulent swordfish dinners and a pair of Caravaggios in the **Museo Regionale,** bus no. 76 to 81 to V. d. Libertà 465 (☎ **090/361-292**); admission is 8,000L ($4.70); it's open Monday to Saturday 9am to 2pm, and again Tuesday, Thursday, and Saturday 4pm to 7pm (October to May 3pm to 6pm); and Sunday 9am to 1pm. But unless you fly or ferry straight to Palermo, Messina will be your introduction to the island. Since you'll be passing through, here's how to get in and out—plus where to stay and dine in case you get stuck. The **tourist office** is to your right as you exit the train station, Pz. d. Repubblica 44 (☎ **090/672-944;** www.aapitme.it/indexen.html). It's open Monday to Thursday 8am to 1:30pm and 3 to 6pm, Friday and Saturday 8am to 1:30pm.

GETTING HERE   By Train   There are five trains daily from **Rome** (8 to 9 hr.; 53,000L/$31.20) that pass through **Naples** (6 hr.; 38,500L/$22.65). Within Sicily there are 12 to 15 trains daily from **Palermo** (3 to 4.5 hr.; 20,000L/$11.75); 14 to 16 trains daily from **Cefalù** (2.5 to 3.5 hr.; 14,000L/$8.25); and hourly trains from **Taormina** (35 to 65 min.; 4,700L/$2.75). Messina's *stazione centrale* **station** (☎ 090/714-935) is handily connected to the ferry docks.

By Bus   There are 12 runs (5 on Sunday) from **Taormina** (60 to 105 min.; 5,000L/$2.95); hourly from **Catania** (90 min.; 10,500L/$6.20); and 6 runs (3 on Sunday) from **Palermo** (3 hr. 15 min; 21,000L/$12.35). There's also an 8pm bus from **Rome** that arrives at 4:30am (65,000L/$38.25). Messina has **SAIS** bus offices (☎ 090/771-914) at Pz. d. Repubblica no. 6 and no. 46.

By Car   Take the A20/SS113 east from **Palermo, Cefalù,** or **Milazzo;** the A18 north from **Taormina.** From the mainland, take the A3 south toward Reggio di Calabria, and get off at Villa San Giovanni for the car ferries across the strait (see above).

WHERE TO STAY & DINE   The central **Nuovo Albergo Monza,** Vle. S. Martino 63 (☎ and fax 090/673-755) is Messina's best simple, modernized hotel, with 59 rooms, 49 with bathroom, but all with phone, air-conditioning, and TV. Doubles without bathroom go for 78,000L ($45.90), those with for 120,000L ($70.60). You'll probably be the only nonregular at **Trattoria Al Padrino,** just below Via G. La Farina at V. S. Cecilia 54 (☎ 090/929-1000), where the food is ultra-genuine, from the excellent *maccheroni* (handmade pasta in a tomato sauce topped with grilled eggplant and toasted ricotta) to Messina's renowned *involtini di spada* (breaded swordfish rolls). It's closed Sunday.

2 Cefalù

165 km (99 mi.) W of Messina, 70 km (42 mi.) E of Palermo

Hemmed in between a towering headland of a mountain and a naturally sheltered harbor, ✪ **Cefalù** is a small, orderly city and a relaxing place to unwind. It has no cars in the historic center, a friendly *passeggiata,* some of Sicily's best Byzantine mosaics, and a sweeping curve of fine beach that has recently attracted some modest resort hotels and expanded the city westward. The 5th-century-B.C. Greeks left a few vases for the museum, and Roger II and his Normans gave the town a mighty cathedral that attracts the crowds and gives us a viable excuse for cooling our heels here for a day or two (though relentless sightseers will be hard-pressed to fill more than a half day).

ESSENTIALS
GETTING HERE   By Train   There are eight trains daily from **Rome** (10.5 to 12 hr.; 64,000L/$37.65); and 10 to 12 trains daily from **Messina** (2.5 to 4 hr.; 14,000L/$8.25). There are at least hourly trains from **Palermo** (45 to 75 min.; 5,900L/$3.50).

By Car   The A20 highway from Messina is incomplete for a 46-kilometer (28-mile) stretch from S. Agata to Castelbuono, so you'll have to drop to the parallel old coastal SS113 (expect traffic). Coming from the other direction **(Palermo),** though, the A20 *is* complete.

VISITOR INFORMATION   The **tourist office** is at Cor. Ruggerio 77 (☎ 0921/ 21050; fax 0921-22-386), open Monday to Saturday 8am to 2pm and 3:30 to 8:30pm. There are info booths at the train station and on Piazza Garibaldi open Monday to Saturday 9am to 1pm and 5:30pm to 9pm (in winter, the hours may be shorter or it may close altogether).

STROLLING THE TOWN, CLIMBING THE MOUNTAIN
Corso Ruggiero is the pedestrianized main drag of Cefalù, awash with the passeggiata and lined with shops and modest *palazzi.* A leisurely stroll down it leads to **Piazza Duomo,** a palm-shaded cafe-lined square that serves as a stage for the monumental twin-towered facade of the ✪ **Duomo** (☎ 0921/922-021), magnificently set against the foot of the towering *rocca* cliffs. Roger II built this first of Sicily's great Norman cathedrals in 1131, supposedly in thanks after his ship found shelter here during a violent sea storm. By 1166, they'd put the finishing touches on the altar-end mosaics, fantastic Greek-Byzantine creations featuring a mighty *Christ Pancrator* in the curve of the apse with outstretched hands and a kindly look on his face. It's open daily 8am to noon, 3:15pm to 8pm.

From the edge of the Duomo square, Via Mandralisca leads down to the **Museo Mandralisca** at no. 13 (☎ 0921/421-547), a small museum whose treasures are a 4th-century B.C. vase showing a tuna vendor and customer haggling, and

✪ **Antonella da Messina's** smirking *Portrait of a Man* (1460s). Admission is 6,000L ($3.55), free under 10; it's open daily 9am to 12:30pm and 3:30 to 7pm (in summer, they stay open 9am to 7pm or later).

Continue down Via Mandralisca to Via V. Emanuele and turn left. Discesa Fiume leads right down to the **Lavatoio,** a medieval Laundromat complete with stone washing and rinsing basins and wedge-shaped scrubbing slabs. Head the other way down Via V. Emanuele to glimpse into the dock-front rooms on the left where fishermen mend their nets, and finally spill left into the little **fishing wharf** itself, where the pebbly beach is filled with sun-bleached wooden boats and (in summer) suntanned swimmers. The famous, uneven row of waterfront boathouses with their yawning Gothic arches was used for scenes in the film *Cinema Paradiso.*

If you've got about 3 hours (early morning is best), you can take a bracing hike 917 feet up the **Rocca.** About halfway up, the path splits. Steps to the right lead the long way up to the overgrown foundations of a 13th-century **Byzantine fortress** at the very top of the mountain. The path to the left leads past ancient cisterns and remnants of medieval houses (and a long, picturesquely crenellated wall), to the so-called **Temple of Diana,** a small, 5th-century B.C. temple made of huge stones fitted together with a few doorways surviving. A path to the right above the temple then leads steeply to that mountaintop fortress.

WHERE TO STAY

Astro. V. Roma 105, 90015 Cefalù (PA). ☎ **0921/421-639.** Fax 0921/423-103. 30 units, all with bathroom. A/C TV TEL. Sept–June 70,000L ($41.20) single, 100,000L ($58.80) double; July 85,000L ($50) single, 130,000L ($76.50) double; Aug 120,000L ($70.60) per person, half-pension required. Rates include breakfast. AE, MC, V. (Turn left out of station. The street ends in 3 blocks at V. Roma and the hotel.)

This modern hotel is in the new part of town, 5 minutes' walk from the *centro storico* and 2 blocks from the beach. The simple, contemporary-style rooms have oils on the walls, nice modular furnishings, a few scattered Persian rugs, and plenty of elbow room. My only complaints are the cranky doorknobs, funny-tasting tap water that never truly gets hot, and considerable noise on the two sides that face streets—especially during morning rush hour. The hotel restaurant is on a terrace off the sidewalk, although the street's so busy this may actually be a drawback.

✪ **La Giara.** V. Veterani 40 (between the Duomo and the harbor), 90015 Cefalù (PA). ☎ **0921/421-562.** Fax 0921/422-518. 24 units, all with bathroom. TEL. 42,000–70,000L ($24.70–$41.20) single, 80,000–130,000L ($47.05–$76.50) double. July 15–Sept 15 required half-pension 87,000–102,000L ($51.20–$60) per person. Breakfast 5,000L ($2.95). AE, MC, V.

The only hotel in the heart of town is the sort of place where repeat guests hug the owners good-bye when they check out. The owners are very proud of the city and its history and traditions, especially in the kitchen, and will be rather unhappy if you don't indulge in the half-pension. The cots in the midsize rooms are in good shape and the functional, wood-plated furnishings very well worn. Accommodations on street are a bit noisier, but most rooms overlook the tiny Arab courtyards and narrow Saracen alleys of medieval Cefalù. The roof terrace gets lots of sun and views of the city roof tiles, with the top half of the Duomo facade rising under the *Rocca* just a few hundred feet away. The bell curve of rates depends on season (peaking in August), and the owners plan to install TV and air-conditioning by 1999.

WHERE TO DINE

✪ **La Brace.** V. 25 Novembre 10 (off Cor. Ruggero). ☎ **0921/423-570.** Reservations highly recommended. Primi 9,000–10,000L ($5.30–$5.90); secondi 10,000–22,000L ($5.90–$12.95). Fixed-price menus 28,000L ($16.50; with wine but no primo) or 48,000L

($28.25; everything but wine). AE, DC, MC, V. Tues–Sun 1–2:30pm, 7–11:30pm. INNOVATIVE SICILIAN.

The dark wood tables covered with black-and-white tooled red scarves and tiny oil lamps evoke Thea de Haan's Indonesian origins while the stone arches and bulk of the menu are firmly Sicilian. Co-owner Dietmar Beckers' Dutch influence must be in the restaurant's efficiency, pleasant attitude, and hearty rib-sticking nature of some of the more innovative dishes such as *involtini di melanzane* (eggplant wrapped around tagliatelle and ricotta *salata* then baked under tomatoes and Parmesan). Other excellent primi include *spaghetti alla crudaiola* (with garlic, capers, tomatoes, basil, and prosciutto) and *rigatoni al rustico* (in a spicy tomato sauce laced with Gorgonzola). Afterward try the *spiedini di pesce spada* (marinated swordfish nuggets skewered with sweet peppers, grilled, and served in a lemon-mustard sauce), or *tournedos La Brace* (rare beef medallions cooked with pancetta under fused butter). Save room for the famous *banana Le Brace* dessert, a banana doused with orange liqueur, baked in foil, then topped with whipped cream.

L'Antica Corte. Cortile Pepe 7 (near the end of Cor. Ruggero). ☎ **0921/423-228.** Reservations recommended. Primi 7,500–13,500L ($4.40–$7.95); secondi 9,500–22,000L ($5.60–$12.95); pizze 6,500–14,000L ($3.80–$8.25). Menù turistico 22,000L ($12.95; with wine). AE, MC, V. Fri–Wed noon–3pm, 7:15–midnight. Open daily June 15–Sept 15; Sat–Sun only in Nov. SICILIAN.

Book ahead for one of the few tables set picturesquely under grape vines in the tiny Arab courtyard—although in the summer heat, you may welcome the long rooms of the air-conditioned interior. The waiters wear red neck bandannas and sashes pirate-style and serve up *casarecci all'arrabbiata* or *agli antichi sapori* (homemade pasta with baby shrimp, limoncello liqueur, and mushrooms), or *pasta con sarde* (with sardines, raisins, pine nuts, fennel, and tomatoes). Fresh fish is always available, or sample the *escalope alle mandorle* (veal scallop flavored with almonds), *couscous di pesce*, or *fileto bisanzio* (beef under a rich gravy studded with peppers and mushrooms).

3 Palermo

70 km (42 mi.) W of Cefalù, 237 km (142 mi.) W of Messina

Sicily's capital is a tough place to love. The dustiest gem of a city in Europe, it contains some of Sicily's greatest sights and museums, but hasn't yet rebuilt whole bombed-out neighborhoods destroyed during World War II. Despite the efforts of a crusading anti-Mafia mayor, Cosa Nostra still strangles the city. But amid the rubble and trash-filled alleys you'll find gloriously stuccoed oratories, glittering 12th-century mosaics, puppet theaters, art museums, and busy fish markets bursting with life and color.

Palermo hasn't had an easy history. Little of the 9th-century Arab city founded by the Saracens remains other than what was adapted by the broad-minded Norman and Swabian rulers like Roger II and Frederick II. Under 6 centuries of Spanish and Bourbon rule, only one king, Charles V, ever set foot on Sicily. This hands-off approach let the city go to pot, or rather to the Mafia, creating problems that have plagued Palermo ever since. To see all the highlights—the churches, markets, and art museum of the Old Center, the Cappella Palatina, and a day trip to nearby Monreale—you'd need 2 to 3 days. But, Palermo is far from the most welcoming of towns, making it tough to stay longer and truly get under its skin, to see what makes this city resoundingly not tick.

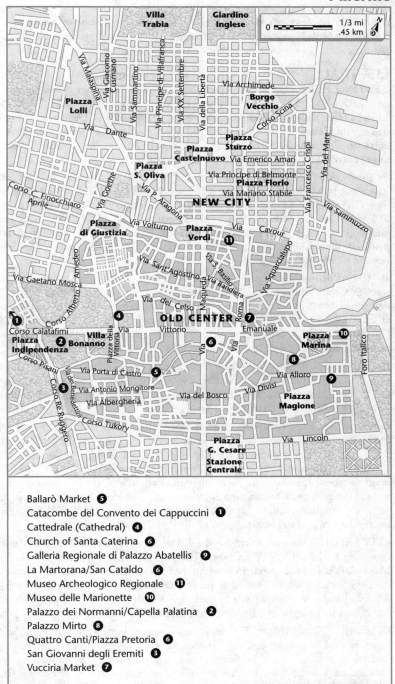

Palermo

0 | 1/3 mi
.45 km

Villa Trabia

Giardino Inglese

Via Malaspina

Via Giacomo Cusmano

Via Sammartino

Via Principe di Villafranca

Via XX. settembre

Via della Libertà

Via Archimede

Piazza Lolli

Via Dante

Borgo Vecchio

Corso Scinà

Piazza Sturzo

Piazza Castelnuovo

Via Emerico Amari

Piazza S. Oliva

Via Principe di Belmonte

Piazza Florio

Via Mariano Stabile

Via Francesco Crispi

Via del Mare

Via Sammuzzo

Corso C. Finocchiaro Aprile

Via Goethe

Via P. Aragona

NEW CITY

Piazza di Giustizia

Via Volturno

Piazza Verdi

Via

Cavour

Amedeo

Via Gaetano Mosca

Corso Alberto

Via Sant'Agostino

Via S. Bandiera

Via S. Basilidera

Via Spraicialupo

Via del Celso

Via Maqueda

OLD CENTER

Via del

① Piazza Indipendenza

Corso Calatafimi

④

Vittorio

⑦

Via Roma

Emanuele

Piazza Marina ⑩

② Villa Bonanno

Piazza della Vittoria

Via

⑥

Foro Italico

Corso Pisani

Via Porta di Castro

⑤

⑧

Via Alloro

⑨

Via Antonio Mongitore

Via del Bosco

Via Divisi

Piazza Magione

③

Via Alberghería

Corso Re Ruggero

Via de Benedettini

Corso Tukory

Via Lincoln

Piazza G. Cesare

Stazione Centrale

Ballarò Market **⑤**

Catacombe del Convento dei Cappuccini **①**

Cattedrale (Cathedral) **④**

Church of Santa Caterina **⑥**

Galleria Regionale di Palazzo Abatellis **⑨**

La Martorana/San Cataldo **⑥**

Museo Archeologico Regionale **⑪**

Museo delle Marionette **⑩**

Palazzo dei Normanni/Capella Palatina **②**

Palazzo Mirto **⑧**

Quattro Canti/Piazza Pretoria **⑥**

San Giovanni degli Eremiti **③**

Vucciria Market **⑦**

A FESTIVAL   Palermo's blowout festival, "U Fistinu," the **feast of patroness St. Rosalia,** takes place on July 14 and is celebrated with costumed processions and a fantastic fireworks display over the harbor.

ESSENTIALS

GETTING HERE   By Train   There are eight trains daily from **Rome** (about 13 hr.; 71,000L/$41.75); three trains daily from **Naples** (about 10 hr.; 56,500L/$33.25); 13 to 16 trains daily from **Messina** (about 5 hr.; 20,000L/$11.75); and at least hourly trains from **Cefalù** (50 to 75 min.; 5,900L/$3.50). Almost all trains pull into the **Stazione Centrale** (☎ 091/616-7514 or 091/616-806) at the foot of Via Roma (***don't*** get off at the suburban *Stazione Notarbartolo*).

By Bus   SAIS lines, V. P. Basalmo 16 or 26 (☎ 091/213-248), runs six buses daily (three Sunday) from **Messina** (3 hr. 15 min; 21,000L/$12.35); and an hourly bus from **Catania** (2 hr. 40 min.; 17,000L/$10). Cuffaro lines, V. P. Balsamo 13 (☎ 091/616-1510), runs seven buses daily from **Agrigento** (2 hr.; 11,500L/$6.75). Segesta lines, V. Balsamo 26 (☎ 091/616-7919), runs 25 buses daily (13 Sunday) from **Trapani** (105 min.; 12,000L/$). From **Rome**'s Tiburtina station, there's a daily 8pm SAIS bus and a daily 9:30pm Segesta lines bus (12 hr.; 65,000L/$38.25).

By Car   Palermo lies on the coastal A20 autostrada that comes from **Messina** through **Cefalù** (though you'll have to detour onto the old SS113 road due to an unfinished stretch in the superhighway). There are **parking** garages at the train station at Pz. Giulio Cesare 43 (☎ **091/616-8297**); near the port at V. Guardione 81 (☎ **091/322-649**); and a 24-hour garage in the new city (between the Politeama theater and Ucciardone prison) at V. Archimede 88 (☎ **091/581-658**).

By Ferry   SNAV runs a 4-hour hydrofoil from **Naples** daily at 5:30pm (120,000L/$70.60 June 26 to September 14; 96,000L/$56.50 September 15 to June 24; no runs in November). The return to Naples leaves Palermo at 9am. Call ☎ **081/761-2348** in Naples, or 091/611-8525 in Palermo.

By Plane   Palermo's **Aeroporto Falcone-Borsellino** (☎ **091/702-0313** for information), also called Punta Raisi, is 30 kilometers (18 mi.) west of the center on the A29 highway. There are daily direct flights in from all of Italy's major cities and London, Barcelona, and Frankfurt. The **Prestia & Comandè bus** (☎ **091/580-457**) heads to central Palermo every 30 minutes and costs 4,500L ($2.65) (downtown, it stops at Piazza Ruggero Settimo and ends/leaves from the Hotel Elena at the train station). If you're laden with luggage, you can catch a taxi for 60,000L ($35.30) (that's the regular fare plus an obligatory and totally legal 15,000L supplement).

CITY LAYOUT   Central Palermo is divided into an **Old Center** to the south and a **New City** to the north by **Via Cavour.** There are two main north-south roads. **Via Maqueda/Via R. Settimo** starts just left of the train station and crosses Via Cavour at the central **Piazza Verdi,** also called **Teatro Massimo** after the theater at its center. Roughly parallel to Via Maqueda to the east is **Via Roma,** a busier and more commercialized boulevard that starts directly across from the train station.

Old Center   Corso Vittorio Emanuele runs east-west through the heart of this area. It crosses Via Maqueda at the **Quattro Canti,** neatly dividing the Old Center into traditional quadrants. To the southeast of this intersection lies **La Kalsa,** once the Saracen Emir's walled quarter for his and other Arab nobles' palaces. These were later replaced with medieval *palazzi* and baroque oratories, but the neighborhood was badly bombed during World War II and is still partly in ruins. Though many of Palermo's central sights are here, it's one of the more dangerous areas after dark and probably not the best place to base yourself.

To the southwest of Quattro Canti lies the residential **Alberghiera,** home to the vast Ballarò market and more bombed-out zones, and also less than safe after dark. The center's northwest quadrant is **Sincaldi,** and aside from the Capo market holds relatively little of specific interest to the visitor. Finally, the northeast **Amalfitani** district is the smallest of the quarters (La Cala harbor intrudes to fill half of it), home to the Vucciria fish market. It's so small that the Via Roma division down its middle helps keep the zone less mazelike, a bit brighter, and more commercially oriented.

New City   The center of this grid of easily navigable, broad roads is **Piazza Castelnuovo/Politeama,** where Via Maqueda (now called **Via R. Settimo**) crosses **Via E. Amari.** We're most interested in the hotel-, bar-, and restaurant-filled southern half of the New City—centered on such streets as the wide **Via Mariano Stabile** to the port and the pedestrian-only **Via Principe di Belmonte**—than the sprawling urban residential section to the north.

GETTING AROUND   By Bus   Palermo's bus system is modern and efficient, with the **major central lines** routed down Via Roma, Via Maqueda, and Corso V. Emanuele. The most useful **hubs** are at the Stazione Centrale/Piazza G. Cesare (the train station), Piazza Indipendenza (behind the royal Palazzo dei Normanni at the end of Corso V. Emanuele), Piazza Verdi/Teatro Massimo, and Piazza Castelnuovo/ Politeama. A **bus ticket,** available at most newsstands and *tabacchi* (tobacconists) costs 1,500L (90¢) and is valid for 60 minutes; an all-day pass is 5,000L ($2.95).

By Taxi   To call a taxi, dial ☎ **091/513-311,** 091/513-374, or 091/682-5441. There are taxi stands at the train stations as well as at Piazza Verdi (Teatro Massimo), Piazza R. Settimo (Teatro Politeama), and Piazza Indipendenza. Taxis cost 6,000L ($3.55), plus 4,000L ($2.35) for the first kilometer and 1,300L (75¢) per kilometer after that. Make sure the meter is always on and running.

VISITOR INFORMATION   There's a **tourist office** in the main train station (☎ **091/616-5914;** www.aapit.pa.it) open Monday to Friday 8:30am to 2pm and 3 to 6pm, Saturday 8:30am to 2pm. Besides the city map, make sure you ask for a copy of *Palermo & Provincia Live,* a bimonthly with lots of handy tourist information plus an events calendar. The main office, at Pz. Castelnuovo 34 (☎ **091/583-847;** fax 091/586-338), is a little less-harried and has a few more pamphlets, as well as lots more information on the province and day-tripping possibilities. There's a branch at the airport as well (☎ **091/591-698**).

FAST FACTS: Sicily

American Express   The local AMEX representative is at Giovanni Ruggieri e Figli, V. E. Amari 40 (☎ **091/587-144**). It's open Monday to Friday 9am to 1pm and 4 to 7:30pm, Saturday 9am to 1pm. To report a lost card, dial ☎ **167/018-839.**

Bookstores   By far the best selection of books in English is at **Feltrinelli,** V. Maqueda 395 (☎ **091/587-785**).

Consulates   The **U.S. Consulate** is at V. Re Frederico 18bis (☎ **091/ 611-0020**). The **U.K. Consular representative** is at V. Cavour 117 (☎ **091/ 326-412**).

Emergencies   For general emergencies, call the Carabinieri at ☎**112.** For the city **police,** dial ☎113; for an **ambulance,** ☎118 or 091/306-644; for **fires,** ☎115; for **road assistance,** ☎116.

Hospitals   The closest emergency room to the center is at the **Ospedale Civico** (☎ **091/606-2207**), off Via Carmelo Lazzaro (in the upper left-hand corner of the tourist office map). Take bus 108 from Politeama or Piazza Indipendenza, or bus 246 from the train station. *A warning:* It's not the most modernized of hospitals, out in no-man's land beyond empty lots and dirt roads. The people at the main emergency desk are the ones who can help you, despite that sign that tells tourists to go to some other office down around the corner (they'll just send you back to the main desk). For an ambulance, dial ☎ **118** or 091/306-644.

Lost Property   Go to one of the police's *ufficio stranieri* (foreigner's office). They're at V. S. Lorenzo Colli 271a (☎ **091/526-037**) and Vle. Strasburgo 180 (☎ **091/526-343**). The main police *questura* (station) is on Piazza Vittoria (☎ **091/210-111**). The train station's *oggetti rinvenuti* (lost and found) (☎ **091/603-1111**) is open 9am to 1pm and (sometimes) 3 to 7pm.

Luggage Storage   The left luggage office (☎ **091/603-3040**) at the train station charges 5,000L ($2.95) per 12 hours, and is open daily 6am to 10pm.

Pharmacies   Other than looking at any pharmacy's door for the posted night-duty rotation list of neighborhood drug stores (or by calling ☎ **192**), pharmacies at the following locations are always open at night (all in the New City): V. Roma 1 (☎ **091/616-2117**), V. Roma 207 (☎ **091/585-869**), V. Mariano Stabile 177 (☎ **091/334-482**), and V. Principe di Belmonte 110 (☎ **091/581-771**).

Police   Dial ☎ **113** for the Carabinieri (national police force), 112 for the city police.

Post Office   The **main post office** (with fax service) is at V. Roma 322 (☎ **091/321-507**), open Monday to Saturday 8:10am to 7:30pm. There are branches at the **train station** (no phone), open Monday to Saturday 8:30am to 1pm; and the **airport** (☎ **091/651-9239**), open Monday to Saturday 8:10am to 1:20pm.

Safety   Palermo is not the safest of Italian cities, with the crime problems of both a big city and a port town, but it isn't much more dangerous than Big Town, USA, either. Yes, there's a strong Mafia presence, but despite splashy headlines and Hollywood imaginations, you're not going to be caught in some kind of good-fellas crossfire. You should be more worried about common thievery and **rampant pickpocketing;** take the necessary common-sense precautions, don't flash valuables, and keep your camera inconspicuous and firmly in hand. Most of the Old Center is a bit dicey, especially after dark—steer clear particularly of the southern half of the Old Center: La Kalsa, the Alberghiera, and around the train station. Stick to Via Roma and Corso V. Emanuele at night. Most of the New City is as safe as any Italian city.

Transit Information   The city bus company is **AMAT** (toll-free ☎ **167/018-378** or 091/321-333).

Travel Agencies   There's a **Wasteels** budget travel counter in the train station (☎ **091/617-2134**). **CTS** has an office 2 blocks off Viale della Libertà at V. Garzilli 28G (☎ **091/325-752**). There are offices of the official **CIT** travel agency in the station (☎ **091/616-9347**), and at Vle. Libertà 12 (☎ **091/586-333**).

Travel Tip

August sees many Palermo sights locked up and the custodians of smaller churches and stuccoed chapels ordered to hang up their keys for a month. However, some of the major sights actually go on longer hours, re-opening in the evenings from 8:30 to 11pm or so; ask the tourist office for a list.

WHAT TO SEE & DO

✪ **Galleria Regionale di Palazzo Abatellis.** V. Alloro 4. ☎ **091/616-4317.** Admission 8,000L ($4.70). Mon, Wed, Fri, Sat 9am–1pm; Tues, Thurs 9am–1pm, 3–5:30pm; Sun 9am–12:30pm. Bus: 103, 105, 139, 225, 824.

This is one of the best art museums in Sicily, well worth an hour or two of your time. The ground floor of this 15th-century, Catalan-Gothic-meets-Renaissance palazzo contains the sculpture collection, including one room devoted to **Francesco Laurana** (look for his bust of Eleonora of Aragon) and another room to a passel of Madonnas by the **Gagini** clan. Also down here is the 1449 fresco of the ✪ *Triumph of Death,* by an unknown but clearly warped hand (possibly Flemish or from the school of Pisanello). The skeleton of death rides an emaciated horse, felling with his arrows an unduly number of bishops and popes.

Upstairs is the painting gallery, starring works by Sicily's greatest Renaissance master **Antonella da Messina,** including his signature masterpiece, the ✪ *Madonna Annunziata.* This is an "Annunciation" scene from the angel Gabriel's point of view, wherein a quiet, delicately featured Mary interrupted at her reading stretches out her hand to us from under the voluminous pyramid of an intensely blue shawl. Also be on the lookout for the incredibly detailed 16th-century *Malvagna Triptych* by Mabuse, Pietro Novelli's early 17th-century Mannerist *Madonna and Child in Glory,* and Francesco Solimena's *Return of Joseph's Brothers.*

Palazzo Mirto. V. Merlo 2 (off Pz. Marina). ☎ **091/616-4751.** Admission 4,000L ($2.35) adults, free under 18 and over 60. Mon, Wed, Fri–Sat 9am–1:30pm; Tues, Thurs 9am–1:30pm, 3–5:30pm; Sun 9am–12:30pm. (Also open some evenings in summer). Bus: 103, 105, 139, 225, 824.

Most of Palermo's glorious and famed 18th- and 19th-century palazzi are rotting behind their massive doors, but this one is open to the public for a glimpse into the lifestyle of Palermo's wealthy caste of centuries past. The noble Filangeri-Lanza family lived in this palace from the 17th century until 1982, and it's furnished exactly as it was in the 19th century, which included many 17th- and 18th-century pieces. Don't miss the tiny Chinese-style room with its remarkable trompe l'oeil ceiling.

✪ **Museo delle Marionette.** V. Butera 1 (off Pz. Marina). ☎ **091/328-060.** 5,000L adults, 3,000L under 18, over 60, and students. Mon–Fri 9am–1pm, 4–7pm, Sat 9am–1pm. Bus: 103, 105, 139, 225, 824.

This is one of the world's largest collections of puppets, documenting a cultural and artistic craft heritage that spans the globe from Javanese stick puppets, Indonesian silhouettes, and Chinese dolls to Neapolitan *Pulcinella* (Punch and Judy) hand puppets and, of course, Sicilian marionettes—many displayed against original stages and backgrounds. Marionette shows were the theater of Sicily's common folk over the past few centuries, telling tales of Charlemagne and the adventures of his knights, as well as swashbuckling Saracen pirate stories and even opera. No visit to Sicily is complete without attending a show; see "Palermo After Dark," below, for show times here and at other Palermo venues.

Quattro Canti/Piazza Pretoria. The intersection of Cor. V. Emanuele and V. Maqueda. Bus: 101, 102, 105.

Quattro Canti (Four Corners) is the nickname for old Palermo's dead-center intersection. The concave corner facades stack on top of their fountains three sculptural levels symbolizing the seasons, above them the four Spanish kings of Sicily, and on top the patronesses of the city. Today, the site is choked by heavy traffic and its facades are black with pollution, but a recent cleaning has uncovered a glimmer of the grandeur the Quattro Canti must have enjoyed during Palermo's theatrical 17th century.

Just south of this intersection, off Via Maqueda, is the raised pedestrian **Piazza Pretoria,** centered on a Mannerist **fountain** sculpted for a Florentine villa in the 1550s but rejected by its commissioners. Palermo bought the thing and set it proudly at city center, though the local populace, scandalized by the racy nude figures and lewd glances these statues were throwing each other across the water jets, promptly renamed it the *Fontana della Vergogna* (Fountain of Shame). This hasn't stopped them from making it a 24-hour sight, dramatically floodlit at night.

If, by divine providence, the church of **Santa Caterina** capping the piazza's east end has finally re-opened when you visit, pop inside for one of the most elaborate baroque marble-and-stucco interiors in Palermo. If it's still closed, content yourself with the grand baroque interior of **San Giuseppe dei Teatini,** on the southwest corner of the Quattro Canti (entered from the front on Corso V. Emanuele or the side on Via Maqueda). Aside from the dome frescoes by Borremans, there's not much to single out inside, but the scale and richness of the decorations make it stand out.

✪ **La Martorana/San Cataldo.** Pz. Bellini 3 (next door to Pz. Pretoria). ☎ **091/ 616-1692.** Admission free. La Martorana open Mon–Sat 9:30am–1pm, 3:30–6:30pm, Sun 8:30am–1pm; San Cataldo open Tues–Sat 9am–5pm, Sat–Sun 9am–1pm (if it's closed; get key in La Martorana). Bus: 101, 102.

La Martorana (aka Santa Maria dell'Ammiraglio) may have a baroque facade, but this mosaic church and its next-door neighbor San Cataldo—that of the little dark pink eraser-head domes—are both Norman and date from the 1140s to the 1150s. Enter **La Martorana** by heading up the stairs to its right and ducking under the surviving 12th-century bell tower of lithe columns and corrugated archways. Aside from some minimal baroque redecoration and 1717 frescoes by Borremans, the interior is pure glittering gold-back mosaic, courtesy of early 12th-century Greek artists who gave Christ kindly eyes and quoted the Bible in flowing Arabic script on the dome.

In sharp contrast, the little church of **San Cataldo** beyond the palm trees got for decorations only those pink, mosquelike domelets and some crenellations ringing the top before the man who commissioned its construction died in 1160. Although San Cataldo served for a time as a post office in the 18th century, today the interior has been stripped wonderfully bare again, a quiet stony vault whose trio each of aisles, apses, and domes are lit through the stone latticework of small windows.

Cattedrale (Cathedral). Pz. d. Cattedrale/Cor. V. Emanuele. ☎ **091/334-376.** Admission to church free; crypt 1,000L (60¢); treasury 1,000L (60¢). Church Mon–Sat 7am–7pm, Sun 8am–1:30pm, 4–7pm; treasury Mon–Sat 7–11:30am, 4–6:30pm. Bus: 104, 105.

Palermo's cathedral is not the city's greatest church. It is a hodgepodge of styles rather uncomfortably knitted together, from the original 1185 Norman structure (visible in the towers and apses at the east end), through the 15th-century Catalan-Gothic overhaul, to the incongruous 1801 baroque dome inflicted upon it by Ferdinando Fuga (who also revamped the interior).

You enter partway down the right aisle, through the well-crafted **Catalan-Gothic porch,** with 15th-century wooden doors and a column on the far left, salvaged from the 9th-century mosque that once stood here (carved with a worn Arabic inscription from the Koran). Once inside, to your left are the dark, gated-off chapels containing a little congregation of the **Norman royal tombs,** housing the mortal remains of, among others, Emperor Frederick II in the left front sarcophagus, and Roger II under the mosaicked canopy tomb behind him.

The first chapel to the right of the entrance (technically, the fourth chapel on the right aisle) sports a Pietro Novelli altarpiece, while the **former High Altar** sculptural ensemble by Antonello Gagini has since been dismantled and dispersed throughout the church: Its statues line the nave, a bit still serves as the main altar, and three reliefs and an *Assumption* reside in the second chapel of the left aisle. The seventh chapel on the left has a nice *Madonna* statue by Francesco Laurana.

Don't bother paying to visit the boring collection of tombs in the **crypt,** but the **treasury** is worthwhile for the nifty, 12th-century bejeweled caplike crown that Frederick II's wife, Constance of Aragon, was wearing when her tomb was opened in the 18th century.

✪ **Palazzo dei Normanni/Capella Palatina.** Pz. Indipendenza. ☎ **091/705-4317** palazzo, 091/705-4879 Cappella Palatina. Admission free. Palazzo open Mon, Fri, Sat 9am–noon; Capella Palatina open Mon–Fri 9am–noon, 3–5pm, Sun 9–10am and noon–1pm. Bus: 104, 105, 108, 109, 110, 118, 304, 305, 309, 318, 327, 339, 364, 365, 368, 380, 389.

Most of the royal palace itself—built by the Saracens and enlarged by the Normans (Roger II and Frederick II both held court here) and again later by the Aragonese—has been closed to visitors for years. If this policy changes—as they insist it soon will—the royal apartments are little to write home about, but don't miss the mosaicked *Sala di Re Ruggero.*

Even with the palace part closed, the tour buses still line up at the back, bringing visitors to file into Palermo's most stunning sight, the Byzantine Greek mosaics of the ✪ **Cappella Palatina,** built by Roger II in the 1130s. It takes the form of a tiny basilica, every inch swathed in rich religious mosaics that symbolically glorify the enlightened reign of Roger II. The craftsmanship is exquisite, using not only gold-backed tessere but also silver mosaic tiles to cause the softly lit surfaces to sparkle and gleam in a kaleidoscope of saints and Old Testament characters. The mosaics on the nave walls date from a bit later (1150s) and exhibit a more Roman styling, while the mosaicked *Christ with Sts. Peter and Paul* above the Norman throne are 15th century.

San Giovanni degli Eremiti. V. d. Benedettini (at V. A. Mongitore). ☎ **091/651-5019.** Admission 4,000L ($2.35). Mon–Sat 9am–1pm and 3–7pm, Sun 9am–1pm. Sometimes closed Sun in winter. Bus: 109, 108, 305, 318, 368.

One of the city's most romantic spots is this ruined 12th-century church and monastery complex on the Albergheria's western edge. The simple church with its five unmistakable Arabo-Norman red domes is set amid luxuriant gardens of palm, Indian fig cacti, and jasmine, where little paths lead to the evocative remains of 13th-century cloisters and into a small rectangular building that was once a mosque.

✪ **Catacombe del Convento dei Cappuccini.** V. Cappuccini 1 (many blocks up from Pz. Indipendenza). ☎ **091/212-117.** Admission 5,000L ($2.95). Daily 9am–noon, 3–5pm. Bus: 327.

This is one of the most macabre yet fascinating sights in Italy, a plaster-walled network of high, naturally lit tunnels in whose niches lie or stand the fully dressed, mummified bodies of some 8,000 dead Palermitani. Some were preserved in lime or arsenic, most were simply dried out by the natural controlled climate down here. The monks began preserving their dead here in 1599, but it soon became fashionable, and sections were created for the wealthy (men and women separate), priests, professors, and

---

Street Markets—The Best Free Sightseeing in Town

Markets are an integral part of Palermo life and a colorful, unmissable sight where vendors hawk piles of silvery fish, Levi's jeans, spiny sea urchins, bootleg CDs, olives from barrels, and steaks carved directly from the swordfish. Bring your camera (but little else) and guard it well. There are close to a dozen markets in town; here are the best.

Even if you're in town for just a day, drop down into the **Vucciria** for photo ops at dozens of fish stalls and vegetable stands, and 500L (30¢) wine in an enoteca. The market is sunk below the surrounding streets (head down the stairs just up Via Roma from its intersection with Corso V. Emanuele), and there are some good old-fashioned trattorie hidden here that serve the freshest fish in town (see Shanghai under "Where to Dine," below). This most famous of Palermo's markets has gotten a bit touristy in recent years, but the Vucciria is still a sight to behold.

More ebullient these days is the sprawling **Ballarò,** in the Albergheria quadrant, spreading roughly from Piazza Carmine to Piazza Casa Professa and Piazza S. Chiara. It, too, is mainly a food market, but with a better balance of veggies, meat, cheese, and dry goods mixed in among the fish stalls, plus a section selling cut-price clothing and toys.

The **Capo** market has two parts: a long line of mainly **clothing** stalls snaking down the middle and sides of Via Bandiera/Via S. Agostino in the city center; and the Via Porta Carini/Via Beati Paoli **food** section off Via Volturno, where many of the streets have been reduced to dirt roads between the buildings and awnings, and sometimes it's hard to tell whether you're indeed in a major European city or a North African Casbah. Lastly, a treasure trove of **antiques** stalls await in the short, shady **Piazza Peranni,** behind the bishop's palace off Corso V. Emanuele.

---

children. The last entombment was in 1920, when 2-year-old Rosalia Lombardo was mummified using a secret chemical injection method that has kept her almost perfectly preserved (if a little sallow), so remarkably undeathlike she's dubbed the "Sleeping Beauty."

Museo Archeologico Regionale. V. Bara all'Olivella 24 (between Pz. Verdi and V. Roma). ☎ **091/611-6805** or 091/662-0220. Admission 8,000L ($4.70). Mon, Thurs, Sat 9am–1:45pm; Tues, Wed, Fri 9am–1:45pm, 3–7:45pm; Sun 9am–1:30pm. Bus: 101, 102, 103, 104, 107, 122, 124.

Palermo's archaeology museum gathers artifacts from across Sicily, from prehistoric times through the Romans. The highlights are the ✪ **metopes of Selinute,** a series of decorative friezes that show a development from the 6th-century B.C. archaic style to the more classically inspired 5th-century B.C. metopes from Temple E. Also in this room is the **ephebe of Selinute,** a 460 B.C. bronze tomb statuette. Among the rest of the collections look for the 6th-century B.C. **oinochoe vase** from the Tuscan town of Chiusi, one of the most elaborate pieces of Etruscan *bucchero* (blackened earthenware) in existence. Among the Roman bronzes are a 3rd century B.C. **ram** and a **Heracles fighting a stag** that may have served as the centerpiece for a Pompeiian villa's fountain.

Sanctuario di Santa Rosalia/Monte Pellegrino. V. Pietro Bonanno (north of the city center). ☎ **091/540-326.** Admission free. Daily 7:45am–6pm (you have to pop in between frequent masses). Bus: 812.

Looming impressively over north Palermo and thankfully protected as parkland, the sheer cliffs and green cradles of trees covering the 2,000-foot **Monte Pellegrino** headland make it look more like it belongs at Yosemite or in some Japanese silk painting than in Sicily. This mountain has seen Paleolithic cave art (casts of which are in the archaeology museum), a 3-year battle during the first Punic War between Rome and Carthage, and hordes of Christian pilgrims for the past four centuries.

St. Rosalia, a niece of William II, lived and died as a religious hermit here on the mountain. In 1624 during a vicious plague, she appeared in a vision to a man and showed him the cave where her remains lay unburied. Palermitani carried these relics through the town to give them a consecrated burial, whereupon the plague stopped and Rosalia was swiftly granted patron saint status. Her cave was outfitted with pews and a baroque foyer to become the popular pilgrimage chapel **Sanctuario di Santa Rosalia,** where the holy water flows from plastic cooler jugs and all the merchandise in the gift shop has been blessed for your convenience. In the cave sanctuary itself, thin spikes of flattened steel cobweb hang from the ceiling like some conceptual modern sculpture—they're to channel the watery mineral drippings from would-be stalactites away from the heads of the devout and collect them as a holy, miraculous liquid.

WHERE TO STAY

Gardenia. V. Mariano Stabile 136, 90139 Palermo. ☎ **091/322-761.** Fax 091/333-732. 16 units, all with bathroom. A/C TV TEL. 80,000L ($47.05) single, 120,000L ($70.60) double. MC, V. Parking 25,000L ($14.70). Bus: 101, 102, 103, 104, 107, 122, 124.

The Gardenia offers serious comfort and amenities at good prices for what you get. The wonderfully firm beds in midsize rooms are surrounded by modular furnishings and brand-new bathrooms. It's up on the 7th floor, with double glazing on the windows and balcony doors, so little noise filters up from the busy road below. Back rooms are even quieter, but don't get the view of Monte Pellegrino. Actually, Via Mariano Stabile is a veritable mine of hotel possibilities; this building alone has four other (more basic) inns, including the joint **Boston/Madonia** (☎ **091/335-364**), with 90,000L ($52.95) doubles; the **Elite** (☎ **091/329-318**) whose 95,000L ($55.90) doubles have comforts similar to the Gardenia; and the skyscraping 10th-floor **Libertà** (☎ **091/321-911**), with a panoramic terrace pub and 80,000L ($47.05) doubles.

Petit. V. Principe di Belmonte 84 (at the corner with V. Wagner), 90139 Palermo. ☎ **091/ 323-616.** Fax 091/581-156 only Mon–Fri 9am–1pm and 3:30–7:30pm, Sat 9am–1pm (they use a nearby copy center). 7 units, 6 with bathroom. TEL. Single without bathroom 35,000L ($20.60), single with bathroom 50,000L ($29.40); double with bathroom 65,000L ($38.25). AE. Free parking on street. Bus: 101, 102, 103, 104, 107, 124, 824, 837.

Nothing if not aptly named, this tiny hotel of tiny rooms is perfectly placed in the middle of Palermo's most hip pedestrian street. Accommodations are utterly basic but tidy, and while the beds could be firmer, the welcome from Signora Salvatrice Nasello and her staff are friendly and prices just right. Rooms on the back are considerably quieter, devoid of the convivial noises wafting up from the bars and cafes below. A few odd quirks to add to those weird fax hours: although the phones are direct dial, you have to ask for the line each time, and you can pay by credit card only between 9:30am and 7:30pm.

Posta. V. A. Gagini 77 (parallel to V. Roma, between Pz. S. Domenico and V. Cavour), 90133 Palermo. ☎ **091/587-338.** Fax 091/587-347. 27 units, 22 with bathroom. TV TEL. 80,000L ($47.05) single, 120,000L ($70.60) double. Rates include breakfast. AE, DC, MC, V. Parking 15,000L ($8.80) in enclosed boxes (must book). Bus: 101, 102, 103, 104, 107, 122.

This favorite of Italian actors and writers (including Nobel prize-winner Dario Fo) has been family-run since 1921. As of 1998, everything is brand new, from the sparkling white tile floors to the modern wood veneer and white lacquer furniture units. Almost all accommodations are comfortably large and the beds are nice and firm. The downsides to this excellent central choice are that a few rooms have yet to be retiled, paint and lacquer is chipping in spots, and with the city's major thoroughfare just a narrow block away there is some background traffic noise mixed with those Palermo sirens—but at least it isn't right under your balcony. Also, there's no air-conditioning, although table fans are available to help combat the summer heat.

✪ **Principe di Belmonte.** V. Principe di Belmonte 25 (near corner with V. Principe di Scordia). ☎ **091/331-065.** Fax 611-3424. 17 units, 14 with bathroom; 6 apts, all with bathroom. TEL. 40,000L ($23.55) single without bathroom, 70,000L ($41.20) single with bathroom; 91,000L ($53.55) double with bathroom; 100,000L ($58.80) apt. AE, DC, MC, V. Free parking in street. Bus: 101, 102, 103, 104, 107, 124, 824, 837.

It's got firm beds, ample-size ultraclean rooms, and a friendly owner, all in the best part of town. It's also on one of modern Palermo's less-trafficked streets, 1½ blocks down from a cafe-lined pedestrian mall. The time-bitten furnishings are plain but sturdy, the bathrooms are large (though some are of the hold-your-own-shower-nozzle variety), and almost all rooms have TV and balcony. However, hot water can run scarce, and the lamps have iffy wiring. The high-ceilinged miniapartments are great values, with compact kitchens, large bedrooms, and a dining niche (and three have air-conditioning). For once, hotel prices on breakfast items are as cheap as at a bar.

Sausele. V. E. Errante 12, 90127 Palermo (exiting the train station, turn left then left again onto V. Oreto, then right). ☎ **091/616-1308.** Fax 091/616-7525. 36 units, all with bathroom. TEL. 75,000L ($44.10) single, 115,000L ($67.65) double. Breakfast 10,000L ($5.90). AE, DC, MC, V. Parking 15,000L ($8.80). Bus: any to Stazione Centrale.

This family-run inn stands out amid the depressing station-area hotels—heck, it would anywhere in Palermo, with its high ceilings, globe lamps, strikingly clean linoleum or tile floors, and spanking new wood modular furnishings. To greet you are an amicable staff, modern art on the walls, and Eva, the resident St. Bernard. Rooms on the street can be a bit noisy, so light sleepers should request one overlooking the peaceful courtyard. There's a living room–style TV lounge, rustically pretty little breakfast room, and tiny museum of artifacts collected by the late Sig. Sausele on his travels through Asia and Africa.

Sole. Cor. Vittorio Emanuele 219, 90133 Palermo. ☎ **091/581-811.** Fax 091/611-0182. 150 units, all with bathroom. A/C TV TEL. Oct–June 100,000 ($58.80) single, 150,000L ($88.25) double; July–Sept 150,000L ($88.25) single, 200,000L ($117.65) double. Breakfast included. AE, DC, MC, V. Parking 10,000L ($5.90) in walled lot. Bus: 101, 102, 104, 105.

It's the closest hotel to Palermo's epicenter, mere steps east of the Quattro Canti—and quite a sight cheaper than its fancier neighbor the Centrale Palace (below). It is drearily modern inside, but while the hotel is unexceptional in appearance, the staff is friendly and courteous, prices and location a dream, and it's so gosh-darn huge that plenty of rooms are often available. Accommodations are fairly large, furnished with built-in units (a few rooms mix in antique pieces) and comfy chairs to watch TV in. While rooms right on the Corso are noticeably noisier, some enjoy a peekaboo view of the Fontana Pretoria across the street. Don't miss the roof terrace—360° of downtown Palermo rooftops, domes, the fountain and Quattro Canti below, and the mountains that ring the city beyond.

WORTH A SPLURGE

Centrale Palace Hotel. Cor. Vittorio Emanuele 357 (a few steps west of the Quattro Canti), 90134 Palermo. ☎ **800/528-1234** in the U.S., or 091/336-666. Fax 091/334-881. www. bestwestern.com/thisco/bw/98153_b.html. E-mail: centrale@palermo.pandora.it. 63 units, all with bathroom. A/C MINIBAR TV TEL. 200,000L ($117.65) single, 295,000L ($173.55) double; 385,000L ($226.50) suite. Rates include breakfast. AE, CB, DC, MC, V. Bus: 101, 102, 104, 105.

Palermo's best splurge is also one of its most central inns, a 17th-century palazzo converted to a hotel in 1892 and recently modernized by the Best Western group. Furnishings are mostly discreetly functional and modern, with a few period or Empire antiques and Oriental rugs to liven up the decor. Most doubles are medium-sized, while spacious suites come with contemporary wood furnishings and fainting couches. All the bathrooms are brand new with built-in hair dryers. The quietest rooms are on the *cortile* or side streets, but the double glazing on the front windows block traffic noise fairly efficiently, plus on the first and second floor these Corso-side rooms have balconies with askance views of the Quattro Canti. The top floor breakfast room has a vista over Palermo rooftops to Monte Pellegrino.

WHERE TO DINE

✪ **Antica Focacceria San Francesco.** V. A. Paternostro 58 (on Pz. San Francesco d'Assisi). ☎ **091/320-264.** Panini & primi 3,000–7,500L ($1.75–$4.40). No credit cards. Daily 10am–midnight. Bus: 103, 105, 225. SANDWICHES/LIGHT DISHES.

This Palermitano institution has been stuffing customers with stuffed *focaccia* sandwiches and other cheap eats since 1834 in a high-ceilinged, marble-floored space that resembles nothing so much as an old-fashioned train station waiting room. A huge central counter proudly displays trays of deep-dish *focaccie* fresh from the oven and a bubbling cauldron of steaming *milza* (spleen). Regulars usually order a beer and two dishes each, the most popular being *arancie* (giant fried rice balls filled with ragout, peas, and cheese) and split, stuffed *focaccie,* best served *maritata* (with spleen, heart, ricotta, and hard caciocavallo cheese), *schietta* (with ricotta and hard caciocavallo cheese), or *con panelle* (with chickpea fritters).

Bellini. Pz. Bellini 6 (off V. Maqueda). ☎ **091/616-5691.** Reservations recommended. Primi 8,000–15,000L ($4.70–$8.80); secondi 13,000–18,000L ($7.65–$10.60); pizze 7,000–12,000L ($4.10–$7.05). MC, V. Tues–Sun noon–3:30pm, 7pm–midnight. Open daily June–Sept. (Note: might close Wed instead of Mon.) Bus: 101, 102, 104, 105. SICILIAN/PIZZA.

The Bellini has one of the choicest settings in Palermo: tables spread on the piazza in front of the floodlit domes of La Marotana. Set into the entryway of the defunct Bellini theater, it's undoubtedly most popular for its pizza (not bad, but not outstanding) and live keyboard music on summer evenings. Bigger appetites will enjoy the *pasta con sarde,* couscous smothered with squid, shrimp, and mullet, or *rigatoni pomodoro e melanzane* (pasta tubes with tomatoes and eggplant), to be followed by a *costata di maiale* (pork chop), fresh fish of the day, or *involtini* of swordfish or veal. Friday lunches, there's a seafood-based tasting menu that's a steal at 40,000L ($23.55; reserve ahead).

Hosteria Al Duar. V. A. Gravina 31–33 (between V. P. Scordia and V. L. Massa). ☎ **091/ 329-560.** Primi 6,000–9,000L ($3.55–$5.30); secondi 3,000–16,000L ($1.75–$9.40). Completo Tunisiano 16,000L ($9.40). MC, V. Tues–Sun noon–3pm, 7pm–midnight. Bus: 101, 102, 103, 104, 106, 107, 108, 124, 134, 164, 806, 812, 824, 833, 837. TUNISIAN/ITALIAN.

Homesick Tunisians and hungry Palermitani come for one thing only—the gut-busting *completo tunisiano,* perhaps Palermo's best dining deal. They crowd the long, air-conditioned room hung with battered pots and pans and brightened by hand-painted Tunisian plates, waiting to dig into a conga line of North African specialty stews and couscous dishes. If you're not in a Tunisian mood, there's plenty of standard Italian fare as well.

✪ Osteria Fratelli Lo Bianco. V. E. Amari 104. ☎ **091/585-816.** Reservations not accepted. Primi 5,000–6,500L ($2.95–$3.80); secondi 8,000–10,000L ($4.70–$5.90). No credit cards. Mon–Sat noon–3pm, 7:30–10pm. Bus: 101, 102, 103, 104, 106, 107, 108, 124, 134, 164, 806, 812, 824, 833, 837. SICILIAN CASARECCIA.

This local bastion of shopkeeps and dock workers is a no-nonsense osteria of wood paneling, fluorescent lights, and wine on tap. Hustle to a communal table where Signor Barone bustles over to announce "We got ravioli or spaghetti," as if this were news after 90 years and no menu changes. This is your cue to choose a primo, the ravioli in tomato sauce, the spaghetti *alla ragù*, a garlic-and-parsley *carrettiere*, or *verdure* veggie sauce. Service is fast and efficient; you might be in and out in half an hour. The recited list of secondi might include a well-grilled *trancia di pesce spada* (swordfish steak), *polpette* of tiny, local fish, or a *bistecca* (steak). If *involtini di pesce spada* is among the offerings, snap up these tasty swordfish rolls immediately.

Pizzeria Italia. V. Orologio 54 (off Pz. Verdi). ☎ **091/589-885.** Reservations not accepted. Primi 6,000–10,000L ($3.55–$5.90); secondi 7,000–13,000L ($4.10–$7.65); pizze 5,000–12,000L ($2.95–$7.05). No credit cards. Tues–Sun 7pm–midnight (or later). Closed Aug. Bus: 101, 102, 103, 104. PIZZA/SICILIAN.

There's no sign and usually a long wait at this popular but tiny joint serving what is widely acclaimed to be Palermo's best pizza. In June and July, you can escape some of the crowding inside for tables out on the little side street. The *pizza Italia* with tomato, mozzarella, and spinach is excellent, as is the *pizza rustica*, with tomatoes, spicy salami, capers, smoked scamorza cheese, and oregano. For 3,000L ($1.75) extra, you can get fresh *bufala* mozzarella. For a pizza parlor, the *tagliolini del contadino* (with raw prosciutto, onions, carrots, celery, butter, and Worcestershire sauce) and *filetto con olive nere* (beef fillet covered with black olives, tomatoes, and brandy) are pretty good.

✪ Santandrea. Pz. Sant'Andrea 4 (south of Pz. S. Domenico). ☎ **091/334-999.** Reservations highly recommended. Primi 12,000L ($7.05); secondi 15,000–21,000L ($8.80–$12.35). MC, V. Wed–Mon 1–3pm, 8pm–midnight. Closed Jan. Bus: 101, 102, 103, 104, 107, 122. INNOVATIVE SICILIAN/SEAFOOD.

Family-run and casually classy, Santandrea is all about candlelit tables on a small, Palermo piazza of half-decayed buildings and a forgotten church facade (in winter, they retreat under terra-cotta ceilings). Instead of a menu, Annamaria recites in delicious detail the daily offerings based on the freshest ingredients from the nearby Vucciria market. The excellent *antipasto misto* is heavy on the seafood. Their *spaghetti con bottarga e aragosta* (lobster and dried, grated fish eggs) is excellent, as are fresh tagliatelle with mullet, shrimp, capers, and black olives, or in a pesto of zucchini leaves, toasted pine nuts, and sun-dried tomatoes. Roasted or grilled fish is the most popular main course, although a mix of grilled meats or those *involtini di pesce spada* are also tempting. Desserts are all made in-house. Still little-known among foreigners, this place is popular with Palermitani, so book ahead, especially in summer.

Shanghai. Vc. Mezzani 34 (on Pz. Caracciolo). ☎ **091/589-702.** Reservations not accepted. Primi 3,500–5,000L ($2.05–$2.95); secondi 6,000–12,000L ($3.55–$7.05). No credit cards. Mon–Sat noon–3pm, 6:30–10:30pm. Bus: 101, 102, 103, 104, 105, 107, 122, 225. PALERMITANO.

A bit of a shabby Palermo institution, this terrace trattoria overlooking the Vucciria market serves mediocre but dirt-cheap food in a tumultuous setting. The name supposedly comes from the sea of stall awnings below, reminiscent of Shanghai. The entry is basically someone's living room with platters of fish displayed on a table, beyond which locals at a long central table wolf down plates of spaghetti and drink wine straight from the bottle. The terrace is reserved for the tourists, most of whom get intimidated into springing for the *misto di golfo* (mixed fish fry). Although I've heard rumors that you can pick a fish from the stalls below, I've only seen the restaurant cook up what's on the menu: *pasta con broccoli integrame* (with broccoli and saffron), or steaks of *tonno naturale* (tuna) or *pesce spada* (swordfish) garnished with shrimp.

WINE & DESSERTS

Palermo is still filled with old-fashioned **wine shops**. The market areas are great places to search these joints out. My own Palermo favorite watering hole is in the Vucciria, the **Taverna Azzurra,** V. Maccheroni 9 (no phone), where Nino will hook you up with a 500L (30¢) shot of wine or a 66-centiliter bottle of hearty, frosty Forst beer for 2,000L ($1.20).

You can find great Sicilian **pastries**—including the rich Sicilian candied fruit *cassata* cake and treats made of *marzipan* almond paste that for centuries has been artistically shaped to mimic in miniature fruits, vegetables, and other foods (sometimes even whole plates of spaghetti)—at **Peccatucci di Mamma Andrea,** V. P. di Scordia 67 (☎ 091/334-835), or **Spinnato il Golosone,** Pz. Castelnuovo 16 (☎ 091/329-220). For ice cream, head to a legendary favorite in the city wall across from the harbor front turned fun park, **Gelateria Illardo,** V. Foro Umberto 1, 12 (☎ 091/616-4413).

PALERMO AFTER DARK

I won't kid you: You just won't want to be hanging around after dark in many parts of Palermo—including most of the old center, especially the Kalsa, the Alberghiera, and around the train station or first few blocks of Via Roma (once, simply waiting for the bus here, I received six offers from prostitutes, two for drugs, and two solicitations from guys who pulled over and winked).

Still, many parts of the New City are perfectly safe, and Piazza Verdi and Piazza Castelnuovo are both generally full of people. If you fancy a night at the **opera, ballet,** or **modern dance,** check out what's playing at the **Politeama Garibaldi,** Piazza R. Settimo (☎ 091/605-3315), and the **concert** hall of the Sicilian Symphonic Orchestra, **Teatro Golden,** V. Terrasanta 60 (☎ 091/305-217). The newly restored **Teatro Massimo, Piazza Verdi** (☎ 091/605-3315), presents **theater, music,** and **operettas.** The tourist office has detailed schedules of everything going on in town (pick up the *Palermo & Provincia Live* pamphlet here), including lists of restaurants and cafes presenting live music in the summer.

If all you want to do is kick back with a beer, head to **Via Principe di Belmonte** (between Via R. Settimo and Via Roma), a pedestrian strip lined with **bars and cafes,** many of which have outdoor seating in nice weather, a few with live pianists.

For an early evening of traditional fun for all ages, hunt down a *teatro dei pupi* (**marionette theater**) to watch professional puppeteers stage elaborate stories from the Charlemagne/Orlando sagas or tales of Saracen warriors (for a long time, this was the poor Sicilian's version of theater). The **Museo delle Marionette** (see listing under "Seeing Palermo's Sights," above) puts on shows every Friday at 5pm, September to July. Otherwise, the Cuticchio siblings are the only artists currently really active in Palermo; Mimmo puts on 5:30pm shows Saturday and Sunday on **V. Bara all'Olivella 95** (☎ 091/323-400), while his sister, Anna, does 9pm performances in winter (but irregularly of late) at the **Teatro dei Pupi,** Vc. Ragusi 6—the second block off Corso V. Emanuele west of the Quattro Canti (☎ 091/329-194). Also check with the **Teatro Bradamente,** V. Lombardi 25 (☎ 091/625-9233), to see if the free 10pm Friday performances are still on.

✪ A SIDE TRIP TO MONREALE'S MONASTERY

In a church on a hillside 8 kilometers (5 mi.) south of Palermo lies the greatest medieval mosaic cycle in Europe. The polychrome scenes on a shimmering gold background literally carpet the walls, arches, and apses of mighty ✪ **Monreale,** the last and greatest of Sicily's Norman cathedrals. When Palermo's British bishop Walter of the Mill started building the downtown cathedral, young William II decided in 1174 to flex his independence from that ecclesiastical potentate by raising his own cathedral outside the city. It's one of the most visually sumptuous day trips you can take anywhere in Italy. Even if you have only one day in Palermo, spend half of it here; nothing in town can compare.

Few people do not gasp in awe when they enter this cathedral, swathed with 68,472 square feet of luminous ✪ **mosaics.** The interior is like the Cappella Palatina writ large; it competes with St. Mark's of Venice as the most mosaicked church in Christendom—only less well lit, since few visitors arrive with a bag of coins to feed the many 1,000L light boxes. Although not the pinnacle of the Greek craftsmen's artistic prowess, they are nonetheless excellently executed and many panels do stand out, none more magnificently than the 66-foot-high, kindly eyed, and all-embracing *Christ Pantocrater* in the main apse. The two side apses are dedicated to St. Paul (left) and St. Peter (right) respectively. The restored **wood ceiling** of the nave is gorgeous, too, and don't forget to look down once in a while at the marble inlay work on the **floor.**

The attached monastery preserves the beautiful and serene ✪ **cloisters,** a festival of pointed arches supported by twin columns, each pair different from the last: some carved or twisted, some plain, and many inlaid with colored marble and gold mosaic chips in geometric patterns. Every column capital, too, is unique, carved in a beautifully symbolic medieval style with mythological figures and religious scenes. Even with the bused-in tour groups, these cloisters manage to retain a relaxed, contemplative air, helping make this day trip a double escape from the urban chaos of Palermo.

The **Duomo** itself (☎ 091/640-4413) is free, and open daily 8am to noon and 3:30 to 6:30pm. Admission to the cloisters (☎ **091/640-4403**) is 4,000L ($2.35). They're open Monday 9am to 1pm, 3 to 7pm; Tuesday to Saturday 9am to 1pm, 3 to 7pm, and 8 to 11:30pm; Sunday 9am to 12:30pm.

For ridiculously huge portions of home cookin' at remarkably low prices, the huge **La Fattoria** restaurant, just below town on the main road from Palermo at V. Circonvallazione di Monreale 26 (☎ **091/640-1134**), serves up an excellent *cannelloni alla casalinga* (homemade pasta leaves wrapped with meat and ricotta, topped with tomatoes and cheese, then baked) and tasty *pollo al forno* (oven-roasted chicken). They also serve pizza, and stay open Tuesday to Sunday noon to 1am (daily in July and August). Credit cards are not accepted.

GETTING HERE   Take **bus 389** from Palermo's Piazza Indipendenza right to the cathedral. Monreale has a **tourist office** to the left of the cloisters entrance on Piazza V. Emanuele (☎ 091/646-6070), open Monday to Saturday 8:30am to 1:30pm, and Tuesday and Thursday again from 3:30 to 5:30pm.

THE GREEK RUINS OF SEGESTA EN ROUTE TO ERICE

The temple and theater of ancient Egesta are two of the most beautifully sited classical monuments in the world, set in the lush middle of nowhere of the Sicilian countryside. Egesta adapted Greek ways early on, using the ✪ **Doric temple** design to build a house of worship in the 5th century B.C. The squat, pale honey-colored temple perches at the lip of a gorge surrounded by a high natural amphitheater of verdant hills. The nearby theater is chipped out of a mountaintop with a sweeping vista across the landscape to the Gulf of Castellammare. It's best appreciated on a summer night when **classical plays** are staged almost daily around 8:45pm. Tickets run from 11,000L ($6.50) to 44,000L ($25.90); call ☎ **0924-951-131** for information. Even with the tour-bus crowds and modern highways nearby, Segesta remains one of the most magical, romantic corners of Italy.

VISITOR INFORMATION   The site is wedged between the A29dir autostrada from Palermo to Trapani and the old SS113 road (exits from both).

Both the train (four daily; 2 hr.; 8,200L/$4.80) and the hourly bus (75 min.; 8,000L/$4.70) from **Palermo** stop at the train station *Segesta Tempio,* about a 1-kilometer (0.6-mi.) walk from the site. **Tarantola** (☎ **0924/31-020**) runs four direct buses daily (one Sunday) from **Trapani** (60 min.; 4,500L/$2.65) direct to the site entrance.

There's a cafe/ticket office/souvenir stand at the entrance (☎ 0924-952-356). The site is now enclosed; admission is 4,000L ($2.35) and it's open 8:30am to an hour before sunset (until 6pm on show days in summer).

4 Erice

112 km (67 mi.) W of Palermo

✪ **Erice** is the most enchanting and stoniest medieval city you'll find in Sicily. It's often compared with a Tuscan or Umbrian hill town, but this ancient seat of mystical power is pure Sicilian, established more than 3,000 years ago by the native Sicani with the city laid out by the Elymians in a magical triangle shape. From its thrilling mountaintop setting, two sheer cliffs drop 2,478 feet to open up vistas across the plains of Trapani and down the west coast of Sicily. On a clear day, you can even see Cape Bon in Tunisia, but this Sicilian aerie is more often shrouded in a mist that only adds to the mystique (or, especially in winter, the misery, when temperatures can really plummet below Sicilian norms and snow or hail is not uncommon).

Erice's quiet beauty has put it firmly on the package tour map, and caused the prices to spike to some of Sicily's highest outside Taormina. But an afternoon wandering the medieval streets and drinking in the vistas will help you readily see beyond the tourism industry to fathom why, for thousands of years, people have flocked here to worship at the temple of one of the ancient world's most famous and powerful earth goddesses, known to the Romans as *Venus Erycina.*

FESTIVALS   On Good Friday, there's a street **procession of the *misteri,*** sculpted scenes of the Passion. In late July, the churches around town host a **festival of medieval and Renaissance music,** and in December a Sicilian **folk music festival** comes to town.

ESSENTIALS

GETTING HERE   By Train or Bus   To get to Erice by public transportation, you must head to the provincial capital of Trapani 14 kilometers (8.4 mi.) below Erice on the coast. There are eight to nine trains daily from **Palermo** (2 to 4 hr.; 12,100L/$7.05) to Trapani. Segesta (☎ **0923/20-066**) runs 25 buses daily from **Palermo** (105 min.; 12,000L/$7.05). Lumia (☎ **0922/20-414**) runs four buses (two Sunday) from **Agrigento** (3 to 4 hr.; 17,400L/$10.25). From Trapani, there's an AST bus (☎ **0923/21-021**) up to Erice at least every 2 hours (40 min.; 3,000L/$1.75).

By Car   Follow the A29dir from Palermo or Segesta to the first Trapani exit, then continue along the signposted switchback road up the mountain.

VISITOR INFORMATION   The tourist office at Vle. Conte A. Pepoli 11 (☎ **0923/869-388;** fax 0923/869-544), is open July to August Monday to Saturday 8am to 8pm, Sunday 9am to 1pm; September to June Monday to Saturday 8am to 2pm.

STROLLING THROUGH ERICE

Erice has few technical sights, but plenty of stony hill town character, and the best way to enjoy it is simply to wander the back streets and alleys set with strategically placed flowering vines and pots, baroque balconies, and medieval shop fronts (today private home entrances).

If you need some destinations for your ambles, head first to the **Chiesa Matrice,** built in 1314 with a fine Gothic porch. The neo-Gothic interior, open 8am to noon and 4 to 7pm, has a Domenico Gagini *Madonna* on the right aisle. You can climb the 15th-century bell tower for 1,000L (60¢) to get a great view over the town in one direction and a panorama across the gulf of Trapani and Egadi Islands on the other.

Make sure you head to the southwest corner of town where you'll find the ilex-shaded **Villa Balio gardens**—laid out in the 19th century when Count Agostino Pepoli reconstructed the Norman castle in their midst. Beyond the gardens, a path is slung along the cliff edge to lead up to Erice's highest point, the ✪ **Castello di Venere,** today little more than crumbling Norman-era walls surrounding the sacred site where the Temple to Venus once stood. Piercing the walls are several windows and doorways with spectacular views across the countryside.

WHERE TO STAY

Edelweiss. Cortile Padres Vincenzo. ☎ and fax **0923/869-420.** 15 units, all with bathroom. 100,000L ($58.80) single, 130,000L ($76.50) double. For stays of longer than 1 day in Aug, obligatory half-pension runs 120,000L ($70.60) per person. Rates include breakfast. MC, V.

Comfortable, friendly, and family run, this pensione tucked away in a quiet corner of town off Piazza San Domenico is pricey Erice's best value. It's a simple place whose large rooms have patterned rugs on tile floors and sometimes a few choice architectural elements like a massive wood beam or column-flanked archway. Beds aren't the firmest, but will do. Some accommodations come with an adjacent room for a third bed—great for families. Six accommodations have sea views, four from balconies (though the vista itself is best from the top-floor rooms 115 and 118). Some rooms have minibars, most have TVs, and they all should have phones by 1999.

WORTH A SPLURGE

✪ **Moderno.** V. Vittorio Emanuele 63, 91016 Erice (TP). ☎ **0923/869-300.** Fax 0923/869-139. 40 units, all with bathroom. TV TEL. Nov–Feb 120,000L ($70.60) single, 170,000L ($100) double; Mar–June and Oct 130,000L ($76.50) single, 190,000L ($111.75) double; July–Sept 140,000L ($82.35) single, 200,000L ($117.65) double. Half-board 120,000–150,000L ($70.60–$88.25) per person. Rates include breakfast. AE, DC, MC, V.

If price is less of a concern, the Catalano family's modernized hotel with 19th-century roots is the best place to book. Traditional hand-woven runners line the halls and stairs, and room furnishings are bent wood and wicker, with brass bedsteads with antique dressers. Floors are tiled or, as in the 14 rooms of the "new wing" (still an old building) across the street, carpeted, and almost all have a minibar. Those with balconies on the street have the best people-watching but the most noise (not that it's raucous). Their dining room is actually the best-regarded restaurant in town, although a meal will set you back a good 60,000 to 70,000L ($35.30 to $41.20) à la carte, making that half-board deal quite attractive.

WHERE TO DINE

Almonds feature prominently in Erice cooking, which is otherwise dominated by Trapanese cuisine like couscous covered with fish.

Monte San Giuliano. Vicolo S. Rocco 7 (off Cor. V. Emanuele). ☎ **0923/869-595.** Reservations highly recommended. Primi 11,000L ($6.50); secondi 13,000–18,000L

($7.65–$10.60). AE, DC, MC, V. Tues–Sun 12:30–3pm, 8–11pm. Open daily July–Aug. Closed Nov 3–16 and Jan 7–16. TRAPANESE/SEAFOOD.

Tucked away in a stone courtyard beyond a medieval double gate is Monte San Giuliano, serving some of the best food in Erice. It's perhaps a hair below the Moderno in quality, but its considerably lower prices and terrace setting make it stand out. Book ahead for a seat on the walled flagstone terrace to enjoy the *pasta con sarde, busiati S. Giuliano* (in an almond pesto with tomatoes, eggplant, and pecorino added), or the ubiquitous *cuscus alla Trapanese* (doused in fish broth and ladled with the meat of various white fish). Follow it up with *pescespada al salmorgiano* (swordfish with marjoram), or a *zainetto dello chef* (beef rolled around tomatoes, mozzarella, and eggplant then roasted).

Osteria di Venere. V. Roma 6 (at Pz. S. Giuliano). ☎ **0923/869-362.** Reservations recommended. Primi 10,000–13,000L ($5.90–$7.65); secondi 10,000–20,000L ($5.90–$11.75). No credit cards (yet). Thurs–Tues 12:30–3pm, 8–11pm. SICILIAN/TRAPANESE.

This one-room restaurant has a touch of refinement that makes it popular with locals who turn out in groups for the finely observed Sicilian cooking. Luckily, you can sample much of it via the *tris di primi*, a trio of pastas that may include papardelle with shrimp and tuna, ravioli in a cream sauce, or *casarecce* prepared *all'Ericino* (an almond/tomato pesto) or tastily *alla venere* (with eggplant, tomatoes, swordfish, and mint). Secondi run from the expected *involtini alla siciliana* (veal rolls) and fresh fish to more inventive dishes like *calamari ripieni* (stuffed squid). By the time you visit, you should be able to pay by credit card.

PASTRIES & RUGS

Erice is renowned for two products: pastries and hand-woven rugs. The former is a craft developed and refined by various orders of nuns based in Erice from the 14th to 18th centuries. These convents' tradition is carried on by the *pasticceria* founded by **Maria Grammatica** in 1950, V. V. Emanuele 14 near Piazza Umberto (☎ **0923/ 869-390**). For 10,000L ($5.90), you can get half a kilo (about a dozen) of her various sugary almond treats kissed with lemon or citrus juices and made famous by *Bitter Almonds,* the cultural cookbook she co-wrote with Mary Taylor Simetti.

Rugs, about 2 feet wide with colorful basic geometric designs in zigzags and diamonds, were traditionally woven from textile leftovers. The best weavers still use scraps on their hand-worked looms, although they also turn their artisans' hands to more innovative designs using first-rate threads and a kaliope of dyes. **Maria La Sala** works the loom in her little shop at V. V. Emanuele 80 (no phone); Anna weaves inside **Ceramica Ericina** at V. V. Emanuele 7 (☎ **0923/869-140**). At either, rugs 2 to 3 yards long cost between 100,000 and 200,000L ($58.80 and $117.65).

5 Selinute

120 km (72 mi.) S of Palermo, 98 km (59 mi.) SE of Erice, 90 km (54 mi.) NW of Agrigento, 88 km (55 mi.) SE of Trapani

Founded by Greeks in the 7th century B.C., Selinute was named after the *selinon*, or wild celery, that still grows in abundance alongside wild capers. Although relatively short-lived as an ancient capital, Selinute got rich quick, built the temples to prove it, and then was defeated by Carthage and faded into malaria-borne obscurity until the 16th century so that little modernity has corrupted the gorgeous archaeological site. Today, the few re-erected rows of columns stand against the bright green grass and the deep blues of the sky and the sea, perched picturesquely on a pair of plateaus overlooking the Mediterranean between two small rivers. Selinute's modern support town is **Marinella,** a fishing village-cum-modest beach resort that has in the past decade boomed from a single road with a few hotels to a thriving little town filling the area east of the site.

Selinute's archaeological site (☎ 0924-46-277) is split between two zones: the **East Hill** temples right at the ticket office—nearest to Marinella and boasting the largest temples—and the **West Hill/Acropolis** picturesquely sited overlooking the sea. All the temples are known simply by letters, since no one is certain to which god any one was dedicated, and all have descriptive plaques to provide background. Admission is 4,000L ($2.35); hold on to your ticket to get in the separately fenced West Hill. Selinute is open daily 9am to one hour before sunset.

A FESTIVAL In summertime, there is a series of **nighttime performances amid the ruins,** usually at Temple E. These can range from Classical plays like *Oedipus Rex* to southern U.S. gospel, and productions of *Chorus Line* to modern dance. Call ☎ 0924/904-555 for information and tickets.

ESSENTIALS **Getting to Castelvetrano by train or bus** The gateway to Selinute is Castelvetrano, a lackluster city about 23 kilometers (14 mi.) inland from the ruins. There are 13 **trains** daily (7 Sunday) from **Trapani** (68 to 83 min.; 6,700L/$3.95); five to seven trains daily (one direct, the others entailing an iffy change at "Alcamo Diramazione" with just a 3-minute window to transfer) from **Palermo** (2 hr. 45 min.; 10,100L/$5.95).

To **bus** it, contact **AST** (☎ 0924/47-392 in Castelvetrano), which runs three daily buses from **Trapani** (95 min.; 8,500L/$5). **Lumia** lines (☎ 0922/20-414) makes the same run four times Monday to Saturday, none on Sunday. Lumia will also carry you here from **Agrigento** three times daily (2 to 2.5 hr.; 11,000L/$6.50) and lets you off near the hospital on Via Marinella (wait for the bus to the ruins across from the "Bar Selinus"). **Salemi** (☎ 0923/981-120) has a direct bus from **Palermo** to Castelvetrano eight times Monday to Saturday, two on Sunday (2 hr.; 10,000L/$5.90).

Getting to the Site From Castelvetrano's train station, six **buses** (four on Sunday) make the 20-minute run to Marinella/Selinute, dropping you off across from the site entrance. Purchase tickets on the bus for 4,000L ($2.35) round-trip (*andata e ritorno*). The last bus back to Castelvetrano is at 8pm Monday to Friday, 2:30pm weekends. By **car,** just take Via Marinella out of town, which becomes the SS115, branching left into SS115d.

Tourist Information There's a visitor information cabin (☎ and fax 0924/46-251) at the parking lot/site entrance, which hands out a good site plan. It's open Monday to Saturday 8am to 8pm, Sunday 9am to noon and 3pm to 6pm.

WHERE TO STAY & DINE

Albergo Lido Azzurro. V. Marco Polo 98, 91020 Marinella (TP). ☎ **0924/941-000.** Fax 0924/46-256. 14 units, all with bath. TEL. July–Aug 65,000L ($38.25) single, 95,000L ($55.90) double; Sept–June 60,000L ($35.30) single, 85,000L ($50) double. Rates include breakfast. AE, DC, MC, V. Free parking.

This modern hotel sits at the heart of Marinella's commercial main drag, across the street from its own beach and restaurant/pizzeria. The management is decidedly mellow in an amiable way, and the bulk of the basic rooms—spruced up with tiny Matisse prints—have balconies with views of the Mediterranean. It's kept tolerably clean, the beds aren't *too* soft, the modular furnishings not too worn yet, and the prices are quiet agreeable. By 1999, you can expect in-room TVs. C-minus for the bathrooms, though, where the sink's hot water tap seems to be there merely for decoration and—although this may have been a temporary plumbing problem—the bathroom in my room emitted an entirely unpleasant odor.

Pierrot. V. Marco Polo 108. ☎ **0924/46-205.** Reservations recommended. Primi 9,000–12,000L ($5.30–$7.05); secondi 9,000–12,000L ($5.30–$7.05); pizze 6,500–12,000L ($3.80–$7.05). Tasting menus 32,000–40,000L ($18.80–$23.55; no wine), light meal menus 12,000–20,000L ($7.05–$11.75; no wine). AE, DC, MC, V. Wed–Mon noon–3:30pm, 8pm–midnight. Open daily in Aug. Closed Jan–Feb. SEAFOOD/PIZZA.

This second-story terrace restaurant overlooking the coastal commercial drag of Marinella and the Mediterranean scant feet away has excruciatingly slow service but arguably the best food in town. On the run you can make do with a pizza, or settle in for a primo such as *spaghetti con zucchine fritte* or *con vongole veraci* (with tiny clams), *casarecce cappa e spada* (homemade pasta with capers and swordfish), a *couscous di pesce* on Friday evenings, or splurge on *spaghetti all'aragosta* (with lobster) for 18,000L ($10.60). Follow it up with a *frittura da re* (abundant fry-up of seafood), *sogliola alla mugnaia* (sole meunière), or *cotoletta panata* (breaded veal chop).

6 Agrigento

129 km (80 mi.) S of Palermo, 175 km (109 mi.) SE of Trapani, 90 km (54 mi.) SE of Selinute, 256 km (154 mi.) W of Siracusa

Ancient Greek *Akragas*, founded around 581 B.C., is lucky enough to retain a ridge below the city lined with 5th-century B.C. Doric temples, one of which, the ✪ **Temple of Concord**, is one of the two best preserved Greek temples in the world. The vista from the city of the temple ridge with the sea beyond is one of Italy's most breathtaking sights—notwithstanding the eyesore of 600 concrete condominium monstrosities illegally erected by the Mafia. There are few spots more magic or beautiful to spend a sunset than in Agrigento's Valley of the Temples. It's a long, full day to see the museum, Insula Romana, and the temples themselves. If your time is limited, just hit the temples. There's nothing of consequence to see in the city itself.

A FESTIVAL   The early February **Festival of Almond Blossoms** is a celebration of local folklore with music, flag tossing, and traditional foods held in the temple zone.

ESSENTIALS

GETTING HERE   By Train   There are nine trains (four on Sunday) from **Palermo** (2 hr.; 12,100L/$7.10); and five to eight trains from **Catania,** direct or with a transfer at Caltanissetta Xirbi (4 to 5 hr.; 16,000L/$9.40). The **Agrigento centrale station** (☎ 0922/26-669) is on Piazza Marconi, just down the steps from Agrigento's central Piazzale A. Moro. Don't get off at the suburban station *Agrigento Bassa.*

By Bus   Agrigento's depot is on Piazza V. Emanuele, above Piazza A. Moro. **Lumia** lines (☎ 0922/401-494) runs a bus that runs three times Monday to Saturday from Castelvetrano (the **Selinute** stop; 2.5 hr.; 11,000L/$6.50). Cuffaro (☎ 0922/5961-490) runs seven daily buses from **Palermo** (2 hr.; 11,500L/$6.75). SAIS has 11 runs (6 Sunday) from **Catania,** just north of Siracusa (2 to 3 hr.; 17,500L/$10.30); their office is behind the booth on V. Ragazzi del 99 (☎ 0922/595-933).

By Car   Agrigento lies on the coastal SS115, which you can follow from Castelvetrano near Selinute or from Siracusa. From Palermo, take the SS121/SS189.

VISITOR INFORMATION   Agrigento's **tourist office** (☎ and fax 0922/20-454) is just behind Piazzale A. Moro at V. C. Battisti 15, your first left off Via Atenea. It's open daily 8:45am to 1:15pm and 4:30 to 6:30pm. There's another information office at V. Empedocle 73 (☎ 0922/20-391; fax 0922/20-246). For a **taxi,** call ☎ 0922/26-670 or 0922/21-899.

ATMs in Agrigento

The only ATM in town that will accept American bankcards or credit cards is the San Paolo branch at the northeast corner (far left as you exit Via Atenea) on Piazza Vittorio Emanuele, across from the cinema and post office.

THE VALLEY OF THE TEMPLES

GETTING HERE   Buses 1, 2, and 3 run from in front of the train station down Via dei Templi into the Valley of the Temples. You can get off at the Museum/Insula Romana or stay on all the way to the Posto di Ristoro, a pricey cafe/souvenir stand at the entrances to the two temple zones.

MUSEO ARCHEOLOGICO REGIONALE   You enter the museum (☎ 0922/ 497-111) through a little garden and a catwalk over the *Ekklesiasterion,* a 4th-century B.C. assembly arena. The museum's room 3 contains an outstanding collection of superbly painted vases spanning the 6th to 3rd centuries B.C., some Attic but many from Agrigento itself. Room 6 is devoted to the Temple of the Olympian Zeus (see below), with models of how it once might have looked and the museum's most striking exhibit, a reconstituted ✪ *telamon*—sculpted male figure—stacked up against one wall. This weather-worn, 25-foot giant used to be part of the temple's decoration. In the rest of the museum, look for the 2nd-century B.C. alabaster sarcophagus of a child, carved with happy childhood moments and a touching death scene, and the 5th-century B.C. painted krater from Gela showing a battle with the Amazons. Admission is 8,000L ($4.70). It's open Monday to Saturday 9am to 1:30pm and 2:30 to 7:30pm, Sunday 9am to 1:30pm (in August, also Sunday 2:30 to 5pm).

INSULA ROMANA   Across the street from the museum is the Roman-Hellenistic Quarter, a few excavated blocks of the Roman city that thrived here from the 2nd century B.C. to the A.D. 4th century with some peachy polychrome floor mosaics under those glass huts. Admission is free; it's open daily 9am to 1 hour before sunset and is across the street from the Museo Archeologico Regionale.

✪ TEMPLES   Down the road, you'll arrive at the true draw of Agrigento—a series of 5th-century B.C. Doric wonders surrounded by olive and almond trees (☎ 0922/ 20-014). To the right of the road, past the ticket booth, are the massive, jumbled remains of the **Temple of Olympian Zeus,** or **Olympieion.** At 363 by 174 feet, this is the largest Doric temple ever attempted, begun in 480 B.C. but left unfinished when the Carthaginians invaded in 409. Earthquakes and wars brought most of it down, and in the 18th century much of its stone was quarried to build the nearby port of Porto Empedocle.

It's hard to fathom the sheer size of the thing—little remains other than a weedy mound of ancient cut rubble—but here are some ciphers to help. Each column was over 55 feet high and 13 feet thick at the base—there's half of one capital sitting near the top of the rubble pile. Lying in the dust nearby is a worn replica of one of the *telamones,* or columns carved as a man (the original's in the museum up the road). This 25-foot giant took up less than half the height of the columns (never mind adding in

---

The Valley's Hours & Admission

Oddly enough, you have to pony up 4,000L ($2.35) to get into the least interesting section—that with the ruinous Temple of Olympian Zeus—but the rest of the valley's temples are free and gateless. The site is open daily, 8:30am to 1 hour before sunset.

---

the steps, pediment, and roof). Beyond is a pile of cut blocks with U-shaped grooves, which were used to help haul them into place.

THE TRIO OF TEMPLES   The postcard trio of temples are up off the east/left side of Via dei Templi, balancing atop a wide ridge with a wash of olive groves spilling down on the Agrigento side, and a cliff falling off toward the sea on the other. When you first clamber up into the area on some steps chipped out of the stone, you find yourself climbing into the ruins of the **Temple of Heracles,** the oldest shrine here (500 B.C.). Most of it is tumbled down, but eight, 33-foot-high columns have been reerected and you can scramble about the remains of the cella.

Just up the road, past a **paleochristian necropolis** with tombs honeycombed into the rocky ground and tunnels under the road, is the spectacular ✪ **Temple of Concord.** Raised in 430 B.C., this is the best-preserved Greek temple outside of Athens itself—largely because Agrigento's bishop turned it into a church in the A.D. 6th century. In the more classically minded 18th century, all the churchiness was stripped away. The cella and 34 Doric columns all still stand, supporting an architrave and miraculously complete entablatures on both ends. The temple's in such good shape, they've fenced it off for preservation reasons.

The road continues to slope up, passing the remains of the ancient city walls on the right set with some Byzantine tombs, to the broken-toothed **Temple of Hera,** also incorrectly called the Temple of Juno. It was built around 450 B.C. at the very edge of the cliff. Twenty-five of its 34 columns remain standing, with bits of the entablature intact on one end. At press time, it was partially scaffolded, and remains temporarily closed to visitors for fear of another landslide at its edge like they had in 1976. A low, stepped wall on the far side makes (wind notwithstanding) an ideal spot to picnic with the panorama of temples before you.

WHERE TO STAY

If you can't find space at the hotels below, rooms 32 to 35 at the **Belvedere,** V. S. Vito 20 (☎ and fax **0922/20-051**), has vistas over the Valley of Temples. There are no amenities, but it's clean, if a bit down at the heels. Doubles run 65,000L ($38.25) without bathroom, 90,000L ($52.95) with private bathroom.

Bella Napoli. Pz. Lena 6, 92100 Agrigento. ☎ and fax **0922/20-435.** 46 units, 23 with bathroom. 35,000L ($20.60) single without bathroom, 40,000L ($23.55) single with bathroom; 55,000L ($32.35) double without bathroom, 75,000L ($44.10) double with bathroom. Breakfast 5,000L ($2.95). AE. Walk to the far end of V. Atenea, then turn right past the funky chamber of commerce and immediately right again to double back up the short, steep street.

It's not a bad budget joint, but it's a far cry from the stellar Concordia (below). The almost cell-like rooms are exceedingly plain, with functional furnishings of various ages and states of disrepair, and ceiling lamps that look like leftovers from the *War of the Worlds* film set. The tile floors are clean, though, and it's in a quiet part of town at great, *pensione* prices. However, the cots' springs are on their last legs.

✪ **Concordia.** Pz. S. Francesco 11, 92100 Agrigento. ☎ and fax **0922/596-266.** 28 units, all with bathroom. TV TEL. 30,000L ($17.65) single, 75,000L ($44.10) double. Rates include morning coffee. AE, DC, MC, V. Take V. Pirandello (left parallel to V. Atenea), which becomes V. S. Francesco; the hotel's about 500 feet down on the left.

If you aren't ponying up the dough for the Villa Athena (below), call here first. The Concordia is the eternally favorite inexpensive inn of Agrigento. It's family-run and it feels like it, with by far the warmest reception in town. And although the cots are lazy-springed and the bathrooms cramped, the modestly sized rooms are kept clean, the modular veneer furnishings nice enough, and the stuccoed walls repainted regularly. Best of all, you get to take advantage of a 20,000L ($11.75) lunch menu at their terrific trattoria La Forchetta (see below).

WORTH A SPLURGE

✪ **Villa Athena.** V. d. Templi 9, 92100 Agrigento. ☎ **0922/596-288.** Fax 0922/402-180. 40 units, all with bathroom. A/C MINIBAR TV TEL. 180,000L ($105.90) single; 250,000L ($147.05) double without view, 300,000L ($176.50) double with view. Rates include breakfast. AE, DC, MC, V. Take V. Petrarca (or bus 1, 2, or 3), following signs into the archaeological zone; it's a private drive off to the left after the museum (ask bus driver to let you off).

Splurge shmurge, this 18th-century villa would be a steal at any price. It may have the most fantastic location of any hotel in Italy: within the Valley of the Temples archaeological park, directly across an olive grove from the Temple of Concord, whose practically perfect Doric profile is framed by the windows of half the rooms (best from rooms 302 to 304 or 202 to 206). If you can tear your eyes off the ancient splendor of your next-door neighbor, you'll see the carpeted rooms are smallish but very comfortable, with genuine beds and mattresses and mild-mannered functional pieces. There are several restaurant and bar spaces set into terraced gardens that look over at Concord, and a green pool at the base for washing off the dust of a day at the temples. Book far in advance for this romance, especially during summer, when even Zeus would have a hard time securing a room.

WHERE TO DINE

If you're planning on a day at the temples, pack a lunch, as the sandwich bar at the site is ridiculously expensive.

✪ **La Forchetta.** Pz. S. Francesco 11. ☎ **0922/596-266.** Reservations recommended. Primi 7,000–10,000L ($4.10–$5.90); secondi 8,000–20,000L ($4.70–$11.75). MC, V. Mon–Sat noon–3pm, 7–11pm. In summer, also Sun 7–11pm. AGRIGENTESE/SICILIAN.

La Forchetta has grown from its humble osteria roots, but one thing hasn't changed: It still serves the best food in town at prices that can't be beat. Gone is the bare room where locals filed in and grabbed their own bread from the kitchen. Now we get a bona-fide decor (of pine paneling and historic photos) to go with our meal, and tourists have become the majority of clients, at least in summer. The prices, however, have stayed low, and if anything, the food's improved. The judiciously spicy *penne pirandello* (tomatoes, sausage, pepperoncino, and cream) is delicious, as is the *pasta del giorno* (pasta of the day), which is usually made with fish or eggplant. Secondi are simple, be it a *panata siciliana* (breaded steak) or a *cotolette si agnello arrosto* (tasty roast lamb chop).

Le Caprice. V. Panoramica d. Templi 25 (a road leading around the east side of the archaeological zone, south of town). ☎ **0922/26-462.** Reservations recommended. Primi 10,000L ($5.90); secondi 15,000–25,000L ($8.80–$14.70). AE, DC, MC, V. Sat–Thurs 12:30–3pm, 7:30–11pm. Closed July 1–15. SEAFOOD/SICILIAN.

Come here for the fantastic second-story view of the Valley of Temples beyond olive groves—although rushing traffic below your feet distracts from the idyllic scene. It's a splurge, but so long as you don't do anything foolish like order the 7,000L ($4.10) green salad, you can enjoy that view *and* a full meal for under 40,000L ($23.55) alongside regulars who eat here two or three times a week. The menu is limited, but each dish is usually excellent, from risotto with seafood to *cavatelli della casa* (macaroni mixed with fried eggplant, tomato, ricotta, mozzarella, and basil, then baked in foil). If you prefer a meaty secondo, try the tasty *involtini all siciliana* (grilled breaded stuffed veal rolls), though you may offend the staff if you don't want seafood like *pesce spada* (swordfish) or a *fritto misto* fresh from their gulf.

Lumie di Sicilia. Cortile Contarini 3 (off V. Atenea). ☎ **0922/595-520.** Reservations recommended. Primi 6,000–15,000L ($3.55–$8.80); secondi 9,000–20,000L ($5.30–$11.75). Menù turistico 12,000–32,000L ($7.05–$18.80). MC, V. Thurs–Tues noon–3pm, 7:30pm–midnight. AGRIGENTESE/SICILIAN.

Under new family ownership as of May 1998, the real draw of the Lumie is the hidden, canyonlike courtyard, with a wooden deck and hanging lights for meals al fresco. The new owners aren't sure yet how they'll change the menu, but they plan to stick to hearty Sicilian concoctions like *tagliatelle alla francescana* (with tomatoes, mushrooms, ground veal, and eggplant) and *orecchiette alla rabbatiddisi* (pasta with pork, fennel, and other earthy aromas). For a main course, try the excellent fresh fish or seafood *fritto misto* (fry-up of calamari, shrimp, mullet, hake, and so on).

EN ROUTE TO SIRACUSA:
PIAZZA ARMERINA'S ROMAN MOSAICS

In the hamlet of Casale outside the small city of Piazza Armerina lies the ✪ **Villa Romana del Casale** (☎ **0935/680-036**), an A.D. 4th-century villa whose 40 rooms are carpeted with some 37,800 square feet of the most extensive, gorgeous, and colorful ancient mosaics in western Europe. This was the hunting lodge of Maximanus, Diocletian's co-emperor, and the remarkable mosaics were probably the work of north African craftsmen. They're remarkable not only for their Technicolor variety and sheer extent of preservation, but also for their masterful craftsmanship.

This being a hunting lodge, many of the scenes involve big game hunting and other sports, no more spectacularly than in the **Great Hunt,** a mosaic scene undulating for 200 feet in a catalogue of animals found throughout the ancient empire. Most are shown being captured alive and herded onto the ships that will carry them to Rome to be used in stadium spectacles (look for the North African lion, rendered extinct by such Roman excesses). Nearby in the *palestra* (gym) you'll see a **Chariot Race** held at Rome's Circus Maximus, complete with cheering fans. But the most famous scene is hands-down the **Ten Bikini Girls,** apparently female athletes either working out at the gym or competing in various events and, yes, wearing strapless bikinis. The kiddie's rooms are especially amusing, featuring pint-size versions of the main halls' majestic scenes. Also be on the lookout for the mosaic **erotic couple** sneaking a kiss in one side room, her toga slipping off for a gratuitous bottom-shot. Admission is 4,000L ($2.35). The site is open nonstop 8am to 30 minutes before sunset, but the ticket office closes between 1 and 3pm.

GETTING HERE From Agrigento, take one of four SAL buses (none Sunday) to Gela (90 min.; 8,000L/$4.70) where you can transfer for one of two to four daily Etna buses to Piazza Armerina (30 to 60 min.; 5,500L/$3.25). Once in Piazza Armerina, the B bus makes the 15-minute run out to the Villa Imperiale at Casale hourly from 9 to 11am and 4 to 6pm (return trips hourly 9:30 to 11:30am and 4:30 to 6:30pm).

VISITOR INFORMATION Piazza Armerina has a friendly **tourist information office** inside the *palazzo* at the top of Via Cavour (☎ 0935/680-201, fax 0935/684-565), open Monday to Saturday 8am to 2pm. **Ristorante Hotel Mosaici da Battiato** (☎ and fax **0935/685-453**) is a fairly good restaurant with basic but serviceable guest rooms outside town and right at the turnoff for the ruins (follow the signs toward "i mosaici"). Doubles run 80,000L ($47.05), half-pension 65,000L ($38.25) per person, no credit cards, and it's closed November 20 to December 25.

7 Siracusa

256 km (154 mi.) E of Agrigento, 87 km (52 mi.) S of Catania, 330 km (198) miles SE of Palermo, 182 km (110 mi.) S of Messina

Siracusa (Syracuse to some) was settled by Greeks in 733 B.C. and was the major power in Sicily from 480 B.C. through the Roman occupation. With a perfect location at the center of the Mediterranean world, the heritage of this powerful trading port has left the modern city with everything from fantastic ruins—including one of the world's largest intact Greek theaters—and a baroque old quarter to one of Italy's finest archaeological museums and the only stands of papyrus that grow in Europe (supposedly a gift from Egyptian ruler Ptolemy II). Siracusa makes a great base and good spot to slow down for a day or two, for while it has plenty of top-notch sights to keep you busy, it also sports a relaxed atmosphere, with pleasant cafes, seaside walks, and open-air restaurants to while away the hours.

FESTIVALS & MARKETS   Siracusans parade relics of their **patron Santa Lucia** around with pomp and ceremony on December 13 and again the first two Sundays in May. The city also sponsors summertime **performances in the ancient Greek theater.** These tend to be of classical plays translated into Italian (some of which even premiered in this very theater—2,500 years ago). Contact the tourist office for specifics.

ESSENTIALS
GETTING HERE   By Train   From **Agrigento,** take one of nine daily trains to Canicatti (45 to 60 min.; 4,700L/$2.75), where you transfer for one of four trains (two on Sunday) to Siracusa, usually changing trains again in Gela or Modica (4.5 hr., not including transfer; 22,000L/$12.95 total). From **Noto,** there are five to eight trains (30 min.; 3,900L/$2.30). From **Palermo,** you can take one of six daily trains to **Catania** (3.5 to 4 hr; 20,000L/$11.75), from which there are at least hourly runs (85 min.; 7,400L/$4.35) on to Siracusa. From **Messina,** there are at least hourly runs (3 to 4 hr.; 16,000L/$9.40). **Siracusa's station** (☎ **0931/67-964** or 0931/66-640) is on the mainland, west of Ortigia and south of the archaeological zone.

By Bus   Two lines service Siracusa. **AST** has its depot and ticket office (☎ **0931/ 462-711**) on Piazza della Posta just over the bridge on Ortigia. **SAIS** has a depot on Riva Nazario Sauro just above Piazza della Posta and office nearby at V. Trieste 28 (☎ **0931/66-710**).

Both companies run buses from **Catania** about twice an hour (60 to 75 min.; 6,500L/$3.80). From **Agrigento,** take one of four daily SAL buses to Gela (90 min.; 8,000L/$), where you can change for one of four to five daily trains (3.5 hr.; 16,000L/ $9.40) or two AST buses Monday to Saturday to Siracusa (2 hr.; 13,500L/$7.95). AST also runs two daily buses from **Piazza Armerina** (4 hr.; 11,500L/$6.75). From **Noto,** SAIS runs nine buses, two on Sunday, (60 min.; 4,500L/$2.65). From **Taormina,** SAIS runs two buses Monday to Saturday (2 hr. 45 min.; 12,500L/$7.35).

By Car   From **Piazza Armerina,** follow the scenic, twisty SS124 through the mountains. From **Agrigento,** take the SS115 all the way. From **Palermo,** take the A20 autostrada east toward Cefalù, exiting onto the A19 through Enna and the interior to where it hits the SS114 just south of Catania and follow that into Siracusa. From **Messina**, you can follow the coastal SS114 all the way through **Taormina** and **Catania** to Siracusa.

GETTING AROUND   City **buses** cost 600L (35¢) and make circular routes. Most start/end at Piazza della Posta just over the bridge on Ortigia. Although lines 21 to 23 stop at the train station and continue to Ortigia, these run infrequently; you're better off turning left out of the station and walking a few blocks to Piazza Marconi (aka Foro Siracusiano), where just about every line passes. But from here, you're just a 5-minute hike down Corso Umberto from Ortigia. For a **taxi,** dial ☎ **0931/69-722,** 0931/69-735, or 0931/64-323.

VISITOR INFORMATION   The most helpful tourist office is on Ortigia at V. Maestranza 33 (☎ **0931/464-255;** fax 0931/60-204), open Tuesday to Friday 8:30am to 2pm and 4:30 to 7:30pm, Monday and Saturday 8:30am to 2pm (Easter to September open Monday afternoon as well). There's also an office on the mainland at V. S. Sebastiano 45 (☎ **0931/67-710** for the desk, 0931/482-100 for the main office; fax 0931/67-803) across from the San Giovanni catacombs, open June to September Monday to Saturday 8am to 7pm, Sunday 9am to 1pm; October to May Monday to Saturday 8am to 2pm and 3 to 6pm. Finally, there's an info kiosk at the entrance to the archaeological zone at **Largo Anfiteatro** (☎ **0931/60-510**), open daily 8:30am to 7pm (they may close during *riposo* in winter).

THE ARCHAEOLOGICAL ZONE ON THE MAINLAND

✪ **Archaeological Park of Neapolis.** Lgo. Anfiteatro, off Cor. Gelone/Vle. Teracrati. ☎ **0931/66-206.** Admission 4,000L ($2.35). Daily 9am to 2 hours before sunset. Bus: there 1, 4, 8, 11, 12, 15, 21, 22, 23, 25; back 2, 3, 8, 11, 12, 14, 26.

This vast archaeological park contains Siracusa's greatest concentration of ruins. It's divided into three main sections: the *latomie* (stone quarries), the Greek theater, and the Roman amphitheater, all of which you can see in about two hours. The first two are together beyond the main gate. Hold on to your ticket, for upon exiting the Greek theater/*latomie* area you backtrack up the souvenir stand–lined road to enter the amphitheater area.

After the ticket desk, veer right onto the path down to the **Latomia del Paradiso,** an ancient quarry now planted with a jungle of orange and lemon trees. In the back wall is a narrow cavern 76 feet high, 214 feet deep, and only about 25 feet wide. It was dubbed by Caravaggio the "Ear of Dionysius"—either due to its pointy shape, like the ear on a satyr, or its remarkable acoustics, allowing you to stand at one end and hear a whisper spoken at the other (Dionysius' name enters the picture from a local legend that the tyrant used this cave as a prison and its acoustics to spy on his captives). Next door to the "ear" is the pretty *Grotta dei Cordari* ("ropemaker's cave"), a wide quarry fissure romantically filled with water and maidenhead ferns; its preservation is in a precarious state, so it is roped off.

Return to the ticket office and take the left path, which leads to the stark white curve of seats comprising the ✪ **Greek theater,** one of the largest in the world at 455 feet in diameter. Built in the 5th century B.C. and later expanded, its 42 rows of seats were hewn directly out of the living rock, and probably saw the first productions of some of Aeschylus' plays. The Romans, who felt serious drama was to be taken only in moderation, adapted the thing so they could occasionally flood the stage and stage tiny mock sea battles.

The theater still stages summertime productions (mostly classical plays)—wonderful if you can attend one, but the modern stage and fill-in-the-gap aluminum grandstand seating spoils the antique mood for daytime sightseers. At the top of the *cavea* are niches that once contained little votive altars, plus a little niched pond that collects the cold water flowing from an ancient aqueduct—great for dipping your tired feet.

On the path down into the Roman amphitheater area you'll see on your left the few columns still standing and the long stone base of the 3rd-century B.C. **Altar of Hieron II,** at 653 by 75 feet, the longest altar ever built. The A.D. 1st-century **Roman**

amphitheater was where Siracusans held bloody gladiator fights and the like when they tired of the plays at the Greek theater. It, too, is used today for productions (mainly musical) in the summer, when bright red poppies bloom against the green wash of the overgrown seating sections.

✪ **Museo Archologico Paolo Orsi.** Vle. Teocrito 66. ☎ **0931/464-022.** Admission 8,000L ($4.70). June–Aug Mon 3:30–7:30pm, Tues–Wed 9am–7:30pm, Thurs–Sat 9am–11pm, 1st and 3rd Sun of month 9am–1pm; Sept–May Tues–Sat 9am–2pm, 1st and 3rd Sun of month 9am–1pm. Bus: there 1, 4, 8, 11, 12, 15, 21, 22, 23, 25; back 2, 3, 8, 11, 12, 14, 26.

This fantastic museum is one of Italy's top archaeological collections, and by far the best in Sicily. It'd be a worthwhile stop simply for the aesthetic beauty of many pieces, and the well-documented exhibits make it invaluable for understanding the Greek and other cultures of ancient Sicily.

Section A takes care of the island's southeastern corner during prehistoric times, kicking off with a pair of articulated dwarf elephant skeletons found in nearby caves; looking at the skulls it's easy to see why many academics believe that their odd shape and large central nasal passage led the local ancients—who surely stumbled across them—to invent the myth of one-eyed, cave-dwelling giants called Cyclopes. But the best part of the prehistoric section is the remains left by humans, a collection of tools, ceramics, and sculptures that open a window onto the richness of Stone and Bronze Age cultures.

Section B covers Siracusa and its province in all its ancient Greek glory. The highlights include a terra-cotta statue of a goddess nursing twins (550 B.C.); the headless *Venus Landolina,* an Imperial Roman copy of a 2nd-century B.C. statue that's a lesson in both anatomy and aesthetics; the museum's mischievous mascot of a 6th-century B.C. terra-cotta Gorgon, grinning and sticking his tongue out; and cases full of 5th- and 4th-century B.C. votive statuettes dedicated to Demeter/Ceres and Kore/Persephone, to whom there was apparently a temple across the street (workers breaking ground for the huge Sanctuary of the Madonna discovered it a few decades back).

Section C contains the best remains from Magna Graecia settlements across eastern Sicily, including decorated vases from Gela spanning the 6th and 5th centuries B.C.; an enthroned goddess from 6th-century B.C. Grammichele; and a trio of rare 7th-century B.C. wooden statues found near Agrigento. Lookout for the spectacularly carved 4th-century sarcophagus from the San Giovanni catacombs.

Catacombs of San Giovanni. V. San Giovanni alle Catacombe (between the archaeological park and museum). ☎ **0931/67-955.** 4,000L ($2.35) adults, 2,000L ($1.20) under 10. Wed–Mon 9am–12:30pm, 2:30–6pm. Bus: there 1, 4, 8, 11, 12, 15, 21, 22, 23, 25; back 2, 3, 8, 11, 12, 14, 26.

What is now the ruined church of San Giovanni was a potters' cave in Greek times, but after St. Paul preached on the spot it became serious holy ground. A 6th-century basilica here was knocked down by the Saracens then rebuilt by the Normans in the 12th century. After the 1693 earthquake shook it to the ground, a baroque structure was grafted onto the ruins, but the 1908 quake destroyed that. Siracusans gave up and left the roofless Norman walls and half an apse as they were, romantically sprouting flowers and weeds. It's still consecrated, and marriages and summer Sunday services take place around a sarcofagal altar.

The bored guide will whisk you through the original 6th-century Greek-cross crypt, with remnants of frescoes and capitals from the Byzantine and Norman eras, including the purported column where Siracusa's first bishop, San Marziano, was flogged to death. But the real treat are the catacombs, the only set of Siracusa's many subterranean burial grounds currently open to the public. There are some 20,000 tombs down here, niched into tunnels that honeycomb the earth connecting former Greek cisterns (recycled by early Christians into chapels). Along with cornrows of graves that once housed extended families, you'll see a few faded frescoes and early Christian symbols etched into stone slabs.

EXPLORING ORTIGIA

Just across the Ponte Umbertino bridge to Ortigia is the long, shaded Piazza Panciale, the end of which opens up into Piazza XXV Luglio, a traffic circle bounded on the east by a sunken archaeological zone the sprouts a few Doric columns stumps, a long low set of stairs, half a wall, lots of weeds, and a few palm trees. This is what remains of the early 6th-century B.C. **Temple of Apollo,** the first Doric temple in Sicily.

The star of the oblong, cafe-lined Piazza del Duomo at Ortigia's center is the ✪ **Duomo** (open 8am to noon and 4 to 7pm), adapted by the Byzantines and then the Normans from a 5th-century B.C. Temple to Athena. The interior is marvelously simple, a honey-colored world of sacred quiet that feels about as close as stepping back in time and into an ancient temple as you're ever going to find. To convert the Greek temple to a church wasn't hard: They just punched archways through the *cella* (the sacred central chamber of the temple) to make it into a nave, and filled in between 19 giant Doric columns from the temple's peristyle—all a bit askew from a 1542 earthquake—to make the outer walls of the aisle. Aside from Andrea Palma's 1728–54 baroque facade, the cathedral remains essentially medieval and plain (a baroquing of the interior was yanked off in the 1920s). Look in the first chapel on the right for a baptismal font recycled from an ancient marble font resting on 13th-century bronze lions. Along the left aisle there are four statues by the Gagini (three in between the second to fifth columns and a *Madonna delle Neve* up near the end of the aisle).

Just down Via P. Picherali from the south end of the piazza you'll find the harborside Lago Arethusa, whose centerpiece is the lovely little sunken pond containing the **Fonte Aretusa,** Siracusa's most famous mythological site. Half a dozen Greek poets wrote the tale of the nymph Arethusa, who was bathing in the Alpheus River in Greece one day when the god of that river took a liking to her. She begged for deliverance from his advances, and Artemis in pity turned the nymph into a spring, allowing her to escape underground. She traveled under the sea to emerge here, in Siracusa. Alpheus, though, was hot on her heels, and came gushing out in the same spot, mingling his waters with hers for eternity. They used to say you could toss a goblet into a spring at Arcadia in Greece and it would pop up here. Today, the font still flows softly from its grotto into the pond, planted with puffy-headed, willowy papyrus and swimming with fish and ducks. Shops selling sheets of papyrus "paper" pigeonhole the surrounding streets, especially Via Capodieci.

The **Palazzo Bellomo,** just up Via Capodieci at Via Roma, was built between the 13th and 15th centuries. It features a Catalan-Gothic staircase and courtyard, and is home to the **Museo Regionale di Arte Medievale e Moderna** (☎ 0931/69-617). Its two stellar works are Antonello da Messina's highly ruinous but still exquisitely painted *Annunciation* (1474), and Caravaggio's moody *Deposition of S. Lucia* (1608). Other standouts include medieval and Renaissance sculptures on the ground floor—among which a *Madonna* by Domenico Gagini—and a comical early 17th-century painting of angels ferrying the Madonna's house across the sea to Loreto with baby Jesus perched on the roof. The collections are rounded out by 18th- and 19th-century carriages, livery, furnishings, and ceramics, including a 15th-century Spanish/Moorish faience plate patterned in metallic reddish gold. Admission is 8,000L ($4.70). It's open daily 9am to 2pm (last entry 1pm), with July and August afternoon hours Tuesday to Saturday of 3:30 to 7:30pm, and evening hours Thursday to Saturday of 8:30 to 11pm.

WHERE TO STAY

Aretusa. V. Francesco Crispi 75 (near the train station), 96100 Siracusa. ☎ and fax **0931/24-211.** 52 units, 12 with bathroom. 40,000L ($23.55) single without bathroom, 47,000L ($27.65) single with bathroom; 60,000L ($35.30) double without bathroom, 70,000L ($41.20) double with bathroom. Breakfast 5,000L ($2.95). No credit cards.

Tiny, bare, and functional, this is a budget last resort, but not bad for what you get. What the rooms lack in style and lighting they make up for in general cleanliness and a sound night's sleep in orthopedic cot frames. The neighborhood's a drag—not dangerous, just dull and a long hike from anything interesting—but when other hotels are full, you'll probably find a room here, and it's nicer than most of the other squalid dumps between the station and Ortigia.

Bellavista. V. Diodoro Siculo 4 (off Vle. Tunisi, north of the Latomie near the coast), 96100 Siracusa. ☎ **0931/411-355.** Fax 0931/37-927. www.infoservizi.it/hotels/siracusa.htm. 47 units, all with bathroom. TV TEL. 94,000L ($55.30) single, 148,000L ($87.05) double. 10% discount if book via Internet. Rates include breakfast (if you ask for no breakfast, knock 9,000L/$5.30 per person off rate). AE, DC, MC, V. Bus: 1, 2, 3, 4 to Vle. Tunisi and turn right; or 7 to Lgo. Latomie and walk up Vle. Tunisi.

It's removed from the action, but only about a 10-minute walk from the archaeology museum and park. The functional, comfortable rooms have firm beds, and amenities you won't find nearer the center at these prices (there' no air-conditioning, but fans help keep the rooms cool). Aside from a distant sea view from the balconies of some upper-floor accommodations, there's little exceptional about the Bellavista, but nothing to complain about either; a solid choice for those who don't mind a bit of walking.

✪ **Gran Bretagna.** V. Savoia 21 (on Ortigia, near Pz. XXV Luglio), 96100 Siracusa. ☎ **0931/68-765.** Fax 0931/462-169. E-mail: mcapill@tin.it. 12 units, 4 with bathroom. 52,000L ($30.60) single without bathroom, 62,000L ($36.50) single with bathroom; 86,000L ($50.60) double without bathroom, 98,000L ($57.65) double with bathroom. Rates include breakfast. AE, DC, MC, V. Closed mid-Nov to early Dec.

This is the only reasonably priced hotel on Ortigia itself, cheap and run by a family that keeps it immaculate. First-floor rooms are older and bathless, but are larger than ones above, with big carved wooden furnishings and high vaulted ceilings. A few even have frescoes—no. 2 and 3 just around the light fixture, but in huge, family perfect no. 7 the whole ceiling is painted. Upstairs rooms were more recently redone and most have bathrooms, but they're cramped with less attractive modular furnishings. The best is no. 8, with a spiral staircase up to a little terrace from which you can sea the sea on both directions. Posters and prints from Euripides's plays and wonderfully firm beds on wooden bases or new, stiff cots round the place out.

WORTH A SPLURGE

Domus Mariae. V. V. Veneto 76 (on the east side of Oritiga, just below V. Mirabella), 96100 Siracusa. ☎ and fax **0931/24-858.** 12 units, all with bathroom. A/C TV TEL. 150,000L ($88.25) single; 200,000L ($117.65) double. Breakfast included. AE, DC, MC, V.

Finally, another hotel has opened on Ortigia itself, albeit a pricey one. In 1995, the Suore Orsoline turned part of their old convent into a quietly stylish, modern hotel, where half the room's balconies look over the sea. The building backs onto the quiet coastal road on the far side of Oritigia. The large rooms with built-in units have patterned rugs on the tile floors and marble-top sinks in the modern bathrooms. A few feature fold-out couches that make them great for families. Those sea-view rooms, kindly reception, and all these comforts make this upscale nunnery worth the splurge.

WHERE TO DINE

Il Cenacolo. V. d. Consiglio Regionale/Corte degli Avolio 9–10 (just north of Pz. Duomo).
☎ **0931/65-099.** Reservations recommended. Primi 8,000–18,000L ($4.70–$10.60); secondi 10,000–22,000L ($5.90–$12.95); pizze 5,000–20,000L ($2.95–$11.75). AE, MC, V. Daily noon–3pm, 7pm–1am. SICILIAN/PIZZA.

You don't really come for the food—which isn't half bad—or the prices, which are slightly overblown. You come to "The Last Supper" for the relaxed setting under dwarf palms in a pocket of a piazza hidden at the very heart of Ortigia. That and the theological exercise of matching the pizzas' biblical names with their toppings (the "Lazarus" comes with the mushrooms of decay, "Judas" with the sting of hot peppers). There's also the standard array of Sicilian dishes like spaghetti alla bolognese or *ai ricci di mare, zuppa di cozze e vongole verace, bistecca alla pizzaiola* (steak covered in pizza sauce and mozzarella), but we encourage you to "discover the pleasure of variety" by calling ahead and ordering something special like *paella valenciana* (a Spanish rice dish rich with seafood) or couscous (with meat or fish).

✪ **La Foglia.** V. Capodieci 29 (south of Pz. Duomo). ☎ **0931/66-233.** Reservations recommended. Dishes 12,000–20,000L ($7.05–$11.75). AE, MC, V. Wed–Mon noon–3pm, 7–10pm. MEDITERRANEAN/VEGETARIAN.

"The Leaf" has a vegetarian slant toward delicious soups and veggie concoctions, but you can also have basic meat and fish dishes. The decor seems torn between South Seas and Sicilian peasant, and rather than hand you a menu, the artist/owner will amble over in his Panama hat to give you the "panorama" of what's available today. The soups may be *funghi* (mushroom), *lenticche* (lentils), or broccoli. Pastas like *tagliolini* (eggless tagliatelle) or ravioli come in sauces of *burro e salvia* (butter and sage), ripe tomatoes, *alle verdure* (mixed chopped veggies), or fish (only on the tagliolini). For secondo you can get a huge mixed salad or *verdure alla griglia* (eggplant, zucchini, mushrooms, and various other local vegetables grilled), *tonno alla mattalotta* (tuna steak with tomatoes, capers, and olives), grilled veal or pork, or *sarde al beccafico alla catanese* (large sardines split, cleaned, and sandwiched around a frittata of egg and cheese).

Spaghetteria Do Scogghiu. V. D. Scinà 11 (just off NW corner of Pz. Archimede, at Cor. Matteotti). No phone. Primi 6,000–8,000L ($3.55–$4.70); secondi 8,000–13,000L ($4.70–$7.65). No credit cards. Tues–Sun noon–3pm, 7pm–midnight. Closed Dec. SPAGHETTI/SICILIAN.

It's a simple, crowded and noisy room with locals and budgeteers crammed into communal tables for 20 excellent varieties of spaghetti with few frills. Most sauces are mix-and-match combinations of *pancetta aff.* (like smoked bacon), *pepe rosso* (red peppercorns), *melanzane* (eggplant), *pomodoro* (tomato), and olive. Two personal faves are alla carbonara and *spaghetti piccanti* (with smoked pancetta, tomatoes, and red peppercorns). Steak, fresh fish, and frozen calamari or shrimp roasted or fried constitute the limited set of secondi, but don't hold a candle to the filling plates of spaghetti.

WORTH A SPLURGE

Jonico-'A Rutta 'E Ciàuli. Riviera Dionisio II Grande 194 (just down from Lgo. Latomie). ☎ **0931/65-540.** Reservations highly recommended. Primi 8,000–12,000L ($4.70–$7.05); secondi 15,000–28,000L ($8.80–$16.50); pizze 5,000–10,000L ($2.95–$5.90). AE, DC, MC, V. Wed–Mon noon–3pm, 5pm–2am. Bus: 3, 7. SIRACUSAN.

This splurge is one of Sicily's best restaurants, certainly Siracusa's finest, and so staunchly traditional that the menu's written entirely in dialect. The setting is especially romantic: on a curving terrace lined with blown-glass lamps 50 feet above the soft surf lapping against the rocks with a sweeping vista of the Ionian sea and Ortigia. Try the traditional Siracusan *spaghetti c'a muddica e anciovi* (with grated bread

---

The Forge of Vulcan

Mt. Etna is the biggest, baddest volcano in Europe and one of the largest in the world, 10,990 feet of massive molten energy that dominates eastern Sicily like an earthborn storm cloud.

Etna's summit constantly smokes, and every few years it goes into a volcanic fit. In 1989, at the summit, a new crater grew over 330 feet in just a month. From 1991 to 1993, it erupted almost continuously, and in 1998, eight months of violent activity culminated in an eruption on July 12 that spewed ash almost a mile into the air, closing Catania's airport and covering the mountain with a fresh layer of pumice and lava. Even as this book goes to press, Etna's begun spewing lava again—and making the locals rather nervous. Its lava flows have threatened, and occasionally actually swallowed, several of the small towns that brave the danger to take agricultural advantage of the rich volcanic soil.

From the A18, a road leads up through the town of Nicolosi and then winds up the mountain to the *Rifugio Sapienza* souvenir-driven snack bar/way station at 6,300 feet (☎ **095/911-158** for cable car and conditions information). You can catch an early morning AST bus (☎ **095/746-096**) from Catania, currently leaving Catania at 8:15am (8am Sunday); the return bus leaves the *Rifugio* at 4:15pm (2.5 hr.; 7,000L/$4 round-trip). At the *Rifigio* you can buy a ticket to cover one, two, or all three stages to the top. The *funvia* cable car to 8250 feet is 17,000L ($10) one way, 32,000L ($18.80) round-trip. Add in the Jeep from that point to the *Bar di Ristoro,* an espresso stop at 9,636 feet, for 55,800L ($32.80) round-trip. Or get both plus the guide who'll walk you from *Bar di Ristoro* to as close to the top as it is currently safe to get for 62,000L ($36.50). On a clear day, the vistas from up here encompass all of Sicily.

On the Jeep ride back to the cable car the driver pulls over so you can gaze down into the spectacular **Valle delle Bove,** an enormous yawning cleft measuring 11 miles around and almost 4,000 feet deep scooped out of the southeast slope. Much of the lava flows this century have found their way safely into this channel, away from inhabited soil. Back down at the *Rifugio,* you can explore some nearby extinct craters more fully. The *Rifugio* also offers spartan rooms (☎ and fax **095/911-062**) for 32,000L ($18.80) per person, 60,000L ($35.30) with half-board.

---

and anchovies), or the specialty *spaghetti co tunnu friscu* (with fresh tuna, tomatoes, and capers). The kitchen's best secondi are *bistecca a siciliana* (steak smothered with tuna, onion, and cheese) and *orata 'c'aranciu* (gilt-head bream cooked with orange juice, orange zest, and white wine). Meat eaters may prefer the *custati ri agneddu panate* (breaded mutton chops). There's a less formal pizzeria up on the open-air roof.

8 Taormina

134 km (80 mi.) N of Siracusa, 48 km (29 mi.) S of Messina

Sicily's most famous resort town remains an enchanting corner of the island despite the tourist hordes. It's a jasmine-scented ridgetop escape that marries the drama of a Greek colony established here in 403 B.C., a medieval air of Sicilian *palazzi* and tiny churches, and the modestly hedonistic atmosphere of a latter-day resort village that draws famed names and package tours alike. It sticks the lot together with liberal amounts of bougainvillea, seascape vistas, and a laid-back take on life.

In the 20th century its role as a haven for homosexuals on holiday has meshed well enough with the local traditionalist peasantry, the middle-class crowds of latter-day mass tourists, and the jet set of famed writers and Hollywood glitterati, all of whom continue to show up in droves. Taormina's been a fave over the years of everyone from Greta Garbo, who returned every spring for 30 years, to D. H. Lawrence, who found here the inspiration for his feverishly sensual *Lady Chatterly's Lover,* a story based, according to local rumor, on his own wife's dalliances with a Sicilian mule driver.

FESTIVALS & MARKETS   In May there's a festival to show off **traditional Sicilian carts and costumes.** There are **concerts and performances in the Greek theater** and churches around town from June to September. And in July and August, Taormina hosts an **international film festival.** There's a daily morning **market** in Via Cappuccini.

ESSENTIALS

GETTING HERE   By Train   There are 12 to 13 trains daily from **Siracusa** (2 to 2.5 hr.; 12,100L/$7.10), and hourly ones from **Catania** (45 to 50 min.; 4,700L/ $2.75) and from **Messina** (35 to 65 min.; 4,700L/$2.75). There are also three daily trains from **Rome** (9 hr.; 56,500L/$33.25) that pass through **Naples** (6.5 hr.; 42,000L/$24.70). The train **station, Taormina-Giardini** (☎ **0942/51-026** or 0942/51-511), is down on the SS114 coastal road. There's a left luggage open 6am to 10pm that costs 5,000L per bag per day. A local bus makes the 15-minute trip up to Taormina itself three times an hour for 2,000L ($1.20).

By Bus   There are two buses (none Sunday) from **Siracusa** (2 hr. 45 min.; 12,500L/ $7.35); and at least hourly runs from **Catania** (60 to 90 min.; 6,000L/$3.55), and from **Messina** (60 to 110 min.; 5,000L/$2.95). There's a bus ticket booth at the bus station just outside the town gate on Via Pirandello (☎ **0942/625-301**)

By Car   Taormina is above the coastal A18 autostrada (and its parallel, the SS114 highway) from Messina to Catania and Siracusa.

VISITOR INFORMATION   The tourist office is in the Palazzo Corvaja on Largo S. Caterina (☎ **0942/23-243;** fax 0942/24-941; www.taormina-ol.it).

PASSEGGIATA DESTINATIONS

The single most popular activity in Taormina is simply strolling up main drag **Corso Umberto,** window-shopping and people-watching. The east end of Corso Umberto is anchored by Largo S. Caterina, home to **Palazzo Corvaja,** a fine 14th-century example of local masonry style, which highlights gray limestone walls with black and white lava trim. The staircase in the pretty little courtyard leads up to the **Museo Siciliano d'Arte e Tradizioni Popolari,** a small collection of Sicilian folk art and crafts. Admission is 5,000L ($2.95) adults, 2,500L ($1.50) under 12 or over 55 (women) or 60 (men). It's open Tuesday to Sunday 9am to 1pm and 4 to 8pm.

Via Teatro Greco leads to Taormina's only required sight, the 3rd-century B.C. ✪ **Greek theater** (☎ **0942/23-220**), a drama in and of itself. It was rebuilt by the Romans in the A.D. 2nd century, and when you stand at the top of the *cavea* (the curved seating), Taormina's prime postcard vista opens out before you, sweeping down to the coastline and encompassing the mountains of Calabria across the straight and mighty Mt. Etna in the near distance. This panorama is partly blocked by the half-ruined wall and columns of a *scena* erected by the rather unromantic Romans who used the place for gladiator combats. Admission is 4,000L ($2.35); it's open 9am until an hour before sunset.

Walk back to Largo S. Caterina and around the right side of its eponymous church to see a section of curving seats belonging to the **Odeon,** a modest Roman-era theater currently growing weeds. Continuing up Corso Umberto, turn left down Via Numachie to see the **Naumachie,** a 400-foot brick wall of 16-foot-high niches that formed a wall between an Imperial Roman gymnasium and an ancient cistern. A bit farther up the Corso is the town center, **Piazza IX Aprile,** a communal living room built as a terrace with a view over the Ionian sea from the railing bounding one side. Lined with pricey cafes and brimming with visitors and caricature artists, it's the best place to sit back with a cappuccino and enjoy the relaxed resorty ambience of Taormina.

Pass under the 12th-century **clock tower** and you'll be in the medieval section of town, where Corso Umberto eventually spills into **Piazza del Duomo.** The battle-mented Duomo sports six huge antique pink marble columns inside and free concerts many summer evenings. The square's centerpiece is a fantastical 1635 fountain atop which perches a copy of the odd two-legged female centaur, a Greek mythological creature whose meaning or function no one quite seems to understand—so Taormina made it the town mascot.

HITTING THE BEACH

On Via Pirandello, between the bus depot and the gate into town, lies a *funivia* (cable car; ☎ **0942/23-906**) that runs every 15 minutes and costs 3,000L ($1.75). It carries you down to **Mazzarò Beach,** where an umbrella and chair run 10,000L ($5.90) per day and paddle boats rent for 15,000L ($8.80) an hour. To the right, past the Capo Sant'Andrea headland, is the region's prettiest cove, where twin crescents of beach sweep from a sand spit out to the minuscule **Isola Bella** islet. You can walk here in a minute from the bottom of the *funivia,* but it's more fun to paddle a boat from Mazzarò around Capo Sant'Andrea, which hides a few grottoes with excellent light effects on the seaward side.

North of Mazzarò are the long, wide beaches of **Spisone** and **Letojanni,** more developed but less crowded than **Giardini,** the large built-up resort beach south of Isola Bella. There's also a local bus that leaves Taormina for Mazzarò, Spisone, and Letojanni, and another that heads down the coast to Giardini.

WHERE TO STAY

It's hard to believe a town so obscenely crammed with hotels can fill up, but in summer it does. If the tourist office can't find you anything up here, they can help get a room in a beach resort below town (Mazzarò is closest and small enough to be charming; sprawling, modern Giardini will always have room).

✪ Villa Belvedere. V. Bagnoli Croci 79, 98039 Taormina (ME). ☎ **0942/23-791.** Fax 0942/625-830. www.eniware.it/villabelvedere. E-mail: hotbelve@tao.it. 50 units, all with bathroom. TV TEL. 70,000–134,000L ($41.20–$78.80) single, 108,000–205,000L ($63.50–$120.60) double. Breakfast 21,000L ($12.35). MC, V. Parking 8,000L ($4.70). Closed Nov 15–Mar 13 (sometimes open Dec 18–Jan 10).

Christian Pécaut's hotel has remained a favorite for three generations due to its friendly reception, professional maintenance, and old-fashioned style. The terra-cotta floors support firm beds and a variety of furnishings, all functional but with a touch of class. Most rooms have slivers of balconies to enjoy views over the neighboring public gardens to the sea, and top floor rooms have small terraces from which you can glimpse Mt. Etna (these are also air-conditioned, as are rooms on the back, which have double-paned windows to block noise from the street above). The flowering property is terraced down the hillside, with the pool sprouting a palm tree from its center.

✪ Villa Gaia. V. Fazzello 34/Pz. Carmine 6 (turn up Salita Badia Vecchia staircase from Pz. d. Duomo), 98039 Taormina (ME). ☎ and fax **0942/23-185.** 8 units, all with bathroom.

45,000–60,000L ($26.50–$35.30) single, 80,000–120,000L ($47.05–$70.60) double. Rates include breakfast in Aug; otherwise 5,000L ($2.95). No credit cards.

Staying at this cozy little hotel in the heart of town is like moving in with a local family for the night. The beds are a little soft, but not bad, and almost all rooms have a terrace or balcony: the view from no. 5 gets in a bit of the sea and Mt. Etna, while the long terrace shared by no. 1 through 4 will soon be divided so each room has a private one. You take breakfast in a teensy garden shaded by mandarin orange and grapefruit trees. By 1999, the management should accept Visa and MasterCard, and will have put in phones (and air-conditioning in some rooms). They've applied for two-star status, so book early—these prices are hard to beat; rates reflect season.

✪ **Villa Nettuno.** V. Pirandello 33, 98039 Taormina (ME). ☎ **0942/23-797.** Fax 0942/626-035. 13 units, all with bathroom. TEL. 60,000–73,000L ($35.30–$42.95) single,, 90,000–126,000L ($52.95–$74.10) double. Rates include breakfast. MC, V (only July–Aug). Parking 7,500L ($4.40). Closed some weekdays in Jan.

It's a bit creaky and worn with a patina of loving care, but the Nettuno's got a hefty dollop of Taormina's 19th-century class. The location is handy—between the bus stop and town gate, across from the cable car to the beach. In 1953, Maria and Vicenzo Sciglio, now assisted by son, Antonio, turned the family house into a pensione. I only wish the accommodations, where basic furnishings reign, had as much atmosphere as the antique-filled salon and the wandering paths and stairs of the colorful and surprisingly extensive statue-studded gardens. The beds aren't firm, but everything's as tidy and clean as can be, and the view up the coast is stupendous. Climb to the top of the lush gardens for an outstanding vista from Etna across the sea to Calabria.

Villa Schuler. Piazzetta Bastione/V. Roma, 98039 Taormina (ME). ☎ **0942/23-481.** Fax 0942/23-522. www.infoservizi.it/hotels/taormina.htm. E-mail: schuler@cys.it. 26 units, all with bathroom. TV TEL. 98,000L ($57.65) single, 145,000L ($85.30) double. 10% discount if booked via Web site. AE, DC, MC, V. Parking 5,000–15,000L ($2.95–$8.80). Closed mid-Nov–mid-Mar. Turn left off Cor. Umberto on Scesa Morgana just before Pz. IV Aprile.

Nestled within its own fragrant terraced gardens, the Villa Schuler looks over the Ionian Sea from a premier site below Piazza IV Aprile. Gerardo Schuler's grandfather built it to be a private home, but the family's run it as a hotel since 1905. Sea-view rooms look across the flowery and palm-shaded gravel terrace where most guests take their breakfast. (Via Roma runs directly below this terrace, meaning garden-view rooms are slightly quieter, though smaller and less attractive.) Accommodations are fitted with modular furniture mixed with characterful antiques. Most rooms have balconies; no. 29 through 32 on the top floor share a terrace with a vista from the Greek Theater to the coast. There's access to nearby tennis courts for 10,000L ($5.90), and a free chair and umbrella available at the beach (May to November).

WHERE TO DINE

Al Giardino. V. Bagnoli Croci 84. ☎ **0942/23-453.** Reservations recommended. Primi 8,000–10,000L ($4.70–$5.90); secondi 8,000–17,000L ($4.70–$10). MC, V. June–Sept daily noon–2:30pm, 7:30–11pm; Oct–May Fri–Wed noon–2:30pm, 7:30–11pm. Closed Nov. SICILIAN/ITALIAN.

Friendly Sebatiano Puglia really cares about his simple, tasty dishes. There are only a dozen small tables scattered on the patio out front, shaded by an awning dripping with flowers, so call ahead if you want one. The only drawback is the occasional car that whizzes by (but other than that, the sole sound is birdsong from the public gardens across the street). His spaghetti alla carbonara is great, as is the *paglia e feino alla bolognese* (strands of green and yellow pasta tossed with a ragù). For secondo I recommend the *omlette al prosciutto* and *involtini alla rusticana* (veal rolls stuffed with cheese and skewered with lemon slices and Sicilian sausages before being grilled).

Il Ciclope. Piazzetta S. Leone 1 (on Cor. Umberto). ☎ **0942/23-263.** Reservations recommended. Primi 7,000–14,000L ($4.10–$8.25); secondi 12,000–20,000L ($7.05–$11.75). AE, DC, MC, V. Daily noon–3pm, 7–10:30pm. Closed Tues in winter. SICILIAN/ITALIAN.

Salvatore Sturiale's restaurant is right on the main drag, but in the medieval part of town beyond the gate, so there's less of a log-jam of tourist traffic passing the shaded terrace fronting the street. The people-watching, however, is still great. Although it looks awful touristy, Il Ciclope is actually quite good, serving delectable dishes such as *rigatoni alla ciclope* (just spicy enough with ham, tomatoes, hot and black peppers, and oil), *fettucine con pescespada* (with swordfish, olives, and pistachios), *cuscinotto alla polifemo* (a veal rolled with mozzarella, prosciutto, and mushrooms, breaded, and coated with an herbed cream sauce), and *bocconcini di vitellina alla turiddu* (almost a veal stew, with olives, tomatoes, pancetta, onions, pepperoncino, and basil).

La Botte. Pz. Santa Domenica 3 (*not* Pz. San Domenico; this square's near the Greek Theater). ☎ **0942/24-198.** Reservations recommended. Primi 8,000–17,000L ($4.70–$10); secondi 12,000–25,000L ($7.05–$14.70); pizze 10,000–16,000L ($5.90–$9.40). AE, DC, MC, V. Daily noon–3:30pm, 7pm–1am. Closed Mon Jan–May. From the east end of Pz. S. Caterina, take the little street parallel to and sunk below the right of the road to the Greek theater. SICILIAN/PIZZA.

La Botte is a bit more expensive than it should be, but the setting's terrific—either in stuccoed rooms lined with photos of noted patrons or in nice weather under umbrellas on a quiet, breezy little piazza off Taormina's beaten passeggiata path. The antipasto buffet is a prodigious spread, and one of La Botte's main draws—that and quite good pizza to be washed down with Messina beer. *Pasta fresca al cuore di carciofo* (homemade pasta with artichoke hearts), *maccheroni alla Norma*, and *zuppa di cozze* are all good ways to round out the menu.

✪ U' Bossu. V. Bagnoli Croci 50. ☎ **0942/23-311.** Reservations recommended. Primi 7,000–10,000L ($4.10–$5.90); secondi 13,000–18,000L ($7.65–$10.60). DC, MC, V. Tues–Sun noon–3pm, 7–11:30pm. Closed Nov 15–Dec 20, Jan 10–Mar 20. Open Mon evenings mid-June–Aug. SICILIAN.

It mystifies me that Enzo's hole-in-the-wall isn't better known. It has killer prices (especially for Taormina), a friendly and helpful staff, an almost excruciatingly quaint trattoria decor—plants, garlic ropes, and bunches of peppers hanging from wood beams in a single candle-lit room with opera playing—and rather excellent food. Still, the tourists manage to find it, so book ahead for one of the nine tables arranged around a great antipasto buffet. The primi are flavorful works of art, from the *spaghetti alla mafiosa* (with tuna and tomatoes) to the *casareccia alla turiddu* (homemade pasta with tomatoes, cream, capers, olives, baked ricotta, and eggplant). The best secondo is *involtini "U' Bossu"* (veal rolls), though the mixed fresh fish grill isn't bad either. By all means don't miss Enzo's terrific homemade pepperoncino liqueur.

Appendix: Glossary of Useful Terms

A Basic Vocabulary

English	Italian	Pronunciation
Thank you	**Grazie**	*graht*-tzee-yey
You're welcome	**Prego**	*prey*-go
Please	**Per favore**	pehr fah-*vohr*-eh
Good morning or Good day	**Buongiorno**	bwohn-*djor*-noh
Good evening	**Buona sera**	*Bwohn*-ah *say*-rah
Good night	**Buona notte**	*Bwohn*-ah *noht*-tay
How are you?	**Come sta?**	*koh*-may *stah*
Very well	**Molto bene**	*mohl*-toh *behn*-ney
Good-bye	**Arrivederci**	ahr-ree-vah-*dehr*-chee
Excuse me (to get attention)	**Scusi**	*skoo*-zee
Excuse me (to get past someone on the bus)	**Permesso**	pehr-*mehs*-soh
Where is. . . ?	**Dovè. . . ?**	doh-*vey*
the station	**la stazione**	lah stat-tzee-*oh*-neh
a hotel	**un albergo**	oon ahl-*behr*-goh
a restaurant	**un ristorante**	oon reest-ohr-*ahnt*-eh
the bathroom	**il bagno**	eel *bahn*-nyoh
To the right	**A destra**	ah *dehy*-stra
to the left	**A sinistra**	ah see-*nees*-tra
straight ahead	**Avanti (or sempre diritto)**	ahv-vahn-tee (*sehm*-pray dee-*reet*-toh)
How much is it?	**Quanto costa?**	*kwan*-toh *coh*-sta?
The check, please	**Il conto, per favore**	eel kon-toh *pehr* fah-*vohr*-eh
When?	**Quando?**	*kwan*-doh
Yesterday	**Ieri**	ee-*yehr*-ree
Today	**Oggi**	*oh*-jee
Tomorrow	**Domani**	doh-*mah*-nee
Breakfast	**Prima colazione**	*pree*-mah coh-laht-tzee-*ohn*-ay
Lunch	**Pranzo**	*prahn*-zoh

Dinner	Cena	*chay*-nah
What time is it?	Che ore sono?	kay *or*-ay *soh*-noh
Monday	Lunedì	loo-nay-*dee*
Tuesday	Martedì	mart-ay-*dee*
Wednesday	Mercoledì	mehr-cohl-ay-*dee*
Thursday	Giovedì	joh-vay-*dee*
Friday	Venerdì	ven-nehr-*dee*
Saturday	Sabato	*sah*-bah-toh
Sunday	Domenica	doh-*mehn*-nee-kah

NUMBERS

1	**uno** (*oo*-noh)	22	**venti due** (*vehn*-tee *doo*-ay)
2	**due** (*doo*-ay)	30	**trenta** (*trayn*-tah)
3	**tre** (tray)	40	**quaranta** (kwah-*rahn*-tah)
4	**quattro** (*kwah*-troh)	50	**cinquanta** (cheen-*kwan*-tah)
5	**cinque** (*cheen*-kway)	60	**sessanta** (sehs-*sahn*-tah)
6	**sei** (say)	70	**settanta** (seht-*tahn*-tah)
7	**sette** (*set*-tay)	80	**ottanta** (oht-*tahn*-tah)
8	**otto** (*oh*-toh)	90	**novanta** (noh-*vahnt*-tah)
9	**nove** (*noh*-vay)	100	**cento** (*chen*-toh)
10	**dieci** (dee-*ay*-chee)	1,000	**mille** (*mee*-lay)
11	**undici** (*oon*-dee-chee)	5,000	**cinque milla** (*cheen*-kway *mee*-lah)
20	**venti** (*vehn*-tee)	10,000	**dieci milla** (dee-*ay*-chee *mee*-lah)
21	**ventuno** (vehn-*toon*-oh)		

B Menu Terms

Abbacchio   Roast haunch or shoulder of lamb baked and served in a casserole and sometimes flavored with anchovies.

Agnolotti   A crescent-shaped pasta shell stuffed with a mix of chopped meat, spices, vegetables, and cheese; when prepared in rectangular versions, the same combination of ingredients is identified as **ravioli.**

Amaretti   Crunchy, sweet almond-flavored macaroons.

Anguilla alla veneziana   Eel cooked in a sauce made from tuna and lemon.

Antipasti   Succulent tidbits served at the beginning of a meal (before the pasta), whose ingredients might include slices of cured meats, seafood (especially shellfish), and cooked and seasoned vegetables.

Aragosta   Lobster.

Arrosto   Roasted meat.

Baccalà   Dried and salted codfish.

Bagna cauda   Hot and well-seasoned sauce, heavily flavored with anchovies, designed for dipping raw vegetables; literally translated as "hot bath."

Bistecca alla fiorentina   Florentine-style steaks, coated before grilling with olive oil, pepper, lemon juice, salt and parsley.

Bocconcini   Veal layered with ham and cheese, then fried.

Bollito misto   Assorted boiled meats served on a single platter.

Braciola   Pork chop.

Bresaola   Air-dried spiced beef.

Bruschetta   Toasted bread, heavily slathered with olive oil and garlic and often topped with tomatoes.

Bucatini   Coarsely textured hollow spaghetti.

Busecca alla Milanese   Tripe (beef stomach) flavored with herbs and vegetables.

Cacciucco ali livornese   Seafood stew.

Calzone   Pizza dough rolled with the chef's choice of sausage, tomatoes, cheese, and so on, then baked into a kind of savory turnover.

Cannelloni   Tubular dough stuffed with meat, cheese, or vegetables, then baked in a creamy white sauce.

Cappellacci alla ferrarese   Pasta stuffed with pumpkin.

Cappelletti   Small ravioli ("little hats") stuffed with meat or cheese.

Carciofi   Artichokes.

Carpaccio   Thin slices of raw cured beef, sometimes in a piquant sauce.

Cassatta alla siciliana   A richly caloric dessert combining layers of sponge cake, sweetened ricotta cheese, and candied fruit, bound together with chocolate butter-cream icing.

Cervello al burro nero   Brains in black-butter sauce.

Cima alla genovese   Baked fillet of veal rolled into a tube-shaped package containing eggs, mushrooms, and sausage.

Coppa   Cured morsels of pork fillet encased in sausage skins, served in slices.

Costoletta alla milanese   Veal cutlet dredged in bread crumbs, fried, and sometimes flavored with cheese.

Cozze   Mussels.

Fagioli   White beans.

Fave   Fava beans.

Fegato alla veneziana   Thinly sliced calves' liver fried with salt, pepper, and onions.

Foccacia   Ideally, concocted from potato-based dough left to rise slowly for several hours, then garnished with tomato sauce, garlic, basil, salt, and pepper and drizzled with olive oil; similar to a deep-dish pizza most popular in the deep south, especially Bari.

Fontina   Rich cow's-milk cheese.

Fritto misto   A deep-fried medley of whatever small fish, shellfish, and squid are available in the marketplace that day.

Fusilli   Spiral-shaped pasta.

Gelato (produzione propria)   Ice cream (homemade).

Gorgonzola   One of the most famous blue-veined cheeses of Europe—strong, creamy, and aromatic.

Gnocchi   Dumplings usually made from potatoes (*gnocchi alla patate*) or from semolina (*gnocchi alla romana*), often stuffed with combinations of cheese, spinach, vegetables, or whatever combinations strike the chef's fancy.

Granita   Flavored ice, usually with lemon or coffee.

Insalata di frutti di mare   Seafood salad (usually including shrimp and squid) garnished with pickles, lemon, olives, and spices.

Involtini   Thinly sliced beef, veal, or pork, rolled, stuffed, and fried.

Minestrone   A rich and savory vegetable soup usually sprinkled with grated Parmesan and studded with noodles.

Mortadella   Mild pork sausage, fashioned into large cylinders and served sliced; the original lunchmeat baloney (because its most famous center of production is Bologna).

Nervetti   A northern Italian antipasto made from chewy pieces of calves' foot or shin.

Osso buco   Beef or veal knuckle slowly braised until the cartilage is tender, then served with a highly flavored sauce.

Pappardelle alle lepre   Pasta with rabbit sauce.

Pancetta   Herb-flavored pork belly, rolled into a cylinder and sliced—the Italian bacon.

Panettone   Sweet yellow-colored bread baked in the form of a brioche.

Panna   Heavy cream.

Pansotti   Pasta stuffed with greens, herbs, and cheeses, usually served with a walnut sauce.

Peperoni   Green, yellow, or red sweet peppers (not to be confused with pepperoni).

Pesci al cartoccio   Fish baked in a parchment envelope with onions, parsley, and herbs.

Pesto   A flavorful green sauce made from basil leaves, cheese, garlic, marjoram, and (if available) pine kernels.

Piccata al marsala   Thin escalope of veal braised in a pungent sauce flavored with marsala wine.

Piselli al prosciutto   Peas with strips of ham.

Pizza   Specific varieties include *capricciosa* (its ingredients can vary widely depending on the chef's culinary vision and the ingredients at hand), *margherita* (with tomato sauce, cheese, fresh basil, and memories of the first queen of Italy, Marguerite di Savoia, in whose honor it was first made by a Neapolitan chef), *napoletana* (with ham, capers, tomatoes, oregano, cheese, and the distinctive taste of anchovies), *quatro stagione* (translated as "four seasons" because of the array of fresh vegetables in it; it also contains ham and bacon), and *siciliana* (with black olives, capers, and cheese).

Pizzaiola   A process whereby something (usually a beefsteak) is covered in a tomato-and-oregano sauce.

Polenta   Thick porridge or mush made from cornmeal flour.

Polenta de uccelli   Assorted small birds roasted on a spit and served with polenta.

Polenta e coniglio   Rabbit stew served with polenta.

Polla alla cacciatore   Chicken with tomatoes and mushrooms cooked in wine.

Pollo all diavola   Highly spiced grilled chicken.

Ragu   Meat sauce.

Ricotta   A soft bland cheese made from cow's or sheep's milk.

Risotto   Italian rice.

Risotto alla milanese   Rice with saffron and wine.

Salsa verde   "Green sauce," made from capers, anchovies, lemon juice and/or vinegar, and parsley.

Saltimbocca   Veal scallop layered with prosciutto and sage; its name literally translates as "jump in your mouth," a reference to its tart and savory flavor.

Salvia   Sage.

Scaloppina alla Valdostana   Escalope of veal stuffed with cheese and ham.

Scaloppine   Thin slices of veal coated in flour and sautéed in butter.

Semifreddo   A frozen dessert; usually ice cream with sponge cake.

Seppia   Cuttlefish (a kind of squid); its black ink is used for flavoring in certain sauces for pasta and also in risotto dishes.

Sogliola   Sole.

Spaghetti   A long, round, thin pasta, variously served: *alla bolognese* (with ground meat, mushrooms, peppers, and so on), *alla carbonara* (with bacon, black pepper, and eggs), *al pomodoro* (with tomato sauce), *al sugo/ragù* (with meat sauce), and *alle vongole* (with clam sauce).

Spiedini   Pieces of meat grilled on a skewer over an open flame.

Strangolaprete   Small nuggets of pasta, usually served with sauce; the name is literally translated as "priest-choker."

Stufato   Beef braised in white wine with vegetables.

Tagliatelle   Flat egg noodles.

Tiramisu   Richly caloric dessert containing layers of triple-cream cheeses and rum-soaked sponge cake.

Tonno   Tuna.

Tortellini   Rings of dough stuffed with minced and seasoned meat and served either in soups or as a full-fledged pasta covered with sauce.

Trenette   Thin noodles served with pesto sauce and potatoes.

Trippe alla fiorentina   Beef tripe (stomach).

Vermicelli   Very thin spaghetti.

Vitello tonnato   Cold sliced veal covered with tuna-fish sauce.

Zabaglione/zabaione   Egg yolks whipped into the consistency of a custard, flavored with marsala, and served warm as a dessert.

Zampone   Pig's trotter stuffed with spicy seasoned port, boiled and sliced.

Zuccotto   A liqueur-soaked sponge cake, molded into a dome and layered with chocolate, nuts, and whipped cream.

Zuppa inglese   Sponge cake soaked in custard sauce and rum.

Index

Page numbers in italics refer to maps.

General Index

FROMMER'S® COMPLETE TRAVEL GUIDES

Alaska
Amsterdam
Arizona
Atlanta
Australia
Austria
Bahamas
Barcelona, Madrid & Seville
Beijing
Belgium, Holland & Luxembourg
Bermuda
Boston
Budapest & the Best of Hungary
California
Canada
Cancún, Cozumel &
  the Yucatán
Cape Cod, Nantucket & Martha's Vineyard
Caribbean
Caribbean Cruises & Ports of Call
Caribbean Ports of Call
Carolinas & Georgia
Chicago
China
Colorado
Costa Rica
Denmark
Denver, Boulder & Colorado Springs
England
Europe
Florida
France
Germany
Greece
Greek Islands
Hawaii
Hong Kong
Honolulu, Waikiki & Oahu
Ireland
Israel
Italy
Jamaica & Barbados
Japan
Las Vegas
London
Los Angeles
Maryland & Delaware
Maui
Mexico
Miami & the Keys

Montana & Wyoming
Montréal & Québec City
Munich & the Bavarian Alps
Nashville & Memphis
Nepal
New England
New Mexico
New Orleans
New York City
Nova Scotia, New Brunswick &
  Prince Edward Island
Oregon
Paris
Philadelphia & the
  Amish Country
Portugal
Prague & the Best of the Czech Republic
Provence & the Riviera
Puerto Rico
Rome
San Antonio & Austin
San Diego
San Francisco
Santa Fe, Taos &
  Albuquerque
Scandinavia
Scotland
Seattle & Portland
Singapore & Malaysia
South Africa
Southeast Asia
South Pacific
Spain
Sweden
Switzerland
Thailand
Tokyo
Toronto
Tuscany & Umbria
USA
Utah
Vancouver & Victoria
Vermont, New Hampshire
  & Maine
Vienna & the Danube Valley
Virgin Islands
Virginia
Walt Disney World & Orlando
Washington, D.C.
Washington State

FROMMER'S® DOLLAR-A-DAY GUIDES

Australia from $50 a Day	Hawaii from $70 a Day	New Zealand from $50 a Day
California from $60 a Day	Ireland from $50 a Day	Paris from $85 a Day
Caribbean from $70 a Day	Israel from $45 a Day	San Francisco from $60 a Day
England from $70 a Day	Italy from $70 a Day	Washington, D.C.,
Europe from $60 a Day	London from $85 a Day	from $60 a Day
Florida from $60 a Day	New York from $80 a Day	

FROMMER'S® PORTABLE GUIDES

Acapulco, Ixtapa & Zihuatanejo	Dublin	Puerto Vallarta, Manzanillo & Guadalajara
Alaska Cruises & Ports of Call	Hawaii: The Big Island	San Diego
Bahamas	Las Vegas	San Francisco
Baja & Los Cabos	London	Sydney
Berlin	Maine Coast	Tampa & St. Petersburg
California Wine Country	Maui	Venice
Charleston & Savannah	New Orleans	Washington, D.C.
Chicago	New York City	
	Paris	

FROMMER'S® NATIONAL PARK GUIDES

Family Vacations in the National Parks	National Parks of the American West	Yellowstone & Grand Teton
Grand Canyon	Rocky Mountain	Yosemite & Sequoia/ Kings Canyon
		Zion & Bryce Canyon

FROMMER'S® GREAT OUTDOOR GUIDES

New England	Southern California & Baja
Northern California	Washington & Oregon

FROMMER'S® MEMORABLE WALKS

Chicago	New York	San Francisco
London	Paris	Washington D.C.

FROMMER'S® IRREVERENT GUIDES

Amsterdam	London	New Orleans	Seattle & Portland
Boston	Los Angeles	Paris	Vancouver
Chicago	Manhattan	San Francisco	Walt Disney World
Las Vegas			Washington, D.C.

FROMMER'S® BEST-LOVED DRIVING TOURS

America	Florida	Ireland	Scotland
Britain	France	Italy	Spain
California	Germany	New England	Western Europe

THE COMPLETE IDIOT'S TRAVEL GUIDES

Boston	Ireland	Paris
Chicago	Las Vegas	San Francisco
Cruise Vacations	London	Spain
Planning Your Trip to Europe	Mexico's Beach Resorts	Walt Disney World
Florida	New Orleans	Washington, D.C.
Hawaii	New York City	

THE UNOFFICIAL GUIDES®

Bed & Breakfast in
  New England
Bed & Breakfast in
  the Northwest
Beyond Disney
Branson, Missouri
California with Kids
Chicago

Cruises
Florida with Kids
The Great Smoky &
  Blue Ridge
  Mountains
Inside Disney
Las Vegas

London
Miami & the Keys
Mini Las Vegas
Mini-Mickey
New Orleans
New York City
Paris

San Francisco
Skiing in the West
Walt Disney World
Walt Disney World
  for Grown-ups
Walt Disney World
  for Kids
Washington, D.C.

SPECIAL-INTEREST TITLES

Born to Shop: France
Born to Shop: Hong Kong
Born to Shop: Italy
Born to Shop: New York
Born to Shop: Paris
Frommer's Britain's Best Bike Rides
The Civil War Trust's Official Guide
  to the Civil War Discovery Trail
Frommer's Caribbean Hideaways
Frommer's Europe's Greatest Driving Tours
Frommer's Food Lover's Companion to France
Frommer's Food Lover's Companion to Italy
Frommer's Gay & Lesbian Europe
Israel Past & Present
Monks' Guide to California

Monks' Guide to New York City
The Moon
New York City with Kids
Unforgettable Weekends
Outside Magazine's Guide
  to Family Vacations
Places Rated Almanac
Retirement Places Rated
Road Atlas Britain
Road Atlas Europe
Washington, D.C., with Kids
Wonderful Weekends from Boston
Wonderful Weekends from New York City
Wonderful Weekends from San Francisco
Wonderful Weekends from Los Angeles